ISSN 0276-8178

Volume 107

Twentieth-Century Literary Criticism

**Criticism of the
Works of Novelists, Poets, Playwrights,
Short Story Writers, and Other Creative Writers
Who Lived between 1900 and 1999,
from the First Published Critical
Appraisals to Current Evaluations**

Linda Pavlovski
Editor

Scott Darga
Assistant Editor

GALE GROUP
★
THOMSON LEARNING

*Detroit • New York • San Diego • San Francisco
Boston • New Haven, Conn. • Waterville, Maine
London • Munich*

STAFF

ynn M. Spampinato, Janet Witalec, *Managing Editors, Literature Product*
Kathy D. Darrow, Ellen McGeagh, *Product Liaisons*
Linda Pavlovski, *Editor*
Mark W. Scott, *Publisher, Literature Product*

Jennifer Baise, Marie Lazzari, *Editors*
Thomas Ligotti, *Associate Editor*
Scott Darga, *Assistant Editor*
Jenny Cromie, Mary Ruby, *Technical Training Specialists*
Deborah J. Morad, Joyce Nakamura, Kathleen Lopez Nolan, *Managing Editors*
Susan M. Trosky, *Director, Literature Content*

Maria L. Franklin, *Permissions Manager*
Margaret Chamberlain, *Permissions Specialist*

Victoria B. Cariappa, *Research Manager*
Sarah Genik, *Project Coordinator*
Ron Morelli, Tamara C. Nott, Tracie A. Richardson, *Research Associates*
Nicodemus Ford, *Research Assistant*

Dorothy Maki, *Manufacturing Manager*
Stacy L. Melson, *Buyer*

Mary Beth Trimper, *Manager, Composition and Electronic Prepress*
Carolyn Roney, *Composition Specialist*

Michael Logusz, *Graphic Artist*
Randy Bassett, *Imaging Supervisor*
Robert Duncan, Dan Newell, Luke Rademacher, *Imaging Specialists*
Pamela A. Reed, *Imaging Coordinator*
Kelly A. Quin, *Editor, Image and Multimedia Content*

Library of Congress Catalog Card Number 76-46132
ISBN 0-7876-4567-2
ISSN 0276-8178
Printed in the United States of America

10 9 8 7 6 5 4 3 2 1

Twentieth-Century
Literary Criticism

Guide to Gale Literary Criticism Series

For criticism on	Consult these Gale series
Authors now living or who died after December 31, 1999	*CONTEMPORARY LITERARY CRITICISM (CLC)*
Authors who died between 1900 and 1999	*TWENTIETH-CENTURY LITERARY CRITICISM (TCLC)*
Authors who died between 1800 and 1899	*NINETEENTH-CENTURY LITERATURE CRITICISM (NCLC)*
Authors who died between 1400 and 1799	*LITERATURE CRITICISM FROM 1400 TO 1800 (LC)* *SHAKESPEAREAN CRITICISM (SC)*
Authors who died before 1400	*CLASSICAL AND MEDIEVAL LITERATURE CRITICISM (CMLC)*
Authors of books for children and young adults	*CHILDREN'S LITERATURE REVIEW (CLR)*
Dramatists	*DRAMA CRITICISM (DC)*
Poets	*POETRY CRITICISM (PC)*
Short story writers	*SHORT STORY CRITICISM (SSC)*
Black writers of the past two hundred years	*BLACK LITERATURE CRITICISM (BLC)* *BLACK LITERATURE CRITICISM SUPPLEMENT (BLCS)*
Hispanic writers of the late nineteenth and twentieth centuries	*HISPANIC LITERATURE CRITICISM (HLC)* *HISPANIC LITERATURE CRITICISM SUPPLEMENT (HLCS)*
Native North American writers and orators of the eighteenth, nineteenth, and twentieth centuries	*NATIVE NORTH AMERICAN LITERATURE (NNAL)*
Major authors from the Renaissance to the present	*WORLD LITERATURE CRITICISM, 1500 TO THE PRESENT (WLC)* *WORLD LITERATURE CRITICISM SUPPLEMENT (WLCS)*

Contents

Preface vii

Acknowledgments xi

Preface

Since its inception more than fifteen years ago, *Twentieth-Century Literary Criticism* (*TCLC*) has been purchased and used by nearly 10,000 school, public, and college or university libraries. *TCLC* has covered more than 500 authors, representing 58 nationalities and over 25,000 titles. No other reference source has surveyed the critical response to twentieth-century authors and literature as thoroughly as *TCLC*. In the words of one reviewer, "there is nothing comparable available." *TCLC* "is a gold mine of information—dates, pseudonyms, biographical information, and criticism from books and periodicals—which many librarians would have difficulty assembling on their own."

Scope of the Series

TCLC is designed to serve as an introduction to authors who died between 1900 and 1999 and to the most significant interpretations of these author's works. Volumes published from 1978 through 1999 included authors who died between 1900 and 1960. The great poets, novelists, short story writers, playwrights, and philosophers of the period are frequently studied in high school and college literature courses. In organizing and reprinting the vast amount of critical material written on these authors, *TCLC* helps students develop valuable insight into literary history, promotes a better understanding of the texts, and sparks ideas for papers and assignments. Each entry in *TCLC* presents a comprehensive survey on an author's career or an individual work of literature and provides the user with a multiplicity of interpretations and assessments. Such variety allows students to pursue their own interests; furthermore, it fosters an awareness that literature is dynamic and responsive to many different opinions.

Every fourth volume of *TCLC* is devoted to literary topics. These topics widen the focus of the series from the individual authors to such broader subjects as literary movements, prominent themes in twentieth-century literature, literary reaction to political and historical events, significant eras in literary history, prominent literary anniversaries, and the literatures of cultures that are often overlooked by English-speaking readers.

TCLC is designed as a companion series to Gale's *Contemporary Literary Criticism,* (*CLC*) which reprints commentary on authors who died after 1999. Because of the different time periods under consideration, there is no duplication of material between *CLC* and *TCLC*.

Organization of the Book

A *TCLC* entry consists of the following elements:

- The **Author Heading** cites the name under which the author most commonly wrote, followed by birth and death dates. Also located here are any name variations under which an author wrote, including transliterated forms for authors whose native languages use nonroman alphabets. If the author wrote consistently under a pseudonym, the pseudonym will be listed in the author heading and the author's actual name given in parenthesis on the first line of the biographical and critical information. Uncertain birth or death dates are indicated by question marks. Single-work entries are preceded by a heading that consists of the most common form of the title in English translation (if applicable) and the original date of composition.

- A **Portrait of the Author** is included when available.

- The **Introduction** contains background information that introduces the reader to the author, work, or topic that is the subject of the entry.

- The list of **Principal Works** is ordered chronologically by date of first publication and lists the most important works by the author. The genre and publication date of each work is given. In the case of foreign authors whose works have been translated into English, the English-language version of the title follows in brackets. Unless otherwise indicated, dramas are dated by first performance, not first publication.

- Reprinted **Criticism** is arranged chronologically in each entry to provide a useful perspective on changes in critical evaluation over time. The critic's name and the date of composition or publication of the critical work are given at the beginning of each piece of criticism. Unsigned criticism is preceded by the title of the source in which it appeared. All titles by the author featured in the text are printed in boldface type. Footnotes are reprinted at the end of each essay or excerpt. In the case of excerpted criticism, only those footnotes that pertain to the excerpted texts are included.

- A complete **Bibliographical Citation** of the original essay or book precedes each piece of criticism.

- Critical essays are prefaced by brief **Annotations** explicating each piece.

- An annotated bibliography of **Further Reading** appears at the end of each entry and suggests resources for additional study. In some cases, significant essays for which the editors could not obtain reprint rights are included here. Boxed material following the further reading list provides references to other biographical and critical sources on the author in series published by Gale.

Indexes

A **Cumulative Author Index** lists all of the authors that appear in a wide variety of reference sources published by the Gale Group, including *TCLC*. A complete list of these sources is found facing the first page of the Author Index. The index also includes birth and death dates and cross references between pseudonyms and actual names.

A **Cumulative Nationality Index** lists all authors featured in *TCLC* by nationality, followed by the number of the *TCLC* volume in which their entry appears.

A **Cumulative Topic Index** lists the literary themes and topics treated in the series as well as in *Classical and Medieval Literature Criticism, Literature Criticism from 1400 to 1800, Nineteenth-Century Literature Criticism,* and the *Contemporary Literary Criticism* Yearbook, which was discontinued in 1998.

An alphabetical **Title Index** accompanies each volume of *TCLC*. Listings of titles by authors covered in the given volume are followed by the author's name and the corresponding page numbers where the titles are discussed. English translations of foreign titles and variations of titles are cross-referenced to the title under which a work was originally published. Titles of novels, dramas, nonfiction books, and poetry, short story, or essay collections are printed in italics, while individual poems, short stories, and essays are printed in roman type within quotation marks.

In response to numerous suggestions from librarians, Gale also produces an annual paperbound edition of the *TCLC* cumulative title index. This annual cumulation, which alphabetically lists all titles reviewed in the series, is available to all customers. Additional copies of this index are available upon request. Librarians and patrons will welcome this separate index; it saves shelf space, is easy to use, and is recyclable upon receipt of the next edition.

Citing *Twentieth-Century Literary Criticism*

When writing papers, students who quote directly from any volume in the Literary Criticism Series may use the following general format to footnote reprinted criticism. The first example pertains to material drawn from periodicals, the second to material reprinted from books.

George Orwell, "Reflections on Gandhi," *Partisan Review* 6 (Winter 1949): 85-92; reprinted in *Twentieth-Century Literary Criticism,* vol. 59, ed. Jennifer Gariepy (Detroit: The Gale Group, 1995), 40-3.

William H. Slavick, "Going to School to DuBose Heyward," *The Harlem Renaissance Re-examined,* ed. Victor A. Kramer (AMS, 1987), 65- 91; reprinted in *Twentieth-Century Literary Criticism,* vol. 59, ed. Jennifer Gariepy (Detroit: The Gale Group, 1995), 94-105.

Suggestions are Welcome

Readers who wish to suggest new features, topics, or authors to appear in future volumes, or who have other suggestions or comments are cordially invited to call, write, or fax the Managing Editor:

Managing Editor, Literary Criticism Series
The Gale Group
27500 Drake Road
Farmington Hills, MI 48331-3535
1-800-347-4253 (GALE)
Fax: 248-699-8054

Acknowledgments

The editors wish to thank the copyright holders of the excerpted criticism included in this volume and the permissions managers of many book and magazine publishing companies for assisting us in securing reproduction rights. We are also grateful to the staffs of the Detroit Public Library, the Library of Congress, the University of Detroit Mercy Library, Wayne State University Purdy/Kresge Library Complex, and the University of Michigan Libraries for making their resources available to us. Following is a list of the copyright holders who have granted us permission to reproduce material in this volume of *TCLC*. Every effort has been made to trace copyright, but if omissions have been made, please let us know.

COPYRIGHTED EXCERPTS IN *TCLC*, VOLUME 107 WERE REPRODUCED FROM THE FOLLOWING PERIODICALS:

—*The American Poetry Review,* v. 14, July-August, 1985. Copyright © 1985 by World Poetry, Inc. All rights reserved. Reproduced by permission.—*American Psychologist,* v. 23, 1968; v. 53, October, 1998. Copyright © 1968, 1998 by the American Psychological Association, Inc. Reproduced by permission.—*The Centennial Review,* v. XXXVII, Spring, 1993. Copyright © The Centennial Review, 1993. All rights reserved. Reproduced by permission.—*Contemporary Literature,* v. X, Spring, 1969; v. XXII, Winter, 1981. Copyright © 1969, 1981 by the Board of Regents of the University of Wisconsin System. Reproduced by permission.—*Great Plains Quarterly,* v. 8, Winter, 1988. Copyright 1988 by the Center for Great Plains Studies. Reproduced by permission.—*The Grosseteste Review,* v. 6, 1973. © Donald Davie.—*The Hudson Review,* v. XV, Winter, 1962-63. Copyright © 1963 by The Hudson Review, Inc. Reproduced by permission.—*Journal of American Culture,* v. 14, Summer, 1991. Copyright © 1991 by Ray B. Browne. All rights reserved. Reproduced by permission.—*Journal of American Studies,* v. 31, August, 1997. © Cambridge University Press 1997. Reproduced by permission.—*The Massachusetts Review,* v. VI, Autumn-Winter, 1964-65. Copyright, 1964, by The Massachusetts Review, Inc. Reproduced by permission.—*The Midwest Quarterly,* v. XXII, Summer, 1981. © Copyright 1981 by The Midwest Quarterly, Pittsburg State Univeristy. Reproduced by permission.—*Modern Fiction Studies,* v. 36, Spring, 1990. Copyright © 1990 by the Purdue Research Foundation. All rights reserved. Reproduced by permission.—*The Modern Language Review,* v. 40, July, 1945. Reproduced by permission.—*The Nation,* New York, v. 209, November 24, 1969. Copyright 1969 by the Nation Associates, Inc. Reproduced by permission.—*The New York Times,* November 9, 1958; November 24, 1991. Copyright 1958, renewed 1986, 1991, by The New York Times Company. Reproduced by permission.—*Paideuma,* v. 7, Winter, 1978; v. 10, Spring, 1981. Copyright © 1977, 1981 by the National Poetry Foundation, Inc. Reproduced by permission of the authors.— *The Paris Review,* v. 33, Fall, 1991. Reproduced by permission of Russell & Volkening as agents for The Paris Review. Copyright © 1991 by *The Paris Review.*—*Perspectives USA,* no. 1, Fall, 1952. Reproduced by permission of the author.— *Poetry,* v. XLIV, July, 1934. Copyright, 1934, by Harriet Monroe. All rights reserved. Reproduced by permission.—*Prairie Schooner,* v. 53, Summer, 1979. Copyright © 1979 University of Nebraska Press. All rights reserved. Reproduced by permission.—*Raritan,* v. 14, Fall, 1994. Copyright © 1994 by Raritan. Reproduced by permission.—*Sagetrieb,* v. 12, Winter, 1993. Copyright © 1993 by The National Poetry Foundation. Reproduced by permission of the authors.—*Saturday Review of Literature,* v. X, March 24, 1934. Reproduced by permission.—*The Sewanee Review,* v. LXV, 1957. Reproduced by permission of the editor.—*South Dakota Review,* v. 20, Autumn, 1982. Reproduced by permission.—*Studies in Philology,* v. LXIX, July, 1972. © 1972 by the University of North Carolina Press. Reproduced by permission.—*Studies in the Novel,* v. XVIII, Spring, 1986. © 1986 by North Texas State University. Reproduced by permission.—*The Times Literary Supplement,* n. 2737, July 16, 1954; n. 2794, September 16, 1955; n. 2896, August 30, 1957. Reproduced by permission.—*The Yale Journal of Criticism,* v. 9, Spring, 1996. © 1996 by Yale University and The Johns Hopkins University Press. Reproduced by permission.—*Western American Literature,* v. XXIII, Summer, 1988; v. XXV, Spring, 1990; v. XXXI, Winter, 1997; v. XXXIII, Spring, 1998. Copyright ©1998, 1990, 1997, 1998, by the Western Literature Association. Reproduced by permission.

COPYRIGHTED EXCERPTS IN *TCLC*, VOLUME 107, WERE REPRODUCED FROM THE FOLLOWING BOOKS:

Aldridge, John W. From an interview in *Conversations with Wright Morris: Critical Views and Responses.* Edited by Robert E. Knoll. University of Nebraska Press, 1977. Copyright © 1977 by the University of Nebraska Press. All rights reserved. Reproduced by permission.—Cassidy, John D. From *Robert W. Buchanan.* Twayne Publishers, Inc., 1973. Copy-

Gordon Bottomley
1874-1948

English poet and playwright.

INTRODUCTION

As a writer of verse drama, Bottomley emphasized poetic language over theatrical concerns. Many of his plays were offered without costumes or props, and the lines recited rather than conventionally acted out. Stylistically and thematically, his works resemble those of the great Irish modernist William Butler Yeats.

BIOGRAPHICAL INFORMATION

Bottomley was born February 20, 1874, in Yorkshire, England, where his education began. However, he suffered from a chronic bleeding disorder, which took him away from a banking career and greatly reduced his activity. He relocated to Silverdale, a Lancashire village near the Scottish border, and in 1905 married Emily Burton from a nearby town. The two were said to have had a profound bond, enjoying literature and the arts.

Bottomley published his first collection of poetry, *The Mickle Drede and Other Verses*, in 1896 but later attempted to destroy all copies of this book, which he considered to be immature. With *The Crier by Night* (1902) and *Midsummer Eve* (1905), he turned to verse drama, setting out to revive the art in England. His early plays were respected for their poetic qualities but did not result in long-lasting productions. His *King Lear's Wife* (1920), however, was produced by the Birmingham Repertory Theatre and became a success despite negative reviews from the critics. *Gruach* (1921), similar to *King Lear's Wife*, was written as a prelude to a Shakespeare tragedy. The play was performed at the Atheneum Theatre in Glasgow in 1923 and the St. Martin's Theatre in London in 1924.

Bottomley told an interviewer from *Bookman* magazine, "I have no biography. Nothing ever happened to me," and, indeed, he ventured out very little, spending most of his adult life taking pleasure in the paintings and finery that surrounded him. Given the limitations of his physical condition, Bottomley still managed to kindle associations with leading literary figures of the era, including John Drinkwater, Lascelles Abercrombie, and Paul Nash. He also served as president of the Scottish Community Drama Association and vice-president of the British Drama League. Bottomley's last published work was *A Stage for Poetry: My*

Purposes with My Plays (1948), in which he expounded on theatrical concerns and recounted his close associations with two drama teachers, Marjorie Gullan and Duncan Clark.

MAJOR WORKS

Bottomley found inspiration in the literature of the past. Besides Shakespeare, he looked to classical Greek and Roman literature, William Morris, and Oscar Wilde for the material from which he formed his plays. *The Riding to Lithend*, written in 1907 but not produced until 1928, is based on a Norse saga. The hero refuses to join his fellow Icelanders in battle and is ostracized. *Britain's Daughter* (1921) takes place at the height of the Roman Empire. The English heroine defies the invaders and is taken to Rome as a prisoner.

The two plays based on Shakespeare are regarded as Bottomley's finest works. In *King Lear's Wife*, Bottomley portrayed the life and death of Lear's neglected wife Hygd

1

in a drama rife with betrayal and greed. *Gruach* is the tale of Lady MacBeth before she became Lady MacBeth, at the time in her life when she is about to marry a different Scottish nobleman before the man she is destined to wed finally appears.

Encouraged by Yeats's success, Bottomley wrote a great many short verse plays dealing with the extremes of human experience. He felt the influence of Jacobean drama and Japanese Noh theater, and the resulting dramas are said to contain a sense of history and a moral outlook comparable to what is found in Yeats's verse dramas *The Shadowy Waters* and *Deirdire.*

CRITICAL RECEPTION

Critics who read Bottomley's plays tended to appreciate them more than those who saw them performed. William S. Braithwaite described *The Riding to Lithend* as "vigorous with passion and character." Abercrombie called Bottomley "a poet who certainly ought to be better known than he is." On the other hand, the headline of a newspaper review of *King Lear's Wife* called it "a Gifted Mistake."

From a modern perspective, Bottomley's plays are considered poetic successes but dramatic failures. The language is rich and noble, but the characters are not convincing and the plots are not coherent. William V. Spanos described Bottomley as a transitional figure; Bottomley's use of verse cleared the way for later work by the modernists, including T. S. Eliot's *Murder in the Cathedral.* Some critics have noted that virtually all of Bottomley's protagonists are female. In this, too, he is a transitional figure, but his efforts do not compare favorably with those of George Bernard Shaw in his *Saint Joan* and *Pygmalion.*

PRINCIPAL WORKS

The Mickle Drede and Other Verses (poetry) 1896
Poems at White Nights (poetry) 1899
The Crier by Night (drama) 1902
The Gate of Smaragdus (poetry) 1904
Midsummer Eve (drama) 1905
Chambers of Imagery (poetry) 1907
Laodice and Danaë (drama) 1909
The Riding to Lithend (drama) 1909
A Vision of Giorgione: Three Variations on Venetian Themes (poetry) 1910
Chambers of Imagery, 2nd series (poetry) 1912
King Lear's Wife and Other Plays (dramas) 1920
Gruach and Britain's Daughter: Two Plays (dramas) 1921
Littleholme (poetry) 1922
Prologue (poetry) 1922
Poems of Thirty Years (poetry) 1925
Frescoes from Buried Temples (poetry) 1928

Gordon Bottomley [also published as *Selected Poems*] (poetry) 1928
A Parting and The Return (poetry) 1928
Scenes and Plays (dramas) 1929
Festival Preludes (poetry) 1930
Lyric Plays (dramas) 1932
The Acts of Saint Peter (drama) 1933
Choric Plays and A Comedy (dramas) 1939
Deirdire (drama) 1944
Kate Kennedy (drama) 1945
A Stage for Poetry: My Purposes with My Plays (drama) 1948
Poems and Plays (poetry and dramas) 1953
Poet and Painter, Being the Correspondence of Gordon Bottomley and Paul Nash, 1910-1946 (letters) 1955

CRITICISM

Anna Benneson McMahan (review date 1910)

SOURCE: A review of *A Vision of Giorgione,* in *The Dial,* Vol. XLIX, No. 579, August 1, 1910, p. 69.

[*In the following excerpt, McMahan offers a favorable review of* A Vision of Giorgione.]

[A] beautiful specimen of book-making is Mr. Gordon Bottomley's *A Vision of Giorgione,* which has all the dainty features we have learned to expect in a Mosher book. There is scarcely another painter of equal rank with Giorgione of whom we know so little. Vasari mentions his fondness for music and his love for a lady. This furnishes Mr. Bottomley the inspiration for his sequence of three poems (rather than dramas) called **"A Concert of Giorgione," "A Pastoral of Giorgione,"** and **"The Lady of Giorgione."** The poet has caught the Venetian atmosphere very perfectly in his charming verse; perhaps he has also caught the secret of the painter's method in a passage such as this:

> I pose models no more,
> But find adorable ladies with such fair minds
> They may be trusted to express themselves
> Graciously, perfectly in perfect gowns;
> I ask them to come here quite half in secret,
> Wearing the gowns they think for quiet joy;
> Sometimes I play them music of subtle discords,
> Or tell them casual fragmentary stories
> About the sudden things women do
> Which no man understands. And I watch,
> I paint and watch; they think they are but broidering,
> Or wondering, or resting from their fate.

O. W. Firkins (review date 1916)

SOURCE: A review of *Laodice and Danaë,* in *The Nation,* New York, Vol. 103, No. 2676, October 12, 1916, p. 348.

[*In the following excerpt, Firkins reviews* Laodice and Danaë.]

In *Laodice and Danaë* an Oriental queen of sunken authority kills a maid of honor who has saved her conspiring lover from the penalties of his transgression. Mr. Bottomley takes the homicide very calmly; what excites him is the picturesqueness of the attendant ceremony. What he aims to do is to show fell passions, wrath, revenge, hatred, wandering luxuriously amid arcades, braziers, carpets, divans, unguents, roses, coffers, lamp-chains, brocades, jewels, lattices of cedar, and broidered curtains. This equalization of passion with setting, this pitting of the luxurious against the fiendish, is fairly original, not unimpressive, intensely exotic, and irreparably morbid.

Mr. Bottomley utilizes as instruments a dreamy, sensuous imagination quick to image this delaying, voluptuous, fastidious hate, and a blank verse, which, in spite of inexcusable perversities, I should like to twist into a pastille and burn in a brazier, holding my nostrils to the flame:

> Needing me he turned.
> Was it not best to die still needing me,
> And save the amount of kingdoms for my boy,
> The climbing vine of gold up Shushan's front,
> The cedar palaces of Ecbatana?
> Though Berenice sits in Antioch
> Safe with her suckling in her suckling's
>   name . . .
> Winds, bring to me a ship from Antioch.

O. W. Firkins (review date 1922)

SOURCE: A review of *Gruach and Britain's Daughter*, in *The Yale Review*, Vol. XII, No. 1, October, 1922, p. 194.

[*In the following excerpt, Firkins reviews* Gruach and Britain's Daughter.]

Mr. Gordon Bottomley in his early British plays [in *Gruach and Britain's Daughter*] takes us so very far in so short a time that we are surprised to perceive that in a much longer time he has taken us so very little farther. He is shaggy where Mr. Yeats is threadlike, and there is a good growl in his verse, which, however, shows itself less and less susceptible of reduction to a tune. *Britain's Daughter,* the second play, hardly counts, but in *Gruach,* a story of the Shakespearean Macbeths in the pre-Shakespearean moment of their first meeting and almost instant troth-plight, the signals and harbingers of power are as irresistible as ever. Gruach, the future Lady Macbeth, is very well indeed as long as she remains a rumor, a contour, and a voice; it is only when she becomes a person that she dwindles. Drama, unfortunately, is rather dependent on persons. But if Mr. Bottomley hardly gets beyond the threshold of drama, few things of our day are better worth while than the impressiveness of his dusky figure as it halts in the gloom of the doorway.

Storm Jameson (review date 1922)

SOURCE: A review of *King Lear's Wife and Other Plays,* in *The Yale Review,* Vol. XI, No. 2, January, 1922, pp. 426-27.

[*In the following excerpt, Jameson discusses strengths and weaknesses in* King Lear's Wife.]

Mr. Gordon Bottomley is . . . a poet. *King Lear's Wife* is a poem, arranged in the form of dramatic dialogue. The verse has a sombre beauty. In the song of Goneril over her dying mother, it has a sharp edge. In such moments as Goneril's scorn of Regan it flashes, suddenly and briefly:

> Does Regan worship anywhere at dawn?
> The sweaty, half-clad cookmaids render lard
> Out in the scullery, after pig-killing,
> And Regan sidles among their greasy skirts,
> Smeary and hot as they, for chaps to suck.

The speech of all the characters is overburdened with adjectives. They are like the touches of an artist's brush. They are not the natural gestures of the speaker's thoughts. Goneril tells her mother that she "sped as lightly down the dewy bank as any mothering owl that hunts quick mice." Woven in this thread of words, the figures of the lustful King, of Goneril, the fierce young virgin, of Gormflaith, the King's mistress, of the dying Queen, of the child Cordeil, who is only a child's voice and a child's hands, are the figures of an old tapestry, angular, stiffly beautiful, clothed in dim colors, fashioned with an ancient cunning. Sometimes the colors blaze as if a shaft of light had fallen across them through a half-open door.

The Lear and Goneril of this play are at once more primitive and infinitely more sophisticated than the Shakespearean conception. When they are primitive they reach back to that Anglo-Saxon mind of rage and lament, childlike in fear and courage, savage in hate and lust. Where they are modern they are subhuman. They stand at the beginning of a road which leads to the monstrous figures of *Petrouchka,* those grotesque, frightful beings who are not dolls but living things below humanity—the maimed, thwarted desires and feelings buried in the human mind, evil, menacing, like words spoken out of a dead and frightful past.

It would be foolish to withhold from Mr. Bottomley the admiration due him. *King Lear's Wife* is full of delicate beauties. It would be impossible not to recognize that these beauties are of a picture and not of a drama. *King Lear's Wife* is not a drama, a tale told "in mimic hour," wrought to a moment of illumination and understanding. It is static, a cloudy vision, a seeming. The Queen, Gormflaith, the King, and Goneril, are at the end what they were at the beginning. There has been no drama, but there have been some poignant moments and also a strange loveliness of words.

Theatre Arts Magazine (review date 1922)

SOURCE: A review of *Gruach and Britain's Daughter,* in *Theatre Arts Magazine,* Vol. VI, No. 4, October, 1922, p. 347.

[*The following review offers a positive assessment of* Gruach and Britain's Daughter.]

How large Mr. Bottomley's audience for his verse dramas is going to be, either in the theatre or in the library, will depend largely upon how many there are among the people who have the good fortune to come upon his work who, having visual imagination themselves, enjoy adding it to the imagination of a poet to recreate stories on great and universal tragic themes. Mr. Bottomley's audience must play his plays with him, to make them live. These are distinguished plays, with a strong personal quality, definitely superior to almost all of that mass of contemporary material being added to our stage literature, so much so that it is a temptation to speak extravagantly of them. But it is a greater compliment to Mr. Bottomley not to do that but rather, ranking the plays with the verse dramas that have lived through generations, to say that they are not, for example, Marlowe or Shelley. Perhaps the best method of comparison for this later volume is with Mr. Bottomley's other plays. One may say that **Britain's Daughter** is not so convincing as **Gruach** and that **Gruach,** in spite of its more perfect first act, its fine characterization, its steadier line, both of verse and story, does not do—as a background for *Macbeth*—what **King Lear's Wife** did for *King Lear.* The book is a welcome volume to lovers of the theatre. **Gruach** should be played. It would add lustre to good acting.

Arthur Bryant (review date 1923)

SOURCE: A review of *A Vision of Giorgione,* in *The Bookman,* London, Vol. 64, No. 379, April, 1923, pp. 45.

[*In the following excerpt, Bryant reviews* A Vision of Giorgione.]

These poems of Mr. Bottomley's—stories of Giorgione—were published in a collected edition twelve years ago in America. They now appear for the first time in this country [as **A Vision of Giorgione**]. As the works of Gordon Bottomley they have a passport to any country, but alas! there are no **"Cartmell Bells"** among them. It is a book of long emotional utterances on music, philosophy and love, but the startling clarity that Mr. Bottomley's admirers have learnt to expect of him is curiously lacking. And the use of expressions such as "porfection comes but once" gives one to think furiously; Jove nods outrageously sometimes.

Occasionally the old spark lights. At the beginning there is a charming dedication to his wife:

> Where all is yours,
> What virtue hes in giving?

> Though nought endures,
> In writing as in living
> I have given myself to you,
> And, as you take me,
> My poems grow more true,
> More true you make me.

That, I think, is the best thing in the book. If I seem a little hard on this collection it is because I am forced to judge the man, who wrote the great dedication to "some English ironmoulders," by a very high standard—the highest there is.

C. Henry Warren (essay date 1925)

SOURCE: "The Poetry of Mr.Gordon Bottomley," in *The Bookman,* London, Vol. 68, No. 405, June, 1925, p. 176.

[*In the following essay, Warren reviews* Poems of Thirty Years.]

Perhaps one of the best known of Mr. Bottomley's poems is **"The End of the World."** In frozen phrases, light as the flakes that drift down from the closing sky, it pictures the desolation of the End. The cow-house where hitherto the snow had always melted "with yellow stains from the beasts' breath inside," is quite thatched over now; the snow slides from the over-weighted leaves (or is it a dead bird falling?); inside the house the clock has stopped and a butterfly drops from the ceiling's shadow, dead; the rails of a broken bed lie charred in the grate:

> And when he touched the bars he thought the sting
> Came from their heat—he could not feel such cold.
> She said, "Oh, do not sleep,
> Heart, heart of me, keep near me! No, no; sleep!
> I will not lift his fallen quiet eyelids,
> Although I know he would awaken then—
> He closed them thus but now of his own will
> He can stay with me while I do not lift them."

I have purposely recalled this poem in some detail because it seems to me typical of the whole of Mr. Bottomley's work. The quietness of its rhythm, the deftness of its pictures, its mournful remoteness—all are typical of that dream world whereof his poems treat. It is a world set apart from this world of ours that is so bathed in the light of common day. There move those ladies of old time, Helen and Bathsheba, Kassandra and Rosamund; and there too are David and King Avelin, Moses and Hadrian. There the apple trees bloom endlessly against a dewy sky; and there in the cloudy turrets are bells that ring out soft and clear. It is a static world, shut in an iridescent bubble; or a gorgeous frieze in a mighty circular room; or a world of ice and flame, marvellously carved, marvellously twining.

For Mr. Bottomley (save in the successful exception of **"To Ironfounders and Others"**) holds aloof from our soiled and turbulent days. His mind is truly its own resting-place. He is the cloistered poet. It is enough for him that, out of the storied past, he can fetch beauty and fashion it for our inspiration. He is the craftsman of the immaculate word and the immaculate phrase, chiselling his poems endlessly (so it seems to me), and carving his pictures with endless care. Not that the labour behind his work is too evident; like the studied prose of **"Elia"** (that has been aptly described as seeming but the overflow of good talk), it hides its abundant technique under the graceful ease of inevitability.

Yet although Mr. Bottomley is the cloistered poet, he has had a most considerable influence upon modern verse. In him there is a strange union between the last century and the present one. Two of his books were called *Chambers of Imagery*; and they almost founded a school. They took as their unit the dexterous phrase, the pure-drawn image; and in pictures, as meticulously hammered as Francis Thompson's snowflake, they envisioned some delicate emotion, some hesitant sentiment for our delight. Here, in a poem called **"Sanctuaries,"** is an instance:

> There is a chamber in the dawn
> 　Sought by a bird alone—
> A cloud, a gleam, a veil withdrawn
> 　On brighter veils beyond,
> Glistening with one far ringing tone,
> 　One fluttering mote and blond.
> There is a chamber in the night
> 　Sought by a girl alone—
> A secret place, white after white,
> 　With inner walls more dim,
> And farther places whitely strown
> 　As though with thoughts that swim.

He is modern also in the intellectual content of his verse; and his shy paganism belongs utterly to our time. For all that, however, there are poems that reach back in this book to a day that is now over-past. Such particularly are the quasi-dramatic poems like **"Kassandra Prophesies"** and **"Solomon's Parents."** From this strange marriage in his poetry of the past with the present springs a queer paradox. I feel in reading him to-day that I am thrown beyond the experimental and feverish tendencies of the "Georgians" into a statelier and less querulous time; yet I feel also that I am in the presence of one entirely sympathetic with our present yearnings and indeed a participant in them. Perhaps this is due to the fact that apparently Mr. Bottomley has enjoyed the friendship of so many of our "younger" moderns; or perhaps he has that best gift of never growing with the years.

This beautifully produced volume [*Poems of Thirty Years*] seems to represent all of Mr. Bottomley's lyrical output to date; or at least all that part of it he is anxious to preserve. Here is the lovely **"New Year's Eve, 1913,"** from which, for its own sake and for the personal joy I have in it (since it was by this poem, in *An Annual of New Poetry, 1917,* that Mr. Bottomley first swam triumphantly into my ken), there comes a double pleasure in quotation:

> O, Cartmel bells ring soft to-night,
> 　And Cartmel bells ring clear,

> But I lie far away to-night,
> 　Listening with my dear . . .

> The loveliness, the fruitfulness,
> 　The power of life lived there
> Return, revive, more closely press
> 　Upon that midnight air.

> But many deaths have place in men
> 　Before they come to die;
> Joys must be used and spent, and then
> 　Abandoned and passed by.

> Earth is not ours; no cherished space
> 　Can hold us from life's flow,
> That bears us thither and thence by ways
> 　We knew not we should go.

> O, Cartmel bells ring loud, ring clear,
> 　Through midnight deep and hoar,
> A year new-born, and I shall hear
> 　The Cartmel bells no more.

Here you will find those dew-drenched and moonlit poems of apple-orchard days, poems joy-worn and weighed down with their own loveliness; here you will find that clean-cut and alien poem, **"Babel: The Gate of the God,"** where "the orgulous king Nimroud stands up conceiving he shall live to conquer God," and where words lose themselves in inarticulate gasps reaching out to "curves of immortal thought"; here you will find again those three majestic Hymns to Touch, Form and Imagination:

> Imagination is acceptance wrought
> When things beyond ourselves with faint sounds press
> Upon the limits of our consciousness;

and here too you will find all the songs out of Mr. Bottomley's several poetic plays—not forgetting that sardonic realist song, from *King Lear's Wife*:

> A louse crept out of my lady's shift—
> 　Ahumm, Ahumm, Ahee.

I do not know, when historians come to reckon up the poetry of our day, with what date they will mark the coming in of Georgian poetry; but it is a most heartening thought that they cannot exclude Mr. Bottomley from their count. Mr. Hardy we must grudgingly forgo; and the Poet Laureate. But Mr. Bottomley (though the earliest of his poetry here dates back to 1896) is certainly ours. The thought is a comforting one.

Hoxie Neale Fairchild (essay date 1962)

SOURCE: "More Mavericks," in *Religious Trends in English Poetry,* Vol. V: 1880-1920, *Gods of a Changing Poetry,* Columbia University Press, 1962, pp. 306-311.

[*In the following excerpt, Fairchild discusses major themes and ideas in Bottomley's poetry.*]

Born in 1874, Gordon Bottomley published two immature and derivative volumes of verse in the nineties, the first depending mainly on Rossetti and the second mainly on Yeats. In *The Gate of Smaragdus* (1904) he began to walk alone, and in *Chambers of Imagery* (1907) he emerged as his uneven, restlessly searching true self. But by 1912, when a second series of *Chambers* appeared, he had already begun to devote himself chiefly though not exclusively to verse dramas which treated legendary tragic themes with a harshly primitive realism which some people found rather shocking. Such readers preferred the impressionistic incantatory lyrics in which he emulated and sometimes rivaled De la Mare, or the more numerous nature poems which exhibited an almost Wordsworthian simplicity, directness, and economy. On the whole, however, he never won much fame with the general public although he was respected by many of his fellow poets. A chronic invalid whose life often hung by a thread, he was no less unable than temperamentally disinclined to bustle about in the literary market place or to attach himself to a coterie.

In 1925 he asserts that his "most cherished pilgrimage" has been "The quest of beauty by word and sound."[1] His maturer work, however, frequently implies a more intellectualized, less trivially sensuous conception of poetry than that which he had cultivated in the nineties. Not enough attention, in fact, has been paid to his more seriously reflective nondramatic poems. After reading De la Mare it is refreshing to turn to a poet who so often wants to use his brains. He dislikes the world in which he lives no less intensely than De la Mare, but except in occasional fantasy-vacations he shows no disposition to shrink from it into dreamland. Sometimes more aggressively loyal to the romantic faith than De la Mare, at other times he can be sharply critical of it. Neither an escapist nor a pseudorealist of the Gibson type, he aspires to be a poet of *intellectual* engagement. But the technical problems involved in this endeavor are not satisfactorily solved. The poems in question show an extremely modern mind seething uncomfortably within the confines of traditional forms. The struggle to discover and express ideas without lecturing about them too often results in a contorted, incoherent style. Nevertheless the ambition is honorable and the achievement at least interesting.

In **"The Embarkation,"** the way in which the limited land ends and the limitless sea begins *just here* raises the question of what may lie beyond. The speaker will seek an answer:

> Let me enlarge my world and know what verge
> Escapes this mass of earth for balance thrown:

> Embark, my heart: the lip of all the land
> Is under flamelets that outlive the dark;
> Lost figures with white vacant faces stand,
> Hand moves to hidden hand;
> Rope slips; the near thwart sinks . . . My heart, embark.[2]

Here as sometimes elsewhere, Bottomley is ambiguous. Is this *Crossing the Bar* or *Ulysses*? The voyage from mortal to immortal life or the onward drive of creative imagination into a romantically conceived infinitude? In either case we may infer that the wisdom sought by Bottomley must offer not only intellectual but spiritual satisfaction. Mere pagan humanism, as he makes Hadrian confess while musing over the dead body of Antinous, is good but not good enough. On the other hand, this religious-minded poet is also a skeptic. "Gods live but in their worshippers" is the theme of **"A Passing of Faith."** The god Set, being of course bull-headed, insists that Christ has not conquered *him*; but the other gods of the Egyptian pantheon tell him that he and they are dead simply because no one now believes in them.[3] The implication is that Christianity will not prove exempt from the same principle.

Unlike many of his contemporaries, however, this son of a devout Swedenborgian father knows that Christianity is still very much alive. Although he rejects it he pays it the compliment of taking it seriously. That he draws the usual contrast between Christ and the Christian creed is to be expected. More interesting are the paradoxes of **"In Church,"** a more aggressive version of Cory's *Mimnermus*. While

> The priest, in thoughtless daily use,
> Delivered the fairy tale of Eve,

the poet gave a fresh twist to the *felix culpa* theme:

> I thanked the God for all the joy
> Ordained for me by Eve's best sin:
> Except for God she might have been
> Stainless and ever a garden-toy.

And hearing the parable of the sower,

> Yet most I praised the stony soil
> That did so rare and great a thing,
> Spending its power to serve its King
> Unmasked by man's officious toil.

At times he seems engaged in a systematic attempt to naturalize the "fairy tales" of Christianity. Moses, soliloquizing in *Sinai*, says that his power over men lies not in his knowledge of God but in his knowledge of nature. His miracles are those of science:

> I understand how water stratifies:
> Smiting, I change the balance of its force.

By calling his scientific knowledge "God," he can impose his will upon men who do not yet realize that such knowledge, regarded simply as what it is, would give not enslavement but freedom and mastery.[4]

In a lighter, more sophisticated vein not unlike that of Anatole France, he amuses himself with David and Bathsheba and with Abishag as the consolation of David's senility. But these poems are preceded, and in a sense prepared for, by **"Rosamund Grief,"** a searchingly serious study of pious erotomania in which a modern girl bereaved of her lover adopts with insane literalness the illusion of being "the bride of Christ." But this skeptical essay in psychiatry is preceded in turn by the more sympathetic **"Calvary-Talk."** With the dead Jesus still hanging on the Cross, the three executioners discuss the affair. One says that in doing such jobs on real criminals he feels no pity;

> But to nail a rough-tongued prophet up,
> A harmless drone and clean—
> You might have wiped the shame from my face
> As I drove the cold nails in;
> 'Twas only work for priests or their wives,
> For men too spiteful and mean.

While the talk continues,

> Up the hill and over the hill,
> With cloths on a bier spread,
> The pitiful mourners came again
> Who thought their God was dead.[5]

Again an ambiguity: are the mourners mistaken in supposing that He is God, or in supposing that He is dead? Probably the former, but we cannot be quite sure.

We cannot be quite sure, for Bottomley's skepticism is inseparable from a wistful desire to know. A Hardyesque sexton explains that he is ringing the passing bell on the *birth* of a child because

> when a child is born
> A spirit must leave God's house;
> And is not that the blindest death,
> Numbest, most piteous?

To the question, "And how many years do you toll?" he replies:

> Ah God, if I only knew
> I might learn the place where Heaven is,
> And a light-swift path thereto.

"Babel: The Gate of the God" represents man's endeavor to reach "the place where Heaven is" by the force of imagination.

> Nimroud stands up conceiving he shall live
> To conquer god, now that he knows where god is.

Meanwhile "Little men hurrying, running here and there," chatter their bigoted disagreements as to precisely where in the tower an altar should be erected and precisely what it should look like. From their petty notions about God, not from Nimroud's mad but noble ambition, result the confusion of tongues and the collapse of the great work of art. Nimroud's failure was humiliating, but also partly encouraging, to the romantic faith. Here man was,

> In the last courses, building past his knowledge
> A wall that swung—for towers can have no tops,
> No chord can mete the universal segment,
> Earth has no basis. Yet the yielding sky,
> Invincible vacancy, was there discovered.[6]

The discovery that Heaven is vacant leaves man free to fill it with his own imaginative creations, secure in the knowledge that they are as true as anything can be true in this world of illusion.

Within the realm of art, then, man is the Creator. But the limits of that realm must scrupulously be observed: there must be no pretense that the illusion possesses extra-aesthetic validity. This is the price that the twentieth-century romantic must pay for the privilege of autonomy. In **"A Hymn of Imagination"**, Bottomley insists on the distinction between "Imagination," whose "murmurings" within us constitute "The only conscience that is not pride," and "Baseless Invention," which "sets man to believe himself his guide." The operative word is "baseless."

> The nourishing of religions in Invention,
> Wonders and furbishings;
> There merchants of the incredible, in contention,
> Postulate Divinity apart
> From knowledge or perception; crude desire
> Seeks an Unknown for gaping at, a mart
> Where virtue whips God's first debentures higher:
> . . . . .
> Imagination does not thus devise
> Wilful and rootless miracles.

Its essence, on the contrary, is

> Ability to conceive the nature
> Of every creature, every stature,
> Ability to live in every form,
> To know the passions that have passed,
> Stillness or storm,
> In nobler hearts or hearts of sin—
> All things without at last
> Answering to things within.[7]

In short Imagination seeks not to deny outward reality, still less to dominate it, but to enter into empathetic union with it. This is the gospel of Keats, not of Blake or Shelley.

Bottomley would disentangle poetry from its traditional supernatural associations. In **"Atlantis"** he declares that the Platonic ideal of Beauty may or may not abide everlastingly "in Nirvana or the Heavenly courts," but that

> Its body of poetry, as the body of man,
> Is but a terrene form, a terrene use,
> That swifter being will not loiter with;
> And when mankind is dead and the world cold,
> Poetry's immortality will pass.

"A Hymn of Touch" lauds the earthiest, most immediate, least subject to sentimentalizing of the senses. Contact is the vitalizing element in *all* sense-experience.[8]

Still more revelatory of his aesthetic philosophy is **"A Hymn of Form."** Form is "eternal father of existence," "The holy virtue of living, the soul's delight,"

> The change of a short season,
> Nude rhythm, no growth, no lesion,

That makes a worm be earth, wet earth be a tree:
The building of deity, and then
The unbuilding of deity again
And calling God by a new name
To keep Him yet awhile the same:

      . . . . .

By dark recurrence alone we grow
Endless, immortal, godlike, bare,
And do not care.

      . . . . .

This is the instinct of our perfecting:
The lust of creation, the ache for forming,
The mathematic beauty warming
As intellectual exact ardours sting
Till proud inevitable solutions spring.[9]

Coherence is not the salient characteristic of this hymn in praise of aesthetic order. Nevertheless Bottomley's emphasis on a free creativity whose ardors are restricted but also validated by the precision of mathematical beauty suggests that if the circumstances of his life had been different he might have played an important part in formulating the doctrine of the "modern poem." He clearly illustrates the quasi-religious motivation of that desperate stronghold of the romantic faith.

Notes

1. *Poems and Plays*, p. 23. The whole body of Bottomley's work has never been collected. By far the most comprehensive volume of selections is the *Poems of Thirty Years*, brought together by Bottomley himself in 1925. It includes everything that I have quoted. But Professor C. Colleer Abbott, the poet's literary executor, grants me permission to quote on condition that whenever possible I cite his own selective edition, *Poems and Plays* (1953). References in this section to *Poems of Thirty Years* pertain to poems not included in Professor Abbott's edition.

2. *Ibid.*, p. 31.

3. *Poems of Thirty Years*, pp. 31-33, 79.

4. *Poems and Plays*, pp. 41, 63.

5. *Poems of Thirty Years*, pp. 84-94 *passim*.

6. *Ibid.*, pp. 26-29, 81.

7. *Poems and Plays*, pp. 42-43.

8. *Ibid.*, pp. 25, 46-48.

9. *Ibid.*, p. 50.

William V. Spanos (essay date 1967)

SOURCE: "The Historical Pageant: The Rhetoric of Action," in *The Christian Tradition in Modern British Verse Drama: The Poetics of Sacramental Time*, Rutgers University Press, 1967, pp. 58-63.

[*In the following excerpt, Spanos focuses on the religious pageant* The Acts of Saint Peter.]

Like the post-Romantic poetic Histories, the pre-Canterbury Pageant drama sought to infuse poetry into Biblical events by locating the action, through verbal and visual decor, in a remote past. It achieved instead a "charming medievalism" and a pious sentimentality. Charles Clay's famous *The Joyous Pageant of the Holy Nativity,* written in the early twenties, is a notable example.[1]

Gordon Bottomley's pageant, **The Acts of Saint Peter,** written for the octocentenary celebrations of the consecration of the Cathedral Church of St. Peter at Exeter a decade later (1933), represents a significant advance over these and, in some respects, over his own earlier efforts. There is in the sequence of action a symbolic significance and in the verse a contemporaneity traceable to the pressure of an embryonic conception of sacramental time that is utterly foreign to the great majority of earlier religious plays. Yet insofar as the concept of sacramental time is imperfectly conceived, Bottomley's pageant fails to achieve the special dramatic rhetoric that depends on a sense of the continuity of past and present actions. It provides therefore an instructive example of a transitional Christian verse play.

Conceived in epic terms, the pageant is divided into twelve loosely connected episodes in the life of the Apostle. More important, however, is the broader structural division into two equal parts: the first culminating in the Crucifixion (Episode VI), following Peter's denial of Christ; and the second, in Peter's final acceptance of Christ's burden and his own crucifixion in Rome (Episode XII). Preceding each episode a Chorus representing the modern church (though it is not clearly projected) comments omnisciently on the action directly to the audience.

This outline immediately suggests that Bottomley conceives the double action figurally. Peter's crucifixion is analogous to Christ's, and both establish a recurrent redemptive pattern that, with the interpretive commentary of the Chorus, is to engage the imagination of a contemporary audience. The suggestion of the recurrent pattern is further emphasized by the fact that during each crucifixion the Chorus modulates into a funereal chant employing the same three-stress rhythm and the same opening line. Thus after John expresses his desperate hope that Rome's wisdom, in the person of Pilate, will save Christ, the Chorus introduces the moving Crucifixion scene:

    Rome's wisdom failed
    Cold, secure, blind.
    The spent night paled;
    Earth's heavy mind

    With dawn woke in gloom
    And dark fierce flame.
    With whips, cross, tomb
    His Kingdom came.[2]

And following the Roman soldiers' binding of Peter to a cross, the Chorus again breaks out:

Rome's wisdom failed,
Hard, secure, blind.
Although not assailed;
Heedlessly, undesigned.

An old, unknown man
Out of obscurity
In innocence began
A state no eye could see.

                                                                    [p. 81]

The significance of these choruses becomes more clear when it is seen that this striking verse pattern is used only for these scenes.

To enhance further the sense of historical continuity, the several episodes are given at least a modicum of psychological realism. Episode I, for example, depicting Andrew's and Peter's departure from home to follow Jesus, is projected as a relatively realistic family situation in which both mother and wife (Peter's), each in her own way, obstinately and bitterly refuse to understand the brothers' call. On occasion, however—Episode XI for example, which presents the conversion of the gay Roman prostitutes—the narrow bounds of the scene inhibit the full development of characters and result in a violation of probability.

Finally the verse represents a movement in the direction urged by the concept of sacramental time. Though on the whole it fails to achieve distinction, it does have at least the negative value of avoiding the archaisms of diction and rhythm that give so many of the pre-Canterbury religious and secular history plays the hothouse aura that alienates a contemporary audience. At its best, as in the moving Crucifixion scene, the dialogue achieves a restrained and poignant dramatic power. This scene, because of Bottomley's adroit management of point of view, has been called "the best, as well as the most economical dramatization" of this phase of the Christian narrative "in our time."[3] As the light begins to fail and Christ's voice and the derisive shouts of the mob assail the remorseful Peter, who has just denied Jesus for the third time, the guilt-ridden Judas enters to demand his company as a right:

JUDAS: Peter . . . Peter . . .

PETER: *as though awakening*: Who is it?

JUDAS: I . . . Judas . . .

     (PETER *returns to his concentration of anguish*.)

JUDAS: You will have to speak to me.
I shall wait until you do: it is my right.
You denied Him: you cannot reject my company.

PETER: My punishment begins.
It is true. What then? Do you dare
To come where He is dying, as I dare?

JUDAS: You and I have only each other now.
We dare not go to the others, or even go home.

We have each forsaken Jesus: He is dying yonder:
It is uniting us for ever, Peter
I cannot let you go.

                                                                    [pp. 37-38]

The great difference in the diction between this and the pseudo-Shakespearean echoes of, say, Laurence Housman's *Little Plays of St. Francis* ("Sweet night, how we have fouled thee! Into thy fold / Have come like wolves, and all the flocks of peace / Into a howling wilderness have scattered!"[4]) or even of Bottomley's earliest work, is obvious. It only remains to point out that the traditional blank verse line becomes in *The Acts* a freer structure, modulating according to the dramatic situation between a primary 5-stress and a secondary 3-stress pattern (each containing an indefinite number of syllables) that, in its suggestion of contemporary speech rhythms, points toward the later experiments in dramatic verse of T. S. Eliot and other post-World War I Christian dramatists, particularly Ronald Duncan and Anne Ridler.

And yet, in the last analysis, because he does not follow through the implications of sacramental time, Bottomley fails to absorb the temporal into the eternal, the concrete into the universal, and thus to give a genuine poetic significance to the Biblical action he is imitating. A fundamental contradiction exists between the two actions that should be analogical. In the first part, the drama centers around the irony of Peter's own denial of Christ after his censure of others (his mother, his wife, and Judas) for not believing. In the second part, however, though the action ends in his own martyrdom, Peter's unwillingness to seek safety from the Romans suggests his failure to fulfill the commitment to the burden of the Cross which he undertook in repenting his apostasy. Rather, he gives himself up to the Romans' persecution out of a kind of world-weariness—"I cannot stay with you always. It would not be long, / And I desire the end of this endless living. / Let it come now. . . . Here. . . . Alone . . ." (p. 78). This, like the "angelic" attitude toward the ravages of the temporal of Bottomley's drama of the pagan British past, runs counter to the sacramental view of time. His crucifixion, therefore, does not convey a sense of redemptive force. Indeed, the general emotional tone of the play works against nature. It suggests not only that the world is a sad, even terrible, place but also that life is a futile ordeal better avoided. This is the theme, for example, of the episode of Lazarus and the daughter of Jairus (Episode II), both of whom have been resurrected from the dead. Lazarus recognizes that they have been revivified by

The still indifference that denies
All that it looks on in vain
Desire to see again—again—
Places, presences, lights, all strange
By beauty never due to change.

                                                                    [p. 15]

The implication, of course, is that one comes to heaven by rejecting nature rather than through nature.

Furthermore, though the function of the Chorus is apparently to engage a modern audience in the contemporaneous significance of the action, to relate the past action and the present audience in an act of communion celebrating the continuity of history, it does so only on occasion. The choric commentary following Peter's departure from home, where it excuses modern man for his failure to affirm because "Dark powers have interfered" (p. 10), is one of these occasions, but on the whole the choric commentary focuses too consistently on the specific past action instead of enlarging its sphere of significance. The lack of modern references, in itself a negative attribute, is symptomatic of this basic failure.

Despite its innovations, **The Acts of Saint Peter** is thus a play about a weak man who, too weary to continue the temporal struggle of Christendom, commits a kind of suicide in order to get to heaven, where he can find the rest he ardently desires. As such, the play fails to fulfill the poetic potential implicit in the sacramental aesthetic.

Notes

1. Terence Vale, "Lest One Good Custom," *Christian Drama*, I, 5 (February, 1948), 11. Vale's article reviews the twenty-fifth anniversary of Clay's pageant. His criticism of its flamboyance and its aura of pastness reflects the new approach to religious drama. But his interpretation of the new movement to achieve a truly timeless mode of experience as one leading toward a highly "stylized, conventionalized, and abstract" drama analogous to the Byzantine mosaics of San Appollinaire is misleading. Though it does reflect a tendency of the Christian drama movement, it does not recognize the operation, even in the early plays, of the sacramental aesthetic. His argument assumes the separation of time and eternity that sacramentalism reconciles and thus is a manifestation of the angelic imagination.

2. Gordon Bottomley, *The Acts of Saint Peter: A Cathedral Festival Play* (London, 1933), pp. 34-35. Further page references will be incorporated in the text in parentheses.

3. E. Martin Browne, in a review of *Poet and Painter, Being the Correspondence of Gordon Bottomley and Paul Nash, 1910-1946*, ed. Colleer Abbott and Anthony Bertram (London, 1955), *Drama*, 37 (Summer, 1955), 6-7.

4. Laurence Housman, *Little Plays of St. Francis: A Dramatic Cycle from the Life and Legend of St. Francis of Assisi* (New York, no date), p. 19.

FURTHER READING

Criticism

Clarke, Austin. Review of *Lyric Plays*, by Gordon Bottomley. *Life and Letters* 8, No. 47 (December 1932): 488-89.

Favorable appraisal, concluding that with the works in the volume "Bottomley has revolutionized the form of verse drama."

————. "Gordon Bottomley." *The London Mercury*, XXXIX, No. 234 (April 1939): 658.

Favorable review of *Choric Plays*, identifying *Dunaverty* as "the most powerful example of the new form in which Mr. Bottomley has been working."

Kendon, Frank. "Three Poets of Today." *The Bookman*, London, LXXVI, No. 456 (September 1929): 302-03.

Review of *Scenes and Plays*. Kendon concludes that the "poetry here is purposely flattened, and all the dramatic active quality is taken away. Yet it goes without saying that Mr. Gordon Bottomley's plays are, in their mode, effective; as poetry they are strangely and remotely beautiful, though entirely unreal."

Mason, Eugene. Review of *Gruach and Britain's Daughter*, by Gordon Bottomley. *The Bookman*, London, LXI, No. 363 (December 1921): 2-3, Christmas supplement.

Highly appreciative assessment.

Meyer, John H. "The Too Easily Lost." *Poetry*, 86, No. 6 (September 1955): 363-65.

Discusses the strengths and limitations of Bottomley's poetry and drama in a review of *Poems and Plays*.

Squire, J. C. Review of *A Vision of Giorgione*, by Gordon Bottomley. *The London Mercury*, VIII, No. 44 (June 1923): 206.

Brief favorable notice of the British edition of *A Vision of Giorgione*.

Twitchett, E. G. Review of *Scenes and Plays*, by Gordon Bottomley. *The London Mercury*, XX, No. 119 (September 1929): 528-30.

Praises Bottomley's concept of chamber-drama.

Additional coverage of Bottomley's life and career is contained in the following sources published by the Gale Group: *Contemporary Authors*, **Vol. 120; and** *Dictionary of Literary Biography*, **Vol. 10.**

Robert Buchanan
1841-1901

English poet, novelist, playwright, and critic.

INTRODUCTION

A controversial figure in Victorian literature, Buchanan was out of sympathy with the leading figures of his age, chiefly the Pre-Raphaelites Dante Gabriel Rossetti and Algernon Charles Swinburne. Deriding the efforts of what he termed "the fleshly school of poetry," Buchanan wrote work expressive of his fluctuating moral views and his strong opinions on social and political matters. The chief influences on his literary style were the Romantic poets John Keats, George Gordon, and Lord Byron. Buchanan, out of financial need, penned a number of plays and novels of decidedly inferior quality.

BIOGRAPHICAL INFORMATION

Born in Staffordshire, England, to a Scottish socialist and a woman whose father was a prominent radical lawyer, Buchanan inherited his parents' political convictions. By the time he moved to Glasgow for his university studies, however, he also had developed a taste for poetry. With his friend David Gray, he moved to London with the intention of living the life of a poet. Instead, he found himself acting, writing journalism, and married to a sixteen-year-old girl whose younger sister he adopted. (Harriett Jay, the adopted daughter, went on to write Buchanan's biography.) He eventually managed to publish short stories and verse; a collection of poems titled *Undertones* was issued in 1863. The book was well received by Robert Browning, George Eliot, and Eliot's mentor and partner George Henry Lewes, and Buchanan developed a particularly close association with Thomas Love Peacock.

Buchanan reportedly suffered a nervous breakdown after his father's death in 1866. The disturbances he underwent accentuated his displeasure with what he considered the amoral excesses of Swinburne and Rossetti. This displeasure extended to the poets' lives as well as their works, and Buchanan vented his feelings in *The Fleshly School of Poetry and Other Phenomena of the Day* (1872). The book created a stir in London literary circles and left its author alienated from those who had been his friends and supporters. He then lived for short periods in Scotland and Ireland.

Buchanan returned to London in 1878, founding a short-lived literary journal called *Light*. By this time his poetic aspirations were constantly put aside for his desire to be

heard on political interests and his ambitions toward popular, rather than distinguished, achievement in the theater. He wrote editorials on numerous issues of the day, including vivisection, the rights of women, and, in 1890, the fate of the Irish nationalist leader Charles Stewart Parnell, whose career had been derailed by an illicit affair. Five years later, Buchanan spoke up on behalf of Oscar Wilde when the controversial poet and dramatist became embroiled in a ruinous lawsuit. He also championed the poetry of Walt Whitman and traveled to meet the American poet in New Jersey in 1884.

After a series of theatrical successes with such melodramas as *Alone in London* (1885) and *Sophia* (1886), his adaptation of Henry Fielding's novel *Tom Jones*, Buchanan began to take risks on careless productions, and his confrontational style often stood in the way of business matters. The playwright met with financial ruin in 1894, and bankruptcy proceedings began the same month his mother died. After repeated struggles to set his financial life in order, Buchanan suffered a stroke in 1900 and died the following year.

MAJOR WORKS

Best remembered for his critical attack on the Pre-Raphaelite poets, Buchanan produced great amounts of poetry, drama, and fiction that have not approached a comparable level of fame. *Undertones*, written as a series of dramatic monologues set in ancient Greece and Rome, was followed by *Idyls and Legends of Inverburn* (1865), which practiced the same technique but transferred the setting to Scotland. He was, however, capable of other styles: *Saint Abe and His Seven Wives: A Tale of Salt Lake City* (1872) was a satire on Mormon polygamy; *Effie Hetherington* (1896) presented a fictional consideration of prostitution. Buchanan's collected works also include detective stories and speculative fiction.

CRITICAL RECEPTION

After the promise of his first published works, Buchanan's literary reputation was uneven at best. William Michael Rossetti, writing in defense of his brother Dante, jeered at Buchanan as a "poor and pretentious poetaster," although given the circumstances this judgment is clearly biased. However, when *The Spectator* labeled Buchanan's novel *Stormy Waters: A Story of To-Day* (1885) "unworthy of the merest literary hack," there is no indication that the harshness of the judgment was due to personal animosity.

PRINCIPAL WORKS

The Rathboys [with Charles Gibbon] (drama) 1862

Storm Beaten; or, Christmas Eve at the "Old Anchor" Inn [with Charles Gibbon] (drama) 1862

Undertones (poetry) 1863

The Witch Finder (drama) 1864

Idyls and Legends of Inverburn (poetry) 1865

Ballad Stories of the Affections: From the Scandinavian (poetry) 1866

London Poems (poetry) 1866

David Gray and Other Essays, Chiefly on Poetry (essays) 1868

North Coast and Other Poems (poetry) 1868

The Book of Orm: A Prelude to the Epic (poetry) 1870

Napoleon Fallen: A Lyrical Drama (poetry) 1870

The Drama of Kings (poetry) 1871

The Land of Lorne 2 vols. (essays) 1871

The Fleshly School of Poetry and Other Phenomena of the Day (essays) 1872

Saint Abe and His Seven Wives: A Tale of Salt Lake City (poetry) 1872

Master-Spirits (essays) 1873

White Rose and Red: A Love Story (poetry) 1873

A Madcap Prince (drama) 1874

The Poetical Works 3 vols. (poetry) 1874

Corinne (drama) 1876

The Shadow of the Sword (novel) 1876

Balder the Beautiful: A Song of Divine Death (poetry) 1877

The Nine Days' Queen (drama) 1880

A Child of Nature (novel) 1881

The Exiles of Erin (drama) 1881

Foxglove Manor (novel) 1881

God and the Man (novel) 1881

The Shadow of the Sword (drama) 1881

Ballads of Life, Love and Humour (poetry) 1882

The Hebrid Isles (essays) 1882

Love Me Forever (novel) 1882

Lucy Brandon (drama) 1882

The Martyrdom of Madeline (novel) 1882

Selected Poems (poetry) 1882

Annan Water (novel) 1883

Lady Clare (drama) 1883

The New Abelard (novel) 1883

A Poet's Sketch-Book: Selections from the Prose Writings of Robert Buchanan (essays) 1883

A Sailor and His Lass [with Augustus Harris] (drama) 1883

Stormbeaten (drama) 1883

Bachelors [with H. Vezin] (drama) 1884

The Poetical Works 2 vols. (poetry) 1884

Agnes (drama) 1885

Alone in London [with Harriett Jay] (drama) 1885

The Earthquake; or, Six Days and a Sabbath (poetry) 1885

The Master of the Mine (novel) 1885

Matt: A Story of a Caravan (novel) 1885

Stormy Waters: A Story of To-Day (novel) 1885

Sophia (drama) 1886

That Winter Night; or, Love's Victory (novel) 1886

The Blue Bells of Scotland (drama) 1887

A Dark Night's Bridal (drama) 1887

Fascination [with Harriet Jay] (drama) 1887

A Look Round Literature (criticism) 1887

The Queen of Connaught (drama) 1887

The City of Dream: An Epic Poem (poetry) 1888

The Heir of Linne (novel) 1888

Joseph's Sweetheart (drama) 1888

Partners (drama) 1888

Roger-la-Honte (drama) 1888

The Man and the Woman (drama) 1889

The Old Home (drama) 1889

On Descending into Hell: A Letter Addressed to the Right Hon. Henry Matthews, Q.C., Home Secretary, Concerning the Proposed Suppression of Literature (essay) 1889

That Doctor Cupid (drama) 1889

Theodora (drama) 1889

The Bride of Love (drama) 1890

Clarissa (drama) 1890

The English Rose [with G. R. Sims] (drama) 1890

Miss Tomboy (drama) 1890

The Moment After: A Tale of the Unseen (novel) 1890

The Sixth Commandment (drama) 1890

The Struggle for Life [with Frederick Horner] (drama) 1890

Sweet Nancy (drama) 1890

Come, Live with Me and Be My Love (novel) 1891

The Coming Terror and Other Essays and Letters (essays and letters) 1891

The Gifted Lady (drama) 1891

Marmion (drama) 1891

The Outcast: A Rhyme for the Time (poetry) 1891

The Roll of the Drum [with G. R. Sims] (drama) 1891

The Wedding Ring: A Tale of To-Day (novel) 1891

The Lights of Home [with G. R. Sims] (drama) 1892

The White Rose [with G. R. Sims] (drama) 1892

The Black Domino [with G. R. Sims] (drama) 1893

The Piper of Hamelin: A Fantastic Opera in Two Acts [with F. W. Allwood] (opera) 1893

The Wandering Jew: A Christmas Carol (poetry) 1893

The Woman and the Man (novel) 1893

The Charlatan (drama) 1894

Dick Sheridan (drama) 1894

Lady Gladys (drama) 1894

Rachel Dene: A Tale of the Deepdale Mills (novel) 1894

Red and White Heather: North Country Tales and Ballads (poetry and short stories) 1894

A Society Butterfly (drama) 1894

The Charlatan [with Henry Murray] (novel) 1895

Diana's Hunting (novel) 1895

Lady Kilpatrick (novel) 1895

The Strange Adventures of Miss Brown [with Harriett Jay] (drama) 1895

The Devil's Case: A Bank Holiday Interlude (poetry) 1896

Effie Hetherington (novel) 1896

Is Barabbas a Necessity? (essay) 1896

A Marriage by Capture: A Romance of To-Day (novel) 1896

The New Don Quixote [with Harriett Jay] (drama) 1896

The Romance of the Shopwalker [with Harriet Jay] (drama) 1896

The Wanderer from Venus [with Harriett Jay] (drama) 1896

The Ballad of Mary the Mother: A Christmas Carol (poetry) 1897

The Mariners of England [with Harriett Jay] (drama) 1897

Father Anthony: A Romance of To-Day (novel) 1898

The New Rome: Poems and Ballads of Our Empire (poetry) 1898

The Rev. Annabel Lee (novel) 1898

Two Little Maids from School [with Harriett Jay] (drama) 1898

Andromeda: An Idyll of the Great River (novel) 1900

The Voice of "The Hooligan": A Discussion of Kiplingism [with Walter Besant] (criticism) 1900

Complete Poetical Works 2 vols. (poetry) 1901

CRITICISM

The Nation (essay date 1866)

SOURCE: A review of *Poems*, in *The Nation*, New York, Vol. 2, No. 27, January 4, 1866, pp. 22-4.

[*The following essay offers a review of* Undertones *and* Idyls and Legends of Iverburn.]

One has not to read far in this collection of Mr. Buchanan's poetry to see that he is a poet, but one should read it through before deciding on his defects and merits. This is due to him as well as to most young poets, the present transition school of verse reflecting so positively the characteristics of two or three of its masters that originality is about the last thing we look to find in a new disciple. Mr. Buchanan is an original poet, the reader will discover, but not to any great extent in his first volume, **Undertones,** which contains nineteen poems on what may be carelessly considered classical subjects, exclusive of the poet's prologue, **"To David in Heaven,"** and his epilogue, **"To Mary on Earth."** The former of these superfluous productions is commemorative of David Gray, the young Scottish poet, who came up to London with Mr. Buchanan some half-a-dozen or more years ago, with the wildest notions of what he would accomplish, looking for nothing less than immediate reputation, and, finally, a monument in Westminster Abbey, but who, poor fellow, soon died, leaving his unpublished verse to the tender care of Lord Houghton, Mr. Buchanan, and the pity of the English public. As a tribute to the memory of his friend, the prologue does honor to Mr. Buchanan's feelings; as a poem, it is scarcely more than a bad compound of the mannerisms of both the Brownings, particularly of the peculiar cadences and rhythms of Mrs. Browning, the jarring imperfection of whose double rhymes it caricatures. What can be worse, for instance, than such rhymes as "also" and "falls so," "you thought" and "truth ought," and "silence" and "mile hence?" The enthusiasm of the poem is of a cheap order, and, of course, vastly overrates the dead poet who is its subject.

About one-half of the classical poems are on mythological themes, and it is not so much the fault of the poet as of the time that they are not informed with the true Greek spirit. A good deal of supposed Greek poetry has been written in England within the last forty or fifty years, but we can recall only two poets who seem to have been Greeks by nature—John Keats and Walter Savage Landor, the latter a perfect pagan in more senses than one. We should include, perhaps, in this catalogue the Tennyson of "Enone" and "Ulysses," Mr. Matthew Arnold, whose little-known tragedy of "Merope" is a noble antique, and Mr. Algernon Charles Swinburne, whose "Atlanta in Calydon" is a notable production for a young man. As these poets, however, and others who might be named, have achieved their greatest successes in the school of romantic art, they can hardly be added to the list of really Greek poets. What the present rage for Homeric translation will end in cannot be foreseen, but hardly, we conjecture, in a new race of Greek poets in England. The defect of most of the modern attempts at Greek poetry comes from what may be called the reflective character of the modern mind, which is not content to exercise itself upon the simply sensuous element of Greek literature—the beautiful fictions of its divinities and the more or less historical legends of its heroes—but is fain to find something deeper in both, to impart some of its own tendencies to them; in short,

"To point a moral and adorn a tale."

This is a grave mistake, however skillfully it may be concealed, and, of course, Mr. Buchanan shares it in common with his contemporaries. The first of his semi-mythological poems, **"Proteus,"** is not an endeavor to embody the old Greek ideal of a for ever changing deity, as the reader might naturally expect from its title, but an attempt to indicate on a broader scale the play of the eternal law of change, especially as shown in human creeds. Even in this it is not successful, since it is too brief to touch upon even the strong points of the ancient and modern mythologies. The theme of the next poem, **"Ades,"** is much finer, but its execution is in no sense Greek, though it is certainly meritorious from the stand-point of the present schools of verse. Its chief faults are an entire absence of the dramatic, and an overwhelming presence of the descriptive, faculty—Ades, the speaker, never for a moment reminding us of himself, but always of the poet, whose puppet he is, and who makes him describe, in detail, his subterranean kingdom, the appearance of Persephone above him, how the earth looked around her, how he felt, what she did, etc., etc., through forty pretty stanzas. So abundant, indeed, are the details that the poem, as a whole, leaves no definite impression on the mind.

"Pan," which is in a higher mood, is a fair specimen of Mr. Buchanan's blank verse, which flows smoothly, after the luxuriant models of the day. It is picturesque as a matter of course. **"The Satyr"** would be a genuine Greek poem but for an occasional gleam of the over-refining modern element. The wild, rambling melody of its verse is well handled.

"Polypheme's Passion" contains some very clever writing, but can hardly be considered successful. The trivial part of Silenus is much better done than the more ambitious one of Polypheme, who may have been "spoony" on Galatea, but not to the extent that Mr. Buchanan portrays when he makes the grim old Cyclops say:

> "That I have learned to tremble and to blush,
> To drop this eyelid modestly, to flush
> All over at the tiniest whispering sound,
> To pick small dainty steps upon the ground,
> As if I saw, and, seeing, fear'd to crush
> Some crawling insect or the crimson-crown'd
> Small daisy-flower that, wheresoe'er I pass,
> Shuts up its little leaves upon the grass,
> And thinks the shadowy eve has stolen down."

This is pretty poetry, certainly, but it does not suit the mouth of Polypheme even in love. Note, too, the excessive detail of this description of himself, which illustrates a vicious species of elaboration now very much in fashion:

> "Unto the beach
> I wearily strode, with great head bowed, and dragg'd
> Foot echoes after me; and with no speech
> On yonder shore, weedy and wet and cragg'd,
> I stood, and in an agony of pain,
> Look'd out with widening eyeball on the main."

Equally false and absurdly Gothic for a Greek poem is this picture of a sea-nymph, who is clearly the modern mermaid:

> "I saw, far down upon the brown sea-strand,
> A nymph, who held aloft in pearly hand
> A white-toothed comb, and comb'd her locks of gold
> Over a dank and shipwreck'd sailor lad."

"Penelope" is, perhaps, the best sustained of all Mr. Buchanan's would-be classical poems. The blank verse is often majestic, though it lacks compactness, and occasionally lets the reader down with such atrocious lines as these:

> "Grown like the sampler coarse-complexionéd."

> "Of tannéd haycocks and of slanted sheaves."

> "And not a marinere, or man, or boy."

And such patent Tennysonisms as these:

> "The ships
> Have dipt up moistly from the under-world."

> "Hast pluckt upon the windy plain of Troy."

Excellent as **"Penelope"** is, on the whole, an American poet—Mr. E. C. Stedman—has managed the same theme more artistically in a volume of "Lyrics and Idyls," published by him some five or six years since, and to which we refer the reader who may wish to compare his mode of treatment with Mr. Buchanan's.

"The Siren" is the most melodious piece of versification in the *Undertones,* its minor ditties being as perfect of their kind as the exquisite little lyrics which Shelley seemed to write so easily. The conception of **"Pygmalion the Sculptor"** is, in some respects, fine, but the execution is quite bad, suggesting the earlier poetic writings of Mr. Alexander Smith. The fourth section, which depicts the awakening of the statue unto life, is much the best portion of the poem. **"Fine Weather on the Digentia"** is a rollicking bit of heathenism, which is very pleasant reading, though we are not certain that we like its over-fluent measures.

Enough, however, in the way of quotation from, and quotation upon, Mr. Buchanan's *Undertones,* which we leave to his readers for whatever they choose to think them worth; except as poetical promises they have no value in our eyes. Very different are his *Idyls and Legends of Inverburn,* a series of short pieces, mostly in blank verse, and on the commonest of themes, pages and chapters selected almost at random from that large and never-finished volume of tears and smiles,

> "The short but simple annals of the poor."

We can recall nothing precisely like them in English poetry, and we have not forgotten the early idyllic flights of Wordsworth in such poems as "The Brothers," and one or two episodes in "The Excursion," the few good blank verse pieces of Coleridge, as "The Nightingale," "Frost at Midnight," etc., and the idyls of the Laureate, who has surpassed both these poets in idyllic writing, as he has most of the singers of his time, delineating the ordinary life of the English people with Flemish fidelity in "Dora," and that of the upper classes with almost an Italian richness of color in "The Gardener's Daughter." To say that Mr. Buchanan's idyls can be read with pleasure after Tennyson's, is to bestow high praise upon them. It speaks well, too, for his poetic growth since the *Undertones,* and for the native strength of his genius, that his manner of handling his subjects is entirely his own, and generally just what a correct artistic taste would have dictated. His verse is fresh, natural, and apparently unstudied, flowing along as musically as a country brook. A slight flavor of his native tongue, in the shape of a few expressive Scottish phrases, which hardly need the glossary that he has given, adds, we think, to its charm, and imparts an air of reality to his creations, the best of which are invariably those which are the least ambitious. **"Willie Baird,"** for instance, the story of an old Scottish schoolmaster whose favorite pupil, Willie Baird, was lost in the snow, is a model of the simple and pathetic in narrative verse; as is likewise **"Poet Andrew,"** a touching idyl on the life and death of David Gray; and, better still, **"The English Huswife's Gossip,"** a bit of cottage-chat about a weak-witted, tender-hearted natural, crossed in love. As a faithful study of character, we know of nothing finer in the whole range of English poetry. Admirable, also, is **"The Two Babes,"** in which we have a glimpse of the canny side of the Scottish character, and **"The Widow Mysie,"** which is the best thing in the way of humor that Mr. Buchanan has yet done. The more romantic pieces—as **"Lord Ronald's Wife,"** **"White Lily of Weardale Head,"** **"The Fairy Fostermother,"** **"The Green Gnome,"** **"The Legend of the Stepmother,"** **"The Minister and the Elfin,"** and **"The Legend of the Little Fay"**—please us less, partly because they do not seem to have come so naturally as the idyls, and partly because they suggest other poems and poets. They are better, however, than any of the rhythmical pieces in the *Undertones,* and show that Mr. Buchanan is learning the musical part of his art with commendable rapidity. **"A London Idyl,"** which the American publishers have added to their reprint from the pages of the *Fortnightly Review,* is a remarkable poem, in which the poet has completely triumphed over the difficulties of his subject—the vexed question of "the social evil"—producing a worthy companion-piece to Hood's famous "Bridge of Sighs," if not, indeed, surpassing that pathetic work of art.

That we think highly of Mr. Buchanan the reader may, perhaps, infer from what we have written, despite the fault which we found with him at the beginning. He seems to us one of the few young singers of the day who is really a poet, and who has a future before him.

The North American Review **(review date 1866)**

SOURCE: A review of *Poems,* in *The North American Review,* Vol. 102, No. 210, January, 1866, pp. 555-56.

[*In the following review, a critic discusses strengths and weaknesses of* Poems.]

The invasion of ancient Hellas from the East by force of arms seems to have been no less distinctly a failure, than the modern attack from the West by force of imagination. Her new strategy is a masterly inactivity; strangers may come to her shores and she makes no resistance; they may climb her hills, may listen to her brooks, may peer into her caves, but the Gods and Muses are not there, and no invader can find the living source of the old poetry. When men worshipped, the Gods fought side by side with them in native strength and thunder; but they scoff at those who ransack their temples and kneel at their shrines for spoils, and remain veiled.

We doubt if it be possible for a modern to treat classical literary subjects in the classical manner; for it is not by the power of imitation, but of total change in mind and heart, that such a triumph of genius can be attained. For how shall a gentleman of the last half of the nineteenth century, who moves by steam, learns by gas, writes by telegraph, fights with gunpowder, reads print, sails by the needle, knows of political economy, electricity, and comparative philology, teaches his children that the sun does not rise in the east, that the moon is a mirror, and that the whole universe is an illusion, conceive of the world without these things? To reproduce the first Olympiad he must have a mind capable of believing the earth supported by a tortoise, of peopling the trees, rivers, and winds with gods and demigods, and a heart so formed that it can worship beings combining divine power with the meanest and most brutal passions, for it is to worshippers, not sceptical philosophers, that the Muses sing.

If Mr. Buchanan has not done this, he has done the next best thing, and, feeling the impossibility, has abandoned the attempt. A Scotch Eumolpus, in the clutches of the Siren, he says,

> "Where am I, where?
> Where is my country, and that vision olden?"

and with better fortune than Eumolpus, has the luck to be able to bid the Siren firmly, though politely, farewell, and return to the land of his birth. Not but that he has brought back some very pretty poetry, but it is not Grecian poetry.

Indeed, now that Mr. Buchanan has got back to Scotland, he must himself wonder how he could ever have been such a gad-about; for he belongs peculiarly to Britain, and the Britain too of our day. In his poetry may be continually traced the effect upon English literature of his predecessors and contemporaries. He has studied the expression of simplicity under Wordsworth, of force under Browning, of sentiment under Tennyson, while he shows the delicate dramatic power in the portraiture of character which an age of analytic novel-writing has produced. We do not speak of him as a copyist,—he apes no one; but he is limited as yet by those bounds of time and space which original and greatest genius does not know; and the die of his age has left its impress on him,—a die making him current for the time. His poems are not the pure nuggets of gold as they come from the mine, but after they have passed through the mint, and become national by having a little home-made alloy put in them.

Mr. Buchanan has imagination and humor, a great deal of very pretty fancy, and has shown in one or two poems—as, for example, **"Hugh Sutherland's Pansies"**—an excellent perception of form. He has genuine faith, tenderness, and manliness, and shows self-command in his choice of dramatic rather than lyrical forms. The great genius which can use to the highest purpose all these qualities he has not yet shown; but let those who doubt whether he may show it at least give him the benefit of their doubt.

The Nation (review date 1867)

SOURCE: A review of *North Coast and Other Poems,* in *The Nation,* New York, Vol. 5, No. 130, December 26, 1867, pp. 524-25.

[*In the following review, a reviewer identifies strong points and shortcomings in* North Coast and Other Poems.]

Mr. Buchanan's strength as a writer seems to lie almost wholly in the fulness and tenderness of his sympathy with the poor, the unfortunate and the criminal, the lowly and the low. He says in the prelude to his miscellaneous poems:

> "My full heart hungers out unto the stainèd."

So it does. We may add that this hunger is not often expressed with much more of force or beauty than in the verse above quoted. We should not send any one to his poetry for anything more than the pathos of the facts of daily life in "the cottages where poor men lie"; the huts and cells where men and women lie whom poverty has driven into crime or error. And we should beforehand advise the reader not to expect that Mr. Buchanan either greatly heightens the pathos of the facts or beautifies it by the charm of his imagination. He does not, to our apprehension. There is the narrative; he invented it or he discovered it—to do the one is as easy as to do the other—and besides this there is not much. Yet there is something besides this. He is not destitute of humor or of imagination, and his pitying sympathy has given him insight into the motives and feelings of the class of people which he has most studied. There is something more than sympathetic presentation of facts in the **"Scottish Eclogue,"** in **"The Ballad-Maker,"** and in parts of **"Meg Blane."** Imagination had a finger, if not a hand, in the production of them. We copy a passage from the last-named poem. Meg Blane has been seduced, twenty years since, by a lover who deserted her, promising to return. She, meantime, lives as a fisherwoman, rearing her son, an idiot, to man's years. "Bearded," Mr. Buchanan very often calls him, for he has a way of repeating favorite words which would seem to prove his vocabulary limited. He, meantime, forgets her and marries another. He is cast ashore, by shipwreck, near Meg's hut, and she speedily finds that the hope she has been so long cherishing is a vain one. The dying out of her love for him is thus told:

> "Over this agony I linger not,
> Nor shall I picture how upon that shore
> They met and spoke and parted yet once more,
> So calmly that the woman understood
> Her hope indeed had gone away for good.
> But ere the man departed from the place,
> It seemed to Meg, contemplating his face,
> Her love for him had ne'er been so intense
> As it had seemed when he was far from thence;
> And many a thing in him seemed little-hearted
> And mean and loveless; so that ere they parted
> She seemed unto her sorrow reconciled.
> And when he went away she almost smiled,
> But bitterlie, and turned to toil again,
> And felt most hard to all the world of men."

This seems true to nature everywhere, among high and low, and it would not be fair to the author to say that he found it in the story. Meg sickens, losing all her courage; her life died with her love, and she pines away. Her witless son waits on her in her illness; and the poet has well imagined the effect on his behavior of his mother's woes. Or, as one may say—seeing how in other things, when facts cannot help him, his imagination mostly fails him—he has closely studied and sympathetically reproduced all the features of a case which actually fell under his observation. In the other case the sympathetic imagination seems to have been at work, and in this one sympathetic observation. We may as well say here that in the **"Battle of Drumliemoor," "The Saint's Story,"** the very disagreeable **"Poem to David,"** and certain other pieces [in *North Coast and Other Poems*] where Mr. Buchanan escapes wholly from facts and trusts himself to his unaided powers, he makes a bad failure. This is the description of the idiot son's imitative sadness:

> "And now there was a change in his sole friend
>   He could not comprehend.
> But, lo! unto the shade of her distress
> His nature shaped itself in gentleness;
> And when he found her weeping, he too wept;
>   And if she laughed, laughed out in company.
> And often to the fisher-huts he crept,
>   And begged her bread, and brought it tenderly,
> And held it to her mouth, and, till she ate,
>   Would touch no piece, although he hungered sore.
> And these things were a solace to her fate,
>   But wrung her heart the more.
>
>   . . . . .
>
> Something had made the world more sad and strange,
> But easily he changèd with the change.
> For in the very trick of woe he clad
> His features, and was sad since she was sad,
> And leant his chin upon his hand like her,
>   And looked at vacancy and when the deep
>   Was troublous, and she started up from sleep,
> He too awoke, with fearful heart astir;
> And aye the more her bitter tears she shed
>   Upon his neck, in woe to mark his woe,

The more in blind, deep love he fashionèd
His grief to hers, and was contented so."

Giving to the best pieces of the book the praise we have given it, and adding to that the further praise that it has passages of natural reflection well enough expressed, and some not excellent but good descriptions of natural scenery, we will say, on the other hand, that frequently the poet is heard speaking through the personages of his story instead of letting them speak for themselves, and that he too exclusively gives himself up to the harrowing. Both are artistic faults, and both have the same origin. Close adherence to his original, accurate and comprehensive portrayal of the life he tries to paint, would have saved him from the one and the other; then his farmers would never talk Buchanan, nor would all his low life be low life made—to the sacrifice of truth—on the single theory which the poet has chosen as most effective on the reader's feelings. Of his usual matter and manner the passages we have quoted above afford a specimen rather favorable than otherwise. But we have already sufficiently described the book. Mr. Buchanan is, so far as he is at all valuable, a poetical preacher of love and charity, enforcing his text by moving examples. Thus he does a noble work; and he does it more than tolerably well, but is hardly a poet, or he would not have chosen themes that might better have been treated in prose; at the utmost, would have treated them less prosily. The binding of the volume, a heavy octavo, is elaborately fine, red and green and gilt cloth, with bevelled edges; the paper is tinted and heavy; the type is large and clear; the illustrations are many—most being ugly— and altogether the book, as regards inside and outside, is good enough to constitute a pretty and valuable holiday gift.

The London Quarterly Review (review date 1870)

SOURCE: A review of *Book of Orm,* in *The London Quarterly Review,* Vol. XXXIV, April & July, 1870, p. 525.

[*In the following excerpt, a reviewer presents a mixed appraisal of* The Book of Orm.]

Buchanan's **Book of Orm** has been written, as appears from a note of the author's, whilst ill-health has weighed upon him. This has prevented the volume from being published in a complete form. **"A Rune Found in the Starlight,"** **"The Songs of Heaven,"** are written, but cannot, in Mr. Buchanan's present state of health, "be made perfect for press." **"The all-important 'Devil's Dirge,'"** also, we are informed, is wanting in the present edition.

The body of the volume is divided into ten sections, each section being made up by a number of poems, mostly very short. **"Orm the Celt"** and his **"Visions"** appear, in a shadowy, uncertain, phantasmatic way throughout the book, the outline or method of which it would be very difficult to describe. Much of the writing is exceedingly beautiful, though full of sorrow, doubt, and unrest; but more of

it is misty and mystical. The old and insoluble problems of the world are perpetually recurring, Mr. Buchanan's gospel being universalistic. Altogether the tone of the book is so troubled and morbid, that we can well understand that ill-health has given an infection of misery to it throughout. Its obscurity also is almost as pervasive as its sadness.

Our readers do not need any specimens to be given them of the poet's power of word-painting, or of the exquisite melodiousness which frequently distinguishes his verse. It is more to the purpose to remark that he has in this book allowed himself in not a few instances to follow Mr. Arnold's bad example in publishing so-called poems, which are altogether *lege soluta,* which have neither rhyme, nor metre, nor rhythm. Furthermore, Mr. Buchanan has, unfortunately, no classical culture. Even this, however, is hardly sufficient to account for such a solecism in all ways as that which occurs in the first lines of those we are about to quote:

> "Now an evangel
>   Whom God loved deep,
> Said, 'See! the mortals,
>   How they weep!
> They grope in darkness,'" &c., &c.

The Nation (review date 1870)

SOURCE: A review of *The Book of Orm,* in *The Nation,* New York, Vol. 11, No. 266, August 4, 1870, pp. 76-7.

[*The following review offers an unfavorable assessment of* The Book of Orm.]

In previous volumes, Mr. Buchanan has published verses which were not precisely good poetry, and which were not very agreeable reading, but which, nevertheless, showed that he had in him something of poetic power. The imagination in them was of the purely sympathetic order, and was unaccompanied by any but a weak and futile way of thinking, and was unaccompanied, too, so far as appeared, by any perception of the beautiful or sense of the humorous. The impression given was of a thoroughly Scotch mind and nature, flushed with a good deal of that hectic which has consigned a great many young Scotchmen to poetry and an early grave. But for all that—though he was conceited and bumptious, pragmatic, unideal, of unrefined taste, not well educated in the higher sense of the word, nor perhaps in the lower—he nevertheless had the genuine insight which sympathy gives into the sufferings and joys, but especially into the sufferings, of certain of the humbler of his fellow-creatures, and was able to express it in a form that made it effective upon others. A consumptive artisan in an alley pining for green fields; a prostitute in her chamber, with a heart hardened but sore and sick; a fisher-wife, deserted by her seducer; an old couple who lament in their cottage the loss of the son that was to be a scholar—people like these Mr. Buchanan gives us, or used to give us, with real power. It was not, one thought, a very good choice of subjects; but it was, one saw by many signs, a wise enough choice if the man who made it was to do his best, or was to do anything worth while in literature. Nor was it absolutely bad either; if not the best, it was still not bad, and many of the poems produced when our author was working this vein are of value and capable of giving pleasure.

But in the volume before us Mr. Buchanan goes out of the field in which he has had success, and makes exhibition of all his faults and of no one of his merits. A more laborious and ambitious attempt at doing something beyond one's strength—or rather entirely foreign to one's nature—and a more decided failure, is not often made.

The author's intention in *The Book of Orm*—which is styled *"A Prelude to the Epic"*—would seem to be to state in a poetical manner his notion of the old, old problem of man's relations to God. What does it all mean; how is this important soul of mine, this gifted soul of mine, to discern the inner reason of things and also be saved; why am I thus tormented; is not this deep sadness of mine a proof that I am a being of immortal brightness; why then am I thus sad; wherefore is there death; what is this mystery of sorrow; how comes it to pass that knowledge is vain, that human wisdom is to know human ignorance and confess human weakness; is evil really evil, or is the devil one day to be dead, or else converted; why cannot we look into the unseen; why does not a personal God reveal himself to man, who hungers and thirsts for him, and is not sure that he exists and would so much like to be sure; what is the ocean saying; what mean these eternal stars that shame our puny and transitory race?—these questions, which have been stormed about and wailed about and groaned about by the weaker poets of the last twenty or thirty years as if they were new questions, and have caused public wringing of the hands and beating of the breast and slapping of the brow and dashing back of the hair and avowed anticipations of the tomb, to an extent that most people have regretted to see or hear, are the questions which Mr. Buchanan, in the *Book of Orm,* dashes back his hair about, and stamps about, and fixes sad eyes on the stars about, and over which he becomes moody and sulky and resigned and impious and trustingly pious, and all the rest of it.

Such is the weightiness of the book considered as thought. If its manner and method of presentation be considered, the result will be equally unfavorable to Mr. Buchanan's reputation. Everything is hollow and forced and artificial; and there is as much fluent life of the imagination in it as in wooden waves or in toy forests carved in Nuremberg. Yet there is a most offensive strenuousness of effort to be grand and fine. There is an expensive machinery of hoary pilgrims, and star-voices, and Voices within the Temple, and Spirits, and Spirits of Sorrow, and Veils, and Shadows; but all comes to nothing, and serves only to suggest how hide-bound is the imagination of the poet when to be sublime he must fall back on capital letters and on stage

properties long worn-out in the service of "Festus" and other persons much afflicted by the universe.

The Book of Orm appears to be poems written by a certain bard called Orm the Celt, who, however, in spite of the mythic and ancient look of his designation, must be conceived of as a Celtic bard of our own time:

> "There is a mortal, and his name is Orm,
> Born in the evening of the world, and looking
> Back from the sunset to the gates of morning.
>
> "And he is aged early, in a time
> When all are aged early,—he was born
> In twilight times, and in his soul is twilight.
>
> "O brother, hold me by the hand, and hearken,
> For these things I shall phrase are thine and mine,
> And all men's,—all are seeking for a sign.
>
> "Thou wert born yesterday, but thou art old,
> Weary to-day, to-morrow thou wilt sleep—
> Take these for kisses on thy closing eyelids."

This dismal prelude is the appropriate antechamber to the poems that follow; but perhaps better as showing more clearly the unhealthy frame of mind in which the book was planned, and as foreshadowing the pretentious feebleness of it, is the affected and melancholic **"Inscription"**:

> "Flowers pluckt upon a grave by moonlight, pale
> And suffering, from the spiritual light
> They grew in: these, with all the love and blessing
> That prayers can gain of God, I send to thee!
>
> "If one of these poor flowers be worthy thee,
> The sweetest Soul that I have known on earth,
> The tenderest Soul that I can hope to know,
> Hold that one flower, and kneel, and pray for me.
>
> "Pray for me, Comrade! Close to thee I creep,
> Touching thy raiment: thy good eyes are calm;
> But see! the fitful fever in mine eyes—
> Pray for me!—bid all good men pray for me!
>
> "If Love will serve, lo! how I love my Friend—
> If Reverence, lo! how I reverence him—
> If Faith be asked in something beautiful,
> Lo! what a splendor is my faith in him!
>
> "Now, as thou risest gently from thy knees,
> Must we go different ways?—thou followest
> Thy path, I mine;—but all go westering,
> And all will meet among the Hills of God!"

We had supposed the fashion had gone out of being publicly sad-eyed and ruined in hopes. It is going out certainly, if it has not quite gone, and this performance of Mr. Buchanan's will help it to its burial. Nothing could well be in worse taste.

Orm sings first of The Veil:

> "In the beginning,
>   Ere Man grew,

And through the music of the languid hours,
They hear like ocean on a western beach
The surge and thunder of the Odyssey,

they discern, on closer acquaintanceship, a significance even when under the sensuous influence of the 'surge and thunder,' its supreme significance lying in its truth to the state of the civilisation which it reflects, 'the description of its daily acts and the motives which make individuals act in the sense of their character and of their race.' Again, what is the significance of such men as Dante or Shakespeare? To quote Victor Hugo, 'Dante incarnated the supernatural, Shakespeare incarnated Nature.' But we must not forget, in indicating the significance of a seer or a teacher, that circumstances and influences are capable of modifying the possibility of permanency in the quality of the significance. Instance, for example, the fact that 'Milton lost much of his significance under the influence of modern thought, and that Virgil suffered from the influences of the Renaissance.'

From this host of great lights let us come to our poet, and attempt to indicate his significance. Passing out of our memory for the present the thought of his earlier poems, we call into view the series of epics and odes, carols and ballads, which extended from the publication of *The Book of Orm* to that of *The New Rome*. Throughout the whole of this work several ideas are reiterated. In the first place, that man is continually searching for a solution of life's meaning, and in that search calls to the God-Father for light. To this cry there never comes an answer. The face of God is for ever hid behind the veil; the law of God, stern, inexorable, working on unchanged, is never broken—that law expressed in terms of science as the struggle for existence and the survival of the fittest. To ameliorate the suffering of mankind, human love springs supreme and eternal, together with a belief in a future life of reconciliation in the celestial ocean, in which some recompense shall be found for earthly inequalities. The essence of this human love is the Christ—the Jew, Jesus of Nazareth—and in his protest against the inexorable law of the Father, he, representing all the time the ambition of the human soul, is, in a sense 'ά θεός'—atheist—that is, apart from God. All this we have indicated as we proceeded. The sublimity of Jesus lies not in his claim of divine fatherhood, or in his unfulfilled dream of the world's salvation, but in his recognition of the despair of humanity under the cruelty of a despotic egoism. In this sense, God the Father is the Grand Egoist; Jesus, and with him Humanity in general, the Sublime Altruist. Oppressing the fair face of Christ's noble altruism is the cloud of the Churches, and in striking contrast to the loving freedom of soul which is the essence of the teaching of the Nazarene, is the attempt by the theologies to strangle the Christ in creeds. Having accepted the evolutionary spirit in most of its bearings, the poet is consistent enough to conclude that if the records of miracles and the so-called historical documents are not to be trusted as scientific evidence, then it follows that some other explanation must be found to account for many of the details of Jesus' life. This position being adopted, there is nothing then of an abhorrent nature in the view the poet presents

of the early life of Mary the Mother as it is found in the **"Ballad."** Only one conclusion could be drawn, and it adds to Mr. Buchanan's significance that he seized hold of this matter and treated it boldly. The poet or seer must always discern the truth sooner than other men, and granting the acceptance of the eclectic position as it is conveyed, for instance, by Mr. Huxley, and there can be no future for any literary movement careless of science, the time will come when the logical sequence will be a question of commonplace acceptance.

Mr. Buchanan's significance lies then in the fact that he has used, as a subject for poetry, the great truths Science has taught, and those his own speculative imagination seemed to discern behind the cloud of conventional belief. Disdainful of using the mighty medium of poetry as a simple reflector of things as they are in a conventional sense, he has used these great truths, or attempts at truth, as the bases of his poetical aspirations, and in so doing has accomplished what he longed to see attempted in his earlier outlook on life. It is another question whether in so doing he has been true to literature and to history. Truth to literature is a much more difficult question to solve than truth to history. History is a record of facts; literary methods are evanescent. They are born, they evolve, die, are renascent, and so on. We are not talking of metre or the mere grammar of literature, but of the method, dramatic or otherwise, used by the seer. Taking a man who has used similar material, though in a totally different spirit and with a totally different object in view, it would be as absurd to compare Milton and Buchanan, as it would be to compare, say, Offenbach and Wagner. There is a kind of gospel of grammar, metre, and rhythm, but none of the method by which any particular form of truth shall be presented in literary shape. Truth to history is easier. Here we are dealing with a comparison of facts.

There is another form of truth less exact and less definite, varying in regard to the point of view. That is the truth of deduction—the inferences to be drawn from ascertained fact. If this aspect of the question is to be considered, the poet,—and there is nothing unnatural in this—clears away much of that nebulosity of doubt which the scientist is unable to do by the methods at his disposal. The poet is not content with the simple view of the concrete facts of nature; he is prepared to accept the longings of the soul as something as palpably true as those more material facts. Science, replying that it has a theory of the evolution of these longings which might relegate them to mere responses to sensuous emotions, depending for their basis on acquired knowledge and prejudices, gets no sympathy from the poet, who sees in these yearnings the promise of the full light of the Celestial Ocean, and the joys of human reconciliation. Science, accepting the principle of the survival of the fittest as the only basis on which the higher evolution can be reached, and recognising that the struggle between natural forces, between the strong and weak, between health and disease, is the only means to secure the prolongation of natural vitality in its highest form, is passed by the poet, who demands from the All-Father the reason of this cruel principle. The same spirit makes him protest against all forms of investigation that necessitate injury to lower organisms, and against wars between creatures of the same instinct, the same possibilities, and the same aspirations.

In this we venture to indicate the criticism of science; the criticism of the theological position is evident, and need not be insisted upon.

To this must be added Mr. Buchanan's very significant study of the Devil, the parallels of which we have already considered. If the Devil is to be referred back to the original Daēvas of Zoroastrian Scriptures as the Spirit of Evil working conjointly with the Spirit of Good in the organisation and evolution of the nature of man, then Mr. Buchanan's Devil is both sophistical and paradoxical, and loses in being so, much of its significance. But if we are to study him as he was viewed by the Churches, and as in later days made responsible for an appearance as the serpent in the Mosaic story of the Garden of Eden, then the poet's Devil, claiming to be the spirit of knowledge and the spirit of progress, is logical and consistent enough. In this case he comes to be the Æon of Science, the herald of light, he who, in face of the direct and indirect opposition of ecclesiasticism, fought for centuries at the head of the great army of secularists, an army which went to war for the sake of the great principle of eclecticism, that is,—absolute freedom of thought, and for the sake of emancipation from those superstitious fears which kept mankind from facing the truths of nature, and using them for its own purpose. Viewed from this point of view, there is a deep significance in the poet's conception of the æon, who added to his schemes, not the defiance of the laws of nature, but the discovery of the means by which the apparent cruelty of these laws might be modified. In this sense he becomes the pioneer of scientific altruism.

This love of altruistic action, and this hatred of the cruel egoism of nature, which latter is, after all, reply the scientists, ultimately altruistic, are the essentials at the base of all the poet's work. 'God shall cast away no man' is the continued note of his most impassioned writing, whether found dramatically expressed in **"The Ballad of Judas Iscariot," "The Vision of the Man Accurst,"** or in the tragedies of common life as they are conveyed in his *London Poems*—the later of which, in their sublimity in surrounding tragic commonplaces with a spiritual halo, add a fresh significance to Mr. Buchanan as a poet.

As we have indicated, there are in many of the poet's more brilliant attempts evident signs not only of anachronisms, but of sophistries and paradoxes; yet the underlying principle of Revolt in the name of mankind against the Father of suffering and death, set to poetical expression, cannot fail to individualise the work of Mr. Buchanan. The failure of his significance cannot be prophesied, or if prophesied, relegated with any definiteness to futurity. Whatever he has failed to do, he has at least satisfied the standard set up for himself—he has given us fearless truth

and imagination, applied to the great phenomena of creation; he has not rehabilitated creeds that are indeterminate. He has faced fearlessly the problems that must come to all of us, however cynical, sceptical, or dilettante we may be, concerning man's relation to man, and to the revelations of the Godhood in nature. However inadequate has been his expression, however partial his view, however sophistical his general expression, he has at least faced truth fearlessly and eclectically, and in so doing has laid claim to the highest intellectual morality. For let it not be forgotten by those who are startled by the poet's eclecticism, who even shudder at his view of what has been to them truth sacred in the holy of holies of their soul, that to men of speculation and of fearless outlook, the unforgivable sin is intellectual immorality. The eclectics can only lift up their faces fearlessly to mankind, they can only express their prayer to a God-Father by speaking the truth as they find it; and however wrong they may be, however far they may drift away from the white throne where Truth sits in her lonely splendour—espied occasionally, but never reached, by poet or thinker—yet in the very sincerity of their search they find their salvation and their justification. And it is necessary to remind mankind occasionally with regard to the question of susceptibility, that those of orthodox faith do not hold a monopoly either of conscience or of feeling. The constant reiteration of inconsequent and illogical dogmas is as distasteful to an eclectic searcher after truth, as are the fearless analyses of doctrine and dogma at the hand of the eclectic distasteful to the faithful adherent of the venerable creeds. The susceptibilities of the one deserve as much consideration as those of the other. In the words of Carlyle, 'He who builds by the wayside has many masters,' and members of a church militant need not be surprised if the enemy they are attacking use as effective, or even more effective, weapons than they use themselves. Reverence can be monopolised by no particular theology or particular school of thought. The eclectic thinker demonstrates his reverence not only by the use of the abilities which Nature has assigned to him, but also by the very fact that he is suspicious of systems which parochialise the worship of the supreme λόγος by cramping it in creeds. The universal recognition of that simple fact will go far to bind humanity by the bond of a common love. As for our poet, although ecclesiastics may say that he has acceded too much to the autocracy of reason, and even though scientists may be suspicious inasmuch as he has demanded an equal right for the spiritual emotions, yet the poet will reply that spiritualism and naturalism—using them here conventionally as distinctive terms—are necessary elements of every work of art, and the predominancy of one over the other has no certain or unchangeable ratio. Finally, let it be remembered to Mr. Buchanan's honour that he has never attempted to humour his reputation, and has never been led to follow the false gods of those who ensured him a certain place in contemporary estimation if he would but promise to sing a poem occasionally to the gods of the moment, however much he suspected their divinity. His methods of dealing with these deities were not always pleasant or delicate; but having at a very early stage of his career been driven into the wilderness, he could not, as an

Ishmael, use the methods of a pampered Isaac. It will probably be found that the poet will not come to his own till the remembrance of these, what may appear to some as, literary blasphemings is forgotten, and certainly not till contemporary thought comes up to the point reached by the seer.

Nor must we omit the significance of Mr. Buchanan apart from his more prophetic and speculative utterances. The author of **"The Ballad of Judas Iscariot,"** of *White Rose and Red,* and of **"Poet Andrew,"** must always be regarded with serious attention by students of poetry, even if neglected by many of the petulantly ignorant collectors of anthologies and their numerous friends. The foremost Scoto-Celtic poet of our time, as he is called by Mrs. Sharp in the 'Lyra Celtica,' can allow his phantasies and realities in verse to be independent of the indifference of cliques, as long as they touch the larger heart and the more far-seeing criticism. 'His deep insight into Nature, and his fine interpretation of the mystical sentiment bred of man's contact with her, his delicate fancy, his semi-Celtic phantasy,' to quote Dr. Japp, 'which in his treatment of certain themes impart such glow and glamour of colour, and weird witchery of impression, as no other poet of the time has approached, not to speak of his realistic, dramatic perception, as seen in such ballads as **"Liz"** and **"Nell"** and **"Meg Blane,"** combine to place him apart amid the select few, the best of whose work is to "live." He touches the most commonplace things with the light that never was on sea or shore, and yet nothing of truth is sacrificed. This is the true test of poetry. Then in his *Book of Orm* he translates us to a world of dream, yet a world in which the grand realities of life stand out bold, like vast mountains whose lofty heads are lost in mist, yet faintly outlined. You are moved to a sense of some vast, vague, shadowy presence, which, felt or unfelt, is weird, fateful, and inevitable, hovering over all life, and touching it with awe and wonder. The manner in which Mr. Buchanan traces out and justifies, in a poetic sense, the bliss of gradual dissolution is at once elevated and powerful. The picture of the void left on the sense and the imagination by the sudden disappearance of all trace, even of the poor body, as the dewdrop melts in the sun, the horror, as of some awful fate for ever hovering above and around, is suffused with the sense of mystery and awe, and the recovery, as if from some nightmare, is equally fine. In Mr. Buchanan's genius,' says Dr. Japp, 'is wedded the grace and witchery of delicate phantasy with the directest and boldest realism. Nature and man stand between the two, as it were, and the force of his sympathies unites them, and brings them into accord. . . . He is alive to every thrill of the intellectual, social, and moral atmosphere, and translates, as his genius dictates, the impression into art. . . . He is in touch with all that makes men feel, that makes men suffer, and that makes men lonely, dissatisfied, and despair and doubt.'

Let Mr. Buchanan be tested on well-defined lines, and what is the result? If the question of pure human Drama is concerned, excluding altogether *The Drama of Kings,* of which the poet himself is suspicious, let us take such po-

ems as **"Fra Giacomo"** and **"Hakon of Thule."** In each of these we have a single idea, presented in a perfect dramatic fashion, fearlessly true to the central 'motif,' without any critical intrusion to mar the simple directness of the idea. In 'ballad metre,' let the severest and most academically critical spirit be applied to **"The Battle of Drumliemoor"** and **"The Ballad of Judas Iscariot,"** and let the result be realised. When simplicity of character and equal simplicity of surroundings are to be spiritualised in poetic expression, what is more perfect than **"Willie Baird"**? Among genre and pastoral pictures, **"The Churchyard"** and **"Down the River"** must always occupy a notable position; and although Mr. Buchanan has written few lyrics, his lyric-descriptive poems, of the type of **"Spring Song in the City,"** contain some of his finest work, and are in every sense worthy of more than mere contemporary estimation.

It has been suggested more than once, that all Mr. Buchanan's 'aberrations' have sprung from a want of the sense of humour. It is this sense, certainly, which gives us, more than any other, the sane, the healthy estimate of life; but a civilisation which charges a man with the want of a virtue should be certain, first, of its own righteousness. 'My critics,' says the poet, 'presume, I suppose, that I ought to perceive the joke of the Nonconformist conscience and latter-day Christianity.' Let us prove to our own mental and spiritual satisfaction that modern civilisation and the concurrent pursuit of an idealised religion are compatible, and then we may be free to talk of the want of sense of humour in others. If we face facts as they are, and acquiesce in the charges that the essential elements in modern, political, and social life are incompatible in their practice with the Faith of which our Royal master is the defender, we may then be justified, by our intellectual honesty at any rate, in viewing the want of humour in one who is mortal like the rest of us, yet perceives the hollowness of making an eternal compact between the rush for power and the worship of show, and the doctrines of abnegation and humility as preached on the Mount of Olives. We recall, in this instance, what the present Laureate wrote to Mr. William Watson at the time when the latter was calling upon his countrymen to risk international complications by plunging into a piece of vague, benevolent altruism in favour of a suppressed people. Mr. Austin reminded Mr. Watson that if he 'were but with him in his pretty country-house, were but comfortably seated by the Yule-logs' blaze, and joining with him in seasonable conviviality, the enigmas of Providence and the whole mysteries of things would become transparent to him.' That is what we are virtually saying to our poet—'God is in His heaven, all's right with the world.' There is still laughter, and love, and song, and although we have not yet discovered the universal tabloid for natural egoism and 'original sin,' at any rate out of this mixture of personal egoism and social altruism, the love of war and the gospel of peace, worship of strength and love of weakness, essential Materialism and professed Christianity, social purity and organised vice, legalised monogamy and polygamy in camera, we have made an excellent social broth that will warm the national conscience, and make us forget the submerged dissatisfaction in the general sense of good-fellowship that this mess of pottage inspires!

The present writer firmly believes that the point of view of the poet is often neither absolutely true to history, nor, in a few cases, to his own personal experience, but at the same time, he doubts whether the test of humour can be applied in the case of the poet's more serious efforts, for the very reasons he has been attempting to indicate. If there is a want of the sense of humour, it springs from a belief that there is a likelihood of any radical changes taking place in human paradoxes. The poet himself owns that the law of God is never broken, and therefore he is unlikely to get much help from Nature, and if he but recall that there is little evidence to show that the altruistic spirit is evolving, he may rest satisfied that the advance to human salvation will continue to be a slow one, and checked by many retrograde steps. Despite Mr. Herbert Spencer, man is born an egoist as of yore. The change, if there be one, lies not in the evolution of an altruistic spirit, but in the accumulation of altruistic ideas, which become the capital of Society. Man does not come into his legacy in the mere process of being born; he inherits it as a member of a social state. 'That man is susceptible of a vast amount of improvement by education, by instruction, and by the application of his intelligence to the adaptation of the conditions of life to his higher needs, I entertain not the slightest doubt. But so long as he remains liable to error, intellectual or moral, so long as he is compelled to be perpetually on guard against the cosmic forces, so long as he is haunted by inexpugnable memories and hopeless aspirations, so long as the recognition of his intellectual limitations forces him to acknowledge his incapacity to penetrate the mystery of existence, the prospect of attaining untroubled happiness, or a state which can, even remotely, deserve the title of perfection, appears to me to be as misleading an illusion as ever was dangled before the eyes of poor Humanity.'[1]

For the paradoxes and inconsistencies of social life, what is wanted is not rhetoric but ridicule, not passion but satire. And although the poet in much of his work seems to lose sight of this fact, he discerned at one time its essential truth: 'It has been repeatedly forced upon me of late, that of all things wanted by the present generation, a satirist is wanted most; one who would tell the world its sins and foibles, not with the sneaking snigger or familiar wink of a society journalist, but with a voice loud and clear enough to reverberate from Land's End to John o'; Groat's. It would matter little where the voice was first heard. It might be in the pulpit, it might be on the stage. It might sound as the voice of one crying in the wilderness, or it might be heard, as more than once heretofore, from the very heart of the crowd. Since Dickens dropped the scourge, satire has been sadly at a discount, and we are in reality worse off for "censores morum" than were our prototypes, the prosperous "bourgeoisie" of the Second Empire. . . . Meanwhile Society, Mænad-like, twines flowers in her hair, and goes from bad to worse. The only indi-

viduals who tell her of her vices are those who flourish through them, and the cue of these is to lament over the ideals they first overthrew, and to pretend that goodness is useless, since there is no power but evil left. Well, even a comedy of the Empire would be better than this. . . . The only straight-forward and truth-telling force at present at work is modern Science, but it is not sufficiently aggressive in the social sphere to be of much avail. So the feast goes on, so the soothsayer is put aside, and the voice of the prophet is unheard. Some fine day, nevertheless, there will be a revelation—the handwriting will be seen on the wall in the colossal cipher of some supreme Satirist. How much of our present effulgent civilisation will last till then? How much will not perish without any aid from without, by virtue of its own inherent folly and dry-rot? Meantime, even a temporary revelation would be thankfully accepted. Such satire as Churchill suddenly lavished upon the stage would be of service to Society just now. Even satire as wicked as that with which Byron deluged the "piggish domestic virtues" of the Georges would not be altogether amiss. Only, it must come in simple speech, not in such mystic dress as that worn by St. Thomas of Chelsea when he gave forth his memorable sartorial prophesies.' That embodies the spirit of wisdom. When angry rhetoric is but a douche of hot, and indifference a douche of cold water, and reason a slow lethal process, ridicule and satire are deadly poisons. A fuller recognition of this fact might have led Mr. Buchanan nearer to that 'sense of humour' without which life, whether we view it on its social, moral, or intellectual sides, becomes a very anarchic concern. But the sense of humour is a two-edged sword, and many people are apt to take it by the blade, and not by the handle. If it brings us nearer to sanity, it also may tend to paralyse our holiest convictions. In fact, in an age when human ambitions and human aims drift easily into social and conventional moulds, when materialism and the principles of social compromise are the fashionable gods, there is a tendency to blur the face of aspiration, to reduce the purple of hope and ambition to a dull grey of indifferent acquiescence. And those who preach control and sanity most fervently see most clearly the dangers which lie before us if this control and sanity are allowed to be systematised into a gospel. After all, control as a virtue is only of a negative sort; and sanity does not mean mediocrity and tameness, it simply means wisdom. When we pursue the normal level of living, let us not despise the man on the look-out; while we hew stones and draw water, let us not sneer at him who interrogates the stars. And is it wise, in the ease of our own calm sanity, to cherish a hatred of that hot blood and indomitable persistence which inspire the dreamer, the poet, and, in a more vicious sense, the fanatic?

It is this blood that has inspired forlorn hopes, this spirit which may drive a man to be crucified for his belief. It would be a black day for the world when emotion had fuller sway than reason, when sensibility became a higher virtue than sense, and passion a nobler pursuit than sanity; but it would be a blacker when the worship of the evident in life and the pursuit of the commonplace were raised to such a pitch that the dreamer or the impassioned poet, voyaging on seas for which Science has no chart, nor Experience any compass, were counted as men free from their wits, or, to come back to the phrase we beg, 'wanting in the sense of humour.' Mr. George Meredith—always rapid as the dart to pierce the heart of things—holds that it is the first condition of sanity to believe that our civilisation is founded on common sense, and taking his fellowmen to be as wise as himself, he stepped no further into the elaboration of his terms. But might it not be judicious to suggest that it is wise always to understand that the essence of the word, that is 'sense,' is to have a more emphatic emphasis than the prefix 'common,' and that in the aggregate, common sense is not necessarily the philosophy of mediocrity. And it is wise also to remember that there is more in the scheme of life than mere foundations. And even when we are allowed to turn our minds to the gods, we must not be accused of worshipping alone that Spirit of Comedy which the genius of Mr. Meredith has idealised in godhead—that spirit with its brows flung up like a fortress lifted by gunpowder, which looks humanely malign, and roars with laughter whenever men wax out of proportion, are self-deceived and hoodwinked, and are given to run riot in idolatries, and drift into vanities. The older gods command our worship, and although we may not discern them in the market-place, let us not limit the world by the boundaries of the bazaar, but let us recognise a world in which poets may dream and voyage forth to catch the message which they tell us the gods hold for mortals; a message which it will do us no harm to hear, if not to embody in our philosophy. Keats, in a memorable sonnet dedicated to Homer, reminds the poet:

> For Jove uncurtained Heaven to let thee live,
> And Neptune made for thee a spermy tent,
> And Pan made sing for thee his forest-hive.

And though Wordsworth, keenly alive to the sanity which the pursuit of things as they are only can bring, reminds us that 'to the solid ground of Nature trusts the mind that builds for aye'; yet he, like all seers, was conscious of the deadening power which a life in the fair paths of common truths tends to have upon the human soul:

> The world is too much with us; late and soon
>   Getting and spending, we lay waste our powers:
>   Little we see in Nature that is ours;
> We have given our hearts away, a sordid boon,
> This sea that bares her bosom to the moon,
>   The winds that will be howling at all hours,
>   And are up-gathered now like sleeping flowers.
> For this, for everything, we are out of tune;
> It moves us not—Great God! I'd rather be
>   A pagan suckled in a creed outworn;
> So might I, standing on this pleasant lea,
>   Have glimpses that would make me less forlorn,
> Have sight of Proteus rising from the sea,
>   Or hear old Triton blow his wreathèd horn.

The true humour, in fact, is reached by a knowledge of good and evil evidenced from fact and comparison with a beatitude derived from an inspiratory fervour which comes to us at those times when, 'from the songs of modern speech, men turn and see the stars.'

Finally, to the poet, belief and living are twin conceptions, and his faith is

> Not far away
> In the void Heaven up yonder, not on creeds
> Upbuilded 'mid the ever-shifting sands,
> Not in the Temple of God's sycophants,
> But here, among our fellows, down as deep
> As the last rung of Hell.

Hatred of mankind and love of God cannot exist together:

> Hate Man, and lo! thou hatest, losest God;
> Keep faith in Man, and rest with God indeed.

He who has gone with us with any care, to view the poet's outlook, will have a clear enough vision of his philosophy. It is in the long-run a glorious optimism, inasmuch as it implies belief in the eternity of living, in the holiness of human love. His distaste for creeds springs from a simple belief that the last word of the soul can never be written, and that an ever-winged bird, soaring higher and higher in the eye of God, cannot be brought to earth to sing in the dreary cage wherein every note is formulated and catalogued.

He believes in Love, but not as it is painted by the creeds. He finds no love in the great struggle for life—therefore he sees none in the will of the God-Father. He can praise and he can pray, but he cannot love. God sends nothing but agony, a struggle, and death.

> Walk abroad; and mark
> The cony struggling in the foumart's fangs,
> The deer and hare that fly the sharp-tooth'd hound,
> The raven that with flap of murderous wing
> Hangs on the woolly forehead of the sheep
> And blinds its harmless eyes; nor these alone,
> But every flying, every creeping thing,
> Anguishes in the fierce blind fight for life!
> Sharp hunger gnaws the lion's entrails, tears
> The carrion-seeking vulture, films with cold
> The orbs of snake and dove. For these, for all,
> Remains but one dark Friend and Comforter,
> The husher of the weary waves of Will,
> Whom men name Peace or Death.

But he believes in human Love, and cries out his belief in the ears of priests and ascetics. 'Is there any honest man that doubts that Love, even so-called "fleshly Love," is the noblest pleasure that man is permitted to enjoy; or that sympathy of woman for man, and of man for woman, is in its essence the sweetest sympathy of which the soul is capable. Only one thing is higher and better than Love's happiness, and that one thing is Love's sorrow, when there comes out of loss and suffering the sense of compensation, of divine gain.'

After all, the wisest of men have occasionally to wipe away the dew that dims the glass of their philosophy. All efforts are comparative, all Truth is comparative. Good and bad are not yet writ on the scrolls of the absolute, and to the present writer Mr. Buchanan's merit lies not so much in that he has dreamed often, and has fluttered his poetical wings often, but in that he has dared to bring the charm of poetical expression to bear on themes which were originally considered the sole property of philosophers and speculators. While Tennyson is the mirror of the present age, Carlyle its censor, and Macaulay its panegyrist; while Herbert Spencer is its recording angel, and George Meredith the true discerner of its comic spirit, Robert Buchanan is the herald of its revolt, the mouthpiece of a sphinx-like woe, which, as a seer, he knows is buried deep down in the heart and soul of contemporary thought, and he realises that at the last.

> God and the gods shall abide, wherever our souls seek
>   a token,
> Speech of the Gods shall be heard, the silence of
>   Death shall be broken,
> And Man shall distinguish a sign, a voice in the mid-
>   night, a tremor
> From every pulse of the Heavens, to answer the heart
>   of the Dreamer!
> Faces of gods and men shall throng the blue case-
>   ments above him!
> Heaven shall be peopled with throngs of Spirits that
>   watch him and love him!

Mr. Linley Sambourne in a moment of inspiration[2] has depicted the idealised figure of the New Century springing from the wing of Time, and buoyant and unconscious of the 'shades of the prison-house,' straining forward with inquiring, fearless, inspired gaze into the meshes of the veil that hides the future. In her hand the staff of Faith and the lamp of Science. No longer do we espy an allegory of twin souls, Reason and Faith; Reason with his eyes fixed to the 'solid ground of nature,' groping, in the shadows, his uneven way with difficulty to Truth; and Faith with eyes to heaven, sailing in the full light of inspiration, unchecked to the Sungates. Faith and Reason now unite in the spirit of Imaginative Science, in the ideal of the aspiring Searcher after Wisdom. In the Ideal figure we see personified Imagination guided by Reason, Prophecy lighted by Science. This is what the Nineteenth bequeaths to the Twentieth Century. Hereafter, Superstition must creep warily and be an outcast from the newer Heaven, and Sacerdotalism assume a lower grade in the temple of human aspiration. For the construction of this Ideal, which is to lead mankind to the brink of the Celestial Ocean, Robert Buchanan has ever been an impassioned advocate, appealing not with the mere egoism of rhetoric, but with a yearning desire to bring human hopes and aspiration to a higher level than what to him appears to be the parochialised methods of the Churches, and the paralysing doctrines of mere materialism.

In the gradual reconstruction of human hopes and human ideals, parochial truths will fade, yet flicker on for a while, whilst Eternal Truth will flash up anew to guide nations in the process of time to the basis of a common ideal and a common religion. The methods that shall assist in the em-

bodiment of this ideal and this religion will differ widely, and may continue to be the ground of strife and dissension, yet in the evolutionary process the teaching of Jesus will gain new life and a new significance, whilst Christian theology will lose its supremacy and its vitality. The tendency will be to combine the essential truths of all great ethical systems, and in the attainment of that combination the process of the survival of the fittest will continue to have its legal sway. Not for the first time shall Jewish, Greek, Roman, and Hindu thought meet on the banks of the Jordan. With a tenderer reconciliation in view shall the priests of the newer gods rouse from their slumber their older brethren. No longer shall Christ walk in the wilderness, where despair, melancholy, and gloom dwell, but in the purified groves of Pan; and at the gateway of the new heaven Apollo, Prometheus, Balder, Bhudda shall sing with the Nazarene a new song of Hope. That song may sound clearer in the East than in the West, in that Far East, perhaps, where a young nation is springing eagerly forward to grasp and use what is best in the garden and storehouse of the world. Yet clear against the sky of human endeavour shall be written that sign which Mr. Buchanan discerned so clearly in his later days: 'The Law of God is never broken.' With that Truth impressing itself upon human reason and human imagination, no man, however inspired, will attempt to break or suspend that Law.

With the dead century the pen of the poet is laid aside. Ending as he began, he takes his final steps towards the brink of the Valley of the Dark Shadow, with few of his contemporaries to give him the grand hailing sign of sympathy. But the militant poet has had the last bay leaf snatched from his brow, and hereafter must begin to take an assured place amongst the poets that he loved of English race. The present writer, standing as he does by training, by instinct, and in the general conduct of life, at nearly opposite poles to Mr. Buchanan, lays this introduction to his poetry with affection at the side of his bed of sickness, with the hope that it may serve to reveal to many a new aspect of a man who is known to them only as a novelist, playwright, and publicist, believing that a sympathetic study of the poet will light at least one new fire in the temple of human aspiration, and add one more interpreter for the mystic language of the human heart.

> For lo! I voice to you a mystic thing
> Whose darkness is as full of starry gleams
> As is a tropic light; in your dreams
> This thing shall haunt you and become a sound
> Of friendship in still places, and around
> Your lives this thing shall deepen and impart
> A music to the trouble of the heart,
> So that perchance, upon some gracious day,
> You may bethink you of the song and pray
> That God may bless the singer for your sake!

Solemn before the poet, as before all of us, is veiled the dark portal, and until that is passed, we know not if all the glory and the dream of the poet be merely the rainbows of his sorrow, or 'whether in some more mystic condition the

Gods sweep past in thunder,' and if the Immortals are re-membering all the melodies and the ideals that we on earth have forgot, and are plucking again the living bloom from the rose-trees of life's Maytime. Though that riddle of the gods cannot be answered by Seer or by Dreamer—

> Yet shall the River of Life wander and wander and wander,
> Yet shall the Trumpet of Time sound from the Sun-gates up yonder,
> Yet shall the fabled Sphinx brood on the mystic To-morrow,
> While newer Cities arise, on the dust that is scatter'd in sorrow!

Notes

1. Huxley.

2. 'Punch's Almanac,' 1901.

Arthur Symons (essay date 1901)

SOURCE: "Robert Buchanan," in *Studies in Prose and Verse*, E. P. Dutton & Co., 1922, pp. 121-23.

[*In the following essay, originally published in 1901, Symons comments on the combative tone of many of Buchanan's writings.*]

Robert Buchanan was a soldier of fortune who fought un-der any leader or against any cause so long as there was heavy fighting to be done. After a battle or two, he left the camp and enlisted elsewhere, usually with the enemy. He was, or aimed at being, a poet, a critic, a novelist, a play-wright; he was above all a controversialist; he also tried being his own publisher. As a poet he wrote ballads, lyr-ics, epics, dramas, was realist and transcendentalist, was idyllic, tragic, pathetic, comic, religious, objective, subjec-tive, descriptive, reflective, narrative, polemic, and jour-nalistic. He wrote rhetorical and "Christian" romances be-fore Mr Hall Caine; his plays were done entirely for the market, some of them in collaboration with Mr G. R. Sims; his criticism was all a kind of fighting journalism. "Lack-ing the pride of intellect," he has said of himself, "I have by superabundant activity tried to prove myself a man among men, not a mere *littérateur*." And, indeed, his ca-reer shows an activity not less surprising than superabun-dant. He took himself so seriously that he considered it le-gitimate to "stoop to hodman's work"; thinking, he tells us, "no work undignified which did not convert him into a Specialist or a Prig." He never doubted that he might have been "sitting empty-stomached on Parnassus," if he had cared for the position. He defended himself, perhaps un-necessarily, for not having done so. "I have written," he said, "for all men and in all moods." He took the day's wages for the day's work, but was not satisfied. From the first his books were received with serious attention; they were considered, often praised greatly, often read largely. Whenever he had anything to say, people listened. When

he hit other men, the other men usually paid him the com-pliment of hitting back. "For nearly a generation," he la-mented, ten years ago, "I have suffered a constant literary persecution." Well, it is difficult to do justice to one who has never done justice to another. But persecution is hardly the word to be used for even a hard hit, when the hit is re-ceived by a fighter of all work.

Like most fighters, Buchanan fought because he could not think, and his changing sides after the fight was neither loss nor gain to either cause. It was at most the loss or gain of a weapon, and the weapon was often more danger-ous to friends than foes. He liked playing with big names, as childen play with dolls and call them after their dreams. He took God and the devil into his confidence, very pub-licly, and with a kind of lofty patronage. He used the name of God to checkmate the devil, and the devil's name to checkmate God. "And absolutely," he tells us, "I don't know whether there are gods or not. I know only that there is Love and Lofty Hope and Divine Compassion." There are more big names to play with, and he wrote them, even their adjectives, in capital letters. The capital letters were meant for emphasis, they also indicated defiance. He gave many definitions of what he meant by God, the devil, Love, Hope, and Compassion. The definitions varied, and were often interchangeable. I find some of them in a book written in his honour, called *Robert Buchanan, the Poet of Modern Revolt*. From this book I gather that Buchanan was himself an example of the "divine" and the "lofty" virtues. His weakness, he admits, was too much brotherly love. "With a heart overflowing with love, I have gathered to myself only hate and misconception." Whatever he at-tacked, he attacked in all the sincerity of anger, and anger no doubt is the beginning of all avenging justice. He has said (so Mr Stodart-Walker's book tells me, and though I gather that it was said in verse, I am unable to reconstruct the lines in metrical form) "I've popt at vultures circling skyward, I've made the carrion hawks a byword, but never caused a sigh or sob in the breast of mavis or cockrobin, nay, many such have fed out of my hand and blest me." There is hardly a contemporary writer whom he did not at-tack, but it is true that he recanted with not less vehe-mence, and with a zest in the double function which sug-gests the swinging impartiality of the pendulum. When he insulted an idea, it was with the best intentions and on be-half of another idea. If he spoke blasphemously of God, it has only been, he assures us, in his zeal for religion, and when he "lifted his hat to the Magdalen," in a famous phrase, it was all in the cause of chastity. With infinite po-etic ambition, he had a certain prose force, which gave his verse, at times, the vehemence of telling oratory. He at-tempted in verse many things which were not worth at-tempting and some which were. In all he aimed at effect, sometimes getting it. He was indifferent to the quality of the effect, so long as the effect was there, and the mere fact of his aiming at it disqualified him, at his best, from a place among genuine, that is to say disinterested artists.

Harriett Jay (essay date 1903)

SOURCE: "Play-Writing," in *Robert Buchanan: Some Account of His Life, His Life's Work and His Literary Friendships,* T. Fisher Unwin, 1903, pp. 231-49.

[*In the following essay, Jay surveys Buchanan's plays.*]

It was not till he had passed the forties that Mr. Buchanan obtained any real success upon the stage. From the time of the production of the *Witchfinder* he had never ceased to regard it as a possible means of livelihood, knowing as he did that in this connection far greater prizes were to be obtained than from the mere writing of books, even of novels, but for many years the life he led was not conducive to his being able even to make a bid for theatrical success. The state of his health made it impossible for him to live in London, so he was unable either to familiarise himself with stagecraft or to be in touch with those who might have aided him in this branch of literature. During what may be termed his years of exile, he never ceased to work at play-writing, devoting to it all the time which he could comfortably spare from his other arduous tasks, and thus it may be said, that for ten or fifteen years, he was gradually perfecting himself in the art, from which, in the autumn of his life, he reaped such great rewards.

The first play which he produced after the *Witchfinder* was a little costume comedy in three acts entitled *A Madcap Prince.* This piece was staged in 1875 at the Haymarket Theatre, then under the management of the late J. B. Buckstone. Though it had the advantage of an exceptionally fine cast, which included such names as Mr. and Mrs. Kendal, the late Mr. Buckstone, Mrs. Chippendale, Mr. Howe, and Mrs. Fitzwilliam, and on its initial production scored a distinct success, it never had the slightest chance of a prosperous London run. It was produced at the close of the London season, and was put up as a *bonne bouche,* for the benefit of the manager of the theatre, and though it was announced that the piece would be played by "the Haymarket company during their tour, and would reopen the Haymarket in October," it was never afterwards performed in London. This fact, however, could not be attributed to the non-success of the play, the reception of which was enthusiastic. "Prince Arthur was present, and at the end called Mr. Kendal to his box and congratulated him on the play, which he declared to be one of the best he had ever witnessed." It was, however, taken on tour, and although Mr. Buchanan had some difficulty in obtaining his fees ("I have to issue a writ against Buckstone for what he owes me, confound him!") the piece was phenomenally successful. In Liverpool they "refused money in all the more expensive parts of the House." In Edinburgh it was presented with every possible success, while in Glasgow it attracted "the largest audience seen in the Theatre Royal for a long time. The house was crammed to the door with a fashionable audience, and one important source of the eagerness of the great assembly was the fact that a new comedy was to be produced from the pen of one whose youth was spent in Glasgow, and whose name is now well known all over the world." The comedy met with a "decidedly brilliant reception from the whole audience, who were hearty and unstinted in their demonstrations of satisfaction. Greatly charmed, they cheered again and again." Yet, as I have said, *A Madcap Prince* did not form the opening attraction at the Haymarket Theatre on the return of the company to London, the principal reason for this, I fancy, being the fact that its author was driven to the necessity of "issuing a writ against Buckstone for the fees."

His next production was a play entitled *Corinne,* and again the circumstances were such as to preclude any chance of success. The play was bought by a lady, who, beyond having acted as an amateur, had had little or no experience upon the stage. She took the Lyceum Theatre for a month in the off-season, in order to exploit herself in the leading part, and the result of this experiment was disastrous to everybody concerned. "The lady's acting" (wrote Mr. Buchanan) "was simply *awful,* and a strong acting piece was lost through her incompetence. So far as the literary merits of the play went, the critics were right perhaps—it was merely meant to be a *theatrical* success. Fortunately, I had secured my full money beforehand, or I should have been a heavy loser. As it is, though I have gained nothing in reputation, this very failure has brought me two heavy offers or commissions from London managers, all of whom saw *why* the piece could not run."[1] Though the play failed to draw the public to any great extent, it held the stage during the lady's tenure of the Lyceum Theatre, and later on it was evidently taken on tour, for in a subsequent letter to Mr. Canton Mr. Buchanan said: "I see *Corinne* is to be played in Glasgow. Between ourselves, I am very sorry for it; for the lady (*entre nous*—don't whisper it abroad) is quite incompetent. It is a play of the French romantic school, and wants perfect acting to do any good."

But so far from daunting him these failures only acted as an incentive to fresh efforts, and his next bid for theatrical success came in the shape of a dramatic version of my first novel, *The Queen of Connaught.* There are one or two circumstances in connection with this play which it may be interesting to relate. The book, which was issued anonymously, was received most kindly by the critics, and met with great and instantaneous success. "You will observe with amusement" (wrote Mr. Buchanan) "that all the writers think the author is a 'he.'" This indeed was the case, and in many quarters the book was spoken of as the work of Charles Reade. Fearing the great author's anger, I wrote him a letter of apology, telling him that I was only a beginner in the art which I had adopted under circumstances so auspicious, and finally assuring him that I had had no hand whatever in the circulation of the reports which connected the book with his name. The reply which I received was courteous and kindly in the extreme. Mr. Reade began by congratulating me on the success which I had obtained so early in my career. He urged me not to lose my head over it, or to be too eager to rush into the market with another book. "Rest on your laurels," said he, "and be careful to fill up the teapot before you pour out again." Finally he confessed that the report had not made him angry in the least; it had, in fact, sent him to the book (he was not a great reader of fiction). But having read this particular work, he could only say he would have been proud to acknowledge it as his own.

Some time later, when I was dining with him at his house in Knightsbridge, our talk reverted to the subject which had been the means of making us personally acquainted, and he showed me a note-book in which he had scribbled the following: "*Queen of Connaught*—good for a play." I told him that Mr. Buchanan had had the same idea; that, as a matter of fact, he had sketched the play, and had begun the writing of it, but that so far he had been unable to see in it the makings of a theatrical success. At this Mr. Reade became keenly interested, and was so good as to say that in the event of Mr. Buchanan going on with the work he would be only too pleased to help him with his criticism and advice. I related all this to Mr. Buchanan, who, spurned to fresh efforts, reviewed his notes and returned to the writing of the play. As the work proceeded we went, on Mr. Reade's invitation, from time to time to Albert Gate, to read him certain scenes and talk over others, and many delightful evenings were so spent. One evening, I remember, while Mr. Buchanan was reading a scene in the last act, the great novelist became so excited that he could not keep in his seat. He paced the floor ejaculating "Good!" "Very powerful!" "Go on, my boy!" and on the conclusion of the reading he rang the bell, announcing, in his most delightful manner, that the act was quite good enough to warrant the opening of a bottle of champagne. The play, on its completion, was accepted by Mr. Henry Neville, and was produced by him at the Olympic Theatre (then under his management), Mr. Neville himself appearing as the hero John Darlington, while the late Ada Cavendish sustained the part of the Queen of Connaught. Though the piece drew fair business, and could not by any stretch of the imagination be called a failure, it never rose into what may be called a great theatrical success.

Following this came *The Nine Days' Queen,* produced for a short run at the Connaught Theatre in 1880, *Lucy Brandon* at the Imperial, and *The Shadow of the Sword* at the Olympic in 1882; but the dramatisation of his novel, *God and the Man,* which, as I have said, was produced at the Adelphi Theatre under the title of *Stormbeaten,* brought him a far greater monetary reward than he had reaped from all his other dramatic productions put together. The successor to *Stormbeaten* was the version of *Le Maître de Forges,* and entitled *Lady Clare.* For this production Mr. Buchanan took the Globe Theatre. The play ran for over a hundred nights, and was taken off to a good margin of profit, Mr. Buchanan also receiving considerable sums for it from America. But the play which made the most money was *Alone in London,* the very one for which he cared the least; indeed, he could never bring himself to speak of it with anything but contempt. However, it has never failed to make money for everybody connected with it, but the money so earned brought him no satisfaction, for he was always ashamed of the source from which it sprang, and so, taking my consent for granted, he sold the piece for an absurdly small sum to Messrs. Miller and Elliston, and so parted with the goose which laid the golden eggs.

It was during the first provincial tour of *Alone in London* that Mr. Buchanan began a connection which was destined to bring him much pleasure, no little profit, and considerable reputation as a writer for the stage, for in that year Mr. Thomas Thorne (then the sole manager of the Vaudeville Theatre) read and accepted his comedy of *Sophia.* The first performance of this play was a triumph for everybody concerned in it—for the management, the company, and the author. A brilliant representative audience was assembled, and prominent in a private box was Mr., now Sir, Henry Irving, who, directly the comedy began to "move," was liberal both with laughter and applause, and who sent round a cordial "Bravo, Tom!" to Mr. Thorne directly the play was over. The author was called and recalled, and made his bow in the midst of the performers instead of before the curtain. Immediately after the descent of the curtain the stage and the manager's dressing-room were crowded with friends of the management, who came to offer their congratulations, for Mr. Thorne was justly popular in private life as well as with the appreciative public.

Sophia had waited exactly ten years for a production, and had been declined with thanks by several leading London managers. Mr. Wilson Barrett, however, had read it some years before, and had written to this effect: "I like it. Will the public stand it?" and had paid a small deposit for the right of doing it within a year. A little later it was almost staged by the late Mr. Edgar Bruce, then managing the Prince of Wales's Theatre in Tottenham Court Road, but the question of the expensive costumes finally decided him against it, and he produced the *Colonel* instead. It had been offered in vain to Mr. Bancroft in England and to Lester Wallack in America—neither thought that it would be successful. As a matter of fact it ran consecutively for over five hundred nights, or close upon two years, and it has been more than once revived. Towards the end of its run, and after the author had been receiving fees for its performances from the beginning, he sold the acting rights to Mr. Thorne for £600.

The day after production the newspapers were full of enthusiastic notices, one of the warmest and most cordial being from the pen of Mr. Clement Scott and published in the *Daily Telegraph.* Yet, in spite of such encomiums, the fate of *Sophia* hovered in the balance for about a month, so much so indeed that the piece was actually withdrawn for a short time during the heat of the summer. It was not till its revival to open the autumn season that it began the career of prosperity which, as I have said, lasted for nearly two years.

The production of *Sophia* at the Vaudeville was the beginning of a very happy theatrical experience. After it came *Joseph's Sweetheart,* the dramatisation of *Joseph An-*

drews, in which Mr. Thorne appeared as the humorous country parson. This play was produced at the Vaudeville in March, 1888—as usual at an afternoon performance—and on the succeeding night it was placed in the evening bill. Before the comedy began Miss Vane, in the character of Lady Booby, spoke the following prologue:—

"Ladies and gentlemen—behold in me
A wicked dame of the last century,—
Just brought to life again before your gaze,
To hint the fashion of forgotten days,
When Garrick, bent to woo the comic Muse,
Changed his high buskin for soft satin shoes,
And frolicking behind the footlights, showed
Love *à bon ton* and marriage *à la mode!*
La, times are changed indeed since wits and lords
Swagger'd in square-cut, powder'd wigs, and swords!
Picture the age!—a lord was then, I vow,
A lord indeed (how different from *now*)
And trembling Virtue hid herself in fear
Before the naughty ogling of a peer.
Abductions, scandals, brawls, and dissipation,
Were rich men's pleasure, poor men's consternation,
While Fashion, painted, trick'd in fine brocade,
Turn'd Love to jest, and Life to masquerade!
Well, 'mid the masquerade, the pinchbeck show,
When Folly smiled on courtesan and beau,
Some noble human Spirits still drew breath,
And proved this world no hideous Dance of Death
Sad Hogarth's pencil limn'd the souls of men,
And Fielding wielded his magician's pen!
Off fell the mask that darken'd and concealed
Life's face, and Human Nature stood revealed!
Then rose Sophia at Fielding's conjuration,
Like Venus from the sea—of affectation.
Then madcap Tom showed, in his sport and passion,
A man's a man for a' that,'spite the fashion.
Then Parson Adams, type of honest worth,
Born of the pure embrace of Love and Mirth,
Smiled in the English sunshine, proving clear
That one true heart is worth a world's veneer!
And now our task is in a merry play,
To summon up that time long past away;
To bring to life the manners long outworn,
The lords, the dames, the maidens all forlorn—
A *tableau vivant* of the tinsel age
Immortalised on the great Master's page!
Hey, Presto! See, I wave my conjuror's cane!
The Present fades—the dead Past lives again—
The clouds of modern care dissolve—to show
Life *à la mode,* a hundred years ago!"

This comedy, which was in five acts, had a reception quite as enthusiastic as that of its predecessor. Admirably put upon the stage, the scenes of Lady Booby's Boudoir (realising Hogarth's picture in his "Marriage à la Mode") and of Parson Adams's Cottage being wonderfully solid sets for so small a theatre. A new recruit came to the already excellent company in the person of Mr. Cyril Maude, whose foppish *roué,* Lord Fellamar, was admirably conceived and executed.

Joseph's Sweetheart ran for over a year, or, speaking literally, for three hundred and fifty odd nights. It was succeeded in 1889 by a practically original comedy from the pen of the same author, entitled **Dr. Cupid**—a fantastic bit of imagination, the scene of which was laid in the eighteenth century. The cast included Winifred Emery, Cyril Maude, Fred Thorne, and Thomas Thorne. The run of **Dr. Cupid** was briefer than that of its predecessors, but it drew excellent houses for over six months.

By this time Mr. Buchanan had succeeded in establishing at the Vaudeville a sort of vogue for costume comedies and dramatisations of masterpieces of English fiction. The difficulty, of course, was to keep the ball rolling—in other words, to find new subjects founded on old masterpieces or imbued with the spirit of old comedy. *Tom Jones* and *Joseph Andrews* were all very well, but where were their successors to come from? *Amelia* was out of the question for many reasons, quite apart from its inferiority as a work of art, and the works of Smollett were at once coarser and more chaotic than those of his mightier contemporary. When the names of Fielding and Smollett were spoken, only Richardson remained among the great masters of eighteenth century fiction, for *Tristram Shandy* was not exactly a story, but a succession of amusing incidents dealing with the surroundings of a hero only just born. While the author was speculating what work he should produce next for the little theatre in the Strand, a French melodrama, founded on a French feuilleton, was placed in his hands for adaptation for the English stage. This was *Roger la Honte,* better known to English playgoers as Robert Buchanan's famous play, **A Man's Shadow.** The adaptation of this work was not an easy task, for the original was in innumerable acts and episodes, and it had been offered to and refused by nearly all the managers in London, while Mr. Beerbohm Tree, who went to Paris to see the French play, gave it as his opinion that there was not a penny in it. Mr. Buchanan's version, however, was at once accepted by Mr. Tree. Produced at a critical moment for the management of the Haymarket Theatre, it became an enormous success, playing to crowded audiences from early autumn to the following summer, and enabling Mr. Tree to distinguish himself in the dual *rôle* of the hero and the villain Luversan, the latter a masterly bit of characterisation. Previous to the production of **A Man's Shadow,** Mr. Tree had obtained no little success in a play from Mr. Buchanan's pen entitled **Partners**—an adaptation of Daudet's *Fromont Jeune et Risler Ainé.*

Mr. Buchanan was now in the high tide of success as a popular dramatist, and naturally his hands were very full of work. The triumph of **A Man's Shadow** led to an offer from Messrs. Gatti, asking him to collaborate with Mr. G. R. Sims in a new play for the Adelphi, and in an evil moment he accepted. I do not use this expression to convey the fact that it was in any way derogatory to him to write melodrama for the most melodramatic house in London, especially in combination with a writer so thoroughly strong and human as Mr. Sims; but, in point of fact, he was doing too much, and overloading himself with work, which, at the very best, could only be perfunctory. This the result proved, for during the next three or four years he produced a large quantity of dramatic work of exceedingly mixed quality, and began to grow tired of play-writing altogether. Up to date, in spite of all his success, he had not obtained the object which made him write for the stage at all—that of securing enough money to enable him to devote the rest of his life to pure literature, more particularly to poetry. He certainly made large sums—sums far greater than any he could possibly have made by the mere writing of books—but with his increased income came increased expenditure, and he soon found that what he earned melted rapidly away. It is a curious fact that, despite his many struggles, he never could master the art of compound addition, so that whatever his income was he always managed to be a little in arrear. He could no more help being prodigal with his great gains than the sun can help shining. I have known him to go to Trouville with two hundred pounds in his pocket and return at the end of a week without a penny of it, even although that two hundred pounds happened to be his last, and the spending of it meant that he had to shut himself up in his study and work incessantly till the deficiency could be made good. But it must not be supposed that all his money went in the purchase of mere personal pleasures. His generosity was without parallel, and he never refused a request for help if it was in his power to grant it. If a friend happened to be in "Queer Street" he would lend him a hundred pounds with as little hesitation as he would lend ten, and it was a peculiarity with him that he never looked for the return of such money, no matter how large the sum might be, but always regarded it as so much to the good if it happened to come his way again.

For four years he collaborated with Mr. Sims in plays for the Adelphi. Their first production, *The English Rose,* was a considerable success, and after it had been running for some time Mr. Buchanan sold out his share in it for two thousand five hundred pounds. Its successor, *The Trumpet Call,* was even more popular, but Mr. Buchanan sold out for a lesser sum. Next came the *White Rose*—a costume drama produced in the summer season. This was only moderately successful, in spite of some superb acting. Two other plays followed—*The Lights of Home* and the *Black Domino*—but neither of these equalled their predecessors in popularity.

For the production of the *Trumpet Call* the authors had the assistance of that charming actress Mrs. Patrick Campbell, and the first night was memorable for an incident, or rather for an accident, which might have wrecked the play. Mrs. Campbell played the part of Astrea, a gipsy girl, and in one of the later scenes, that of a low lodging-house, she had to appear in rags. As she crossed the stage the skirt of her dress became loose, and descended slowly towards her knees. A low murmur, deepening to a groan, arose from the audience; but with wonderful presence of mind the actress, quite calm and not in the least disconcerted, gripped the garment with one hand and drew it upward, fixing the spectators at the same time with one long look, a sort of "Peace be still" expression in her great black eyes. The roar of horror changed into a tumultuous roar of applause, and a disaster was averted.

Afterwards, in the *White Rose,* Mrs. Campbell played, with extraordinary sweetness and pathos, the part of Cromwell's daughter.

But in turning his attention to the Adelphi Mr. Buchanan was not forgetting his former love, the little Vaudeville. Here, at a *matinée* in March, 1890, was produced *Miss Tomboy,* a quite new version of Vanbrugh's *The Relapse,* formerly used by Sheridan in the *Trip to Scarborough.* It was received with complete enthusiasm, the impersonation of the heroine by Miss Winifred Emery being quite the most perfect thing this versatile actress had done in comedy. In the same year Mr. Buchanan staged at the same theatre his version of Richardson's *Clarissa Harlowe,* with Miss Emery as the hapless heroine, Mr. Thalberg as Lovelace, and Mr. Thomas Thorne in a quasi-serious *rôle*—that of Bedford. No play of Mr. Buchanan's ever held an audience under so complete a spell, but the final act was almost too pathetic for the public taste of that moment, especially at a theatre so closely associated with broad comedy.

Meantime, not satisfied with his ventures at the Vaudeville and the Adelphi, he had produced on his own responsibility at the last-named theatre, for a *matinée* performance, a poetical play founded on the story of "Cupid and Psyche," and called the *Bride of Love.* It was written in blank verse throughout, and was highly poetical and imaginative, too much so for the English public, who will only tolerate such experiments when they are made the occasion for gorgeous scenery. The scenery at the Adelphi, though correct and adequate, was inexpensive. In this production I myself played the part of Psyche, Miss Letty Lind that of Euphrosyne, Mr. Thalberg that of Eros, Mr. Lionel Rignold that of Zephyr, and the late Miss Ada Cavendish that of Venus Aphrodite. The reception of the *Bride of Love* on its first production was so encouraging that Mr. Buchanan was induced to take the Lyric Theatre and to reproduce the play there for a "regular run." This was a serious mistake, as he made no attempt to improve the scenery, but trusted to the mere poetry of the piece to draw the public. After his long experience of the stage he ought to have known better.

There is no modern instance, I think, of a poetical play attracting audiences on its own merits apart from the arts of the showman and the tricks of the scene-painter. This experiment cost him some thousands of pounds, nor was he much consoled, I fancy, by the almost daily receipt of letters from unknown admirers congratulating him on the work. One of these letters was so remarkable in the tone of its compliments as to be almost unique. The writer said that he had long ceased to find in the theatre the enjoyment and the interest of his early years; the glamour had all passed away, as he thought, for ever; but in witnessing the *Bride of Love,* he said, all the charm and all the glamour had returned, and he felt again the delight and enthusiasm of his boyhood. The signature to this letter was that of the distinguished American dramatist, Bronson Howard.

I may remark in passing that the *Bride of Love* was not a Greek play in the strict sense of the word, but rather a dramatisation of a Greek fairy tale. Whatever its merits as an acting piece might be, it certainly contained passages of real poetry.

Two exquisite choral odes were composed for this play by Sir Alexander Mackenzie and sung by Stedman's choir. Other incidental music, some of it of bewitching beauty, was written by Mr. Walter Slaughter, now so widely known to the public as a musician of the finest gifts. Before passing on to other matters I may mention that on the occasion of the opening of the Glasgow Exhibition in May, 1888, the great representatives of poetry and music were Robert Buchanan and Sir Alexander (then Mr.) Mackenzie.

"The fine ode which Robert Buchanan had written was worthily set by Mr. Mackenzie, and was worthily sung . . . . No one who heard it will soon forget its noble swelling harmonies, and assuredly few more striking and impressive scenes have been witnessed than when the vast audience stood with bowed heads while the massive strains were pealed out by the organ, orchestra, and chorus. Immediately after the conclusion of the Ode, just as the large assembly was bursting into cheers, the Prince of Wales stepped forward and declared the Exhibition open."[2]

Before resigning the tenancy of the Lyric Theatre Mr. Buchanan produced there, under the title of **Sweet Nancy**, his dramatisation of Miss Rhoda Broughton's most popular book, and the reception of this play was so favourable that he took the Royalty Theatre in order to continue the "run." Never was a comedy of the kind better played; indeed, Mr. John Hare, witnessing the performance at the Royalty, averred that the acting was the very best he had seen for years. Miss Annie Hughes was inimitable as Nancy, almost equally delightful were the Algy of Mr. H. V. Esmond, and the Tow-Tow of Miss Beatrice Ferrer. Everything was going well and the piece was giving promise of a successful run when Miss Hughes was taken ill and had to resign the leading part. An attempt was made to find a substitute for this delightful *comédienne,* but the only possible one was Miss Norreys, who was not at that time available. Without Miss Hughes **Sweet Nancy** was absolutely worthless, so perfect in its captivation had been her rendering of the character, so the piece was withdrawn, and that was Mr. Buchanan's last experience of theatrical management on his own account and with his own money.

So far, mainly as I have shown through disastrous speculation, his work for the stage had not left him one penny the richer. He grew reckless, and the next few years, from 1890 to 1894, were lived at headlong pace. Never perhaps was a man so busy, so full of affairs, and his marvellous power of rapid writing now became his bane, for besides a succession of plays which were more or less successful, he was contributing a great deal to the Press, and in such leisure as he could find he was putting the finishing touches to his poetical writings. The present chapter, however, is concerned solely with his work for the stage. Among the productions of those years was the **Sixth Commandment,** which was a version of Dostoievski's *Crime and Punish-*

ment. This play failed to attract the public, but it was noteworthy for two pieces of magnificent acting on the part of Mr. Herbert Waring and of Mr. Lewis Waller. Later on **The Charlatan** was written for Mr. Beerbohm Tree at the Haymarket Theatre, and although it was most warmly received it just fell short of a great financial success. **Dick Sheridan** was produced at the Comedy Theatre and also met with an adverse fate, and running simultaneously with it, for afternoon performances only, was the **Pied Piper of Hamelin.** This little play, which was acknowledged by the Press to be almost perfect of its kind, also failed from some reason or other to draw the public.

I am now approaching the end of this brief summary of his dramatic work. By this time he was not only far off independence, but heavily in debt. His last stake was a comedy of which he was part author, and for which he engaged the famous Mrs. Langtry, then anxious to return to the stage. Having secured a small financial backing, quite inadequate as the issue proved, he took the Opera Comique, and produced there in June, 1894, the **Society Butterfly,** with Mrs. Langtry in the chief female part, and such excellent artistes as Mr. Fred Kerr and the late Miss Rose Leclercq to support the leading lady. All would have gone very well, but for one unfortunate *contretemps.* The fate of the play absolutely depended on a certain dance to be performed by the leading actress at the end of the third act, but at the last moment Mrs. Langtry was unable to do the dance, and some ineffective *tableaux vivants* had to be substituted in a hurry. These *tableaux* provoked a stormy reception and led to very adverse criticisms in the Press. The play, however, ran for some weeks to very fair business, and was actually promising to develop into a popular success when the managerial exchequer was found to be empty. At that moment a creditor served Mr. Buchanan with a petition in bankruptcy. His house of cards collapsed, and a few months later he was standing in the bankruptcy court, a practically ruined man.

Looking back upon that experience, I think now that the man whom I then regarded as his bitterest enemy, since he brought about his financial disaster, was in reality a friend in disguise. For several years he had been living in a fool's paradise, veritably gambling away the best hours of his life. What part had he, who from first to last was a Poet with the deep poetic heart, among the worldlings of finance? All his thoughts and dreams were of higher and nobler things, and *au fond* all his daily prayer was to escape again into solitude and to be alone with his first love. It was only half a heart he could give to money getting. He awoke from his folly disillusioned, wretched, dispirited, but the punishment he had received was really given to him in mercy, for from that time forth he saw both himself and the world with very different eyes.

Notes

1. Letter to Mr. Canton.

2. *Scotsman.*

Lafcadio Hearn (essay date 1922)

SOURCE: "A Note on Robert Buchanan," in *Pre-Raphaelite and Other Poets*, edited by John Erskine, Dodd, Mead and Company, 1922, pp. 386-406.

[*In the following essay, Hearn offers a laudatory overview of Buchanan's poetry, focusing on the* "Ballad of Judas Iscariot."]

Among the minor poets of the Victorian period, Robert Buchanan cannot be passed over unnoticed. A contemporary of all the great singers, he seems to have been always a little isolated; I mean that he formed no strong literary friendships within the great circle. Most great poets must live to a certain extent in solitude; the man who can at once mix freely in society and find time for the production of masterpieces is a rare phenomenon. George Meredith is said to be such a person. But Tennyson, Rossetti, Swinburne, Browning, Fitzgerald, were all very reserved and retired men, though they had little circles of their own, and a certain common sympathy. The case of Buchanan is different. His aloofness from the rest has been, not the result of any literary desire for quiet, but the result, on the contrary, of a strong spirit of opposition. Not only did he have no real sympathy with the great poets, but he represented in himself the very prejudices against which they had to contend. Hard headed Scotchman as he was, he manifested in his attitude to his brother poets a good deal of the peculiar, harsh conservatism of which Scotchmen seemed to be particularly capable. And he did himself immense injury in his younger days by an anonymous attack upon the morals, or rather upon the moral tone, of such poets as Rossetti and Swinburne. Swinburne's reply to this attack was terrible and withering. That of Rossetti was very mild and gentle, but so effective that English literary circles almost unanimously condemned Buchanan, and attributed his attack to mere jealousy. I think the attack was less due to jealousy than to character, to prejudice, to the harshness of a mind insensible to particular forms of beauty. And for more than twenty years Buchanan has suffered extremely from the results of his own action. Thousands of people have ignored him and his books simply because it was remembered that he gave wanton pain to Rossetti, a poet much too sensitive to endure unjust criticism. I suppose that for many years to come Buchanan will still be remembered in this light, notwithstanding that he tried at a later day to make honourable amends to the memory of Rossetti, by dedicating to him, with a beautiful sonnet of apology, the definitive edition of his own works.

But the time has now passed when Buchanan can be treated as an indifferent figure in English literature. In spite of all disadvantages he has been a successful poet, a successful novelist, and a very considerable influence in the literature of criticism. Besides, he has written at least one poem that will probably live as long as the English language, and he has an originality quite apart and quite extraordinary, though weaker than the originality of the greater singers of his time. As to his personal history, little need to be said. He was educated at Glasgow University, and his literary efforts have always been somewhat coloured by Scotch sentiment, in spite of his long life in literary London.

Three volumes represent his poetical production. In these are contained a remarkable variety of poems—narrative, mystical, fantastic, classical, romantic, ranging from the simplest form of ballad to the complex form of the sonnet and the ode. The narrative poems would, I think, interest you least; they are gloomy studies of human suffering, physical and moral, among the poor, and are not so good as the work of Crabbe in the same direction. The mystical poems, on the contrary, are of a very curious kind; for Buchanan actually made a religious philosophy of his own, and put it into the form of verse. It is a Christian mysticism, an extremely liberal Unitarianism forming the basis of it; but the author's notions about the perpetual order of things are all his own. He has, moreover, put these queer fancies into a form of verse imitating the ancient Celtic poetry. We shall afterward briefly consider the mystical poetry. But the great production of Buchanan is a simple ballad, which you find very properly placed at the beginning of his collected poems. This is a beautiful and extraordinary thing, quite in accordance with the poet's peculiar views of Christianity. It is called **"The Ballad of Judas Iscariot."** If you know only this composition, you will know all that it is absolutely necessary to know of Robert Buchanan. It is by this poem that his place is marked in nineteenth century literature.

Before we turn to the poem itself, I must explain to you something of the legend of Judas Iscariot. You know, of course, that Judas was the disciple of Christ who betrayed his master. He betrayed him for thirty pieces of silver, according to the tradition; and he betrayed him with a kiss, for he said to the soldiers whom he was guiding, "The man whom I shall kiss is the man you want." So Judas went up to Christ, and kissed his face; and then the soldiers seized Christ. From this has come the proverbial phrase common to so many Western languages, a "Judas-kiss." Afterwards Judas, being seized with remorse, is said to have hanged himself; and there the Scriptural story ends. But in Church legends the fate of Judas continued to be discussed in the Middle Ages. As he was the betrayer of a person whom the Church considered to be God, it was deemed that he was necessarily the greatest of all traitors; and as he had indirectly helped to bring about the death of God, he was condemned as the greatest of all murderers. It was said that in hell the very lowest place was given to Judas, and that his tortures exceeded all other tortures. But once every year, it was said, Judas could leave hell, and go out to cool himself upon the ice of the Northern seas. That is the legend of the Middle Ages.

Now Robert Buchanan perceived that the Church legends of the punishment of Judas might be strongly questioned from a moral point of view. Revenge is indeed in the spirit of the Old Testament; but revenge is not exactly in the spirit of the teaching of Christ. The true question as to the fate of Judas ought to be answered by supposing what Christ himself would have wished in the matter. Would Christ have wished to see his betrayer burning for ever in the fires of hell? Or would he have shown to him some of that spirit manifested in his teachings, "Do good unto them that hate you; forgive your enemies"? As a result of thinking about the matter, Buchanan produced his ballad. All that could be said against it from a religious point of view is that the spirit of it is even more Christian than Christianity itself. From the poetical point of view we must acknowledge it to be one of the grandest ballads produced in the whole period of Victorian literature. You will not find so exquisite a finish here as in some of the ballads of Rossetti; but you will find a weirdness and a beauty and an emotional power that make up for slenderness in workmanship.

In order to understand the beginning of the ballad clearly, you should know the particulars about another superstition concerning Judas. It is said that all the elements refused to suffer the body to be committed to them; fire would not burn it; water would not let it sink to rest; every time it was buried, the earth would spew it out again. Man could not bury that body, so the ghosts endeavoured to get rid of it. The Field of Blood referred to in the ballad is the Aceldama of Scriptural legend, the place where Judas hanged himself.

> 'Twas the body of Judas Iscariot
>   Lay in the Field of Blood;
> 'Twas the soul of Judas Iscariot
>   Beside the body stood.
>
> Black was the earth by night,
>   And black was the sky;
> Black, black were the broken clouds,
>   Though the red Moon went by.
>   . . . . .
>
> Then the soul of Judas Iscariot
>   Did make a gentle moan—
> "I will bury underneath the ground
>   My flesh and blood and bone.
>   . . . . .
>
> "The stones of the field are sharp as steel,
>   And hard and bold, God wot;
> And I must bear my body hence
>   Until I find a spot!"
>
> 'Twas the soul of Judas Iscariot
>   So grim, and gaunt, and grey,
> Raised the body of Judas Iscariot
>   And carried it away.
>
> And as he bare it from the field
>   Its touch was cold as ice,
> And the ivory teeth within the jaw
>   Rattled aloud, like dice.

The use of the word "ivory" here has a double function; dice are usually made of ivory; and the suggestion of whiteness heightens the weird effect.

> As the soul of Judas Iscariot
>   Carried its load with pain,
> The Eye of Heaven, like a lanthorn's eye,
>   Opened and shut again.
>
> Half he walk'd, and half he seemed
>   Lifted on the cold wind;
> He did not turn, for chilly hands
>   Were pushing from behind.
>
> The first place that he came unto
>   It was the open wold,
> And underneath were pricky whins,
>   And a wind that blew so cold.
>
> The next place that he came unto
>   It was a stagnant pool,
> And when he threw the body in
>   It floated light as wool.
>
> He drew the body on his back,
>   And it was dripping chill,
> And the next place he came unto
>   Was a Cross upon a hill.
>
> A Cross upon the windy hill,
>   And a Cross on either side,
> Three skeletons that swing thereon,
>   Who had been crucified.
>
> And on the middle cross-bar sat
>   A white Dove slumbering;
> Dim it sat in the dim light,
>   With its head beneath its wing.
>
> And underneath the middle Cross
>   A grave yawned wide and vast,
> But the soul of Judas Iscariot
>   Shiver'd, and glided past.

We are not told what this hill was, but every reader knows that Calvary is meant, and the skeletons upon the crosses are those of Christ and the two thieves crucified with him. The ghostly hand had pushed Judas to the place of all places where he would have wished not to go. We need not mind the traditional discrepancy suggested by the three skeletons; as a matter of fact, the bodies of malefactors were not commonly left upon the crosses long enough to become skeletons, and of course the legend is that Christ's body was on the cross only for a short time. But we may suppose that the whole description is of a phantasm, purposely shaped to stir the remorse of Judas. The white dove sleeping upon the middle cross suggests the soul of Christ, and the great grave made below might have been prepared out of mercy for the body of Judas. If the dove had awoke and spoken to him, would it not have said, "You can put your body here, in my grave; nobody will torment you"? But the soul of Judas cannot even think of daring to approach the place of the crucifixion.

> The fourth place that he came unto,
>   It was the Brig of Dread,
> And the great torrents rushing down
>   Were deep, and swift, and red.

He dared not fling the body in
　　For fear of faces dim,
And arms were waved in the wild water
　　To thrust it back to him.

There is here a poetical effect borrowed from sources having nothing to do with the Judas tradition. In old Northern
folklore there is the legend of a River of Blood, in which
all the blood ever shed in this world continues to flow;
and there is a reference to this river in the old Scotch ballad of "Thomas the Rhymer."

　　It was mirk, mirk night, and there was nae light,
　　And they waded in red blude up to the knee,
　　For a' the blude that's shed on earth,
　　Rins through the springs o' that countrie.

Judas leaves the dreadful bridge and continues his wanderings over the mountain, through woods and through great
desolate plains:

　　For months and years, in grief and tears,
　　　　He walked the silent night;
　　Then the soul of Judas Iscariot
　　　　Perceived a far-off light.

　　A far-off light across the waste,
　　　　As dim as dim might be,
　　That came and went like a lighthouse gleam
　　　　On a black night at sea.

　　'Twas the soul of Judas Iscariot
　　　　Crawled to the distant gleam;
　　And the rain came down, and the rain was blown
　　　　Against him with a scream.

　　　　　　.　.　.　.　.

　　'Twas the soul of Judas Iscariot,
　　　　Strange, and sad, and tall,
　　Stood all alone at dead of night
　　　　Before a lighted hall.

　　And the wold was white with snow,
　　　　And his foot-marks black and damp,
　　And the ghost of the silver Moon arose,
　　　　Holding her yellow lamp.

　　And the icicles were on the eaves,
　　　　And the walls were deep with white,
　　And the shadows of the guests within
　　　　　　Passed on the window light.

　　The shadows of the wedding guests
　　　　Did strangely come and go,
　　And the body of Judas Iscariot
　　　　Lay stretch'd along the snow.

But only the body. The soul which has carried it does not
lie down, but runs round and round the lighted hall, where
the wedding guests are assembled. What wedding? What
guests? This is the mystical banquet told of in the parable
of the New Testament; the bridegroom is Christ himself;
the guests are the twelve disciples, or rather, the eleven,
Judas himself having been once the twelfth. And the guests
see the soul of Judas looking in at the window.

　　'Twas the Bridegroom sat at the table-head,
　　　　And the lights burned bright and clear—
　　"Oh, who is that," the Bridegroom said,
　　　　"Whose weary feet I hear?"

　　'Twas one look'd from the lighted hall,
　　　　And answered soft and slow,
　　"It is a wolf runs up and down
　　　　With a black track in the snow."

　　The Bridegroom in his robe of white
　　　　Sat at the table-head—
　　"Oh, who is that who moans without?"
　　　　The blessed Bridegroom said.

　　'Twas one looked from the lighted hall,
　　　　And answered fierce and low,
　　"'Tis the soul of Judas Iscariot
　　　　Gliding to and fro."

　　'Twas the soul of Judas Iscariot
　　　　Did hush itself and stand,
　　And saw the Bridegroom at the door
　　　　With a light in his hand.

　　The Bridegroom stood in the open door,
　　　　And he was clad in white,
　　And far within the Lord's Supper
　　　　Was spread so long and bright.

　　The Bridegroom shaded his eyes and looked,
　　　　And his face was bright to see—
　　"What dost thou here at the Lord's Supper
　　　　With thy body's sins?" said he.

　　'Twas the soul of Judas Iscariot,
　　　　Stood black, and sad, and bare—
　　"I have wandered many nights and days;
　　　　There is no light elsewhere."

　　'Twas the wedding guests cried out within,
　　　　And their eyes were fierce and bright—
　　"Scourge the soul of Judas Iscariot
　　　　Away into the night!"

　　The Bridegroom stood in the open door
　　　　And he waved hands still and slow,
　　And the third time that he waved his hands
　　　　The air was thick with snow.

　　And of every flake of falling snow,
　　　　Before it touched the ground,
　　There came a dove, and a thousand doves
　　　　Made sweet sound.

　　'Twas the body of Judas Iscariot
　　　　Floated away full fleet,
　　And the wings of the doves that bare it off
　　　　Were like its winding-sheet.

　　'Twas the Bridegroom stood at the open door,
　　　　And beckon'd, smiling sweet;
　　'Twas the soul of Judas Iscariot
　　　　Stole in, and fell at his feet.

"The Holy Supper is spread within,
    And the many candles shine,
And I have waited long for thee
    Before I poured the wine!"

It would have been better, I think, to finish the ballad at this stanza; there is one more, but it does not add at all to the effect of what goes before. When the doves, emblems of divine love, have carried away the sinful body, and the Master comes to the soul, smiling and saying: "I have been waiting for you a long time, waiting for your coming before I poured the wine"—there is nothing more to be said. We do not want to hear any more; we know that the Eleven had again become Twelve; we do not require to be told that the wine is poured out, or that Judas repents his fault. The startling and beautiful thing is the loving call and the welcome to the Divine Supper. You will find the whole of this poem in the "Victorian Anthology," but I should advise any person who might think of making a Japanese translation to drop the final stanza and to leave out a few of the others, if his judgment agrees with mine.

Read this again to yourselves, and see how beautiful it is. The beauty is chiefly in the central idea of forgiveness; but the workmanship of this composition has also a very remarkable beauty, a Celtic beauty of weirdness, such as we seldom find in a modern composition touching religious tradition. It were interesting to know how the poet was able to imagine such a piece of work. I think I can tell a little of the secret. Only a man with a great knowledge and love of old ballads could have written it. Having once decided upon the skeleton of the story, he must have gone to his old Celtic literature and to old Northern ballads for further inspiration. I have already suggested that the ballad of "Thomas the Rhymer" was one source of his inspiration, with its strange story of the River of Blood. Thomas was sitting under a tree, the legend goes, when he saw a woman approaching so beautiful that he thought she was an angel or the Virgin Mary, and he addressed her on his knees. But she sat down beside him, and said, "I am no angel nor saint; I am only a fairy. But if you think that I am so beautiful, take care that you do not kiss me, for if you do, then I shall have power over you." Thomas immediately did much more than kiss her, and he therefore became her slave. She took him at once to fairy land, and on their way they passed through strange wild countries, much like those described in Robert Buchanan's ballad; they passed the River of Blood; they passed dark trees laden with magical food; and they saw the road that reaches Heaven and the road that reaches Hell. But Buchanan could take only a few ideas from this poem. Other ideas I think were inspired by a ballad of Goethe's, or at least by Sir Walter Scott's version of it, "Frederick and Alice." Frederick is a handsome young soldier who seduces a girl called Alice under promise of marriage, and then leaves her. He rides to join the army in France. The girl becomes insane with grief and shame; and the second day later she dies at four o'clock in the morning. Meantime Frederick unexpectedly loses his way; the rest I may best tell in the original weird form. The horse has been frightened by the sound of a church bell striking the hour of four.

Heard ye not the boding sound,
    As the tongue of yonder tower,
Slowly, to the hills around,
    Told the fourth, the fated hour?

Starts the steed, and snuffs the air,
    Yet no cause of dread appears;
Bristles high the rider's hair,
    Struck with strange mysterious fears.

Desperate, as his terrors rise,
    In the steed the spur he hides;
From himself in vain he flies;
    Anxious, restless, on he rides.

Seven long days, and seven long nights,
    Wild he wandered, woe the while!
Ceaseless care, and causeless fright,
    Urge his footsteps many a mile.

Dark the seventh sad night descends;
    Rivers swell, and rain-streams pour;
While the deafening thunder lends
    All the terrors of its roar.

At the worst part of his dreary wandering over an unknown and gloomy country, Frederick suddenly sees a light far away. This seems to him, as it seemed in Buchanan's ballad to the soul of Judas, a light of hope. He goes to the light, and finds himself in front of a vast and ruinous looking church. Inside there is a light; he leaps down from his horse, descends some steps, and enters the building. Suddenly all is darkness again; he has to feel his way.

Long drear vaults before him lie!
    Glimmering lights are seen to glide!—
"Blessed Mary, hear my cry!
    Deign a sinner's steps to guide!"

Often lost their quivering beam,
    Still the lights move slow before,
Till they rest their ghastly gleam
    Right against an iron door.

He is really in the underground burial place of a church, in the vaults of the dead, but he does not know it. He hears voices.

Thundering voices from within,
    Mixed with peals of laughter, rose;
As they fell, a solemn strain
    Lent its wild and wondrous close!

'Midst the din, he seem'd to hear
    Voice of friends, by death removed;—
Well he knew that solemn air,
    'Twas the lay that Alice loved.

Suddenly a great bell booms four times, and the iron door opens. He sees within a strange banquet; the seats are coffins, the tables are draped with black, and the dead are the guests.

Alice, in her grave-clothes bound,
    Ghastly smiling, points a seat;

All arose, with thundering sound;
  All the expected stranger greet.

High their meagre arms they wave,
  Wild their notes of welcome swell;
"Welcome, traitor, to the grave!
  Perjured, bid the light farewell!"

I have given the greater part of this strange ballad because of its intrinsic value and the celebrity of its German author. But the part that may have inspired Buchanan is only the part concerning the wandering over the black moor, the light seen in the distance, the ghostly banquet of the dead, and the ruined vaults. A great poet would have easily found in these details the suggestion which Buchanan found for the wandering of Judas to the light and the unexpected vision of the dead assembling to a banquet with him—but only this. The complete transformation of the fancy, the transmutation of the purely horrible into a ghostly beauty and tenderness, is the wonderful thing. After all, this is the chief duty of the poet in this world, to discover beauty even in the ugly, suggestions of beauty even in the cruel and terrible. This Buchanan did once so very well that his work will never be forgotten, but he received thereafter no equal inspiration, and the **"Ballad of Judas"** remains, alone of its kind, his only real claim to high distinction.

The poetry of Robert Buchanan is not great enough as poetry to justify many quotations, but as thinking it demands some attention. His third volume is especially of interest in this respect, because it contains a curious exposition of his religious idealism. Buchanan is a mystic; there is no doubt that he has been very much influenced by the mysticism of Blake. The whole of the poems collectively entitled *The Devil's Mystics,* must have been suggested by Blake's nomenclature. This collection belongs to ***The Book of Orm,*** which might have been well called *The Book of Robert Buchanan.* Orm ought to be a familiar name to students of English literature, one of the old English books also being called "The Ormulum," because it was written by a man named Orm. Buchanan's Orm is represented to be an ancient Celt, who has visions and dreams about the mystery of the universe, and who puts these visions and dreams, which are Buchanan's, into old-fashioned verse.

The great Ernest Renan said in his *Dialogues Philosophiques* that if everybody in the world who had thought much about the mystery of things were to write down his ideas regarding the Infinite, some great truth might be discovered or deduced from the result. Buchanan has tried to follow this suggestion; for he has very boldly put down all his thoughts about the world and man and God. As to results, however, I can find nothing particularly original except two or three queer fancies, none of which relates to the deeper riddles of being. In a preface in verse, the author further tells us that when he speaks of God he does not mean the Christian God or the God of India nor any particular God, but only the all-including Spirit of Life. Be that as it may, we find his imagery to be certainly borrowed from old Hebrew and old Christian thinkers;

here he has not fulfilled expectations. But the imagery is used to express some ideas which I think you will find rather new—not exactly philosophical ideas, but moral parables.

One of these is a parable about the possible consequences of seeing or knowing the divine power which is behind the shadows of things. Suppose that there were an omnipotent God whom we could see; what would be the consequences of seeing him? Orm discovered that the blue of the sky was a blue veil drawn across Immensity to hide the face of God. One day, in answer to prayer, God drew aside the blue veil. Then all mankind were terrified because they saw, by day and by night, an awful face looking down upon them out of the sky, the sleepless eyes of the face seeming to watch each person constantly wherever he was. Did this make men happy? Not at all. They became tired of life, finding themselves perpetually watched; they covered their cities with roofs, and lived by lamp light only, in order to avoid being looked at by the face, God. This queer parable, recounted in the form of a dream, has a meaning worth thinking about. The ultimate suggestion, of course, is that we do not know and see many things because it would make us very unhappy to know them.

An equally curious parable, also related in the form of a dream, treats of the consolations of death. What would become of mankind if there were no death? I think you will remember that I told you how the young poet William Watson took up the same subject a few years ago, in his remarkable poem, "A Dream of Man." Watson's supposition is that men became so wise, so scientific, that they were able to make themselves immortal and to conquer death. But at last they became frightfully unhappy, unutterably tired of life, and were obliged to beg God to give them back death again. And God said to them, "You are happier than I am. You can die; I cannot. The only happiness of existence is effort. Now you can have your friend death back again." Buchanan's idea was quite different from this. His poem is called **"The Dream of the World without Death."** Men prayed to God that there might be no more death or decay of the body; and the prayer was granted. People continued to disappear from the world, but they did not die. They simply vanished, when their time came, as ghosts. A child goes out to play in the field, for example, and never comes back again; the mother finds only the empty clothes of her darling. Or a peasant goes to the fields to work, and his body is never seen again. People found that this was a much worse condition of things than had been before. For the consolation of knowledge, of certainty, was not given them. The dead body is a certificate of death; nature uses corruption as a seal, an official exhibit and proof of the certainty of death. But when there is no body, no corpse, no possible sign, how horrible is the disappearance of the persons we love. The mystery of it is a much worse pain than the certain knowledge of death. Doubt is the worst form of torture. Well, when mankind had this experience, they began to think, that, after all, death was a beautiful and good thing, and they prayed most fervently that they might again have the privilege of dying in the old way, of putting the bodies of their dead into beautiful tombs, of being able to visit the graves of their beloved from time to time. So God took pity on them and gave them back death, and the poet sings his gratitude thus:

> And I cried, "O unseen Sender of Corruption,
> I bless thee for the wonder of Thy mercy,
> Which softeneth the mystery and the parting.
>
> "I bless Thee for the change and for the comfort,
> The bloomless face, shut eyes, and waxen fingers,—
> For Sleeping, and for Silence, and Corruption."

This idea is worth something, if only as a vivid teaching of the necessity of things as they are. The two fantasies thus commented upon are the most original things in the range of this mystical book. I could not recommend any further reading or study of the poet, except perhaps of his **"Vision of the Man Accurst."** But even this has not the true stamp of originality; and only the **"Ballad of Judas Iscariot"** is certain not to be soon forgotten.

Hoxie N. Fairchild (essay date 1952)

SOURCE: "The Immediate Source of *The Dynasts,*[1]" in *PMLA,* Vol. LXVII, No. 2, March, 1952, pp. 43-64.

[*In the following essay, Fairchild traces evidence that suggests Buchanan's* The Drama of Kings *as a source of Thomas Hardy's* The Dynasts.]

In my opinion Robert ("Fleshly School") Buchanan's **The Drama of Kings** (1871) exerted so strong an influence on Hardy's *Dynasts* that it deserves to be regarded as the immediate source of that work. The contention would appear to be virginal.[2] The biographies and critical studies of Abercrombie, Blunden, Brennecke, Chakravarty, Chew, Duffin, Florence Emily Hardy, Hedgcock, Holland, McDowall, Rutland, Southworth, Symons, Weber, and Webster provide, in their greatly varying degree, suggestions as to the philosophical and literary background of Hardy's trilogy. None of them, however, suggests any relation between *The Dynasts* and **The Drama of Kings.** In fact none of them even mentions the name of Robert Williams Buchanan with the exception of Edmund Blunden, who notes the interesting fact that Buchanan dedicated to Hardy his novel, **Come Live with Me and Be My Love.**[3] He might also have observed that Buchanan elsewhere devotes a laudatory poem to Hardy and warmly praises "Tom Hardy" in another poem.[4]

When the Hardy scholars speak of "influences" they are merely suggesting that certain works, each of them admittedly different from *The Dynasts* in almost all other respects, might have contributed this or that element to the masterpiece. The consensus of scholarly opinion is that the work is essentially unique. Rutland, who provides the most elaborate and by far the most fruitful discussion of

the problem, asserts: "In the literature of the nineteenth century after Shelley, there is nothing to which it is even remotely related. . . . It appears then, that had England, in the three-quarters of a century before *The Dynasts* was written, produced no imaginative literature, Hardy's masterpiece would still be what it is. Such independence would surely be hard to parallel."[5]

The thesis of this article by no means excludes the possibility that *The Dynasts* was *also* influenced by some or all of the background works mentioned by the authorities. The situation is complicated by the fact that **The Drama of Kings** seems to have been influenced by Aeschylus, Goethe, Shelley, Hugo, and Swinburne—all of whom are alleged by one scholar or another to have influenced *The Dynasts.* Hence I must not too confidently trace back to Buchanan some element for which both he and Hardy may be independently indebted to an earlier source. Rutland says that "Hardy's continual use of semichoruses was clearly modelled upon Shelley's practice" in *Prometheus Unbound,* and that "Hardy saw in *Hellas* how choral poetry might be grafted on to events in history."[6] Now Buchanan uses semichoruses no less continually than Shelley, and he grafts choral poetry on to historical events which were more interesting to Hardy than the Greek Revolution. Perhaps Shelley alone is responsible for the presence of these elements in **The Drama of Kings** and *The Dynasts.* This possibility, however, does not diminish the significance of the fact that Buchanan's work embodies *in a philosophical-historical drama on the Napoleonic tradition* not only these but several other features which scholars have hitherto sought up and down the centuries and all about the Western world.

Let me also note in passing that Rutland's hesitant suggestion (not, I believe, anticipated or echoed by other scholars) of a faint similarity between *The Dynasts* and the work of the Spasmodics is highly gratifying to me. Buchanan was a belated Spasmodic[7] and a close friend of Sydney Dobell. If Rutland had moved onward from Dobell's *Balder* (1854), which he mentions, to Buchanan's **Balder the Beautiful** (1877), he might well have come upon **The Drama of Kings.**

The scholarly works consulted by me, the merest neophyte in this field, constitute only a minute fraction of all the books and articles devoted to Hardy. In answer to my appeals for guidance, however, Ernest Brennecke, Samuel C. Chew, and Carl J. Weber replied that so far as they knew the question had never been discussed. Having looked into the small amount of Buchanan material pretty thoroughly, I can say that nothing published about him between the appearance of Part I of *The Dynasts* and the present (May 1951) has any bearing on our problem. Here, of course, Dr. Cassidy's agreement is conclusive. It seems safe to assume that if, in the teeth of the leading authorities, anyone had contended that Hardy was influenced by Buchanan the fact would be known to my kind advisers at Bryn Mawr, Colby, and Columbia. If the question has ever been raised, it has certainly never entered the main stream of scholarship.

Of course Hardy himself never published a word that intimated any obligation to Buchanan; and there is no evidence that he ever spoke such a word on the many occasions when pilgrims to Max Gate persuaded him to talk of *The Dynasts*. Buchanan, as we have seen, warmly admired his writings and said so in print on at least three occasions. Even without the evidence which will be adduced later, the antecedent probability that Hardy would have read a widely-reviewed treatment of a Napoleonic theme by this well-known man of letters is strong.

For our purposes the question of whether the two men were personally acquainted is interesting but not at all crucial. The familiar "Tom Hardy" would be good affirmative evidence if Buchanan had been a less impudent fellow. The words of the dedication of **Come Live with Me and Be My Love** (1892) are so formal as to suggest only slight, if any, acquaintance: "To Thomas Hardy. Dear Sir,—Will you permit me to inscribe with your name a tale of English country life, with no claim to any higher merit than that of extreme simplicity both of subject and treatment? The author of 'The Woodlanders' needs no tribute from me, but I venture to tender it, nevertheless, in memory of many happy hours passed in the Arcadia of your creation, and in token of my admiration for one of the few remaining masters of English fiction. I am, Dear Sir, Yours truly, Robert Buchanan."[8] In Dr. Cassidy's opinion, "personal acquaintance is probable." He observes that they were "almost exact contemporaries, Hardy being born in 1840 and Buchanan in 1841"; that they were both in London from 1862 to 1866; that they were both interested in positivistic philosophy, evolution, and the humanitarian movement. Their paths could easily have crossed, but on the whole we had better say that we simply do not know and that it does not greatly matter.

Dr. Cassidy concerns himself with a more important question when he avers that Hardy made wholly legitimate use of **The Drama of Kings**: "Certainly he had not plagiarized; he had adopted a plan which suited his purpose and had broadened and ennobled it beyond Buchanan's rather crude and hastily written work. And if he had any lingering doubts or twinges of conscience, he could always silence them by recalling Buchanan's flagrant plagiarization of his novels." On the other hand Professor Weber strongly urged me to broaden my article into what would amount to a general discussion of Hardy as a plagiarist, using **The Drama of Kings** as the most striking of rather numerous examples. This task I prefer to leave to Professor Weber, who has already published several articles on this wider theme and whose special field I do not wish to invade. Suffice it to say here that there seems to be a good deal of evidence against the assumption that Hardy was incapable of deliberately concealing a literary debt.

In this instance, furthermore, he would have particularly strong motives for remaining silent. Buchanan, an egotistic, bad-tempered, and jealous man, had many acquaintances but few friends in literary circles. He lost most of the latter in 1871, the year in which **The Drama of Kings** was published. "It was reviewed," says Dr. Cassidy, "within a few weeks after Buchanan had won for himself almost universal disapproval by his Fleshly School article attacking Rossetti in the *Contemporary*. Rossetti's friends were powerful and held positions of influence in the critical world. They were not slow to seize the opportunity to belabor the 'scrofulous' Scotchman who had attacked Dante Gabriel." It would have been humiliating for Hardy, in his most ambitious work, to acknowledge indebtedness to one of the least popular productions of this unpopular second-rater.

As early as June 1877 Hardy's intention for his Napoleonic project had shifted from his 1875 idea of a series of ballads "forming altogether an Iliad of Europe from 1789 to 1815" to "a grand drama, based on the wars with Napoleon."[9] The Preface to *The Dynasts* seems to imply that the work was "outlined" about 1897.[10] Hardy had been gathering material and making plans for about a score of years before that, but by 1897 he may have felt that the unsuccessful **Drama of Kings** lay so far in the past that he could outline in good earnest. Buchanan himself had helped to dismember and bury his own Napoleonic trilogy, for Dr. Cassidy's manuscript informs us that in the collected **Poetical Works** of 1874 "he cut it so drastically as to destroy its identity, publishing in the second volume some selections from it under the general title 'Songs of the Terrible Year' and in the third a few more titled 'Political Mystics'."[11] As my fellow-discoverer suggests, Buchanan's repudiation of his own work might have led Hardy to feel "that he had carved his epic out of the cast-off block of marble, and that, therefore, there was no necessity of an acknowledgment."

In his closing years, furthermore, Buchanan was thought of as a novelist, playwright, and miscellaneous journalist rather than as a poet.[12] But besides Hardy there was certainly one person who remembered the **Drama,** and his name was Robert Buchanan. In 1901 that obstacle was removed by death, and in 1902 we find Hardy for the first time at work on the actual composition of *The Dynasts*.[13] I do not know in what month of 1903 Buchanan's sister-in-law, Harriett Jay, published her memoir, *Robert Buchanan,* but it is extremely unlikely that she had seen the rare first issue of *Dynasts I*. In any case she said next to nothing about Buchanan's writings. Hardy could safely proceed to finish his own trilogy. Since he transformed a mess of Schwärmerei into something like a masterpiece we may, if we choose, say the usual things about the privileges of genius. Or we may insist that although Hardy was fully entitled to make creative use of **The Drama of Kings,** he should have said "Thank you" to the querulous shade of poor Robert Buchanan. I hold the latter opinion, but I am not undertaking an investigation of the professional ethics of Thomas Hardy.

So far we have been assuming what remains to be proved. It is not impossible that some Hardy experts may already have considered the hypothesis which I am about to advance but have tacitly rejected it as unworthy of serious consideration. For the differences between the two books are immense, and I do not wish to ignore them. In playing my hand I shall lead from weakness, holding back the ace.

The Dynasts, with all its faults, is a monument of English literature; *The Drama of Kings* is one of the least successful major efforts of a poet who always overstrained the real but limited talent which he possessed. Credibly and charitably, Dr. Cassidy suggests that the faults of this particular work may be ascribed partly to the conflicting emotions aroused in Buchanan by the debacle of the Franco-Prussian War at a time when he had not yet fully recovered from a nervous breakdown caused by overwork and by sorrow at his father's death. The *Drama,* though unbearably long, is a mere triolet in comparison with the huge bulk of *The Dynasts.* The historical fields of the two dramas overlap but do not coincide. Only Part I of Buchanan's ("Buonaparte, or France Against the Teuton") directly concerns the first Napoleon. Part II ("Napoleon Fallen") deals with Napoleon III in his downfall, and Part III ("The Teuton Against Paris") with Wilhelm and Bismarck in their hour of triumph. Buchanan, indeed, derives his "inspiration" less from an interest in Bonaparte than from humanitarian indignation at the Franco-Prussian War and humanitarian hopes aroused by the deposition of Napoleon III and the proclamation of the Third Republic.[14] In Part I, furthermore, there is nothing about England, the true hero of Hardy's drama: the theme is "France Against the Teuton." The action opens at Erfurt after the victory of Jena and corresponds, very roughly, to that of Part II, Act I, Scenes iii-viii of *The Dynasts.* Unlike Hardy, Buchanan cares little about history for history's sake: it merely provides opportunity for rhetoric on the part of the human characters and for lyricism on the part of the Chorus.

Buchanan talks about destiny, but he is less bleakly necessitarian and mechanistic than Hardy. He seems to assume that the general course of history is the working-out of an incomprehensible law but that the characters are more or less free agents. But although he is enthusiastic about Humanity, he takes almost no interest in individual human beings. Hence his historic personages, theoretically freer than Hardy's, do not exhibit even the puppet-individuality possessed by those of *The Dynasts.* In the *Drama* we find nothing about an unconscious Immanent Will which may or may not eventually acquire consciousness. The mysterious force which directs the actions of men is called "God" and referred to as "He," not "It."

The Drama of Kings is written entirely in verse. It possesses not one gleam of humor. The entire *Dynasts* cannot be staged in a theatre; but it can very impressively be staged in the reader's mind, and many of its scenes are admirably dramatic. *The Drama of Kings* is not a play in this or any other sense. Buchanan treats the downfall of Bonaparte in a "Choric Interlude" sandwiched between Parts I and II. Here Waterloo is not even mentioned, much less spread before our eyes. A Voice representing Humanity merely keeps informing a Voice representing Bonaparte that his hour has struck, and the Chorus sings its exulta-

tion and finally its pity. Even in the main body of the work, where closet-drama conventions are more faithfully observed, there is hardly any attempt to convey an illusion of reality through concrete detail. One finds a few stage directions such as "Clouds rise" and "A confused noise," but nothing that could have suggested to Hardy his elaborate descriptions of actions and scenic effects or his dumbshows.

In the main body of the *Drama* the only supernatural spectators are the Chorus. They are more consistently spectators than Hardy's, who sometimes mingle in the human action.[15] They frequently divide into Semichoruses I and II and possess soloists who speak as separate Voices. These Voices, however, are not differentiated Spirits of this and that as in Hardy.[16] Essentially Buchanan's Chorus is a unit which expresses, without opposition or mockery from other Spirits, the sorrows and hopes of Hardy's Pities. *The Drama of Kings* has no Recording Angels. Its choric portions display much less prosodic variety and resourcefulness than those of *The Dynasts.* We shall see later that there are significant verbal resemblances, but here it must be granted that they are very few and difficult to discover except by the closest reading.

In short it would be nonsense to say that Hardy is a mere imitator of Buchanan. Great as they are, however, the differences are no greater than those which exist between many other literary works and their acknowledged sources—say between Shakespeare's *Measure for Measure* and Whetstone's *Promos and Cassandra.* *The Drama of Kings* is a poetic trilogy in closet-drama form concerning Bonaparte and the heritage of his ambition. It deals sympathetically with the sufferings of the common people beneath the feet of dynasts. It is local and cosmic, natural and supernatural, historical and philosophical. It regards nineteenth-century European history as merely a phase in the endless martyrdom of humanity:[17] in dedicating the work "to the Spirit of Auguste Comte" Buchanan calls it "this Drama of Evolution," a phrase that would have interested Hardy. The historical events are commented upon by a chorus of "celestial spectators" who view the play from seats in "the Heavenly Theatre." Until we find another work anterior to *The Dynasts* which shares with it *all* of these essential characteristics, the hypothesis that Buchanan influenced Hardy is not to be rejected without serious investigation.

The action of Part I of the *Drama* takes place at Erfurt after the victory of Jena. It opens with a despairing dialogue between Baron Stein and an Officer. Their dejection is then rendered lyrically by the Chorus, hopelessly longing for the ever-receding "Golden Year" of freedom. It should be noted that the Chorus is not a group of German soldiers or war-widows but a group of heavenly watchers. Stein, Arndt, and Jahn, less dejectedly, discuss their hope that Austria and Russia will come to the aid of "the Teuton soul," which Buchanan rashly identifies with the freedom-loving Spirit of Man. The Chorus sings of how the noble passion for liberty aroused by Washington and Lafayette has been perverted by Napoleon into a new tyranny.

There follows a scene (in the Continental sense) which is at least rather Hardyesque in personnel: "Buonaparte; the Czar; Jerome Buonaparte; Louis Buonaparte; the Kings of Saxony, Bavaria, Wurtemberg; the Hereditary Princes and Dukes of the Rhenish Confederation."[18] Enter to them, with historical inaccuracy admitted by Buchanan in a note (p. 454), Louisa of Prussia. The scene which she now plays with Napoleon and the Czar has none of the rich sardonic humanity of the corresponding scene in *The Dynasts* but might have suggested to Hardy the dramatic possibilities of such a confrontation. Louisa, left alone, spouts a pathetic soliloquy. Enter to her Stein, who cheers her with such remarks as

> The legions of the conqueror are weak
> Against the strength of the Free Thought of Man.

> (p. 75)

He sounds like the Marquis of Posa in Schiller's *Don Carlos*. Taking their cue from him, the Chorus sings more sanguinely of Liberty, whose betrayer, Napoleon, must and will be destroyed.

Then a scene between Bonaparte and a Cardinal in which the conqueror spurns the authority of the Pope and threatens him through his emissary. The Chorus, growing more and more Shelleyan as its hopes rise, says that earth, ocean, air,

> All liberated things that leap and roll
> Unfetter'd under yonder heaven, await
> The one free voice triumphant over Fate,
> The one free voice of Man, the Life, the Soul.

> (p. 107)

Next comes an endless speech by Napoleon to his "Famulus." The Famulus says nothing, does nothing, and is presumably invisible. Napoleon is the "Avatar," the sadly corrupted mortal manifestation of the "Titan," the freedom-loving Spirit of Man. The Famulus, whom Bonaparte addresses as "Soul within my Soul" (p. 120), is a sort of spiritual link uniting what the conqueror has become with what he originally was. Napoleon tells the Famulus of his ambition to be "King of all Humanity." He has advanced to his present height by enlisting in his service the Titan Man, to whom he has represented himself as "Child of the Revolution" and champion of Liberty, the *princesse lointaine* whom the Titan is constantly seeking. But herein he has deceived Man, for "she he seeks I know to be a dream." His one fear is that the Titan, who is infinitely mightier than he, may discover the trick, "put out his frightful strength again" as in the Revolution, and destroy him. At all events he must die some day, and then what will become of his empire? "I must have a child." Hence he tells the Famulus of his plan to divorce Josephine and arrange a match with Princess Anne of Russia (pp. 113-127 passim). Concluding Part I, the Chorus calls upon the Titan to arise in his might. He obliges in the misty "Choric Interlude" to which I have already referred.

The possibility that all this might have provided the crude stuff which Hardy's imagination metamorphosed into *The*

Dynasts is rendered less remote by certain specific points. Hardy informs us through his wife: "By November of 1887 he had outlined another plan for *The Dynasts,* in which Napoleon was represented as haunted by an Evil Genius, or *Familiar,* whose existence he has to confess to his wives."[19] Perhaps, then, Hardy considered and abandoned the notion of using Buchanan's Famulus in a way of his own. In abandoning his own conception, however, he returned to something very like Buchanan's. In Part I of *The Dynasts* the Spirit of the Pities says that Napoleon

> Professed at first to flout antiquity,
> Scorn limp conventions, smile at mouldy thrones,
> And level dynasts down to journeymen!—
> Yet he, advancing swiftly on that track
> Whereby his *active soul, fair Freedom's* child,
> Makes strange decline, now labours to achieve
> The thing it overthrew.[20]

Buchanan had already implied that Napoleon's *"Soul within my Soul"* is the child of freedom.

The lines just quoted from *The Dynasts* also show that Hardy agrees with Buchanan in regarding Napoleon not as a mere tyrant, but as a corrupted champion of liberty. The Chorus of the Pities echoes the insistence of Buchanan's Chorus that Napoleon must be crushed,

> . . . For the large potencies
> Instilled into his idiosyncrasy—
> To throne *fair Liberty* in Privilege' room—
> Are taking taint, and sink to common plots
> For his own gain.

> (p. 4)

And the Spirit of the Pities later whispers in the conqueror's ear:

> Lieutenant Bonaparte,
> Would it not seemlier be to shut thy heart
> To these unhealthy splendours?—render thee
> To whom thou swarest first, *fair Liberty?*

> (p. 56)

The epithet "fair," attached to personified and capitalized Freedom or Liberty in all three of the foregoing quotations, accords with Buchanan's basic metaphor of Liberty as a beautiful woman, constantly attracting and constantly eluding Man her suitor.

Since Parts II and III of ***The Drama of Kings*** do not correspond to the historical matter of *The Dynasts,* no detailed discussion of them is needed. A few specific points are worth noting. In Hardy's memorandum of 21 September 1889 we read: "A spectral tone must be adopted. . . . Royal Ghosts."[21] Throughout both works, of course, the choric material provides a spectral tone, though far more successfully in Hardy's. But as for Royal Ghosts, in Part II of the ***Drama*** the sleeping Napoleon III is reproached by various ghosts among whom the shades of Julius Caesar, Napoleon Bonaparte, and the Emperor Maximilian qualify as royal. In *Dynasts III,* Bonaparte is similarly haunted, but by his dead soldiers and generals rather than by royalty.[22] Of course this device is at least as old as Shakespeare's *Richard III,* and the parallel is inconclusive. But perhaps by "Royal Ghosts" Hardy means that the kings should be portrayed—and they are so portrayed in *The Dynasts*—as merely phantasmal shadows of mysterious realities which transcend their petty mouthings and struttings. In that case we should note that Buchanan's personified figure of Time speaks in the "Epilogue" of the *Drama* of "these *Ghosts of Kings*" (p. 428). The phrase means "these kings who are mere phantoms."

The third part of Buchanan's trilogy contains a scene between a Deserter and the Chorus, which here uniquely and absurdly abandons its celestial-spectator status to become a "Chorus of Sisters of the Red Cross." At first they reproach the Deserter for his cowardice, but his recital of what he has suffered in this war between rival kings arouses their pity (pp. 321-333). The scene, though feeble enough, might have suggested the remarkable scene of the deserters in *Dynasts II.* Buchanan's Deserter does not say, like Hardy's, "Good Lord deliver us from all great men, and take me back again to humble life" (II.120), but that is what he means.

Our inquiry grows more fruitful when we turn to the supernatural machinery of the two works and the more or less philosophical ideas for which it is the medium. After a dedicatory poem **"To the Spirit of Auguste Comte"** and a lyric **"Proem,"** both written in Buchanan's own person, *The Drama of Kings* opens with a "Prelude Before the Curtain." The scene is "The Heavenly Theatre." "The Lord" and "The Archangels" are present but say nothing. Much less taciturn are "The Celestial Spectators," who will constitute the Chorus throughout the work except when the Red Cross Sisters briefly usurp their function in Part III. Unwilling to commit himself as to the heavenly status of his Spirits, Hardy in his Preface (pp. vii-viii) calls them "*supernatural spectators*" or "*Phantasmal Intelligences.*" Looking forward for a moment to Buchanan's "Epilogue," we note that the personified figure of Time speaks of the

> . . . host
> Of *strange Intelligences* who behold
> Our Drama.
>
> (p. 430)

"Phantasmal" is a great improvement on "strange." In the "Prelude" the only philosophizing is provided by the celestial Chorus, who mystically declare that when at last the Rose of Heaven fully unfolds, the Heart of the Rose will prove to be identical with the Heart of Man. Lucifer now appears, but he cuts an even feebler figure than that least successful of Hardy's Phantasmal Intelligences, the Spirit Sinister. Here he is simply Buchanan in masquerade, making an uneasily jocular little speech about what the spectators (actually the modern readers) are to expect.

The "Prelude" is followed by a "Prologue" (Buchanan is cloyingly generous in such matters)[23] which consists

wholly of a speech by a "cloaked and hooded" figure who introduces himself as "that *ancient* Shadow men call Time" (p. 13). The closely corresponding character in *The Dynasts* is of course The *Ancient* Spirit of the Years. After some remarks which we must glance at later, Time suddenly "Unhoods—shows the mask of a Caput Mortuum," and announces:

> . . . My name
> Is Death; and I am deathless. I
> Am Time and most eternal. I am he,
> *God's Usher,* and my duty is to lead
> The actors one by one upon the scene,
> And afterwards to guide them quietly
> Through that dark postern when their parts are played.
> They come and go, alas! but I abide,
> And I am weary of the garish stage.
>
> (p. 17)

Observe his hoary weariness and disillusion, prominent characteristics of Hardy's Spirit of the Years. Less fond of pseudo-mystical paradoxes, Hardy does not identify this Spirit with Death but makes him refer familiarly to "*The Will's* old *Tipstaff,* . . . my good friend *Death*" (II.15). For Hardy the Immanent Will is the only God, and in this context "Usher" and "Tipstaff" are perfect synonyms. Time ends his speech by sketching the historical situation at the beginning of Part I, thus foreshadowing the function performed by Hardy's Recording Angels.

Buchanan's "Prelude" and "Prologue," taken together, correspond to Hardy's "Fore Scene." At the close they are balanced by an "Epilude" and "Epilogue" which similarly correspond to the "After Scene." Where the "Epilude" takes place is hard to say, for those present include not only The Lord and all the Spirits but Chancellor Bismarck, the dominating figure of Part III. We may safely assume, however, that the location is one suitable for disclosing the higher truth of things; for Bismarck, unmasking, reveals himself as Lucifer, who explains that he had also played Bonaparte in Part I and Napoleon III in Part II. The Lord urbanely says that under all his disguises Lucifer has "wrought for good" (p. 435). The Chorus hymns its vision of that Heavenly City of the future which shall be ruled by the Soul of Man—"Last of the fruits of Earth, first of the fruits of Heaven" (p. 447). Finally comes the "Epilogue," which consists of a summary and peroration by Time.

The Drama of Kings has no preface, but Buchanan appends an essay **"On Mystic Realism: A Note for the Adept."** He has tried, he explains, "to combine two qualities which the modern mind is accustomed to regard apart—reality and mystery, earthliness and spirituality" (p. 465). Hardy has more successfully achieved that combination. Like Hardy in his Preface, Buchanan in his essay speaks rather diffidently of his spirit-personages, fearing that perhaps "the supernatural machinery of Prelude and Epilude is a defect, like all allegory. . . . But if it serves to keep before the reader the fact that the whole action of the drama is seen from the divine auditorium, he [the author] will not regret its introduction." At least he "may plead the example of the greatest poetic sceptic of modern times. No one did fuller justice to mystic truths than the great positivist who wrote the first and second 'Fausts'" (p. 470). The formula of poetic scepticism or mystical positivism might be applied to *The Dynasts*. We also recall Hardy's description of his Spirits as "supernatural spectators of the terrestrial drama" (p. vii). Rutland praises Hardy for "his creation of a form new in literary technique. He places a drama within a drama." This critic grants the probable influence of *Faust* but believes that Hardy made much more thorough-going use of this conception.[24] Buchanan, however, has anticipated Hardy by staging in "the divine auditorium" his "royal puppet-shows" (II.302), which in themselves are merely episodes in the eternal mystery-play of human life (p. 428). Buchanan's readers, like Hardy's, are spectators of the spectators of a play.

Buchanan contributed little or nothing to the realistic and historical aspects of Hardy's long-meditated scheme. But he did, I believe, suggest the possibility of substituting philosophico-historical closet-drama of "mystic realism" for straightforward narrative poetry and of placing the whole action under the gaze of celestial interpreters. Buchanan would probably not have influenced Hardy in this respect unless there had been some community of thought and feeling between the two men. The "philosophies" of *The Drama of Kings* and *The Dynasts* are not so different as a hasty reading might lead one to suppose. Of course I am not suggesting that Hardy's characteristic view of life, which had taken form under other influences as early as 1866, was shaped by Buchanan. My contention is rather that Hardy found in the *Drama* certain congenial ideas and an example of how they might give cosmic sweep and loftiness to his own Napoleonic project. *The Dynasts,* predominantly pessimistic, clings stubbornly to a hope, and the hope is that of Buchanan expressed less sentimentally and flamboyantly. *The Drama of Kings,* predominantly optimistic, is shadowed by pessimism, and the pessimism is very similar to Hardy's.

Within the straitened limits of an article it would be impossible to give a detailed account of Buchanan's complex, inconsistent, constantly veering philosophical and religious views as revealed by the two stout volumes—small print and double columns—of his *Complete Poetical Works* (London, 1901). Briefly, he was a perfect specimen of the Victorian believing unbeliever.[25] If you asked him to believe anything in particular he would talk like the village atheist. If you asked him to deny the existence of God and the hope of immortality he would talk like an enraptured seer. He felt at home with Leslie Stephen (also a friend of Hardy's), Lecky, and Lewes; he felt equally at home with Sydney Dobell and Roden Noel.[26] He wished to resemble his picture of Goethe—a poetic sceptic, a mystical positivist. He enjoyed being gloomy, and he hankered after roseate illusions.

God, he says in *The Book of Orm,* has hidden His face behind the veil of the sky, which He has woven for that purpose. Our constant longing to behold that face is therefore constantly thwarted. When Buchanan feels sentimentally pessimistic, he emphasizes the futility of the quest; when he feels sentimentally optimistic, he cries:

> Yet mark me closely!
>   Strongly I swear,
> Seen or seen not
>   The Face is *there!*[27]

In the latter mood he can even credit Christianity with "The higher truth of poesy divine" and apostrophize *Pilgrim's Progress*:

> O fairy Tale Divine! O gentle quest
>   Of Christian and the rest!
> What wonder if we love it to the last,
>   Tho' childish faith be past,
> What marvel if it changes not, but seems
>   The loveliest of dreams?[28]

Compare the wistful "Hoping it might be so" mood of Hardy's *The Oxen* and *The Darkling Thrush*—or the cry of the Spirit of the Pities:

> Something within me aches to pray
> To some Great Heart, to take away
> This evil day, this evil day.
>
>   (II. 276)

It might be added that Buchanan was strongly opposed to vivisection and to every other sort of cruelty to animals. If Hardy wrote *The Sheep Fair* and *The Blinded Bird,* Buchanan wrote **"The Song of the Fur-Seal."**[29]

Although he dedicates **The Drama of Kings** to the spirit of Comte, Buchanan is by no means an orthodox positivist. Nevertheless he represents that vague, loose, sentimentalized English refraction of Comte's creed which may be called the Religion of Humanity. It provided a link between the unbelieving and the believing sides of his nature. It enabled him to spurn the illusions of supernaturalism and yet to bow in reverence before the concept of **"God Evolving"**:

> No God behind us in the empty Vast,
>   No God enthroned on yonder heights above,
> But God emerging, and evolved at last
>   Out of the inmost heart of human Love![30]

Similarly in the **Drama** the Chorus is sustained by the faith that when at last we behold the face of God we shall find it to be none other than the the the face of perfected Man.

But what has all this to do with Hardy? If on one occasion he assured Clive Holland that he would prefer not to have been born, on another occasion he told the same friend "that his books were not 'the gospel of pessimism' that one American critic had described them, 'but one continued plea against man's inhumanity to man—to woman—and the lower animals'."[31] The two statements express inseparable elements in Hardy's psychology. His pessimism was the outcry of a tender heart. Like his early mentor

John Stuart Mill, he could not reconcile the religious hypothesis with the fact of pain in nature and in human relations. His response to the mystery of evil was mainly pessimistic, but not unrelievedly so. His friend Swinburne says of man in the "Prelude" to *Songs Before Sunrise,* "Save his own soul he hath no star"; and Hardy uses the line as a motto for Part II of *Jude the Obscure.* This thought was the source of his despair, but it was also his only reliance. "My practical philosophy," he assured William Archer, "is distinctly melioristic."[32] In *The Dynasts* as in the whole body of his work the softer, more sanguine side of his nature is never wholly subdued by his sadness and irony. The Pities voice his own sympathy with human suffering, his indignation at tyranny, his melioristic hopes:

> Yet is it but Napoléon who has failed.
> The pale pathetic peoples still plod on
> Through hoodwinkings to light!

> (III. 158)

We misinterpret Hardy if we suppose that he expresses such aspirations merely to enjoy the cynical pleasure of mocking them through the Spirit of the Years and the Spirits Ironic and Sinister. In their gentle, wistful, groping way the Pities are indomitable, and they are granted the last word. Partly because Buchanan is more of a sentimentalized Comtian than Hardy and partly because he is much less of an artist, he talks more about Humanity and less about human beings. Nevertheless his Chorus, philosophically even more than technically, is a crude preliminary sketch of the Pities.

It may be objected that the Pities are sustained by an idea which finds no parallel in Buchanan—that the unconscious Immanent Will may some day acquire consciousness. But all this can actually mean for Hardy is that men may gradually become decent enough to treat their fellows with something like the beneficence which they used to impute to God before they learned that God does not exist. In other words, it means that the unconscious Will may become perfected human *good*-will. Wishing to be very "deep" in this most ambitious of his works, Hardy borrows from Hartmann an impressive metaphysical cloak (like pre-existence in Wordsworth's *Immortality*) for the dim aspiration which he usually expresses in straightforward humanitarian terms. Fundamentally, all he offers here is what he offers in *A Plaint to Man*:

> The fact of life with dependence placed
> On the human heart's resource alone,
> In brotherhood bonded close and graced
> With loving-kindness fully blown,
> And visioned help unsought, unknown.

This is what Buchanan is saying in his more sanguine, highfalutin, "mystical" way when he identifies the Heart of the "fully blown" Rose of Heaven with the Heart of Man.

It is true that Buchanan, stirred by the proclamation of the Third Republic, is more inclined to embody his aspirations in the language of political revolt.[33] Nevertheless Hardy, as we have seen, makes a good deal of the fact that Bonaparte is the betrayer of "fair Liberty." The Greek motto shows that Hardy did not draw his final title from the Magnificat without thinking of its context, "He hath put down the mighty from their seat"; nor would he object to our adding, "and hath exalted the humble and meek." Professor Chew has reminded me, indeed, that the entire passage from St. Luke's Gospel is quoted in a note to the After-Scene. Hardy often says with grim realism what Buchanan says with the rhetoric of Shelley or Hugo. Thus the Spirit Ironic at Waterloo:

> Warfare mere,
> Plied by the Managed for the Managers;
> To wit: by fellow-folks who profit nought
> For those who profit all!

> (III. 337)

In their milder way, the Pities express the same thought after the interview between Napoleon and the Emperor Francis:

> Each for himself, his family, his heirs;
> For the wan weltering nations who concerns, who cares?

> (I. 208)

But the gentle Pities do more than lament and dream. They are reformers who think that Napoleon should be crushed. In his place, they say to the Spirit of Earth,

> We would establish those of kindlier build,
>   In fair Compassions skilled,
> Men of deep art in life-development;
> Watchers and warders of thy [Earth's] varied lands,
> Men surfeited of laying heavy hands
>   Upon the innocent,
> The mild, the fragile, the obscure content
> Among the myriads of thy family.
> Those, too, who love the true, the excellent,
> And make their daily moves a melody.

> (I. 4-5)

Such worthies would be qualified to establish and direct that "perfect State" of which Buchanan's Chorus sings:

> 'Tis where the home is pure,
> 'Tis where the bread is sure,
> 'Tis where the wants are fewer,
>   And each want fed;
> Where plenty and peace abide,
> Where health dwells heavenly-eyed,
> Where in nooks beautified
>   Slumber the Dead.

> (p. 272)

Of course Hardy is incapable of such bathos. I am not trying to represent *The Dynasts* as a sanguine poem. I observe merely that it includes, as a persistent *subordinate* theme, that melioristic humanitarianism, that hope of "life-development," which provides the *main* theme of Buchanan's *Drama.*

On the other hand, if *The Dynasts* is not all gloom **The Drama of Kings** is not all sunrise. It contains much that accords with Hardy's darker, more characteristic mood. Consider these lines from the "Famulus" scene, where Napoleon asks why he should bemuse himself with peering into the future

> Like some purblind philosopher or bard
> Asking stale questions of the Infinite
> Dumb with God's secret? questioning the winds,
> The waves, the stars, all things that live and move,
> All signs, all augurs? Never yet hath one
> Accorded answer. "Whither?" Death replies
> With dusky smile. "Wherefore?" The echoes laugh
> Their "wherefore? wherefore?" Of the time unborn,
> And of the inevitable law, no voice
> Bears witness. The pale Man upon the Cross
> Moan'd—and beheld no further down the Void
> Than those who gather'd round to see him die.
>
> (p. 119)

In such turbidly Spasmodic passages Hardy would have found a view of life much like his own. The inevitable law—the Immanent Will.

The figure of Time in Buchanan's trilogy is a curious mixture of the Spirit of the Years and the Spirit of the Pities, with a slight touch of the Recording Angels. We have already observed the patient weariness which Time displays in the "Prologue":

> How far these feeble feet may wander yet
> I know not. All is dark before my steps.

Like Hardy's Spirit of the Years, he has seen everything but does not pretend to understand anything. Once again, as so often in the past, he hears men's voices crying "Liberty,"

> But whom they call by that mysterious name
> I say not, nor can any angel say,
> Nor one thing under God.

Toward the close of his speech, however, he becomes much more cheerful. He tells the spectators that although the play will show how the Soul of Man was betrayed by leaders who merely pretended to serve the cause of Liberty, it will also show

> how from sorrow came mysterious good,
> Seeing Man's wrong'd Soul hoarded its deep strength
> In silence, making ready for that day
> When God Himself, who knows the secret only,
> May bless it with that single truth it seeks.
>
> (pp. 13-16 passim)

In the "Epilogue," on the other hand, Time *begins* in the optimistic vein of the lines just quoted, saying that

> these Kings whom ye have seen
> Were God's unwilling servants, but for whom
> The Titan soul of Man were still asleep,

> Trancëd to sorrow and forgetfulness;
> And now that Soul is waken'd, now, O friends,
> Begins the serious matter of our play,
> For scene by scene we purpose to set forth,
> To the same audience and on other nights,
> The mighty spiritual brightening,
> And the last laying of these ghosts of Kings.

At the very close, however, we find him taking like the Spirit of the Years:

> Ay, but I weary. O I weary. Sleep
> Were better. Would the mighty play were o'er!
> Again and yet again the same old scenes,
> The same set speeches, the same blind despairs
> And miserable hopes, the same sick fear
> Of quitting the poor stage; so that I lose
> All count of act and scene and speech, confuse
> Scenes present and scenes past, actors long still
> With actors flaunting now their little hour. . . .
> . . . Ay, I weary! O to see
> The great black Curtain fall, the music cease,
> All darken, the House empty of its host
> Of strange Intelligences who behold
>
> Our Drama, till the great Hand, creeping forth
> In silence, one by one puts out the lights.
>
> (pp. 429-430)

Strange, that the pessimistic *Dynasts* should end on a note of hope and the optimistic **Drama** on a note of gloom! It seems clear, however, that the Spirit of the Years is developed from Time. Hardy assigns Time's incongruous optimism to the Pities, his expository function to the Recording Angels, and preserves and points up his tired sadness and disillusionment.

Let us also observe that **The Drama of Kings** and *The Dynasts* share a peculiar idea which might be described as the absent-mindedness or entrancement or self-hypnotizing of God. The Chorus of the Years refers to the Immanent Will as "the *rapt* Determinator" (II. 302). "It works unwittingly" in "a fixed foresightless *dream*. . . . Like a potter *rapt* in panning" (III. 341). This idea is not quite consistent with Hardy's official theory that the Will is completely unconscious: absent-mindedness implies the possession of a mind. What we have here is a mind which has been "rapt" or self-hypnotized *out* of consciousness by absorbed concentration on its own mysterious tasks. Compare the following very Hardyesque lines from the concluding chorus of Buchanan's Part II:

> Under the Master's feet the generations
>   Like ants innumerably come and go:
> He leans upon a Dial, and in patience
>   Watches the hours crawl slow.

The glories of heaven blaze all about him, yet

> He heeds them not, but follows with eyes yearning
>   The shadow men call Time.
> Some problem holds Him, and He follows *dreaming*
>   The lessening and lengthening of the shade.

Under His feet, ants from the dark earth streaming,
Gather the men He made.

He is heedless of these insects:

How should He care to look upon such creatures,
Who lets great worlds roll by?

It is useless to ask His help or to seek His face, for "The problem holds Him."

So hath it been since all things were created,
No change in the immortal Face may fall;
Having made all, God paused and *fascinated*
Watch'd Time, the shade of all.

(pp. 257-259)

Here God is entranced by the contemplation of time rather than of His own activity; but what after all is time but the endlessly turning wheel of the Divine Potter? The thought is the same.

Is the reader still sceptical? Only one card remains in my hand, but it is the ace. I quote in full Hardy's memorandum of 21 September 1889, already quoted in part: "For carrying out that idea of Napoleon, the Empress, Pitt, Fox, etc., I feel continually that I require a larger canvas. . . . A spectral tone must be adopted. . . . Royal Ghosts. . . . Title: *A Drama of Kings.*"[34] The chance of coincidence is infinitesimal. It is especially significant that Buchanan's title should appear at the precise point where Hardy feels the need of giving his historical realism breadth and "spectral" impressiveness by means of supernatural machinery. This evidence, added to the many other similarities which have been noted and validating some which might otherwise be regarded as accidental, would seem to be conclusive.

The absolute proof may lie hidden behind those ellipsis-periods. Was it Hardy or his wife who omitted from his original notes words which we shall never read?[35] Probably Hardy, for when Cyril Clemens asked him in 1925 whether he intended writing an autobiography he replied: "I will tell you something in confidence. . . . I intend to write my autobiography through my good wife. Each day I slant my memoirs, as though my wife were writing them herself. After she has copied the day's stint on the typewriter, we hold a discussion, and she makes invaluable suggestions which are almost always incorporated in the text. Then my original manuscript is given to the flames. Thus is insured absolute accuracy. My idea, of course, is to have the work appear after my death as a biography of myself written by my wife."[36]

It seems astonishing that Hardy should have thought of appropriating a title which had been used for a similar work by a well-known contemporary. Conceivably, feeling that what he intended was very different from Buchanan's trilogy, he briefly thought that he might adopt the title with some prefatory acknowledgment, perhaps after obtaining permission to do so from his admirer. But it is even more astonishing that in his old age he should have authorized his wife to publish so significant a clue to his otherwise unrevealed indebtedness. Why did he not cover his tracks completely? Did he sardonically decide, with a faint twinge of conscience, to leave *one* hint for a source-hunter who might have read Buchanan's work?

However this may be, there seems to be little room for doubt that **The Drama of Kings** exerted a stronger influence upon *The Dynasts* than any other work that has been mentioned by scholars in this connection. Personally, I am willing to go even further: as my rash title indicates, I feel no hesitation in describing Buchanan's work as Hardy's immediate source.

Notes

1. The article by John A. Cassidy on "Robert Buchanan and the Fleshly Controversy," which immediately follows, was accepted for publication on 8 June 1951, and Professor Fairchild's article was accepted on 20 June. On 21 June a letter arrived from Dr. Cassidy asking if *PMLA* would be interested in considering an article on the source of the *Dynasts*. Recognizing an ironic coincidence, the Editor wrote on 21 June to ask that the article be sent "at once," explaining that an article on the same subject had just been accepted, Dr. Cassidy's essay arrived promptly and proved to be, in most essential respects, a duplication of Professor Fairchild's argument. In view of the chronology of events—and after an agreeable interchange of letters with both authors—the Editor eventually suggested that the second article be sent to Professor Fairchild, with a covering letter form Dr. Cassidy permitting the use, with acknowledgments, of any pertinent materials not already present in the first article. This was done, with results here evident.—ED.

2. But see the Editor's note on the interesting coincidence by which the maiden topic has divided her favors between Dr. Cassidy and me. Dr. Cassidy informs me that he became convinced of Hardy's indebtedness to Buchanan in the fall of 1950; I stumbled upon the same fact in March 1951. Thus although, for reasons which the Editor of *PMLA* explains, I have been granted the privilege of making the announcement, Dr. Cassidy should be recognized as the first discoverer. I am extremely grateful for his kind permission to use his MS. article, "Buchanan's *Drama of Kings* and Hardy's *Dynasts*," in revising the paper which I originally submitted to this journal. References to his findings in my text and footnotes indicate precisely the extent and nature of my indebtedness to his expert knowledge of Buchanan. They do not, however, adequately express my appreciation of the generous spirit which he has shown in this complicated affair.

3. *Thomas Hardy* (London, 1942), p. 95. Blunden probably gathered this fact from the description of Item 30 in the catalogue, *Thomas Hardy, a Collection of Books from His Library at Max Gate* (London:

Maggs Bros., 1938). I have not read Buchanan's novel. Dr. Cassidy describes it as "a downright plagiarism of *The Woodlanders* and *Far from the Madding Crowd.*"

4. Buchanan, *Complete Poetical Works* (London, 1901), II, 400, 403.

5. William R. Rutland, *Thomas Hardy: A Study of His Writings and Their Background* (Oxford, 1938), pp. 284, 288.

6. Ibid., p. 289.

7. Ibid., pp. 285-286. Corroboration is supplied by Dr. Cassidy, whose MS. article shows that at least one reviewer associated *The Drama of Kings* with the qualities of the Spasmodic school.

8. I am obliged to my daughter, Anne Fairchild, who transcribed this dedication for me from a copy in the Widener Library.

9. Florence Emily Hardy, *The Early Life of Thomas Hardy* (New York, 1928), pp. 140, 150. These and all other passages quoted from this book are used by permission of the publishers, the Macmillan Company. My statement does not necessarily imply that Hardy first read *The Drama of Kings* between May 1875 and June 1877. He may well have read it soon after its appearance in 1871 but tried at first *not* to do something that in any way resembled this work on a subject which had fascinated him since boyhood. And as late as March 1881 (ibid., p. 191) he has not quite abandoned the ballads idea, which of course is reflected in several of the *Wessex Poems.*

10. (New York, 1936), p. vi.

11. I had already observed this curious dismantling of *The Drama of Kings* in the *Complete Poetical Works* of 1901. That edition, however, is in two volumes, in the first of which "Songs of the Terrible Year" and "Political Mystics" constitute successive sections. Hence the identity of the *Drama* is less completely obscured than in the three-volume 1874 *Poetical Works* more properly used by Dr. Cassidy, where the two batches of selections are printed in different volumes. Since the *Drama* is a comparatively rare book, these bibliographical details may help to explain why Hardy's indebtedness has so long remained unnoticed. Nevertheless it was a reading of the 1901 *Complete Poetical Works* which made me feel certain that the *Drama,* which I had not yet read in its entirety, would reveal a connection with Hardy.

12. Archibald Stodart-Walker, *Robert Buchanan: The Poet of Modern Revolt* (London, 1901), p. 332. This book was written when Buchanan was still alive but known to be dying of an incurable disease. Stodart-Walker devotes an entire chapter (pp. 89-111) to *The Drama of Kings* but hardly does more than summarize it. The title-essay of Henry Murray, *Robert Buchanan: A Critical Appreciation, and Other Essays* (London, 1901), was written, or at least completed, after Buchanan's death. It does not mention the *Drama.*

13. Florence Emily Hardy, *The Later Years of Thomas Hardy* (New York, 1930), p. 100.

14. Part II, "Napoleon Fallen," was separately published in 1871 before the appearance of the entire *Drama of Kings.* Using dates of reviews as evidence, Dr. Cassidy suggests January for the former and November for the latter, in which "Napoleon Fallen" was considerably revised.

15. Dr. Cassidy, however, instances a case (*Drama,* p. 83) in which Buchanan's Chorus directly warns Napoleon.

16. Of course their moods vary with the circumstances to which they respond. Dr. Cassidy would trace Hardy's sharper classification of his Spirits to the shifts of feeling in Buchanan's Chorus, but as to this point I feel rather sceptical.

17. The curious jumble of optimism and pessimism in Buchanan's thought reminds one of Winwood Reade's *Martyrdom of Man,* which was not, however, published until the year after the *Drama.* But Buchanan knew Charles Reade and may have had opportunities to converse with his nephew. See Harriett Jay, *Robert Buchanan* (London, 1903), p. 175.

18. Buchanan, *The Drama of Kings* (London, 1871), p. 55. Subsequent page references given in my text are to this edition.

19. *Early Life,* p. 266 (italics mine). Throughout the remainder of this article italics will be used to call attention to verbal resemblances.

20. Thomas Hardy, *The Dynasts* (New York, 1936), Part I, 53. Quoted, like all my other quotations from his work, by permission of the publishers, the Macmillan Company. References are to pages of the three Parts, separately paginated in this one-volume edition.

21. *Early Life,* p. 290.

22. *Dynasts* III. 254. On another occasion Napoleon is addressed in his sleep by the Spirit of the Years (ibid., p. 344).

23. Dr. Cassidy's manuscript shows that two of Buchanan's reviewers objected to this pretentious superfluity.

24. Rutland, *Thomas Hardy,* p. 319.

25. Especially for this reason I hope that Dr. Cassidy's dissertation on Buchanan may be published as a book.

26. Harriett Jay, *Robert Buchanan* (London, 1903), pp. viii, 21, 66, 76, 104ff., 118 ff., 120 n., 127, 228.

27. *Complete Poetical Works,* I, 258. Italics are Buchanan's.

28. Ibid., II, 52.

29. Dr. Cassidy enables me to say further that Buchanan became an active member of the Humanitarian League in 1894, and that a letter of Hardy's to the Secretary of the League in 1910 suggests that he also

was either a member or strongly interested in its work. See *Later Years,* pp. 141-142.

30. Quoted by Harriett Jay, op. cit., p. 151.

31. Clive Holland, *Thomas Hardy, O.M.* (London, 1933), pp. 12, 13.

32. Quoted by Blunden, *Thomas Hardy,* p. 111.

33. Buchanan's father was a disciple of Robert Owen both as atheist and as socialist. In his Glasgow boyhood the poet "had become acquainted with the French socialists, Louis Blanc and Causidière, during their visits to the home of his father and from them he had developed an abiding admiration for the French people and their struggles for liberty." (Thank you again, Dr. Cassidy.)

34. *Early Life,* p. 290. Italics mine. Ellipsis-periods as in source.

35. Conceivably, however, he used ellipsis-periods or dashes in his original notebook to separate his rough jottings, in which case it would not be necessary to suppose that he had deleted anything from his memorandum.

36. *My Chat with Thomas Hardy* (Webster Groves, Missouri: International Mark Twain Society, 1944), p. 26. Professor Carl J. Weber, who supplied the Introduction to Clemens' brochure, kindly sent me this reference in response to my appeal for help on the point in question.

John A. Cassidy (essay date 1952)

SOURCE: "Robert Buchanan and the Fleshly Controversy," in *PMLA,* Vol. LXVII, No. 2, March, 1952, pp. 65-93.

[*In the following essay, Cassidy discusses Buchanan's role in the Fleshly Controversy—a literary conflict ignited when Buchanan published a scathing assessment of the poetry of Dante Gabriel Rossetti.*]

In the long history of literary polemics none has been more savage or more far-reaching in its consequences than the Fleshly Controversy, which raged in Victorian England during the 1870's with Robert Buchanan on one side and Swinburne, William Michael Rossetti, and the unfortunate Dante Gabriel Rossetti on the other. The literary importance of the latter three and the intensive study devoted to their careers have thrown a revealing light upon their activities in the Controversy. Robert Buchanan has fared quite differently. Although widely heralded in the 1860's and '70's as a young poet of promise, he subsequently suffered such a literary eclipse that by the time of his death he was relatively little known. Today almost everything he wrote has been forgotten and his sole claim to fame is the negative one of being the man who attacked Dante Gabriel Rossetti and brought about his premature death. This paper is devoted to an examination of his ca-

reer before, during, and after the Controversy in order to throw some light upon the role he played in that melee and to show that his attack, while reprehensible, was not made without some provocation.

As in the case of larger human conflicts, it is impossible to say just when the Fleshly Controversy began and what was its specific incitement, but it may have been a mutual antipathy experienced by Robert Buchanan and Swinburne. It would be strange indeed if the two had not been thrown together at some time during the 1860's, for both were living in London as ambitious young men of letters, both knew Lord Houghton and were befriended by him, and both came to prominence during the middle years of the decade.[1] Indeed, it may have been at Lord Houghton's home, sometime between 1862 and 1866, that the groundwork for the Controversy was laid, for that nobleman was fond of bringing opposite personalities together, introducing subjects on which he knew them to disagree, and then watching the sparks fly.[2] He would not have found it difficult to set two such gamecocks as Swinburne and Buchanan upon each other. Swinburne was known as a literary representative of the Pre-Raphaelites, a cultural and artistic coterie to whose foreign flavor Buchanan's sturdy Scottish spirit was naturally opposed. As early as 1862 he expressed some of his contempt by satirizing them in ***Temple Bar*** in his farcical novelette, **"Lady Letitia's Lilliput Hand,"** in the character Edward Vansittart, whom he described as a painter "whose 'Donkey feeding on Thistles' was so much commended by Mr. Buskin for the Pre-Raphaelite vigour of its drawing" (IV, 554). If they did meet, Swinburne, with his halo of red hair, his birdlike mannerisms of hopping on and off articles of furniture when he was talking, and the flutelike tones of his voice, probably affected Buchanan unfavorably. Swinburne's outspoken pride in his French ancestry would not have moved him to admiration, while his better circumstances and aristocratic connections would have earned Buchanan's envy. Temperamentally, both were vain, opinionated young men with little tolerance of any opposition to their beliefs and theories and no disposition to heed the advice of their elders.

But whatever may or may not have taken place behind the scenes, the printed war begins properly with the publication of Swinburne's *Poems and Ballads* near the end of July 1866. Two reviews written from advance copies were published before the book was available in the bookshops, John Morley's in the *Saturday Review* (XXII, 145-147) and Buchanan's in the *Athenaeum*.[3] Morley regarded the volume with horror, but Buchanan's personalized remarks verged close to insult:

> When . . . we find a writer like the author of these 'Poems and Ballads,' who is deliberately and impertinently insincere as an artist,—who has no splendid individual emotions to reveal, and is unclean for the mere sake of uncleanness,—we may safely affirm, in the face of many pages of brilliant writing, that such a man is either no poet at all, or a poet degraded from his high estate and utterly and miserably lost to the Muses. How

old is this young gentleman, whose bosom, it appears, is a flaming fire, whose face is as the fiery foam of flowers, and whose works are as the honeyed kisses of the Shunamite? He is quite the Absalom of modern bards,—long-ringleted, flippant-lipped, down-cheeked, amorous lidded. He seems, moreover, to have prematurely attained to the fate of his old prototype; for we now find him fixed very fast indeed up a tree, and it will be a miracle if one breath of poetic life remain in him when he is cut down. Meantime he tosses to us this charming book of verses, which bears some evidence of having been inspired in Holywell Street, composed on the Parade at Brighton, and touched up in the Jardin Mabile. Very sweet things in puerility . . . fine glaring patterns after Alfred de Musset and Georges Sand,—grand bits in the manner of Hugo, with here and there a notable piece of insertion from Ovid and Boccaccio. Yet ere we go further, let us at once disappoint Mr. Swinburne, who would doubtless be charmed if we averred that his poems were capable of having an absolutely immoral influence. They are too juvenile and unreal for that. The strong pulse of true passion beats in no one of them. They are unclean, with little power; and mere uncleanness repulses. Here, in fact, we have Gito, seated in the tub of Diogenes, conscious of the filth and whining at the stars.

(4 August 1866, pp. 137-138)

The description of Swinburne, caricature though it is, furthers the conjecture that Buchanan was personally acquainted with him. The note of personal animosity is strong, and unfairness of comparing him to Gito Buchanan admitted privately (Jay, p. 161). The patronizing manner in which he refers to Swinburne's immaturity contains a grain of sardonic humor in that Buchanan was three years younger than the "young gentleman" he was advising to mend his poetical ways.

There can be little doubt that literary gossip must have made known to Swinburne the name of at least one of his detractors. Buchanan implied this when he said later that this review led to Swinburne's slur on David Gray (Jay, p. 161). Further proof is the slight on Buchanan contained in William Rossetti's defense of Swinburne published later in 1866 and titled *Swinburne's Poems and Ballads,* a slight otherwise so gratuitous that it can be explained only on the ground that Rossetti knew Buchanan to be one of the offending reviewers (p. 7). If Swinburne entertained any doubts on the personal bias of his assailant, they were dissipated when Buchanan let fly another shaft at him in his mocking poem, **"The Session of the Poets,"** published in the *Spectator* on 15 September 1866 and an obvious imitation of Sir John Suckling's "A Session of the Poets" (XXXIX, 1028). In Buchanan's version Browning, Arnold, Lytton, Bailey, Patmore, Alford, Kingsley, and Ingelow are dealt with lightly. Of himself Buchanan says:

> There sat, looking moony, conceited, and narrow,
>   Buchanan,—who, finding, when foolish and young,
> Apollo asleep on a coster-girl's barrow,
>   Straight dragged him away to see somebody hung.

Buchanan's poem differs from Suckling's in that he deals more severely with himself than does the older bard—

possibly the better to preserve his anonymity—and in that, whereas Suckling's barbs are scattered impartially among his brethren, Buchanan's most telling blows are directed at Swinburne, whose actions furnish an unmistakable climax.

VI

> What was said? What was done? was there prosing or
>   rhyming?
>   Was nothing noteworthy in deed or in word?—
> Why, just as the hour of the supper was chiming,
>   The only event of the evening occurred.
> Up jumped, with his neck stretching out like a gander,
>   Master Swinburne, and squeal'd, glaring out thro'
>   his hair,
> "All Virtue is bosh! Hallellujah for Landor!
>   I disbelieve wholly in everything!—There."

VII

> With language so awful he dared then to treat 'em,—
>   Miss Ingelow fainted in Tennyson's arms,
> Poor Arnold rush'd out, crying "Soecl' Inficetum!"
>   And great bards and small bards were full of
>   alarms;
> Till Tennyson, flaming and red as a gypsy,
>   Struck his fist on the table and utter'd a shout;
> "To the door with the boy! Call a cab! He is tipsy!"
>   And they carried the naughty young gentleman out.

VIII

> After that, all the pleasanter talking was done there,—
>   Who ever had known such an insult before?
> The Chairman tried hard to rekindle the fun there,
>   But the Muses were shocked and the pleasure was
>   o'er.
> Then "Ah!" cried the Chairman, "this teaches me
>   knowledge [sic]
>   The future shall find me more wise, by the powers!
> This comes of assigning to younkers from college
>   Too early a place in such meetings as ours!"

> Caliban.

That Buchanan realized Swinburne would regard the **"Session"** as a deliberate insult is shown by his use of the pseudonym, when for several years all his poems had been signed. Further reasons for wishing to conceal his identity probably lay in his unwillingness to anger Lord Houghton, Swinburne's literary sponsor, and in his fear of reprisals from the powerful Pre-Raphaelites. At any rate, Swinburne soon learned that the inimical poet and the *Athenaeum* reviewer were the same.[4]

In his defense published late in 1866 as "Notes on Poems and Reviews," Swinburne displayed, for him, remarkable forbearance, for though he styled his critics "vultures," his times an "age of hypocrites," and retorted that his poems were not meant to be read by girls, he chose to overlook personalities and treat the matter as a question of literary criticism.[5] Not so, however, William Michael Rossetti, who chose to enter the fray by publishing at about the same time as Swinburne's "Notes" his defense of *Poems and Ballads.* In his very first sentence he went out of his way to deal Buchanan a malicious blow; in his second he praised Swinburne: "The advent of a new great poet is sure to cause a commotion of one kind or another; and it would be hard were this otherwise in times like ours, when the advent of even so poor and pretentious a poetaster as a Robert Buchanan stirs storms in teapots. It is therefore no wonder that Mr. Swinburne should have been enthusiastically admired and keenly discussed as soon as he hove well in sight of the poetry-reading public" (p. 7). Had William Michael foreseen the far-reaching consequences of his slur at Buchanan it is doubtful that he would have written it. Coming from Swinburne, Buchanan would not have relished it certainly, but he would have had to acknowledge it as not unearned. As the work of Rossetti, a man who was not directly concerned in the quarrel, Buchanan could have viewed it in no other light than as the stiletto blow of a meddlesome and treacherous bystander. In this instance the bystander was all the more a *persona non grata* because of the foreign flavor of his name. With a horizon no broader than that of most Victorians, Buchanan saw anything British as basically good and honorable, while that which smacked of the foreign was to be distrusted and attacked. This concept is borne out in his novels, where the foreigner is often the villain, thoroughly treacherous and despicable. From here on, Buchanan regarded any member of the Pre-Raphaelites as fair game and certainly the name Rossetti was singled out for special attention (Jay, pp. 161-162).

The "storms in teapots" was undoubtedly a reference to the popularity of Buchanan's **London Poems**, which had been published in 1866 and had met with considerable enthusiasm in the critical press. His rise to fame had not been easy. Almost penniless and friendless, he had arrived in London in 1860 as a boy of eighteen with no more than a fair education from the University of Glasgow and with a consuming ambition to win literary renown. By dint of hard work and a dogged determination which refused to give up he made his way slowly up the literary ladder with an occasional helping hand from Charles Dickens, George Lewes, and Hepworth Dixon, who admired his courage and thought they discerned in the young Scotsman an inherent literary ability. His **London Poems** marked the apex of his career and was hailed as the work of budding genius which would certainly achieve great things (Jay, pp. 44-124). Small wonder that he regarded Swinburne and his friends as poseurs who sought to conquer the literary world by subterfuge and the mutual assistance of a coterie rather than by merit and hard work (pp. 161-162).

His reply to Swinburne and Rossetti would probably not have been long in appearing had not his attention been diverted by other and more pressing affairs. The death of his father in the spring of 1866 together with the strain of overwork and mounting family responsibilities precipitated toward the end of the year a nervous breakdown which amounted to a light stroke. In search of health he moved his family from London to the resort town of Oban, a gateway to the Hebrides on the northern coast of Argyle. Here he lived the life of a recluse from 1866 to 1873, with only occasional short visits to London for business rea-

sons. His recovery was discouragingly slow and was complicated by a disposition to brood on religious questions. Since his father had been an avowed atheist, his death had brought a whole host of morbid imaginings and fancies with which Buchanan wrestled in a vain endeavor to develop for himself a solid philosophy and faith. He continued to write sporadically in order to meet his mounting expenses and sought relaxation by sailing his small boat among the islands of the Hebrides. In 1869 two attempts to supplement his earnings by public readings of his poems in London brought about so severe a recurrence of his nervous disorders that he was forced to return to Oban and to refrain from work of any kind (pp. 129-158).

In the meantime the Controversy languished. Swinburne's essay on Arnold's poetry was published in the *Fortnightly* in October 1867, with a remark in connection with his disapproval of Wordsworth's doctrine that if a poet were inspired he did not need to master the technique of his craft that "such talk as this of Wordsworth's is the poison of poor souls like David Gray" (N.S. II, 414-445). There was hardly any malice intended in such a statement and it is difficult to believe that Buchanan could have had his ire aroused by it. But when Swinburne republished this essay in his *Essays and Studies* of 1875 much fuel had been added to the Controversy and Swinburne's temper was at such a heat that he appended to this reference to Gray a lengthy footnote in which he attacked the dead poet with the utmost scorn and ill-feeling. In later years when Buchanan was laboring to find some explanation for his attack upon Dante Rossetti he cited this footnote as his provocation (Jay, p. 161). He is unquestionably in error, for his attack antedated the footnote by four years. That his feeling toward Swinburne in 1867 and 1868 had simmered down to little more than aversion is evidenced by a letter to his friend Roden Noel in 1868 in which he admitted that his failure to appreciate Swinburne's work was probably attributable to an artistic blind-spot in himself more than to any fault in the poetry (p. 155). In 1868 Buchanan published an essay **"On My Own Tentatives"** in his **David Gray and Other Essays** in which he said regretfully that "a gifted young contemporary, who seems fond of throwing stones in my direction, fiercely upbraids me for writing 'Idyls of the gallows and the gutter, and singing songs of costermongers and their trulls'" (p. 291). In his "Under the Microscope" of 1872 Swinburne admitted that he was the offending critic.

Buchanan finally got around to evening accounts with Rossetti in 1870 in another *Athenaeum* review, this time of William Michael's edition of Shelley. Again the review was unsigned, as was the custom of the *Athenaeum,* but Rossetti was not long in ferreting out the author (*Family Letters,* I, 295). The article was lengthy and in a more scholarly tone than Buchanan was in the habit of using when discussing his enemies, but his opinions were almost entirely negative. He stated that Rossetti had neither sufficient material, critical insight, nor the good taste requisite for such a task. He accused him of misinterpreting the facts and objected to his attempts at revising the juvenilia.

His conclusion was quite patronizing: "Mr. Rossetti has, in our opinion, mistaken his vocation in undertaking the role of commentator. Still, there can be no doubt that he has pointed out a considerable number of errors in the existing text; his book therefore cannot fail to have a certain value in the eyes of future editors, and of readers who are fond of textual criticism" (29 January 1870, pp. 154-156).

Here the Tragic Muse took a hand in what had hitherto been only light comedy. Another actor entered the scene in the person of William Rossetti's brother, Dante Gabriel. He, in a precarious condition of mind and body from overdoses of laudanum and alcohol, suffered himself in 1869 to be persuaded to resuscitate the verses which, in an act of self-imposed justice, he had buried in his wife's coffin in 1862. In 1870 after insuring a favorable reception for the volume by arranging that members of his circle should review it in most of the prominent critical journals—he seems to have been warned by William Michael and Swinburne that his book would probably be attacked by Buchanan—he published it.[6] The venture fared exceedingly well. The reviews, paced by Swinburne's eulogy in the *Fortnightly,* were predominantly favorable; the looked-for attack by Buchanan did not materialize; and Rossetti found himself in short order in the first rank of contemporary poets.

The reasons for the delay in Buchanan's expected attack are not difficult to find. A reliable barometer of his physical condition during these years is his contributions to periodicals, and a survey of these shows that throughout 1869 and 1870 he did very little. For another reason, his collapse had prompted his friends, and probably chief among them Lord Houghton, to plead his case with Gladstone for a Civil List pension, and this matter was quite evidently under consideration during 1869 and 1870. Because his breakdown took place during the early part of 1869, and because of the general slowness of governmental machinery, it was probably not until late in 1870 that he was placed on the Civil List for a pension of a hundred pounds a year for life. Even one of Buchanan's impetuous nature would reason that discretion was the better part of valor, at least until the pension was safely his; for Lord Houghton was a friend to the Swinburne faction as well as to Buchanan, and even had he not been so, literary polemics, had they come to Gladstone's attention, would hardly have recommended Buchanan as a worthy recipient of a pension. A third reason lay in the fact that his ailment had brought an intensification of the religious doubts which had plagued him since the death of his father in 1866. In the solemn fastnesses of the Hebridean mountains he went into a morbid communion with himself and nature to try to arrive at some solution. His ruminations and soul-searchings he published in rough, inchoate verse which he hoped would mean as much to his fellowmen as the experiences leading to its composition had to him. This book, *The Book of Orm,* came out within a few weeks of Rossetti's *Poems* and with a preface which indicated that Buchanan considered he had achieved something new and great in poetry. Early in 1871 he rushed into print with his

hastily conceived and even more hastily written interpretation of the Franco-Prussian War, *Napoleon Fallen,* done in the same rough, abstruse style as the *Orm.* Then he sat back to await the accolade he felt certain would be his (Jay, pp. 136, 139-140).

How rude was his awakening, when the critical returns began to come in, to find that while his own ambitious offerings were ridiculed as formless and meaningless, those of Rossetti were eulogized! To add gall to the wormwood, often the notices were in such juxtaposition that they appeared on the same page. The *Westminster Review* dismissed the *Orm* with a curt and unfavorable paragraph, and right beneath it compared Rossetti's *Poems* favorably with those of Shakespeare and Goethe (XCIV, 107-108). The *North British Review* drew an odious comparison of the *Orm* with Swinburne's "Atalanta" by saying, "In these unfortunate verses Mr. Buchanan has exceeded the irreverence, while he has none of the fiery and fitful music, of the choruses of *Atalanta in Calydon.*" Then it immediately turned its attention to Rossetti with, "Mr. Rossetti's Poems have the unwonted and personal qualities of all really original work. The sense of strangeness is soon lost in admiration of the great beauty of the verses, of their wide range of subject, their various and appropriate music, their lyric fire, their lofty tone, and their high level of common perfection" (LII, 596-601). In April 1871, the *Westminster Review* extolled Swinburne's *Poems and Ballads* as approximating the verse of Shelley and Chaucer and harshly castigated Buchanan for writing his *Orm* and *Napoleon Fallen* too rapidly (XCV, 275-276).

Buchanan was quick to discern a plot in all this. It appeared to him that his enemies had gained control of nearly all the critical journals and that they were determined to exalt Rossetti while debasing him. In an angry mood and still sick mentally and physically, he secured a copy of Rossetti's *Poems* in the summer of 1870 and read it. Seen through his jaundiced eyes and against the beautiful natural backdrop of sea, sky, and mountains of the Hebrides, these verses struck him as the work of "an affected, immoral, and overpraised writer" (Jay, pp. 159, 162). In 1871 his health improved to the point that he resumed his writing for the periodicals; in the fore part of the year he was occupied with seeing his *Land of Lorne* through the press, but in the fall he finally got around to his belated attack on all his enemies by striking at Dante Gabriel Rossetti. Although Dante Gabriel had given Buchanan no offense he bore the name and was the brother of one who had; and although Buchanan's attack upon Dante was unwarranted, so had been William Michael's attack upon Buchanan. One unwarranted attack deserved another in Buchanan's code, and so he set about his work with a will.

"The Fleshly School of Poetry; Mr. D. G. Rossetti" appeared under the pseudonym Thomas Maitland in the *Contemporary Review* for October 1871, and filled some seventeen pages of that journal (pp. 334-350). Buchanan began by imagining the poets of the day as the cast of *Hamlet* with Tennyson and Browning alternating as the immortal Dane, himself as Cornelius, Swinburne and Morris as Rosencrantz and Guildenstern, and Rossetti as Osric. Then he accused the Pre-Raphaelites of overplaying their parts in a vain attempt to rival Tennyson and Browning. The Fleshly School he found to be a grotesque offshoot in style and matter from two of Tennyson's poorer poems, "Maud" and "Vivien." He disparaged Rossetti's paintings and added that his poetry was equally thin and uninspired. He found him inferior to Swinburne, even though extolled by his family and friends. He clearly showed his bias and his recollection of William Rossetti's slight of 1866 by remarking that Dante had dedicated his *Poems* to William Michael, "who . . . will perhaps be known to bibliographers as the editor of the worst edition of Shelley which has ever seen the light." Marvelling that Dante had not been taxed with sensuality as Swinburne was in 1866, he condemned Rossetti's as the worse offense because he was a mature man, whereas Swinburne had been a boy in 1866. Of Rossetti's "Nuptial Sleep" he said: "Here is a full-grown man, presumably intelligent and cultivated, putting on record for other full-grown men to read, the most secret mysteries of sexual connection, and that with so sickening a desire to reproduce the sensual mood, so careful a choice of epithet to convey mere animal sensations, that we merely shudder at the shameless nakedness."

This attack was manifestly unfair. As Buchanan said later, he had no idea he was assailing an unwell man—a man who today would be put under the care of a psychiatrist—or that he was causing untold pain by unwittingly heaping obloquy upon Rossetti's marriage relationships (Jay, pp. 166-167). He saw in Rossetti the same kind of an affected esthete he later scorned in George Moore, an esthete surrounded by a powerful group of friends who were determined to laud his works far above their true worth. To him Rossetti's poems were of a piece with those of Swinburne's *Poems and Ballads,* and his onslaught upon Rossetti was not more severe than his berating of Swinburne in 1866.

He realized, however, that he had to do with powerful foemen who would not be slow to retaliate if they learned his identity. William Rossetti claimed he had evidence to prove Buchanan was urged to sign the article but refused (*Family Letters,* I, 294). Harriett Jay said Buchanan meant to acknowledge it sooner or later, but this is doubtful (p. 163). Buchanan himself implied that the signature "Thomas Maitland" was not his idea, but had been affixed by Alexander Strahan, editor of the *Contemporary,* without Buchanan's knowledge.[7] This, too, is doubtful. There is in the literature of Scotland a dissertation titled *De Jure Regni apud Scotos Dialogus* published in 1579 by George Buchanan and dedicated to King James VI of that country. The whole thing took the form of a debate or flyting between Buchanan and his friend Thomas Maitland and advanced the then daring thesis that all law originates with the people and that a tyrannical king who refused to obey it could rightfully be killed. The underlying premise, the peril of men being corrupted by evil influences, is somewhat akin to the central thesis of the **"Fleshly School"** article. It is

hardly likely that a business man like Strahan would have known of this recondite work or would have used the pseudonym without Buchanan's consent if he had. It is more probable that Buchanan had come across the old flyting in his browsing around the British Museum reading room, had looked into it, noted the association of the names, and had filed away "Thomas Maitland" for future reference. This is, of course, conjecture and cannot be proved; there is, however, no other association of the names Buchanan and Thomas Maitland in literary history prior to the Fleshly School article, and this fact alone adds considerable weight to the supposition.[8] Added to this is the point that Buchanan did not at first unreservedly deny that he had conceived of the pseudonym and suggested to Strahan that it be used. He simply said, ". . . the pseudonym 'Thomas Maitland' was affixed to my article when I was out of reach—cruising on the shores of the Western Hebrides."[9] He could have written the name on paper, left it with Strahan or mailed it to him, and suggested its use. This would be quibbling of course, but such quibbling he could have justified to himself as a fair enough expedient in the war in which he was engaged. Actually, although the Rossetti faction made much of the pseudonym and fastened upon it as incontrovertible evidence of Buchanan's perfidy, there was no literary law, written or unwritten, which prohibited its use, even in a journal where the articles were usually signed with the author's name. English literary history affords numerous instances of similar employment of the pseudonym. True enough, to throw his enemies off the scent he assigned himself the insignificant role of Cornelius in the literary cast of *Hamlet* with which he opened his article, but this was for reasons of camouflage rather than from egoism.

His article had the effect of a bombshell among his enemies. The man he attacked was in no condition to bear such blows with equanimity and when he learned that the assailant was the hated and feared bogey, Buchanan, his rage was Homeric (Doughty, p. 103). Fear of legal reprisals, however, prevented all-out warfare upon Buchanan until he could be driven from ambush and forced to acknowledge his guilt. Here the resources of the far-flung Rossetti clan were employed. On 2 December 1871 the *Athenaeum* printed a short paragraph in its "Literary Gossip" column stating that Sidney Colvin was shortly to publish an answer to "'**The Fleshly School of Poetry,**' by Thomas Maitland, a *nom de plume* assumed by Mr. Robert Buchanan" (p. 724). To this, one week later, Colvin printed a disclaimer couched in language so ironic that it was obviously designed to flush the quarry from his hiding place.

> You learn . . . that the same Mr. Buchanan is himself the author of this spirited performance, only he has been too modest to acknowledge it, and has had the happy thought of delivering his thrust from behind the shield of a putative Thomas Maitland. Still, what then? Do you "prepare an answer"? Rather you stand off, acknowledging it out of your power to accost Mr. Maitland-Buchanan on equal terms. You admire his ingenious adaptation of the machinery of candour to the purposes of disguise; you inwardly congratulate a perti-

nacious poet and critic on having at last done something which his friends may quote concerning him; and you feel that his achievement need only be known to be appreciated. If your announcement, together with this disclaimer, may in any way contribute towards such publicity, I shall the less regret the original inadvertence in your columns.

(9 December 1871, p. 755)

The ruse worked even better than its perpetrators could have hoped. Quite evidently, Buchanan and Strahan had agreed to maintain silence, and Strahan accordingly sent this letter to the *Athenaeum:* "In your last issue you associate the name of Mr. Robert Buchanan with the article **'The Fleshly School of Poetry,'** by Thomas Maitland, in a recent number of the *Contemporary Review.* You might with equal propriety associate with the article the name of Mr. Robert Browning, or of Mr. Robert Lytton, or of any other Robert." Buchanan was not so circumspect. With a characteristic flash of anger he penned a heated letter to the *Athenaeum* defiantly admitting his authorship. His letter is dated 12 December, the publication date of the issue which contained Colvin's letter, an indication that Buchanan wrote in hot haste and without deliberation.

Russell Square, W., Dec. 12, 1871.

I cannot reply to the insolence of Mr. "Sidney Colvin," whoever he is. My business is to answer the charge implied in the paragraph you published ten days ago, accusing me of having criticized Mr. D. G. Rossetti under a nom de plume. I certainly wrote the article on **'The Fleshly School of Poetry,'** but I had nothing to do with the signature. Mr. Strahan, publisher of the *Contemporary Review,* can corroborate me thus far, as he is best aware of the inadvertence which led to the suppression of my own name.

Permit me to say further that, although I should have preferred not to resuscitate so slight a thing, I have now requested Mr. Strahan to republish the criticism, with many additions but no material alterations, and with my name in the title-page. The grave responsibility of not agreeing with Mr. Rossetti's friends as to the merits of his poetry, will thus be transferred, with all fitting publicity, to my shoulders.

Robert Buchanan.

The *Athenaeum* was not slow to capitalize upon this windfall. At the end of Rossetti's "Stealthy School of Criticism" in the issue for 16 December 1871 it printed first Strahan's denial, then Buchanan's admission, and finally its own acrimonious comment:

Mr. Buchanan's letter is an edifying commentary on Messrs. Strahan's. Messrs. Strahan apparently think it is a matter of no importance whether signatures are correct or not, and that Mr. Browning had as much to do with the article as Mr. Buchanan. Mr. Buchanan seems equally indifferent, but he now claims the critique as his. It is a pity the publishers of the *Contemporary Review* should be in such uncertainty about the authorship of the articles in that magazine. It may be only a matter of taste, but we prefer, if we are reading

an article written by Mr. Buchanan, that it should be signed by him, especially when he praises his own poems; and that little "inadvertencies" of this kind should not be left uncorrected till the public find them out.

(p. 794)

With the identity of the enemy clearly established, the way was open for a shot at him. Dante composed a pamphlet in answer to Buchanan's accusations, but, fearing a charge of libel if it were printed, suppressed it (Doughty, p. xxxix). From the pamphlet he made up a letter called "The Stealthy School of Criticism," which he published in the *Athenaeum* on 16 December 1871. Written in a quiet tone of gentlemanly protest, it contrasted favorably with the angry vitriol of Buchanan's attack (pp. 792-794). Not contented with this, he composed a ballad ridiculing his enemy which he intended to publish in the *Fortnightly,* but on Colvin's advice changed his mind and suppressed it.[10]

Clearly uncomfortable because the *Athenaeum* had caught him in a falsehood, Alexander Strahan printed in *Pall Mall* on 23 December 1871, one week after the *Athenaeum*'s damaging arraignment, a letter of defense (p. 3). His weak expostulations were about as effective as those of a small boy caught with his hand in the cookie jar. He protested that his "short and hurried note" was not meant to enter into the question of authorship, but "was simply intended as a protest against the intolerable system of gossipmongering to which our firm has been so frequently subjected." He complained that the *Athenaeum* had done him an injustice by printing his letter with Buchanan's so that "by putting the two together, an appearance of contradiction could be established, and Strahan and Co. be thus made to look ridiculous." He based his complaint on the childish contention that since he had written his letter earlier than had Buchanan, it should have been printed earlier. This blustering retort was seconded by one from Buchanan which was equally blustering and which had enough in common with Strahan's to indicate that they had profited from their former blunder of writing independently of each other. The issue of the *Athenaeum* for 23 December 1871 contained an angry letter from Buchanan in which he denied the statement of the editorial comment upon his letter of the week before. He pointed out that he had not praised his own poetry, but had instead disparaged it. He added a vainglorious insult to the editor which could do him no good with impartial readers: "It is in vain, perhaps, to protest against the comments of such a judge as you, but for every one who reads your journal a dozen will read my reprinted criticism, and will be able to see you in your true colours" (p. 887).

True to his defiant promise, Buchanan published his long-heralded book, *The Fleshly School of Poetry and Other Phenomena of the Day,* early in 1872, this time under his own name. Strahan was the publisher of what turned out to be the magazine article revised and blown up to three times its original size. The more inclusive title is significant of the broadening of the base of his attack which accounts for most of the additions. In his preface he reviewed the history of the original article, reiterated his contention that the pseudonym was used without his knowledge, and then added grandiloquently, ". . . *in order that the criticism might rest upon its own merits and gain nothing from the name of the real writer.*" He defended himself from the charge of vanity by saying that whereas he took the character of Cornelius, who speaks only one line in *Hamlet,* he might have taken that of Fortinbras or the First Gravedigger. He said that the charge of vanity was but a red-herring to distract the attention of the public from the real issue, and exclaimed in disgust that, because Rossetti's poems were labeled "nuptial," they seemed to "have actually become favourites with that prude of prudes, the British matron; and several gentlemen tell me that their aunts and grandmothers see no harm in them!" The conclusion of the preface served notice that he had taken the bridle off his pen and permitted it to gallop at will through invective and savage insult, for he insisted, "Animalism is animalism, nevertheless, whether licensed or not; and, indeed one might tolerate the language of lust more readily on the lips of a lover addressing a mistress than on the lips of a husband virtually (in these so-called 'Nuptial' Sonnets) wheeling his nuptial couch out into the public streets." From this he proceeded to his attack, which was so farfetched, so ridiculous and phantasmagoric that the only conclusion one can reach is that it was the product of an abnormal mind. The record of his physical and mental troubles from 1866 to 1874 shows that he was neurotic and unstable; the **Fleshly School** pamphlet is proof that he had gone far toward catastrophe. His notes to the pamphlet are interesting. They include an excerpt from an article in the *Quarterly Review* in condemnation of "Jenny" and another called "Coterie Glory" from the *Saturday Review,* which took Rossetti and his friends to task for praising each other's works under the guise of criticism. Finally, there was a lengthy note praising Whitman and explaining that although he had written a few lines of indecent verse, he was by no means a fleshly poet.

The reactions to the Controversy were many and varied. One of the earliest replies to Buchanan appeared in R. H. Horne's preface to his poem *Orion,* written in November 1871, and published in 1872. Deprecating the recurrence of prudery, Horne argued that since the body came from the Creator it and its appetites could not be denied. Henry Buxton Forman, a scholarly friend of William Rossetti, published in *Tinsley's Magazine* in February 1872 an answer to the *Contemporary* article (pp. 89-102). In it he replied patiently and painstakingly to Buchanan's charges one by one, explaining the background and context of each one of Buchanan's quotations. *Temple Bar* agreed with Buchanan's viewpoint: ". . . Mr. Rossetti and his admirers have been told a few wholesome truths. There is in all the writings of this school a *fleshliness* which is meant to be natural, but is exaggerated and unwholesome . . ." (XXXIV, 99-100). It agreed that the system of friends writing approving criticism of the work of friends was evil and should not be condoned. The consensus, however, was against Buchanan. *The Illustrated News,* noting that a current issue of *St. Paul's Magazine* contained several of

Buchanan's sonnets, sneered: "Mr. Buchanan, having quarrelled with Mr. Rossetti, appears ambitious of proving that he can write sonnets too, and has produced a string of these compositions, which assuredly run no risk of being mistaken for the production of his rival" (LX, 490). *Fraser's,* after a scholarly discussion of the merits of the poetry of Rossetti, Swinburne, Morris, and Tennyson, said of Rossetti: "Mr. Rossetti has come nearest to the embodiment of the heart's desire of the school; but though he is often artificial, fantastic, and wilfully obscure, he has a real power which cannot be explained away by calling him fleshly, sub-Tennysonian, or any other names" (N.S. V, 588-596). The *Athenaeum* reviewed the matter of the pseudonym, calling it an alias and implying that Buchanan had lied in his disclaimer (25 May 1872, pp. 650-651). It deplored his lack of judgment in republishing his charges and the ridiculous lengths to which he had gone in expanding them. It concluded that "malicious friends" must have advised him to publish the pamphlet, and quipped: "Mr. Buchanan tells how the miasmic influence of Italy 'generated madness even far north as Hawthornden and Edinburgh.' What influences may have generated so much foolishness even as far north as the Hebrides we cannot tell; but only that the foolishness is there, and has ended in a worthless and discreditable treatment of what might have been made a perfectly just and interesting question of criticism."[11] The *Saturday Review* began by agreeing with Buchanan's accusations that Rossetti and Swinburne resented all adverse criticism, that their poetry was "fleshly" and effeminate, and their influence "mischievous." Then it lashed Buchanan for his egoism and bad taste in printing the pamphlet. Ironically, it observed of his excuse that the pseudonym was used to avoid giving the article the added power of his name:

> In the old romances we occasionally read of a knight of tremendous prowess and overpowering reputation, who found it necessary, in order not to alarm antagonists too much, to enter the lists with closed visor and borrowed shield; but Mr. Buchanan is hardly a combatant of this description. There is no reason to suppose that his name carries with it an oracular authority which would be fatal to the free exercise of private judgment; and, on the other hand, it is conceivable that the general reader would appreciate the necessity of examining his dicta more cautiously when aware of the peculiar relations of the critic to the objects of his criticism.

It satirized his morbid imagination in fancying sensuality in everything about him, and thought that most of the trouble lay in his own head. It scoffed at the inconsistency of his admiration for Whitman and concluded: "There is unhappily a spreading taint of sensualism, which may be traced in various directions at the present moment, but it may be seriously doubted whether such productions as this pamphlet are not calculated rather to minister to than to check it" (XXXIII, 700-701). The *Graphic* thought that the pamphlet contained "more objectionable stuff than in anything we have seen lately" (V, 606). It was of the opinion that Buchanan had forfeited his right to a serious hearing by the ridiculous lengths he had gone to in proclaiming some of the most beautiful poetry in English literature tainted with sensuality, and then praising Walt Whitman and Paul de Kock.

Buchanan fired one last shot at Rossetti in an article published in *St. Paul's Magazine* in March 1872 (pp. 282-303). His main object was patently to repair the slight on Tennyson in his article and pamphlet, for he flattered the Laureate by eulogizing him for the nobility of his verse as exemplified in his "The Parting of Arthur and Guinevere." Then, by way of contrast, he appended a footnote with several illustrations of what he considered Rossetti's affected language and concluded: "Here is Euphues come again with a vengeance, in the shape of an amatory foreigner ill-acquainted with English, and seemingly modelling his style on the 'conversation' of Dr. Samuel Johnson." The epithet, "an amatory foreigner," betrays Buchanan's prejudice and reveals the reason why he set upon the Rossettis with such savagery, while by comparison his style of address to his arch-foe, Swinburne, is almost courteous.

Buchanan soon learned that the *Athenaeum* had spoken with the voice of prophecy and that the publishing of the pamphlet had been a grave error. He had expected powerful forces to rally to his support, but none did. Although he insisted that Tennyson and Browning gave him their verbal support and said that he received encouraging letters from such unlooked-for sources as Cardinal Manning, Lord de Tabley, and others not so well known, no one took the lists publicly in his behalf. Friends of long standing fell away from him. There is no mention anywhere of his having any further contact with Lord Houghton. When they met him on a stroll in Regent's Park, George Eliot and G. H. Lewes snubbed him openly, Eliot refusing to stop at all and Lewes only so long as Buchanan held fast to his hand. When Buchanan wrote to ask the reason for his coldness, Lewes replied that Buchanan had shown for the rights and feelings of others a disregard of which he should not have believed him capable. Buchanan's angry reply terminated one of his earliest and most profitable literary friendships (Jay, pp. 109-110). The effects upon his literary work were immediately apparent. Many of his magazine contributions through 1872 and his **White Rose and Red** of 1873 were published anonymously to escape the onslaught of his enemies. In 1873 his magazine work dwindled to almost nothing, either because of illness or his lessened popularity. Reviews of his signed works became noticeably more caustic. The *London Quarterly,* for instance, which had praised his **London Poems** and his **Orm,** was downright insulting in its review of his **Poetical Works** of 1874, a general collection of his poetry (XLIII, 213-214). The same trend is observable in the reviews by the *Athenaeum, Academy,* and *Westminster Review.* A futile attempt to stem the tide was the obvious "puff" given him in the pages of the *Contemporary* by George Barnett Smith (XXII, 872-892).

Matters went even worse for the man he had attacked. He attempted suicide with an overdose of laudanum in 1872, and from that date until his death in 1882 he lived a broken man whose course, though he occasionally revived sufficiently to do a little painting and writing, was steadily downward.

But although Rossetti was incapable of answering his attacker, Swinburne was not. In 1872 he wrote and published his "Under the Microscope," one of the most savage lampoons in the language, inspired principally by Buchanan's taunts. He did not honor his foe by deigning to argue with him as Rossetti had done in "The Stealthy School"; he belabored him with epithets, insults, and scurrilous insinuations; he left him not one shred of dignity as a human being; but cast him aside at the conclusion as a foul serpent too loathsome to touch. To do justice to Swinburne, it must be noted that he had had ample provocation for his reprisal and that he, too, having begun the bibulous practices which were to lead almost to his undoing, was by no means in complete possession of himself. In "Under the Microscope" he more than evened the score for anything Buchanan had said or done. With some justice Buchanan could say in later years that, had he not been made of sturdy fibre, he might have suffered a fate like that of Rossetti.[12]

Although his armor was dented and his head reeling from Swinburne's doughty blows, he still had spirit to fight back. In *St. Paul's Magazine* he published his retort, **"The Monkey and the Microscope,"** in which he once again satirized Swinburne's vanity and amorous proclivities:

> Once, when the wondrous work was new,
> I deemed Darwinian dreams untrue,
> But now I must admit with shame
> The caudal stock from which we came,—
> Seeing a sight to slay all hope:
> A Monkey with a Microscope!
>
> A clever Monkey—he can squeak,
> Scream, bite, munch, mumble, all but speak;
> Studies not merely monkey-sport
> But vices of a human sort;
> Is petulant to most, but sweet
> To those who pat him, give him meat;
> Can imitate to admiration
> Man's gestures, gait, gesticulation;
> Is amorous, and takes no pain
> To hide his Aphrodital vein;
> And altogether, trimly drest
> In human breeches, coat, and vest,
> Looks human, and upon the whole
> Lacks nothing, save perchance a Soul.
> For never did his gestures strike
> As so absurdly human-like,
> As now, when, having found with joy
> Some poor old human Pedant's toy,
> A Microscope, he squats to view it,
> Turns up and down, peers in and thro' it,
> Screws up his cunning eye to scan,
> Just like a clever little man!
> And from his skin, with radiant features,
> Selecting small inferior creatures,
> Makes mortal wonder in what college he
> Saw real Men study entomology?
> A clever monkey!—worth a smile!
> How really human is his style;
> How worthy of our admiration
> Is such delicious imitation!—
> And I believe with all my might

Religion wrong and science right,
Seeing a sight to slay all hope:
A Monkey use a Microscope! (XI, 240)

The controversy lay dormant through 1873 and 1874 and might have expired altogether had it not been for Swinburne, who published his *Essays and Studies* in 1875 with the addition of the ill-natured footnote on Gray in his "Matthew Arnold's New Poems" (p. 153). While outwardly interested only in identifying Gray, he called him "a poor young Scotchman" who received aid from Dobell and Houghton, referred to his poems as "his poor little book," accused him of plagiarizing "some of the best known lines or phrases from such obscure authors as Shakespeare and Wordsworth into the somewhat narrow and barren field of his own verse . . ." and railed upon his "hysterical self-esteem." By way of explaining why he used Gray to illustrate his point, he added unconvincingly: "I may add that the poor boy's name was here cited with no desire to confer upon it any undeserved notoriety for better or for worse, and assuredly with no unkindlier feeling than pity for his poor little memory, but simply as conveying the most apt and the most flagrant as well as the most recent instance I happened to remember of the piteous and grievous harm done by false teaching and groundless encouragement to spirits not strong enough to know their own weakness." Buchanan could hardly have doubted that Swinburne's prime objective was himself. If knowledge of Buchanan's sentimental relationship to the deceased Gray had not come to him through his association with Lord Houghton, Buchanan's memoir of Gray published in 1864 would have apprised him of the fact. The footnote was unworthy of Swinburne and shows that on his side also the Controversy was being conducted without any pretense to literary sportsmanship. This is the note which Buchanan erroneously said led to his original *Contemporary* article of 1871. One point which cannot be doubted is Buchanan's assertion that the note enraged him to the point of desiring revenge. The blows at himself in the essay of 1872 he had taken, but this attack on his dead and innocent friend was another matter. He sought eagerly for an opportunity to strike back and subsequent events gave his enemy into his hands.

In the summer of that same year, 1875, was published an anonymous poem entitled *Jonas Fisher.* The author was actually James Carnegie, the Earl of Southesk, but it is not surprising that it was attributed by Swinburne and the Rossetti circle to Buchanan because Buchanan had announced that his *Orm* was a prelude to an epic poem which was to follow, after the manner of Wordsworth; *Jonas Fisher,* while it is not called an epic, is a poem which fills a book of 243 pages and is as prolix and verbose as the *Drama of Kings*; also, the style of the verse closely resembles Buchanan's: it is of a rough and unfinished quality and is really only prose set to rime with many stumbling lines and marks of hasty and inept composition. In content the resemblance is even closer. The entire poem is a versified criticism of the times, much after the manner of the *Spectator* of Addison and Steele and in the same vein as the *Fleshly School* pamphlet; particularly, it deplores

the immorality of current literature and hints at France as the fountain-head of all such pernicious tendencies. If Swinburne required any further proof that *Jonas* was Buchanan's handiwork, he found it in its appearance at exactly the right time for the expected riposte to his thrust at Gray. He was quick to retaliate with four lines of scornful verse in the *Examiner* on 20 November 1875, which show to what depths a great poet could descend when under the joint influence of malice and alcohol:

> He whose heart and soul and tongue
> Once above-ground stunk and stung,
> Now less noisome than before,
> Stinks here still, but stings no more.

> A. C. SWINBURNE [p. 1304]

A week later the same paper came out with a review of *Jonas,* devoting its first long paragraph to speculating that Buchanan was the probable author:

> This anonymous poem is said by the "London Correspondents" to be the work either of Mr. Robert Buchanan or of the Devil; and delicate as may be the question raised by this double sided supposition, the weight of probability inclines to the first of the alternatives. That the author, whichever he is, is a Scotchman, may be inferred from one or two incidental sneers at the characteristic virtues of his countrymen. If a prophet has no honour in his own country, it must be said on the other hand that a country seldom gets much honour from its own prophet; the worst things said about countries have been said by renegade natives.

> (27 November 1875, p. 1336)

That the review had come to Buchanan's attention is evidenced by his printing in the *Athenaeum* on 4 December 1875 a flat denial that he had even seen *Jonas Fisher* (p. 751). The denial brought forth an acrid retort from the *London Quarterly* that since the real author had not signed the poem, he "thus afforded Mr. Robert Buchanan a favourable opportunity (not altogether lost) of getting up another fuss about himself" (XLV, 527-528).

Either the disclaimer did not convince Swinburne, or he chose to overlook it in his desire to use the opportunity to burlesque the whole matter of the original *Contemporary* article and the pseudonym. In the *Examiner* for 11 December 1875, he printed a letter titled "The Devil's Due" and signed "Thomas Maitland" (p. 1388). The letter opened with a long paragraph imitating the style of Buchanan's critical essays with a bewildering number of reservations, insinuations, and definitions; after some scornful references to the poem it came to an end with the pseudonymous signature and the date-line "St. Kilda, December 28, 1875," all of which was, of course, directed at Buchanan's excuses for the use of the original pseudonym. That his readers might not overlook the implication of dishonesty, Swinburne added a postscript purporting to be Buchanan's instructions to his publisher: "P. S.—On second thoughts, it strikes me that it might be as well to modify this last paragraph and alter the name of the place affixed; adding at the end, if you please—not that I would appear to dictate—a note to the following effect:—" What follows is a malicious parody of both Buchanan's and Strahan's notes to the *Athenaeum*:

> The writer of the above being at present away from London, on a cruise among the Philippine Islands, in his steam yacht (the Skulk, Captain Shuffleton master), is, as can be proved on the oath or the solemn word of honour of the editor, publisher, and proprietor, responsible neither for an article which might with equal foundation be attributed to Cardinal Manning, or to Mr. Gladstone, or any other writer in the *Contemporary Review,* as to its actual author; nor for the adoption of a signature under which his friends in general, acting not only without his knowledge, but against his express wishes on the subject, have thought it best and wisest to shelter his personal responsibility from any chance of attack. This frank, manly, and consistent explanation will, I cannot possibly doubt, make everything straight and safe on all hands.

Buchanan took his time about entering suit, perhaps because he was living in Ireland and did not wish to undertake an unpleasant winter journey to London to set legal machinery in motion. However, his intentions were advertised early enough to bring about the immediate suppression of Swinburne's pamphlet of "The Devil's Due," which he had published concurrently with the newspaper article.[13] With the advent of summer he proceeded to bring his tormentor to justice by suing Mr. P. A. Taylor, owner of the *Examiner,* for five thousand pounds for libel done him in the review of *Jonas Fisher* and in the anonymous "The Devil's Due," with most of the charge resting upon the latter. The formal charge read: ". . . that the said letter was written . . . with the malicious intention of injuring the plaintiff's position and abusing his personal character . . ."[14] The hearing began on Thursday, 29 June, and lasted until Saturday, 1 July 1876. It was held in the Common Pleas Division of the High Court of Justice before Justice Archibald and a Special Jury. Charles Russell and a Mr. MacClymont represented Buchanan, while Taylor retained as his attorneys the Messrs. Murphy, Nathew and Hawkins, and Williams.[15] Despite considerable dodging about England to avoid being dragged into the trial, Swinburne was subpoenaed on 18 or 19 June, he and the Earl of Southesk being the only witnesses called. Because Swinburne freely acknowledged the letter, Taylor's counsel attempted to save their man by suggesting that the suit against the publisher be dropped in favor of one against the author,[16] but Swinburne had a friend in the enemy's camp in MacClymont, who prevailed upon Buchanan not to change his suit.[17] In response to the Justice's question as to why they were unwilling to do this, Counsellor Russell replied for Buchanan, irritating Swinburne by stating that he "was a man of straw who presumably could not be made to pay up, and therefore they had fallen back on the proprietor of the paper as a scapegoat . . ."[18] This last is Swinburne's angry interpretation of the attorney's answer rather than the actual words used in court.

With this point settled, the trial proceeded and entered upon some amusing ramifications. In order to prove the li-

bel Buchanan's attorneys had to review the facts attendant upon the original *Contemporary* article. Their man, they said, "in the course of his public duty as a critic and writer had had occasion to examine the works of certain writers of English verse, and to point out that some of the works of those writers were obscene, indecent, and offensive to sound moral and religious taste." This gave the defense attorneys an opportunity they quickly seized. Reading excerpts from "The Session of the Poets," Hawkins tried to prove that Swinburne had had ample provocation for his letter; and when Buchanan unblushingly offered the makeshift excuse that his poem had been directed at Swinburne's writings and not his person, even the Judge was moved to comment incredulously. Finally, to prove Buchanan's insincerity in his attack on the Fleshly School, Hawkins forced him to acknowledge his praise of Whitman's poetry; whereupon the attorney, producing an unexpurgated edition of those poems, triumphantly submitted them to the Judge and the jury for silent examination because they were considered too evil to read aloud. To this poser Buchanan replied that he still considered Whitman a "colossal mystic" and fundamentally "a spiritual person."[19]

In his summation to the jury, Justice Archibald indicated rather clearly that he sided with Taylor. He carefully defined libel and warned that something written simply in bad taste could not be construed as libellous. Although he pointed out that Taylor was responsible for anything printed in his paper, he advised that if the jury was of the opinion that Swinburne rather than Taylor should have been sued, this point might affect the amount of damages charged against Taylor. Then he blandly stated that the matter of Buchanan's provoking the alleged libels could not affect the case of Taylor since it had not concerned the publisher but only Swinburne, *who should have been sued in his stead.* Turning his attention to the two poets, he observed that many of the works of the so-called "Fleshly School" would have been better unwritten; but since they had been written, "they were not to be rebuked except in a grave and serious way; and if, instead of this, they were made the excuse of a sensational essay, and the same faults were reproduced by repetition and unnecessary quotation, such a mode of treatment must be taken into account by the jury in assessing damages" (*The Times,* p. 13). He followed this by reading passages from the *Contemporary* article and "The Session of the Poets," commented adversely upon Buchanan's defense of Whitman, and asked the jury if they thought the author capable of honest criticism of the Pre-Raphaelites.

The jury, however, were of a different mind and stood upon their constitutional rights to arrive at their own verdict. The *Athenaeum* summed up the trial by explaining that they were swayed by Swinburne's unsavory reputation, by Taylor's being a radical and his paper having radical and deistic principles, and by the fact that Buchanan was poor and Taylor rich. They deliberated only twenty minutes before awarding Buchanan damages of one hundred and fifty pounds.

The trial created a sensation in London literary circles and, by virtue of the humorous comments upon it, was viewed as somewhat of a comedy. Only *The Times* dignified it with a long, detailed report. The *Illustrated News* regarded it as a "dolorous lawsuit" of quarrelling poets which made nobody happy, not even Justice Archibald, because he wore a white hat and a quotation was read from one of Buchanan's poems ridiculing judges in white hats (LXIX, 42). *Once A Week* agreed it was a mistake for poets to attack each other and that the trial had done only harm in advertising a deal of obscene poetry (IV, 265). The *Athenaeum* regarded Buchanan's triumph as a hollow victory brought about by a biassed jury and inept counsel rather than by the merits of his case (8 July 1876, pp. 50-51). *Pall Mall* made its report in the form of a dialect poem in which an imaginary cockney named Samuel Perkins—a lineal descendant of Dickens' Sam Weller—used the incident as the basis of a lengthy sermon to his son on the evils of writing poetry and the futility of human strife. After reviewing the history of the Controversy and the incidents leading to the trial, Perkins said:

> That you see's what comes of printin' what a hangry
>   poet writes.
> Lor! what larks to see them lawyers overaul Buchan-
>   an's lines
> Dippin' in their scoops to try 'em like my cheeses,
>   through the rines!
> Tastin' this and smellin' t' other. "Isn't this a little
>   strong?"
> "Call that pure?" "Well, what of this now, for a ham-
>   matory song?"
> Yes, by George, I never laughed so 'earty, nor I never
>   shall,
> As at 'earing Mr.'Awkins read about that Injin gal,
> And the cuddlin' in the forest! Well, per'aps it meant
>   no harm,
> Still the author owned hisself the scene was just a
>   trifle warm.
> Then, of course, Buchanan's counsel—he was not a
>   goin' to fail;
> So he dropped upon the "fleshlies" right and left and
>   tooth and nail!
> "Grossly senshal," "most indecent," "hanimal passion
>   consecrated."
> Says the judge, "A style of poitry 'ighly to be depre-
>   cated!"
> Well, the upshot was Buchanan gets his verdic safe
>   and sound,
> And he comes on Mr. Taylor for a hundern-fifty
>   pound.
> But, Lord love you, my dear Dudley, what a foolish
>   price to pay!
> What a terrible exposy for the poets of the day!
>
> (3 July 1876, p. 5)

The trial ended all activity along the fleshly front until 1881 and the appearance of Buchanan's novel, *God and the Man,* some six months before Rossetti's death. It is impossible to delineate the circumstances which led up to Buchanan's apology to Rossetti contained in the dedication of his novel, but it is probable that in the intervening years since his pamphlet of 1872 he heard rumors and gossip in literary circles of the pitiable condition of the man he had attacked. Always tenderhearted toward any unfortunate, his conscience must have plagued him with the thought that he had contributed to Rossetti's unhappiness. More accurate and detailed reports of his enemy's condition probably came to him from Westland Marston, who was a long-term friend of both Rossetti and Buchanan, and from Hall Caine, who became intimate with Rossetti in 1879. There was at least one other factor involved: in 1881 Buchanan was a very different man from the neurotic and psychotic disputant of 1871 and 1872. Not only had he regained most of his mental stability, but the impeding death of his wife sharpened his sympathies with his fellowman, especially a fellowman who, like Rossetti, had more than an ordinary claim upon his commiseration. The result of all these influences is the two verses with which he dedicated his novel of hatred and forgiveness:

> I would have snatch'd a bay leaf from thy brow,
>   Wringing the Chaplet on an honoured head;
> In peace and tenderness I bring thee now
>   A lily-flower instead.
>
> Pure as thy purpose, blameless as thy song,
>   Sweet as thy spirit, may this offering be:
> Forget the bitter blame that did thee wrong,
>   And take the gift from me.
>
> **"To An Old Enemy"** (p. iii)

Before his death Rossetti had heard of the verses and was moved by them as he was also by Buchanan's poem, **"The Lights of Leith,"** which Caine read to him (Caine, p. 293). After his death Buchanan added two more stanzas for a later edition, this time placing Rossetti's name above them:

> Calmly, thy royal robe of Death around thee,
>   Thou sleepest, and weeping Brethren round thee
>   stand—
> Gently they placed, ere yet God's crown'd thee,
>   My lily in thy hand!
>
> I never knew thee living, O my brother!
>   But on thy breast my lily of love now lies;
> And by that token, we shall know each other,
>   When God's voice saith 'Arise!'[20]
>
> **"To Dante Gabriel Rossetti"**

Not satisfied even with this, he prostrated himself at his enemy's feet in a final prose paragraph:

> Since this work was first published, the 'Old Enemy' to whom it was dedicated has passed away. Although his name did not appear on the front of the book, as it would certainly have done had I possessed more moral courage, it is a melancholy pleasure to me to reflect that he understood the dedication and accepted it in the spirit in which it was offered. That I should ever have underrated his exquisite work, is simply a proof of the incompetency of all criticism, however honest, which is conceived adversely, hastily, and from an unsympathetic point of view; but that I should have ranked myself for the time being with the Philistines, and encour-

aged them to resist an ennobling and refining literary influence (of which they stood, and stand, so mournfully in need), must remain to me a matter of permanent regret.

In a somewhat different tone is the letter written to Caine by Buchanan after Rossetti's death and published in a footnote in Caine's *Recollections* (pp. 71-72). Here he reviewed the quarrel, confessing his error and not in any way rescinding his apology to Rossetti, but defying "the horde of slanderers who hid within his shadow" and left no epithet unturned to injure Buchanan. Quite evidently his forgiveness and apology did not extend to Messrs. Swinburne, William Rossetti, and others of the enemy forces.

His final word on Rossetti was said in his **"A Note on Dante Rossetti,"** an essay published in 1887 in his *A Look Round Literature,* wherein he showed how far he had moved with his times under the impact of Zolaism and Ibsenism by boldly stating that all love, even the fleshly variety, was the highest human pleasure (pp. 152-161).

But Buchanan was to discover he had raised a genie he could not command. Within a few months after Rossetti's death the staid *British Quarterly* in a review of Rossetti's "House of Life" sonnets described him as coarsely sensual and everything he had been called in the **"Fleshly School"** (LXXVI, 54-63). This so angered Buchanan that he reiterated his apology with added emphasis in *A Look Round Literature.* Again in 1882 in a review of his novel, *The Martyrdom of Madeline,* the *Academy* mistook what was probably an attack upon George Moore and the cult of aestheticism for a ghoulish lampooning of the dead Rossetti (XXI, 428-429). This brought a speedy and bitter denial from Buchanan in a letter to the *Academy* in which he remarked that Swinburne had now forsaken fleshliness and Morris and Rossetti had never embraced it. Sarcastically he asked the readers of the *Academy* to reexamine his novel "to compare the lineaments of my Blanco Serena, a society-hunting, worldly minded, insincere, but good-humoured, fashionable painter, with the literary image of Mr. Rossetti [,] a solitude-loving, unworldly, thoroughly sincere and earnest, if sometimes saturnine man of genius, in revolt against society. The blundering of windmill-criticism could surely go no further" (XXII, 11-12).

Strategically Buchanan's several apologies were the worst thing he could have done for his own cause. Rossetti's friends might have blamed his death upon Buchanan even so, but the unreserved admission of error, instead of placating them by its manliness and straightforwardness, brought them down upon him in a veritable avalanche of accusation and imprecation. The incongruous fact that Rossetti's demise did not take place until a full ten years after the *Fleshly School* pamphlet, was overlooked. They were quick to clothe him in the white robes of a martyr and to cast Buchanan in the sinister garb of executioner, pointing to his recantation as conclusive proof of his guilt.

The various matters of provocation given Buchanan by William and Swinburne were conveniently relegated to the background or forgotten altogether. Minimized were the long and increasing use of chloral and alcohol by Dante Gabriel, his haunting memory of his wife's death with the corroding suspicion that his neglect had caused her to commit suicide, the subsequent desecration of her grave to recover his poems—all of which were certainly factors in the poet's catastrophe. His defenders stubbornly insisted that Buchanan's attack was the major cause of his collapse, probably from a desire to cover up Rossetti's shortcomings on the one hand and to damn a common enemy on the other. The melodramatic quality of their claims undoubtedly appealed to the Victorian audience, trained as it was to love melodrama and to think in its terms. Another propaganda device was employed in that the story was told so often and with such vehemence by so many different persons that even the skeptical were convinced. As for Buchanan, his several apologies had robbed him of the power to speak out in his own behalf without appearing to give the lie to himself, so he was forced to endure in silence the slings and arrows of his outrageous fortune which pelted him from all sides from Rossetti's death in 1882 until his own passing in 1901.

Within a year after Rossetti's death Theodore Watts published an article in the *Nineteenth Century* comparing the attack upon him with those upon Keats and Poe and calling upon the poet's friends to stamp out any lingering traces of the charge of sensuality which yet might cling to his name (XIII, 404). In its review of *Foxglove Manor* the *Spectator* sneered that no member of the Fleshly School had ever done anything more morally obnoxious (LVII, i, 652-653). George Moore aimed a cut at the old wound in his passage at arms with Buchanan in 1889, when he described Buchanan as a failure rejected by Moore and all other true descendants of Rossetti and Swinburne.[21] William Rossetti in his book, *Dante Gabriel Rossetti As Designer and Writer,* published in 1889, implied that Buchanan should have admitted his error much sooner than he did and pointed to the apology as complete justification for William's having labeled the attack unfair and uncalled for all along (p. 156). In the same year William Bell Scott published in his *Autobiographical Notes* his account of the events leading up to and following the **"Fleshly School."** While he admitted the precarious condition of Rossetti's mind before 1871, the use of chloral and alcohol, and the controlled criticism of the *Poems,* he stated flatly and arbitrarily that Buchanan's onslaught was the deciding factor in the artist-poet's breakdown (II, 161-181). Tenacious and unimaginative William Rossetti re-entered the fray in 1895 with a *Memorial* to his brother which is chiefly remarkable for its display of that strong family loyalty not uncommon to people of Italian blood. Denying the truth, that Dante had shepherded the criticisms of his *Poems,* he argued that Buchanan's own words in his apology proved his attack a "miserable" and "disgraceful" matter inspired only by jealousy of Dante's success. He insisted his brother had been a well man until 1872, that the attack had brought on increased use of chloral, and that it had been a direct cause of Dante's subsequent misfortunes and torments (*Family Letters,* I, 289-290, 301-306). His version was accepted without question by Buchanan's old enemy, the *Saturday Review,* which observed venomously and illogically:

> What caused the tragic downfall of Rossetti's mind and temperament? His brother conclusively proves, what other writers have surmised, that the signal for it was given by the attacks made upon him in 1871 and 1872 by a malignant and pseudonymous poetaster. How deeply those attacks were felt by Rossetti, more deeply, perhaps, than the reader of his brother's studiously moderate narrative would suppose, is within the personal recollection of many, and among them the writer of this review. That he became for a while insane under the wicked insinuations of "Thomas Maitland" is not to be questioned, and equally little that his mind never recovered a perfect equilibrium. But why did such results follow such trifling cause? Rossetti's fame was never lessened, even for a moment, by the insinuations of his "scrofulous Scotch" critic; he was surrounded by a bodyguard of ardent and effective friends; he was, or should have been, conscious of his own rich and elastic genius. It has always seemed to us highly humiliating that such an insect could have stung to death so great a king of men. The fact is that "Thomas Maitland," though his murder of Rossetti is his chief claim to human recollection, need boast of it but little. The health of Rossetti was deeply under-mined long before this trifle threw it finally off its balance.

(LXXX, 838-839)

In this completely biased statement the *Saturday Review* saw no need to recall that in 1872 it had supported the essence of most of Buchanan's charges against Rossetti and Swinburne. William repeated his accusations in the preface to *The Works of Dante Gabriel Rossetti,* first published in 1894. In 1906, irritated by the account of the Fleshly School in Harriett Jay's *Robert Buchanan,* he tediously and querulously retrudged the old road in his *Reminiscences* to prove that Buchanan had been entirely at fault and his brother entirely guiltless (II, 521-525).

If Buchanan found a grain of comfort in the entire matter it must have been in the reflection that fortune had done him at least one good turn in Theodore Watts's intervention in Swinburne's affairs in 1879 to save him from the consequences of his alcoholism; otherwise his death would certainly have taken place in the 1880's and would in all probability have been laid at Buchanan's door. As it was, Buchanan suffered his Gehenna manfully. He did not break his silence, though with the passing years he developed a conviction that his career had been blasted by the unfair criticism heaped upon his literary offerings as a direct result of the animosities engendered by the Controversy. The *Westminster Review* corroborated his opinion by stating in 1882 that the friends of the Fleshly School had lampooned his works on every opportunity (CXVIII, 135). Impartial testimony was offered by Roden Noel, a friend to both Buchanan and the Pre-Raphaelites, who hailed Buchanan as one of the leading poets of his day, appreciated widely

"except by a clique, and perhaps by here and there a small literary buccaneer."[22] In a review of Noel's book, the *Spectator* concurred with this statement "because we think that Mr. Buchanan's really noble poetry has met with scant justice from critics of repute" (LIX, i, 755-756).

The Fleshly Controversy passed into history with most literary people holding the view crystallized by William Rossetti and the *Saturday Review*: that the death of Dante Rossetti had been brought about by the action of a disagreeable and envious man who had had none but the basest of motives for his attack. Buchanan's later polemics against a variety of people and institutions did much to solidify this opinion. With the advent of modern realism in all forms of art and with the progress of science, the mind of the times became more frank and liberal, so that subjects which had called forth shocked revulsion in the 1860's and 1870's were regarded with equanimity in the '80's and '90's. Buchanan's attack, therefore, assumed a more and more ridiculous aspect even to periodicals which had agreed with him in 1871 and 1872.

The stigma stuck to his name as though it had been fastened there by Merlin's curse. In remarking upon Buchanan's death in 1901, both the *Academy* and the *Spectator* printed excerpts from his "session of the Poets," but the most unkindest cut was struck by the arch-conspirator in the Fleshly Controversy, the *Contemporary,* which, in its review of Harriett Jay's biography, remarked anent the matter of Buchanan's reading his Greek Testament at the race track, "Truly, the 'Fleshly School' of poets was revenged" (LXXXIII, 452-454).

Notes

1. Samuel C. Chew, *Swinburne* (Boston, 1929), p. 35; Harriett Jay, *Robert Buchanan* (London, 1903), n. to p. 61.

2. Georges Lafourcade, *La Jeunesse de Swinburne* (Paris, 1928), I, 177.

3. Lafourcade (I, 242) ascribes this review to "Lush," but gives no supporting evidence. In her *Robert Buchanan* Miss Jay includes a quotation by Buchanan in which he states flatly that the review is his (p. 161). It is unthinkable that Buchanan would have admitted that he had struck the first blow in the Controversy had he not done so, or that Miss Jay would have included such a damaging admission had she not been convinced of its validity.

4. William Michael Rossetti, *Dante Gabriel Rossetti, His Family Letters with a Memoir* (London, 1895), I, 295.

5. Sir Edmund Gosse and Thomas J. Wise, eds. *The Complete Works of Algernon Charles Swinburne* (London, 1926), VI, 353.

6. Oswald Doughty, ed. *The Letters of Dante Gabriel Rossetti to His Publisher F. S. Ellis* (London, 1928), p. 5.

7. Buchanan, "The Stealthy School of Criticism," *Athenaeum,* No. 2305 (30 Dec. 1871), 877.

8. It is possible that the alert Swinburne had discovered the association of the two names and was hinting of it when, in a footnote to his "Under the Microscope," he referred to his enemy as "this classic namesake and successor of George Buchanan." See n. to p. 440 of "Under the Microscope," *The Complete Works of Algernon Charles Swinburne,* VI (Bonchurch Edition).

9. "The Stealthy School of Criticism," p. 877.

10. William Rossetti, *Dante Gabriel Rossetti as Designer and Writer* (London, 1889), p. 158.

11. This raises the question as to what part Strahan may have played in urging Buchanan to write the pamphlet as a defense of Strahan, who had certainly lost caste as a result of Buchanan's delivering him into the hands of the *Athenaeum* by his ill-timed admission of authorship. It is significant that whereas Strahan had been Buchanan's chief publisher up to the Controversy, from 1876 until the end of his life there is not a single instance of his entrusting one of his books to him. It is not unlikely that Buchanan came privately to the *Athenaeum*'s viewpoint that for him the publishing of the pamphlet had been folly into which he had been urged by the importunacy of Strahan.

12. T. Hall Caine, *Recollections of Dante Gabriel Rossetti* (Boston, 1883), n. to p. 71.

13. Thomas Hake and Arthur Compton-Rickett, *The Letters of Algernon Charles Swinburne* (London, 1918), p. 120.

14. *Athenaeum,* No. 2541 (8 July 1876), 50-51.

15. *The Times* (London), 3 July 1876, p. 13.

16. Thomas J. Wise, *A Bibliography of the Writings in Prose and Verse of Algernon Charles Swinburne* (London, 1927), p. 134.

17. Georges Lafourcade, *Swinburne: A Literary Biography* (London, 1932), pp. 247-248.

18. Gosse and Wise, *Complete Works of Swinburne,* XVIII, 260.

19. *Athenaeum,* No. 2541 (8 July 1876), 50-51.

20. Buchanan, *God and the Man* (London, 1883), p. iii.

21. Buchanan, "Imperial Cockneydom," *Universal Review,* IV (1889), 90.

22. "Robert Buchanan," *Essays on Poetry and Poets* (London, 1886), pp. 282-303.

George G. Storey (essay date 1953)

SOURCE: "Robert Buchanan's Critical Principles," in *PMLA,* Vol. LXVIII, No. 5, December, 1953, pp. 1228-32.

[*In the following essay, Storey discusses evidence of personal animosity on the part of Algernon Swinburne and William Rossetti for Buchanan that predates Buchanan's controversial review of Swinburne's* Poems & Ballads *(1866).*]

John A. Cassidy's recent article, "Robert Buchanan and the Fleshly Controversy" (*PMLA,* LXVII, 65-93), is the first complete and wholly impartial account of the celebrated quarrel to be published. Mr. Cassidy has showed that the attack on Rossetti, "while reprehensible, was not made without some provocation" (p. 65), and that despite his later apology to his "old enemy" Buchanan was subjected to unrelenting harassment by Rossetti's friends. In his study Cassidy emphasizes the personal side of the controversy. But if, as seems certain, personal animus was not the sole motive on Buchanan's side, an additional note will perhaps be helpful to clarify our understanding of the unsavory affair.

At the outset it may be pointed out that there is interesting evidence (not mentioned by Cassidy) of bitter hatred for Buchanan on the part of Swinburne and William Rossetti even before Buchanan reviewed *Poems and Ballads* in August 1866. The source is two letters between Swinburne and William Rossetti in Mr. Wise's collection, from which extracts were printed by Georges Lafourcade in his essay on Swinburne and Keats. In the first of the letters Swinburne expresses contempt for an edition of Keats which Buchanan had prepared for the series of Moxon's Miniature Poets. Early in 1866 Swinburne had just completed his Byron for the same series, and in writing to William Rossetti to ask his advice about the sum he should demand for his work he said: "An illustrious Scotch person of the name of Buchanan has done, it seems, a like office for Keats, and received £10 in return. This sum the publisher is willing to lose, and to cancel the poor devil's work, if I will do Keats instead on those terms; and won't I? and wouldn't I gratis? This forthcoming Scotch edition of Keats, who hated the Scotch as much as I do . . . has long been a thorn in my side; and apart from the delight of trampling on a Scotch poetaster, I shall greatly enjoy bringing out a perfect edition of Keats with all his good verses and none of his bad." In reply, Rossetti remarked, "I confess a peculiar abhorrence of Buchanan, and satisfaction that his Caledonian faeces are not to bedaub the corpse of Keats."[1] What Buchanan had said or done to arouse such abhorrence it is impossible to say. Swinburne's remarks suggest, however, that Swinburne, at least, was not personally acquainted with Buchanan at that time. They also suggest a possible motive on Buchanan's side for the virulence of his review of *Poems and Ballads.*

Whatever personal differences there were between Buchanan and the Pre-Raphaelites before the summer of 1866, it is certain that there were irreconcilable differences in their artistic convictions. When Buchanan ridiculed Pre-Raphaelite painting in "Lady Letitia's Lilliput Hand" (see Cassidy, p. 66), he expressed a principle that he was to maintain throughout his life; namely, that in the economy of arts and letters, the aesthete is not worthy of his hire. As regards poetry, the creed which Buchanan accepted is enunciated in three essays published between 1866 and 1868, and it is illustrated in three volumes of his poems: *Idyls and Legends of Inverburn* (1865), *London Poems* (1866), and *North Coast and Other Poems* (1868). The aversion of the Pre-Raphaelites to this creed is typified in Swinburne's scornful description of *London Poems* as "idyls of the gutter and the gibbet."

Buchanan's theory of poetry, as set forth in the three essays mentioned above, was neither original nor important in itself, but because it supplies part of the explanation for his attack on the Pre-Raphaelites it deserves a brief summary. Most revealing of the essays is one entitled **"The Poet, or Seer."**[2] In it the poet is defined as one "who sees life newly, assimilates it *emotionally,* and contrives to utter it *musically*" (p. 3). Poetry, then, is a compound of three elements—vision, emotion, and music. The first is by far the most important: a profound insight into truth is "the rarest and most important of all gifts; so rare, indeed, and so powerful, that it occasionally creates in very despite of nature the other poetic qualities" (pp. 3-4). Let a man but see some truth clearly and express his vision sincerely, and his work will possess the one essential characteristic of all poetry—namely, spiritualization. "The specific aim of art, in its definite purity," Buchanan asserts in typical Victorian phraseology, "is *spiritualization*; and pleasure results from that aim, because the spiritualization of the materials of life renders them, for subtle reasons connected with the soul, more beautifully and deliciously acceptable to the inner consciousness" (p. 17). Hence, while not aiming at moral teaching, the poet produces something which is moral in the highest sense. Significantly, Buchanan adds, "An essentially immoral form, a bestiality, a lie, an insincerity . . . has no permanent place in art, because spiritualization is fatal to its very perceptibility" (pp. 19-20).

A view of poetry similar to that just summarized is presented in the essay **"On My Own Tentatives,"** which appeared in the same volume with **"The Poet, or Seer."** In a third essay, first printed in September 1866, the question of "Immorality in Authorship" receives separate attention.[3] Here Buchanan equates morality and sincerity: "Morality in literature is, I think, far more intimately connected with the principle of sincerity of sight [i.e., insight] than any writer has yet had the courage to point out. . . . Wherever there is insincerity in a book there can be no morality" (*David Gray,* p. 240). The paramount moral responsibility of an author is to be true to his inner vision. If he contemplates writing something which he does not earnestly believe or which he does not fully understand, what Buchanan calls the "moral mind" will register a protest. Admittedly, the "moral mind," defined vaguely as "one consistent with a certain standard accepted by itself, and situated at a decent height above prejudice" (p. 240), is conditioned by prevailing ethical standards. Therefore, much that was moral for Chaucer or La Fontaine would not be so for a Victorian author, for it could not be written in the nineteenth century with the full acquiescence of the "moral mind."

Buchanan reiterated these principles in numerous essays to the end of his life. In his last book of essays as in his first, he declared that spiritual insight is "the one prerogative and proof of genius."[4] To Buchanan this meant that an art-ist must not merely reproduce life as it is nor withdraw from life to luxuriate in his own sensations. Hence he battled the naturalism of Ibsen and Zola and the aestheticism of Gautier, George Moore, and the Pre-Raphaelites with equal fervor and indiscrimination. His novel *The Martyrdom of Madeline* (1882) and essays entitled **"The New Gironde"** (1887) and **"The Modern Young Man as Critic"** (1891) may be cited as evidence that the apology to Rossetti betokened no alteration in Buchanan's general critical principles.

It cannot be maintained, of course, that Buchanan applied his principles consistently and dispassionately. But it can be asserted that a critical issue was involved in the Fleshly controversy; the issue is discernible in the articles on Swinburne and Rossetti, intermingled with the insults and vulgar rant. The basic charges that Buchanan brought against Swinburne in 1866 were insincerity and imitation. Swinburne's poems were immoral, said Buchanan, because the poet had tried deliberately to shock his readers: he had been unclean merely for the sake of uncleanness. Besides, he had imitated miracle plays, French lyrical poets, and Mr. Browning; he had offered no original insight into human experience. Similarly, in 1871 Buchanan alleged that Rossetti had deliberately disguised his animalistic sensations as operations of soul, and that he was therefore guilty of a most offensive kind of insincerity. Furthermore, Buchanan missed in Rossetti's poetry the sympathy for humanity which he so much admired in Whitman. He saw in the English poet only a morbid preoccupation with his own exquisite sensations. The charge that Rossetti was insincere was the tragic error for which Buchanan later tried to make amends; the charge that Rossetti was morbid and oppressively sensuous was partially just, but it was obscured in the smoke of the battle that Buchanan's first blast touched off.

In his apology to Rossetti, Buchanan admitted that his article and pamphlet had not been objective criticism. The article, he said, in the dedication of *God and the Man,* was conceived "hastily and from an unsympathetic point of view." And he had already confessed to Browning that the attack had been prompted by "the instinct of recrimination."[5] But may we not accept as equally honest his assertion in 1891 when, recalling the quarrel, he wrote, "I really believed that Rossetti was an affected, immoral, over-praised writer"?[6] Probably Buchanan was not entirely clear as to what his motives had been, and we cannot hope to answer the question for him. But we can observe that his attacks on Swinburne and Rossetti were not isolated instances of his condemnation of artists who espoused the doctrine of *l'art pour l'art.*

Taking all available evidence into the account, we may conclude that Buchanan's most notorious pieces of criticism, though spiteful and malicious, were not mere outpourings of spite and malice, but that they were founded upon a view of poetry which Buchanan held throughout his life—a view which could not but produce an imperfect sympathy, even in an unprejudiced critic, for much of the poetry of Swinburne and Rossetti. In applying his principles to the Pre-Raphaelites, therefore, Buchanan was not altogether wrong; but he disqualified himself as a critic by his deviousness and by his extravagance. It is ever to be regretted that he treated so unworthily what, in the words of the *Athenaeum*, "might have been made a perfectly just and interesting question of criticism."[7]

Notes

1. G. Lafourcade, *Swinburne's Hyperion and Other Poems with an Essay on Keats* (London, 1928), pp. 30, 31.

2. Printed in Buchanan's *David Gray and Other Essays* (London, 1868) and again in *A Poet's Sketch-Book* (London, 1883). In all three essays which discuss literary principles Buchanan repeats, with slight alterations, ideas expressed by his friend and benefactor George Lewes in Lewes' series of articles entitled "The Principles of Success in Literature" (*Fortnightly Rev.,* May to Nov., 1865).

3. *Fortnightly Rev.,* VI, 289. The essay was reprinted in *David Gray* under the title "Literary Morality."

4. *The Coming Terror* (London, 1891), p. 246.

5. From a letter to Browning quoted by Gosse in *The Life of Algernon Charles Swinburne* (New York, 1917), p. 205.

6. Quoted by Harriett Jay, *Robert Buchanan* (London, 1903), p. 162.

7. *Athenaeum,* 25 May 1872, p. 651.

Hoxie Neale Fairchild (essay date 1957)

SOURCE: "Buchanan and Noel," in *Religious Trends in English Poetry,* Vol. IV: 1830-1880, *Christianity and Romanticism in the Victorian Era,* Columbia University Press, 1957, pp. 216-39.

[*In the following essay, Fairchild compares the treatment of religious subjects and themes in the works of Buchanan and Roden Berkeley Wriothesley Noel.*]

Although several of the Seers and Seekers are writers of some literary as well as historical interest, none of them occupies so important a position on the main highway of English poetry as to deserve a separate chapter. Two of them, however, are so rewarding to the student of spiritual pathology that they are worth particular attention. It will not be inappropriate to couple the names of Robert Williams Buchanan (1841-1901) and Roden Berkeley Wriothesley Noel (1834-1894).[1] They were personal friends and sympathetic interpreters of each other's work.[2] To some extent both were continuators of the Spasmodic tradition—Buchanan more obviously than Noel.[3] They both tried to write authentic poetry and sometimes succeeded. Noel did so more frequently than Buchanan or at least

abused his gift less wantonly. As regards religion they followed related though not identical paths of thought and arrived at much the same conclusions.

They differed markedly, however, in background and personality. Buchanan was the son of a freethinking Glasgow tailor who left his trade to become an editor of obscure socialist journals. The son obtained a Glasgow B.A. but never knew enough to justify his intellectual pretensions. He was neurotic and sickly. Although he possessed a good deal of sentimental generosity, the **"Fleshly School"** imbroglio bears witness to his jealousy, bad temper, and professional irresponsibility. Noel, son of the Countess of Gainsborough, seems to have been a rather noble person by nature as well as by birth. Buchanan, reared in an atmosphere of radicalism and aggressive secularism, nevertheless developed religious aspirations which he was unable to satisfy. Noel intended to take Orders after receiving his Trinity M.A.; but German philosophy and foreign travel broke down his orthodoxy, and his service as Groom of the Privy Chamber to Queen Victoria may have helped to make him a republican with socialistic leanings.

Noel was an almost pure romantic who, except in occasional moments of despairing scepticism, was able to regard himself as a Christian by identifying Christianity with the romantic faith. Buchanan's case-history is more complicated. Within the straitened limits of this chapter it is impossible to give a full account of the constantly veering philosophical and religious views revealed by the two stout volumes—small print and double columns—of his *Complete Poetical Works.* He was a perfect specimen of the Victorian believing unbeliever. If you asked him to believe anything in particular he would talk like the village atheist. If you asked him to deny the existence of God and the hope of immortality he would talk like an enraptured seer. He felt no less at home with Leslie Stephen, Lecky, and Lewes than with Dobell and Noel. He wished to resemble his picture of Goethe—a poetical sceptic, a mystical positivist.[4] Hardly less antagonistic to the rampant infidel than to the orthodox Christian, he attacks materialism and rejoices in the death of Nietzsche:

> Poor gutter-snipe! Answer'd with his own prayer,
>   Back to primeval darkness he has gone;—
> Only one living soul can help him there,
>   The gentle human god he spat upon!

That even Nietzsche may hope for the human god's pardon is suggested by **"The Ballad of Judas Iscariot,"** one of Buchanan's most effective poems, where Christ admits the soul of the humbled, repentant Judas to communion with Him in heaven. In his softer moods this positivist can credit Christianity with "the higher truth of poesy divine" and apostrophize *Pilgrim's Progress:*

> O fairy Tale Divine! O gentle quest
>   Of Christian and the rest!
> What wonder if we love it to the last,
>   Tho' childish faith be past,
> What marvel if it changes not, but seems
>   The loveliest of dreams?[5]

Several of Buchanan's more ambitious works—*The Book of Orm, Balder the Beautiful, The City of Dream*—suggest a comparison with Bunyan in being allegories of man's quest for God. But the difference is far greater than the similarity, for the deity sought in these poems is not the Hebraic Jehovah, nor any god of the Greeks or Teutons or Hindus,

> . . . nor the Man Divine,
> The pallid rainbow lighting Palestine;
> Nor any lesser of the Gods which Man
> Hath conjured out of Night since time began.
> I mean the primal Mystery and Light,
> The most Unfathomable, Infinite,
> The Higher Law, Impersonal, Supreme,
> The Life in Life, the Dream within the Dream,
> The Fountain which in silent melody
> Feeds the dumb waters of Eternity,
> The Source whence every god hath flown and flows,
> And whither each departs to find repose.

This God, he says in *The Book of Orm,* has hidden Himself behind the veil of the sky, which He has woven for that purpose. Our constant longing to behold His face is therefore constantly thwarted.

> Yet mark me closely!
>   Strongly I swear,
> Seen or seen not,
>   The Face is *there*!

But if the veil were lifted the revelation would be unbearably terrifying. For Buchanan all intellectual clarity is associated with unbelief, and all belief with inscrutable mystery. God owes His very existence to the fact that He is "the Dream within the Dream." Our only justification for seeking Him is the certainty that He can never be found. For this very reason, however, there is something to be said for all man-made religious symbols:

> No creed is wholly false, old creed or new,
>   Since none is wholly true.[6]

But Buchanan's inherited rationalism forbids him to cultivate the sentimental latitudinarianism which this relativistic position would otherwise have encouraged. He remains quite enough of a freethinker to insist that men should not call themselves Christians unless they affirm the doctrines of Christianity. To the genuine secularist, nothing is more infuriating than the refusal of self-styled believers to specify their beliefs. Hence this Gilbertian chorus from **"The Devil's Sabbath"**:

> To all us literary gents the future life's fantastical,
> And both the Christian Testaments are only "wrote
>   sarcastical";
> They're beautiful, we all know well, when viewed as
>   things poetical,
> But all their talk of Heaven and Hell is merely theo-
>   retical.
> But we are Christian men, indeed, who, striking pious
>   attitudes,
> Raise on a minimum of creed a maximum of plati-
>   tudes!

> For this is law, and this we teach, with grace and with
>   urbanity,
> That whatsoever creed men preach, 'tis essential Chris-
>   tianity![7]

Despite his nostalgic affection for Bunyan's fairy-tale, the same honesty makes it impossible for him to profess any serious belief in the historic faith. He is a little perplexed that so genuinely Hellenic a pagan as Noel should also be "a true Christian." Eager not to misrepresent his friend he hastens to explain:

> Not that I conceive for one moment that he accepts the whole impedimenta of Christian orthodoxy—he is far too much of a pagan still ever to arrive at that. But he believes, as so many of us have sought in vain to believe, in the absolute logic of the Christian message: that logic which is to *me* a miracle of clear reasoning raised on false premises, and which to others is false premises and false reasoning all through.[8]

The peculiarities of Noel's interpretation of the Christian message will emerge gradually as we proceed, but his address to Byron may serve as an introductory sample:

> A fierce, glad fire in buoyant hearts art thou,
> A radiance in auroral spirits now;
> A stormy wind, an ever-sounding ocean,
> A life, a power, a never-wearying motion!
> Or deadly gloom, or terrible despair,
> An earthquake mockery of strong Creeds that were
> Assured perversions of calm earth and sky,
> Where doom-distraught pale souls took sanctuary,
> As in strong temples. The same blocks shall build,
> Iconoclast! the edifice you spilled,
> More durable, more fair: O scourge of God,
> It was Himself who urged thee on thy road;
>
>   . . . . .
>
> May all the devastating force be spent?
> Or all the godlike energies be shent?
> Nay! thou art founded on the strength Divine:
> The Soul's immense eternity is thine!
> Profound Beneficence absorbs thy power,
> While Ages tend the long maturing flower.[9]

As we see, Noel is moved not only by Byron's "fierce, glad fire" but by his "terrible despair." The Victorian poet feels a Byronic melancholy when he gazes upon a storm at sea:

> O hymn sublime, confounded, infinite
> Of Tempest, how the chaos in my soul
> Responds to your appeal, and drifts with cloud!
> I too am worn with many moods at war,
> Wind thwarting tide; stern duty, passion, love,
> Wrestle while, unresolved to harmony,
> They urge me blindly, violent, confused.

He has read not only *Childe Harold* but *Morte d'Arthur* and *Stanzas from the Grande Chartreuse,* for he adds:

> The old-world order passeth, and the new
> Delaying dawns, one crimson, loud with voices

We know not, with wild wars in earth and heaven;
The fountains of the great deep are broken up,
Threatening deluge; our firm earth goes under.

At such times nature seems merely to deride "the ideals of our childhood." The caves in a sea cliff look like huge church windows

Which Time, the old Iconoclast,
While the centuries rolled by,
Slow-fashioned there in irony
Of Gothic minster, Gothic creed,
Human worship, human need.

Our life is like **"The Merry-Go-Round"** revolving at night on the shaky old pier at Fowey, "Over all the silent stars! beyond, the cold grey wave." It whirls round and round "To a loud monotonous tune that hath a trumpet bray." This bright spot in the darkness is meaningless and transitory:

I know that in an hour the fair will all be gone,
Stars shining over a dreary void, the Deep have sound
    alone.
I gaze with orb suffused at human things that fly,
And I am lost in the wonder of our dim destiny.[10]

Noel's darker moods are shared by Buchanan. A Hardyesque passage in *The Drama of Kings* portrays his *deus absconditus* as too completely self-hypnotized by His contemplation of the passage of time to care anything about His world. The glories of heaven blaze all around Him, yet

He heeds them not, but follows with eyes yearning
    The shadow men call Time.
Some problem holds Him, and He follows dreaming
    The lessening and the lengthening of the shade.
Under His feet, ants from the dark earth streaming,
    Gather the men He made.

. . . . .

How should He care to look upon such creatures,
    Who lets great worlds go by?[11]

A world without death, says Buchanan, would be unbearable, since in such a world man's painful quest of the Absolute would be endless. Orm therefore blesses God "for Sleeping, and for Silence, and Corruption." Three pages later, however, he thinks that death releases the soul from the flesh-prison which prevents it from uniting in love with other souls. But eighteen pages further on, death is associated with absorption into external nature rather than with benevolism, for Orm prays:

In the time of transfiguration,
Melt me, Master, like snow;
Melt me, dissolve me, inhale me
Into thy wool-white cloud;

. . . . .

And melt and dissolve me downward
In the beautiful silver Rain

That drippeth musically,
With a gleam like Starlight and Moonlight,
On the footstool of Thy Throne.

In *The City of Dream,* grim old Death, who has dogged the footsteps of the hero throughout life's pilgrimage, turns at last into a "radiant child" who seems to promise that all the great questions will be answered. But Satan, in **"The Devil's Case,"** admits:

Death alone I cannot vanquish—
Death and God, perchance, are One!

Yet throughout the pretentious muddle of his speculations on death Buchanan never quite lost the hope expressed in the lines which he chose to print last of all among his collected poems:

Forget me not, but come, O King,
And find me softly slumbering
    In dark and troubled dreams of Thee,
Then, with one waft of Thy bright wing,
    Awaken me![12]

Either of these men might have written:

Ah! for a vision of God! for a mighty grasp of the
    real,
    Feet firm based on granite in place of crumbling
sand!

But in this case the poet is Noel, whose longing to solve the mystery of life and death was sharpened by the loss of his little son. The early primrose budded while the child lay ill; he hoped he would be up to see it open, but he died on the very day it bloomed.

I wonder if he saw it,
Saw the flower open,
Went to pay the visit
Yonder after all!
I know we laid the flower
On a stilly bosom
Of an ivory image;
But I want to know
If indeed he wandered
In the little garden,
Or noted on the bosom
Of his fading form
The paly primrose open;
How I want to know![13]

The power of some bad poems to move us is one of the anomalies of literary criticism.

In groping toward answers to such questions Noel's chief support is a romantic pantheism which should be studied not only in his poems but in his highly revealing critical essays. "I believe," he declares,

that Rousseau, Wordsworth, Byron, Shelley, Keats, Coleridge, were verily prophets, to whom a new revelation was entrusted. In a time when . . . the angels of Faith and Hope seemed to be deserting forever the desecrated shrines of mankind—then it was that these Prophet-Poets, as very ministers of Heaven, pointed men to the World-Soul, commanding them once more to veil their faces before the swift subtle splendour of Universal Life. . . . "The light that never was on sea or land, the consecration and the poet's dream," is indeed a new revelation, made peculiarly in the modern poetry of true spiritual insight, and of this Poetry of Nature Wordsworth is the High Priest. . . . In seeking for a *note* of this peculiar modern nature-worship, I think we must set down as a principal one, *Pantheism,* either overt or implicit. For it is a *worship*—precisely as the Scandinavian and Greek Mythologies are *worships*—only in a modern form.[14]

One is tempted to say that Noel is more like John Middleton Murry than anybody but John Middleton Murry.

The Wordsworthian nature-faith is "modern," Noel insists, even in the sense of being strictly up-to-date. Mechanistic science has by no means destroyed it: the notion that nature can be known "correctly" only by the scientist is giving way before the realization that "Spiritual Imagination alone knows Nature." By the use of this faculty James Hinton has reconciled science with a pantheism which is consistent with a deeply religious awe. Noel admiringly cites Hinton's theory

> that, as atoms we name inorganic are compelled, by some unknown power, to resist the law of chemical affinity and combine into vital organisms—into human bodies, whereunto pertains consciousness and thought, so these world-atoms of the void yonder, together with this our own world-atom, may form greater living organisms endued with grander thought. Then we should ourselves be to these as the living monads of our own blood, as the parasites of our tissues to us.

With sanguine feelings which we now find difficult to share, he appeals also to

> recent investigations into the nature of ultimate elementary atoms by Thomson, Clerk-Maxwell, and Clifford; how these hypothetic entities pulsate and radiate, whirl and travel, just like planets and suns. May not these too be worlds with life and thought in them, if one could only comprehend? . . . What rational vital unity then pervades solid granite rocks, the Atlantic that rebels against their boundary, solar systems yonder, and ourselves who wonder!

Such a vitalistic interpretation of the universe is further encouraged, and somehow harmonized with essential Christianity, by Hegel and Robert Browning. *A Grammarian's Funeral* teaches us that

> Things are not in their momentary appearances . . . they are fulfilled in their disappearances even, and their living again in richer form. . . . "That which thou sowest is not quickened except it die: and God giveth it a body as it hath pleased Him." So a rather discredited old book says. Three great writers see and teach this very distinctly—Hegel, Hinton, and Browning.[15]

Noel's attitude toward nature is not without a tincture of genuinely religious objectivity and humility. He does not *consciously* wish to think of man as master of the physical universe. For him, nature-worship would not be a religion unless it entailed *worship.* One thinks of Spinoza when Noel says: "He who loses his own personality in Nature, who lays down before her . . . his own private wrongs and griefs and fevered aspirations, hereby redresses the balance so unduly weighted with the self-will and momentary longings of one restless man." Not without some confusion between two meanings of the term "law," he declares that in nature "the harmony of inviolable laws appears coöperant to an end. But I think that this inevitableness of a universal order involves the idea of rightness, that of some fulfilled obligation tinged with morality, or what is akin to it. I know this cannot be proved, but I think it may be felt." He himself feels it so strongly that except in a few unusually despairing moments he cannot believe that nature is completely alien to human aspirations. "All that is profound, eternal, impersonal in us, goes forth to wed with the profound, eternal, impersonal Heart of all. It is beyond our good and right, more than our ideal, yet justifies, sanctions, transcends, absorbs it."[16]

Thus when he sees huge waves thundering fiercely into a cave he asks:

> Of Demiurgic Powers, afar from the man and the
>   woman,
> Are these dim echoing chambers the mystical veiled
>   thought,
> Indifferent, aloof, or enemy to the human?
> How, then, are they a haven for minds and hearts o'er-
>   wrought?
> Ah! many and many an hour in your sublime com-
>   munion
> I pass, O Gods unknown, of ocean, wind, and cloud;
> I find profound repose, refreshment flow from the
>   union.

But even this communion with the human though more than human Heart of all is not sufficient when Noel "wants to know" what has become of his little son. He is thinking of the dead child in *A Southern Spring Carol*:

> Ah! Nature never would have power
> To breathe such ecstasy of flower,
>   · · · · ·
>
> If *he* were turned to common earth!
> If a child so fair, so good,
> Were a waif on Lethe's flood,
>   · · · · ·
>
> She [Nature] would reel dissolved, and faint
> With deep dishonour of the taint!
> The very girders of her hall
> Crushed, her stately floor would fall.
> Ourselves are the foundation-stone;
> If thought fail, the world is gone.

Needless to say, thought does *not* fail. In response to the incantation of this verse the vernal landscape reveals all its latent humanity:

> Nature rises on immortal wings!
> And soaring, lo! she sings! she sings!

There is no death!
She saith.
O Spring! O Spring! O Southern Spring!
What a triumphal song you sing![17]

In Noel's opinion such flights of imagination are authenticated by philosophy and even by science. In his essay, *The Poetic Interpretation of Nature,* he declares that "since Berkeley, Kant, and modern physiology, it is no longer permissible to doubt that . . . what we call 'laws of nature' are merely the interpretation which our sensible and mental constitution enables us to put upon the language of the Kosmos."[18] This is a drier version of his statement that "Spiritual Imagination alone knows Nature." And so the inviolable laws which we are to regard with such deep self-surrendering reverence are after all the product of our own minds. "Ourselves are the foundation-stone." The worshipper of nature is the maker of nature, and the circularity of the romantic faith—from man to nature to man—is once again made manifest.

On this theme Buchanan is much less fruitful. As we shall see later, he feels a theoretical reverence for evolving nature as the matrix of Man's loving heart; but since he can conceive of no religion (other than the religion of humanity) which is more than mere emotional guesswork about unfathomable mystery, his dabbling in nature-worship is inconsistent and half-hearted. Unlike Noel, he seldom tries to philosophize about nature because, though he wants to believe, he associates reason exclusively with unbelief. In the thirty-four **Coruisken Sonnets** he begins by lamenting that he can find God neither in the city, where human misery seems to deny His existence, nor in the country, where we are like children waiting in a fair house for a father who never comes. If God really *is* present in the hills about Loch Coruisk, He should be ashamed of Himself: He should be in London helping the poor. Since He seems to care nothing for suffering men, He Himself should be judged at the Last Day. The beautiful hills are changeless and impassive and indifferent to humanity—like God. It would be better to be unhappy and imperfect and passionate than to be a mountainpeak deity. But the little brook which "murmurs 'God made me!'" reminds Buchanan of "the happy hearts of Earth," and he asks God to forgive him for his fretfulness. In the last sonnet a rainbow appears—"Art thou a promise?" This is feeble stuff compared to Noel. In **The Book of Orm,** "Earth the Mother" had beheld God's face in the days before He hid it behind the veil of the sky, but now the senile crone hardly remembers how He looked. Feeling that she knows the great secret, men question her, but they get either no answer or an answer which makes them deny God's existence. Again there is a rainbow, however. As the poem continues, Orm not only enjoys nature but sometimes detects beneath its beauty "An understream of sober consecration." These Wordsworthian intimations, however, are disappointingly evanescent:

Yet nought endured, but all the glory faded,
And power and joy and sorrow were interwoven;
There was no single presence of the Spirit.

Later on, Orm declares that he will worship God when the mountains and rivers and clouds do so—which they obviously don't.[19] In short the super-God, "the Dream within the Dream," is not to be found in nature. It is axiomatic with Buchanan that He is not to be found at all.

Let us return to Noel. Despite his reverence for the romantic poet-prophets, some of his most seriously philosophical nature-poetry is more deeply indebted to the Greeks than to Wordsworth. There was of course nothing incongruous in using Greek mythology as a vehicle for romantic pantheism: Wordsworth himself, not to mention Shelley and Keats, had done the same. The great romantics, according to Noel, were the revivers, not the inventors, of the true faith. Of course he has no literal belief in the symbols of pagan myth, but he holds that the Greeks "were not far from the truth when they formulated their conviction that our spiritual kinship with Nature testifies to some spiritual beings like ourselves behind the phenomena of Nature—the elements, and so-called inanimate objects, being only their expression, body, or vesture. . . . Modern Nature-poetry is reverting . . . to this primal conception of the ancients." And quite rightly, since no other religion is fit for a true poet: "For as Science . . . affords no help to the poetic feeling of life and spirit in Nature,[20] so neither does a theology which teaches that there is a God external to the world, who once made, and still possibly sustains it. Poetry demands God immanent in Man and Nature." After quoting Wordsworth's "I'd rather be a pagan" sestet he pays one of his tributes to the wise Germans: "But the philosophy of idealism supplies for the logical faculty the conception needed to lift it into some harmony with the vision of children, poets, and the more primitive, less sophisticated races."[21] It is interesting that he should value transcendental idealism as a rationalization of the intuitive wisdom of childhood. The gap between romantic primitivism and romantic transcendentalism is not so wide as Professor Lovejoy would have us think.

The long poem entitled *Pan* is Noel's contribution to the widespread and rather tedious debate, initiated by Miss Barrett's retort upon Schiller, as to whether Pan is dead or alive. Noel of course supports the latter thesis:

Pan is not dead, he lives for ever!
Mere and mountain, forest, seas,
Ocean, thunder, rippling river,
All are living Presences.

Science (of the wrong sort) is impotent to tell us "whence all the vision flows." It flows from a Pan-spirit at the heart of everything.[22] The poem reaches the conclusion that Christ came not to destroy Pan but to fulfill him—a point which must be reserved for later examination.

Buchanan admires his friend's Neo-Hellenic paganism but seldom emulates it: his myths are usually homemade or, as in **Balder the Beautiful,** Scandinavian. Nevertheless he also writes a **"Pan."** It advances the heterodox idea that Pan is dead in his old rural haunts but still alive in the city, where his spirit gives our drab existence "the gleam of some forgotten life."[23]

The two poets, however, stand shoulder to shoulder as humanitarians and advanced socio-political liberals who associate their views with spiritual values. We have already noted that Buchanan disapproves of God's indifference to social service. The poet's sympathies embraced the lower animals as well as man. Like Tennyson, Browning, Christina Rossetti, and many other eminent Victorians, he opposed vivisection. He belonged to the Humanitarian League, among whose members his **"Song of the Fur Seal"** was much admired.[24] The aristocratic Noel's *Poor People's Christmas,* contrasting the message of the herald angels with the actual life of the poor, might have been written by one of the plebeian social-protest poets. In *Livingstone in Africa* the great missionary desires to manifest the spirit of Christ by rescuing the blacks from the horrors of the slave trade rather than by "saving souls" in the ordinary sense.

Noel's personal tragedy made him especially sensitive to the sufferings of children, for

> Where 'er there comes a little child,
> My darling comes with him.

A display of toys in an arcade makes him love outward from his lost son to other men's living children:

> I will be a minister
> The fountain of their joy to stir,
> In such resorts, and by such measures,
> As were wont to yield him pleasures;
> Or where little hearts may ail,
> Love's yoke-fellow, I will not fail,
> Where are tears and visage pale,
> To quell the tyranny of Fate,
> Or man, that renders desolate:
> And I deem he will approve
> In the bowers of holy Love,
> Near and nearer to me move.

His memories of that little boy drew him to the verge of Christianity, but he could never bring himself to take the leap. In *The Children's Grass,* he juxtaposes the children of the poor and of the rich, bitterly asking,

> Are not these thy children, Father?
>   These—or only those?
> Are we not all orphans rather
>   Of whom—none knows?[25]

Buchanan could look back to boyhood days when the home of his father, disciple of Robert Owen both as atheist and as socialist, was visited by the pioneer French socialists, Blanc and Caussidière. The mature poet subscribed to no fixed political or economic creed but retained a warm affection for the French people and for the ideals of the Revolution. Victor Hugo influenced him strongly. *The Drama of Kings* (1871) was an outburst of indignant sympathy for France and an attack on the German pretense of fighting "in the name of the Lord." But the first part of this work deals with Bonaparte, the pretended champion and real betrayer of fair Liberty. At last he is overthrown by the "Titan," Liberty's faithful lover, the "Spirit of Man," for

> The legions of the conqueror are weak
> Against the strength of the Free Thought of Man.

Now, in 1871, the martyrdom of man[26] is being repeated, with Bismarck in the oppressor's rôle. But the poet's hopes are revived by the deposition of Napoleon III and the proclamation of the Third Republic. At last he permits the Chorus to predict that the liberated Spirit of Man will eventually establish the "perfect State":

> 'Tis where the home is pure,
> 'Tis where the bread is sure,
> 'Tis where the wants are fewer,
>   And each want fed.
> Where plenty and peace abide,
> Where health dwells heavenly-eyed,
> Where in nooks beautified
>   Slumber the dead.[27]

Noel also sympathizes with France in her struggle with Germany and believes that England and America should enter the war on her side. This is no time to prate of international amity:

> Arm, England, arm! The halcyon hour must wait
> When Love and Righteousness shall vanquish Hate.
> Jesus of old was royal hailed in scorn:
> Now the world crowns Him—still it is with thorn!
>
>   . . . . .
>
> Fair is our dream of universal peace;
> But there be wolves, and lambs of tender fleece.

Economic competition—compare Tennyson's *Maud*—is in itself a kind of war, and a baser kind than an armed crusade for liberty. Noel's long socialistic poem, *The Red Flag* (1872), rebukes the nominally Christian world in the name of the Crucified Carpenter, to whom he prays:

> Friend of the lowly, fainting on the wood,
> Behold thy poor upon a golden rood!

He tells those decorous well-fed churchgoers who are shocked by *The Origin of Species* that their own behavior exemplifies the struggle for existence:

> Lift up your pious eyes at Darwin's creed;
> And try to prove him right about your breed,
> Dear fellow-Christians! who live as though
> Not even yet you'd struggled from below.
> For beasts of prey with all their savage strife
> Are still the cherished models of your life.
>
>   . . . . .
>
> Ah! what if some unshamed iconoclast,
> Crumbling old fetish-remnants of the past,
> Rouse from dead cerements the Christ at last?
> What if men take to following where He leads,
> Weary of mumbling Athanasian creeds?

The same religious-revolutionary hope is expressed in *Poor People's Christmas,* where the widow of a man who has been goaded to suicide by economic injustice has a vision of Jesus in the guise of "a common workman." He consoles her, saying:

My servants fashion even now
Justice for the commonweal;
From toilers with the hand, the brow,
Idle men no more may steal;
My servants seek; I whisper how
They may find the remedy,
Save my little ones who cry:
For I am poor Myself, you know;
The Poor are Mine, and I will heal!—
Already dawns millenium;
Soon My holy reign will come.[28]

The connection between Noel's pantheism and his religion of social reform is clearly revealed by *The Spirit of Storm,* a poem which manages to be both Shelleyan and Spencerian:

I send my spirit adrift upon the storm,
Careering along the triumph of the blast,
Exultant! well I know the living God,
God the creator, for destroyer too;
Who purifies by hurricane, evolves
From birth-throes of rebellion, fraught with fear,
Perplexity and pain, the common weal,
Raised to a higher excellence.

Out of the evolutionary-revolutionary turmoil symbolized by the storm arise, as Spencer taught, organisms not only more complex but more altruistic and cooperative. The final outcome will be "the nobler type of Man," Noel's version of the Tennysonian "Christ that is to be." Mother Nature is a good Utopian Socialist:

Lo! the World-Soul commandeth to emerge
From dead, resolved, more simple forms the higher
Through pain, defeat, death, folly, sorrow, sin,
Compelleth all to be themselves, through all.
From thee, O mystic Mother, deeply dark,
From thee, O mother Nature, impulse floweth,
Urging mankind to launch, like wintering bird,
Upon the unknown dim airs, by faith to find
Fair undiscovered realms beyond the dawn![29]

For reasons already explained, Buchanan's faith in the ultimate triumph of the Spirit of Man is less deeply rooted in nature-mysticism. Even for him, however, that triumph is the result of the evolutionary process. He is more of a positivist than Noel. *The Drama of Kings* is dedicated "To the Spirit of Auguste Comte" as "this Drama of Evolution." Buchanan is by no means an orthodox worshipper in the temple of the Great Being—he was never an orthodox anything. Nevertheless he represents that looser, vaguer, more sentimental reverence toward Collective Humanity which most Englishmen associated with the name of Comte. It provided a link between the unbelieving and the believing sides of Buchanan's nature, enabling him to spurn the illusions of supernaturalism and yet to bow his head before the concept of **"God Evolving"**:

No God behind us in the empty Vast,
No God enthroned on yonder heights above,
But God emerging, and evolved at last
Out of the inmost heart of human Love.[30]

Noel has much the same idea, but he steeps it more deeply in romantic pantheism and tries harder to identify it with Christianity. "Pan is not dead," he answers Mrs. Browning, "save in this sense—that God manifest in Nature is now, since the revelation of our Blessed Lord Jesus Christ, felt to be less worshipful than God manifest in Divine Humanity."[31]

Such language is too pious for Buchanan's taste, but he knows that his friend means no harm by it. He and Noel, he says, fully agree that "The atheist and the Christian, the believer and the unbeliever, meet on the platform of a common beneficence. Faith in Love is all-sufficient, without faith in any supernatural or godlike *form* of love." He credits Noel with a "fully reasoned-out faith in the divine destiny of Man."[32] Despite some verbal differences, then, both poets worship the Divine Humanity—the God of William Blake. What we mean when we say "God" is simply "Mercy, Pity, Peace, and Love," the highest qualities of perfected Man. Man is God because man loves and Love is God. God does not yet fully exist, for the absolute identity of Man and Love is still to be achieved; but He *will* exist when completely loving Man emerges as the final product of the evolving universe. God, then, depends on Man. Does not Man in turn depend upon the laws of nature? Yes, in a sense—that is what makes it all so "scientific." But we must remember Noel's statement that "what we call 'laws of nature' are merely the interpretation which our sensible and mental constitution enables us to put upon the language of the Kosmos."[33] It is from Man's love that nature derives her power to produce loving Man—again the romantic circularity. Man is the Alpha and the Omega. In worshipping God, as Feuerbach taught, he worships only himself.

Thus in the **"Ode to the Spirit of Auguste Comte"** prefixed to *The Drama of Kings,* Buchanan declares that

. . . God is multiform,
Human of heart and warm,
Content to take what shape the Soul loves best;
Before our footsteps still
He changeth as we will—
Only—with blood alone we gain Him, and are blest.

The idea that humanity assumes divinity through martyrdom may be a Christian heresy or, as has already been suggested, a reflection of Reade's *Martyrdom of Man.* It reappears in lines which support the latter hypothesis:

The creeds I've cast away
Like husks of garner'd grain,
And of them all this day
Does never a creed remain;
Save *this,* blind faith that God
Evolves, thro' martyred Man.

"The Last Faith," says Buchanan, is faith in man, the one faith without which we perish:

Hate Man, and O, thou hatest, losest God;
Keep faith in Man, and rest with God indeed.

And what if, after all, the God thou seekest
Were here, not yonder,—God in act to be,
To find and know Himself for evermore.

Orm's closest approach to fulfillment of his quest occurs
when

At last in a Garden of God
I saw the Flower of the World.
This Flower had human eyes,
Its breath was the breath of the mouth.[34]

And in *The Drama of Kings* the Chorus is sustained by
the belief that when at last we behold the face of God we
shall find it to be none other than the face of perfected
Man.[35]

Noel, as we have seen, is not thoroughly satisfied with
faith in man unless he can associate human love either
with the love of Christ or with the love which permeates
both the World Soul and the Spirit of Man and binds them
together. The latter sort of love is celebrated in the lines:

Find the birthplace of sweet Love;

. . . . .

Find his nest within the grove
Of mystic manifold delight,

. . . . .

Discover hidden paths of Love!
Explain the common miracle,
Dear abundant treasure-trove,
Celestial springs in earthly well,
In human vase Heaven's ænomel!

Like so many men who completely discard divine transcendence in favor of divine immanence, he is rather vague
as to the distinction between *eros* and *agape*. His prone-
ness to confuse the two is aggravated partly by his Neo-
Hellenic paganism and partly by his admiration for Hinton's theory that the all-pervasive cosmic energy is sexual.
The Secret of the Nightingale is the bird's "holy love" for
its mate:

Behold the chosen one, the bride!
And the singer, he singeth by her side.
Leap, heart! be aflame with them! loud, not dumb,
Give a voice to their epithalamium!
Whose raptures wax not pale or dim
Beside the fires of seraphim.
These are glorious, glowing stairs,
In gradual ascent to theirs:
With human loves acclaim and hail
The holy love of the nightingale!

Elsewhere two lovers fail to cooperate with nature by seiz-
ing upon what Browning would call their "good minute":

Spring confused her lovers all,
Each obeyed the sacred call;
Only we refused to fall,

Surely, calmly, self-incurled
'Mid such sweet madness of the world!

. . . . .

And we are still apart, alone!
Might our clashing kindle Hell?
Ask no more, I cannot tell;
Was it well? was it well?

Noel's answer is obvious enough. But such a poem as
Passion is less Browningesque than Swinburnian:

O pale my lady, and were you death,
Kissing away the soul's own breath,
I would follow, for all cold Reason saith,
Even where Ruin raveneth![36]

Remembering Buchanan's attack on "The Fleshly School,"
we shall not expect his conception of love to be so concrete and full-blooded. He tenderly cared for his invalid
wife, but he seems to have been more deeply devoted to
his mother, who lived far too long for his good.[37] Thinking
perhaps of the conclusion of *Faust* and perhaps of Comte,
he sometimes rationalized his fixation into a doctrine of
salvation through womanhood and especially through
motherhood. He tells the Virgin Mary that if he could worship at any Christian shrine it would be at hers, since

Holiest and best of all things, holier far
Than Godhead, is eternal Motherhood![38]

In the essay **"On Mystic Realism"** appended to *The
Drama of Kings* (1871) he writes of himself that "The
personal key-note of all his work is to be found in *The
Book of Orm,* and most of all in 'The Man Accurst'."[39]
This concluding section of *Orm* (1870) presents a vision
of Judgment. Everybody has been saved except one utterly
vile, defiantly unrepentant man. As a last resort God asks
if any of the redeemed is willing to leave heaven and
share the wretch's exile. There are two volunteers—his
mother and his wife, both of whom he had treated basely.
The man weeps, whereat God admits him. *Orm* is an early
though thoroughly characteristic work, but in one of his
last poems Buchanan asserts:

I reverenced from the first
The Woman-Soul divine
(Mother, that faith was nurst
On that brave breast of thine!)
Pointing the heavenward way,
The angel-guide of man,
She seems to me today
As when my faith began![40]

Some readers may be reluctant to accept the conclusion
that these poets represent the complete submergence of
Christianity in romantic nature-worship and man-worship.
Does not Noel profess belief in "the revelation of our
Blessed Lord Jesus Christ"? Must we demand of so ardent
a lover of mankind any *particular* interpretation of those
words? And do not *The Man Accurst* and *The Ballad of
Judas Iscariot* suggest that Buchanan was mistaken in

thinking that he was not a Christian? Both poets cherished the *Christ-ideal,* and that is what really matters. It may be so. Instead of debating the point let us examine more closely what these men actually say concerning Jesus Christ.

"To me," says Buchanan, "the historical Christ, the Christ of popular teaching, is a Phantom, the Christ-God a very Spectre of the Brocken, cast by the miserable pigmy Man on the cloudland surrounding and environing him. I conceive only the ideal Christ, as an Elder Brother who lived and suffered and died as I have done and must do; and while I love him in so far as he is human and my fellow-creature, I shrink from him in so far as he claims to be Divine."[41] Jesus, then, is a nonhistorical ideal personification of loving and suffering humanity. But despite Buchanan's frequent use of the "martyrdom of man" idea, Orm shudders when he beholds a vision of God in heaven with the bleeding Lamb at His feet:

> All the while it cried for pain,
> It could not wash away the stain.

Orm is relieved to awaken from "that pale Dream of Pain." For Buchanan, furthermore, Christ is by no means a unique symbol of loving self-sacrifice. In **Balder the Beautiful** he explicitly compares the relations between Odin and Balder to those between God the Father and God the Son. Balder prays to Odin:

> As the blood of a sacrifice is shed,
> Let me die in my brethren's stead.

He would be "Thy Son who dies that men may live." Meeting Christ at the close of his wanderings, Balder hails Him as "elder Brother." Christ in turn greets Balder as one of "The golden Sons of God." There are, he explains, many other "Paracletes," such as Buddha, Prometheus, and Hiawatha;

> And whosoe'er loves mortals most
>   Shall conquer Death the best,
> Yea, whosoe'er grows beautiful
>   Shall grow divinely blest.

The unexpected lugging in of beauty might be a reminiscence of *Hyperion,* though the first two lines suggest Coleridge's "He prayeth best who loveth best." Essentially, however, Christ is at most one of various man-made symbols of George Eliot's "Choir Invisible." Walt Whitman apparently qualifies for membership in this company: in one poem he is told that there is "something Christ-like in thy mien," and in another he is described as a Christlike iconoclast who believes in Man.[42]

In a very late poem entitled **"A Catechism,"** Buchanan summarizes his beliefs. Asked if he is a repentant sinner, he answers:

> . . . If Sin be blent
> Into my nature as its element,
> Then 'tis my God's as surely as 'tis mine;

> But since I know my Father is Divine,
> I know that all which seemeth Sin in me
> Is but an image and a mystery.

To the question *"Who is God?"* his response is especially revealing:

> . . . He is I;
> Impersonal in all that seems to be,
> He first and last grows personal in me.

"Hath He no Being, then, apart from thee?" "None," responds the catechumen. *"Yet abideth through Eternity?"* "As *I* abide." *"Yet is He Lord of Death?"* "Yea, and if I should perish, perisheth." *"Is He not more than thou?"*

> . . . He is the Whole
> Of which I am the part, yet this my Soul
> Is He, and surely through this sight of mine
> He sees Himself, and knows Himself Divine.

Asked to list God's attributes, Buchanan insists that His only attribute is Love, which is manifested "In me, / And in mine other self, Humanity." Asked if he believes in Jesus Christ, the Son of God, he responds:

> In Him, and in my Brethren every one:
> The child of Mary who was crucified,
> The gods of Hellas fair and radiant-eyed,
> Brahm, Balder, Gautama, and Mahomet,
> All who have pledged their gains to pay my debt
> Of sorrows . . .
>
>   . . . . .
>
>   . . . the wise, the good,
> Inheritors of Nature's godlike mood;
> In these I do believe eternally,
> Knowing them deathless, like the God in me.

"How many sacraments hath God ordained?"

> None; since all sacraments in Man are blent,
> And I myself am daily sacrament.[43]

Particularly important for us is Buchanan's insistence that although the Divine Humanity is greater than any single man, the difference is more quantitative than qualitative. The divinity of Collective Humanity is the sum total of the divinity of individual men: the Great Being would not be God unless Buchanan, along with every one of his fellows, were godlike. "He is I . . . He first and last grows personal in me." One sees how easily a cult of humanity, divorced from belief in objective godhead, can be used to satisfy the romantic desire for self-deification.

Noel is of course more ambiguous. He has a more religious nature than Buchanan and takes fuller advantage of the circumstances which enabled a poet of his generation to identify with Christianity any sort of nonmaterialistic attitude toward nature and any sort of enthusiasm for the welfare of mankind. Buchanan, we know, regards him with some surprise as an authentic Christian who "embraces in full affluence of sympathy and love that ghostly godhead [Christ] and credits *him* with all the mercy, all the knowledge, all the love and power which we [Buchanan] believe to be the common birthright of Humanity,— the accumulation of spiritual ideals from century to century."[44] Several of Noel's poems, considered in isolation from the general drift of his thought, could be used to support this description of him. For example, these lines from *Suspiria*:

> 'Tis only a little we know; but ah! the Saviour knoweth;
> I will lay the head of a passionate child on His gentle breast,
> I poured out with the wave, He founded firm with the mountain;
> In the calm of His infinite eyes I have sought and found my rest.
> O to be still on the heart of the God we know in the Saviour,
> Feeling Him more than all the noblest gifts He gave!
> To be is more than to know; we near the Holy of Holies
> In coming home to Love; we shall know beyond the grave.[45]

What more could be demanded of any Christian poet?

But the further we read in his work the more it becomes apparent that for him "Christ" is merely a passionate, imaginative, personalized way of expressing that love which is the essence of the pantheistic World Soul. In *Pan*, Jesus is identified with the love-goddess

> . . . who is the heart of all,
> Uranian Aphrodite, whom
> The world laid in a Syrian tomb
> Under the name of Jesus.

For Venus and Pan and the other gods of Greece are not truly dead: it is only that Jesus more worthily embodies the holy truth which they symbolized before His coming. The principle involved is precisely that of *Hyperion*:

> For while the dawn expands, and lightens,
> Greater Gods arrive to reign,
> Jupiter dethrones the Titans,
> Osiris rules the world again,
> But in a more majestic guise;
> Sinai thunders not, nor lightens,
> Eagle, sun-confronting eyes
> Veils before mild mysteries!
> Balder, Gautama, full-fain
> Pay humble tribute while they wane;
> All the earlier Beauty prone is
> Before a lovelier than Adonis!

We are not to suppose, however, that Christ is the final goal of the evolution of love. The purpose of the World Soul will not be attained

> Till even the Person of our Lord
> In yonder daylight of the Spirit,
>
> . . . . .
>
> Will fade in the full summer-shine
> Of all grown Human, and Divine,

> And every mode of worship fall,
> Eternal God be all in all;
>   Pan lives, though dead![46]

Eternal God can only be the Divine Humanity, which has nothing to worship but itself, and Christ is a provisional man-made symbol of that ideal. Spiritual progress consists in learning to get along without Him. Meanwhile He derives solely from human love whatever temporary sacredness He may possess. Noel, who shared Buchanan's admiration for Whitman and devoted an essay to him, quotes these lines from the American romantic's *To Working Men*:

> We consider Bibles and religions divine—I do not say they are not divine;
> I say that they have all grown out of you, and may grow out of you still;
> It is not they who give the life; it is you who give the life.

"Does it not breathe the very spirit of Christ?" demands Noel.[47]

"Christianity" is a noise produced by the organs of speech, and there is nothing to prevent any man from using that noise in connection with any conceivable affirmation or denial. But our efforts to engage in rational discourse with one another are considerably hindered when we insist on using the same noise as a means of pointing toward referents which are not merely different but incompatible. Whatever semantic signs we adopt, the fact remains that the religion of Noel and Buchanan is approximately the same religion as that of Mr. Middleton Murry. It is a quite different religion from that of George Herbert, of Christopher Smart, of Gerard Hopkins, of T. S. Eliot. Perhaps more clearly than any other poet whom we have yet considered, Noel and Buchanan illustrate the chasm which separates what I choose to call Christianity from what I choose to call the romantic faith. Although my own preference is glaringly obvious, nothing in this series of studies necessitates the conclusion that either religion is "truer" than the other. I insist only that they are radically different, and that the difference is important for the history of ideas. Perhaps the contrast will become even more obvious if we now turn to a group of poets who say, with Leslie Stephen's rustic churchwarden, "You see, sir, I think there be a God."[48]

Notes

1. Although their careers run considerably beyond the terminus of this volume they are Victorian poets in the sense in which I am using that term. Both began to publish verse in 1863 and were steadily productive thereafter.

2. Noel wrote an essay on *Robert Buchanan's Poetry*; Buchanan edited, with a substantial "Prefatory Notice," a volume of selections from Noel's poems for the Canterbury Poets series.

3. But although Buchanan more frequently reminds us of his close friend Sydney Dobell, Noel's *A Modern Faust* (1888) is distinctly Spasmodic in theme if not in style.

4. *The Drama of Kings,* p. 470.

5. *Complete Poetical Works,* I, 287, 494ff.; II, 52, 380.

6. *Ibid.,* I, 257, 280-284; II, 52.

7. *Ibid.,* II, 411. The penultimate line suggests that he is glancing at Matthew Arnold.

8. Roden Noel, *Poems,* p. xix (Buchanan's "Prefatory Notice").

9. *Ibid.,* pp. 310-311.

10. *Ibid.,* pp. 41-42, 84, 89.

11. *The Drama of Kings,* pp. 257, 259. The comparison with Hardy is not aimless. See my article in *PMLA,* LXVII (1952), 43-64, which identifies the *Drama* as "The Immediate Source of *The Dynasts.*"

12. *Complete Poetical Works,* I, 269, 272-273, 290; II, 158, 273, 432.

13. *Poems,* pp. 99, 343.

14. *Essays on Poetry and Poets,* pp. 1-2, 4, 88.

15. *Ibid.,* pp. 4, 279, 343, 344. For Hinton see above, p. 187.

16. *Ibid.,* pp. 2, 3.

17. *Poems,* pp. 79, 119-120.

18. *Essays on Poetry and Poets,* p. 5.

19. *Complete Poetical Works,* I, 248ff., 259-260, 277.

20. He means unenlightened *materialistic* science. A moment later he cites Hinton as providing scientific support for the vitalistic-pantheistic faith. The romantic may either fight science head on or reinterpret it romantically and then stand forth as its champion.

21. *Essays on Poetry and Poets,* pp. 7, 8, 9.

22. *Poems,* pp. 65, 68.

23. *Complete Poetical Works,* I, 185.

24. See the special chapter on Buchanan as a humanitarian in this narrower sense contributed by Henry S. Salt to Harriett Jay, *Robert Buchanan,* pp. 144-152.

25. *Poems,* pp. 144, 345, 350.

26. The jumble of negation and affirmation, pessimism and optimism, in Buchanan's thought reminds us of Winwood Reade's *Martyrdom of Man.* It was not published until the year after the *Drama,* but Buchanan knew Charles Reade and may have had opportunities to converse with his nephew.

27. *The Drama of Kings,* pp. 75, 272.

28. *Poems,* pp. 31, 34, 138, 145-149 *passim.*

29. *Ibid.,* pp. 91-92.

30. Quoted by Harriett Jay, *Robert Buchanan,* p. 151.

31. *Essays on Poetry and Poets,* p. 8.

32. Noel, *Poems,* pp. xx, xxiv (Buchanan's "Prefatory Notice").

33. See above, p. 225.

34. *Complete Poetical Works,* I, 280; II, 382, 432.

35. *The Drama of Kings,* pp. 5-6.

36. *Poems,* pp. 8, 9, 18, 21, 159.

37. Harriett Jay, *Robert Buchanan,* p. 2.

38. *Complete Poetical Works,* II, 300.

39. *The Drama of Kings,* p. 467.

40. *Complete Poetical Works,* I, 290-294; II, 431.

41. Noel, *Poems,* p. xix (Buchanan's "Prefatory Notice").

42. *Complete Poetical Works,* I, 279, 425, 471, 476-477, 479; II, 395ff. While traveling in America Buchanan saw something of Whitman in Camden and Washington. For other poems to or about Whitman see I, 380; II, 398.

43. *Ibid.,* II, 302-305.

44. Noel, *Poems,* p. xix (Buchanan's "Prefatory Notice").

45. *Ibid.,* p. 103. See also pp. 121-122 for another apparently heartfelt expression of belief in the Christian Saviour.

46. *Ibid.,* pp. 70, 73-74.

47. *Essays on Poetry and Poets,* p. 325.

48. See above, p. 68.

William D. Jenkins (essay date 1972)

SOURCE: "Swinburne, Robert Buchanan, and W. S. Gilbert: The Pain that Was All but a Pleasure," in *Studies in Philology,* Vol. LXIX, No. 3, July, 1972, pp. 369-87.

[*In the following essay, Jenkins identifies Buchanan as the model for Archibald Grosvenor in Gilbert & Sullivan's* Patience.]

The middle-aged spinster as an object of ridicule in the Gilbert and Sullivan operas has been the subject of much inconclusive controversy. Many commentators have interpreted Gilbert's frequent use of the "old maid" joke as indicating a streak of cruelty in his character; the word "sadism" has been specifically applied.[1] However, at the very worst, Gilbert was only mocking a recognizable type of woman. Apparently no one has charged Gilbert with using a living individual as a model for Ruth, Lady Jane, or Katisha.

On the other hand, some of the male figures of fun bore a remarkably close resemblance to living contemporaries. There was W. H. Smith, for example, a politically-appointed First Lord of the Admiralty who stuck close to his desk and had never been to sea. Then, of course, there was Oscar Wilde, lampooned as Bunthorne, in *Patience;* or so it has been generally supposed.

Sweet were the uses of publicity for Wilde in 1881, and he was willing, indeed eager, to identify himself with Bunthorne. The future author of *The Importance of Being Earnest* had a Gilbertean sense of humor of his own and found nothing personally objectionable in the benign mimicry of his poses and posies. His poesy, as such, was spared, because almost nobody had read it. Wilde was twenty-five years old, just down from Oxford, and his private life had not yet become a public scandal. So much could not be said for another literary figure of the day. Persistent emphasis, over a period of eight decades, on the harmless mockery of Wilde has minimized recognition of the more subtle witticisms directed at a much greater and more vulnerable man—Algernon Charles Swinburne. Although several commentators on *Patience* have mentioned Swinburne's name in passing, it seems that only three, Frances Winwar,[2] Audrey Williamson,[3] and John B. Jones,[4] have emphasized Swinburne as the primary figure in the composite of Victorian aesthetes that constitutes the "Fleshly Poet," Reginald Bunthorne.

Since the subject of Miss Winwar's book is Oscar Wilde, it is understandable that she did not discuss the Swinburne-Bunthorne identity at length. Both Miss Williamson and Mr. Jones have developed the argument with convincing evidence. But both stop short before considering a hypothesis which adds another intriguing dimension to *Patience*: Bunthorne is primarily Swinburne; ergo, Bunthorne's hated rival, Grosvenor, is primarily Swinburne's bitter antagonist in the Fleshly Controversy, Robert Buchanan. Both Williamson and Jones suggest that the appellation, "Fleshly Poet," for Bunthorne derives from "The Fleshly School of Poetry," an essay by Buchanan which, as Williamson says, "was a direct attack on Rossetti and Swinburne, made on the grounds of the alleged immoral tendencies of their verse." There is much evidence, in the polemics of Swinburne and Buchanan, and in the final text of *Patience,* suggesting that the appellation, "Idyllic Poet," for Grosvenor derives from the same source. Furthermore, since the point at issue in the Fleshly Controversy was Swinburne's "immoral tendencies," I suggest, as an added hypothesis, that Gilbert inserted several subtly disguised private jokes on this subject (specifically sado-masochism) into *Patience*.

The most recent analytical study of *Patience* is Jane W. Stedman's detailed account of the earliest known extant draft, a fragment of Act I, deposited in the British Museum. Miss Stedman points out that "at this stage the rival poets of the final version are still the competitive clergymen whom Gilbert borrowed from his own Bab Ballad, 'The Rival Curates.'"[5] However, Miss Stedman also notes that the identity of the leading characters in *Patience* "seesawed between the Grosvenor Gallery and the Anglican church for some six months. Gilbert's original intention seems to have been to make aesthetes of Bunthorne and Grosvenor (long before these names had been settled upon)." Like other commentators, Miss Stedman cites part of a letter (November 1, 1880) from Gilbert to Sullivan: "I mistrust the clerical element. I feel hampered by the restrictions . . . and I want to revert to my old idea of a rivalry between two aesthetic fanatics . . . instead of a couple of clergymen."

Only one of the rival clergymen appears in the fragment discussed by Stedman. He bears a poet's name, "The Reverend Lawn Tennison," and he recites Grosvenor's two ridiculous verses, "Gentle Jane" and "Teasing Tom." Despite such sports as Donne, Swift, and Lewis Carroll, the writing of verse (even idyllic verse) is not a commonplace accomplishment among the clergy. Hence it may be reasonable to believe that this aspect of the Reverend Lawn Tennison is a holdover from Gilbert's "old idea of a rivalry between two aesthetic fanatics."

In view of the many identifications of Bunthorne and Grosvenor (Wilde, Swinburne, Whistler, Burne-Jones, Morris, etc.) made by various exegetes, the composite theory advanced by Leslie Baily,[6] Williamson, and Jones, seems the most reasonable. Indeed, to attempt to exclude any of Gilbert's artistic contemporaries from the composite picture is to move to unsafe ground. Jones, for example, suggests that the "Idyllic Poet," Grosvenor, is a composite of Coventry Patmore and William Morris; Tennyson, composer of *Idylls of the King,* is "summarily dismissed as the object of Gilbert's satire since none of Grosvenor's characteristics jibe with the popular impression of Tennyson." Whatever the "popular impression" may have been, Gilbert, apparently, was not greatly concerned with it when he wrote Lawn Tennison into his early draft. I suggest further, that Gilbert was no more concerned with consistency in creating his rival aesthetic fanatics. Thus Williamson finds a touch of Morris in Bunthorne, Jones finds a touch of Morris in Grosvenor; both are probably correct. Isaac Goldberg finds a touch of Swinburne in Grosvenor;[7] the slight evidence for this view does not negate the primary Bunthorne-Swinburne identification.

The essential point is that *Patience* was written at two levels. The average Victorian theater-goer, like the average reader of *Punch,* viewed the rival poets as comic figures who wore funny clothes and said ridiculously funny things. He could not know, and did not care, whether the originals were Swinburne or Wilde, Postlethwaite or Maudle. That the jokes about specific identity were not intended to be generally understood appears in the earnest work of the students who have addressed themselves to the problem. Neither Gilbert nor Sullivan ever dropped a single extra-theatrical hint on the subject. The astute Richard D'Oyly Carte was similarly close-mouthed, despite his exploitation of the willing Wilde for promotion purposes. Such discretion may well have been dictated by the element of "other-Victorian" bawdry in the principal private joke.

It has been noted that W. S. Gilbert was a gentleman of good taste and sensibility, who adapted his discourse to his company. Among his male peers, Gilbert's off-stage humor was heartily Rabelaisian.[8] On the other hand, his opera librettos were written to be appreciated by "the young lady in the dress circle."[9] Goldberg cites a declaration made by Gilbert many years after *Patience*:

I am so old-fashioned as to believe that the test whether a story is fit to be presented to an audience in which there are many young ladies, is whether the details of that story can be decently told at (say) a dinner party at which a number of ladies and gentlemen are present.[10]

This attitude is decidedly different from that expressed by Swinburne in an 1866 essay, "Notes on Poems and Reviews," which contributed to the Fleshly Controversy:

Who has not heard it asked, in a final and triumphant tone, whether this book or that can be read aloud by her mother to a young girl? whether such and such a picture can properly be exposed to the eyes of young persons? If you reply that this is nothing to the point, you fall at once into the ranks of the immoral.[11]

Perhaps Gilbert did protest his purity too much. However, his precept was not violated in *Patience*. The joke about Swinburne's sexual deviation is not only "too French," it is told in a language that "the young lady in the dress circle" did not understand; she was not sophisticated enough to be shocked. Perhaps Gilbert could not resist the opportunity of applying his unique topsy-turvy logic. Was it a case of letting "the punishment fit the crime"? Or was it rather, since it is not cruelty to be cruel to a masochist, "a most ingenious paradox"?

In any case, the theme of sado-masochism in *Patience* begins with the very first chorus of the twenty love-sick maidens who revel in their misery. The meaning is clear to the simple milkmaid, Patience, who observes that "love is a thorn . . . love is a nettle that makes you smart." Patience is thus led to believe that true love must be painful, and later she voluntarily subjects herself to the ordeal of loving Bunthorne, as she says: "With a heart-whole ecstasy that withers, and scorches, and burns, and stings!" And she sings: "Love is a plaintive song, / Sung by a suffering maid." Like the Marquis de Sade's innocent Justine, Patience suffers "The Misfortunes of Virtue." A more direct reference to Swinburnean masochism appears in Gilbert's sextette with the repeated chorus identifying pain with pleasure:

I hear the soft note of the echoing voice
    Of an old, old love, long dead—
It whispers my sorrowing heart "rejoice"—
    For the last sad tear is shed—
The pain that is all but a pleasure will change
    For the pleasure that's all but pain,
And never, oh never, this heart will range
    From that old, old love again!

Yes, the pain that is all but a pleasure will change
    For the pleasure that's all but pain, etc.

The linkage of pleasure and pain in Swinburne's poetry scarcely needs comment. It is especially notable in "Rococo," a poem about dead love, which may have been the model for Gilbert's parody. Here is Swinburne's third stanza:

Time found our tired love sleeping,
    And kissed away his breath;

But what should we do weeping,
    Though light love sleep to death?
We have drained his lips at leisure,
    Till there's not left to drain
A single sob of pleasure,
    A single pulse of pain.[12]

The concluding two lines of half the stanzas of this ten-stanza poem refer to pleasure and pain. Equally characteristic of Swinburne is the structure of Gilbert's lines: "The pain that is all but a pleasure . . . the pleasure that's all but pain." Such repetition, but inversion, of the key words has been called by Cecil Y. Lang, "the purest Swinburnese—'simple perfection of perfect simplicity.'"[13]

However, it is the poetry of Reginald Bunthorne which offers the most amusing parodies of Swinburne—in style, in content, and, in one instance, in circumstances of inspiration. Here is a passage from Act I, wherein Patience says that she does not like poetry and rejects Bunthorne's love:

PA. I only ask that you will leave me and never renew the subject.
BUN. Certainly. Broken-hearted and desolate, I go.
    (*Recites.*)
        "Oh, to be wafted away
            From this black Aceldama of sorrow,
        Where the dust of an earthy today
            Is the earth of a dusty tomorrow!"
It is a little thing of my own. I call it "Heart Foam." I shall not publish it.
Farewell! Patience, Patience, farewell!

Gilbert seems to have crammed several Swinburnean references into the four lines of "Heart Foam," including the repetition-inversion of "dust" and "earth." Additionally, there is a close resemblance to "The Garden of Proserpine," described by Swinburne in "Notes on Poems and Reviews" as expressing "that brief total pause of passion and thought, when the spirit, without fear or hope of good things or evil, hungers and thirsts only after perfect sleep."[14] Stanza ten reads:

We are not sure of sorrow,
    And joy was never sure;
Today will die tomorrow;
    Time stoops to no man's lure;

Bunthorne as the rejected poet and lover suggests "A Leave-taking," wherein Swinburne plays a similar role: "Let us go hence, my songs; she will not hear. . . . Let us go seaward as the great winds go, / Full of blown sand and foam." The seemingly meaningless title, "Heart Foam," is perhaps explained by Swinburne's fondness for the word "foam," notable even in a poet who loved sea imagery. Thus the bitterly hostile Buchanan commented: "I attempt to describe Mr. Swinburne; . . . men and women wrench, wriggle and foam in an endless alliteration."[15] Whether the point deserves criticism is immaterial; the fact is readily documented. The disappointed lover "foams" frequently in "The Triumph of Time"; in "We have seen thee, O Love"; in "Rococo"; and in "Dolores" no fewer than eight times, e. g., "By the lips inter-twisted and bitten / Till the foam has a savour of blood."

The first and third stanzas of Bunthorne's other poem, "Oh, Hollow! Hollow! Hollow!" suggest passages from "Dolores" and "Felise" respectively:

> What time the poet hath hymned
> The writhing maid, lithe-limbed,
>   Quivering on amaranthine asphodel, (Hollow)
>
> Thou wert fair in the fearless old fashion,
>   And thy limbs are as melodies yet,
> And move to the music of passion
>   With lithe and lascivious regret. (Dolores)
>
> Is it, and can it be,
> Nature hath this decree,
>   Nothing poetic in this world shall dwell?
> Or that in all her works
> Something poetic lurks,
>   Even in colocynth and calomel?
>   I cannot tell. (Hollow)
>
> For many loves are good to see;
>   Mutable loves, and loves perverse;
> But there is nothing, nor shall be,
>   So sweet, so wicked, but my verse
>   Can dream of worse. (Felise)

The "Hollow" title, and the flowers that "are only uncompounded pills" in Bunthorne's second stanza, may derive remotely from "The Garden of Proserpine": "Where summer song rings hollow / And flowers are put to scorn." Patience's confusion of the alliterative "Hollow! Hollow! Hollow!" with "a hunting song," perhaps hints at "a hymn from the hunt that has harried the kennel of kings," the concluding line of Swinburne's self-parody, "Nephelidia," published in *The Heptalogia*, 1880. In November of that year Gilbert completed the libretto of *Patience*. Although *The Heptalogia* was published anonymously, it seems probable that Gilbert knew the identity of the author and admired the wit of a fellow-parodist.[16] Bunthorne confesses: "There is more innocent fun within me than a casual spectator would imagine." Note the names of the humorous weekly, *Fun*, for which Gilbert had written his *Bab Ballads*, and the literary journal, the *Spectator*, which was strongly anti-Swinburne on moral grounds and which figured in the Fleshly Controversy.[17]

The Swinburne-Buchanan feud began with unfavorable reviews of Swinburne's poetry, suggestive references to the poet's private life, and even unflattering comment on Swinburne's personal appearance. Typically, these Buchananisms were unsigned. An early skirmish was Swinburne's mildly defensive "Notes on Poems and Reviews," in the *Fortnightly Review*, 1866. The poet conceded that his work was not necessarily written for young ladies, but demanded that it be judged on aesthetic grounds exclusively. (Bunthorne: "They find me too highly spiced, if you please! And no doubt I *am* highly spiced.") He paid tribute to Tennyson, but decried the Laureate's less talented imitators:

> Thus with English versifiers now, the idyllic form is
> alone in fashion. . . . We have idyls good and bad,

ugly and pretty, idyls of the farm and the mill; idyls of the dining room and the deanery; idyls of the gutter and gibbet.[18]

Buchanan, author of a volume of verse entitled *Idyls and Legends of Inverburn,* interpreted Swinburne's anti-idylism as a direct affront. The animosity smouldered until 1871, when it flared into white heat with publication in the *Contemporary Review* of a critical article, **"The Fleshly School of Poetry."** Using the pseudonym "Thomas Maitland," the mean-spirited Buchanan attacked Swinburne and D. G. Rossetti for the immoral sexuality of their poetry. Buchanan criticized Rossetti's rhyming technique; "accenting the last syllable in words which in ordinary speech are accented on the penultimate . . . 'Between the lips of Love-Li*lee*.'" (Bunthorne: "I shall have to be contented with a tulip or li*ly*!") Swinburne was chastised as "only a mad little boy letting off squibs. . . . 'I *will* be naughty!' screamed the little boy."[19] Finally, Buchanan noted Swinburne's "foaming" ("Heart Foam," above).

If Buchanan's condemnation helps identify Swinburne as Bunthorne, the "Fleshly Poet," Swinburne's response is equally suggestive of Buchanan as Grosvenor, the "Idyllic Poet." In a pamphlet, *Under the Microscope,* 1872, Swinburne recalled his "Notes on Poems and Reviews" of 1866:

> From a slight passing mention of 'idyls of the gutter and gibbet' in a passage referring to the idyllic schools of our day, Mr. Buchanan . . . is led even by so much notice as this to infer that his work must be to the writer an object of special attention.

In *Patience*, Grosvenor recites two examples of his "idyllic" verse, "Teasing Tom . . . a very bad boy," and "Gentle Jane . . . as good as gold." Swinburne uses both names, Tom and Jane, in referring to Buchanan. Because Buchanan concealed his identity under the pseudonym, "Thomas Maitland," Swinburne observes that it was "not the good boy, Robert, for instance, but the rude boy, Thomas," who was throwing stones and shooting off a popgun. Elsewhere Swinburne asks: "How should one address him? [Buchanan] 'Matutine pater, seu Jane libentius audis?' As Janus, rather, one would think, being so in all men's sight a natural son of the double-faced divinity."[20]

Grosvenor's "Teasing Tom" reflects not only Swinburne's idea of the hypocritical Buchanan, "the rude boy Thomas" with his stones and popgun, but even more pointedly Buchanan's idea of Swinburne, "a mad little boy letting off squibs."

> Teasing Tom was a very bad boy,
> A great big squirt was his favorite toy;
> He put live shrimps in his father's boots,
> And sewed up the sleeves of his Sunday suits;
> He punched his poor little sisters' heads,
> And cayenne-peppered their four-post beds,
> He plastered their hair with cobbler's wax,
> And dropped hot halfpennies down their backs.
>   The consequence was he was lost to*tally*,
>   And married a girl in the *corps de bally*!

How the ribald inner Gilbert must have chuckled when he wrote Grosvenor's introduction of this priapic young sadist! "I believe I am right in saying that there is not one word in that decalet which is calculated to bring the blush of shame to the cheek of modesty." To which Angela, echoed by "the young lady in the dress circle," affirms: "Not one; it is purity itself." Swinburne never married, "single he did live and die"; but in 1867 he did contract a notorious liaison with a "girl in the *corps de bally*." She was the beautiful actress and courtesan, Adah Isaacs Menken. The brief affair was arranged by Swinburne's friends and was eagerly accepted by the poet; in his case it was good publicity to let it be thought that he indulged in anything so normal as keeping a mistress. The window dressing was so successful that a photograph of Algy and Adah together was sold in London stationery shops.[21]

In contrast to "Teasing Tom," Grosvenor's "Gentle Jane" is pointedly uninterested in sadistic pastimes. Neither does she foster "a passion for alcohol," another of Swinburne's well-known failings.

> Gentle Jane was as good as gold,
> She always did as she was told;
> She never spoke when her mouth was full,
> Or caught bluebottles their legs to pull,
> Or spilt plum jam on her nice new frock,
> Or put white mice in the eight-day clock,
> Or vivisected her last new doll,
> Or fostered a passion for alcohol.
> And when she grew up she was given in marriage
> To a first-class earl who keeps his carriage!

The style of Grosvenor's dreadful doggerel is a more-than-fair approximation of some of the highly moral stuff Buchanan contrived to publish. As Swinburne commented: "In effect there were those who found the woes and devotions of Doll Tearsheet or Nell Nameless as set forth in the lyric verse of Mr. Buchanan calculated rather to turn the stomach than to melt the heart."[22] We recall Bunthorne's scorn of Grosvenor's "placidity emetical." However, except for his titles, Grosvenor's verse is not really a parody of Buchanan. Totally without style, Buchanan, at his worst, defies parody. Perhaps this passage from **"Attorney Sneak"** represents Buchanan at his worst:

> "Tommy," he dared to say, "you've done amiss;
> I never thought to see you come to this.
> I would have stopped you early on the journey
> If I had ever thought you'd grow attorney.
> Sucking the blood of people here in London;
> But you have done it and it can't be undone.
> And Tommy, I will do my best to see
> You don't at all disgrace yourself and me."[23]

One wonders on what grounds the rhymer of "London" with "undone" could cavil at Rossetti's "Love-Lil*ee*." Also compare Grosvenor's "to*tally*" and "bally." Here's another; **"The Widow Mysie: An Idyl of Love and Whisky"**:

> O Widow Mysie, smiling soft and sweet
> O Mysie buxom as a sheaf of wheat!

> O Mysie, widow Mysie, late Monroe
> Foul fall the traitor face that served me so!
> O Mysie Love, a second time a bride,
> I pity him who tosses at your side—
> Who took, by honied smiles and speech misled,
> A beauteous bush of brambles to his bed![24]

The last line recalls the complaint about Swinburne's "endless alliteration." It also recalls the song of Patience: "If love is a thorn, they show no wit / Who foolishly hug and foster it." One more example; Buchanan's **"Kitty Kemble,"** a girl from the *corps de bally*:

> You pertly spake a dozen lines or so,
> While just behind you, glaring in a row,
> Your sillier sisters of the ballet stood
> With spleen and envy raging in their blood!
> Thus, Kitty Kemble, on and up you went,
> Merry, yet ill content;
> And soon you cast, inflated still with pride,
> Your city man aside
> Cut him stone dead to his intense annoy,
> And like a maiden coy,
> Dropt, blushing crimson, in the arms scarce vital
> Of an old man of title![25]

Unlike Gentle Jane, Kitty did not marry her man of title; the consequence was she was lost to*tally*. A comparison of these moral idyls with those ascribed to Grosvenor reveals Gilbert's vastly superior technique, which Swinburne specifically noted. In a letter entitled "The Devil's Due," signed "Thomas Maitland" (*The Examiner,* 1875), Swinburne called Buchanan "the multi-faced idyllist of the gutter," and advised him:

> . . . to study in future the metre as well as the style and reasoning of the "Bab Ballads." Intellectually and morally he would seem to have little to learn from them; indeed a careless reader might easily imagine any one of the passages quoted to be a cancelled fragment from the rough copy of a discourse delivered by "Sir Macklin" or the "Reverend Micah Sowls," but he has certainly nothing of the simple and perfect modulation which gives a last light consummate touch to the grotesque excellence of verse which might wake the dead with "helpless laughter."[26]

It can hardly be doubted that Gilbert was amused and gratified at Swinburne's appreciation, and that the letter intensified his interest in the Fleshly Controversy. Both "Sir Macklin" and the "Reverend Micah Sowls," from two different *Bab Ballads,* are long-winded clergymen who deliver boring, moralizing sermons. A certain line in *Patience* concerning Grosvenor, "Your style is much too sanctified—your cut is too canonical," has been called by Williamson, "a rather obscure gibe as applied to a poet."[27] Jones agrees that this point "has long troubled critics."[28] I suggest that the obscurity is readily dissipated if the line is read as a paraphrase of the gibe at Buchanan. Swinburne's use of Buchanan's alias, "Thomas Maitland," also gives point to another of Bunthorne's lines: "I'll meet this fellow on his own ground and beat him on it." This threat immediately precedes the "canonical" gibe.

In his earlier essay, *Under the Microscope,* Swinburne had loosed a lengthy (and somewhat twisted) satirical shaft at the sanctified style and canonical cut of his adversaries:

> . . . in place of the man of God at whose admonition the sinner was wont to tremble . . . perhaps a comic singer, a rhymester of boyish burlesque; there is no saying who may not usurp the pulpit when once the priestly office and the priestly vestures have passed into other than consecrated hands. For instance, we hear, in October, say, a discourse on Byron and Tennyson . . . we stand abashed at the reflection that never till this man came to show us did we perceive the impurity of a poet who can make his heroine "so familiar with male objects of desire" as to allude to such a person as an odalisque "in good society"; we are ashamed to remember that never till now did duly appreciate . . . the depravity of the Princess Ida and her collegians.[29]

The quotation recalls a passage from Tennyson's *The Princess*: "Our statues!—not of those that men desire, / Sleek Odalisques, or oracles of mode." And if we have "the keen penetration of Paddington Pollaky," perhaps we may find a recollection of Swinburne's sarcasm among the elements that make up a Heavy Dragoon in *Patience.* These include "Tupper and Tennyson" (but not very much of him) and the "Grace of an Odalisque on a divan." It cannot be denied that this effeminate grace stands out in startling incongruity to the other attributes of a Heavy Dragoon. Did Gilbert throw it in merely for want of a better rhyme?

Lang has commented on certain financial arrangements between Swinburne and one of his publishers, John Camden Hotten: "Swinburne co-operated (collaborated might be a more precise word) with Hotten in the issue of certain books from which both publisher and poet seem to have derived both satisfaction and income—*Flagellation* and *Romance of the Rod* are the two named by Swinburne."[30] It so happened that Hotten was also W. S. Gilbert's first book publisher. In 1869 Hotten reprinted from *Fun* a collection of *Bab Ballads.* The last four pages of this edition carry advertisements for other Hotten books, the final item being: "*Romance of the Rod*—An anecdotal History of the Birch in Ancient and Modern Times. With some quaint illustrations. (In preparation.)" The advertisement does not mention the author of this obviously unpoetic work. Not included in the Hotten *Bab Ballads* is the prototype of Archibald Grosvenor's "Teasing Tom," a ballad called "The Story of Gentle Archibald." Archibald's behavior is even more reprehensible than Tom's:

> With irresistible attack
> He jumped upon her aged back,
> Pulled off the poor old lady's front,
> And thrashed her while she tried to grunt,
> . . . . .
> Was loved by an Ape, in the days gone by.
> . . . . .
> He bought white ties, and he bought dress suits,
> He crammed his feet into bright tight boots—
> And to start in life on a brand new plan,
> He christened himself Darwinian Man! etc.

> The change had really turned his brain;
> He boiled his little sister Jane;
> He painted blue his aged mother;
> Sat down upon his little brother; etc.

"Gentle Archibald" appeared in *Fun,* May 19, 1866, and it may not be unreasonable to speculate that Gilbert, realizing the possible association of ideas, withheld it from Hotten because of the publisher's known pornographic ventures.[31] Goldberg, commenting at length on "Gentle Archibald" as one of the "lost" *Bab Ballads,* has remarked that Gilbert never acknowledged the relationship with "Teasing Tom."[32] Nevertheless, the name "Archibald" was eventually bestowed on Grosvenor. It is certain that Gilbert originally intended to use the name "Algernon" for at least one of his poets. A stage direction from an early draft of the libretto reads at a certain point: "Algernon Bunthorne enters followed by ladies." Elsewhere in the same draft, Patience, speaking to Grosvenor, says, "Farewell, Algernon!"[33] The final choice for Bunthorne's Christian name is equally significant. It was apparently no secret that Swinburne used "Reginald" as a *nom de plume* in his lewd correspondence. Clyde Kenneth Hyder notes that as early as 1871 a novel introduced "Reginald Swynfen, obviously a defamatory caricature of the poet."[34] Nevertheless, Swinburne defiantly called himself "Reginald Harewood" in *Love's Cross-Currents,* published in 1877 as *A Year's Letters,* and later gave the name "Reginald Fane" to a flogged schoolboy in *The Whippingham Papers.*

Swinburne's paternal grandfather was a baronet; his mother, Lady Jane Swinburne, was the daughter of the Earl of Ashburnham. Bunthorne lives in a Castle, and Grosvenor also "comes of noble race." But the proper swell in *Patience* is Lieutenant The Duke of Dunstable, who explains significantly that he joined the Dragoons because he might be "perhaps even bullied, who knows? The thought was rapture." (In 1854 the youthful Swinburne, fresh from the flogging block and bullying of Eton, expressed the desire to join a cavalry regiment, a project firmly vetoed by his father.[35]) At this point in the libretto Gilbert had written a solo for the Duke which was eliminated before the opening performance. However, it survives in the British Museum in the manuscript which had been submitted to the Lord Chamberlain for approval. The Duke sings in part:

> . . . Scandal hides her head abashed,
> Brought face to face with Rank and Money!

> Society forgets her laws,
> And Prudery her affectation,
> While Mrs. Grundy pleads our cause
> And talks "wild oats" and toleration;
> Archbishops wink at what they think
> A downright crime in common shoddy,
> Although Archbishops shouldn't wink
> At anything—or anybody![36]

The reference to scandal is intriguing, but the song seems to have no thematic relevance to *Patience,* whether the context be curates or poets. We can understand its deletion, but why was it written in the first place? Is it possible that Gilbert had heard a garbled version of an anecdote related by Edmund Gosse? Lady Ritchie, Thackeray's daughter, met Swinburne at Lord Houghton's home in 1862. The company included her father, her sister, and the Archbishop of York, to whom the poet read his "The Leper" and "Les Noyades." According to Gosse, the Archbishop did not wink. On the contrary, his Grace was silently horrified, while Thackeray and his daughters were enchanted by poet and poetry alike.[37] Manifestly, Swinburne's rank and money did not protect him from scandal, although he did have a few influential apologists. Lady Ritchie, the highly respectable Edmund Gosse, and others remained Swinburne's life-long friends. So, of course, did the very model of a Victorian factotum general, Theodore Watts-Dunton, described by Lang as "the dingy old nursemaid who, irresistibly, excites the satirist in every man."[38] (Bunthorne, introducing his solicitor: "Heart-broken at my Patience's barbarity, / By the advice of my solicitor . . . I've put myself up to be raffled for!")

Although some of the evidence is tenuous, the sum suggests that it was W. S. Gilbert himself who, in 1881, walked to stage center, glanced furtively about, and whispered conspiratorially:

> This costume chaste
> Is but good taste
> Misplaced!
>
> Let me confess!
> A languid love for lilies does *not* blight me!

The musical ear of "the young lady in the dress circle" was insufficiently attuned. She did not catch the faint counterpoint of one of Swinburne's most frequently quoted lyrics:

> Men touch them, and change in a trice
> The lilies and languors of virtue
> For the raptures and roses of vice.

Notes

1. Leslie Baily, *The Gilbert & Sullivan Book* (London, 1966), p. 218, cites various comments.

2. Frances Winwar, *Oscar Wilde and the Yellow Nineties* (New York, 1940), p. 60.

3. Audrey Williamson, *Gilbert & Sullivan Opera* (London, 1953), pp. 79-87.

4. John B. Jones, "In Search of Archibald Grosvenor: A New Look at Gilbert's *Patience*," *Victorian Poetry*, III (1965), 45-53.

5. Jane W. Stedman, "The Genesis of *Patience*," *Modern Philology*, LXVI (1968-9), 48-58.

6. Baily, pp. 201-6.

7. Isaac Goldberg, *The Story of Gilbert and Sullivan* (New York, 1928), p. 261.

8. Baily, p. 422.

9. Goldberg, p. 495.

10. William Archer, quoted by Goldberg, p. 492.

11. *Swinburne Replies,* ed. Clyde Kenneth Hyder (Syracuse, 1966), pp. 29-30.

12. Swinburne, *Poems and Ballads,* First Series (London, 1866). All the poems herein suggested as models for Gilbert's parodies are from this collection.

13. *The Swinburne Letters,* ed. Cecil Y. Lang (New Haven, 1959), I, xvi.

14. *Swinburne Replies,* p. 24.

15. Robert Buchanan, *The Fleshly School of Poetry* (London, 1872), p. 80. Gilbert was not the first parodist to make fun of Swinburne's "foaming." (Mortimer Collins, "Salad": "Anchovies foam-born, like the Lady / Whose beauty has maddened this bard." Lewis Carroll, "Atalanta in Camden-Town": "When the foam of the bride-cake is white, and the fierce orange-blossoms are yellow.")

16. Swinburne and Gilbert had the same book publishers, John Camden Hotten, and his successor, Andrew Chatto, who published *The Heptalogia*. Gilbert could hardly fail to recognize "Nephelidia" as a parody of Swinburne's style. Did he also recognize the allusive content of the concluding line? (*Atalanta in Calydon:* "Amid the king's hounds and the hunting men," etc.)

17. John A. Cassidy, *Algernon C. Swinburne* (New York, 1964), pp. 128-44, gives a detailed account of the Fleshly Controversy.

18. *Swinburne Replies,* p. 31.

19. Buchanan, *The Fleshly School,* pp. 36-48.

20. *Swinburne Replies,* pp. 71, 76-7. The Latin is identified by Hyder as a quotation from Horace: "O father of the morning, or Janus, if you would prefer to be so addressed."

21. *The Swinburne Letters,* I, 295.

22. *Swinburne Replies,* p. 72.

23. Buchanan, *London Poems* (London, 1867), p. 168. "Attorney Sneak" was first published in 1866, two years after W. S. Gilbert became an impecunious young barrister.

24. Buchanan, *Idyls and Legends of Inverburn* (London, 1866), p. 157. The "beauteous bush of brambles" was altered to an unalliterative "Delilah" in some later editions.

25. Buchanan, *Poetical Works* (Boston, 1874), pp. 299-300.

26. *The Swinburne Letters,* III, 91-2. Swinburne's delight in Gilbert is evident in several letters. To D. G. Rossetti, 1870: "By the way what a splendid 'Bab' that was in the Graphic for Christmas Day about the shipwrecked men and their common friend—I thought it one of the best—and it took me about an hour to read out en famille owing to the incessant

explosions and collapses of reader and audience in tears and roars of laughter" (II, 106). To Andrew Chatto, 1886: Ordering two copies of "Gilbert's comic operas," published that year by Chatto & Windus; a third copy in 1888 (V, 154, 237). He also wrote three letters to Chatto requesting separate copies of the libretto for *Ruddigore* (V, 195, 201, 237). *Ruddigore*, produced in 1887, includes these lines:

> As a poet I'm tender and quaint—
> I've passion and fervor and grace—
>   From Ovid and Horace
>   To Swinburne and Morris
> They all of them take a back place.

Did Swinburne ever attend a G&S performance? Lang notes that during his Putney retirement, the poet "came to loathe the theater, partly as a result of encroaching deafness" (I, xxxi).

27. Williamson shares the view that this line is a hold-over from the "Rival Curates" version of *Patience*. I would argue that the gibe is even more obscure as applied to a curate; in fact it is no gibe at all. A curate is expected to be canonical, as a poet is expected to be poetical, not canonical.

28. In line with his theory that Grosvenor is primarily Coventry Patmore, Jones holds that the line refers to the "popular notion" of Patmore's prissy character: "For the purpose of public satire, the popular notion of the poet's personality is a fitter subject than his real character." I would argue that the "popular notion" is manifestly irrelevant since, in eighty years, Jones is the first man to appreciate the joke. If "public satire" of anybody was intended, this must surely be Gilbert's most spectacular failure.

29. *Swinburne Replies*, p. 39. Perhaps Gilbert remembered this passage in 1883, when he wrote (or rewrote) his own *Princess Ida*. Buchanan's response to *Under the Microscope* was "The Monkey and the Microscope," 1872, a scurrilous rhyme directed at Swinburne:

> A clever Monkey—he can squeak,
> Scream, bite, mumble, all but speak;
> Studies not merely monkey-sport
> But vices of a human sort;
>
> · · · · ·
>
> Is amorous and takes no pain
> To hide his Aphrodital vein;
> And altogether trimly drest
> In human breeches, coat and vest,
> Looks human, and upon the whole
> Lacks nothing, save perchance a Soul.

Cf. *Princess Ida*:
A Lady fair of lineage high,

30. *The Swinburne Letters*, I, xlviii.

31. Steven Marcus, *The Other Victorians* (New York, 1967), p. 68.

32. Goldberg, pp. 90-1, 253.

33. Reginald Allen, *The First-Night Gilbert & Sullivan* (New York, 1958), p. 166.

34. *Swinburne Replies*, p. 10. The novel was *Two Plunges for a Pearl*, by Mortimer Collins.

35. Cassidy, p. 33.

36. Kenneth Carrdus, "The Duke's Song in 'Patience,'" *The Gilbert & Sullivan Journal*, May 1967, pp. 97-8.

37. Edmund Gosse, *The Life of Algernon Charles Swinburne* (London, 1927), p. 90.

38. *The Swinburne Letters*, I, xliii.

John A. Cassidy (essay date 1973)

SOURCE: "The Victorian Novelist," in *Robert W. Buchanan*, Twayne Publishers, Inc., 1973, pp. 137-49

[*In the following essay, Cassidy surveys major themes in Buchanan's novels.*]

As a novelist, Buchanan displays the same extraordinary productivity we have seen in his poems and plays. In the twenty-four years, beginning in 1876 and ending in 1900, he published twenty-five full-length novels, or better than one a year. These figures tell once again the story of writing too rapidly and too much, and they result from the same combination of unfortunate circumstances that plagued Buchanan throughout his career. He was forced into novel-writing by his ever increasing need for money to support his family, as well as by his personal follies of betting on horse races and of permitting himself to be a "soft-touch" for impecunious friends and acquaintances.

Buchanan left no written complaint against the restrictions upon the novelist as he did against those upon the playwright; but, as always, he quarreled with adverse critics here also. While publishers could and often did refuse to publish novels which they deemed offensive to the public taste, they were generally much more lenient than the theater managers or the Lord Chamberlain's Licenser of Plays. Furthermore, since Buchanan wrote all but one of his novels himself, he did not have to compromise with collaborators as he often did in the dramas. He was, therefore, freer to choose his materials and to express his own opinions. The novels, consequently, break into viable categories; and it is in these categories that I propose to discuss them: the novels of purpose, those dealing with the supernatural, the religious novels, and the "new" novels—those written after the catastrophe of 1894 that reveal a new view of life and character.

I THE NOVELS OF PURPOSE

As might be expected, the Owenite Victorian is clearly discernible in many of Buchanan's novels. Where he could do so, Buchanan used them as sounding boards for many of the social causes and views that were close to his heart. These are the same strains that reverberate throughout his poetry and some of the plays: the evils of war, the belief in the fundamental goodness of mankind, the social injustice wreaked upon woman by unequal laws and the lust of unscrupulous men, the evils of alcohol. These subjects form the basic themes of seven of the novels which are so structured as to drive home Buchanan's convictions with considerable force.

In two novels—*The Shadow of the Sword* (1876) and *That Winter Night* (1886)—Buchanan labors to expose the utter folly and the futility and barbarity of war as a curse perpetrated upon mankind in the name of patriotism by the forces of tyranny and greed *The Shadow of the Sword* is substantially the same story which he adapted to the theater five years later in 1881. The plot was in reality nothing more than a real-life story which Buchanan had come upon during a vacation spent at Étrétat in Normandy, the tale of a young Frenchman, Rohan Gwenfern, who had so strongly hated war that he had gone to great lengths and had suffered great privations in order to avoid being conscripted into the armies of Napoleon I. The story was one with which Owenite Buchanan was bound to sympathize; moreover, since he wrote most of it during 1875, just a few years after the Franco-Prussian War, his personal reaction to the horrors of that conflict—set forth in detail in *The Drama of Kings*—strongly reinforced his Owenite antipathy to war. The result was the novel, which he serialized in the *Gentleman's Magazine* in twelve monthly installments. For the serial rights alone, Buchanan asked and presumably received one hundred and eighty guineas, not a bad price for a first novel.

The chief difference between the novel and the play is that, although the play ends with the defeat of Napoleon at Leipzig, the return of the Bourbons, and the public proclamation of Rohan's pardon just as he is about to be executed, the novel includes Napoleon's escape from Elba, which forces Rohan once more to go into hiding. Convinced that he will never have peace until he personally slays Napoleon, Rohan hides himself in the garret of a cottage in which the Emperor spends the night. But as Rohan stands with his dagger in hand, looking down at the sleeping Napoleon, he sees only the face of a weary, careworn old man who sleeps as trustfully as a child. Rohan realizes that his intended victim, bloody though he is, is also God's creature and he decides to leave him in God's hands for punishment. He escapes and returns to his hiding place. Napoleon goes to Waterloo. This scene is an effective re-sounding of the theme of "The Vision of the Man Accurst," that no man is completely evil or deserving of eternal damnation.

Of poorer quality is *That Winter Night, or, Love's Victory* (1886), the next antiwar novel, not published until a full ten years after *The Shadow of the Sword.* The basic theme is the same that Buchanan used later in his play *Lady Gladys*—antagonism between man and woman turning into true love. Here again the Franco-Prussian War furnishes the basis of the story, and the theme centers around the hatreds aroused in otherwise good people by the cruelties

and barbarities of war, also an idea which Buchanan had stressed in the earlier novel. In the plot—as lively as any devotee of light fiction could wish—a young French maiden of good family is befriended by a young German officer, one of the invaders of her country. Later, when he is wounded near her home, she takes him in and nurses him in repayment for his kindness to her and also because she finds herself half in love with him.

While nursing the German, she worries about her father, who is serving in the French army, and from whom she has not heard for several weeks. Her sympathy for the German turns to violent hatred when she discovers that he has the locket and chain she had given her father and when he confesses in a delirium that he had killed her father several weeks previously in battle. Her first impulse is to take up the helpless man's sword and slay him, but religion and her father's teachings prevent her. After an inner struggle, she can even bring herself to administer the necessary medicine to save his life. This tangled situation is resolved by the reappearance of her father with the news that, though he was thought wounded beyond hope, the German Red Cross had nursed him and saved his life. All, therefore, becomes clear and comprehensible. The German had not hated her father when he shot him: he was simply carrying out his orders as a soldier. And the anonymous Frenchman who had shot the German had done it for the same reason. All were victims of the barbarity of war.

The moral is pointed up in the last scene, two years later, with the marriage of the French girl to her German lover, who has now become a French citizen. At the wedding he announces his determination to fight no more wars for any reason whatsoever. Precisely how he intended to carry out this resolution in the event that his newly adopted country declared war and asked him to serve in its forces is not discussed. Obviously, he had not expressed these sentiments to the French officials to whom he had applied for citizenship, or they would hardly have granted it.

Akin to Buchanan's sermon preached against the inanity of the hatreds engendered by war is his impassioned plea against all personal human hatreds which forms the theme of *God and the Man* (1881). This is the novel, discussed in Chapter 2, which contained his dedicatory apology to Dante Gabriel Rossetti, and which he adapted to the stage as *Stormbeaten* in 1883. In a short preface Buchanan makes clear that this is the second novel in a proposed trilogy. *The Shadow of the Sword* was an attack upon the evils of war; this one was designed to emphasize the folly of hatred between individuals; the third, later entitled *The Martyrdom of Madeline,* was to have as its theme "the social conspiracy against Womankind."[1]

As we have noticed, Buchanan was emotionally overwrought by the long illness and the death of his wife in November, 1881. *God and the Man,* with its heartfelt apology to Rossetti, was the fruit of his anguish and soul-searching. Even more notable than the apology is the strong affirmation of belief in God and in a personal immortality with which Buchanan closes the story. Nowhere else in any of Buchanan's writings is there so positive a statement of faith. For the second time in his life the loss of a dear one had brought him face to face with the great questions of life and death. The death of his father had plunged him into despair; the parting from his wife led him at least into a temporary hope and belief in better things than his peering eyes had ever before been able to discern.

The novel exhibits the same faults that we noted in the play. Its overdone melodrama and its extravagances of emotional fervor weary the reader. The chief fault is its too-easy solution to a profound human problem. Transporting two enemies to a new environment will in itself hardly turn them into friends, though it is entirely reasonable that their becoming better acquainted might do much to improve their relationship. Conceivably, this closer acquaintance could have happened in England as well as in the Arctic regions.

Buchanan's third social thesis, woman as the victim of man's injustice, cruelty, and lust, was one that lay equally close to his heart. Not only was it an Owenite credo practiced and preached by both Buchanan's parents, but the movement for woman's rights was a ground swell that mounted ever higher throughout the Victorian period in both England and America. Buchanan, an avowed proponent of the cause, overlooked no opportunities to advance it, as we have seen in many of his poems and plays. His first novel in this direction was the third novel of his trilogy, *The Martyrdom of Madeline* (1882), in which he makes his heroine an actress; and he attacks through her, as he had in the play *Corinne,* the age-old assumption that actresses are immoral and cannot be admitted to the better circles of society.

But the main theme is concerned with more than the plight of the actress; it portrays a social system in which formidable forces unite, almost in a conspiracy, to the great disadvantage of womankind. Some of these forces are the predatory male who victimizes the naïve young girl, the unequal marriage laws slanted in favor of the husband, the gossip columnists who are always eager to believe and to insinuate the worst about an actress, and the stubborn Victorian mores that gave no quarter to the fallen woman, no matter how extenuating the circumstances of her fall.

The gist of the plot is that Madeline, the heroine, a young English girl in a French boarding school, falls into the hands of the villainous French esthete, Gavrolles, who, with the hackneyed device of a fake marriage, seduces her and makes her his accomplice in crime. From her predicament, she is rescued by a kind Englishman and returned to England, where her guardian welcomes and provides for her. Since her guardian is also a playwright, through his influence she secures leading roles in his plays and soon becomes one of the leading actresses on the London stage. Unfortunately, the details of her past life become known to unscrupulous journalists and appear as insinuations in the

gossip magazines. Nevertheless, she finds love and marriage with a wealthy English widower; and, leaving the stage, she settles down to a quiet married life.

Disaster strikes when the rascally Gavrolles reappears, convinces her by a bogus marriage certificate that she and he were legally married, and torments her so cruelly that she flees from home, husband, and nemesis to seek safety in anonymity. The same benevolent Englishman who had before rescued her from Gavrolles discovers the part he has played in her disappearance, follows him to France, and kills him in a duel. Returned to England, this good angel finds Madeline in a home for reformed women of the streets and restores her to her husband. Shortly afterward, she and her husband migrate to America, where, Buchanan observes—mistakenly, we must admit—"the viperous journal of the period has not yet begun to crawl."[2]

The weakness of this novel is that Madeline's "martyrdom" is not a martyrdom; her problems are the natural consequences of her own recurring folly. She runs away from the finishing school with Gavrolles not because she loves him but because of a pique she has developed against the headmistress. Again, when the rascal approaches her in England, she does not confide in her husband, whom she has fully informed of her past, but chooses to deal with the situation herself. Furthermore, completely aware of the rascality of Gavrolles as she is, she permits herself to be hoodwinked a second time by his claims of marriage and to be driven to the brink of suicide by his bogus certificate. In short, the novel is melodramatic in its plot, in its characters, and in the unrestrained quality of the writing.

The best portions of the novel are those scenes in which Buchanan satirizes the cult of estheticism; for, to point up his case, he makes his villain an esthete. These are done with a light touch and a delicious mockery that are in sharp contrast with the melodrama. In connection with the attack on estheticism is Buchanan's berating of the critics that I have discussed in Chapter 3 in relation to his two anonymous poems, *St. Abe and His Seven Wives* and *White Rose and Red.* This lampoonery, too, is cleverly done and adds considerable interest to the novel.

Buchanan's second novel about the wronged woman was *Annan Water* (1883). Published less than eighteen months after *The Martyrdom of Madeline,* this story is along parallel lines except for a few minor differences. Omitted are the attacks on the press, estheticism, and the critics. The locale is changed to Scotland; a wealthy Scottish lady turns out to be the mother of the unfortunate heroine; the French rascal this time is really married to the heroine, who has a child by him, thus complicating the situation considerably. But all turns out well in the end when the villain is slain, clearing the way for the Scottish hero to wed the heroine, who inherits a fortune from her mother.

Buchanan's third novel about the woman-victim theme was *The Heir of Linne* (1888). This narrative is also set in Scotland, but the plot varies considerably from that of

Annan Water. The victimizer this time is the crusty old Laird of Linne, who, years before, had seduced a Scottish peasant girl and had had a son by her. Refusing to marry her, he had sent her and the baby to Canada; but news arrived that the ship had foundered, and they had been lost. An eccentric ex-clergyman of the neighborhood, Willie Macgillvray, takes the Laird to task for his sins and brings him to repentance. Part of his atonement is to adopt an orphan girl of the village and rear her as his daughter. He makes her his chief heir, but adds a clause to his will that, if the lost illegitimate son should reappear, he is to have the bulk of the estate. Of course, the son appears incognito, wins the love of the orphan, outwits a rascally nephew of the old Laird who complicates the plot, and settles down with his bride to enjoy his title and his fortune as the new Lord of Linne.

The best features of this novel are the authentic touches of Scottish life and character Buchanan works into it. Willie Macgillvray is so delightfully eccentric and yet realistic in his homely philosophy and in his pithy language that he may well have been drawn from someone Buchanan knew intimately; but, even so, the portrait is a genuine work of art. The stubborn old Laird, too, is quite convincing and original. The warm friendship of the two old men enriches an otherwise ordinary novel. In relation to Buchanan's own history it is worth noting that Willie had been one of Robert Owen's missionaries until alcohol had cost him his position. Now a confirmed teetotaler, he lectures to all who will listen on his two favorite themes of the love and reverence a son owes his mother and of the evils of drink. The two themes are associated in Willie's mind because his own alcoholism had sorely distressed his mother.

The Woman and the Man (1893) sounded once more the same theme but with the emphasis on the injustice to a woman of the marriage laws and customs. Otherwise, there are no important changes in plot, characterization, or viewpoint; for the novel is only an adaptation of his play *The Man and the Woman* of 1889. We wonder why Buchanan transposed the two nouns in the title unless it was to avoid legal action by whoever had purchased the play. The novel affords evidence of hasty writing and of the use of extraneous material, possibly to fill the requisite number of pages. Since it was published toward the end of 1893, while Buchanan's bankruptcy took place in 1894, it is probable that the book represents a desperate attempt to stave off financial disaster.

Buchanan's last venture on the woman-victim concept was *Lady Kilpatrick* (1895). Although this tale is set in Ireland with Irish characters, it employs the same plot that he had used in *The Heir of Linne.* This time, however, Moya Macartney, the wronged peasant girl, is allowed to return with her son to take her rightful place as Lady Kilpatrick. This change is accomplished by having the supposedly spurious priest who performed the supposedly fake marriage—Buchanan's usual gimmick for explaining why his heroines permit themselves to be seduced—turn out to be a real priest and the marriage to be valid. But this novel is

written with such ease and charm and is so free of the inanities and absurdities that mar its four predecessors of the woman-victim theme that it lends substance to Harriett Jay's claim that Buchanan's bankruptcy was a disguised blessing which shook him out of his mad race for money and forced him to take a more realistic view of himself and the world.[3] Certain it is that there is little that is extraneous in *Lady Kilpatrick.* The plot unfolds swiftly and moves as surely to its climax and dénouement. The characters come to life with an immediacy lacking in *The Heir of Linne* except for Willie Macgillvary and the Laird. Best of all, the melodrama of the earlier novels is completely absent.

In both *The Heir* and *Lady Kilpatrick* Buchanan touches upon the evils of alcoholism. But in *Rachel Dene* (1895), he preaches a fervent sermon on the havoc that can be wrought in even a good man's life by drinking and gambling. Since the gambling in this case is horse-betting, we have to suspect that he was using some of his own personal experiences which resulted in bankruptcy. Buchanan's hero is a young man in a textile mill who wins the favor of the owner because he invents a machine which promises to increase profits. The owner's daughter, Rachel Dene, regards him with interest and affection. But he takes to liquor and gambling and worsens so rapidly that he is suspected and sent to prison for a murder of which he is innocent. All is solved when the real murderer confesses. The hero, who has learned his lesson, is freed. He marries Rachel and succeeds her father as owner of the mill. The weakest feature of this novel is the hero's too sudden change from virtue to drinking and gambling, a fault which originated in the impatience of Buchanan's own nature and which prevented his mastering the technique of portraying gradual developments in character. Otherwise, the novel is well written, and the characterizations are generally authentic.

The final novel of purpose, *A Child of Nature* (1881), launches a protest against the deleterious effects of English absentee landlordism upon the Scottish Hebrides. This novel Buchanan adapted to the theater in 1887 as *The Blue Bells of Scotland.* In the novel, the English lord is not the rascally seducer that he is in the play, nor does he die in India as punishment for his sins. He lives, marries the heroine, discharges his cruel overseer, and lives in peace and amity with his tenants. This conclusion in no way solved the basic economic difficulties of the impoverished Highlanders, but it did furnish a satisfactory close for the novel.

II NOVELS OF THE SUPERNATURAL

Buchanan's incessant probing into the mystery of God and of death resulted in two novels dealing with the supernatural. The earliest of these was given the fanciful title of *Love Me Forever,* and it was first published in the Christmas number of *The Illustrated London News* for 1882, appearing in book form in 1883. Essentially, this book contains the same material that Buchanan cast into poetry nine years later in *The Outcast,* the story of *The Flying Dutchman* and its blasphemous Dutch captain, Philip Vanderdecken, who, enraged by his inability to round Cape Horn, calls down God's vengeance by his vain oath to keep trying until Judgment Day. And of course it is also the story of Charles Maturin's *Melmoth the Wanderer*; for, by Christ's intercession, Vanderdecken is permitted to spend one year in every seven ashore seeking a maiden whose love will free him from the curse. Buchanan achieves a happy ending to this gloomy tale by having the hero turn out to be a descendant of Vanderdecken and by having the love of the heroine inspire him to reform his life of crime and brigandage. The real Vanderdecken never appears except in a nightmarish dream of the heroine.

The central idea of *The Moment After* (1890) might well have been suggested to Buchanan by Browning's poem, "An Epistle," for it, too, deals with a man who has been dead, or nearly dead, and then has revived. Buchanan's protagonist is a man convicted of murdering his adulterous wife and her lover. When he is hanged, the rope parts slowly, strand by strand, and his body falls to the ground. Revived by the prison authorities, he insists that he has been in the other world, that he there met and became reconciled with his murdered victims, and that all three journeyed to the gates of a heavenly city where they were greeted by Christ. Just as they were about to be judged, he awoke to find himself once again on earth. He begs for the execution to continue so that he may rejoin his comrades, for he is convinced that, until he does so, they must remain outside the gates of Heaven. However, the authorities commute his sentence to life imprisonment. Shortly afterward, when he is found dead with a blissful expression on his face, the prison chaplain is certain that he has found eternal happiness, the promised happiness of his dream; but the prison physician remains skeptical. Thus Buchanan, having once again posed the question of immortality, leaves the matter just where he leaves it in his poetry—squarely on dead center.

The whole matter of the occult claims of spiritualism is examined in *The Charlatan* (1895)—nothing more than a recasting in novel form of Buchanan's play of the same title of 1894. Since the novel was a collaboration with Henry Murray, and since it shows no significant changes from the play, it needs no discussion.

III Novels On Religious Matters

During 1884 Buchanan published two novels which represent an attack on the Anglican Communion because they focus upon the vagaries and the frailties of two Anglican clergymen who are highly discreditable to the Establishment. The first, *The New Abelard,* appeared in March, followed by *Foxglove Manor* in September. Ambrose Bradley, the titular figure of *The New Abelard,* is a vacillating weakling who has broadened his religion to the point that he scarcely knows what he believes. His attempts to reconcile science, art, and religion cause trouble with his

Bishop and lead to his resigning his living. Having fallen in love with a wealthy young parishioner, he marries her even though he has learned that his faithless first wife, whom he had long supposed dead, still lives. His bigamy is exposed, and he confesses all to his new partner. She, saddened, becomes a Roman Catholic and dies, leaving her fortune to an order of nuns. The heartbroken Bradley journeys to Oberammergau, where his faith is restored by the famous Passion Play shortly before his own death.

Foxglove Manor is even more dastardly, for the young clergyman is a liar, a lecher, and a coward named Charles Santley, a name that is possibly intended as a pun on the adjective "saintly." After seducing and nearly causing the death of his church organist, he directs his attentions to a married woman of the neighborhood, and has nearly accomplished his purpose when her husband learns of what is going on and so terrifies Santley that he leaves in frantic haste for parts unknown. Some time later, religious papers carry the news that he has entered the Church of Rome.

Of the two novels, *The New Abelard* shows the better writing, better depiction of scene and character, and more sympathetic handling of materials. *Foxglove Manor* is so marred by an improbable plot, poorly drawn characters, and so many instances of bad taste that it is a regrettable performance. Although Buchanan prefaced both stories with a disavowal that either was an attack upon the clergy, most of the reviewers were not beguiled. A few admired his courage for daring to express a negative view of the clergy, but most thought his time and talents should have been better employed.

The Rev. Annabel Lee (1898), a futuristic novel set in England of the twenty-first century, is designed to show the inadequacies of Comtean Positivism. Positivism has replaced all the old religions, and people calmly accept its dogma that all life ceases with death. But with the death of her brother in her girlhood, Annabel Lee realizes the emptiness of such doctrines. When she discovers some Christian documents of 1890, she is so inspired that she goes about England preaching the Christian gospel. A great earthquake aids her in combating Positivistic intolerance and bigotry. The novel concludes with her denunciation of Positivism and with her prophecy that Christianity will overcome all opposition. Because Buchanan was more interested in his philosophical premises than in telling a story, the novel suffers. The plot is patently designed to suit his purposes, and his characterization is equally contrived.

IV The "New" Novels

The new Buchanan who emerged from the financial chastening of 1894 is clearly evident in three of his very best novels—*Diana's Hunting* (1895), *Effie Hetherington* (1896), and *Father Anthony* (1898). Like *Lady Kilpatrick,* they are almost entirely free from melodramatic fustian; they reflect a deeper understanding of life and character, especially that of women; they show a restrained, refined style of writing that is in sharp and welcome contrast to Buchanan's earlier ranting; best of all, the dialogue is suited to the character and subtly reveals nuances of meaning that greatly enrich and deepen the story. All three books probe depths of life and complexities of character almost totally absent from the earlier novels. Even more remarkable is it that none of them is concerned with advancing an Owenite tenet.

Diana's Hunting deals with the predatory activities of the young actress, Diana Meredith, who stalks the playwright, Frank Horsham, with all the determination of the ancient Greek deity for whom she is named. Not at all deterred by his being married and the father of a little girl, she leaves no wile untried in her efforts to entice him away from his family; and she is only thwarted in the end by a friendly drama critic who finally brings Horsham to realize that his true happiness lies in remaining in England with his wife and child instead of following Diana to America. Diana is one aspect of the new woman, a sister to Becky Sharp, Hedda Gabbler, and Nana. In creating her, Buchanan uses throughout the novel the objective method of Ibsen. Through her deeds and her words he reveals her motivation with a crystal clarity. The other characters are very well done, but Diana is an artistic gem.

The same fundamental theme and a corresponding artistry are employed in *Effie Hetherington*—another story of the havoc wrought by a selfish, vain coquette upon the lives of others. Minor variations from *Diana's Hunting* are effected by using the love-triangle motif, with Effie pursuing the husband of another woman and turning a deaf ear to the wooing of the hero, an admirable young man who would make her an excellent husband. Psychological complexity is added by the fact that Effie's pursuit of the husband springs not from her love of the man but from a malicious desire to embarrass and wound his wife.

No better illustration could be given of what Buchanan's new artistic vision meant to his work than the third of the new works, *Father Anthony.* For this novel is only a reworking of his and G. R. Sims's collaborative play of 1890, *The English Rose,* a rather low-grade Adelphi melodrama. But with what difference, with what more profound perception, with what greater artistry is the novel written! The focus of the story is on Father Anthony Creenan, a shy, diffident young Irish priest who, on the surface, appears to be cast in the same mold as Ambrose Bradley of *The New Abelard.* Underneath, however, he is made of true steel; and he remains faithful to his priestly vows even at the cost of his own life. Equally fascinating is Father Anthony's clerical superior, Father John Croly. Genial and bibulous, he wins the affectionate friendship of his flock by his camaraderie and his good-natured raillery, while the solemnity and earnest reverence with which he conducts the rites of the church earn their respect and obedience. He casts an emollient glow over the novel, relieving, yet blending with, yet in contrast to, the tragic pathos

of Father Anthony. The tender affection of the two priests for each other and their loving concern for their flock cause us to wonder if this novel could be the work of the same hand that wrote *Foxglove Manor.* The same hand, perhaps, but certainly not the same person. Buchanan had indeed changed.

Unfortunately, the change was not perceived by most of the reviewers. Buchanan's frequent potboilers, both on the stage and in his novels, had so damaged his reputation that these three excellent works received indifferent notice from the critics. The *Spector* and the *Outlook* praised the artistry and the power of *Effie Hetherington*;[4] the *Academy* thought *Diana's Hunting* "neither edifying nor amusing";[5] and the *Westminster Review* slighted *Father Anthony* as a fairly good Irish novel with an artificial plot.[6] If Buchanan could have had ten more years of high-quality work, he might have redeemed the reputation he had lost. But his life was near its end, and the opportunity was denied him.

For the sake of completeness I list here six novels that I do not intend to discuss because they are only potboilers. Their publication dates cover a span from 1885 to 1900, for even in his "new" period he did write two of them. Most of the six are hastily and poorly written; those that show better writing have such hackneyed plots and characters that they must be categorized as potboilers. Since they cannot be included in any of the classifications I have used in this chapter, I am placing them here. Their titles and publication dates are as follows: *Stormy Waters* (1885), *The Master of the Mine* (1885), *Matt: A Story of a Caravan* (1885), *Come Live with Me and Be My Love* (1891), *Marriage by Capture* (1896), and *Andromeda* (1900).

One of the very last works to come from Buchanan's hand, *Andromeda,* is of biographical interest because it depicts the agony a playwright undergoes on the first night of his play until the audience reaction finally reaches a pitch of enthusiasm that tells him he has achieved success. Of significance also is a prefatory notice to the novel warning that Buchanan reserved to himself all future dramatic rights. Clearly, his intention was to have another fling at the theater, but death prevented its fulfillment.

Notes

1. Buchanan, *God and the Man* (London, 1883), p. iii.

2. Buchanan, *The Matyrdom of Madeline* (London, 1884), p. 200.

3. Jay, pp. 248-49.

4. *Outlook,* I (June 18, 1898), 630. *Spectator,* LXXVI (June 27, 1896), 927-28.

5. *Academy,* XLVIII (December 28, 1895), 564.

6. *Westminster Review,* CL (December, 1898), 713.

FURTHER READING

Criticism

Blodgett, Harold. "Whitman and Buchanan." *American Literature* 2 (1930-31): 131-40.

> Traces Buchanan's enthusiastic critical endorsement of Walt Whitman.

Purcell, E. Review of *The Martyrdom of Madeline,* by Robert Buchanan. *The Academy* 21, No. 528 (17 June 1882): 428-29.

> Notes numerous weaknesses in the novel, chiefly discussing implausible characters and plot details.

Review of *London Poems,* by Robert Buchanan. *The Spectator,* 39, No. 1,987 (28 July 1866): 832-34.

> Favorable assessment locating Buchanan's particular strength in "the union of lyrical with dramatic conceptions."

Review of *North Coast and Other Poems,* by Robert Buchanan. *The Spectator,* 40, No. 2,052 (26 October 1867): 1201-04.

> Appreciative review, concluding that "this book will greatly raise Mr. Buchanan's reputation as an original poet of high imaginative power and a singularly pure art."

Review of *Stormy Waters,* by Robert Buchanan. *The Spectator,* 58, No. 2,970 (30 May 1885): 733-34.

> Unfavorable assessment of the novel. According to the reviewer, "It is bad enough when a man of Mr. Buchanan's capabilities and attainments condescends, under any pressure less severe than that of actual necessity, to give himself up to the production of potboilers; but it is much worse when he shows himself so cynically indifferent to his reputation as not to care whether he reaches even the low average of potboiling work."

Review of *The City of Dream,* by Robert Buchanan. *The Spectator,* 61, No. 3,127 (2 June 1888): 752-54.

> Praises "much fine poetry" in *The City of Dream,* but finds it lacking as a history of the development of spiritual doubt and particularly faults its depiction of the Roman Catholic and Protestant churches.

Wright Morris
1910–1998

(Full name Wright Marion Morris) American novelist, photographer, short story writer, essayist, memoirist.

INTRODUCTION

For more than half a century, beginning in the late 1930s with his "photo-texts," which incorporated written character sketches and photographs, Morris was a limner of American consciousness, a chronicler of American experience, and a biographer of American character. Mixing allegory and symbol, realism and absurdity, cliches and gallows humor, characterization and caricature, his novels probe persons and places, consciousness and perception, memory and imagination, desire and resignation over plot development and action. He frequently wrote about the Midwest, particularly Nebraska, his home state, and about the pioneer stock who wrought out of the land a culture, and out of their relation to the land an identity. In a score of novels and more than two dozen short stories, in photographs, essays, and in memoirs, Morris explored the effects of the values these Midwesterners created, the conflicts they endured, the accommodations they accepted, the follies they committed, the losses they suffered, and how they came to terms with the past and coped with a present he usually characterized as lonely and empty.

BIOGRAPHICAL INFORMATION

Within a week of Morris's birth in Central City, Nebraska, his mother died and he was left in the care of a neglectful and vagabond father, who became a prototype for many of the men in his books. Morris lived with his father in Omaha and Chicago, and, in his teen years worked on an uncle's farm in Texas. In the early 1930s he enrolled in Pomona College in California, but left in 1933 before graduating and went to Europe, seeking adventure, with dreams of becoming a writer. Bicycling through fascist Italy he was briefly incarcerated for being a spy because of the camera he had picked up in Vienna. In Paris, his money was stolen. In 1934, he returned to the United States, married his first wife, and began writing and taking pictures in earnest. He held his first photo exhibit at the New School in Manhattan in 1941, and was awarded the first of his three Guggenheim fellowships in 1942. (Two, in 1942 and 1946, were in photography; one, in 1954, was in literature.) He was a prolific writer, and published steadily from 1942, the date of publication of his first novel, *My Uncle Dudley,* until a few years before his death

in 1998. He was a lecturer in literature and writing at Haverford, Princeton, Sarah Lawrence, Swarthmore and several other colleges, and taught at California State College in San Francisco from 1962 to 1975.

MAJOR WORKS

Morris has the reputation not only for being a prolific writer, but for having written so many first-rate books. His first novel, *My Uncle Dudley,* is a picaresque story of a car trip through the Western United States. *The Home Place* (1948) sets photographs and text on facing pages in order to form a work whose completion comes from the interactivity of the parts in the reader's perception. He developed the novel *Man and Boy* (1951) from his short story "The Ram in the Thicket" (1948), and then rewrote the novel, reconsidering the character of "Mother," in *The Deep Sleep* (1953). *The Huge Season* (1954) employs subjective and objective narration contrasting 1920's hero worship with the realities of McCarthyism in the 1950s; he dealt with the violation of sexual conventions in *Love Among the*

Cannibals (1957); and with sexual vitalism in *In Orbit* (1967). Although it garnered mixed reviews when it was published, *The Field of Vision* (1956), a complex study of character, meaning, truth, and justification set in Mexico at a bullfight, won the National Book award in 1957, and has come to be regarded as one of Morris's major works. His last novel *Plains Song* was the American book award winner in 1981. Because defeated men dominated by frigid women had been one of Morris's characteristic themes, *Plains Song* is regarded as another major achievement both for its presentation of three generations of women struggling with the frontier experience, and with their own definition as women. The novel also demonstrates the ongoing development of Morris's vision and of his craft in complexity, variety, and range. Although Morris opposed the hyper-consciousness of the twentieth century, which he believed abstracted people from an immediate and essential "non-conscious" relation with nature and each other, his essays on art, society, writers and writing reveal he was a most conscious and conscientious craftsman.

CRITICAL RECEPTION

Morris has been the recipient of numerous honors and awards for his books and photographs, including a retrospective of his photography at the San Francisco Museum of Modern Art, a Life Achievement Award from the National Endowment for the Arts, the Mark Twain Award, the Distinguished Achievement Award from the Western Literature Association, a Senior Fellowship from the National Endowment for the Humanities, and a National Institute Grant in Literature. His stories have been printed in magazines including *Harper's Bazaar, Esquire* and *The New Yorker,* and his books have always found major publishers, and have been kept in print after first publication by presses such as the University of Nebraska and Black Sparrow. Nevertheless, his books, with the exception of *The Field of Vision* and *Love Among the Cannibals,* have enjoyed little popular success. Reviews of his books at the time of publication often were mixed, but in a large body of criticism, which has grown up around his work, Morris's work is seen as a unified and interdependent whole. Morris is studied as one of the major American writers and photographers of the twentieth century.

PRINCIPAL WORKS

My Uncle Dudley (novel) 1942
The Man Who Was There (novel) 1945
The Inhabitants (photo text) 1946
The Home Place (photo text) 1948
The World in the Attic (novel) 1949
Man and Boy (novel) 1951
The Works of Love (novel) 1952
The Deep Sleep (novel) 1953
The Huge Season (novel) 1954

The Field of Vision (novel) 1956
Love Among the Cannibals (novel) 1957
The Territory Ahead (essays) 1958
Ceremony in Lone Tree (novel) 1960
What A Way To Go (novel) 1962
Cause for Wonder (novel) 1963
One Day (novel) 1965
In Orbit (novel) 1967
A Bill of Rites, A Bill of Wrongs, A Bill of Goods (essays) 1968
God's Country and My People (photo text) 1968
Green Grass, Blue Sky, White House (short stories) 1970
Fire Sermon (novel) 1971
Love Affair: A Venetian Journal (photo text) 1972
War Games (novel) 1972
Here Is Einbaum (short stories) 1973
A Life (novel) 1973
About Fiction: Reverent Reflections on the Nature of Fiction with Irreverent Observations on Writers, Readers, and Other Abuses (essays) 1974
The Cat's Meow (short stories) 1975
Real Losses, Imaginary Gains (short stories) 1976
Wright Morris: Structure and Artifact: Photographs 1933-1954 (photography) 1976
The Fork River Space Project (novel) 1977
Earthly Delights, Unearthly Adornments: American Writers As Image Makers (essays) 1978
Plains Song: For Female Voices (novel) 1981
Will's Boy: A Memoir (memoir) 1981
Picture America [with James Alinder] (photo text) 1982
Photographs and Words (photo text) 1982
Solo: An American Dreamer in Europe: 1933-1934 (memoir) 1983
Collected Stories 1948-1986 (short stories) 1986
Time Pieces: Photographs, Writing, and Memory (photo text) 1989
A Cloak of Light: Writing My Life (memoir) 1993

CRITICISM

Edwin Seaver (review date 1942)

SOURCE: A review of *My Uncle Dudley,* in *Direction,* Vol. 5, No. 2, April-May, 1942, p. 19.

[*In the following review, Seaver finds Morris's first novel* My Uncle Dudley *lacking in depth.*]

American is the word which emerges immediately from this story [*My Uncle Dudley*] of a young man's trip across the country with a remarkably shrewd and yet casual Uncle, who is able to inveigle a number of other men to come along as paying guests, to cover the expenses of the trip. The tale is certainly realistic, but it has not the variety nor originality of other work by Mr. Morris. The characters he has chosen are convincing but have little to make them linger in the mind. Tire trouble and the continual breaking down of the car they ride in make an artificial drama, rather than a human one. We know that Mr. Morris has a much deeper feeling for American types of men and women than he has put in this book.

Harvey Breit (essay date 1951)

SOURCE: "Talk with Wright Morris," in *The New York Times,* June 10, 1951, p. 19.

[*In the following essay, Breit reports on a conversation in which Morris distinguishes between the processes of revealing and exposing.*]

Wright Morris, author of the recently published novel, **Man and Boy,** is a fully matured, civilized, hard-thinking, friendly 41-year-old fellow. He is the possessor of a compact, stocky frame, as well as of a hazardously upright and virile thicket of hair that must be, beyond any shadow of a doubt, the cynosure of all wearers of toupees. This crowning glory may have something to do with the fact that Mr. Morris comes out of Nebraska (sometimes known as the Tree Planter State) and attended Pomona College (in mythology, Pomona is the goddess of fruit trees). The symbol of growth, at any rate, seems to have chosen Mr. Morris for a friend—and it may very well be that Mr. Morris, through good works, will help dispel the notion that American writers invariably fail to exhibit the lineaments of growth. (*Give praise.*)

Man and Boy is 'Mr. Morris' sixth book. Two of the earlier works combined photographs and text. What was Mr. Morris? Why should he be allowed to be two things? What was his pigeonhole? "I'm a writer first, then a photographer," Mr. Morris said. "I'm primarily a writer, but already I'm lying because I'm also a photographer. In those books I tried to arrive at a balance between the picture and the writing; each had to stand alone, autonomous, yet related. I tried to free each medium of the environment of foreign matter."

Was Mr. Morris contemplating another such book? "I'm detached from it somewhat now." Mr. Morris said. "My next book will be a straight novel too. But I suppose I do look at things a little more photographically than if I hadn't used a camera." Mr. Morris leaned back in his chair as a painter leans back from his canvas. He matted his hair down with the palm of his hand and when he took his hand away the hair rose up higher than ever.

"Photography," Mr. Morris said after he had settled down a bit, "presents the realistic dilemma in absolute purity. Exposure becomes confused with expression. The real creative problem is to reveal. Say it is the problem of revelation versus exposure. It is practically a problem of the American temperament. Americans feel that if a thing exists it is important, if it happened to *me* it is important, and all I have to do is to record it. But this recording, or exposure, is not really relevant to the problems (alas, we have to say it) of art."

Most photography was merely "exposure," according to Mr. Morris. Which, if any, wasn't? "Walker Evans," Mr. Morris said, "is a fine example of a man who uses realism for revelatory purposes. Documentary has always been the wrong word for Evans. In Stephen Crane," Mr. Morris said, passing over from the camera to the scrivener, "the devices of realism are used for revelatory purposes. The *charge* of the writing is always more important than the literal content. Stephen Crane and Frank Norris are both regarded as realists, but Crane was revelatory and Norris was not. To my mind, the difference is summarized in them. From Norris we get a documentary; from Crane we get an esthetic experience."

For Mr. Morris, then, realism was some sort of a mistaken notion? "Anything," Mr. Morris said, "anything that takes us back to realism as the real thing is a retrogression. As I said before, it's almost a national problem of temperament. In the name of so-called realism writers like James Jones are victimized by the notion that absolute photographic realism is an art form. What they're employing is exposure. The very techniques of exposure require use of shock which invariably cancels out the depth and wider meaning of the subject or the experience. The author suffers the most from this; he is cut off from the depth and fullness and significance of his own material."

Would a man at the turn of the century feel the limitations of realism so strongly then as now? "I think our satisfaction with realism has always been relative and partial. The good realists are writers in spite of themselves."

Mr. Morris' favorites were Tolstoy's "The Death of Ivan Ilyitch," Melville's "Benito Cereno," Camus' "The Stranger"—all short novels. Mr. Morris nodded. "My feeling is," he said, "that we are going to need more short books. The long book involves us in the very thing we have to get away from."

Lists and catalogues? That was true, it turned out. "The short book imposes on the author a facing up to the major problems of his craft. No lists, itemizations, accumulations. In the short novel the limitations of realism become evident."

Mr. Morris' **Man and Boy**: 212 pages (twenty lines to a page as against the average 30 lines), a short novel it most certainly was.

Delmore Schwartz (review date 1951)

SOURCE: A review of *Man & Boy,* in *Partisan Review,* Vol. XVIII, No. 5, September-October, 1951, pp. 575-76.

[*In the following review, Schwartz focuses on Morris's treatment of the domineering and indomitable mother figure in* Man & Boy.]

The attack on the American Mother attains a new intensity and dimension in Wright Morris' **Man & Boy.** Mrs. Ormsby, the mother of the novel, rules with an iron hand not only in the region of emotions and *mores,* but she commands and transforms language as well. Mr. Morris has dramatized the extent to which much of her power comes from a mastery of language, an aspect of the American mother which has been neglected in most descriptions of her. Mrs. Ormsby uses language to make her own values devastating tabus. She is the absolute monarch, through her fund of formulation, of decorum, rectitude, prohibition, inhibition, and permission. She has at ready hand and for all occasions any number of Latin tags, Biblical maxims, and glittering generalities, distorting them invariably to suit the purposes of her own overwhelming and annihilating femininity. Once we remember how often the mother has first been a schoolmar'm, we recognize the cleverness and the justice with which Mr. Morris has exhibited the perfidious alliance of maternal tyranny and verbal glibness.

Man & Boy deals with a single important day in the life of Mr. and Mrs. Ormsby, the day on which the mother is going to launch a ship named by the Navy in honor of their dead son. In restricting himself to one day, and in his use of a modified interior monologue, Morris makes a fine and original use of some of the leading techniques in *Ulysses.* Indeed the father resembles Leopold Bloom as well as Caspar Milquetoast, and the climax of the book is his meeting with a young soldier who adopts a filial role toward him and who protests with much eloquence against the supremacy of mother over father. The young soldier, Private Lipido, declares that there would be "less heroes if the boys had known the old man would get a deal like that!"; and he adds that "I don't know this kid of yours, but if I had a nice old man like you this *Dear Mrs. Ormsby* would damn near make me sick." Subsequently Private Lipido succeeds in striking Mrs. Ormsby from behind with a suitcase as she goes up an escalator, an action which suggests the extent to which existence and literature have begun to imitate the comic strip and slapstick comedy. But this vain action as well as the directness of the young soldier's verbal attack serve chiefly to reveal how the Mother survives all kinds of attacks, unscathed and secure. She is a fact of society as irreducible and unconquerable as a fact of nature. She is superb, superior, indifferent, and in the end untouchable and opaque. Although she is literate, she would not understand a word of Mr. Morris' wit and observation.

Albert J. Guerard (review date 1952)

SOURCE: A review of *The Works of Love,* in *Perspectives USA,* No. 1, Fall, 1952, pp. 169-70.

[*In the following excerpt, Guerard praises* The Works of Love *as a "vision of American loneliness."*]

The America of Wright Morris might seem, at a glance, as remote from a European consciousness: the Midwest and West of the early twentieth century, the baked plains and lost towns and snowy wastes of Nebraska. How explain to this European consciousness the romance of a freight train seen thirty kilometers away? Or the glamour attached to even the smallest restaurant and hotel? Or the very fact that a distant cloud of dust may mean a small town, other human beings? *The Works of Love* is (like Lewis' *Babbitt,* Fitzgerald's *The Great Gatsby* and West's *Miss Lonelyhearts*) a vision of American loneliness. Yet the loneliness is as depersonalized as that of Ivan Ilyích. Will Brady is the Anonymous Man. He is capable of giving love but not of receiving it; he drifts through life but is never *in* it. Hence the appropriateness of his two marriages with prostitutes, from whom companionship can be purchased. Such a man, coming from such a place, would almost certainly not have married these prostitutes so casually . . . as any "realist" would know. Yet the marriages are symbolically true; almost, one might argue, inevitable. "All men lead lives of quiet desperation," but quietness may be even more common and more sinister than despair. An obvious point perhaps, yet this is a genuinely original book. Wright Morris does not always achieve the degree of stylization and distortion he wants, and there are times when his grim jocularity seems forced. He too, moreover, lacks that final dramatic sympathy with the foolish and the damned which the major novelist shows. But he has written a very intelligent book and one which—for all its modesty and its local character—is not bound to the present time.

Delmore Schwartz (review date 1952)

SOURCE: A review of *The Works of Love,* in *Partisan Review,* Vol. XIX, No. 3, May-June, 1952, pp. 357-58.

[*In the following excerpt, Schwartz argues that* The Works of Love *is an incompletely realized novel.*]

Innocence is the theme of Wright Morris' new novel, **The Works Of Love.** The hero is the truly good and truly pure man who is doomed to give all that he has and to love all that he can without receiving gift or love in return. Morris has a beautiful sympathy for this kind of human being, and he masters more and more, in each new book, the gift of a colloquial poetic style. Unlike Sherwood Anderson and Gertrude Stein, who often wrote from the point of view which Morris has adopted in this book, he is always vivid and concrete (he has a wonderful eye for the purely American detail) where they tended to become increasingly vague or abstract or private. But something goes wrong in the middle of **The Works Of Love**: the innocent hero is too weak and too passive to be entirely admirable, at least in the way in which the author wants us to admire him. We have only to compare Morris' prairie saint with Dostoevsky's Prince Myshkin, a comparison which Morris' intention and ambition suggests, to recognize how there is too little temptation, too little struggle, and too much acceptance of rejection and desertion. And the reader cannot help but wonder how, under many circumstances, one can distinguish between innocence and ignorance, between purity of heart and stupidity. Moreover, as the book goes forward, the author intervenes to underline and emphasize the meaning of situation and episode, and to make his hero merely the mouthpiece of his own convictions: a voice from the sky, a book about a trip to the moon, Ralph Henry Barbour's books for boys, a trip to Hollywood, and Santa Claus are all introduced to make possible formulations on the hero's part which are not so much out of character as too conscious, too glib, and too fluent.

Nevertheless, [there is a] depth of sympathy and [a] love of experience—of existence itself—throughout *The Works Of Love.*

The Times Literary Supplement (review date 1954)

SOURCE: A review of *The Crossroads,* in *The Times Literary Supplement,* No. 2737, July 16, 1954, p. 453.

[*In the following excerpt, the unnamed reviewer notes the importance of the American landscape and "the terrible American female" in Morris's fiction.*]

To read an American novel after several English ones is to rediscover with a sort of surprise the sense of place. While our own writers for the most part develop personal relationships or states of mind in a vacuum, the Americans present their vivid background almost as a *deus ex machina* moulding and controlling their characters' lives. Thus Mr. Wright Morris, one of the most interesting and personal of American novelists, far indeed from being simply a descriptive reporter like many of his countrymen, yet seems to suggest that the American landscape and social organization are the prime factors in his people's fate.

[In *The Crossroads*] scene is the household of a judge and public benefactor during the twenty-four hours after his death; the theme, the effect on a family of a matriarch's rule. In turn, the judge's wife, his daughter, his mother, his son-in-law and general factotum, meditate, according to their several capacities, upon Howard Porter's real character and the profound isolation imposed on him by the wife's bleakly puritanical cast of mind. The mystery to be solved is the durability of this strange and uncompanionable marriage. "Thou shalt not give a particle of gratification" says Webb, the son-in-law, summing up the atmosphere of this all-American home. "Thou shalt drive from the Temple the man who smokes . . . and thou shalt drive from the bed the man who lusts . . . and thou shalt drive from the parlour the man who feels . . . for the man who feels undermines the Law of the House." It is the terrible American female celebrated by Thurber and by countless others of her compatriots who is the story's centrepiece. Yet she has been formed, a reader feels, by her environment. With great subtlety and economy of language, Mr. Wright Morris, who extracts from stark premises a warm conclusion, suggests that beneath her formidable reserve this woman loved her husband and did what she could.

Louis O. Coxe (essay date 1954)

SOURCE: A review of *The Huge Season,* in *Partisan Review,* Vol. XXI, No. 6, November-December, 1954, pp. 690-91.

[*In the following review, Coxe argues* The Huge Season *is a failure.*]

Mr. Morris' new novel [*The Huge Season*] begins auspiciously with a strong evocation of atmosphere and a promise of exciting events to come. The reader feels that here is a real attempt to explore the secret, the power, of those fabulous men of the '20s he has read and heard so much about. One of the first pictures Mr. Morris limns is the shadowy one of a figure before a Congressional investigating committee, a figure who will become, one is made to feel sure, of crucial importance. One cannot help asking Who is he? was he a Communist? why? what has happened in the past that must work itself out thus and set this man before us with the TV cameras on him? I for one found that though Mr. Morris raised these questions and many others like them, he never really answered them, and not because the questions were explored so excitingly as to render answers superfluous; no, I felt cheated. Mr. Morris went about in his book seeming to tell me he was going to give me answers—good, pungent, longed-for answers. I never got them.

The failure, I think, derives from two weaknesses: stylistic and structural. The author speaks in two voices in alternating chapters, the one being that of the protagonist, Foley, and the other that of the effaced narrator telling about what happened on that crucial day in Foley's life. I do not think Mr. Morris ever brings these two disparate methods together, with the result that Peter Foley remains a device rather than a person, and the other characters (all of whom are associated with Foley) are hopelessly split: what they were is no clue to what they are. Mr. Morris cannot bring the past and present together and his technique simply drives them farther apart. As for the style, there are further devices and techniques which irritated me: the early-Auden technique of omitting all articles, for no reason that I could discover, and the tendency to lapse into a Fearing-esque ironic catalogue of urban and suburban materialistic fetishes. Finally, the over-clever talk of some of the characters, notably Dickie, palls after a while. I think Mr. Morris defeats his purpose here, just as he does in his over-use of symbolism.

I believe Mr. Morris has failed in this novel because he attempted a big job without sufficient attention to the main task involved: that of really showing the how and the why of a man like Lawrence or Dickie or Proctor. He has been too hasty and counted on style, evocation and symbolism to do that which only patient thought, imagination and analysis can do.

The Times Literary Supplement (essay date 1955)

SOURCE: A review of *The Huge Season,* in *The Times Literary Supplement,* No. 2794, September 16, 1955, p. 546.

[*In the following unfavorable review of* The Huge Season, *the reviewer concludes that Morris's "pretentiously culti-vated climate contains more air than imagination."*]

The Huge Season is a kind of study of the effects of hero-worship, and for a hero Lawrence seems as good a name as any other, though in this book the name is more apt than the character is convincing. Lawrence is the son of a Barbed Wire tycoon, compact of the usual virtues and vices of such sons, who soon takes himself off to Europe to see the sights and get the feel of things, including Life; he ends by getting a horn in the groin from a very Spanish bull. We see Lawrence as a sort of bright sun, round whom the lesser planets, in the person of Foley, Lundgrum, and Procter, revolve; and he is such a hero that he is able to hold lesser men in moral captivity for many years of their lives. We follow these worshippers through their school days, and so down to the present; after 250 pages have been worked through we realize that we have been skin-close to the youthful moral reflections of Foley and com-pany, now considerably matured, and one is startled only by the fact that none of it seems very important. The book is poorly constructed, the reader often embarrassed by the self-consciousness of the writing. The book is intense without being original, and general feeling has a fugitive existence. Before one is half-way through the climate is apparent, and Hemmingway thuds and Fitzgerald-like ech-oes abound. Mr. Morris's pretentiously cultivated climate contains more air than imagination.

Wayne C. Booth (essay date 1957)

SOURCE: "The Two Worlds in the Fiction of Wright Mor-ris," in *The Sewanee Review,* Vol. LXV, 1957, pp. 375-99.

[*In the following essay, Booth examines the roles and the meanings of heroism, imagination, and love in Morris's novels.*]

Wright Morris has published ten books, all of them critical successes. Many would agree with Mark Schorer that he is "probably the most original young novelist writing in the United States." Yet nothing seems to happen, nothing, that is, of the kind that ought to happen. His books have never been taken up by "the wider public"—assuming that there is still such a thing for serious literature—and critics have left his praise almost entirely to isolated, and frequently misleading, reviews.[1]

There is perhaps little point in fussing about the popular neglect; though he provides no murders, rapes, or bed-room scenes, his great gift for evoking the recent Ameri-can past and for playing upon the humor and poignancy of

life as felt by Americans since the turn of the century will ensure that his book, in the long run, will make their way. But we ought to take a first step toward critical justice now by recognizing the richness of the vision which oper-ates beneath the engaging surface of his "realistic" novels and stories.

I

One need not attempt to go beneath that surface to dis-cover his preoccupation with the problem of what is real and what is "phony." "Just what the hell isn't bullshit?" the young Foley asks in **The Huge Season,** and he spends the rest of his life trying to outgrow the effect on his imagi-nation of Lawrence's answer: a foolhardy act of unmistak-able physical courage. In the latest novel, **The Field of Vi-sion,** the lesson is somewhat different, but the problem is the same. "It's deader," the middle-aged failure, Boyd, says to his friend's grandson, "than that coonskin hat."

> The boy wiped it from his head to look at it. Had he thought it was alive?
>
> "It's a *real* one," he said. "It's not a phony."
>
> "Is that so?" said Boyd. "How do you know?"
>
> The boy stroked the tail on it, and said, "It cost more. It cost four dollars."
>
> "That's how you can tell?" said Boyd.

He then grabs the hat, gets the matador to put it on his head, and returns it to the boy. "It's a real hat now," went on Boyd, "because it's been on the head of a hero. That makes it real."

But even Boyd knows that that is not enough. Still trying to give to the boy the touch of reality which, for Boyd, only his own lost sense of the heroic can give, he throws the cap into the bull ring and sends the boy after it. And it works. A few moments later the boy is walking with his grandfather, and they pass a man selling black paper bulls.

"'You can have a bull,' said McKee [the grandfather] to the boy. 'You want a bull?' 'It's not a bull if you buy it,' said the boy." And McKee, annoyed and baffled by his own sense that nothing he touches is any longer real, says, "Okay—since you're so smart I'll just buy a little bull for myself. And while I'm at it I think I'll buy myself a pair of these real horns." But he seems to know that they won't be real if he buys them.

As a final example, toward the conclusion of **The Huge Season,** more than twenty years after Foley learned from Lawrence to recognize what was real, he overhears the following conversation between two characters who, like himself, have been unable to free themselves of the "strange captivity" of the twenties.

> "Mesdames et Messieurs," Dickie said, raising his hand for attention. He stepped forward and bowed to Lou Baker, took her hand in his own, kissed it. "Doll, it's been *real.*"

"Oh, Christ!" said Lou Baker.

"That's the way they're doing it now," said Dickie.

"I can't believe it," said Lou Baker. "I *won't* believe it."

"You think we're different, eh?" Dickie said.

"I think we *were* different," Lou Baker replied. Under her gaze Dickie lowered his eyes, flicked the levers on his watch. "They *say* it's been real, but we *were* real," Lou Baker said.

Such passages may look deceptively matter-of-fact, even naive, out of context. But they are a manifestation of a highly sophisticated dialectic that flows throughout Morris's works. The real world, gruesome as it is, is not as real as it looks. To endure it, indeed to live at all, a man must, as Brady discovers in *The Works of Love,* find a more genuine reality by getting "out of this world." The novels indicate at least three main ways of doing so.

HEROISM: THE MOMENT OF REAL ACTION

The three passages already quoted all indicate, at least indirectly, the same way to reality—the way of heroic intensity. Whatever else may be phony, the man who can do the big thing, with transcendent vitality or courage or even foolhardiness, is not. In a world in which things tend to fall apart at the seams, in which most people are dead on their feet and hardly know who or where they are, the hero is at least *really there.* The dead hero of Morris's second book, *The Man Who was There,* was much more real than any of the living characters whose lives were affected by his having been *there.* Similarly the "rainmakers" in *The Huge Season* are able to "make rain" to water the wasteland of the twenties mainly because they see themselves in the large, they cannot be contented with anything less than some sort of greatness. Lawrence, the tennis player, is satisfied only with championship, and he drives toward that championship with a style that in more ways than one never allows the ball to hit the court; forced to stop playing tennis by an accident, he takes up bullfighting, is badly gored and shoots himself. Proctor, wanting more than anything else to be a great runner, shoots himself through the foot in order to prove to Lawrence that a Jew can do the great thing, can not only take it but "can give it up." Foley finds that he cannot free himself from the impact that such total living, now gone from his world, has made. He writes a book about his obsession with those times when heroism in the midst of despair still meant something.

"Young men are a corn dance, a rite of spring, and every generation must write its own music, and if these notes have a sequence the age has a style."

Who said that?

Peter Nielson Foley.

Where could it be found?

Near top of last, or next to last, page of manuscript now lying in grate of his fireplace, unpublished, unfinished, and tentatively titled "The Strange Captivity."

Above statement led up to the following:

"The great style, the habit of perfection, united George Herman Ruth and Charles A. Lindbergh, Albie Booth and Jack Dempsey, Juan Belmonte and Jay Gatsby, and every man, anywhere, who stood alone with his own symbolic bull. He had his gesture, his moment of truth, or his early death in the afternoon."

Foley does not find the world of the fifties obsessed with the habit of perfection; in losing the sense of the heroic, the world has lost a great deal. Morris makes it clear that the heroic dreams of the bullfighters and the tennis players and the great Gatsbys pursuing the green light were never enough in themselves. Foley's whole effort is, in fact, to find an escape from the limitations of the heroic ideal without losing the imaginative transformations it could effect. On the one hand, they really did make rain in that huge season, and the wasteland was not a complete wasteland because they were there. Yet much as Foley has lost, it is clear that he must lose even more, if he is to free himself of the strange captivity. The danger of the heroic is that it can freeze the imagination as well as liberate it.

Boyd, in *The Field of Vision,* has learned all this the hard way. All his life he has been obsessed with a romantic desire to be the ultimate hero. As a young man he drove toward the great success, even at one point nearly drowning himself by trying to walk on the water: if one is going to be a real hero, certainly only Christ is ultimately satisfactory as a model. When it becomes clear to him that he will never succeed in becoming a positive hero, he takes the next logical step of trying to become a heroic failure.

In a prologue to a play that was never produced, Boyd advised his public that he *hoped* to fail, since there was no longer anything of interest to be gained in success. He went on to speak of culture as a series of acceptable clichés. A photographer's salon where ready-made frames, hung on the walls of rustically historical gardens, lacked only the faces of succeeding generations in the ready-made holes. This hand-me-down world defined the realm of the possible. The impossible—become a cliché itself—had been ruled out. This left the artist—Boyd himself, that is—with only one suitable subject, and life itself with only one ironic result. This was Failure. Such as Boyd, from the beginning, had practiced himself.

Now in his fifties he still carries about with him an old pocket he had torn, as a boy, from the pants of his hero, Ty Cobb. That pocket had once worked a transformation, had raised his sights, had given him the habit of perfection, and was so far so good. But somehow Boyd, a man of "promise," got stuck with an inadequate dream. The problem, he says to himself as he watches the heroic transformations of the bullfight, was "how not."

How *not* to be embalmed in a flannel pocket, how *not* to be frozen in a coonskin hat. How to live in spite of, not because of, something called character. To keep it open, to keep the puzzle puzzling, the pattern changing and alive.

To make a flannel pocket into "Gordon Boyd's piece of the Cross" is to lose oneself in the past, rather than using that past imaginatively. There is no question but that even this is better than the almost total imaginative failure of McKee, the grandfather. But it is not enough.

IMAGINATION: THE MOMENT OF TRUTH

The heroic can never be an end in itself; it is only a means to the imaginative transformations it can effect, the moments of truth it can yield. The insight itself is what is important, and it is therefore not surprising that although all the novels can be said to move toward or through moments of revelation, the heroic is far from being necessary to those moments. Anything that can capture and hold the imagination will do. In the earlier novels the precipitant is often a single physical object with no heroic associations, an object that can show, if looked at closely, what life really is for those who made the object and have used it. Though the objects shift from book to book, from milieu to milieu, ranging from old croquet balls, kitchen stoves, and Swiss watches to new Davy Crockett hats and sombreros, there is always a tremendous sense of the human meaning of the things as conveyed by their visual reality.

The man who can really see an object used by human beings can in the process see something about them that even the closest look at their faces could not yield. It is thus no accident that two of his first books were "illustrated," though that is hardly the word, with his own photographs. In *The Inhabitants* and *The Home Place,* the texture of the overalls, the feel of the broken plow handle, the heat and weight of the kitchen stove are made to belong to us more really, in a sense, than they did even to the people who actually used them: they have been made into art by the imagination of the author and photographer.

It is also no accident that Morris chose as the epigraph to *The Home Place* Henry James's vivid statement of his own feeling for the object:

> To be at all critically, or as we have been fond of calling it, analytically, minded—over and beyond an inherent love of the general many-colored picture of things—is to be subject to the superstition that objects and places, coherently grouped, disposed for human use and addressed to it, must have a sense of their own, a mystic meaning proper to themselves to give out: to give out, that is, to the participant at once so interested and so detached as to be moved to a report of the matter.
>
> [*The American Scene*]

In that book, the narrator, having returned to the home place, surveys the ugly, worn objects in the weatherbeaten house, and wonders why they have the effect on him that he would expect only from beautiful objects. "Everything in its place, its own place, with a frame of space around it. Nothing arranged. No minority groups, that is. No refined caste systems for the furniture." And he concludes that their singular power lies in their ability to carry him, as

genuine art works do, out of himself: they evoke, they suggest, they carry their own weight in a way that will not allow the sensitive viewer to go his own way without taking them into account. Clyde Muncy's moment of truth comes when, in the abandoned house, he goes through the old relics and suddenly feels their essential "holiness."

> For thirty years I've had a clear idea what the home place lacked, and why the old man pained me, but I've never really known what they had. I know now. But I haven't the word for it. The word beauty is not a Protestant thing. It doesn't describe what there is about an old man's shoes. The Protestant word for that is character. Character is the word, but it doesn't cover the ground. It doesn't cover what there is moving about it, that is. I say these things are beautiful . . . this character is beautiful. I'm not going to labor the point, but there's something about these man-tired things, something added, that is more than character. . . . Perhaps all I'm saying is that character can be a form of passion, and that some things, these things, have that kind of character. That kind of Passion has made them holy things. That kind of holiness, I'd say, is abstinence, frugality, and independence—the home-grown, made-on-the-farm trinity.

Useful as objects can be, however, in stimulating the imagination to its task of creating the real world, they have their limitations. They tend, for one thing, to lead the author into relatively private evocations, and thus to an almost plaintive rhetorical appeal to the reader to share what the author feels as he contemplates them (e.g., "I say these things are beautiful, but I do so with the understanding that mighty few people anywhere will follow what I mean. That's too bad." [*The Home Place*]). Morris has shown steady growth in the "size" of the objects receiving his attention, and he has shown increasing ability to pack them with the meaning he intends by surrounding them with the characters, actions, and events necessary to make the evocation public. In some of the earlier works one is occasionally left wondering why in the world he thinks these things are so charismatic; I should think that for readers who have never shared the small-town experience they would be even more frequently unintelligible than they are for me. But more and more he has developed the technique of centering on heroes and saints who are heroic and saintly just because they have the "holy" ability to create reality out of what is not yet real. "The man" who "was there" re-created everything and everyone he touched when alive by the intense vitality of his imaginative life. In *The World in the Attic,* those who live in the mundane world have their only real life in the "attic," the house where the romanticized Caddy Hibbard acts upon their imaginations like a magnet working on iron filings, "supplying the town with energy and direction, like a dynamo." In *Man and Boy,* Ormsby struggles, almost without knowing it, for some kind of imaginative clarity that will make it possible for him to cope with his domineering wife and the empty, dry life she has forced, as he thinks, on himself and his dead son. Thinking of that dead son, and of the charge that his son's life was worthless, that he "went phooey," Ormsby says to himself:

"*The* Boy and *the Ormsby*" [the ship named for the heroic son] he continued, which certainly meant nothing whatsoever, or considerably more than anything he had ever said. "There goes the Ormsby," men would say, just as he had always looked and said to himself: "There goes the Boy." *The* Boy and *the Ormsby*—it was a very strange thing that they both had the definite article. There was something impersonal and permanent about both of them. . . . There goes the *Ormsby,* men would say, without ever knowing, as he knew, how absolutely right it was. Without ever knowing that this was proof that his plans went right.

Other men had lost boys—but until he met a man who had *found* one, he could hardly talk about this thing. . . . And then it would depend on whether the man thought of his son as the Boy, or as something that belonged to him.

Will Brady in *The Works of Love,* dim as his vision is about most matters, sees and feels one thing clearly: the hopeless, helpless need for love in "this world" which does all it can to stifle love; in taking on the role of Santa Claus he re-creates, re-imagines the ideal of disinterested love.

In *The Deep Sleep* Webb, son-in-law to the dead judge, struggles throughout for what he calls "the picture," the picture of the judge, sane, kindly, wise in his public life, harried, driven to secrecy and loneliness by his wife. Throughout most of the book Webb feels nothing but hatred for the domineering female; it is hardly surprising that some readers have accused Morris of hating women. In his half-drunken apocalyptical vision, Webb shouts at his wife:

> "The first and last Commandment of the House reads— Thou shalt not give a particle of gratification. Thou shalt drive from the Temple the man who smokes, and he shall live in a tent behind the two-car garage, and thou shalt drive from the bed the man who lusts, and he shall live in tourist camps with interstate whores, and thou shalt drive from the bathroom the man who farts, and he shall sit in a dark cubby-hole in the basement, and thou shalt drive from the parlour the man who feels, and he shall make himself an island in the midst of the waters, for the man who feels undermines the Law of the House!"

It is true enough that Mrs. Porter sins by drying up the sources which water the creative imagination. But she is herself the victim of a world which forces the female into an unimaginative role as the defender of the House. The deep sleep that falls on the male in the presence of Eve can also be read as the sleep that makes Eve what she is. Thus the epigraph of this work, "And the Lord God caused a deep sleep to fall upon Adam . . ." should be read with that of *Man and Boy,* from Donne: "If man had beene left *alone* in this *world,* at first, shall I thinke that he would not have *fallen*? If there had beene no *Woman,* would not man have served, to have beene his own *Tempter*?" Webb's discovery of forgiveness at the end of the book, as shown by his coming to the point of restoring the Judge's watch to Mrs. Porter, even though the Judge had hid it from her,

is almost unintelligible if we try to explain it by ordinary standards of character motivation. Only if we see that the mere act of "getting the picture" is for Morris a holy thing does his reversal make sense. And Katherine, his wife, after years of hatred for her mother, is able to forgive when she finally understands: "Her mother, God knows, understood nothing, neither her husband, her son, nor her daughter, but perhaps it was not beyond reason to understand her. Perhaps *that* was just what her husband [the Judge] had done. Perhaps that explained what could not be explained about him."

The fullest expression of the role of the creative consciousness is given, however, in the last two works. We have already seen how Foley, in *The Huge Season,* is trapped in a strange captivity of the imagination. He escapes from that captivity only by capturing in his imagination the meaning of the past. In his consciousness, that past is

> Suspended in time, like the ball that forever awaited the blow from the racket, or the upraised foot that would never reach the curb. A permanent scene, made up of frail impermanent things. A lover like Lou Baker, a saint like Lawrence, a martyr like Proctor, and a witness like Foley . . . in the burning they gave off something less perishable. How explain that Lawrence, in whom the sun rose, and Proctor, in whom it set, were now alive in Foley, a man scarcely alive himself. Peter Foley, with no powers to speak of, had picked up the charge that such powers gave off—living on the field of the magnet, he had been magnetized. Impermanent himself, he had picked up this permanent thing . . . the bones of Peter Foley would go on chirping in a time that had stopped. No man had given a name to this magnet, nor explained the imperishable lines of force, but they were there, captive in Peter Foley— once a captive himself. . . . He took out his watch, started to wind it, and saw that the time—the captive time—had stopped. At two o'clock in the morning, the first day of his escape from captivity.

Similarly the whole structure of *The Field of Vision* can be described as that of the concurrent search, by a small group of American tourists in Mexico, for some kind of vision that will lead them out of their unreality. Only Boyd and Lehmann, through their capacity to think and feel, come close to the condition of being real human beings, and even they are seriously maimed. Everyone else suffers more or less unconsciously, gropes more or less blindly, lives if at all only in the life provided by some other more vital consciousness. Old Scanlon, the great grandfather, lives in the events of his father's past (not, as at least one reviewer has said, his own past) having retreated from his drab and meaningless existence in Lone Tree to a more heroic, and hence more visitable, age. McKee, the aimless grandfather, hardly lives at all, but there are signs that he once almost lived, like his son and grandson, in the light reflected from Boyd's vivid imagination. Mrs. McKee, like Mrs. Porter frozen into the half-life of the American middle-class matron, unloving and unloved, seeing and feeling nothing but what her own conventions impose on the life around her, still remembers the one moment when she was really kissed by a man who was, at least at the time, *there,* in the kiss: by Boyd, of course. Paul Kahler, now Paula, frustrated in his attempts to find a meaningfully creative life as a male, "lives" through having imagined himself, transformed himself, into a totally harmless—though totally ineffectual—woman.

Boyd and Lehmann both see, in different ways, the nature of the imaginative act that alone can give redemption from these uncreated worlds. For Boyd, the problem is to find a picture of himself that is not so thoroughly padded with clichés that it is not a picture at all.

> Neither going to pot, throwing in the sponge, or even working at it had brought him failure. How achieve it? It had to be imagined, like everything else. It had to undergo a sea change, a transformation, that would indicate that failure had *happened* . . . to the man behind the front. The armor of clichés [all of the trappings of failure, unconsciously accepted as the real thing] kept him from touching bottom, or from being touched.

Thinking about what must happen to his young namesake, the grandson, before he will find himself, Boyd describes the process more clearly than he can when dealing with himself.

> . . . he would not know its meaning until the pattern itself appeared. And that he would not *find.* No, not anywhere, since it did not exist. The pattern—what pattern it had—he would have to create. Make it out of something that looked for all the world like something else . . . a tireless shifting of the pieces . . . until the pattern—the imagined thing—began to emerge.

Lehmann, finally, the half-fraudulent and half-inspired "psychoanalyst," sees much more clearly than anyone else what is required, what the imaginative act must be. Why, he asks, are things so seldom what they seem?

> They were not *meant* to be. They were meant to seem different—each according to the nature that was capable of seeing, behind the spectacle of lights, the constellation in his own roof brain. The universe in the process of being made. . . . Emerging and dissolving patterns of meaning, seeding the world's body with cosmic rays that each according to his nature would absorb, resist, or lightly dust off. Each according to his lights, such as they were, if and when they came on. . . .

> *"Mehr licht,"* Lehmann said, softly. . . .

LOVE: THE MOMENT OF COMPASSION

If the world of our imaginings is the universe in the process of being made, it might be inferred that *what* is given reality in that world would be a matter of indifference. If the activity of the creative consciousness is itself of supreme value, one might suppose that distinctions between good and bad, beauty and ugliness, and even truth and falsehood, would disappear into a relativistic, but "realized," universe. Some writers for whom the sensitive vision is the greatest value have indeed aimed for neutrality toward all other values: most notably Joyce. And there are times when Morris seems to imply, momentarily, that for him there is no objective order of values which in any sense controls the worth of particular imaginings. But whatever he might *say,* his novels reveal a world full of distinctions of value, full of love and hate, of Good and Evil, of Heaven and Hell.

We have already seen him using terms like "holy" and "religious" in talking about the feelings which come with the moment of truth. Such terms thicken whenever he deals with love. It was not clearly so in his earliest works; love did not figure in that holy trinity, "abstinence, frugality and independence," in *The Home Place.* The value of love as compassion, however, as the charity that alone makes us capable of imagining ourselves into other people's lives, has been implicitly important from the first. And since *The Works of Love* (1952), his characters have wrestled constantly with the problem of how to find "connection" with their fellows; the quest for the moment of love has thus become the most frequent particular form of the general quest for the moment of truth.

The longest sustained and most explicit quest for love is that of Brady in *The Works of Love.* Brady is an ordinary, confused, helpless man, engaged in a blind search for love in a world that provides no love. The hell of his existence, referred to in the epigraph from Blake, is only occasionally relieved by hints of possible "connection" with one or another of his fellows (another epigraph to this book is Lawrence's, "We cannot bear connection. That is our malady"). There is, briefly and dimly, his mother. There is the whore who likes to talk with him and to whom he proposes marriage, only to be laughed out into the street. There is the other whore whose baby he adopts, and there is the baby itself, "the boy." There is his first wife, the terrified, hopeless and lonely bride, whose fear of physical connection delays their spiritual connection until it is too late: they must return to "this world." There is a second wife who marries him because he *is* hopeless, because he "knew how to give" but didn't know how to receive anything. There is a woman who reminds him of his mother, and there is an assortment of other lost souls. He loves all of them, in the only fashion he knows; he finds real connection, genuine reciprocal love, with none. His world is not geared for love; he has not been trained for it. And like the madman he meets in the California park, who is happy only when he is being poured like a teapot, and who thanks kindly anyone who will pour him, or like the many "holy men" in Morris's works who feed pigeons with bread soaked in their own spittle, he is forced to find inadequate substitutes for the real thing. Yet even these substitutes are the only thing approaching reality in his life. Shut off, because of his meagre consciousness, from any of the other paths to reality, he has only the path of love.

The meagreness of Brady's consciousness is, I suppose, the greatest hurdle to comprehending what Morris is about in this work, and may account for its having been less enthusiastically received than most of the others. But Brady's blindness is necessary—even though the technical problem of how to portray that blindness without limiting the book itself unduly might have been better solved. Where is there, in Brady's world, any source of better information about love than he has been given? Who is there to tell him what is wrong with his marriages? Where, in the towns he passes through on his gradual movement eastward, can he hope to find someone who will tell him what is wrong with the lives that touch his and with his own.

> It all seemed to Will Brady, there in the moonlight, a very strange thing. A warm summer night, the windows and the doors of most of the houses were open, and the air that he breathed went in and out of all of them. In and out of the lungs, and the lives, of the people who were asleep. They inhaled it deeply, snoring perhaps; then they blew it on its way again, and he seemed to feel himself sucked into the rooms, blown out again. Without carrying things too far, he felt himself made part of the lives of these people, even part of the dreams that they were having, lying there. . . . Men had been there [to the moon], it was said, but where was the man who had traveled the length of his own house? Who knew the woman at the back—or the boy at the front who lay asleep? . . . What about the man who stood in the dark eating cornbread and milk? What about the rooms where the blinds were always drawn. . . . What writer, what traveler, could explain the woman who rolled herself up in the sheet, like a mummy or the man who came home every night and undressed in the dark? All one could say was that whatever it was it was there in the house, like a vapor, and it had drawn the blinds, like an invisible hand, when the lights came on. As a writer of books he would have to say that this vapor made the people yellow in color, gave them flabby bodies, and made their minds inert. As if they were poisoned, all of them, by the air they breathed. And such a writer would have to explain why this same air, so fresh and pure in the street, seemed to be poisoned by the people breathing it. . . . What the world needed, it seemed, was a traveler who would stay right there in the bedroom, or open the door and walk slowly about on his own house. Who would sound a note, perhaps, on the piano, raise the blinds on the frontroom windows and walk with a candle into the room where the woman sleeps. A man who would recognize this woman, this stranger, as his wife.
>
> But if books would put a man in touch with the moon, perhaps they would put him in touch with a boy. . . .

And still groping, he tries to discover in *Penrod* and *Tom Sawyer*—where else?—some clue to his failure with his own son.

Finally, crushed by what looks like a total failure with every human being he has ever tried to "get in touch with," he lands in Chicago, "In The Wasteland," kept alive by meagre memories, meagre letters from what he has forgotten is only his adopted son, meagre conversations with only half-real, half-living acquaintances in the city, meagre clichés about providing his son with "the best." In a final

uncomprehending desperate grasp at love, he takes a job as Santa Claus—"Oh how they will love you," says one of his friends—and, blinded by a sunlamp which he uses to make his cheeks rosier for the children, he walks into the heart of the city—into the canal where earlier he has imagined, in the only really apocalyptic "imagining" he ever attains to, that all the souls of all the people who really "have faith" have gone to get "out of this world." His all-encompassing pity, fed by the acrid human smell from the city below him, makes of the smell the "breath of life."

> He leaned there on the railing, his eyes closed, but on his face the look of a man of vision—a holy man, one might even say, as he was feeding the birds. But when the lantern dropped down . . . he did a strange thing. He went down the turning stairs toward the water, toward the great stench, as if he would grasp it, make it his own before it could blow away from him. Or as if he heard above the sound of the traffic, the trains in the yard, and the din of the city, the tune of that Piper—the same old Pied Piper—over the canal [the one who had led all the people of faith away, in his earlier dream]. The one that had drawn him, time and again, into the streets.

His death is thus a final attempt at an embrace, an embrace this time of the whole of pitiable humanity.

Brady's salvation through love, through his realization of a common bond with all other helpless, hopeless men, is simply the extreme form of what one finds throughout the novels: in love thus broadly conceived, one discovers reality. And it is significant that with Morris as with E. M. Forster in *A Passage to India* and *Howards End* the bond of love does not extend simply to other human beings. Proctor and Foley saving the helpless cockroach, Lehmann in *The Field of Vision* resuscitating the fly, the natural enemy, simply because it is helpless, are doing the works of love just as truly as is the young Ormsby when he sends off ten dollars to help save Floyd Collins trapped in a mine. There are of course instances of strong personal love in Morris—fathers and sons, husbands and wives, heroes and hero-worshippers, and just plain lovers. But he has never been willing to forget that such loves are only local manifestations, as it were, of a general problem, a general problem which is illustrated perhaps even better by impersonal compassion on the one hand and by relatively impersonal hero-worship on the other, than by grand passion or even by deep personal affection.

In *The Field of Vision* the love felt for the hero as strong aggressor, the male, the bull, the "goddam fool" who compels our dreaming, is contrasted with the tender love of a Paula Kahler who, in a rejection of all aggression, all brutality, has rejected her own maleness and "transformed" herself to a woman. Both kinds of love, love as admiration and love as pity, can compel the imagination many days and many hours, but in this last novel the helpless pitiable flies are perhaps even more important than the more prominent bulls. (Even the bulls are symbolic as victims as well as heroes. One of McKee's chief associations with the killing in the bullring is his childhood experience of shooting a friendly pig). One night Lehmann, the only one in the book who approaches to wisdom, the man who has, out of pity, attempted to save Paula Kahler only to find that she is in a sense saving him, goes to her room and discovers her lying with eyes wide open but apparently unconscious.

> He was still in the doorway when she suddenly cried out HELP! There had been no mistaking the word, or the fact that she needed it. Gulped it out, as if choking, a last cry before going under, and he had felt that the corpse had spoken of the life beyond the grave. Needing *help*. So that both sides of life were the same. HELP WANTED was the big need in both of them. There was no trap door, no escape through a hole in the floor, or a door in the ceiling, on earth as it was in heaven and hell, a man needed help. This was his human condition. This was the basis of his brotherhood. . . . It was a need shared by all men. . . . To the question, *Where was Paula Kahler?* a simple answer. Everywhere. Everywhere that any living thing needed help. Among those who knew it, like Lehmann and Shults, among those who feared it, like Boyd and the McKees, and among those who knew as little as the fly that had dropped on Lehmann's chest. Few would need it so badly they would change their nature for it, but all of them would one day advertise for it.

The ambiguity of love as admiration and love as pity is partially resolved as Lehmann thinks further about the meaning of man's helplessness. Just as the bull, goring the matador, lifts them both to a moment of flight, a transformation into one thing, man-and-bull, a transformation that could not have occurred without both, so the mind of man is totally dependent on its links with the animal, its "connections" with the lowest, least human, life. Paula's rejection of everything but her own kindly light is, then, while a beautiful transformation in itself, not unambiguously a good thing; it is at best both good-and-evil, and at worst it is a flat denial of the truth.

> There was no mind if the lines to the past were destroyed. If the mind, that is, was nothing but itself. . . . There had to be connections, the impulse had to ooze its way through light years of wiring. . . . It was why Leopold Lehmann had emerged at all. Why he was as he was, criminal by nature, altruistic and egocentric by nature, merciless and pitiful by nature, but up there at the front of the bull, forked on his horns, as well as wagging his tail. In Leopold Lehmann the inscrutable impulse was reaching for the light. . . . But the thrust, even in reaching for the light, must come from behind. Out of the shoulders of the bull, on the horns of this dilemma, against the current that must always determine his direction, in reaching for more light man would have to risk such light as he had. It was why he needed help. It was why he had emerged as man. It was according to his nature that he was obliged to exceed himself.

It is this passage, I think, which explains the seeming inconsistency in calling Paula Kahler a saint, because of her absolute devotion to the teachings of Christ, and calling the tennis player Lawrence a saint, in *The Huge Season.* They are holy not only in the loves they inspire but also in their absolute embodiment of that part of man's nature which obliges him to exceed himself and reject the very world that made him.

II

Out of this World

If the act of heroism is made important only by being transformed in the consciousness to something more fundamental than heroism itself, if the creative consciousness makes a reality which is inevitably permeated with a sense of love, we still have to account for how Morris manages to make all this seem more "real" than the drab real world which it redeems. Why should moments of awareness be so important, to art as to life? What is there about awareness even of pain, of captivity, of death in the afternoon, that is "religious"? It is in answering this question that one comes to what is thematically the most important element in Morris's work. Without announcing any specific religious dogma, his novels, more successfully than any other American novels in this century, render the mystical relation of time and the timeless. Like Proust and Mann, among others, Morris is attempting the fictional voyage of discovery into the nature of reality itself, and as one might expect, he discovers the real in whatever is permanent in a world of change. The permanent is permanent by virtue of being outside of time—and yet as human beings we discover it only in time, only in the world of impermanent things. Fiction itself, being an instrument for fixing materials which otherwise would remain impermanent, is thus a bridge between the two worlds, the world of time which always disappoints, always cheats us in the end, and the timeless world which, as for all Platonists,[2] is more real. The three themes traced above can be seen, therefore, as no accidental roads to the "holy": whatever has been "really" *done, imagined,* or *felt* has been, in fact, re-created, transformed from one world into another. Ormsby's boy is permanent, because he did something that means something. Brady has found a way "to live in this world, so to speak, and yet somehow be out of it," "to be mortal and immortal, at the same time"—by imagining and performing an act of love. Foley knows that even after the final bomb falls, "according to Foley's Law, what had been loved or created would be untouched," that what "had been hammered out on the forge of art could be hammered to pieces, burned, bombed, or ignored, but it could not be destroyed. The outward form could be shattered, become smoke and ashes, but the inward form was radioactive, and the act of disappearance was the transformation of the dark into the light. Metamorphosis. The divine power of art."

Foley cannot himself complete his attempt at a work of art; there is no reason to believe that he will ever finish his novel. But he can achieve what is, in fact, an equivalent: he can bring his past experience into an imaginative unity and thus remove it from the ravages of the unreal world. As the book ends, he is faced with the likelihood of being investigated by a Senate committee, and he is thus likely to become more closely involved in "this world" than for many years. At the same time, he has moved to a revelation of "a permanent scene, made up of frail impermanent things."

The solution, if it can be called that, is an uneasy one, full of the paradoxes that plague any mystical solution in "real" life. Achieving timeless triumphs does not really deal with the world, "the world of men here below." Attempts to deal with "this temporal kingdom, this bloody cockpit," inevitably involve a man in evil: "all action was blended with evil, but one could *be* good, one could only be good, by sitting on one's hands." Yet attempts to escape the "battleground" leave the victory to "the Prince of Darkness." There is no escape from the paradox, except for the paradoxical fact that to understand the paradox, to see the trap for what it is, is in a sense to escape it.

But only in a sense. One cannot even understand it except by moving through experiences in time; like most writers on the timeless world, from Plato to Eliot, he sees that only the world of time can yield the necessary materials for the ascent into the world of ideas. "If you want to go to heaven, you got to go to hell *first*," old Scanlon teaches his grandson. Boyd cannot succeed without utter failure, without really "touching bottom"; "the bottom was a long way down—as it was also a long way up."

The way up and the way down are the same way—it is not surprising to find that in this poetry of the two worlds Morris should quote frequently from Eliot's poetry on the same theme. As early as *The World in the Attic* (1949) he used a quotation from "Burnt Norton" as an epigraph, and he has apparently gone on absorbing the whole of *Four Quartets* until Eliot's language now permeates his own whenever he attempts to deal with the still world.

> And the matador? At this point he had turned away. As from a still life, an arrangement that would remain as he had left it, the scene transformed into a frieze of permanence. The matador a magician, holding the wand to which was attached the magic cloth, behind which the double transformation had taken place. Word into flesh, and the flesh itself into myth. . . . [The praise] created a vortex, a still point where he stood alone with himself. . . .

> Boyd could see the still point where the dance was. The man rooted to it. . . . In controlling . . . the still point, he dominated the bull. Except for the still point there would be no dance. . . . The moment of truth was at that moment, and not at the kill.

Writing a book is, or should be, another such dance at the still point out of time, another act of permanence in a world of change. Everything Morris does shows this effort for permanence, this passion for transforming through the creative imagination the flat, lifeless, unreal materials— what he has come to call the clichés—into a living world. In style, subject matter, and structure, his books are thus running battles with cliché. I would have thought, for ex-

ample, that nothing more could or should be done with the clichés about the twenties, growing out of Fitzgerald's originally fresh vision—until I read *The Huge Season*. I would have thought that nothing more could or should be done with the clichés about bullfighting, growing out of Hemingway's originally fresh portrayal—until I read *The Field of Vision*. In transforming these clichés of situation, as in twisting dead phrases into new life, he exemplifies his aesthetic theory: when you see something truly, and give it a name, it is taken out of time, where it suffered all the ills that flesh is heir to, and placed in a permanent world where time must have a stop. You cannot do this, of course, by talking about mysticism, as Huxley often attempts to do. You must render the transformation. And in the renderings effected by our creative imaginations, we can make a permanent world—according to our lights, such as they are, if and when they come on.

III

Heroism, imagination, and love, as forms of action, thought and feeling that lead "out of this world," by no means exhaust the intellectual content of Morris's works. There are other persistent themes, and there are of course other topics under which his ideas could be treated. The original "holy trinity," abstinence, frugality and independence, could be expanded, for example, to account for much that escapes my formulation. "Independence," particularly, could be made to explain some elements of the free imagination which do not fit easily into the new trinity. There are times when sheer audacity or spontaneity seem almost more important than truth itself, when the ability to create, to create anything regardless of how quixotic the creation, seems more important than the ability to "get the picture" as it really is. Foley has discovered his cat and a chipmunk playing a fantastic sort of dancing game, a game incredibly inventive and "unnatural," which they repeat again and again throughout the summer.

> . . . the chipmunk [grew] fat and [had] to be carried by the neck, like a kitten, and after putting on her dance [lay] . . . with panting sides, like a fat ballerina. . . . To be believed it had to be shared with one of [Foley's] species. . . . It finally led Foley to look into Darwin . . . and to spend nights brooding on a creative evolution of his own. Founded on what? Well, founded on audacity. The unpredictable behavior that lit up the darkness with something new. That in some audacious moment of the lunar past, at the mouth of some cave, had resulted in man. A turning on the hinges of his own dark past, toward the light. Through some jeweled chink in Mother Nature's own armor, through some flaw in her own habit of perfection, the glint in some creature's eye shot new rays into the dark. . . . The Origin of a species based on charm, on audacity, on the powers of the dance, and the music that soothed whatever needed soothing in the savage breast. . . .

This passage, like many others, contains a good deal more than is comprehended in my systematic formulation.

What is more, to deal with Morris's ideas in this way leaves most of the major critical questions untouched. Even if his ideas are, as I believe, richer and more profound than the ideas of most contemporary novelists, they are not original by any means—at least in my account of them. And it is possible that a novelist could make use of all of them without being a great novelist.

But it is hard to see how he could fail to be an important and symptomatic one—that is, a novelist who must be given our sustained attention. Even his bare ideas, extracted brutally from their fictional context, show an honest and penetrating mind at work. And perhaps enough of the fictional embodiment of the ideas comes through in the above account to indicate that he has created a truly impressive variety of fictional worlds, made up of living characters facing real problems in a contemporary setting, surrounded by objects that tell the truth about those characters and their problems. We may want to claim that the characteristic form of Morris's novels—the more or less blind quest for permanent values in a world that, like our own real world, seems to deny those values wherever it can—is no more his own invention than are his ideas; it is a form that certainly bears strong resemblance to a long tradition that reached one kind of culmination in *Remembrance of Things Past*. But the above account should have made clear, what only a different sort of critical essay could do justice to: the fact that Morris gives to that tradition a new and important turn.

Such unsupported claims, however, merely illustrate the point that many of the important critical questions have not been asked here. Morris has many faults, or what look to me like faults, and a fully helpful criticism must sooner or later ask the questions that will lead to a discussion of those faults. But it should do so only after looking closely enough at his virtues to recognize what a fault would be in the distinctive context he provides. Certainly our first job is to see what it means to us to have a novelist of his gifts and his integrity coming now after fourteen years of steady, impressive growth, into what can hardly fail to be his greatest years.

Notes

1. Since the writing of this article Mr. Morris has been given the National Book Award for *The Field of Vision*.

2. The philosophical validity of Morris's ideas is of course not in question here, though any novelist who is as much concerned with conceptual ideas as he is must ultimately be held more directly answerable to philosophy than novelists like Jane Austen or Hemingway or even Henry James, whose "mind was never violated by an idea." The fact that Morris's "Platonism" is closer in detail to Plotinus than to Plato does not matter at this point, since his fictional effects come from rendering the struggle to ascend from one world into the other, a struggle that is common to all forms of Platonism, including, of course, the Christian.

   Similarly, detailed comparisons of Morris's moments of truth with strikingly similar moments in other fic-

tion, like Proust's moments of heightened memory, Joyce's epiphanies, or Virginia Woolf's moments of vision, would not be appropriate here. The whole problem of the various types of epiphany and the technical difficulties raised by trying to realize them in fiction has scarcely been touched by modern criticism, in spite of—or perhaps because of—its concern with symbolism and self-expression.

The Times Literary Supplement (review date 1957)

SOURCE: A review of *The Field of Vision*, in *The Times Literary Supplement*, No. 2896, August 30, 1957, p. 517.

[*In the following review of* The Field of Vision, *the uncredited writer criticizes Morris for the novel's diction and "elaborate symbolism."*]

Mr. Wright Morris's **The Field of Vision** won the 1957 American National Book Award, whose judges wrote, "he is the voice and conscience of provincial America." If undistinguished prose and jargon constitute their provincial voice and conscience, they are right. Or it may be that American and English writing are now so far removed from one another that an Englishman cannot appreciate American provincial life, when described in thousands of sentences of this kind, ". . . you would think in a town of twelve hundred people what kids there were would all know each other, but they didn't and that was the thing about Polk . . ."; or, "what he felt was, when he began to feel something, that it was an old feeling and he had felt it many times before. He recognized that feeling. . . ."

Once the English reader has adapted himself to reading twelve words where six will do he will find something authentically American in **The Field of Vision.** As a determined "creative" novelist, Mr. Wright Morris is not frightened of trying to say things in a new way. For instance, his subject is a bull-fight, but only because a bull-fight has elaborate overtones for his hero. "The durable fragments of his memory seemed to gather round the bull-ring as round a magnet, and his mind was compelled to come to imaginative terms with them." In spite of some agreeable portraits of rustic types, old Uncle Sams, &c., this elaborate symbolism demands too great an effort on the part of the reader who reads for pleasure.

R. W. Flint (review date 1957)

SOURCE: A review of *The Field of Vision*, in *Partisan Review*, Vol. XXIV, No. 1, Winter, 1957, pp. 142-43.

[*In the following excerpt, Flint dismisses* The Field of Vision *as overblown and empty.*]

Wright Morris, says John W. Aldridge, is "the most important novelist of the American middle generation" and *The Field of Vision* "brilliantly climaxes his most creative period. It is a work of permanent significance. . . ." Well, leave us face it, as the TV comics say. It just ain't so. Morris handles the romantic figures of tabloid legend and the mythical *Reader's Digest*-reading average man with a star-struck wonder that's just a wee bit hollow and fake. His real gift, on the basis of a chapter called "Scanlon," seems to be for action narrative and hallucinated horror. I don't say he cannot be amiable, nor that he doesn't deserve to make a comfortable living as a writer. But this particular "novel" (the only one of his I have read) is all signification and no significand. A group of middling folks watch a bull-fight in Mexico (you expected Spain?). Sometime in the past one of them, said to be as charming and as doomed as Orson Welles, has ripped a pocket off Ty Cobb's uniform, which talisman is meant to be a comic Golden Fleece (or something), and has kissed somebody's frigid, blue-eyed wife in a moment of sheer insight into her true character. This—plus some bull-ring monkey-shines and some Blood in the Afternoon—comprises the novel's whole action. So help me God! Oh yes—there's a funny foreign psychiatrist with (vast mine of symbolism) a transvestite in tow! The rest is mostly a busy, fussy tying-together of a lot of portentous details, in a short-winded Faulknerian rumination I found mildly amusing, though not exactly the glory of the middle generation.

Wright Morris (essay date 1957)

SOURCE: "Letter to a Young Critic," in *The Massachusetts Review*, Vol. VI, No. 1, Autumn-Winter, 1964-65, pp. 93-100.

[*In the following letter, originally published in 1957, Morris talks of his own work, and of other writers.*]

> David Madden was in 1957 a graduate student at San Francisco State College contemplating a master's thesis on the novels of Wright Morris. In December of that year he sent Morris a list of questions relating to the novels. This letter is Morris's reply to most of those questions. It has been edited slightly by Morris and Mr. Madden, whose questions and comments are noted within brackets.

Wayne, Pennsylvania

December 7, 1957

Dear David Madden:

On the assumption, gratefully assumed, that you have made your way both in and out of Darkest Morris, I greet you at the edge of the clearing with a bottle of cherry phosphate and some fatherly advice. I take it you have a copy of your map in hand, so let's begin at the beginning:

> [What is your estimation of Wayne C. Booth's essay ("Two Worlds in the Fiction of Wright Morris," *Sewanee Review*, Summer 1957, 375-399) on your novels?]

Booth's report strikes me as sound, in the essentials, and it had much of interest to say to the author. The theme of audacity, as I would describe it, in one or several disguises, and many variations, emerges from all of the books. We begin with it in *Uncle Dudley,* and we last confront it in *The Cannibals,* where both Horter and the Greek improvise on the "act of bolting." *The Cannibals* seems to have thrown you off stride, as it did many of my readers, who were happily nested in the groves of Nostalgia. It is the purpose of that book to shake the sentimental leaves from all those mythic limbs. You will not find this achievement of much interest until you have processed your own past, and come to terms with your inheritance of raw material. Having written ten books on this subject, I can appreciate your engagement. But there can, and in my opinion, should, be an end. In **"The Territory Ahead,"** [incorporated into a book with the same title published by Harcourt Brace in 1958] an essay in *The Living Novel,* just published by MacMillan, you will find a summarizing statement on American writing and writers, on technique and raw material, that will answer many of the questions you have about Morris—and raise others. Insofar as my books and opinions interest you, I cannot urge it on you too strongly. It should serve as a statement, to which these notes may be appended.

> [Are your novels in the "realistic" genre?]

Realistic etc.—all of my books testify to the function of *verisimilitude*: the life-like look that conveys the sense of life. No theories here: this is how the mind works, or how it doesn't. What I want is a sense of life so real it evokes a little more than life.

> [You use some of the same character names, and indeed some of the same characters, throughout the novels; different characters have some of the same very particular memories, sometimes almost verbatim. How intentional is this common memory store?]

In putting my puzzle together—a fairly literal description—I began with no conception that a pattern might emerge, or that this emergence was a latent, groping form of conception. (See **"Territory."**) The pieces of the jigsaw that keep turning up (figures like Tom Scanlon; the unemployed heroes, Charles Lawrence, Boyd, etc.; men who feed birds, open cans with forks; bowls that contain the past, like an urn; paper weights where it is forever snowing, and clearing, and snowing)—these are the keys to the house of fiction. A writer shapes them to open doors with them. The room and the view will be different, but the key is the same. In *The Field of Vision* you see me arranging familiar pieces in a new pattern. A beginning. Much still to be done. It could not be done at all, however, while I was trapped in my own material. In those self-dug graves lie the bearded giants—face down.

On this subject we might prattle happily forever. It is both denser and more complex (the life of these fragments) than is evident in the published books. *The Works of Love,* a key book in this matter, in an early, wonderfully incoherent draft, contained the gist of all these potsherds in a flow reminiscent of Bridie Murphy. By the way—and a very *large* by—the University of California at Berkeley has a quantity of Morris manuscripts in their library, just waiting for the likes of Madden. . . . In the many drafts of the key books you will find some questions answered, others raised. But there, my boy, is the site of Morris-Troy. Bring up your wooden horse!

> [One of your finest qualities is the subtlety of your un-
> derwriting, by which some large feelings and ideas are
> generated; but sometimes one gets lost. For instance,
> Dudley's audacious behavior is often enigmatic.]

Dudley is caught in the Morris field of vision, that magnet that buzzed in Lawrence, Boyd, [Agee] Ward, and [Earl] Horter, obliging him to be something of a damn fool in order to be himself. Blake plagiarized me here, as he does elsewhere, when he said that a fool who persists in his folly will become wise. I know that what you want to know is WHY—the simple, bare-faced motives, and indeed they are bare. The old fool merely wants to show himself a man. Underwriting—which seems to be a species of underwater swimming—has its many disadvantages, and that is one. Is the pool empty? That is how it often looks. I still have, in my possession, a *very* early manuscript that appears to be in Hindu. It is also *very* long. There were giants in the earth in those good old days.

> [Why do so many characters—the Boy and Lipido in
> *Man and Boy,* for instance—resemble birds? Is this
> motif related to the image of the wetting of the bread
> with spittle before feeding it to the birds?]

I seem to find birds a sympathetic and lucid form of symbolism. The old man and the spittle is an instance. Fact and imagination, dream and reality, the caged and the uncaged—flight with feathers on it.

> [And eggs. The novels are well-stocked with eggs. The
> theme of Sherwood Anderson's "The Triumph of the
> Egg" seems dominant in *The Works of Love,* which
> you dedicated to Anderson.]

And EGGS. Let us, my dear Boswell, clear this matter up. That damn Anderson EGG has long haunted me. Long before either Morris or Anderson hoped the egg would triumph or break, my father had the dream—à la Brady—of a chicken farm in Nebraska. About 1916. *The Works of Love* is true to the atmosphere. The egg—from which all birds come (see above) entered my life the HARD way, and that is very much the way it is working out. HARD. I will NOT say we have seen the last of them. It may seem hard to credit, with my affection for Anderson, but I had never read "Triumph of the Egg" until a review of *The Works of Love* called it to my attention! So there we have it. The small, small world, the large, LARGE egg. I suppose it was the dedication to Anderson that encouraged the tie-in. Well, HE would love it. What egg could triumph better than that?

> [What other writers have influenced you?]

On the subject of writers and influences—very tricky at the best—a clarifying point. I read madly in college (where I discovered books) but nothing at all contemporary. (To correct this oversight a dear overseeing lady gave me a copy of *The Fountain* by Charles Morgan!) I began to write without a model or style, without *any* useful notion of form and conception, which will help to explain a very long five years of apprenticeship. I wrote novels of childhood, several of them, then I began to write the dense, prose-poem sort of things . . . that eventually appeared in such a book as *The Inhabitants,* facing the photographs. It is writing that led me to photography—and you will see why if you study the prose pieces. I was trying to lay my hands on the object *itself.* The photograph seemed the logical way to achieve such ends. It was *one* way, of course, but a writer's way is another, and these artifacts, thousands of them, go on turning up in my books. That *Uncle Dudley,* my first published novel, resembles no other book so much as itself, is due to the background I have described. Your nostalgia, I'm afraid, kept you from sensing the close affinity, both in style and substance, that *Love Among the Cannibals* has for *Uncle Dudley.* We have come full circle—I came, that is, full circle without being aware of it—and *The Cannibals* marks a fresh engagement with the present, rather than the past, which has now been re-experienced. I am not, in any sense, through with it—*The Field of Vision* is the first act of organization—but I am finished with immersion. In the waters of my fathers I have been dipped. This may be the great American baptism, since all our writers of consequence have to go through it. In my opinion (vide **"The Territory"**) damn few survive. Immersion is immolation.

I admire writers as diverse as Hemingway and Camus, Mann and Joyce, Kafka and Lawrence, but I observe, increasingly, that this admiration is remote from imitation, and may have little to do, as in the case of Lawrence, with the major novels, or the public figure. One book, or a few pages, may suffice to include a man in the personal pantheon. The writer who writes more than he reads, as I do, will develop the faculty of appraising, in a short exposure, what it is that he seeks, and what it is that nourishes him. Whether the twig bends to water or not, the writer bends to the currents that feed him. All others are merely distractions. He truly *learns* only what he can use.

In this matter, as in many others, I refer you again to **"The Territory Ahead,"** where I have stated, as clearly as I know how, relevant opinions on writing and writers.

> [One of your major and unique abilities is to achieve
> dramatic intensity and interest without the crutch that
> action often becomes in American literature. Why do
> you eschew action and focus retrospectively upon a
> few memorable events?]

The notion of what is dramatic, novelistically speaking, is apt to be either fashionable or clichéd: the meaningful object, or the meaningful event, is precisely what the writer must imagine, and in this *act of the imagination* are such elements of drama as he finds necessary. It is the *imaginative act,* not the action of events, that reveals the artist of stature—the action of events can be learned by formula, and often is. My problem as a writer is to dramatize my conception of experience, and it may often exclude, as it often does, the entire apparatus of dramatic action. The impassive life of Brady is instructive in this point. His life, for me, is full of meaningful action on the level of awareness. This is also true of *The Cannibals*—with its pattern of surface action—as it is of *The Works of Love,* where the action is submerged. (See Chapter 3 of **"The Territory."**) What a writer *does,* not what he should do, not even how well or badly he does it, is the only imaginative fact of any consequence. This is now all but forgotten. It is assumed books are written to provoke discussion. Actually, they are conceived to make discussion irrelevant.

[Even while you were a photographer, did you feel yourself becoming a writer?]

This is answered in my remarks on an earlier question. I began as a writer. In my effort to possess the *ding an sich* I tried the resources of photography. They are considerable but limited. Reality is not a *thing* but a *conception,* and the camera cannot conceive. I tried to overcome this limitation by a marriage of sensations in the mind of the beholder: *The Home Place* and *The Inhabitants.*

[A dirty question, but one raised emphatically by your works: how do you regard women in our society?]

Women? A very dirty question, indeed. But *Woman,* that is another matter. My opinions on this subject have been formulated, with my problem in mind, by Henry James. (Vide: *The American Scene.*) Betrayed by Man (deprived of him, that is), woman is taking her abiding revenge on him—unconscious in such figures as Mrs. Ormsby [in *Man and Boy*] and Mrs. Porter [in *The Deep Sleep*], where she inherits, by default, the world man should be running. Since only Man will deeply gratify her, the Vote and the Station Wagon leave something to be desired. One either sees this, or one doesn't. As of now both man and woman are tragically duped: the Victor has no way of digesting the spoils.

[What explains Webb's very moving act of kindness in *The Deep Sleep* when he lays the watch where Mrs. Porter can find it?]

Webb's act reflects his respect for the forces that both salvage human life and destroy it: the pitiless compulsion that testifies, in its appalling way, to the spirit's devious ways of survival.

[Your novels declare that you are haunted by Nebraska, the region of your childhood. Not since Thomas Wolfe has such lucid and meaningful nostalgia pervaded a body of work.]

Not since Thomas Wolfe? My dear Boswell, Mr. Wolfe tried to do the impossible—and failed, naturally. Mr. Morris is much more ambitious. It is the possible he wants, and sometimes he gets it. . . .

[How have your novels been received outside the United States?]

Too early to say. German editions just now appearing. *The Deep Sleep* seems to be the most exportable. It did very well in England, and has been translated into German and Italian. The English critical scene has a familiar incoherence. *The Field of Vision* was the object of considerable irrelevant abuse. . . .

[In what direction are you now heading in your work? *Love Among the Cannibals* doesn't seem to begin a direction that you would be likely to follow very long.]

I have been dropping hints all along the way. The biggest hint you preferred to ignore, since it didn't suit your pattern. *The Cannibals.* A deliberate putting aside of the familiar nostalgic pattern. An effort to confront, in Lawrence's terms, the poetry of the present, where the strands are all flying, and the waters are shaking the moon. When a writer does that rare thing—stops doing what he knows how to do, and endeavors to do something more—it is instructive that those who hold an interest in his work should be the first to cry havoc. When we are less engaged with the nature of our pasts, and have unreeled our minds to come to terms with the present, we will, I suspect, find *The Cannibals* a much different book. If I should prove to be a writer of some interest, it will prove to be one of my most interesting books.

Ray B. West Jr. (review date 1957)

SOURCE: "Six Authors in Search of a Hero," in *The Sewanee Review,* Vol. LXV, 1957, pp. 498-508.

[*In the following review, West uses Morris's* The Field of Vision *as a touchstone for evaluating several other novels published contemporaneously with it.*]

Reading as many as six novels at a time cannot fail to give one a generalized sense of what might be happening to the novel form. When all six are by American authors and when they all appeared within a few months of each other, the impact is likely to be more concentrated and, we might hope, more trustworthy. The impression may be of hope or of disappointment, without regard for the merit or failures of individual works. In the case of the present six books, the impression was distinctly good. There is not a really bad book among them. Some are more limited than others. At least one is slightly disappointing when seen in terms of the author's previous works. Yet the general impression is one of health, and for reasons which I, for one, was not prepared to expect.

We have become accustomed in the past few years to feel that the American novel was in a kind of slump. It has been attacked for its thematic insignificance and for its preoccupation with technique and form. Inevitably, it has been subjected to comparison with our modern masterpieces—such novels as *A Farewell to Arms, The Sun Also Rises, The Sound and the Fury, Light in August,* even *Studs Lonigan* and *U.S.A.,* to say nothing of *The Great*

Gatsby. Even so skillful a contemporary as Robert Penn Warren has suffered from such comparisons, and the question has arisen: Where can our younger novelists turn to find their own voice and subject matter?

I do not intend to suggest that the present group of novelists have answered that question. It was less the achievement of these novels that impressed me than it was that so many of them seemed to be working towards the same thing. In a superficial sense, they are not too different from other groups of novels I have read in the past few years which have left me with a sense of depression. They are still for the most part novels of definition, which means that much of their effort has gone to survey (to limit and examine) their subject matter. Such a method, in the recent past, has led to the construction of thin, sophisticated works, which made often insignificant comments upon American life, or it has led to the writing of overly clever and ingenious social comedies, where no comment was intended, unless it were to suggest the author's superiority to his subject.

If, as I say, the present six novels are still working towards a definition of their subject matter, they do nevertheless do something rather unusual in this decade—they turn their focus away from the general aspects of modern society and aim it towards the singular and the unique. Instead of showing concern for the alienated individual, lost in a lonely crowd, and suggesting that he should be one with the mass, they consider the possibilities of singularity, not as a course, but as a possibility for greatness. In at least five of these novels, there is a hero (or a concept of heroism), either on the periphery or hovering behind the scenes, who serves to concentrate the meaning and to define the subject matter in terms to which we have been long unaccustomed, at least with the proficiency with which it is accomplished here.

The clearest instance of this tendency is Wright Morris's novel, **The Field of Vision,** where a group of Americans are brought together at a bull fight in Mexico, and where each is somehow transformed momentarily by the nature of the spectacle before him. As the author expresses it early in the book:

> What a crazy goddam world, Boyd was thinking—and so made room for himself. Also for Dr. Lehmann, the celebrated quack, with nothing to recommend him but his cures, and Paula Kahler, the only sort of failure he could afford. Also for old man Scanlon, the living fossil, for McKee, the co-inventor of the dust bowl, for his wife, the deep-freeze, and her grandson who would live it all over again. Here gathered at a bullfight. The sanded navel of the world. Gazing at this fleshy button each man had the eyes to see only himself. This crisp sabbath afternoon forty thousand pairs of eyes would gaze down on forty thousand separate bull-fights, seeing it all very clearly, missing only the one that was said to take place.

The focussed attention of the bull-ring serves to return a group of mediocre, small-town characters to their own moments of small triumph in a Nebraska town where they grew up together and to reveal to them, briefly, the extent of their lost opportunities. To oversimplify what is presented through an exceedingly skillful portrayal, we might say that Mr. Morris raises, and in part answers, the question: What has happened to the hero in our time? Americans, he says through one of his characters, are by profession heroes, but they are by situation unemployed. Their heroism is all of the past or of the future. Yet, simply by raising the question, he also suggests that the potential for greatness exists in taking the risk: "Man, his arms spread wide, could only take wing on the thrust of his past, and at the risk of toppling forward on his face." "To eliminate the risks," he says, "you simply did not run them. . . . The object was to *be* the champ, not to meet him. That entailed risk."

What Mr. Morris does with these tantalizing hints, I should like to defer until later, because the important thing for the moment is that he raises the question of the nature of heroism in our time. Equally important is the remarkable similarity of most of the remaining novels of this group to his, at least in their preoccupations. Elizabeth Spencer's *The Voice at the Back Door* presents the reaction of a small Southern town to an attitude which can only be called heroic. It presents incidents in an election for sheriff, where the campaign explodes dramatically over two issues; the enforcement of prohibition and equal rights for Negroes. In terms of local customs, one of the candidates, Duncan Harper, almost achieves the stature of hero in his stubborn determination to protect the rights of the Negroes and to insist on the enforcement of the state's liquor laws. But the true hero is not at the center of the action, as Duncan is, and he exists more as a point of measurement—as a means of defining—the actions of the other characters. He is a Negro, Beck Dozer, and his is the "voice at the back door," of the novel's title. He is, indeed, more of a voice than a character, but a voice which arouses the complex emotions of a town confronted by a problem with which it cannot deal except in the old way of violence and terrorism. Beck is the son of an educated Negro who lost his life in a cold-blooded massacre years before, and Beck's father has become a symbol, not only of the white man's guilt, but of the black man's danger. Beck himself has felt impelled to carry on what he considers an advance towards equal rights for Negro and White made by his father, even though every gesture he makes constitutes a risk of his life. The realization of Beck Dozer's dream (to use an expression common in recent American fiction) would, if successful, represent a break-through from the world of mediocrity into a world of idea as compelling as that of most traditional heroes (consider Captain Ahab's attempt in *Moby Dick* to break through the mask of nature that confined him), had the author chosen to treat it as such. But the point is, Miss Spencer almost willfully withholds the role of genuine hero from him. Beck Dozer is less a symbol than are Wright Morris's shadowy bull-fighters, but since the intent of the novel is rather to define the other characters than to display Beck's heroism, it is primarily as a symbol that he functions.

Similar to the manner of Miss Spencer's novel, almost to the point of incredibility, are the events of Harris Downey's less pretentious novel, *Thunder in the Room.* Here, where the situation is also set in a Southern town, the author deals not with the Negro problem, but with common justice and the community's attitude towards it, exemplified by the separate reaction of individuals towards the fate of a condemned man. David Yancey has been sentenced to death for the killing of his superior officer on the police force in a fit of passion, and his impending execution touches the lives of the principal characters of the novel: Governor Madden, who might have granted the reprieve, and his wife, Stella, whose almost-total energy is devoted to adorning the governor's mansion and who believes that he should be protected from those who would waste his time and energy, as well as Lucy Warren, a former school teacher of the condemned man, who is convinced an injustice is being done. That Mr. Downey was interested in more than what his publishers claim for him ("insights into human limitations insights fused with forgiveness and love") is suggested by several specific references in the text. At one point, he has one of his characters say, "A leader of the people is a conformist. . . . He has no insight of his own; therefore, no courage. Oh, tomorrow, perhaps. Who knows when a leader will arise? But not today!" Later, the same character remarks, "A leader must be original; but be willing, even eager, to accept the responsibility for decision. Like the artist! . . . Like the hero!" The question of artist as hero is one that needn't detain us, except to remark that it is pertinent to events in Mr. Downey's novel, for the governor's daughter, who is in a kind of adolescent rebellion against him and his world, hopes to become a musician, while Lucy Warren's dead husband, whose presence permeates the book, has been a promising writer; but the important reference points clearly to the governor's failure in the Yancey case, on a simple level, even to Yancey himself, as potential or symbolic hero. In fact, Yancey is reminiscent of a much greater symbolic hero, Billy Budd, in Melville's final allegory dealing with the nature of heroism, for both are destroyed by an act of passion, unlawful, but not necessarily unjust. Yet Yancey is not at the center of this novel as Billy Budd is in Melville's, and it is rather the lack of heroism in the governor that is exploited, not the potential for it in the condemned man. Like the bullfighters of Morris's novel and the Negro of Miss Spencer's, Yancey serves merely as a force to trigger the events.

In a slighter work than any of these, Mark Harris's *Bang the Drum Slowly,* the world of baseball is examined in a not too dissimilar manner. Harris's story is told from the point of view of a successful pitcher in one of the major leagues, Henry Wiggen, in a manner somewhat too reminiscent of Ring Lardner's *You Know Me, Al* stories, but it deals less with Wiggen than it does with the whole team's reaction to the fatal illness of another player, Bruce Pearson, who is dying of Hodgkin's disease. It is Pearson's illness, known at first only to himself and Wiggen and Wiggen's wife, Holly, that serves to transform the little world of competition and jealousy into a scene of warmth and compassion without becoming overly sentimental. Harris prefaces his work with a quotation from an earlier Wright Morris novel to the effect that a book containing scenes of bullfighting is not necessarily a book *about* bullfighting. *Bang the Drum Slowly* deals almost exclusively with baseball players, but its author is correct in his implication that it is a book about something more. How much more depends, in part, upon how one views the possibility of baseball to convey that larger and more universal world that it is designed to image. As symbolic hero (and despite Hemingway's use of Dimaggio in *The Old Man and the Sea*), the baseball player is at least once removed from the bullfighter, who is not merely playing a game but is facing possible death each time he steps into the ring. Nevertheless, Harris's style, comical in its exaggeration, does create a pathetic situation in the events surrounding Pearson, and he shows the compassion of Pearson's teammates, not so much as a quality of the novel's setting in the baseball world, but as a quality of general human compassion. In its own terms, *Bang the Drum Slowly* is skillfully done, but its terms are slighter (if not unrelated to our central problem, through the transformed baseball squad; transformed, be it said, as a kind of response to Pearson's minor form of heroism) than are the terms of most of the novels here under consideration.

The most unabashedly pretentious of these novels (and I do not mean the term in a bad sense) is Mary Lee Settle's *O Beulah Land.* In her portrayal of the settlement of the eastern frontier of America in the eighteenth century, the author seems to me to be returning to subject matter of great promise and complexity and treating it with a skill that is not uncommon in American novelists today, but which is exceptional in most novelists who have dealt with American historical subject matter. After a somewhat blurred opening, where chronology seems to have been unnecessarily violated, Miss Settle brings her many characters together to depict the development of western lands in the days preceding the Revolutionary War. Heroism is not too large a word to use in describing many of these events, for the complications of settlement in a territory claimed by the Indians, administered from across the ocean, and desired by men and women of more than the usual ambition demanded courage and devotion to a dream no less intense or valid than that which we have asked of traditional heroes. Miss Settle makes no attempt to "debunk" or limit her characters, as has been so common in the historical novel of recent years, nor does she treat them sentimentally; she portrays them in all their primitive nature, somehow without detracting from their heroic stature. In fact it is their heroism which transforms them and raises them above their generally commonplace origins. T. K. Whipple once defined heroism "to mean strong in the primitive virtues—the animal virtues, if you like—physical vigor, physical courage, fortitude, sagacity, quickness, and the other qualities which enable man to survive in an uncivilized environment." Given these qualities, as Miss Settle has them in her novel, and given too the fact that the Western settlement of America has become almost a national myth, the subject matter alone of *O Beulah Land* is exceedingly promising. Yet to say that Miss Settle has achieved a national epic would be to claim too much— more, perhaps, than the author herself would care to maintain.

In this novel, the action is too dispersed, there are too many characters and not a strong enough focus upon a single one. The method of its telling (despite what I have said about the necessarily confused chronology) is a little too documentary and explanatory, thus limiting the events too much to their particular area and never quite raising them to their mythical potentiality. We are told by the publishers that Mary Lee Settle has planned a whole series of "American historical novels," and it may be that this series may turn out to be a single novel—an epic of the American drive westward—and this we can at least hope for, because *O Beulah Land* as it stands now, gives the impression of being a lengthy fragment of a very long and very important story.

What is significant about this novel, to my mind, is the manner in which it lays the groundwork for the heroic novel, not merely attempting to define its conditions. Compared with its conception, such a novel as Saul Bellow's *The Adventures of Augie March,* despite Mr. Bellow's more competent execution, seems a mere exercise in social comedy. Mr. Bellow's name is not irrelevant here, not only because when it appeared *The Adventures of Augie March* seemed a daring move away from the predominantly self-investigatory novel, but because we are called upon also to consider a more recent work of his, a collection of one short novel and three short stories titled *Seize the Day.*

In considering the short novel, which appeared originally in *Partisan Review* and which gives the collection its name, it may be unfair to demand too much, for it seems likely that this is a volume put together and offered to the public, more to keep its author's name alive between more important projects than as a manifestation of Mr. Bellow at his best. Yet, put forward it has been, and here it is now, fortuitously gathered together with these five other novels for review. Such an accident may be Mr. Bellow's misfortune, or it may be my own, for in the context of this review it can serve only as contrast.

The principal character of *Seize the Day,* Tommy Wilhelm, seems almost perversely unheroic. The events of his day, which make up the story of the novel, although rendered with Mr. Bellow's usual skill, consist of an accumulation of small worries and small meetings, none of them very important in itself, but all of them together combining to effect a sense of almost absolute frustration. In some respect Wilhelm is a composite of the weaker characteristics of Augie March, without Augie's ingenuity or ambition. Caught in a web of failure in business, in marriage, and in relations with his family and friends, he succumbs finally to a kind of (not genuine grief but) boundless self-pity. After the final event, which is the loss of his money in a stock gamble, Wilhelm joins a crowd of anonymous

mourners at the funeral of a man unknown to him, where he gives himself up to his frustration and weeps openly, protected by the occasion where he is mistaken for some member of the grieving family.

The ironic point that Bellow seems to be making is that Tommy, submerged in the public mourning, is protected from the glare of the isolation into which he has been forced by his failures; or, to put it another way, that man in isolation is more open to public responsibility (the grand failure) than is he who merges with the public mass. As a kind of case study of mediocrity, then, the story of Tommy Wilhelm has its own interest, and in Bellow's handling of it, a certain pathos. Despite the seriousness with which I have stated its intentions, the story is essentially comic, perhaps even consciously patterned upon those traditional comedies where the foibles and fables of mankind are parodied by the actions of a character of a low order. In such terms, *Seize the Day* may be granted its small success. What is most disturbing about such a success, however, is that it represents a return on Bellow's part to interests nearer to those of his first two novels, *The Dangling Man* and *The Victim* than to the more significant concerns of *The Adventures of Augie March.* What I mean is that Bellow made his initial reputation as a novelist by the force of his portrayals of what has become known, rather tiredly, as the alienated man—attempts, presumably, to depict and examine the lot of modern man, dissociated from society. In his third novel, *The Adventures of Augie March,* he appeared almost to reverse his direction, for Augie, although he remained an isolated figure in many respects, was one who gloried in his differences, thus suggesting the possibility that such an American character, if he could not obtain true epic stature, could at least enjoy the fulsome stature of a mock hero.

Tommy Wilhelm is neither of these, nor was he intended to be, and it may even be unfair to ask that Mr. Bellow, in so slight a work, demonstrate the direction his career is going. Nevertheless, it would be asking too much of a reviewer to demand that he give up the attempt to find out, particularly when, in this particular group of novels, he finds Mr. Bellow lagging behind authors of lesser experience and reputation. Of all these novelists, Mr. Morris is the only one who might conceivably be considered the peer of Saul Bellow in this respect, and it is because I should like to suggest what seems to me to be the superiority of Mr. Morris's present concerns to those of Mr. Bellow that I have reserved the right to conclude this review with a further consideration of *The Field of Vision.*

I suppose what it all boils down to, finally, is that Mr. Morris seems to be working toward a definition of the hero, with a suggestion lurking that there might yet be a place in contemporary writing for the emergence of the epic novel (and in this he would seem to be supported in one degree or another by four of the novelists examined in this review), while Mr. Bellow appears to suggest the futility of heroism in our time, and to suggest that the greatest need is for some means of public communion. Because

I have already, by implication here and in statements elsewhere, taken sides on this question, I will not go into the relative merits of the two positions, but rather point out more specifically what appear to be the qualities and the virtues of Mr. Morris's theme.

As I have said, *The Field of Vision* is not a novel *of* heroism, but in subject is the idea of heroism. None of his spectators at the bullfight is a hero, yet as they view the spectacle before them, each of them does reach back somewhat wistfully into his own past for memories of courage and passion: the failed writer, the unsuccessful farmer and his convention-ridden wife, the young son who wears the trapping of heroism in his Davy Crockett hat, the disillusioned psychiatrist, and the withered pioneer. "What had happened?" one of the characters asked His reply:

> The neatest trick of the week. All that one had to do to tame the bull was remove the risks. Along with the means, that is, the meaning dropped away from it. Instead of bulls, prime rib on the hoof; instead of Crockett, nurseries full of records; instead of frontiers a national shortage of coonskin hats.

In other words, he goes on to say, "You eliminated . . . the amateur. He ran the risks, he made all the errors . . . and in every instance he lacked the professional touch. . . . What [you] saw might be vulgar or cruel, botched like the amateur's kill in the bullring, but the passion behind it, the force in the blow, the absurd risks, the belief in lost causes, had in it something that struck him as beautiful. What was it? Until he saw a bullfight he didn't know."

Yet this character, who is the defeated writer, recalls less his failure as an artist than he does the time when he ran with a group of young boys onto the baseball field and ripped the pocket from Ty Cobb's uniform, for this was a moment of genuine excitement when the risk did not matter. It was, as he acknowledges in the telling, a kind of mock heroism, contrasted with the true heroism of the bullfighter, but the elements were the same. Heroism was not art, it was in a sense, foolishness, but it reminded him of "the origin of species."

> In New York he had often watched children, spied on them, that is, since it seemed to him that children, and only children, led passionate lives. The life, that is, that Boyd—once a prodigy of action—no longer lived himself. They struck out blindly, they laughed and cried, they cheated, hooted, looted, heartless and generous, at the same time. They *represented the forces he felt submerged in life* (my italics). All the powers that convention concealed, the way the paving concealed the wires in the street, the sewage and the waste, were made visible. The flow of current that kept the city going, the wheels turning, the lights burning, and the desires that made peace impossible in the world.

Mr. Morris does not use my term, heroism, in describing his intentsions, which are given as a kind of combined preface and blurb on the jacket. "The range and nature of the plains imagination," he writes, "—its audacity, however ill advised, and its practicality, however illusive—contain elements that are peculiarly American. Out of this tension grows one of the durable dreams of American life." Mr. Morris does not so much utilize the dream as he defines it in this novel—contrasts its aspirations with the facts. Since his own imagination is, presumably, the "plains imagination" he mentions, perhaps this work represents a kind of exploratory searching out of the subject, the staking of a claim, so to speak, for a work of truly heroic proportions. At least, this is the promise that seems to hover over *The Field of Vision.* It hovers, too, to a lesser degree, in all of the novels of this group, and it is the sense I got of a group of authors searching for a hero, or for the source of heroism in our day, that gave rise to the very real, if very unusual, general effect they created.

Robert Gorham Davis (essay date 1958)

SOURCE: "Readers and Writers Face to Face," in *The New York Times,* November 9, 1958, p. 4FF.

[*In the following essay, Davis reports on a symposium discussing the writer's role in mid twentieth-century America, in which Morris was one of the participants.*]

Recently *Esquire* magazine and the Writers Club of the School of General Studies, Columbia University, both celebrating anniversaries, joined in inviting four highly articulate writers to take part in a two-day symposium at Columbia. The results were dramatic but puzzling. The writers expressed very vividly feelings of alienation, feelings they found difficult entirely to explain.

At such symposia, which flourish in the colleges, the topics are always impossibly broad ones. This means that intellectually nearly anything goes. One posture is as relevant as another. The topic this time was "The Role of the Writer in America." The participants were Wright Morris, Leslie Fiedler, Saul Bellow and Dorothy Parker, all successful writers and sharp observers of the native scene, all serious humorists for whom humor is a mode of truth.

The audience, though a sophisticated one, well used to such affairs, was in for a shock. It found itself on trial. Instead of being the audience, it was the accused. The first two speakers, Wright Morris and Leslie Fiedler, took the offensive at once. They talked not of an America in the abstract, but an America sitting in front of them in the auditorium. They criticized the way this America regarded writers and writing. What they particularly disliked, apparently, was exemplified by the present symposium. They distrusted the motives that led people to ask writers to get up in public and talk about the role of the writer.

Public recognition of the writer is harmful, they said, if it is the wrong kind of recognition. Grants from foundations, professorships in colleges, invitations to appear in symposia, feature stories in weekly magazines, even making the best-seller lists—none of this is any good, if the writer is not read as he wants to be read, if no one really hears what his works are actually saying. "Never," said Mr. Fiedler, "has serious writing been less relevant to people's lives and decisions than in America today."

Audiences turn up at symposia because they are interested in the writer rather than the writing. They know the writer from what they have read about him, not what they have read by him. "The purpose of the book review," Mr. Morris said, "appears to be to dispense with the book." Praising the feature of *The New York Times Book Review* called "And Bear in Mind," he wondered whether the books listed were not more often borne in the mind than in the hand—if, indeed, a mind existed. How much mind for books was there in this "mindless America, preoccupied with adolescence and obsolescence"?

Mr. Fiedler was even angrier at what is being done to the writer by those who pretend to value him most. The public role of the American writer is "not tragic or pathetic, but simply absurd." His position combines "a maximum of alienation with a maximum of recognition, a maximum of irrelevance with a maximum of security." The contemporary novel, Mr. Fiedler said, is taught in the classroom, and once it has become a classroom experience, it is something to be lived down, grown away from, regretfully abandoned, like fraternity parties.

"Loving writers, however, is *chic,* like philosemitism or driving foreign cars. People want to love writers—or rather they want to *seem* to love writers." He cited Dylan Thomas, and said that if Thomas had not been very acute, his experience might have fooled him into thinking that this country was full of people who spent their time reading his work.

People want the writer, Mr. Fiedler said, to be the symbol of an alternative way of life. The further he departs from the conventional stereotype, the more he fascinates the public, as happened with Dylan Thomas, Jack Kerouac, the Angry Young Men. But this is humiliating. When the writer begins to disappear into his public role, then the joke is on the artist himself. At that point it is time to stop laughing.

Messrs. Morris and Fiedler were the principal speakers at the first session of the symposium. But time had been left for comment from Saul Bellow and Dorothy Parker, and for questions from the floor. Mr. Bellow and Miss Parker dissented politely. Perhaps the amount of attention and material support writers were receiving had been exaggerated somewhat by the previous speakers—at least *they* had not received so much—and perhaps America was not quite so mindless as Mr. Morris suggested.

The emphatic response, however, was from the floor. Mr. Fiedler had declared belligerently that the writer's proper role is a nay-saying, a destructive one. He should not hesitate to bite the hand which feeds him.

In the audience a forest of bitten hands began waving. The listeners, who thought that they valued literature, were baffled and exasperated. Yet just because they took writers seriously, they were troubled by what they heard. Why destructiveness? What was really wrong? How did America figure in all this? Before anything could be straightened out, the session had to end.

When the symposium reconvened the next evening, there was obvious tension. Everyone was aware that a confrontation had occurred, the kind of I-thou confrontation the existentialists talk about. Writers had met readers and made serious charges against them. The readers were troubled, but so were the writers. Nearly every speaker referred to after-thoughts and a restless night.

Saul Bellow, the first speaker, began gently, asserting that when he was writing, he was absorbed in his story, and felt no antagonism to society. He criticized writers who, in the tradition of Flaubert, cut themselves off from society, suffered over their writing, and let that suffering and isolation darken the vision of life their fiction expressed. But if the secretary of a foundation came to him and offered him ideal conditions for his work, what would he ask for? He realized that he would be tempted to ask for nothing less than a new society, free from the appalling falsehoods of the present one. In it the people as a whole, including writers, would be more open and communicative, more finely consious. Figuratively speaking, men would "eat persimons, and sing ballads, walk on stilts."

As it is, Mr. Bellow said people expect writers to create a rich life for them. But how many writers in America lead a public or private life in which there is richness they can pass on? Too many of them suffer in isolation within social forms they are tired of.

Miss Parker in her prepared talk, did not think that the writer should complain, or expect privileged treatment. His function is to write; he is a worker like any other. The question is: How good is his work? When an audience is interested in him for any other reason, it is the audience which is absurd. Spokesmen for the Beat Generation, "Jack Kerouac and all the little kerouacs, going about in their lumbermen's jackets, saying 'New, new' and turning sex into the dreariest of calisthenics" may receive a lot of attention. But this is quite irrelevant, since what is printed by them does not come under the category of writing at all.

The serious writer, Miss Parker said, has to take blows and not complain. Otherwise he should not be a writer. The writer is an Aesop traveling through a forest in the dark of evening. Out comes a wolf who runs after him, bites him in the leg, and says, "There, Aesop, go home and write a fable about that!"

Miss Parker's acceptance of her lot did not satisfy Messrs. Morris and Fiedler, whom she had mildly spoofed. Wright Morris agreed that he had met appreciative readers. There were others who asked him which of his books he would recommend their reading. But mostly he found Americans in a state of distraction which breeds a deep fatigue that they seek to remedy with further distraction. In this state they cannot read the book; they want the writer to be the book for them.

Mr. Fiedler, who had waited a long time, came up boiling with eloquence. He, too, had had afterthoughts. He, too, wanted to clear up misunderstandings, by making even more emphatic what he had said the afternoon before. The writer as nay-sayer must attack not only society in general but especially those who seem closest to him in their allegiances. As father, citizen, he may join the P. T. A. or a political party, and work within their partial truths, their partial lies. As writer he can accept nothing but total truth. To everything else he must say, like James Joyce and the Devil, "Non serviam." The Jew must be false to Judaism, the liberal to liberalism.

The writer, Mr. Fiedler went on, must "assert the values of the impulsive life, the Id, against all ego ideals, he must engage in a holy war of destruction, not against values, but against the illusion that society is living by any values at all. He must say 'No' in thunder. Knowledge even of what is terrible and sordid and disgusting is itself beautiful."

The audience, which had been stirring angrily, as if it might be moving to lynch Mr. Fiedler, relaxed a little at hearing the word "beautiful."

When Fiedler was calling for destructiveness, Saul Bellow had suggested that Hollywood and TV are the real destroyers. "Then we must destroy their destructiveness," Fiedler replied.

But what, Saul Bellow asked, about love? "Human feelings also lead to truth, and one of these feelings is love."

The audience greeted the long-awaited word with relief. "What about Tolstoy?" someone shouted. "Did he write out of destructiveness or out of love?"

Mr. Fiedler knew about Tolstoy. Tolstoy, he said firmly, put forward the most life-denying set of ethical principles ever formulated. In fact, Tolstoy thought that the human race should cease propagating itself.

As for love—and here Mr. Fiedler paused, pained that so highly charged a word had been used, as if someone had talked of the hydrogen bomb—as for love, "We ought to be able to assume that we all love certain things—life, the truth. But for the final love, Homer believed in one kind only, *amor fati,* love of fate, the ability to embrace existence, however terrible."

The audience drew in its breath sharply at this peroration, but its mood had changed. All the right symposium words had been used, "love," "truth," "beauty," "existence," even if in unfamiliar ways. Of the evangelical seriousness of the writers, of their sense of the importance of their role, there was no shadow of doubt. In this they were very American. But what the most emphatic writers were asking for, what

they thought was really wrong remained troublingly unclear. It had to do with America, with the American condition, but it remained finally undefined, unexplained.

Benjamin DeMott (essay date 1960)

SOURCE: "Fiction Chronicle: Wright Morris," in *Partisan Review,* Vol. XXVII, No. 4, Fall, 1960, pp. 754-59.

[*In the following excerpt, DeMott praises Morris for showing the "quality of life" of mid twentieth-century midwestern America.*]

The Nebraska plains and towns where much of his [Morris's] fiction is situated have little on the capacity of metropolis for suggesting the uncontrollable. On those occasions (*The Deep Sleep* or *Man and Boy* are examples) when Morris approaches the city, he does so only to concentrate on middle figures whose awareness of crisis ranges from minimal to non-existent. And as for his voice: it is invariably relaxed, wry, patient. "Come to the window," his new book says quietly as it opens:

> The one at the rear of the Lone Tree Hotel. The view is to the west. There is no obstruction but the sky. Although there is no one outside to look in, the yellow blind is drawn low at the window, and between it and the pane a fly is trapped. He has stopped buzzing. Only the crawling shadow can be seen. Before the whistle of the train is heard the loose pane rattles like a simmering pot, then stops, as if pressed by a hand, as the train goes past. The blind sucks inward and the dangling cord drags in the dust on the sill.

The tranquility of tone, the care of the composition, the evident desire to make even the most trivial event *occur*— these seem to stand in themselves for a total withdrawal from urgency.

Yet Morris's evocation of middleness, rural and other, has from the beginning had its allusion to ominousness, its hints of monster crabs seething noiseless and invisible in clipped, rose-bordered lawns. The suggestion of comical wars of nature is less misleading than might be thought. A notion of what surrounds and destroys the homely old objects of the Nebraska scene is brilliantly (and modestly) set forth in the jacket design of *Ceremony in Lone Tree*— red, brutal, bladelike wedges thrown down on the weathery wood spokes of a cart wheel. (The design is the work of Harry Ford.) But in Morris's writing the hum of the machine of otherness, incomprehensibility, seems in its subtle pervasiveness more like nature than nature itself, an encompassing, un-isolatable, half-comic force. The novel at hand, like *The Works of Love* and parts of *The Field of Vision,* is an ironic celebration of Scanlon, a 90 year old plainsman who knew Buffalo Bill. Newspaper agitation issues in a birthday celebration for the old man in a ghost town—an affair to which his family returns from suburbs everywhere in the land. The book is told in Morris's usual manner: a long view of the empty way station where the party is to be held; a series of static, more or less undramatized, shifts from consciousness to consciousness; and then one "galvanizing" event—an effort to enliven the ceremony that kills the pioneer with a paroxysm of joy.

There is more comic invention in this tale than in anything its author has done before—but the hilarity conceals neither the disabilities of the celebrants nor the elements of culture that are responsible for them. Boyd, a writer who left town young, is a self-acknowledged cripple; the impotency of the others is revealed indirectly. McKee, the plainsman's son-in-law, sits in his garage reading the paper outwardly "undisturbed," but inwardly trembling at the ferocity of the new youth (GIRLS KIDNAP HUMBOLDT FARMER). "Where did they come from? Were they born the way normal children were born? What troubled [him] was . . . the knowledge that nothing he could say or do would ever change their belief that he was their mortal enemy. Every time [he] entered a corner drugstore or blinked his eyes in a movie lobby he saw these youngsters gazing at him with their sightless eyes." McKee's wife, the plainsman's daughter, cannot believe in her own reality except when she is fumbling a grown grandson who terrorizes her. One of the plainsman's older great grandsons, Lee Roy Momeyer, works in a garage (it bears a sign that announces: "HAVE GUNS—WILL LUBRICATE") and shoots his grease gun at college boys who come too close to the pit, or uses it to "pin the flies to the wall. . . ." The sister of this figure, Etoile (Eee-toal) Momeyer, the plainsman's great granddaughter, keeps a card file on bust development ("Under Jayne Mansfield Etoile had written, *Not so hot*"). The father of the two, another of the plainsman's sons-in-law, is a postman who reads *Popular Mechanics* half the night, spends years working on a self-filling fountain pen, drives an old Fire Department Hupmobile with a dead red bulb on its roof, comes home daily from his route to "pick and dress half a dozen chickens," and then "goes off with his bow and arrow . . . until dark." Nor are the other inheritors of the past less sick or less mad.

It is said of their creator that he is the darling of the Litry—and *Ceremony in Lone Tree* does show signs, like Morris's earlier books, that he has read other writers beside himself, including Faulkner and perhaps even Nabokov (Morris is the latter's equal or superior on the subject of The American Road). It is also said of him that his people are weightless and insignificant, and as the foregoing catalogue indicates, the charge is just: Bud Momeyer the postman stirs only laughter, the burial procession of the quasi-heroic Westerner stirs only the sense of pathos—there are no giants on this writer's plains. The defense of Morris need not rest, however (as it has done in the past), entirely on his wit, or on his power to create out of emptiness a living scene, or even on his eye for such boondocks of the age as the castrating Female. His strongest claim is that alone among American writers he has an intuitive sense of the present quality of that life of the middle that has been spoken of here: a sense of waves of *kitsch*, buried Calvinism, bogus hatred (of the city), bogus

love (for the tough old mountain men, The Pioneers), fear of the bomb and disbelief in the bomb that now torment and now titillate the millions who still sit on kitchen chairs instead of on kitchen bar stools, who still play pinochle on Wednesday nights, who still think they themselves are bringing up their children. His accomplishment is that of persuading his reader that the doom of these characters is not different from, nor less a matter to be soberly felt than, the ruin of Village speech, the decay of Bar Harbor, or even (extravagant as it appears to say) the misery of 104th Street. It is probably fair to ask whether the present middle culture ought not to yield something better than a letter-carrying Robin Hood, and it is possible that the man who answers with a violent affirmative is a genius rather than merely another somnambulist "utterly removed from contemporary reality." But the possibility is hardly vivid enough to discourage a firm impulse of gratitude for the singer of Lone Tree. He is less than Tolstoy like many others, but he is alive, and were it not for what he has snatched from the Chiclet-dripping jaws of our hell, the Schooner State, these faint visions of real buffalo on real plains, and all trustworthy trace of the vanishing, self-destroying class might even now have disappeared.

Alan Trachtenberg (essay date 1961)

SOURCE: "The Craft of Vision," in *Critique,* Vol. 4, Winter, 1961, pp. 41-55.

[*In the following essay, Trachtenberg argues that Morris's work as a photographer informed his technique as a writer.*]

> Again, the mind must think of itself, of the conditions
> of its existence (which are also conditions of growth),
> of the dangers menacing its virtues, its forces and its
> possessions, its liberty, its development, its depth.
>
> —Paul Valery

The American literary inheritance has not been a comfortable one for modern writers. Often a burden with its preponderance of metaphysical themes, its shadowy people, and its eccentric styles, the native tradition has amounted to a free and robust language, and nothing more. For Wright Morris, however, that tradition is a good deal more than a down-to-earth sentence style. Morris has tried to make his literary past usable by inventing new forms for the old themes of innocence and corruption. His craft is his response to tradition. In Morris's view, expressed in *The Territory Ahead,* American literature has been dominated by the notion that the "raw material" of experience is more important than technique or the way in which that material is processed "for human consumption." Even though writers like Whitman and Mark Twain achieved their best work through a first-rate technique, they always preferred the "facts" of actuality to the "mind" of technique. This split between mind and fact, Morris points out, is based on the American version of primitivism, the belief that nature is real and purifying while society is artificial and corrupting. Starting with Emerson and Thoreau, Americans have behaved as though nature has its own pristine order which society (the world of Huck Finn's Aunt Sally) gets in the way of; reality, therefore, always lies somewhere else, where life is raw and unprocessed. Our culture has tended to place its hopes in "the territory ahead," which, as Mark Twain demonstrates, lies behind us in the pastoral idyll of childhood. The most American trait of our literature, Morris believes, is a lament for the loss of innocence and harmony, the "naturalness" of the past. Scratch beneath the hard-boiled and sophisticated disguises of Hemingway, Fitzgerald, and Faulkner, and you will find the Big Two-Hearted River, the green world in the eyes of Dutch sailors, and the freshly-cut clearing in the woods.

For Wright Morris, the pastoral dream-lament has lost its integrity. Huck Finn has been copyrighted into a pastel dream by Norman Rockwell. The "raw material myth" has become a soft-focus vision, tinted with nostalgia which the writer, and every man, must resist. The antidote to the American Dream that selfhood lies waiting fully formed in a "territory ahead" is hard and clear vision. As a writer, Morris has made vision a dominant theme. The craft of vision, at the same time, is his technique.

Morris's technique, I want to show, owes a great deal to the art of photography. Morris was a photographer before he became a novelist and, in an original way, remains a photographer in his novels. To call his works "photographic," however, is misleading. He is not mainly a pictorialist, although physical description of a high order is a mark of his style. Rather, photography has given Morris a rich sense of the technical and symbolic possibilities of sight in fiction. Throughout his work we find references to photographs and pictures and to images of lenses and sight; see, for example, the opening sections of **The Works of Love, The Deep Sleep, The Huge Season,** and **Ceremony in Lone Tree.** Two of his most interesting books, in fact, join picture and text in imaginative ways. But the clearest evidence of a creative incorporation of the lessons of one art form to the requirements of another is **The Field of Vision,** the National Book Award winner in 1957. In this novel, vision defines both theme and technique, and to understand their complexities we must first learn what vision in the photographic sense has meant to Wright Morris.

I

Photography has been a significant educator of artists for almost a hundred years. Perhaps most obvious and somewhat overemphasized has been its influence against naturalism in painting. "If the camera can see the real world better than I can," we suppose Picasso to have thought, "then why should I compete?" But the important movements in painting since impressionism have not been simply anti-photographic; they have been instead concerted efforts to represent more of the world than had been seen through traditional conventions. With Cézanne, sight itself became a new order of conception as well as perception,

of mind as well as eye. In the movement toward a reconstruction of the visual field according to its hard-rock components, the camera was an important ally; it helped defeat the old conventions, not by capturing them, but by showing, scientifically and mechanically, their inadequacies. First of all, through its ability to record the world of appearances more accurately than the hand, the camera gave painters a useful instrument for studying the details of form. Then too, and more important, the camera showed that the process of vision itself is more complex, more analytical, than the academic conventions had allowed. It showed that the eye does not merely record, but that it creates. Vision begins in the head.

For literature, the lessons were not as plain and dramatic. The wealth of detail in naturalistic and impressionistic prose is mistakenly called photographic, on the assumption that the details reconstruct themselves in the reader's mind to form a picture as accurate as a photograph. But this is a misuse of the adjective "photographic." If photography is a process of creation as well as selection, then the finished print of a serious artist is an accurate record *only* of the maker's vision, not of an honorific reality which awaits, fully composed, before the eye. The print, as Alfred Stieglitz more than anyone else convinced his fellow artists, is as much a contrived artifact, a created thing, as a cubist painting or a poet's metaphor (Picasso, in fact, recognized that he and Stieglitz were working in the same spirit). Writers like Dos Passos in his "camera eye" reveries and his montage technique, and Hart Crane in his visionary metaphors, are closer to a literary use of photography than naturalists like Farrell. But few writers so far have incorporated photography into their work with as much careful thought as Wright Morris.

Curiously enough, Morris's uses of photography are illuminated by his literary debt to Henry James. James is for Morris the only American writer who remained undamaged by the "raw material myth." If Norman Rockwell is the technician of latter-day pastoralism, creating the sweet illusion that our culture still has its young innocence, then Henry James, the "restless analyst" of *The American Scene,* is the technician with an alternative. James was the sole American writer able to face the present moment without "the consolations of the past, without recourse to the endless vistas of optimism." Morris simplifies James a good deal to make him useful, and what he admires, it seems to me, is less a philosophical outlook (James indeed had his own consolations) and more the craft which James founds on the "faculty of attention." This faculty for James is the ability to confront our immediate experience, in art or life, with all our capacities intact; attention is the way we make our experiences vibrant with meaning. This is the faculty which made James such a keen *observer* and which is displayed nowhere with more acumen and poise than in *The American Scene.* From that book of unparalleled insight into American manners and scenes, Morris has taken this passage as a classic formulation of the Jamesian point of view he wishes to adopt:

> To be at all critically, or as we have been fond of calling it, analytically minded—over and beyond an inher-

ent love of the many-colored picture of things—is to be subject to the superstition that objects and places, coherently grouped, disposed for human use and addressed to it, must have a sense of their own, a mystic meaning proper to themselves to give out: to give out, that is, to the participant at once so interested and so detached as to be moved to a report of the matter.

(New York, 1907, 263)

Here James describes a point of view toward "objects and places" which anyone familiar with the art of photography will recognize. Here is a point of view—an esthetic—we find in the memorable prints of Stieglitz, Paul Strand, Edward Weston, Walker Evans, and Morris as well. The "straight photography" of these artists is based precisely on James' "superstition" that, first of all, the objects which occur in the field of vision contain their own life, their own "sense," which has only to be *seen* to be known; second, that the camera is an excellent instrument for *seeing* in this sense of knowing (which makes the act of sight an act of participation); and third, that through the camera, what is seen can be kept at enough distance from the personality of the seer, to permit a "report of the matter." In photography, the enforced objectivity makes possible the passionate subjectivity of vision we feel in the prints of masters. The artist in photography gives us not copies of a real world, but the world *as it is seen* by the artist; the seeing makes the world real. In the hands of a "restless analyst," the camera transforms the idle sensations of sight into the "mystic meaning" of vision. The effect that one gets from the pictures of, say, Walker Evans (who collaborated with James Agee in *Let Us Now Praise Famous Men*) is a sudden arrestment of time, a jolting of the mind into a state of attention. He forces us to look and to see as we have never done before, and what he shows us in the faces and textures of his rural and city scenes is a "mystic meaning" almost too much to bear. Does any man have the right to look so closely? We ask this, not because privacy has been invaded (it has not; his portraits are posed, not "candid"), but because our own flabbiness of vision has been provoked and challenged. We are forced to experience a report of things with a sense of their own. Evans's pictures, and Morris's, are not invitations; they are imperatives.

In what was, I suspect, an effort to discover what lessons his photography had for his fiction, Wright Morris produced two unique books about fifteen years ago. *The Inhabitants* (1946) and *The Home Place* (1948) combine, each in its own way, words and pictures. These books are based on the photographic outlook toward the world which I have just described. In neither book are the pictures illustrations of the text, although they appear to be so in *The Home Place.* This is a short novel about the return of a Nebraskan to his childhood home after a thirty year absence. *The World in the Attic* (1949) continues this story, whose point is that "home is where you hang your childhood." (67) In *The Home Place,* the pictures are a dimension of the action separate from, but equivalent to the events of the narrative. If the theme of the book is the return of a "rural expatriate" and his efforts to revive the

past, then the pictures pursue this theme on the level of graphic reminiscence. The pictures of farm equipment, corners of rooms, sewing baskets, old chairs and stoves and shoes and newspaper clippings, beds and shaving mugs and lace curtains are all rich with associations, and together they reconstruct a "home place" on the visual level just as the hero tries to reconstruct it for himself on an emotional level. The narrative is in the first person, and the hero says, "I'm trying to get my bearings. I'm trying to feel at home out here." Each picture is a phase of past experience rediscovered; the entire sequence comprises a visual metaphor of the hero's emotional life.

One weakness of this book is that the pictures, which are all direct and straightforward, with an occasional close-up, compete with the narrative for our attention. Seeing them on alternate pages of the text, we cannot always experience them and the narrative simultaneously. This is avoided in *The Inhabitants,* a more successful and, for his fiction, more useful synthesis. This book has an entirely different principle. The work is structured on three separate levels, a brief monologue of an "I" who meditates on the theme of what an "Inhabitant" is, a sequence of pictures of vacant houses, and a short prose "voice" with each picture. The theme of the book is that objects and people have their own "look" about them, which comes from something that "inhabits" them. This something is, in James' words, their "mystic meaning," the "sense" they give out to the interested yet detached participant. The pictures of vacant houses are the "look;" the prose voice, sometimes third person, sometimes first person, sometimes dialogue, is a verbal translation of what "inhabits" the house. It belongs to the picture. "An Inhabitant is what you can't take away from a house. You can take away everything else—in fact, the more you take away the better you can see what this thing is." (2) The first person monologue, which announces the theme and pursues it through the book, referring to people and places he has known across America (mainly rural America), is the argument of the book. A section of the monologue (sometimes a sentence, sometimes more) and the prose voice (entirely separate from the monologue) face each picture. All three levels, then, are available at once to the reader.

This triangular structure creates a rich complexity in the book and looks forward to the narrative devices Morris has developed in his fiction of the last ten years. The monologue provides a narrative frame in the present tense (it is not an action, but an address to the reader, conveying a dramatic immediacy); the voices are taken as moments in the past stirred up by the pictures, which are in a present simultaneous with the monologue. Each picture and voice, meanwhile, is a separate moment of consciousness, in which a mind (the voice) confronts its own experience in the form of a visual equivalent. The voices, which, taken in their entirety, are disconnected, do not comment upon the pictures, nor explain them, nor are they in any obvious way related to the pictures. Rather, the voices emerge from the pictures metaphorically as vernacular translations. At the same time, the entire sequence of picture and voice comprises the consciousness of the "I" of the book; it is that upon which he meditates. In other words, the "I" (whom the reader both watches and joins) perceives his own mind by perceiving the picture and the voice, and the entire sequence, all at once. In *The Field of Vision,* the "I" has disappeared, or more accurately, it has been transformed into the implicit continuity of the work; while the voices, each confronting its own past and present experience, carry the entire narrative. Each voice is a segment of the entire action, which the reader reconstructs in his own mind's eye.

II

In *The Field of Vision,* Wright Morris assembles his characters at a bullfight in Mexico. There is a family group, consisting of eighty-seven year old Tom Scanlon, his middle-aged daughter Lois and her husband Walter McKee, and their young grandchild, Gordon McKee. Also at the bullfight is the McKees' old friend, Gordon Boyd, an ex-playwright who has been living precariously for several years. He is accompanied by two exotics, a Dr. Leopold Lehmann, Boyd's analyst, and the ambiguous Paula Kahler, another patient of Dr. Lehmann. The entire novel takes place during the two and a half hours of the bullfight. The characters are spectators, relatively stationary; the real action of the novel takes place in the consciousness of each character. Varieties of sight, including blindness, provide the major symbols of this highly symbolic work. Morris shows that each character, looking at the events of the bullfight, sees only himself. However, because they are unable to focus beyond the narrow rim of their own pasts, they do not really see themselves. Unable to see each other and to see themselves in the eyes of each other, they are figuratively blind. Their limited vision expresses their limited self-knowledge.

Morris exploits the symbolic suggestions of sight by means of a complex narrative form. The book is divided into twenty-four sections, each given over to an account of a single character's mind as it confronts the action occurring in the present (the bullfight). Morris lets us see the immediate action through the minds of his five sentient characters (Paula Kahler and Gordon McKee are presented only through the eyes of the others); from their references and cross-references to the events in the bull ring, the reader, functioning like an eye assembling particles of light into a coherent picture, can reconstruct a whole event which obeys the unity of time. The bulls come in, the ceremony begins, a man on horseback moves toward the center of the ring, then backs off, a boy from the stands suddenly springs into the ring and is gored by a bull, Mrs. McKee faints and Mr. McKee takes her to their car outside, Boyd squirts pop at a bull, and so on. The reader does not perceive these actions in a sequential form; rather, the action occurs as events of consciousness in the minds of the characters. The reader, in other words, perceives the character as he receives the event through the web of associations that comprise his mental life. These associations return to various moments in the past, both the immediate

past of the day before, sightseeing in Mexico, or the distant past of childhood. The time dimension of the novel is even further complicated by the presence of four generations, from Tom Scanlon to his great-grandson, Gordon Boyd. Also, Mr. and Mrs. McKee and Gordon Boyd share several experiences in childhood and young adulthood, and these experiences form yet another level of narrative.

Morris's use of several intersecting *personae* differs from the interior monologue technique in that each mind is presented in the third person. This consistent third person point of view keeps the reader at enough distance, we might say photographic distance, from the character so that he can see the character in several contexts at once, the contexts of the immediate action, of memory, and of the entire community of consciousness. The reader, then, is simultaneously aware of past and present, individual and community. He has the materials for an act of consciousness of his own, which is the perception of the "mystic meaning" in the groups of minds "disposed for human use" before him.

Some readers may find this method of structuring a novel especially trying since no single character serves as a central focal point. But Morris has tried to convert this difficulty into an advantage. The journey into the past becomes not only a psychic one, but a communal one as well. Through several novels in the fifties, Morris has been breaking away from the familiar disconnected hero who has made both the picaresque and stream of consciousness techniques so popular in recent fiction. In this novel, Gordon Boyd does have the lineaments of such a hero, and he does in fact become the character we care most about; however, his life in the novel is inseparable from the community of consciousness which creates a web of connection between him and the world. It is quite obvious that Morris intends to bring the dangling American hero back into a society, not to give him a comfortable social role to play but, instead, to confront him with his image in the minds of others, and by so doing, to teach him something about the nature of the mind itself.

III

As an epigraph to *The Field of Vision,*[1] Wright Morris quotes Satan's famous lines,

> A mind is its own place, and in itself
> Can make a Heav'n of Hell, a Hell of Heav'n.

Although this is a vain boast on the part of the fallen Lucifer, there is a great deal of "romantic agony" in these lines. The rebellious hero who cuts himself off from the source of his being, full of pride in his self-sufficiency and blindly confident of his powers to create a world in his own image—this is the familiar romantic hero of western culture. For Milton, of course, the fierce pride and unremitting egotism is an unerring measure of Satan's damnation. But in spite of the inevitable self-destruction of this hero-figure, his appeal persists. We find him throughout American literature, on the high seas and the open roads, as well as in the tailored estates of Long Island. Throughout Morris's work we find heroes of this sort whose huge capacities seem to bestow life upon their captivated followers; the others in their worlds are either witnesses or victims. In *The Field of Vision,* Gordon Boyd is such a hero; or at least he was. His heroics as a youth have left him stifled and empty as a man. As a boy, he had his earliest glory by ripping Ty Cobb's pocket from his pants after a game. Twenty-five years later, the pocket is still with him, now a rag he cannot lose, "the portable raft on which he floated anchored to his childhood." (61) As a young man, he stole a kiss from Lois Scanlon, while Walter McKee, her fiance who had not yet kissed her, stood by, smiling helplessly. Then Boyd dashed off with Walter to an old sandpit, boasting that he could do the impossible and walk on water. "Right up till he failed, till he dropped out of sight, McKee had almost believed it himself." (9) Neither Boyd nor McKee nor Lois has ever quite recovered, each in his own way, from Boyd's heroics. Even after years of not seeing Boyd, Mrs. McKee at the bullfight "didn't trust her own senses, and the ground kept shifting beneath her feet" (31) in his presence. But Boyd, alone of the three, struggles to release the hold of the past. In this novel, he succeeds as far as divesting himself of his personal myths, and touches "bottom." In *Ceremony in Lone Tree,* a sequel to *The Field of Vision,* he and the McKees, after a series of subtle re-enactments of the past, reach a certain harmony and peace.

What Boyd learns during the course of the bullfight is the necessity of "transformation." The world is not what it *seems*; sight is only the beginning of vision.

> What had *he* seen? How long would it take him to puzzle it out? He was now a jigsaw loose in its box, the bullfight one of the scarlet pieces, but he would not know its meaning until the pattern appeared. And that he would not *find.* No, not anywhere, since it did not exist. The pattern—what pattern it had—he would have to create. Make it out of something that looked for all the world like something else. . . . It called for transformation. Out of so many given things, one thing that hadn't been given. His own life. An endless sequence of changes, a tireless shifting of the pieces, selecting some, discarding others, until the pattern—the imagined thing—began to emerge. Death would fix the outlines. Frame the picture as no man would ever see it himself.
>
> (138)

Boyd's search for "his own life" begins when he realizes that having failed to do the impossible, to "walk on water," no other heroics remained. He says of himself, "Profession: hero. Situation: unemployed." Boyd found himself something like Huck Finn, who is left at the end with the spurious Tom Sawyer clichés of heroism on one hand, and "the territory ahead" on the other. Boyd had chosen as new territory the field of failure. When he came to Dr. Lehmann, he was a "dedicated no-man, one who had turned to failure as a field that offered real opportunity for success." (61) Lehmann recalls a prologue to one of Boyd's unproduced plays, in which

Boyd advised his public that he *hoped* to fail, since there was no longer anything of interest to be gained in success. He went on to speak of culture as a series of acceptable clichés. A photographer's salon where ready-made frames, hung on walls of rustically historical gardens, lacked only the faces of succeeding generations in the ready-made holes. This hand-me-down world defined the realm of the possible. The impossible—become a cliché itself—had been ruled out. This left the artist—Boyd himself, that is—with only one suitable subject and life itself with only one ironic result. This was Failure.

(62-63)

Through failure Boyd had hoped to reach his true self. He lived in poverty, unkempt and disheveled. But through Lehmann he discovered, sometime before the events of the book, that this too was a cliché, the reverse side of the Norman Rockwell coin. "The cliché of failure, like that of success, hung on the walls of the room he decayed in, and through the hole in the ready-made frame he popped his own head." (63) Because of his "armor of clichés," Boyd had actually failed to fail; he had failed, that is, "to touch the floating bottom of himself." He had come to Mexico with Lehmann to observe, and maybe write about, one who had indeed failed, had touched bottom, and who came up radically transformed and radically crippled. I am referring to Lehmann's other patient, Paula Kahler, the man who had willed himself into a woman.

Through Paula Kahler, the Tiresias-sphinx who poses the riddle of life but can tell no answer, and through Tom Scanlon, Wright Morris portrays the wider dimensions of Boyd's problem. Both had succeeded in transforming themselves, yet at the sacrifice of their ability to live fully. The ultimate self-awareness, which is self-creation, leaves its scars. In each, the mind has become so much "its own place," that it has closed the world out. Both are blind to the events of the world and of the bullfight; their sight turns only inward. Their blindness, then, is metaphoric. In Tom Scanlon, the paradox of transformation, being both self-creation and self-destruction, is particularized as American; in Paula Kahler, it is universalized. Scanlon, an old Nebraskan plainsman, lives only in a fantasy world of the frontier past. "When the century turned and faced east, he stood his ground. He faced the west." (38) Paula Kahler has gone even further; she has eliminated the past and all time. She lives completely in a sightless present. Also, both characters "died" sometime in the past—Scanlon in a recurring fantasy in which he sees himself lying dead on the western desert and Kahler in a serious illness ("She had been sick to the death—she had died, that is—and passed over to the other side. From there all things looked the same." 100-101) In their recreated worlds, sight in the usual sense is unnecessary. Paula Kahler sits wide-eyed and sees nothing; her head lolls to the side. Scanlon, in fact, "didn't know he was so blind until they came for him. In Lone Tree, where nothing had changed, he saw things in their places without the need to look at them. They were in their places without the need to look at them." (45)

In Scanlon's fantasies, Wright Morris recreates his own version of the American frontier experience. The divestment of civilization on the journey across the desert is a bizarre event; it is a symbolic journey through the inferno of self-discovery. According to the familiar legend, the inessentials are stripped away. But the legend is transformed in the imagination of Tom Scanlon who, although he reenacts in his dreams the crossing of the desert, had never been west of Lone Tree, Nebraska. And by making the crossing an imagined act, Morris is able to suggest its symbolic scope. Here is Scanlon's imagination working:

> The wagons were like ants in the neck of a bottle, and all along the trail, wherever you looked, they were busy putting something down, or picking something up. Everybody seemed to have a lot more than they needed, and right beside the trail, where you could reach out and touch them, were sacks of beans and sugar, and slabs of bacon stacked like cords of wood. Back on the plains people would trouble to hide it, thinking they would come back for it later, but there in the canyon they just dumped it beside the trail. Anything that was heavy, that would lighten the wagon, they dumped out first. Some had brought along every fool thing they owned, rocking chairs, tables, and barrels of dishes, and others had big framed pictures they would like for setting up house. Some had brought along books, trunks of fine linen, all the tools they might need for building a home, and you could see what a man valued most in his life from where he put it down. Towards the last you began to see people, friends who had sworn they would never part, or relations who had got too old, or too weak, left to shift for themselves. They weighed too much. So they were just dumped like everything else.

(85)

To see how accurately Morris has gotten to the heart of the frontier journey, compare this passage, with its grotesque humor, to the stagecoach scene early in Mark Twain's *Roughing It*. In both cases, the dumping of books and the paraphernalia of civilization is a necessary ritual. But Morris shows, more than Mark Twain, the ambiguous implications of the ritual. Here, the discarding of civilization means the discarding of people, of community. Tom Scanlon's imagined pioneers are unaware of what they are up to. "No matter where it was people had been, or where it was they thought they were going, they wanted it to be the same as wherever they were from." (85-86) What was dumped by one party was picked up by another, so that people would see, "ahead on the trail, what they had put down themselves a day's ride back." But no one stopped to pick up people.

In Scanlon's fantasy, the crossing of the desert is a journey through the hell in which a man must lose himself in order to find himself. Out there, while he is desperately searching for water in the hot sands, Scanlon stumbles on a dead body—his own. It does not surprise him. "There were two men within him, and he knew for sure that one of them had died." (167) And it was the better man of the two who had died, he believes, leaving the other man to

spend out his days dreaming of the first death. Scanlon, unlike his fellow pioneers, had touched bottom on his imaginary frontier and never recovered. But although the old plainsman had sacrificed the present to his fantasy of the past, his lesson is clear: the shortest way to heaven is straight through hell, and "the thing about Hell was that you had to go in, if what you wanted was out." (168) Paula Kahler, whose disconnection from actuality is more extreme than Scanlon's, makes this lesson universal and at the same time shows with what expense the knowledge is bought. Unable to endure the world, Paul Kahler merely changed his nature, making himself Paula and closing his mind into itself. The peace he—or she—finds is the peace of catatonic insanity. In her death-like sleep, she cries out, "Help!" Her transformation has taken place outside the community of men; by recreating her self so totally, she has destroyed herself. Her loss is a warning against so thorough a change. As Lehmann, who hears her cry and devotes himself to her, remarks, "There was no mind if the lines to the past were destroyed. If the mind, that is, was nothing but itself." (182)

During the course of the bullfight, which intrudes upon the characters as reenactments of past events or as metaphors of present conditions, the McKees, solid and average citizens of Nebraska, do nothing more than suffer in their own narrow visions. Happily married in appearances, they are ironically the least connected of the entire group. They fail to see each other. The book ends as McKee's wife gazes at him through the car window with what he misunderstands as her "serene blue eyes." He senses, however, that they are "ice-blue." But his sight ends with that perception. McKee, with his unseeing eyes, is a foil for Boyd; as McKee fails to see himself in his wife's eyes, Boyd, looking into the eyes of McKee's grandson, suddenly "detected a change in himself." This change is the critical psychological event of the novel. The boy's gaze takes Boyd back to a moment in his recent past, when, watching the "passionate lives" of scampering children in a New York playground, he dozed off on a bench.

> When he awoke the bullring was empty, the swings and teeter-totters idle, but a small child leaned against the heavy wire fence, her eyes to one of the holes. So absorbed with what she saw, or what she thought she saw, she gazed into Boyd's face as if he were blind. As if she could see into his eyes, but he could not see out of them. He felt himself—some self—in the midst of a wakeful dream. Had he dozed off with his own eyes wide open, seeing nothing? Had this child stood there for some time, gazing in? This child—for that was all she was, a soiled faced, staring little monkey—seemed to have seen in him what Boyd could not see himself.

(176)

The child, Boyd feels, "had run up the blind on his true *self,*" and he is unable to move or to close his eyes. He thinks he is mad or, perhaps, sane for the first time in his life. "Able to see, at that moment, from the other side. Behind appearances, such as the one he made himself." This is Boyd's moment of truth: by smiting his sight the innocent child, in short, has restored his vision. In this moment, the unity of Morris's theme and technique is perfectly clear. The act of seeing, with both passionate interest and detachment, is the appropriate symbol for the act of knowing.

Vision, Boyd has learned, is an austere form of consciousness. To see the real self through the veil of clichés requires the flexing of muscles flabby with habit. But the mind, Morris shows, is a perilous place. In striving to know itself, it runs the risk of knowing nothing else. Blindness, as for Paula Kahler, is the consequence of a too subjective sight. There is no way of avoiding the risk. Tiresias must lose his eyes to gain his sight. Americans, as a rule, have supposed that the gain can be made without the loss. Like his master, Henry James, Morris is an exception to the rule. For him, the gain of truth is the loss of illusion—and painful. That gain, for Boyd as for Strether, is the perception of oneself as a figure in a landscape with a "mystic meaning" all its own. Integrity of mind depends upon this vision of one's place in the composition.

Morris deserves our attention because he has thought deeply about man's dilemma in a New World which has promised the end of all dilemmas. In spite of its minor failings, such as an excessive symbolic contrivance, *The Field of Vision*—and this seems to me to be the highest praise—occasions serious thought by Americans about themselves as human beings. Morris's craft of vision focuses upon the community of men in America searching for a way to convert the loss of pastoral innocence into a gain of personal integrity. Vision itself is both the instrument and the substance of this transformation.

Note

1. All page references to *The Field of Vision* are to the Signet edition, New York, 1957.

Paul Levine (essay date 1962-63)

SOURCE: A review of *What a Way to Go,* in *The Hudson Review,* Vol. XV, No. 4, Winter, 1962-63, pp. 601-02.

[*In the following excerpt, Levine praises Morris's novel* What A Way to Go *as "shrewd, funny, and beautifully written."*]

Twenty years separates Wright Morris' first novel, *Man and Boy,* from his eleventh, *What a Way to Go.* Why in those two decades Morris' distinctive talents have been enjoyed by only a small coterie remains a mystery to me. Perhaps the secret lies in his great versatility which allows him the freedom continually to change his focus but denies us the liberty of ever pinning him down. More likely it has something to do with that slightly cock-eyed world of his, a world definitely mad but with a special madness that may be as difficult to appreciate as it is to depict.

A novel of innocents abroad, *What a Way to Go* describes the reluctant wooing of a forward American teenager by a retiring professor of English. The man is Arnold Soby, searching among the artifacts of Venice and Greece for his vanishing identity. The maid is Cynthia Pomeroy, finding amid the relics of Greece and Venice her emerging identity. Other travellers include Cynthia's two chaperones: Miss Winifred Throop, who affects a wig, indulges a weakness for tippling, and presents to the world "a face like that of Boswell's Johnson," and Miss Mathilde Kollwitz, a health fiend who approaches life with a Germanic thoroughness and about whom "there was no nonsense." Also on board are a slightly decadent Italian painter; a clutch of German *Wandervogel* including a miniature Austrian photographer who misses being *echt deutsch* by being 3/7 Jewish; a professor from Basel; and a roguish cat named Aschenbach after the hero of Mann's *Death in Venice.*

A bit of an Aschenbach himself, Soby is part Prufrock and part Strether, appearing "sensible, respectable, invulnerable," researching in libraries his life's work on "The Wisdom of the Body." Cynthia, on the other hand, is all things to all men: Primavera to the Italian, Nausicaa and Miss Liebfraumilch to the *echt deutsch*; Tadziu and Lolita, perhaps, to Soby. But whether "Primavera in Venice or Lolita in Winnetka," Cynthia is woman incarnate—a sort of Venus with braces—and the wisdom of the body which she imparts to Soby is of the kind that cannot be found in books. "Everyone his own Pygmalion," observes Miss Throop, and Soby, playing creator, finds himself created.

On the one hand, Morris is concerned with the differing aspects of creating beauty. "Was it not strange," Soby reflects, "that only lovers could compete with artists? Transform the object, that is, according to taste?" On the other hand, he is concerned with the differing aspects of perceiving beauty. "Or had that first glimpse of beauty," Soby wonders while watching Cynthia, "the word made flesh, established in man the two poles of his nature—to materialize and to spiritualize? To pass away in a delirium within sight of the beloved object, like Aschenbach, or to sit and stare like cannibals at the grape-stained lips."

In its central relationship between an aging man and a young girl, *What a Way to Go* is reminiscent of Morris' earlier work, *Love Among the Cannibals.* But it is a measure of his versatility that the two novels are so different, the one dealing with Aschenbach's delirium and the other with the cannibal's delight. As a satire of tourist manners in the old world and a travel guide to courtly love in the new, *What a Way to Go* is shrewd, funny, and beautifully written. May it bring to Wright Morris a measure of the popular success that he has deserved all along.

Wright Morris with John W. Aldridge (interview date 1977)

SOURCE: "The American Novelist and the Contemporary Scene: A Conversation Between John W. Aldridge and Wright Morris," in *Conversations with Wright Morris:*

Critical Views and Responses, edited by Robert E. Knoll, University of Nebraska Press, 1977, pp. 14-33.

[In the following interview, Morris discusses his place in mid twentieth-century fiction.]

[Aldridge]: In your critical book, **The Territory Ahead** *[1958], you talk about the American writer's difficulty in turning his experience into usable literary material; and you imply that he simply has too much material. I'd suggest that this has been the problem for American writers right up to your generation, but that now we have many novelists—people like Barth, Pynchon, Hawkes, Vonnegut—who don't seem to be making much direct use of American experience. They are turning more and more to what has been called fabulation, the creation of fables, the creation of fictions of fictions, parodies of fiction, and so on.*

I want to ask you: Do you think that this indicates that these writers can no longer cope with American experience? About ten years ago Philip Roth said that one of the difficulties with American life is that it is so grotesque, so outlandish, that it outdoes the writer's inventiveness. In effect it nullifies his power of imagination. Do you think this movement away from the direct or realistic reflection of experience indicates these writers are in that difficulty, or have we in some way used up certain essential experiences so that they have become so clichéd that you can't really get back to them?

[Morris]: It is almost twenty years since *The Territory Ahead* appeared. I was at that time concerned with an overuse of raw material, simple American experience or regional experience or the personality that seemed to be present in most of it. Faulkner was doing something with one part of America. Who else?

I think of Thomas Wolfe and Willa Cather.

Something had to be substituted for the regional experience that had already been processed into fiction. When I was asking the question, America had been "literally" discovered. Though not seen clearly by me at the time, young writers in 1955 were taking different directions. The whole concept of what could be interesting had changed for them. As members both of the American and the world community, they had begun to feel more than simply American sentiment. That question of raw material had already been bypassed.

Why do you think these novelists who are now about forty-five moved away from this realistic, impressionistic attempt to reflect and define the essence of American experience? Would you credit Roth's statement with any truth?

Well, it has truth for the satirist. A certain type of humorist is handicapped by the extravagance of the American scene. The satirist forces his experience into the grotesque in order to deal with it. If his work is anticipated by events, then he has nothing that is going to shock. He must anticipate the public, not follow along after it. It is idle to attempt to caricature American life if the caricature is already there. I am appreciative of the grotesque in the American, but I draw short of making it unsympathetic. For me behind this caricature is an element that is essentially appealing, no matter how abused or distorted it has become.

Don't you think that Bellow and Roth, to name two of the better Jewish writers, have an advantage in being able to draw on either childhood ghetto experience or idiosyncratic urban characters? I think Bellow tends to populate his novels with grotesques, people who are incredibly manic, tormented, angry, and so on. They just don't seem real to me—I don't know people like that. Black writers also have a very colorful, vital, intense experience to draw on. They have an advantage which most Anglo-Saxon writers do not have.

Then there is this other group—and they would be highly offended to be put into a group!—who are working in black humor and the surreal; John Hawkes in particular. You, Wright, have a steadily larger element of black humor, a very gentle black humor. Maybe yours is only gray humor. You've always had a sense of the preposterous, of the comic possibility in the rather rough-hewn types that we encounter in your novels. But there is some point, maybe in **Ceremony in Lone Tree** *[1960], where you begin to be more and more preoccupied with the outlandish; and in* **Cause for Wonder** *[1963] and* **What a Way to Go** *[1962], the whole landscape gets a little gothic. Some of your characters become almost as idiosyncratic as Bellow's. Do you feel conscious of this increasing grotesquerie?*

What you identify as "grotesquerie" is largely a question of moment and circumstance. *Man and Boy* [1951] is the first overt instance of this type of characterization, but that's early. I wrote that in 1948. If I'd written the same thing ten years later there would have been more edge in that portrait of mother. That portrait undergoes the complexity of a full-scale reconsideration in *The Deep Sleep* [1953]. There I take what I felt was something of a caricature, a grotesque, and I say, Wait a minute! There's something lacking in this! That woman represents something that is absolutely inexhaustibly mystifying to me, something that is both individual and, in another sense, American. She represents a continuation of the notion of default in the male. Henry James talks about the default of the man in America and how the American woman picks up the pieces.

I felt in rereading **The Deep Sleep** *that there is more of the real malevolence here than I see in your later work. I think Mrs. Porter is not made hateful enough. You were too kind to her.*

Your judgment there is at a great remove from the substance of my fiction. My fiction is not judgmental. I thought that in *Man and Boy* I had indulged myself at the expense of the human personality. It was too easy to make an absurdity out of Mrs. Ormsby—so Mrs. Porter in **The Deep Sleep** is a reconsideration of this woman. What her motivations are defy my analysis. She is not an assembly of human characteristics, and she is not merely a generic type. Mrs. Porter is unique.

She resembles a distinct middlewestern type of a pioneer. Some of my relatives are like that woman.

This is not my conscious intention, but in being just to my responses, to my intuitions, I produce an authentic terror, one which you can not dismiss as ridiculous and absurd. She is fundamentally different from similar figures that the Jewish writers observe in urban life.

They are caricatures.

Yes. Bellow used to be quite sensitive to the fact that characterization could become so facile that it would go over into the grotesque. But I sometimes feel that his talent as a writer, as an image maker, is at the expense of his characterization.

He has much talent for characterization, or at least for creating characters; whether he really characterizes deeply doesn't matter. He's so fecund that he comes up with character after character who is strange and colorful and melodramatic.

Much of what Bellow writes about comes directly out of his own experience. In fact, it strikes me that much fiction now comes unabashedly from first-person experience. Almost always the persona-narrator is indistinguishable from the author—he becomes a sort of conduit down which wash the author's fears, and torments, and longings.

Once the conduit is opened up, the flow continues. This identification of writer and narrator seems to be where Bellow feels at home. He has seldom departed from it.

The conduit really opened up in Augie March.

Yes. Where the writer and the narrator are the same persona, the writer waits for the experience to accumulate, then he processes it. For one reason or another this type of fiction is much appreciated today, and gratifies both the writer and the reader. It's a kind of confessional memoir that appeals on the level of the *roman à clef* to the intellectual, and the truth, the whole truth, and something more than the truth to the general reader. These readers do not want fictive distance. In fact, they want this "distance" eliminated. If they turn to my fiction it is this "distancing" that disturbs them. It is not the *other,* the fictive character they want, but the discovery or the confirmation of themselves.

They want confession?

Well, they want the facts, the nitty-gritty. They want to dispense with the intermediary—but the intermediary is the heart of fiction. Through it the author reveals, rather than exposes, even about himself. On the evidence the modern reader-viewer prefers exposure, and that is what he gets. It may be a subtle way of reassuring us about our "immediate present." The distanced experience is something else.

Does the first-person or pseudo-first-person writing these days exist because people feel that they can trust only their own experience; or if not that, somebody else's self-revelatory experience? Is this partly the result of the isolation people suffer now, their sense of solipsism? Generalizations aren't conceivable anymore.

The fact that we have a rash of this sort of thing indicates that there may be several areas of motivation. In a way I feel that the cause is not as complicated as you're inclined to make it. I think of the frailty of our ability to concentrate. We can bring very little intelligent energy to bear on an artistic experience now, and so we want the artistic experience to be immediate. We can easily justify our choices by saying we don't trust generalizations. We want somebody saying I, I, I—but a sophisticated reader knows that no one is less trustworthy than an I. In all of fiction absolutely nothing is so ambiguous and so ambivalent. In fact the only time the I-voice is really useful in fiction is when it is deliberately used ambivalently, as Camus uses it in *The Fall,* and there you ponder the whole novel to discover who the I is. Is it the author? We take delight in the perplexity.

This is ironical, isn't it? In the heyday of the New Criticism people were saying that what we want in fiction is not life *but* form—*that is, the ordered impression of life. And now we come all the way back to a demand for life as immediate and as raw as possible.*

And yet this is just an exchange of illusions. No one is working so hard at illusion as Bellow. He knows, as any writer knows, that you provide one illusion of reality over another which, for the moment, seems to have lost its appeal; but both are fictions. I worked on this in **About Fiction** [1975]. We should be free of any idea that one decade is going to be closer to reality than the next.

The appeal of this immediacy is, I think, tied up with the competitive spirit. Let's take a character like Mailer—such personalities introduce our problem right away. Mailer, through his natural gifts and those sympathies which are modeled on characters like Hemingway, comes into literature with the established, built-in assumption that fiction is essentially an ego projection, a platform. So why in the hell should Mailer talk about *he* when what he is really talking about is *I*? And with his characteristic effort to be candid Mailer gets into problems because he is also a promoter. Basically he is interested in furthering the simplification of the *I*. He makes "advertisements for myself" into an accepted art form; and he asks, Why the hell trouble with the whole fictive pretense?

He's not really a novelist. He's a fine writer, but I don't think he's a novelist.

He's a hell of a good writer. But what we're asking really is, Why should this mode prove to be so attractive? Mailer will be able to read Bellow, because he feels that he's getting less fiction through Bellow than he gets through other writers. Mailer does not read me because my writing is fiction, not well-or-ill disguised autobiography. I suspect that he no longer relates to "fiction." Somebody with a small talent but the ability to suggest "I'm giving it to you straight!" will persuade Mailer to sit down and read.

When he writes about his contemporaries, he tends to favor people who are much like himself.

And a tide is running in that direction. There is no patience now for distancing in fiction: the illusion that we can dispense with complexities by simply saying *I* instead of *he* is our most abused conceit. The long history of literature suggests that only when we learn to say *he* do we learn to see *I*.

Maybe most people are anxious for the authentic because they have so little in their own lives. They have so little sense of other people that to hear one man confessing something real—preferably agonizing—reassures them that experience is still out there and that it can be dealt with. We have a harder and harder time finding experience for ourselves, projecting ourselves imaginatively into somebody else's fictive experience. It is only when we feel that this story is not fictive, that this is right from the horse's mouth as you are fond of saying, that it can be acceptable to us.

This is an urbanized, sophisticated predicament. People in general do not participate in it. If I take a sampling of young people at random, if I dip hands that are tipped with honey into a group of people and come up with several dangling, if I did this in a non-urban environment these people would respond in a traditional manner. They would *not* put a story aside if they lacked instant recognition. They would *not* demand an instant serving. There's a parallel between hamburger chains and fiction—both strive to provide the instant servicing of need.

Now it was Bellow's particular gift to be able to meet this acute urban need. *Herzog* was read by writers and by readers who identified with Herzog. It was seldom read as fiction. The great pleasure it provided Bellow's generation was that of self-justification, self-recognition. God knows how many *Herzogs* were being written, and how many were put back in the drawer. Bellow wrote their story. Who needed fiction? What one wanted was what one felt good after.

Bellow's first two books were highly fictive in the Camus sense, not in the classic way; but he departed from all this and has never gone back to it.

Right. And why should he? *Herzog* was a mandate from the reading public, Bellow's public, that this was what they wanted, and it was what he could give them. It takes

a great talent. If he tripped, the pack at his heels would trample him to death. In many respects Bellow seems to write the novels Mailer has in mind, but does not write. Bellow is surely one of his inhibitions. The urban drama of Jewish life is the only intellectual drama we have. But that may be changing. The "intellectual" content of even urban life is now too thin and faddish to be of dramatic substance.

This is especially so when people are not sure what the real thing is any more. And it explains, to some extent, the popularity of the nonfiction novel which has been blown up into a major category these days. People want to be thrust into real events in an imaginative way. Normally they cannot comprehend the shape of events as they come through TV and the newspapers. When they get a sensitive person writing a nonfiction novel about, let's say, the march on the Pentagon, then they understand the event.

This is the most plausible audience-author relationship that exists. Capote touched on it in *In Cold Blood.* I am not like that. If I happen to write a novel about an assassination, everything that bears on the immediacy of the experience is irrelevant. I make that event instantly impenetrable, difficult to apprehend, impossible to find handles on: I muck it up into a novel; and it proves to be just as difficult to get at as fiction, even when it is presumably an immediate event.

I think this is a fashionable crisis, but the cinema has contributed its inestimable effect on what we take to be real. The cinema presents us with a look which both the sophisticated and the unsophisticated can accept as how things are. We feel when we look at a film that we're getting authenticity which does not require an intermediary. And so we come to the matter of psychic energy. Psychic energy is necessary to enable us to experience something that is *new,* or real; and energy that is used by the cinema can't be used for fiction. At one time anyone who was worked up, distraught, or bored had only the consolations of fiction. He might have had one or two other activities if he didn't read—possibly he could collect pictures or go to museums or study bugs or something of the sort, but the type of intelligence that was self-aware enough to want to *know* had limited options.

All those standing in line waiting for the next installment of Dickens have been stolen away from the novel by the film.

They're gone, and they'll never come back, not in our time.

You too probably saw a lot of films when you were growing up, didn't you? I did.

I didn't.

In the thirties and forties we knew a movie was going to give only one very incomplete, largely fantasy vision of ex-

perience, so I did not find any conflict in going home from a film and picking up a novel. The novel was giving me the real thing, while the films fed my daydreams. That is no longer the case.

This is one more aspect of the complicated reality that diminished faculties have to deal with, or so we sometimes feel. Instead of developing more faculties to deal with more difficulties, we find our faculties are becoming more constrained—in some ways even exhausted—while the difficulties with which they must deal are multiplying. The other day I was talking in the faculty club about **The Works of Love** [1952]. We have a young poet here, a very good young poet, a very attractive personality. Like many young people, he speaks out directly and competently, but he was stumbling around over some of these questions. Suddenly he made the reasonably obvious but nevertheless important observation that among his neighbors he didn't know anybody as well as he did the people in **The Works of Love.** He said, Here I know all these people, but I really don't know them, whereas the only people I know are in art! Well, that's why we have fiction; and that, in the last analysis, will keep it alive.

Then the other thing: He had seen a Bergman movie. What was it, *Scenes from a Marriage?* I've not seen it, but it had made a great impression on this young man. Here was the question that any writer today asks when he sees a great film: Is the film threatening me? Even if you're not a film maker, you say, Hey this is blowing on my neck! So here it is. The film is not a substitute for the novel because the film experience is elusive and you cannot return to it instantly. But the writer must consider in his own way: here is a competitor.

Don't you think the novel has benefited by appropriating filming techniques? You see them again and again in contemporary novels. Whether this is an imitation of one medium by another or some sort of simultaneous flowering of certain ideas, I don't know.

The film lived off the novel brazenly for half a century, and now it's become adult, so possibly some of this debt can be repaid. Up until recently the film had little for the writer—except for a few like Faulkner who could appropriate film technique. Of course anyone can see how to incorporate certain forms of experience from a Chaplin film; but in the main, film had simply been a distraction. Now we can't help but be affected by a great film. If the writer sees a good film, he incorporates that experience as he would an actual experience and it becomes part of his psychic equipment. Sometimes technically he may say, Ah ha! and then modify his narrative methods. Consider the increased ease with which the dissolve takes place in most of the young writers. They don't trouble with transitions at all. You're just there, and there's no problem. An older writer might say, Here's a transition problem; but the young are already finished with it. They just drop it. I am not much of a filmgoer, and I am too critical, as a "writer," to see film as clearly as I should. I may have an instant sense of challenge, but I am slow to absorb what is useful to me as a writer.

I think you've been absorbing film techniques for a long time, without direct imitation. You resort to a lot of filming devices.

You must remember that I'm a photographer, and in a certain sense I have anticipated film. I see in ways that are very filmlike without having been a film maker.

I see a lot of montage effect in your fiction, and a kaleidoscopic rendering: glimpses, glimpses, glimpses everywhere, more than one thing going on at once.

Even reasonably obvious multilevel narration is actually filmlike. The film *does* what I have to simulate. The writer ponders how to achieve a film effect without getting into what is technically audacious but not really convincing. He can do what Robbe-Grillet does, you know. He writes as though he were translating a scenario.

He makes a novel out of the filmlike experience.

Yes. He says, Let's see now, the car comes around the corner, and it comes and now it's a little closer; I'm beginning to pick up the sound; now it's gone; now look over here, oh yes, look at that shadow; it's just moving, oh, here it comes . . . here's the car now; it's a little, etc. He just gives us this, and he's intelligent and skillful, and the writer reads that with a sense of discovery, of more than novelty. It's fresh, it's there, but it was soon over.

Yes, those experimental people have gone far on that one insight and I'm a little tired of it.

I think Robbe-Grillet's *Jealousy* gets through to the writer-reader on the imaginative level. He comes out of it, I think, on a slightly different level of consciousness than when he entered. An enlargement, largely on the technical level. The writer who turns from Robbe-Grillet to his own work will sense that he is making a nice accommodation of what he has experienced to what he is now doing. In short, he's learned something. Even though briefly. In this writer's other volumes his theories about fiction reduce his practice to clever exercises.

*We have talked about your kind of characterization in other contemporary writers, and we have touched on the relation of the film to the novel. We perhaps ought to deal with the relationship of the world around you to the subject matter of your fiction. I think, for example, that as your work goes on, beginning maybe with **The Huge Season** [1954], you have become much more aware of violence in contemporary life. That book is haunted by the bomb, and so is **Ceremony in Lone Tree.** Perhaps crescendoing in **In Orbit** [1967] you get a much more direct confrontation with the really ugly violence that we've all become so aware of in the last ten or fifteen years. There are instances in which you're dealing quite explicitly with that.*

Is this new violence connected with the violence of the frontier to which you've recurred in your fiction? Are you suggesting that the new violence is the result of frustration people feel in not having a place to move on to, new challenges that the frontier once gave? The violence in those days somehow had almost a moral sanctity. We were bringing virtue to the aborigines, even if we killed them off in such numbers. Do you feel, when you're writing about these things, that there is a kind of metaphysic behind it? Are you saying that this is America without frontier?

Actually I am not that kind of writer. I'm not essentially a social commentator who looks around and perceives an emerging situation and then says, This requires my attention. What I have are preoccupations. The violence we sense emerging in my fiction is as unpremeditated in me as it is in the violent persons I write about. I deal with it thematically. I can't do anything but try to come to terms with it. I am part of the novel's predicament.

There are some interesting things here which I think will be true for me but not of many American writers, including the Jewish writers we were speaking of a moment ago. I am not an urban novelist. I am a son of the Middle Border; and however concealed, I represent a sensibility like Mark Twain's, right down the center. I will accept the absurd if I can see it in reasonably human terms, humanized essentially by humor. I will accept the absolute grotesque if I can see it in a context that makes it human. And in a sense that is what Twain did, but increasingly it has become an implausible way of handling American experience. When I began, it was still acceptable. We can see this in **My Uncle Dudley** [1942] and in some of my earlier fiction.

But those are cheerier books, you know, than the later ones. You have a dark strain that's getting more and more to the surface.

Those early books grow out of my acceptance of the varying types of American "humors." These are not just midwest types. They run the whole gamut of American experience. The violence is essentially historical and it's not excessive, given the melodramatic situations. It's accepted as a fact.

God knows violence was not new—either to me or America—but the energy released in the postwar incidents, like the war itself, was on a new scale. I discussed it with my friends. One of them would have been Loren Eiseley. We often talked about this in both the loose and specific way of two men who don't have to explain their terms. And right smack at that time—we're both midwesterners—comes the Starkweather incident in Nebraska. We had read about these different cases, but we had accepted them as some type of social or let us say psychological maladjustment that really did not concern the culture as a whole. Two or three people had been under too much pressure, say, and so they crack up and shoot eight people in Brooklyn; or somebody shoots seven people in South Carolina; or somebody shoots six people in Alabama, and so forth.

But the Starkweather case occurred in a place and among people where it was almost pointless to use facile psychological explanations. It forced a reexamination of the clichés associated with violence. Most of our reflections were anguishing reflections. We were distressed in a way that the violence on the television and in newspapers did not touch us. What had been rather easily accepted became a problem. It was on my mind, and on the minds of my characters.

You remember **Uncle Dudley**? A nostalgically comic and picaresque situation—a car full of picturesque vagrants on the high road to adventure—suddenly shifts to the interior of a southern jail. I had been there just the year before. It had given me much cause for wonder. As the open road adventure wound itself down, I was aware that it needed to wind itself up as it closed. The jail scene would provide Uncle Dudley with a chance, I hoped, to redeem lost time. This is what we find him doing in the novel. For most Americans of my time "bad" experiences, like wars, occurred to be put into books. Evils could be exorcised by writing about them. Perhaps the writer will never be wholly free of that naiveté. I had been badly scared—as Huck Finn had been scared—but I knew in my bones I would survive it. Wasn't this America? Didn't everything happen for the best? To move from this state of ignorance to that state of disorder revealed by Charles Starkweather has been the mind-quaking move of my generation. Violence can be a life-enhancing release.

But I think that the violence, if you can call it violence, in **My Uncle Dudley** *is much cheerier. It's more remote. I don't think you feel the horror anything like the way you come to later.*

Do you remember when the jackets of books described the author as anything *but* a writer? He was a dishwasher, a hobo, a "soldier of fortune," a migrant worker, a bus driver, anything but a writer. To *be* a writer, all of these real-life adventures had to happen to him. Jail was such an adventure, one of many often cited; war was also such an adventure, if the writer survived it. Love, too, hopefully, was an adventure that might be experienced at home, as well as in exile. These and other ordeals that writers are born to survive were necessary to the prospective author. A little late, I left college and went to Europe. It more than measured up to my expectations, and I returned as a young man authorized to write—in my own mind. This ceremony of innocence passed away with Gatsby and Malcolm Lowry's Consul in Cuernavaca. Most writers now know that events do not occur with them in mind.

Don't you find that you're getting to be more aware of the psychopathic nature of violence as the years go on? Take **In Orbit**. *There you're dealing with a psychopathic adolescent.*

I don't think of him as psychopathic.

How do you see him?

I see him as a rather ordinary, ignorant, open-ended American juvenile. He has an opportunity to do what we think of as irrational. I consider him absolutely normal and his seeming psychopathic elements are introduced by the options within his situations. These options gradually prove him to be distressed and to possess an element of violence almost equal to the storm that appears in the book. The situation creates the violence. He is not violence-prone at all. He is merely another young man on a motorcycle, full of beans, and he's young, and he's ignorant, and outside of that he's Huck Finn. He's anybody that you're likely to find who suddenly one day walks through a door and says, I feel like something is going to happen today. I wonder what it's going to be. Maybe I'll get on my little old bike and go out and see what's going to happen. And then life begins to roll.

And what happens is what happens.

To me, *In Orbit* gives a good—if small—measure of American life.

I keep seeing more sinister elements in your work.

I think there's plenty sinister in *In Orbit,* but I don't start with it, you see. This is crucial.

Is that a commentary on the whole generation? I saw this boy much more like a figure from A Clockwork Orange, *completely mechanical.*

Yes, the book excites that image in the first two or three pages, so it's almost unavoidable. But then I take the trouble to say, Look, that is how he *appears* but this is how he really *is.* He's just an ignorant kid, but let's see what happens.

You take artifacts from life which are clichés or have become encrusted with cliché, and you freshen and individualize them. You take this boy out of the newspaper headlines and you make him into that *boy. This revivification of stereotypes is prominent in* **Love Among the Cannibals** *[1957]. You consciously used clichéd material there.*

Yes, that was very deliberate and becomes acceptable because it had the enthusiasm of romp, and I enjoy that. That book should have a great sense of energy in it. It's a book that should carry you along. You should not feel that the writer is skillfully setting up pins to be knocked over.

There is a darkening strain as well as much playfulness in that book. The same rollicking occurs in **Cause for Wonder,** *and in* **What a Way to Go,** *but I wasn't aware of it in your earlier things. You were never morbid, malevolent, but you were awfully serious.*

I like to *think* the early books were laced with humor. They reflected my temperament, at the time sanguine, and my pleasure in experience—*any* experience. America seemed disorderly to me, but beckoning and rich. It had its brutal, its depressed, its disgusting side, but on the other hand it beamed with promise. It's the "but on the other hand" that dominates the early fiction. The first humorous touch of doubt is in **Man and Boy** [1951] where I am

dealing with the mystique of the well-emerged Mother image. Then come the complications. Have you read **War Games**? That book was written in 1951, but not published until recently [1972]. I think it's full of surprises, even for the author. More than any other book it supports your feelings about the "darkening strain" in my later fiction. This strain is so obvious, and yet so novel, I was advised not to publish it at the time it was written. It features both black and charcoal gray humor.

And that was certainly not in vogue in those days.

I can't tell you how unvoguish it was. That is hard to understand now. But out of that state of mind, we get these extremes of response that emerge with Boyd and Paula Kahler in **The Field of Vision** [1956]. Uncle Dudley's effort to become another person is a prelude to Paula Kahler's effort to become a completely different person, even to changing her sex. Now these are, in their way, extraordinary responses to American life.

This state of mind that makes itself felt a little bit in Twain was more felt in Melville, and in other American writers. There is a feeling that there is a force in American life; for all of its extraordinary buoyancy, for all of its sun, there is this yearning for darkness, for blackness. And even for a person of my temperament, which is as I say essentially sunny, this *other* makes itself felt with great persistence. Conceivably I would be the blackest black humorist—if I were not a son of the Middle Border. This is what spares me the essentially intellectual, essentially sophisticated, response. I start from scratch and build my mud figures and live in my mud huts, and then the storms come.

My concern is not to have these things in my novels brought to a conclusion, but to indicate that they represent states of American sensibility, of the American soul; and just as I am brooding over the alternatives, I want the reader to brood, too. I do not want to present anybody with a settled conclusion. The novels simply exist, like people you know outside the novels, like the writer himself.

And that's enough. That's quite enough.

G. B. Crump (essay date 1978)

SOURCE: "Introduction: The Two Sides of Wright Morris's Fiction," in *The Novels of Wright Morris: A Critical Interpretation,* University of Nebraska Press, 1978, pp. 1-27.

[*In the following essay, Crump discusses the conflict between the ideal and the actual, the relationship of time, memory, and imagination to each other, and the influence of Henry James and D. H. Lawrence in Morris's fiction.*]

Granville Hicks begins his introduction to *Wright Morris: A Reader* with a familiar lament: "Those of us who strongly admire the work of Wright Morris . . . are always wondering why everybody doesn't see his writings as we see them, as one of the most imposing edifices on the contemporary literary horizon. We, who look forward to each book of his as it is announced, and talk about it with excitement when it appears, cannot understand why so many pulses remain calm."[1] Indeed, the continued public and scholarly indifference to Morris, whose career as a novelist, essayist, and photographer now stretches over more than thirty years and twenty-five volumes,[2] is epitomized by the fact that *Wright Morris: A Reader* (1970) has pointedly not done for him what *The Portable Faulkner* did for Faulkner. If this neglect were deserved, of course, it would not be worth mentioning, but I believe, with Hicks, that Morris is an important writer. In an effort to demonstrate his importance and clarify his contribution to modern fiction, I begin this study by looking at some critical comments made about him which help to isolate significant features of his work. Since I believe that these comments represent an incomplete and sometimes inadequate view of Morris, I offer a new theoretical groundwork for criticizing his fiction. Specifically, I distinguish two broad currents in Morris's art, both of which must be taken into account in order to arrive at a satisfactory picture of it. When both are considered, I believe one can see that Morris's fiction encompasses a wider range of human experience than has generally been thought.

In a brief judgment, Alfred Kazin goes to the heart of what many readers must feel on opening a Morris novel for the first time:

> I confess that I have never been able to get very much from Wright Morris, though he is admired by influential judges. In reading Morris's **The Field of Vision,** I thought of George Santayana's complaint that contemporary poets often give the reader the mere suggestion of a poem and expect him to finish the poem for them. Morris's many symbols, his showy intentions, his pointed and hinted significances, seem to me a distinct example of the literary novel which professors like to teach and would like to write: solemnly meaningful in every intention, but without the breath and extension of life.[3]

Presented without illustration, this one-paragraph assessment (of a book which won the National Book Award) would effectively quench any reader's desire to look at the novel itself. The core of Kazin's indictment, the sense of incompleteness related to the presence of "significances" both "hinted" and "pointed," is unquestionably discernable in *The Field of Vision* (1956). In the following passage, depicting the failed artist Boyd's memory of a scene in a children's playground, the narrative voice is distinctively Morris's:

> A small child leaned against the heavy wire fence, her eyes to one of the holes. So absorbed with what she saw, or what she thought she saw, she gazed into Boyd's face as if he were blind. As if she could see into his eyes, but he could not see out of them. He felt himself—some self—in the midst of a wakeful dream. Had he dozed off with his own eyes wide open, seeing

nothing? Had this child stood there for some time, gazing in? This child—for that was all she was, a soiled-faced, staring little monkey—seemed to have seen in him what Boyd could not see himself. What she saw moved her to pity. Pity seemed to be all she felt. But what *Boyd* saw, and what *he* felt, was something else. He could not seem to close the eyes that she stood gazing in. He could not speak to her, smile or wink, or indicate to her that *he* was now present. He could do nothing. If the child had run up the blind on his true *self,* he could not run it down. He seemed to be fixed, with his eyes wide open, a freshly mounted trophy with the pupils of the eyes frozen open so the passer-by could look in.

> Had he been mad? For the length of that moment he might have been. Or had he been—as he had come to think—for once in his life sane. Able to see, at that moment, from the other side. Behind appearances, such as the one he made himself. Eagle Scout Boyd, the pocket snatcher, turned inside out like a stocking, so that the underside of the stitching showed.

> [p. 198]

There is definitely a quality of Joycean epiphany here, an intimation that something very important to and about the character is being revealed. Superficially Morris's method is more direct and explicit than Joyce's often is in *Dubliners*; unlike many of Joyce's characters, Boyd is a sensitive artist of whom we get a candid inside view. The passage contains relatively little of the dramatic irony and few of the external dramatic details Joyce frequently relies on to establish character and situation. The images in the passage are Boyd's own, deliberately chosen from his own experience, and if he knows to choose them, he should also know what they mean. Yet the full significance of his epiphany constantly eludes us, always escaping into the next sentence and the next, and the passage never seems to come to any resolution. Readers might very well feel that Morris expects them to finish the paragraph for him.

Nevertheless, I would suggest that while Kazin perceives an effect that is certainly present, he misses its purpose and its true character. The real quality of this passage is not incompleteness, but tentativeness. The rhetorical questions substituted for statements, the qualifying adverbial clauses beginning with *if* and *as if,* and the complete thoughts broken into two or more sentences—all capture the mind in the process of thinking, an effect readily recognized in more conventional stream of consciousness ("direct quotation" of the flow of thought using free association, a high concentration of figurative language, materials from prespeech levels of consciousness, and syntactic distortion), but often missed in the works of writers like Morris or D. H. Lawrence, where the narration is third-person limited omniscient and the syntactic distortion is slight.

It is especially important to recognize the tentativeness implied in Morris's style for what it is because the style reflects his deeper conviction that the truth of the passage remains relative, tentative, and a product of process, rather than an absolute. This explains why the prominent verbs are *seemed* and *might,* and it also explains why the novel as a whole is narrated through the eyes of several characters who perceive reality differently from one another. This feeling that truth is tentative is tied to Morris's belief that life, experience, and the universe itself exist in a state of constant becoming, a belief fundamental to an understanding of his work.

A second critical judgment illustrates that the nature and scope of Morris's fiction is not completely understood. In a recent book surveying contemporary American literature, Ihab Hassan lists Morris among several "prominent" novelists and yet seems uneasy with a sizable portion of his work:

> Satire and nostalgia mingle in Morris's work. However, in such later fictions as **What a Way to Go** (1962), a kind of lightness, an amusing triviality, begins to show. Hoping to catch the new mood of erotic comedy, he shifts his focus; his locale ranges from Italy to Mexico. But his lasting contribution lies elsewhere. Trained initially as a photographer, Morris composes in his best novels a montage of static scenes through which the lost life of Americans may be glimpsed.[4]

Since Hassan's book is a broad introduction, we cannot expect him to be an expert on every writer he mentions. Thus, he can be excused for repeating the common misconception that Morris turned to fiction after first being interested in photography,[5] and probably Hassan ought not to be held too accountable for the overall gist of his remarks. However, this comment does reflect a view, widely held even among Morris specialists, that only his American novels (often only his midwestern novels) and those with "static scenes" are of any account. "Nostalgia" is the war cry of this group. Their predilections are evident in a recent, more extended and specialized treatment, which occasionally sounds as if only the midwestern novels exist: "In **The Field of Vision** Morris finally hit upon the technique of developing several centers of consciousness within a novel, each representing a particular 'field of vision.'"[6] Actually, the technique first appears in mature form in **The Deep Sleep** (1953), one of Morris's best novels, although it is set in Pennsylvania.

The problem with this attitude is not the judgment it leads to on the relative worth of the midwestern novels; the judgment may even be correct. Rather it is that the work of a writer is no more divisible than his sensibility. What T. S. Eliot once wrote in an essay on Yeats is true of Morris: "You cannot divide the work of a great poet. . . . When there is the continuity of such a sensitive personality and such a single work, the later work cannot be understood, or properly enjoyed, without a study and appreciation of the earlier; and the later work again reflects light upon the earlier, and shows us beauty and significance not before perceived."[7] To see Morris steadily, we must see him whole, and the real challenge facing his critics is not to decide which books he should have written and which not, but rather to arrive at a perception of his career which

can accommodate them all—good and bad, those set in Nebraska and those set in Europe, those that are nostalgic and those that are farcical.

One critic to accept this challenge has been Wayne Booth. In an important article entitled "The Two Worlds in the Fiction of Wright Morris," Booth argues that Morris's fiction is structured around a cardinal distinction between the "phony" and the "real," between the everyday, time-bound world of "reality" in the ordinary sense and the timeless world of a deeper, more perfect platonic reality.[8] In Booth's words, Morris believes that "the real world, gruesome as it is, is not as real as it looks. To endure it, indeed to live at all, a man must . . . find a more genuine reality by getting 'out of this world'" (p. 377). There are three "bridges" available to him: "Imagination: the moment of truth" (p. 380), "Heroism: the moment of real action" (p. 377), and "Love: the moment of compassion" (p. 387). Thus, "whatever has been 'really' *done, imagined,* or *felt* has been, in fact, recreated, transformed from one world into another" (p. 395). Morris, then, is "attempting the fictional voyage of discovery into the nature of reality itself, and . . . he discovers the real in whatever is permanent in a world of change. The permanent is permanent by virtue of being outside of time and yet as human beings we discover it only in time, only in the world of impermanent things" (p. 394).

Booth's two worlds have special meaning for Morris's theory of art, but of more immediate interest is their relevance to his conception of time and, through that, to the theme of nostalgia mentioned by Hassan. For Morris, proof that an act transcends the real world is its power over the imagination, and the proof of that power is the vividness of its impression on the memory. Thus, the central tension between time and timelessness often resolves itself into a tension between the perceived present and the imperishable memories of the past.

The force of Booth's observations is best seen by applying them to a particular work. The first manuscript of **Cause for Wonder,** a relatively late novel (1963), dates from 1935,[9] making it one of Morris's earliest works in conception. The prolonged gestation demonstrates the power the book had over his imagination, and perhaps as a result of this power, it is Morris's most explicit and schematic examination of time and memory and is especially useful for purposes of illustration. Read in the light of Booth's observations, **Cause for Wonder** becomes a testament to the power of the imagination to rescue life from the depredations of time. The protagonist Warren Howe had spent an unforgettable winter at Schloss Riva in Austria, thirty years before the present time of the novel. He associates this stay with an artifact from his childhood, a castle in a snow-filled glass ball, which becomes a symbol of the past. Howe characterizes the castle in this paperweight as being "both in and out of this world" (p. 9), a concrete existent in the "phony" world of becoming which, by virtue of its power over the imagination, is preserved from time in a platonic realm of ideal reality (the ice-snow image applied to that which has escaped life as process is one of Morris's favorites).

In *Cause for Wonder* and several other Morris novels, movement in space is equated with movement in time. The novel's two-part structure follows Howe from California and "Time Present" to Schloss Riva and "Time Past." The trip to Riva, actually made in the present time of the novel, symbolizes the power of memory to recapture the past and produce a sense of time similar to that in the opening lines of Eliot's *Burnt Norton*: "Time present and time past / Are both present in time future, / And time future contained in time past." In *Cause for Wonder,* time, as experienced in the consciousness, amounts to "skull-time. . . . A form of daylight time salvage, a deep-freeze where time was stored like the mammoth in the Siberian cakes of ice" (pp. 268-69).

For Howe, the past is in one sense not unredeemable, not already behind him where the dark fields of the republic rolled on under the night. Nevertheless, both Morris and his critics have been concerned with Jay Gatsby's problem, the typically American nostalgia for a mythicized personal and historical past which no longer exists in fact. Nostalgia becomes a problem when, as for Gatsby and to a certain extent Howe, it interferes with man's functioning in the present.

Before attempting a critique of Booth's view, I think it would be useful to look at some of its further ramifications, as worked out in the four articles and one book by David Madden.[10] These constitute the most sizable body of criticism on Morris. Drawing on the theories of Booth and of Joseph Campbell in his study of myth, *The Hero with a Thousand Faces,* Madden argues that Morris's novels center around a "hero," who generally has transcended Booth's real world through "audacity," "improvisation," and "transformation." The terms are taken from Morris's own criticism. Audacity denotes the brazenness to try anything; improvisation, the talent for implementing one's audacious impulses with the materials of the moment; and transformation, the conversion of reality into fiction or ideal reality. The first two are tools, the last the product. But "the uncommon men exist for the edification of the common" (p. 28). Every hero has his witnesses, and it is sometimes they who achieve transcendence as their imaginations transform the heroics they have observed. For Madden, the interaction of hero and witness is at the heart of Morris's fiction: "A central, recurring theme in Morris' novels, around which many other themes revolve and through which his vision is often focused—is the relationship between the hero and his witnesses . . . who become in some way transformed as a result of their relationship with the hero" (p. 34). The Nebraska plains along the ninety-eighth meridian become Campbell's world navel, the source of mystic life to which the hero penetrates and whose power of transformation, traditionally represented as the elixir of life, he imparts to his witnesses. In these plains Madden also perceives opposite poles of the American culture and character; they mark the meeting point of

East and West, realism and idealism, agrarian novel and western romance (p. 28).

Again *Cause for Wonder* is useful for illustration: Castle Riva receives its imaginative charge from its resident heroes—the mad caretaker George and his no less mad employer Dulac. During Howe's first stay, George played practical jokes, like sweeping snow from the roofs onto unsuspecting guests below. During the second visit, George paints everything within reach white, symbolically recreating the snow of thirty years before. In this way, he preserves the past in the present. Dulac ensures that he too will remain both in and out of this world, like his ugly wife with the face of a frog and the voice of an angel, by inviting the latter-day guests to Riva for his funeral, even though he is alive when they arrive. Dulac's remaining alive after his death is announced is emblematic of his ability to cheat death through his immortal impression on his witnesses, and when he later throws himself down a hill, he deliberately courts death to cast his lurid charm over the boy Brian: "He had . . . taken the plunge. In what way could he leave a more memorable impression on the boy. . . . Senility had not deprived him of the wisdom of his folly. A dead man, he returned to life in the boy" (p. 189). Like nostalgia, the hero-witness relationship can become a problem since the hero, if the spell he weaves is too strong, can imprison his witnesses in a single heroic moment. Booth acknowledges this problem (p. 180), and it is central to Madden's work.

The criticism of Booth and Madden is so fundamental to a study of Morris that no subsequent criticism can afford to leave them out of account, and the debts I owe to them in this book are frankly ubiquitous. Nevertheless, I would like to suggest some qualifications of their views. Booth admits that transcendence as a response to the unpleasantness of reality is "full of the paradoxes that plague any mystical solution in 'real' life. Achieving timeless triumphs does not really deal with the world, 'the world of men here below.' Attempts to deal with 'this temporal kingdom, this bloody cockpit,' inevitably involve a man in evil. . . . Yet attempts to escape the 'battleground' leave the victory to 'the Prince of Darkness'" (pp. 395-96). In spite of this admission, Booth's choice of the label *platonic* inevitably implies a preference for the timeless. It suggests that reaching for the transcendent world is somehow a higher and better course than trying to live in this world, and both Booth and Madden tend to treat transcendence in itself as an unalloyed good. The main reason for this admiration for the transcendent, aside from whatever internal evidence is available in the fiction, is that they equate all kinds of transcendence with the transcendence of art, which Morris discusses in his critical writings and seeks to accomplish in his own art. Yet to assume, as Booth and Madden do, that Morris is setting up the artist's creation of a transcendental fiction as a model for his characters to emulate is a mistake. Although art is essential in character, realistic art, like Morris's, labors to give a representation of existential life, a sense of how life really is. Yeats perhaps best expressed the dominant sense of modern life when he wrote, "Man can embody truth but he cannot know it."[11] A man or a character does not set out to live with imagination; he sets out to live—to write, to make love, to build friendships, to hate some things and embrace others, to plant crops where there is no rain, in Morris's words, to "face the battle of daily life" (*The Huge Season,* p. 169)—and if in the end he lives with imagination, if his life has a style, it is because of the way he does the other things. No matter how similar the result, Morris and his characters really set out from two different directions. By approaching the novels as if they are primarily intended to illustrate Morris's critical dicta, Booth and Madden inject an unnecessary degree of abstraction into their studies.

Moreover, the Morris who emerges from Booth's essay and from Madden's two early essays is Morris near the middle of his career. He is one Hassan would feel at home with, for this is largely the nostalgic Morris of the midwestern novels.[12] A more comprehensive view of his work, especially one which includes novels like *What a Way to Go* and the novels since *Cause for Wonder,* suggests that, while he recognizes the value of transcendence in art, Morris's feelings about it as a goal for people and characters are ambivalent and subject to change.

I suggest Morris's fiction should be examined using a somewhat different conceptual framework from Booth's. It is one which can be supported in the novels as a whole, which places books like *What a Way to Go* in relation to Morris's overall work, and which also throws new light on the quality of tentativeness observed earlier in the passage from *The Field of Vision.*

Morris's most comprehensive statement about the relation of life to art is in *The Territory Ahead* (1958): "In the novel it is conceptual power . . . that indicates genius, since only conception responds to the organic pressures of life. The conceptual act is the most organic act of man. It is this that unites him with the processes of nature, with the nature of life. If man is nature self-conscious . . . art is his expanding consciousness, and the creative act, in the deepest sense, is his expanding universe" (p. 229). Anyone prepared to find an emphasis on the transcendental character of the creative act will be surprised to find it tied so closely to a nature very much in this world. The stress on conception, consciousness, and the preeminence of the creative act is characteristic, but no more so than the emphasis on nature and process. Art is man's expanding consciousness. Since expansion implies process, it can occur only in time, only in a world which is in a state of becoming. Art represents the evolving consciousness of the artist, unfolding to the eyes of the beholders an ever widening moral horizon, and consciousness, the faculty whereby nature knows itself, is the most advanced product of evolution. Physical and imaginative conception are related acts. Morris's career reflects this world view. The gradual maturing of his craft and the evolution of his attitudes toward

his material are instrumental to the tentativeness in the Boyd passage and have helped to make his fiction the best example of sustained creative growth in modern American literature.

The emphasis on the dynamic and organic is so intrinsic to Romanticism and is still of such great importance today that there is no reason to attribute Morris's ideas to any particular source. The philosophy of Henri Bergson, however, is especially helpful and appropriate to use in studying Morris, first, because Bergson's view of time resembles Morris's so closely, even employing some of the same images, and second, because Bergson's theories demonstrate particularly well the shortcomings of Booth's emphasis on a platonic dualism. To Bergson, there is a reality independent of man's perception of it and readily apprehensible by him. Existing in time-space, this reality is in a constant state of becoming: "There do not exist *things* made, but only things in the making, not *states* that remain fixed, but only states in the process of change."[13] In all living things including man, change is driven by what Bergson calls in one essay "the vital impetus," or the Life Force, which impels living things to evolve into higher and higher forms:

> All organized beings, from the humblest to the highest, from the first origins of life to the time in which we are, and in all places as in all times, do but evidence a single impulsion, the inverse of the movement of matter, and in itself indivisible. All the living hold together, and all yield to the same tremendous push. The animal takes its stand on the plant, man bestrides animality, and the whole of humanity, in space and in time, is one immense army galloping beside and before and behind each of us in an overwhelming charge.[14]

One aspect of the Life Force is consciousness, which the evolution of life requires in order to have some conception of its own needs and direction. Consciousness develops into instinct, in lower organisms, or intellect, in man, according to the differing needs of the various species. But the intellect developed in man is of such a kind that it does more than fulfill narrow and immediate needs. It is like an invention from which "we derive an immediate advantage," but of which it can be said that the advantage "is a slight matter compared with the new ideas and new feelings that the invention may give rise to in every direction" (*Creative Evolution,* p. 201). Indeed, the chief difference between man and the animals is that the intellect is "set free" from consideration of immediate ends and can turn to more philosophical self-contemplation (ibid., p. 203).

The similarity is obvious between these ideas and those in the passage from *The Territory Ahead* quoted earlier. Bergson's view of human awareness and human perception of time also resembles Morris's. Man perceives life as Bergson's "duration," which is the consciousness of time's motion made possible by memory: "There is no consciousness without memory, no continuation of a state without the addition, to the present feeling, of the memory of past moments. That is what duration consists of. Inner duration is the continuous life of a memory which prolongs the past into the present" (*Creative Mind*, p. 211). Man's apprehension of self is an apprehension of his own indivisible duration, which constantly grows as he moves forward in time and accrues more and more memories; the self is "a succession of states each one of which announces what follows and contains what precedes." Further, "it is just as much a continual winding, like that of a thread into a ball, for our past follows us, becoming larger and larger with the present it picks up on its way; and consciousness means memory" (ibid., p. 193). Thus, though time moves in one direction, man's memory makes his perception of it multi-directional, and time is experienced as a subjective state, as in Morris's "skull-time."

The emphasis on memory as defining the individual self and the problems it raises for the consciousness in keeping the past and present in their proper relationship are major themes in Morris's work, as my remarks on *Cause for Wonder* have partly illustrated. "Time might well be my subject. But how does one begin with time?" asks Howe at the opening of the novel. How does one begin with what has no beginning since it has always been? The similarity between Morris's "skulltime" and Bergson's duration is demonstrated by the fact that Howe uses an image very like Bergson's to describe his accumulating impressions as he moves through time and space: "We put everything on tape today, even time. The tape I have in mind is the line that runs down the center of a blacktop highway. . . . At sixty miles an hour time and space seem to wind on the spool beneath me. Or within me, which is more accurate. . . . At the wheel of the car, at sunrise, with the dawn light behind me, the road opening out before me, I sense a dimension of time that otherwise escapes me, the spool of tape being myself" (p. 50).[15]

The paradox of a timeless work of fiction about the subject of time is a central one in *Cause for Wonder*. Bergson's treatment of the same paradox leads me to my major point. The sense of duration, Bergson believed, could not be captured by rational analysis, which "generalizes at the same time that it abstracts" (*Creative Mind*, p. 196), that is, which reduces duration to uniform, discrete, and disembodied concepts. It could only be apprehended through "intuition," a sympathetic identification with the flow of time, which is experienced as "an uninterrupted continuity of unforseeable novelty" (ibid., p. 39). Although words partake of the abstraction of concepts, intuition can be verbally evoked by a "convergence of images" that "direct" the consciousness to a "precise point where there is a certain intuition to seize on" (ibid., p. 195). The value of a verbal structure like a novel is that it constitutes a highly organized pattern of images which stands above the flow of life and time and yet evokes an intuition of it. The novelty of art, made possible by the expanding consciousness of the artist and the accretion of past imaginative triumphs, keeps pace with and makes comprehensible the inexhaustible novelty of life.

I can now make a more formal statement of an earlier observation: Unlike art, life must remain in the flow, and

novels, though verbal constructs, function to provide some intuition of the nonverbal, mobile reality. Booth's characterization of Morris as seeking a platonic reality is finally misleading because for Plato the mobile real was only an imperfect reflection of the static ideal, whereas for Bergson the static concept is only a relatively crude approximation of the mobile real. Although art may be transcendent, it is too strong to argue, as Booth seems to, that Morris always prefers stasis over mobility and heroic transcendence over imaginative engagement with the finite world of concrete existents for his characters. He is a novelist dealing with the world of experience, after all, not a philosopher dealing with the world of concepts, and he is especially a novelist whose developing consciousness of his material has led him to a constantly shifting sense of what constitutes the successful life.

Many of Morris's conceptions about man and his relation to the universe are presented in expository form by his friend the naturalist-essayist Loren Eiseley in *The Immense Journey*. In the course of his evolution, man became "something the world had never seen before—a dream animal—living at least partially within a secret universe of his own creation," which he created in his imagination and through which he "has escaped out of the eternal present of the animal world into a knowledge of past and future."[16] The point of my remarks about Bergson is implied in Eiseley's speculations on man's ability to imagine himself in other people's shoes, a special form of which is the novelist's dramatic identification with his characters. Eiseley sees imagination as the most remarkable testimony to nature's powers of expansion: "This is the most enormous extension of vision of which life is capable: the projection of itself into other lives. This is the lonely, magnificent power of humanity. It is, far more than any spatial adventure, the supreme epitome of the reaching out" (p. 33). As this observation implies, the powers of nature to evolve and man to imagine, though analogous in creative impetus, occupy very different realms, for nature evolves in time and space, while imagination, expressed in the immobile, conceptual images Bergson describes, transcends "any spatial adventure."

In other words, there are indeed two worlds in the fiction of Wright Morris, and any adequate conception of his work must make room for both. The first has an absolute reality; it is a playground of natural forces which do the work of time, destroying each moment in order to create the next. The second is the habitat of a supernatural force, imagination, which nevertheless grows out of the natural process of evolution.

The real-ideal dualism points to an emerging pattern of contrasts, or opposites, which can be found in Morris's work. They include physical conception and imaginative conception, life and art, flow and arrest, process and culmination, text (outside of space but experienced in time) and photo (outside of time but experienced in space), man and nature, hero and witness—all but the last three pairs subsumed under Booth's two worlds. The relative weight

Morris assigns to one side of the dualism or another varies from book to book depending upon the specific situation depicted, the side which other themes happen to give the greater stress, and the point to which his developing consciousness of the world has brought him. His reservation of absolute judgment grows first from an ambivalence toward his subject, an ambivalence which is the only legitimate and truthful reaction to a profoundly ambiguous world, and from his basic premise that life is process. His tendency to think in patterns of opposites on whose relative worth conclusive judgment is withheld is further evidence of his deliberate tentativeness; respect for the unfinished character of the world prevents him from emphasizing once and for all one side of a dualism when tomorrow he may find the other more cogent.

Morris has always been a strong spokesman for the importance of tradition in shaping the individual talent, and his own talent has been partially formed by two very different writers—D. H. Lawrence and Henry James—who are both singled out for praise in *The Territory Ahead.* Morris himself has said that his admiration for other writers is "remote from imitation";[17] it is rather an awareness of literary tradition as part of the total culture out of which any writer must write. Because, as he says, echoing James's judgment, "It is the fiction that shapes the fact,"[18] Morris was "influenced" by Lawrence and James before he ever knew their work.[19] Like any good artist, he was attuned to his time and place, which owed a part of their sense of themselves to these men. The debt to James has received more attention perhaps because it involves technique, especially in the well-defined matter of point of view. One thing I want to do is at least partially to redress the balance by exploring his debt to Lawrence.

Anyone familiar with Lawrence's expository writings, especially *Apocalypse, Psychoanalysis and the Unconscious,* and *Fantasia of the Unconscious,* will recognize the family resemblance between his world and Bergson's.[20] In *Apocalypse* one finds a close cousin of Bergson's organicism: "The cosmos is a vast living body, of which we are still parts. The sun is a great heart whose tremors run through our smallest veins. The moon is a great gleaming nerve-centre from which we quiver forever."[21] In *Psychoanalysis and the Unconscious* one finds Bergsonian "consciousness" called the "unconscious," made the measure of individual identity, and equated with physiological life processes: "Where the individual begins, life begins. . . . And also, where the individual begins, the unconscious, which is the specific life-motive, also begins . . . this source [of the unconscious] . . . is the first ovule cell from which an individual organism arises. At the moment of conception . . . does a new unit of life, of consciousness, arise in the universe."[22] Such consciousness, for Lawrence, was truly "blood consciousness," the pulse in the heart and sinews of the total man. It resembles what Morris calls in *What a Way to Go* "the wisdom of the body," just as the sexual ethic in that novel and *Love Among the Cannibals* resembles the sexual ethic in Lawrence's fiction.

But these explicit resemblances, striking as they are, are less profound than some subtle affinities between the personalities of the authors. Morris spells out what Lawrence means to him in an interview: "Temperamentally, I now [1958] lean very strongly to such an imaginative figure as D. H. Lawrence, who in his later years defined to me the serious predicament of a man coming to terms with the present and using the past, not abusing it; in an effort to make this imaginative act possible" (Bleufarb, p. 35). To "come to terms with the present" is to recognize creation as an unending process of becoming, to accept what Lawrence called "the immediate present"[23] as the one point at which man, through his choices, can determine the shape of the uncreated future, and to exercise the responsibility thereby incurred. A man's use of the past is to let evolution work through him; he recognizes that in choosing he chooses not only for himself but also for the strange and strangely wise life processes that have devoted a billion years of evolution to producing him. This is his tie to the past; his tie to the future is the imaginative act in life and art which helps to determine what form that future will have. As Morris writes in *The Territory Ahead,* "the man who lives in the present—in his own present—lives to that extent in both the past and the future: the man who seeks to live elsewhere, both as an artist and as a man, has deceived himself" (p. 230).

In Morris's work, the treatment of choice more nearly resembles that of such doctrinaire existentialists as Sartre than that of Lawrence: characters are often confronted with very difficult dilemmas resulting from the nature of the contingent world in which they find themselves. Nevertheless, like Lawrence, Morris senses a creative presence in the universe that comes close to being God and that debars him from the radical states of anxiety, fear and trembling, and sickness unto death usually associated with existentialism. Impersonal forces are working their obscure ends in man, but there are ends, however obscure. Moreover, existentialism is an extremely self-oriented philosophy, while Morris's most sensitive characters, like those of Lawrence, have an instinctive sense of belonging among the larger forces of life in the cosmos and recognize that the universe is not a mere backdrop for their own self-absorbed little dramas.

To Morris, in *The Territory Ahead,* Lawrence is "indispensable" to writers in the immediate American present because he is the modern author whose work most fully expresses the dynamic and organic character of life. While Eliot cultivated familiar gods "to make the modern world possible in art," Lawrence quested after strange gods to make "life possible in the modern world" (p. 225). Eliot required familiar gods to evoke an order and an absolute from the past which would make artistic sense of the chaos of the present. For Lawrence this chaos represented, not disintegration of past order, but unlimited possibilities for choosing a new order. Each man, each day, could become the resurrected Christ of *The Man Who Died,* dead to the old world yet newly awake and alive to a new world. Old gods must be replaced with new, for only eternally changing gods can satisfy the eternally changing nature of life. A strange god, which nevertheless "will bear an astonishing resemblance to the one it displaced" (p. 230), is the visible sign of the new cosmos which Lawrence, with his ever expanding consciousness, perceived and, in perceiving, created.

When Morris takes as his subject "blood consciousness" and its habitat, the life of the present, he has D. H. Lawrence looking over one shoulder. When he turns his own consciousness, in the sense of his shaping imagination, upon moral and psychological nuances in the American present, he has James looking over the other, for the real protagonist in his novels is often the sensitive observer whose consciousness, in the Jamesian sense, expands in perceiving subtler and subtler ramifications of the observed experience. Lawrence speaks for the life in art, its "raw material," its humanly meaningful "object," but, as Morris writes in *The Territory Ahead,* James refined the "object" in art almost out of existence. For him, life, embodied in the author's "experience," and consciousness were one: "Experience is never limited, and it is never complete; it is an immense sensibility, a kind of huge spider-web of the finest silken threads suspended in the chamber of consciousness, and catching every air-borne particle in its tissue."[24] Thus the object is replaced by the subject, raw material by the author's consciousness of his material, or in Morris's metaphor, the sock by the unraveled yarn (*The Territory Ahead,* p. 100): "One thing always leads to another, that in turn to another, and this play of nuances, like ripples lapping on a pond, is the dramatis personae of James, the novelist. His subject was his own ceaselessly expanding consciousness" (ibid., p. 97). It is also, in a very real sense, his technique. In narrating his stories from the point of view of his "lucid reflectors," James placed his readers behind the artist's all-seeing eye and all-comprehending vision and gave the very act of vision a local habitation and a name. If "the material seems missing," Morris says, we find instead "the *im*material . . . in his books" (ibid., p. 95), a result predictable and fitting from a writer who found experience in the artist's "power to guess the unseen from the seen, to trace the implications of things, to judge the whole piece by the pattern" ("The Art of Fiction," p. 35). For Lawrence, his artistic consciousness was in the service of moral perceptions which could renew the world if accepted by all. For James, on the other hand, consciousness was a sufficient end in itself: "It is in the Jamesian moment of experience that one is most alive, most real; for . . . the Jamesian moment leads to full consciousness, through which one's inner, personal reality is achieved."[25]

Morris is deeply indebted to James in countless ways: for his emphasis on the importance of art, for his use of limited narrators rather than an omniscient narrator, for his insistence on the need for technique generally, and, not the least, for his clear-eyed criticism of America in *The American Scene,* which Morris still finds valid fifty years later. Like James, Morris believes that "Life *is* consciousness. Therefore . . . art *makes* life—by extending conscious-

ness" (Cornwell, p. 136). Like James, Morris seems at times to be writing novels in which little happens, in which external action is subordinated to the intense drama of consciousness in the process of perceiving a moral revelation. This effect is best seen in what James thought was the finest moment in *The Portrait of a Lady,* "my young woman's extraordinary vigil on the occasion that was to become to her such a landmark . . . it is but a vigil of searching criticism; but it throws the action further forward than twenty 'incidents' might have done. . . . It is a representation simply of her motionlessly *seeing,* and an attempt withal to make the mere still lucidity of her act as 'interesting' as the surprise of a caravan or the identification of a pirate . . . but it all goes on without her being approached by another person and without her leaving her chair."[26] In *The Territory Ahead,* Morris describes the precise stylistic effect of such a scene: "The mind of James . . . gives off and and receives a series of vibrations that find their resolution in parenthesis. Nothing is closed. Closure means a loss of consciousness" (pp. 96-97). This is a reasonable description of the Boyd passage cited earlier, just as James's comment aptly characterizes *The Field of Vision* as a whole.

Morris associates the organizing power of man's consciousness with metaphors of sight, as James does in the passage quoted above and in one of his most famous statements about fiction:

> The house of fiction has . . . not one window, but a million—a number of possible windows not to be reckoned, rather; everyone of which has been pierced . . . by the need of the individual vision and by the pressure of the individual will. These apertures, of dissimilar shape and size, hang so, all together, over the human scene that we might have expected of them a greater sameness of report than we find. They are but windows at the best, mere holes in a dead wall, disconnected, perched aloft; they are not hinged doors opening straight on life . . . at each of them stands a figure with a pair of eyes, or at least with a field-glass, which forms, again and again, for observation, a unique instrument, insuring to the person making use of it an impression distinct from every other.
>
> [*Art of the Novel,* p. 46]

In places the metaphor suggests paintings on a wall as well as windows, reminding us that both James and Morris use works of visual art in their fiction as devices to suggest the quality of vision in various artist-characters. However, thinking of fiction in terms of an essentially spatial art form has results in Morris it does not have in James.

Lawrence and James serve to isolate and illuminate two distinguishable, though finally inseparable, modes in Morris's fiction. The first mode, built around what can be called "the still-point structure," exhibits qualities which especially show Morris's affinities with James, though occasionally with un-Jamesian results. The best example is also one of Morris's best books, *The Field of Vision.* In novels using the still-point structure, Morris expands a moment of consciousness like that experienced by Isabel Archer to encompass his entire novel. To do so successfully, he must subordinate external action to the inner drama of consciousness; this, in turn, causes the setting to be static and the time which elapses in the work to be drastically shortened (it is about three hours in *The Field of Vision*). The combined result is much more of a sense of a timeless, spatial aesthetic experience than is ever found in James, for all his visual metaphors; like Morris's photos, these novels seem to freeze reality by removing it from time, an effect sharpened by frequent flashbacks suggesting the timeless skull-time of *Cause for Wonder.* Multiple centers of consciousness are used to tell the story in the third person. The ongoing "action" of this mode is not so much movement in time, as a movement from narrator to narrator, with each seeing the action according to his own peculiar psychological angle of vision. As the author returns to the same character a second and third time, he creates the effect of circling the observed action, each time broadening its implications and deepening the reader's understanding. As a stimulant to consciousness, the action becomes a still point, like a mystic world axis, around which consciousness circles. The true still point rests, not in the action itself, but in the locus it provides for a moment of full consciousness in the beholders, an almost mystical moment of intuiting the truth at the heart of reality. One critic has described a similar effect in James: "The development or extension of consciousness was to be achieved by what James termed the 'process of vision': the gradual accumulation of separate moments of experience, 'the happy moments of our consciousness' . . . a succession of lesser moments leading to the moment of vision . . . of full consciousness—a moment of acute, mental and emotional awareness similar to Eliot's timeless moment of illumination" (Cornwell, p. 128). The mystical implications of the phrase *the still point,* used by Morris himself in *The Field of Vision* (p. 111), need to be further explored, but it can best be done later in discussing the kinds of heroes in Morris's fiction.

Although these similarities between Morris and James exist, Morris does not always manage to dramatize in this mode a "development" of consciousness of the sort found in James, a development which convinces us there is a permanent change in a character's moral makeup. Isabel Archer's character seems truly to grow in wisdom because her moment of consciousness is the culmination of a long, slowly developing dramatic action and because it is then tested in the crucible of subsequent action when she must decide whether or not to return to Osmond. By shortening the elapsed time of his novels and using the circular pattern of narration, Morris creates the effect of character not truly developing but serially revealed in a static moment that fills the whole book and approaches the effect of a painting.

Morris's fondness for almost Dickensian caricatures drawn with one or two grotesque traits and his overreliance on symbolic rather than dramatic resolutions for character conflicts further militate against a true sense of character

development. In *The Field of Vision,* the fraudulent psychiatrist Lehmann illustrates the first of these and the resolution of Boyd's problem, the second. If there is development in his mode, it usually comes in a witness's movement from ignorance to wisdom, though there is sometimes doubt even about this. The bullfight in *The Field of Vision* focuses and intensifies the characters' insights, but because so many of these insights are tied to past memories, the effect is that the characters are reviewing what they have always known rather than learning anything new. The real insight may come to the author in writing his novel or the reader in witnessing this heroic act.

The second mode in Morris's fiction, built around "the open-road structure," tends to show his affinities with Lawrence. Considering that the open-road structure has been used in more books than the still-point structure, from his very first, *My Uncle Dudley* (1942), to one of the most recent, *A Life* (1973), the static structure of *The Field of Vision* would seem a late-developing and secondary offshoot of Morris's career. Nevertheless, as the Hassan comment shows, many critics still see nothing but stasis. The open-road structure appears in its purest form in *Love Among the Cannibals* (1957). To capture a sense of life as dynamic, this mode typically deals with a journey from one place to another, the movement in space rendering visible the movement in time. The locales through which the characters travel have symbolic value; for example, the Midwest usually stands for the American past and all that goes with it in the imagination, while California and Pennsylvania represent the present. Thus, even though Nebraska sets up poetic vibrations for Morris as no other place does, all his settings have meaning and importance in relation to the works in which they appear. In contrast to books with the still-point structure, those with the open-road structure employ one or two narrators, cover a longer span of time, and place greater stress on external dramatic action. Although the hero is sometimes spoken of as getting out of this world, this mode emphasizes not transcendence, but immanence: the hero and sometimes the witnesses are manifestations of the creative force immanent in nature and striving to perfect itself through them. This process is expressed in their obedience to their most organic impulses, impulses which can be realized only in time. In the best novels of this type, the change of place is emblematic of a real, dramatically rendered development of character, usually on the part of the narrator-witness who observes and reports the behavior of a hero. Sometimes, though, the change in the witness is again an enlarged awareness of life's shaping forces as revealed by the hero during the journey.

Often a single novel will contain vestiges of both modes. For instance, "The Roundup" and "The Ceremony" sections of *Ceremony in Lone Tree* (1960) adumbrate the open-road and the still-point structures, respectively. As has already been suggested, these two modes point to another distinction to be made about Morris's heroes, in addition to those offered by Booth and Madden. The hero who more nearly deserves to be called platonic is the one whose transcendence of the real world is complete and permanent, either through death or through a resistance to change which cuts him off from life; such transcendence repudiates the world of flux and contingency. The agency whereby transcendence is achieved varies from book to book. A second kind of hero, who may be termed *immanent,* embodies a Dionysian rather than platonic mysticism. He does not reach beyond nature, but feels for once attuned to her: "Nature which has become alienated, hostile, or subjugated, celebrates once more her reconciliation with her lost son."[27] The timelessness of this hero's state consists in its transpiring in the eternal now, that moment of imaginative stasis within the flux of time. The immanent hero resembles the existential hero in that he accepts the responsibility for selfhood in a contingent world, determining his essence by a continuing series of choices in the realm of existence. In doctrinaire existentialism, and at least sometimes in Morris, the transcendence Booth describes amounts to a cowardly evasion of responsibility, for strictly speaking, only man's essence can be transcendent because only it can exist in the past and therefore be complete. The immanent hero's essence is timeless, but he remains in the existential flow. It is only in this sense that any hero is (and thus only the immanent hero who can be), in one of Morris's favorite phrases, "*both* in and out of this world."

The transcendent hero comes to be symbolized in Morris's fiction by the figure of the Minotaur, an out-of-this-world beast inhabiting the labyrinth of the human psyche and barring the way to continued change and development. He frustrates the ongoing process of life. The converse symbol of the centaur stands for the immanent hero. Man above and beast below, the centaur connotes, first, the unified relationship between man's shaping consciousness above and "the wisdom of the body" below and, second, the course of evolution, beginning in the lower forms and eventuating in man. Both kinds of heroes embody transpersonal forces of the cosmos, and both represent special manifestations of American culture. The former is more common in the early Morris and the latter in the recent Morris.

The question now arises whether the Jamesian moment of full consciousness, achieved by the witnesses who register the hero's imaginative charge, is to be identified with transcendence, as Booth seems to argue when he speaks of imagination as a "bridge" out of this world and as Morris implies with the term *the still point.* As the instant when the "material" becomes "immaterial," this moment certainly smacks of mystical apotheosis, and at least one commentator treats it that way in dealing with James: "James offers full, personal consciousness as his source of life, vision, and experience; it is his means of reconciling beauty and ugliness, good and evil, and of bridging the gap between the individual and his fellow men, the individual and his world" (Cornwell, p. 156). Surely, though, the moment of full consciousness, in both James and Morris, is a state of heightened moral awareness, not a meta-

physical experience. Above all, it is a state of being able to make ever finer moral distinctions, not an annihilation of the need to make distinctions. Therefore, it should be distinguished from other kinds of transcendence in Morris's novels. In fact, imagination is sometimes manifested in the witness's heightened consciousness, sometimes in a work of art created by the witness or the hero, and sometimes in the audacious behavior of the hero. If consciousness leads to the production of art or to the performance of a heroic act, the art or the act may be transcendent, but the producer remains immanent so long as he continues to change.

When the distinction between the hero and the witness is regarded as a distinction between the doer and the knower or, in a larger sense, between life as it is and life as it can be understood in the imagination, then one can see that Morris's work is itself a witnessing of his own life and of the American experience. Moreover, as part of the expanding consciousness of nature, Morris's own consciousness of his material remains in process. Consequently, it is a mistake to read as fixed and complete from the first what really constitutes a long process of development. That is, it is a mistake to interpret Morris's early works in terms of his mature pronouncements on fiction. As Morris admits in *The Territory Ahead* (p. 15), these pronouncements grew out of his early failures, which unintentionally display as problems what some critics have treated as consciously dramatized themes. For example, when Morris speaks of nostalgia in connection with *My Uncle Dudley,* he is acknowledging in retrospect his own difficulties in coming to terms with his past, not referring to a conscious theme.

Although an unusually large number of Morris's works are excellent in themselves, they take on greater meaning and power in light of his whole career; his sustained development makes him especially satisfying to read in his entirety, from *My Uncle Dudley* to *Fire Sermon* and *A Life.* For the power and suggestiveness of these last two come in no small measure from the fact that they retell Dudley's story in the light of thirty years of reflection. The difference between the two tellings is a visible lesson in the power of consciousness to transform life and of Wright Morris to process the raw material of his experience into lasting art.

Notes

1. "Introduction," *Wright Morris: A Reader,* p. ix.

2. See Bibliography for the list of editions of Morris's full-length works cited. All further references to works by Wright Morris will be cited in the text.

3. "The Alone Generation," *Contemporaries* (Boston: Little, Brown, 1962), pp. 213-14.

4. *Contemporary American Literature, 1945-1972: An Introduction* (New York: Ungar, 1973), p. 36.

5. Morris was first interested in fiction. See his comments in "Interview," in *Wright Morris: Structures and Artifacts: Photographs 1933-1954,* p. 111.

6. Gerald Nemanic, "A Ripening Eye: Wright Morris and the *Field of Vision,*" *MidAmerica I: The Yearbook of the Society for the Study of Midwestern Literature* (1974), p. 126.

7. "The Poetry of W. B. Yeats," in James Hall and Martin Steinmann, eds., *The Permanence of Yeats* (1950; rptd. New York: Collier Books, 1961), p. 305.

8. "The Two Worlds in the Fiction of Wright Morris," *Sewanee Review* 65 (Summer 1957): 375-99.

9. Jack Rice Cohn, "Wright Morris: The Design of the Midwestern Fiction" (Ph.D. diss., University of California, Berkeley, 1970), p. 72. Further references will be cited in the text as Cohn.

10. "The Hero and the Witness in Wright Morris' *Field of Vision,*" *Prairie Schooner* 34 (Fall 1960): 263-78; "The Great Plains in the Novels of Wright Morris," *Critique* 4 (Winter 1961-62): 5-23; "Wright Morris' *In Orbit*: An Unbroken Series of Poetic Gestures," *Critique* 10 (Fall 1968): 102-19; "Morris' *Cannibals*, Cain's *Serenade*: The Dynamics of Style and Technique," *Journal of Popular Culture* 8 (Summer 1974): 59-70; portions of the first two articles are included in condensed form in his book *Wright Morris,* Twayne United States Authors Series (New York: Twayne Publishers, 1964). Unless otherwise specified, further references to Madden will be to the book and will be carried in the text.

11. W. B. Yeats to Lady Elizabeth Pelham, 4 January 1939. Quoted in Joseph Hone, *W. B. Yeats: 1865-1939* (New York: MacMillan, 1943), p. 510.

12. Neither Booth nor Madden can be included among the critics who ignore the nonmidwestern fiction. Madden's book is the best synthesis of Morris's career yet, and Booth argues for the comic European novels in "The Shaping of Prophecy: Craft and Idea in the Novels of Wright Morris," *American Scholar* 31 (Autumn 1962): 608-26.

13. *The Creative Mind,* trans. Mabelle L. Andison (New York: Philosophical Library, 1946), p. 22. Further references will be cited in the text.

14. *Creative Evolution,* trans. Arthur Mitchell (1911; rptd. New York: Modern Library, 1944), p. 295. Further references will be cited in the text.

15. Another striking similarity of imagery deserves to be noted. The motion-picture imagery of *Cause for Wonder*—still photographs projected twenty-four times per second so that they take on the appearance of movement—dramatizes the tension between organic mobility and conceptual stasis and is related to the snapshot imagery sprinkled throughout Morris's novels. In *Cause for Wonder,* the imagination of young Brian records and preserves the insane antics of his elders as if on celluloid: "For a moment they stood, without movement, as if the voice behind them had cried 'Camera!' and a scene that had long been in preparation was being shot. Behind them, shooting it, was the boy" (p. 262). Bergson employs the same "cinematograph" image to illustrate the abstracting power of intellect and to show how it creates a sense of mobile becoming by putting together a series of static percepts (*Creative Evolution,* pp. 331-34).

16. *The Immense Journey* (1957; rptd. New York: Time Reading Program, 1962), p. 87. Further references will be cited in the text.

17. "Letter to a Young Critic," *Massachusetts Review* 6 (Autumn-Winter 1965): 97. Further references will be cited in the text.

18. "Made in U.S.A.," *American Scholar* 29 (Autumn 1960): 483. Further references will be cited in the text.

19. Sam Bleufarb, "Point of View: An Interview with Wright Morris, July, 1958," *Accent* 19 (Winter 1959): 35. Further references will be cited in the text.

20. There is evidence that Lawrence knew Bergson's work early in his career (before 1913). Rose Marie Burwell, "A Catalogue of D. H. Lawrence's Reading from Early Childhood," *D. H. Lawrence Review* 3 (Fall 1970): 230.

21. *Apocalypse* (1931; rptd. New York: The Viking Press, 1960), p. 45. Further references will be cited in the text.

22. *Psychoanalysis and the Unconscious* and *Fantasia of the Unconscious* (1921, 1922; rptd. New York: The Viking Press, 1960), pp. 13-14. Further references will be cited in the text.

23. "Poetry of the Present," *The Complete Poems of D. H. Lawrence,* ed. Vivian de Sola Pinto and F. Warren Roberts (New York: The Viking Press, 1964), p. 182. See the last chapter of *The Territory Ahead* (pp. 217-31) for the full significance of the term to Morris.

24. "The Art of Fiction," in *Theory of Fiction: Henry James,* ed. James E. Miller, Jr. (Lincoln: University of Nebraska Press, 1972), pp. 34-35. Further references will be cited in the text.

25. Edith F. Cornwell, *The "Still Point": Theme and Variations in the Writings of T. S. Eliot, Coleridge, Yeats, Henry James, Virginia Woolf, and D. H. Lawrence* (New Brunswick, N.J.: Rutgers University Press, 1962), p. 156. Further references will be cited in the text.

26. "Preface to *The Portrait of a Lady,*" in *Art of the Novel: Critical Prefaces by Henry James* (New York: Charles Scribner's Sons, 1934), p. 57. Further references will be cited in the text.

27. Friederich Nietzsche, *The Birth of Tragedy or: Hellenism and Pessimism,* in *Basic Writings of Nietzsche,* trans. Walter Kaufmann (New York: Modern Library, 1966), p. 37.

Randall K. Albers (essay date 1979)

SOURCE: "The Female Transformation: The Role of Women in Two Novels by Wright Morris," in *Prairie Schooner,* Vol. 53, No. 2, Summer, 1979, pp. 95-115.

[*In the following essay, Albers examines the way Morris treats the conflict between desire and repression in* The Field of Vision *and* Ceremony in Lone Tree.]

They came in covered wagons, in buckboards, on horseback, on foot. They ate what they could when they could. They cursed and prayed and fought, their fear and terror overcome by a dream. Many died; some survived. Everything tasted like dust. They left a trail of their possessions and their dead across the land.

"Circle the wagons and trap the past! Women and children in the center! Lord, protect us from the future. Give us this day our daily dream, and forgive us—though we have not sinned."

The struggle to break free of the past is itself the sin that Wright Morris considers in *The Field of Vision* and *Ceremony in Lone Tree.* Behind the picture of the ever-receding frontier embodied in Frederick Jackson Turner's "frontier thesis" lay the Great American Dream: the self-made man. And when the frontier was no more, the dream remained—but with no means of realization. The result: contact with the present became lost in nostalgia for an irretrievable past. The Dream, and everything that went with it, became a cliché—overused and undervalued. Morris writes:

> The battered basin, the bony nag, the old man with the bats loose in his belfry are so many strings around our memory fingers, the unbroken ties we retain with the past. They transport us, rather than transform us, and it is the past, not the future, that beckons.[1]

The past must be transformed. The transforming agent, that which revivifies the cliché, is the imagination. Only the imagination will awaken the American male from the impotent lethargy of his dream. And nowhere are the effects of that lethargy more evident than in his relationship with women. Nowhere, perhaps, will the effects of transformation be so easily discerned as in the altered concepts of male and female roles.

That the relationship between males and females is an index of even more deep-seated ills and that those ills are still being dealt with twenty years after Morris published his novels attests to both the perspicacity of Morris's own vision and the importance of "re-discovering" (as, almost yearly, someone does) the importance of what Morris has had to say in his very large body of work as a whole and, most particularly, in those two novels where the ills are articulated with greatest clarity. *The Field of Vision* and *Ceremony in Lone Tree* exhibit, with Morris's characteristic and compelling understatement, the ways in which personal insecurities infect the web of relationships called society and how the Idea behind that society—behind America, that is—feeds those insecurities further. At a time when we struggle to understand ourselves and deal with some of America's propensity for violence and moral poverty, Morris's voice is one that should be listened to carefully, for he promises, by his own example, a type of salvation in the imagination.

Leslie Fiedler has linked Morris to Hemingway and Faulkner as the "quite serious calumniators of the female."[2] Though, in effect, Morris admits his debt to Hemingway and Faulkner, he would qualify Fiedler's indictment.[3] True, in Morris's novels, women control as much as possible the workings of a not-very-well-run society. They suppress their menfolk. They smother and sexually assault their children. They repress their own emotions and demand the same from those with whom they live. They require obedience from their husbands and security in their environment.

Still, Morris's women are human, believable, not merely plastic caricatures. As such, the woman is not to blame. In fact, it is doubtful that Morris would have his females accept even the larger share of blame. If, as one critic has written, Morris's archetypal woman is a "castrating female,"[4] she is so largely because the male has dropped his drawers. Lost in the sleep of his memories, he has abdicated his right to authority in the present. The frontier was, for better or worse, a male world. As long as the wagons kept moving, the men kept leading. When the wagons stopped, their imaginative quest gave way to the nostalgic memory of that quest, to the ethic of failure.

In his book of criticism, *A Bill of Rites, A Bill of Wrongs, A Bill of Goods,* Morris tells us the effect on the family incumbent upon this abdication of responsibility by the male:

> When the American male defaulted to the woman, relinquishing his role as head of the family, he established the pattern of *default* in family matters of guidance and authority. How—the grown-ups ask—accept the responsibility for their children's lives? Who are they to wield such authority? Having personally failed to do the impossible—pursue and cage the American dream—they are hardly in a position, they feel, to map this adventure for their children.[5]

In other words, as long as the success ethic remains embedded in the consciousness of male and female, insecure parents will choose to convey one of two undesirable extremes of values: either they offer their children the cliché, or they offer no values at all except perhaps Darwinian ones. For Morris, the ethic of success has been introjected most strongly by the male, and it is his insecurity that will be the greatest when failure occurs. Unimaginative as his spouse may be, she is nevertheless forced to accept a role for which she is little prepared and one which she would probably rather not accept. Thus, the battle between the sexes is less the result of culpability on the part of a predatory female than of an inability on the part of the male to escape the paralyzing separation between past and present.

How the cliché of the past may be transformed in the present is the question that Morris attempts to answer in *The Field of Vision* and *Ceremony in Lone Tree.* In a sense, these two books may be seen as one long novel.[6] In them, however, Morris explores the possibilities for transformation in two entirely different ways. *The Field of Vision* deals with the attempt of one man, Gordon Boyd, to understand his own ill-fated process of transformation. In *Ceremony in Lone Tree,* Morris presents a whole group of people who gather to pay homage to the past and who instead are forced out of the past on the strength of a woman's symbolic act. In examining the movement of the two books toward this symbolic act, we may be forced to reevaluate Morris's alleged calumniation of the female.

The action of *The Field of Vision* centers on seven people attending a bullfight in Mexico—five males, one female, and one person of questionable sex. The central character is Gordon Boyd, the self-described failure, the "self unmade man" who carries with him the burden of unrealized potential, the desire for heroism, and the vision of transformation. Morris has noted in an interview that the germ for his novel was based on the "idea of audacity in American life."[7] Boyd is the purveyor of the unexpected, thriving on the element of surprise. His actions represent one alternative to the past-present conflict, the most hopeful and, if unrealized, the most tragic alternative. Time after time in *The Field of Vision,* the hopefulness turns to tragedy or, more correctly, to pathos. Boyd's Maileresque attempts at transformation by audacity, epitomized in his childhood attempt to walk on water, have failed to remove the stigma of the cliché from his life. He has failed at everything he has attempted, failing ultimately in the active pursuit of failure itself; even the "bum," he realized, was a cliché. In the end, much like every other American male, the past, the memory of his audacious attempts, is his only possession. The accumulation of pathetic failures seems to require a final verdict of tragedy. Yet, awake to the dangers inherent in nostalgia, Boyd cannot help but think that even the failure of audacity is preferable to the sleep of stolidity and blindness to the conflict between past and present.

One of those who is "blind" is Scanlon, the old man who has completely immersed himself in the past and who has lost all contact with present reality. Scanlon's past is in fact twice-removed from reality since he is lost not in memories of his own past but rather in the secondhand fantasies of his father's trek west. His is a distinctly male world.

At the other extreme from Scanlon is Paula Kahler, a silent transvestite who is equally absorbed in a private vision. Having killed a man who attempted to molest "her" in an elevator, Paula has slipped into catatonia. He is oblivious and, therefore, protected from the threat of male violence which, as Morris indicates in *Ceremony in Lone Tree,* is a natural outgrowth of the American male's failure. Paula's placidity is the feminine opposition to Scanlon's vision of the wild, male West. We may summarize these two extremes as past-without-present (Scanlon) and present-without-past (Paula's past too painful to remember). Existing somewhere between these two extremes are Walter McKee and his wife, Lois.

McKee is trapped in a separation of the past and present. For him, the attraction of the past rests simply with its opposition to the present. As a child, McKee had adopted the role of a necessary and willing witness to Boyd's audacious acts, a role in which he obtained a great deal of vicarious pleasure. Now he looks upon those days with a great deal of nostalgia; virtually everything he sees in Mexico *reminds* him of something from that carefree childhood. Nevertheless, McKee realizes that the "good old days" are also bygone days, a world apart. He believes in squarely facing the reality that, as Morris has written elsewhere, "hopes dissolve into responsibilities" and that the pursuit of happiness runs smack into the brick wall of the success ethic. By seeing his childhood as bearing little or no relationship to his present existence, McKee neutralizes the effect of the past; he spares himself the painful process of comparing the hopes of his childhood to the failures of his adulthood. That Boyd has never given up childhood audacity puzzles him. He regards this as a failure to accept adult responsibility. Boyd, on the other hand, sees McKee as a man asleep. Lacking imagination, McKee also lacks the power of transforming the excitement of childhood into any meaningful relevance for the ongoing process of living. If Boyd has no illusions about his own failure to realize his potential, he nevertheless sees his own feeble attempts to define his life as far preferable to McKee's sleepwalking or blind denial of his manhood.

Nowhere is McKee's denial more evident than in his relationship with his wife. Lois is the barometer of attraction-repulsion in the confrontation between Boyd's audacity and McKee's stolidity. Thirty years earlier, Boyd had kissed her right in front of McKee's characteristically impotent gaze. For a moment, she felt passion and life stirring in her bones; but she also felt the insecurity, the "craziness." She opted for security and predictability in choosing McKee for her husband, but she has never been able to forget the moment she was almost bewitched into marrying Boyd. She shudders at the uncertainty which would have been brought on by such an act:

> McKee had pointed out, even before she had met [Boyd], and long before it got to be popular, that just hearing about Boyd gave her a feeling of insecurity. The way she put it was, the ground didn't seem to stand beneath her feet. Anything might happen with a person like that, and he had gone out of his way to prove her right. It had almost happened, according to her, the first time she met him. Boyd had kissed her. Up till then she'd never been kissed.[8]

Since that time, she has almost always resisted the attraction of that memory. Clamping an iron-willed control on her emotions, she has, like McKee, neutralized the effects of the past. She sees Boyd as the purveyor of craziness, as a type of chancre threatening the health or peaceful security of comfortable human relationships. She also categorizes such craziness as a distinctly male trait. Even the ever-stoic McKee has his eccentricities (like being *reminded* of things). Having restrained such eccentricities in herself, she feels perfectly justified in demanding self-discipline from her husband. Of course, McKee, in his insecurity, sees that she is right, thus allowing himself to be castrated. Lois fosters the illusion that McKee is the head of his family, but she nevertheless manipulates his every move and will continue to do so until such time as the male purges himself of his Boyd-like craziness and becomes fit to accept authority once again.

Having straitjacketed their emotions, Lois and McKee relate according to a pattern which is archetypal in Morris's depiction of male-female relationships, the pattern of control and evasion. Lois controls; McKee attempts to evade that control. They exist concurrently but separately. Their relationship thus takes on the character of a business arrangement—passionless, pragmatic, lacking communication. They have in fact no love; they are simply companions who have banded together in defense against a world of ever-increasing craziness. The intransigence of their positions is an effective counterpoint to Boyd's fine frenzy.

In stark contrast to the heroic transformations taking place before them in the bull ring, Boyd sees the utter stasis and lifelessness of the McKees' relationship (54). He also sees that the two of them, in their dustiness, represent a covert attack on his own heroic attempts. Their overpowering dullness and repression of feeling are diametrically opposed to his own imaginative audacity. Their simple satisfaction and surface existence contrast with his own yearning for something better:

Mrs. McKee and me couldn't be happier.

That was what he had said. That was what he had meant, so it was naturally what he said.

[57]

Boyd can't help but think of the craziness of it all, but in contrast to their opinion of him, Boyd is much more democratic about the extent of the boundaries to the state of craziness:

What a crazy goddam world, Boyd was thinking—and so made room for himself. Also for Dr. Lehmann, the celebrated quack, with nothing to recommend him but his cures, and Paula Kahler, the only sort of failure he could afford. Also for old man Scanlon, the living fossil, for McKee, the co-inventor of the dust bowl, for his wife, the deep-freeze, and her grandson who would live it all over again. Here gathered at a bullfight. The sanded navel of the world. Gazing at this fleshy button each man had eyes to see only himself.

[59]

For Boyd, the antidote to insanity rests with the ability to reach beyond complacent omphalos, beyond the walls people erect between each other and into the human heart. The prerequisite for such realization is imaginative life.

Boyd's statement conveys the sense of isolation, of loneliness, of being trapped in patterns of relating, that pervades Morris's work. That is, finally, what he means when he says that character has become a cliché, "appallingly predictable." In a lecture delivered at Amherst College, Morris observes, "Character, as I never tire of saying, is primarily an imaginative fact, a fiction to which the flesh is incurably responsive. It is the fiction that shapes the fact." In other words, in order to deal with the raw material of our lives and in order to connect with the present in any sort of coherent pattern, the imagination must be active. If, like McKee, one is trapped in an insipid past, it is only because satisfaction has led to imaginative atrophy. In a man like Boyd, the sense of solitude and aloneness resulting from the destructive capabilities inherent in a multitude of Scanlons and McKees breeds, says Morris, "a passionate need to pin something down, or join something up."[9] *The Field of Vision* is the chronicle of Boyd's attempt to find such coherence. He is forced down and down into himself, stripped of illusions about his grandiose vision in much the same way that the pioneers had stripped themselves of those possessions not absolutely essential to their survival. Going beyond simple opposition to conditioning forces, Boyd struggles to make a real affirmation of his imaginative powers and to find a way of breaking out of the self-perpetuating patterns of "fossilism."

This struggle is the impetus behind Boyd's use of the shocking statement and surprising, unpredictable act as he probes for a chink in the McKee's armor of invulnerability. Their adaptive powers continually surprise him. When Boyd insults him in an attempt to find an emotion beneath the façade, McKee nervously chides him or slumps into smiling speechlessness as he had done on the night Boyd had kissed his girl. Lois's reaction is to simply freeze up. She is careful not to let Boyd know whether he has struck a responsive chord in her. To keep their social and familial machinery running smoothly, the McKees merely assign Boyd to the fringe of society, to the realm of the fascinating failure, and thereby neutralize the threat he represents.

Interestingly, however, despite her outward show of calm, Lois does sense an emptiness and seems almost on the verge of admitting it. Just seeing Boyd has driven her, however unwillingly, back to the past. She is taken back to the time on the porch when Boyd "took advantage of her" and for once in her life made her feel like a woman. Confronted with McKee's nostalgic reminiscences, Lois is only irritated; but seeing and feeling the infectious, imaginative energy in Boyd, she begins to speculate and to compare the real past with that which might have been. Finding the evidence for Boyd's imagination in his magnetic eyes, she comes to a realization: "*That* made her think of old times, it made her wonder, that is, if anything in the world had really happened since McKee's best friend had kissed the girl he hadn't kissed himself" (90). Lois, like Boyd, has a vision of her own transformation—or, rather, lack of it—since that moment on the porch. After that one moment of almost involuntary excitement, she chose stability rather than change:

It wasn't only her father who was trapped in the past, who didn't turn with the century as her mother described it, but also all of the people who had once been young, with dishes to wipe. And after wiping the dishes had stepped, for just a moment, out on the porch. Trapped. If she could believe her eyes, Boyd was trapped there himself.

[92]

She is right. Boyd *is* trapped on the porch. However, unlike Lois, he has not attempted to escape the memory of this one true transformation by marrying an unchanging McKee. On the contrary, Boyd has spent his whole life searching wildly for another such spontaneous, almost existential, moment. Lois embraces the cliché out of the fear of unpredictability. Boyd embraces unpredictability out of fear that his life may become a cliché. One fears what *might* happen; the other fears what *might not.* Both fear for the future.

The future, in *The Field of Vision,* is bound up in the Mc-Kees' grandson and Boyd's namesake, little Gordon. Once again, this time between grandmother and grandson, the male-female relationship develops into one of control and evasion. Lois fights to control her grandson, trying to protect him from the eccentricities of Boyd and McKee. She is unable to see that, like McKee, the boy's natural reaction is to evade the repressive control of overwhelming maternal affection. In his coonskin hat, Gordon attaches himself to the characters of old man Scanlon's dream. He seems destined to search for genuine heroes until overcome by the familiar cliché—failure.

In his Amherst lectures, Morris notes, "The boy who casts himself as Jesse James or Marlon Brando, the girl who casts herself as Jayne Mansfield or Greta Garbo, are those who bear witness to the cliché. We are left with a product rather than a process—a coonskin rather than a Davy Crockett."[10] This is precisely what Boyd begins to learn while watching the bullfight and the boy. His own actions seem always to remain cliché. At one point, he squirts pop in the bull's face. Apparently a spontaneous, unpredictable act, it instead takes on the air of a pathetic, mock-heroic confrontation. The act lacks meaning, is incapable of transforming him, for two reasons: first, it lacks true risk; second, as spontaneous as it may have looked, the act is calculated. Thus, it bears no relation to the kiss on the porch. There, audacity had not been the purpose; it was the result.[11] In controlling and killing the bull "according to the rules," the matador imbues the cape and sword with symbolic meaning. In this confrontation between the man and the bull where the man is armed only with the potential for symbol, Boyd begins to see the reason for the consistent failure of his own acts of audacity.

Though Boyd realizes all of this, he still doesn't know what to do with his insight. However, in the struggle to free the future from Lois's control, he decides to give little Gordon "something to remember." Snatching the lifeless coonskin from the boy's head, he places it on that of the matador who is "a real hero." Then, returning it to the boy, he says that it has now been transformed, given symbolic value: "That makes it real" (226). But it isn't real, as Boyd soon sees, and it won't be until the boy himself transforms the object. Picking the hat off again, Boyd tosses it into the ring and sends the boy after it. For a moment, as he recovers it just ahead of a group of other children, little Gordon is lost in the fantasy of Davy Crockett pursued by Indians. When McKee tries to call him to safety, the boy refuses to respond to the voice of stolidity, preferring instead to remain lost in his imaginative battle. When he finally does return, it is only to Boyd's call for Davy Crockett. For little Gordon, the past has gained a meaning through its contact with the present, a link forged in the imagination.

In an interview with Sam Bleufarb, Morris traces the stages of development in his own attitude toward the past. The four stages through which he passed are: (1) an infatuation with, an immersion in, the past, (2) an initial skepticism as to its value, (3) a serious questioning of the past, and (4) a rise into concern with the present. "The past and present," he states, "play a kind of fugal development in the novels."[12] *The Field of Vision* is one attempt to explore the necessity of coming to terms with the past in order to establish meaning in the present. Morris establishes conflict between Boyd's audacity and Lois's resistance to audacity. McKee is lost somewhere in between, attracted and repelled by both. Though they all reach some measure of insight, they are far from willing to compromise their respective struggles. Boyd has not been transformed himself, but he has nonetheless staked out his claim to the future in little Gordon. To McKee's hollow assertion that "This boy belongs to his grandma," Boyd simply replies, "You're too late" (246). Lois seems to have suffered some form of defeat.

By the end of the novel, however, it has become obvious that whatever victory may have occurred for Boyd in his struggle with Lois over little Gordon, such a triumph may be shortlived. In a sense, the battle for the future in little Gordon was being fought on Boyd's terms and on Boyd's turf—which is, properly, anywhere outside of Lone Tree, Nebraska. One gets the feeling that Lois may be merely biding her time until she gets back to her predictable element. She *expects* craziness in Boyd's territory, and she gains strength for her feat of self-control in knowing that she is only a temporary denizen of his world. Moreover, it seems obvious that not even Boyd may progress any further toward his goal of transformation until he overcomes his own fear of the past. The lessons of the bullfight would have to be tested in the much more "natural" and equilibristic environment of Nebraska. The spectre of Tom Scanlon, presiding over the Lone Tree nothingness, would have to be confronted head-on if the destructive pattern of relationships were to be prevented from breaking the social fabric apart at the seams.

That the destruction has already begun is evident near the outset of *Ceremony in Lone Tree.* A sense of urgency pervades the narrative. Behind the central events of the novel lies the haunting consciousness of an apocalyptic insanity apparently eating away at the smoothly running social machine. The American Dream has already gone flat. It is fast becoming a nightmare. Charlie Munger has killed ten people at random because "he wants to be somebody." Lee Roy Momeyer "just got tired of being pushed around" and ran his car over two of his high school tormentors. The shooting iron that tamed the West in the nineteenth century has found its counterpart in the customized jalopy of the twentieth; they both make a man larger than life. They negate the impotence felt in the American male's unsuccessful attempt to pursue and cage the Dream.

McKee, impotent and satisfied with his own meagre success, just can't understand how the hard-working Lee Roy, the boy who almost became a minister, could possibly summon up enough hate to murder two people—and moreover feel no compunction for the act. Yet McKee forebodingly senses his own attraction to the "forces of Evil," and this leads him to a pessimistic vision of the future.

> McKee had recognized the nameless face of evil—he recognized it, that is, as stronger than the nameless face of good. Everybody talked about Good, but had McKee ever set eyes on it? Had he ever felt pure Good? No, but he had come face to face with evil. He had seen the underside of the rock. What troubled him was not what he saw, but the nameless appetite behind it, the lust for evil in the faces of the beardless boys. McKee felt more life in their life than in himself. He didn't want a showdown. He felt himself beaten at the start. If McKee represented Good, like the Gray Ladies on the war posters, then the forces of evil would carry the day.[13]

The gap between McKee's repressed emotions and Lee Roy's murderous rage at first seems too wide to comprehend. Yet, perhaps it is only a hairbreadth. In terms of the future, the choice seems to be between accession to the "forces of Evil" (by continuing the surrender to the past) and some kind of transformation out of emotional repression-become-habit. The movement of *Ceremony in Lone Tree* is toward the realization that there is, in fact, a *choice* in the matter.

Since the intent and themes of this novel closely parallel those of *The Field of Vision,* our purposes will be better served by examining the way they are handled in a few key scenes than by either scratching the surface of the plot or by attempting an in-depth character analysis.

After an initial setting of scene, the story picks up almost exactly where *The Field of Vision* had ended. It is the morning after the bullfight. The three McKees and Scanlon, loaded with the usual haul of tourist souvenirs, stop to say good-bye to Boyd before heading back to Nebraska. Overnight, McKee has switched once again from repulsion at Boyd's audacity to attraction: "You know, you're closer to me than a brother, Gordon." Already speechless at this overt display of affection, Boyd is floored when Lois touches his arm lightly and says, almost gaily, "Why Mr.

McKee, what a thing to say to Mr. Boyd" (26). At that touch, Boyd realizes that he has never broken out of her control: "After thirty years of exile Boyd was back where his life had begun." Slowly, Boyd begins to see that, if he ever expects to be transformed, he will have to come to terms with "the one real friggin woman" who got away. He will have to return to Lone Tree.

At the bullfight, Boyd has learned that the existential moment, the moment of true heroism, is not to be gained by seeking. Uncertain of what he expects to learn in Lone Tree, he oscillates between feeling that it is sheer madness for him to return—that it would be like working toward a deathful predictability—and at the same time feeling the emptiness and transience of pleasure promised in the embraces of another and yet another Quirina Dolores Lupe Mendoza, the child-whore who is one of the many offspring of Boyd's distinctly unrepressed landlady and who is the exact antithesis of Lois.[14]

The trip from Acapulco to Lone Tree, from Quirina to Lois, initially reflects this oscillation. Traveling in the old Plymouth, which is as mechanically exhausted as Boyd himself is emotionally and physically unsound, Boyd wanders first northward to Nogales and then northwest, further away from Lone Tree, through Phoenix and Las Vegas to a small town in western Nevada by the name of Beatty. It is particularly interesting to note, as Boyd wonders whether the grasp of Lois or the clutch of Quirina represents a greater stranglehold on his future, that Beatty is barely a dozen miles from Death Valley. Though we are not told of this proximity in the story, the location is an ideal choice for the turning point in Boyd's mental state from oscillation to decision. Here, at the edge of an actual and emotional desert, both of which signal death, Boyd finds direction.

He checks into a hotel where the matron tells him that he simply must see the bomb go off during the early morning test. Behind his name in the register, she writes, WAKE BEFORE BOMB! Boyd quickly notes the contrast between these people who live every day with the possibility of destruction and the people of Lone Tree who exist in a comfortably secure sleep:

> No one cried out back there because everyone slept. The old man in the past, the young ones in the future, McKee in his cocoon, and Lois, ever-patient, ever-chaste Penelope, busy at her looming. WAKE BEFORE BOMB? how did one do it? Was it even advisable? The past, whether one liked it or not, was all that one actually possessed: the green stuff, the gilt-edged securities. The present was the moment of exchange—when all might be lost. Why risk it? Why not sleep on the money in the bank? To wake before the bomb was to risk losing all to gain what might be so little—a brief moment in the present, that moment later joined in the past.
>
> [32]

Lone Tree and its inhabitants denied the very existence of the present. Their sleepwalking could never be redemptive. One could only find life by taking the risk of waking before the bomb:

Did these bones live? At that moment they did. The meeting point, the melting point of the past confronting the present. Where no heat was thrown off, there was no light—where it failed to ignite the present, it was dead.

[32]

The bomb might be different for every person, but whatever it was, it involved heat or life. Understanding could only come when the imagination, as catalyst, made the connection of the past with the present in the realm of pure feeling. For the inhabitants of Lone Tree, this means confronting the opposition of all they value. For Boyd, in particular, it means confronting Lois's stoicism with the one event in which he is sure that an emotion was shared. In picking up the woman he calls "Daughter" and bringing her along, Boyd has only a vague idea that she might be the walking embodiment of the passion Lois fears in herself: "For a long time, Daughter, she's expected the worst. Maybe this is the time to let her have it" (38). The appellation *Daughter,* with its suggestion of incest, can only add to the shock waves of the bomb that Boyd is trying to detonate under Lois. Likewise, the name calls to mind the obvious analogue with Quirina, further reinforcing the tension between the futility of passion and the futility of repression in either filling the past with content or shaping the future.

Morris pictures the family which gathers together for Tom Scanlon's birthday as a microcosmic matriarchal society. The women control their emotions and their husbands with equal strength. They encourage their female children, as in the case of Étoile, not to miss out on the sexual fulfillment that they themselves had missed. They smother the male children with a suffocating, almost sexual, love, thereby asserting their authority over them and demanding obedience. Thus, they unwittingly propagate a system of relationships characterized by more and more extreme solutions to the problem of expressing love and hate. The males evade when possible and submit when necessary to the pursuing females. Since moderation is the cardinal virtue, the circle becomes complete as the women complain that they are being forced to grasp for greater control only because the men express so many eccentricities. The men seem to be merely along for the ride. For instance, McKee hides out in the garage and in his memories in order to evade Lois's control. He obviously believes he is guilty of the accusations leveled by his wife and is content to let her manipulate the puppets living in her house. Bud Momeyer has a simpler means of evading responsibility for not living up to the Dream; he simply refuses to "grow up."

While the males sleep, the women take over, thus perpetuating a degenerating system. The women, at any rate, are beginning to panic at this degeneration. Bud's wife, Maxine (perhaps the most pitiably human woman in the book), has nearly reached the end of her patience with the existing order of things:

> If something didn't happen over the weekend—if Calvin didn't speak, or Étoile didn't speak for him, or

Eileen or Lois didn't shoot somebody, or McKee or her father do something crazy—if something didn't happen to change the world, she would do it herself.

[25]

More and more, she is coming to the opinion that everyone is "crazy" or "stone mad." Maxine, like her sister, Lois, invests the greatest share of her efforts in merely keeping the pattern of family dynamics operating smoothly, but the center is failing to hold. The lack of imagination, the lack of depth, and their reliance upon habitual patterns of relating are the unseen sources of their disintegration. As Étoile notes, there exists a pervasive fear of examining sources, perhaps best exemplified by the head-in-the-sand attitude toward Lee Roy Momeyer: "It's because nobody wants to know why. It's because nobody wants to know *any-thing*! Everybody hates everybody, but nobody knows why anybody gets shot" (117). To search for answers behind such acts is to question the very structure of a flimsy system. It would require an act of heroism even to admit that the "gilt-edged" security was being threatened from within. Morris pictures a failure of will and imagination; it is so much more comfortable to remain asleep.

The difference between sleeping and waking is exposed in two major episodes in the novel. The first takes place in the chapter entitled "The Leaves of the Table," or, as it might be more aptly named, "The Forces of Convention Meet Gordon Boyd." Here the matriarchal society gets its first real test. After something over four pages of "surface" conversation, someone asks the uncharacteristically restrained Boyd to say something. He parodies their conversation with a travelogue description of Nebraska and Nebraskans. As the meal gets under way, it becomes apparent that Boyd is mustering all his forces for an attack on that carry-over from pioneer days, emotional control. He points out that "It's okay to show a bit of leg, a bit of bosom and a bit of bottom, but the man who shows the fly of his feelings has to leave the state" (180). When Daughter pops a contact lens onto her plate, Boyd reassures the startled guests: "It's just a show of feelings of an unusual order." Daughter's utter lack of inhibition is exactly what Boyd had hoped would contrast with Lois's "icy" reserve.

Then, Boyd attacks even deeper. He attempts to crack the illusion of happiness, the veneer of self-satisfaction, by telling McKee: "On good authority I have it that you and Mrs. McKee couldn't be happier. You couldn't be, so you haven't been, happier. What scares you pissless is not the fear of death, but the fear of exposure" (181). When McKee retorts by attempting to put Boyd on the "crazy fringe" of their society, Boyd counters with a question: "You awake or asleep?" McKee says nothing, sleeping silently. Finally, Boyd forces the emotion out in the open by pulling his trump card, the incident on the porch thirty-odd years in the past. It works. Lois is visibly shaken. McKee offers an angry but weak defense. Lois attacks Boyd, showing in the process that Boyd's words have reached her through her hitherto impenetrable armor. She dismisses both men with a distinctly value-laden epithet: "Men!" As she walks out of the room, little Gordon appears from behind her dress, as if by magic, holding one of Scanlon's pistols. The image of exposed female emotion in conjunction with the armed innocence of the child presents a picture charged with meaning in terms of the effects on the children of a smothering matriarchal system.

The second episode of importance in the confrontation between Boyd and the matriarchy over the question of sleeping and waking is, of course, Lois's firing of Scanlon's pistol. This is the event toward which Morris's two novels may be said to move. In the chapter entitled "Lois," where the shooting occurs, Boyd's attempt to join past with present has, to some extent, obviously succeeded. The vision of the episode on the porch forces Lois to confront her own past, and she realizes that she has been waiting for something, anything, to happen since that night. She has been waiting in fear, but she suddenly knows that during all those thirty years, she was fearing "not that something might happen, but after waiting so long it might not." Lois has become aware of what she worked so hard to repress, that Boyd's kiss was the one moment she had ever really felt alive.

Seeing this, everything else seems to fall into place for her. She realizes that what she has been terming "craziness" is nothing more than the violent recoil of an emotional spring which, having been wound tighter and tighter every day, finally reaches its breaking point. No longer does she see the problem in their isolated community as being one of the center holding; rather, she sees what Boyd has been trying to tell her all along, that their little world is held together with sealing wax from the *outside*. The thousand little acts of craziness are the expression of a human life which could never be totally squeezed into a straitjacket. Smothered in one place, it would burst out— quite naturally—in another. To leave one's mark was a healthy sign, a sign that one was fighting against the deadly slumber:

> She had never been so wide awake. *That* was the trouble. If the only way to leave an impression was to do something crazy like Boyd, she would do it—she would leave them with one they would never forget.
>
> [267]

She fires the gun. Scanlon wakes up to find that the century has turned—and dies. Like the detonation of the bomb, Lois's firing of the gun signals a transformation, and her father's death signals the end to the Scanlon view of the past.

How complete is the transformation? After the dust settles, McKee asks himself this question:

> How much really had [changed]? They had all grown old with trouble in their legs, their hearts or their heads, but Boyd still tended to get out of control, Mrs. McKee still retired to her room, and Maxine still fried an egg you couldn't dent with a fork.
>
> [293-94]

There still appear to be some certainties. Perhaps nothing really has changed. Yet a bit later McKee muses over the difference between Daughter and Lois, a comparison which, we remember, Boyd had encouraged them all to make: "Not a pretty girl at all, and when he stopped to think, when McKee stopped to think of how Lois once was—well, when he stopped to think of that he couldn't help but marvel how times had changed" (299). Once again, McKee seems to be *reminded* of something. But there is a subtle difference. More than simply nostalgia for a lost past, he consciously compares the past to the present, forcing the past to shed light on the present, and in the process, he sees Lois as she really is for the first time.

As the covered wagon bearing the body of Scanlon pulls out of Lone Tree, Lois yells, "Just remember, McKee—," the end of which is lost in the hee-haw of a mule "as if he had heard what she said." Her injunction cuts two ways. McKee *is* remembering; but he is no longer trapped in those memories. Moreover, the mule's response may signal McKee's own changed attitude toward gynocratic control, a hold which, if it has not been done away with, has at least loosened somewhat.

Neither McKee nor the reader is able to predict the extent of the change. As the dead wagon rounds the hotel, the town disappears from McKee's view. It is as if his static vision of Lone Tree is finally receding into the past. And with this passage, McKee realizes that the "sanded navel of the world" will not be the same when he returns:

> The wall of the hotel, the MAIL POUCH sign peeling, moved in between them and the rest of the town, like an old-style curtain between the movies and the vaudeville. Had one just rung down on something? . . . Tomorrow it would be different. Could anybody say in just what way?
>
> [301]

Lois's act seems to have released them from simple nostalgia for the past. In a nice twist, Morris ends the final scene with Boyd and Daughter fast asleep and McKee looking into the future, wide awake, imagination free, envisioning the possibilities for turning the area around Lone Tree into a land of plenty. He sees a new frontier of corn and wheat and clover. It is a Dream, and yet it differs from that of old Scanlon who, McKee surmises, died in part from the smell of that clover. A thousand acts of transformation would have to be performed by women *and* men if the dream were to be realized. Nonetheless, at least some of them—the riders in the wagon—have made the imaginative leap from the past to the future in the synapse of the present. For awhile, the degeneration of the matriarchal society would be slowed as the Dream took on less insurmountable proportions: "Tomorrow it would be different. Could anybody say in what way?"

If Morris is truly a calumniator of the female, we must, on the basis of these two novels, see that he is equally contemptuous of the male. Most likely, he is contemptuous of a certain segment of either sex—those who exist on the surfaces of life, those who have forgotten what the word *imagination* means, those who are content with the petty games and isolation incumbent upon maintaining order at all costs, those who are content with the stasis of self-satisfaction, those who put their emotions in a box and padlock it shut, those, in short, who succumb to the sterility of success or to the hardness of heart resulting from failure in the distinctly American attempt to "pursue and cage" the impossible, the American Dream. In *The Field of Vision* and *Ceremony in Lone Tree,* Wright Morris makes it clear that transformation is not simply a male prerogative. The leap into the future may be accomplished by the hand of a woman.

Notes

1. "Norman Rockwell's America," *Atlantic* 200 (December 1957): 138.

2. Leslie Fiedler, *Love and Death in the American Novel* (London: Paladin, 1960), p. 316.

3. See Wright Morris, *The Territory Ahead* (New York: Harcourt, Brace, 1957), p. 133-46, 171-86.

4. Jonathan Baumbach, *The Landscape of Nightmare* (New York: New York University Press, 1965), p. 156.

5. Wright Morris, *A Bill of Rites, A Bill of Wrongs, A Bill of Goods* (New York: New American Library, 1967), p. 54.

6. See Morris's comments in a 1959 interview, specifically: "I would say that the last book [*The Field of Vision*] and the book that is to come [*Ceremony in Lone Tree*] are linked imaginatively so that a chain reaction seems to be taking place." Sam Bleufarb, "Points of View: An Interview with Wright Morris," *Accent* 19 (Winter 1959): 38.

7. Ibid., p. 55.

8. Wright Morris, *The Field of Vision* (New York: Harcourt, Brace, 1956), p. 19. Page numbers in the text of quotations from *The Field of Vision* refer to this edition.

9. Wright Morris, "Made in U.S.A.," *American Scholar* 29 (Autumn 1960): 483, 485.

10. Ibid., p. 483.

11. Wayne Booth traces the difference with clarity in his two excellent articles on Morris, "The Two Worlds in the Fiction of Wright Morris," *Sewanee Review* 65 (Summer 1957): 375-99, and "The Shaping of Prophecy: Craft and Ideas in the Novels of Wright Morris," *American Scholar* 31 (Autumn 1962): 608-26.

12. Bleufarb, "Points of View," p. 45.

13. Wright Morris, *Ceremony in Lone Tree* (Lincoln: University of Nebraska Press, 1973), pp. 50-51. (Original date of publication 1960.) All the following quotations are taken from this edition of the text.

14. Note, particularly in relation to McKee's fear of the "forces of Evil," that Quirina is described as the very "flower of evil."

Raymond L. Neinstein (essay date 1979)

SOURCE: "Wright Morris: The Metaphysics of Home," in *Prairie Schooner,* Vol. 53, No. 2, Summer, 1979, pp. 121-54.

[*In the following essay, exploring the interplay of words and pictures, and of fact and fiction in Morris's Nebraska novels, Neinstein argues that Morris's characters taint the perception of the actual with a dreamlike vision.*]

> They say that "home is where the heart is." I think it is where the *house* is, and the adjacent buildings.
>
> —Emily Dickinson, *Letters*

Repeatedly, in the course of Wright Morris's large work (at last count, eighteen novels, three collections of short stories, four photo-text books, and four volumes of essays and criticism), there is a return to the territory of his birth, "the navel of the world," as he calls it, the plains of Nebraska. Morris is not the first writer to try to come to terms with that region in literature; Willa Cather is his most distinguished predecessor. But Morris's experience of Nebraska, as a child in the years 1910-19 and, more important, as an adult rediscovering his home place on several return trips in the 1940s, is different from Cather's. Hers was the world of beginnings, of the pioneer immigrant settlers, those who found "nothing but land: not a country at all, but the material out of which countries are made."[1] Her relationship to the place was one of settlement, of possession. Morris's is one of exodus and attempted repossession. By the time he became conscious of his home place, it was largely a thing of the past. How to return to that place and come to terms with that past in a way that does not cripple but, rather, nurtures the imagination, is the problem posed by that portion of Morris's work which I want to examine: the early Plains trilogy, *The Inhabitants* (1946), *The Home Place* (1948), and *The World in the Attic* (1949); the subsequent trilogy, *The Works of Love* (1952), which Morris calls "the linchpin in my novels concerned with the plains," *The Field of Vision* (1956), and *Ceremony in Lone Tree* (1960); and the more recent *Fire Sermon* (1971) and its sequel, *A Life* (1973).[2]

In his critical essay *The Territory Ahead* (1958), Morris finds the American imagination, as it is revealed through its literature, strangling in the death grip of nostalgia for a past that is largely mythic and definitely over.[3] The only writer who proves an exception, Morris claims, is Henry James, whose definition in *The American Scene* of the artist, the writer, or the critic as "the participant at once so interested and so detached as to be moved to a report of the matter," can stand as the ideal to which Morris aspires. James speaks in the same sentence of "the superstition that objects and places, coherently grouped, disposed for human use and addressed to it, must have a sense of their own, a mystic meaning proper to themselves to give out" (*Territory,* 187). Morris began as a photographer as well as a writer; his early books are experiments combining photographs and written texts. Although his later novels may dispense with photographs, they are still concerned with the act, and the art, of seeing, the possibilities of seeing clearly what is there with a vision rendered by the imagination's taking hold of landscapes and things, finding the "mystic meaning" in "objects and places, coherently grouped, disposed for human use."

The problem of returning to a home place and trying to see nothing that is not there involves grappling with a nostalgia which can easily become what Clyde Muncy, in *The World in the Attic,* calls "home-town nausea." The risk is that what one will see is the nothing that is there. And in Nebraska, again and again in Morris's works, that is exactly what we find, nothing, miles and miles of it, punctuated by an occasional grain elevator.

But that very emptiness, according to Morris, can feed the imagination, forcing it to supply what is otherwise lacking. In *Ceremony in Lone Tree,* he writes: "There is little to see, but plenty of room to look. . . . The emptiness of the plains generates illusions that require little moisture, and grow better, like tall stories, where the mind is dry . . . the plain is a metaphysical landscape" (4-5). Earlier, in *The Works of Love,* Morris has said much the same thing: "In the dry places, men begin to dream. Where the rivers run sand, there is something in man that begins to flow" (3). Thus, the movement of Morris's work is away from nostalgia, from the longing for the Great Good Place we tend to locate in our youth or in the past, and toward an imaginative confrontation with "objects and places, coherently grouped," often toward the most humanly minimal scenes, landscapes, and environments. Out of this confrontation with what is at hand, once what is there is seen clearly, what "mystic meanings" there are will arise in the mind of the witness. That event will constitute the imaginative repossession of the landscape, free of nostalgia or hometown nausea. Turning from Willa Cather's nostalgic evocation of the Nebraska past, the mythic times of the first immigrant settlers, to Morris's effort to repossess Nebraska imaginatively as a territory for his fiction, we may perceive the distinction between a neoregional literature and the prior version of regionalism from which it developed.

The Inhabitants, The Home Place, and *The World in the Attic* form a most unusual trilogy. The first two books are linked in that they are both photo-texts, that is, combinations of writing and photography, but they are otherwise quite different. *The Inhabitants* presents a series of unconnected prose fragments, each one accompanied, on the facing page, by a photograph which sometimes seems to have an unspecified "something" in common with the piece of prose. *The Home Place* presents a continuous narrative, a novel about the return of Clyde Muncy, a Nebraska-born writer now living in New York, with his family, to his hometown of Lone Tree. Facing each page of the text are photographs that seem to be illustrations of the story. Thus, a scene taking place in a barbershop will be matched by a photograph of a barber chair, and when "Uncle Harry" is mentioned, there is a photo of an old man whom we take

to be Uncle Harry. *The World in the Attic* is a narrative sequel to *The Home Place,* taking up the events of the very next day, but lacking photographs.

Morris relates in an interview that he had planned to have photographs in *The World in the Attic,* but was persuaded by his publisher to omit them because they were causing confusion on the part of the public. Those who were interested in fiction found the photographs intrusive, and those interested in photography were not readers of fiction.[4] As there is no reason why it should not, the confusion seems to extend into the realm of criticism. Few critics seem to know what to make of the combination, in one book, of words and pictures. Some find *The Inhabitants* the more successful of the two volumes; some prefer *The Home Place.*[5] Some see the photographs in that volume as "primary," while others see them as illustrations of the story, "lend[ing] reality to the fictive text."[6] But this last is an example of imprecise and unthought-out language. What does it mean, to lend reality to a fictive text? What kind of reality can a fictive text be said to have, except a fictive reality, a reality as fiction? And what kind of reality does a photograph possess? Is a photograph not a fiction of sorts as well, as real (that is, as *un*real) as a picture made of words? Are not both selected, developed, framed images? It is only half correct to say that the photographs "lend" reality to the written text. A loan, unlike a gift outright, implies repayment. The text will have to give up something in return, will find itself giving up *its* reality to the photographs, which seem realer.

What is seldom discussed in Morris criticism is the tension between text and photographs in *The Inhabitants* and *The Home Place.* The tension is not so apparent in *The Inhabitants.* Since the writing is free of specific characters, plot, even place, since it is just writing, or speech, it is free, as the houses, barns, grain elevators, and so on are also set free, not intended to illustrate a story. The two media are in a delicate harmony, on friendly terms. But since *The Home Place* has a story, the photographs are easily seen as illustrations, going along, in some unspecified but generally accepted way, with the text. Critics focus on the characters—Muncy vs. his wife, Muncy vs. his small-town and rural relatives, old folks vs. children. No one discusses the interesting and problematic juxtaposition of two modes of seeing, even though Muncy keeps talking about his "camera eye," his Aunt Clara is conspicuously given a glass eye, and the novel culminates in the whole clan sitting around discussing an old photograph of the family.

The photographs do not "lend reality," whatever that means, to the text; they actually undermine the only reality the text has, a fictive one. They suggest or insist that something out there is real, *really* real, *more* real than the text. They intrude on the written text, which has to fight back to reclaim its preempted or usurped territory by the devious processes of fiction. The text has to try to subvert the photographs and insist on the right to reality of a character or a place in fiction. "It hadn't really occurred to me,"

Clyde Muncy thinks, "that no matter what I said, or how I said it, it would be taken for the truth" (**Home Place,** 38). Muncy is thinking about how his urban deviousness is taken by his ingenuous rural relatives. But the statement could also be Morris's, applied to readers who identify Muncy with Morris and go on to say, "There is such a place as Lone Tree, such a man as Grandpa Muncy. We see them and believe they have an existence outside the book."[7]

Alan Trachtenberg, in his essay "The Craft of Vision," makes more sense and has a more sophisticated idea of photography, vision, and fiction's version of the real. He understands that "vision begins in the head," that "the finished print of a serious artist is an accurate record *only* of the maker's vision, not of an honorific reality which awaits, fully composed, before the eye. The print . . . is as much a contrived artifact, a created thing, as a cubist painting or a poet's metaphor. . . . The artist in photography gives us not copies of a real world, but the world *as it is seen* by the artist; the seeing makes the world real. . . . In neither book are the pictures illustrations of the text."[8]

Another reader of Morris's work touches on, but then passes right by, the interesting problem of the relationship of written text to photographs: "*Who* then, is responsible for the photographs? The narrative is Clyde's; the author of the photographs is totally out of sight behind the shutter."[9] The "author of the photographs" is also, however, "behind" the first-person narrative, which is a device. Muncy is a literary invention, a device by means of which Morris can both reach out to and gain distance from the place, its objects, houses, and people. The photographs are also devices, meeting points for artifacts and the consciousness that is both fascinated by them and wary of the grip of that fascination, held in their grip through nostalgia, and nauseated by their insistent overwhelmingness. Muncy and the shutter are both intermediaries, distancing and framing devices.

Muncy, with his camera eye, sees as if through a shutter: "Everything in its place, its own place, with a frame of space around it" (**Home Place,** 41). His problem of not fitting in back in Lone Tree after thirty years away, his desire to settle in there, to move into his Uncle Ed's house, but his finding it absolutely impossible, the way he sees with his distancing, alienating camera eye what the others hardly see at all, these are all indications that the way in which the photographs seem to lend reality to the text is a subversive, ironic way, that the camera eye is part of the problem and is perhaps one of the central subjects of the book.

Morris, then, near the beginning of his career (there were two previous novels, one of which, **The Man Who Was There,** contains a section of descriptions of photographs)[10] poses a neoregional rather than a regional problem: the problem of place. The very "thereness" of the land, its structures, artifacts, and inhabitants, is called into question through the juxtaposition of two media which seem to exist on, or to report on, two different levels of reality, yet which both prove to be equally artistic, contrived, fictive. Each thus casts doubts on the status of the other; the tension is mutually subversive. We never quite know who or what to believe. Is that old man in the photograph really the Uncle Harry of the novel; is that the Model T they ride to town in; is that really Lone Tree? Really?

These questions come to a head in the last episode of **The Home Place,** in which the whole family gathers around a nineteenth-century photograph of the family and discusses who's who, and who married whom, and who had which children, and who died when and where. On the facing page we also see what is ostensibly the photograph in question. That is, we see a photograph of a photograph in which nine men, five women, and a cat are lined up, side by side, in front of a fence beside a clapboard house. Here, text and image seem to merge, since the text concerns the image, *as image.* It is a different condition than that in which we read about a barbershop and saw a photograph of a barbershop. Here, one frame is exchanged for the other, one text jumps into the reality of the other. As the characters in the novel discuss the photograph and we look over their shoulders, we see them doing what we have been doing all along, i.e., making connections about place and history through an image. It is also what Muncy has been trying to do, to feel connected to a place and its people. His artist's camera eye, which he thought distinguished and separated him from the rest, proves to be the eye through which the family, in this oft-repeated ceremony, maintains its sense of itself, its continuity in time, its relation to a place. That they don't *know* what they are about, and could not discuss, or even want to, the frame-within-a-frame ontological/aesthetic problem they pose, as Muncy would probably enjoy doing, is not the point. The joke is on Muncy, who thought he was so different. The joke is on the reader who fails to perceive the ironic mode of **The Home Place,** which is signalled in Morris's use, as an epigraph, of James's remark about the artist or critic as the interested but detached participant. We are immediately to dissociate Morris, the interested but detached artist, from the all-too-attached Muncy. Muncy, who longs for, but cannot realize, an authentic relationship with the place, never realizes that he is reacting to images, images that provoke in him varied responses, from awe to nausea. Morris, the maker and manipulator of these images, allows us, as readers, to "play Muncy" as we look, supposedly through his camera eye, at the photographs. Muncy has the nostalgic, regional sense of place, the longing for an unrecoverable landscape that neoregionalist Morris shows to be, and always to have been, an image.

The clinical probing of that image, as if it were an abscessed tooth, continues in **The World in the Attic,** in which the Muncy family, having turned east in Lone Tree, passes through the next town down the road, Junction, a town in which Clyde spent a good many years as a boy. The narrative presents the events of two days and the intervening night. On the day of his arrival, Clyde wanders through the town of his memory and looks up a boyhood pal, Bud Hibbard, now married and the father of two children. He also pays a visit to Bud's grandmother, Aunt Angie, who, aged and blind, lives alone at the back of an enormous mansion which her son, Bud's uncle Clinton Hibbard, built for his southern bride, known to the town as Miss Caddy. Clinton Hibbard is long dead; Aunt Angie's husband is dead. Although the two old women live on in the same house, Aunt Angie has sealed off her part from Caddy's, refusing even to speak to her, living on only in the hope of outliving her.

Caddy, whose death is the central event of Muncy's second day in Junction, is presented as having been, for the whole town, a Gatsbyan "dream of Daisy," who long ago brought with her, from the Deep South, a faint touch of romance and elegance, qualities to which the townspeople could only respond, in their fascination, by ostracizing her. Clyde remembers, from his boyhood, Caddy's all-night parties, the Japanese lanterns on the lawn, the games, the laughter, the tinkling of glasses, the elegant buggies that brought handsome young people out from Lincoln and Omaha, the dancing, the music, the "lovely girls and fresh young men." Caddy was the lone representative and is now the lone survivor of the promise of life Junction once, long ago, felt itself to have, a promise it never realized. The town, its main street named Horace Greeley, looked west, while history went east. Junction, as Clyde's New York wife Peggy knows from the start, and as Clyde sees by the novel's end, is a "jerkwater town" which "can't live with this notion of marble stairs, and those girls you used to see, Sunday evenings, in the tasseled lawn swings. Those girls had gone somewhere else. . . . They had gone to the cities . . . now the lawn swings were rusty, the platforms matted with grass." And the town's one streetlight, "hanging where the crossroads had been planned, where the heavy city-traffic would demand it—a fine City lamp" now affords "a full view of the small town dump" (*Attic*, 171-73).

The book, then, is capable of being read as Clyde Muncy's effort to find out "what to make of a diminished thing," that thing being Junction, his youth, its dreams. He knows that his own orientation is clear: "however the world or the poles shifted, my needle still pointed toward the house on the corner where Miss Caddy Hibbard and Aunt Angie were known to live" (*Attic*, 174). What Muncy doesn't seem to see until the end is that it is his nostalgic attachment to that boyhood dream, just as much as the town's repressed but equally firm connection to it, that diminishes, that in fact stifles the possibilities of the present. Bud Hibbard, Clyde discovers, still lives in the Gatsbyan past. Clyde's mention of the pretty girls who had lived next door twenty years ago brings a blush to Bud's cheeks and a "ssshhhhh" to his lips, just as it would have then. But Muncy thinks that he himself is somehow not implicated in the drama in which Junction is the arena and the forces of past and present are in conflict.

What Muncy sees as he walks through town produces in him "home-town nausea." But what he sees and remembers are scenes we first saw and read in *The Inhabitants*.

That book proposed to give us "the look" of a place, and a look, we read, is what a man or a house has when it is "inhabited." And nothing, Morris tells us in book after book, is so inhabited, nothing is so full of the presence of life, as a vacant house, a house which still bears all the traces of human life—the path worn into the rug by the repeated habits of a lifetime, that path the true "figure in the carpet"; the bed shaped into an imprint of its occupants; the basement; the attic; the porch; the privy. Nothing is so vibrant with life, so possessed, as an empty house. The look we see in *The Inhabitants* is a ghostly, vacant one, then: abandoned houses, eroded fields, and unattached, free-floating prose passages, verbal equivalents of the snapshots they accompany, through which Morris tries to evoke the life he feels to be so present, most present, in its absence.

In *The World in the Attic*, some of these prose pieces are repeated, slightly changed, and set in context. The context is that of a man, a writer, returning to his home place, trying to recover its look, the look he remembers, and to show that look to his wife and children. But Muncy is undercut by Morris from the start. The novel opens with a wonderfully ironic incident. Muncy has stopped the car and is giving his son, who has grown up on Fifty-third Street in Manhattan, a lesson on Nebraska, demonstrating the extent to which he is still the native. When the boy calls what he has seen growing in the fields grass, Muncy reproaches him, telling him it's wheat, "Can't you tell wheat from grass?" he asks his son, only to be corrected by a young boy riding a pony, "That's rye, wheat's over there" (*Attic*, 1-6).

Muncy is not the only butt of this joke. He has explained how he and his father had gone through the same business about grass and wheat and how to tell them apart. He had been convinced then, as his son has every right to be now, that his father didn't know what he was talking about. The nostalgic myth of the old-timer, the man close to the land, is punctured. Not Muncy, not his father, probably not *his* father before him. What was there was there only as it was perceived, as we have learned from the crash course in the image that *The Home Place* provided. In that book the pump Muncy remembered as being a block away from the house was, he found, quite close. He never did know wheat from rye from grass. Even as a child on the plains, he lived in "an Omaha house" that his father had built, and ate in a Japanese restaurant. And this, it seems, was the aspiration of the whole town—to be away, somewhere, anywhere else than the plains of Nebraska. This wish was what Miss Caddy, with her southern-belle ways, spoke to in the town. Always living in a world of make-believe, always somewhere else, Caddy was the living embodiment of the town's dream, its romance of placelessness that finally caused (and ended in) the Dust Bowl, when the topsoil of the Plains could be seen in the skies over Manhattan, America's first neoregional event.

Miss Caddy, once the town's secret dream, is now old, sick, crippled, and about to die. Her death awaits only Muncy's arrival. Is it merely a staged coincidence, the bit of drama Morris had to provide, or are there valid structural connections between the two events? Why, on both occasions when Clyde visits Aunt Angie, does she, in her blindness, see the "Dead Wagon" passing by? What does old Mr. Purdy, who lives across the road from Aunt Angie and looks after her, mean when, discussing with Muncy Aunt Angie's vision of the Dead Wagon, he tells Muncy:

> "Would depend . . . who she saw ridin' in it."
>
> "We can take that for granted," I said. "After all, who else would it be?"
>
> "That's where you're wrong."
>
> "Just what do you mean?" . . .
>
> "What you were sayin' yesterday—" he said. "That you were just passin' through." . . .
>
> "Well, let's put it that way," said Purdy.
>
> [Attic, 157-58]

The Home Place, we may recall, had a very similar structure to that of The World in the Attic. Muncy, having left New York City to bring up his children in Lone Tree, is told he can have his dying Uncle Ed's house across the road just as soon as Uncle Ed dies. The rest of the day, and the rest of the novel, is spent in a vulturelike hovering around the house until Muncy's little girl's breathless and ghoulish announcement, "We can have it, Mummy—he's dead" (Home Place, 143). Muncy, at that point, had been in the midst of a silent discourse on the "holiness" and "beauty" of the old man's shoes and bib overalls, how they connote "abstinence, frugality, and independence—the home-grown, made-on-the-farm trinity." His daughter's completely nonnostalgic, realistic pronouncement on the situation provides the ironic counterpoint to Muncy's nostalgic appropriation of the artifacts of another man's life.

Let us now turn our attention back to The World in the Attic. Morris hints that his novel is "like the Platte, with all of its meaning under the ground—out of sight but not quite out of mind" (Attic, 178). David Madden, in his study Wright Morris, claims that "it is appropriate that the day of Caddy's death and of Muncy's return coincide."[11] But he never really explains how or why it is appropriate. His reading of the novel cannot adequately explain it since he sees the event as symbolic of Muncy's liberation from the past, his ability to live, henceforth, in the present. But for Muncy to be so reborn, he needs to understand something more crucial than that Caddy is dead. What he must understand is, in fact, the underground meaning of the novel, the real appropriateness of the timing of the novel's central event. For Aunt Angie has seen, in her senile but oracular blindness, what Muncy and family finally come to understand only at the novel's end, and what seems to have escaped the critical gaze of most of Morris's readers: that it is, of course, Muncy, riding blindly into the ghost town of his own nostalgia, who rides the Dead Wagon, that it is the town itself, collective prisoner of its own nostalgia, that has denied itself any chance at life. When

Muncy, on his way out of town, stops to peek through the windows at the viewing of Caddy's coffin, he sees Aunt Angie emerge, after decades, from her "cave" at the back of the house, unlocking the doors that had long been shut, passing judgment on the whole town: "Facing them, her apron blowing in the draft down the stair well, she felt again what she had known all the time. The folly of it. They were witless. And now they were dead" (Attic, 188). At least this is Muncy's reading of what he sees. When he and his family drive out of Junction at the end of the novel, his daughter says, "'I've been thinking—you want to know what I've been thinking?'" Muncy's reaction is, "Nobody did. It was more or less clear, I guess, to all of us" (Attic, 189). What is clear is that to tell grass from wheat and wheat from rye, to tell alive from dead and past from present, one needs more than a nostalgic, albeit a camera, eye. One needs a kind of moral courage, the courage to take a close and nonnostalgic look, at once interested and detached, at one's place and at oneself:

> Here in the box, at least, one could really look at her. As you would look at your childhood, or the best impression you had of yourself. I knew this as well as any man, and if I did not come for a look at Caddy it was because I knew it, because it privately scared me to death. For I knew that more had died, upstairs, than I had reckoned with. I also had died, and the gist of my life was to be born again.
>
> [Attic, 147]

Muncy does not take the crucial look. But he knows that it is still there for the taking. Driving eastward out of town, the sunset in his rear-view mirror, he understands, in a way that is "more or less clear, I guess, to all of us," the meaning of his overnight stay in Junction. We understand the moral structure of a neoregional novel, and one of the moral imperatives of neoregionalism.

It is the "nostalgic myth," Morris writes in The Territory Ahead, "that now cripples the imagination, rather than the dark and brooding immensity of the continent. It is the territory behind that defeats our writers of genius, not America" (Territory, Foreword, n.p.). As was mentioned earlier, it is Henry James, and specifically the James of The American Scene, who typifies, for Morris, the ideal "seer" of place:

> The heart of the matter is that James is not a victim of nostalgia. Among all of these exiles, he alone is not a captive of the past. James is a free man in the sense that Tocqueville is free. Each can feel confidence in his impressions, knowing that these impressions are not hopelessly betrayed by nostalgic ties, or concealed emotional commitments. . . . [James] returns as a native to repossess, fully, what was both unpossessed and dispossessed.
>
> [Territory, 190]

Morris's Nebraska trilogy provides a lengthy lesson on the dangers of nostalgia, both to the perceiver and, more important, to the perceived. Even a critic like Marcus Klein, whose essay on Morris is one of the most sensible and helpful, sees *The Territory Ahead* as Morris's recognition of "this nostalgia that all but captured his work," i.e., as a critical reading of his own novels.[12] But this is, again, to confuse Morris with Muncy and to risk missing what *The Inhabitants, The Home Place,* and *The World in the Attic* have carefully shown, how a nostalgic view of a place, its people, houses, artifacts, overlooks what is there at the very same time that it appropriates and feeds upon what is there for its own purposes. This is, in fact, the ecological history of America. If our environment today is imperiled, it is largely because our society is caught in a web of nostalgia, riding a Dead Wagon, living by outmoded myths, the myth of the frontier, the myth of inexhaustible resources, the myth of our own national youth, and is consequently oblivious to what is really *there.*

Muncy, in *The World in the Attic,* remembered his pioneer grandfather, "mad all his life with the incurable vagueness, the receding promise of the next frontier" (11). But as we have read in *The Inhabitants,* "the thing about Grandpa is that all you see is where he is from. No matter where he is all you see is where he is from" (9), or, as Morris puts it in *The Territory Ahead,* "for more than a century the territory ahead has been the world that lies somewhere behind us, a world that has become, in the last few decades, a nostalgic myth" (Foreword, n.p.). *The Territory Ahead* only spells out the lessons of Morris's earlier Nebraska trilogy, in which one can see how Muncy's perceptions, on his return to Lone Tree and Junction, how his attempts to repossess his past were, just as the towns themselves had been, "hopelessly betrayed by nostalgic ties and concealed emotional commitments." But by the time Muncy leaves town, thinking "perhaps I looked like a man who had seen something" (*Attic,* 188), we may trust, with a certain degree of confidence, that Muncy is no longer heading for "where he is from."

But a whole new cast of characters is still making this trek. The confusion of one's destination with one's origin, and the consequent blindness and potential for violence to one's own place and time, are all pursued further in Morris's next Nebraska trilogy, *The Works of Love, The Field of Vision,* and *Ceremony in Lone Tree.* David Madden sees the last two of these novels as "parts of a single novel whose third part is yet to come."[13] In fact, *The Field of Vision* and *Ceremony* are the last two works in a coherent vision of the American imagination that begins in *The Works of Love.* Working out from the mind and career of one single individual, Morris proceeds to give us an entire range of consciousnesses (and some nonconsciousnesses), a society in miniature spanning five generations, from the one that opened the West to the ones that now have to inhabit it. The works of love are as much the subject of the latter two novels as of the first, and the central character of the first novel, Will Brady, is resurrected in *Ceremony* in the character of his adopted son, Will Brady, Jr.

In *The World in the Attic,* Muncy remembered his father's story of a man named Tom Scanlon, who lived in a room of the New Western Hotel in Lone Tree, looking out a westward-facing window, at nothing. "No house or store, no building of any kind, lay to the west. . . . Over the years Tom Scanlon saw a good many things, where, as a rule, there was nothing to see" (*Attic,* 41-43). Scanlon reappears in *The Field of Vision,* and is the central character, or focal point, of *Ceremony.* He is an eccentric, stubborn plainsman, now almost ninety, still living alone in the same hotel, now abandoned and set in what is now the ghost town of Lone Tree. Scanlon, as is obvious, and as we are told again and again in *Field* and *Ceremony,* represents the past. When the century turned, Scanlon refused to turn with it. When the westward movement turned east, Scanlon still sat by his window, facing west. By the time we meet him in *Field,* he is a total captive of the past, confusing pioneering stories his father had told him when he was a boy with his own life, believing his father's experiences had actually happened to *him,* blind to the present, literally and figuratively, living not even in his own memory, but in that of another man, long dead.

Scanlon stays put in a ghost town on the Nebraska prairie, gazing west. Will Brady, whose life story is told in *The Works of Love,* starts out on the same western prairie, in a sod hut, and moves east, with the times, to Chicago. He makes money, he makes love to, and marries, several women. But his is a painfully undeveloped consciousness; starting from ground-zero, emerging from a sod hut which is more under the ground than above it, "like a mound or a storm cave," Brady is unprepared for the world, uncomfortable in it, confused by it, eventually destroyed by his inability to live in it and understand it.

Morris links Scanlon and Brady in an essay on the development of his fictional characters:

> Will Brady and Scanlon seem initially to arise from the same impulse, but then Brady, in his story, heads east, down the long road that leads to Chicago. Indian Bow and the view to the west are left to such a character as Scanlon. It is on this ever-receding horizon that his eyes are fixed. If Brady seems to point toward an intolerable future, Scanlon's gaze is fixed on the mythic past. It remains serene and uncorrupted because it keeps itself out of this world.[14]

It is significant, then, that Lone Tree, which was one of the scenes of Clyde Muncy's "home-town nausea," with its barber-shops, feed store, soda fountain, and so on, is now, in *Ceremony,* an abandoned ghost town. Except for Scanlon, there is no one left but Morris's "inhabitants," the ghostly presences that remain and bear the traces of the lives once lived. Both Indian Bow, Brady's origin, and Lone Tree are described in similar ways, as dry, empty places productive of nothing so much as dreams, illusions, imagination. We recall, from *Works,* Morris's opening lines: "In the dry places, men begin to dream. Where the rivers run sand, there is something in man that begins to flow" (3); and, from *Ceremony*: "The emptiness of the plain generates illusions that require little moisture, and grow better, like tall stories, where the mind is dry. The tall corn may flower or burn in the wind, but the plain is a metaphysical landscape and the bumper crop is the one Scanlon sees through the flaw in the glass" (5). Not the clear pane, but the flaw—sitting eye-to-eye with it, Scanlon "sees . . . the scenic props of his own mind" (4). The shift, then, from the homey small town, surrounded by farms, to the deserted ghost town surrounded by arid plains, is more than a shift in locale, setting. It signals a change in consciousness. If the small town is associated with a nostalgia that shaded on nausea, if it was full of sentimental images—old folks, old photographs, old farmhouses, old jalopies—the ghost town is associated with consciousness itself. The setting and the subject of the trilogy is, as announced in the lines from *Paradise Lost* that serve as epigraph to *Field,* "the mind" which "is its own place."

But there is a bitter controlling irony or double vision at work in the description of the plains as a metaphysical landscape, a country of consciousness, since the two characters who are presented as pure products of the plains, Will Brady and Tom Scanlon, are scarcely conscious at all. Will Brady is a dull, passive, confused, plodding man, a man incapable of making connections, perceiving relationships between things, a man never at home in his own houses, but only in hotel lobbies or in the unreal world of Hollywood, "a hotel lobby as big as the great out-of-doors" (**Works,** 191). Looking at a map of Nebraska, Brady hears businessmen talking of how the state is booming, but "eyes open, all he saw was the map" (19). Living in a world of signs, with no understanding that they refer to things, he is a semiological illiterate. Starting from an empty, "out-of-this-world" place that has ill-prepared him for life in this world, and constantly required to "read," to interpret situations, Brady finds himself, wherever he is, lost. To him, things are always exactly what they seem to be. At the novel's end, working as a department store Santa Claus, he believes he *is* Santa Claus. How different is this from Scanlon's belief, in **Ceremony,** that he is Buffalo Bill? Or Scanlon's great-grandson Gordon McKee's conviction, in **Field** and **Ceremony,** that he is Davy Crockett? Or Gordon's brother Calvin's desire, in **Ceremony,** to be old Scanlon, or who he thinks Scanlon was? Or the desire of the teen-age mass-murderer Charlie Munger, in **Ceremony,** to "be somebody"? If the emptiness of the plains generates illusions, they can be deadly ones. Especially since, in the modern wasteland Brady eventually makes his way to, the one which is the background of **Field** and **Ceremony,** so many illusions are available, so many are for sale. Scanlon, in his mind the old frontiersman, wears, as does his great-grandson, a Disney imitation coonskin cap. Gordon Boyd, a central character in **Field** and **Ceremony,** has spent his whole life trying to be someone, anyone. As a teen-ager he tried to walk on water, and has made a subsequent career out of such quasi-grandiose, quasi-bathetic failures, trying, if not to reach the top, at least to "touch bottom," but only in terms of the images, the clichés, of such an attempt. His deterioration is finally so picturesque that he finds his photograph in *Life* magazine. Walter McKee, Boyd's boyhood friend, has spent his whole life watching Boyd, instead of living himself. Bud Momeyer,

McKee's brother-in-law, a mild-mannered mailman and perpetual adolescent, stalks his neighborhood in Lincoln, Nebraska, at night, in **Ceremony,** with a bow and arrows, playing Indian, and killing stray cats.

It is not that there is too much imagination in these characters. There is not enough; there are only clichés. Their problem is that they don't know who they are, or that there is no satisfaction to be had in one's personal identity when one is bombarded with more spectacular ones out of our uncorrupted past: Davy Crockett, Buffalo Bill, or a wild, scalping Indian. The once real "raw material" of our past, as Morris terms it in **The Territory Ahead,** has been used, processed, so many times that by the time we inherit it, it is only as an exhausted cliché, a *Saturday Evening Post* cover by Norman Rockwell. If James may be said to be the hero of **The Territory Ahead,** Rockwell certainly figures as the villain. In his chapter on Rockwell, Morris writes:

> The paradox of our situation might be put like this: having either exhausted, or depleted, the raw material that appeals to us, we needed a technician to create the illusion that it was still there. Rockwell is that technician. He understands the hunger and supplies the nourishment. The hunger is for the Good Old Days . . . sensations we no longer have, but still seem to want, dreams of innocence, as a rule, before they became corrupt.
>
> [**Territory,** 117-18]

Rockwell, as Morris describes him, is the regional artist, the "master of verisimilitude . . . who . . . *heightens* the appearance of reality" (**Territory,** 114), giving people exactly what they want, the assurance that the Good Old Days and the Good Old Places are still there. Morris is determined not to be such a technician of sentiment. The situation he speaks to and demands recognition for, is a neoregional one in which "the *region*—the region in the sense that once fed the imagination—is now for sale on the shelf with the maple-sugar Kewpies; the hand-loomed ties and hand-sewn moccasins are now available, along with food and fuel, at regular intervals on our turnpikes. . . . No matter where we go, in America today, we shall find what we just left" (**Territory,** 22).

That hunger for uncorrupted innocence, for the Good Old Days, is what we find in Scanlon; in fifty-three-year-old but still adolescent Bud Momeyer, with his exclamations of "Dang!" and "Criminenty!" as he slaughters rabbits, cats, and his in-laws' prize bulldog; in Calvin McKee, a nineteen-year-old Gary Cooper look-alike who is happiest prospecting for gold in the Rockies, looking for a world where he can "ride horses, shoot guns and live just as he pleased" (**Ceremony,** 93). But Calvin's stutter, so terrible that he literally cannot speak at all, is the very articulate sign as well as the product of the sexuality that denies that innocence. His world teaches him that proper men and women deny and repress their sexuality in the name of innocence. Calvin's mother, Eileen, tells him, "Calvin, honey, if your mother could cry out loud you wouldn't stutter" (*Ceremony,* 164). As Boyd sermonizes in *Ceremony,* "the state emblem" is a "stiffly pleated upper lip" (179). Calvin's upper lip, twitching and quivering uncontrollably, is almost a character in the novel itself, a most subversive and embarrassing Nebraskan.

Another character who lives in terms of the Good Old Days and also cannot cry out loud is Walter McKee's wife and Tom Scanlon's daughter, Lois. Having once been kissed, for the first time in her life, by the audacious Gordon Boyd, on her own front porch, as McKee, then her fiancé, looked on, never having kissed her himself, she has lived a life dedicated to the repression of the passion Boyd stirred in her. Some forty years later, meeting Boyd quite by accident in Mexico, and attending a bullfight with him, a bullfight which provides the scene for *Field,* the McKees cannot help but relive the past, as they have both been doing all their adult lives. Lois remembers the kiss on the porch and a dream of Boyd she had later that fateful night, so vivid it collapsed her bed. Lois, it is clear, has married McKee so as not to have to worry and wonder any longer about passion. Her "ice-blue" Scanlon eyes have kept McKee always at a safe distance.

The sandy bullring makes McKee think of Boyd's attempt to walk on water in a sandpit on the outskirts of their hometown, Polk, Nebraska, and of all of Boyd's other impulsive, attention-grabbing, grandstand attempts at heroics. Boyd also lives only in dreams of the Good Old Days, still carrying around with him the pocket he tore off Ty Cobb's pants at a baseball game in Omaha forty years before, for him his one real heroic moment. Now, as then, a soiled, dirty rag, it is "the portable raft on which he floated, anchored to his childhood, on the glassy surface of the sandpit where he had failed to walk" (*Field,* 68).

The condition Morris describes of finding, wherever we go, the place we just left, is precisely the frontier experience we see through Scanlon's confused memory. Describing a wagon train heading west along the Platte, he finds that "no matter where it was that people had been, or where it was they thought they were going, they wanted it to be the same as wherever they were from. They brought along whatever they needed to make it that way" (*Field,* 96). This situation is like that of the crowd at the bullfight in *Field*: "What did they feel? What would they see? They would feel and see what they had brought along with them" (*Field,* 54). Will Brady, a boy in Indian Bow, sitting on the roof of his sod house, looking at "the empty world in the valley," felt "that he was the last man in the world" (*Works,* 10). An old man in Chicago, "he felt himself the last man in the world. He was back . . . where he had started from" (239), i.e., out of this world, on the plains of Nebraska, both the metaphysical landscape of the mind and the dead but still unburied past, unburied as long as Scanlon lives on in his father's memories of covered-wagon trains, arid deserts, comrades dying of thirst, and his discovery, in hallucination, of "the light that cast no shadow," the land outside of time, where the dead man, whose body he stumbles across while out scouting for water, is himself (*Field,* 142-51, 186-90).

If Morris is anywhere the antithesis of the Norman Rockwell artist who provides real-life pictures of the past we want so much to be alive, it is in this portrait of Tom Scanlon. The fact that, old and senile, he relives not his own past, but his father's, heard as tall tales over and over in his boyhood, provides an illuminating insight into the nature of nostalgia. We have seen the wagon trains crossing plains, mountains, and desert, trying to transform some new territory into the place left behind. The voyage out is only a long, hazardous attempted return home. Nostalgia (*nostos,* return home; *algos,* pain), the desire for the remote and irrecoverable home, the Origin, is shown to be necessarily incapable of fulfillment, satisfaction. Wherever one is, one locates "home" back still further, elsewhere; to find it, one has to go elsewhere. The journey is circuitous, always doubling back upon itself, because the experience it seeks, we are shown, is only an image, a father's tall tale, an old photograph. Nostalgia is a desire, not for what *was,* but for what is, at each successive stage, presumed to *have been,* for what is desired to have been. It is a desire for a spurious experience, not one's own, not anyone's. Scanlon's father, wandering alone in Death Valley, finds, in his thirst-induced hallucination, the only possible goal of a journey motivated by such a desire—he sees himself, lying dead in the sand, rotting in the hot sun, vultures circling overhead. Morris has shown us the skull beneath the grin of Norman Rockwell.

All these characters, then, Boyd, McKee, Mrs. McKee, Calvin McKee, Bud Momeyer, and Scanlon, are prisoners of their pasts—in Scanlon's case, of his father's past. To remain in that past requires a considerable blindness to and repression of the feelings, emotions, and passions of adulthood, of the present. This blindness and repression, the controlling theme and subject of *Field,* is symbolized most vividly in the character of Paula Kahler. This character, a woman who was once a man, is in the custody of Boyd's Viennese psychiatrist, Dr. Leopold Lehmann. Once Paul Kahler, a gentle, almost saintly boy and young man, Kahler has completely transformed himself into a woman who has excluded all things masculine from her consciousness. Silently, blind to the world around her, she knits and, when not knitting, she dozes.

> Paula Kahler was always in the best of health. Everywhere. Since all places were the same. The same reflection gazed at her from all of the mirrors. She had been sick to the death—she had died, that is—and passed over to the other side. From there all things looked the same. They were small as a rule, thought to be helpless, and of one sex. There were no males in Paula Kahler's brave new world.
>
> [*Field,* 113]

Once, working as a chambermaid in a hotel in Brooklyn, Paula Kahler had strangled an amorous bellhop in the hotel elevator. "She had been a little bruised, physically, but psychologically undisturbed" (74). Living totally in the metaphysical landscape of her own mind, blind to the world and to her own physical nature, Kahler stands as the complete exemplar of repression and its deadly consequences. Dead to the world, but capable of killing, to Dr. Lehmann she stands for "what he saw everywhere he looked" (75).

Blindness and repression are crucial to the maintenance of the carefully preserved Good Old Days; the violence with which what has been repressed can erupt is one of the main concerns of **Ceremony**. Near the beginning of that novel, Gordon Boyd, traveling up from Mexico to Lone Tree on McKee's invitation to a family reunion in honor of Scanlon's ninetieth birthday, stops at a motel in Nevada near a bomb-testing site. The motel owner, an elderly woman with an apron tied at her waist and a radiation-detector dog tag around her neck, a radio behind her playing hymns, asks Boyd if he would like to be awakened to watch the bomb go off just before dawn, "a wonderful sight." "Wake Before Bomb," she writes after his name in the ledger. These words stay with Boyd throughout the novel, and are, if anything is, its controlling theme, the possibility, even the advisability, of waking up before some kind of an explosion, before we all destroy ourselves in our sleep, of waking out of the dream of the past, the playing at Buffalo Bill, Davy Crockett, Santa Claus, and so forth, coming out of the emotional deep freeze.

Smaller versions of the bomb hover around the scene: in little Gordon McKee running about wildly shooting everyone with his toy guns, screaming "bang! you're dead!"; in the teen-age, "mad dog" killer Charlie Munger, who "just wanted to be someone"; in Bud Momeyer, stalking at night with bow and arrows; in Bud's nephew, Lee Roy Momeyer, a quiet Bible student who kills two of his classmates with his hot rod because "he just got tired of being pushed around"; in Lois McKee's displaced and uncontrolled passion for Gordon, her grandson, a passion only deflected from the real Gordon in her life: "[she] drew his body to her, her hands on his hips, feeling the tight grip of his strong little legs . . . shamelessly knowing what she was doing, she would sometimes almost eat little Gordon alive" (**Ceremony**, 57).

The family reunion has in fact been planned to allow Calvin McKee to elope with his cousin, Étoile Momeyer. Their wild midnight return to Lone Tree, in a borrowed mule-drawn wagon, Calvin's attempt to delight Scanlon by reenacting his frontier stories, causes Lois to fire a pistol semiaccidentally, the shot waking Scanlon out of his book-length sleep behind the stove at the hotel, but the shock of the event killing him. The covered wagon he was born in, which had become Lone Tree's Dead Wagon, serves as Scanlon's hearse at the novel's end. Although Scanlon did wake up before dying, it was only to call out the name of one of the characters of his father's pioneering stories. In a real sense, Scanlon never wakes out of his lifelong deep sleep.

Does anyone in the novel "wake before bomb"? It is hard to find grounds for optimism in Morris's work; his fundamental stance seems locked in a double bind. The imagination's power to transform reality, raw material, is pos-

ited, both in **Territory**, and, by Dr. Lehmann in **Field**, as our only means of leaving the fields of nostalgia, of worn-out, overused clichés, of sentimental lingering on the Good Old Days, associated with our national past (the pioneer days) and our own personal past (McKee, Boyd, Bud Momeyer, even Kahler, all refusing to grow up and take on the burdens and responsibilities of adulthood), and entering the territory ahead. "The only regions left are those the artists must imagine," Morris asserts in **Territory**, "the true territory is what [the artist] must imagine for himself" (22, 231). Lehmann, pondering, as he watches the bullfight, Boyd's lifelong futile effort to achieve anything more than the clichés of either heroism or failure, comes to the conclusion that "neither going to pot, throwing in the sponge, or even working at it had brought him failure. How achieve it? It had to be imagined, like everything else. It had to undergo a sea-change, a transformation" (**Field**, 71). Paula Kahler represents, for Lehmann, "what he saw everywhere he looked, but he saw it clearer in the bullring than anywhere else. What did he see? A transformation. He saw it take place. Before his eyes, the commonplace miracle of everyday life. . . . The human thing to do was to transform something, especially yourself" (**Field**, 75-76).

When Lehmann had first shown Paula Kahler to Boyd, Boyd had commented, "Facts are stranger than fiction!" Lehmann replied, "*Fax, wot* fax? If you haf tudge boddom, there are no fax. It iss all viction. Only viction iss a fack!" (**Field**, 228). But if the only "fack" is "viction," where are we, and who but Scanlon and Paula Kahler are the successful artists? Morris is clearly not exhibiting these two cases of the living dead as heroes we should emulate. They have not, and will never wake before bomb. Their misfortune, like Boyd's, was to get stuck. Boyd is stuck with Ty Cobb's pocket, his symbol of transformation, but "a stranger transformation than he had thought. Not merely a foul ball into a pocket, but a pocket into a winding sheet where the hero lay, cocoon-like, for the next twenty years. Out of this world, in the deep-freeze of his adolescent dreams. The object was transformation, but it had stopped where it should have begun . . . each transformation called for another, or the hero remained . . . snug in his flannel winding sheet" (**Field**, 109-10). Like the matador who gets gored, turning his back on the bull he had succeeded in momentarily mesmerizing into stillness, Boyd, and Morris, and we, as readers, become stuck on the horns of a dilemma. The dilemma is that the very act of imaginative transformation can create and trap us in a metaphysical landscape, while, as **Ceremony** shows us, the Bomb, symbol of all the unconscious, pent-up energies that simmer below the tranquility of our nostalgia, threatens to turn the whole world into a metaphysical landscape. The Dust Bowl, and the violence of neglect that created it, is, in its updated version, the Mushroom Cloud. And to wake before bomb might only be to awaken in time to see it go off. "Wake Before Bomb," Boyd thinks, in **Ceremony**. "How did one go about it? Was it, indeed, advisable? If the clock had stopped, if the dreams had crossed, and if one couldn't be happier—only unhappier—why wake?" (232). Is the Nevada motel owner right when she tells Boyd, "Terrible as it was, it was also a wonderful sight" (31)?

That may be all that Morris has, thus far, to offer—that it is better to be alive and awake in *this* world, however violent and grotesque it may be, than to sleep in a state of suspended animation, a repressed, emotional deep freeze, since the Bomb generated by the violence of that repression, that nostalgia for a more innocent time, threatens to annihilate our by now deformed landscape along with the very nostalgia that has helped deform it. But what we are confronted with, if we are awake, is what Morris calls "the nameless face of evil." McKee sees that face when, in *Ceremony,* a gang of hoodlums in a hot-rod drives up next to his newly bought station wagon and proceeds to scratch it up, lighting matches on the hood. McKee, basically an unimaginative and optimistic man, looking into the grinning faces of the young hoodlums

> had recognized the nameless face of evil—he recognized it, that is, as stronger than the nameless face of good. . . . What troubled him was not what he saw, but the nameless appetite behind it, the lust for evil in the faces of the beardless boys. McKee felt more life in their life than in himself. . . . He felt himself beaten at the start. If McKee represented Good, . . . then the forces of Evil would carry the day.
>
> [*Ceremony,* 50-51]

Lois McKee recognizes that nameless Evil in her eight-year-old grandson Gordon, and in a little boy in Mexico whom she saw shoot his own eye out merely because he knew he would thereby hurt his mother. "How well he [i.e., little Gordon] would have understood a shot like that," she thinks. "Men who went around shooting others were just stupid, frustrated children, compared with these little monsters who had learned to shoot themselves" (*Ceremony,* 63-64).

Everywhere one looks in *Ceremony,* there is that grinning face of evil—in little children; in Bud Momeyer, Lincoln's favorite mailman, eating up the Labor Day death toll statistics and then going out into the night with bow and arrows; in the "mad dog" killer Charlie Munger and his only less glamorous friend Lee Roy, Bud's nephew. Etoile, Bud's concupiscent seventeen-year-old daughter, comes closest to naming the evil when, after Munger's killing spree, she bursts out: "You want to know why? . . . It's because nobody wants to know why. It's because nobody wants to know *any-thing*! Everybody hates everybody, but nobody knows why anybody gets shot. You want to know somethin'? I'd like to shoot a few dozen people myself" (117).

But is McKee, looking at the grinning young hoodlums, and Mrs. McKee, looking at her grandson, looking into the future, as they seem to think, at something new? Or are they only seeing, in new forms, displaced and unemployed, the energies that tamed the West, conquered the meta-

physical landscape, and "invented the Dust Bowl," the aggressive male energy of the original Scanlons and Bradys, wearing out mule teams and wives, wearing out the land? When informed that his wife had died, Scanlon asked only who would now feed the chickens. Lois, his daughter, "had never heard him once speak of her mother, who had borne and raised his four daughters. . . . He was more like a piece of nature than a man. A withered slab of cactus, more dead than alive" (*Ceremony,* 69). The wild violence of the hot rodders, the crazed and murderous desire of Charlie Munger to "be somebody," what is it but the frontier spirit with no frontier to conquer, no place to go, nothing to do but ride around Lincoln, Nebraska, all night in "a '37 Ford coupe with Graham wheels, the top shaved off . . . mufflers alongside the windshield" (*Ceremony,* 118)? With no place left to go *to,* one just rides *around.* Is the hot rod not an updated, souped-up version of the Dead Wagon?

"Sweet Jesus," Boyd's young girlfriend says, looking at the original covered wagon that had brought the Scanlons west, that Tom Scanlon had been born in, that had served as Lone Tree's Dead Wagon, and that was now about to cart Scanlon off to the undertaker. "You people come out here in something like that?" Maxine Momeyer, Bud's wife and Lois's younger sister, can only reply in what ought to be the last words of the novel: "I'm afraid they did, Mrs. Boyd. . . . I just wish to God they never had" (*Ceremony,* 292).

Morris is intent, however, on killing off more than just Scanlon. His true death having occurred in the distant past, when his own father had died, Scanlon's death in *Ceremony* is, as Leon Howard remarks, really a posthumous performance.[15] In the latest two Nebraska novels, Morris takes us back to the plains again, back to the iconic Home Place, in the company of another old man, Floyd Warner, and his grand-nephew, an orphaned twelve-year-old, Kermit Oelsligle. Warner is a native Nebraskan who has spent the last twenty years in a small trailer parked in a trailer court in California. The vast emptiness of the prairie has been reduced to a four-by-five "mini-verandah" which is "filled with green gravel, to give a grassy effect" and sheltered by a metal awning (*Fire Sermon,* 19). For the past year, Warner has taken care of Kermit, after the death of the boy's parents in an automobile accident. Upon receiving news of the death of his sister, Viola, back in Nebraska, Warner decides to take the boy to the Home Place, to show him the place that is now his, and to take over the old house. "Aunt Viola could be buried, in one plot or another, and rise as she knew she would to heaven, but there remained the house" (*Fire Sermon,* 64).

Warner is the latest version of the same uncle Morris has been offering up since his first novel, *My Uncle Dudley* (1942). Under the various names of Dudley, Dwight, Fremont, or Floyd, the character invariably has been a Nebraskan by birth, a farmer in Texas (or, as here, in New Mexico), and is given the honor of having "invented the Dust Bowl." Clyde Muncy, in *The World in the Attic,* remembers his Uncle Dwight, as does Mrs. Violet Ormsby in Morris's 1951 novel, *Man and Boy.* McKee, in *Field,* thinks back to his stay on his Uncle Dwight's Texas farm, and in *Cause for Wonder* (1963) Warren Howe pays a visit to his uncle Fremont Osborn, who is retired and living in a trailer court in California. Uncle Dudley, in the 1942 novel, also once a farmer in Texas, is a boy's dream of the perfect uncle, part drifter, part con man, part Santa Claus. Together with his nephew, The Kid, who narrates the story, they drive an old Marmon touring car from Los Angeles toward Chicago, with an assortment of passengers they take along for money. *Fire Sermon* gives us a similar trip east with an old man and a young boy, the old farmer uncle Morris has refined over and over, and his nephew, from whose point of view the story is told.[16]

Floyd Warner is an irascible, surly old curmudgeon, prone to interminable and quite imaginative cursing, not at all fond of children or of the world he has lived long enough, by the age of eighty-two, to be alive in. In *Fire Sermon,* he appears a somewhat comical, absurd-looking, crabby, argumentative, old man. It is only in the sequel, *A Life,* told through Warner's consciousness, that he becomes a truly sympathetic character.

Basically, only two things happen in *Fire Sermon.* Driving to Nebraska, Warner and the boy pick up a young hippie couple who are hitchhiking east. The couple, Stanley and Joy, is not portrayed by Morris with any sympathy or even a touch of life. Their vocabulary consists only of "OM," "groovy," "far out," and lyrics of Beatles songs. Their only activity is sexual. Warner is predictably disgusted by them; the boy is predictably fascinated. When the four arrive at the old house in Chapman, Nebraska, an oil lamp is accidentally knocked over and the house burns to the ground. Warner seems to disappear during the fire, leaving his trailer behind. The boy is left alone and, presumably, will soon leave with Stanley and Joy.

A Life presents, from Warner's point of view, the events of the following day, a day that proves to be his last. Having left Kermit to his new-found friends, he decides to drive to his old sheep ranch in New Mexico. On his way there, he picks up a young Indian, George Blackbird, an ex-GI back, it is implied, from Vietnam. At the old man's now deserted place in New Mexico, that night, Blackbird kills Warner, slashing his wrist with the lid of a can. The killing is described not as an act of aggression, but more as Blackbird's being the agent of the old man's desire for an end to it all, just as the hippie couple in *Fire Sermon* seem somehow agents of a kind of inevitability—no matter how often Warner passed them by on the highway, there they always were up ahead the next day, thumbing a ride, until he finally gave in and picked them up. During the day, Blackbird repeatedly asks Warner, "Old man, what do you want?" Each seems to have met, in the other, on this day, his fate. "It was not Blackbird's intent to do this for him [not *to* him], but Blackbird, too, has been shaped to this moment, the ceremonial opening of the vein in Warner's wrist" (*A Life,* 152).

We are watching, then, in these two novels, the often-repeated attempt to return "home." A figure representing the past and one representing the future travel together in a direction that is backward for one, forward for the other:

> Leaving California, the morning sun in his eyes, he had sensed that he was traveling backward, but that the boy, in the seat at his side, at the same moment was hurrying forward, free as the wind. The same direction in space proved to be the opposite direction in time.
>
> [*A Life,* 30-31]

The boy, at the age of twelve, born and raised in California, his parents dead, his only living relation this relic of days that hold no meaning for him, has nothing to do but look to the future. At one point, Warner asks him what he looked forward *to.* "Just as feared, the boy didn't know. He looked forward, that's all. If it was evening he looked forward to morning. If it was Monday, he looked forward to Saturday, and that sort of thing. He just looked forward. Where else was there to look?" (*Fire Sermon,* 74). Warner had told Kermit how he, as a boy, had once met Buffalo Bill, but Kermit didn't know who that was. The return to the hometown, then, is a different experience for each of the characters; "the old man . . . would see what he remembered, but the boy's squinting eyes saw only what was there. He didn't think it much" (120). In the house, the boy "brought so little to what he saw, he saw what was there" (137).

In a pair of novels in which Morris finally burns down the by now sacred old house, kills off the by now obligatory old uncle, and even has the young boy, the inheritor of what is now gone, disappear with a very dubious set of surrogate parents, one of the informing principles seems to be, once again, vision, perception, vision turned inward by nostalgia, so that one sees only what one remembers, or vision with no relation to the past, so that one sees only what is there, but does not know what it is that one sees. The openings of both novels, and the end of *A Life,* are appeals to our sight, as if a painting or a photograph were being described in each case. Not only is a picture described, but we are told where we, as viewers, stand: "From the highway to the east, where his car is parked to the left of a mailbox propped in a milk can, we can see him standing in the knee-high grass at the edge of a field of grain stubble" (*A Life,* 1). This implication of the viewer in the scene also occurred at the opening of *Ceremony*: "Come to the window. The one at the rear of the Lone Tree Hotel. The view is to the west" (*Ceremony,* 3). The "field of vision" is ours: "If asked if he [Warner] could use a pair of shoes, he would reply, I have a pair of shoes. We see them on his feet" (*A Life,* 1).

Warner twice sees himself and his surroundings as if they were paintings. The first time is when, just before the fire, he sits by a window of the old house in Chapman:

> His impression had been that his eyes, his *own* eyes, hovered above him like a presence, seeing the things of this world about him for the first time. The view from

the window, framed like a painting, impressed him as timeless and unchanging, and the old man seated on the armless rocker was within the scene, not outside of it. For a fleeting, breathless moment he took himself for dead.

[*A Life,* 15-16]

At the very end, dying in the New Mexico desert, the Indian holding his bleeding wrist, Warner sees the scene as "a painting, the title a motto that somehow escapes him, stamped on the frame of the picture he is within" (152). He has "the impression that he was outside, not inside, his own body. . . . One seemed as real to him as the other: to be outside, perhaps, even realer. . . . He thinks, *I have been walking in my sleep, and now I am awake*" (151).

There is the vision, then, that sees only, or mainly, what is remembered, and the vision that, bringing nothing to the scene, sees, but cannot comprehend, only what is there. And there is the mystical, out-of-the-body, visionary experience of seeing the world as if for the first time, and seeing oneself, as if in a painting, as if dead. Warner, defined only through his link to the past, can only die when that link is broken. Time and again, in *A Life,* the question is posed, "Where was he now?" (26), or "Old man, so where are you?" (45). Where he is, mainly, is in his mind, his memory, tied to a place that has gone up in smoke. "There had always been a place," he thinks, but now, "nothing would be gained in going back, since there was, in truth, no place to go back to" (45). "Where he is" is defined several ways. "With the sun on his right, he was driving south on route 183," is one attempt to place him. But he seems to exist more in time than in space: "the past was now coming toward him as the present mysteriously receded. What had happened last night fell away, slipped away, like the road visible in the rear-view mirror, but what had happened in the distant past flowed toward him like the objects approaching on the highway" (26).

There is a meaningful balance in Morris's having hippies burn down the home place in *Fire Sermon* and an Indian kill Floyd Warner in *A Life.* The hippies, who seem to appear out of nowhere, ultimately to claim Kermit as theirs, are citizens of a future Morris, like Warner, distrusts and has no sympathy for. This future is portrayed as being uninterested in its past, basically illiterate, and unaware of its own mortality. Kermit, who could only look forward, is left to the precarious agency of this future. The Indian, George Blackbird, who equally comes out of nowhere to claim Warner, is then, perhaps, an agent of the past. Warner, who could only see the past, is left to die in the arms of this man out of the land's own mythic past. Blackbird's silence is the opposite but balancing term to the hippies' illiteracy, both silence and illiteracy being rejections of language. As Leslie Fiedler argues in *The Return of the Vanishing American,* the "counterculture"—vision-seeking acid heads, rural communards, urban guerrillas—can be seen as a contemporary surfacing of the spirit of the American Indian.[17] Both hippie and Indian stand opposed to the White American Dream of wealth and prosperity in the name of which the West was won, Indian culture shattered, and the land finally depleted.

Morris is doing more than wishing, along with Maxine Momeyer in *Ceremony,* that the westward movement hadn't happened. He is reversing it, putting the sons and grandsons of the pioneers into a 1928 Maxwell coupe, as close as one can come, in the 1970s, to a covered wagon, sending them back on an eastward journey, burning down the old homestead, and delivering them, young and old, into the hands of representatives of cultures far different from that of the pioneers. And this renunciation, it finally seems, is the old man's inner wish, his desire and dream:

> On Warner's mind's eye he saw this scene—one of the last he would see—as if clearly painted. It would bear the somewhat puzzling title "Old man, what do you want?" From the scene it seemed clear it was help that he wanted, but he seemed reluctant to ask for it. What help? All his life he had made it a point never to ask. Everything had happened according to a plan that would prove to be his as much as Blackbird's, so that what he wanted, strange as it might appear, was what he had got.

[*A Life,* 150]

What he wanted, and what he gets, is a terrible justice, almost religious in its ritual working-out. Warner remembers how "his father had taken grass, as he did most things, religiously." His father had taught him "before the land had been plowed, or some would say broken," to distinguish a dozen or more kinds of grasses, "the nameless grasses that kept the soil from washing and blowing away. . . . In his mind, thanks to his father, the word of God is tangled with the names of grasses" (*A Life,* 2-3). At the home place in Nebraska, Warner had shown Kermit an ox shoe nailed to a pedestal sticking up above ground. The boy asked what had pushed it up to its elevated position. Warner's reply was that nothing had pushed it up; the earth had washed away from it. After the fire, Warner having disappeared, Kermit feels the old man's presence, "point[ing] to the ox shoe that the earth has moved away from" (*Fire Sermon,* 155). When Warner returns to his old New Mexico farm, he finds the land "grassless, like a play yard, and strewn with the bodies and parts of wrecked cars" (*A Life,* 119-20). In his house, someone had printed on a towel hanging on the wall, framed by long-tasselled ears of Indian corn: WHEN THE GRASS IS PULLED UP / THE SOD COMES WITH IT" (123). "This place was a graveyard," Warner thinks, and "he was one of the many curious objects" (127).

The wish, then, of this old man with a religious sense of the grass, who has lived the past twenty years in a trailer court full of gravel painted green to look like grass, is to awaken from nostalgic reveries, to see clearly, and to die in the arms of the Indian youth who will kill him. In a mystical vision that clarifies what is seen, Warner feels awakened from sleep. He has had this experience right before the home place burned to the ground, and he has it again as he is dying. Warner has, for the first time in his life, come home, found a perspective toward himself and his place that allows him to be both so "interested and detached" as to see the "mystic meaning" of his experience. The "help" this old plainsman had wanted, and that naturally only a young Indian warrior could render, was to give sense and shape to his pilgrimage:

> One thing led to another, and all of it led to where he had crouched in the yard, as if he had planned it. Wasn't that what he had wanted? That things should go according to some plan? That however they went, they should not be like ditch weeds fitfully blown in the wind stream of a car.

[A Life, 142]

The ending of *A Life* is a dreamlike one, the two men sitting facing each other, silently, on the dark dusty plains, the Indian holding the old man's bleeding wrist, helping him die, the old man awake and aware, seeing it all as if looking at a picture. It is a white man's dream, the dream of a pioneer, a conqueror, an erotic dream of death at the hands of, and in the arms of, the dark stranger, the Indian, one had always known would be there. It is a dream Custer might have had, or Carson, or Buffalo Bill Cody.

Wright Morris's Nebraska novels constitute a consistent and relentless examination of the ways in which we have thought about our "places," our "homes." A photographer in love with the worn artifacts of inhabitation, but wary of the perilous ways in which nostalgia can cloud the vision and destroy both seer and seen, Morris has shown the home place to be an image, has revealed the nostalgia at the core of the westward movement and the death wish at the core of nostalgia. Seeking always to reduplicate, further and further ahead, an irrecoverable place and time of origin, we have moved across the land like an army of sleepwalkers, interested only in keeping our dreams of innocence playing before our lidded eyes. Floyd Warner's last moments in *A Life* are among the rare episodes in Morris's fiction in which a character is "able to see . . . from the other side" (*Field,* 198) with a vision that is both awake and free of nostalgia. At these moments, such characters, and Morris himself, become witnesses to and reporters of consciousness aware of itself, its moment in time, its place in the world.

Notes

1. Willa Cather, *My Ántonia* (Boston: Houghton Mifflin, 1954), p. 7. First published in 1918.

2. With the following exceptions, all references are to Bison Book editions, published by the University of Nebraska Press: *The Inhabitants* (New York: Charles Scribner's Sons, 1946); *Fire Sermon* (New York: Harper & Row, 1971); *A Life* (New York: Harper & Row, 1973). Since *The Inhabitants* is unpaginated, for reference purposes I have numbered each photograph to correspond with the facing text page; thus 9 refers to the text facing the ninth photograph. *The World in the Attic, The Works of Love, The Field of Vision,* and *Ceremony in Lone Tree* will hereafter be referred to, respectively, as *Attic, Works, Field,* and *Ceremony.* Morris's comment on *Works* appears on the back cover of the Bison Book edition.

3. Wright Morris, *The Territory Ahead* (New York: Harcourt, Brace, 1958; rptd. New York: Atheneum,

1963). References are to the 1963 edition, which hereafter will be cited as *Territory.*

4. *Wright Morris: Structures and Artifacts* (Lincoln: Sheldon Memorial Art Gallery, 1975), p. 115.

5. Compare Arther E. Waterman, "The Novels of Wright Morris: An Escape from Nostalgia" with Alan Trachtenberg, "The Craft of Vision," both in *Critique* 4 (Winter 1961-62): 24-40, 41-55.

6. The quotations are from Leon Howard, *Wright Morris* (Minneapolis: University of Minnesota Press, 1968 [University of Minneapolis Pamphlets on American Writers no. 69]), p. 11, and from Waterman, "The Novels of Wright Morris," p. 26.

7. Ibid.

8. Trachtenberg, "The Craft of Vision," pp. 43-45.

9. John W. Hunt, Jr., "The Journey Back: The Early Novels of Wright Morris," *Critique* 5 (Spring-Summer 1962): 52.

10. Wright Morris, *The Man Who Was There* (New York: Charles Scribner's Sons, 1945).

11. David Madden, *Wright Morris* (New York: Twayne Publishers, 1964), p. 63.

12. Marcus Klein, "Wright Morris: The American Territory," in his *After Alienation: American Novels in Mid-Century* (Cleveland: World Publishers, 1964), p. 207.

13. Madden, *Wright Morris,* p. 131.

14. Wright Morris, "The Origin of a Species, 1942-57," *Massachusetts Review* 7 (Winter 1966): 127.

15. Howard, *Wright Morris,* p. 27.

16. Robert J. Guettinger in a useful essay, "The Problem with Jigsaw Puzzles: Form in the Fiction of Wright Morris," *Texas Quarterly* 11 (Spring 1968): 209-20, shows how Morris skillfully and purposefully repeats the same stories and characters with only minor, but telling, variations.

17. Leslie Fiedler, *The Return of the Vanishing American* (New York: Stein & Day, 1968), passim.

David Madden (essay date 1981)

SOURCE: "Character as Revealed Cliché in Wright Morris's Fiction," in *The Midwest Quarterly,* Vol. XXII, No. 4, Summer, 1981, pp. 319-36.

[*In the following essay, Madden argues that Morris's "manipulation of clichés" is at the root of his power to render "the sensibilities of articulate and inarticulate characters" effectively.*]

Morris says, in *The Territory Ahead,* "Every writer who is sufficiently self-aware to know what he is doing, and how he does it sooner or later is confronted with the dictates of style. If he *has* a style, it is the style that dictates what he says. *What* he says, of course, is how he says it . . ." (137). No American writer's style, I think, is as perfectly controlled as Morris's. Everything style has been trained over the centuries to do, Morris makes it do in his novels. If Hodler, one of his more articulate characters, "admits to the frailty of language," Morris forces that frailty to perform amazing feats (*In Orbit*, 14). "In the beginning was the word," says Morris, "and the word was made flesh. American character emerges from the American language, as the language emerges from the shaping imagination" (**"Made in U.S.A.,"** 487). Morris's style—the American language in action—conveys the informal tone and feel of a man talking to men. He makes imaginative use of American slang, clichés, idioms, and especially of midwestern speech patterns and rhythms as a way of getting at the American character. He tunes us in on the resignation, the melancholy overtones, the subtle poetry, the humor, the shrewdness of insight of midwestern speech.

In any work of fiction, the point-of-view technique the writer chooses dictates style. The third person central intelligence point of view that Morris most often uses dictates a conversational, informal tone and style; Morris modulates between a simulation of first-person informality and the more formal syntax, diction, and tone of an omniscient voice. Filtering his character's experiences and reveries through the third person, Morris employs his unique ability to transform the clichés of American language and culture into expressions of wit, satire, and peculiar lyricism. Morris creates a congruence of outer and inner reality—a triumph of style. Examining the immediate emotional and intellectual intuitions and perceptions of his characters from within, as they move from one small, but highly charged moment to another, Morris has evolved a flexible style, based on a manipulation of clichés, that has proved effective in rendering the sensibilities of both articulate and inarticulate characters.

Given the characters he describes, the events he depicts, and the point-of-view techniques he uses, one of the major dictates of Morris's style is his use of clichés. "The cliché told the story," Lehmann thinks, contemplating Boyd's life (*Field of Vision*, 70). To achieve his unique style, Morris consciously improvises upon clichés. "Character is revealed cliché," he says, and character reveals itself through the clichés in which his characters think, speak, and act (**"Made in U.S.A.,"** 487). Each of Morris's novels is an answer, given in the language of the cliché, to Crevecoeur's cliché question, "What is an American?" The cliché is symbolic of the American dream defunct, and it is in this "dead" language of clichés that Morris tells us of the sterility of modern life. But the special contexts he prepares for clichés simultaneously annihilate their phoniness and resurrect their original vitality; he suggests that the dead past can be made to live again.

Morris's characters share his efforts to salvage something from the cliché. "The pathos of things that had served their purpose had a profound appeal for Cowie. And why

not? Chief among them he considered himself. He rather favored clichés. He only picked up a phrase when it has been dropped" (*One Day,* 87). The clichés, with which Americans conceal whatever deep feelings they have, Morris uses to lift lids; for the reader, the glimpses are comic at first, then pathetic, then self-revealing. Manipulating the clichés of our mass culture and language as a witty and humorous function of style, he turns clichés insight out. What makes them tick would set off a home-made bomb.

If "it is style that sets the cliché" (**"Made in U.S.A.,"** 487), what moves us is the charm of the style; the charm of his style enables the mythic figure to exchange his mortal life for immortality. Garbo, Babe Ruth, and Lindbergh had this style, the style of the Lone Eagle. In the twenties, the characters in *The Huge Season* had it, too. But today it is the cliché, not the process of becoming mythic, that proves contagious—those who cast themselves as Mick Jagger, Jack Kennedy, or Ali merely "bear witness to the cliché. We are left with a product rather than a process—a coonskin hat rather than Davy Crockett." That is a paralyzing quality of the cliché, which has its positive qualities, too. "Clichés, bless them, both destroy life and make it possible" (**"Made in U.S.A.,"** 490). In Morris's fiction, events of the past are simple and trite, stereotyped, cliché. If "time past . . . is a mythic land of genial clichés" (**"Origin of a Species,"** 128) and if "culture is a series of acceptable clichés" (*The Field of Vision,* 70-71), Morris's stereotyped characters cannot experience the present until they have come to terms with the clichés that flood their everyday lives, and stripped themselves down to the essentials. If one is audacious enough to confront the real thing, one runs the risk of being abandoned by the safe cliché. The real McCoy is what one has after the cliché has been sheared off. Morris's novels depict the process of improvisation in which the cliché is transformed.

For Morris, the cliché serves the purpose of almost every technical device: it characterizes, enhances mood, evokes time and place, points up dialog, describes it; expresses modes of transformation, revelation, and resurrection; it is revealed in gesture and in informal ritual; and it acts as a structural aid.

Let's look briefly at the novels in chronological order, noting a few of their key clich clichés, each of which Morris uses with variations in most of his earlier and later works. Notice that most of the titles are themselves clichés.

The Kid tells the story of *My Uncle Dudley* in the language of the cliché. Dudley's audacious acts may take their cues from clichés, but only because Dudley's intention is to negate clichés by making them new. The cliché "I'll spit in your eye," though never said, becomes the real thing, a blend of fact and fiction in the hands of an improvisor, a transformer.

> I got out and stood in the ditch grass and he leaned on the running board. He just stayed there looking at Cupid and once Cupid looked at him. . . . The cigar juice was leaking on Uncle Dudley's chin and he looked like

hell yet he looked kind of sporty. He tipped his head and winked at Cupid with his good eye. Cupid thought that was pretty funny and winked back at him—then he closed one eye and opened the other one wide. And right when he did Uncle Dudley spit him, full flush in that eye . . . he reached for the gun, but Biscuit had it, pointing it at the sky. He made motions with it for Uncle Dudley to get in. . . .

Uncle Dudley turned and spit the rest in the road, hitched up his pants. He didn't look at me but climbed inside and closed the door. He sat back behind the side curtain so I couldn't see. Biscuit put the gun on the floor and Cupid kept his head down, just his red neck showing. Biscuit backed the car around and they slowly moved away. In the rear view mirror I could see him looking back at me. They went along with a wheel in the road grass like we had come. The wind was faster now and went by, stirring a kind of dust on the road, getting thick, then petering out where the pavement began. On the turn my Uncle Dudley put out his hand.

(202-210)

That unpredictable, foolhardy, audacious cliché gesture ends the novel, elucidating the meaning of Dudley's relationship with his nephew; preparation for that moment is built up by variations on other, similar, clichés. In their raw-material form, both character and cliché are "inflexible" and "appallingly predictable," but transformed in the characters, they are as resilient as Charlie Chaplin's cane, as unpredictable as that oldest standby of all clichés—the weather. The Kid and Dudley resist the cliché "just passing though." "I said we were seeing the country, not just passing through" (78). That cliché turns up in most of the novels, until it becomes rich in nuance, almost mystical in *A Life.*

In *The Man Who Was There* (1945), Agee Ward turns up missing, as the cliché would have it. But Gussie Newcomb gradually sees that the missing man turns up in the people he left behind—including herself. She intuitively senses mystical implications in the expression "The King is dead—long live the King!" "'He thinks he's missing,'" says Peter Spavic, "'but boy, did we fox him!'" (236). Few people really die in Morris's fiction; they are merely missing, and, in a kind of resurrection, they almost always turn up in the living.

For Norman Rockwell, character is not revealed cliché, simply presented cliché. Clyde Muncy, in *The Home Place* (1948), observes the way his Uncle Harry holds a baby in the barber shop, as though he were a Madonna with child (as though he were a *Saturday Evening Post* cover). "On the one hand I knew that what I saw was unbelievably corny, on the other hand I knew it was one of the finest things I had seen" (*The Home Place,* 107). In Clyde's sensibility, both the cliché and the real thing blend in a moment of revelation.

In *The World in the Attic* (1949), the cliché "the finest living creature on God's green earth" is applied in many variations to Nellie Hibbard and, by implication and more appropriately, to Caddy Hibbard. "The finest of God's living creatures—as she would always be to the man who knew her—might have struck you differently when you passed her in the dime store, or out on the street. First of all, you might not have noticed her" (54). More noticeable is Lois McKee to whom the phrase is applied with even more ironic, sardonic variations in *The Field of Vision* and *Ceremony in Lone Tree.* In *The World in the Attic,* and throughout Morris's novels, characters rename each other with clichés. "Hold it a second, Captain," Clyde Muncy says. "I'm Chief," says Mr. Purdy, "You're Captain" (119). Purdy also refers to himself as "your Uncle Dudley."

Will Brady, a strong silent, self-made man, in *The Works of Love* (1952) manages like many other Morris characters to "live both in and out of this world" (172), because he cannot really feel at home in one place. The house he builds only leads him to the cliché question: "Homelike? Well, that was said to be the word for it" (73).

In *The Deep Sleep* (1953), Reverend Barr says to Paul Webb, the skeptical artist, "The Lord, Paul, is a mighty warrior—" (241). All day Webb has observed in Mrs. Porter the kind of motherly behavior that made her daughter, Katherine, Webb's wife, come to the conclusion, when she was a child, that she and her brother were "orphans of the storm. That Mrs. Porter, a civic-minded person, had adopted them" (111). She is full of bromides, axioms, sayings. Her husband's death is "all for the best" (15). But it is out of Mrs. Porter's mouth that the most moving cliché in all Morris comes. At the end of a day of funeral preparations in which she has seemed to everyone (except Mr. Parsons, the handy-man) to lack feeling, Mrs. Porter stands alone on the back porch, and the moment is perceived from Katherine's point of view:

> The summer night was very lovely, and her mother, while her hands were busy, seemed to be listening to the music of the spheres.
>
> "I don't know what I'd do," her mother said, "if other people didn't go to bed."
>
> Katherine waited a moment, then said, "Is it all right if I go now, Mother?"
>
> "Your father would go to bed, but he never slept until I was there."
>
> "Good night, Mother," Katherine said, and when her mother didn't answer she started for the stairs.
>
> "Which one is Orion?" her mother said.
>
> "I'm afraid I've forgotten it all, Mother."
>
> "I'm going to miss your father," her mother said, and Katherine turned, her hand on the stair rail, as if another person, not her mother, had spoken. A voice, perhaps, from one of the letters she never mailed. Katherine wanted to speak, but now that this voice had spoken to her, broken the long silence, she could hardly believe what she heard. She went on up the stairs, entered her room, then closed the door before she remem-

bered, before she noticed, that Paul wasn't there. Still, she would have called to him except for the fact that she had no voice, her throat ached, and he had been the one who had cried that this was a house without tears.

(302)

Katherine does not know that her husband, Webb the artist, who has spent the day puzzling "over the pattern of the Judge's life" (14), trying to get the picture in a maze of clichés, finally sees the picture he has been trying to get in focus when he finds the watch Mrs. Porter had put in "a safe place" (95), and so misplaced. Webb, who insists on striking down every cliché, responds to the cliché of Mrs. Porter's daylong search for her dead husband's watch with the only truth there is in that situation, a cliché act of compassion. Having accidentally found the watch, he puts it where she will discover it. "That was quite a picture, one that pleased him. . . ." (312).

To describe the effect the hero Lawrence, in *The Huge Season* (1954), has on his witnesses, Foley rubs two clichés together, contemplating "the origin of a species based on charm, on audacity, on the powers of the dance, and the music that soothed whatever needed soothing in the savage breast" (168). Montana Lou Baker captures herself and her hero-witnesses in this cliché: "They *say* it's been real, but we were real" (277). In every work of fiction, there are lines that teach the reader how to hold in his mind the book he holds in his hands. In *The Huge Season,* when Dickie shows the "unloaded" Colt revolver Proctor used to shoot himself in the foot, Mrs. Pierce reminds them that "it's always the empty gun that kills somebody" (224). Empty clichés in Morris's prose often prove to be loaded.

In *The Field of Vision* (1956)—itself a cliché of perception—Morris improvises again upon most of the key cliché expressions he resurrected in previous books. Having played with the clichés "hit bottom" and "walk on water" in *The Huge Season,* he focuses on them in *The Field of Vision.* In *The World in the Attic,* Clyde Muncy muses on the trite painting of The Lone Wolf in the snow and "the never-ending problem of what [he] intended to do" (60). In *The Field of Vision,* McKee compares Boyd the loner with the Lone Wolf. "He could hear the iron creak of Boyd's shoes in the snow. Like that wolf in the picture he had moved in close, then he had turned and run off" (177). Lone Wolf, Lone Eagle, loner are clichés Morris uses with many variations throughout his work. When the bull charges the bull fighter, McKee remembers two cliché events of the past: Boyd charging Ty Cobb to get his baseball autographed and Boyd trying to walk on water. "Don't it take you back?" (77) McKee asks Boyd. Twenty-three pages later, Boyd improvises sardonically upon that cliché: "Don't it take you back, Boyd? He knew sure as hell it did. But to where? And when? And for chrissakes why? Taken back. Always taken back. Never ahead" (100). The cliché phrase "helpless and hopeless" (256) helps to explain the charm of the fool the whole world loves, and that phrase goes through many variations in *The Field of Vision, Ceremony in Lone Tree, War Games,* among others.

In *Love Among the Cannibals* (1957), Earl Horter, the narrator, is immersed, by profession if not by temperament, in the submediocre mass-media culture of contemporary America; he transforms clichés into song lyrics for mass consumption. "If you live in a world of clichés, as I do, some of them of the type you coined yourself, you may not realize how powerful they can be" (92). Horter has become so saturated with clichés that after he meets the Greek in Hollywood, where the phony pitch is strident, he tells her, "Earl Horter, master of the cliché, did not say to you what he thought he was feeling, since he hardly knew, without the clichés, what it was he felt" (227). "What next?" (a question Morris characters often ask) is the title of the song Earl is improvising when he meets the living answer, the Greek. Academic in the beginning, the question, at the end of the novel, is real. The conflict between the cliché and the real thing is one between the inessentials and essentials. By example, the Greek teaches Horter that the "first problem, surgically speaking, is to remove the encrusted cliché from the subject" (**"Made in U.S.A.,"** 487). With the Greek, Horter improvises on the act of "bolting" from the phony. Free of clichés at the end, Horter can explore new possibilities. He has learned that "you've got to take what's phony, if that's all you've got, and make it real" (112). That, of course, is exactly what Morris has been doing from the first novel on, but this is the novel in which he most obviously meditates on the process.

One of the conceptual clichés in *Ceremony in Lone Tree* (1960), sequel to *The Field of Vision,* is "now you see it, now you don't." Another is "the call of the wild." "Mr. Jennings, do you ever feel the call of the wild?" Eileen asks. "Not especially, ma'am," he says, "But I know people who do" (209). Sixty pages later, he sees a sign in the ghost town of Lone Tree: "VISIT THE LYRIC TONITE. And why not?" he thinks. "If the call was wild enough maybe some of them would" (270). The mild cliché "everybody needs a little push" is introduced in this way. "I thought you might need a little push," Daughter says, referring to Boyd's Plymouth. "Didn't everybody need one in the good old days?" A major variant is this: "I just got tired of bein' pushed around," says Lee Roy, who pushes his hot rod into a bunch of bullies, thus stirring up another cliché: "Lost control of it, eh?" a highway patrolman asks Lee Roy. "No, he hadn't lost control. He had been in control for once in his life" (127). Jennings thinks of Lee Roy and the mass murderer Charlie Munger as "Local boys. Local boys who made—or unmade—good" (137). Another local boy, out of the past, a returning creative native, thinks of himself in terms of similar clichés. "Morgenstern Boyd, pop-squirter, water-walker and friggin bore. First and last of the completely self-unmade men" (302). For many reasons, Boyd knows "it's later than you think. I'm clowning it up before the bomb" (172). But heeding the call of the wild, the hometown folks behave in such a way as to leave Boyd speechless and stymied. "It was McKee's look," McKee notices, "on Boyd's face . . . his jaw slack as if he still had adenoids. Stymied. That was how he looked. Never before had McKee seen him speechless" (149). But

Boyd remembers his own speechless response to Lois's charm, forty years ago. Boyd had "mailed a letter enclosing a blank piece of paper. Speechless. For the first and last time in his life" (228). McKee finds that undelivered letter in the Lone Tree hotel mail box, and, wondering what Boyd had written to his wife, not knowing it is blank, almost gives him a heart attack. Such is the power even of the unspoken cliché in Morris's fiction.

In carefully prepared contexts, even simple cliché expletives become highly charged. Private Lipido in *Man and Boy* (1951), Proctor in *The Huge Season,* and Etoile in *Ceremony in Lone Tree,* among others use the expletive "Ha!" to debunk. Bud Momeyer's emotions come out in "Gee Whiz, What the Deuce, and Dang. He never seemed to feel anything those words didn't cover" (76), thinks his wife, Maxine. The young woman Boyd brings with him to shock the folks, says repeatedly, "Sweet Jesus." It becomes so contagious that Maxine, having come to the end of her rope, says, "'Sweet Jesus.' For no particular reason, and hardly caring why" (90).

Even out of simple names Morris conjures connotative values. "Your mother has a headache," Maxine says, referring to herself. "You want to bring her two aspirin?" "When her mother was near the end of her rope," Etoile thinks, "she referred to herself as her mother" (90). The problem of identity is played out most fully in *Ceremony in Lone Tree.* "That you Conley?" (103) Jennings remembers an old man once asked a streetcorner Santa Claus. Almost all the characters are asked a similar question. At the end: "Raising on his elbow, Jennings peered through the moonlight and said, 'That you Scanlon?' just as the old man dropped as if through a hole in the floor" (277).

"What a way to go!" in the 1962 novel of that name, is an apt travel slogan for many Morris characters. In an old world of clichés, in Venice and Greece, Soby observes life imitating art, the relation between fact and fiction becoming ambiguous. Like Horter in *Love Among the Cannibals,* he asks, "What next?" and feels the imperative, "Make it new!" "Feeling no pain," he learns, "the wisdom of the body" (10). Soby attempts to transform these and other clichés: "the new element forged is oneself."

In *Cause for Wonder* (1963), Howe returns to "a combination loony bin and fairy castle" near Vienna that once made him feel "both in and out of this world." When he left, he wonders now, several decades later, "Was I running *for* my life, or was I running away?" Seymour Gatz expresses Howe's own fears. "Know what scares me? A place to hide. What if I liked it?" (20). Howe's Uncle Fremont Osborn tells him, "You can't live in the past, boy. Can't even die in it" (47). These key cliché expressions go through more paradoxical, ironic variations than any other in *Cause for Wonder.* The cliché title *Cause for Wonder* turns up in a different form in *One Day* (1965): to ask the question "What next?" on the day President Kennedy is assassinated is "cause for alarm." Cowie, "a loner who does not want to be alone," "an artful dodger" who early

in life said, "I give up," observes things "get back to normal"—in a world in which the normal proves to be abnormality. Cowie, the thinker, meditates: "One man's small hand had come between all living men and the sun's face, casting a shadow that momentarily darkened the world. What had he cried at such a moment? Look, Ma, one hand!" "The word from Dallas" "dissolved into a bottomless pool of impotence," a gibberish of clichés.

In *In Orbit,* cliché rhetorical questions elicit actual events. "And how is Miss Holly?" Hodler routinely asks Avery, to which Avery always answers, "Who the hell would know that?" But today, "Somebody finally knew." Jubal, the mysterious stranger, is thought to have raped her. "It is a torment to Hodler that this essential knowledge is what he once desired for himself" (20). When the mailman reports that a spaceman raped Miss Holly, Kashperl asks Jubal a typical, kidding question: "Now why's a boy like *you* do that?" (85). Today, just by chance, he asks the right person, and Jubal stabs him. A literary cliché Morris often plays with is most effectively used, with variations, in *In Orbit*: a motorcyclist and a twister hit a small town simultaneously, sending everybody into some kind of dance. "Who can tell the dancer from the dance?" "At the still point, there is where the dance is:" Other clichés enhance this central conceptual cliché. "A dozen or more people are known to be missing." In many more ways than one.

In *One Day,* Cowie anticipates the title of one of Morris's nonfiction books: "A *Bill of Wrongs*—the small print at the bottom of the Bill of Rights." The title of the nonfiction work puns further on the word "rights": *A Bill of Rites, a Bill of Wrongs, a Bill of Goods* (1968).

Morris's characters often pause to turn clichés over in their minds. "'The work here is taxing,' the bellhop said, 'she's all worn out.' The word taxing impressed the Colonel as a strange one, but good. He, too, would like to find things taxing, rather than merely hard" (*War Games,* 1972, 44).

Morris's improvisation upon clichés is less aggressive, less playful, less imaginative, less dynamic in *Fire Sermon* (1971) and *A Life* (1973) than in any of his other novels; he seems to be deliberately muting the cliché voice.

In *The Fork River Space Project* (1977), the imaginative adventures are all meditative flights rather than flights of science fiction action. Imagination is Kelcey's "state of mind"; what he sees and does is less important than what he imagines. What he hears and sees "boggles the mind" and gives "cause for wonder." "I was ripe for the word, but it escaped me," he tells the reader. Dahlberg asks him, "Do you grasp it, Kelcey?" He almost does. In the past, Americans, especially on the frontier, had "great expectations," one of many clichés whose original freshness Morris resurrects in lively contexts. "The word *expected* was so appropriate to Olivia that the Colonel felt obliged to fulfill her expectations."

Morris's use of clichés in *Plains Song, For Female Voices* (1980) is less overt, less intrusive, than in his other novels, with no conceptual clichés repeated in a pattern throughout, as in many of his novels. The clichés are all incidental and arise naturally out of the context of a character's flow of perception. "What *was* on her mind?" "She was as full of life as a box of kittens." Sharon looks at a place where the barn once stood "pondering the imponderable." Into thin air. How did one measure air?" "Sharon was spellbound. Her flesh crawled, an expression she had always found ridiculous." "Just one day before Sharon would not have marveled at the forces that brought such loose ends together, making them one." "Alexandra said, 'Do I look a sight? Who is there to see me but God?'"

Morris's transformed clichés themselves sometimes return to their moribund state through overuse. The phrases "turned as if he might see" and "she lidded her eyes" are two examples. Serviceable rhetorical phrases such as "on the evidence, which is impressive" and "how explain it?" have become perhaps too familiar. Key terms and concepts that Morris develops in his nonfiction and echoes in his fiction, such as "transformation," "raw material," "the immediate present," "permanence and impermanence," "fact and fiction," "life and literature," "conception" run the risk of becoming clichés themselves.

Even when his tone is satirical, Morris's purpose in using clichés is to resurrect, reveal, and transform. In the process of experimenting with phototext techniques, Morris discovered, experienced, the difference between exposure and revelation. In *The Home Place,* the farmer exemplifies the sanctity of individuality and privacy, themes which reach their most heightened expression in the scene in Uncle Ed's house. In the modern world, the idea has grown that at the root of privacy there is something suspect; the private, therefore, is meant to be exposed. Privacy is so rare today, Morris believes, that there is a quality of holiness about it. Morris photographed a bed, symbol of privacy. Under it squatted a chamber pot, cliché of the rural scene.

One may imagine Morris in his darkroom, watching the picture rise toward him out of the solution in the pan, an effect suggested in this passage from *The Home Place*: "I wiped my face on the towel and watched the PILLSBURY stamp come up, slowly darkening," says Clyde Muncy, "like a print in the developer" (27). The sight of the chamber pot, a folksy, Norman Rockwell cliché invasion of privacy, exposure of character, made Morris cringe, there in the dark, with shame. "In the honest guise of telling the facts, this photograph ended up lying, since in such a context the larger statement . . . the revelation could not be heard above this shout." Shock, even comic shock, "is the technique of invasion, and it marks a signal failure of art," the purpose of which is to reveal. Here is a typical instance of Morris's refusal to exploit sensational, comic, or local-color cliché details. He rejected *that* photograph. In the second photograph, the details harmonize with the conception, a portrait not of a habit but of a way of life, an eloquent expression of the atmosphere and the meaning of privacy and the holiness of artifacts.

Looking at that photograph, we know why sarcastic, finger-snapping, scornful Peg, Clyde's wife, reacts as she does. "'That's Ed's room,' I said, and my wife stepped up to look at it. Then she backed away, as if she saw someone in the bed" (135). Had she seen the thunder mug there under the bed, Peg might have barked a laugh, taking her cue from Morris himself. Clyde muses on the implications of the response Peg *did* make: "There are beds with a single image, overexposed. There's an etched clarity about them, like a clean daguerreotype, and you know in your heart *that* was how the man really looked. . . . Without a word, or snapping her knuckles, my wife turned away" (135). Revelation becomes "the problem of stating what remains unsaid," says Morris, and this photograph, with its text, is one of the finest illustrations of what he means. Here is also a good example of the technique of revision that Morris employs in the process of refining his style. That verbal image (and even the photograph itself) goes through several variations throughout Morris's books.

This passage from *Man and Boy* is one of the most revealing examples of Morris's ability to transform the cliché.

The basement toilet had been put in to accommodate the help, who had to use something, and Mother wouldn't have them on her Oriental rug. But until the day he dropped some money on the floor, and had to strike a match, inside, to look for it, Mr. Ormsby hadn't noticed just what kind of a stool it was. Mother had picked it up, as she had told him, second-hand. There was no use, as she had pointed out, why she should buy anything new or fancy for a place that was meant to be in the dark. He hadn't pushed the matter, and she hadn't offered more than that. What he saw was very old, with a chain pull, and operated on a principle that was very effective, but invariably produced quite a splash. The boy had named it the Ormsby Falls. That described it pretty well, it was constructed on that principle, and in spite of the splash they both preferred it to the one upstairs. This was a hard thing to explain, as the seat was pretty cold over the winter, but it was private like no other room in the house. The first time the boy had turned up missing, he had been there. It was that time when the boy had said—when his father nearly stepped on him—*Et tu, Brutus,*" and sat there blowing through his nose. Laughing so hard Mr. Ormsby thought he might be sick. Like everything the boy said there had been two or three ways to take it, and there in the dark Mr. Ormsby couldn't see his face. He had just stood there, not knowing what to say. Then the boy stopped laughing and said: "You think we ought to make one flush do, Pop?" and Mr. Ormsby had had to brace himself on the door. To be called Pop had made him so weak he couldn't speak, his legs felt hollow, and when he got himself back to the stairs he had to sit down. Just as he had never had a name for him— the boy had never had a name for him—one, that is, that Mother would permit him to use. And of all the names she couldn't stand, Pop was the worst. Mr. Ormsby didn't like it either, he thought it just a vulgar common name, a comic name used by smart alecks to flatter old men. He agreed with her completely—until he heard the word in the boy's mouth. It was hard to believe a common word like that could mean what it did. Nothing more had been said, ever, but it remained their most important conversation—so important that they were both afraid to improve on it.

(26-29)

After Morris's use of it, a cliché is never quite the same—it is intellectually demolished and emotionally transformed in the moment of usage, so that the reader feels as Mr. Ormsby did when his son called him by the cliché nickname "Pop": "It was hard to believe a common word like that could mean what it did." Or consider Mother, who asks us to "Consider the Lilies."

> . . . she always seemed to be saying more than she said. He had never seen nor heard of a woman with a greater store of pithy sayings, though it sometimes took a little reflection to figure them out. The saying was plain enough, but Mother always managed to use it, like she did the lilies, in a very original way. It gave what was generally described as depth to everything she said.

(45)

One might say the same of Morris. The tone of the fresh context Morris creates makes the familiar cliché sound strange—it has an aura of having just been coined. It never loses the sense of wonder that gave it birth, the sense of the unique on which it first thrived. "Every cliché once had its moment of truth," says Morris. "At the moment of conception it was a new and wonderful thing" (**"Made in U.S.A.,"** 488). In carefully prepared contexts, Morris revives that "moment of truth" in his use of each cliché.

From the common man's viewpoint, Morris describes people who live in the mode of sentimental clichés. With artful control and contrivance, he creates a unique diction that does with the cliché three things simultaneously: 1) presents them, as such, with a fidelity that reveals their essential emptiness; 2) presents his characters in the language of the clichés by which they live and communicate; but in so doing, he 3) reveals what is genuine and viable. In the same moment that the cliché works against itself, it is transformed and becomes, at times, both eloquent and significant.

Marilyn Arnold (essay date 1982)

SOURCE: "Wright Morris's *Plains Song*: Woman's Search for Harmony," in *South Dakota Review,* Vol. 20, No. 3, Autumn, 1982, pp. 50-62.

[*In the following essay, Arnold discusses Morris's depiction of gender roles and gender conflicts in his novel,* Plains Song.]

Perhaps smarting a little under the criticism that his books rarely center around women, Wright Morris, in his recent novel, ***Plains Song,*** may be trying to correct the imbalance. His title page indicates that the "song" he is present-

ing is "for Female Voices."[1] And indeed it is. The two principal voices are those of Cora Atkins and Sharon Rose Atkins, a niece Cora reared as her own. The first third of the book is given to Cora, the second two-thirds to Sharon, though both figure prominently in the whole book.

Plains Song opens with an introduction to the dying Cora, then jumps back to the story of her courtship and marriage in the early part of this century. From there the novel proceeds chronologically through her life and the lives of succeeding generations of the Atkins family. As a tall, flat, able young woman she gratefully married the stoical Emerson Atkins after a short acquaintance and the two began farming the Nebraska prairie. Sharing their farm and labors was Emerson's brother, Orion, a wilder sort, but more appealing than Emerson. When Orion's wife, Belle, died in childbirth, it was left to Cora to provide a home for Belle's two living children, Sharon Rose and Fayrene.

The book's opening sentence establishes two things—the subject of the book and the narrative attitude the book intends toward that subject. It announces: "It is a curse in this family that the women bear only daughters, if anything at all" (p. 1). ***Plains Song*** is mainly about women and about the fact that in three generations only female children have been born into the Atkins family. That such is considered "a curse" defines an attitude of a time and place toward the relative value of men and women and the nature of their roles and relationships. The essence of this attitude is not only that men are superior, but also that men and women are radically different and have clearly defined, God-ordained roles which are inflexible and binding. John W. Aldridge comments on the causes and consequences of this role distinction. He says this of frontier life:

> [It] demanded so much that whole vital areas of the psychic life . . . had to be repressed, and the need for repression became the basis for a religion of self-sacrifice, endurance, parsimony, and rectitude, a religion trumped up by pioneer expediency in the name of moral virtue. But since in the prairie world it was the men who conquered and the women who secured and maintained, a sexual split was created which became at last a permanent national schizophrenia.[2]

And perhaps there was some justification for establishing binding role definitions. Certainly, in a culture where women must work as hard as men and have little time to practice being "ladies," customary social distinctions among men and women run the risk of being lost. The maintenance of them may require extra effort. Morris is writing in this book about the nature of those role definitions in plains life and the painful, isolating consequences of their imposition. Cora's story is one of tough-minded endurance, of loss of self in the sexual necessity of child conception, of perpetuation of a system she believed providence to have established. She is strong, she is adamant, she endures. Sharon's is the story of fearful, then determined, rejection of a system, of escape from dependent yet estranged relationships, and of a troubled return to what she had left. She is both strong and weak, decisive and vulnerable.

Morris develops his narrative around two key events which surface repeatedly throughout the novel. These events reveal the natures of the two women, set the tone for their lives, and finally merge in an ultimate clarification of Morris's theme. The first of these is alluded to in the opening description of the dying Cora. We are told that this "implacable" woman whose "eyes are open" though her mind is sealed, like a tomb" (p. 1), has "between the first and second knuckle" on her right hand "a scar blue as gun metal" (p. 2), a scar said to have resulted from the bite of a horse. We learn later, however, that the bite was self-inflicted on the night of her first sexual experience with her husband. For her, the experience was like "an operation without anesthesia" in which "horror exceeded horror." Her husband was perceived as "her assailant" doing "what must be done." The morning light revealed that in her shock "she had bitten through the flesh of her hand, exposing the bone" (p. 14).

The second key event occurs some years later. Upon returning from Lincoln where she had gone to enroll at the university, Sharon finds that she is an unwanted third party in the life of Beulah Madge, Cora's oldest daughter and Sharon's childhood friend. Sharon angrily leaves Madge and Ned Kibbee spooning in the buggy and stalks into the house screaming, "Is he looking for a wife or a housemaid?" Cora, who hears her from the screened-in porch where she is ironing, follows her in, grabs her wrist, and whacks the palms of her hands with a hairbrush, crying, "That will teach you" but knowing in her heart that it would not. Cora knows, in fact, that "Sharon Rose meant it even worse than she said it" (pp. 75-76). These passages reveal, of course, the basic conflict between Cora and Sharon, between the woman who is handed her role and then grittily chooses it too and the woman who refuses to accept the role and pities the one who does. And between their defiance, one the defiance of acceptance, the other the defiance of rejection, is Madge who accepts her woman's role because she likes it, who represses troubling questions and lolls through marriage like a fat, contented cow.

The implications behind the two events reverberate through the book as the question of sexual roles is raised in each succeeding generation. Emerson is a stranger to Cora in their sexual union, and he remains so all their lives. In a system that defines roles so strictly, that allows no crossing over, the differences between men and women are stressed to the point that sex is their only meeting ground. In all else, each has his and her place, and the distance between them is not only maintained but widened. Cora and Emerson are very careful to establish territorial rights. She wants grass around the house and he concedes, "I guess it's your yard, but don't you ask me what you plan to do for horsepower." We learn that "she never did. It was her yard, it would be her grass, and she would manage to care for what was hers." She is much more comfortable once "she had determined her own domain," concluding, "It worked better if everybody had their place" (pp. 56-57). Madge and Ned practice the same territorial division, with Ned taking care of the outside and Madge the inside. But even though they seem to find the sexual experience mutually satisfying, they cannot communicate that satisfaction in the light of day. They, too, are strangers.

The same set of rules that divide men from women also divide women from women. This is one thing that Sharon is protesting in her scream, the fact that in accepting Ned, Madge must automatically reject her. Men and women are strangers, but their sexual relationship precludes any other relationships. Nothing but superficial loyalties are allowed among women, and, worse still, they are often taught to mistrust and betray each other. Cora enjoys some things about Belle, but she does not trust her. Cora is also annoyed when Lillian Baumann, Sharon's friend, sends Sharon little gifts through the mail. Madge and Ned are forever urging Sharon into relationships with men, and it is clear that Madge will not feel comfortable with Sharon so long as Sharon is single. Ned even implies that he blows on his baby daughter's tummy so that she will "like boys more than girls" (p. 112). There is also a suggestion that the childhood relationship between Madge and Sharon was acceptable mainly because the two were so different from each other.

In defiance of convention, and implicitly, thus, of Cora, Sharon avoids marriage and settles for limited friendships with women. At one point, she even develops a motherly regard for Madge's oldest daughter, Blanche. The girl seems ready to break out of the conventional mold, but after a brief excursion to Sharon Rose's world in Chicago, she slips back and accepts the role Madge and Ned have set for her. Madge's second daughter, Caroline, however, rejects conventional roles, resenting the expectation "that she should like boys more than she did girls" (p. 177). She becomes an avowed feminist, something Sharon would never have considered. Sharon simply wants independence, and freedom to choose relationships other than those like Cora and Emerson's or Madge and Ned's. Sharon is shocked to learn that Caroline's decision against marriage was prompted by her example.

The hidden message behind the cultural practice that disallows real friendship among women and perpetuates a hopeless rift between men and women is, according to Morris, that women are inferior to men. This being the case, no woman in her right mind would choose a woman for a companion over a man. The habitual assumption that women are less valuable than men is spawned quite naturally on the plains where it is generally agreed that a man needs a farmhand and a housemaid more than he needs a companion, and "that a family of girls you couldn't marry off was hardly a blessing to a marriage" (pp. 108-109). Madge is certain that "Another girl she did not want" (p. 140). The mother of Blanche's friend, Libby, apologizes for her daughter and exclaims that to her great relief, "her other children were boys" (p. 155). Ned refers to his automobile as "she" because that is how he says "a man" would "see it" (p. 125). Emerson's comments and attitudes are sometimes more subtly expressed, but they are no less judgmental. For example, we learn that "politics interested Emerson, but he understood its complexities were beyond the grasp of women" (p. 31). He remarks offhandedly that "the problem with a female child was to shut them up once they start talking" (p. 35), or that Cora has failed him because "what a farm needed was sons" (p. 36). When Belle delivers a daughter, Emerson is "annoyed" (p. 47), and when she delivers a second, the narrator observes in wry understatement that it was not "a cause for rejoicing for Emerson" (p. 51). Later, when Fayrene comes, she is just "one girl too many" (p. 66). Even his compliments are a slap in the face. When Cora buys a player piano with her egg money he assures her "that for a family limited to girls she had chosen right" (p. 63).

Morris's concern, however, is not just with what happens to women in a plains culture that insists on rigid distinctions between male and female roles. He is also concerned with what happens to human beings, to both men and women. Ironically, the cultural system that teaches the limited worth of women diminishes men even more. In this book, the women tend to grow stronger in the face of opposition, and the men grow weaker. The weakest characters in the book are men, not women. The dominant pictures of Emerson, Orion, and Ned portray them as ineffectual failures. Certainly, that is one reason why Sharon Rose is not interested in marrying, because she sees what poor weak creatures the men in her life are. And she despises women for giving up their independence to such creatures. When Sharon screams her bitterness for both Cora and Madge to hear, and receives a whack from Cora's hairbrush in return, Cora reads in Sharon's glance "less anger than pity. Pity for Cora, who felt no pity for herself." Cora understands that "however much Sharon Rose disliked farmers, her scorn for farmers' wives was greater" (p. 76).

Sharon's sense of betrayal in her relationship with Madge and her mixed scorn and pity for Cora have left her with an inner scar to match Cora's outer scar. She fears her own feelings, and backs off from close human relationships. As a musician, Sharon has keen sensitivities and active emotions, but she runs from intimacy. Her friend Lillian apparently wearies of Sharon's evasiveness and terminates their relationship. Her friend Monica is never allowed to get close. Blanche is sent home before she can seriously disappoint Sharon. There is, in fact, only one binding tie in Sharon's life, and that is her tie to Cora, who is at once her rival, her tormenter, her mother, her conscience, and her other self. Sharon goes home to Fayrene's wedding, ostensibly for her sister's sake, but Sharon knows that she is going because she would not dare to be absent "when Cora cried out, 'Where is Sharon Rose?'" (p. 124) Cora is Sharon's past. She is what Sharon has to come to grips with before she can ever be reconciled to her past. In particular, Sharon must reconcile her attitudes and feelings about male and female sexual roles with those of the seeming strangers who people her past. And Cora is both the defender and the victim of those attitudes. She stands for them even though they put her on the rack.

Cora grimly accepts the means by which children are conceived, and she never "doubted that the nightmare she had survived would result in a child. The logic of it was clear and not to be questioned. The gift of life was holy, and one paid for it dearly" (p. 22). She bears the mark of her sacrifice, a "blue-scarred knuckle" (p. 23) on one hand. She ponders the meaning of sexual union and accepts its horror ("In the wild, cats shrieked. In the bedroom Cora had bitten through her hand to the bone," p. 36), and Sharon cannot forgive her for accepting it.

Later, as a very old woman, Cora sometimes forgets that she had bitten herself, and thinks of the wound as having been inflicted by a horse. She remembers the truth, however, and her hand throbs in empathetic recognition, when she sees Emerson treat a stubborn horse with mixed cruelty and affection. The incongruency of Emerson's gestures toward the horse triggers anew Cora's memory of the day Sharon screamed. Time telescopes, bringing the event into the present where "now she knew, as she hadn't before, that Sharon Rose had meant it just as she had said it." Significantly, Cora's next thought is of her bitten hand: "It had not been a horse that bit her; she had bitten herself" (p. 164). In that passage Cora's mind links the two events and thus links Sharon's pain with her own. This is a moment of truth for her, of recognition that Sharon had been justified in screaming against what marriages often meant for a woman on the plains. Cora's own scarred hand is a testimony to the accuracy of Sharon's perception.

Earlier, Cora had not been able to face the truth of what Sharon's scream meant. When Ned and Madge took her with the family to the World's Fair in Chicago, the plan had been for them to meet Sharon one afternoon. But when the appointed time arrived, Cora refused to go: "Cora was possessed by something. She could hear the shrill piercing voice of Sharon, and feel the rage in her body, like that of a trapped animal, when Cora had whacked her palm with the hairbrush." The others went off, "leaving Cora free to sit on a bench facing the animal cages. . . . Seated alone, in this throng of people, Cora was seized with a sadness so great her throat pained her" (p. 143).[3]

Through a lifetime Cora has finally had to come to terms with the meaning of the book's two pivotal events, her own biting of her hand and Sharon's screaming at Madge's betrothal. At the same time, Sharon has had to come to terms with the meaning of her past, and with the meaning of Cora in particular. She makes three trips home, the last two thirty-three years apart, but the reconciliation process does not really begin for her until she learns the difference between independence and freedom. It had been observed that Lillian wanted her independence in order to be free, but that Sharon wanted her freedom in order to be independent. Sharon can never be truly free until she reconciles herself to what Cora and the plains and the others who inhabit the plains of home are, and what they have done to shape her. She cannot free herself by escaping from them. She can free herself only by choosing to accept them. She must finally learn Cora's trick, to achieve freedom by actively choosing what fate has handed out.

It is surely appropriate (if a bit contrived) that as Sharon approaches home to pay her last respects to the dead Cora, she comes face to face with the Women's Liberation Movement, first in the person of Alexandra Selkirk, an international figure in the movement who is bound for a convention in Grand Island, and then in the person of Madge's daughter Caroline. The Movement is, after all, a formal recognition of the male-female rift/dilemma precipitated by growing resistance to restrictive role assignments that exploit and demean women. Had Cora been born in another place and time and convinced that heaven were on her side, she would likely have been at the front of the feminist battle line. Sharon seems to sense this on the plane going home as she looks at the hands of the sleeping Alexandra and observes, almost surprised, that "they were scarless." She remembers that "a similar pair of hands had gripped her in such manner that she could still feel them" (p. 188), Cora's on that long ago day when Cora "had gripped her by the wrists as she whacked her palms with the hair-brush" (p. 190).

Stopping with Caroline and two of Fayrene's grandchildren (one of them a boy—the "curse" has apparently been lifted) at a museum of prehistoric animals, Sharon is prompted to compare the animals' earlier nonchalance in the face of extinction with that of the large, powerful creatures engaged in a football game in the nearby Nebraska stadium. She thinks of "Alexandra Selkirk: the pleasure she would feel in Man's extinction—her sorrow at Woman's loss" (pp. 193-94). Looking at the remains of the extinct beasts, Sharon thinks, "Who could not see in this . . . the future of man in a world of women. . . . Even at this moment the males were gathered in one of their primitive ceremonies, blind as the dinosaur to what was happening. . . . In the diggings of the future, the football coliseum would be the interment site of an extinct species" (p. 193). Sharon admits that she owes this ingenious bit of logic to Alexandra Selkirk.

The problem with the Women's Movement, as Morris sees it, is that it emphasizes differences that have already been given too much attention. It separates men and women even more, sets them against each other. In Caroline, Sharon encounters again an "us against them" attitude, minus Alexandra's largeness of spirit and saving humor. This is the spirit that divides, and Sharon does not want to exemplify that spirit to Caroline, though she is equally uncomfortable with Caroline's veiled charges of cowardice. Sharon's mood now is one of reconciliation, not division, even toward Caroline, who is much like Cora but has never forgiven Cora for stubbornly accepting her role as Emerson's wife.

Through Sharon, Morris deliberately moves outward from considerations of maleness and femaleness to the larger concern of the humanness of all of us. And it is essentially this humanness to which Sharon must finally be reconciled. Earlier, she had cringed with distaste when Avery Dickel (Fayrene's betrothed) had chipped some tartar off a cat's teeth at the dinner table and extended it congenially for her examination. Now, as the dinner following Cora's burial ends, Blanche's pet bird flies into the room and pecks at the bits of food between Blanche's teeth. Sharon's emotions are "confounded," but it strikes her that the bird and Blanche seem to have a natural kinship. Recalling the story of another bird's flight through darkness and light, Sharon admits that contradictory experience is "like life itself" (pp. 212-213). She notices, however, that Caroline sits with her eyes lowered, unable to bear the sight of Blanche and her bird. With all her audacious courage to tell the hidden things, Caroline is silenced by what the open act conceals. What is behind Blanche and her bird Caroline can never know. Sharon realizes that "the most appalling facts were those that burned like gems in the open. Not in the bedroom only, or in the barn, or in the mind's dim recesses, but in the shimmering light" (p. 213). No philosophy about male and female roles and needs, no stance on marriage or women's issues, can explain or even confront the larger question of what it is to be human in this world. The old incident comes to mind again: "On the palm of her hand Sharon felt again the stinging slap of Cora's brush" (p. 213). Sharon recognizes that she and Caroline had blundered in the same way, had shouted out about hidden things. But now she knows what Caroline still has to learn, that only when the tongue is silent in "matters that were secret to the heart" is it "possible to guess at what they were" (p. 213).

These realizations come for Sharon in the context of Cora's death and burial. It follows that when we move beyond considerations of male-female role definitions to confront our mutual humanity, we also confront the fact of our mortality. We confront death. Human beings age and die. Morris underlines this fact by leading us systematically through the lives of several generations of people who age before our eyes. Some, like Belle and her infant daughter Eula, die very young. The fact of mortality and certain death thus overrides considerations of sexual roles and freedom, and there is no lasting stay against such a fact. There is a temporary stay, however, and that lies in the acceptance of our own lives. Sharon realizes at last that to deny her past is to deny what life she has. But in reaching that resolution Sharon has to work through what seems to her death's victory anyway. She sees in Cora's death the erasing of Cora's "works and meager effects" which seems a profound "violation, like a shaking of the earth. . . . Her death was an incident of small importance compared with this ultimate rejection" (pp. 214-15).

Sharon remembers a boy she had met on the train years ago, a boy who was running away, as she had done, to freedom. She wonders, "Had they both grown up and old in order to recover what had escaped them as children?" (p. 215). Sharon at last makes the admission that will ensure Cora some kind of extended life: "As much as or more than the child she had borne, Sharon had been Cora's child" (p. 216). Cora will in some sense survive so long as those in whose past she dwells willingly own that past. Sharon at last accepts her past, knowing that whatever future lies ahead for her, "it would prove to reside in this rimless past" (p. 216). She comes to know the meaning of "mutual kinship" (p. 217) with figures of her past, and seems to recognize that such kinship is the main thing we have. Implicit in this recognition is also the suggestion that cultural expectations about male and female roles are largely an attempt to guarantee human relationship, to ensure binding human ties. Even though they seem sometimes to produce still more painful isolation, they are humanity's attempt at connection, unity. Sharon has to concede that unity is what others are seeking, even though she might be right in perceiving that they rarely achieve it.

The last scene of the novel is in the Crossways Inn where Sharon goes to meet Alexandra Selkirk at the women's assembly. She sees a sign that says "that children under 12, accompanied by their parents, were free," and asks no one in particular, "Is that possible?" (p. 217). Can children indeed be free if accompanied by their parents? What Sharon is coming to learn is that while independence may require severance from family connection, true freedom may depend on that connection. Mutual kinship is essential to the individual life. There is a touch of sly sarcasm in the narrative voice as on the heels of such realizations Sharon enters the motel and breathes "the bracing air of womanly independence" (p. 218). Thus, Sharon meets the old problems again, the separating and dividing into roles and the sloughing off of ties that bind. Then she sees through an open door the performance of a "corrupt" male in concert whose gyrations simulate the sex act and whose lips mouth the words to obscene songs. Here, then, she confronts the image of male-female relationship in its ugliest possible form, a reminder of all she might have hated in what she guessed Cora had to endure and what she herself had run from. She is both horrified and fascinated. This experience is crucial, however, for it presents a graphic view of Sharon's own distorted notions of sexual experience. She must acknowledge what her mind has made of such experience before she can accept the reality of sex and sexual roles.

Morris's insistence that mortals need each other is further substantiated when in Sharon's half-dream that night she sees a child "wearing a blindfold, groping about as if for companions," and "a profound recognition sweetens her sorrow" (p. 221). Sharon's experiences in the last few pages of the book lead her ever more surely to reconciliation—with the past, with Cora's silent acceptance, with humanity, with her own self as a sexual being. She is awakened at 1:20 a.m. and summoned by Alexandra Selkirk. On the way she encounters "an amorous couple, the woman in pajamas, . . . grappling in the warmth of the laundry room," and she marvels at them, "at the forces that brought such loose ends together, making them one" (p. 222). Not long ago, she would have responded very differently to such an incident, but now she accepts the wonder of urges that accomplish union. Next she sees a couple sitting on the stairs, the woman in obvious distress,

the man attempting to give comfort. When she asks, "What can I do?" he replies gently, "Ma'am, what can we do to be saved?" Thus, here in the hallway of the Crossways Inn, Sharon hears perhaps the largest question of all: is salvation possible, and if so, how? The very asking of the question implies that it *is* possible, the "astonishing statement" itself "like a sign of life in something believed dead." Sharon feels an old burden lifting, one she "had been reluctant to acknowledge" (p. 223).

She enters the open door of Alexandra's room to find the flamboyant feminist drying her hair after a bath. Sharon reflexively recalls the time when as a child she had guiltily watched Cora in her tub. The other images of Cora flash into her mind. As Alexandra speaks—asking, "Who said let there be light?" "Who saw that all of it was good?" "Who said let us make him in our own image?" "Who said let them have dominion over the whole shebang?" and answering each question with an emphatic, "*He* did"—Sharon feels "comforted. When she heard the voice of Alexandra she heard *His* voice, and knew she was in good hands" (p. 224). Cora's God, who had assigned male-female roles in the beginning, now appears, of all things, to be speaking through Alexandra's voice. The unity is complete, the abyss bridged. The language of the Biblical creation paraphrased here by Alexandra is absorbed into Sharon's consciousness through her growing sense of a new world beginning for her. When Alexandra asks how her day went, she thinks, "Of the six days of creation, which one had it been?" She then repeats what had been said by the man on the stairs. Characteristically, Alexandra must make the distinction, draw the dividing line. She asks, "Was it a man or a woman?" Sharon's reply refuses the division: "Both, I think." At that moment they hear the brazen crow of a rooster, "shrill with young male assurance" (p. 227), and the chauvinistic sound transports Sharon back to remembered sights, smells, and sounds of her childhood. But the language and imagery of redemption proliferate. Morris not only provides the suggestion of the crucifixion in the name of the motel, but also interjects a "cock's crow" into the scene, restoring a myriad of details from Sharon's past "to the glow of life."

Then, finally, climatically, Sharon perceives in the "flat, skeletal figure" of Alexandra "a resurrection of Cora." And it is Alexandra/Cora who asks, "Do you know the sun is perpetually rising? Every moment somewhere" (p. 228). She invites Sharon to join her in watching it rise on this particular piece of plains. Sharon goes gladly with Alexandra, indicating that she had "not seen a sunrise" since childhood. In the final lines of the novel Morris completes his vision of Sharon's reconciliation with the past, a reconciliation which allows her to inhabit a new world, different from the one she and Cora had created out of a cultural cliche and a distorted view of what sex and human interdependencies are and mean. Alexandra's final remark suggests a final reconciliation with God's scheme for her too, even though he may seem to have given women a bad shake. She senses that in him resides a broad tolerance that somehow makes all his children acceptable. She shrugs off an impulsive concern over how she might look, going out with scruffed up hair, and clad only in a terry towel robe; but she concludes to go anyway, adding, "Who is there to see me but God?" (p. 229).

Notes

1. Wright Morris, *Plains Song* (New York: Harper & Row, 1980). All citations will be noted parenthetically in the text. In a conversation between Wright Morris and Wayne C. Booth titled "The Writing of Organic Fiction: A Conversation," in *Critical Inquiry,* 3 (Winter 1976), 387-404, the question of whether or not Morris has ever "fully portrayed a sympathetic woman" arises. The two discuss the issue, and Morris insists that he has never "calculated [his] position in regard to women or men or anything else" (p. 400).

2. John W. Aldridge, "Wright Morris Country," in Robert E. Knoll, ed., *Conversations with Wright Morris* (Lincoln: University of Nebraska Press, 1977), pp. 7-8.

3. It is worth remembering here, as Cora faces the animal cages and thinks of Sharon, that Sharon habitually likened farm people to animals, despising them for what she regarded as subhuman characteristics.

A. Carl Bredahl (essay date 1986)

SOURCE: "The Outsider as Sexual Center: Wright Morris and the Integrated Imagination," in *Studies in the Novel,* Vol. XVIII, No. 1, Spring, 1986, pp. 66-73.

[*In the following essay on Morris's novel* In Orbit, *Bredahl examines "the outsider" as a sexual force infusing creative energy into the lives of Indiana townspeople who have become static in their habits.*]

When the narrator of Wright Morris' *In Orbit* tells us that his joyfully named protagonist, Jubal E. Gainer, "makes old things new,"[1] he places Jubal in what to Morris is a mainstream of American life: "Pound may have been the first to give the thrust of doctrine to the American instinct to *make it new.* In so doing he gave official sanction to what came naturally to the natives. In the new world where so much had to be made, or remade, making it new was both an aptitude and a necessity."[2] For Morris, the outsider generates energy, and energy—several critics to the contrary—is at the center of Morris' world.[3] "Make it new" has obvious sexual implications as well, and Morris' outsider is at once a destroyer of normative values and a stimulator of life. Gail Crump describes the context for sexual vitality in Morris when she speaks of his "belief that life, experience, and the universe itself exist in a state of constant becoming, a belief fundamental to an understanding of his work."[4] And we begin to understand the importance of Wright Morris' writings for the twentieth-century imagination when we note how easily Alfred North Whitehead's description of "Creativity" relates to Morris' interest in individuals who can make old things new.

[Creativity] is the ultimate principle by which the many, which are the universe disjunctively, become the one actual occasion, which is the universe conjunctively. It lies in the nature of things that the many enter into complex unity. "Creativity" is the principle of *novelty.* . . . "Creativity" introduces novelty into the content of the many, which are the universe disjunctively. The "creative advance" is the application of this ultimate principle of creativity to each novel situation which it originates.[5]

In these terms making it new becomes essential to life processes; for Morris, it is an ability as important to artists as to outsiders, for "each time the writer creates and solves the problems of fiction, he makes it possible for men and women to live in the world."[6] Creating and solving problems of fiction are thus not concerns cut off from experience but ways both of participating in and making it possible for others to participate in the vitality of a dynamic world. Of many fictional problems addressed by Morris, one of the most significant is that of integrating the imagination's potentially divided verbal and visual powers. *The Home Place* (1948) and *In Orbit* (1967) are sufficiently separated in the Morris canon so that a comparison of their common interest in pictures reveals strikingly his effort to resolve a fundamentally life denying divisiveness.

In *The Home Place,* the protagonist, a Nebraska-born writer named Clyde Muncy, arrives at the home place with his city-bred wife and two children. "There is no grass in New York," says Muncy, "no yards, no trees, no lawn swings—and for thousands of kids not very much sky. They live in cages. . . . It's like a big zoo of kids. A cage with windows and bars."[7] The search for freedom and room to move, however, does not adequately explain his motivation. The force of nostalgia also shapes the direction of his vision and life, a force evidenced in the narrative's unusual technique of employing both photographs and prose. The dominant qualities evinced by this photo-text technique are those of division and stasis. Because of the division between the verbal and visual powers of Muncy's imagination, his ability to move is negated; the surviving cliche and fossilized remnant of the past distort his perception of the present. Muncy can only go back, seeking a remembered world at the home place. But the going back will later make possible a going forward: "Stock taking, inventory, is the first effort of the mind to make itself at home," says Morris in *The Territory Ahead,*[8] and indeed in the course of the novel Muncy does obtain enough insight into himself and the home place to leave the home place behind.

The photo-text technique of *The Home Place* exposes the limitations of an imagination dominated by nostalgia.[9] The pictures in the book are stills, freezing a fluid world into stable artifacts. Mary Ann Flood, in an unpublished 1971 master's thesis, examines these pictures, noting that they focus on artifacts rather than human life (we see the human face, for example, only through photographs of photographs), that they are black and white, that they emphasize high-definition closeups, and that they stress man-made vertical and horizontal lines imposed upon natural forms:

> The stress upon lines and the use of black and white composition in the photographs attest to an intellectually controlled vision which desires to construct rules, order, and permanence which run counter to the ever-changing nature of existence. The presence of lines and the black and white, rather than color, photographs connote the world view of the dual nature of existence: the belief in black and white, good and evil, right and wrong. The mind, caught up with abstractions, is divorced from perceiving, and, thereby, from experiencing the thing-in-itself. Externally imposed value systems and abstractions, rather than the concrete manifestations of life, dominate and solidify the picture presented of the home place.[10]

In Orbit also centers on a picture but one significantly different from those in *The Home Place*. Most importantly, with *In Orbit* we are examining a single picture; the book itself results from a union of verbal and visual: "That's the picture. You might want to add a few details of your own," says the narrator after the initial description of Jubal. And on the last pages of the text, he says: "That's the picture: there are those who can take it in at a glance. . . . But perhaps the important detail escapes you. He is in motion." The picture referred to here, the totality of events described, results from the narrative fusion of verbal and visual. And the dynamic quality of the picture is evidenced in its use of line. The photographs from *The Home Place* depend upon horizontals and verticals, but this opening from *In Orbit* develops a different kind of line:

> This boy comes riding with his arms high and wide, his head dipped low, his ass light in the saddle, as if about to be shot into orbit from a forked sling. . . . He is like a diver just before he hits the water, he is like a Moslem prayer-borne toward Mecca, he is like a cowpoke hanging to the steer's horns.

The verticals and horizontals of *The Home Place* imply the possibility of a vector, but the resultant is missing. With no directed force, we simply have two lines and a consequent freezing of motion. *In Orbit,* however, presents a story of force and motion; the picture taken in at a glance is that of the vector itself, the integration of vertical and horizontal forces. Because the subject moves, the details and forces continually change, and the narrative eye capable of perceiving and articulating this dynamic picture must be able to integrate as opposed to that earlier vision, *The Home Place,* limited to freezing and fragmentation. The contentment with nostalgia which generated the fragmentation of *The Home Place* is ultimately life denying. No human faces are seen in the photographs, and there is no evidence in either the verbal or visual text of the energy originally embodied in the pioneers. We see the products, not the process, of settlement which established new life on the prairies. In contrast, it is energy which is the subject of *In Orbit.* In spite of its dispassionate surface, *In*

Orbit is a highly sexual book. A divided imagination denies the possibility of new life, but an imagination which seeks to take in a fluid, thrusting world appropriately sees a story which is at once destructive of the static condition of verticals and horizontals (here imaged in the cutting of the old oak tree) and at the same time explosively creative. When Jubal enters Pickett, we are told that "the words of his song string out behind him like the tail of a kite" (p. 10), imaging as well the tail of a comet or twister or perhaps even the tail of a sperm cell. "As for the overall impression of the boy on the bike, it is that of two cats, piggyback: hard at it" (p. 27). Twister or sperm cell, the thrusting force embodied in Jubal Gainer is, in Whitehead's terms, creative; it explodes internal energies and brings new life to the individuals in Pickett, Indiana. "Nature abhors a vacuum," we are told, and the natural forces of Jubal and twister rush into the vacuum at the center of the town and certain of its inhabitants. The frequently mentioned photograph images a movement into the center. When that center lies within an individual, like a sperm cell driving toward an ovum, the energy brings a stimulus to life.

Little distinguishes Jubal from other teen-agers; the narrator makes every effort to stress Jubal's ordinary characteristics. No knight errant conscious of his direction and in control of his intentions, Jubal has the sniffles. But the special quality about Jubal is not his physical appearance or his intellectual prowess; it is rather the fact that he operates out of the center of himself. Characters in the book accuse him of intention, but Jubal functions naturally, responding boldly to stimuli of the moment. His relations with others are center-to-center, just like human sexual relations, in contrast to the relationships established by the inhabitants of Pickett where impersonal, distancing newspapers and telephones unite the citizens. Jubal almost instantaneously establishes physical, interpersonal contact with his "victims." He seldom speaks, so the contact is not verbal, nor does he impose himself on others. Jubal is welcomed by his "victims" who similarly respond from within themselves.

These implicitly sexual center-to-center relationships occur in a fertile environment awaiting penetration. Two of the most pervasive images, bees and spray, establish an atmosphere of fertility. The events of *In Orbit* occur on May 17, a spring day in Indiana. Warm, overpowering smells of springtime fill the air. Bees swarm in the cloying, pollen-laden atmosphere, a masculine role repeated in frequent scenes of spraying. Pauline Bergdahl hoses down the cinders, a plane sprays for insects, and two Pickett firemen hose the sidewalk. Unlike the bees, each of these human actions consciously seeks to hold back natural forces which might imperil the smooth functioning of an ordered society. But the spraying as well images ejaculation. "Because he is non-fixed, this one also sprays the fireplace and the white sidewalls of Alan's Porsche" (p. 28). That description of one of Charlotte's cats makes clear the connection between sexuality, fixing, and spraying. The book's dispassionate surface reflects the suppressed sexuality of Pickett, but underneath are individuals and a natural world ripe for fertilization. Jubal's "victims" are beings of potential, and his energies either deflate or stimulate what is within. Energy is transferred, as in an electron's jump from one orbit to another, so that when Jubal leaves Pickett "there is no longer much flex in his knees, much spring in his legs. The words of a song do not trail out behind him like the tail of a kite" (p. 152). His potency has been spent and needs time to regenerate.

Given the book's equal and integrated relation between motion and sexuality—to be alive is to move—the frequent uses of the word "fix" are entirely correct. To "fix" is both to pin down and to remove sexual potency. Holly Stroymeyer, we are told, "is a gentle, childlike woman, and like a child she loves to wander. . . . It's the wandering that has led to problems" (p. 12). And Charlotte Hatfield does not have "much sense of place. . . . Charlotte has been trained to live in a house, to use her box, and to purr when petted. But like the cat in her lap, she is a creature who has not been fixed" (pp. 34-35). In contrast to the sexually stimulating and fertile women, the men in Pickett are unwilling or unable to become sexually aggressive. Haffner is "more AC than DC," Alan Hatfield can "place the needle in the groove" but doesn't seem to turn Charlotte on, and Sanford Avery is limited to rubbing his crotch at the *idea* of sex.

The central male figure, other than Jubal, is Curt Hodler, a newspaper editor with possibilities, but an individual who works best in a fixed world:

> But the forecast is less important than the date, May 17th. The date, strange to say, is more important in the long run than anything in the paper. Day in and day out the news is pretty much the same. . . . It is the date that gives it meaning. . . . If the paper loses its dateline it loses its mind. The purpose of the forecast is to pin down the day, whether it rains or not.
>
> (p. 14)

Like Stephen Crane's correspondent or Sherwood Anderson's George Willard, Hodler's occupation indicates his possibilities and his limitations. A man of words in a book whose narrator is keenly sensitive to language, Hodler prefers to fix meaning to words and to stories. He suppresses his potential just as he suppresses his sexual desire for Miss Holly. His envy of Jubal is the envy of action:

> "And how is Miss Holly?"
>
> For more than twenty years Avery's cynical answer had been the same. *Who the hell would know that?* Now thanks to some snooping idler, or passing stranger, that was no longer an idle question. Someone finally knew. It is a torment to Hodler that this essential knowledge is what he once desired for himself. How *was* Miss Holly. Some idle lecher, some wandering pervert, some bored delinquent, some loyal friend or guardian, envied but unknown to Hodler, and still at large, finally knew.
>
> (p. 20)

Pickett's dealer in army/navy surplus, Kashperl, also prefers to fix events although he, too, is fascinated with action. "Is it more than a tree that falls? It falls to give this day its meaning. To give Kashperl a cud for his idle, vagrant thoughts" (p. 75). For Kashperl, meaning is something tangible to cling to in a day when experience appears chaotic. "A preference for the fading title, or the missing author, or better yet the rare volume that proved to lack both, a country waiting to be staked out and mapped by Kashperl" (p. 77) indicates both Kashperl's potential—he deals with the "clothes of men *missing in action*" (p. 74)—and his preference for fixing the unknown. He is content with being sedentary, with vicariously living off the experience of others. Both Hodler and Kashperl find an event food for thought rather than a stimulus for action. Kashperl even shares the desire of Avery and Hodler for Miss Holly: "But that was not what the fat man was waiting to hear. He wanted what Jubal had had without all the trouble. He wanted the cherry" (p. 87).

Structurally, Jubal's encounter with Kashperl—Chapter 5—is at the center of the nine chapter book; in Chapter 5 Jubal is also at the physical center of Pickett. He penetrates the town just as he does individuals, revealing a fertile world ripe for stimulation. The bag of cherries smashed on Haffner's head nicely images the condition of the town and Jubal's effect upon it: "[Kashperl—and Hodler and Avery—] wanted the cherry, which was actually more than Jubal had got" (p. 87). The earlier book, *The Home Place,* breaks in two, a verbal and a visual text; *In Orbit,* however, is a single picture, initially taken in at a glance and then explored more fully. Thus instead of a two or three part structure, *In Orbit* is a verbal/visual whole that seems to be continually moving. It is very difficult, for example, to speak of a beginning, middle, and end. Instead we move into and then out from Pickett and its inhabitants. Chapters 1 and 9 present the picture taken in; 2 and 8 focus on the force that is Jubal; 3/4 (Holly) and 6/7 (Charlotte) narrate Jubal's stimulation of two sexually responsive women; and 5 presents the bloodless puncturing of the town's center. The symmetry of the book is suggestive of the sexual act itself, a penetration that breaks cherries and shatters hollow dreams followed by a withdrawal that ultimately is stimulating rather than deflating.[11]

In Orbit, then, is a picture of a single motion; our efforts as viewer/reader are to see the whole rather than fix by seeking to extract meaning. The picture combines the deceptively simple and apparently static with the powerfully dynamic. Clyde Muncy's vision of the world in *The Home Place* was dominated by division and meaning, but the narrator of *In Orbit* sees a world of motion and unity as evidenced by the picture he describes. His use of language in that description is part of the vision:

> This boy comes riding with his arms high and wide, his head dipped low, his ass tight in the saddle, as if about to be shot into orbit from a forked sling. He wears a white crash helmet, a plastic visor of the color they tint car windshields, half-boots with stirrup heels,

a black horsehide jacket with zippers, levis so tight in the crotch the zipper of the fly is often snagged with hair. Wind puffs his sleeves, plucks the strings of his arms, fills the back of his jacket like a wineskin, ripples the sootsmeared portrait of J. S. Bach on his chest. His face is black as the bottom-side of a stove lid, except for his nose, which is pewter-colored. He has the sniffles and often gives it a buff with his sleeve. He is like a diver just before he hits the water, he is like a Moslem prayer-borne toward Mecca, or he is like a cowpoke hanging to the steer's horns, or a high school dropout fleeing the draft.

(p. 9)

The use of detail and figurative language is particularly striking in this passage, and it characterizes much of the writing in the book. The narrator approaches language as though it were at the same time a visual and a verbal medium. Curt Hodler struggles to perceive shape while the narrator enjoys exploring the motion of an integrated picture. As the narrative and structure are acts of penetration, so is the use of language—thus the fascination with metaphor and simile. In contrast to Hodler's need to use language to fix change, the narrator is sensitive to the power of language to open up, focus, extend, and expand our perceptions. For the narrator, language is not a device to get at meaning. *In Orbit* yields very little "meaning"; rather it describes an event. The verbal medium penetrates, probes that event. The lines which conclude the paragraph just quoted take the crisply detailed opening and put it into motion by allowing the imagination the freedom to work with those details in multiple ways. Thus the opening lines both particularize and set in motion the picture that will continue to be explored. The narrator perceives a world of possibility, and his ability to use language allows him to penetrate, experience, and verbalize that world.

In an early book of critical essays, *The Territory Ahead,* Wright Morris discusses what he sees as the relationship between art and life. "We have a need, however illusive, for a life that is more real than life. It lies in the imagination. Fiction would seem to be the way it is processed into reality. . . . If man is nature self-conscious, as we have reason to believe, art is his expanding universe."[12] The fiction of Morris is a particularly good place to see the expanding universe of one man's imagination.[13] The urge is to live fully in a universe whole and alive. *In Orbit,* then, is only in part the story of Jubal E. Gainer. It is also Morris' imaginative attempt to explore the territory ahead, to conceive and articulate an integrated, dynamic, fertile—in a word, a living—image.

Notes

1. (Lincoln and London: Univ. of Nebraska Press, 1968), p. 80. Further references to *In Orbit* will also be to this edition and will appear in the text.

2. Wright Morris, *About Fiction* (New York: Harper and Row, 1975), p. 79.

3. Critics are divided in their perceptions of the underlying thrust of Morris' work. To many the dominant force is nostalgia, even a T. S. Eliot "still point." See, for example, the [essays by J. C. Wilson ["Wright Morris and the Search for the 'Still Point,'" *Prairie Schooner,* 49, ii (Summer, 1975), 154-163] and Joseph J. Wydeven ["Consciousness Refracted: Photography and the Imagination in the Works of Wright Morris," *Midamerica,* 8 (1981), 92-114]. Gail Crump, on the other hand, stressing dynamics in Morris, sets herself in contrast to Wayne Booth and David Madden whom she describes as tending "to treat transcendence in itself as an unalloyed good." See *The Novels of Wright Morris* (Lincoln and London: Univ. of Nebraska Press, 1978), p. 9.

4. *The Novels of Wright Morris,* p. 4.

5. *Process and Reality* (New York: Macmillan, 1969), pp. 25-26.

6. *About Fiction,* p. 11.

7. (Lincoln and London: Univ. of Nebraska Press, 1968), 6.

8. (New York: Atheneum, 1963), p. 8.

9. Because of the interesting use of the photo-text technique, *The Home Place* is frequently discussed by scholars who seem to be in agreement that the book is one of Morris' weaker efforts. In particular I refer to writings by Alan Trachtenberg ["The Craft of Vision," *Critique,* IV, iii (Winter, 1961-1962), 41-55], David Madden, *Wright Morris* (New York: Twayne, 1964), and Gail Crump (p. 55). *The Home Place,* says Crump, for example, "does demonstrate Morris's increasing insight into his past, but the insight is evidenced only on the conceptual level, not in mastery of his fictional technique" (p. 57); and Madden: "Although the photographs are excellent, their relation to the text is more literal and less interesting than in *The Inhabitants* (p. 52). I disagree with such readings for the reasons I set forth in my essay. The divisive, static world established by the photo-text technique is precisely the problem with which Clyde Muncy's imagination has to deal.

10. "The Hero-Witness Relationship in the Fiction of Wright Morris," University of Florida Master's Thesis, 1971, pp. 16-17.

11. Gail Crump offers an interesting different description of the book's intriguing structure: "The image of orbiting brings together both transcendence (being out of this world) and immanence (being in motion through space-time), and the book's structure—nine brief chapters following Jubal's frenetic rampage through Pickett—suggests the motion of the open road, while opening and closing the book with almost identical framing passages suggests the completion of an orbit" (p. 186).

12. P. 229.

13. See Roger J. Guettinger, "The Problem with Jigsaw Puzzles: Form in the Fiction of Wright Morris," *Texas Quarterly,* II, i (Spring, 1986), 209.

Linda M. Lewis (essay date 1988)

SOURCE: "*Plains Song*: Wright Morris's New Melody for Audacious Female Voices," in *Great Plains Quarterly*, Vol. 8, No. 1, Winter, 1988, pp. 29-37.

[*In the following essay, Lewis discusses Morris's treatment of women and feminism in his last novel.*]

TRIUMPH BY DEFAULT

"Man's culture was a hoax. Was there a woman who didn't feel it? Perhaps a decade, no more, was available to women to save themselves, as well as the planet. Women's previous triumphs had been by default. Men had simply walked away from the scene of the struggle, leaving them with the children, the chores, the culture, and a high incidence of madness." The lines are from Wright Morris's *Plains Song: for Female Voices*; they represent a "brief resume" of the "forthcoming lecture" by Alexandra Selkirk, a feminist who has just arrived in Grand Island, Nebraska, to rally the daughters of the Plains to their incipient liberation.[1] Although the speech is assigned to a fictional leader of the women's movement, the sentiments about the default of man and the corresponding ascent of woman are those of the novelist.

Morris's female characters are often types—the wizened great-aunt or grandmother, the domineering matriarch, the urban huntress, the repressed ice woman, the haunted siren. Those among them who triumph usually do so by default. The pioneering men of previous generations tamed the wilderness, then, through weariness or boredom, left women the less audacious task of maintaining the society and culture, such as they were, that the men had wrought. Morris's indictment of the patriarch in terms of his default can be documented over a span of years. In 1957, Morris stated that man has defaulted in running the world and that woman takes her unconscious revenge by playing the role of tyrannical matriarch.[2] In his 1967 essay, **"Children Are the Best People,"** he claimed that default has undermined the structure of the American family: "When the American male defaulted to the woman, relinquishing his role as head of the family, he established the pattern of the default in family matters of guidance and authority."[3] In a 1975 interview about the novel *One Day*, Morris said his character Evelina Cartwright is *woman* in the mythic sense of the word. "She embodies a certain unpredictableness of temper, a rather ridiculous eccentricity, but she is basically a product of man defaulting in his role as man. The woman is left having to be two personalities in order to replace what the man has failed to provide.[4] And in 1980, the year he published *Plains Song*, Morris stated that women control culture because men default. The men are downtown after business, the women uptown pursuing culture. This latter-day "Jamesian woman," who contributes the cultural embroidery to the canvas man has supplied, appeals to Morris: "Her enigma remains one of the fruitful enigmas of my life."[5]

In the early Morris fiction, the novelist seemed sure that a ruling matriarchy is unnatural and that women who rule their own households spiritually impoverish themselves and their entire families. Since matriarchies are unnatural, Amazons who triumph in victory by default are themselves also victims of a culture that is a hoax—a culture in which men have walked away from the scene of struggle. In the later fiction, however, Morris claimed to be more sympathetic with the new woman than with the old. He rejected the allegation that he was antifeminist and said that in the 1970s he was "shifting over to the female some of the audacity that seemed to be wasted on the males."[6] Morris believed this shift signaled an important new direction in his fiction. *Plains Song: for Female Voices,* published on the author's seventieth birthday, was Morris's first attempt to strike the chords of an audacious new song written entirely for female voices and entirely about women's issues. If it proves to be better than the hoax of man's culture, that new song must be one of consciousness, of the singer knowing who she is, where she came from, and where she is bound.

AUDACIOUS WOMEN

Plains Song begins with the terminal illness of Cora Atkins, mother, grandmother, widow, and pioneer. As the dying Cora recalls the chronology of the Atkins women, the narration evolves as extended flashback. Early in the novel, a matrimonial bargain is struck for Cora, a quiet, solemn, tall, and somewhat plain merchant's daughter of school-marm attire and demeanor. Cora's attributes are her skill at figures, her ability to write in a fine Spencerian hand, and "the virtues of a good hired hand" (p. 5). Cora marries Emerson Atkins, a stranger with a dry sense of humor who has come to Ohio from his homestead in Nebraska to acquire supplies and a wife for his farm, and boldly sets out with him to his government claim on the Plains.

Emerson's honeymoon is a dismal failure, for the awkward bridegroom is neither enlightened nor romantic; when her "assailant" consummates the marriage, the pain for Cora is comparable to an operation without the anesthesia and, to prevent crying out, she bites her clenched fist to the bone. Emerson later conceals her shame by telling the doctor that the wound is a horse bite. As the pastor terms it, the "wages" of Cora's single sexual encounter is the pain of childbirth. Cora's daughter, Beulah Madge, is the first female in a long line of daughters and granddaughters—it being a curse that the women in the Atkins family "bear only daughters, if anything at all" (p. 1). In due course, Emerson's brother, Orion, takes a backwoods bride from the hills of Arkansas; when the somewhat uncivilized Belle Rooney Atkins dies in childbirth and Orion goes off aimlessly chasing after adventure as a hunter and soldier, Cora becomes, by default, the mother of two more girl children. The intelligent and lively Sharon Rose, first-born child of Belle and Orion, is the adored playmate of Cora's listless and lazy Madge. The independent Sharon becomes Cora's second generation counterpart, a figure for the new woman as Cora is for the dying breed of grandmothers.

The first half of the novel depicts Cora's young womanhood; the second half depicts the career of Sharon Rose. Unlike Cora's daughter, Madge, who settles for the conventional female role of marriage and motherhood, Sharon escapes the farm, first for the university, later for the city. In Chicago, she pursues her natural bent as musician. While Cora is growing old in the company of her family, Sharon is growing into middle age avoiding attachment "to persons and places, to kinships, longings, crossing bells, the arc of streetlights, or the featureless faces on station platforms, all of which recede into the past" (p. 137). Unlike Cora, the younger woman is unsure just where she ever will be anchored. Sharon becomes a professor of music; Cora becomes a widow.

Finally, Cora's descendants converge on the home place one last time for her funeral, and the narration in time past catches up to the narration in the present. On her flight to Nebraska, Sharon meets the feminist Alexandra Selkirk, who reminds her of Cora. Selkirk impulsively invites Sharon to join her at a women's convention in Grand Island. After the funeral, Sharon meets the audacious plains women at the convention center, and the final scene of the novel is a tableau of optimism.

There are fifteen females in the novel, spanning four generations. As Joseph J. Wydeven points out, the female voices function through counterpoint, "layers and layers of voices . . . swelling into a chorus."[7] The plains songs are often more cacophonous than harmonious, for the two strongest voices are those of Cora and her niece Sharon, and their voices are among the most discordant melodies of the novel. These two women are only one generation apart in the genealogy of the novel, but their circumstances, values, and world views are poles apart. Cora and Sharon are more alike in character, however, than either would admit. They are representatives of Morris's older female and his new woman. Cora is just as audacious in her way as her young niece who flees the Plains for the East, and Sharon's choices have been just as limited by the constraints of character as Cora's were. The redeeming difference in Sharon is her consciousness. A woman of today, Sharon has come to understand that she is a strong woman precisely because she shares the nature of the audacious women who have preceded her. In Morris's fiction consciousness is among the highest tributes, and Morris would call Sharon's understanding a consciousness of the past without nostalgia.

THE ACQUISITIVE SPIRIT

The midwestern farm novel often focuses upon the pioneer trying to wrest a living from the land and to prosper in a vast and hostile wilderness. Within the settler versus the land theme, the settler is sometimes cast as acquisitive. The goal of the plains farmer is to fill his barns, then build bigger barns. In *Plains Song* the Atkinses turn the temporary house into a granary and build a bigger house. Cora, as plains matriarch, represents the acquisitive spirit. She arrives as chattel on Emerson's farm on the Elkhorn River, but she gradually shapes the place by her own energy and puts her stamp of ownership on everything. Cora is a tireless worker: "That work was never done reassured Cora.

She knew how to work and asked only that she work to an end" (p. 19). First she acquires chickens, and with *her* egg money she buys Christmas-colored linoleum to brighten *her* kitchen, even though she is slightly embarrassed that her purchase borders on ostentation. Then there are *her* garden, *her* storm cave, and *her* sheds that Emerson builds for *her* hens. Finally, an invisible line is drawn between Emerson's farm and Cora's yard, and Cora sets about beautifying "her own domain" as she has her kitchen floor. "It was her yard, it would be her grass, and she would manage to care for what was hers" (p. 56).

The confrontation between male and female is also a theme frequently addressed in plains farm novels. A conflict of values occurs because the female is supposedly seeking security, aesthetics, and the amenities, while, as Leslie Fiedler put it, the typical male protagonist is a "man on the run" trying to escape the "civilization" of sex, marriage, and responsibility, and he considers the new land to be as rugged and wild as he is.[8] In *The Territory Ahead* Morris acknowledged that this confrontation of male and female values is a frequent conflict in the American novel.[9] In *Plains Song,* however, there is only temporary conflict between male and female because Emerson defaults. Morris accepted the stereotypical idea that woman needs to domesticate man. The domestication of Emerson is complete when he bows to Cora's recommendations on farm management and when Cora becomes a more vital and imaginative farm manager than her husband. She shapes Emerson's Madison County homestead as she thinks it should be. "Emerson liked to say when he came in from the field he wondered whose farm it was. People who knew Cora could believe that" (p. 67). Eventually Emerson agrees to drink his buttermilk and do his belching away from the table because it is "Cora's house" (p. 71). Cora's dominance of the household is a more gentle version of the rule of Mrs. Porter in Morris's *The Deep Sleep*:

> The first Commandment of the House reads—Thou shalt not give a particle of gratification. Thou shalt drive from the Temple the man who smokes . . . and thou shalt drive from the bed the man who lusts . . . and thou shalt drive from the bathroom the man who farts . . . and thou shalt drive from the parlor the man who feels, and he shall make himself an island in the midst of the waters, for the man who feels undermines the Law of the House.[10]

Morris's admirers point out that he is taking a new direction in *Plains Song.* For example, Lynn Waldeland calls the novel the best feminist work in the past fifteen years.[11] But the truth is that—although this novel speaks in women's voices—the loss of masculine audacity is just as great a loss, and the female audacity of Cora fills the void.

More than Emerson, Cora has the vision to imagine what the farm can become. She spends not a penny on herself, but she buys a player piano for her house and a new rug for her parlor, and she makes new curtains for her windows with the fabric Sharon sends from Chicago for Cora to have a new dress. When Cora wants electricity, running water, and a flush toilet, she finds a way to acquire them just as she had a gasoline motor to irrigate her garden. When Sharon Rose visits her Nebraska home, she is returning to "Cora's weathered house—one defined it as Cora's" (p. 95). At the end of the novel the aging Sharon, who now teaches music at Wellesley and has not been back on the home place for many years, is met at the airport by Caroline, Cora's granddaughter. On the drive home, the younger woman pulls her car off the side of the road so the two can look at the pitted field and stumps of dead trees that demarcate what is left of Cora's farm. And that is exactly how the women think of the farm—as Cora's farm, not as Emerson and Cora's.

Caroline is capable of seeing the farm only with a pathetic sense of loss, feeling that all of Cora's work adds up to nothing. Her house, lawn, chicken run, and sheds have been torn down to make way for progressive farming techniques, for the new generation to farm the land in new ways. While listening to the hymns at Cora's funeral service, even Sharon thinks that Cora's works and meager efforts have been erased from the earth. Cora's descendants agree that her chores kept her going so long, and that when she could no longer work, Cora lived long enough to see the fruits of her labor disintegrate. Caroline despises the life of her dead grandmother because Cora suffered without complaint, worked until she dropped, and seemingly never questioned what her life as woman should have been.

GRANDMOTHER HECATE

Morris's fiction includes numerous caricatures of the grandmother as a type. He wrote, "Grandmother is my fiction. I know her."[12] His aging pioneer woman, held in a corset of character that makes her inflexible and rigid, is shaped by meaningful chores and does not understand idle distractions. When relegated to the rocking chair, she makes afghans, makes trouble, and sometimes makes hell. Morris believed that he understood why Cora works to exhaustion, shapes the farm to her own personality, refuses to let the people in her life penetrate the rigid corset of her character, and regrets too late (after Emerson is dead) that her husband has been a stranger to her and she to him.

Margaret Atwood pointed out that the strong women of Canadian novels are aged Hecate-crones, figures who, like that goddess of the underworld, preside over death and have oracular powers.[13] With the exception of the claim to prophetic powers, the type that Atwood described is much like Morris's grandmother type, imprisoned in the corset of custom, a frozen harridan audaciously haunting her descendants with her intractable nature and the values by which she has defined her own existence. Women like Cora, with their frugality and self-deprivation, their stoic acceptance of an often cruel universe, and their self-sufficient pride, are common types in both the fiction and the experience of the Plains. Cora Atkins is supposed to remind us of our grandmothers.

The literary character that strikes me as most like Cora is Hagar Shipley of Margaret Laurence's *The Stone Angel,* an example that Atwood cites to support her Hecate-crone thesis. Both Cora and Hagar are large women, Cora six feet tall and thin as a rail, Hagar large and stout—an Amazon, Laurence says. Both are motherless daughters, indulged by storekeeper fathers—although Hagar's father has educated her for better things than being a farmer's wife and disowns her when she marries without his approval; Cora's father, a defaulting gentle man with a "cracked pleading voice," urges her to marry someone who will appreciate her virtues (p. 2). Both women marry farmers several years older than themselves; both hardly know the men they marry and never bother to understand them—Cora, because she requires a shroud of privacy, reciprocates by not seeking to know Emerson's soul, while Hagar arrogantly believes she is better than Bramton Shipley, who is common as dirt or "bottled beer."[14] Both women work like dray horses (Hagar's term), and both put egg money aside to enrich the aesthetic side of life on the prairie—Cora with her player piano and Hagar with a gramophone. Cora and Hagar are both uncommonly strong and stoical; Cora refuses to scream out in pain during childbirth even though the midwife recommends yelling, and Hagar hitches up the horse and drives the buggy to town alone to give birth to her son. Both women lack a natural and demonstrative affection for their children, and both feel guilty that they do not have stronger maternal instincts.

Hagar and Cora exhibit the Hecate archetype that Atwood noted. A nearly senile, ninety-year-old Hagar runs away from the son and daughter-in-law who contemplate sending the incontinent and quarrelsome old woman to Silverthreads Nursing Home. In her exile, Hagar encounters two children whom she frightens away; then she realizes that she has just played the role of witch to their Hansel and Gretel. In *Plains Song,* both Belle and Cora are connected with witchcraft; the voluptuous Belle is said to have "bewitched" Orion, and Cora, with her sharp elbows habitually lifted high, reminds Orion of a witch.

Finally, the protagonists of *The Stone Angel* and *Plains Song* are alike because they have gradually become frozen in their isolation. Both have an intense pride that refuses to allow them to be "beholden" to anyone (and in Hagar's case that includes the Protestant God); both refuse to allow penetration of the stiff and corseted framework of their souls to expose the women inside. Laurence's Hagar is, like the Hagar of *Genesis,* an emotional castaway, and she is finally turned to stone because she can neither ask for nor receive forgiveness and cannot express approval, love, or any kind of weakness. As Hagar says, it is an "awful strength" (p. 59). Though she is not as hardened as Hagar, Cora possesses a similar awful strength. In her final hours, her grandchildren do not call her "Grandma" or raise their faces to be kissed. "Not that she is cold, unloving, or insensible. She is implacable" (p. 2).

If we sense that Hagar is more a flesh and blood woman than Cora, it is because Morris intended that we read Cora as both woman and as myth of woman. She is, he said, an icon for the Plainswoman.[15] She is a type for the female settler who overcame loneliness, poverty, hard times, and her own pride and emerged as something of a heroine to her descendants. The photographer-novelist illustrates Cora as icon by his use of two portraits. The first is an image in Sharon's memory; Cora's "remarkable face had no likeness for Sharon until she saw a book of paintings in the library. The intense staring eyes were those of icons" (p. 88). And in another memory, Sharon realizes that it is "Not her image, not her person, but the great alarming silence of her nature, the void behind her luminous eyes" (p. 200). The second portrait is a cheap photo snapped at the World's Fair in Chicago. The aging Cora observes in her photograph the shrinking head, enlarged ears, and set, pleated lips of an elderly woman, "so bizarre it left no afterimage. . . . She was no longer the person she had been, but something more or less" (pp. 142-43). To her granddaughter Caroline, Cora is less, and to the sensitive Sharon Rose, she becomes more. When Sharon meets Alexandra Selkirk, she recognizes the image recurring in the outspoken feminist, whose bird-like legs and talon-like hands remind Sharon of her dead aunt. For Sharon Rose, as for Wright Morris, Cora represents something beyond the woman she was; with her pride, her work, and her intractable nature, she is an icon for the womanhood of the passing generation.

DAUGHTER OF THE MIDDLE BORDER

Although she is Cora's niece, Sharon is more like Cora than is Cora's daughter, Madge. Madge marries a local carpenter who leaves to his wife all matters that he cannot hammer, saw, and measure. Like Emerson, Orion, and Cora's own father, Ned Kibbee is included in the lineage of defaulting males. The last time Sharon sees him, he has not prospered; he is a silent, stooped old man, furtive as a rabbit. Madge is a stolid person like Emerson, and like her mother, Madge takes infinite joy in work. The smell of washed and ironed clothes, the sight of finished laundry hanging on the line, and the feel of soap and washboard give her pleasure. Like Cora, she runs a household of daughters, but unlike Cora, she takes pleasure in sex; and she regrets that this special bond of love is something she cannot discuss with Sharon, her best friend. Sharon Rose is jealous and resentful of Ned and Madge's relationship, which represents to the celibate Sharon a rupture in the bond she and Madge have known from babyhood. When sisters become wives "thick with child," their sisterhood becomes secondary to the definition of the self. And what is lost between sisters seemingly cannot be restored.

If Cora reminds us of the Hecate-crone of prairie fiction, then Sharon reminds us of another type in plains literature: she is the daughter or son of the middle border who flees in order to escape the ugliness of the Plains. Characterized by adjectives like "tireless," "cunning," and "domineering," the first-born daughter of Belle Rooney declares her self-sufficiency early in the novel. Like Willa Cather, she leaves home and returns with her hair cut short like a man's; like Thea Kronborg in Cather's *The Song of the Lark,* Sharon is a *Wunderkind* who flees the suffocating air

of the West to nurture her musical talent in the East. Sharon's search for refinement and education naturally leads her in the opposite direction from the male characters who follow the Horace Greeley dictum and light out for the territory ahead like a generation of Huck Finns. Retreat to the East is retreat to culture and refinement. As her letters and visits home become more infrequent, Sharon believes that she has abandoned her past. Throughout her life, however, she is merely discovering that she is "Cora's girl" (p. 216). If the first half of *Plains Song* is written for Cora's shrill voice, then the second half is written as Sharon's song.

Sharon moves first to Chicago where she studies piano and works in a library. She finds a cultured friend in fellow musician Lillian Baumann and falls in love with the refinement of the Baumann household, but the relationship becomes strained when Sharon refuses to travel with her new friend at Lillian's expense. Like Cora, she will not be "beholden" to anyone. She deflects the interest of youthful suitors and of Professor Grunlich, who talks to her of art. She briefly takes an interest in Madge's older daughter Blanche and rescues her from the dreary and unfulfilling life on the Plains, seeing to it that the child has a good school and proper friends. But when Sharon discovers that Blanche is susceptible to the attractions of the opposite sex, she quickly loses interest in her young niece and sends her home with the excuse that Blanche misses her family. Sharon believes that Blanche, like her mother before her, can fall prey to the trap that man and nature have set for her, that she will "soon appeal to some loutish youth stimulated by the seasonal fall of pollen, and be thick with child" (p. 148).

Like Cora, Sharon is incapable of the deep "natural" feelings that society insists women are supposed to have for their kin. Cora always felt somewhat guilty for not being more affectionate with her daughter and nieces, and Sharon feels guilty because she neither likes nor dislikes Orion, her father, but is only indifferent to him, and because the strongest feeling she has for Cora is pity. As a music teacher at a women's college, she is carefully aloof from her students; she does not want the kind of emotional attachment that can result in pain. She has had pain over her relationship with Lillian and, like Cora's experience with sex, one event of that sort is quite enough for a lifetime. Lillian is correct when she tells Sharon that her fear of being "beholden" is really a fear of her own emotions.

As Sharon places distance between herself and her family, she begins to feel patronizing toward them. Unlike Hagar Shipley, who feels that she is simply of better breeding than Bramton and his kin, Sharon acts as though aesthetic development and intellectual acquisitions have made her infinitely superior to the people on the Nebraska farm and in the towns of Norfolk and Battle Creek. Morris illustrates Sharon's contempt by her repeated comparisons between the rural Nebraskans and their animals. In either the narrator's voice or the characters' voices, the Morris fiction often remarks upon the similarity between people and beasts. In *Plains Song,* both Belle and Orion are compared to calves and Belle to a rabbit; Sharon Rose is cat-like; babies come in "litters"; and Cora notices that Emerson walks like a horse at ease in harness and that he purses his lips like a fat hen's bottom when he spits. Sharon's analogy, however, is contemptuous rather than picturesque. She says that the Plains people are "like beasts of the field," leading lives "more like that of livestock than aspiring human beings" (pp. 124, 85-86). Avery Dickel, the young man who marries Sharon's sister, Fayrene, plans to become a veterinarian because he likes animals, and Sharon sarcastically tells him that he should love farming because everybody on the farm is an animal. She notices that Avery's teeth grow forward like those of an animal meant to crop grass. To Sharon, Cora is the only person for whom the human and livestock comparison seems natural, not repugnant. "What she admired in Cora, yet disliked in Emerson and Avery Dickel, was that they were less persons than pieces of nature, closely related to cows and chickens" (p. 135). Sharon is especially troubled by the easy-going nature of her former companion Madge, who moves around "like a grazing cow" and "ooz[es] creature comfort" and whom Ned pats as he would the rump of a horse (pp. 130, 133).

The Wright Morris hero is frequently a fictional study of the question of whether one can go home again. *Plains Song* is a departure for Morris because a daughter of the middle border asks and answers the same question. Sharon Rose cannot go home again because she is changed in a manner and to a degree that makes home no longer habitable to her; she is no longer of the same domesticated breed.

Sharon is redeemed by an enlarged sense of consciousness that results from her final visit to Cora's home. During her brief stay, Sharon is confronted with a series of memories, but the most important is an epiphany of sorts in which she remembers a whack with the hairbrush that Cora administered when, as a young girl, Sharon denounced Madge's beau. Reflecting on that image, that no-win confrontation between stubborn mother and willful child, makes Sharon conscious that an audacious woman's character is not lost in death and that the living woman carries within herself the character of her mother. No matter how much we might admire Cora, the sturdy pioneer woman, for her endurance and strength, Morris believes that the unexamined life is missing something. Caroline Kibbee and her generation present yet another extreme. They have followed Sharon's example and "don't get married anymore unless [they] want to" (p. 196). Caroline's viewpoint on the subject of male/female relationships and feminism is also an unexamined view, but her conclusion is the opposite of Cora's. In Sharon, Morris presented a woman limited by the pride and inhibitions of the audacious pioneer women who preceded her, but one who finds and affirms the past that is the key to understanding both present and future.

SONG OF CONSCIOUSNESS

In *About Fiction,* Morris wrote that the new fiction of America may be fresh or it may be stale, but that the difference "will be a matter for our enlarged or diminished consciousness."[16] In *The Territory Ahead,* he compared writers like Whitman, Melville, Thoreau, and Twain who light out for the open road, the open sea, the deep woods, or the territory ahead, but he concluded that all directions are forms of nostalgia. An admirer of Henry James, Morris maintained that only James bridged the past and present in a way that makes sense and that the bridge is consciousness. While the other writers of his age were going West, James went East—taking to the wilderness of culture instead of the wilderness of romantic nostalgia—and only he faced the crisis of the modern imagination without resorting to nostalgia. James opted for living in the present; to live elsewhere is a deception.[17] Morris's interest in the enlarged consciousness of the artist applies also to the audacious female voice that we hear in the novel's final pages. Sharon Rose also takes to the East. Like James's retreat to Europe, her escape is a search for refinement and culture. Yet her epiphany does not occur in the East but on a trip to the place of her childhood. In revisiting the scenes from her past Sharon successfully marries the world of the West (the pioneering spirit of the stiff upper lip) and the world of the East (culture, refinement, and education).

Morris pointed out that culture itself may be a wilderness, and in Sharon's case it does not bring consciousness. In the final scenes of *Plains Song: for Female Voices,* Sharon is shocked by Caroline's outspoken rejection of the past in her rejection of Cora. Then Sharon joins Alexandra Selkirk at the Grand Island Crossways Inn where the feminist convention is underway. There Sharon merges with a bustling throng of women—some fleeing the internment camp of marriage and some seized with the mania to be many people. The consciousness-raising Women World Wide group gathered in Grand Island contrasts with the "primitive ceremony" of males that Sharon and Caroline had noticed just a few days earlier at the football stadium in Lincoln, the men as "blind as the dinosaur to what was happening" (p. 195). At the appropriately named Crossways Inn, Sharon is confronted with a troubling collage of images of womanhood and manhood: an androgynous punk rocker in the club's bar, his microphone a phallic symbol thrusting upward and outward from his crotch; an amorous couple grappling in the motel's laundry room and looking like a single two-headed monster; a woman suffering Valium withdrawal symptoms and her male companion asking Sharon, "Ma'am, what can we do to be saved?" (p. 223); and Selkirk, an exotic, stork-legged reincarnation of Cora Atkins, carping about the masculine gender of the creator who made everything in His image. From the confusion and noise of the convention center—complete with the Oneida Marching Band at practice—Sharon and Alexandra escape together to witness the dawn. As she watches her first sunrise since childhood, Sharon finally knows that the spirit of Cora has made its peace with things and that—for both good and ill—the legacy of her pioneer aunt-mother has made her what she is. With a renewed consciousness Sharon takes her place in the contemporary world because she has finally confronted her past without either contempt or nostalgia.

If Morris's fiction has changed as he claimed it has, the change is merely that he has finally decided female audacity is acceptable. The audacity of Cora is the vitality and perseverance of our grandmothers; Cora is an icon of the world that is gone, and her voice been stilled. The audacity of Sharon's song, the song of consciousness, is the voice of the daughter of the 1980s.

Notes

1. Wright Morris, *Plains Song: for Female Voices* (New York: Harper & Row, 1980), pp. 188-89. Further references will be included parenthetically in the text.

2. Wright Morris, "Letter to a Young Critic," *The Massachusetts Review* 6 (1964-65): 99. Examples of Morris's tyrannical matriarch include Mrs. Ormsby in *Man and Boy* and Mrs. Porter in *The Deep Sleep*.

3. Wright Morris, "Children Are the Best People," *A Bill of Rites, A Bill of Wrongs, A Bill of Goods* (Lincoln: University of Nebraska Press, 1967), p. 54.

4. Wayne C. Booth and Wright Morris, "The Writing of Organic Fiction," in Robert E. Knoll, ed., *Conversations with Wright Morris* (Lincoln: University of Nebraska Press, 1975), p. 97.

5. Robert Dahlin, "*PW* Interviews: Wright Morris," *Publishers Weekly* 217 (22 February 1980): 7.

6. Booth and Morris, "The Writing of Organic Fiction," p. 100.

7. Joseph J. Wydeven, "Wright Morris, Women and American Culture," in Helen Winter Stauffer and Susan J. Rosowski, eds., *Women and Western American Literature* (Troy, N.Y.: Whitston Publishing, 1982), p. 219.

8. Leslie A. Fiedler, *Love and Death in the American Novel* (New York: Stein and Day, 1966), p. 26.

9. Wright Morris, *The Territory Ahead* (Lincoln: University of Nebraska Press, 1978), pp. 88-90.

10. Wright Morris, *The Deep Sleep* (Lincoln: University of Nebraska Press, 1958), pp. 278-79.

11. Lynn Waldeland, "Plains Songs: Women's Voices in the Fiction of Wright Morris," *Critique: Studies in Modern Fiction* 24 (Fall 1982): 7.

12. Wright Morris, "Going Crazy in Miami," *A Bill of Rites, a Bill of Wrongs, a Bill of Goods*, p. 67. Morris's "grandmothers" include Miss Caddy and Aunt Angie in *The World in the Attic*, Grandmother and Aunt Elsie Herkimer in *The Man Who Was There*, and Aunt Clara in *The Home Place*.

13. Margaret Atwood, *Survival: A Thematic Guide to Canadian Literature* (Toronto: Anansi, 1972), pp. 199-210.

14. Margaret Laurence, *The Stone Angel* (New York: Alfred A. Knopf, 1964), p. 43. Future references will be included parenthetically in the text.

15. Robert Dahlin, "*PW* Interviews," 6.

16. Wright Morris, *About Fiction* (New York: Harper & Row, 1975), p. 134.

17. Morris, *The Territory Ahead*, p. 230.

Joseph J. Wydeven (essay date 1988)

SOURCE: "Focus and Frame in Wright Morris's *The Works of Love*," in *Western American Literature*, Vol. XXIII, No. 2, Summer, 1988, pp. 99-112.

[*In the following essay, Wydeven offers a "photographic reading" of, and shows the operation of "photographic strategies" in Morris's novel* The Works of Love.]

> *Through the dusty lace curtains at my hotel room window I spied on passersby I secretly envied, as Sherwood Anderson spied on his neighbors in Winesburg. They were dream-drugged, these people, and I envied the depth of their addiction.—Wright Morris*

The passage above, from *Photographs and Words* (28), might well serve as a critical epigraph to *The Works of Love,* a novel which has given readers and critics considerable difficulty. That Morris called this work "the linchpin in my novels concerned with the plains" is appropriate, not so much because *The Works of Love* encapsulated his themes, but because the novel developed the groundwork for his more ambitious project of probing the American psyche. Further, as will be argued here, the narrative method of *The Works of Love* was shaped by Morris through an imaginative fusion of his dual preoccupations as fiction writer and photographer: through his own practice of photography Morris introduced a motif of intersubjectivity and potential violation of consciousness which runs through much of his fiction.

Morris experimented with the relations between photographs and words over two decades—from the mid-1930s to the mid-50s. His first publication, **"The Inhabitants"** (1940), was a photo-text which juxtaposed photographs and brief prose sketches, and several of Morris's novels over the next fifteen years—especially *The Man Who Was There* (1945), the photo-text *The Home Place* (1948), and *The Deep Sleep* (1953)—included explicit references to photographic epistemology as well as carefully described "photographic" images.

That Morris had photography much on his mind throughout the writing of *The Works of Love* is obvious from the chronology of his creativity at that time. *The Works of Love* went through seven drafts between 1946 and 1951, when it was finally published in severely shortened form. The first draft was composed in 1946, the same year as the publication of his first photo-text book, *The Inhabitants* (enlarged and modified from the 1940 **"The Inhabitants"**). About the time of the second and third drafts, Morris paused (with the help of a Guggenheim) to write and take the photographs for **The Home Place** (Cohn 178-79, 230). Then, in the same year that **The Works of Love** was published, Morris contributed an essay to *The Magazine of Art* entitled **"Privacy as a Subject for Photography,"** a plea for photographic "revelation" as opposed to "exposure" (Morris's term for intrusive violation in photography).

Dedicated in part to Sherwood Anderson, **The Works of Love** continues Anderson's analysis of men and women subjected to peculiarly American failures of communication. But whereas Anderson often dealt with damages to the self caused by psychological trauma, Morris seems to develop his protagonist, Will Brady, as a person moved paradoxically by an *absence* of motivation: Brady seems to exist at times as little more than a receptor of sensual stimuli, unable to convert perception into conception in the interests of a better life and fuller consciousness. It is true that Morris suggests Brady's "redemption" through the inclusion of mystical insights which hover about this character's consciousness, but throughout the book Morris emphasizes the more mundane processes of Brady's perception. **The Works of Love** is obviously an ironic novel, and the chief irony is how little knowledge Brady achieves from so many detailed acts of perception. Unable to cope with the hostilities of environment, Brady retreats from the world, transcending it only within his imagination, where he seeks "mystical" escape from reality.

The Works of Love follows Will Brady from his birth in Indian Bow, Nebraska, to his death in Chicago: dressed in a Montgomery Ward Santa Claus suit, he plunges to his death in a sewage canal. The novel follows Brady's eastward course as he leaves the sandhills behind; we see him accept as his own a child, dropped off the eastbound freight and tagged simply *"My name is Willy Brady,"* and we observe the pathos of his first marriage, to Ethel Bassett, and later the bathos of his marriage to Gertrude Long. In the country he builds a huge city-house but "forgets" to put into it either a furnace or a stove. His chicken empire (5000 laying hens) collapses, his relationship to his "son" is strained, his wife runs off with a "Hawayan." Unable to "connect" with wives or child, Brady makes his way to Chicago, where he ages, amidst elaborate attempts at self-deception, living alone, once a year receiving a dutiful letter from Willy. In the end, taking on the role of Santa Claus, Brady dies—ambiguously, for readers cannot be certain if his death is accidental or deliberate.

This synopsis of **The Works of Love** must leave out a great deal, but it is not plot which is the novel's strong point; rather, its chief success is its style, the way in which Morris uses language to show the processes of thought, or what passes for thought carried through the senses. Just as Brady is "a man with so much of his life left out" (4), the authorial voice in **The Works of Love** is extraordinarily selective in the knowledge it chooses to provide for the reader. No wonder critics complain that Brady is both un-

comprehending and incomprehensible: Granville Hicks, for example, complains that Brady is a "mere nothingness, a great blank" (10). The novel proceeds by anecdote, vignette, epiphany—fragments of Brady's reality with few transitions to link them clearly to meaning.

Certainly it is the style of **The Works of Love** which has given readers the most difficulty. G. B. Crump appears to be a representative reader when, acknowledging the source of Brady in Morris's father, he writes:

> Perhaps because [Morris] was so emotionally bound to the Brady character, Morris's tone is sometimes out of control in the book; his sympathy for Brady threatens to become sentimental and his commentary, condescending. Moreover, Morris never quite solves the technical problem of sympathetically communicating to his readers the consciousness of a character whose major problem is his inability to communicate.
>
> (63)

Crump makes two important—although as I want to argue, debatable—points: first, Morris is unable to control authorial tone; second, **The Works of Love** fails in its portrayal of Brady's limited consciousness.

Regarding the form of **The Works of Love,** Wayne Booth observes that the novel's narrative technique is "simply one version of the *erlebte Rede* or *style indirect libre,* or free indirect style that . . . enables modern authors to convey a counterpoint of two or more voices at once" (56). This explanation supports one effect of the style, but it does not sufficiently explain Morris's method. Another reader, Roy Bird, concludes that "The voices of author and narrator are so carefully mixed that the reader must enter into the authorial enterprise." Bird believes that Morris is himself "[u]nable to unravel the enigma of Will Brady's personality," and thus "forces the reader to draw his own conclusions—or admit his own uncertainty—about the meaning of the life of this strange plainsman" (77).

What all these interpretive difficulties suggest is that the fragmented story of Will Brady is extraordinarily similar in concept to the kinds of evidence presented in family photograph albums—with their frustrating gaps in the chronology of weeks, months, or years; tantalizingly unexplained costumes, gestures, and facial expressions; and maddening silences about all those strange pictured incidents. In effect, what Morris seems to employ subtly in **The Works of Love** is a device he used explicitly in **The Man Who Was There**: in that novel Morris includes a photograph album (described in close and detailed prose) from which his characters deduce information as they make sense of the life of Agee Ward, the "missing" protagonist (63-83). In **The Works of Love** Morris removes the explanatory context but nonetheless seems to place Brady within the covers of a family album—from which both narrator and audience extrapolate possible meanings. If the photo album model provides the novel's form—with the pictures based on what Alan Spiegel might call "a photograph of a duration" (72n) or Max Kozloff "a still photograph of narrative import" (143)—the extrapolations are themselves the major effects of style.

Coming to terms with the stylistic ambiguities of *The Works of Love* might be facilitated by an inquiry into Morris's need to come to terms with his father, who had died a few years before. Morris says about the inception of *The Works of Love*: "I was pondering [his father's] life, and how little I knew him. This led me to think about origins. In point of fact I knew very little." In the interests of putting his past in order, he was intent on creating, as he says, "a mythic past of my own, gratifying to my own needs and imaginings" (**"Writing of Organic Fiction"** 76). This myth is continued in one of Morris's three published volumes of memoir/autobiography, *Will's Boy* (1981), which covers much of the same ground (as "memoir") as does *The Works of Love*: both focus on relations between father and son, often in similar language. Roy Bird echoes other critics when he notes that all of Morris's work is "a reprocessing of the same material" (92). That material is the outline of Morris's own early life, and the reprocessing involves an obsession to reclaim his past and end his search for a father.

The evolution of *The Works of Love* shows clearly that Morris had great difficulty in getting the book right. As shown above, Morris clarified his intentions and adjusted his focus through experimentation and extensive revision. This extraordinary care suggests that the novel had a crucial problem which evaded easy solution. As the book involved his father's life, Morris had to *imagine* that life as accurately as possible, but as he writes of Brady, "What is there left to say of a man with so much of his life left out?" At the core of the book, then, he found a paradox and a dilemma: how to make public through art—and so to honor—the essential human bond between father and son *against* the available evidence that in the reality of his own case there was hardly a bond at all. *The Works of Love* is thus indeed a work of love, unified by Wright Morris's sympathetic desire for his father's mutual regard. One can understand Morris's problems with getting the novel right. More important, one can comprehend the sometimes torturous quality of Morris's awareness of the perils of intersubjective exchange, a frequent concern of both his fiction and his essays on photography.

Artistic requirements for *The Works of Love* led Morris to a style founded on what might be called a *strategy of ambivalence*: from this perspective the style itself is an instrument which not only justifies ambivalence, but in fact exploits it to make the novel artistically coherent. How to deal with a neglectful father and nevertheless to accept him with the care and compassion implied through artistic encoding? How to reconcile the absent father of reality with the artistic coherence required of novelistic form?

One way is to design a novel called *The Man Who Was There* (1945)—about a man who is "there" only through his influence. Another solution, that of *The Works of Love*,

is to confront the issue of the father directly but to create a narrative instrument which allows the author to temper the cruelty of social judgments with the mercies of irony; to rationalize failures of will by calling on psychic, social, and geographical determinisms; and to balance his father's failures of daily social intercourse with veiled suggestions of timeless mystical fulfillment. Morris developed a means paradoxically to approach his subject closely and yet to maintain a reverent distance. The method allows Morris both to mock his character's entrapment in time and to suggest the paradox that Brady's very helplessness is the essential condition for his transcendence. When his earthly models—such as T. P. Luckett—fail him, Brady turns to the likes of Teapot, a man who understands that he "was meant to be poured": "Now, there were people who would class Teapot as odd, or even downright wacky, but Will Brady had acquired a different feeling about such men. Put it this way: he felt right at home with them" (199).

Morris derived this method in large part from his intimate involvement with photography: the camera provides his model for comprehending and structuring an appropriate narrative strategy. Although the camera is a crucial instrument for showing us the world, it is silent in explaining what events *mean*. It is precisely the camera's inability to *explain*, however, that Morris turns to advantage: what he presents in *The Works of Love* is a series of pictures of Brady "posed" in his world; the "explanations" of meaning are the responsibility of the carefully crafted narrative voice. It is photography, too, which allows Morris to be both behind the camera as observer and recorder and at the same time sympathetically involved in the proceedings. Readers may be reminded of the photo showing Morris's shadow leaning in towards a Model T Ford, of which John Szarkowski notes "a quality of ceremony and ritual . . . heightened by the inclusion of the photographer's shadow" (*Looking* 148); Peter Bunnell refers to the shadow as Morris's "self-portrait presence" (**"Photography and Reality"** 149). The camera yields Morris what hotel lobbies offer his character Brady, the opportunity to "be both in, that is, and out of this world" (172).

In *The Works of Love* perception is primary, and the role of perception is most carefully worked out through Morris's use of point of view. Morris developed a narrative method which might tentatively be called "participatory third person," in which Morris deliberately involves the narrator as one who *points out* what others are urged to observe—much as one might point to and make observations about the images of people held captive to time in photograph albums. This method allows the narrator continuously to question Brady's consciousness, occasionally to mock its severe limitations, and frequently to defend its pathos. The narrative shifts rapidly back and forth between these various modes of presentation, sometimes sympathetically, more often critically. In this way there is a kind of collusion between narrator and reader, through which the reader is constantly involved in *looking upon* this character Brady and being encouraged to hold certain attitudes regarding him. Morris's irony ensures that the audience will not always agree with the narrator, and thus the audience adds a creative counterpoint which is essential to the narrative strategy. Occasionally, when the narrator seems to "load the case" against the protagonist, the reader is encouraged to Brady's defense.

In these album pages, Morris consistently shows us Brady's responsiveness to his environment: he details what Brady sees, hears, smells, tastes, feels—little of what he *knows,* for he appears to know very little. The reader also finds described photographs as part of Morris's text—for example, the photo that Brady's father has made to send to marriageable women in the East, and the worn snapshots of his son that Brady later shows to his acquaintances in Chicago. But nowhere in that novel is there any attempt to use the *practice* of photography as *direct* referential support for Morris's metaphysics or method. Morris had, however, employed such imagery in early drafts of the novel, as in the following example:

> So many postcards, so many women, and so many scenic views. In some of these shots he stood there with a woman, in some of them with the boy. . . . This snapshot of some father and his son. The father with a softly blurred face, as if he had moved just as the picture was snapped, and a small, overdressed boy with a book under his arm. . . . Could that be Will Clayton Brady and his son? No wonder people kept albums to see who it was that had died.
>
> (Qtd in Cohn 244-45)

Notably, however, such extrapolations disappear entirely from the final version of *The Works of Love*; in fact, none of the photographs described in the published novel are of Will Brady. It appears, then, that Wright Morris deliberately excised specific references to photographic method, possibly because such extrapolations are too self-conscious and conceptual to be carried by the narrative voice.

Nevertheless, in order to support his deliberately fragmented method, Morris introduced photographic strategies into the final version of *The Works of Love.* Two of these are of particular significance: Morris's focus on photographic detail and his emphasis on windows and mirrors as framing devices. (These strategies as Morris used them in his photography are copiously illustrated in all of his photo-texts and other photo books; *The Home Place* is perhaps the most accessible text.)

John Szarkowski has written that closely observed detail is one of the essential elements in photography: the photographer, he says, can only document truth as it is found

> in nature in a fragmented and unexplained form—not as a story, but as scattered and suggestive clues. The photographer [can] not assemble these clues into a coherent narrative, he [can] only isolate the fragment, document it, and by so doing claim for it some special significance, a meaning which [goes] beyond simple description.
>
> (8)

In *The Works of Love* Morris uses frequent prose descriptions: objects in Brady's world are closely, "photographically" observed. One example will suffice, although there are many in the text. In this description we are given details of Brady's final room in Chicago:

> To get from the stove to the sink it was better to drop the leaf on the table and then lean forward over the back of the rocking-chair. On the shelf over the sink were four plates, three cups and one saucer, a glass sugarbowl, two metal forks, and one bone-handled spoon. On the mantelpiece was a shaving mug with the word SWEETHEART in silver, blue, chipped red, and gold. In the mug were three buttons, a roller-skate key, a needle with a burned point for opening pimples, an Omaha street-car token, and a medal for buying Buster Brown shoes. At the back of the room were the folding doors that would not quite close.
>
> (216-17)

The room is obviously closely observed, and yet, as Szarkowski says about photography, the details serve another purpose "beyond mere description": in observing the room, Morris suggests its cramped size and the pathetic nature of the kept objects. Morris also exercises his prerogative as a writer by providing more information than a camera lens would provide. We would not be likely to see in an actual photograph (from the perspective Morris provides) the contents of the cup, and we would have to infer necessary body movements "from the stove to the sink."

Photographic detail, however, is hardly unique to Morris (although he refined the practice in his photo-texts). Alan Spiegel—among others—notes "adventitious detail" as one of the commonplaces of fictional technique since Flaubert (90-108). More important to *The Works of Love* is Morris's use of a number of framing techniques.

A lengthy quotation from the "In the Wasteland" section may help make this point; here Brady is about to make his way to Chicago, deciding to ride the train to the end of the line rather than to get off at his proper destination, Omaha. Morris quite deliberately shows how Brady "wiped a small hole in the frosted glass" in order to see out the window. We are given the scene through Brady's eyes:

> He could see the winter dawn, a clear ice color, and far out on the desolate plain, like the roof of the world, were two or three swinging lights. He could make out the dry bed of the river, and as the train was stopping for water, he could hear, down the tracks, the beat of the crossing-bell. . . . As the train slowly braked to a stop, he could see the frame of the cattle loader, and then, suddenly, the station along the tracks.
>
> (212)

Peering through the hole he has made, Brady sees the telegraph operator in the station, and Morris gives us a detailed description of the man; then, however, Morris takes us into Brady's perceptual imagination: like Brady, the telegraph operator perceives in turn, and Brady sees him staring, absently, into the windows of the passing cars. . . . Will Brady saw all of this as if it were a picture on a calendar. Nothing moved, every detail was clear. He could smell the odor of stale tobacco, and the man's coat, wet with snow, gave off the stench of a wet gunny sack. . . . [A]nd as Will Brady gazed at his face he raised his head, suddenly, as if a voice had spoken to him. He gazed into the darkness where Will Brady lay on the berth. And Will Brady fell back, he held his breath, and as his hands gripped the side of the berth, he heard again the mechanical throbbing of the crossing-bell. He seemed to see, out there on the horizon, the snout-like mound of the buried soddy [the place of his birth and childhood], where he had been, even then, the last man in the world.

(212-13)

This descriptive narration warrants close examination.

First, the passage is typical in its emphasis on perception itself. Morris focuses on three senses—hearing, smell, and most important, vision—and he does so by emphasizing a passive use of the senses: "he could see," "he could make out," "he could hear," "he could smell," and so on. Such phrasing, appearing on page after page of the novel, gives the impression that Brady is a waiting receptacle for stimuli. That is, Brady is like a camera without a motivating human agent as operator: without human volition, the camera can only record the scene "objectively." Brady responds to what he perceives, but only rarely does he conceptualize patterns which might allow him to control his environment.

The second point to be made about the quotation is that Morris is extremely deliberate in the use of framing devices. First we see Brady wiping a hole allowing him to see through the frosted glass of the window. It would be sufficient for Morris simply to show Brady looking through the window, but he obviously wants to emphasize this device. To have Brady clear a peep-hole in the glass is to assert that the hole is like a lens, which is an aid to vision and is clearly limited by its frame. The hole allows Brady to focus and to look through yet another framing device—for the telegraph operator is himself framed by the station window. Thus Brady believes that the telegraph operator, with his own "lens" of consciousness, is gazing at him.

The carefully structured frames which Morris places around these two men emphasize the intersubjectivity of Morris's approach to his craft and to his characters. Through these frames, Morris shows Brady not merely embarrassed, but actually in dread of *being seen and studied*; believing himself under examination through a frame/lens, he experiences a self-conscious distortion of self, and thus he is reduced, dehumanized—to use Morris's word for photographic violation, "exposed." Although Morris eschewed the photographic portrait in practice, insisting that "people, as I knew them, were the subject of my fiction" (Preface, *Inhabitants*), he exploits the problematics of the photographic pose in his fiction. Indeed, discussions of "the pose" in photography often stress the exchange be-

tween subject and object as a struggle for equilibrium: Harold Rosenberg, for example, writes of "a silent wrestle of imaginations" between sitter and photo portraitist (n. pag.).

In the exchange of looks imagined between Brady and the telegraph operator, Brady clearly fears being reduced to a studied object; he appears to be involved precisely in "a silent wrestle of imaginations." When he perceives that he is being perceived, Brady panics, as if in fear of psychic violation. He falls backwards, holds his breath, and grips the berth tightly—all actions resulting from his perception that the telegraph operator's eyes have penetrated him. This psychic penetration informs Brady that *he is visible to others*—that is, that others can "see *through* him." Indeed, his reaction to being seen would be better explained if Brady were a fugitive from justice whose anonymity has been uncovered, his face recognized. But Morris uses this double framing device to clarify Brady's guilt simply as a human being, not as a fugitive. What Brady feels when he remembers the place of his childhood is that in the intervening years he has made little human progress. This is an appropriate response for a man who has abandoned (or who has been abandoned by? We are not sure) his second wife and is now in flight to "the end of the line," Chicago.

Other such devices are frequent in the novel. One explicit example of a frame is the window in the tower room of the freight yards where Brady works in Chicago:

On one side of the room was a large bay window that faced the east. A man standing at this window—like the man on the canal who let the drawbridge up and down—felt himself in charge of the flow of traffic, of the city itself. All that he saw seemed to be in his province, under his control.

Even more emphatically, when Brady sees life outside the window, Morris says, "The bay window in the tower room was a frame around this picture" (237-38), an obvious reference to photographic vision as well as a suggestion that the life outside, framed by borders, is of particular significance, as is any (necessarily framed) photograph which a person *chooses* to take and display. The window in these examples becomes a lens; the frame around the resulting picture both emphasizes the picture's importance as a subjective perception of reality and portrays that subject as vulnerable to psychic reduction by viewer-readers.

One more observation might be made about the concept of frame. When Brady wipes the frosted glass to see through the train window, we must imagine Brady "peering through" the hole he has created. This action of "peering" recurs frequently throughout the novel, usually to show characters looking *through* something at something else. For example, in hotel lobbies, Brady "would peer through the palm trees at the clock" (200); Manny Plinski is often found "peering in" Brady's room through the frame of the doors "that would not quite close" (223); Brady finds his son more interested in "peering out through" a catcher's mask than in the game of baseball itself (141). When Brady has his last view of Mickey Ahearn (the girl who refuses his offer of marriage but who gives him a "son"), she is standing on a caboose platform:

> Mickey Ahearn looked straight down the tracks toward the sawmill until the caboose passed the hotel, when she turned her head sharply as if she had thought of him. But the sun was on the window, *and besides he was behind a potted plant.*

(32; italics added)

The idea of "peering through" something seems to me to be directly related to Morris's frequent repetition in his fiction that there is "no place to hide" on the plains, for to peer out through something implies a desire to be hidden from the eyes of others; with "no place to hide" on the plains, the best substitute is to find a means to reduce one's vulnerability by reducing visibility. The psychological ramifications of having "no place to hide" are hereby worked metaphorically into *The Works of Love.* (Morris's photography itself provides many examples of such a pattern, as even a hurried glance at *The Home Place* reveals: many photographs in that novel have the camera lens directed at objects, and the picture taken, through a physical frame or through windows covered by curtains, so that the process of framing is thoroughly linked to the role of perception as well as to the thing seen. See pages 63, 147, and 161 for obvious examples.)

Another intersubjective device borrowed from photography which Morris uses frequently in *The Works of Love* is the mirror as reflector and lens. One example occurs when Brady first begins to take notice of his future wife, Ethel Bassett, who works in the Hotel Cafe. They exchange looks frequently through the reflecting glass doors of the cafe pie case, and the looks become gradually more pointed—in the following instance through the device of a mirror:

> On the wall behind her was a mirror, so that Will Brady saw her both front and back, in the round so to speak, while she looked him straight in the face. Which was odd, as she never seemed to see anything.

(24)

Later in the "relationship," Brady catches Ethel, "her eyes wide," observing him in the reflecting glass of the pie case:

> He saw that this blank expression, this look she gave him, was meant to be an open one. He was meant to look in, and he tried, but he didn't see anything.

(46)

The reflectors are intended to be indicators of consciousness, used ironically to heighten both intersubjective failure and Brady's personal inability to comprehend—or to resist—Ethel's Motives. As their eyes meet only indirectly, their subjective isolation is intensified.

Perhaps Morris's most complex example of the mirror as an ironic guide to reality occurs in the store where Brady buys his clothes:

> In Fred Conley's private fitting-room [Brady] would see himself in the three-way mirror, and it was there that he saw the new expression on his face. While he was talking—at no other time. While he talked this man in the mirror had a strange smile on his lips. This smile on his lips and a sly, knowing look about the eyes. Something shrewd he had said?

(148)

It is the three-way mirror, showing Brady in dimensions not otherwise available to him, which gives him an "objective" identity that he can use, an exaggerated sense of himself which renders him heroic to his own eyes. This point is emphasized later in the novel, when Brady seeks self-assurance in hotel lobbies. Brady muses that in the hotel lobby a man is transformed into something more important than his usual self:

> He took on the air of a man who was being fitted for a new suit. A little bigger, wider, taller, and better-looking than he really was. And on his face the look of a man who sees himself in a three-way glass. In the three-way mirror he sees the smile on his face, he sees himself, you might say, both coming and going—a man, that is, who was from someplace and was going somewhere. Not the man you saw, just a moment before, out there in the street.

(171-72)

The mirror here is used as agent of (false) self-discovery, and is comparable to discoveries about self people make when they study photographs of themselves. The conclusions drawn from studying such images are generally biased by what we want to see. Brady is exceptional only in the vastness of his need for a sense of personal value. He allows the visual evidence to tell him what he needs to hear. Thus he drifts, a man attuned to experience but not to reflective assessment; a man unable to put the past to use in shaping a future, and consequently forced to the imagination to serve his needs.

This analysis might be extended to include other examples of Morris's method—for example, his use of light (that necessary photographic medium): his frequent references to venetian blinds deliberately drawn to keep light out; and the final irony of Brady's near-blindness from overexposure to the NU-VITA sunlamp. Such evidence for a "photographic reading" is found in abundance in *The Works of Love,* and it suggests that viewing the novel from the perspective of Morris's photography yields proof of considerable technical mastery—of fiction drawn subtly from "photographic" observation.

What Carol Schloss says of the works done by writers associated with photography seems particularly applicable to Wright Morris:

> For [these works] show the conduct of art as a process of life, the making of literature and photography as a constant transposition of values enacted in the world. To think about frames in this context is not to think

about museum walls but to remember a negotiation or approach to the subject, which joins history, personal history, and aesthetics.

(21)

In *The Works of Love,* more than with any of his other novels, Morris struggled to find an appropriate "negotiation or approach to the subject"—and in finding it, Morris used art to clarify his own relationship to a world once inhabited by his father. In a sense, then, *The Works of Love* may be viewed as a rite of passage opening into Morris's artistic maturity—indeed, making that maturity possible.

Criticism of *The Works of Love* has sometimes been divided between those who insist that Brady is excessively passive and thus unworthy of empathy, and those who argue that Brady triumphantly transcends his environment through some kind of mystical fulfillment. I suggest, however, that both of those arguments are misleading, presenting us only with unnecessary either-or choices: I have tried to suggest that Morris gives us both options—and more. As a condition of his novel's complex fulfillment, Morris insists on *empathizing with both* passivity and transcendence in his protagonist. In developing a method founded in the "aesthetics" of the photograph album, Morris found a way to fragment Brady's existence artistically, and thus to view his protagonist in many of the contradictory poses which make up his reality. These poses are probed through an investigative method involving an ironic narrator and a participating audience. I have suggested that Morris developed this method in order to come to grips with conflicting emotions towards his father, that through photography he discovered a strategy which harmonized his emotional and aesthetic needs, and that in this way he preserved both his own and his father's right to privacy.

Works Cited

Bird, Roy K. *Wright Morris: Memory and Imagination.* New York: Peter Lang, 1985.

Booth, Wayne C. "Form in *The Works of Love.*" *Conversations with Wright Morris: Critical Views and Responses.* Ed. Robert E. Knoll. Lincoln: U of Nebraska P, 1977. 35-73.

Cohn, Jack Rice. *Wright Morris: The Design of the Midwestern Fiction.* Diss. U of California, Berkeley, 1970. Ann Arbor: UMI, 1971. 71-20,788.

Crump, G. B. *The Novels of Wright Morris: A Critical Interpretation.* Lincoln: U of Nebraska P, 1978.

Hicks, Granville. *Literary Horizons: A Quarter Century of American Fiction.* New York: New York UP, 1970.

Kozloff, Max. *The Privileged Eye: Essays on Photography.* Albuquerque: U of New Mexico P, 1987.

Morris, Wright, *The Deep Sleep.* 1953. Lincoln: U of Nebraska P, 1975.

——. *The Home Place.* 1948. Lincoln: U of Nebraska P, 1970.

——. "The Inhabitants." *New Directions in Prose and Poetry 1940.* Ed. James McLaughlin. Norfolk, Connecticut: New Directions, 1940. 145-80.

——. *The Inhabitants: Text and Photographs,* 2nd Ed. New York: DaCapo P, 1972.

——. *The Man Who Was There.* 1945. Lincoln: U of Nebraska P, 1977.

——. *Photographs & Words.* Carmel, California: The Friends of Photography, 1982.

——. "Privacy as a Subject for Photography." *Magazine of Art* 44.2 (1951): 51-55.

——. *Will's Boy: A Memoir.* New York: Harper & Row, 1981.

——. *The Works of Love.* 1951. Lincoln: U of Nebraska P, 1972.

Morris, Wright, and Wayne C. Booth. "The Writing of Organic Fiction." *Conversations with Wright Morris: Critical Reviews and Responses.* Ed. Robert E. Knoll. Lincoln: U of Nebraska P, 1977. 74-100.

Morris, Wright, and Peter Bunnell. "Photography and Reality." *Conversations with Wright Morris: Critical Views and Responses.* Ed. Robert E. Knoll. Lincoln: U of Nebraska P, 1977. 140-152.

Rosenberg, Harold. "Portraits: A Meditation on Likeness." *Portraits,* by Richard Avedon. New York: Farrar, Straus and Giroux, 1976. N. pag.

Schloss, Carol. *In Visible Light: Photography and the American Writer: 1840-1940.* New York: Oxford UP, 1987.

Spiegel, Alan. *Fiction and the Camera Eye: Visual Consciousness in Film and the Modern Novel.* Charlottesville: UP of Virginia, 1976.

Szarkowski, John. *Looking at Photographs: 100 Pictures from the Collection of the Museum of Modern Art.* New York: Museum of Modern Art, 1973.

——. *The Photographer's Eye.* New York: Museum of Modern Art, 1966.

A. Carl Bredahl (essay date 1989)

SOURCE: "Wright Morris: Living in the World," in *New Ground: Western American Narrative and the Literary Canon,* The University of North Carolina Press, 1989, pp. 126-34.

[*In the following essay, Bredahl examines how Morris "establishes contact with the energy of living processes" in his novels.*]

Poststructuralist criticism responds to the modernist sense of alienation by rejecting the assumption of essential individuality. Replacing the belief in essences has been the assertion of codes and texts with and within which man operates. From that perspective, the effort of Ernest Hemingway or Harvey Fergusson to place the individual within a world of creative force is both invalid and naive.

However, . . . not all American imaginations operate on the basis of eastern assumptions. In the West and the Midwest, where land and life in a physical world are central, individuals seek to align the patterns of their lives to complement the patterns within the environment. To Wright Morris (1910-), one of the most productive contemporary writers, realignment is what the narrative imagination always seeks to do: "Each time the writer creates and solves the problems of fiction, he makes it possible for men and women to live in the world."[1] Breaking through artificial, enclosing constructs and establishing contact with the energy of living processes is the story of western and midwestern writers. This effort initially has to struggle with frustration, which can become despair, or with nostalgic longing, which can produce stasis.[2]

"If we should ask ourselves," says the Nebraska-born Morris in *The Territory Ahead* (1978), "what it is that the common and the uncommon American have in common, the man in the street and the sophisticate, the hillbilly and the Ivy Leaguer, I think we have an answer. Nostalgia. . . . Stock taking, inventory, is the first effort of the mind to make itself at home."[3] When Clyde Muncy, the protagonist and narrator of Morris's *The Home Place* (1948), moves his family from their apartment in New York City to his boyhood home outside Lone Tree, Nebraska, both nostalgia and desire for freedom motivate him. "'There is no grass in New York,' says Clyde, 'no yards, no trees, no lawn swings—and for thousands of kids not very much sky. They live in cages. . . . It's like a big zoo of kids. A cage with windows and bars.'" During the course of his story, Clyde discovers the obvious, that you can't go home again; but his act of return initiates the process of "stock taking" that enables him to abandon nostalgia.

Clyde Muncy's problems are reflected in the divided narrative that is *The Home Place,* in this case a divided narrative with unusual divisions. On one side of a page is Clyde's first-person verbal narrative; on the facing page is a series of photographs with their own story. At numerous points, the two texts interrelate, but the division between the verbal and visual worlds mirrors a division in Clyde between his head and his eyes. That division stymies Clyde's impulse to move. He is stuck in nostalgia somewhere between New York and Lone Tree, the urban and the rural, the verbal and the visual. "Each time the writer creates and solves the problems of fiction, he makes it possible for men and women to live in the world." *The Home Place* presents us with an obvious fictional problem in the separation of image and word; the effort to solve that "problem" so that men and women can "live in the world" is both the story of Clyde Muncy and that of the Wright Morris canon.

The photographs in *The Home Place* are black-and-white stills, which have the effect of freezing a fluid world of color into isolated artifacts.[4] The pictures lack human life (we see the human face, for example, only through photographs of photographs), are high-definition closeups, and stress man-made vertical or horizontal lines. A drab angularity in the pictures emphasizes the fact that natural and human life are missing. Because of the interest in closeups, we also lack context. We are presented with pieces and made to speculate about the environment in which those pieces exist(ed).

The use of vertical and horizontal lines imposed on natural backgrounds—a fence post driven into barren ground, for example—calls attention to the human forces that broke the Nebraska ground and built the farms and town. These forces countered those in the natural world which would have driven away most people. The lives are therefore testaments to strength; but the unbending quality of the verticals and horizontals testifies both to a stubbornness and to a pride that led to the great dust bowls and a world now lacking color and life.

Given the effect of the pictures, one begins to see a division between what Clyde Muncy wants to find in his return to the home place—a world where his kids can learn to live—and the actual place to which he is returning. There is remarkably little sky in the photographs, for example, and it was sky that Clyde particularly missed in the cages of New York City. We begin with a story that was motivated by nostalgia but that quickly discovers the discrepancy between that impulse and the reality of "home."

But there is more to this story. As the viewer lives with the photographs, something else begins to happen. Even though no human and remarkably little natural life exists in the pictures, they do not image a dead world. There is "life" here, the felt lives of the people who built the fences, slept in the bed, wrote the poems, or sat in the barber's chair. Though not a life one can return to or recapture, it is real all the same. The discovery of that life coincides with Clyde's discovery of life where he least expected it. When he and his wife, Peggy, visit a neighboring house, he wonders, "What is it that strikes you about a vacant house? I suppose it has something to do with the fact that any house that's been lived in, any room that's been slept in, is not vacant any more. From that point on it's forever occupied. With the people in the house you tend to forget that. . . . But with the people gone, you know the place is inhabited." The empty spot on a wall where a calendar used to hang or the old caning in a new chair establishes what Clyde comes to see as "connections" between his world and the life no longer visibly present. When Clyde makes that connection, he is ready to leave the home place, for he has taken stock of his own life.

We do not know where Clyde Muncy goes after he leaves Lone Tree, but we can watch Wright Morris work to solve "the problems of fiction" in the books that follow *The Home Place.* Indeed, Morris's effort is to integrate the verbal and the visual, to put life into motion, and to draw on energy inherent in the natural world.

In Orbit (1967) is a particularly appropriate text to compare with *The Home Place* because *In Orbit* also centers on a picture. This picture, however, is significantly different from the pictures in the earlier book: "That's the picture. You might want to add a few details of your own," says the narrator after the initial description of his protagonist, Jubal E. Gainer. Later, in the last pages of the text, the narrator comments, "That's the picture: there are those who can take it in at a glance. . . . But perhaps the important detail escapes you. He is in motion." The picture referred to, the totality of events described, results from a narrative fusion of verbal and visual, and the dynamic quality of the picture is evidenced in its use of line. The photographs in *The Home Place* emphasize horizontals and verticals, but the opening of *In Orbit* develops a different kind of line: "This boy comes riding with his arms high and wide, his head dipped low, his ass light in the saddle, as if about to be shot into orbit from a forked sling. . . . He is like a diver just before he hits the water, he is like a Moslem prayer-borne toward Mecca, he is like a cowpoke hanging to the steer's horns." The verticals and horizontals of *The Home Place* imply the possibility of a vector, but the resultant is missing. With no directed force, we simply have two lines and consequent freezing of motion. *In Orbit,* however, presents a story of force and motion; the picture taken in at a glance is that of the vector itself, the integration of vertical and horizontal forces. Because the subject moves, the details and forces continually change, and the narrative eye capable of perceiving and articulating this dynamic picture must be able to integrate, whereas the earlier vision was limited to fragmented freezing.

The contentment with nostalgia, which generated the fragmentation of *The Home Place,* is ultimately life denying. No human faces are seen in the photographs, and there is only indirect evidence in either the verbal or the visual text of the energy originally embodied in the pioneers. We see the products, not the process, of the settlement that established new life on the prairies. In contrast, energy is the subject of *In Orbit.* In spite of its dispassionate surface, *In Orbit* is a highly sexual book. A divided imagination denies the possibility of new life, but an imagination that seeks to take in a fluid, thrusting world appropriately sees a story that is destructive of the static condition of verticals and horizontals (here portrayed in the cutting of the old oak tree) and at the same time explosively creative. When the joyfully named Jubal E. Gainer enters Pickett, "the words of his song string out behind him like the tail of a kite" or like the tail of a comet or the tail of a twister or perhaps even the tail of a sperm cell. "As for the overall impression of the boy on the bike, it is that of two cats, piggyback: hard at it." Twister or sperm cell, the thrusting force embodied in Jubal Gainer is creative because it explodes internal energies and brings new energy to the individuals in Pickett, Indiana. Nature abhors a vacuum, we are told, and the natural forces of Jubal and twister rush into the vacuum at the center of the town and its inhabitants, as imaged in the frequently mentioned phonograph record. When that center lies within an individual, the energy stimulates life as a sperm cell drives toward an ovum.

Little distinguishes Jubal from other teenagers; the narrator in fact makes every effort to stress Jubal's ordinary characteristics. No knight-errant conscious of his direction and in control of his intentions, Jubal has the sniffles.[5] But Jubal's special quality is not his physical appearance or his intellectual prowess; it is rather the fact that he operates out of the center of himself. Characters in the book accuse him of intention, but Jubal functions naturally, responding directly to stimuli of the moment. Like human sexual relations, his relations with others are center to center, in contrast to the relationships established by the inhabitants of Pickett, where impersonal, distancing newspapers and telephones unite the citizens. Jubal almost instantaneously establishes physical, interpersonal contact with his "victims." He seldom speaks, so the contact is not verbal, nor does he impose himself on others. Jubal is welcomed by his victims, who similarly respond from within themselves.

These implicitly sexual center-to-center relationships occur in a fertile environment awaiting penetration. Two of the most pervasive images, bees and spray, establish an atmosphere of fertility. The events of *In Orbit* occur on May 17, a spring day in Indiana. Warm, overpowering smells of springtime fill the air. Bees swarm in the cloying, pollen-laden atmosphere, their masculine activity mirrored by frequent scenes of spraying: Pauline Bergdahl hoses down cinders, a plane sprays for insects, and two Pickett firemen hose the sidewalk. Unlike the bees, however, each of these human actions consciously seeks to hold back natural forces, which might imperil the smooth functioning of an ordered society. The spraying also connotes ejaculation. "Because he is non-fixed, this one also sprays the fireplace and the white sidewalls of Alan's Porsche." That description of one of Charlotte Hatfield's cats makes clear the connection between sexuality, fixing, and spraying. The book's dispassionate surface reflects the suppressed sexuality of Pickett, but underneath are individuals and a natural world ripe for fertilization. Jubal's victims are beings of potential, and his energies either deflate or stimulate what is within. Energy is transferred, as in an electron's jump from one orbit to another, so that when Jubal leaves Pickett "there is no longer much flex in his knees, much spring in his legs. The words of a song do not trail out behind him like the tail of a kite." His potency has been spent and needs time to regenerate.

Given the book's interest in both motion and sexuality—to be alive is to move—the frequent uses of the word *fix* are entirely correct. To fix is both to pin down and to remove sexual potency. Holly Stroymeyer "is a gentle, childlike woman, and like a child she loves to wander. . . . It's the wandering that had led to problems." And Charlotte Hatfield does not have "much sense of place. . . . Charlotte has been trained to live in a house, to use her box, and to purr when petted. But like the cat in her lap, she is a creature who has not been fixed." In contrast to the sexually stimulating and fertile women, the men in Pickett are unwilling or unable to become sexually aggressive: Haffner is "more AC than DC"; Alan Hatfield can "place the needle in the groove" but doesn't seem to excite Charlotte; and Sanford Avery is limited to rubbing his crotch at the *idea* of sex.

The central male figure, other than Jubal, is Curt Hodler, a newspaper editor with possibilities, but an individual who works best in a fixed world: "But the forecast is less important than the date, May 17th. The date, strange to say, is more important in the long run than anything in the paper. Day in and day out the news is pretty much the same. . . . It is the date that gives it meaning. . . . If the paper loses its dateline it loses its mind. The purpose of the forecast is to pin down the day, whether it rains or not." Like Stephen Crane's correspondent or Sherwood Anderson's George Willard, Hodler and his occupation indicate his possibilities and his limitations. A man of words in a book whose narrator is keenly sensitive to language, Hodler prefers to fix meaning to words and to stories. He suppresses his potential just as he suppresses his sexual desire for Miss Holly. His envy of Jubal is the envy of action:

"And how is Miss Holly?"

For more than twenty years Avery's cynical answer had been the same. *Who the hell would know that?* Now thanks to some snooping idler, or passing stranger, that was no longer an idle question. Someone finally knew. It is a torment to Hodler that this essential knowledge is what he once desired for himself. How *was* Miss Holly. Some idle lecher, some wandering pervert, some bored delinquent, some loyal friend or guardian, envied but unknown to Hodler, and still at large, finally knew.

Pickett's dealer in army/navy surplus, Kashperl, also prefers to fix events, although he, too, is fascinated with action. "Is it more than a tree that falls? It falls to give this day its meaning. To give Kashperl a cud for his idle, vagrant thoughts." For Kashperl, meaning is something tangible to cling to in a day when experience appears chaotic. "A preference for the fading title, or the missing author, or better yet the rare volume that proved to lack both, a country waiting to be staked out and mapped by Kashperl," indicates both Kashperl's potential—he deals with the "clothes of men *missing in action*"—and his preference for fixing the unknown. He is content with being sedentary, with vicariously living off the experience of others. Both Hodler and Kashperl find an event food for thought rather than stimulus to action. Kashperl even shares the desire of Avery and Hodler for Miss Holly: "But that was not what the fat man was waiting to hear. He wanted what Jubal had had without all the trouble. He wanted the cherry."

Structurally, Jubal's encounter with Kashperl—chapter 5—is at the center of the nine-chapter book; in chapter 5 Jubal is also at the physical center of Pickett. He penetrates the town just as he does individuals, revealing a fertile world ripe for stimulation. The bag of cherries smashed on Haffner's head nicely images the condition of the town and Jubal's effect upon it: Kashperl—and Hodler and Avery—"wanted the cherry, which was actually more than Jubal had got." The earlier book, *The Home Place,* breaks in two, a verbal and a visual text; *In Orbit,* how-

ever, is a single picture, initially taken in at a glance and then probed. Instead of a two- or three-part structure, *In Orbit* is a verbal/visual whole that seems to be continually moving. It is very difficult, for example, to speak of its beginning, middle, and end. Instead, we move into and then out from Pickett and its inhabitants. Chapters 1 and 9 present the picture taken in; chapters 2 and 8 focus on the force that is Jubal; chapters 3 and 4 (Holly) and chapters 6 and 7 (Charlotte) narrate Jubal's stimulation of two sexually responsive women; and chapter 5 presents the bloodless puncturing of the town's center. The movement of the book is suggestive of the sexual act itself, a penetration that breaks cherries, shatters hollow dreams, and is followed by withdrawal.[6]

In Orbit, then, is a picture of a single motion; our effort as viewer or reader is to see the whole rather than to extract meaning. The picture combines the deceptively simple and apparently static with the powerfully dynamic. Clyde Muncy's vision of the world in *The Home Place* was dominated by division and meaning, but the narrator of *In Orbit,* as evidenced by the picture he describes, sees a world of motion and unity. His use of language in that description is part of the vision:

This boy comes riding with his arms high and wide, his head dipped low, his ass tight in the saddle, as if about to be shot into orbit from a forked sling. He wears a white crash helmet, a plastic visor of the color they tint car windshields, half-boots with stirrup heels, a black horsehide jacket with zippers, levis so tight in the crotch the zipper of the fly is often snagged with hair. Wind puffs his sleeves, plucks the strings of his arms, fills the back of his jacket like a wineskin, ripples the soot-smeared portrait of J. S. Bach on his chest. His face is black as the bottomside of a stove lid, except for his nose, which is pewter-colored. He has the sniffles and often gives it a buff with his sleeve. He is like a diver just before he hits the water, he is like a Moslem prayer-borne toward Mecca, or he is like a cowpoke hanging to the steer's horns, or a highschool dropout fleeing the draft.

The use of detail and figurative language, particularly striking in this passage, characterizes much of the writing in the book. The narrator approaches language as though it were at the same time a visual and a verbal medium. Curt Hodler, the newspaperman, struggles to perceive shape, while the narrator enjoys exploring the motion of an integrated picture. Like the narrative and the structure, the language is an act of penetration—thus the fascination with metaphor and simile. In contrast to Hodler, who needs to use language to fix change, the narrator is sensitive to the power of language to open, focus, extend, and expand our perceptions. For the narrator, language is not a device to get at meaning. *In Orbit* yields very little "meaning"; rather, it describes an event. The verbal medium penetrates, probes, that event. The lines that conclude the paragraph quoted above take the crisply detailed opening and put it into motion by allowing the imagination the freedom to work with those details. Thus the opening lines both particularize—"This boy"—and set in motion the picture that will continue to be explored. The narrator perceives a world of possibility, and his ability to use language allows him to penetrate, experience, and verbalize that world.

In an essay entitled **"The Immediate Present,"** from a book of critical essays, *The Territory Ahead,* Wright Morris discusses what he sees as the relationship between art and life. "We have a need, however illusive, for a life that is more real than life. It lies in the imagination. Fiction would seem to be the way it is processed into reality. . . . If man is nature self-conscious, as we have reason to believe, art is his expanding universe." The fiction of Morris is a particularly good place to see the expanding universe of one man's imagination. The urge is to live fully in a universe whole and alive. *In Orbit,* then, is only in part the story of Jubal E. Gainer. It is also part of Morris's imaginative attempt to explore the territory ahead, to conceive and articulate an integrated, dynamic, fertile—in a word, a living—image.

Notes

1. Morris, *About Fiction,* p. 11.

2. Critics are divided in their perception of the underlying thrust of Morris's work. On the one hand, many consider the dominant force in his writing to be nostalgia, even an Eliotic "still point"; see, for example, J. C. Wilson, "Wright Morris and the Search for the 'Still Point,'" and Wydeven, "Consciousness Refracted." Gail Crump, on the other hand, stresses dynamics in Morris and contrasts his views to those of Wayne Booth and David Madden, whom he describes as tending "to treat transcendence in itself as an unalloyed good" (*The Novels of Wright Morris,* p. 9).

Morris has commented in an interview that nostalgia is a starting point from which the individual moves forward.

> Nostalgia, the past, which I first had to rediscover as a matter of personal self-discovery, can be traced in the novels, I think. First the infatuation with the past, a conviction that the past was real and desirable, and should be the way life is. Then a somewhat scrutinous and skeptical attitude toward the past. After which the present begins to come into the picture. . . . Then the past begins to be questioned, and over a period of eight novels, the past first dominated, then was compelled to recede. . . . In a way my books show a development of an escape from nostalgia.

(Bleufarb, "Point of View," p. 45)

See also Waterman, "The Novels of Wright Morris."

3. Morris, *The Territory Ahead,* pp. 19, 25.

4. Because of its interesting use of the photo-text technique, *The Home Place* is frequently discussed by scholars, who seem to agree that the book is one of Morris's weaker efforts. I refer in particular to Alan Trachtenberg, who writes that "one weakness of this book is that the pictures, which are all direct and straightforward, with an occasional close-up, compete with the narrative for our attention. Seeing them on alternate pages of the text, we cannot always experience them and the narrative simultaneously" ("The Craft of Vision," p. 46); to David Madden, who states that "although the photographs are excellent, their relation to the text is more literal and less interesting than in *The Inhabitants*" (*Wright Morris,* p. 52); and to Gail Crump, who says that the novel "does demonstrate Morris's increasing insight into his past, but the insight is evidenced only on the conceptual level, not in mastery of his fictional technique" (*The Novels of Wright Morris,* p. 57).

I disagree with such readings. The divisive, static world established by the photo-text technique is precisely the problem with which Clyde Muncy's imagination has to deal. More helpful, I think, is Mary Ann Flood's Master's thesis, "The Hero-Witness Relationship in the Fiction of Wright Morris" (1971).

5. About Jubal Gainer, Morris says, "I see him as a rather ordinary, ignorant, open-ended American juvenile. He has an opportunity to do what we think of as irrational. I consider him absolutely normal and his seeming psychopathic elements are introduced by the options within his situations. . . . The situation creates the violence. He is not violence-prone at all. He is merely another young man on a motorcycle, full of beans, and he's young, and he's ignorant, and outside of that he's Huck Finn" (*Conversations with Wright Morris,* p. 30).

6. Gail Crump offers a different description of the book's intriguing structure: "The image of orbiting brings together both transcendence (being out of this world) and immanence (being in motion through space-time), and the book's structure—nine brief chapters following Jubal's frenetic rampage through Picket—suggests the motion of the open road, while opening and closing the book with almost identical framing passages suggests the completion of an orbit" (*The Novels of Wright Morris,* p. 186).

G. B. Crump (essay date 1990)

SOURCE: "Wright Morris: Author in Hiding," in *Western American Literature,* Vol. XXV, No. 1, Spring, 1990, pp. 3-14.

[*In the essay, Crump analyzes the significance of Morris's image, in his memoir,* Will's Boy, *of himself hiding under a porch as a psychological key to Morris's work as a photographer, and to his narrative strategies as a novelist.*]

In *Earthly Delights, Unearthly Adornments* [hereafter abbreviated as *EDUA*], Wright Morris presents a telling portrait, or at least thumbnail sketch, of the artist as a young child, and he repeats it at the start of *Will's Boy* [hereafter abbreviated as *WB*], the first of his three volumes of memoirs: *"The small creatures of this world, and not a few of the large ones, are only at their ease under something . . . in the Platte Valley of Nebraska, street culverts, piano boxes, the seats of wagons . . . the dark caves under the front porches were all favored places of concealment. With Br'er Fox I shared the instinct to lie low. Seated in dust as fine as talcum . . . I peered out at the world through the holes between the slats"* (6). The adult writer's decision to give this sketch of the author as child such a primary place in his memoirs underscores its importance to his mature thinking about the nature of the artist and the imaginative process. Indeed, the image of the child peeking out at a prospect framed like a picture by the porch slats reflects some of Morris's central aesthetic pre-occupations and points both to his interest in photography and to the situation of many of his characters—from Brady, looking out through the window of a sleeping car in *The Works of Love,* to the tourists staring at the center of the bullring in *The Field of Vision.*

The image of the hidden child appears prominently in Morris's memoirs—*Will's Boy, Solo,* and *A Cloak of Light* [hereafter abbreviated as *CL*]—where its psychological roots in his experience are revealed and its implications for some of his characteristic themes and narrative methods are illustrated. The image has two sets of connotations in Morris, one clustering around the nature of the view seen from hiding and mixed up with his feelings about his mother, and the second clustering around the situation and character of the viewer and linked to his feelings about his father. It therefore provides an important unifying thread in his autobiographical writings.

The framed tableau observed by the child so clearly evokes Morris's experiments with photographs and "photographic" narrative style that it is like a signature. Those familiar with the author would recognize that "Will's Boy" is Wright Morris upon reading the passage where the boy "rub[s] a hole in the frosted window and peer[s] out" at the black and white world of a Nebraska December night (*WB* 8). The significance of such observed scenes soon becomes apparent: "If I had faculties of a different order" (*WB* 10), Morris writes, he would have pondered the Doppler effect of a train whistle, "but I preferred the shimmering fragment of suspended time that I saw through the porch slats where the train had just been, but was no more" (*WB* 11). The Doppler effect and the speeding train exist in and confirm the reality of time, but the child-viewer longs for the illusion of "suspended time" created by focusing on a segment of framed space so narrow that motion and thus time seem to be excluded from it. *Will's Boy* turns out to be an "Intimations Ode" with an arid plains flavor. It opens with a jumble of such "fragments of suspended time," rendered in the present tense to suggest the illusion of timelessness conveyed in photos, and near the end of Chapter One, as the child Morris sits in a doctor's window waiting for tapeworm medicine to work, he contemplates a "serene tableau, [which] like those I observed through the side slats of the porch, will join the select views that grow brighter rather than dimmer" (*WB* 16).

The serene tableau, as recollected years later, seems "brighter," more vivid and permanent, than the products of adult experience because it is pure and untroubled experience, uncontaminated by the world which is too much with us as adults and unencumbered by the analytical consciousness and mature cares that world arouses in us.

Readers of Morris the man will recognize the child who fathered him: the efforts to freeze time and salvage the past pervade his work. But, like Wordsworth before him, Morris the man discovers that the suspension of time is fitful and illusory, for as the memoirs record, life is nothing less than a fall into time. How else explain the youthful Morris's suggestive fascination with watches which is mentioned several times in the memoirs? (*WB* 69, 97; *Solo* 160). A fall into time entails a fall into loss, with the result that, as the author says, "much of my life would be spent in an effort to recover losses I never knew, realized or felt, the past that shaped yet continued to elude me" (*WB* 6). For Morris the primal loss is that of his mother, who died when he was born. Since he never knew his mother Grace, she is a nebulous figure in the memoirs, experienced only in her absence, but she broods over them in the form of the author's abiding sense of loss. The affective charge associated with this loss is apparent when, at seventeen, Morris meets a mother surrogate, his aunt Winona. When Winona vows she loves him (becoming the first woman in his life to offer such an assurance), the young Morris experiences a surge of feeling as a sense of all that has disappeared into the past comes flooding home to him: "My eyes brimmed with tears . . . my heart almost bursting with the knowledge of my own losses" (*WB* 162). Since Morris usually makes a virtue of being reserved, this (for him) extravagant outpouring of feelings signals a moment of great emotional significance.

The adult Morris's life-long search for "imaginary gains," often identified with timeless tableaux, scenes, objects, and suspended moments glimpsed in imagination as if from under the porch, expresses his need to recover the mother he never knew, and the memoirs link the loss of the mother to the loss of the past in all its manifestations. In *A Cloak of Light,* for instance, Morris, now a novelist, is shocked to find his old Omaha public school has been torn down: "The success of this 'vanishing act' stunned me" he says; "[of] a part of my life. . . . Nothing at all remained" (*CL* 92). An episode in *Will's Boy* explains the depth of his reaction to the disappearance of the school by associating it with his need to be the favored object of a nurturing female. Left ailing with one of his several unsympathetic stepmothers, the young Morris thinks of a classroom at the school as the only place "where I would feel safe" (*WB* 84) because it is identified with Miss Healy, a teacher he has a crush on: ". . . I longed to be back in my seat at the front, so close to Miss Healy I could smell her perfume when she walked up and down" (*WB* 85). Although the dust jacket of *A Cloak of Light* calls it "the concluding volume of his memoirs," Morris ends it about 1960, omitting the last one third of his life. But his need to recover the female love he feels he lost at birth imparts a sense of emotional completeness to the otherwise truncated autobiography. It begins with the death of his mother, moves on to his childhood experiences with various "new mothers" and his adult relations with women whose emotional reserve disqualifies them as replacements for Grace (such as his first mother-in-law and first wife, a woman he feels so remote from that he mentions her by name only in a caption to one of the photos in *A Cloak of Light*), and triumphantly concludes with his recovery of love in his second marriage, to Jo (whom he feels close enough to that he almost always refers to her by her first name).

In an early reminiscence, Morris explicitly associates mother love with his desire to recapture the past, as his child's love for an unidentified maternal figure moves the author to ask, "Not knowing the nature of the longing I felt, would it persist and reappear as a poignant yearning for what it is in the past that eludes me?" (*WB* 6). Casting a crucial sentiment in the form of a question, as Morris does here, is a stylistic mannerism found throughout his work. The unusual guardedness it implies about making direct statements illustrates a second aspect of the view from under the porch—the viewer's desire to remain hidden from the world's gaze; and just as Morris's concept of the view was influenced by his feelings about his mother, so his concept of the viewer is influenced by his feelings about his father. The figure of the concealed viewer represents a condition of the self. Profoundly lonely but deliberately chosen, the isolation under the porch allows the self to attain a paradoxical state of simultaneous fullness and emptiness, of total selfhood combined with complete escape from self. What Morris later calls "the exposed but uncritical soul of the child . . . who accepted the world before he analyzed it, and accumulated a large ticking store of impressions" (*CL* 226) has its being both authenticated and effaced by its role as a locus of keen and permanent impressions. The hidden self is acutely there, stuffed with perceptions, and yet is only a passive, neutral recorder of what it witnesses (and incidentally remains intact and secure from the torment of self-examination triggered by relationships with others): "Such incidents as I remember," Morris writes, "are uniformly free of the impression, if any, I made on my companions. I am a camera, but who it is that clicks the shutter I do not know" (*WB* 10). Indeed, *Will's Boy* stresses the absence of self-revealing views: "In all my childhood no mirror or window returns a reflection [of the young Morris] I remember" (*WB* 10).

Morris's contradictory needs to preserve and efface the self are bound up with his ambivalence about his father. The most prominent external force in *Will's Boy,* the agent of time as it were, is Will Morris, who abruptly shatters the serene tableaux of Chapter One when he shows up with Gertrude, the first of Wright's "new mothers." Morris's treatment of his father is understated, with little commentary or explicit criticism. When Morris does comment, his remarks are often at odds with the effect created by the account of his father's behavior. In many ways, Will Morris emerges as every boy's nightmare of a father, and Morris's reluctance to say so makes the impact of the baldly narrated facts all the more withering. In one scene, Will—elsewhere characterized as "genial," "jovial" (*CL* 82), and a "talker" (*WB* 34)—decides for once to do some talking to his son: "That was new," Morris writes. "He had always been too busy a father, when he saw me, to give me anything but money" (*WB* 64). The son's strongest explicit criticism of Will Morris is preceded by devastatingly faint praise: "He was a kind man, and I think he really liked me, but I was repelled by his ways with women" (*WB* 120). The father frequently disappears for months at a stretch, only to turn up at the most inopportune time to drag the boy away from a place he has come to feel at home in or an activity of benefit to him. When Wright is well along in high school, for instance, his father wants to take off for California because he "had lost his feeling that his future was in Chicago," but as the son adds, "it was Chicago that had given me the expectations that I was now looking up to . . ." (*WB* 128). In Omaha, the father humiliates the son by bouncing a check for the boy's room and board (*WB* 61), and in Chicago the son loses a cartoon contest because his father is never home to answer the phone call breaking the news the boy has won (*WB* 122). Still later, as recounted in *A Cloak of Light,* the father's response to a letter announcing Wright's marriage is to invite the young man to join him in the egg business, an enterprise the elder Morris repeatedly failed at, often at the expense of his partners (82).

No wonder then that the son's response to what threatens and repels him in his father's behavior is to turn away, to hide under the porch figuratively and sometimes literally. Only hidden can the self feel secure from the father's indifference, manipulation, and repulsive "ways with women." When the boy, aged seven or eight, returns home to find Gertrude has run off leaving the house in shambles—his response is familiar: "I didn't want to be home when my father returned, so I hid under the bleacher seats in the park. . . . [Later] I crawled into the sandbox and slept with the lid down" (*WB* 32). Eventually, the child's "instinct to lie low" like Br'er Fox develops into the teenager's determination "to go my own way" (*WB* 120), and the dark cave under the porch begins to connote self-sufficiency and independence. This self-sufficiency is manifested on the return from California when the car breaks down in Arkansas and the sixteen-year-old Morris makes his way back to Chicago by himself. It is manifested again in what, as an adult, he calls "my long-ingrained habit of going solo" (*CL* 162)—a habit evident in the European trip chronicled in *Solo,* in his photo safaris, in his pacifism during World War II, and finally in his career, one of the most singleminded demonstrations of going one's own way in recent American letters.

Nevertheless, the impulse of the self to take refuge under the porch contains overtones of fear and evasion, which are also implied in Morris's less direct strategies for coping with the father and the external world. For instance, Roy K. Bird has discussed how the author's life-long reluctance, evident in his novels and memoirs, to speak openly about sex is rooted in his repudiation of his father and his father's philandering (46-47). The teenaged Morris turns away and the adult writer's narration turns away in a passage relating what happens when the boy inadvertently comes in on his father having sex with a waitress: ". . . my father [was] hoarsely breathing, as if unable to stop the machine he had started. I ran back down the stairs, got into the car, [with high school friends] and we all drove around . . . until it was time for the first matinee. If we liked the vaudeville, which we usually did, we would stay and see it twice" (**WB** 114-15). Many authors would devote a chapter to the effects this primal scene has on an impressionable boy (else why mention it at all?), but with Morris the matinee pre-empts the waitress episode, about which nothing more is said. Later, in *A Cloak of Light,* when Morris, now a married man, stumbles on a couple copulating on a beach, "I took off and ran, as if I had witnessed a crime . . ." (**CL** 37). The memoirs display the same reticence about expressing any strong feelings: in middle age, courting his second wife, Morris confesses, "I may have said I did not want to go on without her, an extravagant admission for a lad with my background. I not only said many of these things, but I mailed the letter off" (**CL** 277).

Morris's desire to shield the self from the trauma of facing the father's flaws is complemented by an urge to escape the burden of selfhood, by dissolving his personality in the scene visible from the porch. This longing for self-dissolution arises, at least in part, from his apprehension that he may be too much like his father. An emotional high point in **Will's Boy** comes when the teenaged Morris, riding on a streetcar with his girl friend and wearing a new hat purchased to impress her, is laughed at by his father, whom the girl does not know. The boy's excessive shame stems from his anxiety that he may be falling into his father's despised ways with women. It is aroused by the fact that "he was wearing a hat so much like mine we probably looked like a vaudeville act. . . ." Furthermore, his anxiety about his new-found identification with his father seems justified when "she said I didn't like her as much as I used to. The moment she said it I knew that I didn't and it increased my shame. I lied and said that I really liked her better than ever . . ." (**WB** 152). Later, the hat that exposed the son's link to the father is the target on which the young Morris discharges his budding self-hatred: "I saw my reflection in the window, the big hat tilted on my head, and that I looked like a fool. I took that hat off . . . and left it. . . . I could no more wear it after what had happened than I could a dunce cap, or a nightpot" (**WB** 152-53). The same identification with the father appears when Morris admits, "I did not like the way he . . . ogled waitress . . . [but] I was not superior to sitting in the darkened bathroom . . . to watch a shapely neighbor, in silhouette, step from the tub to dry herself . . ." (**WB** 120).

A Cloak of Light reveals elements of Will Morris in the adult author. The son's very impulse to run and hide is a version of the father's habit of dealing with problems by moving to a new town. Will's restlessness is reflected in Morris's travels to Mexico, in the European trip related in *Solo,* in his frequent moves from East to West and back, and most of all in what he calls a "lyrical euphoria when exposed to new places" (**CL** 57). Morris explicitly treats travel as a form of psychological escape and release similar to the release of writing: "The great and intricate secret of the open road . . . is the way it provokes and sustains image-making, the supreme form of day-dreaming. . . . What dreams seem to do for so many others, a long car trip does for me" (**CL** 213). As was the case with his father, the escape is often from the girl he left behind. When the author complains about his first wife's "need for the companionship of older women," he blames his own self-preoccupation and adds "to keep my mind on my work, I would wangle ways to be gone" (**CL** 229). Even earlier, when the marriage was still going well, he left his wife to go on a photo safari, commenting that "to be free in this manner, free in my mind and on wheels, yet captive of an abiding and pleasurable enthusiasm [the adult equivalent of the hidden child's ecstatic fullness] . . . this seemed to me one of the best of possible worlds" (**CL** 53).

The reference to wheels recalls that in **Will's Boy** the glamorous appeal getting away had for Will Morris is often displaced onto the colorful cars he gets away in, and vehicles such as the bicycle in **Solo** sometimes throw an irresistible spell over the son too. About buying the bicycle, Morris admits, ". . . my action had been mad, but like that of a foolhardy lover, fated. I could not help myself" (**Solo** 36). He employs a similar language of irrational compulsion to describe his purchase of the most important vehicle in his adult life, the green Jaguar he buys in California not long before his divorce. He was in a "vulnerable state" when he bought it and does not comprehend his own "folly" (**CL** 249). The parallel to his father, who sometimes used cars to run away *with* (as well as from) women, suggests the Jaguar expresses his unconscious wish for a woman with whom to "bolt" from his unsatisfactory marriage—a woman such as the "attractive poetess" he takes to the beach in the car (**CL** 249) or Jo, whom he later drives all over Mexico in it and eventually marries.

Behind these other traits of the father which Morris fears to discover in himself lurks the principal trait of coldness, lack of feeling. In *Earthly Delights, Unearthly Adornments,* he seems to want to make a virtue of the fact that "for my father, intimate knowledge of another person was a form of forbidden knowledge. He would have found self-revelation, as it is now practiced, indefensible" (**EDUA** 8). But intimate knowledge of a sort is just what Will had of numerous women, and the son's characterization sounds suspiciously like an attempt to rationalize his father's apparent indifference to him (as well as a projection of Morris's own distaste for revealing himself). Moreover, Morris sometimes perceives such indifference in his own character. In describing the funeral of his father-in-law—a man of "solid, reassuring, expansive presence, [and] easily given affection" (**CL** 144), the antithesis of Will Morris in fact—he castigates for lack of feeling the dead man's mother and wife (models for the grandmother and Mrs. Porter in *The Deep Sleep*). Yet Morris's own emotions are disturbingly disengaged: "What I felt the most intensely was that I had been cut, but proved to be a poor bleeder" (*CL* 142). "At once sorrowful, saddened, and shamefaced," he seeks to explain to himself and the reader his lack of emotion, blaming his "too-great self-sufficiency" and reverting to a familiar image: "My family ties had been on the fringe of other families, from where I spied on them from pantries, or concealed by the cloak that draped the dining room table" (*CL* 142).

In spite of the pathos this image evokes about the life of Morris the child, Morris the writer's eloquent novel about the family, *The Deep Sleep*, proves the concealed child's view can be very clear. Indeed, since Morris claims that "many [writers] have their beginnings under something" (*EDUA* 1), he clearly regards the perspective from under the porch as empowering and thus making possible the vision of the artist. For one thing, the lonely independence concealment brings with it can encourage an author's originality and in Morris's case, kept him doggedly pursuing his own aesthetic ends through decades of poor sales, publishers' rebuffs, and critical neglect. In contrast to his reserve and evasiveness about his feelings toward people in the memoirs, the author pulls no punches about his work and its lukewarm reception. He concedes without resentment or apology, "*The Field of Vision* . . . mirrored the conscience of the writer, but did not deceive him into thinking that the preoccupations revealed in his writing were shared by his contemporaries. . . . In a really quite tiresome way, he appeared to be a throwback to those 'loners' . . . compelled to do what we find them doing . . ." (*CL* 223).

In a more significant way, the view from under the porch affords the author the distancing from his subject required to achieve that which he insists "the reader wants" but which may in fact be what the author needs—namely "the impersonal narration that . . . is crucial to the craft of fiction" (*CL* 137). The need for impersonal distancing in Morris is bound up with the same psychological needs which required the child who became the writer to withdraw under the porch in the first place. In effect, Morris attributes what he thinks is the failure of *The Works of Love*, his novel about his father, to its violation of the emotional distance from Will which the child required to keep his threatened self intact: ". . . the author increasingly identified with his [the father character's] nature to the extent of becoming a double agent, speaking in one voice for both of them." The book thus made "explicit and painful appeals to the reader's sympathies. . . . A more sophisticated writer than I was at the time would have . . . spared *both the author* and the reader" (*CL* 158; emphasis mine). The contemplation of the space visible through the porch slats, on the other hand, is Morris's model for a more successful and less emotionally perilous aesthetic performance. With the view suspended in time, the concealed, child-like psyche establishes a consoling

"connection," but one which is drained of potentially disturbing personal and subjective contents. Following the lead of Henry James, Morris concludes that the properly sensitive perceiver of a scene experiences a sensation like that of the artist: "detached" yet a "participant," the perceiver is attuned to a "mystical" transpersonal aura present in the scene, and his mental picture of it has numinous and inviolable qualities associated in the romantic tradition with works of art: "The space beneath the porch . . . provides the child with his own magical trappings, and I am impressed . . . with how closely they resemble the more orthodox holy places" (*CL* 226). In spite of the stress on the sensibility of the viewer, the illusions of impersonality and magical timelessness largely depend on the nature of what is viewed. Since events occurring before the opening in the slats, like the train with its Doppler effect, disrupt these illusions, it is permissible and even necessary for the writer following this creative model to omit or deemphasize them: "On such a participant as myself," confesses Morris, "actual events, casual or dramatic, are of relative unimportance. They might be likened to the blurs in a photograph, indicating time's passage" (*CL* 226). What is left (in the theory well known to Morris readers) is the objects or places "*disposed for human use* . . . [with] *a mystic meaning proper to themselves to give out*" forming the subjects of Morris's photographs (Henry James qtd. in *CL* 226).

One striking thing about the creative model formulated here and expressed in the hidden-viewer metaphor is how convenient it is for a lad with Morris's background. To get rid of events, he must get rid of people, who have a habit of turning up in events; and to get rid of people, to have them present in the work only by proxy in objects and scenes they have placed their imprints on, is to get rid of the danger of too close identification with them. This aesthetic model also protects the author from self-exposure. Since he is present only in the act of seeing and seeing only objects, he is relieved of the obligation to analyze the psychology of characters and comment on their moral condition, to do anything but describe the scene and let it do the talking. In art conforming to this model, then, the people are magically both there and not there and the author is magically both disclosed and concealed at the same time. This paradox is evidenced in the memoirs as a whole: they express both Morris's deep reluctance to show his feelings openly and the impulse toward self-revelation implicit in the act of composing memoirs.

A second striking point about this formulation is how unnovelistic it is. Morris has probably gone as far as any contemporary writer in making setting a pivotal conceptual element in his novels and in devoting care and space to the description of scene. Yet the prose form this artistic model brings most immediately to mind is the sketch, not the novel, and the art form it most nearly suggests is still photography. It is photography which speaks without speaking and which Morris believed early in his life would provide the thing itself ("**Letter to a Young Critic**" 97), the pictured subject, without the mediation of an artist. It is photography which most closely conforms to the often-cited aesthetic ideal articulated by Morris in 1951: ". . . the important things are those that remain unsaid and . . . the problems of art are concerned with how we hint at them. The bold front, the bare-faced statement, give the lie to both the heart and the mind" (Qtd. in Hutchens). Even so, as his anecdote about eliminating a chamber pot from one of his Nebraska photos illustrates (**"Privacy as a Subject of Photography"** 54), Morris especially favors a photography of exclusion which reveals the author in as oblique a manner as possible, by what he leaves out rather than what he puts in.

Morris's preference for hints and intimations is everywhere apparent in his theoretical statements about writing and in his fictional practice. For instance, it lies behind his judgment in *A Cloak of Light* that the forces shaping southern culture are "at once unavoidably visible and subject to instant falsification" (56), as if visibility invited falsification. The preference has had the positive result of forcing the author to develop a sensibility more attuned to nuance and implication than that of many contemporary novelists, an especially valuable asset in writing about the plains, where the keynote is emptiness and invisibility. Nevertheless, Morris's success as a novelist has hinged on his growing beyond the front porch model of the creative act and embracing ends and means more characteristic of fiction. An example is his increasing interest in such purely verbal matters as fictional voice, the vernacular style, and the role of clichés, especially linguistic clichés, in culture, Morris's growth as a writer has hinged in turn on his ability to emerge from hiding and close the gap between himself and the figures who people his experience. Just as the memoirs clarify the psychological basis of his preference for hinted truths, they also suggest that his imaginative struggle to come to terms with his experience in his fiction was instrumental in helping him transcend his personal isolation. In the course of that struggle, he came to recognize that the artist's self is inescapably revealed in the work of art, no matter how detached he tries to be, detachment or engagement being merely different manifestations of authorial presence. He replaces the concept of art as static tableau with a concept of art as "image," a comprehensive term connoting something like the objective correlative; the image is an aesthetic figuration of an entire state of being and feeling which makes communication with others possible and encompasses fictional expressions. If his father found "self revelation, as it is now practiced, indefensible," the son comes to believe that, "If the image is right, is appropriate, what is revealed is acceptable" and capable of narrowing the gap between people (*EDUA* 8).

In order to transform people like his father and mother-in-law into intelligible fictional creations, Morris was compelled to analyze and identify with them, with the result that his portraits of such characters as Will Brady and Mrs. Porter manifest a degree of understanding and compassion significantly beyond what he can bring himself to show for their real-life counterparts in the memoirs. In his fiction, evasion, willed isolation, and failure of feeling—flaws the memoirs sometimes uncover in Morris himself—come to be perceived as major sins, while engagement, imaginative identification, and compassion are treated as life-enhancing avenues to salvation. The memoirs depict the key experiences which Morris, boy and man, had to work through in order to function as a person and an author. They testify to his ability to reach an author's imaginative mastery of his particular experiences, at once threatening and empowering, and to exercise that mastery in the creation of significant "images" like that of the child hidden under the porch and peering out at a timeless scene.

Works Cited

Bird, Roy K. *Wright Morris: Memory and Imagination.* New York: Peter Lang, 1985.

Hutchens, John K. "On an Author." *New York Herald Tribune Book Review,* 3 June 1951: 2.

Knoll, Robert E., ed. *Conversations with Wright Morris: Critical Views and Responses.* Lincoln: University of Nebraska Press, 1977.

Morris, Wright. *A Cloak of Light: Writing My Life.* New York: Harper, 1985.

———. *Earthly Delights, Unearthly Adornments: American Writers as Image-Makers.* New York: Harper, 1978.

———. "Letter to a Young Critic." *Massachusetts Review* 6 (Autumn-Winter 1964-65): 93-100.

———. "Privacy as a Subject for Photography." *Magazine of Art,* 44 (1951): 51-55.

———. *Solo: An American Dreamer in Europe.* New York: Harper, 1983.

———. *Will's Boy: A Memoir.* New York: Harper, 1981.

Reginald Dyck (essay date 1990)

SOURCE: "Revisiting and Revising the West: Willa Cather's *My Ántonia* and Wright Morris's *Plains Song,*" in *Modern Fiction Studies,* Vol. 36, No. 1, Spring, 1990, pp. 25-38.

[*In the following essay, Dyck discusses attitudes towards the pioneer experience of the American west as depicted in Willa Cather's* My Antonia *and Morris's* Plains Song.]

The best days are the first to flee.

—Willa Cather

Is the past a story we are persuaded to believe, in the teeth of the life we endure in the present?

—Wright Morris[1]

Revisionist Historian Patricia Limerick opens *The Legacy of Conquest* with a photograph, quotation, and commentary about tin cans, hardly a heroic entrance into the his-

tory of the West. From these apparently ubiquitous artifacts of the frontier she draws this conclusion: the past,
like tin cans where there are no garbage collectors, remains to affect the present; the Old West is connected with
rather than cut off from the New (18). Wright Morris'
Plains Song: For Female Voices also mentions cans in
Ned Kibbee's dinner comment, "I like canned peas better
than fresh ones, always did" (210), which suggests the ba-
nality of Morris' modern, Midwest characters.

On the other hand, turn-of-the-century historian Frederick
Jackson Turner makes no references to tin cans. Neither
do Willa Cather's pioneer women open any. Instead, they
do their own canning. In one of Cather's most famous
scenes, Ántonia's children emerge from the cave that holds
all the produce she has canned for her family. This self-
reliance, Turner claimed, was fostered by the American
frontier. Canning rather than cans represents his West, as it
does Cather's.

Both see a gap between the frontier past and the present
that was emerging. Behind Cather's famous quotation,
"The world broke in two about 1920, and I belong to the
former half," is her resentment against the standardization
and conventionality that she felt characterized the lives of
the pioneers' children (Bennet 146, 148). Turner, proclaiming that the frontier had closed in 1890, also saw his
present in terms of loss. The postfrontier West seemed to
have lost its optimism and character. Historian Elliot West
explains, "The region that once seemed endlessly bounti-
ful and forever wild has become a land of narrowing limits" (quoted in Athearn ix).

Turner and Cather were not alone in finding their present
troubling enough that they shaped the western past into a
world as they wished it to be. "The notion that the West
was succumbing to both a material and cultural standardization during the twenties was noted with increasing frequency in eastern periodicals" (Athearn 53). As doubts developed about the new direction the nation was taking,
many began to resent the changes taking place in the part
of America closest to the pioneer past. Therefore, they
wanted the West set aside as "that frozen-in-time land of
breath-taking sunsets and living folklore" (Athearn 65).

Establishing a gap between past and present provided
Cather and Turner with similar ideological gains. First, it
allowed them to maintain a sense of innocence regarding
what had taken place on the frontier because they could
ignore the consequences of pioneering for native inhabitants and the environment. Second, both Cather's fiction
and Turner's analysis could present individual character as
central because a past cut off from the present could be
imagined as a world existing prior to hampering social
structures. Thus Turner concluded his famous 1893 essay,
"The Significance of the Frontier in American History," by
stating:

> to the frontier the American intellect owes its striking
> characteristics. That coarseness and strength combined
> with acuteness and inquisitiveness; that practical, in-

ventive turn of mind, quick to find expedients; that
masterful grasp of material things, lacking in the artistic but powerful to effect great ends; that restless, nervous energy; that dominant individualism, working for
good and for evil, and withal that bouyancy and exu-
berance which comes with freedom—these are traits of
the frontier.

(37)

Cather celebrates many of these same traits in the vivacious, independent, and determined Ántonia, whose obstacles are either personal or natural. Social and economic
problems received little attention; crop prices are mentioned only when one of Ántonia's daughters tells Jim
Burden that "they were going to have a new parlor carpet
if they got ninety cents for their wheat" (347). Neither
Cather nor Turner adequately acknowledges the impact of
banks, corporations, or the federal government on pioneer
life. In their pioneer world of heroes, aspects that would
diminish the role of the individual receive little recognition.

Instead of social structures, Cather and Turner emphasize
the relationship between individuals and their environment. Earl Pomeroy, noted western historian and critic of
Turner, explains a significant cause for this: "The environmental interpretation appealed to Americans in a national-
istic and ostensibly democratic era, even though the nation
was visibly becoming more like Europe in its drift to industrial power and an urban orientation of society" (580).
Belief in a nation shaped by the frontier environment reassured its citizens of American exceptionalism. When that
belief came into question, a new historical and literary interpretation was required.

Writing sixty years later, Wright Morris presents a vision
shaped by a different social context, one that includes
skepticism about individual or national heroism. Morris
rejects the longing look back to an idealized past that excludes the present. His critical work, **The Territory Ahead,**
warns against its crippling effect on writers for whom "the
present exists—in so far as it exists—in order to heighten
the comparison. . . . It is the past that is real" (19). Although he only mentions Cather once in his critical writing, Morris' continuing criticism of the nostalgic look
back, which he sees as having preoccupied American literature, contains an indirect attack on his Nebraska precursor. He also challenges Cather by rewriting the story of
My Ántonia in his last novel, **Plains Song.**

Both novels open with approximately the same setting,
central Nebraska at the time near the end of the frontier
and the completion of settlement, when immigrants and
Americans were struggling to establish farms and a new
way of life on the plains. Both novels focus their description of pioneer life on a strong woman who by overcom-
ing hardships establishes a place for herself and her family. The first ends with Ántonia enjoying the fruit of her
efforts, whereas **Plains Song** takes us further beyond the
pioneer struggle so that we see its legacy. At the end Cora

is dead, and neither her children nor grandchildren have any interest in preserving her way of life. The two novels, however, differ not only because in one the dream is richly fulfilled and in the other it is somewhat meagerly realized and then destroyed by a new social reality. The definition of the dream itself creates an underlying difference.

This difference deeply marks each presentation of the character who arguably is the main protagonist and who must try to reconcile the past with the present.[2] Both Jim Burden and Sharon Rose Atkins grow up on farms near the end of that special transition time, but they leave to attend the University of Nebraska and then to find careers in the East. They return when they are middle-aged because of the woman who represents their rural past. Through Jim and Sharon, Cather and Morris set forth their attitudes toward both the plains and the past.

If the parallels between the two novels suggest that Morris has rewritten a borrowed script, he has clearly transformed it into his own. The novels' similarities occur within the context of quite different characterization and narrative strategies. Morris uses characters and actions having much in common with Cather's, but he adapts them to his own vision. Harold Bloom in *The Anxiety of Influence* claims that because imagining necessarily means misinterpreting, all poems are antithetical to their precursors (93). Although his explanation is reductive and refuses to acknowledge the social forces shaping the misinterpretation, it does alert us to an important source of generative power in **Plains Song.** The novel needs to be understood as a misprisioning or willful misreading of its Nebraska precursor. Bloom also suggests that readings should be made in the opposite direction. Not only can we see a precursor's influence in the follower's struggle for power, but we also need to see how the follower, through his misreading, provides a new way of understanding the precursor's work (*Map* 54, 60-61). By understanding Morris' work, we gain a perspective for seeing the omissions and contradictions in *My Ántonia* that cast doubt on its common interpretation as a celebration of the pioneer past.

In creating Jim as a sensitive, indecisive, and largely passive narrator, Cather establishes an appropriate voice for expressing her own attitudes toward the place she herself idealized but left. Jim Burden leaves the plains because he has no place there. He is enough of an insider to understand and enough of an outsider to be able, through comparison and dissatisfaction with another way of life, to have a heightened appreciation of Ántonia's world.

Yet Cather unwittingly warns the reader to be wary of Jim's attitude by exposing it as untenable. Through Ántonia, Cather celebrates the pioneer values: determination, love of the land, and human rather than materialistic concerns. But Jim's relation to Ántonia calls Cather's presentation of those values into question. Unlike Ántonia, Jim must confront the present. As we finish reading the novel and see the comparisons suggested between them—frustration/contentment, restlessness/sense of place, bar-

renness/fruitfulness—we sense the failure of Jim's success and the success of Ántonia's failure.[3] Ántonia's life judges Jim's, which in turn represents the emerging American culture.

Jim's present life is defensively described in the Introduction. The narrator of this section suggests that although Jim has moved to the East and has become a part of the new materialistic world, his heart still belongs to the rural plains of his past, and so he has not been corrupted. Two considerations are made. First, his marriage is a failure because his wife (according to the narrator of the Introduction) is shallow, vain, "temperamentally incapable of enthusiasm," and clearly an Easterner—no match for Ántonia who "seemed to mean to us the country, the conditions, the whole adventure of our childhood" (ii). However, this is exactly the problem. The narrator, caught up as much as Jim is with visions of Ántonia, cannot give us a reliable picture of Jim's wife, and, more important, neither can we imagine Jim seeing his wife clearly. He has never resolved his relationship with Ántonia as a woman he desires or as a symbol of his own past. The manuscript he brings the narrator attests to this, as does his failure to know what he wants from Lena and his reaction when he first sees Ántonia as an older woman. "The eyes that peered anxiously at me were—simply Ántonia's eyes. I had seen no others like them . . ." (331). Although it appears that the present causes Jim's failure, Cather actually indicts the past, or more specifically, his longing for the past.

Jim's profession, the second consideration, includes a similar conflict between past and present. Being a lawyer for a great Western railroad is not recognized as important in itself; and this absence, here and during his return visit to Nebraska, helps explain why Jim must give up his present identity in order to rejoin the world that he has left but through which he still largely defines himself. Because the rural, innocent past offers no place for a lawyer, Jim must sacrifice that identity to be accepted by Ántonia and her family. However, the narrator of the Introduction, having broader experience, can find a more accepting way of considering his profession, stating that Jim still "loves with a personal passion the great country through which his railway runs and branches."[4] Not only that, "His faith in it and his knowledge of it have played an important part in its development" (ii). What the narrator does not state is that in helping to develop that great country, Jim's railroad is destroying it. In order to be a safe place for Ántonia, the country must be preserved, because development will force it into the present with its values that Cather abhorred.[5] Again, Jim is trapped because of the gap that Cather, Turner, and others of their generation saw between the heroic past and the mundane present.

Sigmund Freud has written that to be psychologically healthy a person must love well and work well. Jim fails at love because he cannot resolve his relationship with Ántonia. And he cannot pursue his profession for the fulfillment it might give him because it has no place in the world he idealizes. This interpretation does not rest on the Introduction alone. In the last section, to be discussed later, Cather also shows the destructive consequences of clinging to the past.

Morris in **Plains Song** presents the tension between past and present more explicitly than Cather does. Although both Jim and Sharon try to escape this tension through repression, Jim represses the present while Sharon represses the past. Another difference is that Sharon changes: she deepens her self-awareness by recognizing the continuity of past and present. Cather, although she has created Jim as a sensitive character, has not made him a self-reflective narrator. Therefore his concluding insight, that life is a circle, is not a metaphor for growth.

Both characters leave rural Nebraska to attend the university in Lincoln. Sharon's attitude in leaving, unlike Jim's, resembles Cather's own when she made a similar move from Red Cloud.[6] Seeing the people she is leaving as only half-conscious, Sharon looks back with the same rebelliousness that Cather shows in early short stories such as "On The Divide." To both, the plains seem a wasteland that crushes rather than nurtures a fully human life. For Sharon, that life is epitomized by her Aunt Cora. The narrator sums up Sharon's attitude as she left: "However much Sharon Rose disliked farmers, her scorn for farmers' wives was greater. She pitied Cora, who seemed to lack the sense to pity herself" (76). However, when she returns after a thirty-eight-year absence, Sharon comes to Cora's defense. Although she does not develop Jim's idealizing attitude, she does make a change.

In creating a character who comes to recognize the problem of confronting the past, Morris demonstrates an option other than a retreat into the myths of the past. He shows what Sharon gains by leaving a place where she does not belong, whereas Cather only shows Jim's losses. Also, Morris demonstrates more clearly the consequences of Sharon's failure to understand how much her past continues to affect her. Using Cora's coping strategy, independence (which really means abstinence or "not beholding"), Sharon misses much of life, a loss she realizes in reflective times during her return. Because she has this awareness, her insider/outsider stance becomes more integrated, whereas Jim's two worlds remain estranged.

This difference is heightened by each author's decision to make the central character an orphan, a situation which highlights the problem of belonging. Although Jim lives with his grandparents, he never has a role on their farm beyond running errands. Later, when they move to town, his love of country life keeps him from belonging to that life either. Jim leaves for the university, and later for the East, at the instigation of his grandfather, a professor friend, and others. He seldom anticipates the new life each move brings. Because the old life no longer holds a place for him, he yields to the pressure of others, a pressure that pushes him farther and farther from the place he loves. It is no wonder that he feels the best days are the first to flee.

Sharon's situation is less easily defined. Her parents do not belong on their Nebraska homestead; they are too free-spirited to fit in a pioneer world that seems to require Cora's stolid steadiness. After her mother dies, Sharon is reared by her Aunt Cora, who has no patience for initiating either Sharon or her daughter Madge into the life of a farm wife. Neither does Sharon have an interest in learning. Her emotional break with this life comes in a scene that haunts her throughout the rest of the book. As Madge and her boyfriend remain "spooning" in the buggy after dropping her off, Sharon calls out for them and Cora to hear, "Is he looking for a wife or a housemaid?" (75), her indictment of the life she wants to escape. Not surprisingly, however, her escape is only partial, just as her belonging had been.

Sharon, like Jim, remains emotionally connected to the place of her childhood, although she is active in leaving whereas Jim is passive. The difference in their attitudes results from the depth of consciousness that the authors give them. Jim's feeling for Nebraska remains a steady, one-dimensional longing because Cather did not choose to explore an ambiguous response to the plains. He makes no emotional commitments except to his rural past. Sharon at first is also ineffectual in making attachments. Nevertheless, she engages in an uneasy process of deepening awareness that leads to a greater connectedness and has an important effect on her sense of identity.

This issue, the problem of identity, opens the final section of both books, and again the differences strikingly reveal the conceptions of the authors. Questions of identity cause Jim's and Sharon's apprehensions about returning to Nebraska as adults. Jim has a great deal at stake when he meets Ántonia. He understands his dilemma exactly.

> Perhaps it was cowardice that kept me away so long . . . I did not want to find her aged and broken; I really dreaded it. In the course of twenty crowded years one parts with many illusions. I did not wish to lose the early ones. Some memories are realities, and are better than anything that can ever happen to one again.
>
> (327-328)

Not surprisingly, as soon as he meets Ántonia, Jim's doubts are erased.

For Sharon the question of identity is not Jim's question of whether or not the past has survived into the present but rather a question of her own identity in relation to the past. Thus she is not so easily reassured. Morris somewhat heavy-handedly introduces the issue through two characters who mistake Sharon for someone else. The second woman becomes connected in Sharon's mind with Cora, whose funeral she is returning to attend. Alexandra Selkirk,[7] the new Cora who is a pioneer in the feminist movement, grabs one of Sharon's wrists as they talk. "A coincidence, surely, but Sharon was reminded of the confrontation with Cora, who had gripped her by the wrist as she whacked her with the hairbrush" (190). The original incident represents Sharon's emotional turning away from the life that Cora stands for; the repetition signals the uneasy beginning of reconciliation with her past. This is possible because Morris has created a character who becomes aware of the complexities of her relationship with the past.

Jim, on the other hand, simply recreates his boyhood life. As he leaves the Black Hawk railway station and drives out to the Cuzak farm, he enters a realm isolated from the world he has had to confront since traveling east as a young man. He finds a family living in harmony with itself and nature. There have, of course, been hardships, but Cather establishes the situation so that we see triumph rather than deprivation.

Sharon finds a modern world filled with tension and dissatisfaction. On returning, she first confronts the confusion of a football Saturday in Lincoln. Then, while taking her nephew and niece to a museum display of dinosaurs, she faces the troubling question of survival. Soon she finds that a way of life has become extinct. With Cora's death, the farmhouse Sharon grew up in has been destroyed, and the farm is being transformed from a homestead into an agribusiness for which success is determined less by character than by government policies. Sharon finds herself pushed into defending Cora, looked upon with suspicion as an outsider, and not respected for what she has accomplished. Making it more difficult, Sharon is not sure where she stands. With new maturity she perceives that the old, clear judgments about her past are impossible.

Although Jim has no trouble making his judgment after his initial uncertainty—his childhood world has been preserved—Sharon's uncertainty is never eased. No living past is available for her to escape into because Cora is dead, the homestead is destroyed, and the remaining family members all have a petty, small-town narrowness. Unlike Jim, Sharon is not welcomed as an old friend but is treated with suspicion; this is hardly surprising because her attitude toward their lives has always been judgmental.

Cather simplifies the return in *My Ántonia*; during half of the description, Ántonia's husband, "our papa," is away, allowing Jim and Ántonia to reestablish old connections more easily.[8] Morris creates a more complex situation. Sharon first confronts an antagonistic younger generation when her niece Caroline picks her up at the airport and questions her about marriage, independence, wife-beating, Sharon's unwillingness to face life, and the welcome loss and failure of the past. Soon after she must face the extended family at dinner. There are no plates of kolaches, pitchers of milk, and rows of orderly children. Here, children are excluded from the main table; the only attention given them is, "Shut your trap" and "Don't make a face at me!" (208, 214). This world of adult conflicts is not diverted by the presence of charming, polite children.

Later at Cora's funeral service, Sharon is troubled by the hymn she listens to, "Abide With Me": "She pondered the meaning of the words. But what, indeed, had abided? The liberation from her burdens, the works and meager effects

of Cora had been erased from the earth" (214). What a contrast this sense of loss makes with Jim's experience. He returns to find his childhood world essentially unchanged. The new inhabitants give him a hero's status and are ready to provide a future that will keep his old world alive: hunting on the plains with the boys and trips to the old world with Ántonia's husband. Jim could hardly imagine a more successful trip.

The life Sharon returns to might seem to justify the disgust Cather expressed about the present that she saw overtaking the world she had known. Cather's pioneers are like Malinda Matlock in the *Spoon River Anthology*, who says to the younger generation, the equivalent of the family assembled at the end of *Plains Song*:

> What is this I hear of sorrow and weariness,
> Anger, discontent and dropping hopes?
> Degenerate sons and daughters,
> Life is too strong for you—
> It takes life to love Life.
>
> (202)

Morris' reconsideration of this old complaint does not provide a more ennobling understanding of the present generation but instead questions the idealized qualities of the past one.

Cather can sustain the world that Jim returns to only by isolating it. For example, Ántonia raises her family to speak only Bohemian, which keeps them from the changing world around them. The only outside contact mentioned is the old world fair at Wilbur. A possible intrusion would have been Ántonia's oldest daughter, who owns a car. However, because she is an adult who apparently is making a transition into the present, she is barely mentioned. Also, because this daughter represents a part of Ántonia's past that is not idyllic, for Jim she is better forgotten. In contrast, the other children enthusiastically bring Jim back to the past by asking him for clarifications about the old stories. They ask no questions about life in the East, his travels, or his work with the railroad. Cather keeps the focus clearly on the past.

The only embarrassing moment of the visit occurs when Ántonia brings up his present life: "Oh, we don't have to work so hard now! We've got plenty to help us, papa and me. And how many have you got, Jim?" (335). The answer is none. And with that, the topic of his present life is closed. Because that life has no place in this world, Jim must become a boy again. Therefore, he helps bring home the cows, relives the old experiences represented by photographs, sleeps in the hayloft with the boys, and finds that he "felt like a boy in their company" (345). His relationship with Anton Cuzak is really no different from his relationship with the boys because it will be set in the old world of Anton's youth. Not surprisingly, Ántonia is no longer a significant part of this world. She fades into the background when the reminiscing is finished, because an adult friendship would prevent Jim from becoming a boy again.[9]

The visit succeeds only because Jim willingly denies his present life. This perspective reveals that Cather has created an ambiguous conclusion acknowledging both success and failure: not the success of the past and the failure of the present but the failure resulting from successful disintegration. At the end of *My Ántonia,* Jim discovers a section of the old road Ántonia and he traveled that night when they first got off the train in Black Hawk. As he remembers back, he comments on the "little circle man's experience is" (372) because that early life has shaped all they have done. The last sentence reads, "whatever we had missed, we possessed together the precious, the incommunicable past" (372). Jim's emphasis does not rest on what they have missed because the novel offers no room for the type of self-reflection that would threaten to undermine the past they possess. Also, he does not acknowledge that they possess it much differently. Ántonia has found a way to possess the past by living it, although this does impose limitations. Jim can claim the past only marginally by splitting his life into two irreconcilable parts.

Morris precludes a response such as Jim's by embodying the past in Cora, a character not easily idealized. She came to Nebraska not as an immigrant child but as a young American woman waiting for an offer of marriage. The offer comes, but the result is less a union than a mutual co-existence as two worlds become established on one homestead. Cora's biting her knuckle to the bone in her one sexual encounter with her husband represents Morris' confrontation of marital failure, as compared with Cather's evasion by picturing Ántonia's marriage as a friendship. Finally, Cora's death symbolizes the end of the old life, whereas the life represented by Ántonia lives on. The image Cather creates of children rushing out of the cave, the womb of the earth, assures us that the past will survive. These children are the focus of life for Ántonia, whereas Cora's life centers on her house, her chickens, and her yard. Not that these concerns make Cora materialistic; rather, they provide a way for her to create order in a difficult place. Morris shows Cora's inner struggle to cope with both a land and people that do little to nurture the spirit.[10] Consequently, although Ántonia can embrace and find harmony with the plains, Cora endures by limiting her awareness to what she can manage and by making improvements that are more an act of colonization than an act of belonging.

That endurance does not prepare Cora well for the ultimate test Morris puts her through, a test Cather carefully excludes. Cora is forced to confront the outside world of the present when she is taken to the Chicago World's Fair. Her strategy of denying what she cannot face is severely challenged and given physical embodiment: "Seated on the stool in a rented room, Cora could do nothing whatsoever but sit there. All her functions had stopped" (140).

These contrasts between the characters who represent past life on the plains demonstrate Morris' and Cather's differing attitudes toward that life and help establish the dynamics of the interaction between these characters and the two

who must confront the present. Whereas Ántonia is a quasi-lover for Jim, Cora is a surrogate mother for Sharon. She rebels against Cora in her pity for her, but, upon her return, she defends Cora, and in doing so acknowledges how much they are alike. With developed maturity Sharon sees Cora as a woman to be respected, although in only certain ways emulated.

Jim's admiration for Ántonia results from his own inability to grasp life in the present. Sharon's reaction has been the opposite. Earlier the narrator, speaking for Sharon, says, "Giving oneself to the past was even more fruitless than giving oneself to others" (182). Sharon discovers, however, that her escape has never been complete and that in trying to evade the past through her independence, she has paid the price of restlessness and loneliness. What else does she have besides being "into" music? In realizing this, Sharon comes to understand that she has followed Cora's pattern of survival. "As much as or more than the child she had borne, Sharon had been Cora's girl. Abstinence was something she understood; indulgence she did not." This new awareness frees her to feel for the first time "a sweet sadness, a longing touched with dread . . . a tender, pleasurable self-pity" (216). Unlike Jim, Sharon does not capitulate to the past in her longing; her sense of loss is a sign of a new connectedness. Although she is drawn back emotionally as her brother-in-law drives her from Cora's funeral, Sharon chooses to move forward.

A remarkable statement follows that echoes Jim Burden's observation about life being a circle. "Whatever life held in her future for her, it would prove to reside in this rimless past, approaching and then fading like the gong of a crossing bell" (216-217). Again Morris seems to be rewriting Cather's story. However, Sharon's movement back is an act of maturity rather than of denial. Morris is suggesting that a rejection of the past is as constricting as an immersion in it. The past needs to be confronted imaginatively so that one can shape its influence rather than be overpowered by it. This requires more strength than Jim has developed. He never rebels against his grandparents, teachers, or wife. Applauded and pushed along, he has his way smoothed out for him. Sharon does rebel; she takes risks in leaving and breaks new ground. Through this she develops the strength to confront her past and establish a new relationship with it. For Jim the circle means only a return to a starting place; for Sharon it means an encompassing of all experience so that wholeness, at least to some extent, can be achieved.

After leaving Ántonia's farm, Jim has an unfulfilling day in Black Hawk. The town never had caught his imagination, and whatever good memories he has cannot be relived because the town has changed. After Sharon leaves the funeral, she is driven to the Crossways Inn to meet Alexandra, the speaker at the Women World Wide convention. Although Sharon now feels connected to her past, the present it has become in rural Nebraska has no appeal. Entering the motel, "she breathed the bracing air of womanly independence" (218). In Alexandra she has found a new

Cora, a synthesis of past and present. At least on a thematic level, this justifies the book's ending, an early Sunday morning walk to witness the sunrise, which contrasts with Jim's autumn, sunset walk into the open prairie that takes him back to "the incommunicable past" (372).

Wright Morris has reacted against the epic vision of the pioneer past that Willa Cather seems to celebrate.[11] By rereading *My Ántonia* in the light of its misprisioning or misreading by Morris in **Plains Song,** we see that Cather herself, through her novel's contradictions and omissions, calls into question that vision. Cather was a part of a social milieu symbolized by Frederick Jackson Turner's thesis of an America in decline as it entered a postfrontier era. Morris, like historian Patricia Limerick, looks back on the frontier past from a different context and sees a world not so different from the present that has emerged from it.

The most significant gain for these new interpreters of the West may not be a more accurate picture of the past than their precursors left them; Limerick herself admits that she is as guilty as Turner was of presentism (31). Rather, they gain a "useable past" and thus free themselves from the longing look back that only can see the present in terms of loss.

Notes

1. Willa Cather, *My Ántonia* 299; and Wright Morris, *Plains Song: For Female Voices* 1.

2. James E. Miller, Jr. in "*My Ántonia*: A Frontier Drama of Time" and Blanche H. Gelfant, among others, have clarified Jim's central role in the novel. Morris' critics are doing what Cather's early critics did, putting the pioneer woman in the center and missing the central role of the more self-conscious character. Sharon does not narrate as Jim does, but much of the novel is told from her point of view.

3. Tiny, a minor character, is Cather's clearest depiction in this novel of the modern materialist. She has the spirited independence of Ántonia, shown in her leading the dancing at the hotel to Blind D'Arnalt's music (189-191). However, because she does not have Ántonia's love of the land, she leaves and becomes corrupted. She is the only character to mock Jim for not being able to break away from his grandparents (215). Her disfigurement—"She lost three toes from one of those pretty little feet" (302)—is a Hawthornesque way for Jim to set forth his cautiously conservative moral stance. Wick Cutter, another character caught up with money, receives more attention but can only sustain the role of a melodramatic curiosity.

4. Blanche Gelfant gives a much darker picture of this, "the railroad penetrating the virgin fields" (64), as does Leo Marx's *The Machine in the Garden.*

5. Annette Kolodny's *The Lay of the Land* extensively develops this idea.

6. Both Sharon and Willa Cather were raised in rural Nebraska but were not a part of farm life, were eager to escape this area and went East to establish careers in the arts; and were strong-minded, independent, unmarried women who fit in well in a cultured society. Morris also created a specific incident that recalls Cather. Sharon at one point goes to Columbus and returns "with her hair cut like a man's" (70-71). Cather also cut her hair short around the time when she was planning to study medicine.

7. This must be an allusion to Alexandra, the strong pioneer heroine of *O Pioneers!*

8. When Anton does return, his relationship with Ántonia does not disturb Jim's visions. As a number of critics have noted, the Cuzak marriage is more a friendship than a marriage; sexuality is absent. James Woodress, in *Willa Cather: A Literary Life,* states that Cather's greatest failing as an artist is her inability to show adult heterosexual relationships positively (299). Critics have also noted Morris' reticence in dealing with sexuality.

9. Gelfant notes that "Jim describes [Ántonia] finally as a 'stalwart, brown woman, flat-chested, her curly brown hair a little grizzled'—his every word denuding her of sensual appeal" (73).

10. Miller, in "The Nebraska Encounter: Willa Cather and Wright Morris," characterizes Cather's and Morris' created worlds by pointing out the central terrors they hold. In Cather's world it is the prairie itself. Morris' world holds terror that is self-made. "His world is the Cather world inverted, made comfortable and prosperous, fatuous and tranquil, but filled with terrors that Ántonia never imagined—terrors of a flaccid modern America that has, somehow, somewhere, misplaced her soul" (167).

11. In using the term *epic,* I have in mind M. M. Bakhtin's explanation in *The Dialogic Imagination*: "In the epic world view, 'beginning,' 'first,' 'founder,' 'ancestor,' 'that which occurred earlier' and so forth are not merely temporal categories but *valorized* temporal categories. . . . All the really good things (i.e., the 'first' things) occur *only* in this past . . . the epic past is called the 'absolute past' for good reason: it is both monochronic and valorized (hierarchical); it lacks any relativity, that is, any gradual, purely temporal progressions that might connect it with the present. It is walled off absolutely from all subsequent times" (15). In contrast, Morris' characters belong more to time than to space. The differences between Cora, Sharon, and Caroline have more to do with the era to which they belong than with the place in which they live.

Works Cited

Athearn, Robert G. *The Mythic West in Twentieth-Century America.* Lawrence: UP of Kansas, 1986.

Bakhtin, M. M. *The Dialogic Imagination.* Trans. Caryl Emerson and Michael Holquist. Austin: U of Texas P, 1981.

Bennet, Mildred R. *The World of Willa Cather.* Lincoln: U of Nebraska P, 1961.

Bloom, Harold. *The Anxiety of Influence: A Theory of Poetry.* New York: Oxford UP, 1973.

———. *A Map of Misreading.* New York: Oxford UP, 1975.

Cather, Willa. *My Ántonia.* Boston: Houghton, 1918.

———. *O Pioneers!* Boston: Houghton, 1913.

Gelfant, Blanche H. "The Forgotten Reaping-Hook: Sex in *My Ántonia.*" *American Literature* 43 (1971): 62-80.

Kolodny, Annette. *The Lay of the Land.* Chapel Hill: U of North Carolina P, 1975.

Limerick, Patricia Nelson. *The Legacy of Conquest: The Unbroken Past of the American West.* New York: Norton, 1987.

Marx, Leo. *The Machine in the Garden.* New York: Oxford UP, 1964.

Masters, Edgar Lee. *Spoon River Anthology.* New York: Macmillan, 1915.

Miller, James E., Jr. *My Ántonia:* A Frontier Drama of Time." *American Quarterly* 10 (1958): 476-484.

———. "The Nebraska Encounter: Willa Cather and Wright Morris." *Prairie Schooner* 41 (1967): 165-167.

Morris, Wright. *Plains Song: For Female Voices.* 1980 New York: Penguin, 1981.

———. *The Territory Ahead.* 1957. Lincoln: U of Nebraska P, 1978.

Pomeroy, Earl. "Toward a Reorientation of Western History: Continuity and Environment." *The Mississippi Valley Historical Review* 51 (1955): 579-600.

Turner, Frederick Jackson. *The Frontier in American History.* 1920. Tucson: U of Arizona P, 1986.

Woodress, James. *Willa Cather: A Literary Life.* Lincoln: U of Nebraska P, 1987.

Joe Hall (essay date 1991)

SOURCE: "Wright Morris' *The Field of Vision*: A Rereading of the Scanlon Story," in *Journal of American Culture,* Vol. 14, No. 2, Summer, 1991, pp. 53-7.

[In the following essay, Hall offers an allegorical interpretation by using a character's story in Morris's novel The Field of Vision.*]*

Interpreters of *The Field of Vision* agree with characters in the novel in dismissing Scanlon as "a mummified effigy of the real thing," more dead than alive (*The Field of Vision* [hereafter abbreviated as *FV*] 101).[1] While these descriptions are correct, they fail to account for Scanlon's

nevertheless remembering a tale which conveys the core of the creative western myth. This core is the vision of new possibilities open to those heroic enough to make a dangerous journey through unfamiliar territory.

Critics usually think of Boyd as the central voice in the novel, partly because he is the contemporary artist and the only adult character whose perceptions change significantly. Yet, his change is only the realization that the "real" things such as schoolhouses are temporal and unreal while the pictures of "real" things in our mind, established in a context by telling stories, are real and lasting (*FV* 232). Although Boyd states this basic Wright Morris thesis, he neither tells a story which can free people from their denials nor does he hear the Scanlon story, which is bristling with possibilities.

The tale Scanlon tells is an imaginative reconstruction of "real" events into a story which can enable its hearers to see much where others see little. That the old man in the novel did not create the story but inherited it from his father and now carries it as the "mummified effigy" of the hero in the story does not distract from the story's power.

Some readers claim that the story is useless because Scanlon failed to turn with the century (*FV* 32, 42-43; Madden 139; Albers 99). Yet, Morris has Scanlon see better than anyone else what the century was going to be like; it turned back toward the East, which is controlled by materialistic definitions of success, and he refused to turn with it.[2] He waited at Lone Tree, where he had been born, not knowing he was waiting, until his daughter came with her grandson, Gordon, to take Scanlon home with her. When Gordon said his name was Davy Crockett, the old man knew he had an audience.

His refusal to turn with the century is more a negative judgment on the century than on Scanlon. The others in the novel ignore him because they turned with the century and so find Scanlon irrelevant. But those who turned are more the frozen ones than Scanlon. Two years after *The Field of Vision,* Morris published *The Territory Ahead,* [hereafter abbreviated as *TA*] a set of essays on American literature. In that book he described the twentieth century as a time of escape from new experience (101-102), a way of closing the possibility of seeing underneath us the chaos of a world dissolving, "too tragic for any words" (*TA* 111). The twentieth century established a business culture "with its downtown men and its uptown women, its out-of-town children, and its mindless cultural problems" (99). Morris follows Henry James in describing the narrowness of the concerns of the business world; it has little use for the hundreds of other relationships possible to man in the civilized world (201-202). "It is not our barbarism," Morris writes, "but our civilization that gave [James] dread" (189). "Progress" is the great demon which excludes the strange gods who lead us to large notions (211-12, 230-31).

The "mindless cultural problems" of the twentieth century are illustrated in the characters in *The Field of Vision* who turn toward the new century. The McKees bought into the century and succeeded; that is, they are cliché-ridden people, having spent thirty years of married life trying to be certain that the one original event in their lives will not happen again. Boyd, who rebelled against the clichés of success, nevertheless has chosen to succeed, though in this case as a failure. Either kind of success is hollow (*FV* 63; also see Morris' discussion in "Wright Morris' *Field of Vision*: A Conversation," 149). Having failed to walk on water after kissing McKee's fiancé, his thoughts circle around the kiss, the failed walk on water, and a stolen pocket from Ty Cobb's baseball pants as measures of what did not work.

The other major character in the novel, Dr. Leopold Lehmann, is observer and interpreter; he understands the sense of risk and change in Scanlon's story, but doesn't have an imaginative fiction that holds his understanding. Lehmann, for example, puzzles over the minotaur image as he watches the bull fight around which all the memories and stories in the novel revolve. In the midst of this labyrinth, he sees the matador gored from behind, blending with the bull for a moment as the minotaur. "Man," Lehmann thinks, "could only take wing on the thrust of his past, and at the risk of toppling on his face" (114). Much of the novel deals with such risky transformations; when the transformation succeeds, facts are transformed into enduring fiction. Yet, no fiction in the novel provides the open-ended experience of risk in life except Scanlon's.

Scanlon's story is at the heart of the novel, but Boyd's observations help describe its significance. Boyd realizes what kind of story is needed as he reflects on the events of the bull fight and the reactions of the others to it. Early in the novel, Boyd recognizes that he has been a fool; he has pursued transformation but failed, then pursued failure. As the matador is gored, someone asks why he was in the ring if he did not expect to be gored. Boyd recognizes then that heroes are made of risks. Further, he knows that life consists of pieces of experience, stories, and reflections, like a puzzle, except that one does not find the solution to the puzzle. He must create the solution. A major problem in living, however, is to avoid creating a solution that embalms the creator; the pattern has to be kept open, the puzzle puzzling (155).

The twentieth century, Boyd recognizes, has no such open pattern, but all is rendered safe, the risks are gone, and nothing is transformed. Everyone wants to think of himself as being something, not becoming someone (194-95). At this point, Boyd recognizes a change in his perceptions: instead of only failure, he sees beauty in the passion behind struggles everywhere, as in the bull fight—when the bull is dead and the cloth is no longer used in the dance at the center of the circles of life, the passion and beauty are gone (199). Finally, Boyd realizes that if passion is to endure, it, like his memories, must be embodied in a living form, such as a story. Memories endure in stories about the memories: he tells the boy about his capturing Ty Cobb's pocket; then, with the story to animate Gordon, Boyd sets him in the bull ring to re-capture his Davy Crockett hat, re-enacting the story, not an event. Yet, with all this wisdom, Boyd does not find a story which enables him to court possibility instead of failure.

The Scanlon story does all that Boyd and Lehmann think a story should do. That is, it provides a context for seeing. Twentieth-century people avoid such stories, since they could cause them to see that they have not lived. To twentieth-century people, Scanlon has a screw loose or "didn't really live in this world" (14). This last judgment, by Scanlon's wife, is correct, though meant to be a criticism. Scanlon lives in his story, but to the extent that the twentieth century has shaped itself by turning east and freezing possibility, the old west story cannot be lived in it. Scanlon "had renounced his children the moment it was clear that they intended to face their future, or even worse, like his daughter Lois, make a success of it" (43). He had determined to stand his ground; Boyd had the insight to note that Scanlon was "a man who found more to live for, in looking backward, than those who died all around him, looking ahead" (44). He grew up listening to his father talk and from that developed the story that nobody but the boy Gordon heard completely.

Morris describes the town Scanlon was born in as having once had some potential, enough to let us know why Scanlon stayed. It might have been a typical turn-of-the-century rural town, built to human scale with the potential of enabling people to live without avoiding most of life. More importantly, Scanlon, listening to his father's stories, "may have thought him immortal, his mind full of deathless deeds" (47). Those imagined deeds cause the twentieth century to seem a betrayal by comparison. Nurturing his story in the bull ring in Mexico, Scanlon hears McKee ask, "Don't it take you back, Gordon?" But Scanlon knows McKee never had a place to which he could go back, since he "had done nothing but try to go forward all of his life" (52).

The Scanlon story creates a past that can launch man solidly into the future as possibility instead of as safety. Lehmann argues that the true thrust forward is not driven by the need to exclude risk and evil, but comes from our evolutionary heritage, a heritage that confuses distinctions between good and evil and notes transformations as the places where life happens (166, 203-205). The Scanlon story, told in mythopoeic language and patterns, is Morris' masterful embodiment of Lehmann's theories. It makes clear why Scanlon, telling his father's timeless story as his own, refused to go forward into the twentieth century.

His story begins with people leaving their civilized homes for the west, where civilized conventions are irrelevant. In the west, new gods need to be conjured from the landscape; only the character that Scanlon comes to think of as himself is able to 1) recognize that he is not in civilization, 2) abandon the old gods and values in favor of those which seem appropriate to the desert, and 3) die to the self that knew good and evil in the old life. Once these events have happened, he can journey as a different being through hell in order to reach a new self-understanding.

In the story, Scanlon is the scout for a wagon train. The people have left their homes in the east, carrying furniture that indicates that they expect where they are going will be the same as the place they left. This being the case, Scanlon cannot understand why they left. The further they go in the desert, the more objects they are forced to leave by the trail because of the difficulty of the passage. "You could see what a man valued most in his life from where he put it down" (96). Finally, friends and relations who are old or sick are put out; nevertheless, the process reveals that things are valued more than people, since although things were put off first, people continue to pick up things others had dumped, but "none of the wagons ever stopped to pick people up" (96).

In addition to their materialism and their desire that things be the same where they are going as they were in the place they left, they also expect the same gods to rule the new territory. Yet, to Scanlon, the nature of the desert makes clear that they are entering "the Devil's country." Everything is upside down, "with the Devil upstairs and the Lord in the basement," which might mean the Devil is in control, doing the opposite of what the Lord would be expected to do: he "turned the rivers into sand, and the lakes into salt," and the more the Reverend Tennant prays, "the drier it got" (97). That is, life is no longer divided for Scanlon into the usual evils and goods, since perhaps what the Devil does in his own land is "good." With this concept, Scanlon accepts the nature of the desert they are plunging into and believes that the Devil might have characteristics similar to those which humans have: he is at a "certain disadvantage" in that he wants companionship but cannot seem to take it and has to "tag along, like a kid, to see how it worked out" (98).

Scanlon admits that he has not been in a place like this before and so can respond to the place, whereas the others believe what they want to believe, not what is appropriate to a place in which everything is upside down. They, for example, want to believe in what they saw on Criley's map; therefore, they follow a trail that exists only on the map and in their imagination. They also want to believe things are not as bad as they are (they cannot imagine hell in their future) and that the Lord rules as he always has. Scanlon, on the other hand, knows the nature of this journey and does not try to support himself by believing things are as they have always been or are the way one would like them to be.

The second episode of the Scanlon story begins in present time at the bull fight. Scanlon hears the Mexican crowd shouting for *agua* to wet the matador's cape. Boyd, the eastern adolescent grownup, uses Pepsi-Cola for water and teaches the boy Gordon how to make it spew. For Scanlon, however, *agua* means life-giving water in the desert; eastern fools do not know how to value water. When the boy Gordon, for example, is squirting pop into his mouth he doesn't hear Scanlon tell about the *agua* that gives life; he is captured by Boyd's foolishness. Later when Scanlon ends his account of hell, he spits on the Pepsi stains and

shouts for water as he envisions his own death—again indicating the silliness of playing with Pepsi when life and death are the stakes for those who can see.

The pervasive imagery of the second episode is death. *Agua* has not been found in the desert. No living thing is in the desert other than Scanlon and the others with the wagons. Scanlon can hardly believe that the people in the wagons are alive, not only because the desert is empty of other life, but also because their actions are incongruent with their location. They are in the desert because they want the very things they left in the east, but Scanlon knows they are in a place of death (143-45, 150).

Since only Scanlon senses that the ruler of this place, the Devil, can be something of an ally, and since he knows where they are headed and can admit it, then he does not fear it. Perhaps because he was lonely himself, he identified with the loneliness of the Devil early on, and now that identification is strengthened when Scanlon takes a nap in the desert. He imagines the Devil woke him by sitting beside him, leaving some six-sided stones around a hole to signify his humanness. Scanlon develops further his "shameful liking" for the devil, suspecting he "might even need food and water for himself" (146). He puts the rocks in his canteen, not because they do any good, but because they remind him that the Devil might be for him more than he is against him. This indicates that Scanlon is the only one in the party who trusts the situation as it is and finds some comfort in it. For the others, sheer hostility is arrayed against them; they pray to the wrong power to save them, and they gain any comfort they can scrape together by thinking of places they left.

After Scanlon stores the stone amulets, he climbs a mountain and sees hell, a large black part of the desert, ahead. When he sees it, he also sees the way out of it. There, running through hell, is a canyon. Once one is in the canyon, the only way out of hell is straight through it, following the canyon (146-48). The other men on the journey refuse to believe they have to go into hell to get out of it. They expect a way around.

As Scanlon scouts the canyon to find a way to get the wagons down into it, the identity of the place becomes more clear. Huge rocks have been thrown about "as though some giant had been playing with them." A shadow, one with wings, seems to accompany him, reminding him of the smelly, croaking bird he has been associating with the Devil. He "has a pretty good idea" that the canyon leads to the heart of hell, but he is not frightened; he knows where they have to go, so "if it was hell they were going to, he wanted a look at it" (147-48).

When they begin to lower the wagons down the slope into the canyon, they encounter the strangeness more fully. After two wagons have been lowered into the canyon, the rope snaps and the third wagon crashes. A young woman, Samantha, then shoots the bird, as if it were to blame, and it falls on the shattered wagon, as if that were its target.

The other women, seeming to relish the stink as animals would, clean it and cook it. They seem no longer human: one woman who used to fear death seems pleased by it now, and "nobody troubled to thank the Lord" for the bird—perhaps because they are acting like animals and because they at last sense that the bird is not from the Lord—at least not from the one to whom they usually pray.

While the bird is being cooked, a strange wind starts where they are and sucks out the fire. A "crazy-looking cloud" scrapes up the canyon and drops dry rain on them which "scared Scanlon worse than no rain at all"; then a mule died as if the wind had sucked his life out (149-50). These signs suggest death, but Scanlon is not afraid of dying. He is, however, afraid his fellow humans will eat him after he is dead. He leaves them in order to die by himself (being off by himself made him feel so good that he "ran around like crazy, hooting like a kid" [150]) and comes into the black place, which is like a dead sea. This unearthly place disorients him:

> He couldn't tell you if he walked backwards or forwards, or to the right or the left. He couldn't tell you if he thought that was right or wrong. As a matter of fact, he didn't care, but the one thing he could tell you, if you asked him, was exactly where he was. He was in Hell. Knowing that, he didn't seem to mind it so much.
>
> (151)

Right and wrong are ambiguous now, as is direction. He has ventured into hell and so is open to any possibility now.

The only thing that concerns him is that he cannot know what time it is so he can know "when he had done what he could" and therefore "ought to give up" (186). Finally, he stumbles on the body of a man "who had been dead for some time." The wind makes a "ghostly music" come out of his mouth, "a wild hollow sound, like a shell. . . . Scanlon had the feeling he had seen the body somewhere, and he had. The crisp yellow beard was his own. The dead man was himself" (187). He was not surprised by this because he knew "there were two men within him, and he knew for sure that one of them had died." He suspected it was the better man who was dead, and that he had died of knowing he was in Hell.

The "better man" in Scanlon is the part that knows the good and evil, as it is in most eastern, settled people. Now the "shadow" no longer haunts him; the part of Scanlon that is left is that which felt a "shameful liking" for the Devil, whereas that in him which was ashamed of this affection, the "better man," is dead. The man who is left is prepared to make the risky passage through hell, knowing what it is he is going through and prepared to meet it for what it is.[3]

The discovery of the death of his better self also gives Scanlon new knowledge which changes his situation. First, the man who had died had made tracks into hell, whereas Scanlon had made only grease spots. The tracks changed the nature of hell: "but it was not the same sort of Hell, with tracks in it, anymore than Scanlon was the same sort of man, now that he knew who had died, and what time it was" (187). The tracks in hell seem to mark it, making it penetrable. In a similar way, Scanlon, knowing his better self has died, is able to orient himself to time. The Devil has already killed everything in him that it could want (his sense of good and evil), so it is too late to try to save these qualities. He is free to journey without fear across hell; there is nothing he can lose.

Back in camp, Scanlon is confronted with three people who live by the old virtues. They believe in themselves as favored, valuable beings, and in the things which they think give them value. The two men encourage the most "civilized" woman to put on all the clothes and jewelry she can so they can take it with them as they leave to save themselves. Since they do not recognize where they are, they will not listen to Scanlon, who knows that "the thing about Hell was that you had to go in, if what you wanted was out" (189). They try instead to skirt around hell and all three die. When Scanlon finds the woman's remains, "no one had taken the rings from her fingers, the money from the purse at her throat, or the gold from the extra teeth she had brought along." Those like Scanlon who know they are in Hell and that it is time to make the passage through it have no use for this kind of extra baggage. He, with his better self dead, is not intimidated and does not insist that something is wrong with his fantastic view of what is happening. He takes the women, children, and Reverend Tennant straight into hell. When they are well into it, they discover "water cupped in a rock, and one of those little six sided stones at the bottom of it" (190). Since Scanlon connects the stones with the protective nature of the Devil, he takes this as a sign that the Devil has brought them through, just as he led them in.

Scanlon's story does not represent a dead end, but is a tale of courageous risk-taking that is a theme of the best of the frontier stories, passed down, reformulated, and finally handed to people who seem ready to hear it. The Scanlon story, far from representing a failure to feel or to commit oneself (Crump 120), proposes a hero for the next century, the person who has died to his expectations and thus is prepared to meet the strange gods waiting for him if he has the courage to go through the deserts of hard experience instead of trying to skirt comfortably around. The bearer of this story, Scanlon, is only an "effigy of the real thing," but he nevertheless carries a story that can make a creative response to the century possible. Recognizing such stories as guides to seeing can also enable us to distinguish between frontier stories that have the power to encourage a risky thrust into the future and those stories that might freeze us into nostalgia.

Notes

1. Madden, for example, takes Scanlon as proof of what happens if all lines lead to the past. He believes Scanlon failed to build anything for future generations.

Crump appreciates Scanlon's story more than others, naming his dream the "most powerful narrative thread" in the novel, but concludes that this powerful tale is designed to evade the present. He correctly identifies the desert as the intolerable wasteland of the twentieth century, but believes the "real," or morally responsible Scanlon dies in the desert. Consequently, Scanlon fails to commit himself to facing the desert. Crump seems to ignore how the mythical Scanlon fulfilled the story-teller Scanlon's moral: "Shortest way to Heaven's right smack through Hell." Only the Scanlon of the story goes into Hell; the others try to skirt around.

Fullerton believes that Scanlon's "refusal to confront the modern world" leads him to subvert the sensibility of his great-grandson "so completely that the child risks the loss of meaningful life." Albers concentrates on how the characters struggle to break free from the past; the frontier story embodied the self-made man dream with no means of realization in the twentieth century. Whereas Boyd and McKee break free, they are lost in clichés. Scanlon, however, is lost in "the secondhand fantasy of his father's trek west." Albers quotes Morris as stating that "character . . . is primarily an imaginative fact, a fiction to which the flesh is incurably responsive. It is the fiction that shapes the fact." Still, Albers does not recognize that Scanlon's fiction takes on a significant life of its own, providing the "imaginative fact" to which flesh might creatively respond.

2. In an interview, Wright Morris said that Scanlon types are products of a tension in certain "personalities that will almost compel them to believe in the most bizarre types of escape. . . . The small plains community, or the western community, will provide the environment that makes these people possible. In such a community, we make myths about ourselves" ("Wright Morris' *Field of Vision*: A Conversation" 150). The interviewer was not interested in how such myths might help break the grip of the ordinary on those able to push their clichés to deeper sources, so Morris said no more on this subject.

3. See Crump for an interpretation in which the death means that the morally responsible Scanlon is left behind dead. Since this one is dead, Scanlon fails to commit himself; from here on he evades emotional commitments. Crump overlooks the reality of the desert. Only the one open to new moral commitments and not overly tied by emotional commitments can make it "right smack through Hell."

Works Cited

Albers, Randall K. "The Female Transformation: The Role of Women in Two Novels by Wright Morris." *Prairie Schooner* 53 (1979): 95-115.

Crump, G. B. *The Novels of Wright Morris*. Lincoln: University of Nebraska Press, 1978.

Fullerton, Adelyn. "Myth, the Minotaur, and Morris's *The Field of Vision. West Georgia College Review* 16 (1984): 1-8.

Madden, David. *Wright Morris*. New York: Twayne Publishers, 1965.

Morris, Wright. *The Field of Vision*. Lincoln: University of Nebraska Press, 1956.

———. *The Territory Ahead: Critical Interpretations in American Literature*. New York: Atheneum, 1963.

"Wright Morris' *Field of Vision*: A Conversation." *The Black Warrior Review* 10 (1983): 143-55.

Wright Morris with Olga Carlisle and Jodie Ireland (interview date 1991)

SOURCE: "The Art of Fiction," in *The Paris Review,* Vol. 33, No. 120, Fall, 1991, pp. 54-94.

[*In the following interview, Morris discusses his books, his method of composition, and the work of other writers.*]

Morris lives with his wife Josephine in Mill Valley, California, in a small contemporary wooden house tucked into a steep hillside, amidst a profusion of climbing ivy. The house, with its wide balcony, is sheltered by fragrant laurel trees and feels isolated although it is located in the center of Marin County, an area affected by relentless urban growth. Even as the interviewers drove out of San Francisco and across the Golden Gate Bridge, they passed shopping malls where gardens had flourished only last year. The Morrises' immediate neighborhood remains untouched, however, and during the interview birds sang peacefully among the wild forget-me-nots on a bank near their home.

Inside, the house is plain and comfortable. Bookshelves line the living room, where there are deep sofas and piles of newly published art books and magazines. Several photographs by Morris hang on the walls: stark, beautiful images of the plains, the people who once populated them, and the objects they used. Morris also collects prints by the Abstract Expressionists, and a black-and-white Gorky hangs over the mantel. An outsized television set stands to the left of the fieldstone fireplace, near an audio system that brings Bach or Vivaldi into the room with an eerie fidelity. Bright striped fabrics and other mementos of Morris's trips to Mexico are scattered about the living room. One of his books lies on the coffee table: ***Love Affair: A Venetian Journal.*** It is the only one of his photo-texts that does not specifically document the American Midwest, as well as the only one with color photographs.

Wright Morris sat in his favorite vintage Eames chair as he spoke. When the light turned golden at the end of the interview, Jo Morris brought in a tray of tea and cookies and a perfect apple pie.

[*Interviewer*]: *To this day your fiction is considered experimental. Critics have never had an easy time fitting you into any particular group or movement. How do you see yourself? Do you consider yourself a storyteller?*

[Wright Morris]: I can tell a story and often do, but it has never occurred to me to "plot" one. If I'd taken writing courses, as is done today, someone would surely have instructed me in plotting, but I discovered that a narrative could be sustained without plotting, and I have held to that practice.

Since you don't plot, what is it that carries you forward in the narrative?

Let me illustrate: my story, **"Victrola,"** is about an old man and a dog he has inherited from a neighbor. They tolerate—but do not like—each other. The man is ill at ease with the dog's appearance, which he finds prehistoric, the head skull-like, the eyes too small, etc. There is a standoff when they look at each other. Predictably, they will have a confrontation. The origin of this is that one day I had seen this creature at the foot of the driveway. His odd appearance disturbed me. His tail did not wag. His short white pelt had been worn through on the high spots. As I approached he turned and slunk away. Not seeing him again, I often thought about him. In my story the character, Bundy, inherits the dog from his neighbor. They are never at ease with each other. Their daily walk is an ordeal for them both. This walk takes place in Mill Valley, where I live, and follows a prescribed route to the village park. Along this route I am scrupulous about details, but all that takes place on the walk is fiction. This commingling of a real place and imagined events provides the framework for my fiction. There is a narrative line but no plot. I accept what happens (what occurs to me) and imagine an appropriate resolution.

What about "voice" in this setup?

The voice of the narrator—the narration—is crucial. If it is right, the narrative seems effortless, with one incident following another, in the manner of letting out a kite's string. I think I came by this manner, this confidence, in the absence of the old-style linear narration—the time that flowed like a river from the past into the future. That is not the way I comprehended time. My time is cyclical—abstract, yet keenly felt. It seems appropriate to the modern consciousness. Fictive moments contain both the past and the future. Joyce captured this complexity in *Ulysses.* My style of plotless narration is one way of appropriating time to my purposes. All reasonably fully conscious people do this. We have no access to the old time, so we make do with our privately spun new times. I feel a faintly physical vertigo when I hear of jets that fly faster than sun-time—or in the opposing direction. It ain't natural.

Were you aware of what other writers were doing when you started?

I was slow to read my contemporaries, being too busy writing. I read schoolbooks in grade school; in high school, a book that enthralled me was *Literature and Life.* It began with stories from *Beowulf* and the adventures of King Arthur's knights. Books were not part of my home environment. I read *A Boy's Life* and the Tom Swift series. This absence of books, of what we think of as culture, spared me of having a fix on certain writers, which the young reader is prone to do.

Do you think this contributed to developing your own voice and style of narration?

It left me free from the influence of familiar romances, but encouraged me to take an active part in the vernacular for which I showed some early talent. I was a talker, and took part in class productions of *Huck Finn* and *Tom Sawyer.* That my style is profoundly oral I may owe to this circumstance. The sound is crucial. It frequently leads me to take considerable liberties with the syntax. As Yeats said: "As I altered my syntax, I altered my intellect."

When did you make the decision to be a writer? You took a trip to Europe when you were twenty-three. Did you go there to experience Europe as a writer?

In my third year of college I read Richard Halliburton's *The Royal Road to Romance.* It inflamed my desire for adventure. The notion of becoming a writer had been planted, but had not crystallized. In the spring I was in Paris. I sometimes played Ping-Pong at the American Club with a young man from Boston. One day he asked me what it was I was writing. Well, what *was* I writing! I gave it a moment's thought. He went on to say he had connections at *The Atlantic,* in case I had something to submit. Trifling incidents like this can crystallize budding sentiments.

Had you written much at the time?

Not a thing! At that time, however, I was reading a novel by Montherlant, *Les Celibataires,* and I identified with the two aging bachelors. Being moved in this way was new to me. I felt a longing to create lifelike characters myself. This latter impression so reinforced the first that I was nudged from the haze of sentiment to actually think of myself as a writer. What was I about to write? Well, let me think!

So you returned determined to write? Did you come back with a desire to recover your past?

The fact that my past was "missing" proved crucial. Back in California was this void—not my recent adventures in Europe—that proved to be my subject. Insofar as I was able, I began at the beginning, like Joyce's "nicens moo cow" coming down along the road to charm the wits out of "baby Tuckoo!" Considering my ignorance it was a bold start. I had both the memory and the words for it. Joyce, of course, covered this ground in a few pages, but I was drilling the well for my past; three hundred pages later I was still preteen, in Nebraska's Platte Valley. I had left the plains, as a boy of nine, with few emotional ties. My mother died at my birth. I had an absentee relationship with my father, who was a kind and affectionate man, and as baffled by me as I was by him. He had married a young Omaha woman closer to my age than to his own. We were soon in Omaha, where I had a *Penrod and Sam* boyhood very dear to a writer of fiction. Five years later we moved to Chicago—another move that I feel to have been destined, and have never exhausted—and from there to college in California. Each of these moves was a form of exile and gifted me with new resources.

Do you see exile as a positive experience for the writer?

Yes. Both the idea and the fact of exile are critical, and especially for me. California has been the beckoning cloudland, to which I often return.

Yet you seem to have proceeded from a sense of life and adventure, rather than from the idea of exile in the service of art.

Yes, that's right. I have been spared the level of sophistication that came naturally to Europeans. Joyce at eighteen, for instance, was more self-aware than I was at forty. I had the advantage of living forty years as a naïf.

You consider that a literary advantage?

It is, unless you have Joyce's talent. Though nothing happened to Joyce after he left Dublin, his lifework was already laid out in his extraordinary mind. In this respect Joyce was unique even in that very self-conscious era. He was ahead of them all in self-confidence. There's the story about him going to visit Yeats. He hadn't published anything. Yeats says: "Well, how are you, young man?" He waits to be admired, and Joyce just treats him like a has-been.

Are Southern writers an exception to the notion of writers and exile?

Perhaps for the Southern writer the complex problem of being a Southerner is adequate. They too are researching the past. They become exiles through the mere fact that the South is no longer what it was.

Did it ever occur to you to go back to Europe and write over there?

It would have been impossible. Traveling was expensive, and moreover I was never drawn back to Europe for the same reasons that I was drawn elsewhere. With Europe I have only ties that have developed from later interests and tastes, a taste for Venice for instance. Then, of course, the war sealed Europe off.

When you came back from Europe with your mind made up to write, what did you work on?

Curiously, not a word about my European adventures, though it was material tailored to the needs of a young writer. I turned away from this windfall to recall my boy's life on the plains, a cross-country drive, and the few weeks I had spent on a horse-and-buggy farm. I began with the short, untutored but poetically dense sketches in the manner of the *Spoon River Anthology*—a book I actually had yet to read. Even in the first of these pieces the style and concerns of a lifetime are revealed. They speak with a documentary economy, as if the writer had seen too many Farm Security photographs. I had actually seen none. But on the long drive from New York to California we had crossed the dust bowl of Nebraska, desolate farms, bedraggled remnants of cattle, defeated men and women with the aspect of sharecroppers, towns with idle farmers congregating in squares, or under the shade of trees, or in domino or billiard parlors, where they chewed on four-cent cigars and bore little kinship, it seemed to me, to the people I had seen from the top of a freight car just a year before, traveling east. Many of these men would join the stream of Okies headed for California. I saw them only briefly. I did not fully understand what I was, but it left on my mind's eye the images I would see when I sat down to write. Back in the mid-twenties I had been on the road with my father on our first trip to California, and the reservoir of those impressions awaited me on my return from Europe.

Being on the road seems to be an important source of material for you.

Driving has been an important motif in my life and in my work. My first wife's people lived in Cleveland and we drove there once with a dog—a wonderful beast we were taking care of for a friend. We had to fix him up with goggles because he rode with his head out the window, and within twenty-five miles his eyes were watering and he was barking like a fiend. The trick was to get the goggles on while he was otherwise occupied. That dog was all soul. I used this story in several books.

When did you write your first novel, **My Uncle Dudley***?*

In the fall of 1940 I took a cross-country photo-safari, collecting *Inhabitants*. By January, I was in Los Angeles, where I holed up in a room near Echo Lake Park, very dear to my past, and in six weeks wrote a draft of *My Uncle Dudley,* a relatively uncluttered retelling of a bizarre and wonderful car trip to California in 1926, just far enough in the past to enhance the nostalgic haze. The book, quite literally, was a retrieval of that piece of my past.

Did the next book come more easily?

The writing of *Dudley* was an act of liberation. For several years I had compressed paragraphs to sentences, and turned away from narrative. *Dudley* is still overly compressed, but it does tell a story in a tradition about which, at the time, I knew nothing. It is so *oral* it is better recited.

Were your circumstances especially favorable for a young writer?

My wife taught school, which made it possible for me to work. She accepted the fact that the writer we both hoped I would be would find it slow going—that's how we found it. If a manuscript was returned, and many were, I applied myself and wrote another. I never doubted that when I wrote a good enough book, it would be published. Nor did I lack for any encouragement. William Faulkner's editor, Saxe Commins, waded through my early efforts and urged me to send him more, which I soon did. Some of this self-assurance was hardly to my advantage. I was in no way a student of the novel, who would learn the tricks of the trade and then perform. Each of my manuscripts proved to be a publishing problem. My first editor, Lambert Davis, of Harcourt Brace, gave me everything a young writer should have, including some great lunches. One day in 1945, my agent, Diarmuid Russell, reported that Maxwell Perkins had read *My Uncle Dudley* and liked it. So I was not without a welcome. The advantage of a long apprenticeship is that the writer is spared the sunburst of success when he might not be prepared for it. He is also spared fashionable opinions, and free to make or break them on his own terms.

How did you work at that time? Did you do many drafts?

I did. Perhaps too many. One more draft seemed a small thing for the slopes of Olympus. In the fifties, a very productive period, I seldom wrote less than three or four drafts, the first three single-spaced to save paper. Writing drafts, I soon learned to compose while writing, and this soon reduced their number.

Could you tell us something about your work habits?

I am a creature of habit. As soon as I was able to establish my writing habits—which are to start work in the morning and write until hungry, then again in the afternoon until tired—I stuck to this routine most of the days of the week. Once I had learned to compose as I wrote—to make corrections as I went along with a crayon or marking pencil—I would average eight to twelve pages a morning. In time I learned that random breaks—walking around, having a smoke, saving the house from woodpeckers—were creatively helpful. They jogged the mind from its rut, resolved impasses, opened up unforeseen vistas. Since all of my books are closely related, thirty or forty pages into a new book, I would begin to have glimpses of where it was going, and what would follow. *Ceremony in Lone Tree* grew like a branch from a passage in *The World in the Attic, The Field of Vision* from *War Games,* and so on. The disadvantage of these links is that I was never encouraged to stop and take stock, or consider what the public was reading. For better or for worse I was on a time schedule I had invented, doing work I had assigned to myself. Recycling was part of the next step forward, or backward. The loop back before the step forward began with *God's Country and My People,* a book of reappraisal before *Fire Sermon* and *A Life.* The multivoiced fiction of the fifties gave way to a relatively simple narration—the indulgently prodigal writer returning to beginnings.

Do you always work on a typewriter?

Seeing what I have done is important, seeing the way the words fall out, and how I mean to pace them. Seeing the word reassures me about it—as I am reassured or troubled when I pronounce it.

You have said that you have not been working as strenuously, but a great many books have come out in the last five or six years.

I continue to work because I'm a writer. No cliché is truer than that which says that the writer does not feel fully alive when he isn't writing. He doesn't always feel fully alive writing, but he feels more alive.

Except for that early break when you took photographs, was there ever a period when you did not write?

No, there never was such a period. All that training has turned me into a person with a particular type of consciousness—one made up of a great deal of what I'd call "fictive presence." Often it's the voice I'm working with which dominates; at other times it's one suggested by the events of the day. Whenever I take a walk I become involved in this fashion. It happens almost every day, and it contributes to short stories, which I've been doing recently. I'll see or hear something which will cause me on the instant to experiment with a "narrating voice." A few sentences will get me started. The character and tone of this voice will establish the nature of a story.

Do you find that characters develop in this same way, suggested by someone you see or meet?

Oh yes. For instance, I had no conception of the Indian, Blackbird, in *A Life.* I was teaching at Princeton and I encountered an Indian boy from the Hopi tribe. There he was, the real McCoy—not the kind of person to whom you could say, "Let's have a Coke!" I don't think I saw him more than three times. Then he was gone—an isolated memory.

Do you find that people take root more solidly in your imagination when you meet them fleetingly?

Absolutely. This kind of encounter carries within it the virus of suggestion that dreams have. It's the brush you have with death that scares you; certain brief encounters catalyze the imagination in the same way. Fortunately, I think, I'm perfectly willing to let them lie until they ripen.

Don't you note things down?

Constantly, if I am not seated at the typewriter. I once thought I'd use a small tape recorder, but my thinking about the work at hand is closely tied to the physical act of writing—even when the writing proves to be illegible! I could never dictate a work of fiction.

If things are "ripe," as you say, then they resurface when you need them?

Yes. I have never kept a journal. The unavoidably self-conscious tone of a journal is inappropriate to ongoing writing. The attentive reader would sense this instantly, like the change of pitch in a train whistle. Katherine Anne Porter kept a journal, but seldom found that her observations would mesh with what she was writing. In her journal she reported seeing a small boy on a train in Texas with an inverted night pot stuck on his head. His mother was taking him to town to have it removed. He was not in pain, but profoundly humiliated. She described this unforgettably in her journal, yet it was something she never found a place for in her fiction. I would have shaped a new story around it. Perhaps it was, in its pathos, more my sort of material than hers.

Do you think the short story boom has something to do with the proliferation of writing programs?

Without question. Stories are something the talented student can learn to write, but he cannot learn to write a novel, which requires wide resources of experience. Short stories provide a chance for a writer to take certain risks with his own talent.

Is it possible to teach writing?

It is often possible for one writer to help another. I went without this help at my own peril, and it was costly. Yet it is also part of the furrow I plowed—I did it the slow way, and this shaped me as a writer.

What books do you like to teach?

Lawrence's *Women in Love,* Camus's *The Stranger*—but only the first thirty or forty pages!—*The Fall,* the perfect novel of the modern conscience: ambivalent, self-deceiving, self-serving. Something of Thomas Mann, Stein's *Three Lives,* Rilke's *Journal,* Frisch's *I'm Not Stiller* and samplings from *Winesburg, Ohio,* a book created out of "voice," out of vernacular.

It sounds as though you are interested in teaching sections of books.

The whole interests me less than the expressive part, those moments where the writer finds the bloom of his talent. Joyce's story "The Dead" is an example. Much that I love about Joyce is in it, free of the orchestrated performance which I admire but do not reread. This is profoundly unfair to many writers, but it brings out the essence of others. I see life in moments, grasp it in moments, and think this is pretty much our modern lot. Wholes escape us, unless we perceive them in a grain of sand. Increasingly, for me, the ambivalence of words is tiresome. They will prove whatever needs to be proved at the moment, and I am weary of these verbal irresolutions. It has led me to take

refuge in music. I push a button, and I am overwhelmed with the worlds of Vivaldi, Mozart, Stravinsky. Wordless resolutions to wordless impressions.

My generation, especially, was oversold on the power of words. That's not difficult to understand when you look at the writers who were doing the selling—Eliot, Joyce, Proust, Woolf, Mann, Stein, Lawrence, James. They were convinced that words had the power to resolve our problems. Words and more words—they created a new priesthood of selfhood.

Could you elaborate on that?

James epitomized the principle of being fully conscious with his artistic credo: "To be one on whom nothing is lost." I've always been affected by the sincerity of James's feeling in this matter, yet how could a man with such acute sensibility, with such intuition, ever imagine that "to be one on whom nothing is lost" is a bearable human situation? As acute as his response was to his own social milieu, he had no intuition of what the twentieth century was going to be. Within a few years he was to suffer the full torment of that particular conceit. He was brought to his knees by the First World War, and he never recovered from the shock of it, largely because, as he later realized, he had been living in a cuckoo land of his own sensibility. Yet most artists responded to his notion of being one on whom nothing is lost. Except that plebeian, philistine Wells, who was right there to say to James: "You old fraud. You're an amazing man, but really you are quite impossible." My heart goes out to James, but Wells was right.

As I see it, this coincided with Freud's plumbing of the subconscious. I see Freud as a fiction writer, an inspired fiction writer. Words have no other substance—they either convince you by their artistry or else there's nothing there. So here were Freud and James, just in time to cut the last nonconscious ties of man to his time, to his place, to his sense of nature. The fully conscious person became as free and as disconnected as words could possibly make him.

The culmination of James's credo can be seen in Proust's enshrinement of the involuntary memory. At the end of his book Proust's attack on realism and cinematography is an extreme example of the artist displacing life with his own subjective impressions of it. Involuntary impressions take precedence; they become the more ultimate reality. Joyce and Proust and Woolf and dozens of others are figures in the cult of self-consciousness. Ironically their lives were not really equal to the burden of self-fulfillment. Joyce's life, for instance, was a tragic life; he paid a price for his self-involvement and he knew it. But it does show the extent to which, in a culture of words, the idea of a supreme self-consciousness was undisputed.

Do you think Joyce was the first artist to see himself exclusively in terms of his art?

I think the notion of men who give themselves to writing as to a mistress began with the romantic poets—Shelley, Keats, Byron. They saw the poet as legislator, but of what?

The climax of this notion in western sensibility was a vision of the artist moving towards the summit of Olympus. By the time Joyce was published in this country, the concept of Olympus was a rather common one. I don't know of any writer who gives himself entirely to this notion who is not ridiculous.

Lawrence was unique in his ability to bring his perceptions to living, to the here and now, rather than just to the craft of writing. His exile was an escape from literature rather than an escape from life—with the exception of the Great War, when he really became a man in flight. But then he sought to reestablish connections, the same ones he'd gone to such pains to sever, he said: "We cannot bear connection, but we must." His self-consciousness had come full circle.

One man who knew what was happening was Knut Hamsun, a Scandinavian maverick, who wrote *The Growth of the Soil.* It is very long and may seem dated today, but it's one hell of a book about how the obsession with total freedom of the soul is not a resolution of the human condition but rather a predicament. Hamsun was deliberately rejecting the kind of sophistication he felt was destroying Europe. Unfortunately, this led him into the pitfall of sympathy with fascism—as so often happens he backed away from one pit only to fall into another.

In the late thirties, in California, I came upon Hamsun's book and also upon Hermann Broch's *The Sleepwalkers.* Both impressed me profoundly, though Broch's wears better because of his intellectual brilliance. I wrote to him— the first novelist I ever wrote to.

Did he respond?

Many months later I received a letter. Broch was living in Princeton, New Jersey, with the scholar Eric Kahler, and Kahler's family, just two blocks away from Albert Einstein. He said that if I came east, I should visit him. Now this was of course just a courtesy letter, but five years later we were living in Haverford, just an hour's ride away, and I called on him. Broch, Kahler, and several of their Austrian friends were sharing a large house, a haven for central European exiles. I had brought along a folio of my *Inhabitants,* photographs and texts. It seemed to me they would find the interlocking of my photos and texts bizarre, but they were responsive to the concept. Broch, in particular, was excited. He insisted I go to New York and show my work to Kurt Wolff of Pantheon Books, though whatever Wolff thought of the concept, he did not see the material as publishable. He was right, of course. Two years later I would persuade—the exact term—Maxwell Perkins of Scribner's to publish the volume by lining the walls of his office with the mounted photographs and texts.

*When you speak of connections reestablished, might the end of **Plains Song** be an example?*

Yes. Sharon Rose has spent her life severing ties. But she is devastated when she finally returns to her homeplace to find it bulldozed away, the family dispersed. What can she do to be saved? She can try to reestablish consciously the ties to place and people that she has cut. Exile and return for the writer are crucial replays of the flight from constraints and the need for their recovery.

The irony of that phrase of James's, "To be one on whom nothing is lost," lies in the fact that the word "lost," which gives it its power, is somehow incongruous with the notion of total consciousness; the essentially euphoric idea that one is not going to forget anything—the very idea that one could bear such a state—is incompatible with the reality of loss. The moment when one is truly aware of loss— loss through death, betrayal, the loss of friendship or self-esteem—that's the moment when one is really beginning to be fully conscious. And there is no cultural accommodation to help me or anyone else deal with these losses.

Do you remember some of the first books you bought?

Yes, because there were so few of them. In a bookstore in Waterbury, Connecticut, I bought Katherine Anne Porter's *Pale Horse, Pale Rider.* An extravagance at the time, but I bought it. I did the same on another occasion with Faulkner's *The Sound and the Fury.* I still have both of these books. They may have constituted virtually all of my new-book buying. I had become a confirmed used- and remaindered-book buyer. Most of the books I wanted were soon remaindered.

Has publishing changed since you started writing?

Literate men, as well as scholarly men, are giving way to businessmen. The exception proves the rule. And that is one hell of a difference. A big sale for Virginia Woolf was three or four thousand copies. If a book sold that well she was grateful. There's a story about Lawrence that touched me: in a letter he described how he had been able, after many years, to gather together $7,000, the most money he had ever had. I experienced a brief season of affluence from the paperback sale of *Love Among the Cannibals,* about $12,000. I remember thinking, what would Lawrence have thought of such a windfall?

Why do you think people read books today?

The Book-of-the-Month Club used to print an advertisement showing elegant people at a cocktail party discussing books. People have not discussed books at parties for years, unless book promotion is their business. We discuss movies, because movies are discussable. For one thing, everybody has seen them. Books of interest are complex, and few people are competent to discuss them. One need not have seen a movie, however, to discuss the stars, the director, the reviews. Movies and crime have much in common.

Do you have any comments about contemporary criticism?

Criticism is in the hands of the analysts. Perhaps they feel it is their turn. They too are writers of fiction, but they are no longer readers of it.

Do you read criticism of your own work?

If it is favorable.

Who would be the perfect Morris reader?

I get letters from many of them. A sense of humor is essential. I am often a very funny writer. A soft spot for pathos. A tolerance for the ironic. A well-established and chronic inclination to read slowly, and reread the line you just slipped by. The writer gave it his full attention. Let the reader do the same.

You've written a lot about the difficulties of the relationships between men and women. Do you see love as a failed myth in our culture today?

I would say that love "American style" is a myth whose origins we have forgotten. Sex is what we remember. The myth is not completely discredited, but I feel the way love is practiced in our culture is destructive. It feeds solely on illusion and doesn't generate any of the energy it should.

Do you see this as a particularly American problem?

God only knows what the consciousness of a central European has become since the Second World War. The psyche has been dislodged, battered, abused. A writer like Kundera is concerned with these things, but I fail to respond to his writing. For me, the energy of sex is powerfully romantic, a notion that is discredited in Kundera's books.

We saw the movie *Swann in Love* the other night. Proust, of course, is a remarkable analyst of romantic love. He feels its essentially destructive nature—everybody being just in love with his or her own illusion of love. A Buñuel film, *That Obscure Object of Desire,* deals with this boldly—a marvelous accounting of infatuation, which makes the sensibility of Proust seem somewhat remote.

Kundera shows how a romantic love evolves when it is used for political power.

That's exactly why the central European experience is so profoundly different from ours. Our way of treating love is perhaps an attempt to reactivate something that is dead, whereas he at least is looking at the reality of that sentiment's decay. It gives his fiction on this subject a substance which American fiction cannot reach; it's on another plane. In American fiction, stories of defeated romance are just tiresome. The characters experience emotion, but their self-delusion is not interesting. With Kundera they reach the stage of transformation.

Many of your characters experience dramatic transformations.

The idea of transformation captivates me. In a world of change, what other change is so magical, what other change compares with it? When all other options seem closed, transformation provides an escape hatch. In the case of Paul Kahler, for example, first in *War Games,* then in *The Field of Vision,* it seemed to be the lifesaving alternative. I found this both gratifying and plausible because of some hint or vibration of transfiguring changes, *mutatis mutandis,* that are present in much of my fiction. Storytelling, indeed, may have had its origin in such marvels.

In your recent novel, **Plains Song,** *there are no successful male-female connections, but there seems to be hope in the possibility of women connecting with each other. Are men less comfortable with the kind of intimate relationships that women find with other women?*

Absolutely. The man does not want intimacy. It's hard to say if that is cultural, or something more profound. Lawrence fought his inability to connect with men all his life. It drove him almost to the point of a breakdown. He had his homoerotic tendencies, but basically what he wanted was simple friendship, and he couldn't get it.

In an interview in 1975 you made a comment about the women in your fiction taking on some of the audacity previously assigned to men. Does that mean you have more faith in the potential of women?

I was enthusiastic at that time because women were beginning to represent an authentic and different force in American life instead of simply echoing or supporting the old ways. I think my first enthusiasms were like any enthusiasms—you're cheering for the side you believe in. I did believe in that side, but I was blind to the fact that for women the very need to compete would prove to be a Trojan horse.

Surely, though, man is more at sea than woman. A woman is less foolish than a man, more of a biological being. She is related to an authentic biological past in a way that man isn't. Woman has had the task of nurturing for a million years. She has a biological self-assurance that makes her a little less subject to the fits of despair that seize man, because he is just not rooted in life as she is.

Has being a photographer influenced your writing?

Very much. I sometimes have a "camera-eye voice." I attempt to perceive what the camera would see. In the opening line of **Ceremony in Lone Tree** I said to the reader, "Come to the window, and presumed to see only what the camera would see, without intrusive sentiments or observations. I sought neither to describe nor to arouse emotion, following the aesthetic of the camera and relying solely on the emotion I felt was present in the photograph.

Does this happen naturally, or is it a conscious artifice?

Once I had written the words "come to the window," the scene arranged itself. I became preoccupied with what I was seeing and not thinking of it as a novel. The scene I described was the culmination of my long brooding, an artifact rooted in my imagination, a still life carefully assembled to be photographed. This is not recommended novelistic practice, but a very good example of my obsession with places and artifacts—both the words and many photographs grew from the need I felt to materialize them—a retrieval of the past with a vengeance.

Have you ever used actual photographs you've taken as the basis for descriptions in the novels?

I never actually incorporate existing photographs but I use imaginary ones. My way of seeing may be conditioned by the photographing I have done; the imagery is processed by the tone called for by the situation at hand. For instance, there is a scene in *A Life,* about a part of New Mexico which I visited as a boy. There is a rather primitive photograph of my aunt and uncle in front of a shack that figures in a scene of the book, but I did not look at that photograph at the time I was writing the piece. Otherwise I would have been tempted to elaborate in the book on actual visual details. The tone, the manner in which that scene is done in the fiction, is so casually right that any elaboration would have been a mistake.

Do you find that when a character is closely modeled on a real person it inhibits you?

Yes. Yet the inhibition is part of the atonement, and eases the feelings of guilt. I could not get Gordon Boyd, in *The Field of Vision,* clear of the authorial shadow. In speaking for the author, as he frequently does, he is tied to the author in a way that permanently flaws the portrait. He exists, it seems to me, but I am not pleased with him, as I am with McKee and Lois, or Lehmann and Paula Kahler, other characters who speak through me, but not *of* me.

Which brings us back to the question of the individual and his awareness. Do you think we count for less as individuals than we used to?

Once the question has been asked, we feel that we do count for less. The root of the feeling is having to do with numbers. Numbers exceed our comprehension. I am one of 6.4 billion people. How do we account for what exceeds counting? The burden of such numbers exceeds the weight of gravity. My guess would be that our folly lies not in what threatens us, or even what eludes us, but in our inability to adapt to it. We can adapt to anything, which is why we are here, wherever we are. To be fully conscious of this, and accept it, is precisely what escapes us.

My image of society is of a huge ball of string, the size of a small planet, made up of pieces too short to tie, too long to throw away. I see it as something painted by Bosch or Breughel, that rises above the landscape like the tower of Babel.

Do you think we're becoming less aware because the losses we face are so great?

Most of the losses we face are on paper, a loss of words. On the plus side, words are still something that we can share with each other. One-on-one, they still serve the purpose for which they were created: to make it possible for us to be human. On the other hand, they also make possible our escape from that responsibility.

Rosemary Ranck (essay date 1991)

SOURCE: "'A Pact with the Bygone'," in *The New York Times,* November 24, 1991, p. 20.

[*In the following review, Franck praises a collection of Morris's Nebraska photographs.*]

The pull of things past is felt at surprising times and in unexpected ways. The act of dipping a small, sweet cake in a cup of herb tea elicited volumes of prose from Proust; the smell of pickling beets coming from a Nebraska kitchen released a powerful longing in the American novelist and photographer Wright Morris, which he spent years transforming into images and words. Mr. Morris has attempted before, not always successfully, to use his photographs to complement his writing, as another way of evoking the rural life he remembers from his Nebraska boyhood. In editing *Photographs & Words,* James Alinder, a photographer and a frequent collaborator with Mr. Morris, has reproduced the photographs in rich black-and-white tones, thereby revealing strengths that earlier publications obscured through cropping and mediocre printing. Mr. Morris briefly recounts his years as a photographer and describes a momentous visit to his aunt and uncle's Nebraska farm in the 1940's. Awakened by his "beet-pickled emotions" Mr. Morris dedicated himself to "a pact with the bygone" and to recording the symbols of a passing way of life. Of the images included here, only the first portrays a living person—his uncle, shown from the back as he wheels his tools into the barn. Mr. Morris searches for human presence in weathered farm buildings, bureau tops and barber chairs. Some of the images show farmhouse interiors with old photographs of family members. Mr. Morris's yearning for a past impossible to recover, and his good eye for revealing detail, are what animate these photos and make them compelling.

Joseph J. Wydeven (essay date 1993)

SOURCE: "Dualism and Doubling in Wright Morris's *War Games,*" in *The Centennial Review,* Vol. XXXVII, No. 2, Spring, 1993, pp. 415-28.

[*In the following essay, Wydeven discusses the use of the doppelganger in Morris's fiction, and especially its use in his novel* War Games.]

> [Colonel Foss] slept, . . . and he dreamt that he carried a small black bag which contained the leg, the arm, and the tongue of a person who was following him.
>
> *War Games* (74)

Where the double is, the orphan is never far away, with secrecy and terror over all.

Karl Miller, *Doubles* (39)

I

At the heart of *The Field of Vision* (1956), perhaps Wright Morris's most representative novel (and winner of the National Book Award), there is a character who refuses to speak and whose thoughts we are never given, yet whose presence in the novel is essential. This character, Paula Kahler, is presented by Morris as having undergone a mysterious transformation which has changed her psychologically from a man into a woman. Morris presents her as a negative and dysfunctional example of imaginative potential. The genesis of this character and her shadowy associates is of considerable interest to Morris's life and work through nineteen novels and assorted photo-text volumes since 1940.

The existence of characters such as Paula Kahler is evidence of Wright Morris's predilection for dualisms, especially in those works in which he is seen coming to grips with his past, such as *The Man Who Was There* (1945), *The Home Place* (1948), and *The Works of Love* (1951). That Morris's thought is dualistic is by now a commonplace,[1] but little has yet been written about Morris's frequent doubling of characters—of which Paula Kahler is such an extreme example. In this doubling, readers find themselves in the company of those mysterious *doopelgänger* figures which appear from time to time in fiction, often apparently with psychological motives all their own—as in Dostoyevsky's *The Double,* Edgar Allan Poe's "William Wilson," and Henry James's "The Jolly Corner."

As the presence of the double in a work of fiction often raises questions of character psychology, it is reasonable to examine the relationship between character and author. In attempting to comprehend this connection with regards to Wright Morris, it will help to keep three things in mind. First, much of what Morris writes is autobiographical—even to the extent that in *The Home Place* he has his protagonist encounter Morris's *own* Uncle Harry and Aunt Clara. Second, despite (or perhaps because of) the autobiographical origins of his work, Morris often places a curtain of ambiguity between character and reader—just as he sometimes views his subjects through physical curtains in *The Home Place* photographs. The third thing to remember is that Morris is repetitive, often re-using scenes and characters from earlier works, many of which emphasize his childhood and adolescent experiences, including his identity as "half an orphan" (*Will's Boy* 35). Morris has said that "the role of recurrence" was "part of my nature before it was part of my reading" (*Cloak of Light* 137).

This apparent need to repeat himself amounts to an obsession: it is as if, because his childhood is so packed with elusive meaning, Morris has to return to it again and again. In this obsessiveness, Morris is very much like his character Hyman Kopfman, who shares his author's need to re-

peat. Hyman Kopfman is described as "[going] over the same material the way a wine press went over the pulp of grapes. But there was always something that refused to squeeze out" (*War Games* 8). Not for nothing does Morris name Hyman Kopfman as one of "the 'possessed' characters . . . toward which I am powerfully drawn" (**"Writing Organic Fiction"** 95), or admit that "The likes of Hyman Kopfman . . . haunt me today as they did at the time of writing" (*War Games* vi). In Freudian terms, this character appears to be an example of overdetermination: a fictional character first of all, Hyman Kopfman also has significance outside of the works in which he figures.

Hyman Kopfman made his first appearance in a short novel entitled *War Games,* without doubt Morris's most astonishing work, unguarded and defiant of rationality. Nothing remotely like the crepuscular atmosphere—or the New York setting—of *War Games* is found elsewhere in Morris. The novel was written in 1951-52, but perhaps because it was "a premature example of what would soon be known as black humor," Morris's editor advised him not to publish it "until my status as a writer had clarified" (*Cloak of Light* 163). As a result, *War Games* was not published until twenty years later, in 1972, then reprinted with an explanatory preface in 1978. There Morris described the novel as "darkly somber, a book of interiors, dimly lighted streets, hallways and lobbies, with glimpses of objects and colors that emerge in subdued lighting" (vii)—in short, a perfect near-gothic setting suited to lurking doubles.

Morris's observation that *War Games* "began with a scene and a character that had sprouted in the compost of *The Works of Love*" (v) is crucial. The metaphor suggests that the novel was an organic by-product of the long gestation and five years of intense writing which culminated in *The Works of Love,* a novel which ambiguously memorialized his father. As I have suggested elsewhere, in that novel Morris grappled "with conflicting emotions towards his father," finding the means to express "sympathetic desire for his father's mutual regard" (Wydeven 111, 103). Coming out of this period, then, *War Games* may be understood as another attempt by Morris to deal with materials from his childhood.

Obviously Morris thinks of it as an important book: "In the absence of *War Games,* many clues to the fiction that followed were missing" (vii). Curiously, however, Hyman Kopfman, that character formed in "the compost of *The Works of Love,*" has only a brief role in *War Games*; by the end of the first chapter he is dead. But his importance is profound, for Hyman Kopfman is at the center of a complex of dualisms which move the actors in *War Games,* then reappears to haunt the themes of *The Field of Vision* and *Ceremony in Lone Tree* (1960). (Hyman Kopfman finally shows up with his "real" name, Herman Unger, in Morris's memoir *Solo* [1983] 26.) Readers have good reason to wonder why Morris returned to this character so frequently and so memorably.[2]

II

When *War Games* opens, Colonel Foss, the protagonist, has been struck by a pie truck and taken to a hospital, "where he hovered between life and death for several weeks" (2). There he encounters Hyman Kopfman, "a small, rabbit-faced little man who belonged in the hopeless ward, but it had been overcrowded" (7); he suffers from a terminal blood disease, resulting in amputation of an arm and a leg. Morris places these two characters in distinct opposition to each other: Hyman Kopfman, an immigrant, remains exuberant about the possibilities of American life; Colonel Foss, wearing his military glasses, sees "a battlefield" wherever he looks and thus has little desire to live. This opposition is resolved in terms typical of tales of the double: as Hyman Kopfman's case worsens, Colonel Foss, who "had been failing, now for no apparent reason . . . began to improve" (17), and when Kopfman dies, the Colonel is well enough to be released.

So ends the first chapter. Morris seems to have wanted this elaborate introduction in order to put forthcoming events into perspective, providing an acceptable rationale for Colonel Foss's subsequent experiences. Upon his release from the hospital, Colonel Foss takes Hyman Kopfman's meager personal belongings to a Mrs. Tabori, thought to be Kopfman's mother (described as having "luminous" eyes), and her apparent husband, Tabori, a bellhop at the Regent Arms Hotel. Then Foss goes home to his wife, in their fourth-floor apartment in Brooklyn Heights. Shortly afterwards Tabori arranges a meeting with him, and as a result, Mrs. Tabori is installed in the Foss apartment as housekeeper. A few days later the janitor in the building is found dead with a broken neck, and Foss makes the discovery that Mrs. Tabori is responsible.

Then the blackmail starts. Tabori tells Foss that he is "willing to handle it for fifty a week" (97), "no money at all considerin' what you got in the house" (99). What Foss discovers he has "in the house"—Mrs. Tabori—is a man, not a woman. The blackmail gives the Colonel a curious sense of satisfaction: "Every man felt, the Colonel was sure, the lurking furtive guilt that he had been feeling, and the need to attach this sense of punishment to some crime" (102). Furthermore, "He had got a lot of blackmail . . . very cheap" (109).

One day, venturing into Mrs. Tabori's room, Foss discovers a photograph linking Mrs. Tabori to a *Paul* Kopfman, "Soldier of Christ" at the Larrabee YMCA in Chicago. Almost immediately afterwards, for no apparent reason, the Colonel identifies himself to a stranger as "Colonel Kopfman." Then a second death is announced: Tabori's body is found at the bottom of an open elevator shaft at the Regent Arms. Colonel Foss suspects Mrs. Tabori has murdered again.

In a strange, contemplative state of mind ("Was he fleeing from, or hurrying toward something?" [123]), Colonel Foss makes his way to Chicago, where he takes a room in a cheap, fly-infested hotel. The flies in his room drive him to distraction and he goes into a frenzy trying to kill them. Then, seeing himself in a mirror, he undergoes a mystifying experience: "The figure in the mirror had the Colonel's body, but not his face. No, the face was new, and the luminous eyes gazed upon the bed . . ." (128). Now it appears that Colonel Foss has come to identify with Mrs. Tabori, of the luminous eyes—preparing us for his discovery, next day at the Larrabee YMCA, that Mrs. Tabori is in reality the missing Paul Kopfman, Hyman Kopfman's brother.

With a Mr. Hoppe at the YMCA, Colonel Foss pieces together Paul's story: he had suffered severe psychological trauma related to the death of his uncle, then disappeared, leaving his former life behind. As for the uncle, he had frozen to death in the snow, and his body was not recovered until the spring thaw. Then, unidentified, the corpse was handed over to a medical school and dissected; one of the hands was recognized by one of the students and brought to the family, including Paul, for identification. Evidently the shock of this event and its disclosure—and the manner in which it occurred and was presented—was sufficient to cause Paul to reject the world and his own male sexuality. (One of the novel's perplexities is that Morris gives no further information to help readers understand the specific form Paul's rejection takes.) Having completed his business in Chicago—his business apparently being to establish the true identity of Mrs. Tabori and to take on a new "identity" of his own—Colonel Foss returns to New York to find that his wife has "fallen" from the balcony of their apartment. On the pad by the telephone he finds a note in his wife's handwriting: "SHOCKING DISCOVERY. COME HOME IMMEDIATELY" (160). Finally, left alone with Mrs. Tabori in the apartment, Foss feels both terror-stricken and "remarkably free," anticipating "change for better or worse" (164).

This synopsis, of course, is quite unsatisfactory, for this odd book refuses to bend to fictional reason, relying on nuance and suggestion rather than on plot; further, there are gaping holes in the plot which Morris either failed to spot or refused to plug—where, for example, are the police in all of this? And what has led Colonel Foss to such measures? But tales such as this need not adhere to the fictional conduct of realism, for they are subject only to the unruly discipline of dreams.

War Games is most intriguing precisely because of its eeriness, and I am tempted to call it an existential gothic novel: it uses more or less gothic fictional devices to conclude with something like an existential sense of freedom: having apparently transcended guilt and found purpose, at the end of the novel Colonel Foss finds himself "remarkably free." But no label will explain the considerable mysteries in *War Games*—nor does Morris's Preface, which focuses on Hyman Kopfman, but says nothing to illuminate the strange "bond" between Colonel Foss and Mrs. Tabori-Paul Kopfman.

To approach the double in literature is always an adventure, for one generally has to deal with a psychological allegory of sorts, where normal rules of social conduct are put aside, replaced by "the deliriums, impasses, and impossibilities which are encountered in these fictions" (Miller vii). Because free will is challenged by a variety of determinisms, characters are not required to make sense, and events, as C. F. Keppler writes, "can never be entirely accounted for by the facts of the case or by logical reasoning about them" (11). There is frequently confusion of subject and object, and we must decide if the double relationships are intended to be hostile (as in Poe's "William Wilson") or helpful (as in Conrad's "The Secret Sharer"). Furthermore, the double implies or imposes patterns where none were seen to exist before: as Colonel Foss observes of one strange phenomenon, "At one time he would have thought it merely a coincidence" (121).

There is some internal evidence to suggest that **War Games** may be indebted to Saul Bellow's *The Victim,* but Morris's novel is considerably more convoluted and quirky.[3] Whereas Bellow's novel consistently focuses on one double relationship—Asa Leventhal's pursuit by Kirby Albee—Morris's **War Games** is shot through with dualisms and doubles—beginning with the oxymoron in the title itself. Morris even has Hyman Kopfman speak of the amputation of his arm as an operation which "balanced him up" (7). And that the toy animals entering Mrs. Tabori's ark are paired not by male and female, but by principles of natural enmity (lamb and tiger, snake and mouse, fox and rooster) may be emblematic of her dysfunction; there are clearly no human males in her collection, no Adam, not even Noah (113).

The doubling of characters in **War Games** centers on Colonel Foss, the "first self" to whom second selves will somehow adhere. At the outset, as already detailed, Colonel Foss is paired with Hyman Kopfman—a relationship I will turn to shortly. In addition, however, Morris develops double relationships between Colonel Foss and three other characters: Milton Ashley, Tabori, and Mrs. Tabori-Paul Kopfman.

Milton Ashley is introduced to show—the extent of Colonel Foss's failure in life—indeed, Ashley is the reason why Foss is a failure, and Foss despises him because of the guilt he makes him feel:

> The Colonel had been born on the same day [as Milton Ashley] (but forty minutes later, as his luck would have it) in the same town, the same year, and just across the tracks from the fine house where Milton Ashley saw the light of day. . . . Very early, the name of Milton Ashley was coupled with that of the Little Lord Jesus, and produced as a rule the same effect on Roger Foss's mind: a sense of having been born with much too little, much too late.
>
> (42-43)

Ashley is the curse of Foss's life, for his mother holds him up as the pinnacle of success. Just as Foss is constantly in Ashley's shadow, Milton Ashley shadows Foss's entire life. Through Ashley, too, we learn of the impossible ex-

pectations of Foss's mother: from his birth he is a victim of his mother's envy of social position. More important, her persecutions of him for not being Milton Ashley may be responsible for Foss's lack of "interest" in women (1). The mother is clearly indicted in this portrayal. No wonder Foss thinks of himself as a "nonidentified man" (124).

The second double relationship, Foss's connection to the bellhop Tabori, involves a more traditional bond between first and second self. When the Fosses offer Mrs. Tabori employment, the bellhop, previously a stranger, intimates a closer relationship, saying that Mrs. Tabori is doing the Fosses a "favor": "she'd only do it for a friend of the family" (63-64). From the outset the Colonel unaccountably gives way to the bellhop's vaguely threatening cajoleries. Then, when Mrs. Tabori kills the janitor and Tabori begins blackmailing Foss, the Colonel feels a sense of fulfillment—he calls it his "Manifest Destiny" (101-02): the blackmail curiously alleviates the Colonel's complex sense of guilt (concepts like original sin and existential dread come to mind here). Further, when Tabori first makes clear that Mrs. Tabori is really a man, the Colonel feels an ambiguous kinship with him: "[H]e put his hand toward the bellhop, who seemed to be living in fear of something. He even felt, strange as it seemed, in league with him." "They were both, the Colonel realized, exalted by the same dread, and at sea in the same boat" (107). The chapter concludes with the following explanation:

> What the bellhop had done was sell him a share of his predicament. This blackmail was not for money at all, but for company. . . . It had been too much for the man to live alone with his fear. So now the colonel had it—he had at least part of it—and perhaps this night the bellhop would sleep as he had not slept in years, while the Colonel lay awake. It made the Colonel smile (he raised both hands to his face as if to hide what he was thinking) as he had been alone himself, and now for fifty a week he, too, had company.
>
> (109-10)

The third double relationship is between Colonel Foss and Mrs. Tabori-Paul Kopfman, perhaps best expressed by their similarities as ineffectual warriors: Claudine Foss refers to the Colonel as "Mr. Army"; Paul Kopfman had been a "Soldier of Christ" at the Larrabee YMCA. It is the existence of Paul which impels the Colonel to his identity as "Colonel Kopfman," and it is Paul Kopfman-Mrs. Tabori's "luminous eyes" that the Colonel finds in his own mirror image in his hotel near the Larrabee YMCA. Finally, the Colonel's existential future is foreshadowed when he and Mrs. Tabori are thrown together at the end of the novel.

But perhaps the most important doubling in **War Games** is that involving Colonel Foss and Hyman Kopfman. Curiously, Foss is "balanced" by Hyman Kopfman, whose *decline* in health is opposed to Foss's *return* to health: "Here you had the Colonel, who had nothing to live for, but nevertheless was getting better, while Hyman Kopfman, who hungered for life, was getting worse" (17). Again, "It became a contest of sorts, as to whether the Colonel would get back on his feet before Hyman Kopfman lost another limb, or managed to die" (19). Their relationship is one of a type C. E. Keppler calls *counterbalance,* "the complementary oppositeness of the two halves of the being whom they together comprise" (11-12). In *War Games* this balance is emphatic, for Hyman Kopfman's death is posited as a necessary condition for Colonel Foss's recovery and return to the "battlefield" of the world.

Finally, the blood disease which afflicts Hyman Kopfman is another crucial connection to the Colonel, for at the conclusion of the novel, Foss feels kinship with Kopfman's "doomed condition—as if the blood that flowed in Hyman Kopfman's veins flowed in his own" (163). This organic simile supports the view that what doomed Kopfman makes possible the Colonel's newly developed sense of human identity—that is, his move from guilt and failure to freedom and responsibility.

But there is yet another side to Hyman Kopfman's role in *War Games*: he is employed to emphasize a recurring phenomenon in Morris that might be called *a ritual of entry*— that is, a ritual which many of Morris's characters experience as a necessary step prior to transformation of self. Joseph Campbell speaks of rituals which involve "formal, and usually very severe, exercises of severance, whereby the mind is radically cut away from the attitudes, attachments, and life patterns of the stage [of life] being left behind" (10). In *War Games* Kopfman appears to be the agent of this purpose: he makes possible the Colonel's "rebirth." When the Colonel leaves the hospital—it is significantly the first day of spring—he finds his lenses of perception changed: "Everything that he saw was unchanged, familiar . . . but now that he was back, within it, something struck him as strange. It was not, that is, as he had left it" (25). The change has occurred in the Colonel, not in the world he perceives.

This motif—of necessary preparation for radical change, the rendering strange of the world to the perceiver's eyes—is emphasized throughout (as well as in most of Morris's mature fiction) by what Morris elsewhere calls "the thrust from behind" which impels one to some form of effective action (*Field of Vision* 205). Colonel Foss is precipitated by many of these thrusts in a causal chain: struck by a truck (from behind), he enters the hospital, where he engages Hyman Kopfman; when Kopfman dies, Foss is led to Tabori, then to Mrs. Tabori—until his final release into dreadful freedom.

Most of the events leading to the Colonel's transformation are not subject to reason or the laws of normal causation. Nevertheless, Foss comes to believe that there is "logic in certain meaningless events," perhaps most clearly expressed through the following extended metaphor:

> The Colonel's temperament being what it was, it led him to conclude that all unforeseen events, if seen in perspective, were in one way or another predetermined, and to this curious circumstance men gave the name of

Manifest Destiny. He observed that most men got along without it, like freight cars parked on a siding, while the course of events, the main forces of history, passed them by. He had even felt himself of this number—in a fairly long life there had been no jolts, or shocks, to speak of—until the pie truck had hit him from behind. In a matter of months his manifest destiny had caught up with him. . . . The moment the Colonel had set eyes on the bellhop, he had heard, as he had on the plains, the whistle of his future blowing thin and wild far down the tracks. The impulse had been given by the pie truck, and now the jolt had finally reached the caboose. This was it. This was the crossing bell he had been waiting for.

(101-02)

Later, after Foss has been led to call himself "Colonel Kopfman" and the bellhop has plunged to his death, he sees himself described in the newspapers as one of Tabori's friends "not as yet identified." The occasion "defined his position, it cast him in a new role, and it revealed a certain order in all the disorder, as he had known for years that he was, above all, a nonidentified man. An accomplice, as yet unnamed, to crimes yet to be discovered. . . . [H]e was the connection, he was the link of order, between these strange events" (118-19).

For what is the Colonel being "prepared"? Into what has he gained entry? The reader has been groomed to accept Colonel Foss's welcome burden: the novel ends with Colonel Foss going forth to meet Mrs. Tabori-Paul Kopfman, the psychotic but "innocent" murderer who kills to maintain her fragile new identity. The Colonel sees as his life project the task of cherishing and protecting her—as well as saving himself from her potential violence. This means that he must avoid revealing to her that he knows her secret. The challenge, full of ambiguities and desperate risks, is to live at the cutting edge of reality where both the stakes and the rewards are high. In effect, the Colonel's new role is to shadow Mrs. Tabori, bonded to her as her caretaker-double.[4]

III

In this way the doubles in *War Games* achieve a curious resolution, with the narrative thrust intending the Colonel's transcendence of failure and guilt. Hyman Kopfman's function in all of this is primarily to make that transcendence possible, to effect the entry to the new experiences which open and expand into Foss's future. The means by which this is carried through is an elaborate counterbalancing of life and death, Foss and Kopfman. At the center of this strategy, however, is a paradox not to be accounted for by the internal needs of the created fiction: Colonel Foss can only live to achieve transcendence if Hyman Kopfman dies. Hyman Kopfman is given power to effect the future, but *only through his death.* Hyman Kopfman is a martyr.

This is an irony which we find frequently in Morris's work, and it encourages inquiry. One explanation may be sought in Morris's biography and autobiographical fictions. When writers compose from personal experience, they often shore up their own identities with fictional constructs, weaving intricate patterns which repeat as if in code the essence of their lives. One important pattern in Morris's work is that of primordial loss: in effect, he is an orphan seeking to repossess mother and father—in bafflement, anger, ritualistic repetition. Morris never knew his mother, for she died six days after his birth, making him, in his own words, "half an orphan" (*Will's Boy* 4, 35). Whereas the father is a shadowy figure who moves in and out of Morris's life—he writes that after one of his father's more egregious absences, "I had become more of a whole orphan than a half one" (85)—the mother in Morris is figured primarily as a perceived lack, an absence.

Although critical attention has been paid to Morris's "search for a father," comparatively little has been done with the mother. G. B. Crump writes that "Morris's lifelong search for 'imaginary gains,' often identified with timeless tableaux, scenes, objects, and suspended moments . . . expresses his need to recover the mother he never knew, and the memoirs link the loss of the mother to the loss of the past in all its manifestations" ("Author in Hiding" 5). Roy Bird asserts: "The absence of the mother helps to account for the darkness of the world view in Morris's novels, just as it helps to explain the yearning for completeness and connection" (57).

It will help to focus on the *specific* terms of Morris's relationship to his mother, for in several places in his work that relationship is seen as a counterbalancing one. In *The Man Who Was There,* for example, readers find the inscription marking the grave of the protagonist's mother:

ETHEL GRACE WARD
1891-1910
She died so that he might live

(132)

In *Will's Boy,* again, we read, "I am born, and a few days later Grace Osborn Morris is dead, having given her life that I might live" (5). There can be little doubt that Ethel Grace Ward is a mother surrogate carried into a fictional role. Roy Bird has remarked on the irony of the gravestone inscription: "the greatest gap in [Morris's] early experience also creates his greatest opportunity for independent expression . . ." (57).

In fictional terms, then, Morris very deliberately converted the death of his mother into myth, and it may be speculated that the dualistic death-life formula accounts for the strategy of counterbalance informing the relationship between Hyman Kopfman and Colonel Foss (both "doubles" for Morris himself). The view that Morris's mother *must* die to make Wright's life possible—as implied in the inscription—is deliberately (if unconsciously?) paralleled in the fiction. This apparent either-or fallacy (*either* the mother *or* the child must die) came to support an elaborate ritualistic pattern in Morris's fiction. This is curious, as it posits that rebirth may only occur through death—not the death of the self, however, but the death of an *other*—or a *mother.*

This apotheosis of mother into martyr is echoed, surely, in Colonel Foss's rebirth through Hyman Kopfman's death, but also in the Agee Ward of *The Man Who Was There,* who helps others live precisely through his absence; and in the character in *The Works of Love* who symbolically "feeds himself to the birds in a eucharistic parallel that Morris has used more than once" (Eisinger 339).

All this may be explained as part of Morris's coming to terms with his identity as an orphan, to find a means to reclaim the past—or rather, to imagine a re-creation of it in which the parts comprising the whole have never been put asunder. This mythic denial of death allows Morris to reclaim his mother by means of a magical solution, one which *always* restores her to life when it is called upon. If this analysis is sound, then the Hyman Kopfman-Colonel Foss relationship may be viewed as a fictional restoration of the golden past before time ruined it forever.

Notes

1. On Morris's dualism see: Wayne C. Booth, "The Two Worlds in the Fiction of Wright Morris," *Sewanee Review* 65 (1957): 375-99; David Madden, "The Hero and the Witness in Wright Morris' *Field of Vision,*" *Prairie Schooner* 34 (1960), 263-78; and especially G. B. Crump, *The Novels of Wright Morris: A Critical Interpretation,* Lincoln: U of Nebraska P, 1978.

2. Morris himself opens the door to critical inquiry when he writes, "*War Games* may well prove to be the seedbed of much more in my fiction than I am aware, since it was the first turning of earth more than twenty years buried" (*War Games* vi). No doubt *War Games* would benefit from a psychoanalytic critical approach that I have not attempted here. Doubles and their relation to narcissism, the potential relation between severed limbs and the castration complex, and questions of sexual orientation and identity are matters, pertinent to *War Games,* that one finds addressed in Freud's "The Uncanny" and Otto Rank's *The Double.*

3. The relationship between *War Games* and Bellow's *The Victim* may deserve critical attention, but I am operating here only at the level of hunch. Both see urban life as grim, and they emphasize release through transformation of character, including life-enhancing insights provided by pushy, obnoxious doubles—who even use the same line, "what's on your mind?" when they wish to advance their own proposals. Again, Bellow's "destiny" is echoed in Morris's "manifest destiny." The two authors' protagonists might even have passed each other in the lobby of the St. George hotel. Surely Morris knew *The Victim* (1947) by the time he wrote *War Games* in 1951-52. Morris appears to have met Bellow in the late 1940s, in a New York bookstore. It may be no coincidence that in *A Cloak of Light* Morris speaks of *War Games* immediately after an extended discussion of his friendship with Bellow (161-63).

4. Paul Kopfman-Mrs. Tabori of *War Games* re-emerges five years later as Paul-Paula Kahler in *The Field of Vision*, where she is under the loving care of Dr. Leopold Lehmann, an eccentric psychiatrist.

Works Cited

Bellow, Saul. *The Victim.* New York: Vanguard, 1947.

Bird, Roy K. *Wright Morris: Memory and Imagination.* New York: Peter Lang, 1985.

Campbell, Joseph. *The Hero With a Thousand Faces* [2nd Ed. 1968.] Princeton UP, 1972.

Crump, G. B. "Wright Morris, Author in Hiding." *Western American Literature* 25 (1990): 3-14.

Eisinger, Chester E. *Fiction of the Forties.* U of Chicago P, 1963.

Keppler, C. F. *The Literature of the Second Self.* Tucson: U of Arizona P, 1972.

Miller, Karl. *Doubles: Studies in Literary History.* [1985.] New York: Oxford UP, 1987.

Morris, Wright. *Ceremony in Lone Tree.* [1960.] Lincoln: U of Nebraska P, 1973.

———. *A Cloak of Light: Writing My Life.* New York: Harper, 1985.

———. *The Field of Vision.* [1956.] Lincoln: U of Nebraska P, 1974.

———. *The Home Place.* [1948.] Lincoln: U of Nebraska P, 1968.

———. *The Man Who Was There.* [1945.] Lincoln: U of Nebraska P, 1977.

———. *Solo: An American Dreamer in Europe: 1933-34.* New York: Harper, 1983.

———. *War Games.* [1972.] Lincoln: U of Nebraska P, 1978.

———. *Will's Boy.* New York: Harper, 1981.

———. *The Works of Love.* [1951.] Lincoln: U of Nebraska P, 1972.

Morris, Wright, and Wayne Booth. "The Writing of Organic Fiction." *Conversations with Wright Morris.* Ed. Robert E. Knoll. Lincoln: U of Nebraska P, 1977. 74-100.

Wydeven, Joseph J. "Focus and Frame in Wright Morris's *The Works of Love.*"

Mary Price (essay date 1994)

SOURCE: "Wright Morris: Three Photographs," in *Raritan*, Vol. 14, No. 2, Fall, 1994, pp. 19-28.

[*In the following essay, Price interprets two of Morris's photographs in the context of his writing.*]

What can be seen in a photograph of corncobs by Wright Morris, the novelist? The problem might present itself as how to respond to the obvious. This photograph is apparently devoid of associations that would make it interesting, and devoid also of the photographic criteria, the chalk whites and deep blacks, that Morris often explicitly aimed for in his photographic work.

John Szarkowski, Director Emeritus of Photography at the Museum of Modern Art, has made familiar a distinction between those photographs that might be said to function as mirrors and those that might be said to function as windows. Thus, in his 1978 book *Mirrors and Windows,* he argues that

> there is a fundamental dichotomy in contemporary photography between those who think of photography as a means of self-expression and those who think of it as a method of exploration.

Self-expression, as the mirror suggests, emphasizes the photographer's characterization of space and its objects, often formal design and abstract simplicity—for example in the photographs of Alfred Stieglitz. Exploration, the photograph as window, might be exemplified by Atget or Robert Frank.

The limits of such comparisons become evident if one tries to apply them to Wright Morris's photographs. "Corncobs" is both a mirror and a window, and it is also a clue to a mystery. All three terms—*mirror, window, clue*—are metaphors for expressing, sometimes determining how to see, the meaning of a photograph. In the case of "Corncobs," *mirror* seems more applicable for Morris's own vision—"Corncobs," that is, has significance available at first only to the photographer. But *window* seems more applicable for viewers because they—or we—seem to be shown some piled up discards from the process of farming.

Because its meaning is not apparent to the viewer, I prefer to direct attention to "Corncobs" as clue. Corncobs themselves play no part in a city life, but they do play a significant, if minor, part in the life of a dirt farmer. *Dirt farmer* is a term that Morris uses, particularly in connection with the dust bowl years of the depression when the dirt literally blew away. It is also a term that is used as if it distinguished the small individual farm from huge machine-run farms.

Morris's imagination focused with intensity on the small farm in Texas or Nebraska where the wind blew so constantly that fences had to be erected to keep the chickens from blowing away. In the farmhouse, behind the kitchen stove, was a basket of the corncobs shown in the photograph. They were dipped in or sprinkled with kerosene and used as kindling. Sometimes a cob was dipped in kerosene, lighted, and used to singe a plucked chicken.

Over and over in Morris's fiction and autobiographical stories the corncobs identify and characterize a way of life. Such a life could be dangerous—a woman in the novel *In Orbit* has no eyebrows and the text admonishes the reader, "Never pour kerosene on a bin of smouldering cobs." But it is also associated with the fire that is the means of warmth and cooking.

In the novel *Ceremony in Lone Tree,* Morris describes the town: "the town sits on the plain as if delivered on a flat-car—as though it were a movie set thrown up during the night." Inside the house, he says, "the mice raised in the basement move to their winter quarters in the cobs behind the stove." In explaining his book *The Inhabitants* to Uncle Harry and Clara in his 1985 autobiographical *Cloak of Light: Writing My Life,* Morris writes:

> I said I wanted to capture what it was like to have lived on a dirt farm for fifty years, to have lived on this farm for half a century. There was no comment. I recall Clara moving her head from one side to the other, to see and appraise the room she sat in. Her shoes were unlaced. The ties of her apron dangled on the floor. I could hear mice stirring in the kitchen's basket of cobs.

In another of Morris's fictions, *Plains Song,* we learn where the cobs were stored:

> A quilting frame with an unfinished quilt was set up in the shade near the back porch. A few old hens pecked around in the dishwater scum near the screen. The shed to the west, the original house, had been painted green with white windows; the cobs inside pressed against the glass.

The cobs signify the virtue and necessity of fire, food, and frugality. They had this significance for Morris when he took the photograph. With the photograph as clue to his narratives, viewers are able to notice the importance of the cobs in the poor dirt farm economy.

When Szarkowski briefly discusses this photograph, he dismisses the Prometheus story as irrelevant to the cobs and their connection with fire. I agree with him in this—Prometheus has no place in Nebraska, Texas, or in the works of Wright Morris. Szarkowski also says, "It is difficult to say more about the picture than that it represents something shrivelled, desiccated, used up." But that seems to me true only if you see the photograph without the Morris texts and thus without any hint of the part cobs played in Morris's imagination and experience.

In this same book, *Plains Song,* the chapter divisions are marked not by titles but by a repeated detail of a photograph called **"Reflection in Oval Mirror, the Home Place, 1947."** The mirror has no frame. It reflects a corner of a room, showing the line where right-angle walls meet, a fragment of ceiling, and a fragment of floor. Family photographs hang on the two walls at head height. On a table in the corner are more family photographs. A cloth covers the table top. A couple of boxes sit on the shelf below. The mirror is etched with a ribbon bow strung on a formalized line of vine and leaf, and the white etched line seems to tie together the patterned curtains that hang straight on either side of the oval. The light falls strongly on a paneled door facing the viewer, in which the lines of the panels waver with the imperfections in the glass of the mirror. It's tacky, it's family, it's home, it's remarkable because it is remarked. And it is part of the house that one of the characters in the book calls "charged with disturbing expectations."

In a 1992 exhibition catalogue from the San Francisco Museum of Art, entitled *Wright Morris, Origin of a Species,* the complete photograph is complemented by a new, obliquely descriptive paragraph on the page opposite:

> Love too was work, the labor pains what it cost you for the pleasure that couldn't be helped, but not every woman had a talent for it. At her funeral the bluffs along the river were grained as clapboards, her children part of the working party. The wind blew a mist of rain along the tracks, the rails glistening like channels of running water. She had once been to Aurora, on the Burlington local, with the butterflies in and out of the coach windows, but all she knew of the Overland Express was the change in the pitch of the whistle as it flashed by the crossing.

Aurora is about 25 miles west of Grand Island, Nebraska, so the trip was a short one.

The first sentence is deliberately, matter-of-factly ambiguous. "Love too was work"—too? Too, yes, because everything on a dirt farm is work, everything is conceived only in terms of work. The woman who is the unseen subject of the paragraph and of the photograph takes for granted that everything in life is work, love included.

The suggestion of love as intercourse, resulting in conception, labor pains, and children, involves, so the sentence reads, "pleasure that couldn't be helped, but not every woman had a talent for it." The implication is left unresolved. Is this a woman who had a talent for that pleasure, or not? As we learn later, she had not. The "pleasure that couldn't be helped" is the man's, the partner's.

The phrase "couldn't be helped" acquires resonance in Morris's account of a wedding night. Cora, a tall gaunt young woman in *Plains Song,* made a marriage arranged by her father. A friend had seemed willing to explain the sexual obligations of marriage to Cora, but Cora "felt it a breach of the marriage vows to openly discuss such a question. First of all, she knew nothing. What she would come to learn was for her alone to know."

Her bridal night, Morris writes, "might be likened to an operation without the anesthesia. Horror exceeded horror. The time required by her assailant to do what had to be done left her in shock. In the dawn light she found that she had bitten through the flesh of her hand, exposing the bone. . . . Nothing known to her had proved to be both so bizarre and so repugnant as the act of procreation, but she understood that it was essential to its great burden of meaning."

Now, when the mirror has been restored to the larger, complete photograph, retrieved from its chapter heading position in *Plains Song,* that woman has died and been buried. Her children were part of the working party; they helped dig the grave. The description of the bluffs along the river "grained as clapboard" is a description of geological strata. The wind and the rain, the "rails glistening like channels of running water," allow us to share the sensory experiences of being at the funeral.

The direction of interest then shifts to what the experience of the living woman had been, limited but intense. The local trip on the train to Aurora was marked by "butterflies in and out of the coach windows," although most train trips before the era of closed windows and air conditioning were marked by cinders blowing around and getting in the traveler's eye. The train that traveled to distant places was known to her only by "the change in the pitch of the whistle as it flashed by the crossing." The mirror is a frame within the frame, and squeezes its contents together in the same way the life of the woman is squeezed.

The photograph, dated 1947, was first published in *The Home Place.* The descriptive paragraph cited from the 1992 catalogue has the woman as central character. The same photograph was published in *God's Country and My People* in 1968 with a similar paragraph describing a *man's* being buried. The emphasis shifts from birth to death. It begins:

> Love, too, was work, childbirth its reward, a task to be performed like seedtime and harvest, the labor pains what it cost you for the pleasure that couldn't be helped.

So far, the childbirth is simply made explicit, and the "you" still a woman. The shift occurs in the next two sentences.

> One paid for the miracle of life with the labor of death. Not everyone had a talent for it, or understood it should not come easy.

The "it" refers to death, in almost the same phrase as, in the catalogue description, the "it" referred to "the pleasure that couldn't be helped, but not every woman had a talent for it." The 1968 passage continues:

> A man should be long suffering, his death long remembered, the funeral a consecrated working party with the shovel handles sticking out of the raw mounds of earth. Over the wide valley a dim thin rain, the bluffs along the river grained like clapboards, the prevailing wind blowing a cloudlike mist along the tracks. The sleeting rain should glisten on the bared heads of the men and drip from the chins of those still beardless, their prayers rising skyward but their eyes on the hole in the earth. They stand tilted on the boards edging the grave and as the first spade of earth falls hollow on the coffin let it be the one moment in their lives they will never forget.

Death is invested with a dignity and finality that are enhanced by insistence on the bare setting, swept with wind and rain. This is true of both descriptions, for both woman and man. The burial ground and the setting are the same.

The photograph, so constricted and enclosed, contrasts with the openness of the setting for the two funerals, as if death were the release from the unending monotonous hard work of farm life.

The photograph is circumscribed by its frame, or edges, and further compressed by the remoteness of the mirror image. The family photographs are a record of the generations as local and specific as the biblical begats, and about as cheerless. The object of greatest bulk and of greatest puzzlement is the door. The door's surface is a beautiful reflector of light, and that is important in the photograph. But you will have noticed that in fact the door is not attached to anything, so what is it doing there? It is leaning against the wall, covering up rather than opening or closing. And just as the necessary tribulations of the farmer's wife were never spoken of, but simply endured, so objects might have been displaced for some reason now lost to memory. The door may have been detached from its hinges to be rehung or fixed in some way, but the job was never important enough to get around to, so there it stayed. The only door removed within any text of Wright Morris's that I have read was removed to allow the body of an enormously fat man to be taken out. But I don't see the immediate relevance of that here, and I shall have to leave you with another mystery, this time without a clue—unless, of course, the door off its hinges suggests the one release and opening imagined as possible, that of death.

John Hollander (essay date 1996)

SOURCE: "The Figure on the Page: Words and Images in Wright Morris's *The Home Place*," in *The Yale Journal of Criticism,* Vol. 9, No. 1, Spring, 1996, pp. 93-108.

[In the following essay, Hollander discusses the relation of the visual to the verbal in Morris's photo-text The Home Place.*]*

Ecphrastic treatments of photographs in modern literary verse and prose construe their images as invented pictures in themselves as well as confronting their documentary status. Until very recently, most photographs to which poems have been addressed have been portraits, and the text speaks to their subjects as rendered, and perhaps to the occasion of the taking of the picture. Indeed, some recent poetry has paralleled the theoretical writing of the past forty years or so by dealing with fashionable intellectual questions concerning the epistemological and moral status of particular photographs.[1] But for the earlier part of this century, it was left to popular journalism to develop formats for captions, and larger blocks of text used in a caption-like way, and significant modes of juxtaposition in layout, that would bring older issues of ecphrastic glossing or interpretation of a pre-existent image into new contexts. Similarly, the technology of photo-reproduction made photographs available for illustration of a pre-existent text in a way that modified or even nullified their documentary status (see for example Henry James's use of photographs as frontispiece plates for the various volumes of The New York Edition (1907-9)).

The publication in 1941 of *Let Us Now Praise Famous Men,* that famous collaborative work of Walker Evans and James Agee, proved important for the work of the major novelist Wright Morris (whose first novel, **My Uncle Dudley,** appeared the following year). In 1946, Morris produced his fascinatingly problematic volume of photographs and layered captions and associated text, called **The Inhabitants,** framing images of his native rural Nebraska in high-modernist formats. But perhaps his most powerful imaginative work involving text and photographs is **The Home Place** (1948). I should like to explore for a bit its extremely original way of presenting word and image in a mode that appears to mix ecphrasis and illustration.

In 1946 Morris got a Guggenheim Fellowship and bought a 4 x 5 view camera to replace his older 3¼ x 4¼; in early May of 1947 he went back to a family farm near Norfolk, Nebraska where his Uncle Harry and Aunt Clara lived and took a great many photographs, as well as several of the nearby house of a recently deceased relative named Ed, which would eventually form the warp of the fabric of **The Home Place.** At the time he was taking them, he hadn't imagined a narrative fiction growing out of them. But in a funny way, a text lay behind them all; just a few weeks before, he later wrote, he had come upon what he called "a statement that gave me, I felt, unlimited access"[2]—not only to the interior of his Aunt's house (this came from her permission) but, we must suppose from the statement, access of another sort entirely. The passage in question speaks of being

> subject to the superstition that objects and places, coherently grouped, disposed for human use and addressed to it, must have a sense of their own, a mystic meaning proper to themselves to give out: to give out, that is, to the participant at once so interested and so detached as to be moved by a report of the matter.[3]

That "participant at once so interested and so detached" could be construed, of course, as the camera. But Morris, a novelist, couldn't but have had a novelistic matter in mind, a particularly Jamesian matter in fact. When he began to plan a narrative to embrace the images—the weft of the fabric—he wanted to deal with "the sentiments and conflicts of a late-returning native."[4] The passage I have just quoted, from Henry James's *The American Scene,* ended up as the epigraph of his book, and as I shall suggest in a moment, a continued meditation on Jamesian images and narrative agendas pervades the writing of Morris's story, which he put together only after he had assembled an ordered array of glossy prints selected from the pictures he had taken.

The Home Place [hereafter abbreviated as *HP*] is an almost unique sort of novel, with—rather than "in"—photographs, each one accompanying a page of text. It opens with a direct invitation to the reader to consider the meaning of objects in pictures. The first photograph, on the left-hand page, is faced with the story's beginning. Here are its first two sentences:

> "What's the old man doing?" I said, and I looked down the trail, beyond the ragged box elder, where the old man stood in the door of the barn, fooling with an inner tube. In town I used to take the old man's hand and lead him across the tracks where horses and men, little boys and sometimes little girls, were killed. Why was that? They didn't stop, look and listen. We did.[5]

The very first question—"What's the old man doing?"—might be the one posed by readers themselves. The second sentence continues the narrative set up by the words "and I looked": it makes it plain that the neutral "the old man" doesn't only refer to that (unidentified) old man in the photograph, but a member of the narrator's family. Another point to note: the book's readers could all have been expected immediately to conjure up a momentary vision of the inevitable—and in those days ubiquitous—railroad-crossing sign, a diagonal cross with the words STOP LOOK LISTEN prominently displayed.

The story records a day during a visit of return, by a man named Muncy with his urban "wife and snotty kids," to a family farm in Nebraska. It is told from the point of view of a man who doesn't see too well, visiting his aunt who has a glass eye, bringing his camera which has a glass eye. (The text itself confirms this relation: "'It's been a long time since we seen you—' Clara said . . . she rocked, her right eye covered, and looked at me. I did not look at her with my camera eye" [*HP* 43].) So that the opening "What's the old man doing?" becomes, in the unfolding of the narrative, a simple bit of *verismo:* Muncy literally can't quite make out what is actually happening, although the camera's sharply focused eye, and that of the reader, immediately can.[6]

The whole narrative text is full of dialogue and persons, but the photographic images are of things and regions of places. The only living person seen in the photographs is his uncle—the old man in the first image—shown three times in subsequent photographs but with a face that is never visible. The only faces acknowledged by the camera in this book are inscribed in objects—in older photographs repictured *in situ.* Indeed, all the images are of objects, invoked by the facing page of text in a wonderful variety of ways, from precise reference—so that the image could be construed as one sort of "illustration"—to a more general allusion. The images are vertically aligned on the page, for the most part (only 16 out of almost 90 are horizontal). They are mostly, but not entirely, bled on the page: in only one instance does the format, by placing a horizontal image across two facing pages, allow text to appear underneath a picture. This may allude somehow to captioning—his earlier book **The Inhabitants** had been pictures with, as has been observed, peculiar captions—but this is the unique case of an image which consists of an old family photograph of thirteen people posed outside a house, nailed by Morris to the exterior shingled wall of a house and rephotographed there, even though, in the story, the photograph is discussed, and its subjects identified, indoors, and the photograph is framed. The caption, moreover, opens with a characteristic glance at visual contingency, and the problematics of memorializing:

> "Lord—it's fadin'," the old man said.
>
> "You wearin' your glasses?" Clara said, and covered her eye to look at him.
>
> (*HP* 154-55)

To consider the relation of text and photograph throughout the book, one might start with the image of the horseshoes. It faces a page of dialogue—a few old men talking (*HP* 80). There is no reference to horseshoes in the text, but consider (a) that this is the sort of conversation that might accompany this innocent and by now pastoralized leisure activity, and (b) the minute particulars of this image—the horseshoes themselves: the men were about of equal skill, and had presumably played a good bit together, the horseshoes are all touching (even as the image is touching or moving for the viewer) and as if in casual but assured conversation: they are synecdoches of their throwers. But it will be seen that this is in no simple way a narrative illustration: nobody has thrown a horseshoe, nor mentioned one, in the story. Whether the image is read as "illustration," or the text as ecphrastic of the image, the mode of adducing and glossing is profoundly oblique.

On the other hand, consider the elegant photograph of grain elevators. The issue of insistently compressed verticality is there in the cropping and placing on the page. This image faces a passage meditating upon the precise nature of the monumentality of grain elevators, as if to provide an example:

> That's the way these elevators, these great plains monoliths, strike me. There's a simple reason for grain elevators, as there is for everything, but the force behind the reason, the reason for the reason, is the land and the sky. There's too much sky out there, for one thing, too much horizontal, too many lines without stops, so that the exclamation, the perpendicular, had to come. Anyone who was born and raised on the plains knows that the high false front on the Feed Store, and the white water tower, are not a question of vanity. It's a problem of being. Of knowing where you are. On a good day, with a slanting sun, a man can walk to the edge of his town and see the light on the next town, ten miles away. In the sea of corn, that flash of light is like a sail. It reminds a man the place is still inhabited. I know what it is Ishmael felt, or Ahab, for that matter—these are the whales of the great sea of grass.
>
> (*HP* 75)

Another striking image is that of the plow (fig. 4), again literally mentioned in the text, although in passing, in a momentary simile. Remembering how the old man, albeit with great courtesy, refused the gift of a brier pipe and an expensive tin of tobacco, the narrator remarks:

> No, you couldn't tell them, show them, or give them anything. They were like the single plow below my window—when the old man had a piece of plowing to

do he hitched up his team of mares, and that is what he used. A foot deep and a yard wide, stopping at the end of the furrow to sit on the crossbar and spit out the white grubs at his feet.

> (*HP* 25)

But this particular photograph shows the long cast shadow indicating the end of the day, and thus that the plow—and the horse that pulls it and the man that follows and guides it—are all at rest. This is a matter and a time of day not literally invoked in the text at all. But the few lines of text immediately following on the mention of the plow suggest a figurative connection with the photographic image of the plow, and what is almost its monumental or commemorative quality:

> "It's men like him," Ivy had said, "who made this goddam dust bowl."
>
> True enough—but it was men like him who were still around when the dust blew away.
>
> (*HP* 25)

One particular photograph is all of texts. A scrapbook page shows a commonplace-book of newspaper clippings, including the particular one referred to, commented on, and read aloud from in the story. It can be seen that among the clippings there is some newspaper verse, some dialect-humor on the lower right, and next to it some instructions for sending amorous messages encoded in the way a postage stamp is placed on an envelope. Next to that is the text called "A Parody," an example of a vanishing genre in which rhymed, jingly verse was printed as prose in newspapers, as much for the exigencies of spacesaving in a column of type as for the minor pleasure of a readerly recovery of the verse from its linear dislocation. The "parody" in question is of the widely-known verses of Elizabeth Akers Allen (1832-1911), entitled "Rock Me to Sleep" and beginning "Backward, turn backward, O Time, in your flight, / Make me a child again, just for tonight . . ." In the text of the story, the jingle is quoted not in the restored verse format, but with the line breaks identical to those in the columnar typesetting:

> Backward, turn backward, oh,
> Time in your flight, and give us a
> maiden dressed proper and right.
> We are so weary of switches and
> rats, Billie Burke clusters and peach
> basket hats . . . etc.
>
> (*HP* 138)

It is hereby indicated that this is the way Muncy half-mockingly reads the newspaper clipping aloud; it also frames a subtle joke—central for the book generally—about the verbal and the visual and their various versions of each other.

The notion of pattern in its relation to surface and depth, that will recur in the book, is introduced by the image of the chair (fig. 6). Facing it is a paragraph that begins:

To sit on a straight-backed chair I have to lean forward, on my knees, and look at my hands or something on the floor. On the floor was a piece of worn linoleum. The center of the pattern had been worn off, and Clara had daubed on one of her own. Brown and green dabs of the brush. Uneven rows . . .

(*HP* 41)

Later on down the page the narrator continues: "I looked at the floor again and decided that the pattern was part of the floor. It was not decoration. That was why she had daubed it on again" (*HP* 43). This gets picked up again in the text on the following page, following the brief observation quoted earlier, in which the narrator says "I did not look at her with my camera eye." It continues: "I looked at the floor and the hole she had worn in the patch of linoleum, and the hole beneath the patch, by rocking and dragging her heel. Every time she rocked forward, the right heel dragged back." A temporal dimension is added here, in a modern revision of the old Renaissance conceit of *Veritas filia temporis*—"truth is the daughter of time"—that makes it problematic: marked by the pendulum-clock motion of the rocking chair, time effaces pattern and deconstructs surface design.

This central issue returns with a notion adapted from an important Henry James story[7] where it refers to a secret but general interpretive key to a novelist's oeuvre. Morris refigures it throughout **The Home Place,** moving from an image of the pattern on linoleum (and, perhaps more deeply), "in" a carpet, to the later patterns of the traces that human activities themselves impose on, or engrave into, these established ones—moving from a question of the meaning of stories to one of the meaning of lives. This emerges in a most crucial passage in the book (almost "illustrated" by a photograph of a tattered jacket, sweater and cap hanging in a row from hooks against a white wall).

> What is it that strikes you about a vacant house? I suppose it has something to do with the fact that any house that's been lived in, any room that's been slept in, is not vacant any more. From that point on it's forever occupied . . . with the people gone, the place is inhabited. There's something in the rooms, in the air, that raising the windows won't let out, and something in the yard that you can't take out of the grass. The closets are full of clothes you can't air out. There's a pattern on the walls, where the calendar's hung and the tipped square of a missing picture is a lidded eye on something private, something better not seen. There's a path worn into the carpet, between the bed and the door, the stove and the table, where the heel drags, the carpet is gone, worn into the floor. The pattern doesn't come with the house, nor the blueprints with the rug. The figure in the carpet is what you have when the people have lived there, died there, and when evicted, refused to leave the house.

(*HP* 132)

This speaks at once to what a camera would notice in recording tokens of absence, and what a novelist's writing would "notice" in its way of mutually confronting fact and fiction, literal and metaphoric constructions of reality (the fine sentence about the wall with the calendar and the "tipped square of a missing picture" is in some sense a sort of verbal photograph).

The very next photograph is of the bed in the empty house in question. In the narrative, the city-dwellers are inspecting it for possible occupancy—old cousin Ed had recently died in it. The bed, and the barely visible shoes placed one slightly in front of the other, as if they were about to take a step, are the subject of a meditation that moves almost inevitably through metaphors of photography itself. It is significant that the prominently discernible figure in the carpet on the floor at the side of the bed—it looks like a good Caucasian tribal rug, hardly the worn Axminster mentioned elsewhere in the book—is totally ignored in the facing text that immediately follows on the turned page after the passage I just quoted, with its very different use of James's trope of the figure in the carpet.

> "That's Ed's room," I said, and my wife stepped up to look at it. Then she backed away, as if she saw someone in the bed. There are hotel beds that give you the feeling of a negative exposed several thousand times, with the blurred image of every human being that had slept in them. Then there are beds with a single image, over-exposed. There's an etched quality about them, like a clean daguerreotype, and you know in your heart that was how the man really looked. There's a question in your mind if any other man, any other human being, could lie in that bed and belong in it. One might as well try to wear the old man's clothes. His shoes, for instance, that had become so much a part of his feet they were like those casts of babies' shoes in department stores. Without saying a word, or snapping her knuckles, my wife turned away.

(*HP* 135)

The book's closing paragraphs face its very last photographic image, that of the old man—again, with his face averted—walking into a barn in what we cannot help but read not so much as an entrance but as an exiting. The text meditates upon transience and decay, but with a wonderful final turn on the metaphor of the pattern that speaks of surface and depth, and of the ghostly presence of traces of what had been life, in a splendidly conclusive way:

> Nothing happens to a man overnight but sometimes what has been happening for years, every day of his life, happens suddenly. You open a door, or maybe you close it, and the thing is done. It happens. That's the important thing. I watched the old man in his nautical hat cross the yard like one of his harrows, the parts unhinged, the joints creaking under a mat of yellow grass. He stopped near the planter to suck on his pipe, tap the bowl on the seat. On the spring handle of the gear was a white cotton glove, with the fingers spread, thrust up in the air like the gloved hand of a traffic cop. The leather palm was gone, worn away, but the crabbed fingers were spread and the reinforced stitching, the bib pattern, was still there.

(*HP* 176)

But the glove in the narration—its most striking "image" in one use of the term—is not shown in the picture, which has its own allegorical work—about walking in, out, and away—to do. Instead, that verbal image must conclude the book, with the turns on the figure from Henry James used throughout it, in a parallel metaphor, acknowledged in the final sentence. "[. . . the bib pattern was still there.] The figure on the front of the carpet had worn through to the back" (*HP* 176).

Notes

1. John Hollander, *The Gazer's Spirit: Poems Speaking to Silent Works of Art* (Chicago: University of Chicago Press, 1995), 67-69.

2. Wright Morris, *Writing My Life: An Autobiography* (Santa Rosa: Black Sparrow Press, 1993), 353.

3. Quoted in Morris, *Writing My Life,* 353.

4. Morris, *Writing My Life,* 356.

5. Wright Morris, *The Home Place* [1948] (Lincoln, Nebraska: University of Nebraska Press, 1968), I. Subsequent citations in brackets are of page numbers in this edition.

6. David E. Nye in "Negative Capability in Wright Morris's *The Home Place*" (*Word & Image* 4.1 [1988]: 163-69) notes this, but seems not to be concerned with the way in which the reader is questioned, in a caption-like way.

7. "The Figure in the Carpet" in Henry James, *Complete Stories 1892-1898* (New York: The Library of America, 1996).

Alan Trachtenberg (essay date 1996)

SOURCE: "Wright Morris's 'Photo-Texts'," in *The Yale Journal of Criticism,* Vol. 9, No. 1, Spring, 1996, pp. 109-20.

[*In the following essay, Trachtenberg attempts to derive the significations of Morris's photo-texts through comparisons with photos by Walker Evans and a poem by Donald Justice.*]

Wright Morris's inspiration in the 1940s to combine words and photographs resulted in several unique works of fiction, "photo-texts," he called them, in which image and text stand to each other in quite unexpected ways.[1] In *The Inhabitants* (1946), *The Home Place* (1948), and *God's Country and My People,* (1968) picture and word cohabitate in a manner of mutual and complex exchange.[2] At a casual glance these works might seem similar to the juxtapositions of word and image in documentary texts popular at the end of the 1930s, but a more careful look and reading makes clear that in spite of some superficial resemblance in depictions of rural scenes they have little in common with works like Erskine Caldwell and Margaret Bourke-White's *You Have Seen Their Faces* (1937) or

Dorothea Lange and Paul Schuster Taylor's *American Exodus* (1939). They belong more properly under the heading of experimental fiction, formal experiments in the telling of stories, the construction of narratives. Moreover, each of Morris's books ventures a different way of setting image in relation to word, either disposing them throughout an actual novel (as in *The Home Place*) or linking them with texts which stand as discrete memories, not stories as such but story-fragments, free associations more on the order of dreams than narratives. Different as they are, each of the three works addresses similar questions regarding the role of images in the making of fiction. And presiding over the three books is the question of photography itself, its work as a medium and its figurative implications for human experience.

How might pictures play a role in storytelling, how might they lend themselves to accounts of character, event, and scene, how might a visual component or dimension contribute to the verbalization of experience, to the crystallization of experience into knowledge? Questions such as these underlie these remarkable and compelling works and account for their fascinating subtexts, their continual hum of meditation and commentary upon photography and experience. For what emerges as most remarkable, most original in Morris's photo-texts is the way they make of photography something more than a collaborative method. Photography becomes a thematic center of its own, a master key to the essential matters undertaken in the fictions: place, time, memory, aura, privacy, loss, and the scruples and compunctions of consciousness in undergoing these experiences.

The thematization of the photograph, more accurately, of the photographic act itself, appears most prominently in *The Home Place,* the book among the three works which most resembles a conventional novel, a continuous linear narrative. Occupying every other page, the pictures might seem supplements more than complements of its action, direct illustrations of the text, though such literalness of reference is usually undercut by the reader's reflection on the multivalent relations between image and text. The story concerns the narrator's uninvited and unannounced visit from the East with wife and child to an old relative's old house in rural Nebraska . . . .

> "That's Ed's room," I said, and my wife stepped up to look at it. Then she backed away, as if she saw someone in the bed. There are hotel beds that give you the feeling of a negative exposed several thousand times, with the blurred image of every human being that had slept in them. Then there are beds with a single image, over-exposed. There's an etched clarity about them, like a clean daguerreotype, and you know in your heart that was how the man really looked. There's a question in your mind if any other man, any other human being, could lie in that bed and belong in it. One might as well try and wear the old man's clothes. His shoes, for instance, that had become so much a part of his feet they were like those casts of babies' shoes in department stores. Without saying a word, or snapping her knuckles, my wife turned away.

(135)

The wife's turning away precedes by a couple of pages the husband-narrator's reaction to an old album of newspaper clippings:

> I put my hand up to my face, as it occurred to me, suddenly, how people look in a *Daily News* photograph. A smiling face at the scene of a bloody accident. A quartet of gay waitresses near the body slumped over the bar. God only knows why I thought of that, but I put up my hands, covering my face, as if I was there, on the spot, and didn't want to be seen. I didn't want to be violated, that is. The camera eye knows no privacy, the really private is its business, and in our time business is good. But what, in God's name, did that have to do with me? At that moment, I guess, I was that kind of camera.
>
> (138)

Even where the text makes no overt mention of cameras or photographs, by use of windows, mirrors, views through openings, and photographs within the photograph, Morris will often insinuate photography as the figure in the carpet, the underlying master trope which informs an ongoing process of self-discovery. The narrator meditates upon his own behavior as a visitor with an irrepressible eye for objects, surfaces, the fall of light, and their implications. What kind of camera-eye am I? Or might I be? Does seeing photographically hold a clue to my situation here, in this "home place"? What are my obligations and duties to the sense of the past such images recover for me, and to my own place within that past, within *this* place? The camera here represents more than an act of seeing, but an act of seeing which arises from and mirrors back to the self an act of being, a way of standing toward others and the privacy inscribed in their ambient objects, the spaces of their houses, the chairs set against walls, the old snapshots arrayed upon mirrors.

Through his photographic work in the 1930s and 1940s Wright Morris seems to have discovered for himself that photographs have a way of inviting or enticing language, not for the sake of completing or specifying a "meaning" (as in photographs with a documentary purpose) but more contingently, as something camera images do, some aspect of their character as traces of a wordly act of seeing. Morris said in an interview in 1975 that photographers all share a common sensibility, a sensibility which moves among us and works simultaneously through many eyes.[3] And in an essay in 1979 he refers to an actually anonymous picture which might have been made by either him or, say Walker Evans, whose 1930s pictures Morris's work often brings to mind. "I recognized with a shock," Morris wrote, "that this anonymous photographer was seeing through my eyes, and I through his. The similarities of all photographs are greater than their real or imagined differences."[4]

What these similarities are, what a photograph possesses in the way of an embodied act of seeing and knowing by virtue of its being a photograph, is what Morris's photo-texts attempt to say. The similarities his work shares with

Walker Evans's, and the differences upon which the resemblances are founded, can lead us to certain discoveries of our own about Morris's thematic deployment of photography in his photo-texts. While Evans, a would-be writer who chose the camera instead, collaborated often with writers, most famously with James Agee, he scrupulously eschewed adding his own words to his pictures, except for laconic identifying captions. How Evans's images can be said to stand toward language might help us see what is distinctive in Morris's play of word and image in the mode of fiction.

Take this picture, which first appeared uncaptioned in the expanded portfolio of pictures in the 1960 edition of *Let Us Now Praise Famous Men,* and hear how the poet Donald Justice recomposes elements of the image into a text both independent and coeval with it . . . :

"Mule Team and Poster"

Two mules stand waiting in front of the brick wall of
  a warehouse,
    hitched to a shabby flatbed wagon.
Its spoked wheels resemble crude wooden flowers
    pulled recently from a deep and stubborn mud.

The rains have passed over for now,
    and the sun is back,
Invisible, but everywhere present,
    and of a special brightness, like God.

The way the poster for the traveling show
    still clings to its section of the wall
It looks as though a huge door stood open
    or a terrible flap of brain had been peeled back, revealing

Someone's idea of heaven:
    seven dancing girls, caught on the up-kick,
All in fringed dresses and bobbed hair.
    One wears a Spanish comb and has an escort . . .

Meanwhile the mules crunch patiently the few corn-
  shucks
    someone has thoughtfully scattered for them.
The poster is torn in places, slightly crumpled;
    a few bricks, here and there, show through.

And a long shadow—
    the last shade perhaps in all of Alabama—
Stretches beneath the wagon, crookedly,
    like a great scythe laid down there and forgotten.

    on a photograph by Walker Evans (Alabama, 1936)[5]

Compare Morris's textualization of an image in *The Inhabitants* . . . :

> All the same. The streets, the stores, the faces, the people—all the same. An all-overmore something added and that was all. More people, more big, more everything, more less at home. More the less alone it seemed the more he was. More people to know than he'd ever dreamed, more people seen than he'd ever know, more left unsaid. All people in windows, not

people you come to know. A girl in a window showing a ring or holding a bottle and tapping the glass, or stripped down some showing even more. Or a man with a corset to melt your pouch or if you hadn't a pouch it would widen your shoulders, lengthen your life. Nobody thought of talking to her or seeing more than the pouch on him, or wondering if whoever they were they were alive. They were just the pouch, or the ring, or the look, or whatever they did. Not somebody to know or like but something to buy. Something to have if you first just had the dough.

(np)

We can take the poem by Donald Justice as an instance of how Evans's images arouse a desire to speak or write, to reassemble the components of the image, including its interior light, into a construct of words independent of the image, addressed *to* (or, as it says, "on") it rather than *from* it. Through the lens of the poem the separate parts of the picture cohere into the vision of a figurative place, an "Alabama," and its interior life. The Morris text, on the other hand, does not so much reconstruct the image as lend the image a voice, an imagined utterance from within, as if the picture were the occasion of a memory rather than the fact of that memory.

And arbitrarily so: Morris's habit of aligning the same image in different books with different texts confirms the point that the voice attached to the image is a fictive voice. For example, in *God's Country* the same image speaks like this:

> With me in mind, my father picked a room with a view of the park. From the window, if the trees were bare, we could lean out and see the statue of Lincoln, green as the bent prong of the fork used to open the hole in a can of milk. In the room only one person could dress at a time, but that was no problem since the father worked nights. He was in bed in the morning when the boy got up. It was the sheets that took a beating since there was always someone between them. One day the boy came running up the stairs to find his father seated in the bed spout, where the springs sagged, with a girl in his lap. Her face was like a clown's mask bobbing on his shoulder; her thighs hugged his waist. And the boy had arrived on the scene too late; the machine would not stop. Coins dropped from the man's pockets to roll about on the floor. No, it was not a good scene. . . .

(np)

The voice of the image is what is imagined on this particular occasion, not the exclusive or even necessary resident of the place of the picture, only what we hear right now, on this occasion, the occasion of this fiction.

With these differences in mind we might say provisionally that Justice's poem reveals Evans's photograph as representing a moment in cultural history, while Morris's photograph represents, or is treated by the author as representing, a story of personal memory. History and story: I mean these terms here to stand for distinctive kinds or modes of narrative articulation. Where the historian gathers evidence of a past, traces of what has been lived and endured and shared by many, a recognizable public past which can be stated in narrative form, the storyteller speaks of and out of experiences of private persons, out of intimate memory. We can say, abstractly and imperfectly, that the historian constructs public memory, the storyteller constructs private memory, always someone's memory, made communally available in the telling but marked by the privacy of its origins.

In the 1975 interview Morris speaks of something hidden within objects in photographs, and the need for language to bring that inner life forward. The similarity of the subject matter of **The Inhabitants** to depression-era pictures, he explained, "distracts many observers from the *concealed* life of these objects." "All, or most, photographs have many faces. The face desired is revealed by the caption. I do not have captions, but the facing text reveals the nature of the object that interests me: the life of the inhabitants whose shell they are." "These objects, these artifacts," he told the interviewer, "are structured with emotion, with implication, toward which I am peculiarly responsive. I see many of them as secular icons. They have a holy meaning they seek to give out."[6]

A meaning they seek to give out: these words echo a passage from Henry James's *The American Scene* (1907) which Morris mentions frequently and had placed as epigraph to **The Home Place**:

> To be at all critically, or as we have been fond of calling it, analytically, minded—over and beyond an inherent love of the general many-colored picture of things—is to be subject to the superstition that objects and places, coherently grouped, disposed for human use and addressed to it, must have a sense of their own, a mystic meaning proper to themselves to give out: to give out, that is, to the participant at once so interested and so detached as to be moved to a report of the matter.

To be sure, James's account of a "mystic meaning" can be claimed as well for the method of Walker Evans. It's not just the desire to witness and preserve as an image the mysterious aura of meaning of a scene or place which points to the distinctiveness of Morris's romance with the "concealed life" of objects.

The difference between Evans and Morris doesn't lie so much in what they identify as holy or mystic but in what they see as meaningful enough to put down as image, to what innuendos of concealment they respond. Morris wrote that Evans's book, *American Photographs* (1938) "had profoundly confirmed my own responses. I did not see through Evans's eye, but I was captive of the same materials."[7] But, of course, the same becomes the different in different eyes. Evans's pictures typically fill their space with implication, one part articulated in dialogue with another, the whole giving out possibilities of meaning, nothing seemingly concealed, everything on the surface, only complexly so. Morris has an eye for objects which release

. . . [and] ground up." Morris plays briefly with Tocqueville's theory that democracies expand the notion of human perfectibility "beyond reason." A sense that humans are moving toward perfection without regard to restrictions of reason or place creates a monster which assumes that progress is always better, making the habits of the past irrelevant (*TA* 210-13).

According to G. B. Crump, Morris represents "one of the most single-minded demonstrations of going one's own way in recent American letters" ("Wright Morris" 7). In the past twenty years, however, a chorus of writers have joined him in realizing the loss of a vital connection in the twentieth-century rush toward urbanization. Perhaps the most widely known among this chorus is Wendell Berry. In Berry's most extended argument, *The Unsettling of America,* he explains how exploiters, in the name of progress and profit, cause the removal of settled nurturers (usually farmers) from the countryside. The removal to cities changes nurturers from community people with choices into consumers dependent on massive industries wrapped in the cloak of progress. Writers like Berry believe that a necessary set of virtues and a sense of connection to a place are lost when a significant part of the population is not rooted, especially in farming communities. "Kindly use [of a place]," according to Berry, "depends upon intimate knowledge, the most sensitive responsiveness and responsibility. As knowledge (hence, use) is generalized, essential values are destroyed" (31). Many writers are making these arguments now.[3]

Although Morris seems in agreement with these arguments, he is a modernist, not an advocate for social change. He is concerned, as Henry James was, with the centrality of art in "expanding consciousness." This consciousness includes Morris's recognition that, no matter *what* we think, humans are the part of the evolutionary process that has developed self-consciousness.[4] Crump, while recognizing that Morris is most interested in creative acts which jar characters out of their illusions, finds these acts "tied . . . closely to a nature very much in this world." She quotes Morris: "The conceptual act is the most organic act of man. It is this that unites him with the processes of nature, with the nature of life. If man is nature self-conscious . . . art is his expanding consciousness, and the creative act, in the deepest sense, is his expanding universe" (Crump, "Wright Morris" 11). The creative act at its best, however, does not create an alternative to what is, but the "expanding consciousness," with wonder and awe, adapts itself to the nature of life. This adaptation might begin when a keen observer senses something "holy" about people who live simple lives partly because they sense that their lives are rightly tied to "the processes of nature." For Morris, such people seldom carry out the creative artistic act, but they can inspire it through the acts and wisdom that follow when their "place" in the natural world is a central source of daily meaningfulness and meditation in their lives.

For over thirty years, Morris has argued that the ability to adapt is central to what humans are, but that modern people are not good at adapting themselves to the actual world. In spite of having the creativity to adapt to almost anything, they instead invent an illusory world designed to suit their desires. Morris, on the other hand, associates adaptation with a conceptual power that enables a person to see how to change *herself* in relation to reality so that illusory concepts can be scrapped (*TA* 229-30). What we as a culture have attempted to invent is a sense of selfhood based on words and freedom from limitations of place; these are accomplished primarily through displacing the image of reality with language constructs.

In a 1991 interview, Morris argued that such an attempt creates "a new priesthood of selfhood" by investing significance in the construction of consciousness through words. Freud and Henry James were the central promoters of the new "priesthood": "So here were Freud and James, just in time to cut the last nonconscious ties of man to his time, to his place, to his sense of nature. The fully conscious person became as free and as disconnected as words could possibly make him" (Morris interview 69). Freud and James assumed that humans were above all social creatures whose most significant concerns engage them in creating and negotiating relationships with other human beings primarily through language. Nonconscious ties to place and a "sense of nature" seemed relics of a primitive past that we were slowly getting over.

In Morris's *Fire Sermon* (1971) and *A Life* (1973), illusions cluster around notions about human freedom and disconnectedness; the disconnected, free people are the hippies, Kermit, and others in the "new" generation who lack attachment to past and place. In contrast, the old man, Warner, having lived in California for decades, is drawn back to the connections that sustained him, first at his sister Viola's house in Nebraska, and finally, following "the wisdom of the body" (a notion Morris borrowed from D. H. Lawrence [Crump, *Novels* 17]), dies at the hands of a Native American, Blackbird. Blackbird appears as a puzzling, rather threatening agent of the past, standing "opposed to the White, American Dream of wealth and prosperity in the name of which the West was won, Indian culture shattered, and the land finally depleted" (Neinstein 151).

Warner, aided in his death by this mysterious oppositional character, does not know the meaning of his life and death, but what he does know is based on what he is not conscious of and is satisfactory. He believes that he chose a life that he can look back on with satisfaction, but just as neither he nor Blackbird quite know that Blackbird is going to provide an easy death for Warner, Warner does not know the most significant truth about his life: "he had been chosen not merely to grow old, but to grow ripe" (*A Life* 152).[5] Morris explains this in relation to his ties with nature:

> [Warner] does not grasp why [he will die], but his nature accepts it: he gives himself to it. This is considered a transcendent experience for "higher forms" of

life, but it is commonplace among most of God's creatures who have not cut their ties with nature. Curious how we assume that such a "natural" experience is mystical.

(Morris, **"Dictates"** 116)[6]

This kind of consciousness does not depend on verbal explanations, but results from accepting a "natural" image of oneself-in-place without attempting to make something more of what is there.

Most humans, however, find "natural" experience difficult to accept. In an essay on photography published a year before *Plains Song,* Morris wondered what cultural aberration "makes it impossible for us to *reside* in, to be at rest with, an image" ("image" here is a photographic presentation of what is, an image of natural experience). His tentative answer was that we "fear that what we see . . . might be all there is." We reject this seemingly flat possibility by turning to words, a discussion of the image, thereby losing the insight that the image itself can provide (Morris, **"Photographs"** 467). At best, Morris argued, remarkable photographs, fully seen by those willing to look, probe our convictions; one of them, serving as icon, might prove to be "a confirmation of the wonder and the shudder of terror that signal an expanding consciousness."

The expanding consciousness deals with the image serving as icon, not with the verbal explanation. An image having such an iconic effect will contain "the necessary destructive element. What it has in mind for us may not be what we have in mind for ourselves" (469). Most of the images Morris chooses to present in his photography seem to have "in mind" for us a sense that "rural artifacts are inhabited and holy" (Madden 52). Although whether Morris has chosen the "right" images is open to question, an observer who is able to reside in his images might find that the images challenge the assumption that the new, or state of the art, is always better than the old. If the image penetrates, the observer has a wider range of choices than before, though he might like these choices less than the ones he invented.

Morris is not opposed to analysis (he has done plenty of it himself) but wants analysis to be based solidly on images that in themselves require little further explanation. Knut Hamsun's *The Growth of the Soil,* which Morris read in the 1930s, is "about how the obsession with total freedom of the soul is not a resolution of the human condition but rather a predicament" (Morris interview 70). The predicament is that to become free, one must cut his ties to place and people and build a world beyond the images presented to us, but this world will be made of words. A result of this concept of images, words, and place has been Morris's consistently terse fictional style and his spare photographs, as well as his forty-year interest in the frugal Clara/Cora character.

II

Since the 1940s, Morris has puzzled over his attraction to people who seemed at peace working and living simply, or frugally, in a rural place. In the 1970s, he began to work out how a key part of such people's relation to place was nonconscious and should be left so. In this work, Morris is, of course, a novelist concerned to get it right, not an advocate of a romanticized version of rural life. If, as Morris proposed, the past is often a story told under the pressure of an undesirable present, it allows us to escape from the past and so avoid the need to adapt, or transform ourselves, in order to deal with realities. This is the point of the question on the first page of *Plains Song*: "Is the past a story we are persuaded to believe, in the teeth of the life we endure in the present?" How, in other words, do we avoid telling about the past romantically, nostalgically, or in a derogatory way that will only relieve our present anxieties, allowing us to avoid knowing the past for what it is and to continue to create illusions about selfhood and "full consciousness"?

Morris has tried for fifty years to tell the story of his Aunt Clara and Uncle Harry, his central image of people on the home place. He recalls a boyhood visit to their farm near Norfolk, Nebraska, in his memoir, *Will's Boy.* Clara and Harry seemed at ease in their lives, not dependent on language or social skills for their well-being and not especially interested in change: Harry "plowed with horses [a practice Wendell Berry advocates] although his son, Will, had told him there was no place for a horse on a farm. Harry had sent Will to the aggie college in Lincoln, then refused to believe anything he had learned" (73). This could be ignorant backwardness, but more likely is a result of Harry's sensing what method of farming on his place flows from rural "ripeness," a sense of doing the right thing for *this* farm. Perhaps living according to what works on his place was more important to Harry than increasing his production and income.

Aunt Clara and Uncle Harry are central characters in *The Home Place* (1948), along with Clyde Muncy, the man longing to return to their "connected" life. The effort fails; he cannot return completely, partly because he is free and disconnected enough to write about that life and longing. Nevertheless, Clyde tries, at least for the moment, to recapture his relatives' sense of connectedness because although "the smart thing is to say there is no connection . . . you can't get over the feeling that your Grandma, or the old man, were very much wiser in the matter than you managed to be" (59). Although he cannot make the connection, he is able to say that "what I saw was unbelievably corny, on the other hand I knew it was one of the finest things I had seen" (107).

Raymond Neinstein believes readers should not associate Morris too closely with Clyde because Clyde is mistaking a set of images for a recoverable landscape, thus falling into a nostalgic illusion about Clara and Harry's life (129). Neinstein is right in maintaining that Clyde cannot return (he has a city wife and children, for one obvious problem), but is off-base in holding that nostalgia prevents his constructing images that reflect what is really there on the farm, such as exhaustible resources, hardship, and silence. On the contrary, that people and resources wear out in hard work done in silence is at the core of what attracts Clyde. For example, Clyde's reflections on the dying Ed's shoes and old poems clipped from publications are a good gloss on many of the photographs on facing pages in the text. The images are often of simple, worn implements or buildings; these suggest hardship and silence, as Neinstein says, but, in the farm world of the Muncys, hardship and silence are unconsciously assumed to be part of living.

As Clyde looks at "these man-tired things," he finds them not beautiful, but capable of touching his emotions and taking him out of himself into a relation with other things. He tries to place what he feels, knowing it is not quiet "character," but maybe a kind of passion: "That kind of Passion has made them holy things. That kind of holiness, I'd say, is abstinence, frugality, and independence—the home-grown, made-on-the-farm trinity. Not the land of plenty, the old age pension, or the full dinner pail. Independence, not abundance, is the heart of their America" (138-41). The story ends with Clyde's reflections about how, on the farm, as things and people wear out, "the Figure" wears in. "The holy thing, that is, comes naturally. After you have lived your own life, you will die your own death and it won't matter. It will be all right. It will be ripe, like the old man" (176). Clyde knows about "man-tired things" that wear out along with the people that use them, but finds a holiness in the process, whereas Neinstein finds nostalgia.[7]

A basic element in Morris's approach is closely related to Loren Eiseley's conception of humankind as part of an evolutionary process, carrying primitive characteristics of the brain and body into the present. For example, when Lehmann meditates on the mind in *The Field of Vision,* he notes that the mind "had the same bit of froth on it that flecked the primordial ooze," so that "if the lines to the past were destroyed," then the mind is only "a cybernetic marvel" which cannot be turned on. The thrust into present thinking must come from the primordial past just as it comes from the unthinking body—cutting the connections leads to misunderstanding, with one major misunderstanding being the supposition that full consciousness can be created without including "the primordial past" and "the unthinking body."

Several Morris characters lose an essential quality of humanity when primeval connections are severed, though Morris has often taken this loss as a sad but necessary characteristic of contemporary life. Will Brady, in *The Works of Love,* for example, "could leave [the prairie], but he would never get over it" (13). In the last section of the novel, called "In the Wasteland," he is in Chicago, something of an isolated religious visionary playing Santa Claus. He was not insensitive or stupid, but perhaps never lived because he could not apply his love to the city, where works of love seem impossible. These works are relatively simple acts, such as holding children's hands and pitying the mass of people who don't know how to die without taking their material things with them.[8] Morris compared Brady to the ancient son of pioneers, Scanlon: "If Brady

seems to point toward an intolerable future, Scanlon's gaze is fixed on the mythic past. It remains serene and uncorrupted because it keeps itself out of this world" (quoted in Neinstein 136). Neither Brady nor Scanlon is able to use the past to transform himself in the present.

As far as Scanlon is concerned, the story he bears from his father's past, "serene and uncorrupted" as it might be, nevertheless tells how, if we are to live in the future, we must transform ourselves by going on the risky journey straight through hell. Those taking such a journey learn to do without the extra conceptual and mental baggage that prevents their recognizing that they are in a place requiring them to abandon their Eastern preconceptions (Hall). Even McKee, the baffled suburbanite of *The Field of Vision,* muddles through his doubts and oppressions in *Ceremony in Lone Tree* until at the end he identifies for a moment with the possibility that Scanlon had died because he had been disturbed by the smell of clover invading the arid prairie. McKee seems to catch a glimpse of how clover, requiring irrigation, signifies the advance of a culture that dominates and transforms its environment in the image of a consciousness separated from the natural world instead of adapting itself to its surroundings.

In *The Fork River Space Project* (1977), a novel whose interest is as much as anything in what it tells about Morris's concerns as he prepared to write *Plains Song,* Morris implicitly attacks people who believe they can change the world by imagining whatever they please without regard to the facts. Kelsey, a writer, tries to make sense of the dreams of Lorbeer and Dahlberg (and of his young wife's fascination with Dahlberg). The Fork River space project is based on their expectation the earth will either be suddenly resurrected or should be written off. If the earth is not restored, those in the know will abandon the earth to live in orbit. Such thinking leads Kelsey to think about what the earth looks like from outer space—he thinks of it more as inviting a landing than as suggesting a departure. In a central passage, Kelsey meditates on time and evolution, speculating that primates see ahead only because "it's less what they see than what they imagine"; there is more, he thinks, to be seen looking backward (155). He wonders why he had confused the history of the planet with the history of man, who is frivolous and fragmentary compared with the earth. Thus, an appropriate perspective is grounded in the pre-human, nonconscious history of the earth, as Lehmann suggested in *The Field of Vision,* not in whether short-term human expectations about the earth are coming to pass.

In a passage that can help explain what Morris means by "nonconscious ties," Kelsey wakes at night as a blast of wind hits his house; he has a sense of night with cosmic winds sweeping the air away:

> Nights speak to us profoundly of what once happened, of what might happen in the presence of darkness. I gripped the sill but I felt no terror until I came back to bed and missed Alice. I chilled all over, as if I had been dipped in a deep freeze. My sensations were so

primal I lacked a word for them. A plant might feel as much, or as little, as I did. There was not a shred of consciousness in it. I was in the world like a stalk of celery. . . . In the morning I would say I had the damnedest dream—and it would be lost. I would not recover the sensation that must be common to everything but people. A purely sensuous being in the world.

(160-61)

Being human, Kelsey does not remain "a purely sensuous being," but uses his consciousness to think over the event, discovering oddly enough that his consciousness is expanded by the event to include a sense of being "in the world like a stalk of celery," or to sense the world as it was before human consciousness emerged. Kelsey, like Clyde Muncy, cannot return to the submerged consciousness of people like Clara and Harry, but can at moments expand his consciousness to include something like primeval connections to the earth.

This is followed by Kelsey's vision of an earth cleansed of man by a healing flood. Morris seems to be thinking here of the damage humankind has done by, for example, creating humans shaped "out of the need millions of cars have to be serviced" instead of imagining themselves into an identity with a tranquil earth (176). On the one hand, people fail to participate in the earth as nonconscious beings participate, but on the other, they lack the imagination to conceive of the earth as a place of tranquility. Instead, for example, they build cars and shape themselves to serve them or build foolish structures that must look like craters from outer space; these are the locations of stadiums at universities. Such stadiums demonstrate that a central function of universities is to train and exhibit football teams. These teams are an example of how males, like dinosaurs, are out of date, now going through "one of their primitive ceremonies" at a football game, unaware of their imminent extinction.[9]

Finally, when Kelsey recalls a visit to his wife's mother in southern Indiana, he describes a forest version of the Clara figure. Like Clara, Mrs. Calley "sat in an armless, wicker-seated rocker, her arms folded at the front like braces, rocking without lifting her feet from the floor." She does without electricity, rugs, bureaus, or decoration, so that "time moved sideways, ticking, or rose in circles." Kelsey senses "something unearthly" about the nights: "Something in my nature is unduly impressed with what has been sheared off, with the ultimately simple. It seemed to me the air I breathed was holy, like a loon's cry at Walden" (52). Kelsey knows that we have suffered "real losses," not only in our separation from the sensibility of the huge bulk of life on this planet, but also from the holy simplicity of "the ultimately simple." Clearly enough, Kelsey is not going to live like Mrs. Calley, though he is working imaginatively with the implications of a consciousness that is not separated from its sources.

Clearly, Morris is working with an ancient consciousness, one which he usually finds in old women settled in their place, and he is still exploring how such a disappearing reality can become imaginatively incorporated into a contemporary consciousness.

III

In *Plains Song* [hereafter abbreviated *PS*] (1980), Clyde's visit to Aunt Clara and Uncle Harry and the meditations of *Fork River* are reshaped with the craftsmanship a reader might expect from one of our most skillful writers pondering and experimenting with parts of the story for thirty-two years. In this novel Morris for the first time fully develops the flickering consciousness of Cora-at-her-place and the tragedy of the "real loss" in her dying. Cora's niece, Sharon Rose, leaves the home place to develop a contemporary consciousness free from its oppressions—but also, she later learns, cut off from its comforts and connections. Thus, late in the novel she finds her consciousness being expanded and transformed once she has imagined the nature of Cora's character. In this way, all three forms of consciousness interact.

In addition, as several critics have pointed out, Morris has given up on the possibility that men will transform themselves; it is significant that Sharon is an unmarried woman, and that her transformation comes through a vision of sorts (an image), which she then meditates upon. So it is that when Cora dies, Sharon returns to "the home place" to find that she has "grown up and old in order to recover what had escaped [her as a child]" and to feel herself relieved of "a burden she had carried" (*PS* 215, 223), perhaps the burden of telling herself a modern story about personhood that prevents her being transformed.

The narrator, beginning *Plains Song* with Cora on her deathbed, asks "Is the past a story we are persuaded to believe, in the teeth of the life we endure in the present?" "The past" in this case is Cora, now completing about twenty years of dying, and her descendants are those who tell her story "in the teeth of the life [they] endure in the present." Morris's central purpose in telling the old Aunt Clara Muncy story once more is to present it as image and icon, challenging stories often told about the rural past she represents. The stories he calls into question take two general forms: they tell us that all rural people are limited, backward, and longing to escape to the city (assuring us that we have progressed), or the stories are thick with a Norman Rockwell-like nostalgia about our collective childhood (as in the television version of *Little House on the Prairie*). Neither kind of story can lead to the admission that the development of a self- and language-based consciousness might leave us enduring a life that fails to incorporate the wisdom of people like Cora.

For example, before Cora's funeral, Caroline Kibbee, one of Cora's adult granddaughters, shouts her story about Cora and her husband Emerson's life as "The two of them together, sleeping and eating together, year in and year out, getting to loathe each other, none of it for the better, all of it for the worse—" (198-99). Caroline, struggling to define herself as an independent woman, can take some bitter comfort in this version of their life, although she is most angry about how Cora couldn't, or wouldn't, complain about such a life. When the farm is plowed under, this seems to Caroline a clear pronouncement that all they did was of little account.

Cora is an implacable, thin, six-foot, essentially sexless woman who walked with her elbows out, "fencing her off from smaller, friendlier people" (4). She lives the best of her life on "her farm" in the first thirty years of the twentieth century, just when modernist notions of consciousness were being most intensely developed and thousands of people were leaving the farm. In the last two-thirds of the novel, several of her descendants living from the 1930s into the 1960s tell stories about her life which assume she wasted her life on the farm and had no better sense than to choose to be satisfied with such a wasted life. Yet Sharon Rose, the niece whom Cora and Emerson raised, first leaves the narrow, spare life that Cora and Emerson lived, but then, in three returns over a period of about thirty-five years, finally affirms the image that was there was for her to see and "reside in." Then Sharon begins to recognize remnants of Cora's way of living in the world around her.

Central to this version of Clara/Cora is a silence which is appropriate as an adaptation to the silent, empty plains,[10] and an implacable sense of what is right and wrong in such a place. In both cases, Cora has seen what is on the plains and little more; not all of what she sees has to be brought to mind and put into words, especially the central reality, a "luminous void" at the heart of things. Although Cora has conventional ideas about God, these are secondary to her wisdom in assuming the "void," but allowing it to remain in silence. This being the case, she has no reason to analyze or justify her satisfaction in working out her life in relation to the specific Nebraska farm to which Emerson brought her and which she helped develop. Cora's satisfaction with her spare life is grounded in the intelligence with which she ponders the rich daily life she lives and makes improvements she considers compatible with her frugal sense of well-being in the place that in some sense chose her.[11]

For those willing to see this image for what it is, she was one of those chosen to become "ripe." At the same time, this is no romance: no one proposes some common spirit between farmers and their land; instead, there is a tie, or relationship between things different in degree of consciousness and volition. In addition, instead of meditating on the virtues of the untouched prairie, Cora and Emerson change it to suit their limited needs. Nor does Morris idealize Cora. Among her other faults, she is not a warm person; she realizes as Emerson is dying that she has hardly looked at him before now. She never quite grasps his death and slowly declines into senility. Still, even the dullest relatives find something compelling about Cora's certainty about her place and how to behave at "her farm"; they cannot conceive of Cora anywhere but at her place, even when she wanders about, unable to take care of herself.

Attempts to take her elsewhere or to interest her in anything beyond what seems appropriate to her farm end in failure.

From her Puritan forebears but more deeply from the hunters and gatherers from whose way of living we have only recently departed (in a Loren Eiseley—like sense of time), she has inherited a feeling that "against the forces aligned against her . . . there were no truces. If for a day or night she faltered, they made measurable gains" (39). This is not paranoia, but is reinforced daily by her experiences, and is tempered by her pleasures, such as watching Emerson come toward her behind a plow, rocking on the porch, buying and secretly admiring a linoleum floor cover, or admiring her lawn with a croquet game set up (a scene Morris repeats in several books), finding on such occasions that her "contentment might be so great it aroused her guilt. What has she done to be favored with such peace of mind?" (70)

Her guilt leaves her believing that these pleasures should be made up for in work. Ironically, the greatest pleasure, arising from these unquestioned sources, is in having unending work to do, yet being able to "see what each day accomplished" (56). These are human qualities, though close enough to seeming animal-like to a believer in personal development that the difference between Cora and less talented rural people may not be at first apparent. Belle Rooney, for example, the "natural" woman from the Ozarks who marries Emerson's brother and lives nearby, amazes Cora and Emerson with her inability to distinguish between right and wrong. Cora and Emerson are outraged when Belle's second child dies and she and her husband bury her without ceremony not far from the house. Adapting well to one's place does not result from acting "natural," but results from an adaptation to human tradition, in this case the Puritan one, and to a sensibility about what is right and wrong in *this* place. The obligation, the effort, and the satisfaction arise from "the void"; sensible people do not, in Cora's world, raise questions which penetrate this void, or silence.

A third of the way into the novel, the focus shifts away from Cora to her niece, Sharon Rose Atkins; then, as Ellen Uffen says, the story "loses its lyricism [and] its sense of dramatic continuity. . . . With the loss of Cora, the wholeness that once defined life is lost" (104). Most of the characters plod vaguely on, distancing themselves yearly from the sources that were deeply satisfying to Cora. These people are mostly the Kibbee family (Cora's daughter Madge, her children and grandchildren, along with assorted spouses), along with Sharon Rose. Three characters manage to do more than vaguely accept Cora's life: Madge's daughter Caroline is angry with Cora for being satisfied with her limitations; another daughter, Blanche, is a silent follower; and Sharon, who believed for most of her life that Cora should be pitied for being a farmer's wife, changes her story. She learns to tell a story about the past that is not driven by "the life we endure in the present"; in the end, she glimpses some strengths of Cora resurrected in the present. As a result, Sharon's consciousness expands to include Cora and her silent, nonconscious connections to her world; such a transformation would not have been possible if she had remained confined to the creation of language-based consciousness that she learned in the university and city.

Cora and Emerson raised Sharon after her mother, Belle, died and her father, Emerson's brother Orion, proved incompetent. When Sharon returns from enrolling at the University of Nebraska, a clash between Sharon and Cora results in years of reflection by both of them; these reflections reveal much of Cora's inner life and allow us to follow how Sharon changes her concept of Cora.

When Sharon returns from the university, Cora's placid daughter Madge is at the station to meet her. To Sharon's dismay, however, Madge, who was always the admirer of the more active, bright, and talented Sharon, not only pays more attention to her boyfriend, Ned Kibbee, than to Sharon, but is planning to marry him. Sharon screams, "Is he looking for a wife or a housemaid?" Cora, hearing this, is "speechless"; she can respond only by whacking Sharon's palm with the back of a hair brush, crying "'That will teach you!' . . . knowing that it wouldn't even as she said it." On reflection, "Cora's numbed, flickering awareness understood" that what she saw in Sharon's eyes was pity, not anger, and the pity was for farmers' wives, especially for Cora, "who seemed to lack the sense to pity herself" (75-76). For Cora, this cry challenges her choice to be the farmer Emerson's wife and to live with few words a life of chores accomplished in relation to their chosen place—and to be satisfied with the choice. In spite of Madge's saying, "Mama, she don't mean it the way you hear it," Cora always chose to believe Sharon "had meant it just as she said it" (164). When Cora hears language, it is not a device used to create a self; it is not and cannot be fiction in her world. Sparse as it is, language is part of an external reality that one must take serious account of and to which she will adapt as she must adapt to the season's rainfall.

Sharon is the family member most exposed to the "higher consciousness" of urban life, where she becomes a musician and teacher. Soon after she graduates from college, the narrator comments (with some irony) that "Sharon had been in Chicago, becoming a different person" (90). From the time Cora slapped her palm, Sharon suspects that farm life demands a half-submerged consciousness that makes people closer to farm animals than to other people. Farm girls like Madge are prepared for marriage as cattle are prepared for market, and when men ask for them, women give up relations to other women with "no thought to the life they rejected for the drab one they had chosen" (86).

Cora chose such a life, but Sharon always recognizes a strength of will and courage in her implacable sense of life not present in the pliable Madge, and Sharon measures herself by Cora's strength. Thus, "it was Cora Sharon thought of in moments of self-concern or self-appraisal"

(88), even though she believed that Cora wasted her considerable will and talents without complaint. Thus, Sharon remembers Cora sitting in her rocker facing the glare of the sun; later, when Sharon sees paintings of icons with "intense staring eyes," she thinks of Cora. The association seems to be with saints whose devotion eliminates concern for self: "it maddened Sharon that [Cora] refused to think of her*self*" (88). Urban persons like Sharon often seek self-fulfillment through thinking about and developing a *self* in isolation from task and place. Cora, in effect, refused, as Scanlon did in *The Field of Vision,* to enter a century that promoted such folly (*FV* 32, 42-44).

During Sharon's first visit back to the farm shortly after she has moved to Chicago, she listens to a conversation in the old house between Cora, Madge, Emerson, and Sharon's father Orion (95–102). On the surface, the content is inane, but when examined explains why, as Sharon approached the house, it seemed "charged with disturbing expectations." After the conversation, the narrator comments:

> When Sharon had left the farm to live in Lincoln, she had emerged from an oppression so habitual she had hardly suspected its existence. On returning she sensed her submergence to that lower level of feeling. As if drowsy with ether, she observed their movements and listened to their voices. Did this partially conscious life offer comforts she would live to miss?
>
> (102)

Morris often intends such questions to be finally unanswerable. Most people dislike oppression and have worked to create a self with a free consciousness—but "comforts" seems positive in this passage and is clearly tied to "partially conscious." For Morris, this is a case of "real losses" and "imaginary gains," with all the ambiguities implied in "imaginary." Sharon at this point has only the question,[12] but the question suggests doubt about the story she has formulated about the past that Cora represents.

During her second visit, for the wedding of her sister Fayrene, her overwhelming impression is that rural people unfortunately behave much like animals (123-35). From her meeting with the groom, Avery Dickel, whom she finds repugnant, to her seeing Ned pat his wife Madge's ample bottom "as he would the rump of a horse," her descriptions are packed with animal imagery. Although she believes people should not resemble animals, her thoughts take an odd turn toward the end of this visit. First, she finds herself thinking of Cora as she meditates on the "unflinching steadiness" of the gaze of Cora's granddaughter Blanche, who might find all these folk strange because she is more intelligent, awkward, and alone. Later, she muses on how she admires Cora for what she dislikes in Emerson and Avery, "that they were less persons than pieces of nature, closely related to cows and chickens."

What is different about Cora? Perhaps it is a high intelligence applying itself to the daily task of adapting to a place in the midst of a primeval silence, out of which, for such a being as Cora is, might arise events before which she stands speechless and amazed. In Cora, Morris imagines an exceptional example of the plains woman in her place. That few such women and men existed does not detract from the image as possibility lost, nor from its power compared to Morris characters such as Sharon who, seeking to find themselves in the city, find themselves lost.

On the way to catch her train back to Chicago, Sharon sits in Ned's truck, where she is, at least for the moment, submerged into the swarming life around her, so that

> Voices, bird calls, a movement of the leaves, the first hint of coolness in the air, were not separately observed sensations but commingled parts of her own nature. Her soul (what else could it be?) experienced a sense of liberation in its loss of self . . . and Sharon Rose, for all her awareness, blew on the wind with the dust and pollen that made her sneeze.
>
> (135)

This passage does not suggest that Sharon has fallen into a shameful state, but instead indicates that "loss of self" and a commingling with the world around her might offer "comforts she would live to miss." Sharon's response to this dulled but liberated sense is confused and might lead a reader to assume that her "inexpressible relief" on boarding the train to leave Battle Creek is only relief at escaping a repressive culture. It is more importantly relief at escaping a challenge to the story she has told about Cora as well as to her sense of selfhood.

This reading clarifies the episode in which Sharon boards the train for Chicago. A young man sits next to Sharon, telling her how he is leaving his home town and hopes that, once they pass it, he will have seen the last of it. Since what he has chosen henceforth is

> his own life, it would not be the life of Battle Creek or Colby, it would not be the trauma of birth and burial, or mindless attachments to persons and places, to kinships, longings, crossing bells, the arc of streetlights, or the featureless faces on station platforms, all of which would recede into the past, into the darkness—wouldn't it?
>
> (137)

If he chooses "his own life," then, as he hopes, the drama of the beginning and ending of life, the "mindless attachments to persons and places" will fade into the past— maybe. Thus, choosing "his own life" can make him "as free and disconnected as words could possibly make him," (Morris interview 69), and he will escape from the "ceaseless humiliations, inadmissible longings, the perpetual chores and smoldering furies, the rites of kinships" (*PS* 136). Perhaps such young men reject the rich, painful, connected life because they have been persuaded to believe it is undesirable, given "the [fully conscious but isolated] life we endure in the present."

On her third visit, described in the last two chapters of the novel, Sharon goes through one of the transformations that for Morris demonstrate human creativity through loss of illusions and adaptation to reality. Asked about whether the end of *Plains Song* might be an example of connections reestablished, Morris replied:

> Yes, Sharon Rose has spent her life severing ties. But she is devastated when she finally returns to her home-place to find it bulldozed away, the family dispersed. What can she do to be saved? She can try to reestablish consciously the ties to place and people that she has cut. . . . The moment when one is truly aware of loss—loss through death, betrayal, the loss of friendship or self-esteem—that's the moment when one is really beginning to be fully conscious. And there is no cultural accommodation to help me or anyone else deal with those losses.
>
> (Morris interview 71-72)

"Beginning to be fully conscious" in this case does not mean creating a self with the fictions of language. It means the beginning of a transformation from one whose first impulse is to sever ties and withdraw into her self-made world of phantoms. She might then become one who is restored to a "kinship with things that come into being and pass nameless away" (217). The first step in this restoration is to recognize the "real losses" that have been replaced by "imaginary gains." Crucial ties to place and people have been cut, perhaps in part because "progress" seemed to require the removal of millions of people from rural life where such ties were unconsciously assumed to compose the heart of life.[13] Whether one can "reestablish consciously" these old ties is not resolved in *Plains Song*. As the title indicates, the novel is above all a lament, a chant about loss.

Sharon's third visit is her return for Cora's funeral. Caroline, one of Madge's adult daughters, meets Sharon at the airport, reflects bitterly on the waste of Cora's life, and stops the car to show Sharon some stumps and land being plowed under—all that remains of Cora and Emerson's farm. Instead of proving Caroline's point, however, the emptiness of the place (or something else)

> evoked the presence of Cora[.] Not her image, not her person, but the great alarming silence of her nature, the void behind her luminous eyes. It had frightened Sharon. Had she sensed a similar hollow in her own being? Cora Atkins had been for silence, and she would not have countenanced impertinent questions. When she felt the deep silence of her soul threatened she had struck out with her hairbrush.
>
> (200-201)

Thus, the silence for which Cora had stood acknowledges an interior void, one which Morris believes humans fear and now try to fill with language and "full consciousness" of the self. Cora's sense of experience was such that the "silence of her soul" needed to be left unstirred; there were questions that were impertinent to raise because they pointed to the void, a blank lying behind human behavior and therefore so obvious and profound that it should be left as unexplorable reality. This being the case, the great human quality is adaptation, to the void as well as to what comes next (Morris interview 93). Efforts to explain what cannot be explained create illusions.

Later, at Cora's funeral, Sharon recognizes that Cora could never have understood that her works were erased, this being the ultimate rejection for one who measured the significance of her days by how much was accomplished. While the congregation sings "Abide with Me," Sharon wonders "what, indeed, had abided?" (214) Although the question seems unanswerable, Sharon senses that Cora's soul had made its peace; it accepted the half-submerged life that came with being tied to her place, work, and people. At the same time, Sharon realizes that she is Cora's child more than Madge is: about herself and Cora she can say, "Abstinence was something she understood; indulgence she did not." For one thing, Cora never found deep emotional relationships necessary; it did not occur to her to indulge herself in them, nor in piling up goods. Sharon, because she was nearly swallowed up in emotional music, was hurt in an early relationship with another woman, and is Cora's spiritual child, has also abstained.

As she remembers the young man thirty-three years ago who hoped he had seen the last of his town, Sharon wonders whether "they [had] both grown up and old in order to recover what had escaped them as children?" Madge's oldest daughter Blanche, now grown up, unmarried, tall, and usually silent, unwittingly helps Sharon "recover what escaped them as children," especially the meaning of Cora's deep silence. Blanche has "Cora's lustrous eyes" (203) and has drawn Cora's house and barn dimly on her faded wallpaper, confusing Sharon with emotions and remembrances of people now beyond recovery. At dinner the first evening, she feels displaced; statements and events take on meanings beyond the ordinary, setting her up for the visionary meditation later. One of Fayrene's daughters says she is going to live life to the full, speaking for those who believe such a thing is possible. Sharon is too surprised to respond to such a statement, wondering "what the fullness of this life might include."

As the dinner goes on, people seem not to hear what others say, or not to be expected to respond. Invited to eat part of Cora's last batch of pickle relish, Sharon hesitates, thinking of this as if it were part of Cora to be eaten, as in a strange Eucharist. Feeling disoriented, she dwells as much on her recollections of Cora's life as on events during the meal. In this context, Blanche, "the child-woman," who has been cooking and serving the meal, is called in to show Sharon how her pet bird will give her a kiss. Blanche, "her eyes wide with delight," allows the bird to pick her teeth, and all fall silent at this wordless demonstration of trust, kinship, and pleasure.[14] Sharon recalls the Venerable Bede's story of the bird as a symbol of the brevity of life, flying from the void outside for a moment through a brightly lit room, then back into the darkness.

The central meditation on silence follows, a meditation that brings together Caroline's cry against the reduced life Cora accepted without complaint, Cora's sense that the most important realities are not to be discussed, and Sharon's dawning awareness that Cora was, at the deepest level, correct in living the way she did.

> Caroline sat with her eyes lowered, as if in thought. She had been fearless in revealing what had been concealed, in resolutely confronting what had been hidden, but the most appalling facts were those that burned like gems in the open. Not in the bedroom only, or in the barn, or in the mind's dim recesses, but in the shimmering light that rose from the fields and buzzed with the drone of insects. On the palm of her hand Sharon felt again the stinging slap of Cora's brush. No matter how fearlessly youthful eyes stared, or youthful voices cried out what should not be mentioned, the tongue would prove to be silent, the eyes lidded in matters that were secret to the heart. In that way—how else?—it was possible to guess what they were.
>
> (213)

Caroline can say that Cora and Emerson loathed each other and can pronounce Cora's life useless, but this does not touch "the most appalling facts." These facts are about how life is a shimmering but brief, unnamed moment arising from the unspeakable void. Wisdom adapts without unneeded discussion; if "youthful voices cry out what should not be mentioned," someone who immediately knows when the great silence in which that truth lives is being invaded will, if the youthful soul who cried out is lucky, slap her hand with a hairbrush.

Sharon, learning how to retell the story of the past, thinks that "Whatever life held in the future for her, it would prove to reside in this rimless past," and what she learns from that past is how people and houses, "works and days," pass away into the thin air. One must make one's peace by adapting to place and work without falsifying "the most appalling facts" or trying to cover them over with diversions such as "the full development of the self." These thoughts leave Sharon feeling "at once incredulous and believing, at one with the world and fearlessly detached," baffled and elevated (215-17), understanding "real losses" and becoming transformed through "imaginary gains."

Back at the aptly named Crossroads Motel, Sharon, awakened to an "expanded consciousness" by the funeral, is alert to forces that bring "loose ends together" (222).[15] Alexandra Selkirk, a speaker at a Women World Wide convention, calls at 1:20 AM to insist that Sharon join her for breakfast. On the way to Alexandra's room, disparate scenes call for interpretation, including a man comforting a weeping woman. When Sharon offers to help, the man asks gently, "What can we do to be saved?" Sharon is startled by the question, sensing possibilities she had thought dead. At the same time, she realizes that she had, on Cora's funeral day, been "relieved . . . of a burden she had long carried, but had been reluctant to acknowledge." This burden seems to have been the need to construct a self in denial of ancient ties, nameless labor, and recognition of the final silence at the heart of life.

In Alexandra's room, images of Cora occur to Sharon as they had when she met Alexandra at the airport in Boston. She senses that whatever strange thing Alexandra might say, to be in her hands was to be in good hands. In a turmoil of feelings, she listens to Alexandra, who, pumped up by her successful speech the evening before, exults in the energy generated by the women's conference (on issues about which Alexandra is enthusiastic but confesses to not believing in). The cock crows, announcing the morning "with young male assurance," transporting Sharon into a flood of memories from Cora's place, "all of it gone, vanished from this earth, but restored to the glow of life in a cock's crow" (227-28).

Thus, with her burden of rejection lifted, Sharon revisits and affirms the kind of living Cora represents. This is clear when Alexandra, remembering that it is Sunday, invites Sharon for a walk. As Sharon watches Alexandra dress, "against the light of the bathroom her flat, skeletal figure appeared to be a resurrection of Cora," and Sharon imagines a syrup pail full of eggs in her hand and glass eggs bulging from the pocket of one of Emerson's sweaters she wore. When Sharon accepts the invitation to see the sunrise, she tells Alexandra that "I've not seen a sunrise since I was a child," asserting not only a return to the time she lived with Cora, but also to a sense of life associated with the rhythms of days and years.

Sharon sees in Blanche and Alexandra how she can affirm and adapt to a luminous silence that is rooted in a void. Cora's life was an expression of that silence and of her dedication to the accomplishment of chores which constitute life grounded in a place. The death of the Claras and Coras and Mrs. Calleys in the 1950s and 1960s suggests the real and irreplaceable loss of people who lived engaged in "the trauma of birth and burial, or mindless attachments to persons and places" (137). The need to know why we do everything we do, to put it into language, and to be assured of its permanence are, this novel asserts, foolish needs which cannot be fulfilled; the effort to create consciousness through language separate from this reality constitutes an "imaginary gain" that is an illusion.

To see the sunrise again, called by the male voice of the cock and the female voice of Alexandra, is to answer an invitation to imagine again the daily round of life connected to people and a place with a mystery that should remain rooted in nonconscious ties, luminous silence, the daily round of work, and a potential for deep pleasure. In the context of **Plains Song,** this means telling a story about the past that recognizes the wisdom of the adaptation that people like Cora made. In making such an assertion, Morris adds his voice to growing numbers of advocates of rural connectedness, though he might doubt that such a life can be recovered, except as an imaginative transformation.

Notes

1. In 1910 (Morris's birth year), a third of the population were farmers; now fewer than one percent are farming (Berry 63; McKibben 42).

2. Much commentary on the novel deals with Morris's belief that he has wasted his writing on males and now chooses to put women at the center. Arnold, for example, believes the novel is mostly about sexual roles and that Sharon's reconciliation with the present means that she can inhabit her new world because she has dealt successfully with the "distorted view of what sex and human interdependencies are and mean" that she had experienced with Cora (61-62). Lewis takes Cora to be an example of a past generation of women who protected themselves from their feelings and so from "the women inside" (33). These lives were unexamined and the novel is a celebration of the emergence of the audacious song of Sharon, which is "the song of consciousness" (37). Wydeven provides one of the best early readings of the novel, though within the context of Morris's attitudes toward women. Still, he recognized that Cora is in a tradition to which she is faithful and is not simply a bizarre adaptation to the plains. He also notes that Cora's strength reminds us of "the 'animal' qualities of the plains people in general [which] speak to traditional forms of faith and endurance which the younger generations are apparently rejecting out of hand" (223). This analysis places Cora in a tradition, suggests that "animal" (read "nonconscious") qualities are within this tradition, and that this tradition is what the novel demonstrates we are losing. Bird and Dyck believe Cora is admirable, though her adaptation to the plains seems bizarre and her stoicism stupid to Bird, and Dyck believes her method of limiting her awareness seems to be a loss, causing her and Sharon (who uses similar coping strategies) to miss much of life. This interpretation misses the point of Morris's treatment of Cora, though Dyck's conclusion is helpful: "Morris is suggesting that a rejection of the past is as constricting as an immersion in it [Cather's mistake]. The past needs to be confronted imaginatively so that one can shape its influence rather than be overpowered by it" (36).

3. Several people currently puzzling over environmental damage believe that our willingness to disregard the effects of our actions on our surroundings might in part be the result of efforts by contemporary people to cut nonconscious ties to place in order to become "the fully conscious person." But a countermovement may be gaining strength. J. Baird Callicott, for example, believes we are in the process of abandoning mechanistic notions of the natural world and replacing them with a sense "that our artificial systems are embedded in a hierarchy of natural systems" (20). He points out that, at the time of European contact, the aborigines in the Americas had "evolved cultural adaptations to their environments that were symbiotic rather than parasitic and destructive," and he (optimistically, I think) believes we can (and must, if we are to survive) learn to make such adaptations today as long as we recognize that humans are not by nature alien to but part of the ecosystems in which we live.

Part of his evidence that this change in thinking is occurring is that "industrial agriculture's eloquent and devastating critic, Wendell Berry, and organic agriculture's equally eloquent and persuasive prophet, Wes Jackson, have become folk heroes and celebrities" (22). Wes Jackson argues that because urban culture promotes "onlooker consciousness," the natural world is thought of as an object that we can control for our own purposes. A result is that "we no longer identify ourselves primarily as tribal members alive in nature in a spiritual cosmos. We have instead a great sense of selfhood, with which have come clear-thinking technical consciousness and control, leading to capacities for autonomous action" (39). This statement is quite similar to Morris's notion that modern consciousness cuts human ties with place and sense of nature.

Richard Critchfield, in a careful study of the loss of village life, suggests that the urban "glorification of material gratification as the way to happiness" has unfortunate consequences for human well-being and the sustainability of the earth. He believes that a viable culture can eventually be invented, but for now we have no workable replacement for the peasant view of the good life: "an intense attachment to native soil; a reverent disposition toward habitat and ancestral ways; a restraint on individual self-seeking in favor of family and community; a certain suspicion, mixed with appreciation, of town life; a sober and earthy ethic" (Robert Redfield, qtd. in Critchfield 427).

This seems to be a burgeoning field. Bill McKibben recently reviewed four new books on the topic in *The New York Review of Books,* and Diane Quantic published a book in 1995 on Great Plains fiction with the defining title, *The Nature of the Place.*

4. Loren Eiseley, a friend of Morris's, often deals with humans embedded in the natural world, but an especially fine example is "The Flow of the River" in *The Immense Journey,* 15-27.

5. Uncle Harry (Emerson's literary ancestor) is also "ripe" at the end of *The Home Place.* Both Harry and Emerson are more responsive and intelligent than readers often think. Re-reading both *The Home Place* and *Prairie Song* to find what they do and say is enlightening.

6. Crump, however, transforms Morris's "void" from which the wind comes into God, and she transforms Warner's submission to what comes next into a causality with a Cause behind it. Neither *A Life* nor other Morris works provide more than fragments of support for anything behind the physical world that is a cause of the fatalism that many of his characters feel. Leon Howard is more correct when he writes that "there is no God in Morris' imaginative universe—and no Satan, in the form of either a serpent or of a social system" (Howard 19).

7. See Madden (52-55) for a similar discussion of *The Home Place.* Bredahl believes that *The Home Place*

is nostalgic and that the photographs, which show no human faces, create a fragmentation with the text that is "ultimately life denying" (68). Clyde, he believes, goes back to learn the limitations imposed on the imagination by such nostalgia and learns enough to leave the Muncys and their farm behind. He contrasts the movement and sexuality of *In Orbit* with the "stable artifacts" of *The Home Place* to show how Morris favors the outsider, who "generates energy, and energy—several critics to the contrary—is at the center of Morris' world" (66). But not only do "outsider" characters such as Boyd often produce nothing, demonstrating their sterility, but in Morris's more recent work, his characters return to the home place in several ways, not to live there, but to find the "real losses" we have suffered by leaving the virtues and attitudes that sustained those who lived there.

8. See Booth's excellent extended discussion of *Works of Love* for further development. Also, Wydeven compares Brady to Sharon Atkins. Both go to Chicago seeking something—the American Dream or emotional fulfillment, but neither can get over having lived on the prairie (225-26).

9. Morris attacks college football four times in *Fork River* and once in *Plains Song.*

10. Critics deal with Cora's silence, but not as Cora's way of living in the presence of an unspeakable void. Bird, for example, writes only about Cora's silent adaptation to the plains, and Wydeven explains "animal" qualities of plains people that might include a silent acceptance of the demands and limitations a physical, temporal place imposes on living creatures, though he does not say so. The best of such people survive uncertainty with a kind of fatalism.

11. Dyck believes that Cora's improvements are "more an act of colonization than an act of belonging" (35). Yet, animal adaptation to place nearly always involves some change to the place; the problem arises when humans, with their powers of abstraction, no longer take account of the place in their construction, or when "need" is defined only as human need. See Callicott and Dubos for arguments that humans can "belong" to a place as they change it. Although the Atkinses plowed up the natural prairie turf and replaced it with a monoculture, their small-scale methods can be readapted to more sustainable methods (such as those Wes Jackson is developing at the Land Institute in Salina, Kansas) after warnings such as the dust bowl. Morris shows some interest in these issues in *A Life* when Warner observes that the grass he's standing on by the road

> might be classed as weeds by the men who farm the land. It's not a grass they mow, or a grain they harvest, so it must be weeds. This man is old enough to know better and remember when it was grass from horizon to horizon. His father had taken grass, as he did most things, religiously. Be-

fore the land had been plowed, or some would say broken, he had distinguished a dozen or more varieties of land cover, the nameless grasses that kept the soil from washing and blowing away.

(2)

12. William Pritchard believes these questions weaken the novel, since they are "questions no character could ever have asked," and that they turn the narrator too much into the whimsical humorist, winking at us from "behind his characters' skirts" (19). For other readers, the questions pose useful, though often unanswerable problems. Robert Knoll, for example, reads Morris as essentially raising questions: "Wright Morris is not judgmental, he does not prescribe. Perhaps we are to conclude that the newest generation is rootless, aimless, godless, and lost, lacking in some of the integrity that Cora had in marvelous abundance. Has it been downhill all the way? Do we live in the decline of the west?" (83)

13. For a short account of such a community, see Wendell Berry's "Does Community Have Value?" in *Home Economics,* 179-92.

14. Around the time Morris wrote *Plains Song,* he also wrote some short fiction about nonconscious, but natural, communication and sympathy between humans and animals. In "The Cat's Meow" (1975), a cat, "his radar beaming," contacts his human owners to announce his presence or desire to go out. This, the narrator, points out is not extrasensory, but natural. In "Fellow Creatures" (1984), a man, sensing his kinship with animals, cannot eat meat. I suspect Morris means to suggest such communication between Blanche and her bird.

15. Marilyn Arnold treats the episode at the Crossroads Motel in detail, concentrating on human connections and gender roles more than on problems of consciousness and connection to the past. Several have commented on the religious imagery in the last two chapters.

Works Cited

Arnold, Marilyn. "Wright Morris's *Plains Song*: Woman's Search for Harmony." *South Dakota Review* 20.3 (1982): 50-62.

Berry, Wendell. *The Unsettling of America: Culture and Agriculture.* New York: Avon, 1977.

———. *Home Economics.* San Francisco: North Point Press, 1987.

Bird, Roy K. *Wright Morris: Memory and Imagination.* New York: Peter Lang, 1985.

Booth, Wayne C. "Form in *The Works of Love." Conversations with Wright Morris: Critical Reviews and Responses.* Ed. Robert E. Knoll. Lincoln: University of Nebraska Press, 1977, 35-73.

Bredahl, A. Carl. "The Outsider as Sexual Center: Wright Morris and the Integrated Imagination." *Studies in the Novel* 18.1 (1986): 66-73.

Callicott, J. Baird. "La Nature est morte, vivé la nature!" *Hastings Center Report* 22.5 (1992): 16-23.

Critchfield, Richard. *The Villagers: Changed Values, Altered Lives.* Garden City, New York: Anchor/Doubleday, 1994.

Crump, G. B. *The Novels of Wright Morris.* Lincoln: University of Nebraska Press, 1978.

———. "Wright Morris, Author in Hiding." *Western American Literature* 25.1 (1990): 3-14.

Dubos, René. *The Wooing of the Earth.* New York: Charles Scribner's Sons, 1980.

Dyck, Reginald. "Revisiting and Revising the West: Willa Cather's *My Ántonia* and Wright Morris' *Plains Song." Modern Fiction Studies* 36.1 (1990): 25-38.

Eiseley, Loren. *The Immense Journey.* New York: Vintage, 1957.

Hall, Joe. "Wright Morris' *The Field of Vision:* A Rereading of the Scanlon Story." *Journal of American Culture* 14.2 (1991): 53-57.

Howard, Leon. *Wright Morris.* Minneapolis: University of Minnesota Press, 1968.

Jackson, Wes. *Becoming Native to this Place.* Lexington: University Press of Kentucky, 1994.

Knoll, Robert E. "A Doubled Vision of Reality." *Prairie Schooner* 54.2 (1980): 82-85.

Lewis, Linda. "Wright Morris's New Melody for Audacious Female Voices." *Great Plains Quarterly* 8.1 (1988): 29-37.

Madden, David. *Wright Morris.* New York: Twayne Publishers, 1964.

McKibben, Bill. "Some Versions of Pastoral." *The New York Review of Books* 11 July 1996: 42-45.

Morris, Wright. *Ceremony in Lone Tree.* 1960. Lincoln: University of Nebraska Press, 1973.

———. *Collected Stories: 1948-1986.* Boston: David R. Godine, 1986.

———. "The Dictates of Style." Conversation with David Madden. *Conversations with Wright Morris: Critical Reviews and Responses.* Ed. Robert E. Knoll. Lincoln: University of Nebraska Press, 1977, 101-120.

———. *The Field of Vision.* Lincoln: University of Nebraska Press, 1956.

———. *Fire Sermon.* New York: Harper & Row, 1971.

———. *The Fork River Space Project.* New York: Harper & Row, 1977.

———. *The Home Place.* 1948. Lincoln: University of Nebraska Press, 1968.

———. Interview. "The Art of Fiction." *The Paris Review.* With Olga Carlisle and Jodie Ireland. 33.120 (1991): 52-94.

————. *A Life.* New York: Harper & Row, 1973.

————. *In Orbit.* Lincoln: University of Nebraska Press, 1968.

————. "Photographs, Images, and Words." *The American Scholar* 48 (1979): 457-69.

————. *Plains Song: For Female Voices.* New York: Penguin, 1980.

————. *The Territory Ahead: Critical Interpretations in American Literature.* New York: Atheneum, 1963.

————. *Will's Boy.* New York: Harper & Row, 1981.

————. *The Works of Love.* New York: Alfred P. Knopf, 1952.

Neinstein, Raymond L. "Wright Morris: The Metaphysics of Home." *Prairie Schooner* 53.2 (1979): 121-54.

Pritchard, William H. "Fictional Fixes." *The Hudson Review* 33.2 (1980): 257-70.

Quantic, Diane Dufva. *The Nature of the Place: A Study of Great Plains Fiction.* Lincoln: University of Nebraska Press, 1995.

Uffen, Ellen Serlen. "Wright Morris's Earthly Music: The Women of *Plains Song.*" *Midamerica XII.* Ed. David D. Anderson. East Lansing, Michigan: The Midwestern Press, 1985, 97-110.

Waldeland, Lynne. "*Plains Song*: Women's Voices in the Fiction of Wright Morris." *Critique* 24.4 (1982): 7-20.

Wydeven, Joseph J. "Wright Morris, Women, and American Culture." *Women and Western American Literature.* Ed. Helen Winter Stauffer and Susan J. Rosowski. Troy, New York: Whitson, 1982, 212-29.

Laura Barrett (essay date 1998)

SOURCE: "'The True Witness of a False Event': Photography and Wright Morris's Fiction of the 1950s," in *Western American Literature,* Vol. XXXIII, No. 1, Spring, 1998, pp. 27-57.

[*In the following essay, Barrett examines the vicissitudes of photographic reality according to Morris, and how Morris uses photography to influence our understanding of the actual world.*]

> The photographer's power lies in his ability to re-create his subject in terms of its basic reality, and present this re-creation in such a form that the spectator feels that he is seeing not just a symbol for the object, but the thing itself revealed for the first time. Guided by the photographer's selective understanding, the penetrating power of the camera-eye can be used to produce a heightened sense of reality—a kind of super realism that reveals the vital essences of things.
>
> —Edward Weston, "What Is Photographic Beauty?"

In 1939, photographer Edward Weston envisioned a future in which images would surpass reality by capturing its essence rather than its surface. Instead of Weston's superrealism, however, we live in a world of hyperreality, defined by Jean Baudrillard as "the disappearance of objects in their very representations" (45). Postmodernists argue that a profusion of images precludes our ability to experience reality directly: the sign has replaced the referent, and the model has supplanted the real. Wright Morris, who has straddled the eras of modernism and postmodernism, evoked by the Weston and Baudrillard quotations, has long recognized that who we are and what we see are predetermined by previous images.[1] Indeed, describing his emotional response to a funeral procession that he witnessed in Mexico in 1958, Morris writes:

> At the somber beat of the drums the procession approached the farther corner, where, in the shadow of a building, a truck had parked, the platform crowded with a film crew and whirring cameras. The director, wearing a beret, shouted at the mourners through a megaphone. This was a funeral, not a fiesta, did they understand? . . .
>
> In my role as a gullible tourist, I had been the true witness of a false event.
>
> (*Time Pieces* 3)

Ironically, a respectful Morris refrained from photographing the ostensibly sorrowful occasion only to discover that the event existed merely for its filmic value.

His encounter with the pseudofuneral reflects a feeling pervasive in his novels of the fifties—that reality is waging a losing battle with its own representations. *The Works of Love, The Huge Season,* and *The Field of Vision* are rife with fictional photographs that symbolize the dangerous potential of images to reduce and replace reality, particularly as sentimental souvenirs of the past or illusive depictions of paradise.[2] With their tendency to frame space and remove episodes from time, photographs engender the illusion of perfection, stability, and permanence, an illusion so desirable in a complicated and fast-paced society that viewers are eager to acquire it by imitating the image, regardless of the fact that perfection, stability, and permanence equal death. It's not surprising that many of Morris's characters are caught between the material and immaterial worlds, between dreams and reality, between immortality and mortality, between falsity and truth, because they have been deceived by images.[3] On the other hand, Morris, himself a photographer, refuses to deprecate the medium of photography which, as seen in his photo-texts, has the power to reveal by resisting platitudes, by refusing to reduce its subjects to a predictable framed space, and, in that respect, his photo-texts are similar to postmodern photographs that deliberately challenge the reader's expectations. Literally, reusing space—Sherrie Levine's appropriations of famous photographs, including *1979 Untitled (After Edward Weston),* a copy print from a reproduction of Weston's *Torso of Neil,* Richard Prince's recycling of magazine and other mass media images in his self-entitled "rephotography," and Barbara Kruger's montages of reused images in dialogue with epigrammatic statements, such as "I shop therefore I am" and "Your money talks" boldly printed on the pictures—forces the reader to consider his/her relation to the images. Thus, Morris's fictional and actual photographs anticipate both the postmodern crisis, with its superfluity of images, and a possible postmodern response, which produces and/or recycles those images with a knowing eye.

The 1950s that Morris explores in his novels was a decade of representations, replicas, and microcosms. Baudrillard argues that hyperreality arose in the 1950s, epitomized by Las Vegas, "the absolute advertising city . . . of the 1950s, of the crazy years of advertising" (91). Disneyland, an amusement area dedicated to replacing reality with better, safer, and cleaner models, opened to the public in 1955, exemplifying Morris's statement that "our only inexhaustible resource at the moment is the cliché" (*Territory Ahead* 12). A standard travelogue realizes Morris's nightmare when it advertises Disneyland's Bear Country with the proviso "inspired by the great outdoors. What better way to see this rugged country than in Davy Crockett Explorer Canoes?" (McGrath 248). The Disneyland microcosm of nature is presented as better than the real thing. Why venture to Yellowstone or Yosemite, already tamed versions of the wilderness, when visitors can see it all without too much work and take home a plastic souvenir for their meager troubles?[4] For those who wanted the pleasures of a miniature world without having to travel to Nevada or California, television delivered the visible world in a small, two-dimensional, black-and-white package while selling a stereotype of the jubilant white-aproned American homemaker smiling amidst her shining kitchen gadgets.

But before Las Vegas, Disneyland, or television dictated the American dream, picture magazines wielded considerable influence on American culture. According to a survey taken in 1950, when *Life*'s circulation was 5,340,300, "Over half the population of America saw one or more issues of *Life* in any three-month period" (Goldberg 165). "*Life*," writes Vicki Goldberg, "the closest thing to a national newspaper America had ever had, gave photography the largest forum in its history" (184). Perhaps because they deal in the nexus of words and photographs, Morris seems to find picture magazines the most odious of the decade's many lamentable products. While his own phototexts of the forties, which united photographs and words to explore the less picturesque aspects of American culture, brought him little economic success, *Life* and *Look,* which relied heavily on the post-World War II financial boom to purvey a brand of homespun optimism and erase the gloom of the depression years, were selling extraordinarily well, marketing a particular vision of American culture largely through photographs. As Roland Marchand observes in *Advertising the American Dream,* consumers relied on advertising not to reflect society but to enhance it, to appeal to popular aspirations and fantasies in a credible form. The result was a "dramatiz[ation] of the American Dream" (xviii). Picture magazines fashioned and sold a paradigm of the American culture which relied on homogeneity and consensus, and much of what Wright Morris finds troubling about American culture is epitomized by the uniform buoyancy of periodicals, particularly Reverend Norman Vincent Peale's column in *Look* and Norman Rockwell's pictures in the *Saturday Evening Post*. To Morris, Rockwell's *Post* covers revel in sentimentality and predictability, satisfying "a hunger . . . for the Good Old Days" (*Territory Ahead* 118) to a generation that increasingly relies on technology and in a magazine in which advertisers "champio[n] the new against the old, the modern against the old-fashioned" (Marchand xxi).

This cultural schizophrenia, a dialectic between a mythicized past and a technological future that is devouring that past, is palpable in Wright Morris's fiction and essays. As he notes in his cultural manifesto, *The Territory Ahead,* "Nostalgia rules our hearts while a rhetoric of progress rules our words" (25). Notwithstanding his own affinity for photography, Morris sees the medium as dualistic, salvaging the fast fading wreckage of the past, but in its salvaging attempts it replaces things with images:

> Just as there are people . . . who can only see clearly what has a frame around it, can we look forward to a generation that will only be at ease with a picture of something? A view, a pet, a loved one, a disaster? The image provides the confirmation that is lacking in the sight itself. Seeing is believing, if what we see is a photograph.
>
> (*Time Pieces* 20)

As early as 1945, in *The Man Who Was There,* Morris depicts photography as a medium that reveals the facts but not the truth as Agee Ward, the enigmatic hero who is missing for most of the novel, explores a family album as a means of securing an identity. His efforts, however, to locate himself through images are unrewarding. Yet, by the 1950s, photographs in Morris's novels are not simply useless; they are misleading, impeding, perhaps even destructive. Beginning in *The Works of Love* (1952), Morris suggests that photographs can offer a dangerously attractive alternative to reality, illustrated by Will Brady's disease with the world that makes him particularly vulnerable to framed and artificial spaces which mimic a photograph's stability. Two years later, in *The Huge Season* (1954), the effects of ubiquitous images are linked to the burden of literary inheritances: by hampering original experience, images and literature can prove deadly. In that novel, Morris suggests that the lack of authenticity in 1950s America began in the 1920s with the rise of advertising and celebrity, exemplified by Greta Garbo, F. Scott Fitzgerald, and Charles Lindbergh. In his final novel of the 1950s, *The Field of Vision* (1956), Morris explores the subjectivity of perception, suggesting that cameras lie by depicting an objective reality while memory offers a greater truth by preserving the inaccuracies of vision. Each of these novels illustrates photography's reductivism, sentimentality, and stasis, its simultaneous proclivity toward materiality and immateriality, but throughout the works the possibility for characters to survive the dangers of an image-laden world increases: *The Huge Season*'s Peter Foley and *The Field of Vision*'s Gordon Boyd learn to form a salutary union of memory and image, while *The Work of Love*'s Will Brady never acquires the imagination necessary to successfully combat the images around him.

Adam Brady of *The Works of Love* inaugurates the connection between image and desire that will eventually ruin his son, Will. Living in a sod house "west of the 98th meridian," he recruits a bride through a deceitful photograph:

> The picture shows Brady standing, hat in hand, with a virgin forest painted in behind him, and emerging from this forest a coyote and a one-eyed buffalo. The great humped head is there, but the rest of the beast is behind the screen.
>
> The picture might have given any woman pause, but there was no indication, anywhere in it, of the landscape through the window that Adam Brady faced. There was not an inkling of the desolation of the empty plain. No hint of the sky, immense and faded. . . .
>
> There was no indication that the man in the picture had on nearly everything that he owned, including a key-wind watch with a bent minute hand.
>
> (5-6)

The photograph lies about the very geography that defines these characters; identities are formed via images even in the wasteland of Nebraska.[5] Though Adam's son attempts to escape his dismal heritage by moving east, he is too busy retrieving the past or envisioning the future to live in the present. The novel traces Will Jennings Brady's flawed attempts to connect with others, evinced in two failed marriages and an unsatisfactory relationship with his foster son, as well as his reliance on images as a vehicle for self-improvement. Will Brady, like his father, puts faith in advertisements, both those he places to secure a wife and those he answers to plan a vacation or to acquire a job. But perhaps the best example of Brady's reduction to a framed space is the coded message he sends his wife and son by having the manager of the Orpheum Theater flash a slide advertising WILL BRADY'S CHICKENS AND EGGS during a movie to announce his presence in the lobby.

Will's disconnection from humanity causes him to feel most alive in artificial places like lobbies of theaters and hotels, which are, like Brady himself, "both in . . . and out of this world" (172):[6]

> The same things go along with lobbies that go along with dreams, great and small love affairs, and other arrangements that never seem quite real. The lobby draws a chalk line around this unreal world, so to speak. . . . For it is the purpose of hotel lobbies to take you out of the life you are living, to a better life, or a braver, more interesting one.
>
> (173-74)

Preferring to glimpse the silver screen through the lobby doors, Brady stands in "the crack" between his world and another. The chalk line of the lobby is akin to a frame separating Brady from the rest of the world.

Hotel lobbies naturalize his constant self-consciousness, approximating the effect of gazing into a three-way mirror, in which "he sees himself . . . both coming and going, a man, that is, who was from someplace and was going somewhere" (172). Three-way mirrors offer Brady the sense of place that he lacks, providing him with three dimensions and making him feel less the impostor that he is.[7] Windows serve a similar framing function by allowing Brady to view the world as a picture. Sorting waybills in a tower room in the freight yards, he "comes to life" while looking out a large window facing east, which provides a view of the city:

> The bay window in the tower room was a frame around this picture. It hung there on the wall. . . . If he was more alive there than anywhere else—if he seemed to come to life when he faced this picture—it had something to do with the fact that he was cut off from it. Which was a very strange thing, since what the tower room made him feel was part of it.
>
> (238-39)

But the frame through which Brady views the world is only the beginning of the containment devices the novel portrays. Gazing through his window, he watches people through theirs; between the cracks of the drawn blinds, he glimpses a woman peering into a mirror. Frame within frame within frame, Brady and the reader are trapped in endless reverberations of vision.

Like lobbies, windows, and film screens, postcards which always bear the same message serve as another framing device for Brady, effectively keeping him simultaneously connected to and disconnected from his foster son:

> Dear Son—
>
> Have moved. Have nice little place of our own now, two-plate gas. Warm sun in windows every morning, nice view of park. Plan to get new Console radio soon now, let you pick it out. Plan to pick up car so we can drive out in country, get out in air. Turning over in my mind plan to send you to Harvard, send you to Yale. Saw robin in park this morning. Saw him catch worm.
>
> (221-22)

As the postcard becomes too battered and the writing smudged, Brady replaces it. No matter when he writes it, it is always spring on the card; the message is always the same. He refrains from mailing it until he can write the new address, the one with a view of the park, the one that never materializes. Brady traps himself in a pastoral convention, a nostalgic future that will never arrive. Experiencing life like frozen episodes, snapshots which defy the flux of time, Brady reduces everything around him to images but lacks the imagination to make them meaningful.[8] Passing through his hometown late in life, Brady sees the scene as a photograph:

> A lamp, with a green glass shade, hung inside. It threw an arc of light on the wide desk, the pads of yellow paper, and the hand of the man who sat there, a visor

shading his face. The fingers of this hand were poised over the telegraph key. . . . He was staring, absently, into the windows of the passing cars. On the table before him lay a bamboo rod, curved at one end like a plant flowering, and a sheet of folded paper was inserted at the curved end. Will Brady saw all of this as if it were a picture on a calendar. Nothing moved, every detail was clear.

(212-13)

The postcard photographs, like the lobbies, are simultaneously real and unreal, in and out of this world, offering the possibility of permanence in a world of constant change. Because life beyond the photograph's frame is unstable, so clearly proven by the perennial gap between the depictions on posters and postcards and reality, the image within the frame can never be a reliable index of the future as Brady seems to believe it is. Akin to Brady's metaphorical three-way mirrors, photographs idealize, promising an undeliverable Eden or safeguarding a paradisiacal past. Brady runs off with his wife and son to Catalina because of a railroad poster of a glass-bottomed boat sailing from a white pier "toward happiness." They get no further than Los Angeles, that "unreal city, a glittering mirage, . . . a show, another mammoth production, [a] hotel lobby . . . as big as the great outdoors" (191). Los Angeles is the source of the pervasive images that the characters mimic. The flirtatious, fluttering eye of Libby, the girl from whom he buys kisses, mimics the Orpheum billboards, and Gertrude, his second wife, confuses reality with film, as she spends eight hours a day in theaters.

In response to the confusion of a world which proffers hotels in lieu of homes, machine-made suntans, and department-store Santa Clauses, and oddly enough despite his attraction to such illusions and idealizations, Will Brady makes it his mission to produce something real: day-old eggs for the carriage trade (not to be confused with their celluloid-collared and false-cuffed impostors). A fresh egg, for Brady, becomes the epitome of the real, but, ironically, the candling-room, where he determines the freshness and perfection of each egg, resembles a photographer's darkroom, in which a streak of light in the midst of darkness gives rise to an image, thereby linking the "real" with the very image that has clouded reality.

The search for reality is equally daunting in *The Huge Season,* a novel which pits the inherent falsity of 1950s America against what initially seems to be a more original decade, the 1920s. A two-part narrative structure reinforces the dichotomy of the decades. Straightforward descriptive chapters entitled "The Captivity," narrated by Peter Foley in generally chronological order, are paired with "Foley" chapters, stream-of-consciousness passages expressed in a third-person-limited point of view with Foley as the center of consciousness. The "Foley" sections are offered in reverse chronological fashion as Foley inversely recalls incidents of his past over the course of two days in 1952. His recollections and the subsequent actions, including a visit to his college friends, Montana Lou Baker and

Jesse Proctor, are triggered by a newspaper photograph of Proctor, who is under investigation by the House Un-American Activities Committee. Similarly, the narrative in "The Captivity" sections is generated out of photographs and illustrations pinned to the sloping ceiling above an adolescent Foley's bed—images of Bebe Daniels, Sappho, Charles Lindbergh in the cockpit of the *Spirit of St. Louis,* and particularly Charles Lawrence on the tennis court. They share the space with the declensions of Latin verbs, memorized on warm summer nights by the spark of trolley cars, providing a white flash in his dark room. Thus, early on, Foley learns to read the world as a negative metamorphosed into a positive through light.

The photographs of the 1920s, those images of heroes pasted above Foley's bed, bespeak possibility. In contrast are the cynical photographs of the 1950s: Proctor's face splashed across newspapers, alleging treasonous sensibilities. Fittingly, the decade in which coonskin hats replace the American frontier, and Disneyland's hyperrealism distracts the nation from the paucity of reality outside of its gates, is also the decade which manufactured the most famous fake photograph in American political history.[9] Senator Joseph McCarthy's 1950 composite image of Senator Millard Tydings and Earl Browder, former head of the American Communist Party, implied, with the assistance of a suggestive caption, that the two were colluding.[10] The photograph effected McCarthy's revenge on Tydings, who had accused the former of perpetrating "a fraud and a hoax . . . on the Senate of the United States and the American people" with his list of alleged active Communists in the State Department. Though the caption confessed that the photograph, which appeared only in a tabloid created for the occasion, was a "composite" (actually two photographs cut and pasted together and rephotographed), the Maryland public, who received complimentary copies of the newspaper several days before an election, did not understand the meaning of the term "composite," and Tydings lost his Senate seat.

The politics of the fifties, like so much else from that decade, is revealed by the novel to be spurious, and so the reader, like many of the characters, is tempted to believe that the 1920s distinguished itself as more genuine and original than later decades by "establish[ing] standards that were hard to follow" (*Huge Season* 23); but that illusion is quickly obliterated by the redundancy of "the huge season" itself. Imitation and replication are revealed as the driving forces of the twenties, in which reality itself is replaced by film and literature. Chasing Montana Lou Baker, a hybrid of Greta Garbo, Fitzgerald's Jordan Baker, and Hemingway's Brett Ashley, through the streets of 1929 Paris, Foley "grabbed the belt across the back, swung her around, took a grip on her short hair as they did in the movies" (17). Like the still and film images that influence fashion and behavior, a history of fiction engenders imitation, thereby contributing to multiplying stereotypes and all but obviating original writing. The novels' manifold literary allusions Dante's (*Inferno, Hamlet, Leaves of Grass, Ulysses, The Waste Land,* many of Hemingway's and

Fitzgerald's novels, especially *The Sun Also Rises* and *The Great Gatsby*) reveal a respect for the authors' craft that is unfortunately fastened to an overwhelming sense of artistic oppression.[11] Jesse Proctor takes only four books to college with him—including *The Sun Also Rises* and a battered copy of *This Side of Paradise,* which bears his own name on the flyleaf "as if he were the author"—and eagerly steps into the Nick Carraway role of biographer to Charles Lawrence's Gatsby (68). Ironically, the three writers in the novel, Jesse Proctor, Lou Baker, and Peter Foley, cannot finish their own novels or live their own lives, haunted as they are by other works and characters, including Charles Lawrence.[12]

Proctor's imitation of Lawrence is, in effect, an imitation of an imitation, since, as Lou Baker observes, even Lawrence isn't original: "Lawrence is worse than anybody. . . . He's never been Charles Lawrence a minute of his life. He's always copied something, and right now he's copying Lawrence. He's waiting for Proctor to give him tips" (284). When not attired in the carelessly elegant collegiate look of leather patches and dusty white shoes reminiscent of Jay Gatsby, Lawrence recalls Walt Whitman, whose form is immediately identifiable to contemporary audiences because he was so often photographed. Indeed, Lawrence's evocation of Gatsby, a literary character who has fashioned himself after magazine images, and Whitman, a historical figure who idealized the democratizing powers of photography, points toward the similarity between literature and photography.[13] The famous daguerreotype of Whitman in the first edition of *Leaves of Grass* is recalled by Lawrence's carriage, described as "nearly feminine, . . . a little insolent" and notable because his right hand, noticeably longer than his left, customarily rests on his hip (48). But Proctor's imitation of Lawrence's Whitman is initially more literary than physical. When Proctor's novel, based on Lawrence's life, awaits only a final chapter, a fiction which the author can't create until his model has determined it, Dickie Livingston prints ten copies of Proctor's unfinished manuscript without the author's name on the cover or the title page: "It was *in* the book, rather than on it, turning up in the dedication, which read: *For* Jesse Proctor / *Without whom this book* / *would not have been* / *written*" (19). We are reminded of Whitman's conspicuous omission of his own name from the frontispiece of the 1855 *Leaves* as well as its unorthodox appearance in a verse of "Song of Myself." Later, serving as a campus guru spinning themes and variations on the word *disinherited,* Proctor, having taught "his educated feet . . . to walk in his proletarian shoes," dons the Whitmanesque role for himself as he poses for snapshots "in his homespun beard, crouched on his haunches like a hillbilly, photogenically dangling or chewing on a spear of long-stemmed grass" (52). Images of Whitman serve as currency for immediate authentication of Proctor's political agenda. The familiar poses of one of America's most recognizable writers enable the aspiring dissident to tap into unlimited political connotations. Though photographs are obviously not responsible for imitation (after all, Foley sees Proctor as Hamlet and himself as Horatio; Lawrence

is Jake Barnes and Jay Gatsby commingled), they have made replication easier and more efficient. While Lawrence has to perform to resemble literary characters, Proctor merely has to pose to resemble the good gray poet.

Peter Foley, the novel's narrator, however, is haunted by more than the ghosts of film and literature. Having followed in his father's footsteps as a classics scholar and gained renown on his college campus for "lifelike impersonations of Buster Keaton," Foley is terrified by his redundancy (16). As early as 1927, before he had even begun college, Foley, "the rubber stamp of some Viking," assumed that his father's past had determined his own future (287). His boss urges Foley to choose his own path, citing Charles Lindbergh as a model of originality and independence, a man planning to do "something that had never been done" (32). Noting Foley's strong physical resemblance to the aviator, Mr. Conklin barrages him with newspaper clippings of Lindbergh and purchases a large signed photograph for his employee, ironically supposing that originality is contagious. Even Foley's chance at an unpredestined future is sapped by the current Lindbergh fad. No such thing as untapped possibilities exists.

The search for "the real thing" thus becomes the mythical quest in the novel, a quest not easily fulfilled because of the proliferation of lies, mostly in the form of advertisements, in twentieth-century America. Advertising has homogenized American culture, selling the same dream to all its citizens. Foley watches a stranger in a park whose "animated face [reveals] well advertised concern and security for loved ones, long vacations with pay, carefree old age in ranch-style home, . . . [collecting] Rock of Ages monthly insurance check," in other words, a man living the proverbial American Dream (188).

> One fine day—as advertised in *Life*—that brook too broad for leaping would be lapping at the door. A heartbreak dream, with the soundtrack by Chaplin, full of young men still fighting Hemingway's war, still loving and seducing Fitzgerald's women, and believing in perfection—a machine-made perfection—if anything at all. A witness to the power, the glory, and the terrible risks of art.
>
> (189)

The collusion between the bromides of American culture and merchandising make it nearly impossible to distinguish which came first. In fact, Lou Baker suggests that "all the raw material . . . that was needed to write the great American novel" could be found in the 1921 Sears, Roebuck catalogue, which supposes that even if literary influences can be ignored in artistic creation, cultural ones cannot (210). What is clear, however, is that advertising taps into all of the culture's sentimental visions of itself, typified by an ad for hand-crafted shoes so trite that it mesmerizes Foley:

> Bench-made by old cobbler in mural-size photo, flashbulb shining on his mussy white hair, honest sweat on his forehead from honest toil, tight-lipped smile due to

nails in his mouth, and frank, folksy glint in his steel-rimmed eyes, old Yankee stock, sleeves rolled on white arms showing sailing ship, a clipper, leaving ever-snug harbor.

(106-7)

In a world of imitation, even the real thing seems counterfeit. Foley describes a "small flock, a covey of water birds, unidentified . . . looking like freshly painted decoys" (13). Colton resembles a college movie of the twenties; even the mountains and the superfluity of blackbirds seem like props. California, however, disappoints Foley because it does not adhere to the image with which he is familiar. The California of Foley's expectations is born of a photograph: "The barren desert that glared in my father's photographs had disappeared" (33).

California initially seems an incongruous setting for a novel about the literary legacy of the lost generation writers, a group who favored New York and Europe; however, the culmination of the nation's westward expansion and the home of Hollywood suits the characters who congregate there, men who willingly exchange reality for its heightened equivalent. The instability of California—one minute a desert, the next a paradise—makes it the ideal setting for a novel about imitation and duplication. California, with its superabundance of wax museums, ostentatious art collections, and theme parks, is clearly America's testament to illusion, a site of unlimited possibility because of its brief history: "The frantic desire for the Almost Real arises only as a neurotic reaction to the vacuum of memories," observes Umberto Eco (30).

Ultimately, the ads that assault Foley and the illusions that define California raise the stakes of reality, demanding that experience conform to images. More than other visual arts, photography provides a heightened equivalent of reality because it captures a moment that has occurred. Beyond representation, photography repeats an instant, an action, a gesture. It offers the seemingly impossible pairing of the transience of life and the permanence of art; in the midst of a palpable world, people move like ghosts, leaving blurred traces of their temporary presence. Foley's ambivalence toward photographs finds a parallel in his confused relationship with time. For him, time, which flowed easily and naturally for his father, is marked by irregularity: "Time, for my father, seemed to be contained in the watch. It did not skip a beat, fly away, or merely vanish, as it does for me. So long as he remembered to wind the watch Time would not run out" (3). The watch, given by grandfather to father to son, ironically bears the inscription *Incipit Vita Nova,* but how does one begin a new life when the same old time passes from generation to generation? Though the watch "still keep[s] very good time" in Foley's day, "the times are out of joint" (3).

The photograph, like a watch, contains within itself the conflict between stability and fluctuation, permanence and ephemerality. Photographs simultaneously locate their subjects in time and remove them from it. Like so many of

Morris's characters, Foley's susceptibility to the concept of the "still point," "a timeless tempest in an ever-threatening sea," a moment provided by memory and art, initially disables him from reconciling fixity and flux (161). Foley recalls the other Peter Foley: "Unfaded, on the fly-leaf of the Latin books on his shelves, . . . [he] did not change, grow up or grow old, marry the right or wrong girl, come to a good or bad end, or merely peter out, as most men seemed destined to do" (185).

But while photographs rescue subjects from change and disappointment, they concomitantly embalm them. In a Manhattan art shop, Foley is arrested by photographs, clearly taken before fast-lens cameras, which juxtapose blurred passersby against a sharply focused background and leave Foley with a

> curious feeling . . . that these people existed, that they were really there, but by now, as was clear from their clothes, short of some unusual miracle, some freak of longevity, they would be gone. . . . Two blurred shadows, caught by the camera, moving in a scene that was itself immortal, or looked immortal, like beetles in amber, in that scene so full of so many timeless objects, the trees and the river, the history-haunted towers, the bookstalls with their freight of what was still surviving—a seemingly permanent scene with these impermanent shadows crossing it. . . . All around them was Paris, the immortal city; the delicate trees cast their permanent shadows, but the feet of this woman—like the wings of time—were blurred.

(161-62)

The postcard image is later resurrected in Foley's recollection of a scene from the twenties: Lawrence, standing, with his hand in a smoking smudgepot.

> Into the flame Lawrence dipped his hand, and with the sightless smile of an antique statue he turned and gazed into Foley's face. The lips silent, the gaze already remote, he peered toward Foley from a sacred wood that slowly receded into the changeless past. A blurred, shadowy figure, caught by the camera, nameless in a scene that seemed immortal, like that woman of mystery in the postcard view of the Seine. Suspended in time, like the ball that forever awaited the blow from the racket, or the upraised foot that would never reach the curb. A permanent scene, made up of frail, impermanent things. . . . But in the burning they gave off something less perishable.

(305-6)

Lawrence himself is a stillpoint, the space of art which offers something that a fleeting life cannot by making the material immaterial. Describing the essence of that space, Morris remarks, "It is the nature of art to be immaterial, the conceptual act must be grasped by the mind: what appears to be solid is transformed into a vapor thinner than air. That, indeed, is its very indestructibility" (*Territory Ahead* 28).[14] As attractive as that space may be, however, it is essential to remember that it is a space inimical to life. The blur of moving figures implies the dynamics of life but ineluctably suggests the ghostliness of death. One of the century's most famous images of death, the mushroom cloud above Hiroshima, provides the ultimate example of the transformation of the material into the immaterial in *The Huge Season*:

> The camera swept around it, saw that it was bare, that nothing made by man remained in it, then returned to focus on several faint shadows on the asphalt slab. And these? These were the shadows of men—the shadows cast by the blast itself. The shadows of men in the light of their own man-made sun.
>
> (170)

The shadows of atom-bomb victims bear an uncanny likeness to photographic images made immaterial by another man-made sun which casts shadows on paper and metal. Like the bomb, the camera is indifferent to, even exploitative of, the suffering around it. And the final image is the photographic shadow of the shadow produced by the bomb.

Foley, unlike Will Brady and Charles Lawrence, recognizes that immortality is stultifying and thus learns how to maintain immortal moments while living a mortal existence. Lawrence's inability to exist in real time is evinced by the photograph of Lawrence above Foley's bed, which provides the model that its subject must follow. Depicting Lawrence in the middle of a tennis serve, the portrait captures all the promise and potential of a young, talented athlete. But by the end of the novel, Lawrence is dead, having committed suicide because he cannot exist outside of perfection, beyond the frame of the photograph. He never learns what Foley does: that one can encapsulate the past without becoming captive to it.

The ability to live both in and out of time, to remember the past and exist in the present, is central to *The Field of Vision* (1956). That ability requires a recognition of the vagaries of vision, an understanding of the conflict between what one sees and what is there. Five characters, witnessing the same bullfight in Mexico, see entirely different events.[15] Ironically, Walter McKee, one of the most obtuse characters, observes the universal phenomenon early in the novel when he notes that Mrs. Kahler, "a woman whose eyes were as good as [his], if not better," sees only what she wants to see because of "some mental trouble" (14). What he doesn't realize is that is all any of them see. As Gordon Boyd, the most perspicacious of the viewers, notes: "Each man had the eyes to see only himself. This crisp sabbath afternoon forty thousand pairs of eyes would gaze down on forty thousand separate bullfights, seeing it all very clearly, missing only the one that was said to take place" (59). Ruminating on what a photograph of the episode would reveal, Boyd claims, "The camera did not lie. A pity, since the lie mirrored the truth. The camera would report what no pair of eyes present had seen" (154). Gordon Boyd learns that material things pass, and one is left with memories: "it was the unreal thing that lasted, the red-brick phantasm in Boyd's mind, complete with fire escape, erasers, and the listening dog in the Victrola horn" (232).

As Foley apprehends the dangers of absolute immateriality, Boyd grasps the hazards of excessive materiality, which lends itself to the reduction of photographs and souvenirs. Gordon Boyd learns that the importance of his boyhood encounter with Ty Cobb in *The Field of Vision* is not inherent in the pocket ripped from the celebrated baseball player's pants, which he discovers is merely a trophy that stultifies the original transformative experience. Though Boyd, for a time, relies on the relic to conjure a sense of his own heroism, eventually he realizes that the power of the moment lies in the story he tells about it, and that story's potential transformative powers, a lesson he teaches to his friend's grandson, who rejects his grandfather's offer to buy him a paper bull after watching a bullfight in Mexico: "'It's not a bull if you buy it,' said the boy" (249). Souvenirs promote America's backward-looking tendency, avowing a temptation to venerate the old because it is old. Their sheer numbers have caused artifacts to lose their meaning. The superfluity of fake coonskin hats in the 1950s worn by both adults and children who have become versions of "Disney's rubber-stamp midgets" are symptoms of an age of artifacts whose mystical dimensions have been effaced by excess and nostalgia (*Field of Vision* 194). Having removed the risks of the frontier, the only danger is "a national shortage of coonskin hats" (*Territory Ahead* 195).

Like relics, photographs tend to idolize the referent while eliding its significance. In the process of ensuring that the masses get a look at paintings and sculptures previously available only to wealthy travelers, photography has diminished modern art to "vest-pocket reminders of reproductions that hung in bus stations, lounge cars, bedrooms for guests, . . . bathrooms with color matching shower curtains" (*Huge Season* 160). The vulnerability of the image to be clichéd is nowhere more evident than in *The Field of Vision,* where a photograph of Boyd in a camera magazine convinces the subject that even his failure is hackneyed:

> The camera had caught every memorable cliché: the coat fastened with a pin, the cut suggesting better days, the sock there to call attention to the calloused heel, in one soiled hand a paper bag, now empty, and in the other a crust. This crust he shared—the autumn sun shining on it—with his sole companion, a moth-eaten squirrel who had plainly suffered the same misfortunes at the hand of *life*.
>
> (69-70)

Photographs prescribe possibility, presenting "culture as . . . [a] photographer's salon where ready-made frames, hung on the walls of rustically historical gardens, lacked only the faces of succeeding generations in the ready-made holes. This hand-me-down world defined the realm of the possible" (70-71).[16] Appearing in the same novel, a photograph of Tom Scanlon provides evidence that the realm of the possible is only stocked with the prefabricated: described as "looking frozen to death, his feet in the oven, wrapped up in buffalo robes and wearing his cane-sided draymen's hat" with a photo caption claiming "MAN

WHO KNEW BUFFALO BILL SPENDS LONELY XMAS," Scanlon, a ninety-year-old man, born and raised in Lone Tree, is fraudulently placed by the image and caption into the prescribed role of frontiersman (48, 217). By reducing multiple perceptions to one perception, the photograph standardizes vision. As advertisements create an American dream, documentaries create American icons. Intention cannot immunize a photograph against the medium's capacity for cliché.

The disparity between Morris's actual and fictional photographs underscores the dual tendency of photography to salvage or corrupt, to represent or manipulate, to suggest or supplant. Morris's own photographs attempt to rescue those icons and artifacts that are passing away, replaced by machine-made objects that roll off assembly lines. His intimate portraits, straightforward frontal views of buildings, rooms, pieces of furniture leave little room for the construction of cultural myths. His photographs evoke a sense of place, intimate spaces which suggest human presence despite the absence of humans: "In all my life I've never been in anything so crowded, so full of something, as the rooms of a vacant house. Sometimes I think only vacant houses are occupied. . . . An inhabitant is what you can't take away from a house" (*Inhabitants* n.p.). Close-up images of tattered clothes on hooks, a newspaper-lined drawer filled with silverware, and a battered comb on a linen-topped dresser allude to nearby inhabitants that rarely appear in Morris's photographs. When they do appear, their faces are turned from the camera; we know them only from their surroundings and their postures.

Human presence is particularly palpable in his landscapes, where an expansive vacuity conveys overwhelming isolation. A school outhouse circumscribed by a fence sits alone on a flat plain. As if to remind us that human engineering is no match for geography and cosmology, a dead-center horizon line cuts through the puny building and its frame, a fence made absurd by its seemingly senseless delimitation in a void. Two lonely mailboxes stand side by side, dwarfed by an enormous tree while distant telephone poles are swallowed by the sky. Here, as in many of Morris's images, vertical objects battle the imposing horizontality of the plains. The erection of barns, windmills, fences, lampposts, grain elevators, mailboxes, homes, and churches seems a defiance of a flat land. In an essay written forty years after most of the images were taken, Morris confesses, "I saw, but did not fully sense, that these constructions were pathetically temporary on the vast exposed landscape" (*Time Pieces* 124). He describes his aim in *The Inhabitants* as accruing "evidence of humankind in the artifacts that revealed individuals' passing. . . . Nothing will compare with the photograph to register what is going, going, but not yet gone. The pathos of this moment, the reluctance of parting, we feel intensely" (*Time Pieces* 112).

Morris's photo-texts predate the typical postmodern predilection for multimedia projects, what Linda Hutcheon has called "border tensions" and Douglas Crimp has termed "hybridization."[17] His first photo-text, *The Inhabitants* (1946), published in a large format, paired two different narrative styles: brief, somewhat aphoristic first-person commentaries on inhabitants and slightly longer narratives given in dialect, seemingly the voices of inhabitants whose vacant dwellings are pictured alongside the text. Full-page photographs, bleeding off the edges of the paper, reject the traditional framing device that generally circumscribes works of art from the rest of the world.[18] For Morris, who dislikes illustrated novels, the photographs do not illustrate the words; both media remain independent.[19] The language does, however, provide a key to a successful understanding of the images, which should be read not as statements of social realism, like the documentary photographs commissioned by the Farm Security Administration, but as remnants of passing objects whose "mystic meaning" would be missed.[20] His second photo-text, *The Home Place* (1948), offers a narration of a single day as told by a returning native. As in *The Inhabitants,* each page of text faces a photograph, which is cropped to fit a smaller format. "These mutilations removed them, as a group, from the context of artworks, as 'images,' and presented them as 'things' and artifacts" (*Time Pieces* 137). Clearly, for Morris, the term *mutilations* does not connote disintegration. His cropped images force us to see "the thing itself," a phrase, probably borrowed from Edward Weston, that Morris has used to signify the historical artifact, and not the aestheticized image. Indeed, in the context of writing, Morris has relied on the word *mutilations* to express the imperative of each generation to reconsider and transform the literary object, to demystify it so that it ceases to be a burden and instead becomes a path to creativity:

> To make new we must reconstruct, as well as resurrect. The destructive element in this reconstruction is to remove from the object the encrusted cliché. . . . The fragment means more to us—since it demands more of us—than the whole. The mutilations are what we find the most provocative and beautiful.
>
> (*Territory Ahead* xv)

Morris's desire to see the image rather than its manufacturer in no way suggests that he is naive to the photographer's "inscrutable presence" in every photograph:

> Would that image restore my original impressions, or would they be replaced by others? To what extent would this new image, cut off from its surroundings, constitute a new structure? How much of the "reality" had it captured? How much had it ignored? Whether or not it had been my intent, I would end up with something *other* than what was here. It would be a new likeness, a remarkable approximation, a ponderable resemblance, but not a copy. This new image would testify to the photographer's inscrutable presence.
>
> (*Time Pieces* 116)

However ingenuous these images may at first appear, evidence of a postmodernist impulse pervades these testimonials to the past. Images of and through doors and windows suggest a self-consciousness about the act of photography. We look over Morris's shoulder into the camera lens, which itself looks out through a lighted window, or we peer through lace curtains into a parlor or gaze into an oval mirror which reflects photographs of faces beside an unhinged door. But windows don't always allow the voyeur visual access; sometimes they merely reflect the external, as in *Model T in Shed,* or more dramatically, *Tombstone, Arizona,* an image of an abandoned, dilapidated building whose intact windows reflect and whose missing window panes reveal a stunning triptych of clouds and mountains. Here, at least, nature has reclaimed the territory, and the taming of the West seems a slight exaggeration. Many of Morris's photographs include other photographs, allowing us to look, obliquely, through two lenses at once: Morris's own and his predecessor's. Time continuously recedes—as the mirror's reflection suggests. Linking time and vision, another photograph juxtaposes a pocket watch, a trio of photographs, two flashlights, and eyeglasses among the myriad contents of a dresser drawer. Like Hawthorne, Morris rarely lets us forget the inherent voyeurism in any gaze, and the reader/viewer is no less incriminated in the spectatorship than the narrator, the writer, or the photographer. Moreover, we are reminded that the photographer's presence unavoidably alters the situation. Attempting to photograph a vacant space, Morris provides a presence, throws a shadow on a wall or floor, or fills a mirror with his reflection, thus reminding the viewer that representations are never transparent or authorless.[21]

An augmented self-consciousness pervades Morris's third photo-text, published in 1968. In *God's Country and My People,* Morris revisits photographs from *The Inhabitants* and *The Home Place* and thus "reconsider[s] . . . material from a later point in time, using essentially the same techniques and the same body of photographs. It was the quality of the repetition that was necessary to this book" (*Time Pieces* 90). A decade later, postmodern photographers would begin recycling images to convey their senses that since the culture was surfeited with images, new ones were unnecessary. Repetition is a critical tool in postmodernism, forcing viewers to examine images which have become cultural icons. Though his agenda is personal rather than social and political, Morris's act of recycling and reviewing his own images raises some of the same issues as postmodern art: how one sees is inevitably a function of one's historical and social context, which invariably mandates a refocusing of old images. In this regard, *God's Country and My People* recalls one of the central issues in *The Field of Vision*: perception is contingent. Morris does not offer slices of life so much as fragments of his own changing vision, for as Gordon Boyd realizes in *The Field of Vision,* objective reality doesn't exist; all we can ever know is what we see, which is later processed through memory. If as Morris notes, "we continue to see what we will, rather than what is there," then his photo-texts document the shift in personal and cultural influences (*Time Pieces* 4).

But recycling his own photographs does more than note the fluxity of vision; it points toward the artifice of all images. The original version of *Model T with California Top,*

Ed's Place shows no traces of the photographer's presence, whose shadow had left its mark on the negative's foreground; Morris cropped out the evidence of his presence. Years later, however, he printed the full negative, acknowledging in visible terms his own presence. By foregrounding the darkroom work, the cropping, editing, burning, and dodging that alters the already personal view, Morris reminds us that photographs are anything but innocent, disinterested reflections of reality.

In contrast to his actual photographs, which suggest that the best portraits omit people, Morris's fictional images are crowded with people. Perhaps for that very reason they aren't particularly useful in depicting their subjects. Much of the plot of *The Deep Sleep* pivots around an unflattering obituary photograph that so distorts the essence of its subject that the deceased's family considers the previously anathematic alternative of waking him in an open casket just to dispel the photograph's residue. The centerpiece of *The Man Who Was There* is a description of a family photograph album which defies representation. Ironically, the best portraits are those whose faces have been blurred by time:

> And yet it is clear that even without faces these figures are good portraits—the absence of the face is not a great loss. Uncle Harry Ward, third from the right, discovered this for himself. When he was a very young man and most of the figures still had faces, the only one he was sure about was himself. Himself and the two girls, that is. But when his eyes weren't so good and all he could see was how they were standing—why, it seemed that he knew them right off. As soon as their faces were gone he knew them right away.
>
> (64)

Agee Ward, the novel's largely missing central character, is indistinguishable in photographs. His face is blurred in one school photo and blocked in another. An unwound shutter and poor aim foil several attempted shots of the character. Even when successfully photographed, his face is covered by a cap, a pith helmet, or racing goggles. Yet the novel's title, like Agee's facelessness, suggests that he is present despite his physical absence as other characters are rejuvenated by his memory and artifacts. Like people in Morris's photographs, Agee Ward is more present for being absent, more real because he is not literally depicted by photographs.[22]

Morris lambastes a demand for the literal in American culture that has endangered everyone's, including writers', more speculative and figurative tendencies: "Obsessed with what is real, . . . [writers] are skeptical of the imagination, idolatrous of the facts" (*Time Pieces* 69).[23] Artists, like Morris's characters, must learn to find a middle ground between the world of facts and the realm of imagination: an artist "must become that paradox, both a visionary and a realist" (*Territory Ahead* 218). His recipe for literary and cultural survival seems to be what Hawthorne called the romancer's "neutral territory, . . . where the Actual and the Imaginary may meet" (Hawthorne 28): "Life, raw life, the kind we lead every day . . . has the curious property of not seeming real *enough*" (**Territory Ahead** 228). Morris's solution is to process raw life through the imagination in order to make it real. Similarly, to gain an authentic and original relationship to the world, we do not need to reject our national and literary past but need to "reconstruct, as well as resurrect" it because art can only survive through transformation: "I seek to make my own what I have inherited as clichés" (**Territory Ahead** xiv).[24]

In **The Huge Season,** Peter Foley gradually realizes that as the flaw of the 1950s is an excessive reliance on a material world, the inverse flaw of the 1920s is an inability to deal with the material world:

> Did they lack conviction? No, they had conviction. What they lacked was intention. They could shoot off guns, at themselves, leap from upper-floor windows, by themselves, or take sleeping pills to quiet the bloody cries of the interior. But they would not carry this war to the enemy. That led to action, action to evil, blood on the escutcheon of lily-white Goodness, and to the temporal kingdom rather than the eternal heavenly one. That led, in short, where they had no intention of ending up. The world of men here below. The godawful mess men had made of it.

> (299-300)

Foley finds a livable space between the material and the immaterial, reality and imagination.[25] Though he is tempted to burn his manuscript, a narrative of the 1920s, at the beginning of the novel, he realizes the need to join reality and imagination and thus to free himself from the past. The final pages of the novel suggest that Foley, by becoming a willing witness in Proctor's trial, will fully enter the real world. Foley's newfound vitality is inspired by the generative boldness of a local chipmunk, "a cat charmer, a lion tamer, a prophet for a new and holy order of chipmunks," who repeatedly escapes death by mesmerizing Foley's cat with a frantic dance (168). The chipmunk exemplifies a "creative evolution . . . founded on audacity [, t]he unpredictable behavior that [lights] up the darkness with something new" (167). Such audacity, which lights up the darkness, is linked both to a camera's flash in a dark space and an enlarger's streak of light in a darkroom. Photography's heretofore destructive elements, akin to the blast of the atomic bomb, are transformed into a productive aesthetic, a magical realm which combines the seen and the imagined:

> What I saw in the darkroom often took precedence over what I saw on the ground glass. For me, the "picture" emerges in the developing solution, and it is the magic of this moment that I find most exciting. I see my subject through the lens, but I conceive the picture in the darkroom. Photography is *camera obscura.*

> (**Time Pieces** 143)

The darkroom, the space of imagination and possibility, contains its own alternative to the stifling, hackneyed images produced in unimaginative minds. In their finest ca-

pacity, photographs reveal "fissures in time's narrative flow . . . [which leave] expanding and disquieting gaps in our perceived notions of reality, of a familiar and stable world" (**Time Pieces** 11). Like fiction, photographs can provide a link between life and art, reality and imagination, the material and immaterial worlds. For Morris, the medium that proliferates hyperreality can also subvert it.

Notes

1. Andy Grundberg argues that "photography suggests that our image of reality is made up of images. It makes explicit the dominion of mediation" (15). Linda Hutcheon posits that postmodernism's "study of representation becomes, not a study of mimetic mirroring or subjective projecting, but an exploration of the way in which narratives and images structure how we see ourselves and how we construct our notions of self, in the present and in the past" (7).

2. As Morris writes, "The Great Depression was real enough in itself, but the hold it still has on our imagination is largely a photographic triumph. . . . The photographs of Walker Evans have helped shape our image of what is real, and as its image hardens to a cliché, it now obstructs the emergence of what is actually there" (*Time Pieces* 62). For many, the depression is epitomized by Dorothea Lange's *Migrant Mother,* a photograph which evokes all the sentiment, politics, and civic responsibility of that time and hence has effectively displaced the actual tragedy, not to mention the fact that the photograph erased the actual family by making its members symbolic.

3. Critics have categorized a variety of Morris's themes in terms of binaries: real/phony, actual/ideal, hero/witness, moment of truth/cliché, material/imaginary.

4. In *Travels in Hyperreality,* Umberto Eco argues that "Disneyland not only produces illusion, but—in confessing it—stimulates the desire for it. . . . Imitation has reached its apex and afterwards reality will always be inferior to it" (44-46). The preference for representations is pointed, for Eco, in a wax reproduction of Leonardo da Vinci's *Last Supper,* touted as better because the "original fresco is by now ruined, almost invisible, unable to give you the emotion you have received from the three-dimensional, which is more real, and there is more of it" (18). Even American museums, which don't simply display historical and artistic artifacts but recreate original spaces, offer "absolute unreality . . . as real presence. . . . The sign aims to be the thing" (7). Holography, also developed in the fifties, succeeds in America because it is "a country obsessed with realism, where, if a reconstruction is to be credible, it must be absolutely iconic, a perfect likeness, a 'real' copy of the reality being represented" (4).

5. Joseph J. Wydeven compares the novel's form, particularly the "interpretive difficulties" of its slippery narrative voice, to family photograph albums, "with

their frustrating gaps in the chronology of weeks, months, or years; tantalizingly unexplained costumes, gestures, and facial expressions; and maddening silences about all those strange pictured incidents" ("Focus and Frame" 102).

6. Later in the novel, when answering an advertisement to act as Montgomery Ward's Santa Claus, Brady believes he is prepared "to live in this world, so to speak, and yet somehow be out of it . . . to be mortal and immortal, at the same time" (265).

7. Numerous references to mirrors occur in the novel, as well as at least three references to three-way mirrors. See pp. 148, 151, 171.

8. In "Focus and Frame in Wright Morris's *The Works of Love*," Wydeven argues that the novel's "chief irony is how little knowledge Brady achieves from so many detailed acts of perception. . . . Brady is like a camera without a motivating human agent as operator" (100, 107).

9. Baudrillard argues that "Disneyland exists in order to hide that it is the 'real' country. . . . [It] is presented as imaginary in order to make us believe that the rest is real, whereas all of Los Angeles and the America that surrounds it are no longer real, but belong to the hyperreal order and to the order of simulation" (12).

10. The caption read: "Communist leader Earl Browder, shown at left in this composite picture, was the star witness at the Tydings Committee hearings, and was cajoled into saying Owen Lattimore and others accused of disloyalty were not Communists. Tydings (right) answered, 'Oh, thank you, sir.' Browder testified in the best interests of the accused, naturally" (qtd. in Goldberg 92).

11. The sense of exhaustion that permeates postmodern theory, the notion that images, concepts and ideas have been depleted, is pervasive in Morris. For years, he argues, art has been shaping life so that we no longer know if we are responding to the raw material of our culture or merely to previous interpretations of it: "What was once raw about American life has now been dealt with so many times that the material we begin with is itself a fiction, one created by Twain, Eliot, or Fitzgerald. . . . The imagination has now left its stamp on all of [America]" (*Territory Ahead* 13, 21).

12. The crossover between the real and the fictional runs throughout the novel. Morris is writing a novel in which people are affected by literary history while his character, Proctor, attempts to write a novel in which characters are based on actual people: "It just so happened, naturally, that there was a mention of an Indiana family, and certain Indiana families might mistakenly think they were the family he meant. And there was also the mention, at considerable length, of a small, swanky college in southern California, but not in just the terms that might please somebody like the dean of men" (229). The interconnection between

life and art becomes pathological for Proctor, who gives Foley a speech about the distinction between real experiences and phony simulations, which has clearly come, word for word, from his book. Moreover, Proctor cannot finish his novel, so clearly based on Lawrence's life, until Lawrence acts.

13. Whitman suggested that written historical records of important leaders and thinkers be replaced by "three or four or half a dozen portraits—very accurate—of the men: that would be history—the best history—a history from which there would be no appeal." In his own review of *Leaves of Grass,* placed anonymously in the *Brooklyn Daily Eagle,* Whitman explained the peculiar replacement of the author's name with his likeness. "The book itself is a reproduction of the author. His name is not on the frontispiece but his portrait, half length, is. The contents of the book form a daguerreotype of his inner being" (both qtd. in Trachtenberg, *Reading American Photographs* 60, 65).

14. Wayne C. Booth and Richard Daverman perceive the material world as one that must be overcome in order to achieve a world that is more real. I, however, agree with J. C. Wilson and G. B. Crump, who argue that physical reality is as important as imagination in Morris's novels.

15. Morris observes: "The multifaceted aspect of reality has been commonplace since cubism, but we continue to see what we will, rather than what is there" (*Time Pieces* 4).

16. A photograph of Lone Tree taken from a balloon on July 4, 1901, reveals the banal limitations of photographs: "The century had just turned. The locomotive in the picture was headed East. It had come from the East—as a matter of fact, it had *backed* in from the East since there was no local roundhouse" (45). Despite the primitive railroad facilities, the picture had been taken to impress eastern businessmen of Lone Tree's economic future. However, fifty years later "not much had changed—in so far as you could tell from the photograph" (47). Intended as an instrument to inspire progress, the image is transformed over time into a historical artifact documenting stasis.

17. Linda Hutcheon cites "border tensions" as the transgression of boundaries between genres, disciplines, discourses, high and mass culture, practice and theory. Douglas Crimp notes that "hybridization," the mixing of heterogeneous media, genres, projects, and materials, violates the purity of modernist art (77), and Andy Grundberg observes that postmodernism's intermingling of media "dispel[s] modernism's fetishistic concentration on the medium as message" (6).

18. According to David E. Nye, "A frame around an image announces its completeness. In the conventions of art, a white border says that the picture is a self-contained statement. Morris's un-named and un-framed images fill the book with glimpses that can-

not be illustrations, stills from a film, or autonomous works of art. By releasing these photographs from definition through language and from closure through framing, he makes them problematic, without a fixed meaning or stabilized relation to the text" (164).

19. For Morris's comments on the combination of photographs and text, see *Time Pieces* 89.

20. Morris's photographic debt to Henry James may even exceed his literary one. Many of his essays refer to the passage in *The American Scene* where James attributes "mystic meaning" to "objects and places, coherently grouped, disposed for human use and addressed to it" (qtd. in *Territory Ahead* 58–59). Morris maintains that such significance no longer inheres in contemporary artifacts. He considers photography's primary function the salvaging of those objects which still contain it.

21. Roy K. Bird argues that Morris's novels, like his photographs, call attention to their fictional status via authorial intrusions and contemplations (2). "Because of the inevitable subjectivity of memory, he sees all history as a fiction imposed by memory on the past" (36).

22. Roy Stryker of the Farm Security Administration was perplexed by the absence of people in Morris's images. The latter, unsuccessfully angling for an assignment, "tried to explain that the presence of people in the houses and barns was enhanced by their absence in the photographs. [Stryker] had heard many things, but nothing so far-fetched as that" (*Photographs and Words* 20).

23. Morris notes a similar defect haunting photographers, who are "obsessed with some concept of actuality" (*Time Pieces* 88).

24. In an unpublished lecture delivered at Amherst College in 1958, Morris states: "From *My Uncle Dudley* to the *Cannibals,* the author's real and imagined commitments to the past, and his gradual escape from its captivity, is recorded, as in a graph, in the various transformations of The Kid. This does not imply a rejection of the Past but an escape from its crippling enthralldom, such as Peter Foley believes he has experienced in his escape from the captivity of Lawrence" (qtd. in Hunt 59).

25. Wayne Booth and David Madden discuss the concept of imaginative transformation as a redeeming force in Morris's fiction.

Selected Bibliography

Baudrillard, Jean. *Simulacra and Simulation.* 1981. Trans. Sheila Faria Glaser. Ann Arbor: University of Michigan Press, 1994.

Bird, Roy K. *Wright Morris: Memory and Imagination.* New York: Peter Lang, 1985.

Booth, Wayne C. "The Shaping of Prophecy: Craft and Idea in the Novels of Wright Morris." *American Scholar* 31 (1962): 608-26.

———. "The Two Worlds in the Fiction of Wright Morris." *Sewanee Review* 65.3 (1957); 375-99.

Crimp, Douglas. "Pictures." *Art after Modernism: Rethinking Representation.* Ed. Brian Wallis. New York: New Museum of Contemporary Art, 1984. 175-88.

Crump, G. B. *The Novels of Wright Morris: A Critical Interpretation.* Lincoln: University of Nebraska Press, 1978.

Daverman, Richard. "The Evanescence of Wright Morris's *The Huge Season.*" *MidAmerica* 8 (1981): 79-91.

Eco, Umberto. *Travels in Hyperreality.* Trans. William Weaver. San Diego: Harcourt Brace Jovanovich, 1986.

Goldberg, Vicki. *The Power of Photography: How Photographs Changed Our Lives.* New York: Abbeville, 1991.

Grundberg, Andy. *Crisis of the Real: Writings on Photography, 1974-1989.* New York: Aperture, 1990.

Hawthorne, Nathaniel. *The Scarlet Letter.* 1850. New York: Norton, 1988.

Hunt, John W., Jr. "The Journey Back: The Early Novels of Wright Morris." *Critique* 5.1 (1962): 41-60.

Hutcheon, Linda. *The Politics of Postmodernism.* New York: Routledge, 1989.

Lyons, Nathan, ed. *Photographers on Photography.* Englewood Cliffs, New Jersey: Prentice-Hall, 1966.

Madden, David. *Wright Morris.* New York: Twayne, 1964.

Marchand, Roland. *Advertising the American Dream: Making Way for Modernity, 1920-1940.* Berkeley: University of California Press, 1985.

McGrath, Nancy. *Frommer's Dollarwise Guide to California and Las Vegas.* New York: Simon and Schuster, 1985.

Morris, Wright. *The Deep Sleep.* 1953. Lincoln: University of Nebraska Press, 1975.

———. *The Field of Vision.* New York: Harcourt, Brace, 1956.

———. *God's Country and My People.* New York: Harper and Row, 1968.

———. *The Home Place.* 1948. Lincoln: University of Nebraska Press, 1968.

———. *The Huge Season.* 1954. Lincoln: University of Nebraska Press, 1975.

———. *The Inhabitants.* 1946. New York: Da Capo, 1972.

———. *The Man Who Was There.* 1945. Lincoln: University of Nebraska Press, 1977.

———. *Photographs and Words.* Carmel, California: Friends of Photography, 1982.

———. *The Territory Ahead.* 1957. Lincoln: University of Nebraska Press, 1978.

———. *Time Pieces: Photographs, Writing, and Memory.* New York: Aperture, 1989.

————. *The Works of Love.* 1952. Lincoln: University of Nebraska Press, 1972.

Nye, David E. "'Negative Capability' in Wright Morris' *The Home Place.*" *Word and Image: A Journal of Verbal-Visual Enquiry* 4.1 (1988): 163-69.

Trachtenberg, Alan. "The Craft of Vision." *Critique* 4.3 (1962): 41-55.

————. *Reading American Photographs.* New York: Hill and Wang, 1989.

Wilson, J. C. "Wright Morris and the Search for the 'Still Point.'" *Prairie Schooner* 49 (1975): 154-63.

Wydeven, Joseph J. "Focus and Frame in Wright Morris's *The Works of Love.*" *Western American Literature* 23.2 (1988): 99-112.

————. "Images and Icons: The Fiction and Photography of Wright Morris." *Under the Sun: Myth and Realism in Western American Literature.* Ed. Barbara Howard Meldrum. Troy, New York: Whitson, 1985. 177-97.

Joseph J. Wydeven (essay date 1998)

SOURCE: "'No Place to Hide': Biographical and Critical Backgrounds," in *Wright Morris Revisited,* Twayne Publishers, 1998, pp. 1-17.

[*In the following excerpt from the introductory chapter of* Wright Morris Revisited, *Wydeven offers a thumbnail summation of Morris's major themes and techniques.*]

Throughout his active career, spanning the half century from 1942 to 1991 (when he stopped writing) and more than 30 books of fiction, commentary, and photo-text, Wright Morris remained resolutely independent, gradually establishing respectable reputations as both writer and photographer. He has resisted labeling as a realist or as a regionalist, and his experimentation has sometimes made his work difficult; he has insisted, particularly in his photo-texts and in his often extraordinarily visual prose, that readers be willing to cross generic borders, attend closely to detail, and draw conclusions from carefully crafted evidence.

Morris is less a storyteller than a brooder on stories he has already told. His work often has a cultivated ambiguity resulting from an understanding of reality as mysterious and complex, revealed through fragments and implications. This makes him, like the Henry James he admires, a novelist of consciousness. For Morris, it is the mind itself that is often at stake: In his photo-texts, Morris imposes a "third view" derived from photograph and written text; in his early fiction, he ponders the relation between memory and knowledge; and in his mature novels, he stresses the *making* of meaning and "meditative" motivations. G. B. Crump's statement that "the central focus of [Morris's]

best prose is often on nuances of consciousness almost too elusive, too fine, to put into words"[1] is helpful in understanding Morris.

Consciousness for Morris means two things. It is first a condition of imaginative awareness in the individual human mind, making possible what he calls *transformation,* an expansion of consciousness. The second meaning of *consciousness* is pertinent to the condition of the national culture, the decline of which Morris mourns. It is the "diminishment of consciousness" that dismays him.[2] Against "unconsciousness" in the 1950s Morris pitted transformation, but he was increasingly alarmed, especially after the assassination of John F. Kennedy, by American cultural problems evidenced by the decline of reading, increasing puerility in popular culture and the media, and a litany of other factors causing the trivialization of the American Dream.

Morris's most momentous writing is autobiographical, much of it evolving in counterpoint to his own experiences. From the beginning of Morris's experimentation with art, he was obsessed with *identity,* needing to comprehend and verify his past in order to anchor himself (and his characters) in space and time. Then, having explored and recreated the past, in the process coming to respect the powers of time, Morris turned to an artistic grappling with the problem of knowledge and *how* knowing takes place in the human organism.

This interest in epistemology is connected to his search for identity, for he recognized later that he had virtually created himself in his writing. The statement that Morris's work is autobiographical, then, must be tempered by a recognition that his conscious artistic purpose was to transform autobiographical facts into fictions. Over time Morris designed an elaborate theory of the relationships among memory, emotion, and the imagination in the creation of fiction. This theory—and its ramifications—is largely responsible for Morris's difficulty. He used his own life as a catalyst for investigations into identity and knowledge, but he was rarely satisfied that he had achieved closure. David Madden believes Morris never wholly solved his emotional problems in dealing with his Nebraska childhood, as evidenced by his need to seek new solutions to the same problems after writing "novels less personally concerned with the Nebraska past."[3]

Morris has often insisted that his novels cannot be fully understood in isolation from each other, conceptualizing his approach as "an up-and-downward spiraling of my preoccupations [that] would prove to lead me away and upward even as it led me back and downward."[4] This is essentially a way of visualizing the relations in his work among what he calls raw material, craftsmanship, and his need to repeat—even reshape—the past. Madden's view that "[i]t is as true of Morris as it is of Faulkner that full appreciation and understanding require a thorough reading of all the novels" (7-8) may be excessive, but it speaks to Morris's obsession to refigure the past. Attempting to explain Morris's autobiographical repetitions, Chester Eisinger suggests, "to use an overworked but precisely accurate term," that "Morris is haunted."[5] Repetition in writing is complicated, but in essence it is symptomatic of a need to *relive* original moments or events—summed up, perhaps, in Morris's perfect phrase "Home is where you hang your childhood."[6] Why relive seemingly insignificant events from the past? Because they were original, revelatory, pure, and often emotionally reducible to an idea—or even a photographic image.

By the time Morris realized his past might be important, it had already receded and could be recalled only with huge inaccuracies and gaping holes. Morris's recognition of this reality was essential. In mining his life, Morris discovered—long before this idea became the linchpin of autobiography study—that the passion for recollection consists as much of imagination as of memory. As he put it later, "If I attempt to distinguish between fiction and memory, and press my nose to memory's glass . . . , the remembered image grows more illusive. . . . Precisely where memory is frail and emotion is strong, imagination takes fire."[7]

As evidenced by such repetition, Morris was truly "haunted" by his Nebraska childhood. His adventures and vulnerabilities there are memorialized in his often repeated phrase "There is no place to hide," which becomes a metaphor for his career. Because on the Plains there is "no place to hide" from the elements, Morris often evokes means of physical and emotional shelter. The open spaces he emphasizes in his early works and the twisters that find their way into his work later are symptomatic of the need for shelter, and Morris's frequent placement of his characters hiding under porches or behind potted plants (as well as his own concealment as a photographer under the camera hood) suggests a desire for invisibility. This idea permeates Morris's work, suggesting both a psychological pattern for which hiding is a release and the basis for the creation of art as solace and solution. Hiding is a form of ritual preparation for the activity of perception.

Notes

1. G. B. Crump, "Wright Morris," in *A Literary History of the American West* (Fort Worth: Texas Christian University Press, 1987), 781.

2. Wright Morris, "Being Conscious," in *Voicelust: Eight Contemporary Fiction Writers on Style,* ed. Allen Weir and Don Hendrie Jr. (Lincoln: University of Nebraska Press, 1985), 23.

3. David Madden, *Wright Morris* (New York: Twayne, 1964), 170; hereafter cited in text.

4. Wright Morris, *A Cloak of Light: Writing My Life* (New York: Harper & Row, 1985), 137; hereafter cited in text as *Cloak.*

5. Chester E. Eisinger, "Wright Morris: The Artist in Search of America," in *Fiction of the Forties* (Chicago: University of Chicago Press, 1963), 330; hereafter cited in text.

6. Wright Morris, *The Home Place* (New York: Charles Scribner's Sons, 1948), 174.

7. Wright Morris, "Of Memory, Emotion, and Imagination," in *Earthly Delights, Unearthly Adornments: American Writers as Image-Makers* (New York: Harper & Row, 1978), 3.

FURTHER READING

Criticism

Quantic, Diane Dufva. *The Nature of the Place: A Study of Great Plains Fiction.* Lincoln: University of Nebraska Press, 1995, 203 p.

A reading of Morris's reading of the West inside a study of the region as a place in literature.

Wydeven, Joseph J. *Wright Morris Revisited.* New York: Twayne Publishers, 1998, 212 p.

An important volume of Morris scholarship: in-depth discussion of individual novels and photographs which also considers the whole work they constitute, with an excellent chronology, biography and annotated bibliography.

Additional coverage of Morris's life and career is contained in the following sources published by the Gale Group: *Contemporary Authors,* Vols. 9-12R; *Contemporary Authors New Revision Series,* Vols. 21, 81; *Contemporary Literary Criticism,* Vols. 1, 3, 7, 18, 37; *Dictionary of Literary Biography,* Vol. 2, 206; *Dictionary of Literary Biography Yearbook,* Vol. 81; and *Major Twentieth Century Writers* 1, 2.

George Oppen
1908-1984

(Full name George August Oppenheimer) American poet.

INTRODUCTION

Oppen was one of the founders of Objectivism, a movement in American poetry during the early 1930s dedicated to extending Imagism by making the poem itself an object. After his first volume, *Discrete Series,* appeared in 1934, Oppen stopped writing poetry and became a labor organizer in the Communist Party. It was not until the late 1950s that he began writing poetry again, becoming a leading figure in a new wave of Objectivism, and a significant influence on the generations of poets who succeeded his. In 1969, his book *Of Being Numerous* (1968) won the Pulitzer Prize for poetry.

BIOGRAPHICAL INFORMATION

Born into a wealthy family in New Rochelle, New York, Oppen endured a painful childhood. His mother, in the midst of a nervous breakdown, committed suicide when Oppen was four. His father's second marriage, when Oppen was nine, "opened upon me," Oppen has written, "an attack totally murderous, totally brutal, involving sexual attack, beatings." When he was ten, the family moved to San Francisco. Six weeks before his high school graduation from Warren Military Academy, apparently drunk, Oppen had a car accident in which another person was killed. He was expelled from school and his family sent him to travel in Europe. Returning to the United States, he finished high school and enrolled in Oregon State University. He studied poetry, and, there, he met Mary Colby. On their first date, they stayed out all night. She was expelled; he was suspended, but elected to leave as well. The two had decided to become poets and set out on a life of travel and experience rather than academic discipline. They married and hitchhiked throughout the United States together and finally settled in New York City, where they met William Carlos Williams, Louis Zukovsky, and Charles Reznikoff. In 1929, supported by a monthly income inherited from his mother, the Oppens moved to France, and visited Ezra Pound in Italy. Oppen wrote and ran To Publishers, the press he established which published the new Objectivist poets as well as Pound and Williams. Because of the poetic radicalism of Objectivism and the reluctance of booksellers to handle paperbacks, the business was unsustainable. Anti-Semitism, the first waves of fascism, and Pound's political allegiance to it contributed to their returning to the United States. In 1935 the Oppens joined

the Communist Party and worked as labor organizers until 1941. At the beginning of the Second World War Oppen worked at Grumman Aircraft, and was, therefore, exempt from the draft. As a Jew, Oppen felt responsible to fight against Nazism; he left that job so he would be drafted. In 1944 he was seriously wounded. After his discharge from the army with a Purple Heart, he and Mary withdrew from political work, but supported Henry Wallace for president in 1948. In 1949, FBI agents began investigating them, and they fled to Mexico to avoid testifying before the House Committee on Un-American Activities, which could force them to name suspected Communists or go to jail. While in Mexico, Oppen managed a furniture factory and still did not write. In 1958, with the demise of McCarthyism, the Oppens were granted passports and returned to the United States. On the trip back, he has told interviewers, after a dream which told him he would not rust, Oppen began writing poetry again. He also maintained his social commitments, marching on Washington in opposition to the Vietnam War, and supporting the Civil Rights movement. Though Oppen continued to write and to publish, to give public readings, and to grant many interviews, he also shunned fame, faced crises of confidence, and turned down more invitations to read than he accepted. He died of Alzheimer's disease in 1984.

MAJOR WORKS

The greater part of Oppen's poetry from *The Materials* (1962) through *Primitive* (1980) was written after his period of political activity and exile. It is nevertheless recognizably like the verse of his first book *Discrete Series*: experimental, laconic, compressed, syntactically disjunctive, sparsely punctuated, and projecting disconnected, not always fully formed images. The subjects of his poems include the dislocation, alienation, and debasement of the individual personally and collectively in a culture in which humane values have eroded, corporate rules and rigid structures are pervasive, the idea of "humanity" itself is dubious, and words have lost meaning. It is a lyric poetry concerned not with the self of the poet, with myth or psychology like so much modern poetry, but with the actualities of the world out of which the self is constructed, and with the concreteness of the words which reproduce the world. Despite the fact that *Of Being Numerous* is often thought of as his major work, it is truer to Oppen's art as well as to his politics to see his work as a collection of separate parts that contribute meaning to each other and derive meaning from the whole. The poems establish themselves as word-objects built to represent the things, the actualities of the world as they are, not to render a preexisting meaning or a narrative discourse about the world or the poet's consciousness. In all his work, Oppen attempted to reveal the phenomenological reality of the world reduced to its essence. As a poet, as much as a political organizer, his concern was to impinge upon consciousness with concrete words as objects in order to challenge reality by charging consciousness with vision.

CRITICAL RECEPTION

Oppen's poetry is more highly esteemed than well known. *Discrete Series* was lauded by Pound and Williams; his 1968 volume *Of Being Numerous* was awarded the Pulitzer Prize. Poetry magazines such as *Ironwood, Paideuma,* and *Sagetrieb* have devoted entire issues to him. Denise Levertov described his art as representing ongoing process rather than achieved work. Donald Davie has called his poetry "earnest, elegant, and touching." Hayden Carruth, however, dismissed Oppen as "having a fine mechanic's sense," and declined to include any of his work in his 1970 anthology of American poetry. Nevertheless, Oppen's poetry is well represented in many anthologies including the Berg/Mezey collection of "American poetry in open forms," and *Voices within the Ark: The Modern Jewish Poets.* There also is a large body of appreciative Oppen scholarship concerned with explicating his poetry, understanding its connection to movements such as Cubism and Abstract Expressionism, relating it to his politics and to his life, and exploring its connection to the work of

philosophers important to him, especially to Heidegger and Kierkegaard. In his last years, Oppen was awarded the PEN/West Rediscovery Award, and was honored by the American Academy of Arts and Letters and by the National Endowment for the Arts.

PRINCIPAL WORKS

Discrete Series (poetry) 1934
The Materials (poetry) 1962
This in Which (poetry) 1965
Of Being Numerous (poetry) 1968
Seascape: Needle's Eye (poetry) 1972
Collected Poems (poetry) 1975
Myth of the Blaze: New Poems, 1972-75 (poetry) 1975
Primitive (poetry) 1980
The Selected Letters of George Oppen (correspondence) 1990

CRITICISM

Morris U. Schappes (review date 1933)

SOURCE: A review of An *"Objectivists" Anthology,* in *Poetry,* Vol. XLI, No. IV, March, 1933, pp. 340-43.

[*In the following review of* An "Objectivists" Anthology, *Schappes attacks Objectivism as esoteric, nihilistic, lacking direction, and without a revolutionary, proletarian ideology.*]

If we are to understand Objectivism, there are three ideas in its program that must be stated and analysed. (1) "An objective," as defined by Mr. Zukofsky first in his poem, "A," and now in his editorial preface, is the "desire for what is objectively perfect." That is, objectivists, like other poets, aim at writing first, poetry ("I believe it possible, even essential, that when poetry fails it does not become prose but bad poetry," says William Carlos Williams), and then good poetry. Objectivists like to think that they differ from other poets and critics in stressing craftsmanship: "poetry defined as a job, a piece of work." In this belief, of course, they are naive: every poet and critic worth his paper emphasizes technical integrity. And here I must report that in almost 200 pages of paper I found only about a half dozen intelligent poems, and those mostly by Mr. Williams. This criticism brings me to point

(2) "*Impossible* to communicate anything but particulars," Mr. Zukofsky asserts with italic force. But nominalism in the psychology of aesthetics is just as inadequate as nominalism in philosophy. There is no artistic communication of particulars only. When Mr. Rexroth confronts us with

"Black / Blue black / Blue / The silver minuscles[!] / In early dawn the plume of smoke / The throat of night / The plethora of wine / The fractured hour of light / The opaque lens / The climbing wheel / The beam of glow / The revealed tree / The wine crater / The soft depth / The suspended eye" and forty more such lines, or (since I may have outraged his typographical sense by printing these horizontally instead of vertically with white huge margins), with

> stones sabers clouds kings nights leaves wishes arbors sparks
> shells wings mouths stars oranges fabrics ewes queens skins vehicles
> accents seeds cinders chutneys mixtures fevers apes eggs corpses

and more—well, Mr. Rexroth disregards a basic need in art: there must be trees (particulars), but you must be able to discern a wood; some woods have no trees, and are thus bad art; good art needs both the trees and the wood. Objectivists, as exemplified in this anthology, lack the power, the intelligence, to organize their poems. Sometimes, because there is only a single observation, organization is impossible. When Frances Fletcher, in a twelve-line twenty-word poem, *A Chair,* informs us that an electric chair differs from the one I now sit on because it has an electric current to burn bodies, I can merely note that I have so many more, and more profound, associations and connections with an electric chair, that Miss Fletcher's observation not only does not integrate my own experience but irritates me because of its essentially frivolous comment on a mighty symbol. And when a reader's rich experience is impoverished by poetry, this poetry is worthless.

But the most important objection to this book is number (3). The next line after Mr. Zukofsky's definition of an "objective" as the desire for good poetry reads: "Inextricably the direction of historic and contemporary particulars." But it is direction that is lacking in all this work. Mr. Zukofsky's "A," because it is the longest poem and therefore contains more particulars, is a good example. Many things are mentioned: Bach's *St. Matthew Passion,* the gay Leipzig audience, the tuxedos in Carnegie Hall, the subway, unemployment, Wobblies, a Pennsylvania miners' lockout, Pope Pius IX, B. V. D., the Chinese Red Army, Rimbaud, and Lenin (called, with esoteric intimacy, "Vladimir Ilyitch"—"Lenin" being reserved for another poem where he rhymes with "queen"). But there is no coherence, no organization, *no direction* in this long but still incomplete poem. There is the MacLeishian wail that The Speech has turned to jargon: "The Speech no longer spoken and not even a Wall to worship." But the rest is anarchy and chaos, spiritual and aesthetic. There can be no direction, nothing but sensationalism and spineless eclecticism, because there is, in the wide world, nothing, nothing, but particulars, hence—nothing. Rexroth's nihilism is plain: "Believe / Nothing / Just believe / Living / Be / Be living." When "believing" has become "be living," without direction, but *mere,* then intelligence, conscious action, *and art* are denied.

At a certain stage in the decay of a class, its artists turn against it in furious vanity. Control by the middle class, its idolization of Business-Profit, make the poet of little importance. He vents his pique by refusing to write for it, and withdraws into rootless esotericism. Scorned, he scorns. But his very method of rebelling against domination by Finance is conditioned by his former roots in the bourgeoisie. In protesting, he nevertheless accepts its premises; instead of questioning its economics, its politics, its morals, its values, he denies that there are values. In practise, Objectivism is such a nominalistic denial of art, of value. Because he has been reduced, in his social status, to Nothing, he thinks All is Nothing. The intelligent alternative, however, is completely to stride beyond these premises of the bourgeoisie: that is, to ally oneself with the revolutionary proletariat. Only there will the deracinated bourgeois poet find the rock from which criticism can be made, and on which are built values that are other than those sanctioned by a decadent middle class.

Let the critics and poets compare *An "Objectivists" Anthology* with Louis Aragon's *The Red Front* (English translation by E. E. Cummings) and they will understand more concretely what I have had to say with enforced abstractness.

William Rose Benét (review date 1934)

SOURCE: "A Serious Craftsman," in *Saturday Review of Literature,* Vol. X, No. 36, March 24, 1934, p. 580.

[*In the following review of* Discrete Series, *Benét pans Oppen's verse and challenges Pound's endorsement.*]

A serious craftsman: [t]hat is what Ezra Pound, in his preface, calls George Oppen, author of **Discrete Series** (The Objectivist Press, 10 West 36th Street, New York City). He appears to think that the hasty reviewer may say that Mr. Oppen writes a good deal like William Carlos Williams. He sees a difference which he does not "expect any great horde of readers to notice." His opinion of Mr. Oppen's work is that here is "a sensibility which is not every man's sensibility, and which has not been got out of any other man's books." If that were literally true. Mr. Oppen would be a paragon indeed. I know of no writer who has not got something out of other men's books. Certainly anyone's sensibility is at first nourished and increased through them.

Mr. Oppen's offering exhibits that extreme parsimony of words that is taken today to imply infinite profundity. I don't believe it implies anything of the kind. Most of Mr. Oppen's observations fail to impress me. His writing is like listening to a man with an impediment in his speech:

This land:
The hills, round under straw;
A house

With rigid trees

And flaunts
A family laundry,
And the glass of windows

But the definition of "discrete" being "separate, individually distinct, discontinuous," and this being a "discrete series," the statements in it fulfil, fairly well, the definition.

Ezra Pound (essay date 1934)

SOURCE: "Preface to *Discrete Series* (1934)," in *Paideuma,* Vol. 10, No. 1, Spring, 1981, p. 13.

[*In the following preface to Oppen's* Discrete Series, *originally published in 1934, Pound praises the poet for his craft and sensibility.*]

I. We have ceased, I think, to believe that a nation's literature is anyone's personal property.

Bad criticism emerges chiefly from reviewers so busy telling what they haven't found in a poem (or whatever) that they have omitted to notice what is.

The charge of obscurity has been raised at regular or irregular intervals since the stone age, though there is no living man who is not surprised on first learning that *Keats* was considered "obscure." It takes a very elaborate reconstruction of England in Keats' time to erect even a shaky hypothesis regarding the probable fixations and ossifications of the then hired bureaucracy of Albermarle St., London West.

II. On the other hand the cry for originality is often set up by men who have never stopped to consider how much. I mean how great a variant from a known modality is needed by the new writer if his expression is to be coterminous with his content.

One distinguishes between young men who have seriously learned the processes of their elders, and who attempt to use extant tools well, or to invent new ones, and those who merely dress up in old clothes.

The need of "reform" depends entirely on the validity or invalidity of the modes in use. At certain times it is necessary to reform it altogether. At others the adequate variation from a known mode of writing is far less visible to the uninitiate.

I see the difference between the writing of Mr. Oppen and Dr. Williams, I do not expect any great horde of readers to notice it. They will perhaps concentrate, or no, they will not concentrate, they will coagulate their rather gelatinous attention on the likeness.

I salute a serious craftsman, a sensibility which is not every man's sensibility and which has not been got out of any other man's books.

William Carlos Williams (review date 1934)

SOURCE: "The New Poetical Economy," in *Poetry,* Vol. XLIV, No. IV, July, 1934, pp. 220-25.

[*In the following review of* Discrete Series, *Williams discusses what makes a poem a poem, what makes a poem good, and praises Oppen for writing good poems.*]

[In *Discrete Series*] Mr. Oppen has given us thirty-seven pages of short poems, well printed and well bound, around which several statements relative to modern verse forms may well be made.

The appearance of a book of poems, if it be a book of good poems, is an important event because of relationships the work it contains will have with thought and accomplishment in other contemporary reaches of the intelligence. This leads to a definition of the term "good." If the poems in the book constitute necessary corrections of or emendations to human conduct in their day, both as to thought and manner, then they are good. But if these changes originated in the poems, causing thereby a direct liberation of the intelligence, then the book becomes of importance to the highest degree.

But this importance cannot be in what the poem says, since in that case the fact that it is a poem would be a redundancy. The importance lies in what the poem *is*. Its existence as a poem is of first importance, a technical matter, as with all facts, compelling the recognition of a mechanical structure. A poem which does not arouse respect for the technical requirements of its own mechanics may have anything you please painted all over it or on it in the way of meaning but it will for all that be as empty as a man made of wax or straw.

It is the acceptable fact of a poem as a mechanism that is the proof of its meaning and this is as technical a matter as in the case of any other machine. Without the poem being a workable mechanism in its own right, a mechanism which arises from, while at the same time it constitutes the meaning of, the poem as a whole, it will remain ineffective. And what it says regarding the use or worth of that particular piece of "propaganda" which it is detailing will never be convincing.

The preface seems to me irrelevant. Why mention something which the book is believed definitely not to resemble? "Discrete" in the sense used by Mr. Oppen, is, in all probability, meant merely to designate a series separate from other series. I feel that he is justified in so using the term. It has something of the implications about it of work in a laboratory when one is following what he believes to be a profitable lead along some one line of possible investigation.

This indicates what is probably the correct way to view the book as well as the best way to obtain pleasure from it. Very few people, not to say critics, see poetry in their day as a moment in the long-drawn periodic progress of an ever-changing activity toward occasional peaks of surpassing excellence. Yet these are the correct historic facts of the case. These high periods rest on the continuity of what has gone before. As a corollary, most critics fail to connect up the apparently dissociated work of the various men writing contemporaneously in a general scheme of understanding. Most commentators are, to be sure, incapable of doing so since they have no valid technical knowledge of the difficulties involved, what has to be destroyed since it is dead, and what saved and treasured. The dead, granted, was once alive but now it is dead and it stinks.

The term, technical excellence, has an unpoetic sound to most ears. But if an intelligence be deeply concerned with the bringing up of the body of poetry to a contemporary level equal with the excellences of other times, technique means everything. Surely an apprentice watching his master sees nothing prosaic about the details of technique. Nor would he find a narrow world because of the smallness of the aperture through which he views it, but through that pinhole, rather, a world enormous as his mind permits him to witness.

A friend sticks his head in at the door and says, "Why all the junk standing around?"

The one at work, startled perhaps, looks up puzzled and tries to comprehend the dullness of his friend.

Were there an accredited critic of any understanding about, he might be able to correlate the details of the situation, bringing a reasonable order into these affairs. But the only accredited critics are those who, seeking order, have proceeded to cut away all the material they do not understand in order to obtain it. Since man has two legs, then so also must the elephant. Cut off the ones that are redundant! Following this, logically, they describe a hollow tail and a tassel sticking out just above the mouth. This is my considered opinion of the position of the formerly alert critic, T. S. Eliot.

Then there are the people who do reviews for the newspapers. They haven't the vaguest notion why one word follows another, but deal directly with meanings themselves.

An imaginable new social order would require a skeleton of severe discipline for its realization and maintenance. Thus by a sharp restriction to essentials, the seriousness of a new order is brought to realization. Poetry might turn this condition to its own ends. Only by being an object sharply defined and without redundancy will its form project whatever meaning is required of it. It could well be, at the same time, first and last a poem facing as it must the dialectic necessities of its day. Oppen has carried this social necessity, so far as poetry may be concerned in it, over to an extreme.

Such an undertaking will be as well a criticism of the classics, a movement that seeks to be made up only of essentials and to discover what they are. The classics are for modern purposes just so much old coach.

And once again, for the glad, the young and the enthusiastic, let it be said that such statement as the above has nothing to do with the abiding excellence of the classics but only with their availability as a means toward present ends. In the light of that objective, they are nostalgic obstacles.

Oppen has moved to present a clear outline for an understanding of what a new construction would require. His poems seek an irreducible minimum in the means for the achievement of their objective, no loose bolts or beams sticking out unattached at one end or put there to hold up a rococo cupid or a concrete saint, nor either to be a frame for a portrait of mother or a deceased wife.

The words are plain words; the metric is taken from speech; the colors, images, moods are not suburban, not peasant-restricted to serve as a pertinent example. *A Discrete Series.* This is the work of a "stinking" intellectual, if you please. That is, you should use the man as you would use any other mechanic—to serve a purpose for which training, his head, his general abilities fit him, to build with—that others may build after him.

Such service would be timely today since people are beginning to forget that poems are constructions. One no longer hears poems spoken of as good or bad; that is, whether or not they do or do not stand up and hold together. One is likely, rather, to hear of them now as "proletarian" or "fascist" or whatever it may be. The social school of criticism is getting to be almost as subversive to the intelligence as the religious school nearly succeeded in being in the recent past.

> The mast
> Inaudibly soars; bole-like, tapering
> Sail flattens from it beneath the wind.
> The limp water holds the boat's round sides. Sun
> Slants dry light on the deck. Beneath us glide
> Rocks, sand, and unrimmed holes.

Whether or not a poem of this sort, technically excellent, will be read over and over again, year after year, perhaps century after century, as, let us say, some of Dante's sonnets have been read over and over again by succeeding generations—seems to me to be beside the point. Or that such a test is the sole criterion of excellence in a poem—who shall say? I wish merely to affirm in my own right that unless a poem rests on the bedrock of a craftsmanlike economy of means, its value must remain of a secondary order, and that for this reason good work, such as that shown among Mr. Oppen's poems, should be praised.

Thomas Merton (essay date 1965)

SOURCE: "The Madman Runs to the East," in *Conjectures of a Guilty Bystander,* Image Books, 1965, pp. 348-50.

[*In the following excerpt, Merton uses some verses of Oppen's as the basis of a homily.*]

Priests and ministers suddenly believe it urgent to assure everyone that "the world" is telling us the truth—not always making clear what world they mean. And often those who insist that "the world" is deceiving us mean only the world which refuses them and their message, not their own world, their own tight system of fragments of the past held together by money and armies.

I think only the poets are still sure in their prophetic sense that the world lies, and George Oppen has said it well:

> They await
> War, and the news
> Is war
> As always
>
> That the juices may flow in them
> And the juices lie.

This psychic and chemical dialogue of news, glands, juices, opinions, combat, self-affirmation, despair: this is "the world" and no poet need be doctrinaire about it. It is there for anyone to see, and they see it. They see how the people act in it.

> They develop
> Argument in order to speak, they become
> unreal, unreal, life loses
> solidity, loses extent, baseball's their game
> because baseball is not a game
> but an argument and difference of opinion
> makes the horse races. They are ghosts that endanger
> One's soul.

News, argument, and the juices flow. We do not want the news, but the flow of juices. Stimulation is the lie, and we cannot get along without it.

> Wolves may hunt
> With wolves but we will lose
> Humanity in the cities, stores
> And offices
> In simple
> Enterprise.

Yet the poet, Oppen again, knows another and more real world, the world not of lies and stale air in the subway, but of life. The world of life is itself manifest in words, but is not a world of words. What matters is not the words but the life. If we listen particularly to the world's speech about itself we will be lied to and deceived, but not if we listen to life itself in its humility, frailty, silence, tenacity. This poem of Oppen's is about a Jewish baby.

> Sara, little seed,
> Little, violent, diligent seed. Come let us look at the
>   world
> Glittering: this seed will speak,
> Max, words! There will be no other words in the world
> But those our children speak. What will she make of a
>   world
> Do you suppose, Max, of which she is made?

Will the words of the children be lies also, like those of our generation—or worse lies still? When one takes this deeper view he does not have to ask. There is the hope, there is the world that remakes itself at God's command without consulting us. So the poet, here, does not ask about lies or worry about them. He sees only the world remaking itself in the live seed, and Max can confidently take the baby to the window to see the false, glittering buildings, about which some speech will probably come later.

The glitter is false? Well, the *light* is true. The glitter has ceased to matter. It is even beautiful.

George Oppen with L. S. Dembo (interview date 1969)

SOURCE: An interview in *Contemporary Literature,* Vol. X, No. 2, Spring, 1969, pp. 155-77.

[*In the following interview, Dembo questions Oppen about his life and his poetry.*]

In February 1931 *Poetry,* under the acting editorship of a young man highly recommended to Harriet Monroe by Ezra Pound, issued an "Objectivist" number. As that young man, Louis Zukofsky, tells it, the term "Objectivist" was little more than a response to Miss Monroe's insistence that he produce a movement and a label to go with it. And Zukofsky is here generally supported by three other poets to whom the term has been applied, George Oppen, Charles Reznikoff, and Carl Rakosi. According to Reznikoff, the main reason a group formed at all was economic, and The Objectivist Press, which grew out of Oppen's To Publishers, was organized simply to facilitate publication of its members and their friends. The fact remains that Zukofsky did write an essay for the February *Poetry* issue entitled, "Program: 'Objectivists' 1931," in which, albeit elliptically, he developed the poetics of "sincerity and ojectification" and took Reznikoff's work as his example. The following year he brought out, under the imprint of To Publishers, An *"Objectivists" Anthology,* which had as its preface "'Recencies' in Poetry," a further elaboration of principles. Although reaction to both of Zukofsky's endeavors was for the most part bafflement (and, on the part of Yvor Winters, outright indignation), the conceptions were formulated with sufficient clarity for Samuel Putnam to devote an issue of his *New Review* to "The New Objectivism" (July 1931). . . .

George Oppen has actually done most of his work since the late 'fifties. After publishing *Discrete Series* in 1934, he gave up poetry to become a political activist and did not begin writing in earnest again until his return from Mexico, where he had fled with his family in 1950 to escape harassment by the McCarthy committee. Far from being a political poet, then, Oppen felt that political action and poetry were to be kept separate and that under certain conditions the former took precedence over the latter. When he returned to poetry, he demonstrated a profound interest in both the philosophy and psychology of "sincerity," a conception that recurs in all four interviews and is one of the main features of an objectivist outlook. Oppen's world is one in which the poet phenomenologically defines objects by defining his experience of them, and his poetry is the rigorous definition of feelings that exist after the failure of discursive knowledge and the evaporation of sentiment. For Oppen, as for Zukofsky, *seeing,* the act of pure perception that results in joy or awe, is one of the primary faculties of the poet and of men in general in an incomprehensible and terrifying world. New Directions has recently published Oppen's meditative poem, ***Of Being Numerous,*** which draws together the themes of the two preceding volumes, ***The Materials*** (New Directions-*San Francisco Review,* 1962) and ***This in Which*** (New Directions-*San Francisco Review,* 1966). This growing canon, with its philosophic subtlety and poetic intensity, reveals no minor talent, and Oppen, I believe, will eventually gain the recognition he deserves.

[*Interviewer*]: *I'd like to begin with some facts about your life, Mr. Oppen. You've lived many years in New York City, haven't you?*

[Oppen]: Yes, although I spent my boyhood in San Francisco. I was born in New Rochelle. My father, having married a second time, moved to California when I was about ten. I guess I was about nineteen when I left college, the University of Oregon, with Mary Colby, my future wife, and eventually hitchhiked to New York. A young instructor by the name of Jack Lyons had given me Conrad Aiken's anthology of modern poetry. It was my discovery that there was such a thing as modern poetry other than what I had been writing. I could say there was nobody at college with whom I could discuss modern poetry—but now I'm not so sure. I think I was afraid that somebody *would* tell me something about it and I didn't want to be told.

Anyway, we got to New York and started looking for people like Sherwood Anderson and even Vachel Lindsay and Carl Sandburg, who still have a kind of importance to me. Mary and I happened to be walking past the Gotham Book Mart one day before going to a party and we dropped in to waste some time. I saw *Exiles,* 3, edited by Ezra Pound, and he was one of the names I knew I was looking for. And I stood there and read the first poem which was called "Poem Beginning 'The'" by Louis Zukofsky, and went on to the party where someone said, "Oh, you're a poet. We have a friend who's a poet; you should meet him; his name's Louis Zukofsky." I said, "He wrote 'Poem Beginning "The,"'" and they said, "That's true, but you're the only person in the world who knows it."

Unfortunately, you're still in the minority.

That's possible, that's possible. Let's see, then. When I was twenty-one, Mary and I went to France to begin what was called To Publishers for reasons which I forget; it became The Objectivist Press. We printed *An "Objectivists" Anthology,* Pound's *ABC of Reading,* and so forth, but financially the undertaking became impossible. The books were paperbacks and the New York bookstores refused them. The customs officers made trouble, too. Louis did the editing and we did the printing. All that The Objectivist Press meant was that people paid for their own books.

Why was it called "Objectivist"? Was there any sense of movement?

That was Louis' term, as far as I know. When we sat down to write a statement on the book covers, Charles Reznikoff, who had legal training, produced at the right moment his statement: "The Objectivist Press is an organization of poets who are printing their own work and that of others they think ought to be printed." It was a little beyond the fact because there were differences of opinion on what should be included.

Were there any criteria for what got published?

Well, Louis put into *An "Objectivists" Anthology* people whom he liked or admired. He was, however, operating on a principle; there was some agreement among the poets. I think that all of us had considerable area of agreement, very considerable, but nobody signed a manifesto, and, as I said, certainly not everybody was of the same opinion. But there is no question that there was a relationship among these poets. The poets Louis liked all held a certain attitude toward poetry.

Just what was that attitude?

Let me see what we thought and whether I can generalize about it. I'll just put it in personal terms. What I felt I was doing was beginning from imagism as a position of honesty. The first question at that time in poetry was simply the question of honesty, of sincerity. But I learned from Louis, as against the romanticism or even the quaintness of the imagist position, the necessity for forming a poem properly, for achieving form. That's what "objectivist" really means. There's been tremendous misunderstanding about that. People assume it means the psychologically objective in attitude. It actually means the objectification of the poem, the making an object of the poem.

Williams, in fact, speaks of the poem as object.

Right. And this existed in the context of the sloppy American imagism descending out of Amy Lowell and a thousand others. The other point for me, and I think for Louis, too, was the attempt to construct meaning, to construct a method of thought from the imagist technique of poetry—from the imagist intensity of vision. If no one were going to challenge me, I would say, "a test of truth." If I had to back it up I'd say anyway, "a test of sincerity"—that there is a moment, an actual time, when you believe something to be true, and you construct a meaning from these moments of conviction.

My book, of course, was called **Discrete Series.** That's a phrase in mathematics. A pure mathematical series would be one in which each term is derived from the preceding term by a rule. A discrete series is a series of terms each of which is empirically derived, each one of which is empirically true. And this is the reason for the fragmentary character of those poems. I was attempting to construct a meaning by empirical statements, by imagist statements.

Each imagist statement being essentially discrete from the statement that followed or preceded it?

Yes, that meaning is also implicit in the word "discrete." The poems are a series, yet each is separate, and it's true that they are discrete in that sense; but I had in mind specifically the meaning to the mathematician—a series of empirically true terms.

In any case, the "discrete" aspect seems to be reminiscent of the cubist approach, if I'm not being far-fetched—hard, sharp fragments of theme or experience joined mosaically rather than integrated organically.

I'm really not sure what troubles the cubists had, but I had trouble with syntax in this undertaking and, as a matter of fact, I still have trouble with verbs. It's not exactly trouble; I just didn't want to put it too pretentiously. I'm really concerned with the substantive, with the subject of the sentence, with what we are talking about, and not rushing over the subject-matter in order to make a comment about it. It is still a principle with me, of more than poetry, to notice, to state, to lay down the substantive for its own sake. I don't know whether that's clear.

Please go on.

A statement can be made in which the subject plays a very little part, except for argumentation; one hangs a predicate on it that is one's comment about it. This is an approximate quotation from Hegel, who added (I like the quote very much): "Disagreement marks where the subject-matter ends. It is what the subject-matter is not." The important thing is that if we are talking about the nature of reality, then we are not really talking about our *comment about it*; we are talking about the apprehension of some *thing,* whether it is or not, whether one can make a thing of it or not. *Of Being Numerous* asks the question whether or not we can deal with humanity as something which actually does exist.

I realize the possibility of attacking many of the things I'm saying and I say them as a sort of act of faith. The little words that I like so much, like "tree," "hill," and so on, are I suppose just as much a taxonomy as the more elaborate words; they're categories, classes, concepts,

things we invent for ourselves. Nevertheless, there are certain ones without which we really are unable to exist, including the concept of humanity.

I'm trying to describe how the test of images can be a test of whether one's thought is valid, whether one can establish in a series of images, of experiences . . . whether or not one will consider the concept of humanity to be valid, something that is, or else have to regard it as being simply a word.

What you're saying now seems to be a part of the view of reality that's presented in your poems: the belief that conceptual knowledge or generalization is inadequate or misleading in man's relation to reality. Your poetry seems to suggest that physical reality or the environment is mysterious and has to be, in a way, sensuously rather than rationally apprehended; the poet's response is the pure awareness of being, so to speak. In **"Psalm"** [**This in Which**]*, for example, you write, "In the small beauty of the forest / The wild deer bedding down—/ That they are there!" And this seemed to be characteristic; the poet does not respond intellectually or discursively, but as a "nominalist," only to the physical tangibility or reality of the object he views.*

Yes, if one knows what "physical" means or what it contrasts with. But responds by faith, as I admitted somewhere, and to his own experience. All the little nouns are the ones that I like the most: the deer, the sun, and so on. You say these perfectly little words and you're asserting that the sun is ninety-three million miles away, and that there is shade because of shadows, and more, who knows? It's a tremendous structure to have built out of a few small nouns. I do think they exist and it doesn't particularly embarrass me; it's certainly an act of faith. I do believe that consciousness exists and that it is consciousness of something, and that is a fairly complete but not very detailed theology, as a matter of fact. In **"Psalm"** I was constructing what I felt to be a pretty emotional poem out of those few little words isolating the deer. And I just said, in this poem, these little nouns are crying out a faith in "this in which" the wild deer stare out. ["The small nouns / Crying faith / In this in which the wild deer / Startle, and stare out."]

What exactly is the faith? Is it in the world as world or is it in man's ability to know the world?

Well, that the nouns do refer to something; that it's there, that it's true, the whole implication of these nouns; that appearances represent reality, whether or not they misrepresent it: that this in which the thing takes place, this thing is here, and that these things do take place. On the other hand, one is left with the deer, staring out of the thing, at the thing, not knowing what will come next.

Yet you do say in **"A Language of New York"** [**This in Which**] *that the world "if it is matter / Is impenetrable."*

Ultimately, it's impenetrable. At any given time the explanation of something will be the name of something unknown. We have a kind of feeling—I described doubts about it—but we have a kind of feeling that the absolutely unitary is somehow absolute, that, at any rate, it really exists. It's been the feeling always that that which is absolutely single really does exist—the atom, for example. That particle of matter, when you get to it, is absolutely impenetrable, absolutely inexplicable. If it's not, we'll call it something else which is inexplicable.

Is that what you meant when you said in "A Narrative" [**This in Which**], *"Things explain each other, / not themselves"?*

That's it.

There's a passage in "Of Being Numerous" that seems to sum up your attitude. Let me quote it:

> The power of the mind, the
> Power and weight
> Of the mind which
> Is not enough, it is nothing
> And does nothing
>
> Against the natural world,
> Behemoth, white whale, beast
> They will say and less than beast,
> The fatal rock
>
> Which is the world—[#26]

That's right. Then, having said that, I went on to something I called "the lyric valuables" somewhere else ["**From Disaster**" in *The Materials*]. I suppose what I'm saying really is that there is no life for humanity except the life of the mind. I don't know whether it's useful to say that to anyone. Either people will have discovered it for themselves or else it won't be true for them.

Well, exactly what do you mean by "the life of the mind" in this sense?

I mean the awareness . . . I suppose it's nearly a sense of awe, simply to feel that the thing is there and that it's quite something to see. It's an awareness of the world, a lyric reaction to the world. "**Of Being Numerous**" ends with the word "curious" partly as a joke on Whitman, but also because men are curious, and at the end of a very long poem, I couldn't find anything more positive to say than that.

Then by "life of the mind" you mean something intuitive, not something analytical.

Yes, or just my word "faith." I said life of the mind and perhaps I spoke a little carelessly. I was anticipating, as its opposite, all the struggles for happiness, all the search for a morality of altruism, all the dependence on the poor to confer value—and eventually the poor might one way or another disappear. I was anticipating the whole discussion of "the good," of an ethic, and leaping ahead. I don't mean that there isn't anything to do right now, but I was thinking about a justification of human life, eventually, in what I call the life of the mind.

I don't quite follow you. Are you suggesting that "the life of the mind" replace social values?

Not "replace," no. There have been certain bases for a purely humanist or secular ethic which have worked—in the first place, the presence of the poor makes possible an ethic of altruism. That is, to want a good job and white-wall tires and a radio and so on is the very symbol of bestiality, isn't it? But if one can go and find that there are people in the South who don't have these things, then a good job and whitewall tires and a radio become positively spiritual values. I don't mean to mock the kids who went to Mississippi; they were heroic and they were doing what needed to be done. But the ethic isn't permanent and it isn't going to answer the problems. However one names that problem—the outcome of the process of humanity—it won't solve it.

One's afraid of the loss of an ethic because, of course, one does have ethical feelings. One does object to the war in Vietnam, for instance. One has trouble coming to terms with these things. We don't actually know if human life is operable without an ethic. There's the wonderful business of Socrates' defense of himself, with the beautifully worked out, entirely rational principle that one behaves ethically because one has to live in society after all and if one injures society, he will be acting against his own interest. For the sake of this doctrine he was about to drink the hemlock—which is a kind of contradiction that my poems often raise. Why do we do it? My last book tries to say that there is a concept of humanity, there is something we want humanity to be or to become, and this would establish the basis of an ethic. But that's pure metaphysical sentiment. It can't be done the way Socrates was doing it.

I'm beginning to see what you mean by sincerity. Your obligation is to your feelings alone. If it so happens that they are ethical, so much the better.

So much the better, or at least so much the more ethical. But of literature surely we both know that a student having once experienced the meaning of sincerity is hooked; he will know what literature is though he may have only that one quotation to prove it all his life long. And out of the same emotion, the same compulsion, one says what he thinks is true, not because he would like it to be true, still less because he thinks it would be good for the reader. I'm just reporting my experiences in life, including the one that when they drop enough jellied gasoline on children, you can't stand it anymore. I'm just stating a fact about what you can and cannot stand. If it didn't bother one to burn children, why say it does? I don't understand inventing an ethic; I'm just trying to understand what the ethic is, how long it can last. An ethic is a funny thing: when it's gone, it's gone and you can't mourn it. You can only talk about what you actually feel.

There is a difference between an ethic that is gone and one that is merely unfulfilled, though. Napalm may represent the failure of an ethic, the failure of a people to meet an ideal, but does it represent the actual passing of a value? We feel guilt in violating it.

Right. Again, I think I did work it out some in *Of Being Numerous* on the basis of pure metaphysics. We care about the idea of what's going to happen to humanity, including after one's death. I think in some other poem I argued it out; it's a little difficult to go through it tactfully in prose. Young people, even people of thirty, have an uninterrupted memory of twenty years of life and their life expectancy is much more than that, an infinity, more or less. They can reasonably expect to live longer than they can imagine. At a certain time of life, that ceases to be true. People know the most distant date on which they will die, and it does not seem far off. If they knew the world was going to end within that length of time, I argue, they would not bother to live their time out. There are other situations any of us could imagine in which people would not be willing to live, would find it impossible to live, without some concept of sharing in history or humanity—something which is happening after their death. Socrates obviously did because he drank the hemlock. I'm still not inventing or trying to be good for anyone. I'm trying to say how or why it is that one does live.

But you feel that you yourself have a commitment to an ethic. You are not just an observer.

Since I have a commitment to it, then I do something about it. If I didn't have the commitment, I wouldn't—the commitment being a sentiment, a something, a "gene." We simply have an ethical motivation and we must deal with that fact; if we didn't have it, it wouldn't be a problem.

Then you're an observer of your own feelings, which are inherently ethical. The idea of sincerity really seems to be the crucial one here. Well, perhaps we can go on to a different kind of subject. I was wondering whether you had any special ideas on prosody. I know that in an early essay Zukofsky talked about "objectification" in prosodic terms.

Yes. Well, I do believe in a form in which there is a sense of the whole line, not just its ending. Then there's the sense of the relation between lines, the relation in their length; there is a sense of the relation of the speed, of the alterations and momentum of the poem, the feeling when it's done that this has been rounded. I think that probably a lot of the worst of modern poetry, and it would be true of some quite good poetry, such as Creeley's, uses the line-ending simply as the ending of a line, a kind of syncopation or punctuation. It's a kind of formlessness that lacks any sense of line measure.

The meaning of a poem is in the cadences and the shape of the lines and the pulse of the thought which is given by those lines. The meaning of many lines will be changed—one's understanding of the lines will be altered—if one changes the line-ending. It's not just the line-ending as punctuation but as separating the connections of the pro-gression of thought in such a way that understanding of the line would be changed if one altered the line division. And I don't mean just a substitute for the comma; I mean with which phrase the word is most intimately connected—that kind of thing.

Do you agree at all with Williams' notion about "breaking the back of the iambic pentameter"?

I don't subscribe to any of the theories that poetry should simply reproduce common speech, and so on. My reason for using a colloquial vocabulary is really a different one. It may be touched by populism as Williams' is, but in general I don't agree with his ideas on the subject.

What do you mean by populism in this sense?

Williams likes to name those objects: wheelbarrow, white chickens, etc. I, too, have a sense—I hesitate to say it because I have no way of defending it—of the greater reality of certain kinds of objects than of others. It's a sentiment. I have a very early poem about a car closed in glass. I felt that somehow it was unreal and I said so—the light inside that car. Shall I read it? It's very short.

By all means.

In fact a lot of the poems talk about that sort of thing.

> Closed car—closed in glass—
> At the curb,
> Unapplied and empty:
> A thing among others
> Over which clouds pass and the
>   alteration of lighting,
>
> An overstatement
> Hardly an exterior.
> Moving in traffic
> This thing is less strange—
> Tho the face, still within it,
> Between glasses—place, over which
>   time passes—a false light.
>
>   [**Discrete Series**]

There is a feeling of something false in overprotection and over-luxury—my idea of categories of realness.

That's very interesting. It reminds me of another poem in which the light is illusory but does not seem to be false, the poem called "Forms of Love" in This in Which.

I suppose I would have to say to you at this point the terrible word "love," which seems to me to have a category of reality too. The car is detached from emotion, from use, from necessity—from everything except the most unconscionable of the emotions. And that lake which appears in the night of love seemed to me to be quite real even though it was actually fog.

But only two lovers—because of their heightened state of mind or heightened sensitivity—would have thought that the fog was a lake.

Yes, I think that's true. Certainly I was assuming that in the title.

So the vision was actually a form of love.

That's right.

*I notice you quote Kierkegaard in **"Of Being Numerous"** 16, and I wonder if his view of life has in any way influenced you.*

I liked the passage I used very much, although out of context it's a little different. I was very moved by the passage, but I don't think Kierkegaard in general has been very important to me.

You also cite Heidegger and Maritain elsewhere.

They have been very important to me. Maritain's *Creative Intuition in Art and Poetry,* not any other work though. Ideas like Heidegger's have been important to me for a long time, as early as the first poem in **Discrete Series.** It says, "The knowledge not of sorrow, you were saying, but of boredom / Is . . . Of the world, weather-swept, with which one shares the century." The word "boredom" is a little surprising there. It means, in effect, that the knowledge of the mood of boredom is the knowledge of what is, "of the world, weather-swept." But these phrases I use here to paraphrase the poem are phrases from Heidegger's Acceptance Speech [of the Chair of Philosophy at Freiburg] made in 1929, the year I was writing the poem. And the words "boredom" and "knowledge" are, in their German equivalents, the words he used. So I feel I have a natural sympathy with Heidegger—that he should use as a philosophic concept a mood of boredom. And the word is rather strange in the poem, too. The statements are identical.

Just what do you mean, he used as a philosophic concept a mood of boredom?

I was referring to one of the major concepts in the Acceptance Speech: the mood of boredom and the recognition of what is.

You also mentioned Maritain.

Yes, well, what I quoted in the first book is the sort of thing I value most in him: "We wake in the same moment to ourselves and to things." That's pretty central to my own thinking. I don't like his religious apologetics, though.

We've been talking about philosophers that interest you; what about poets? I was wondering what your attitude is toward, say, Pound or Williams.

It's true, of course, that Pound and Williams were both extremely important to me. But some people think I resemble Williams and it seems to me that the opposite is true. Pound unfortunately defended me against the possible charge of resembling him in the original preface to **Dis-**

crete Series. The fact has always haunted me. At any rate, my attitudes are opposite those of Williams. Certainly one would have needed a great deal more courage, without his example, to begin to find a way to write. He was invaluable and many of his poems are beautiful, though I've always had reservations about *Paterson*. I think "The Asphodel" is a most beautiful and profound poem.

I was under the impression that one of the basic themes in Paterson*, "no ideas but in things," would appeal to you.*

I have always wondered whether that expression didn't apply to the construction of meaning in a poem—not necessarily that there are out there no ideas but in things, but rather that there would be in the poem no ideas but those which could be expressed through the description of things. I took it that he meant the latter until I found that the expression was frequently understood in a different way. As for Pound, of course, a lot of his things stay in one's mind forever. Again, I have a great many reservations about Pound.

Anyway, if your interpretation of the Williams line is correct, it seems to me you would in fact partly resemble him.

Perhaps.

What about the Cantos*? They seem to be arranged according to a "discrete series," by the "ideogrammic method."*

Pound's ego system, Pound's organization of the world around a character, a kind of masculine energy, is extremely foreign to me. And Pound's root in Browning, which is so much more tremendous than any other root he has, is also foreign to me. What I really read in Pound are passages and lines. Just about the time I'm beginning to consider Pound an idiot, I come to something like the little wasp in the *Pisan Cantos,* and I know that I'm reading a very great poet.

At least a poet capable of great lyricism.

Yes.

Toward what recent writers do you feel the most sympathetic? I know you mention William Bronk in your poems.

I admire Bronk, but I'd prefer not to run down a list of others. I have no system for judging them. I can name the poets who really have been of decisive importance to me—Charles Reznikoff and Zukofsky as a person, his conversation, not his poetry—although, again as with Pound, while I can make an awful lot of objections to parts of A, the opening words, "A / Round of fiddles playing Bach," have rung in my ears for a very long time and always will, I imagine. Reznikoff has been the most important to me, consciously at least. And otherwise—this is what I have to explain—really Blake is more important to me than Williams, and several philosophers may be more important than Pound. The contemporary poets aren't the most important thing in my life, with the exception of those few things that really matter to me. Wyatt's poems, and several Middle English poems, among other antiquities, mean more to me than any except one or two of the contemporary. It must be some habit of life that makes it seem to young poets that all the other young poets are the major factors in his life. At any rate it's not true.

It would seem to be at least partly true of writers like Olson, Duncan, and Creeley. Have you read much of them?

I've read a lot of Olson. I think "In Cold Hell, In Thicket" is a very fine poem. I don't really like the *Maximus Poems* nor accept them at all. I admire Duncan insofar as I can understand him, which is very rarely.

I notice that in the poem called "Route" in **Of Being Numerous** *you devote a whole section in prose to a story about Alsatian men who tried to avoid being conscripted into the German army during the Second World War by hiding in holes. Evidently that story meant a lot to you.*

Yes, and I had to undertell it all the way because it's terribly dramatic and it got hold of me. I really had to tell it as quietly as I could, and, besides, it's a public story, the account of a terrible experience. But that's what these men did: they spent two or three years in a hole in the ground. They could get out of them only once in a while when it was snowing and their tracks would be covered.

Were these holes actually caves or what?

Foxholes or trenches, with logs laid down and covered over with sod after the man had gotten in. Pierre Adam, who told me the story, would help the men and bring them food when he could. It's a painful story to tell. I wrote it down as simply as I could and the language partly reflects the fact that Pierre told me in French and my French is limited. We spoke a very simple language to each other. It's the kind of story any existentialist—Sartre specifically—might tell except that it did happen to me and it was as important to me as the poem indicates. And Pierre knew what he was telling me; he knew the point he was making. He knew that I was very positive about politics, about a social and political morality—very positive about judgments concerning the war.

And this story is related to the rest of the poem?

The poem is about some of the things that have happened to me; the story is part of the meaning of that poem and all of the experiences told in it to record what I learned. **"Route"** is very closely connected to **"Of Being Numerous,"** the learning that one is, after all, just oneself and in the end is rooted in the singular, whatever one's absolutely necessary connections with human history are. The section plays that part in the poem.

*Then even though **"Route"** and **"Of Being Numerous"** seem to be speaking about the general human condition, they are actually very personal poems, aren't they?*

That's right, but I'm also writing about the human condition. All I actually know is what happened to me and I'm telling it. There wasn't any time in my life when I suddenly decided that now I'd write some philosophy. I'm just telling about what I encountered, what life was to me. In places I think I insisted upon this—"the things which one cannot not see," I wrote, and "not the symbol but the scene." I've written about what happened and the place it happened in, and that, I suppose, is the only philosophy I could possibly understand anyway, except for some kind of mathematical philosophy.

I wouldn't, for instance, talk about death with any great intensity unless I thought I was going to die. As close as I come to a philosophic statement is in that poem in which I wrote, "we want to be here"—just to set the fact down because the poems do have a kind of pessimism; and I'm reminding myself that I do want to be here, that I would not lack the courage to cut my throat if I wanted to do so. I don't do so. In fact I enjoy life very, very much. I wrote that poem in case there was any misinterpretation of that. And I set myself again and again, not in the spirit of any medical pragmatism, any philosophy offering to cure everything, nor in any effort to improve anybody, but just to record the fact, to saying that I enjoy life very much and defining my feeling by the word "curious" or, as at the end of **"The Narrative,"** "joy," joy in the fact that one confronts a thing so large, that one is part of it. The sense of awe, I suppose, is all I manage to talk about. I had written that "virtue of the mind is that emotion which causes to see," and I think that perhaps that is the best statement of it.

This is "the life of the mind" again.

Yes, and that's what I really mean by mind. If the virtue of the mind is missing, if somebody is "wicked" in my sense, I have nothing to say to him and it is this fact that causes me to mourn, now and then, for large sections of humanity. I don't know whether I can tell a whole city or a whole college or a whole class full of people that their minds should possess that virtue. If they do not possess it, I really feel despair when I face them, and I do not know what to tell them.

And this virtue is the primary feeling of the poet, a kind of sensitivity?

Yes, it is an emotion. The mind is capable not only of thinking but has an emotional root that forces it to look, to think, to see. The most tremendous and compelling emotion we possess is the one that forces us to look, to know, if we can, to see. The difference between just the neurosensitivity of the eye and the act of seeing is one over which we have no control. It is a tremendous emotional response, which fills us with the experience that we describe as seeing, not with the experience of some twitching nerves in the eyeball. It can only be interpreted emotionally, and those who lack it I despair of. And that's when the poems sort of stagger now and then, when I talk about despair.

But in a sense it's this very sensitivity that isolates the poet or makes him a lonely man, isn't it?

Yes, I quoted from a letter I received from a very young student at Columbia, Rachel Blau: "whether as the intensity of seeing increases, one's distance from them, the people, does not also increase." It was a profound and painful question that I had asked myself in her words. And that's what you are asking me again, for all that I've written a whole poem to establish, if I could, the concept of humanity, a concept without which we can't live. And yet I don't know that poetry is not actually destructive for people, because what you are implying is true. It does lead to the growing isolation of the poet; there's no question in my mind about it. I can only say that for all one's fears and hesitations and doubts, and for my rejection of poetry for twenty or twenty-five years, I think that what we really want is not to establish a definition of the good and then work toward it, but rather to see what happens happen, to go wherever we are going. I think a poet comes to feel that this is all he does—moves us in the direction we are going.

I think it's interesting that for all your desire merely to report your feelings and to repudiate an ethical aim for your poetry, you do have strong ethical convictions to express. But, as you've said, the important thing is that the ethic be felt and not merely constructed. I notice that your poetry does refer to the Depression on occasion, and I imagine that your feelings during this period were particularly intense.

That's true. I think it was fifteen million families that were faced with the threat of immediate starvation. It wasn't a business one simply read about in the newspaper. You stepped out your door and found men who had nothing to eat. I'm not moralizing now—and I've been through this before—but for some people it was simply impossible not to do something. I've written an essay that appeared in *Kulchur 10* in which I explained that I didn't believe in political poetry or poetry as being politically efficacious. I don't even believe in the honesty of a man saying, "Well, I'm a poet and I will make my contribution to the cause by writing poems about it." I don't believe that's any more honest than to make wooden nutmegs because you happen to be a woodworker. If you decide to do something politically, you do something that has political efficacy. And if you decide to write poetry, then you write poetry, not something that you hope, or deceive yourself into believing, can save people who are suffering. That was the dilemma of the 'thirties. In a way I gave up poetry because of the pressures of what for the moment I'll call conscience. But there were some things I had to live through, some things I had to think my way through, some things I had to try out—and it was more than politics, really; it was the whole experience of working in factories, of having a child, and so on. Absurd to ask myself whether what I undertook was right or wrong or right for the artist and

the rest of that. Hugh Kenner interrupted my explanation to him of these years by saying, "In brief, it took twenty-five years to write the next poem." Which is the way to say it.

I probably won't stop writing poetry this time, not because I've changed my evaluation of things but partly because I feel I have only so much time left and that's what I want to do. During those years I was perfectly aware of a lot of time before me and I at no time thought I wasn't a poet. I don't remember saying it clearly to myself, but I never felt that I would never write a poem again.

What did you actually do during the 'thirties?

Oh, well, we were Communists, all right. I don't know whether to say we had philosophic doubts, but we knew that some forms of activity were of very questionable usefulness. We made sure that what we were doing was not politicalizing but something we really intended to do. We were in a way isolated; all our friends were poets and most of them were poets of the right wing. We joined the movement to help organize the unemployed. There're little accounts of it in the poems, which I think I muffed. The story has to be told very forthrightly and somehow I couldn't do it. It was a matter of going from house to house, apartment to apartment; I think we knew every house in Bedford-Stuyvesant and North Brooklyn and all the people in them. We wanted to gather crowds of people on the simple principle that the law would have to be changed where it interfered with relief and that settlement laws would have to be unenforceable when they involved somebody's starvation. And we were interested in rioting, as a matter of fact—rioting under political discipline. Disorder, disorder—to make it impossible to allow people to starve. It also involved the hunger march on Washington as well as local undertakings.

For how long were you active?

Not so many years. Then there's the well-known story of the difficulty of escaping from the Communist philosophy and attitudes and one's Communist friends. And then there came about a situation that made it impossible for us to participate anymore, even after the difficulty with our own thinking. We were under threat by the McCarthy committee and had to flee the United States. I don't think I have to tell the whole story about that. You get questioned as to who you knew and you refuse to answer and you get jailed. We did not want to get jailed; that would have been only a matter of a year—we weren't terribly important—but we had a child and it would have been a bad thing. Mexico wasn't an absolute refuge, but it made it a little more difficult to get us and we knew we needed only to make it a little difficult. Nobody was very excited about us. But we did have to flee. It was actually more dangerous to drop out than not because the McCarthy committee would figure you were ripe for becoming an informer and we needed our friends badly—and there was the fact of the child too. But this is a little difficult for me to say. There is a difference in one's attitude, in what one wants to say and doesn't want to say, doesn't want to put down on paper, when one is speaking to a child—well, I can't say I was speaking to our baby daughter. I'll simply say I was being a father, and fathers don't confess to fears even to themselves. That is in its way political, too. It's part of the whole pragmatism of social and political attitudes, the test of goodness, which extends awhile when one is thinking of a child. But it's much more complex. It was actually sort of a different time of life that I sat down again and set myself, for the first time really, to complete a poem, to really finish a poem and be sure I felt I had completed it. It was as a matter of fact in 1958.

Was this while you were still in Mexico?

Still in Mexico. The first poem I wrote was one of the long ones in **The Materials.** I think it was **"Blood from a Stone."** It was a fairly rough poem which I knew I just had to write. It took three years to write the whole collection. I don't know what proportion of the poems were written in Mexico and what in New York.

Just how long were you in Mexico?

From 1950 to 1958.

That's a long time.

A long time.

Did you get involved with Mexican culture?

Yes, some, unsuccessfully. I think every American's experience is unsuccessful in this regard. I could tell very nice stories about Mexico, but I also have a lot of negative feelings I don't even want to state. The fact is that it's not a very good place for Americans to be.

What bothered you in particular?

I really will be attacking Mexico if I get into that, and there's no particular reason. But it had to do with my sense of being a craftsman, for whatever it's worth, and my sense of not being an executive. In Mexico foreigners are not permitted to produce objects, and the law is rigorously enforced. I set up a small business, which was not easy. One becomes accustomed to paying bribes everywhere and with the greatest possible tact and skill—a situation of infinite corruption, to begin to tell it, a society, a culture really trapped and not the fault of the people. They are trapped by their culture, by the relation of men and women, by the absolute corruption of government, by the habits of bureaucracy, the habits of people. One is forced to change class very sharply in Mexico; if one is a foreigner, one has to be an upper-bourgeois citizen, as a matter of law or necessity. None of these things was easy for us; they were by no means easy.

What kind of a business did you manage to set up?

I made—"made" in the upper-bourgeois sense—furniture. I never touched a tool. I set up with a Mexican partner, a very wonderful man and a very fine craftsman.

Was there any specific reason for your coming back in 1958?

Just that we could; the McCarthy thing was over. We only went to Mexico in the first place because we couldn't get passports. We weren't illegally in Mexico but we were helplessly there, and we paid an infinite series of bribes.

What did you do when you got back to New York?

Sat down and wrote poetry. We just found a place in Brooklyn which was easy enough to pay for, and I started writing again. I knew James Laughlin of New Directions Press would give me some consideration and that Rago of *Poetry* knew my earlier work or at least recognized my name, so I wasn't entirely without connections. I felt that people knew me a little.

Mr. Oppen, I am deeply grateful for your willingness to discuss your poetry and your life.

I have a liking for openness and a willingness to talk and question, and if one says something that is wrong, so one says something that is wrong. One tries not to write anything that is wrong, but conversations are another matter. Sometimes it turns out that people can find common ground or that they have that virtue of the mind I was talking about when they read your poetry—which is just another way of saying that they give a damn.

L. S. Dembo (review date 1969)

SOURCE: "Individuality and Numerosity," in *The Nation,* New York, Vol. 209, No. 18, November 24, 1969, pp. 574-76.

[*In the following review of* Of Being Numerous, *Dembo illustrates his assessment of Oppen as "a poet of the first order" by selected textual explications.*]

When George Oppen stopped writing poetry in the mid-1930s, he had behind him only a small volume of imagistic poems, hardly enough to mark him for the stature he has achieved today. His efflorescence, after twenty-five years of silence, is remarkable. It would be irrelevant to speculate on what Oppen might have done had he been writing steadily just as it would be sentimental to lament his silence. The four volumes that he has completed are in themselves an impressive contribution to American poetry.

There is nothing in his first volume, **Discrete Series,** to suggest that Oppen's social consciousness was strong enough to lead him to abandon poetry and commit himself fully to political activism. Yet that is exactly what he did. He and his wife joined the Communist Party in 1935, not for philosophic reasons, says Oppen, but out of the desire to do something about mass hunger. That this decision was not foreshadowed in **Discrete Series** is characteristic of Oppen's whole way of viewing his art. He never believed that politics could be made into poetry or, conversely, that poetry could have any effect on social conditions. When a poet could no longer tolerate what he saw before his eyes, Oppen felt, poetry was a luxury.

The following two and a half decades were years of activism, military service and exile. Harassed by the McCarthy committee in 1950, faced with the prospect of informing on friends or going to jail, he fled to Mexico with his wife and child and did not return until 1958, after McCarthy's death. By this time he had been working on some new poems. This opened his most creative period. In 1962 New Directions/*San Francisco Review* published **The Materials** and in 1965, **This in Which.** This year, his stature finally recognized beyond a small group of poets and critics, he won the Pulitzer Prize for **Of Being Numerous.**

Just as Oppen's involvement in political activities marked a divorce from poetry, so his return to poetry marked an exhaustion with politics. Unsurprisingly, the latter poems proceed from the same "objectivist" impulse as the earlier even though they are, of course, broader in subject and more profound. While Louis Zukofsky, Charles Reznikoff, and Oppen himself have all denied the existence of a coherent movement called "Objectivism," the label remains useful. It is unimportant, for example, that Zukofsky's manifesto in the February 1931 issue of *Poetry* was as baffling to Reznikoff, whose poetry Zukofsky used to exemplify his theory, as to Oppen and many of the magazine's readers. More important is that each of the poets had a notion of what he himself meant by "objectivist"; and Oppen's interpretation is the key to all his work.

Objectivism begins for Oppen as an attempt to "construct a method of thought from the imagist technique of poetry—from the imagist intensity of vision. He called it a test of sincerity, based on the idea "that there is a moment, an actual time when you believe something to be true and you construct a meaning from these moments of conviction." "Imagist thought," first embodied in **Discrete Series,** is a form of nominalism in which appreciation of the existence of an object, in its tangibility or luminosity, is the primary poetic feeling. The moment of conviction is aesthetic, not philosophic or ethical:

> the thing
> Happening, filling our eyesight
> Out to the horizon—I remember the sky
> And the moving sea.

The world that is impenetrable to the "power and weight of the mind" reveals itself, in its own way, to the man who is capable "of that emotion / Which causes / To see"; that is, to the man who can experience "a lyric reaction to the world." Poetry, then, ought not to have a social or moral intention, any more than the poet should be what Oppen called a "medical pragmatist" offering remedies. What matters is the "sense of the poet's self among things," not a display of "right thinking and right sentiment" which could not "substantiate themselves in the concrete material of the poem."

The aesthetic qualities of objects or events—apprehended not in terms of their associations or conventional meaning but in terms of their form or motion—were considered by Oppen to be "empirical." They nonetheless depend on the point of view of the perceiver. The chief interest in **Discrete Series** is not so much what is observed but how it is observed or experienced. For instance, here is how a woman appears to a nominalist sexually aroused:

> She lies, hip high,
> On a flat bed
> While the after—
> Sun passes.
>
> Plant, I breathe—
> O Clearly
> Eyes legs arms hands fingers,
> Simple legs in silk.

The subject of the poem is not the lady but the poet who, Oppen explains, regards her as though he were a plant closed in on himself. As a matter of fact, the lady is perceived not as a person but as a set of particulars or visual sensations; such constitutes her greatest "reality" for the speaker.

In the later poems Oppen's phenomenological bent becomes unmistakable. "Thought leaps upon us because we are here" he writes in **"World World"** (*This in Which*). Still rigorously reporting only what he has "seen" or truly sensed, he begins to describe a world of alienation and loss—a world lethal and unknowable yet offering moments of intense aesthetic vision. In poems like **"The Return,"** which reflect (but never declare) Oppen's profound sense of estrangement on his return to New York from Mexico: **"Resort,"** in which he views himself as though he were an alien object; or **"Tourist's Eye,"** in which he vainly tries to penetrate beyond the "mineral fact" of the city, and the sheer "numerosity" of men, to a vision of "humanity" and a sense of continuity, Oppen reveals the human, if stark, struggle that underlies the perceptions of the objectivist. Nonetheless, he could still say—and say characteristically—that "we want to be here" and that he himself lived not from lack of courage to commit suicide but in affirmation of life. Again, what redeemed the world for Oppen was the "lyric valuable."

Poetry thus became for Oppen the language of faith in the material world and the means for expressing its ultimate mystery. Commenting on **"Psalm,"** he argued that in uttering small words like "sun" and "shade" one implied an entire cosmos. "It's a tremendous structure," he said, "to have built out of a few small nouns." The noun is the central part of speech in Oppen's universe, since it signifies the existence of an object but provides no knowledge about it:

> There are words that mean nothing
> But there is something to mean,
> Not a declaration which is truth
> But a thing
> Which is.

That reality—as epitomized, for example, by the islands in the polar mist of **"Narrative"**—can inspire the poet with dread and the sense of *Neant,* as well as with joy and the sense of *Being,* points up the profound ambivalence in Oppen's view of the world. The "life of the mind," which Oppen believes to be the only life for humanity, coexists with *Angst* boredom and despair. Yet underlying these opposing responses is the idea that reality in all its manifestations must be respected as truth. Nontruth is represented by the invented ethic, detached from actual feeling, or in objects, by the hollow decorations of an affluent civilization.

Of Being Numerous, with the title poem and its sequel, **"Route,"** gathers up the themes of the preceding volumes into a coherent meditation. Both are major poems which mingle autobiography and metaphysics in an objectivist style that is anything but confessional. Investigating the philosophic implications of his own experiences and, conversely, the experiential basis of his philosophic generalizations, Oppen reveals little of himself except his proclivity to avoid soul searching. Furthermore, if **"Of Being Numerous"** and **"Route"** can be called meditative poems, they are meditative according to the logic of "imagistic thought." That is, each is a mosaic of observations that might justly be considered a discrete series; they are phenomenological rather than psychological renditions of the poet's consciousness, as the opening lines of **"Of Being Numerous"** indicate:

> There are things
> We live among "and to see them
> Is to know ourselves."

"Of Being Numerous" is concerned with individuality and "numerosity." One of the important, if obscure, questions it raises is, Is there such a thing as "humanity," a vital whole that might be its own justification for living, or are men simply numerous, part of a meaningless, "infinite series"? The poem begins with an inquiry into the nature of men's lives in the city. (Many of the sections are taken from **"A Language of New York"** in *This in Which.*) The things we live among are "sad marvels," the "mineral facts" of skyscrapers, that can be seen but not comprehended. The city merely exists; it has no meaningful or recoverable past; life is pure "occurrence"; the poet finds himself incapable of living in any time but the present.

> Frozen in the moonlight
> In the frozen air over the footpath,
>   consciousness
>
> Which has nothing to gain, which
>   awaits nothing,
> Which loves itself

The poet is aware of his own individuality, but it is an, awareness made possible only by the sense of isolation. Undoubtedly Oppen's actual exile lies behind this universal appraisal, and a personal sense of shipwreck gives force to the abstraction:

> The isolated man is dead, his world
>   around him exhausted
> And he fails! He fails, that meditative
>   man! . . .
>
> Obsessed, bewildered
>
> By the shipwreck
> Of the singular
>
> We have chosen the meaning
> Of being numerous.

The Singular Man had the power of seeing intensely but not of communicating; the shipwreck of the singular is really the failure of the poet to reach a community.

Underlying all the tensions of the poem is a crisis of faith in which Oppen posits an idea of humanity but cannot consistently believe in the metaphysic that will transform the infinite series of single lives into continuity and community, "the metaphysic / On which rest / The boundaries / Of our distances." Generations succeed one another, Oppen implies, only to be lost in "the great mineral silence . . . a process / Completing itself." The poem accordingly ends with a quotation from Whitman in which the capitol dome at sunset is described: "it dazzles and glistens like a big star: it looks quite . . . curious. . . ."

"At the end of a very long poem," Oppen remarked, "I couldn't find anything more positive to say than that."

The "first eyes" of the poet can be bedazzled but all they can *know* is "the noon's / Own vacuity." The anticlimactic comment marks the totality of the poet's knowledge of what he beholds. Aesthetic vision must be its own excuse for being, for there is nothing beyond it.

No less intense a poem than **"Of Being Numerous,"** **"Route"** reflects the profound determinism that marks the whole range of Oppen's work. It has a vision of love, but love understood as a biological phenomenon. A matter of chromosomes and genes, it "occurs" no less unknowable an event than any other natural phenomenon. **"Route"** sees aesthetic clarity as the sum of knowledge:

> One man could not understand me
>   because I was saying
> simple things; it seemed to him that
>   nothing was being
> said. I was saying: there is a mountain,
>   there is a lake. . . .

The poem tells a pathetic story, from real life, about Alsatian men who hid themselves in holes to avoid conscription by the Nazis. But the story is presented in understated irony and in a casual tone, as part of the poet's "reportage" of the way men behave and the way things occur. Characteristically, Oppen does not comment on the horrors of war; his real subject in this section is the strength of authentic feelings, the psychological realities that are prior to all intellectual constructions, ethics included:

Wars that are just? A simpler question;
In the event,
will you or will you not want to kill a
German. Because
in the event, if you do not want to,
you won't.

Consistent with his biological and psychological determinism, Oppen does not see war as a form of evil but rather of insanity. And if the genes do not produce love, "we will produce no sane man again."

Oppen is not the kind of man to call attention to himself; he is unpretentious, soft-spoken and, above all, modest. These perhaps are the personal qualities that lie behind his impersonal style, which is never strident, but generates its own kind of power. In his stark, chiseled idiom he frequently achieves a "limited, limiting clarity." His own poetic ideal is that of the existential man in general whose integrity compels him to face down an absurd universe and whose lucidity keeps him from despair. Behind Oppen's impersonal "reportage" there is all the intensity of personal conviction, unjeopardized by sentimentality and romantic egoism. Oppen has realized the full potential of his objectivist allegiance: he has become a poet of the first order.

Donald Davie (essay date 1973)

SOURCE: "Notes on George Oppen's *Seascape: Needle's Eye*," in *George Oppen: Man and Poet*, edited by Burton Hatlen, National Poetry Foundation, Inc., 1981, pp. 407-12.

[*In the following essay, originally published in 1973, Davie considers Oppen's poems on their own merit rather than as representative of a particular movement or tradition.*]

For us to come to terms with Oppen, the time has long gone by—if it ever existed—when it was useful to start plotting his place in a scheme of alternative or successive poetic "schools" or "traditions." Imagism, objectivism, constructivism, objectism: if there was ever any point in shoving those counters about, that time is long gone by. At present, that sort of categorizing only ducks the challenge that the poems throw down: the way of living, and of thinking about living, which they propose to us.

Oppen is not at all a representative American poet. Not only is he in earnest as few poets are, but the nature of his earnestness is not of a sort we think of as "American." In his background and his past there is a good deal of Marxism, and so his attempts to understand the moment in which he writes are a historian's attempts, not (as with most American poets of comparable seriousness) psychological and/or mythopoeic. Not for him, for instance, the naive pastoralism, the harking back to a pre-industrial economy, which is the stock-in-trade of the American po-

ets currently most popular with the American public. And so it is ironical that when Charles Olson responded to Oppen's review of him he should have protested, "I wanted to open mr Oppen to history"; being open to history is one thing, being open to the recorded and unrecorded past is something else. And one may stay closed to that past not because of ignorance or limited imagination, but as an act of willed choice. This is the choice that Oppen seems to make in a recent poem called, **"The Taste"**:

Old ships are preserved
For their queer silence of obedient seas
Their cutwaters floating in the still water
With their cozy black iron work
And Swedish seamen dead the cabins
Hold the spaces of their deaths
And the hammered nails of necessity
Carried thru the oceans
Where the moon rises grandly
In the grandeur of cause
We have a taste for bedrock
Beneath this spectacle
To gawk at
Something is wrong with the antiques, a black fluid
Has covered them, a black splintering
Under the eyes of young wives
People talk wildly, we are beginning to talk wildly,
    the wind
At every summit
Our overcoats trip us
Running for the bus
Our arms stretched out
In a wind from what were sand dunes

(***Collected Poems*** p. 225) [hereafter abbreviated as ***CP***]

Those who know San Francisco know that wind, they know also the ships that Oppen means, and they will share his sense that in the California scene such attempts at historical *pietas* have an air of irrelevant connoisseurship. The poem comes in fact in a sequence with the deceptively modest title, **"Some San Francisco Poems."** But then . . . Oppen is a San Franciscan, once again voluntarily, by choice. He moves about the city and its hinterland seeing it through eyes that have been conditioned elsewhere. It is an Atlantic eye that looks out over the edge of a continent and a cultural epoch, at the Pacific. The beautiful and precarious shallowness of coastal California, treacherously gummed on to the continent across the San Andreas fault, is caught by him as by no native or thoroughly assimilated Californian. He is as much a foreigner there as we might be, and therefore as incredulous, as dubious, above all as apprehensive.

It is possible to think that poetry should be responsible for giving to Californian youth that ballast which we feel that it so perilously lacks—"You were *not* born yesterday!" That was the response of a thoroughly assimilated Californian, Yvor Winters, in poems like "California Oaks." Oppen will have none of it. For him on the contrary sanity is in holding on to

'the picturesque
common lot' the unwarranted light
Where everyone has been

(*CP,* p. 219)

And so "the courageous and precarious children" (*CP,* p. 226), as he calls them, are to be—have to be—trusted, with whatever misgivings. The past will not help them; and perhaps we only thought that it helped us.

That goes also for the past of Art, of poetic art for instance:

O withering seas
Of the doorstep and local winds unveil

The face of art

Carpenter, plunge and drip in the sea Art's face
We know that face

More blinding than the sea   a haunted house   a
  limited

Consensus unwinding

Its powers
Toward the thread's end

In the record of great blows   shocks
Ravishment   devastation   the wood splintered

The keyboard gone in the rank grass swept her hand
Over the strings and the thing rang out

Over the rocks and the ocean
Not my poem   Mr Steinway's

Poem   Not mine   A 'marvelous' object
Is not the marvel of things

                  twisting the new
Mouth   forcing the new
Tongue   But it rang

(*CP,* p. 224)

We have heard something like this before, from William Carlos Williams. The resemblance is real, and Oppen no doubt would acknowledge it. But the differences are striking too. Williams after all was a mythopoeic poet (*Paterson*) and a historian only so far as he could turn history into myth. He was even a systematizer, and in his last years a master or a prophet looking for (and thinking he found) disciples. Oppen has no such hopes or intentions; his tone is ruminative, intimate, domestic. There is no writer to whom a tag like "American expansiveness" is less appropriate. And indeed this goes beyond "tone"; in a very unAmerican way Oppen seems to offer us, as Hardy did, only "disconnected observations." The claims that he makes on us, for himself and his art, are disarmingly modest.

All the same, and in fact even less avoidably than with Williams, the challenge is thrown down to us: the past is irrelevant, a dangerous distraction. Well, *is* it? For in-

stance, the past of our art. . . . Much as we may agree that "a 'marvelous' object Is not the marvel of things," or that the commonplace is fruitfully mysterious in ways that only this sort of poetry can make us see, still, are we Marxist enough, historical determinists enough, to agree that the time is past for so many of the traditional splendours and clarities as this poetry wants us to dispense with? Outside of the San Francisco sequence there is a poem called (and the title is important) **"West"**:

Elephant, say, scraping its dry sides
In a narrow place as he passes says yes

This is true

So one knows?   and the ferns unfurling   leaves

In the wind

. . . sea   from which . . .

'We address the future?'

Unsure of the times
Unsure I can answer

To myself   We have been ignited
Blazing

In wrath we await

The rare poetic
Of veracity that huge art whose geometric
Light seems not its own in that most dense world
  West
       and East
Have denied have hated have wandered in   *precari-
  ousness*

(*CP,* p. 208)

(I break off at mid-point.) "Splendours"—is that the word for what an old-fashioned reader would feel the lack of, in these verses? Hardly; that elephant, so abruptly huge and patient before us, is himself a splendour. "Clarities," then? Well, yes; the suppression of so much punctuation certainly makes for obscurity (though the most obscure poem is one called **"The Occurrences,"** which has no punctuation-stops at all). But the right word, to point for instance to the melodiousness which it seems plain we must not look for in this writing, is still to seek. I suggest: *"braveries."* This writing denies itself certain traditional braveries (rhyme, assonance, determinable auditory rhythm) precisely because they would testify in the poet to a bravery (in the other sense) about his vocation and the art he practises, a bravery that we cannot afford once we have acknowledged that our condition, obscured from us by Western and Eastern cultures alike, is above all "precarious."

Can we agree? I submit that we cannot. For what we are faced with is a sort of illusionism after all. The poem *has* its own splendours, its own clarities, certainly its own audacities. (Consider only the imperious rapidity of the transitions it manages.) It has all the braveries; even the melody that it seems to lack may have been merely lost in the passage from a Jewish-American mouth to a British ear. The object, willy-nilly, *is* "marvelous." It has to be; since it is an articulation in and of the marvel that is human language. That lack-lustre phrase is certainly a shabby rabbit out of any conjuror's hat. But the shabbiness is appropriate as the response to a shabby argument. If we truly want or need to cut loose from our inherited past, then we should discard not just poetic figurations of language but any figurations whatever, including those which make it possible to communicate at all, except by grunts and yelps. Rhetoric is inseparable from language, including language at its most demotically "spoken." And thus, let language be never so fractured and disjointed in order that the saving commonplaceness of common things shine through it, all that is happening is that a new rhetoric is being preferred before an old one. To put it another way, no Mr Steinway manufactured the instrument, language, on which Oppen performs. And, like it or not, a performance is what each of his poems is—as certainly as a sonnet by Philip Sidney.

This is not in the first place an argument with Oppen or with Oppen's poems. It is a quarrel with those of his admirers—I have met some among "the courageous and precarious children—who would explain their admiration by appeal to the untenable positions that Williams's obtuseness trapped him into (from which he later tried to extricate himself by such manifest absurdities as his "variable foot"). Granted that Oppen does not discard rhetoric for non-rhetoric (which last is an impossibility), but rejects an old rhetoric for a newer one, we have to admire what the new rhetoric permits him to do. In the first place it opens up for him, as it sometimes did for Williams, an extraordinary directness and gentleness in intimacy, as at the end of **"Anniversary Poem"**:

> To find now depth, not time, since we cannot, but
>   depth
>
> To come out safe,   to end well
>
> We have begun to say good bye
> To each other
> And cannot say it
>
>   (*CP,* p. 220)

Indeed, in the world that Oppen charts about him as he thinks of approaching his end, so hedged about as it is with apprehension and misgivings, this particular tone embodies so much of what he can still feel grateful for and sanguine about, that the newer rhetoric justifies itself on this count alone. And it is quite true that the older rhetoric cannot compass this tone of voice. It speaks again on the last page of this slim but substantial collection, in a poem called **"Exodus"**:

> Miracle of the children   the brilliant
> Children   the word
> Liquid as woodlands   Children?

> When she was a child I read Exodus
> To my daughter   'The children of Israel . . .'

> Pillar of fire
> Pillar of cloud

> We stared at the end
> Into each other's eyes   Where
> She said hushed

> Were the adults   We dreamed to each other
> Miracle of the children
> The brilliant children   Miracle

> Of their brilliance   Miracle
> of
>
>   (*CP,* p. 229)

I would call that (though the word may give offence) elegant as well as touching. And I would say indeed that the elegance and the touchingness depend upon each other.

George and Mary Oppen with Michel Englebert and Michael West (interview date 1975)

SOURCE: An interview in *The American Poetry Review,* Vol. 14, No. 4, July-August, 1985, pp. 11-14.

[*In the following interview, originally published in 1975, George and Mary Oppen discuss philosophy, politics, and poetry.*]

This conversation took place in 1975 at the Oppen residence on Polk Street in San Francisco.

[*Interviewer*]: *Mr. Oppen, you are known to be among the handful of poets who consistently decline invitations to read their work in public. May I ask why?*

[George Oppen]: Of course, the primary reason is that I don't absolutely have to, and that if a poet possibly can make his living outside poetry, well, it's obviously a certain broadening of experience. In addition, I feel very strongly—not as a theory or an exhortation to anybody else, but for myself—that the poem is supposed to be on the page.

I don't think that audiences have a right to examine the personality of the poet. It's a falsification. In fact, it's dangerous to the *poet* to hear himself reading. He *knows* that he can do it with his voice, he *knows* that he can do it with his personality, but it's very difficult to be sure of the page.

[Mary Oppen]: It seems to me that many people who want to be poets have this latent in them, or it captures them: the ability to perform. And that ambition sometimes, it seems to me, overrides the necessity of finding within themselves what it is they want to say. They get carried away; they become performers.

[George Oppen]: But there can be a sense of . . . it's difficult to describe . . . a sense of the word falling so solidly, so exactly where you want it to fall, that it will do what your voice really can't do. Of course, what one is trying to do is to express meanings which can only be expressed with the aid of music, so that one has a temptation to rely on the voice. It isn't exactly wrong. Ginsberg, and that whole movement, made a tremendous contribution by bringing their own voices, their actual personalities into the reading. I'm not quarreling with those who do. But my own sense of the thing happens not to be that.

And I have another reason, too. It's just a personal sense of drama. My sense of my own drama is really related to David with his homemade slingshot. I enjoyed reading tremendously when I was totally unknown. I knew I would wow 'em. But cast as Goliath, you see, I know what happened to Goliath. I can practically feel the stone on my head when I show up as the guy who won a Pulitzer for reasons unknown.

Could you expand a bit on your comment that for a poet to make his living outside of poetry affords him a broadening of experience?

[George Oppen]: Well, the independence, to a degree, from acquiring the favor of audiences and critics. I think we could make this sound very, very clear. But it's a very cruel thing to say, because there are people who, for various reasons, aren't *able* to make a living in any way not so arduous as to make it impossible to write poetry.

With that in mind, how do you see the teacher/poet? The poet who teaches classes, say, in creative writing or American Literature while trying to work out his or her own poetry?

[George Oppen]: I don't feel I have much right to answer this. I've simply never done it. I've appeared in a number of places and talked to classes, theoretically teaching I suppose, but what I taught was me. Which is relatively easy, though one couldn't do that for a whole semester I suppose. I don't know what teaching would be. It requires a broadening, which is good for one's character. I'm not sure that I tend to be very broad in that sense, having started in the embattled years when Modernism was an issue.

[Mary Oppen]: Well, until recently there was no such thing as the artist/teacher in the institutions. It's a fairly recent development. I don't think we really know yet.

[George Oppen]: It's even possible that the antonyms are 'teaching' and 'learning.' But again, we arrive at the necessity to make a living in a way not so arduous as to make it impossible to write poetry. Do you remember the name Haldeman-Julius? The Little Blue Books? Julius was a European Socialist who came to this country in the early part of the twentieth century and turned out a library of miniature paper books. They sold for five cents and were

very small. They could fit inside a schoolbook, which was a godsend. It's possible that I owe everything to this; certainly all the education I possess. Anyway, he also wrote a story—I think it was the only story written and published by him. It was of a man like himself, an Italian immigrant, who came to this country to escape poverty. He got a job, more or less a sweatshop job, but was determined not to lose his culture or his cultural interests. So out of his very small salary he saved and saved for six months, or a year, in order to go to the opera. And went, with tremendous excitement. And fell asleep. He was tired. And so the story ends as a story of despair.

It is a question of class, finally. And the people we knew made every kind of solution. Williams, Stevens. Reznikoff, who planned very carefully. And also was probably a bit short on sleep.

[Mary Oppen]: Williams could somehow manage with very little sleep. He was an active doctor in his community and wrote between patients.

And yourself? Do you have a system that you employ?

[George Oppen]: I have a technique. I paste. I make corrections by pasting. Without this it would be impossible for me. I would spend all my time typing if I retyped the poem. What I do is I paste in the correction or change until the sheet becomes so thick it is no longer malleable. Then I copy it out straight. So that it may be two hundred versions, three hundred versions. I precisely lack Williams's sense of his own personal grace and the sureness of his own mannerisms. Nor do I want them.

[Mary Oppen]: But what you do have is an ear that is apparently inexhaustible.

[George Oppen]: Inexhaustible. I happen to have that. I can read the same line five hundred times and it doesn't jangle or jingle. I still hear what I want it to be, even though it's not there. Tolstoy, you remember, described the apparently irrelevant necessities for an artist. An opera singer must have a musical sense, but in addition the lungs of a glass blower. I happen to have a characteristic without which I couldn't have written a line. I continue to hear it. It's like tuning a piano. So again, it's necessary to remember that a poem, I would say by definition, undertakes to say what can only be said with the help of music.

How does the impulse to begin that process manifest itself in your experience? What sets you off? An idea? A line?

[George Oppen]: Not an idea. I start with something in my mind for which I have no words at all, and hardly hope to find the words. I have no words when I begin. Or sometimes *a* word, which turns out to be the *wrong* word. But I do know what it is. It's essentially a sense of place. Yes, of place. And as I say, I have this characteristic that I can write it wrong a thousand times and the sense of that existence of something is still there. There is a destiny that shapes our poems, rough-hewn as they are. But I don't begin with words.

*You mention keeping the impulse. Does that explain why, for example in the poem "**Debt**," and then later on in the poem "**Rationality**," there seem to be . . . well, they seem to be almost the same poem.*

[George Oppen]: They are the same poem, yes. That's why I call it **"Debt."** It was the poem I couldn't write. It was about working. The carpenter working in factories—which meant a great deal to me. And suddenly that meaning disappeared. I was writing it too late.

It was also a defense of the mechanic sense. Mechanics; empiricism; as against the various mysticisms and solipsisms. It was a defense of the rational. The excitement of the young worker. I mean, the thing's made! You do it the way you're supposed to, and there it is!

And I think the tragedy of the rational is also there. I meant it to be. The destruction of the man.

[Mary Oppen]: Yes, but when a workman wasn't alienated, when he still made the object, it was . . . when you make it, you're proud!

[George Oppen]: Yes. And then, there it is! You can't believe it. It looks as though someone else had made it. And the strange thing is—we could use that word Objectivism which haunts us so much—that if it's perfect, you're not in it at all. Which is also a tremendous experience. It may be a more emotional experience than the mark of the maker which is often talked about. Because you *did* do it, and yet it's not oneself. It's closer to giving birth than the other concept, I think.

And of course, as is the case with the quality of the craftsmanship on, say, contemporary office buildings, the panelling for instance, no one notices the quality precisely because it is perfect. If it were flawed, perhaps they would.

[George Oppen]: The sentimental bourgeoisie believes—and I remember my father on this point particularly—that the craftsman has a certain manual knack and that he, the bourgeois, has a higher intelligence, but there's something about his *hands* that just won't work. Whereas of course it's not the hands; it has nothing to do with the hands. It has to do with intellectual capacity. The fact is that in spite of all the admiration for the primitive these days, the human mind was not capable of thinking in tenths of a thousandth.

Oh, of course there are many things about mechanization which seem close to being fatal at this moment, that's entirely clear. But several other things are clear. First, that this kind of craftsmanship which is admired depends absolutely on very low paid workmen. It cannot exist other-

wise. And the second is that what's happening is not the disappearance of the hand, but that more and more of the world's matter is being converted into mind.

Could you expound on that?

[George Oppen]: Well, it is the story of our evolution, isn't it? We're assuming an evolution—a lump of matter which in some way became vegetative life, which in some way became. . . . And we can even add the present overcrowding of the world which is precisely this. And the shortage of raw materials which is precisely this.

[Mary Oppen]: You could also take the literacy of the world. You could take note of how many people had gone to college compared to a hundred years ago. Development of thought. No matter how we disparage our universities or how we disparage our problems of unemployment, nevertheless there is a possibility within this population on earth now that did not exist before, and it's mind. The development of mind.

[George Oppen]: We imagine the most primitive man facing, almost in despair, a mineral universe. And now we see a mineral universe shrinking for its life from the onslaughts of mind.

A question of entropy?

[George Oppen]: Yes, it's a question of entropy. A question of direction.

In the face of this distillation process, what do you make of the onslaught of boredom, and of the apparent need among the developed societies of our day to live intensely; to live a kind of revolutionary fervor?

[George Oppen]: The use of the word 'boredom'—that, too, is part of our history. The first poem in the ***Discrete Series*** describes the mood of boredom, and the sense of the world which occurs in the mood of boredom. I wrote that in 1929 and it happens that this was the same moment that Heidegger was speaking of the mood of boredom as a philosophic concept in his acceptance speech at the University. Since I don't know German I couldn't have read it. It hadn't even been translated.

[Mary Oppen]: When Heidegger speaks of boredom he allies it very closely with that moment of awe in which one's mind begins to reach beyond. And that is a poetic moment; a moment in which a poem might very well be written. But for a child who says he's bored, well there's some lack of connection between his feelings, his emotions. Usually there's manifestation almost immediately of anger, fury, violence. Because it can't be tolerated, this boredom.

[George Oppen]: But boredom *can* be a sense of the world. The sense of the expanse. Which is a penetration; the first penetration, probably. Of course, it can also be frivolous. It can also be the desire to be distracted from precisely that sense. Playing cards, for example. The nature of cards is that they narrow the thing down to these little cardboards in front of you.

Distracted from distraction by distraction.

[George Oppen]: Yes, right. Mary hates cards. I've never met anyone who hated them as much as Mary. She hates competitive undertakings. Mary in a fury over some woman who worshipped poets and was taking over, not Mary, but me, in the living room. She won a game of pick-up-sticks or something.

[Mary Oppen]: Scrabble. I'd never played the miserable game before, but it became clear that I was being challenged. So I did it and won. I never played again.

Is the writing of poetry a political act, do you think?

[George Oppen]: It changes the world, doesn't it?

[Mary Oppen]: It probably is the most important way to change the world. Philosophy, after all, doesn't carry the impact, although it may carry the generic idea of the poetry of the period. But the poetry is what carries the emotion and what carries the senses and what makes it communicable from one era to another. At least we say that. Of course we don't know if it's the same reaction.

[George Oppen]: The voice is in it. Somebody's voice. And not in philosophy. Pound, who said something like, "The truth of the poem is that one person, at least, *felt* this." Which is an important political act, to say what you want and what you don't want. On the other hand it is also true that there's a great deal of philosophizing in poetry by people who haven't realized what the philosophers managed to say. Look at the popularity of the word 'meditation,' as against things that Hegel will say. It would be extremely important to know what has been thought, and to erect a standard of clarity.

I think the proposition is this, or rather these: the phenomena of "representiality"—whether or not they misrepresent—and what could be taken as a crude empiricism, more or less from Hegel, that it is impossible to doubt the existence of one's own consciousness. Which means that consciousness in itself and of itself contains the principle of Actualness. The fact that consciousness by itself carries this principle; the principle that something is actual.

[Mary Oppen]: That something *is*.

[George Oppen]: That's the great marvel, you see. People imagine philosophy as a choosing between positions, or arguing a position, but as all philosophers agree, the central fact is the fact of Being. And that, of course, is an inflection of Descartes.

[Mary Oppen]: We have a son-in-law who's a philosopher and teaches philosophy, and he had a little parakeet which he taught to say, "Cogito Ergo Sum." Another thing he taught it to say was, "Publish or perish."

[George Oppen]: The little bird didn't, though.

[Mary Oppen]: No. He died.

Is there an acid test for great poetry?

[George Oppen]: What the poem must have is the thing itself. To carry its own meaning. Of course, what happened was that there was a period—the sixties, I suppose—in which the life style was important. And there was behind it an actual mission to speak of this life style and its possibilities. It had really quite a startling importance. Because there is a danger in lecturing out of philosophy without saying, "What does one want?" And that was the movement of the sixties: to redefine what it is that we do want. And this gave to the confessional and sometimes extremely loose poetry an importance which I think is really very great.

[Mary Oppen]: We wondered, twenty or thirty years ago, what were people going to do with time? with leisure? What were they going to do when affluence released people from the fourteen-hour day? I think we see now. We have a tremendous audience in the arts. Of course, what we want is a higher level in the arts, but how many people in any fifty-year period are great? We could make a list for our lifetime, and it would not be large.

Yet it would probably be one of the largest lists compared to any past set of fifty years.

[George Oppen]: Yes, absolutely.

[Mary Oppen]: That would of course come with the expanding population. I remember up at Oregon Agricultural College where I met George—this was back in 1926 . . .

[George Oppen]: Don't over-awe the people Mary.

[Mary Oppen]: . . . Sandburg was there with his guitar, singing and reciting his poetry. Well, this was tremendous! I didn't know poetry was being written in my lifetime! So I began to write poetry.

[George Oppen]: And there was the message: talk about yourself. It's the only way you know you're telling the truth. Say what you want; say what you don't want.

If the political climate is sympathetic to such candor. As it is not in whole blocks of nations east and south of us; as it was not in our own nation during the McCarthy days, during which you yourself experienced some difficulties, isn't that right?

[George Oppen]: Yes.

Is that, then, where the vision stops? Is that the limit of the power of poetry to change the world?

[George Oppen]: There is a conflict. A thing like the McCarthy period, or for that matter Russian Communism, refuses to hear what any one person actually does want. And certainly it is the function of poetry to say what happiness is, or what happiness could be; what our desires really are. On the Left and on the Right you get a prescription of what you *should* want. It's an issue to be raised openly as to what extent we can be a part of an entity called humanity.

I've made this point over and over again, trying to argue it quite rigorously and possibly failed. I have also tried to make it while talking in universities, apparently without being understood. I've wanted to make the point that the issue of Socialism, or Communism, which likes to present itself as a 'pork-chop' issue; a very tough-minded, economic issue, and calls upon us to fight a revolution for this matter of a better life, of higher wages (and there's great pride in this system that this is a pork-chop issue and not to be confused with philosophy, and certainly not with metaphysics). However, you see, the argument won't hold as a pork-chop issue. The proposition that we should have a revolution in order to earn a dollar an hour more in wages is simply nonsense. This is not a bargain anyone would accept. What is in peoples' minds, I think most obviously, in China—and it would be in my mind if I were a Chinese peasant—is that it is worth sacrificing your life, and sacrificing a whole generation, or three or four generations, in order to feel that there *will* be a time when you do *not* sell your children. . . . In which humanity may be . . . may become . . . what it should be. And this is purely metaphysic. It's a concern beyond the period of one's own life. It's a desire as to the destiny of humanity. It cannot be argued in simply trade-union terms. No, there is something we want humanity to be, or to become, and this is the impulse of revolution. The impulse of trade-unionism is something else.

[Mary Oppen]: There's an Omega point. A disappearing of everything into mind. And I'm not sure if I give myself to that. It's again, what do we mean by mankind? What is the eventual outcome of all this striving?

Could this universal rushing toward that proverbial Omega point explain why there is so much outstanding poetry being written in the world today?

[George Oppen]: It's entirely possible, yes.

Among your contemporaries, which poets had a particular influence on your work?

[George Oppen]: First, and with a box drawn around it, Charles Reznikoff. No longer such an outrageous statement as it was not so long ago. But to me, Reznikoff is *the* poet among the moderns. I brought my manuscript to Reznikoff to look at. And he read it, and he picked out one line. He said, "George, this is the only line that sings." That line happened to be three words quoted from Ben Jonson. I was pleased, nevertheless.

[Mary Oppen]: Just recently Marie Reznikoff negotiated with Black Sparrow for all of Charles's papers.

[George Oppen]: This is the prose thing I wrote that will be on the cover.

> ". . . a girder
> still itself among the rubble."

That line of Reznikoff's, in the poem of which it is a part, and line upon line of his perfect poems have been with me for the forty-eight years since I first came upon them. If we had no other poetry, I think that we could nevertheless live by virtue of these poems; these lines, these small, precise, these overwhelming gentle iron lines and the images of all that is and our love and pride and our small life, which is immeasurable, as these lines which are still themselves among the rubble.

There are some who would insist those terms are suited to describe your own work.

[George Oppen]: I learned from Reznikoff. And from Zukofsky. I learned from a lot of people whom I wouldn't follow.

We arrived in New York, and had discovered simultaneously modern poetry in Oregon. Sandburg and those people. And it was on the strength of that that we lit out together, hitchhiking. It was dramatic doings because I was underage and Mary wasn't. We were both the same age, but there was that law then, remember. We began with that populism and that image. The image clearest, I guess, in Sherwood Anderson, of the person absolutely alone on these fields, wondering how you begin.

So that what is ascribed as a Williams influence on me is . . . actually I knew that populism and that tone before. When I encountered Williams's work I recognized it as being beyond the Vachel Lindsays and so on, but that was not the beginning for me. What I learned from Williams was precisely what you're not supposed to learn from Williams: I learned the importance of form.

[Mary Oppen]: And also there was, as Sherwood Anderson said, "We wanted to know if we were any good at it."

[George Oppen]: Yes. I quoted that to Hugh Kenner. The conversation was very, very interesting. He said (and in fact I've quoted him several times; I thought it was marvelously brilliant and enlightened), he asked about the gap in my career—the change to politics—and he interrupted me to say, "In brief, it took twenty-five years to write the next poem." Which is absolutely so.

It's when the person writing is frightened by the poem that the poem may have begun. The poem is more than the person, you see. Otherwise, why? Why write it?

Mary Oppen (essay date 1978)

SOURCE: "France" and "New York City," in *Meaning a Life: An Autobiography,* Black Sparrow Press, 1978, pp. 117-39, 143-63.

[*In the following excerpt, Mary Oppen describes the life she and her husband led from the late twenties to the beginning of the Second World War, and tells of their transition from avant-garde artists to communist organizers.*]

George and I avoided joining the groups that surrounded the artists and writers we visited. We had found our beginnings in our own roots, and we had found Zukofsky, Williams and Pound; we were twenty-two years old and full of ourselves. We wanted to observe and learn from the impressions we received as well as from the reading we were doing. Attachments beyond these would have been an encumbrance; we were searching for freedom in which to pursue our own truths. We did not claim the people we met, and I think we avoided also any claim on us. We were the "new generation" to Pound, Williams and Brancusi, and we may have seemed to hold the future opinion of their work in our hands. They certainly respected us, and it seemed to us that they looked upon us as their heirs as we looked on them as our precursors. We respected them, but our position was different from those who were expatriates. We were thoroughly children of the United States, and we intended no other allegiance. We claimed the United States, but since our education had been interrupted when we met we intended this travelling to be our education. It must be remembered that we were always *two*; we learned from reading and from what we saw, but conversation never ceases between us, and our critical views of our elders kept us from depending on them for our daily intellectual sustenance. We made our visits brief, but discussion of these visits was long, sometimes lifelong; we have discussed and discussed again in the light of learning more about what we had already concluded. Our rising concern with politics made us more anxious, especially concerning Pound's reference to "The Boss," Mussolini. He also disclosed that he did not understand that the term "The Boss" is not attractive to American workers.

Pound wrote that he'd be in Paris; we were to meet at a restaurant in Rue de l'Odéon. We had to tell him that we could not continue paying for all the expenses of printing unless a return came to us on the books, and letters from Louis indicated that no money would return. Also, we had read Pound's *ABC of Economics* and discussed it between ourselves; we thought it absurd. Pound wrote, "When I gather chestnuts on the hills of Rapallo I step outside the Capitalist system"—Pound trying to circumvent Marx, Pound who couldn't have read Marx and hold the views he aired. Pound, we knew, lived on income derived through capitalism, and without confronting capitalism he was trying to change the system, proposing as an example his grandfather's system of scrip issued to workers for trade at his grandfather's store. To us this seemed to be the company store of the fur-traders or the tenant-farm system of our southern states, in which workers are compelled to trade at the company store at the trader's or the owner's prices. Perhaps Pound could not think clearly about economics; at any rate, we could not agree to publish the book.

In Berkeley in the 1960's we attended a production of Pound's *Villon* lavishly mounted. In a prologue, excerpts from Pound's works were read by two actors outside the curtain, declaiming dramatically Pound's poetry and including the anti-Semitic curses and indecent language blacked out in the Faber and Faber and New Directions editions of Pound's works. George walked out of the auditorium; the usher, a girl student, said, "Sir, if you go out now I can't let you in again until the intermission."

"I have to kill those actors if I don't leave," he replied, "and I think perhaps that would be wrong."

"Perhaps, perhaps," she said.

The *Villon* itself was attractive, and at moments it was beautiful, especially in a lovely duet. We never found out who made that decision to include Pound's invective—someone with his or her own anti-Semitic hates, no doubt. George says, "Every poet who ever talked to Pound or corresponded with Pound or read him has reason to have loved him; though the madness was real, it was not in him, it seemed—but somehow there."

"The Boss," Pound said, "The Boss," with awe translating "Il Duce." It was the sudden intrusion of a madness, for no man has ever been more pure or more generous than Pound.

The year that we lived in the countryside at Le Beausset we had received a subscription to *Time* magazine. We had never read a newspaper every day and had paid little attention to economics or to politics, but we read *Time* magazine each week and discussed what we read. We were shocked and aghast at the schemes carried out in the last year of Hoover's administration—food was being dumped while people starved. Although we were far from the United States, we had perhaps the advantage of that distance, and our friends the butcher and the hotel-keeper had been educating us. We were innocent of preconceived views, and we looked on at poverty in France, at children so thin and tubercular that they were almost transparent, and our minds began to dwell on politics. Our education was conducted each week by *Time*.

George's father left us a small car that we were to bring back to the States when we came home. It had a removable top, and we could ride along; it was almost like riding in the cart with Pom-Pon, the difference being that we no longer conversed with everyone we met on the road. However, we made friends in Paris with students, mostly Americans, who were of our own generation.

Sylvia Beach's book store in Paris had a lending library, and I borrowed Trotsky's *History of the Soviet Union,* which George and I both read. At first political ideas had seemed to concern others and not George or me, but with Jewish refugees pouring into Paris from Germany in 1932, I could not help seeing their distress and feeling the threat to us, too. I had to try to understand the politics that were affecting events all around us.

Among our new acquaintances in Paris was a young woman doctor, Eva Klein, who because of her presentiment of Hitler's horror was an early refugee. She had opened a summer camp for Jewish refugee children in Paris. Through her and her mate Dan, an American medical student, we met her circle of acquaintances among the refugees and had our first experience of the life of refugees. She took us to a party of White Russian refugees from the 1917 revolution in Russia; here we met a Russian prince, a nervous man who had a sort of tic of shuffling used matches in an empty match-box. George asked him, "What do you think of the results of the Revolution in your country?"

"I would be a traitor to all I was born to if I said a good word for it," he replied. At this same party Chaliapin, the singer, arrived in a magnificent full-length black coat, and as he swept it off and into the hands of a servant, I saw that it was lined with sable.

One Sunday we went into the country with Eva and Dan and stopped at the country house of some of her Russian friends. We were admitted by a servant and shown into a parlor to wait; it was a damp, cold, cheerless habitation. Eva sniffed and said, "Smells like goldfish pee."

Dancing in the park one night to the music of a wind-up phonograph, we stopped dancing and were leaping back and forth over a small iron railing beside the road in the Bois de Boulogne. As I vaulted, my feet slipped on the dew-wet grass, and I hit my head on the iron railing. In no time I was covered with blood, and our two doctor friends directed George to a nearby hospital. Dan rushed into the emergency room, washed up, and was treating my wound before the bewildered nurse in charge could forbid him. George was left standing after having driven us all there; no one was watching, but we heard a thud—Eva looked around and saw George lying unconscious on the floor.

Before our return to the United States, we made a trip to Venice and to Florence to visit museums and to see a little of a country other than France. In the Piazza San Marco, we were suddenly surrounded by Black Shirts pouring into the Piazza from all the entrances so fast that we could not escape. We were pinned against the monument at the center of the Piazza by the press of the crowd, crying, "Il Duce—pericolo del morte." Mussolini's life had been threatened, and we were trapped in this sudden, impressive demonstration. We saw no differences of expression on the faces of the young men, only a blind fanaticism, in ecstasy and worship of Il Duce.

Roosevelt had been elected President of the United States in November 1932, and in that winter the Blue Eagle was introduced in the States. Blue Eagle posters were pictured on the front pages of Parisian newspapers, and the military-looking symbol frightened us. We were afraid it meant that fascism was rising in the United States too. Germans in Venice, military men, had said to me as they passed, "Guten morgen mein Taube." ["Good morning, my pigeon."]

It was 1933, and the next war was ominously looming. We could feel more than we could understand of the threat to Jews, to artists, to all freedoms. I was determined that fas-

cism was not going to strike this pigeon! We saw Jews, the lucky ones who had fled early. Born in Germany, they had been citizens, but they were now threatened, bewildered people who did not yet know the worst that was still in abeyance. We began to understand that this threat was portentous for us as well. We returned to Paris and took passage on the first ship home. We had to get home to see what had happened in the two years that we had spent out of our own country.

Eva and Dan came to New York soon after we had returned, and we shared an apartment, a "railroad flat" on Pineapple Street in Brooklyn Heights. All of us were gone from the apartment all day—Dan to work at the Rockefeller Institute and Eva to study for the exams which would qualify her in her second change of country as a doctor. Sharing a living place became our style of living for the following ten years or more. We did not make a rigid system for this sharing; it was conducted very simply, with a piece of paper hung in the kitchen on which each one who spent money wrote down what had been spent. We found it a cheaper way to rent a much bigger and better apartment, we could afford to pay someone to clean the place, and each couple had living rooms and sleeping rooms apart. We shared the kitchen and the cooking duties, and of course we were in agreement as to the amounts to be spent on food, entertainment, etc. I found it a desirable way to live during the years that we were both working, and later, when we had a child, we often shared households in order to extend our family group and to have another child in the group for the sake of our only child. . . .

. . . In France in 1930, from the art of the Louvre, paintings speaking out of different times, from the streets of Paris which make their patterns and take their names from the earliest use the ancients gave them, from a cafe for writers, tourists, artists or students, we looked on and tried to absorb the meaning to us of a culture which accepted living artists, writers and students into the social fabric with a freedom we had searched for in the United States and had not found. I think I travel to ask the questions which are hard to formulate about one's own times because one is in the midst, at home, of all that one has seen so often that one does not receive the jolt that might confront one with the uncomfortable but important question. Not with answers—answers are not possible for one's own times and in one's own place. The answer only becomes obvious after time has passed, and we can see, if we have survived it, the predicament that we have passed through.

In Paris the Impressionists were not yet all dead; in 1930 even their art was not yet in the old established museums, and we went to a private gallery to see Picasso's latest show. I noticed Picasso himself watching us to see our reactions to his paintings, which were the first I had seen of women distorted into their social and emotional meanings, beyond the portraits of previous times. Meanings which were painful to accept I later found to be profound class judgments and beautiful in new ways, in their colors and design. After seeing these portraits, women on beaches and bourgeois women in cafes had a different meaning, in which Picasso had caught and held them. His contribution of fifty years as a painter, most of which time I have been alive, has put him on a list of those who will speak for us to a future time.

Apprehension mixed with elation as we disembarked at Baltimore and began the drive to New York City. As we approached the first stoplight, grown men, respectable men—our fathers—stepped forward to ask for a nickel, rag in hand to wipe our windshield. This ritual was repeated every time we paused, until we felt we were in a nightmare, our fathers impoverished.

Manhattan loomed across the New Jersey flats; it grew into pinnacles as sunset lit the windows, and we entered the long tunnel under the Hudson River. In Brooklyn we rented an apartment on Willow Street, the first of many apartments we have lived in at one time or another in that same neighborhood of Brooklyn Heights.

Zukofsky, the slender dark young man, sloping along on his long stalk-like legs, head forward, shoulders hunched, a little close-visored cap on his head . . . Louis so delicate I didn't think he'd live out five more years, Louis in my mind associated with his own *Mantis* . . . but as his long life has proven, Louis is hardy, more hardy than we knew. He has survived with Celia, refusing the attentions of the young who have come admiring him and his place in poetry. He survives, perhaps strengthened by his bitterness and feeling that he must be the only poet or he will not accept acclaim. Louis had not been to Europe; he had only corresponded with Pound, and I think it was Tibor Serly who spoke to us of the importance of Louis' going to visit Pound. The problem was that Louis had no money; the trip required that Louis' friends help to pay his way. Somehow this was done, and several of us made contributions; Williams, Serly, George and I bore the expenses of travelling, and Pound and Bunting provided housing and meals once Louis was in Rapallo.

Lorine Niedecker, a student of Louis' at the University of Wisconsin, followed him to New York; we invited her to dinner, and after waiting for her until long after dinner-time, we ate and were ready for bed when a timid knock at the door announced Lorine. "What happened to you?" we asked.

"I got on the subway, and I didn't know where to get off, so I rode to the end of the line and back."

"Why didn't you ask someone?"

"I didn't see anyone to ask."

New York was overwhelming, and she was alone, a tiny, timid small-town girl. She escaped the city and returned to Wisconsin. Years later we began to see her poems, poems which described her life; she chose a way of hard physical work, and her poetry emerged from a tiny life. From Wisconsin came perfect small gems of poetry written out of her survival, from the crevices of her life, that seeped out into poems.

When Louis went for a passport for his trip, he had to get a copy of his birth certificate, which had his name as Salikovsky. The certificate had been made out by a midwife who probably did not know English, and she may have unintentionally misspelled Zukofsky, but Louis was understandably upset. Misspellings happened often enough in immigration or in birth records, but it was a blow to Louis' identity, and he was intent on setting the record straight; he finally got his passport in his correct name, Zukofsky.

Walking with Louis when *Discrete Series* was in manuscript, George was discussing it with him before showing it to anyone else. Louis turned and with a quizzical expression asked George, "Do you prefer your poetry to mine?"

"Yes," answered George, and the friendship was at a breaking point.

George gave a copy of the manuscript of *Discrete Series* to Charles Reznikoff, who gravely discussed it the next time we were together. Charles pointed to the lines inside quotation marks, "'O city ladies.'" "Now this," said Charles, "is the only line that sings."

George also sent a copy of the manuscript to Ezra Pound, who replied with a gift: the foreword. ". . . I salute a serious craftsman, a sensibility which is not every man's sensibility and which has not been got out of any other man's books. [signed] Ezra Pound."

George's father (also named George) was accosted one day in 1934 in his club in San Francisco by a man who drew forth *Discrete Series* by George Oppen. "Here," he said, "did you write this?"

"No," answered George's father. "But my son did." The man began to sputter. George's father asked him, "What would you do if your son wanted to write poetry?"

"I'd shoot the bastard."

The Gotham Book Mart bought some of the books; very few were sold, and the rest were stored. Politics were dominant and danger was imminent. In German neighborhoods in New York City and New Jersey, right-wing organizations were drilling in fascist military style. Father Coughlin was using the radio as it had not been used before; every Sunday, especially in working-class neighborhoods, the windows were thrown open, radios were turned up full blast, and the voice of Father Coughlin, the Radio Priest, blared divisive, vituperative anti-Semitic fascist propaganda. Many people in the United States were beginning to think about politics. We had seen the beginnings of fascism in Europe, and now we tried to understand the reasons for the collapse of the economic systems of the western world. We were reading leftist papers, and we asked Jesse Lowenthal, a friend of Louis, to take us to meet the son of Daniel de Leon, the founder of the Socialist Labor Party (S.L.P.). He explained their program: when the workers of the United States arrived at the realization that the answer to the collapse of capitalism was the socialization of the means of production, then the S.L.P. members would present themselves—well-read, educated and ready for the great day. The S.L.P. was doing nothing at the time to alleviate the problems of the workers with whom they planned one day to ride to power. We looked on at Trotskyites who spoke publicly of revolution, and sometimes caused police attacks by their provocative tactics. The unemployed were the victims who had no desire for revolution; what they wanted and were willing to fight for if necessary were jobs, food and rent money.

We found ourselves suddenly involved in these events which swept over everyone. In 1929, when the stock market crashed in New York, a very few men jumped from windows when they found they were no longer rich. By 1934 despair had swept the whole population, from the richest to the poorest, as factories slowed and then stopped production, railroads had no loadings, ships had no cargo, and the country was bursting with products that no one in the United States or elsewhere had money to buy.

The United States was lagging behind many other countries in social legislation. Welfare organizations in the 1920's, before the crash, were mostly philanthropic, and they soon ran out of money in this overwhelming emergency. People were frightened and helpless and in many parts of the country irregular ways of obtaining food seemed the only way to avoid starvation. The propaganda of fascism and the authoritarian state appealed to many who saw no other solution to the economic collapse of the United States. They had been through some hard years with President Hoover—fathers of families had been given apples to sell on street corners instead of useful work or temporary food-orders and rent money. Men felt guilty when they became unemployed and could no longer support their families, and many left their homes in despair. Young men roamed the country.

In the last days of February and the first days of March, 1933, at the moment we returned to the United States, President Roosevelt's first act as President was to declare a bank holiday. In effect the U.S. Treasury was empty as President Hoover went out of office. Depositors had lined up in front of banks to remove their money. Some banks went bankrupt, and the depositors' savings were lost; with no insurance of depositors' funds they quickly ran out of money and closed their doors. Some banks had speculated with depositors' money, and Wall Street had sold them out; but most of them re-opened with the assurance that government would pass legislation as soon as possible to protect deposits in the banks.

During the last days of Hoover's presidency the depression had deepened, and in the election year of 1932, ten to twenty thousand Bonus Marchers, veterans of World War

I, marched on Washington to demonstrate to President Hoover and to the nation their demand for full payment of their bonus certificates. Hoover had vetoed that legislation; there was actually not enough money in the Treasury to pay the veterans' demands. The marchers were held on Anacostia Flats, across from Capitol Hill; they were attacked by troops with fixed bayonets and by tanks, and one was killed while several were wounded.

In the farm country of the middle west, demonstrations prevented foreclosures of mortgages; when the sheriff arrived with an auctioneer to sell the farm and all the farmer's possessions at auction, the neighbors gathered, and with a pre-arranged plan someone bid one dollar for the farm. "Sold!" cried the crowd, and the buyer returned the farm with ostentation to the farmer. All the items were sold the same way, and although the atmosphere seemed festive, the farmers were united and the authorities did not use force. Farmers were tenacious in their hold on their land, they did not intend to be thrown off it, and farm organizations grew apace. . . .

Before his inauguration, Roosevelt proposed that the Blue Eagle symbol on posters be displayed by employers who pledged to comply with him in a promise to keep wages at their previous levels in an attempt to maintain the slipping economy. It was this same Blue Eagle on the front pages of newspapers in Europe that had seemed to us a symbol of possible military significance and had precipitated our return from Europe.

We spent the summer of 1934 in a visit to Mexico with our friends Jack and Nellie from Berkeley. Mexico was the first undeveloped country we had seen, and the steps toward socialization which they had taken seemed an effective way to develop their country. The ten-year-old boys were the first educated generation, and they joyfully fulfilled the responsibilities of being literate. In the square in Taxco, an English lady with a wide shade hat and her watercolor pad in her lap asked a small boy to pose for her. He held us his thumb and forefinger, a little space between them—"Momentito," it meant, I'll be right back. He returned with his watercolor box on his thumb, and he sat for her while he sketched her on his own pad of paper. All the male children of Taxco were artists; Kitagawa, a Japanese artist living in Taxco, helped them to make their own watercolor boxes from gasoline tins. They made their own colors and he gave them brushes. The boy in the square took us to see an exhibit of their works; I still have a program of this show, and the work was beautiful child-art. Kitagawa was concerned that all the boys of the town were artists, and he asked us, "What will become of such a town?" We met these competent children in the public markets, in the streets, in the plazas, beside the adults, helping in any dealings requiring reading, writing, or arithmetic. Children guided us, and they were both avid learners and teachers—neither shy nor bold, they were responsible and proud of their country with a new pride. They were the generation that was taking Mexico from colonialism and "peonage" into equality of nationhood.

We too were learning as we saw the ideas of socialism applied in a poverty-stricken nation. We saw nationalization of oil, railroads and public education; welfare laws that applied to the whole family of the worker; freeing of fallow land held by absentee landlords to give it to impoverished landless peasants, who formed "ejidos," a form of traditional commune, to improve agriculture and to plant forests in a country that had been bereft of its trees. We admired Cárdenas, the President of Mexico, and we observed that Mexico was coming to a new life. I think it is the only time that artists have been the principal carriers of the ideas of a revolution. Rivera, Orozco and Siquieras were political artists whose murals covered walls of government, schools and public courtyards. Hundreds of walls were entirely covered with the message to the people of Mexico of the country's struggles. In the public places in Mexico City, after years of exclusion under the Porfirio Diaz regime, *peones* walked in their traditional white clothes past the murals, stopping until they understood what they saw in the murals. The pictures portrayed the whole pharmocopoeia of Mexico, with the foods which were made available to the rest of the world when this continent was first discovered. Mexico, a gleaming white city such as the *conquistadores* had not seen before, was also pictured in the murals. The *peones* saw foreigners also examining with respect the record of Mexico and her revolution.

We went to California on our return from Mexico. In San Francisco in 1934 a general strike had been called by the Longshoremen's Union, and San Francisco's upper classes were in an exaggerated state of fear. Some had left town, others barricaded themselves in their homes with quantities of food. Gangs of strike-breakers were organized on the Berkeley campus, to break up sympathy meetings and try to frighten families of workers. But on the day we entered San Francisco the bay was quiet—not a ship moved.

For us, this had been a remarkable year. One year before at this same time we had watched sadly as Pom-Pon was led away in Le Beausset. We had visited Ezra Pound and heard him speak of Mussolini as "The Boss"; we had been alerted to the dangers of fascism when we saw Jews fleeing Hitler's Germany, and we had been present at a fascist demonstration in Italy. During this past year we had studied Soviet movies, searching for clues of what socialism might mean in our own lives, and we had just seen in Mexico a degree of socialization applied to the benefit of development in that country. Revolution and socialism were respectable words in Mexico. We returned to New York City from California to find families sleeping on their household goods, piled on the sidewalks in front of their apartments. The city had an air of disaster; the unemployed were the refugees who had exhausted their resources and did not know where to turn.

An appeal was made to intellectuals by the seventh World Congress of the Communist Parties in 1935 to join in a united front to defeat fascism and war. We responded to that call, and in the winter of 1935 we decided to work with the Communist Party, not as artist or writer because we did not find honesty or sincerity in the so-called arts of the left. (I could make an exception for Bertolt Brecht and for some Soviet movies.) We said to each other, "Let's work with the unemployed and leave our other interest in the arts for a later time." Few in the Party or in the Workers Alliance knew anything of our past, and in a short time we were no longer thinking of Paris or of To Publishers, of poetry or of painting. We also left it to our friends and families to keep in touch with us if they chose. We felt that our political decision was not one in which we wished to involve them.

"We are those selfish travellers, happiest in foreign streets." If George and I had come from the working class we would probably never have joined the Communist Party— that was the nearly unanimous decision of the United States working class. We searched for escape from class. George's experience in the class he came from was one of isolation, and to be a poet who knew no more than that was a bleak outlook; my class background had not led me into an intellectual world. Artists and writers have often looked for ways to escape class and the burden of class mores, and while we did not look for an ivory tower, we did search to find and to understand from the grassroots.

The Communist and the Socialist Parties were the only organizations which were organizing the unemployed to do something themselves about their predicament. When we asked to join, a secretary seemed suspicious of us and sent us to a Brooklyn address, where we again asked to join. The two people in the Brooklyn office also seemed to find us queer birds, and they turned us over to Doretta Tarmon.

Doretta had taken part in the many schisms within the radical left; she had joined with Jay Lovestone when he left the Socialist Party, and she broke away from his group to become a Communist. She came to New York where the Movement was her breath, her sustenance, her life. She had intense black eyes behind thick lenses which flashed as she tossed her head in impassioned speech. She held crowds with her speeches at street meetings—words came to her faster than her mouth could say them. "Prize your fellow worker like the skin of your eye," she said once at a street meeting. Conviction made her a great speaker and a remarkable but difficult friend. Doretta told of herself and of her life-long friend Esther who organized on every job they held; two women, they understood each other and the same passions moved them. Arguing with their boss's lawyer once, they held on to his sleeve while they poured words on him; he pulled and they pulled, and his sleeve came off in their hands. Words failed them, and the lawyer took them to court. The judge listened carefully, and said patiently to the lawyer, "But isn't it possible that the tailor only basted your sleeve to your jacket? Isn't it possible that the tailor neglected to sew the sleeve on his machine and it may have come off rather easily?"

Doretta might as well have moved in with us, as we became constant companions. She was new to our experience, and we were continually surprised, confounded and delighted with her. She took us to our first street meeting, which we could have gone to, of course, without permission, but she gave us permission and we went like adolescents to a first grown-up party. Doretta wore a leather jacket and a hat with a long red feather; having come recently from Paris, I was bare-legged and bare-headed, wearing a Paris dress. Doretta cautioned me, "You don't want to be sectarian, comrade."

At the street meeting in an Italian neighborhood nearby, a speaker explained to Italians on their own block that fascism meant dictatorship. Italian families were sending money to Mussolini, and wives were contributing their marriage rings. To the Italians, Mussolini was a hero because he was winning the war against Ethiopia, and he was unifying Italy, where the trains did run on time. It was a difficult audience at the street meeting, but Italians too were out of work and were threatened with eviction or loss of homes; and although a few milk bottles were thrown, the day after the meeting a few Italians came into the Workers Alliance for help. A short time later, George and I created organizations of the unemployed through this same Alliance.

Doretta invited us to join a new-members class in the Communist Party. Of the fourteen people in the class, not one was foreign-born. Several of those new members are still our friends, but with these new friends we found ourselves in a very different world, a world in which we were politically exposed. The Communist Party remained strange to us; we threaded our way in the organization, and even the vocabulary within the Party was a different vocabulary than I had known. The older Communists were wearing leather jackets that had become almost a uniform. Most of the older members were Russian, Jewish or Polish immigrants, and they were not easy to understand.

The Socialist Party had organized the Workers Alliance, and the Communists had organized the Unemployment Councils—these two organizations merged to form one organization, called the Workers Alliance. George began work in the Borough Hall area of Brooklyn, in a neighborhood that contained the Phillipine, Puerto Rican and Syrian-Lebanese population; it included Atlantic Avenue from Flatbush Avenue to the waterfront and from Brooklyn Bridge to Manhattan Bridge, with all the slums that crowded under the El (the elevated railway). Slums pressed in and around the sweatshops that were now closed. Many single men in this population had come to the United States to work, leaving their women behind. It is hard to understand now the way things were then. Almost no one was working, and the people were in their own neighborhoods, at home or on the street in their own block; the activities of the Workers Alliance in every neighborhood where it existed were the immediate concerns of that neighborhood. George tells in a poem of Petra Roja, who called a crowd together by leaning out her tenement window and beating on her dishpan. When no one worked in a family the rent could not be paid, and if a family could not get "the relief" (as it was called), the landlord gave them an eviction notice and called the city marshall, who with several assistants put the furniture in the street and put a lock on the door. If the furniture was not soon taken from the street, the sanitation department hauled it away to the city dump. This was one of the frequent emergencies for which Petra beat her dishpan. She came down the stairs to march at the head of her little army to the apartment of the family that was threatened with eviction. When the marshall struggled up the solidly packed stairs to the apartment, he found Petra and the other Alliance members filling the apartment. "What's going on here?" yelled the marshall.

Petra yelled back, pointing at George, "It's his birthday!"

When the furniture finally reached the street, the neighbors helped by sitting on it to prevent its being hauled away. One man returned to his evacuated apartment with a big bag of plaster-of-Paris, which he mixed and slowly poured into the toilet, and as it went down through the tree of plumbing the plaster solidified in the pipes of the whole building. It was a war for food and shelter.

George had a bodyguard, a big man named Raf who had been a prize fighter in Puerto Rico and who appointed himself to be George's protector. The membership of George's group in the Workers Alliance treasured George and appreciated the organization they had built together, but they did not think that George was well dressed. A committee was organized to go with George to a nearby men's clothing store. Raf asked to see the manager. "We are from the Workers Alliance on Adams Street," he told him. "We want to buy a new suit for our organizer, and it had better be a good suit or we will come back and picket your place."

A short way out Flatbush Avenue, in front of a big Protestant church, George went one morning with leaflets calling for a demonstration at the nearby relief bureau. As the congregation came out of the church and George was handing out a few leaflets, he noticed that a group of men went back into the church with the leaflets, to emerge in a wedge aimed straight at George. They came swiftly and dispersed the other people who were just standing around; a young police officer directing traffic at the corner moved in fast close to George, who was already belabored. He stopped George from handing out the leaflets, and said, "I'm taking you in."

"But I have a constitutional right—" George began.

"Please," said the cop, and he drew George around the corner. "They'd have slaughtered you," he said as he let George go.

Mary Auerbach and I went to the Bedford-Stuyvesant neighborhood in Brooklyn to form a new local of the Workers Alliance in a neighborhood of Jews, Italians and many blacks who had just come from the South. In most of the southern states nothing was done for the hungry, and thousands were on the roads, moving into the industrial areas. New York had more liberal laws concerning the relief of hunger, and many Southerners came and stayed in the city, but the settlement laws made it difficult for these people to obtain food or rent orders when they first arrived, and they did not know where to turn for help. Emergency relief was given only in dire cases. Poor people do not usually keep records, a year's residence had to be proven, and these people had been harrassed on the roads; starvation was real for them and they were frightened. Mary Auerbach and I went through the apartment buildings, knocking on every door and explaining that it was not the fault of the men that they could not find work and bring home a wage at the end of the week. Many men took to the roads looking for work, while others were just not in evidence, as women and children could more easily get aid if there was no man in the house who presumably should be working. Many women were alone with their children, living in misery. We spent hours every day talking to these people in their apartments. We presented ourselves as members of the Workers Alliance, but our intentions were doubted, and only men came to our first meeting; Mary and I went with these men to the relief-bureau, and we did get emergency food and rent orders. We soon had a membership made up almost entirely of young black women with their little children and older women who knew how to run an organization. They collected dues of ten cents a month, visited the sick and talked to neighbors; it was they who really built the organization. We rented a store building next door to the Nostrand Avenue relief bureau, where we talked with clients on their way in to confront the bureau. We found that they usually came to our headquarters after failing to get food or rent orders. The unemployed wanted jobs, and in the demonstrations we asked for jobs, but the purpose of the Workers Alliance was to relieve starvation and to guide people to a realization that government could solve these problems—not with fascism, but with a liberal solution. But as the organization increased in numbers and its successes became apparent to all levels of government there were attempts to break the Alliance.

We "sat-in." I asked George to bring the membership of his Borough-Hall Workers Alliance to picket the sit-in at the Nostrand Avenue relief bureau. We had learned this technique from the auto workers in Detroit; we sat in for a day and a night, holding the relief bureau so that the day's business could not go on. The administration of the bureau decided on the second day to smash the demonstration, and the police came through the big front doors with clubs swinging as our women screamed. I remember watching a young black woman while she screamed, and as the sound continued it seemed to me she screamed that scream for minutes. Manuel, from George's local, was clubbed to the floor and a cop bent over him beating him on the head. I threw myself between Manuel and the cop, Manuel, not knowing it was my hand beside his face bit my thumb! The cop pulled me to my feet by my long hair, and for days after I could not turn my head nor use my thumb.

We were arrested. The plan of the relief administration was to break up our organization by depriving the membership of leadership. The International Labor Defense took charge of our defense; we were accused of attacking the police. The trial began, and it dragged on for two years—a tactic planned to dissipate energy from the organization by making us attend court. The trial was postponed again and again, but every time it was called, our membership escorted us to court. In November of the second year the trial was finally held, and we were charged with felonious assault on the police. As the jury was chosen we watched and speculated about each person chosen, until the defense's challenges were exhausted, and a Jewish manufacturer of flags and emblems was the last jury member called—we would have rejected him. After deliberating for many hours, the jury returned to the courtroom at ten o'clock at night with a not-guilty verdict for all of us except Manuel, who was the only non-white arrested. We went out free to the street, and there, waiting for us, were our Workers Alliance members.

At a later time we met the girl who was secretary to the manufacturer of flags and emblems, and she told us his account of the jury room. The eleven other members had opposed him—they were for a guilty verdict. The compromise was to convict Manuel, and he served nine months in prison.

George and I were twenty-nine years old. The war in Spain had been going on for a year, and George wanted to go, but I would not agree unless I went too. As we did not have any special skills that would have made a difference in the war, we did not try to go to Spain, but friends near us in age or younger, who were single men and women or who had special skills either went to Spain or tried very hard to get there. Mary Auerbach, with whom I worked every day, gave permission for the son of her old age to go; barely eighteen years old, he had never held a gun. In Spain he was rushed into the lines the very day he arrived, and he was killed in his first battle. . . .

Of 3000 who went to Spain from the United States, 1500 died there. Little news came to us of the war in Spain. The United States government joined with France and England in an embargo of all arms to Loyalist Spain; meanwhile Hitler and Mussolini were supplying Franco with men, arms and planes.

In 1937 George went to a Party training school for a period of study and discussion. I went to see Pete Cacchione, who was chairman of the Communist Party in Brooklyn, and said to him, "You sent George to school, and now you must send me too." Pete felt pressured, but he agreed, and I went for the next three months to the school. George went on to Utica, where we had agreed to go after finishing the school, which was held in the Catskills at a resort hotel. In the wintertime this hotel was the center for lectures on Marxist economics and political theory, discussions of the women's movement, Negro history in the United States and trade union tactics.

Pop Mindel was the teacher I loved. Pop was Russian-born, Jewish, a scholar of Marxism. He was acutely intuitive in his understanding of each one of us, and he is the only person I ever met in the Party who I am sure loved each one of us. A young Negro boy from the deep South who wanted to be an artist drew with his pencil every chance he had. Pop Mindel finally told him, "It's the wrong time for you to be an artist—you have set your foot on the path to help your people, and you can help them more in politics than you can with your art."

To me he said, "There are times in your life in which you might choose to be a revolutionary, but there are also times, as when you marry or when you have children, that this is impossible."

George and I had been unaware of our being a special kind of couple until Hitler and fascism made being Jewish a pointed issue of survival. Our interest had been to understand a class not our own and to be part of sweeping changes in the United States. We held close a belief in ourselves as artists, and we intended to find our way back to a life in poetry and the arts. If there had not been a clear need for people like us to defeat fascism, we would probably have dropped the politics as the depression eased, and we would have resumed a life in the arts. But fascism, socialism or a more liberal form of republicanism were the choices: Germany, Italy, Japan and Spain became fascist, France had a People's Front government, Russia was socialist and the United States had embarked upon a more liberal form of republicanism with the election of Roosevelt and his cabinet of Keynesian economists and politicians. Events moved us with them, and we believed that fascism meant death to us along with the other Jews of the world, and death to millions who would be caught in the war which actually came to pass. Communists were still, at the end of the Depression, the ones who warned most consistently against this danger.

In Utica George and I found ourselves in an industrial area, where workers were either foreign-born or the first generation born in the United States. A strong thread of radical ideas ran through workers in the foundries and in the arms, copper, textile and shoe factories. In opposition to this working-class population, a politically organized upper class of owners and elected officials ruled the area. Traditionally, the cities voted Democrat whereas the surrounding counties voted Republican, and Oneida County was no exception. Utica had a Democratic mayor while the congressman and the senator, with district-wide votes, were right-wing Republican. Hamilton Fish was "our" congressman.

Small groups of Communists were in the towns, and scattered about the countryside were people who in some other time or place had been involved in leftist politics or in trade union actions. George and I set ourselves to find and to talk to every one of these scattered radicals. George began by calling a convention of all the Communists to elect a new leadership; and, of course, George was elected chairman. He then organized meetings open to the public with speakers known to these old-time radicals; these meetings were well-attended and drew people who were interested

in political events in Europe—Italians from the copper mills of Rome, New York Polish women who worked in the textile mills and who were militant, their men who worked in the foundries, Russians who had come to the United States to work in the mines and coal fields of Pennsylvania and who were now farmers in Oneida County, Czechs who worked in the Remington-Rand arms plant. Friends found friends at these meetings, and there was an awakening in this neglected area. A liberal doctor, three or four ministers, a few businessmen and liberal intellectuals found us, or we found them. All these people endangered their livelihoods by their interest in the left, but nevertheless they were interested in defeating fascism. The group also attracted people who were accustomed to being alone with their ideas, and they met together and heard reports of the neighboring areas, where young people similar to George and me in age and background were working in other upper New York State communities. These intellectuals joined the League of Women Voters or the League against War and Fascism, or one of the many groups in the more liberal churches. The election of Roosevelt and the work done to alleviate the Depression had stirred people, and a strong liberal tendency was growing throughout the country, due not only to Roosevelt but to all of us who were opposed to fascism.

Usually the vote is more radical in the United States than the apparent opinion of the people, and we met surprises when we went out door-to-door selling the Communist Sunday paper. People were not afraid of us in their own homes—the fear was for loss of jobs—and they asked us in. We made friends, and they trusted us not to expose them. These people knew at first hand the long and frustrating struggle for trade unions and the continuing struggle to keep those unions honest. The CIO was organizing in this area at this time, and it was making sweeping inroads into the old craft unions of the AFL, which accepted the skilled workers but left the rest of the workers in the same plant unorganized. We were a small force with few allies, and yet we saw first-hand that we obtained results and that achievement came—slowly, but it came. Working in New York City had been frustrating because we lost touch with people and did not see the results directly as we did in this smaller city.

A Methodist minister, an ebullient man from a neighboring church community, came to see us regularly just to talk with us, for he shared similar political ideas and preached his ideas as much as he dared. A Quaker invited us to Quaker meeting which was really an anti-war group and asked us to take over his little group, but we said that although we shared political ideas and that we opposed fascism, we were neither religious nor pacifist, and in sincerity we could not join his group. Both of these men had graduated from Union Theological Seminary, where Harry F. Ward, a loved and respected teacher, had imprinted his liberal mark on many who passed through his classes.

A minister on the staff of the Episcopal cathedral in Utica came to call late at night, a man with five children who was sure of his job only so long as one of the higher-ranking priests needed him. He was ghost-writing the memoirs of this priest. Our caller was the son of a coal miner, who had been educated into the priesthood, and he risked too much if he raised his voice at the cathedral; but he came to tell us that we were in danger. Hamilton Fish, the Republican congressman, was warning the upper bourgeoisie of the town against us, and George's and my name headed the list that Fish wrote on the blackboard in the cathedral. We were not frightened; on the contrary, we were encouraged to know that we had made such an impact on the town.

Farmers were protesting the prices that they received for their milk from the Borden and Sheffield milk companies, which held a grip on the milk market in the milk-sheds all over the country. Upper New York State was one milk-shed, and there were others wherever there was big dairy production. Some farmers formed a Farmers' Union and held their milk, to pour it in protest in the streets of Boonville, where the road ran white with milk in front of the milk receiving depot. I went to visit Archie Wright, leader of the Farmers' Union. Archie welcomed me and suggested that I help by visiting farmers and asking them to withhold their milk, to join the Farmers' Union, or at least not to endanger the farmers' strike. The farmers in the valleys where the soil was rich and deep were not seriously affected by the reduction in the price of milk; their farms were paid for, and they could weather the price-cutting and perhaps even benefit by the wiping out of the small hill-country farms. Enclaves of Welsh farmers in the valleys, whose ancestors had come to the United States in whole village groups to be weavers in the textile mills and who had in a later generation left the factories to take land in the valleys, had forgotten their fathers' struggles as workers, and were now entrenched conservative rich farmers. I made no progress in talking to them about the milk strike, and after a few attempts I went to the "higher tiers," as the hill country was called. Most farmers in the hills had been industrial workers for years in the mines of Pennsylvania, in the steel mills or foundries, or in arms plants or shoe factories. They had dreamed of retirement to a farm, but they could afford only marginal lands, and they still owed money on their land, for which they depended on the sale price for their milk. They had to oppose the price cuts.

These farm families usually consisted of a farmer and his wife and as many of their sons as could be supported by the operation of the farm. Extra cash came from sons who went to work in the factories. These farmers supported the milk strike, but their idea of action was to pick up their rifles. They took a few pot-shots at tank cars carrying milk, and they frightened strike-breaking farmers with occasional armed threats. They were accustomed to acting on their own, and it was a delicate line that Archie Wright trod in holding the strikers to dumping their milk, while at the same time persuading them not to go out and shoot their enemies.

In the higher tiers I met a strange household. A young German immigrant, alone on his farm, had desperately needed a workmate, a woman. He advertised in a farm journal for a woman housekeeper, and from Florida a stranded circus performer answered the ad. She had been born in Bavaria to a bourgeois family, from which she had run away to join the circus because she loved horses. She was an accomplished horsewoman and had also been the lady who got sawed in half; she had lived twenty years in circus life. She and the German farmer married soon after she came to the farm; she wanted a child and the farmer wanted a son, so they adopted a little boy, a scrawny, pitiful small child. They were, I thought, severe with him, but it may have been that their accents in English made their speech seem rough. They were a strange little family and very lonely. They begged me to sleep at their farm when I was in the vicinity, and I slept on a straw tick on the floor. Supper was boiled potatoes with skim milk to drink and maybe onions to eat raw, but I had found that this was usual fare on the hill farms, except that sometimes a bowl of boiled eggs was set out to eat with the potatoes and onions. One farmer, born in the Ukraine, had earned the money in the mines for the down payment on his farm and had moved to it with his wife and five children. All the children died in a diphtheria epidemic; their graves were near the house. But now there were five more, who sat at table with us.

The women worked as hard as the men; they kept house, ran the dairy and kept a kitchen garden if they could find time and strength. Electricity was used to run machines— not for reading, there was little time for reading. Farmers rose at dawn and went to bed early. Poor farmers kept twenty cows, the limit the farm could feed, but fewer cows made a dairy farm uneconomical to run. Rich farmers kept a hundred and twenty cows, with electric milkers and conveyors to bring feed to the cows and to convey manure out of the barn. While I was at one hill farm a cream separator was purchased, and they were using it for the first time. These were radicalized people, still very close to their European backgrounds in Germany, Italy, Czechoslovakia, Poland and Russia, and I found a skein of ideas which intertwined with mine and made these people dear to me. This was not placid country of rolling meadows, but rough country with forest patches where land was too steep and earth too thin for anything but wood-lot. I was driving down out of this country when I passed the local Catholic priest, who motioned me to stop. I stopped and we talked; we were far away from any habitation. He told me that I should get out of this country, that I was not wanted here, and that the farmers were benighted in their demands against Borden and Sheffield milk companies— that I was an arm of the devil and that I was surely headed for hell. I said, "Well, suppose we both go to the Farmers' Union meeting tonight and ask the membership whether you or I should leave this country."

I drove on, but I was angry and drove slowly because it had been a violent, virulent attack. We both were at the union meeting that night. I spoke, then the priest spoke, in the style of Father Coughlin the Radio Priest. Archie defended me and spoke of the divisive role the priest was playing in the strike. He called for a vote, and although the union membership was predominantly Catholic, they voted resoundingly for me to stay.

Charles Tomlinson (essay date 1978)

SOURCE: "Objectivists: Zukofsky and Oppen, a Memoir," in *Paideuma*, Vol. 7, No. 3, Winter, 1978, pp. 429-45.

[*In the following memoir, Tomlinson recalls his relation to Oppen and Louis Zukovsky, and describes their relationship to each other.*]

'It pays to see even only a little of a man of genius.' Thus Henry James, of Flaubert. I saw Louis Zukofsky four times, corresponded with him—on and off—for seven years and edited in 1964 what was, I suppose, one of the earliest Zukofsky numbers of an English review for *Agenda*: I was by no means the first islander to discover Zukofsky—Ian Hamilton Finlay had brought out over here *16 Once Published* in 1962 and that had given one something to think about. Indeed, those sixteen poems promised a way in, whereas the translations from Catullus and the sections of *"A"* I had already seen in *Origin* had left me more puzzled than enlightened. Gael Turnbull who early on had confronted me with Williams, Creeley and Olson, was also puzzled, though he spoke of Zukofsky the man and also of the holy trinity, Louis, Celia and son Paul in a way to arouse curiosity. In 1961 Robert Duncan's poem *After Reading Barely and Widely* had caught one's eye in the *Opening of the Field*—

> will you give yourself airs
> from that lute of Zukofsky?

But the book was simply not available on which to judge that lute, and it was not until August 1963 that I came to own No 132 of the three hundred copies in which edition *Barely and Widely* was printed—in a facsimile of Louis Zukofsky's handwriting and published by his wife. 1963 proved in many ways an *annus mirabilis*. I met both 'objectivists,' Zukofsky and George Oppen. And those meetings were preluded by two others—with Robert Duncan and Robert Creeley.

Yet it was not to these previous meetings that I owed my introduction to Zukofsky's poems: the meetings confirmed what I was now ready for. What remains difficult to explain in retrospect—in any retrospect—is the way one's scattered awarenesses suddenly fuse and focus. Perhaps it was further talk with that indefatigable and indispensable negotiator between cultures, Dr. Turnbull, whom I had last seen in Gloucestershire and who now turned up in Albuquerque where I was teaching at the University of New Mexico. At all events, in the autumn of 1962, I began to realise once more the extent of my ignorance about the work of Zukofsky and about what had been going on when in 1930, as Williams tells us in his biography, 'With Charles Reznikoff and George Oppen in an apartment on

Columbia Heights, Brooklyn, we together inaugurated, first the Objectivist theory of the poem and then the Objectivist Press. . . . The Objectivist theory was this: we had had "Imagism" (Amygism, as Pound had called it), which ran quickly out. That, though it had been useful in ridding the field of verbiage, had no formal necessity in it. . . . It had dribbled off into so called "free verse" which, as we saw, was a misnomer. . . . Thus the poem had run down and become formally nonextant. . . . The poem being an object . . . it must be the purpose of the poet to make of his words a new form. . . . This was what we wished to imply by Objectivism, an antidote, in a sense, to the bare image haphazardly prescribed in loose verse.' Present at that meeting on Columbia Heights (the apartment in question had been George and Mary Oppen's) was Louis Zukofsky, and it fell to him to outline in his essays a set of working principles. Since then he had gone on writing but was still largely unread.

Late in 1962 I tried inter-library loan and early in 1963 the system disgorged a pristine copy of *Some Time*. This was the handsome edition put out by Jonathan Williams in 1956 and one thing a quick glance confirmed was that, though this was the seventh year of its existence, no one had ever cut the pages. This realisation blinded me—quite literally as I was to discover in a few minutes—with sudden anger, and rushing into the kitchen for a sharp knife, I carved the pages apart in a crescendo of fury: such was the fate of poetry in a public library—once obtained, it was left unread. When calm returned and I sat down to lose myself in the book, I was surprised to discover that every time I turned the page two blank pages appeared. Anger and surprise, combined, had so reduced my faculties that it was quite some minutes before I realised that what I had carved apart was Jonathan Williams' beautiful intentions, and that the immaculate candour of these backs of pages printed on only one side had never been intended to be read. Shame replaced surprise, then shame too gave way as my eyes were invaded by the lovely and exact pleasure of

> Not the branches
> half in shadow
>
> But the length
> of each branch
>
> Half in shadow
>
> As if it had snowed
> on each upper half

—as visually precise as, over the page (or rather over the page and two blanks), the following was aurally meticulous:

> Hear, her
> Clear
> Mirror,
> Care
> His error.
> In her

Care
Is clear

—a weighing of tones to be re-echoed, perhaps, in the 'Ears err for fear of spring' passage from Bunting's *Brigg-flatts* ten years on.

In these two pieces, one had both sides of Zukofsky's gift, as stated (in reverse order) in *"A" 6*:

The melody! the rest is accessory:

My one voice. My other: is
An objective—rays of the object brought to a focus
. . .

I had the clue and so I read on, but it is difficult to disentangle the effect of that reading from the experience of another book which came unexpectedly and almost immediately after to hand. This was George Oppen's *The Materials*—his first for twenty-five years. Was this dual discovery what Breton meant by objective chance? In actuality, it was a treble discovery, for out of the same, largely depressing pile of books that lay on my desk for review, emerged Reznikoff's *By the Waters of Manhattan*. I could begin now to reconstruct what had happened in those far off days in Brooklyn and to see how it was still an active, though temporarily forgotten force in the America of the sixties. Zukofsky and Reznikoff had gone on publishing, but their books had been hard to come by. It was Oppen who was the real mystery—a mystery that has subsequently been explained—since all that one could find out about previous publication was that volume of 1934 ('Oppen's first book of poems' as it said on the cover of *The Materials*) which had earned the praise of Ezra Pound: 'a sensibility . . . which has not been got out of any other man's books.' The existence of that first book—instanced but unnamed on the cover—tantalized more and more as I prepared to write the review. On the track of Zukofsky, I had come upon Oppen whose work showed something of the same terse lineation and exactness I had discovered just before in Zukofsky's 'Not the branches / half in shadow.' On an impulse I wrote to Oppen who, in replying, offered me one of his three remaining *Discrete Series,* that first book of poems, and said of the writing of *The Materials* (his unaffected eloquence struck me as one of the classic statements of modern poetry):

I was troubled while working to know that I had no sense of an audience at all. Hardly a new complaint, of course. One imagines himself addressing his peers, I suppose—surely that might be the definition of 'seriousness'? I would like, as you see, to convince myself that my pleasure in your response is not plain vanity but the pleasure of being heard, the pleasure of companionship, which seems more honorable.

Those last two sentences so held my mind, I wanted in some sense to appropriate them, as one does when learning a passage by heart. They were so close to being a poem, I could both appropriate them to my own need and leave them in the hands of their author, simply by arrang-

ing them as lines of verse, changing only the pace yet leaving every word intact. This poem ("To C. T.") was to appear ultimately in Oppen's third volume, *This In Which.* It drew the immediate response from him:

I find myself entranced by the poem with which you have presented me. I see myself—slightly the elder of the two of us—talking to myself—and smoking *my* pipe, which is a shock. I congratulate the three of us on the whole thing.

Another letter, in which he outlined for me the history of the objectivists—an account he much amplifies in an interview for *Contemporary Literature,* Vol 10, No 2—contains the following:

We were of different backgrounds; led and have led different lives. As you say, we don't much sound alike. But the common factor I think is well defined in Zuk's essay.[1] And surely I envy still Williams' language, Williams' radiance; Rezi's lucidness, and frequently Zukofsky's line-sense.

My mind went back continually to a phrase in that first letter—'I was troubled to know I had no sense of an audience at all.' If Oppen's sense of an audience had been an absence, what was Zukofsky's in the poems of *Some Time*? Occasionally it seemed to be almost wholly domestic—as witnessed by those valentines and the frequent family references. But, as I was to learn later, Zukofsky could count on an audience among the circle around *Black Mountain Review,* and its editor Robert Creeley was one of his most convinced readers. When Creeley returned from British Columbia to teach at the University of New Mexico in June 1963, I asked him in a conversation which we taped, what he felt had been Zukofsky's principal lesson for the younger poet. Creeley responded to that question in terms rather different from Oppen's own stressing of the value of Zukofsky's critical sense and the stimulus of his conversation, which were what his letters mainly dwelt upon. For Creeley, Zukofsky chiefly ratified in his poetry one side of the teaching of Ezra Pound:

What Zukofsky has done [said Creeley] is to take distinctions of both ear and intelligence to a fineness that is difficult. . . . It's extremely difficult to follow him when he's using all the resources that he has developed or inherited regarding the particular nature of words as sound. . . . If you read his translations of Catullus in which he is trying, in effect, to transpose or transliterate, or whatever the word would be, the texture of Latin sound into American language, it's an extraordinary *tour de force*. No, I find that in this whole thing that Pound came into—the tone leading of vowels, the question of measure, the question of the total effect in terms of sound and sight of a given piece of poetry—these aspects are tremendously handled by Zukofsky as by no one else.

A couple of days after talking to Creeley, I set out for Kiowa Ranch, on a mountainside beyond Taos. It had been the gift of Mabel Dodge Luhan to D. H. Lawrence and now belonged to the University of New Mexico. In the period I was to spend there, from June 22 to July 27, I had ample time and quiet to absorb the books Creeley had lent me—Zukofsky's *Anew* and *"A" 1-12.* I copied by hand most of the former and parts of the latter—mainly *"A" 7* and *"A" 11,* which still seem to me Zukofsky's two most impressive sections from that long poem. Kiowa Ranch, the sea-wash sound in its pinetrees, the slightly inebriating sense of height, the long horizons, the slow withdrawals of the sunset to a band of deep orange above the far mesas, all these entered into and penetrated my reading and copying. I found myself composing a poem to Zukofsky and enclosed in my first letter to him

TO LOUIS ZUKOFSKY

The morning
spent in

copying
your poems

from *Anew*
because that

was more
than any

publisher would
do for one,

was a
delight: I

sat high
over Taos

on a
veranda

Lawrence had
made in

exile here
exile

from those
who knew

how to write
only the way they

had been
taught to:

I put aside
your book

not tired
from copying but

wishing for
the natural complement

to all the
air and openness

such art
implied:

I went
remembering that

solitude
in the world

of letters
which is yours

taking
a mountain trail

and thinking
is not

poetry
akin to walking

for one
may know

the way that
he is going

(though I did not)
without

his knowing
what he

will see there:
and who

following on
will find

what you
with more than

walker's care
have shown

was there
before his

unaccounting eyes?

In a letter of 1964, Louis was to suggest emmending '(though I did not) / without / his knowing what he' to '(though I /did not) / not knowing / what he', in order to 'make it even lighter': 'Give it a thought—or more than one—if you reprint in a volume—I may very likely be wrong.' Then he added with characteristic elusiveness: 'I just hope eels will never eat electrons or they might end up in my mad house.' The reply to the poem suggested a meeting in New York on my way back in August. It also told me that he had been reading my work since 1957 'and I find it valid. I can read it—which is to be moved—as Ez used to say. And for the rest Prospero had better shut up about Miranda's accomplishments—just go ahead and prosper.' But he was to continue trying to improve Miranda's accomplishments. A later poem, *Gull*—it emerged from seeing one over Brooklyn harbour—which I dedicated to Louis and Celia, was thoroughly re-lineated and compacted by him from its first version, so that the poem as it now stands is as much a work of collaboration as Oppen's **"To C.T."** In fact, it so bears Louis' stamp, I have wondered sometimes whether it ought not to ride one day in his *Collected:*

> Flung
> far down,
> as the
> gull rises,
> the black
> smile of
> its shadow
> masking its
> underside
> takes
> the heart
> into the height
> to hover
> above the ocean's
> plain-of-mountains'
> moving quartz.

The letter which contained his revised version bore the apologetic 'about *Gull*—I probably shouldn't be doing this, but what do you say?'—this ran vertically down the right hand-side of the poem, then vertically down the left: '(And I'm not so sure about alignment, but who's "sure"?)'. And beneath the poem: 'Anyway you moved me to do it fast.' I thanked him. He replied:

> Thank me for? If you hadn't made it in potential, the stroke [axshually, as the weather girl says, I did it very fast] of genius (?) wouldn't have been actual. *No* time wasted, considering you agree—to be perfectly bumptious about it, considering your gratitude makes me happy—and I never take any credit from the prime mover. Don't tell anybody I still do such things, however, or I'll be flooded who knows with rafts of stuff from "pouncers".

I wasn't entirely sure what pouncers within inverted commas implied. The idiom and rhythm of the letter are very much those of Louis' speaking voice. The bits you didn't understand in his rapid patter (he was often extraordinarily comic) left you feeling you ought to have, but there was no lingering for regret or greater comprehension, because what he had gone on to say now demanded your whole attention. You couldn't afford to miss it. And just as you had to read his lettered at all angles for the tiny parentheses, you often had to strain to hear his low-toned voice. His whisper might be as funny as the minute post script down the back of an air letter: 'C just bogged in income tax reports calls from downstairs to ask if we can claim for being *blind*.'

I was to hear that voice for the first time in August. To begin with there had been doubts—doubts that made me realise that Louis was already a frequently sick man ('I'm ill so I can't move my head to left or right, but just to say it

will have to improve by August 4, when you pass through.') There were to be several mentions of 'the aches', not further defined, and three years later, in a letter saying that he had refused some teaching at Buffalo, I read the ominous words: 'The emphysema won't bear the traffic.' There had been more than doubts about seeing the Oppens that summer: it was a certainty they would be on Little Deer Isle, Maine. Then, suddenly, their plans were changed and they intended to be in Brooklyn. And, just as suddenly, our postal search for a New York apartment achieved success—that also was to be in Brooklyn. And though Brooklyn is a large place, as we soon knew, it was sufficiently the one place in which we would all coincide, the Zukofskys, the Oppens and the Tomlinsons.

In *Kulchur 5* Jonathan Williams has an imaginary movie cast to play the modern poets—Edward Everett Horton as T. S. Eliot, Lon Chaney Jr., as Robert Frost, Adolph Menjou as Edward Dahlberg, Cary Grant as James Laughlin. As Louis Zukofsky he casts Fred Astaire. There was an uncanny accuracy about this. Still showing signs of recent illness, Zukofsky had a curious dancing lightness in his build, movement and talk. There was also a touch of elegance, given sartorial precision when ten days after our visit to 160 Columbia Heights, he turned up complete with bow tie at our apartment on Ocean Avenue. What did not fit Jonathan Williams' casting was the densely black thick line of the eye-brows, the continuously re-lit cigarette, the nervous puckering of the forehead as the face flickered from anxiety to humour, the voluble, mercurial, ceaselessly inventive talk. That tenth story of Columbia Heights gave on to a view of the harbour. It was the same spot more or less that had seen the meeting of objectivists—not yet named—on that day in 1930. Through the window, behind Manhattan Bridge, loomed the trajectory of Brooklyn Bridge. You could see it, but only just. The Statue of Liberty rose clear in the sultry August afternoon in the opposite direction. On the balcony the traffic noises floated up from below, often drowning out Zukofsky's soft voice.

We spoke of many things, including the funeral of William Carlos Williams the previous March ('The nicest funeral I ever went to,' said Louis). But what most remains with me is the music of the occasion. By this I do not mean to reduce it to symbolist essence. 'The greatest satisfactions of conversation are probably musical ones,' as Ted Hughes has said. 'A person who has no musical talent in ordinary conversation is a bore, no matter how interesting his remarks are. What we really want from each other are those comforting or stimulating exchanges of melodies.' The music of meeting Zukofsky was exactly right, and one was encouraged to play one's few bars of accompaniment with a sense of satisfaction at having come in at the right place. His stream of talk was not exactly a monologue—he was too aware of one's presence for that—but it flowed and flashed and glowed in such a way that one hesitated to interrupt it. Or, to change the metaphor, one suggested themes on which Zukofsky variated, very much for one's benefit and delight. There was a mutuality in this process which he evidently appreciated and remembered when two years later he wrote to me: 'Hugh Kenner finally got to see us last week—just dropped in on a chance that I'd be at home, and we spent two afternoons together talking, the first talk of its kind I guess since you and I last talked. (The aches have been such we see almost nobody.)'

The talk at Columbia Heights gave place to his reading for us from his Catullus translations. As he did so, one realised that it was not only Pound that lay behind this venture, but principally the Joyce of *Finnegan's Wake*. And Joyce came to mind in the quality of his vocal execution which compared with that light tenor rendering of the Anna Livia Plurabelle passage on gramophone record. The *Cats* as he called them came over as beautifully comic, though I could not help wondering whether, without the help of his expert vocalising and extended from half a dozen to one hundred and sixteen plus fragmenta, these transliterations could hold the mind and not bring on a feeling of eels eating electrons. Here, he had pushed what he always called 'the noise' of poetry about as far as it would go. Tune was his other favourite word:

> The lines of this new song are nothing
> But a tune making the nothing full

Do the tunes of the *Cats* survive in their author's voice? Did the Library of Congress perhaps tape some of them, when he recorded there? He would surely have wished them to be heard his way, the noise bringing to the surface a ghostly Roman gabble. He had written to Alfred Siegel in 1957 concerning Siegel's transliteration of the Chinese through Canto 97, 'you mean the English *noises* [?], that would interest me.'

The Zukofskys regale us with trifle and cake, washed down with root-beer, then walked with us through the twilight to find the bus stop. Louis was saying that his last communication from Ezra Pound was about a rabbi, then went on to define his attitude to the world of regular publishing from which he, Zukofsky, was as yet still excluded. 'I don't care,' was his frequent refrain, though I doubted that. There was a certain undertow of bitterness, though it never dominated the conversation. As we walked through the grimy yet reassuring streets of Brooklyn and finally took up our stand under the pole of the bus stop, it was gaiety that prevailed. We must have talked for half an hour before we realised that no buses intended to halt there and that the notice on top of the pole read 'No Parking.'

George Oppen is a man who came difficultly by knowledge—which makes his Jewishness a very different thing from that of Zukofsky. I recognised the latter's as soon as we had entered his apartment. It had the same flavour that had given point and aliment to my adolescence, when the refugees from Hitler's Germany arrived in the English midlands. Here were people who had records of Bruckner and Brecht's Dreigroschenoper at a time when both were unknown to us. Among them I had heard Kant's categorical imperative explained as if it were a fact of daily life, had listened to a description of Thomas Mann glimpsed

paring an apple 'with surgical intentness,' had discovered that Heine, Kafka, Rilke could still exist among the coal dust and the fumes from pottery chimneys. In this Jewishness one experienced a familial sense at once secretive and hospitable, subtly tenser than one's own involvement in the painful day to day of family bathos, where lack of money and lack of imagination had produced a stale stoicism. That experience of an eagerly tense intellectuality returned as one met the Zukofskys. Not so, with the Oppens.

To gain their apartment in Henry Street, one passed the ground floor window where a pleasant-looking young man sat writing, as George later told me, pornographic fiction. The scarred hallway and stair led up to the top of the house and at the stairhead stood a man with a lined and weathered face like a Jewish sea-captain—a man who, as it transpired, owned a sailing boat but no car. This was George Oppen. Like Zukofsky he saw the humorous side of things, but he listened more. His speech was less fluent, more meditative; it was exact with a pondered exactness like his poetry.

We talked much of Mexico that evening—for we had been there earlier the same year—and of the Oppens' phase of exile in Mexico City and his joinery shop there. In his talk one warmed to a union of the passionate and the deliberate: there was accuracy and there was economy in this, and somehow, in one story he told us, he had managed to carry these to a point where they seemed like miracle or luck. Tired of the way Mexican drivers aimed their cars at you, George, crossing the Zocalo, had once refused to submit to this humiliation and, as the projectile approached, planted his fist square in the windshield: it was not the fist but the windshield that shattered. 'A stupid thing to do,' said George. The owner of the car got out, apparently for the show-down, but looking first at Oppen and then at the shivered glass, could find no way in which *machismo* could account for, admit or take action against such folly, shrugged, re-ascended and drove off. George has a genius for such inevitabilities. They need not always be the fruit of happy violence. In England, nine months after our meeting, the Oppens were at Ozleworth on an afternoon when the vicar called. Conversation turned on the New English Bible and I expended a good deal of wasted wrath on our pastor's admiration for this moribund document. He explained that in order to make sure that its idiom was truly current the committee had consulted a bishop's secretary. George was far more of a marksman than I with my incoherent rage. As the vicar was about to leave, George said with a sort of courteous finality, 'The next time you translate the Bible, call in a carpenter—and make sure he's a Jewish carpenter.' Later, walking down the nave of Wells Cathedral, he gave vent to another unexpected apophthegm: 'I guess I'm a Christian,' he said, 'but with all the heresies.'

The apartment in Henry Street was very much a presence in our conversation on that first encounter. As we sat eating, the evening moved into possession of the scene outside. High above Brooklyn, we watched the sun go down to the right of the Statue of Liberty, swiftly like a coin into a slot. Light shone from the Statue's torch and from the windows of Manhattan—these of a strange greenish hue as if an effect taken up from the water in the summer dusk. Across the bay the Staten Island ferry switched back and forth, a trail of lights above the milky turquoise it was travelling over. The television antennae on the near roofs of Brooklyn looked like ships' masts drawn up before the harbour below. This was a room and a view we were to revisit several times before the Oppens left for San Francisco in 1969 when Henry Street was threatened with demolition. The place seems a cell in a larger aggregate from which memory picks out the building in a street close by where Whitman printed *Leaves of Grass,* now a Puerto Rican restaurant; the commemorative plaque on its wall (stolen, sold and then recovered); what **The Materials** calls 'The absurd stone trimming of the building tops'; the site of the old Brooklyn Ferry and behind its delapidated stakes the line of Brooklyn Bridge—Whitman superimposed on Hart Crane.

As the shapes of Manhattan hardened into black that evening, I began to realise that all was not well between Oppen and Zukofsky, and the impression deepened on subsequent meetings with them both. I think I may now speak of this, for George's poem with which I shall close, makes no secret of the matter. When I reviewed Reznikoff's and Oppen's books I had wondered why there was no Zukofsky in the series, a joint publication of *New Directions* (James Laughlin) and *San Francisco Review* (June Oppen Degnan, George's half sister). His exclusion there clearly rankled with Louis. Even before I had met him, I realised the situation was an uneasy one for, after sending my review to Oppen, I had received the following reply:

> I enjoyed very much reading your review . . . I will have a copy made for New Directions-SF Review for the mention of Zuk. . . . The first year's poetry schedule consists of Oppen, Reznikoff and William Bronk, in which my advice is obvious enough. My recommendation of course included Zuk, but the suggestion—as you see—has not been acted on. It is by now too awkward for me to discuss the matter with Zuk at all, but it is my impression that they would be more likely to do a Selected than a Collected poems, if only for budgetary reasons. I can't really urge Louis to submit a ms. since I have no assurance at all that they would accept it. But you might urge him to try it if you think it worth the risk—to him—of a rejection. If they had a ms. under consideration I could re-open the discussion.

When I arrived in New York, I had some illusory hopes that I might perhaps be able to negotiate on Louis' behalf. As I stayed on, this hope extended to the possibility of somehow reconciling the estranged friends. But the longer I stayed the more I realised that neither project could be easily accomplished. In the first place, not only his self-respect but also Louis' belief that all his life he had been writing *one* poem (and he was very decided about this) stood in the way of my ever persuading him to submit a Selected and secondly, his feelings towards George had

curdled to such an extent that any reconciliation must lie far in the future if it were feasible at all. From hints and suggestions, I gathered that he imagined George had simply failed to act for him, which was not the case. Yet one could not simply *state* this to Louis. He did not live in the atmosphere of simple statement and his aggravated nerves pushed him into more suspicion than was good for him. He was a gentle man, yet his own character and long neglect had created a thorny hedge of self-defence and of self-injury. Years of teaching what he called 'my plumbers' at the Brooklyn Polytechnic Institute cannot have helped: 'My own mess of school etc is proverbial,' he wrote, complaining of chalk-fights and 'kids of seventeen who cannot sit on their asses.' 'All I need is to be away from the "job" I guess—the eel-lectermonickers, curs, curse.' Perhaps he even resented the fact that George was at last free from the job grind. It is hard to be certain. At all events, he made it clear that no interference however delicate would help repair the situation. I unwillingly resigned myself to this fact.

On returning home, I set about sharing my new found knowledge of things American with my fellow countryman, or as many of them as read the little magazines. For *the Review,* January 1964, I edited a Black Mountain number in which Louis figured as one of the founding fathers. Ian Hamilton, the regular editor, added his own characteristic postscript: 'The editorial motive of *the Review* in this project has been a documentary rather than, necessarily, a critical one. We believe that the movement ought at least to be known about.' So much for English caution, incapable of surrendering itself to surprise. The following December appeared the Louis Zukofsky issue of *Agenda.* All this time I kept up a regular correspondence with Louis and an exchange of books. He was an excellent critic and immediately perceptive about where another poet's strengths lay. His method of instruction by letter consisted of copying out the individual phrases which had struck him as centrally strong. I mentioned one poem of mine which he had not touched on and he replied, 'I was trying to point at *that* in your work which might be more useful to you as "craft," when you've extended it *past* your forefathers.' On my *Peopled Landscape* he wrote: 'As for prosody a little nearer Hardy in impulse of song rather than for all I revere his integrity the thought metres of Crabbe—and so on, the old guy's talking too much.' He emphasized that it was 'the "pure" of the craft,' he was interested in revealing to one and on the poem to which I had drawn his attention: '"Craft" as "invention" etc. In itself the poem is nothing to be neglected and in a work like my Test of Poetry would do very well alongside of Crabbe and Marvell. . . .' He could respond unexpectedly to poems whose premises were very unZukofskyan, as when he pointed to one of mine called *The Impalpabilities* and added '[would be your best defence against *Bottom*]'. His square brackets managed to be at once intimately playful and also defensive of another's interests, a typical example of the atunement of his epistolary style and also of his conversation (he was a man who could *speak* square brackets) to the needs of a friend. Of friends' needs he was always studious. His caring ranged from minute, attentive sympathy (on hearing my father was ill, he inquired about him for many letters after) to a sense of troubles taken on his own behalf. It could be simply a question of a meal. Or it could be a friend's luck that brightened his feelings, as when Bunting finally achieved publication with Fulcrum Press: 'I hope Basil gets the garter or sumpin—anything to save him from the dogged silence he's lived. It makes him happy—at any rate he writes cheerfully—to have some attention. *Loquitur* is a beautiful book, and *Briggflatts* is a delayed extension of it.' And there were friends missed. Of Williams he spoke with great affection, for Williams while not quite getting what Louis was at, had always written of him with generosity. One document of their literary relations I discovered while editing the *Agenda* issue—this was a signed statement of Williams' of June 29, 1948 which stated: 'I hereby grant formal permission to Louis Zukofsky to use whatever he wishes to use of my published literary works as quotations in his writings.'

In the winter of 1964 Louis began to talk of retirement. They were to move to two and a half rooms: 'Kitchen, living room with an L for sleeping. We've been living to pay the rent and income tax. The idea is to get down—to something like a bare table top—and maybe something of the feeling of 30 years ago where we wandered the streets of the same neighbourhood, rather young, will come back to us.' By August I heard: 'We're delighted to be in Manhattan again after 25 years . . . the streets have all the interest of a foreign city to provincials.' The same letter contained the news of acceptance by Norton of his poems ('First publication of poetry since they did Rilke in 1938 . . .') and of a further bonus that Reznikoff had just telephoned to read out a long and positive review of *Bottom* in the *TLS*—'very careful and painstaking. . . . So your country gets there ahead of mine.' I hesitated to confess (those were the days of anonymity) that I had written it.

Though Louis continued to feel the loneliness of his position, a period of respite seemed to be ensuing for him. Not that all was plain sailing now. The advance from Norton hadn't, as he wrote, 'covered half the medico's bill.' Yet there was freedom from the plumbers and there was a December visit to Yaddo in 1965 to finish the Cats: 'Silence helps—only a handful of reticent respectful guests—so far we can stand the cold. Pines, trails, waterfalls, high views from the foothills of the Adirondacks, and altogether too many good books around with no time to read if I'm to get through with that Guy (Gai).'

In the meantime I had been planning an anthology. If I could not help to reconcile George and Louis, at any rate I could surely get them together inside the covers of one book. And this book would show English readers an area of American poetry with which they were not as yet familiar. The title, *Seven Significant Poets,* embraced the objectivists (Oppen, Zukofsky, Reznikoff and Rakosi), Lorine Niedecker (characterized in *"A" 12* as a rich sitter') James Laughlin and William Bronk.

I was in New York in the spring of 1966 and so able to speak with Louis about this idea. Our meeting took place at 77 7th Avenue. 'You must come to the biggest Vermeer you've ever seen and you'll find us,' he said over the telephone. The Vermeer proved to be an enormous blow-up of one of his paintings used as a mural decoration for the downstairs vestibule of the apartment building. It still looked solidly composed but uncomfortably stretched. The apartment was overheated, at least for English susceptibilities, and Louis seemed ill, though still full of inventive talk. The meeting was attended by a lingering uneasiness. We were staying with the Oppens a fact not easy to declare, and when the Zukofskys invited us to remain to dinner the awkwardness arose of phoning our hosts from the one room that we would not be back for an evening meal. This I accomplished with absurd secretiveness and put down the phone, having mentioned no names. 'So you're staying with the Oppens,' said Louis. Yet the awkwardness passed and a pleasant meal followed. Louis seemed interested by the idea of the anthology, though he didn't care for the work of Bronk—'All that Stevensian bothering. You either think with things as they exist, or you give up.' 'Is Oppen in it.' called Celia from the kitchen. Louis seemed to accept that fact as inevitable also. I was not so sure that Celia did. But the way ahead looked clear and there was even a sort of geniality in Louis' contemplation of the prospect.

Back in England I put several months' work into the book and Fulcrum expressed their wish to publish it. When they approached Louis for permission to reprint, there came back a firm no in reply. It wasn't entirely unexpected, but one had hoped that, if reconciliations were not possible in daily life, perhaps literary works could still lie down amicably side by side. I never discussed the matter further with Louis, though obviously, without his presence in the book, it must remain a total impossibility. I'd simply spent a great deal of time to little effective end. We continued to correspond with perfect cordiality though we never met again. I should have foreseen the difficulties in the light of George's letter three years before concerning Louis' diatribes against him to innocent visitors: 'But perhaps I had better say that Louis really had no grievance against me, nor has the world, or no greater grievance than it has against anyone in these times of population explosion. And Louis no greater grievance against me than against anyone who "gets printed." Awkward for me, the. And overwhelmingly ironic to discuss my position as "a success" . . . I doubt that I'll produce another book within quite a few years. Maybe that'll heal things.'

That was after **The Materials.** Other books followed and finally a **Collected.** But so did books by Louis, including the two volumes of *All.* Clearly he was right to have resisted a selection. He got what he wanted, but what a time it took. And time didn't, in George's words, 'heal things'. When George gave me his **Collected Poems** in San Francisco in 1976 I found in it, towards the close, a poem I had not read before. I thought perhaps I had missed it in his previous collection, **Seascape: Needle's Eye** but, no, it is not there. The title is *The Lighthouses* and the subtitle for LZ in time of the breaking of nations':

> *if you want to say no say*
> *no if you want to say yes say yes in loyalty*
>
> to all fathers or joy
> of escape
>
> from all my fathers . . .

and the poem modulates into George's seabord world where lighthouses flash and the coastal waters are rock-pierced. He recognises the kinship with Zukofsky—for Zukofsky was in a sense one of his fathers too, a brilliant exemplar and talker in the early days of objectivism. He recognises also the racial kinship as a motif returns, previously used in the poem *Semite*:

>   my
> heritage *neither Roman*
> *nor barbarian* . . .

I do not know whether Louis ever read the piece or whether, had he done so, he would have recognised George's continuing plea for clarity in relationship. *The Lighthouses* is a final document in a long and saddening history of misunderstanding, a misunderstanding which a common experience of a time, place and race might have outweighed but did not. It reminded me of the fact that from both their windows in Brooklyn they had shared the view of the same 'lighthouse'—the beam from the Statue shining back in the dusk towards the windows of Manhattan.

Note

1. 'Sincerity and Objectification.'

Rachel Blau DuPlessis (essay date 1981)

SOURCE: "Oppen and Pound," in *Paideuma*, Vol. 10, No. 2, Spring, 1981, pp. 59-83.

[*In the following essay, Blau DuPlessis discusses Pound's influence on Oppen's poetry, and examines their poetic and political dissimilarities.*]

> . . . poetry must be at least as well written as prose, etc. It must also be at least as good as dead silence.[1]

In a review of Ginsberg, McClure and Olson, published in 1962, as he was publishing the poems of his return, George Oppen strongly suggests that each of these poets exemplifies a tendency in current writing which he must reject; by this review, Oppen tacitly situates himself in relation to some significant contemporaries. On a line between "histrionics and . . . openness," Ginsberg's mode is often "declamatory"; indeed "to quarrel with that is simply to quarrel with the heart of his work." McClure's mode reduces poetic desire to "excitement, intoxication, meaning-

lessness, a destruction of the sense of oneself among things."[2] But Olson's case is less quickly adjudicated. Oppen cites and he ponders, but at the end reading Olson "is simply not an encounter with a new poetry."[3] What, in a word, has impeded Olson's voice and vision? It is Pound. For

> granting once and for all that Olson is worth reading if anyone at all is worth reading, the problem remains for the reviewer and for any reader that it is impossible to confront Olson's poems without first of all acknowledging the audible presence of Pound in them. Not that Olson has not openly and handsomely acknowledged the debt to Pound in the text of the poems, but if we look to poetry as a skill by which we can grasp the form of a perception achieved, then nothing can so deaden the impact of poetic discourse as to be uncertain which of two men is speaking, to half-hear other words paralleling the words we read.[4]

In his assessment of Olson, Oppen makes manifest a fundamental choice for his own poetry: Oppen will not be Pound. Nonetheless, Pound is ubiquitous, a major creator of the poetics and meanings of twentieth century poetry. For Oppen to make the treacherous but enabling equation "Oppen ≠ Pound," he has to situate his vision and voice at a measured remove from this decisive, and unavoidable, influence which had, at the same time, shaped the poetic context in which Oppen could become Oppen. For Pound is the twentieth century poet who formulated most briskly, and promulgated most tirelessly, the aesthetic of visual and aural accuracy, and whose editorial grasp of the clearest word, the most succinct statement, the colloquial turn, and the lightning illumination made a broad path for his peers in his own generation, in the next—and the next. In their objectivist poetics, then, Oppen and Pound are in fundamental agreement. In the carrying out of that poetics, they divide.

Charles Altieri has defined the symbolist and the objectivist world views of modern poetry in ways pertinent to the discussion of Oppen and Pound. The romantic-symbolist approach values the mind's shaping and interpretive capacities as it reflects upon the meaning of perceptions; this mode increases "the distance between the empirical and a realm of imaginative values."[5] The objectivist begins with the detail, the seen or perceived unit, sometimes (and with a certain questionableness) called a fact, and proceeds by "thinking with the things as they exist" and as the mind registers them. In this process, the poet abstains from "predatory intention," and proceeds without teaching, converting, or hectoring the reader.[6] Presentations—not the rhetorics of self-expression or confession—become the poet's most exacting and comprehensive task. In the purest objectivist poetics, there is a continual interrogation of the self and of any stated position or system, a questioning which compels poets to begin as if perpetually prior to their own poetry and their own poetic careers. Such a poet's test of vocation may then be that s/he is always beginning in "poverty" once again, that poetic closure is unstressed, and that the closure of idea into system is avoided, for all would distort the poet's task. An example is the characteristic bewildered pleasure of Oppen "left with the deer, staring out of the thing, at the thing, not knowing what will come next."[7]

One may test Pound against what Altieri calls "the temptations of closure—both closure as fixed form and closure as writing in the service of idea, doctrine, or abstract aesthetic ideal."[8] Certainly *The Cantos* is an endless poem in formal terms, presenting "complex" by "instant" in a spatial network which fuses with the temporal articulations of the self in its changing preoccupations. Yet insofar as certain values or discoveries are treated as settled, Pound's poetry too can settle into his own repeating codes, with only perfunctory engagement with the tactic of beginning from poverty over again. From the inter-war period on, I would argue, while the collaged form of the poem did not change, the meaning which Pound gave to his formal acts did indeed alter. In the midtwenties, that is, *The Cantos* modulated from an early concern for re-illuminating moments of full cultural and emotional achievement (moments of renaissance), to the concern which controls the bulk of the poem: making a new and total culture by the didactic analysis of certain verities.[9]

Before and during World War I, Pound thought that the modern renaissance, for which he had long been preparing himself, was arriving. The War, to his shock and terror, made him see how easily that renaissance could be broken by political and social forces. He therefore turned to the problem of finding a favorable political context for art—investigating with which of the two parties (communist or fascist) the Poundian "Party of Intelligence" would affiliate.[10] In the 1934 Postscript to the 1916 Gaudier memoir, a rare reassessment which indicates his change, Pound feels that the revolution in art, in which he and Gaudier participated, was a prefiguration of a "volitionist" social revolution. The artists had been, gratifyingly, at the revolutionary vanguard. Reassessing the earlier manifesto in this light, he writes that Vorticist formal ideas really had an ideological function; Vorticism

> meant a complete revaluation of form as a means of expressing nearly everything else, or shall we say of form as a means of expressing the fundamentals of everything, or shall we say of form as expressing the specific weights and values [of?] total consciousness.[11]

The Cantos, then, takes on this function; it offers "a complete revaluation of life in general. . . ."[12]

The double meaning of Pound's term *paideuma* can also indicate the play between the historical and the static in Pound's poetics from the late twenties on. An organic culture comprising the values, attitudes and assumptions held in any historical period, along with their interrelations and their products, Pound (following Frobenius) described as "paideuma," "the tangle or complex of the inrooted ideas of any period."[13] In Pound's view, a new paideuma—cultural or social change—can be achieved through historically rooted realizations. However, Pound also used "paid-

euma" to mean a universal, transhistorical set of values in action, which are kept alive by an elite group. Not organic in the sense of being "inrooted," they are instead perpetually reaffirmed, the "recurring decimals" of wisdom and good government.[14] The arithmetical analogy conceals the religious structure. For Pound eventually explains the existence of these ideas in mystical terms, and their believers become initiates in a mystery which unifies the elites of many times and places. "A conspiracy of intelligence outlasted the hash of the political map."[15] When Pound reaches this point in his poetics, *The Cantos* is increasingly based on pre-existing convictions of will and desire, rather than on the investigation of a field of densely inrooted particulars. This is the moment that Oppen will reject Pound.[16] Because of his moral and political convictions, Pound the objectivist became Pound the symbolist, intent—in Altieri's words—on "raising particulars to the level of universals whereby they come to provide models for experience."[17] Hence the purpose Pound ascribes to poetry, and the actual texture and struggle of his poetry are in major contradiction.

As Pound once asked in a parallel context, "Pourquoi nier son père?"[18] This is the question to ask of Oppen, and the Pound-Oppen relation provides several answers—in biography, in poetics, and where these join, as in the nature of their approaches to conflict itself.

The compact between George and Mary Oppen, fairly fresh at the time they met Pound in Rapallo in 1930, was a primary bond of defining importance. The couple took risks for it; they fought its disruption. This will help measure the force of what occurred then, as they remember it now. "There were two of us, and in Pound there is no feminine."[19] Pound had strong male bonding relations with Zukofsky and Bunting. There was no reason in Pound's mind why Oppen should not fit this pattern of discipleship, especially as Pound thought that TO press was prepared to publish his collected works. It bothered the young couple that Pound excluded Mary from conversation, also, as Oppen said, that "he invited me to call, not Mary." But in having extricated themselves from Oppen's family, by whom they were financially and emotionally "seduced," the Oppens had affirmed their "resistance" and self-sufficiency.[20] They were not to give any individual "father" power over them. Hence Oppen resisted the proferred attractions of personal affiliation with Pound. By immersion in political activity and by paying its political cost, Oppen sought a forum for his instruction outside literary tradition; one need not assume that a sense of cultural authority can alone come from the consideration of texts, from discipleship in education, or from the apostolic succession of poet to poet. Immersion in collective struggles (the milk strike, Depression organizing, the War) and saturation in the felt experience of every social class were what the Oppens selected as their cultural instructors.

For the Oppens, trying to read *The Cantos* might well have been like experiencing Pound's magisterial sweep out to the water at Rapallo: "From there came the Greek ships."[21] Too much of a gesture, for he was pointing in the wrong direction. "We weren't wowed by *The Cantos*. We saw that it was magnificent poetry; it was as if someone had played the piano. Didn't mean we had to buy a grind organ."[22] Even though Oppen distances himself from *The Cantos,* still, references to Pound do appear, especially in his recent work. He seems to have been completely moved by Pound's apologia, in which a fragmented reading of the major poem is favored, and in which Pound reveals that he wants, and has always wanted, yet is forced by circumstances to renounce an ending of major proportions. Pound pities himself bravely:

> But the beauty is not the madness
> Tho' my errors and wrecks lie about me.
> And I am not a demigod,
> I cannot make it cohere.
> If love be not in the house there is nothing.[23]

Oppen refers to these lines in **"The Speech at Soli,"** asking Pound "what do you want/to tell." He posits Pound's answer as the intolerable alternative "as against the Populism in my poem"[24]:

> mad kings
>
> gone raving
>
> war in incoherent
> sunlight it will not
>
> cohere it will NOT that
> other
>
> desertion
> of the total we discover
>
> Friday's footprint is it as the sun moves[25]

Here Pound's position is qualified as "desertion / of the total," while the immersion in time and the commonplace light of human need for fellowship are Oppen's response.

For Oppen as for Pound the quest for the initial light of the image was a fundamental, a "primitive" goal. Light appears in each poet as that which fills the world with the possibility of knowing:

> to "see again,"
> the verb is "see," not "walk on"
> i.e. it coheres all right
>   even if my notes do not cohere.
>
>   . . .
> A little light, like a rushlight
>   to lead back to splendour.[26]

Pound's *splendour* is like Oppen's *brilliant, shining, transparent*—terms indicating clarity recur in their work. Yet the words "lead back" remain Pound's keynote. For there is a difference in the activities associated with light in each poet. In Pound's poetic universe, light is not primarily a beginning or an opening to the world that enables

something to be thought; light is the end: an illumination, a halo, a cleansing as occurs after the Hell cantos when the heroes stand in the sunset. Light prevails in Pound as a principle or an absolute—"light tensile immaculata"—which, after it is achieved, can be dispensed as a virtue, a presence, even a judge.[27] This is a religious vision, and he begins *The Pisan Cantos* in the dark night of the soul as "as a man on whom the sun has gone down." That set of cantos is based on the re-establishment of centered vision, through the intervention of generative goddesses and women, and through memories of what his kind has accomplished. In the post-Pisan Cantos, light is treated in two alternative ways, as *karitas* (love, pity, tolerance) and as the absolute sense of rightness, which would have a clear and cutting meaning in *praxis*:

> pity, yes, for the infected,
>   but maintain antisepsis,
> let the light pour.[28]

or

> Muss., wrecked for an error,
> But the record
>   the palimpset—
> a little light
>   in great darkness—[29]

Pity is associated with women, with goddesses, with healing, with a panther sated with sensual glory and pleasure in beauty. But women are too soft—"marshmallow" not "fulcrum"—and the kind of light associated with women has, therefore, the problem of not being sufficiently unbending or touch.[30] As he would often do when faced with an antithesis, Pound chose to disallow, as best he could, the force of the contradiction.

The initial light of the image is both inner and outer in Oppen's poetic universe; it is the "intensity of seeing" which matches "the intensity of what is."[31] Because light is from within and without, its consideration can be filled with movement, conflict, meshing. This light is Oppen's test for the products of mind and craft and is the reason he must turn from a certain statue in a gallery with the words

> Useless!
> Useless! Thick witted,
>
> Thick carpeted, exhilarated by the stylish
> Or the opulent, the blind and deaf.[32]

Instead, Oppen meditates on a pulsing "it": "the intensity of what is," which Oppen poses as a principle by which to test artists, and which has, at the same time, contradiction built into its very nature:

> 'It has been good to us,'
> However. The nights
>
> At sea, and what
>
> We sailed in, the large
> Loose sphere of it

Visible, the force in it
Moving the little boat.

Only that it changes! Perhaps one is himself
Beyond the heart, the center of the thing

And cannot praise it
As he would want to, with the light in it, feeling the
　　long
　　　helplessness
Of those who will remain in it

And the losses. If this is treason
To the artists, make the most of it; one needs such
　　faith,

Such faith in it
In the whole thing, more than I,
Or they, have had in songs.

If Pound, then, is quintessentially bound to the artistic heritage and to artists (as the litany of *The Pisan Cantos* shows), Oppen, as not-Pound, means to make a song that returns not to art but to a world of material relationships and elegiacally factual statements about the "abyss / of the hungry."[33] Treason to the artists. Treason to the tradition—*pourquoi nier son père?* Because one must always begin as if fatherless, begin as if artless: this much is obvious. That Oppen is stating, in a typical moment of almost offhand intransigence, that the artist must end there, end beyond all the institutions, situations and ambitions of art, is more difficult to recognize. But—and it is Oppen's tightrope—not beyond "the level of art"[34]:

> Poetry seems to me a thing to do when it is absolutely beyond, out of sight beyond the me-too of art. And whether the poems are perfect, the leap is made at the first sight of "the girder, still itself among the rubble" (which is quoted from Charles Reznikoff).[35]

When Pound and Oppen met, at New Directions in 1969, the two wept on each other's shoulders. Oppen's poem **"Of Hours,"** first published in *Seascape: Needle's Eye* (1972) explores that oppositional contact and mutual grief in the context of Pound's work, especially *The Pisan Cantos.* I propose to meditate further on the relation of these poets with this poem as guide.

Everyone who has experienced him mentions the "pounding" of Pound. This forms part of H.D.'s memories in *End to Torment.* Oppen evokes this feeling also in the citation with which he begins **"Of Hours"**:

> '. . . as if a nail whose wide head
> were time and space . . .'
>
> at the nail's point the hammer-blow
> undiminished[36]

These lines could serve as an elegy for Pound's intense and brilliant force and the grandeur of his ambition. The passage which Oppen is citing comes from Simone Weil.[37] With the sense of mutuality in meeting (for Pound is both

"old friend" and "father"), the pounding may also come from Oppen's own critical heart, approaching the case of Pound again, perhaps in fear, that

> Holes　　pitfalls open
> In the cop's accoutrement
>
> Crevasse
>
> The destitute metal
>
> Jail metal
>
> Impoverished　　Intimate
> As a Father did you know that

Pound's several confinements—political and psychological, from the post-war detention center to the Washington hospital—are engaged in these lines. Oppen's challenge to Pound is based, interestingly, on paternity. He could be asking whether Pound ever saw the way the role of "cop," of keeper of order, would tend. Are not the "pitfalls," the "holes" in the argument visible? Didn't you know, he asks Pound obliquely, what fascism was (all that "destitute metal," all the trappings, the terror)? And if you knew, why did you believe? Pound was not unaware of the tactics of the Fascists in Italy. The Matteoti murder (1924, the year Pound settled in Rapallo) caused a crisis in Italy; Mussolini responded by a rightward move. Within the next few years, the fascists established totalitarian control. In commenting on this period, Pound saw internal terror as an aberration which he was willing to justify because of his hope that the renaissance for which *he* had long been ready had, in fact, arrived. His letter to Basil Bunting from 1938 evinces, in the curious analogy he chose to explain fascist terror, a forceful blindness:

> You will never get the hang of fascism if you persist in the habit of regarding every act as a precedent.
>
> Surgeon amputates leg / NOT as a precedent / he don't mean to go on amputating the patient's leg every week or year.
>
> Operations to save life / ONLY in an emergency / What are called CONTINGENT. Things to be done ONCE and not erected into a system.[38]
>
> Old friend　　old poet
> Tho you'd walked
>
> Familiar streets
> And glittered with change the circle
>
> Destroyed its content
> Persists　　the common
>
> Place　　image
> The initial light　　　　Walk on the walls

After touching on the lust for social transformation so great that it turned Pound's poetry inside out, Oppen suggests those aspects of Pound's work which he loves—not the palimpsest of paraphrasable argument but the clarities: the smell of mint, clover, the wasp, the moon. There is something telling about the space between the compound noun "commonplace" (a tactic which Oppen uses in other words beginning with *common,* such as *commonwealth*); the isolation of the elements calls attention to the many interesting meanings of the word *common*—public, shared, ordinary—and emphasizes a rootedness in such sights and sites:

> The walls of the fortress   the countryside
> Broad in the night light the sap rises
>
> Out of obscurities the sap rises
> The sap not exhausted

This passage recognizes the tremendous energy of Pound's poetry, the lines and brilliant conjunctions that flare up. Oppen says "obscurities" to suggest both the night setting and the magisterial poem which cannot always be read.

In the next lines, Oppen lists those elements of Pound's poem which he considers the living part:

>   Movement
> Of the stone   Music
> Of the tenement
>
> Also this lonely theme   Earth
> My sister
>
> Lonely sister my sister but why did I weep

The stones bring to mind all the cities and the buildings in *The Cantos*: the stones pulled into place at the sound of a harp, the Tempio, and walk through Alyscamps, the hidden city "moving upward," the watery white columns seen shimmering.[39] Also there are voices present in the sharply articulated accents and macaronic dialects; *The Cantos* are filled with aural precision "as per / 'doan' tell no one I made you that table" in *The Pisan Cantos.*

Two goddesses center *The Pisan Cantos*; one is Aphrodite and the other Gea Terra. At the deepest level, the two are one, for art, ethics, religion, agriculture and economics have the same center: the living force of nature expressed in sexuality and fertility. Aphrodite arrives at the climax of a mid-book vision as if in a masque or a grottoesque renaissance border: "The Graces have brought Aphrodite / Her cell is drawn by ten leopards."[40] In Pound's view, artists are the most privileged hierophants of the goddess of beauty and sensuality. *The Pisan Cantos* celebrate the special grace afforded those who serve beauty, and those with the moral courage to rebuild "stone after stone of beauty cast down." Like an old jongleur, Pound sings to Beauty of those who have given themselves utterly to her service. Their grace is to achieve or to witness the love of beauty manifest in the sexual consummation of male poet and female goddess.

Ideal beauty seen as a female figure and goddess completely echoes the high, old tradition of the female icon and the male worshipper. Hence, in the enumeration of artists which is one of the binding concerns of *The Pisan Cantos,* the women artists and female companions whom Pound did in fact know are never mentioned by name, as are Yeats, Beardsley, Williams, Eliot, Joyce, Symons, Hulme, Lewis, and so forth. Rather, women are encoded into the names of goddesses and mythological figures (as Dryad is H.D.), or are nameless, healing presences seen in vision. Needing this ideal, Pound preserves a division between idealized female figures and real men, their demanding worshipers. Even in the triple conjunction of eyes seen in the tent, identified with three particular women, the women in the poem are a force of being (the process, sanity, forgiveness) which is first outside him, and then, with a great loosening, is absorbed into him. He is able to achieve stability through their palpable presence, but nonetheless retains a peculiar reticence about naming the women to grant them historical or biographical place.[41]

The second climax in *The Pisan Cantos* centers on Gea Terra, but this goddess is less specified, in fact hardly named, and, unlike Aphrodite, is therefore less like a manifestation of a set of traits or accoutrements. Towards the end of *The Pisan Cantos,* there is a "connubium terrae," a marriage of earth and poet consummated in a mystery, so that as he lies flat on each, feeling his chthonic connection with earth and the creatures born here, he suffers the price of such connection with the life force—death and the "loneliness of death." Ignoring Aphrodite, with her more baroque trappings, Oppen picks one of two female forces to comment on, and, significantly, ignores the one whose access is achieved only, or best, via the elite which rescues and sustains beauty.[42] Oppen's phrase for this theme of Pound, "Earth my sister," humanizes the nymphs and goddesses who populate the pages of *The Cantos* by emphasizing a personal and even tragic relation with a natural force.

In Pound, finally, for every problem in history, the solution is myth. A search for moments of transpersonal and transhistorical meaning and certainty takes place in the cantos, which return again and again to the brilliance and unambiguous clarity of visionary experiences which are associated with the gods of nature, with fertility and light. Pound's aim is to find, in history, those incarnate moments when "vortices of social power coincided with vortices of creative intelligence" which coincided with natural understandings.[43] Summarizing his search for this moment, Pound used the breathtaking phrase "We think because we do not know."[44] At the moment of knowing, then, discrimination and judgment will become moot, and there will remain only contemplation of what has been discovered. For Oppen, the problem is understanding value in history, and the solution is clarity within a historical saturation by the process of naming one's strange common condition. Given this difference, one might suppose that Oppen would view Pound's many mythological references as dispersal of force, rather decorative at times, with categories of feeling and response too readily to hand. Pound, in contrast, would view them as the many ways of naming the one mystery, proof that because there are many, in fact there is only one.

For myth does appear in Oppen, although not with Pound's populous texture, but rather as basic activities of meditation, readiness, centering, quest. There is the Blaze and the Tyger:

> Tyger still burning in me burning
> in the night sky burning
> in us the light[45]

But for Oppen myth is not a way of escaping history; rather, myth is a way of entering it. Thus, Oppen's important (and as yet unstudied) saturation in what Judaism means historically, which is virtually inseparable from its myths. The formation of a covenant community, a painful sense of re-iterated election and fallings-away, the nomadic Semite, the mystery of immanence in history—these the binding experiences of Exodus, not to speak of the voice of prophetic intransigeance, and references to anti-Semitism—all appear powerfully in Oppen's work.

But in general, and in his statements, myth is a category of reference and analysis which is at least two, or possibly more, steps beyond what Oppen thinks possible to consider. The taxonomy of language—for the words themselves, he points out, are a kind of category—has enough mystery and resonance to stand, in Oppen's poetic universe, as objects of consideration in the place of maelids and bassarids. For these words are at once objects of faith and of desire, awe and need:

> The little words that I like so much, like "tree," "hill,"
> and so on, are I suppose just as much a taxonomy as
> the more elaborate words; they're categories, classes,
> concepts, things we invent for ourselves. Nevertheless,
> there are certain ones without which we really are un-
> able to exist, including the concept of humanity.[46]

The idea that poetry tests these words to see whether they sustain value is, if you will, the objectivist's (or possibly the Jew's) form of myth, grounding a text or statement in the examination of the word, and shrugging away the rhetorical, the sublime, and the traditional evocations which myth can provide:

> Who
> so poor the words
>
> *would   with   and*   take on substantial
>
> meaning   handholds   footholds
> to dig in one's heels   sliding
>
> hands and heels beyond the residential
> lots   the plots   it is a poem[47]

This recent poem—an almost jaunty exposé, with its pun on plots—curiously reiterates something Zukofsky said in a more irracible tone, probably because it was addressed into the air towards T. S. Eliot's epigones after the *Quartets* were beginning to make their impact on American poetry:

> The poet wonders why so many today have raised up
> the word "myth," finding the lack of so-called "myths"
> in our time a crisis the poet must overcome or die from,

as it were, having become too radioactive, when instead a case can be made out for the poet giving some of his life to the words *the* and *a:* both of which are weighted with as much epos and historical destiny as one man can perhaps resolve.[48]

> Lonely sister my sister but why did I weep
> Meeting that poet again what was that rage
>
> Before Leger's art poster
> In war time Paris perhaps art
>
> Is one's mother and father O rage
> Of the exile   Fought ice
>
> Fought shifting stones
> Beyond the battlement
>
> Crevasse   Fought

That the mechanisms of the high bourgeois art world, the shows, the buying and selling of vision for praise occur irrespective of the crisis of fascism and genocide—this Oppen rejected, loathed. Interestingly, whatever his politics, Pound rarely sold his vision for praise (a clear exception is the "Ma questo" passage at the beginning of Canto 41); left and right join in feeling the depth of a historical crisis. So here Oppen's and Pound's rage—equally in exile from the "me-too of art"—can be imagined as one. This identification with Pound's scrupulous and demanding vocation is one view that Oppen could hold; but another view enters to evoke the fundamental irreconcilable conflict in Oppen's feeling toward Pound.

During the war, Oppen was once whisked from the front lines because of a little piece of luck: he'd won a raffle.

> George walked through Paris to the Boulevards, where
> he looked on, incredulous, at the Boulevardiers, who,
> momentarily safe behind Allied front lines, sipped er-
> satz coffee and nibbled delicacies concocted of saw-
> dust; as they daintily continued their cafe lives, on the
> kiosk were large, beautiful, extravagant posters adver-
> tising Leger's latest exhibit. George says, "I nearly
> went beserk; there was no way to express my anger at
> these Parisians who could care about such mediocrity
> at such a time."[49]

This political rage is translated, interestingly, to family terms. If "art is one's mother and father," one will have several irreconcilable, intense and conflicting relationships with it, as with one's poetic parents: grieving over art; seduced by art; never being as good as art; living in the house of art; leaving the house of art; offering filial piety to art; distancing oneself from art with the cool space of once febrile love. Pound is companion—"old friend"; Pound is the wrong-headed, dying "father"; Pound is the "old poet" so right about poetics, so strained in what he makes his poem do. These double-edged epithets express the contradictory force of Oppen's feelings toward Pound.[50]

> Art's face
> We know that face

More blinding that the sea   a haunted house   a limited

Consensus unwinding

Its powers
Toward the thread's end[51]

This is a poem about finding a destroyed piano over the
cliffs, thrown away. And it is a poem about the collision
between two valuations of art, two poetics, where one is
powerful and seductive and the other is difficult and un-
generous, apparently too suspicious of the blandishments
of art which have, after all, a resounding cultural mandate.
In this poem, Oppen rejects the last holdout of a symbolist
poetics, one shared by most artists even at this minute: the
idea that art is a substitute for religion, and that culture is
a sign of grace.

In the record of great blows   shocks
Ravishment   devastation   the wood splintered

The keyboard gone in the rank grass swept her hand
Over the strings and the thing rang out

Over the rocks and the ocean
Not my poem Mr Steinway's

Poem   Not mine   A 'marvelous' object
Is not the marvel of things

              twisting the new
Mouth   forcing the new
Tongue   But it rang

This negative declaration of his poetics, defensive, even a
little carping with those quotation marks, is precisely what
is wanted to record the pain of severing from this seductive sound. And the *it* which rang is most certainly the piano, speaking its piece for a sonorous, consoling poetics.
In contrast, that implacable "marvel of things" in which a
destroyed piano can be shoved and broken, has trouble
formulating a sound. The shove which gets the piano over
the cliff recalls in "devastation" the "Crevasse" of destruction which is alluded to in **"Of Hours."**

In **"Of Hours,"** Oppen considers the war:

            Fought
No man
but the fragments of metal
Tho there were men there were men   Fought
No man but the fragments of metal
Burying my dogtag with H
For Hebrew in the rubble of Alsace

When the metal which is being fought becomes, in the
repetition of that line, one's own identity, the metal tag
which characterizes oneself as anathema, then the war and
fascism live in the sword against oneself, and in the degree to which one fears one's own identity because it is
one's otherness.[52] So Oppen remembers the war, remembers thinking

that the lives of all Jews were endangered by fascism;
our lives were in danger, and not to fight in the war
was to ask of others what we would not do for ourselves.[53]

It is hard to be kind to Pound here, although in the recently published "Addendum for Canto C" he states that
usury is "beyond race and against race."[54] There are, over
all, too many nasty quotations, despite the honorably, but
rather oft-repeated assurances that he lacked *personal* anti-
Semitism. In some curious way, this is not as exculpatory
as it has sounded, for it isolates the good Jews (my friends,
the elite) from all the others (the enemy). The political
anti-Semitism of fascism—a universal pogrom—was not
Pound's solution; he simply wanted a limited antisepsis, at
the top. But besides Pound's prescriptions, those poor,
much maligned Jews in Pound's cantos are symptomatic
of a mode of thought far removed from Oppen's and which
makes another distinction between them. A conspiracy
theory is, after all, so monocausal as to almost miss being
termed analytic. And the degree to which a conspiracy
theory, with its familiar scapegoats, is injected into
Pound's poem is the degree to which he could be one of
the secret objects of Oppen's brief manifesto:

We, the poets, change the accents, change the speech.
We change the speech because we are not explaining,
agitating, convincing: we do not write what we already
knew before we wrote the poem.[55]

But Pound does indeed write what he knew before the
poem. For Oppen, this represents a failure to create poetry
out of the objectivist poetics which Pound had, in effect,
invented.

Syntax in poetry, like narrative choices in fiction (e.g. co-
incidences, the nature of beginnings, what is resolved or
excluded at conclusions), is the area where ideology or
world view is most keenly revealed. What then is it like to
read *The Cantos,* to read **Seascape,** or **Primitive**? What
world view does the poetry convey?

On site, inside the poem page by page, *The Cantos* are the
location of tremendous poetic conflicts pulling the work in
opposite directions. The major stress comes between the
ideogram and the summary category, that is, between structuring by the presentation of particulars in a field and by
the representation of statement. A field structure is heuristic and process-oriented, its paratactic arrangements allowing an intimate relation between reader and writer, sustained by the poet's tact and by a deep commitment to
equalizing access to information and vision. Capitalizing
on Fenollosa's analysis of syntax, Pound developed that
poetic structure by dissociating the energies of words
(interpreted as variants of verbs) from the presumably limiting and deadening patterns of sentences in which words
were enclosed. Yet as Pound's political ideas became more
fixed, the poet violated or drastically modified this poetic
procedure by summarizing or asserting ideas. Thus he limited his words in their meaning, while attempting to free
them by his structure. For instance, *The Cantos* often
makes shorthand allusions to and summaries of arguments

already presented elliptically in his prose. In practice, therefore, many words appear to the untutored reader as if in a code. Pound compels at least temporary discipleship for this reason; only by learning Poundean references as if learning a foreign language can a reader fully comprehend key words and thematic references in the poem. For instance, the word METATHEMENON, whenever it appears, indicates a passage in Aristotle which discusses the altering of currency values. In order to read this contextless word, one must search for the anecdote, connotation or reference in other works by Pound. So the unit of composition of the poem approaches being a unit of language: a poundeme. A good number of words do not yield meaning until a special referent is discovered for them.

Pound's cantos certainly present a horizontal vista of multiple potential relations created by the juxtaposition and thematic resonance of lines. In this he is like the *Paterson* poet. But while both poets create an endless poem about change and of change, Williams was committed to a process of decreation and invention, while Pound desired that his poem should show change—once and for all. Terms such as "totalitarian synthesis" and "hierarchy of evaluation" testify to the rich verticality and didactic intention of Pound's coordinates.[56]

Pound took these risks for his poem because he wanted it to have a social function, to make the old world new. If one may properly speak of a historical time of transition, perhaps *The Cantos* are the first poem to function as a "text of transition" in a period of historical crisis. Pound's work is problematic because of its tremendous and insistent direction: he wanted to allow for the use of the work—"that I tried to make a paradiso terrestre."[57] Not, that is, the paradise of a finished or thoroughly consistent work, but a living society adumbrated, a new and total culture which existed in reality. So Pound risked the poem for the world.

Indeed, by the late thirties, Pound seems to have lost interest in the general reader, and to have wanted to use his poem as a tool to build up and fortify the new elite, which he sometimes termed *le beau monde*. This became Pound's main political reform, done through the screening process of the poetic text itself. He seems to have viewed his fragmented lines, clear images, and key facts as a special shorthand message to the elite. And the form of work is then not a fiction or story, but a series of true statements, functioning as directives to the men on the job.[58] The poetics of the ideogram gets assimilated to the politics of a real, earthly paradise. The "detached phrase"—really the syntactic unit of *The Cantos*—is the means of communication "half way between writing and action," and gives the elite "condensed knowledge"[59]:

> *Le beau monde* governs because it has the most rapid means of communication. It does not need to read blocks of three columns of printed matter. It communicates by the detached phrase, variable in length, but timely.[60]

Pound grew to justify his use of juxtaposition and fragmentation by its political usefulness to select and train an audience, and he staked all on the validation of the poem through the future historical realizations and changes which he desired. The poem is literally dependent on the future for its ending and its coherence.

Therefore the tragedy of Pound who staked too little on his poem *as* poem and too much on a narrow understanding of the historical realities with which he was confronted. Pound's *Cantos* have the shape and meaning they do because Pound's political desires overrode and negated his poetic practice. And this gradually intensifying encapsulation of the poem was the result of a profound choice made in the inter-war years in response to the disaster of World War I. Thereupon follow a series of tragic ironies. The poet who wanted the end of a symbolist poetics, the end of a hermetic poetry, the end of ivory-tower seclusion becomes more hermetic, more arcane and inaccessible than he had ever desired. The poet who wished to convert readers and energize them into action ends by sapping the readers' strength, or at least preoccupying them permanently in the very consideration of the poem. And the poet who wanted to educate a politically active elite has educated a far more inturning elite of Poundians.

But Pound's legacy is neither the hierarchy of values nor his own hectoring insistences which could be written as mottos on half a page. Rather it is the flat, vast, uncoordinated canvas of poetry into which one steps as into world itself. Pound's legacy, then, is not his content, but his struggle, recorded on the level of syntax. He is such fecund soil for poetry because he struggled so hard with the seriousness of his poetics and of his political vision, and *The Cantos* are a ragged and bloody record of that struggle—between imposed categories and immanent experiences, between kinesis and stasis, between the totalitarian and the democratic worlds, between the imposition of knowledge and the discovery of knowledge. For myself, Pound's conflict is not really reconciled in anything, least of all in his didacticism, which is finally wearying. The fact that no formula or structure can resolve Pound's major conflicts of purpose does create the formal endlessness of his poem, which is of itself interesting for contemporary poetics.[61] Yet Pound, unlike Williams, would have liked to solve that endlessness; Williams, in contrast, embraced it, stepping out of the reiterating cycles of Paterson IV into the fifth book, with the male satyr/poet and unicorn fruitfully caught in that fecund web of a thousand beautiful things—the mille fleurs. And Williams even left scattered notes for a sixth section. As for *The Cantos,* its epigraph may well be that it has "the defects inherent in a record of struggle."[62] Pound the grappler with the enormity of a vocation and an ambition—this is Oppen's Pound: the Pound of struggle itself.

The formation of meaning in Oppen occurs in linearity or forward movement, as the formation of meaning in Pound occurs by networks clotted around category. In Oppen, the reader experiences a forward pulse of language (especially marked in *Seascape* and *Primitive* which is ur-syntactic, seeking connectedness, yet asyntactic because suppressing certain conventions for connection:

> That most complex thing of syntax, of those connections which can't be dealt with outside the poem but that should take on substantial meaning within it.[63]

Oppen's poetry is built with strongly marked line breaks and a rejection of terminal punctuation in sentences: this takes place on a canvas with an uncompromising use of white space to solemnize the encounter between the chosen and the void. By consistently placing the first words of a subsequent thought on the same line with the end of the last thought, a simultaneous hovering-over and forward-pulsing is created on the scale of the smallest unit. Also, a ratio or metonymic resonance is created between the words on any given line.[64] Further, there is virtually no descriptive amplification of any unit of meaning. These tactics engender three feelings in the reader: mental weightlessness, physical density or pressure, and a sense of the void.

The mental weightlessness of this syntactic movement occurs because no thought "closes" before it gets pushed past the possibility for such closure or terminus. Freedom and terror of risk are embraced. Things are combined to create a new thought on the page: this is, of course, the stated intention of the poetics of the ideogram, or of metonymy as a production of meaning, and may indeed occur in reading Pound.

When I think about the physical density of the experience of reading Oppen, I do not mean the richness of a cultural and historical circuit, the Poundian periplum, but rather a sense of navigation itself. Say when we sailed in the boat, going from Sunset Cove to Eagle Island. George handed me the tiller. Not sure what I expected, but the sea pulled hard in every which direction. It was heavy and it pulled. The poem is then the person on the sea, steering, the sea pulling: the poem changes force and weight at every word but moves on its way, forward. Indeed, many of Oppen's poems have the sea as that force or element against which and in which all is tested. Syntactically and intellectually, the poems create a tension-filled vector: "trying to find the thought that will take us somewhere."[65]

A sense of the void is, of course, hard to describe. I am talking of the illuminated blankness before an image, an accident, an event. This is a defining moment in which the self is elected (out of its own resistances) as the explorer of that silence in which it is also dissolved. And from which it may emerge, stammering the relation of poetry to aphasia. This is the point at which Oppen's "take" on Pound (that poetry should be at least as well written as silence) becomes a serious matter of approaching a mystery of being without having to populate it with opinion and strained hope. Pound was, finally, not a poet of negative capability, for he did not want to wait:

Clarity

In the sense of *transparence,*
I don't mean that much can be explained.

Clarity in the sense of silence.[66]

An exacting and tender guide to the void occurs in a recent review by Gustaf Sobin; I will modify his terms to fit Oppen. Linearity or a sense of forward movement is achieved with the knowledge of contradictory pulls of

meaning or possibility, and by the excision of traditionally binding elements, whether in syntax, in explanation, or in ideas which might be good for the reader to absorb. This procedure creates

between or even "behind" the words an emptiness, a "void." The use of this void as *dimension* completely modified the expression of man's relationship with the world. . . .[67]

Part of what Oppen achieves is a constant set of contradictions created within syntax itself, and these are, at the same time, enactments of the ethical experiences he proposes: love and rage, alienation and populism, the singular and the multitude, the "level of art" and the "me-too of art," the children and the cataclysm. These contradictions simply continue, unresolved.[68] It is a world view quite different from Pound's. In his, one side is consciously chosen; both sides are not maintained except as dualistic and highly contrasted elements: "we know that there is one enemy."[69] In Oppen, the movement from word to word, the question where a sentence ends or whether it ends, the hovering created by removing a question mark from a syntactically created question, the multiple readings possible with intonation shifts—these are some of the syntactic ways that contradiction is organized and sustained. The contrast Pound/Oppen begins with an apocalyptic poet who thought he discovered the truth in (reactionary) revolution, who wanted to effect the sudden ending of one world and the beginning of another, and whose poem, in consequence, reads like a manifesto. He is opposed to a historical poet who inhabits time by writing as if navigating a vector of conflicting forces, whose morality it is to work for statements fit to be tested as truth, and whose poems, in consequence, read like gnomic, but lyric, philosophy.[70]

And so Oppen's poem to Pound, **"Of Hours"**—of the pulse of time moving forward—gathers force as it states the doubleness of revulsion and love at the moment when the two faced each other, almost forty years after their first meeting.

I must get out of here

Father he thinks *father*
Disgrace of dying

Pourquoi nier son père? On matters of irreducible principle, as, on the uses of the poem, on the uses of vision. And so here Oppen dramatizes his final question to Pound before the painful last word:

Old friend   old poet
If you did not look

What is it you 'loved'
Twisting your voice   your walk

This quoted word can refer to two essential moments in Pound's *Cantos*. It may evoke almost the last words on the last page of *Drafts & Fragments*.

M'amour, m'amour
        what do I love and
            where are you?

That I lost my center
        fighting the world.
The dreams clash
        and are shattered—

and that I tried to make a paradiso
            terrestre.[71]

Given Pound's realizations, one may project several responses from Oppen. One certainly is tears of empathy and grief. Another might be tears of rage. As, unkindly?—it's a little late in the game to be asking the question "what do I love."

And that the word "loved" may refer to the climax of *The Pisan Cantos* startles with the critical edge of Oppen's question and his assertion: Pound did not really look, with the acute perception which was his gift to poetry, and therefore how could he know what he loved?[72] The turn away from Pound's poetic diction (*lov'st* to *loved; thou* to *you*) may be deliberate.

What thou lovest well remains,
            the rest is dross
What thou lov'st well shall not be reft from thee
What thou lov'st well is thy true heritage
Whose world, or mine or theirs
            or is it of none?
First came the seen, then the palpable
    Elysium, though it were in the halls of hell,
What thou lovest well is thy true heritage[73]

What did Pound love? Beauty; order; the earth. But also a political order that sculpts the masses like art. And as well, a social hierarchy which privileges the artifax (leader or artist). The past, and the attempt to restore such values in the present. Understanding—but how garnered? With the exasperated tone of the autodidact, Pound has used his whole life and much of his poem to tell us: "with one day's reading a man may have the key in his hands."[74]

For Oppen, the idea of any "key" to knowledge is equally exasperating.

Wet roads

Hot sun on the hills

He walks twig-strewn streets
Of the rain

Walks homeward

Unteachable

Notes

1. George Oppen, Letter to Rachel Blau [DuPlessis], 20 October 1965. The Pound to which this unceremoniously refers is in Letter 60, to Harriet Monroe, January 1915: "Poetry must be *as well written as prose.*" *The Letters of Ezra Pound, 1907-1941,* ed. D. D. Paige (New York: Harcourt, Brace & World, Inc., 1950), p. 48.

2. George Oppen, "Three Poets," *Poetry,* 100:5 (August 1962), 330, 329, 333. This is Oppen's only review.

3. "Three Poets," p. 332.

4. "Three Poets," p. 331. Oppen does seem to be using Olson mainly to measure his own danger, for he also states that "even the poems in which one is most aware of Pound assert their own musical and intellectual life," p. 332.

5. Charles Altieri, "The Objectivist Tradition," *Chicago Review,* 30:3 (Winter 1979), 9.

6. Louis Zukofsky, "Sincerity and Objectification" (1931), cited by Altieri, p. 6; Louis Zukofsky, "An Objective" (1930, 31), *Prepositions* (London: Rapp & Carroll, 1967), p. 26.

7. For the word "poverty," see George Oppen, *Collected Poems* (New York, New Directions, 1975), p. 213. For the deer, L .S. Dembo, Oppen Interview, "The 'Objectivist' Poet: Four Interviews," *Contemporary Literature,* 2 (Spring 1969), 163. J. Hillis Miller's formulation in *Poets of Reality* (Cambridge, Mass.: Harvard University Press, 1966), p. 8, is deservedly classic, if based on that saturating sexual plunge most characteristic of Williams: ". . . the mind must efface itself before reality, or plunge into the density of an exterior world, dispersing itself in a milieu which exceeds it and which it has not made."

8. Altieri, "Objectivist Tradition," p. 15.

9. "New and total culture" is a citation from Pound which I unfortunately cannot locate.

10. In the *Exile* period, Pound proposed that there were three "parties": Marxist, Fascist, and his own, the Party of Intelligence, which was investigating both. By the mid-thirties, the Party of Intelligence had chosen fascism for various reasons, among them that "Mussolini is the first head of state in our time to perceive and to proclaim *quality* as a dimension in national production" ("Murder by Capital" [1933], *Impact: Essays on Ignorance and the Decline of American Civilization,* ed. Noel Stock [Chicago: Henry Regnery Company, 1960], p. 87). Pound personally identified with Mussolini as late as *Drafts & Fragments*; he felt Mussolini achieved in the political sphere what Pound achieved in the aesthetic, and essentially saw himself as Mussolini's corresponding half.

11. Ezra Pound, *Gaudier-Brzeska, a Memoir* (New York, New Directions, 1970), p. 144. First published 1916. I have supplied a conjectural word for the missing one.

12. *Gaudier-Brzeska,* p. 144.

13. Ezra Pound, *Guide to Kulchur* (London: Peter Owen, 1938), p. 57. Another historical definition occurs in

"For a New Paideuma," *The Criterion* X VII, 67 (Jan. 1938), 205: "the active element in the era, the complex of ideas which is in a given time germinal. . . ."

14. *Guide to Kulchur,* p. 249.

15. *Guide to Kulchur,* p. 263.

16. Hence when Dembo asked Oppen about a resemblance between the idea of a discrete series and the ideogrammic method, he received a response criticizing Pound's organization of the poem by ego; Dembo, Oppen Interview, *Contemporary Literature,* p. 170. As a further note: the Oppens met Pound at a juncture which was defining in both their political lives. By 1930, as I have already indicated, Pound was well into the romance of fascism. Mary Oppen has commented how eye-opening it was to hear Pound talk about Mussolini as "the Boss." Putting Oppen next to Pound also creates, in little, a most defining confrontation in twentieth century history: the right reactionary philo-fascist and the left revolutionary communist (later, populist).

17. Charles Altieri, "From Symbolist Thought to Immanence: The Ground of Postmodern American Poetics," *Boundary 2,* 1:3 (Spring 1973), 611.

18. Referring to Browning in a letter to René Taupin, May 1928, in Pound's *Letters,* p. 218.

19. "Talking with George and Mary about Pound," author's notes, made 16 May 1980, San Francisco.

20. These words come up in conversation as they come up in Mary Oppen, *Meaning a Life* (Santa Barbara: Black Sparrow Press, 1978), pp. 132-136.

21. Mary Oppen, *Meaning a Life,* p. 132.

22. "Talking with George and Mary." How then did Oppen "get" his Pound? To some degree it was through Zukofsky. For the Oppens and Zukofsky were the strongest and deepest friends at the time when Zukofsky was writing the important study of Pound which appeared in *The Criterion* in 1929. Further, Oppen "gets" Pound in "passages and lines. Just about the time I'm beginning to consider Pound an idiot, I come to something like the little wasp in the *Pisan Cantos,* and I know I'm reading a very great poet." Dembo, Oppen Interview, *Contemporary Literature,* p. 170.

23. Ezra Pound, Canto 116, *Drafts & Fragments of Cantos CX-CXVII* (New York: New Directions, 1968), pp. 25-26.

24. Kevin Power, "An Interview with George & Mary Oppen," *Montemora* 4 (1978), 200.

25. "The Speech at Soli," *Collected Poems.* The Friday/Crusoe reference is central to the poem "Of Being Numerous," as in sections 6, 7 and 9.

26. Pound, Canto 116, p. 27.

27. Pound, Canto 74, *The Pisan Cantos,* p. 7.

28. Pound, Canto 94, *Section: Rock Drill, 85-95 de los cantares* (London: Faber & Faber, 1957), p. 95.

29. Pound, Canto 116, p. 25. Pound continues the thought, and his personal identification with Mussolini, two pages later: "Many errors, / a little rightness, / to excuse his hell / and my paradiso."

30. See the end of Canto 93, *Rock Drill,* p. 92.

31. "Intensity of seeing," "Of Being Numerous," *Collected Poems,* p. 152; "intensity of what is," from "Giovanni's *Rape of the Sabine Women* at Wildenstein's," *Collected Poems,* pp. 91-93. In the *Montemora* interview, Oppen states, "I suppose I use the word light to mean that emotional response in that internal space" [to the light from the visible world]. (*Montemora* 4, p. 188.)

32. *Collected Poems,* p. 92.

33. "To Make Much," *Primitive* (Santa Barbara: Black Sparrow Press, 1978), p. 15.

34. "Of Being Numerous," *Collected Poems,* p. 168.

35. George Oppen, letter to Rachel Blau [DuPlessis], Sept. [Oct.?] 1965.

36. H.D., *End to Torment: A Memoir of Ezra Pound* (New York: New Directions, 1979); "Then, there is a sense of his pounding, pounding (*Pounding*) with the stick against the wall," p. 8. Oppen's poem appears in *Collected Poems,* pp. 210-212. I will cite it without subsequent reference.

37. "The phrase from Weil is, maybe, better than the poem. What she said was: 'When a hammer strikes a nail the whole force of the blow is delivered undiminished to the point of the nail. The head of the nail is the whole of infinity and the point of the nail is held against the human heart.'" *Montemora* 4, p. 199.

38. Pound's letter to Bunting, *Impact,* p. 263. "Matteotti, an exceptionally brave Socialist Deputy, exposed the electoral practices by which the Fascists had gained some 65 percent of the vote. He was murdered by Fascist toughs. The response of the still relatively free press, public and parliament was such as to shock Mussolini into the realization that he could not expect to rule without total controls." Consequently, "the one-party state moved to total control over press, judiciary, educational, trade union, cultural, propaganda, and youth activities." John Weiss, *The Fascist Tradition: Radical Right-Wing Extremism in Modern Europe* (New York: Harper & Row, Publishers, 1967), xxi-xxii. Especially pertinent is Pound's tacit confession that he did know, without learning from, the terror tactics; the reference here is to a famous one—forced diarrhea: "Nobody hit me with a club and I didn't see any oil bottles." *Jefferson and/or Mussolini* (New York: Liveright, 1935), p. 51.

39. In fact, Guy Davenport has noted that each of the first thirty cantos "either ends with the image of a city wall or tower or contains such an image. . . ."

("Persephone's Ezra," in Eva Hesse, ed., *New Approaches to Ezra Pound: A Co-ordinated Investigation of Pound's Poetry and Ideas* [Berkeley, University of California Press, 1969], p. 142).

40. *Pisan Cantos,* p. 69.

41. Wendy Stallard Flory, "The 'Tre Donne' of *The Pisan Cantos,*" *Paideuma,* 5:1 (Spring 1976), 45-52.

42. I still cannot say why Oppen uses the term "Earth my *sister*" except as "sorella la luna" had been a continual presence in the Pisan sequence, and as the wasp at the end, thought to be a Brother, is really female (and therefore, perhaps, a Sister).

43. "Arnold Dolmetsch" (1918), *Literary Essays of Ezra Pound* (London: Faber and Faber Limited, 1954), p. 436.

44. "A Visiting Card" (1942), *Impact,* p. 57.

45. "The Poem," *Primitive,* p. 14. John Taggart's essay "Deep Jewels" provides a subtle analysis of the Oppen-Blake connection. *Occurrence,* 3 (1975), pp. 26-36.

46. Dembo, Oppen Interview, *Contemporary Literature,* p. 162.

47. "Song, The Winds of Downhill," *Collected Poems,* p. 213.

48. Zukofsky, "Poetry *For My Son When He Can Read,*" (1946), *Prepositions,* p. 18.

49. Mary Oppen, *Meaning a Life,* p. 177.

50. Also to Zukofsky. With Zukofsky, Oppen sought literary comradeship, which Zukofsky later and bitterly tried to remake into a paternal-filial drama; of course Oppen resisted.

51. "Some San Francisco Poems," *Collected Poems,* p. 224.

52. In his essay on Edmond Jabès, Maurice Blanchot cites Robert Misrahi, *La condition réflexive de l'homme juif* (ed. Juilliard): "'To be a Jew' is something that cannot be defined for the cultured, assimilated Jew, except paradoxically and circuitously: by the *mere fact* of always being susceptible to gratuitous murder 'because of being Jewish' . . . ," *Montemora* 6 (1979), 80. In the *no man,* Oppen is rehearsing the otherness of Jewishness, the anonymity of war, and reparsing Pound's capture of the Odyssean moment in *Pisan Cantos:* ΟΥ ΤΙΣ is *no man,* wittily teasing his giant captor Polyphemous.

53. Mary Oppen, *Meaning a Life,* p. 173.

54. Pound, *Drafts & Fragments,* p. 28.

55. Oppen, "A Letter," *Agenda* (1973), 59.

56. *Guide to Kulchur,* p. 95; *Impact,* p. 177.

57. *Drafts & Fragments,* p. 32.

58. As in this passage from the essay "We Have Had No Battles But We Have All Joined In And Made Roads," *Polite Essays* (London: Faber and Faber, 1937), p. 55: "It may be even that the serene flow of a sentence is more exciting to the reader than are words set down in anger. But when one is not narrating? When one specifies the new life or the new temple? When one talks to the capo maestro, that is to the building foreman as distinct from making architectural pictures that one knows will remain for ever (or for ages) unrealized, one may have other criteria? Risking the END of the reader's interest when the house or palace is up?" (Il Capo was a name for Mussolini.)

59. *Impact,* p. 40; *Literary Essays,* p. 408.

60. *Impact,* p. 50.

61. What is interesting about the "abandonment" of *The Cantos* (Hugh Kenner's word on the final pages of *The Pound Era* [Berkeley: University of California Press, 1971]) is that Pound did not permanently accept the moral and emotional stance in *The Pisan Cantos,* yet could not negotiate the rest of the poem in the way he had planned. For I think the paradiso was to be a paradiso *cum* Mussolini; hence, after World War II, he was "stuck." That word, of course, comes from Donald Hall's interview with Pound, *Paris Review,* no. 28 (1962).

62. *Guide to Kulchur,* p. 135. These summary pages on Pound were written in 1975. Now Wendy Stallard Flory's just-published book has this title. My comments may be construed to "second" her use of that phrase. Any overlap in our conclusions is unintentional.

63. *Montemora* 4, p. 198.

64. "The meaning of many lines will be changed—one's understanding of the lines will be altered—if one changes the line-ending. It's not just the line-ending as punctuation but as separating the connections of the progression of thought in such a way that understanding of the line would be changed if one altered the line division. And I don't mean just a substitute for the comma; I mean with which phrase the word is most intimately connected—that kind of thing." Dembo, Oppen Interview, *Contemporary Literature,* p. 167.

65. Mary Oppen, *Montemora* 4, p. 203.

66. *Collected Poems,* p. 162.

67. Gustaf Sobin, "Review of *L'Ecriture Poétique Chinoise* by François Cheng," *Montemora* 5 (1979), 248. Zukofsky noted this "void" at the very beginning of Oppen's career. In a letter to Pound (6 March 1930) which I am citing from an unpublished paper by Tom Sharp, Zukofsky says: "[Oppen] seems to me to handle a kind of void in a way all his own—so that one excuses the posited negatives, the occasional Cummings and confused perceptions."

68. In his desire to pursue the non-ironic presence of full contradiction, Oppen recalls the Enzensberger of "Summer Poem": "Literary language has a tendency

to tie down anything that can be said. This text opposes the tendency by breaking up sentences. That is why the poem is dominated by a kind of syntax which classical grammar calls *apo koinou*: four sentence parts are related in such a way that the sentence can be read in several different ways. The repetitions in the poem serve to subject the experiences dealt with to doubt, to contradiction, to questioning." Hans Magnus Enzensberger, *Selected Poems* (Harmondsworth: Penguin Books Ltd., 1967), p. 90.

69. *Guide to Kulchur,* p. 31.

70. "It is part of the function of poetry to serve as a test of truth. It is possible to say anything in abstract prose, but a great many things one believes or would like to believe or thinks he believes will not substantiate themselves in the concrete materials of the poem." Oppen, "The Mind's Own Place," *Montemora* 1 (Fall 1975), 133. (Originally published in *Kulchur* 10, 1963). Every time Oppen talks about truth, he raises the spectre of the absolute idea; one must, I think, read the word as true-at-the-time or truth as "moments of conviction," as he said in the interview, *Contemporary Literature,* p. 161.

71. *Drafts & Fragments,* p. 32.

72. In his criticism of Pound, Oppen has emphasized the visual impact of things in the world; Zukofsky, at a similar juncture, takes up the aural: "When [Pound] asked me [in 1939] if it were possible to educate certain politicians, I retorted, Whatever you don't know, Ezra, you ought to know *voices*" ("Work/Sundown," *Prepositions,* p. 157).

73. Canto 81, *Pisan Cantos,* pp. 98-99.

74. Canto 74, *Pisan Cantos,* p. 5.

Norman M. Finkelstein (essay date 1981)

SOURCE: "Political Commitment and Poetic Subjectification: George Oppen's Test of Truth," in *Contemporary Literature,* Vol. 22, No. 1, Winter, 1981, pp. 24-41.

[*In the following essay, Finkelstein argues that Oppen resolves the conflict between his social ethics and objectivist aesthetics in his poetry through the "interpenetration of the subject's reaction to the object."*]

As an heir of modernist poetics, George Oppen, like all poetic inheritors, appears simultaneously as disciple and iconoclast. For Oppen, Pound is a fairly remote mentor and Williams is an older pioneer. The ground they broke becomes the foundation of a literary venture that both reinterprets and challenges modernist poetics on formal and ideological grounds. Oppen and his fellow objectivists may be seen as the followers of a well-established modernist tradition, a view best expressed by Hugh Kenner: "They are the best testimony to the strength of that tradition: to the fact that it had substance separable from the revolutionary high spirits of its launching. None of them makes as if to ignite bourgeois trousers. All that was history. They simply got on with their work."[1]

But while Oppen did "get on with his work," we must also consider what he brought to it: a profound knowledge of left-wing politics heightened by years of activism. When we consider his own remarks, we find that, grounded in the tradition as they may be, they also denote a position of ethical concern that is usually foreign to earlier modernist utterance: "I'm trying to describe how the test of images can be a test of whether one's thought is valid, whether one can establish in a series of images, of experiences . . . whether or not one will consider the concept of humanity to be valid, something that is, or else have to regard it as being simply a word."[2] In such statements as this, and in the whole of Oppen's poetic opus, the direct confrontation with exterior reality crucial to Pound's version of imagism and Williams' version of objectivism undergoes subjectification in explicitly moral terms. This is not to say that Pound and Williams are not concerned with the moral impetus behind the development of exteriorizing poetics. But for Oppen, refining imagist techniques and developing an objectivist poetic begins with what he calls "a part of the function of poetry to serve as a test of truth."[3]

This at first seems an odd stance for a modernist heir to assume, and indeed, the ideological quandary it presents to Oppen at the outset of his career compels a drastic solution. For the subjectivity of Oppen's concern with truth, or at least personal sincerity—"a moment, an actual time, when you believe something to be true, and you construct a meaning from these moments of conviction"[4]—goes hand in hand with extreme forms of nominalism and empiricism that demand concrete evidence for abstract assertions, especially in the field of the poem. This attitude is at its height in the early poems, when Oppen's empiricism places reality in the poem as a "discrete series," fragmented and unrelated to itself except through the poet's consciousness. As L. S. Dembo points out, "While the poet aimed to be empirical, the best he could be in actuality was true to his own perceptions—not necessarily true to the thing as it was but true to it *as encountered.*"[5] This is the paradox of objectivism, a dialectical impasse in which the goal of objectivity directs the poet back on himself and his faith in his own perceptions. Williams discovered this when he sought an objective poetry that could deal with complex political issues,[6] and Pound certainly discovered it when he departed from imagism into an increasingly more confused quest for historical truth.

But for Oppen, the young rebel determined to break with his bourgeois background, the harsh political realities of the thirties make the question of objectivity a moot point: the poet's immediate perceptions were of "fifteen million families that were faced with the threat of immediate starvation."[7] Previously, Oppen and his wife Mary had studied Trotsky's *History of the Russian Revolution,* and, on their visit to Pound in Rapallo, were chagrined by their mentor's support of Fascism and economic naiveté. Despite their youthful involvement with the arts, the next step in their careers was becoming clear. As Mary writes in her autobiography, "An appeal was made to intellectuals by the seventh World Congress of the Communist Parties in 1935 to join in a united front to defeat fascism and war. We responded to that call, and in the winter of 1935 we decided to work with the Communist Party, not as artist or writer because we did not find honesty or sincerity in the so-called arts of the left. . . . We said to each other, 'Let's work with the unemployed and leave our other interest in the arts for a later time.'"[8]

The Oppens' decision to abandon what was essentially a Bohemian existence and instead attempt to organize the unemployed as members of the Communist Party indicates one direction that the poetic consciousness may take when confronted with the ethical imperative of social action as a response to the immediate conditions of reality. There comes a point when poetry is no longer serviceable; it becomes a luxury, and therefore antithetical to its origins in the poet's thought and emotions: "There are situations which cannot honorably be met by art."[9] Oppen knows that ultimately, man formulates his political vision through an artistic response. As he says, "the definition of the good life is necessarily an aesthetic definition."[10] This "definition" is implicit throughout the poetry as a rigorously controlled but still vital Utopian impulse, quietly visionary despite the poet's professed distrust of such "subjective" matter. But in the midst of actual political struggle, the aesthetic decision upon which the creation of art is contingent must be set aside. When the circumstances change, and the poet returns to his calling, the reverse becomes true: he must "declare his political non-availability,"[11] an attitude that certainly dates back to Sidney's assertion that "the poet, he nothing affirms."

This split in Oppen's poetic identity is the legacy of the socialist realist aesthetic that dominated the artistic policy of the Communist Party when Oppen was politically active. Obviously, the young objectivist could have no truck with such an aesthetic: "The situation of the Old Left was the theory of Socialist Realism, etc. It seemed pointless to argue. We stayed carefully away from people who wrote for the *New Masses*."[12] This explains Oppen's thirty year silence, extending from his initial political involvement, through his military service in World War II, and into his self-imposed exile in Mexico during the McCarthy years.

The long silence that Oppen felt it necessary to impose upon himself can be explained in aesthetic, that is, poetic terms, as well as in the sociological terms that Oppen himself offers. Indeed, such an explanation is a necessary adjunct to what has been summarized above. Oppen argues that a desire for political efficacy must be satisfied by political action rather than being channeled into an artistic response. Yet Oppen's poetry, in that the impetus behind it is the same impetus that caused him to give up poetry, is thoroughly political, and grapples with some of the most basic and significant ethical issues that have informed political action in our time. How does the individual, locked

within his own consciousness, reconcile himself to the contradictions of contemporary society's "numerosity"? Is such a loss of subjectivity possible, or even desirable? Oppen struggles to find the ethical answers to these questions in the face of overwhelming skepticism, a skepticism justified by his immediate perceptions of the society in which he lives. For Oppen, as for Williams, the poem is a field of action, and if the action with which Oppen is concerned is political in nature, then politics perforce enters the poem. Along the same lines, Oppen condemns any notion of "the poet-not-of-this-world" and declines exhorting the poet to face reality only with great reluctance.[13] Clearly, it is in the poems, so intimately bonded to Oppen's social experience, that a resolution is sought to the dialectical tensions of skepticism and commitment the poet has confronted all his life. The totality of the poems within the life is Oppen's test of truth.

The test begins with the modernist premises of which Oppen has spoken, the moment-by-moment test of poetic integrity that the imagist position offers. *Discrete Series* (1934) is arguably the most extreme example of the imagist and objectivist tendency to isolate and examine discrete objects within the field of experience, allowing the poet to scrutinize both the object in itself and the inextricably connected reactions of the observer to that object. The loss of subjective consciousness in the diffusion of objective reality is never actually achieved, but Oppen approaches this state through the use of a highly compressed and fragmented language indicative of the willingness of the poetic consciousness to be as much dispersed among the objects it perceives as it believes the objects themselves to be. Subjective reactions to objects, such as assertions of their significance, remain in the poem, but are placed at the same fragmented level as more immediate perceptions:

> She lies, hip high,
> On a flat bed
> While the after-
> Sun passes.
>
> Plant, I breathe—
>
>   O Clearly,
> Eyes legs arms hands fingers,
> Simple legs in silk.[14]

Rachel Blau DuPlessis has schematized the philosophical movement of the typical Oppen poem, and even in such a brief lyric as this, the poet's *modus operandi* may be seen:

> The ideal relationship between perceiving subject and the perceived, real object in Oppen's poetry could be schematized as first, minimization of subjectivity, then the presence of the object, and finally, the subject's belief that the formulation the object has taken expresses some basic fact or configuration of the object. While this radical imagist or objectivist position ideally holds to total empiricism, in fact, the perceiver is only capable of a strong tendency toward that extreme.[15]

Compressed in the space of a few lines, subjectivity is reduced and the object is engaged on its own terms. Typically, the short lines break off as thoughts are left incomplete, articles and pronouns are eliminated to further the sense of immediacy, and the subject, when he does appear, merely exists, like a plant. But what is truly remarkable about this poem is its erotic subject matter, which has rarely been treated by a poet in such a spare manner. Oppen's "reportage" of emotionally charged subjects is masterful from the beginning of his career, and even when he wishes to report a subjective impression, his depiction of the situation, including his own thoughts, assumes a sense of discreteness that goes beyond even his intended irony:

> 'O city ladies'
> Your coats wrapped,
> Your hips a possession
>
> Your shoes arched
> Your walk is sharp
> Your breasts
>   Pertain to lingerie
>
> The fields are road-sides,
> Rooms outlast you.

(*Collected Poems* pp. 12–13) [hereafter abbreviated as *CP*,]

In this poem, the ladies are denoted as a series of physical characteristics, culminating in the wonderfully empirical observation "Your breasts / Pertain to lingerie." The final two lines open the poem to much wider geographical, social and historical contexts, but again, simple declarations of stated "facts" mark the piece as rigorously objectivist.

When Oppen takes his early poetic beyond the personal, he confronts the limitations of his willful reduction of subjectivity. Empirically observed fragments of reality are forced to assume meaning beyond their capacity for signification, as in the following brief poem:

> Bad times:
> The cars pass
> By the elevated posts
> And the movie sign.
> A man sells post-cards.

(*CP*, p. 13)

If Oppen is to hold to his poetic beliefs, at this point he can say no more. But the depth of feeling implied in these few lines actually demands much greater development, given the historical conditions under which they were written. Perhaps the best gloss for the poem is Mary's brief account of the Oppens' return from France in 1933: "As we approached the first stoplight, grown men, respectable men—our fathers—stepped forward to ask for a nickel, rag in hand to wipe our windshield. This ritual was repeated every time we paused, until we felt we were in a nightmare, our fathers impoverished."[16] In terms of the poem's relationship to reality, we have reached on a formal level what is equivalent to Oppen's admission of the limitations of art. The objectivist can only state the case; if that does not fulfill his purpose, he must find another means of treating the matter at hand. Hence the underlying tones of isolation and frustration in *Discrete Series*:

> From a train one sees
> him in the morning, his morning;
> Him in the afternoon, straightening—
> People everywhere, time and the work
>   pauseless. . . .

(*CP*, p. 13)

Like the passenger on the train moving through the awakening town, the poet can only catch glimpses of the life around him: he stands apart, reporting what he sees in a muted but desperate attempt at connection. In one of the few metaphorical declarations in the volume, Oppen abruptly cries, "O what O what will / Bring us back to / Shore, / the shore" (*CP*, p. 13). For a long time, the answer does not lie within the bounds of the poem.

Discrete Series is the culmination and dissolution of extreme objectivist poetry, in which the moral impetus of the objectivist stance confronts the boundaries beyond which the aesthetic it demands cannot go. When Oppen resumes his poetic career in the late fifties, a decidedly new note enters his work: the poems are imbued with a new sense of subjectivity. While the immediate experience remains the proving ground of sincerity, the poetic consciousness deliberately, even provocatively ranges through such experience, testing its perceptions against "the materials" of circumstance. Oppen's closest model for such poetry is Williams, who, in his poetry in the thirties, imbued flat description with a sense of political commitment that could be detected given the social contexts in which the poems were written, and yet kept the poems true to immediate perceptions. Hence, a piece like "Proletarian Portrait," from *An Early Martyr* (1935), which we may compare to the first section of Oppen's **"Blood from the Stone,"** in *The Materials* (1962):

> A big young bareheaded woman
> in an apron
>
> Her hair slicked back standing
> on the street
>
> One stockinged foot toeing
> the sidewalk
>
> Her shoe in her hand. Looking
> intently into it
>
> She pulls out the paper insole
> to find the nail
>
> That has been hurting her[17]
>   . . . . .
>
> In the door,
> Long legged, tall,
> A weight of bone and flesh to her—
>   Her eyes catch—
> Carrying bundles. O!
> Everything I am is
> Us. Come home.

(*CP*, p. 31)

In the first poem, description operates in such a way as to imply sympathetic concern; we see the young woman as somewhat squalid, but capable and nonchalant in the face of bourgeois propriety. The title stirs one's class consciousness, and a political value judgement is inevitable after a statement of the case. In Oppen's poem, the same kind of abbreviated portrait is followed by the poet's subjective reaction. It is a carefully reported moment of sincerity that leads to the political meditation in the rest of the poem.

Oppen modifies Williams' poetics in order to establish a style of lyric poetry in which the object and the subject's reaction to the object totally interpenetrate, thus resolving the conflict he encountered at the outset of his career. With thirty years of political experience behind him, Oppen can venture to accommodate the objectivist poem to his personal knowledge and belief. His refinement of the objectivist mode may account for his ambivalent feelings toward Williams. When questioned about the dictum "No ideas but in things," he replied: "I have always wondered whether that expression didn't apply to the construction of meaning in a poem—not necessarily that there are out there no ideas but in things, but rather that there would be in the poem no ideas but those which could be expressed through the description of things. I took it that he meant the latter until I found that the expression was frequently understood in a different way."[18] Oppen's interpretation of the phrase seems to be operative in the poems written after he broke his silence, as objects engender appropriate ideas within each poem. Oppen does not believe, as did Williams, in the simple reproduction of common speech (a fact that becomes quite clear in his recent work), but he does praise Williams for his "insistence on 'the American idiom,' on the image derived from day to day experience, on form as 'nothing more than an extension of content,' who shows a derivation from populism."[19] Oppen's quest for a poetry rooted in populism leads him to his finest work.

"Blood from the Stone" is a case in point. The poem is one of Oppen's many attempts to come to terms with his long period of poetic inactivity, and the circumstances to which the poem refers are personal reminiscences. As Williams was content to record immediate perceptions, trusting in the integrity of his vision, so Oppen is content to record his memories of events, and judge them in the light of his skeptical but sympathetic knowledge:

> As thirty in a group—
> To Home Relief—the unemployed—
> Within the city's intricacies
> Are these lives. Belief?
> What do we believe
> To live with? Answer.
> Not invent—just answer—all
> That verse attempts.
> That we can somehow add each to each other?
>
> —Still our lives.

> (*CP,* p. 31)

Here, the poet attempts to equate the moral force behind his verse with the force that impelled the organization of the unemployed in the thirties. The validity of such a comparison is left in doubt, but the conclusion, flatly stated, is still held to in faith. The final section of the poem reflects the same decision in purely ontological terms:

> Blood from a stone, life
> From a stone dead dam. Mother
> Nature! because we find the others
> Deserted like ourselves and therefore brothers. Yet
> So we lived
> And chose to live
>
> These were our times

> (*CP,* p. 33)

To make a life, to make poetry even from a "stone dead dam" may seem futile. But the decision is made, and, indeed, for Oppen there is no other choice.

The unending conflict between desire and the insufficient or repressive social formations that desire must endure in order that it may be realized increasingly becomes Oppen's central concern, both in *The Materials* and even more so in *This In Which* (1965). At times, Oppen will look into history to find the proper images for this conflict. In **"Chartres,"** the "bulk" of the cathedral becomes the all-encompassing object that has subsumed the collective desire of the generations that have sacrificed their lives to its completion. The cathedral is a monument to their desire's endurance, "Because a hundred generations / Back of them and to another people // The world cried out above the mountain" (*CP,* p. 56). But when he casts his eye on contemporary culture, he frequently sees nothing but the makings of a second "Ozymandias." As he ironically comments: "And down town / The absurd stone trimming of the building tops // Rectangular in dawn, the shopper's / Thin morning monument" (*CP,* p. 38). While the vulgarity of popular culture fails to outrage Oppen—he does not rant against it as does Pound—he cannot celebrate it either, as does Williams. Perhaps Oppen's best comment on the dilemma is the subtle **"The Bicycles and the Apex,"** from *This In Which*. Here, the "pure products of America" are contrasted with the material and spiritual detritus of latter-day capitalist society. Oppen does not simply condemn this society, however, for he realizes the dialectical necessity for progress contingent upon such a way of life. Such enlightened recognition (lacking in nearly every other recent political poet) creates a verse of wonderful delicacy and refinement:

> How we loved them
> Once, these mechanisms;
> We all did. Light
> And miraculous,
>
> They have gone stale, part
> Of the platitude, the gadgets,
> Part of the platitude
> Of our discontent.

Oppen is capable of stark moral judgements, yet his dis-criminating sense of poetic as well as political dialectics maintains a thoughtful and decidedly undidactic tone:

> Let us agree
> Once and for all that neither the slums
> Nor the tract houses
>
> Represent the apex
> Of the culture.
> They are the barracks. Food
>
> Produced, garbage disposed of
> Lotions sold, flat tires
> Changed and tellers must handle money
>
> Under supervision but it is a credit to no one
> So that slums are made dangerous by the gangs
> And suburbs by the John Birch Societies
>
> But we loved them once,
> The mechanisms. Light
> And miraculous . . .

                                              (*CP*, p. 125)

The poem vacillates; a line of thought breaks off as an-other is taken up. Oppen knows that there is no poetic resolution for such contradictions, and he is content to rep-resent the contradictions clearly, for only then does an aes-thetic totality present itself.

Clearly, in the brief lyrics of *The Materials* and *This In Which,* Oppen deals with subject matter that gradually de-mands a more expansive treatment, in which the antitheti-cal moments that the individual poems embody may in-form each other more completely within a single form. Of the two poems in series in *This In Which,* one, **"A Lan-guage of New York,"** will be expanded into Oppen's mas-terpiece, **"Of Being Numerous."** The other, **"A Narra-tive,"** may be regarded as a tentative statement of Oppen's most important theme: the reclamation of some ground of human values in the face of seemingly inevitable cultural fragmentation. This may actually be considered the domi-nant concern of all major modernists, but for Oppen the case must be stated in personal and immediate terms, out of which may emerge political and philosophical asser-tions. Thus Oppen may observe that

> . . . we will lose
> Humanity in the cities
> And the suburbs, stores
>
> And offices
> In simple
> Enterprise.

                                              (*CP*, p. 135)

The result is "The constant singing / Of the radios," a world that will not cohere even to Oppen's modified em-piricist stance, "In which things explain each other, / Not themselves" (*CP*, p. 134). Such confusion is ultimately le-thal; it leads to the most basic existential doubts, in which the isolation of subjective perceptions in a seemingly cha-otic world assumes universal, even cosmic proportions:

> But at night the park
> She said, is horrible. And Bronk said
> Perhaps the world
> Is horror.
> She did not understand. He meant
> The waves or pellets
> Are thrown from the process
> Of the suns and like radar
> Bounce where they strike. The eye
> It happens
> Registers
> But it is dark.
> It is the nature
> Of the world:
> It is as dark as radar.

                                              (*CP*, p. 138)

"Bronk" is William Bronk, as fine a poet as Oppen but with as different a sensibility as can be imagined, a poet who can declare, in "The Mind's Limitations Are Its Free-dom," that

> The mind has a power which is unusable
> and that is its real power. What else but the mind
> senses the final uselessness of the mind?
>
> How foolish we were, how smaller than what we are,
> were we to believe what the mind makes of what
> it meets. Whatever the mind makes is not.[20]

Bronk's aggressively philosophical skepticism represents only one tendency in Oppen's work, and his appearance in **"A Narrative"** serves as a reminder of the interior world of discourse that is as valid a reaction to the world as Op-pen's more dominant politicized stance. What Oppen fi-nally offers in **"A Narrative"** is the potential for "a sub-stantial language / Of clarity, and of respect" (*CP*, p. 140), thus reaffirming his belief that direct statement of an issue, at the moment of the mind's first encounter, will yield a form of integrity in a world otherwise rife with horror.

Again, however, the question arises as to the possibility of achieving such clarity, and the cost of its achievement in terms of one's relationship to the mass of humanity. This is the dilemma at the heart of Oppen's finest volume of poems, *Of Being Numerous* (1968), particularly the long title poem. Previously, in **"Psalm"** from *This In Which,* Oppen had posited the essentials of his faith in "the small nouns," the basic but isolated presences of things which in themselves deserve praise. But it is imperative for Oppen to go beyond such a quietistic position, though even in **"Of Being Numerous"** it is there to offer solace and calm. For it is ultimately an intensely personal, even isolated po-sition, and Oppen continues to dwell on the possibilities of greater community, even for the "singular" or "meditative man," the poet's projection of himself as the man who stands outside the mass but sees its circumstances more clearly. Oppen quotes from a letter he received from Rachel Blau DuPlessis, which in a sense summarizes his predicament:

'Whether, as the intensity of seeing increases, one's
   distance from Them, the people, does not also increase'
I know, of course I know, I can enter no other place

                                   (*CP,* p. 152)

But entering that place is no longer viable, either as an artist or as an erstwhile political activist:

Obsessed, bewildered

By the shipwreck
Of the singular

We have chosen the meaning
Of being numerous.

                                   (*CP,* p. 151)

The result of this "shipwreck" is actually the entrance into
an ideological no man's land where the inadequacy and
alienation of capitalist social relations are recognized, but
a genuinely communistic vision remains problematic. Such
a crisis of faith is oddly reminiscent of those experienced
by the Victorian poets, such as Arnold in "Stanzas from
the Grande Chartreuse" and Tennyson, who must move
through a series of tortuous meditations in the lengthy *In
Memoriam* before he achieves spiritual reconciliation. Oppen too must move in such a manner, and it is the cumulative power of the series poem that allows him to consider
the many possibilities of the people's "numerosity" without entirely losing his faith to his omnipresent skepticism.
Thus even the form of the poem implies a means by which
the discrete philosophical moments of the earlier lyrics
(themselves the work of a "singular" man) may be transcended in a work that is, if not "organically" whole, at
least more encompassing in the range of its politicized
meditation.

This may be seen when Oppen addresses the value of art
in the poem. He admits that the art of the singular man is
exhausted, but that what could be considered the art of the
crowd likewise lacks creative potential:

Or, in that light, New arts! Dithyrambic, audience-as-
artists! But I will listen to a man, I will listen to a man,
and when I speak I will speak, tho he will fail and I
will fail. But I will listen to him speak. The shuffling of
a crowd is nothing—well, nothing but the many that
we are, but nothing.

                                 (*CP,* p. 153)

The time-honored myth of the isolated artist and the myth
of a "people's culture" seem equally futile. Instead, the
poet turns his attention to the aesthetic experiences of others, which in reality are social experiences as well:

Coming home from her first job
On the bus in the bare civic interior
Among those people, the small doors
Opening on the night at the curb
Her heart, she told me, suddenly tight with happi-
   ness—

                                 (*CP,* p. 154)

Oppen can respond to such an experience; it is part of "the
materials" in which he has placed his love: "I too am in
love down there with the streets / And the square slabs of
pavement—// To talk of the house and the neighborhood
and the docks // And it is not 'art'". The rhetoric becomes
one of anti-art, against both the over-insulated, ultra-
refined artist, and the undifferentiated mass of experiences
of "the people." The individual's response to the mass, his
personal involvement, becomes of the utmost importance,
and Oppen speaks from experience when he declares:

Stupid to say merely
That poets should not live their lives
Among poets,

They have lost the metaphysical sense
Of the future, they feel themselves
The end of a chain

Of lives, single lives
And we know that lives
Are single

And cannot defend
The metaphysic
On which rest

The boundaries
Of our distances.

                                 (*CP,* p. 165)

Here is a potential solution to the poet's inability to reconcile himself to the aesthetic and social experience of numerosity. Not only must the poet live among the people,
as opposed to a Bohemian coterie, but he must also recognize himself and his art as part of a self-subsisting chain
of continual human creativity, despite the boundaries that
he perceives before him. No other attitude is defensible. If
the poet can locate this experience in "the one thing," the
unique image, he has attained "the level of art."

We have approached the point in Oppen's argument at
which politics, philosophy, and poetics reflect each other
so closely that he seems to speak of the three simultaneously—an achievement unmatched in contemporary
verse. Oppen's struggle to achieve a sense of identity with
the people is heroic, and such heroism is congruent with a
poetic tradition in which the poet-hero's greatest act is the
dissolution of the self into the greater selfhood of community. As Oppen confesses,

I cannot even now
Altogether disengage myself
From those men

With whom I stood in emplacements, in mess tents,
In hospitals and sheds and hid in the gullies
Of blasted roads in a ruined country . . .

How forget that? How talk
Distantly of 'The People'

Who are that force
Within the walls
Of cities

Wherein their cars

Echo like history
Down walled avenues
In which one cannot speak.

(*CP,* p. 157)

Yet Oppen can speak, and in recognition of both the human creativity he celebrates and the equally human forces of negativity he acknowledges, he declares "If to know is noble // It is ennobling," as the strength of the mind enlightens all endeavor. In a kind of rapture, the poet chants "Only that is should be beautiful," and asserts, in one of the final sections of the poem, "Surely infiniteness is the most evident thing in the world"—an idea that will manifest itself strongly in the later poems. But here, Oppen acknowledges the need to struggle for such Utopian insight. This struggle devolves on the "new generation":

How shall one know a generation, a new generation?
Not by the dew on them! Where the earth is most torn
And the wounds untended and the voices confused,
There is the head of the moving column

(*CP,* p. 166)

In a sense, the dialectic remains unresolved, for the struggle constantly renews itself, as consciousness yearns for its object, and the people yearn for a way of life whose outlines, in the midst of change, can hardly be articulated. The hope of the future, the new generation, remains forever in question, but this recognition is itself a major advance, an implicit reconciliation of Oppen's political and poetic identities.

Thus Oppen's stance is continually open, a continual confrontation with the real. Ultimately this confrontation is itself a cause for celebration, as in **"Ballad,"** one of his most beautiful lyrics, often overlooked among the more monumental poems in *Of Being Numerous*. But **"Ballad"** gains from the accumulated wisdom of the series poems. Traveling with "A poor lobsterman" and his wife, the poet realizes that "The rocks outlived the classicists, / The rocks and the lobstermen's huts" (*CP,* p. 202). The endurance and faith of these simple people express in miniature the point to which Oppen's political, philosophical, and poetic endeavors have brought him: "She said // What I like more than anything / Is to visit other islands. . . ."

In Oppen's work of the last ten years, this sense of openness has expanded to embrace his entire poetic, creating a formal situation reminiscent of *Discrete Series* but actually its philosophical antithesis. For in *Seascape: Needle's Eye* (1972), *Myth of the Blaze* (1972-75), and *Primitive* (1978), the objects of experience seem to be continually subsumed into the diffusion of the subjective consciousness, so that objects seem lost in the self, even as the self began by being lost among objects. The highly elliptical

syntax of the late volumes also resembles Oppen's earliest work, and Oppen has actually expressed some doubts as to its efficacy: "I'm a little troubled by this feeling of incoherence. I think the syntax holds, I'm not sure . . . I'm troubled by it because it's taken as being complex."[21] The verse is indeed complex, but it is a complexity not of totalizing syntax but of highly concentrated fragmentation:

Out of obscurities the sap rises
The sap not exhausted   Movement
Of the stone   Music
Of the tenement

(*CP,* p. 211)

This is from the moving **"Of Hours,"** addressed to Pound, who stands behind these recent poems as an *éminence grise,* a ghost whose own later work grew diffuse in the burden of its vision. It is perhaps too early to judge, with Oppen's opus still incomplete, whether the poet can achieve the needed "Sanity to redeem / Fragments and fragmentary / Histories . . ." (*CP,* p. 226). What remains of the balance in *Of Being Numerous* must be sought when Oppen chooses to address the most pressing and personal questions of poetic identity. In the literally scintillating **"To the Poets: To Make Much of Life,"** he follows Pound and Williams into what has become a modernist tradition, the great realm of light that stands for the overwhelming strength of immediate experience:

'come up now into
the world' no need to light

the lamps in daylight *that passion
that light within*

and without   (the old men were dancing

return
the return of the sun)   no need to light

lamps in daylight working year
after
year the poem

discovered

in the crystal
center of the rock image. . . .

(*CP,* p. 254)

With exquisite poignancy, what seems to be the entire objectivist endeavor dissolves into the greater poetic tradition, as if a purely poetic reality could for once assert itself over Oppen's resolute grasp of tangible experience.

Notes

1. *A Homemade World* (New York: Alfred A. Knopf, 1975), p. 169.

2. The 'Objectivist' Poet: Four Interviews," *Contemporary Literature,* 10 (1969), 162.

3. "The Mind's Own Place," *Kulchur,* 3 (1963), 4.

4. "Interviews," p. 161.

5. "The Existential World of George Oppen," *Iowa Review*, 3 (1972), 65.

6. See Robert von Hallberg, "The Politics of Description: W. C. Williams in the Thirties," *ELH*, 45 (1978), 132, for an analysis of Williams' political poetry that serves as a foundation for my own analysis of Oppen's relation to Williams. Von Hallberg's essay thoroughly examines the poetry of *An Early Martyr* through a skillful synthesis of formal and historical methodologies. It is the only piece I have seen on Williams to successfully locate his ideology within the framework of objectivist poetics.

7. "Interviews," p. 174.

8. *Meaning a Life* (Santa Barbara: Black Sparrow, 1978), p. 151.

9. "The Mind's Own Place," p. 7.

10. "The Mind's Own Place," p. 8.

11. "The Mind's Own Place," p. 8.

12. "A Conversation with George Oppen," *Ironwood*, No. 5 (1975), 23.

13. "The Mind's Own Place," p. 7.

14. *The Collected Poems of George Oppen* (New York: New Directions, 1975), p. 9; hereafter cited in the text as *CP*. Copyright 1934 by The Objectivist Press. Copyright © 1962, 1965, 1968 by George Oppen. Reprinted by permission of New Directions.

15. "George Oppen: 'What do we believe to live with?'" *Ironwood*, No. 5 (1975), 65.

16. *Meaning a Life,* p. 144.

17. *The Collected Earlier Poems* (New York: New Directions, 1951), p. 101.

18. "Interviews," p. 170.

19. "The Mind's Own Place," p. 3.

20. *To Praise the Music* (New Rochelle: The Elizabeth Press, 1972), p. 12.

21. "An Interview with George and Mary Oppen," *Montemora* 4 (1978), 201.

Constance Hunting (essay date 1981)

SOURCE: "'At Least Not Nowhere': George Oppen as Maine Poet," in *Paideuma*, Vol. 10, No. 2, Spring, 1981, pp. 53-8.

[*In the following essay, Hunting surveys the effects of several geographies on Oppen's poetry.*]

Oppen is such a *good* objectivist. Besides supplying money for the movement's early publishing efforts, he has remained true to its tenets as set forth by Williams and has made his poems artifacts "consonant with his day." Yet

Oppen is very much present in his poems—even if sometimes by his seeming absence. Over them, through them, broods a personality at once anguished and delicate, cryptic and open, terribly vulnerable to experience and sensation and thus occasionally brutal. It is in his Maine poems that these tensions are eased, not entirely resolved, but allowed an alleviation and hence a naturalness of expression less often permitted in Oppen's other land- and seascapes.

Why should this be so? If it is so, indeed? Or is the notion that geography affects the poet and his art merely fanciful, sentimental? Oppen is a traveller, a wanderer; is the eye of the traveller changed by what he looks upon? Here is Oppen in New York:

> The roots of words
> Dim in the subways
>
> There is madness in the number
> Of the living
> 'A state of matter'
>
> There is nobody here but us chickens
>
> Anti-ontology—
>
> He wants to say
> His life is real,
> No one can say why
>
> It is not easy to speak
>
> A ferocious mumbling, in public
> Of rootless speech

(***Collected Poems***, p. 159) [hereafter abbreviated as ***CP***]

It's all here, layer on layer, crafty vertical piling of pain ("It is not easy to speak") like stones for a tilting building. Oppen in San Francisco:

> The ocean pounds in her mind
> Not the harbor leading inward
> To the back bay and the slow river
> Recalling flimsy Western ranches
> The beautiful hills shine outward

(*CP,* p. 216)

—the lines moving in, around, and out with masterful technique and then becoming in the city itself even as the city, disjunctive, forcing:

> To naked eyes
> This city died young
> You too will be shown this
> You will see the young couples
> Leaving again in rags

(*CP,* p. 216)

And Oppen at Chartres:

> The bulk of it
> In air
>
> Is what they wanted.

(*CP,* p. 56)

In these three opening lines, in this first sentence, he begins the structure. "The bulk of it"—yes—"In air"—exactly—"Is what they wanted." Precisely. The mix of tenses in the third line could not be simpler or more effective: time resonates like a bell.

These examples seem to show that Oppen's eye adjusts itself to geography not automatically but through willed effort. He makes the geography; it does not make him. The stress is enormous and accounts for much of the power of such poems. What about Oppen in Maine? Here is the opening line of **"Product"** (*CP*, p. 40):

> There is no beauty in New England like the boats.

Again:

> There is no beauty in New England like the boats.

The line lies on the page like the horizon. If spoken, it must be in a level voice—not a monotone, for a horizon is not perfectly level. This one curves very slightly over the word "beauty." I am not going to suggest that this line was "given" to Oppen, but I will go so far as to say that its effect and its simplicity of statement indicate that he was not feeling compelled to comment on the scene before him or to manipulate his artistic binoculars or to choose an adversary or a partisan stance. It is as though the line has seen him first; has offered itself to him. What will he do now?

He is not nervous, but he is cautious. "Each itself," he begins after the necessary pause of acceptance:

> Each itself, even the paint white
> Dipping to each wave each time
> At anchor . . .

Still a bit tentative, still taking it slowly. Each by each.

> At anchor, mast
> And rigging tightly part of it
> Fresh from the dry tools
> And the dry New England hands.

The "ideas" in the "things" of the last two lines of this first section release the poet to the rest of the poem, which begins to move, motion made possible by the very freshness of "dry tools," "dry New England hands."

> The bow soars, finds the waves
> The hull accepts.

Even as "The bow soars," so the poem rises with emotional implementation of that early implicit acceptance:

> Once someone
> Put a bowl afloat
> And there for all to see, for all the children,
> Even the New Englander
> Was boatness.

First, "the boats"; then each separate boat, then one boat ("The bow soars")—then this "bowl" imagined, superimposed upon scene and recognized by us children, for we are all suddenly children under this suddenly universal sky, "Even the New Englander," that supreme dour specimen. And if "bowl," then poem, coconut shell, life represents "boatness," the essence of which is that it floats. And as each is "itself," so Oppen in and by the poem:

> What I've seen
> Is all I've found: myself.

What he's found is all he's seen; quite simply, his life, his poem.

From the indirect "New England" to plain Maine, which Oppen realizes is more complicated than it appears. In **"Penobscot,"** Oppen explores the territory with, as it were, a dowser's stick. Because of its form, rather typically Oppen in its cannily broken lines with pauses for mingling of thought and sound, the poem seems tentative:

> Children of the early
> Countryside
>
> Talk on the back stoops
> Of that locked room
> Of their birth
>
> Which they cannot remember
>
> In these small stony worlds
> In the ocean . . .
>
> (*CP*, p. 105)

Actually he is following right along behind his wand, moving towards and among such statements as "I think we will not breach the world / These small worlds least / Of all with secret names"; "Penobscot / Half deserted, has an air / Of northern age"; "It is a place its women / Love, which is the country's / Distinction." While it is true that these statements can be as complicated as we wish to make them—"breach" is a brutal word, "deserted" contains a Maine pun, "It is a place its women" sets in sound the women of Maine on a pedestal, and so on, all good poetical fun—they are also straightforward in their whole sense. They stand out like trees in the forest, or, rather, like trees in the fine mist that winds so often among them by the shore. Oppen attempts to find the source of Penobscot's essence by alternating means—to take it by surprise, perhaps. The poem is not progressive but eddying, and its ending circles towards its beginning:

> One sees their homes and lawns,
> The pale wood houses
>
> And the pale green
> Terraced lawns.
> 'It brightens up into the branches
>
> And against the buildings'
> Early. That was earlier.
>
> (*CP*, p. 107)

What is this "'It'"? The green of the lawns? The light of early morning? The quotation that was spoken earlier? By one of those women who love the place, the country distinguished by love? "That was earlier." In a sense Oppen has assimilated Penobscot; in another sense it must elude him, for the essential Penobscot of the secret name is always and forever "earlier." Oppen is not responsible for it, which is a relief to the poem and accounts for the extraordinary transcendental quality which pervades it.

The danger to the poet who is not a native, and to those lesser ones who are, is that Maine can seem simple as well as noble. When in **"Penobscot"** Oppen writes of "these innocent / People / In their carpentered / Homes," he runs the risk of sentimentality. Quaintness hovers; the faintest condescension. So in **"Ballad"** (*CP*, p. 201), which begins with the splendid "Astrolabes and lexicons / Once in the great houses—" and immediately thrusts before this vision of the past "A poor lobsterman / Met by chance / On Swan's Island," "A poor lobsterman / His teeth were bad." Upon reading these lines, a Maine native snorted, "'A *poor* lobsterman'? Huh!" Innocent people? But this is not fair to the poem:

> He drove us over that island
> In an old car . . .
>
> His wife in the front seat
>
> In a soft dress
> Such as poor women wear
>
> She took it that we came—
> I don't know how to say, she said—
>
> Not for anything we did, she said,
> Mildly, 'from God.' She said
>
> What I like more than anything
> Is to visit other islands . . .

What saves the poem, if indeed it needs saving, is the word "Mildly." A poet's choice. "Astrolabes and lexicons" is a hard act to follow, which is something of what **"Ballad"** is about; but by letting what (clearly) actually happened do most of the work, Oppen does not completely avoid the noble-simple wonder-trap. Maine can be cruel when seeming to be kind, at least to poets.

The poem **"Workman"** does not mention Maine; but it may represent the best result of Oppen's Maine experience in that it at once subsumes and releases large concerns while keeping its language of images literal and its form calm:

> Leaving the house each dawn I see the hawk
> Flagrant over the driveway. In his claws
> That dot, that comma
> Is the broken animal: the dangling small beast knows
> The burden that he is: he has touched
> The hawk's drab feathers. But the carpenter's is a cul-
>   ture
> Of fitting, of firm dimensions,
> Of post and lintel. Quietly the roof lies
> That the carpenter has finished. The sea birds circle
> The beaches and cry in their own way,

> The innumerable sea birds, their beaks and their wings
> Over the beaches and the sea's glitter.

> (*CP*, p. 41)

The carpenter is a crafter, a joiner. The hawk is a predator. The sea birds are scavengers and criers. What is the relationship among them? Say that the carpenter is the poet. The poet is a crafter, a joiner, his "is a culture / of fitting." As a human being he is between life and death, and recognizes that "dangling small beast" as a synonym for himself one day. The hawk is not a shadow but is "flagrant," caught out in his business. The sea birds may or may not be gulls, with all that the word implies wisely omitted, but they are certainly attractive in flight over the "glitter" of that symbolic sea. The poet, like them, gives utterance in his own way. The scene, then, is highly emblematical—but it is founded in actuality, rests on granitic support. The poet is a "workman," a "carpenter": Oppen suggests that such work is solemn, almost holy. Its satisfactions are implicit in the deliberate cadences of Oppen's description of his work. Craft becomes art, *is* art: solid syllables, alliteration, succession of vowels, tools building "firm dimensions."

In the poem **"Technologies"** (*CP*, p. 71), Oppen remarks, "Like hawks we are at least not / Nowhere, and I would say / Where we are." That is what poets are always saying in one way or another. In his Maine poems, Oppen also listens. Something healing in that exchange of generous geographies.

Ron Silliman (essay date 1981)

SOURCE: "Third Phase Objectivism," in *Paideuma*, Vol. 10, No. 1, Spring, 1981, pp. 85-9.

[*In the following essay, Silliman discusses Oppen's relation to several postwar movements in American poetry.*]

Objectivism's third or renaissance phase, from 1960 onward, is the most problematic of that literary movement's periods, simultaneously its most influential and least cohesive time, mixing a resurgence of interest in existing texts with the production of new writings, altering the very definition of that curious rubric as it was being used to rewrite the literary history of the thirties and forties. Its absence, the long second phase of neglect, had been marked clearly by the extremism, both in form and content, so many of the New American poets of the fifties had found necessary to bridge the distance between themselves and those twin sources of a rigorous, open-form, speech-based poetics, Ezra Pound and William Carlos Williams. Not surprisingly, the return of the Objectivists was to coincide with a tempering and toning down of just this extremism, and the formation of not so much a neo-objectivist movement as a kind of "middle road" half-way between the New American writers and those academics who'd moved on their own toward a poetry founded on speech, both in open form and syllabics. This middle road, which was first to reach the public through the *San Francisco Review,* the third series of *Origin, Poetry* during the last seven years of Henry Rago's editorship, and later through a series of tightly-edited little magazines, including *Maps, Ironwood, Occurrence,* and most recently *Montemora,* has substantially altered the contours of American verse, although it has received relatively little attention as a phenomenon in its own right.

That the revival period of Objectivism would prove less cohesive was to have been expected. Men and women in their sixties, their aesthetics and work fully formed (and, in some instances, largely behind them), have fewer needs for peer group response than do writers in their twenties. Nor, unlike first phase Objectivism, did they now have to rely on one another for publication and the other support services which normally characterize any collective literary activity.

The actual products of Objectivism's third phase are not many, but they are significant: Bunting's addition of *Briggflatts* to an essentially completed *oeuvre*; Zukofsky's return for only the second time in twenty years (there had been a period of work between 1948 and 1951) to the great poem "*A,*" composing 11 new sections and adding Celia Zukofsky's *L.Z. Masque* to finish it; Rakosi's return as a writer of short, witty, lyrical poems; and 95% of the works of George Oppen. It is this last fact, the "return" of George Oppen from decades of silence to a place *beyond* that which he had taken during the earlier periods, which fundamentally defines third phase Objectivism, transforming it from the aesthetically radical and oppositional poetry of the early thirties to a more conservative (*not,* however, politically) phenomenon which then serves as the foundation for the ensuing middle road. This transformation is registered most clearly in the recent *Chicago Review* feature on Objectivism, which is incoherent from the perspective of the first phase, but consistent with this much later view.

But there is more to this evolution than the mere addition of new poems giving one writer greater weight within a collective whole. Oppen's works, from *The Materials* to the present, are decisively different than *Discrete Series,* his first phase volume. This shift is precisely one of stance, and it may well be that a quarter century of struggle, with the constraints of daily life, marriage, parenting, with war and exile, with capitalism and its Frankenstein, fascism, render the later position inevitable. However, it is not difficult to demonstrate that it falls outside the original, loosely-held program of phase one Objectivism.[1] It is only necessary to constrast the recent work with a piece such as the review of *Discrete Series* written by William Carlos Williams (more a father figure to the Objectivists than a member) for *Poetry* under the title of *The New Poetical Economy,* which reads in part:

> The appearance of a book of poems, if it be a book of good poems, is an important event because of relationships the work it contains will have with thought and accomplishment in other contemporary reaches of the

intelligence. This leads to a definition of the term "good." If the poems in the book constitute necessary corrections of or emendations to human conduct in their day, both as to thought and manner, then they are good. But if these changes originated in the poems, causing thereby a direct liberation of the intelligence, then the book becomes of importance to the highest degree.

> But this importance cannot be in what the poem says, since in that case the fact that it is a poem would be a redundancy. The importance lies in what the poem *is.* Its existence as a poem is of first importance, a technical matter, as with all facts, compelling the recognition of a mechanical structure. A poem which does not arouse respect for the technical requirements of its own mechanics may have anything you please painted all over it or on it in the way of meaning but it will for all that be as empty as a man made of wax or straw.

> It is the acceptable fact of a poem as a mechanism that is the proof of its meaning and this is as technical a matter as in the case of any other machine. Without the poem being a workable mechanism in its own right, a mechanism which arises from, while at the same time it constitutes the meaning of, the poem as a whole, it will remain ineffective. And what it says regarding the use or worth of that particular piece of "propaganda" which it is detailing will never be convincing.

Beginning with *The Materials,* Oppen, contrary to the admonitions of this highly partisan piece of writing, has demonstrated himself to be a master in calling attention to *the importance in what the poem says.*

This he achieves through a variety of devices, the sheer number of the techniques employed making it evident that this is, in fact, a difference in position and not (as rigid adherence to the tenets of phase one Objectivism might lead one to conclude) a decay in skills brought about by decades of disuse: (1) a formal rhetorical tone, sometimes utilizing inversions of syntax or the parallel construction of examples, each punctuated with an *and,* implying a sobriety of context; (2) the use of adjectives which, value-laden, impart as much of *judgment* as they do description; (3) the use of repetition, which in Oppen's work nearly always carries the tone away from that of speech, positing a supplement of emotion beyond the content of the repeated term itself; (4) the use of spacing and silence to cast certain terms and phrases into a highly defined frame; (5) the placement of key terms at critical locales on the line itself (no one in Oppen's generation has been so sensitive to the fact that placement itself alters semantics, that the last word in a line carries the greatest weight, but that the first word carries the next, so that any line beginning *and* or *of* carries a formality beyond that of the words themselves); (6) the use of plurals or mass nouns, rather than particulars or individuals, as objects for description and discussion; (7) the actual utilization of judgmental statement in the midst of description. Several of these can be observed simultaneously in the two-stanza, fourth section of the sequence "**Tourist Eye**":

> The heart pounds
> To be among them, the buildings,

The red buildings of Red Hook! In the currents of the
   harbor
The barn-red ferries on their curving courses
And the tides of Buttermilk Channel
Flow past the Brooklyn Hardware stores

And the homes
The aging homes
Of the workmen. This is a sense of order
And of threat. The essential city,
The necessary city
Among these harbor streets still visible.

   (*Collected Poems,* p. 45) [hereafter abbreviated as *CP,*]

They are even more visible in the later poem **"Exodus"**:

Miracle of the children   the brilliant
Children   the word
Liquid as woodlands   Children?

When she was a child I read Exodus
To my daughter   'The children of Israel . . .'

Pillar of fire
Pillar of cloud

We stared at the end
Into each other's eyes   Where
She said hushed

Were the adults   We dreamed to each other
Miracle of the children
The brilliant children   Miracle

Of their brilliance   Miracle
of

                                 (*CP,* p. 229)

Note that final lower case *O.*

It is not as if no other Objectivist poet employed such devices, even to the same ends. Consider "*A*" - 10, for example. Yet none went so far as to make of them the
grounds for an entire poetics, which the Oppen of third
phase Objectivism has. One can imagine that the response
of the partisan Williams of the thirties to this stance at its
most extreme would not be positive. Who, for instance, is
the first of the two voices in the 38th section of *Of Being
Numerous,* a character created wholly out of the placement of the word *last,* the rhetorical closure of the statements via the repeated terms *You* and *Nurse,* and the increased formality gained by the final use of the word *him*
in the third stanza?

You are the last
Who will know him
Nurse.

Not know him,
He is an old man,
A patient,
How could one know him?

You are the last
Who will see him

Or touch him,
Nurse.

                                 (*CP,* p. 178)

But one must remember that Williams was a partisan to a
particular cause, that there was an entire other tradition in
American poetry which was then much more prevalent
and substantial than anything he, Pound and these young
followers had going for them. There was, in short, a battle
being waged which had largely been settled, if not forgotten, by the time *The Materials* was published, a year before Williams' death. The problem which confronted
George Oppen in the early sixties was not one of either/or,
but rather the possibility of showing that alternate, always
conservative, tendency in poetry *how it might be done better by other principles,* specifically Objectivist in their origin.

So it is not surprising that Oppen should be the bridge-
poet between the tradition known as the New American
poetry and those I have been referring to as the middle
ground, a specific accomplishment of third phase Objectivism which restructured the entire field of American
verse. Third phase Objectivism, unlike the first, was always a social fact, never a literary movement, the consequence of the resurrection of the work of Oppen, Zukofsky, Bunting, Rakosi, Reznikoff and Niedecker to public
attention achieved during a very concentrated period of
time. It is essential, in discussing any of these individuals,
to contextualize every element, its time of composition, its
time of publication, the relations between these people and
toward others, if we are to have anything other than a homogenized hodge-podge understanding as to what Objectivism, in any sense, might mean.

                              Note

1. Hopefully, in 1980, the possible counter-argument
    that Objectivism was never anything other, or more
    important, than a justification for devoting a single
    issue of *Poetry* to their work, and hence never had a
    program, is not seriously to be raised. Phase one Ob-
    jectivism (1930-35) had *all* the essential features of
    any literary movement: personal contact, a shared
    tradition, the publication of one another, even their
    own manifestoes. In fact, 50 years of practice on the
    part of Objectivists has yielded a much more unified
    corpus of literary production than that of the Projec-
    tivists, a movement whose existence is seldom if
    ever questioned. What the Objectivists lacked was
    not a movement, but *its immediate success,* and even
    here literary history has belatedly obliged them.

Hugh Kenner (essay date 1982)

SOURCE: "Oppen, Zukofsky, and the Poem as Lens," in
*Literature at the Barricades: The American Writer in the
1930s,* edited by Ralph F. Bogardus and Fred Hobson, The
University of Alabama Press, 1982, pp. 162-71.

[*In the following essay, Kenner discusses the early Objectivist poetry of Oppen and Louis Zukovsky in relation to
the socio-economic circumstances of the 1930's.*]

It was a bleak year, 1931, the breadlines hardly moving. "The world," George Oppen wrote at about that time, ". . . the world, weather-swept, with which one shares the century."[1] It was a world in which someone approaching the window "as if to see / what really was going on" saw rain falling. All of which seems easy, pictorial, the Pathetic Fallacy in fact: a rainy day as emblem for a rainy time. Oppen's poem, though, encloses the falling rain amid many syntactic qualifications, and our first sense of it is apt to be not of an image but of a single sentence so intricate we're never quite sure we've grasped it whole.

> The knowledge not of sorrow, you were
>   saying, but of boredom
> Is—aside from reading speaking
>   smoking————
> Of what, Maude Blessingbourne it was,
>   wished to know when, having risen,
> "approached the window as if to see
>   what really was going on";
> And saw rain falling, in the distance
>   more slowly,
> The road clear from her past the window-
>   glass————
> Of the world, weather-swept, with which
>   one shares the century.

This is the untitled first poem in Oppen's **Discrete Series** which the Objectivist Press published in 1934, and having just carefully copied it out I'm aware anew that it's virtually impossible to reproduce it from memory with perfect accuracy, although it clings to the memory. It is full of seemingly arbitrary decisions. How many lines has it? Seven? Fourteen? I was about to say it had seven capital letters, making the other seven elements look like runovers, but even that isn't true, since "approached," in a flush-left position, lacks a capital. And the dash after "Is," like an open parenthesis, promises a mate it never finds, the poem's other two dashes being twice as lengthy. We may eventually want to elide all the poem's middle, and read for its kernel sentence just the first twelve words and the last ten:

> The knowledge not of sorrow, you were
>   saying, but of boredom
> Is . . .
> Of the world, weather-swept, with which
>   one shares the century.

When we do that we're aware of three persons, the speaker, "you," and "one," to which cast of characters the elided middle section adds a fourth, Maude Blessingbourne (someone we know?—perhaps) and even a fifth, whoever spoke the words, carefully attributed by quotation marks, that say how Maude moved, having risen. To be told that Maude Blessingbourne is to be found in Henry James's "The Story in It" makes less difference than you'd expect.

I'll not labor this, though I could linger on the syntax, its careful engineering, its look of improvisation. I'll say only in summary that more and more comes out of the poem as we linger with it, and that though at first glance it's apt to

seem built around a glimpse of someone at the window glimpsing emblematic rain, it turns out to create a populous, complex, difficult world for its gray mood to pervade. A Discrete Series, Oppen later explained, is a series of numbers wherein no rule permits one to guess the next term; his example was 14, 18, 23, 27, 33, which looks arbitrary but in fact corresponds to the stops of the uptown Manhattan subway: the numbers, you see, dictated not by numerical laws but by history, by long-forgotten accidents of city planning. So the poem's words, this analogy implies, are specified neither by prosodic laws nor by syntactic, but by a complex reality to which it is faithful. And this is why it is so difficult to memorize its local accuracies, since mnemonic systems are guided by poetic symmetries this poem invokes only to evade them.

The February 1931 *Poetry* printed Louis Zukofsky's "Sincerity and Objectification," with its homemade lexicography:

> *An Objective: (Optics)—The lens bringing the rays*
> *from an object to a focus. That which is aimed at.*
> *(Use extended to poetry)—Desire for what is objec-*
>   *tively*
> *perfect, inextricably the direction of historic*
> *and contemporary particulars.*

This is worded to guide future dictionaries, and among other things states that the poem deals with particulars, among which the historic and the contemporary are inextricable, like those forgotten Manhattan determinations, commercial, social, architectural, which today's subway stops register.

"Each word," Zukofsky went on to say, "in itself is an arrangement, . . . each word possesses objectification to a powerful degree." A one-word poem, even, seems thinkable, and not the least strange moment in that anthology of strangenesses, Zukofsky's long poem "A," is the appearance, after fifteen movements spread through several hundred pages, of a sixteenth movement that has only four words, carefully disposed on white space.[2] "The objectification which is a poem, or a unit of structural prose, may exist in a line or very few lines," Zukofsky had written in 1931; still, "the facts carried by one word are, in view of the preponderance of facts carried by combinations of words, not sufficiently explicit to warrant a realization of rested totality such as might be designated an art form." That nevertheless the one-word poem is a thinkable lower limit is a fact to remind us that words, one by one, encapsulate "historic and contemporary particulars." Speaking of his collected short poems, Zukofsky said, "The words are my life." And he said in the same statement that the poet's form "is never an imposition of history, but the desirability of making order out of history as it is felt and conceived."

For the endlessly surprising thing about Zukofsky and Oppen, ministering to the bewilderment that has attended them from their first publication until now, is their balance between verbal algebra and the demands of what they could not pretend to control. The predominantly verbal poet, of whose ways Swinburne may serve as example, feels obligated to no such balance, writing for instance "in a land of sand and ruin and gold" with no need to imagine that land, its time, its name, its geography, content so that word leads into word, offsets word. On the other hand, writing enthralled by a subject's particularities may be graceless, settling for lurid fact: "The blown-up millions— spatter of their brains / And writhing of their bowels and so forth." (That is Browning.) Still, either convention is clear and gives readers no difficulty. The exacting objectivist ambition was to keep the poem open to the entire domain of fact, and simultaneously to keep it a thing made of words, which have their own laws.

The domain of fact, moreover, had received its exegete in Karl Marx, and of nothing were Zukofsky and Oppen more fully persuaded in 1931 than of the pertinence of dialectical materialism to all human experience. They had what hindsight discloses to be complementary but classic revolutionary backgrounds. Oppen (who had the money for a while to grubstake their publishing activities) was born in 1908 into a family sufficiently affluent for repudiating affluence to seem a matter of conscience, while Zukofsky was born in 1904 into a working-class, Russian Jewish family—its only member to be born in America—and in due course got radicalized at Columbia College in the 1920s. He was close to Whittaker Chambers, in whose *Witness* he figures as "the guy with the eyebrows," after the suicide of Chambers's brother "Ricky" wrote an elegy that is now the third movement of "*A*," and was recruited by Chambers for the party.

There followed a Keatonian comedy. He was taken to a meeting like a scout for induction and aroused the suspicions of shrewd Ma Bloor herself. She had vehement doubts of his proletarian credentials ("My father pressed pants all his life," he would interject, telling the story). He was a bourgeois intellectual, was her verdict. Willow-slim, pulled forward as if by the weight of his own eyebrows, he seemed an implausible stormer of any moneyed Bastille, not even a forcible pusher of leaflets. Ma Bloor's verdict was final, and Zukofsky, debarred from membership, soon cooled in fervor though he retained a lifelong respect for Marx's intelligence. As for Oppen, after *Discrete Series* (1934) he dropped poetry for a third of a century, organized workers, also moved to Mexico, where he lived as a cabinet worker and tool and die maker.

Anyhow reality, for these young men when they were in their twenties, was dialectical materialist reality: the sensible, physical world interacting with physical brains. How to make poems from that? Hymns to The Worker might have been acceptable, but bombardment of the senses by particulars disclosed no apotheosizable Worker—what Walter Lippman, in a genial gibe at John Reed, had called "a fine statuesque giant who stands on a high hill facing the sun." Poetry, moreover, existed, like all things, in history, which by 1931 had disclosed certain things about its nature.

Words move, exist, in time; and the formal problem of the poem may be described in this way: How may a work strung out in time justify its beginning, its ending, and its progress from its first word to its last? There appear to be several main ways. The poet can tell a story, like Homer or Wordsworth. He can construct an argument, like Lucretius or Donne. He can follow the promptings of a tune, like Sappho or Swinburne.

A fourth, less canonical way is to make as if to describe a picture, as Rossetti did in "The Blessed Damozel"; continue till its detail is accounted for; then stop. This had been a satirical mode; it is related to the ancient convention of the character sketch and underlies Chaucer's portraiture in the General Prologue. More than one satire of Marvell's is headed, "Instructions to a Painter."

The story, the argument, the tune, the picture. But novels had long since preempted the story, making versified stories seem quaint (one senses that Edwin Arlington Robinson in *Tristram* is struggling with a dead convention). And the knack of interesting argument in verse was long ago lost, perhaps with the mathematicization of argument, which made verbal equivalents seem either cumbersome or slick. Music—the tune—had been Ezra Pound's recourse, the poem prolonged till it fills out and resolves a melodic figure its first words imply, and in the long run it was to be Louis Zukofsky's guiding analogy likewise. But in 1931 he pointed out what was to be the underlying procedure for the short "Objectivist" poem, writing "An Objective (Optics)—The lens bringing the rays from an object to a focus." As the first great decade of social photography opened, the decade of Dorothea Lange, Walker Evans, Margaret Bourke-White, the poem was directed to work, with leisured sophistication, like the photograph.

This seems, in retrospect, a natural development of the dominant verbal movement of two decades before, socalled imagism, in 1931 only eighteen years in the past. "An Image," Pound had said, "an intellectual or emotional complex in an instant of time." He had probably not been thinking of the snapshot, but nothing in his formulation precludes it. Imagism, William Carlos Williams was to remark, had, however, "no formal necessity implicit in it." By the 1930s it had long since "dribbled off into so-called 'free verse,'" and the poem had become "formally nonextant," stopping arbitrarily after being shaped haphazardly.[3]

To think of rays being brought to a focus, though, is to think of a necessary configuration, its geometry obligated by physical laws. Through the lens stream photons responsive to the randomness of the physical world, the world that is simply *there*: "historic and contemporary particulars." They impinge on the plate, arriving (if all is well) at a focus when they are just where the plate is. Not all of the random given world is entailed, only what the geometry of circular ray-cone and rectangular plate can comprise together. And the resultant image, fixed in chemicals, drained of color, is arrayed in massed patterns of mono-chrome, with, however trivial the subject, the special au-thority of law. And, for the camera as not for the painter, there are no trivial subjects: it receives all equally, accords equal status to all. And resolving the patterns of mono-chrome into a "picture" is a culturally learned skill: sav-ages cannot do it, and typically see in photos "of" them-selves about what the casual reader sees in a Zukofsky poem.

The "image" of imagism, for Pound an almost mystical perception, was apt in lesser hands to degenerate into a picture. Objectivist intuition forfended that particular de-generation—Zukofsky is the least pictorial poet one can think of—because its analogy for the poem was not the photograph but the photographic process, recreated in slow motion. This process is restricted to today's world (there were no photographs before there were cameras), and to-day's world's prime realities, though technological, may receive mysterious inflection from human presence: you can tell an Oppen poem as you can tell a Dorothea Lange photograph, though neither Oppen nor Lange in the old declaiming way has made a statement, and Lange's kind of camera is available to anyone much as Oppen's brain is anatomically indistinguishable from anyone else's ("nerves, glandular facilities, electrical cranial charges," wrote Zukofsky of the organism—his own—that shaped the words we are reading about it).

Photographs introduced representational art to a new theme, the indifference of the subject. Zukofsky's "To my wash-stand" (1932) is a sharp-focus monochromatic study of something that would no more, once, have attracted po-ets than a plumbing fixture would have attracted painters:

> To my wash-stand
> in which I wash
> my left hand
> and my right hand
>
> To my wash-stand
> whose base is Greek
> whose shaft
> is marble and is fluted
>
> To my wash-stand
> whose wash-bowl
> is an oval
> in a square
>
> To my wash-stand
> whose square is marble
> and inscribes two
> smaller ovals to left and right for soap . . .

We can imagine all that in a fine glossy black-and-white eight-by-ten: it is part of the new sensibility of the 1930s. And so is the close-up of a cracked tile that can look like a face:

> . . . so my wash-stand
> in one particular breaking of the

> tile at which I have
> looked and looked
>
> has opposed to my head
> the inscription of a head
> whose coinage is the
> coinage of the poor
>
> observant in waiting
> in their getting up mornings
> and in their waiting
> going to bed
>
> carefully attentive
> to what they have
> and to what they do not
> have . . .

The poem ends,

> an age in a wash-stand
> and in their own heads

—"inextricably the direction of historic and contemporary particulars." Neither the poem nor the fugue of attention it reenacts would have been thinkable before that decade: a decade partly characterized by poor folk who rise and go to bed and have maybe no amenity for keeping themselves clean—not even anything as simple as that. This wash-stand comes to seem a luxury, even, and one operative word, emphatic as early as the first line, is "my." Zukof-sky's cosmos pivots on little worlds.

Oppen in *Discrete Series* was less hermetic if not less subtle; the poems go by like snapshots in an album.

> Bad times:
> The cars pass
> By the elevated posts
> And the movie sign.
> A man sells post-cards.

And:

> It brightens up into the branches
> And against the same buildings
> A morning:
> His job is as regular.

And:

> Town, a town,
> But location
> Over which the sun as it comes to it;
> Which cools, houses and lamp-posts,
>   during the night, with the roads——
> Inhabited partly by those
> Who have been born here,
> Houses built—. From a train one sees
>   him in the morning, his morning;
> Him in the afternoon, straightening——
> People everywhere, time and the work
>   pauseless:
> One moves between reading and re-reading,

The shape is a moment.
From a crowd a white powdered face,
Eyes and mouth making three——
Awaited—locally—a date.

These glimpses, carefully composed and accented, enforce nothing save a certain emptiness. Men exist in the physical world, always have: but exist now aimlessly, going as their machines go, their images going as their glass surfaces go:

Closed car—closed in glass——
At the curb,
Unapplied and empty:
A thing among others
Over which clouds pass and the
        alteration of lighting,
An overstatement
Hardly an exterior.
Moving in traffic
This thing is less strange——
Tho the face, still within it,
Between glasses—place, over which
        time passes—a false light.

That was how it was; and as to how the poems were, they bespoke the 1930s in a certain necessary thrift, using every word impartially, notably the little monosyllables: *place, over, which, time, passes, a, false, light.* . . . That semantic monotone declares a decade, marking such poems off sharply from the shaggy diction of Williams a decade earlier, with his "reddish, purplish, forked, upstanding / twiggy stuff of branches and small trees," much as their lenslike objectivity has replaced Williams's brio and zest.

Small words of course were part of the young century's mystique. Perhaps remembering how Stephen Dedalus feared "those big words which make us so unhappy," Ernest Hemingway made his Lt. Henry declare that words such as *glory, honor, courage, hallow,* were obscene. Hemingway implied that small words were more honest because closer to the testimony of the senses. Oppen thought rather that little words were potent because we are sure what we all agree about when we use them: without them, he has said, we really are unable to exist. "I believe that consciousness exists and that it is consciousness of something," and we share consciousness most fully in words like *sun* and *stone* and *grass.* He wrote in the 1960s of how we manage with less substantive words, making do as we always must:

The steel worker on the girder
Learned not to look down, and does his work
And there are words we have learned
not to look at,
Not to look for substance
Below them. But we are on the verge

Of vertigo.

There are words that mean nothing
But there is something to mean.

Not a declaration which is truth
But a thing
Which is. It is the business of the poet
"To suffer the things of the world
And to speak them and himself out."

"But there is something to mean:" yes: and Oppen is always accessible because some substantial perceived thing is always there. Zukofsky, more philosophically inclined by far, a lifelong reader of Spinoza and in later years a connoisseur of the spiky Wittgenstein, was fascinated by the little words that do not even name: the prepositions, the articles. "To my washstand:" *my* is a pivot word, and so is *to,* commencing as in "An Ode to . . ." and altering its import part way through the poem. At twenty-three, perhaps remembering that Pound had begun the *Cantos* with "And," Zukofsky wrote "Poem beginning 'The'" and got Pound to publish it in the *Exile.* That was perhaps a mite cheeky. But his lifelong work called "*A,*" a poem fascinated for close to fifty years by the intimate processes of language, pours the public and private events of half a century—"inextricably the direction of historic and contemporary particulars"—through an intricate grid of rules as austere as Euclid's, dominated by the taxonomies of the indefinite article, which says of everything that it is "a" something, itself yet one of a kind. As late as 1938 Marx was still supplying "*A*" with materials, but by then no hope lingered, if there had ever been any, that the poem would make a difference to the masses. Zukofsky had by then become the most hermetic poet in the American language: as hermetic as Mallarmé: an odd destiny for a poetic that had once meant to register objectively the social and material world of the dialectic. Oppen's poetry, though less difficult, has no more hortatory relevance. When he turned full time to activism he simply gave writing up, for decades.[4]

How poetic language may be related to social change remains an unsolved question. It may be that there is no such thing as social change, that such a phrase gets uttered only in the throes of romantic dream, that only details can change, and techniques, and formulations. Still, Ma Bloor was clearly right to reject the guy with the eyebrows, and Oppen to choose years of silence. The only American poetry that had its roots in the 1930s brought the premises of the decade—objectivity, comprehensiveness, literature exact as science—to conclusions no one intuited any better than Ma Bloor, and that histories still pass over in baffled silence.

Notes

1. Oppen's poems are found in George Oppen, *Collected Poems* (New York: New Directions, 1975).

2. Louis Zukofsky, "*A*" (Berkeley and Los Angeles: University of California Press, 1979). See also Louis Zukofsky, *All, 1923-58* (New York: W. W. Norton, 1965).

3. William Carlos Williams, *Autobiography* (New York: Random House, 1951), p. 264.

4. For further light, see L. S. Denbo's interviews with both poets in *Contemporary Literature* 10 (1969): 159-77, 203-19; L. S. Denbo, "The Existential World of George Oppen," *Iowa Review* 3 (Winter 1972); and special issues devoted to Oppen and Zukofsky respectively by *Ironwood* 3, no. 1 (1975) and *Maps* 5 (1973).

Michael Heller (essay date 1985)

SOURCE: "The Objectivist Tradition: Some Further Considerations," in *Conviction's Net of Branches: Essays on the Objectivist Poets and Poetry,* Southern Illinois University Press, 1985, pp 97–106.

[*In the following essay, Heller explores the poetics of Objectivism.*]

George Oppen states in the opening passage of *Of Being Numerous*:

> There are things
> We live among 'and to see them
> Is to know ourselves.'[1]

Among "things" we live with, see, and come to know ourselves by are the poems of our time. For poetry, Heidegger reminds us, is an act which founds whole historical worlds. An Objectivist poetry, involving a poetics more or less subscribed to by a group of poets labeled Objectivists, who were in constant contact with each other over three or four decades, founds its Heideggerian historical worlds in "rested totality," Zukofsky might claim, in sincerities and objectifications as fields of possibility rather than in strictures on form. For we live in an age, Zukofsky tells us, "that will not bear too regular a form," an age saturated with the revolutionary thought of Einstein and Heisenberg pressing at our backs, an age in which our Nietzschean "eternal recurrences" manifest themselves as variations on an as-yet-to-be-revealed theme. Poetry in such a time is the music of indeterminacy; George Lukacs warns us in *Soul and Form* that it now "consists of the dominance of the accompaniment over the solo voice."[2] Poems and poetries no longer successfully enter into our lives as wisdom, as they did in the nineteenth century, but as occasions and registrations of being wise or unwise, lucky or unlucky, within time and event. Our poems require a resemblance to instantaneously gathered *sensibilia,* contradictory and competing gestalts, perspectives, apprehensions in time. They seek to express what D. H. Lawrence called "poetry of that which is at hand: the immediate present." Judgment has a lighter hand in these matters.

And therefore, we are right to conjure the contemporary poet nearly as a kind of relativist, operating within a field of relations, a relativist, that is, until the poem finds its moment of closure and the absolute of "this is what it meant to me" is pronounced. And how different is this absolute from the wisdom-dispensing poems of the past, from the hectoring urge of moral applicability.

With Aristotle, then, we may conjecture that a distinction exists between the orderings of the historian or scientist and those of the poet. But this too is no longer the simple case of being subject to different laws and different mental operations. Rather, what we must say of the poem, finally, is that it is subject to different intentions. For if the historian's or scientist's world is an arrangement, an ordering with "order" in mind, i.e., something of a *fait accompli,* an articulated design, the "historical" world founded by the poem is a gratuitous array, a mixed field of forces across the human disciplines, a product of the poet's willing entrance or submission to the world and to its mutually compelling systems of thought. It seeks out, again in Lawrence's words, "the pure relationship with the living universe." The poem then, to the extent that it is less constrained than the disciplines, is the result of the interaction between the live poet and random or inarticulate promptings of both world and language. The poem, in this sense, is before the fact, created by virtue of a methodological difference with other forms of knowledge.

This difference is explored and lived through, in one way or another, with the Objectivist poets. Oppen, for example, claims in *Notes on Prosody?* that "the poem is NOT built out of words, one cannot make a poem by sticking words into it, it is the poem which makes the words and contains their meaning."[3] Where then is the representation, the "thing" (the scientific formula or history's image of an age) to be represented? If we follow Oppen, what we seem to arrive at is a new compact between poet and poem, not new as an invention perhaps but as a discovery; for the Objectivist poem does not enact a mimesis but mediates between representational systems. It is subject, like the King's subject, to thought; it is, to modify Heiddegger's influential phrase, the clearing house of other knowledge. Objectivist practice would seem to be a constant shunning of any systematic ethos; having fallen under the sway of our newest understandings, it is part of what Géfin calls, in *Ideogram,* "the accurate artistic expression of this posthumanist reality."[4] The Objectivist poem lacks the soundingboards of even our recent poetic past, the agrarian backtracking of the Fugitives, for example, or the politicized Anglicanism of Eliot. It foreswears the archaic as an idealized poetic world, thus marking itself off from the works of Olson and the ethnopoetic poets. Yet Objectivist poetry is not at all comfortable with the deterministic Freudianism of so much contemporary domestic poetry either. The Objectivists, and this is a critical if not poetic difficulty, lean into uncertainty. The test qua test of their poetry, applied by the poet, is in this feeling of being on the edge. Oppen sums it up precisely: "When the man writing is frightened by a word, he may have started (writing a poem). . . ."[5] This is to be composing poetry at the horizon of knowledge, never out of touch with thought but at what Heidegger refers to as "the boundary of the boundless."

Objectivist poetry is, therefore, not a thought *about* something but thought itself (language, statement, poem), already "perfect" in the sense Wittgenstein once used the word as a synonym for completed, i.e., something in accordance with Oppen's "that which cannot not be understood."

Zukofsky's procedures may be said to take up this same problem in another way, for Zukofsky's attentiveness is, in a sense, spatial; his poems are a compositional space, a place for the interaction of a multiplicity of thoughts, feelings, and facts, which are, in the poem, continually weighed, checked, and balanced. The poem is not an afterthought concerning these materials, but the very process of their mediation. The English critic Eric Mottram writes of Zukofsky that "his experience is order because the poem articulates it."[6]

Out of such "order" come new possibilities of knowledge. Just such a point and its concomitant implications are developed by William Carlos Williams in his *Embodiment of Knowledge*. And Aristotle's denigration of history, that is, "poetry is graver," before the poet's workings seems to involve a similar consideration.

Objectivist poetry, in the argument I am constructing here, is, first of all, a test of other articulations, of other lingual expressions. And since it is not *a priori* thought out in the realm of other discourses, its issuance, when laid alongside other discourse, is violent and creative. For, like all significant poetry, Objectivist poetry is an uncertain element, a slightly foreign body, brought into relation with existing world-views, knowledge and other poetries. Its perturbation with respect to other thought, its disturbance in the data-bank, is two-fold: not only will the poem, nonconforming as it is, be difficult to categorize or rationalize, but the knowledge, which may be said to radiate from it once it is taken up as both literary artifact and lived occasion, may displace or alter already existing knowledge. Perhaps the only test of poetry in this age of proliferating poets and shrinking numbers of readers, a test surely applicable to the Objectivists, is to consider whether the poem, no matter how self-harmonized its parts, creates disharmony, disquiet, openings or irruptions in conceptual knowledge.

True, this idea, proposing contrasts in the orderings of poetry and science, has its own oddity. For poems, of course, are the conspiratorial intertwinings of man and *logos*; this latter word is used here instead of "word" or "language," as with Heraclitus, to suggest large-scale inspirings or to recount, as the philosopher Hans-Georg Gadamer wishes to remind us, that "our finitude as human beings is encompassed by the infinity of language."[7] The writer (poet) then is not a user of the tool "language" but is a kind of idiom (Merleau-Ponty's formulation) or a genre. And the production of the poet, whose only law is the questioning of his own habit of mind, can be distinguished from that of the scientist because the latter's agenda involves an attempt to rationalize lived experience into law. In Merleau-Ponty's words, "science manipulates things and gives up living in them."[8]

What can be said of science may also be said of conventional notions of the poetic tradition: the typology of canon formation, the classification of authors, and so forth, like the generalizing and abstracting laws of science, present the history of authorship as the history of repertoires of devices and effects. The Objectivist sense of tradition, most clearly enunciated by Zukofsky, is a history not of old or new cookiecutters but of articulated mind-body states, of capacities to "tune in" on the "human tradition." This tradition, a response to felt needs, to "keeping time with the pulse of existence," and not to the representations of the classroom or writing workshop, is what informs an individual poetic talent. We do not stand, as we discover, on Dante's *terza rima,* but on Dante himself.

It is here that the dynamic tension of past-present becomes interesting. For what distinguishes Objectivist work is its sensitivity to the spirit of the tradition as a whole, not to any particular instancing of it. The poet does not choose between techniques, genres, stances, fashions, for such choosing would be self-limiting. Rather, rightness or aptness of craft entails or involves the largest of aspirations since, for the Objectivist, in this case Zukofsky, "the scientific definition of poetry can be based on nothing less than the world, the entire humanly known world." Craft then means an aspiration which would make it possible that "the whole art may appear in one line of the poet or take a whole life's work in which to appear."[9] Thus, Zukofsky, in "An Objective," disassociates himself from the ordinary concepts of taste and canon-making to embrace the largest possible meaning of tradition.

> Only good poetry—good an unnecessary adjective—is contemporary or classical. A standard of taste can be characterized only by acceptance of particular communication and concerned, so to speak, whenever the intelligence is in danger of being cluttered, with exclusions—not with books, but with poetic invention. The nothing, not pure nothing, left over is not a matter of 'recencies', but a matter of *pasts,* maybe *pasties.*
>
> It would be just as well then dealing with 'recencies' to deal with Donne or Shakespeare, if one knew them as well as a linguistic usage not their own can know them.[10]

The informing elements of a new tradition, its particular "recencies," knowledge, a sense of history and the prior traditions of which one is a part, are gathered as a unique occasion of work and thought in the Objectivists. This tradition, as it too becomes visible and so enters into dialogue with our various poetries, is particularly powerful and suggestive. We could call this the tradition's "conviction," its believability not as truth but, as Oppen defines it in **"Of Being Numerous,"** as

> Clarity
>
> In the sense of *transparency,*
> I don't mean that much can be explained.
>
> Clarity in the sense of silence.[11]

The mind is quieted in its peace, in the poem's "rested totality," which, though true to the "science" of poetic tradition, may not amount to much as Science or Reason. Oppen further maintains that the poem seeks to satisfy "not truth but each other." Its form is closer to love than intellectual dominance. Thus, the sense of conviction which it bears emerges not out of the older, human-centered sense of mastery of experience, a kind of humanist arrogance, but out of its show of vulnerability, out of the poet's willingness to enter experience disarmed and to relinquish the dictates or niceties of form when form threatens the sincerity of expression. As in the throes of love, the poet not only breaks with received forms (in this case, of the poem) but with the form of his own mind-set, his self-image as poet. This is not avant-gardism but blunt need or desire for clarity. At the level of the poem, this is a willingness, as Oppen has written, "to refuse the trick of gracefulness."

In this sense, the Objectivists can be said to work against the twin notions of the poem as autonomous object and indeterminate artifact. Objectivist art, both as theory and practice, is an art always *in relation*. The cadence of a Zukofsky or Niedecker poem, for example, its urging to sing or say "out of deep silence," implies not a telegram to or from the void, but a formalized wish to bridge the difficult gap between poem and reader. The poem's tight rhythms, as they animate the reader, interfere with the urge to distance or symbolize the "contents" of the poem. Objectivist poetry, with its leaps of thought and perception, as in Oppen or Rakosi, often requires the reader to "fill in" the gap, to extrapolate or think around the materials of the poem's images. In Reznikoff, the denial of conclusiveness, the desire to be resolutely evidential, opens the space for the reader's judgment or interpretation. The gap or lacuna, the leap across linguistic space, is not simply a flag or marker to indicate how the material of the Objectivist poem is to be read but is, in effect, the arena for discourse and participation. In such a discourse, history is again a form of knowledge and interpretation (an object of knowledge which can be approached) rather than a form of destiny or dictatorial mandate. The Objectivist poem does not aspire to autonomy but to something closer to the "I—Thou" connection put forth by Martin Buber: "Primary words do not signify things but they intimate relations. Primary words do not describe something that might exist independently of them, but being spoken they bring about existence.[12] Conviction, then, is a net of branches, an entangling in music (Zukofsky and Niedecker), or an expression of lines of sight made lingual (Oppen and Rakosi). Thus, Objectivist poetry rescues the image from both its literary theatricality and from its implied status as a datum of science by transforming the "out there" into Zukofsky's sense of "living with things as they exist." Such a poetry adds to sight the burden or savor of communication, of intersubjectivity, of words as human arousal (my self, my other).

In Objectivist poetry, Aristotle's vexed views concerning history and poetry are mediated and in a sense reconciled. The relationship between history and poetry has always been a troubling one. The example of Pound . . . is useful to contemplate here. According to Kenner, in his discussion of the Objectivists and Pound in *A Homemade World,*

the "requisite objectification" was present, in Pound, nearly from the beginning, but the "sincerity," the felt weight in pain and loss, the cost of historicizing, of Pound's imagining, appeared only with the *Pisan Cantos*. (This is, of course, a critical shibboleth, but the cliché has its core of hard truth.)

Pound, until the *Pisan Cantos,* reorders and displays historical elements until "all ages are contemporaneous," until his poem "contains history." Objectivist "history," by contrast, is cumulative, embedded in the meanings behind words and signaled by the cadence or music in which they are embedded; the poem, not history, is accurately "tuned" as a result of the poet's knowledge of the historical "association" in the word. History is less like a lesson than a pressure; as with the terminology of Objectivist poetics, it is meant to translate man for the present. The backward "golden age-ism," the quest for the archaic or primordial moment, the Adamic speech act, is conspicuous because of its absence in Objectivist poetics. Instead one confronts a present dynamic awareness of historical accretion in which no outcome is assured, no particularized rule, model, or standard is issued by which to live. The contemplation of history, as with Rakosi's contemplation of form, leads ultimately to "the existential world."

Objectivist poetry, it seems, would substitute for the historical lesson a kind of time-bound adeptness. The poet's precise function is in arriving at—not in dictating—some language (the poem) which embodies a skillfulness in apprehending the present. Thus, one can look at Objectivist poetics as honing insight, as refusing the nostalgia of a past time's modality, as ever uncertain.

Ever uncertain. How then are we to understand in the light of this sense of uncertainty, the notion of "rested totality," the ultimate goal or attainment of the Objectivist poem. For "rested totality," we are told by Zukofsky, is synonymous with "the mind's perfect peace." These two terms seem utterly at odds with the sense of uncertainty we have just discussed, and also with the idea . . . of Objectivist poetry as a peculiarly interactive poetry. The contradiction is significant.

We can perhaps take a clue from George Lukacs' remarks on the notion of "composition" in *Soul and Form*. A "composition," Lukacs tells us, is something "you cannot enter into, you cannot come to terms with it in the usual way. Our relationship to a composition—to something that has already taken form—is clear and unambiguous, even if it is enigmatic and difficult to explain: it is the feeling of being both near and far which comes with great understanding, *that profound sense of union which is yet eternally a being-separate, a standing outside. It is a state of longing*" (my italics).[13] The Objectivist poem, the product of an Objectivist poetics, registers its "rested totality" as an instance of completed form; that is, all its elements and all its exclusions have been accounted for and considered, not only against the weight of tradition but against the weight of our time. In this, it is synonymous with Lukacs' "composition." It engenders longing—and here the poem is nearly a stand-in for its poet—because, like persons, it arouses the attractive possibilities of uncertainty and desire. And like these possibilities, it is ever alive, ever capable of evoking one's creativity, of evoking the deep transformations which are at the center of life and poetic art. In this way, the openness of Zukofsky's poetics, Oppen's and Rakosi's situating of form as a question, and the varied though formal reticences of Reznikoff and Niedecker propose a poetics of workability, a relation to tradition that seems to combine depth and ease and intellectual rigor. This study, then, has come full circle, for the sense of workability is, in itself, an open and unfettered prophecy.

Notes

1. Oppen, *Collected Poems,* p. 147.

2. George Lukacs, *Soul and Form,* trans. Anne Bostock (Cambridge, Mass.: MIT Pr., 1971), p. 85.

3. Oppen, "Notes on Prosody?," *Ironwood 5* (1975), back cover.

4. Géfin, *Ideogram,* p. 137.

5. Oppen, *Ironwood 5* (1975), back cover.

6. Eric Mottram, "1924-1951: Politics and Form in Zukofsky," *Maps 5* (1973): 76.

7. Hans-Georg Gadamer, *Philosophical Hermeneutics,* trans. and ed. David E. Linge (Berkeley: Univ. of California Pr., 1977), p. 67.

8. Maurice Merleau-Ponty, *The Primacy of Perception,* trans. James M. Edie (Evanston, Ill.: Northwestern Univ. Pr., 1964), p. 159.

9. Zukofsky, *Prepositions,* p. 9.

10. *Ibid.,* p. 16.

11. Oppen, *Collected Poems,* p. 162.

12. Martin Buber, *I and Thou,* trans. Ronald Gregor Smith; 2nd ed. (New York: Charles Scribner's Sons, 1958), p. 3.

13. Lukacs, *Soul and Form,* pp. 91-92.

Joseph M. Conte (essay date 1991)

SOURCE: "The Subway's Iron Circuit: George Oppen's *Discrete Series*," in *Unending Design: The Forms of Postmodern Poetry,* Cornell University Press, 1991, pp. 121-41.

[*In the following essay, Conte discusses the relation of parts to whole in Oppen's* Discrete Series.]

When The Objectivist Press was inaugurated at the Brooklyn apartment of George Oppen in 1933, a few blocks from the site where Walt Whitman first printed with his own hands a book called *Leaves of Grass,* it was agreed that the authors would pay for the publication of their own

work, alternative financing being unavailable. The advantage to George Oppen, acting as editor and publisher of his *Discrete Series* in 1934, was that this slender green book of thirty-seven pages was made as he wanted it: one poem, however short, to a page.

In an interview, George and Mary Oppen frequently answer for one another, finish sentences the other has begun, and occasionally speak the same words in unison; so it can be assumed that Mary registers George's discontent with the "poetical economy" with which New Directions reprinted his first book in *The Collected Poems of George Oppen*: "Well, Jay Laughlin just got a little bit too Scotch and wouldn't give a whole page to each poem and the way they've been reprinted makes some people think that if there are three little bits on a page, that's one poem, whereas that wasn't the way the *Discrete Series* was printed."[1] This edition, black and white as an old TV, emphasizes a commercial publisher's parsimony and not the true economy of words which William Carlos Williams marks in the title of his 1934 review. The serial form of the book is the unfortunate casualty of the confusion over which "lumps, chunks,"[2] as Oppen calls his verse, constitute poems and which do not. Like the steel cables that are at once the structural support and the aesthetic appeal of the Brooklyn and Golden Gate bridges (landmarks of two of Oppen's *residencie en la terra*), an essential structural tension of the serial poem occurs between the series as relational system and the autonomy of each poem: the whole must act as a taut mechanism, just as the parts must have their independent sway. Oppen chose not to number his poems consecutively, 1 through 31, as Robert Duncan has, until recently, numbered his *Passages*; so it is critical to the book as a discrete series that his decision be respected to isolate the poems, each on its own page, as Creeley has done in his *Thirty Things*.

In an interview with L. S. Dembo, Oppen stresses the structural tension between the series and the individual poem as he defines the title of his book:

> My book, of course, was called *Discrete Series*. That's a phrase in mathematics. A pure mathematical series would be one in which each term is derived from the preceding term by a rule. A discrete series is a series of terms each of which is empirically derived, each one of which is empirically true. And this is the reason for the fragmentary character of those poems. I was attempting to construct a meaning by empirical statements, by imagist statements.
>
> Q. Each imagist statement being essentially discrete from the statement that followed or preceded it?
>
> A. Yes, that meaning is also implicit in the word "discrete." The poems are a series, yet each is separate, and it's true that they are discrete in that sense; but I had in mind specifically the meaning to the mathematician—a series of empirically true terms.[3]

Oppen attempts to "construct a meaning" as one might build a bridge: should he impose a too rigid "rule," his serial structure will snap in a high wind. Each poem is neither derived from the preceding nor does it generate the next—each must be, as he says, "empirically true." This discretion is also contained in Jack Spicer's house-room analogy for serial structure: each room has its functional place in the house as a whole, yet the poet discretely douses the light from each room before proceeding.

In a letter to Rachel Blau DuPlessis, Oppen makes a late addendum:

> I thought too late—30 years too late—that the fly leaf should have carried the inscription
>
> 14, 28, 32, 42
>
> which is a discrete series: the names of the stations on the east side subway.[4]

These four numbers are a mathematical example of a discrete series, but they also function analogously: the stops on a subway line which they indicate offer, as one rises out of the dark tunnel onto the cross-streets of Lower Manhattan, a series of empirically derived observations. Hart Crane shares Oppen's experience of New York in the section of *The Bridge* (1930) which he calls "The Tunnel":

> The intent escalator lifts a serenade
> Stilly
> Of shoes, umbrellas, each eye attending its shoe, then
> Bolting outright somewhere above where streets
> Burst suddenly in rain. . . .[5]

For Crane as well as Oppen, the enormous metropolis offers itself to the individual view only in discrete parts.

After the neo-Jamesian proem to the book, whose source in Henry James's "The Story in It" has been perhaps too thoroughly researched—down to the additional *e* that clings to Oppen's version of Maude Blessingbourne's surname—the second poem of the series offers a more characteristic example of Oppen's mechanism, if one can find the machine in the rubble of his syntax:

> White. From the
> Under arm of T
> The red globe.
>
> Up
> Down. Round
> Shiny fixed
> Alternatives
>
> From the quiet
>
> Stone floor . . .

> (**Collected Poems** 3) [hereafter abbreviated as *CP*]

Charles Tomlinson, the British ally of the Objectivists, first suspected that the empirical object (which this poem does not, finally, represent) is the control handle of a circa 1929 elevator.[6] The scene could easily be the floor of the New York Stock Exchange, white ticker tape strewn about, strangely quiet after the stocks, their precipitous rise com-

plete, had suddenly crashed: "Up / Down." My own ignorance of economics, by which all stocks appear enigmatic alternatives, seems to support this interpretation. But the more salient question is, do we need to know what the referential object of this verbless poem is, and if we entirely satisfy our curiosity upon learning what it is, is the poem then a good one? William Carlos Williams, in his review of **Discrete Series,** answers this question in the following extended argument. The importance of a poem

> cannot be in what the poem says, since in that case the fact that it is a poem would be a redundancy. The importance lies in what the poem *is*. Its existence as a poem is of first importance, a technical matter, as with all facts, compelling the recognition of a mechanical structure. A poem which does not arouse respect for the technical requirements of its own mechanics may have anything you please painted all over it or on it in the way of meaning but it will for all that be as empty as a man made of wax or straw.
>
> It is the acceptable fact of a poem as a mechanism that is the proof of its meaning and this is as technical a matter as in the case of any other machine. Without the poem being a workable mechanism in its own right, a mechanism which arises from, while at the same time constitutes the meaning of, the poem as a whole, it will remain ineffective. And what it says regarding the use or worth of that particular piece of "propaganda" which it is detailing will never be convincing.

> (*MP* 267–68)

The preceding statement has been brought to you by a counterrevolutionary modernist intent on eradicating the weed of romantic organicism. Oppen is not so interested in compelling our recognition of some machine in an urban landscape, whether elevator, ticker-tape machine, or as one critic rather perversely suggested, a shower stall, as compelling our recognition of the poem itself, the series itself, as mechanical structure. As critics, we would be a good deal too smug to think that, having exhumed Maude from the collected tales of Henry James or, like urban archaeologists tunneling under New York City, having unearthed the elevator car, half a century old at the bottom of its shaft, our job was done.

How, then, does the poem work? White and red are dialectical adjectives, the colors of the two globes, round, shiny, and fixed, which indicate alternatives of movement. As such, these adjectives are signifiers of an opposition. Lacking a verb, the poem relies heavily on prepositions to convey a sense of movement. The central pair, "Up / Down," reinforces the opposition of the color adjectives. The syntactical impulse of the poem depends almost entirely on prepositional phrases: "From the / Under arm of T," where "Under," disassociated by a space from the anatomical description "underarm," functions more as a reduplicated preposition. It may well be that the poet stands in an elevator, making an empirical observation of the white-up, red-down indicators of his own or other cars, noting the hush of a large, marbled lobby of an office building. But the prepositions that govern this poem are relational—like the lights, they are signs of an opposition. They are gears that, as they mesh, turn in opposite directions. We never *get* the referential, substantive noun—and if we agree with Williams that the poem is to *be* an object among the other objects of the empirical world, it cannot assume a secondary, representational relationship with the world.

How good is this poem? TO Publishers, begun in France by the Oppens and the forerunner of The Objectivist Press, included the poem in *An "Objectivists" Anthology* (1933) with the title **"1930's."** The title implies that the referent of the poem is the entire Depression era, a formidable task for a poem of such modest means. We can propose, as Louis Zukofsky did of Charles Reznikoff's contribution to the Objectivist number of *Poetry,* that the particulars of the poem function metonymically to suggest the larger contexts: "It is a salutary phase of Reznikoff's sincerity that the verbal qualities of his shorter poems do not form mere pretty bits (American poetry, circa 1913) but suggest . . . entire aspects of thought: economics, beliefs, literary analytics, etc."[7] But, as Robert Creeley has said of his own early work, the poem strains under the obligations of being an anthology-bound "hit single." The poem becomes good, in a sense, when Oppen sees fit to drop the unwieldy title and to include the poem in a discrete series, not an anthology; numbered 1, it is paired with the third poem in the series, numbered 2 and located on the facing page. The poem succeeds, not *solus,* but as a part of the whole series, its small gears meshing with larger; at the same time, it is discrete, requiring neither a substantive referent nor the rule or information of any preceding or following poem in the series.

The poetry of the Objectivists is predominantly metonymic; Oppen in particular is concerned with the relationship of part to whole. In one of his few essays, he rejects, with a nod to both Williams and Pound, the metaphors of nineteenth-century romanticism: "It is possible to find a metaphor for anything, an analogue; but the image is encountered, not found; it is an account of the poet's perception, of the act of perception; it is a test of sincerity, a test of conviction, the rare poetic quality of truthfulness."[8] The third poem of **Discrete Series,** and the partner of the poem just discussed, illustrates the metonymic concerns of the Objectivists:

> Thus
> Hides the
>
> Parts—the prudery
> Of Frigidaire, of
> Soda-jerking———
>
> Thus
>
> Above the
> Plane of lunch, of wives
> Removes itself
> (As soda-jerking from
> the private act

> Of
> Cracking eggs);
>
> big-Business

(*CP* 4)

Metaphors, of which there are none in this poem, are no better than refrigerator cases, glossy and white, which prudishly cover the nuts, bolts, and flywheels of the machine; the metonymic "parts" are what is real and functioning in the Objectivist poem, the rest is all appearance. To the general public, metaphors are synonymous with poetical writing; to the consumer of the quick lunch in a bourgeois capitalist society, the corned beef hash emerges with its poached egg already nesting in the center. The Objectivist poet is an Apex Tech repairman not afraid to get his hands dirty.

Unlike the previous poem, this one supplies its context, or whole; the abstract noun subject is detained until the final line—"big-Business." As Williams indicates in his review, unless the poem is first "a workable mechanism in its own right," it will never be a convincing piece of "propaganda." Oppen's gentle Marxism succeeds because of the poem's precise metonymic style, free of the bombast and sweeping gestures of condemnation which he found in much of the poetry of the Left.[9] No soda-jerk, (and here Oppen departs from Pound) he does not make his poetry a service industry for any political party or economic program; it is a "private act," like cracking eggs, which one can and should do for oneself.

Oppen has praised William Bronk' poems as "a permanent part of literature," saying that his is "a poetry of the use of his own senses, for the universe is not an abstraction . . . it cannot be derived by abstracting."[10] One of Bronk's poems provides expert commentary on the Objectivist's metonymic approach to poetry and the world:

> Metonymy as an Approach to a Real World
>
> Whether what we sense of this world
> is the what of this world only, or the what
> of which of several possible worlds
> —which what?—something of what we sense
> may be true, may be the world, what it is, what we
>   sense.
> For the rest, a truce is possible, the tolerance
> of travelers, eating foreign foods, trying words
> that twist the tongue, to feel that time and place,
> not thinking that this is the real world.
>
> Conceded, that all the clocks tell local time;
> conceded, that "here" is anywhere we bound
> and fill a space; conceded, we make a world:
> is something caught there, contained there,
> something real, something which we can sense?
> Once in a city blocked and filled, I saw
> the light lie in the deep chasm of a street,
> palpable and blue, as though it had drifted in
> from say, the sea, a purity of space.[11]

Bronk's promotion of the pronoun "what" to a substantive in line 2 and the lurching "which what?" of line 4—a precarious suspension of syntax—demonstrate a stylistic and epistemological affinity for what Oppen refers to as "the little words that I like so much"—that one knows the world only through a series of particulars, met and connected. While Oppen's verbless snippets and Bronk's fully formed clusters might not, at first, indicate an alliance of poetics, both poets recognize, as T. S. Eliot could not, that the form of the whole world is not within the circumference of the poet's perception. Charles Altieri codifies this distinction: "Where objectivist poets seek an artifact presenting the modality of things seen or felt as immediate structure of relations, symbolist poets typically strive to see beyond the seeing by rendering in their work a process of medi[t]ating upon what the immediate relations in perception reflect."[12] Or as Bronk says more simply: we can make a world, but does what we make contain something of the real? Only the poem that employs metonymy as an approach to the real world can meet Oppen's "test of conviction, the rare poetic quality of truthfulness."

Bronk's travelers, eating foreign foods and adjusting to local time, could comfortably appear in the eleventh poem of Oppen's series:

"Party on Shipboard"

Wave in the round of the port-hole
Springs, passing,—arm waved,
Shrieks, unbalanced by the motion——
Like the sea incapable of contact
Save in incidents (the sea is not
    water)
Homogeneously automatic—a green capped
    white is momentarily a half mile
    out——
The shallow surface of the sea, this,
Numerously—the first drinks——
The sea is a constant weight
In its bed. They pass, however, the sea
Freely tumultuous.

                                (*CP* 8)

The effect of a "party on shipboard" is conveyed in the first three lines with an economy possible only through the contiguity, or tangency, of two perceptions: a single wave seen through the porthole (with its implied context, the sea); and, abruptly, a flailing arm (with its implied context, the remainder of the body of, the general group of, party-going passengers unbalanced by their "first drinks" and the white-capped waves). The wave and the "arm waved" are metonymies that, in a contiguous relationship, establish a complex scenario—revelry on the open sea.

The lines "Like the sea incapable of contact / Save in incidents" introduce an epistemological investigation which Oppen claims was not fully engaged until the series **"Of Being Numerous"** (1968). Contact, or empirical observation, is basic to the Objectivist program and to the method of *Discrete Series* itself. Williams, in the journal called *Contact,* claims as the essential quality in literature "contact with an immediate objective world of actual experi-

ence."[13] Although the poet can know parts of the real world in incidents (the splash of a wave against the porthole, or someone's drink against your arm), how can anyone, by direct contact, know the whole sea or the whole of humanity? Oppen collapses the terms of the simile, which in line 4 is syntactically detached, in his discussion of the poem with L. S. Dembo:

> You see the separate waves but somehow there is *the sea,* just as you see people and somehow there is, or could be found, *humanity.* . . . The waves are the individual person. Humanity can't be encountered as an incident or something that has just happened. But all one has is "this happened," "that happened"; and out of this we try to make a picture of what a man is, who these other people are, and even, what humanity is. . . . I left it as a contradiction, that I *know* there is such a thing as "the sea," the whole. But the poem doesn't manage to see it, and it records the poet's—my own—inability to see it.

                              (*MP* 201-2)

As Bronk says, "conceded, we make a world"; so Oppen recognizes that out of discrete incidents we make a picture of what humanity is, hoping something real is contained there. A metonymic poetics is then the most tightly fitting wrench for this epistemological nut.

The epistemological "contradiction" that Oppen "left" in **"Party on Shipboard"** is closely related to the structural tension of a discrete series of poems. Oppen is "attempting to construct a meaning by empirical statements." Each poem is an autonomous, discrete observation, but the poet recognizes that each poem, as a *part,* must participate in the relational system of the *whole,* the series, if he is to construct a meaning. He also recognizes that if each statement remains discrete, empirically derived, he will not be able to see the whole from any one part; the individual poem will not depend on the information of the whole, what precedes or follows it, for its meaning. How can the poet "construct" a meaning from statements that are "empirically," separately, valid? The epistemological contradiction between the empirically encountered part and the implied but unverified whole finds its structural equivalent in the discrete series; if metonymy is the wrench, the series is the engine itself.

How can we know, from its "shallow surface," that "the sea is a constant weight / In its bed"? The adverb "Numerously," itself syntactically afloat, suggests that one approaches the whole through a multiplicity of separate incidents; it also directs us, for further inquiry, to the later series **"Of Being Numerous,"** which begins:

> There are things
> We live among 'and to see them
> Is to know ourselves'.
>
> Occurrence, a part
> Of an infinite series. . . .

                              (*CP* 147)

Oppen, aware that a discrete series is a structural reinforcement of the epistemological contradiction between the encountered part and the implied whole, considers whether, through the numerosity of occurrences in an infinite series, he may come to know himself as an object among other objects—that is, both himself as an individual and "ourselves," humanity. The process, though, is still metonymic; each occurrence is only a part of that infinite series which might include the whole of a person's life. In these forty consecutively numbered poems, Oppen contemplates the relationship of a discrete, or finite, series (which emphasizes the separate validity of the individual poems) to an infinite series (which emphasizes the continuous process and the multiplicity of poems which find their validity in that process). In this endeavor, he approaches the poetics of Robert Creeley, whose infinite series, *Pieces,* was published in 1969, one year after the collection *Of Being Numerous.*[14]

Metaphor has been the traditional mode of language for those poets, from Coleridge to Eliot, who aspire to a comprehensive view of the world; they are able, as Oppen claims, to find an analogue for anything. The circumference of their perception is coextensive with the world, and their esemplastic imagination, with which they scope the field of similarities, is located at the focus of this one great circle. The "vehicles" of each metaphor orbit the central "tenor," held by the centripetal force of the poet's imagination. This metaphoric mode of language is especially suited to the single, well-made lyric.

Metonymy as a mode of language is, by contrast, most appropriate to the structure of the series. Contiguity, the method by which metonymies combine to make larger structures, rather neatly describes the tangent and yet autonomous relationship of the individual poems of the series. The poems are like gears which, as they mesh, are only in contact one tooth at a time. Each metonymy is a point on the periphery of some whole or context; the force upon it is centrifugal, and so not directed toward a central poetic ego. Williams provides the graphic illustration in his essay on Marianne Moore: "There is almost no overlaying at all. The effect is of every object sufficiently uncovered to be easily recognizable. This simplicity, with the light coming through from between the perfectly plain masses, is however extremely bewildering to one who has been accustomed to look upon the usual 'poem,' the commonplace opaque board covered with vain curlicues. They forget, those who would read Miss Moore aright, that white circular discs grouped edge to edge upon a dark table make black six-pointed stars."[15]

Or compare this image of "faces in a crowd" at the train depot, from the twenty-first poem of *Discrete Series* (closer, actually, to the semiotic apprehension of Creeley's "Numbers" than to Pound's painterly "Metro"):

> The shape is a moment.
> From a crowd a white powdered face,
> Eyes and mouth making three———
>
> (*CP* II)

A number of similar things, like modular seating or penny rolls, will stack up, paradigmatically, for easy storage. "Numerous" metonymies will form chains, contiguously linked, their contexts like "circular discs grouped edge to edge," or to put it more sociably, like the bronze rings of the old Ballantine beer label. For this reason, the metonymic mode of language finds its structural correlative in the serial poem. Oppen approaches "the whole" through the numerosity of occurrence, not the comprehensiveness of the ego; his chosen form, with a postmodern humility, is the discrete series, not the epic (*The Waste Land* or *The Cantos*) or the sequence (*Four Quartets* or *Hugh Selwyn Mauberley.*)

The nineteenth poem of *Discrete Series* illustrates the combinatory aspect of metonymic poetry:

> Bolt
> In the frame
> Of the building———
> A ship
> Grounds
> Her immense keel
> Chips
> A stone
> Under fifteen feet
> Of harbor
> Water———
> The fiber of this tree
> Is live wood
> Running into the
> Branches and leaves
> In the air.
>
> (*CP* 10)

Three discrete metonyms, bolt, keel, and fiber, combine to give form to the poem. The three contexts, while diverse, are not distressingly scattered or in any way surreal; it would certainly be possible, though not required, to find a pier in Lower Manhattan from which one could observe a building, a ship, and a tree. Such a referential justification is not the true test of poetry. Rather, we ask, is the construction of the poem sufficiently adroit that, as with a machine or system, there is nothing redundant or superfluous? In answer to this question, Williams states in his review: "Oppen has moved to present a clear outline for an understanding of what a new construction would require. His poems seek an irreducible minimum in the means for the achievement of their objective, no loose bolts or beams sticking out unattached at one end or put there to hold up a rococo cupid or a concrete saint, nor either to be a frame for a portrait of mother or a deceased wife" (*MP* 269).

Certainly Oppen's disposition of his nouns on the line is as careful as a grand master's placement of his rook or queen; the three punctuation marks in the poem are like the best of a spot-welder's craft. The larger contexts, building, water, and air, close each of the three sections. At the same time, they interact with the opening noun of the next section: we move from one human construct, "building," to another, "a ship"; "water" keeps the nutrients running through "the fiber" of the tree. The metonyms themselves, though discrete, are also seen to be related: the bolt in the frame of the building is not decorative but structural; a sturdy keel is such a *sine qua non* that it is the traditional metonymy for a ship; and the fiber is that which gives form to all plant life. In short, these three metonyms are the indispensable items in their respective structures. Interestingly, none of them can actually be seen by the poet, like the parts of the Frigidaire. They are not decorative, "vain curlicues," but structural elements, both in the empirical object from which they are drawn as well as in the poem-as-construct in which they now occur.

A discrete series is a closed system; it is, to provide an analogue, "the subway's iron circuits" (*CP* 46). The poet and his metonymic mode of language are "the welder and the welder's arc," joining part to part, rail to rail. In a later series, **"A Narrative,"** from ***This in Which*** (1965), Oppen acknowledges the necessity of a closed system when he says, "things explain each other, / not themselves" (*CP* 134). In agreement with this statement, Saussurean semioticians might don Oppen's "firm overalls," since they too recognize that the link between the signifier and the signified, between word and thing, is arbitrary and not intrinsic; as a result, the single sign cannot explain itself and things cannot name themselves—they can only be accounted for in terms of an internally coherent system. A discrete series, then, is a hermetic rather than an orphic poetry.

In his interview with L. S. Dembo, Oppen admits, "The little words that I like so much, like 'tree,' 'hill,' and so on, are I suppose just as much a taxonomy as the more elaborate words; they're categories, classes, concepts, things we invent for ourselves" (*CW* 175). His preference for the concrete, substantive nouns, like Zukofsky's obsession with the particles "a" and "the," results in poems that Hugh Kenner has called "systems of small words." Kenner elucidates Oppen's confession to Dembo:

> This is important; it avoids Hemingway's implication that the small words have a more intrinsic honesty. It is cognate to Mallarmé's famous realization that nothing is producible of which we can say that "flower" is the name. ("I say, 'a flower,' and musically, out of oblivion, there arises the one that has eluded all bouquets.") That the word, not anything the word is tied to, is the only substantiality to be discovered in a poem gave Mallarmé ecstatic shivers. . . . Oppen prefers to note that whatever words may be, men cannot survive without them.[16]

This knack of survival is indicated by the ninth poem of **"A Narrative":**

> The lights
> Shine, the fire
> Glows in the fallacy
> Of words. And one may cherish
> Invention and the invented terms
> We act on. But the park
> Or the river at night

> She said again
> Is horrible.

(*CP* 138)

In a dark and meaningless world ("And Bronk said / Perhaps the world / is horror," as quoted in the eighth poem), even the word, an invented term arbitrarily linked to its signified, is warmth and comfort; we may act on words *because* we trust in the coherence of the system.

Kenner grants absolution to Oppen for his false faith in the little words: "We need not suppose that abstract nouns are empty whereas there is virtue in concrete ones. Rather, all nouns, all words, exist in a network of trust."[17] But Oppen is not so eager to do penance for his sin. In the Dembo interview, he says, "I, too, have a sense—I hesitate to say it because I have no way of defending it—of the greater reality of certain kinds of objects than others. It's a sentiment" (*CW* 180). Although he recognizes that the little words are just as much a "taxonomy," he cannot suppress a yearning for the elemental word and the colloquial object; the contradiction, as he has said, is "left" in the poem.

Again, as in **"Party on Shipboard,"** the contradiction that Oppen leaves stranded—his sentiment that the little words are more closely attached to the real and his acknowledgment that language is a system whose signifiers are arbitrarily assigned—is closely related to the structural tension of a discrete series. On the one hand, each term of the series, each individual poem, is to be empirically derived. He claims that "it's been the feeling always that that which is absolutely single [separate, discrete] really does exist," and that it is "absolutely inexplicable" (*CW* 176). Oppen insists on empirical truth: "That they are there!" (*CP* 78). However, he can no more present in words the "absolutely single" than Mallarmé can present a flower from a real bouquet. He attempts, instead, to construct a meaning (i.e., the series itself) from these empirical statements. So the series, as an internally coherent system, allows these discrete observations, which cannot explain themselves, to explain each other. The structural tension, then, between a discrete observation and a closed system of relations is in part a manifestation of the contradiction in Oppen's thought regarding language itself—which he rather amiably, and productively, preserves.

Williams, like any economical building contractor, commends Oppen for the "irreducible minimum in the means" with which he constructs ***Discrete Series***; there are no loose bolts or unattached beams "to be a frame for a portrait of mother or a deceased wife." ***Discrete Series*** does, however, include several "portraits" of a young and very much alive Mary Oppen, not as sentimental ornaments, but as essential components in the structural economy of the work. Their eroticism is not a diversion from the urban realities of crane operators, tug boats, or elevators. These love poems function according to the same rigorous principles of composition as any others; they are objects "empirically derived" which nevertheless "explain each other."

These poems are not, in any sense, a group, implying some thematic development or dependence of one on the other. But neither are they randomly distributed through the series, any more than a carpenter could randomly space 2 × 4 studs under a plasterboard wall. To be thorough, we would need to consider what similarities exist among these poems (their paradigmatic value), their pro- and antagonistic interaction with other contexts in the series, and their syntagmatic relations (the points of tangency or combinative effect of one poem and another). This examination would be fairly exhaustive, and so I have chosen, somewhat arbitrarily, the twenty-fourth poem of the series as a focus for discussion.

Oppen claims to be "a fairly passionate mechanic" (*MP* 205), and this passion seems to enhance the pleasure he finds in a photograph that juxtaposes a woman and a car:

> No interval of manner
> Your body in the sun.
> You? A solid, this that the dress
> >   insisted,
> Your face unaccented, your mouth a mouth?
> >   Practical knees:
> It is you who truly
> Excel the vegetable,
> The fitting of grasses—more bare than
> >   that.
> Pointedly bent, your elbow on a car-edge
> Incognito as summer
> Among mechanics.
>
> >   (*CP* 12)

Flattery is not the intention of this poem; twice he questions whether the image is actually of his lover. The woman is an unaccented solid—the dress does nothing for her figure, the photographer has caught her, as happens, expressionless. She has, like any Econo-Car, "practical knees." And finally, it is as an elemental solid that the poet praises her: "you who truly / Excel the vegetable." She is, like the other subjects of Oppen's poetry, and the poems themselves, unornamented by the traditional metaphorical blandishments, "more bare than / that."

Oppen has said that he has a sense of "the greater reality of certain kinds of objects than of others. It's a sentiment," perhaps the only sentiment he allows himself. He continues, "I have a very early poem about a car closed in glass. I felt somehow it was unreal and I said so—the light inside that car." In the ninth poem of the series, that car, a limousine, elicits "a feeling of something false in overprotection and over-luxury" (*CW* 180-81). The "sentiment" to which Oppen refers is partly Marxist, a distaste for the accumulation of wealth; he assigns to such objects a lower level of veracity—the car appears in "a false light." So the unflattering portrait of a woman in bright sun, "among mechanics," not chauffeurs, is a positive counter in his argument, true praise.

The sixteenth poem in the series can be related to the twenty-fourth poem; their points of contact are very precise and easily evident.

> She lies, hip high,
> On a flat bed

> While the after-
> Sun passes.

> Plant, I breathe——
> >   O Clearly,
> Eyes legs arms hands fingers,
> Simple legs in silk.
>
> >   (*CP* 9)

This is a more private scene, charged with a passive eroticism; only the master mechanic himself is present, pretending to be a houseplant. The bright sun continues to shine on his lover; we notice that the "noon" of "afternoon sun" has fallen away under the scissors of Oppen's cut-and-paste method of revision. The two most discrete lines of the poem, "Plant, I breathe——/ O Clearly," flower with a gentle sprinkle of Oppen's own explication: "My own presence is like a plant, just breathing, just being, just seeing this. Well, no, I was talking about eroticism, just internal sensations, like a plant. I don't exist otherwise. It's the closure of eroticism within oneself. It's two things, the tremendously sharp vision of erotic desire, together with a kind of closing of one's self, within oneself emotionally" (*CW* 203). "O Clearly," a syntactically detached exclamation, is then a marker for the empirical observation of the Objectivist campaign, brought to the intensity of an erotic passion. When we consider that the poet's lover "excels the vegetable," she may then be said to be more open to an emotional-physical exchange (certainly her posture indicates this), in contrast to the poet's solipsistic pleasure. The concluding metonymic list of body parts (might they not include a fender, exhaust manifold, or head-light?) stops, like "practical knees," on "simple legs." They are, however, adorned with silk, since Oppen claims that he hoped it would be "an erotic poem . . . a dirty poem" (*MP* 203).

Another circular disc that can be placed edge to edge with the first love poem we examined is the twenty-second poem of the series:

> Near your eyes——
> Love at the pelvis
> Reaches the generic, gratuitous
> >   (Your eyes like snail-tracks)
> Parallel emotions,
> We slide in separate hard grooves
> Bowstrings to bent loins,
> >   Self moving
> Moon, mid-air.
>
> >   (*CP* 11)

In "'The Shape of the Lines': Oppen and the Metric of Difference," Marjorie Perloff takes a moment in the midst of her exacting prosodic analysis of this poem to note that "'Love at the pelvis' is hardly a very pretty image, despite the near-rhyme of 'Love' and 'pelvis,'" and that the poet, "perceiving his beloved's eyes quite unromantically as 'snailtracks,'" attempts a rather desperate simile (*MP* 224-25). Although this poem is the most sexually explicit one in the series, concluding in an active engagement, it is curiously similar to the twenty-fourth poem in its unflattering images of the woman. This poem and the sixteenth are joined, like Siamese twins, at "hip high" and "pelvis"; both focus our attention to the erogenous zones without much prior ambient description. The initial conjunction of eyes and pelvis, the parallel and yet separate grooves of the lovers, and their "self moving / Moon" shape suggest the less conventional, less "generic," "69" position. But then the design of the poem, the positioning of the predominant noun phrases, is more significant than the finally undiscernible bodies of the lovers. Oppen is, after all, an Objectivist poet, not the casting director for a blue movie.

About this positioning, Oppen has said, "I do believe in a form in which there is a sense of the whole line, not just its ending. Then there's the sense of the relation of the speed, of the alterations and momentum of the poem, the feeling when it's done that this has been rounded" (*CW* 180). As Kenner has said, casually embracing Mallarmé and Oppen, the words, not the bodies of the lovers, are the only substantiality to be discovered in the poem. Or there is Williams's desire, with one eye on Juan Gris, to write a poem that is "pure design."[18] So Oppen is concerned that each poem, and the series entire, be a made thing, "rounded," with no sense of an undone.

Although "bent loins" provides an erotic charge missing from the twenty-fourth poem's "Pointedly bent, your elbow on a car-edge," in the most intimate of poems Oppen consistently gives priority to the design of the poem, the form of his lines, and a cubist's attention to geometrical shapes, ignoring the flattery or sentimentality attendant upon mere subject. (We might even say that he mocks the traditional "your eyes are like limpid pools" encomiums.) His hip high, bowstrings, and bent elbows are all bolts in the frame of his series, points of tangency which demonstrate that these are not single lyrics but poems at once discrete and related.

Oppen claims that in **"Drawing,"** the twenty-ninth poem of the book, he was "talking about form . . . primarily, since that's a major preoccupation of this whole volume."[19] **"Drawing"** and the last poem of the series are explicit comments on the form of *Discrete Series*; they are the construction foreman's blueprints.

DRAWING

Not by growth
    But the
Paper, turned, contains
This entire volume

(*CP* 14)

The organic form of romantic poetry, like the growth of a plant in which the form of the bud is preceded and determined by the form of the seed or stem, is rejected; instead, with epigrammatic brevity, Oppen describes the mechanistic program of the Objectivists—each page turned as one would, at the start of a new day, turn over the engine of

one's car. "Each term is empirically justified rather than derived from the preceding term."[20] The car either starts or it doesn't. The effect of this formal description relies heavily on the 1934 edition of *Discrete Series,* in which each page, turned, revealed a separate but related poem.

But Oppen, who employs so few finite verbs, says that the turning of pages "contains" the entire volume; we assume that his careful choice of the verb has formal implications for the series. A discrete series is a finite series, a system of containment. Oppen has said that "discrete" means "empirically true" and "separate." This containment, then, indicates the Objectivist preference for the finite series, or "rounded object," over the unbound and ongoing process of the infinite series. Oppen constructs a system of containment with his pages; he does not, as we have mentioned, try to encompass *all* the world. Nor does he endeavor to take, as Creeley does in his infinite series *Pieces,* "a common audit of days." The Objectivist selects discretely from the incidents of the day, and it is only in the combination of these separate pages, turned, that he constructs a meaning, contains his empirical observations in a closed structure.

The last poem of the series also concerns itself with formal arguments:

Written structure,
Shape of art,
More formal
Than a field would be
(existing in it)——
Her pleasure's
Looser;
'O—'

        'Tomorrow?'—

Successive
Happenings
(the telephone)

(*CP* 14)

Oppen will not let us forget that the poem is a made thing, a construction; it is, like a machine, assembled, so that there are no redundant, nonfunctioning parts, no loose bolts. As in the twenty-ninth poem, he contrasts his structural approach to poetry with the organic: a field and a woman's pleasure are "looser" than the forms of art. Williams records in his *Autobiography* the first meetings of the Objectivists in George Oppen's apartment—or, at least, he records their arguments for an implicit formal necessity in the poem:

The poem, like every other form of art, is an object, an object that in itself formally presents its case and its meaning by the very form it assumes. Therefore, being an object, it should be so treated and controlled—but not as in the past. For past objects have about them past necessities—like the sonnet—which have conditioned them and from which, as a form itself, they cannot be freed.

The poem being an object (like a symphony or cubist painting) it must be the purpose of the poet to make of his words a new form: to invent, that is, an object consonant with his day.[21]

In *Discrete Series,* Oppen has invented an object, a new form consonant with his day; only the series, not the sonnet sequence, responds to the current necessities of "Successive / Happenings / (the telephone)." Each call is discrete, not derived from the information provided by a preceding call. Calls can be entirely unrelated (a wrong number), or fairly intimate: "'O—' / 'Tomorrow?'" And until recently, "G Oppen" was assigned a number in the Pacific Bell System's San Francisco telephone book. The telephone, which did not exist when the sonnet was invented, becomes the contemporary analogue for a poetic form in which individual poems are at once separate and part of a system of communication.

The binding of my New Directions Paperbook 418, *The Collected Poems of George Oppen,* is already beginning to loosen around the few pages allotted to *Discrete Series.* When they finally fall out, I will cut and paste the poems, much as Oppen revised and edited his manuscripts, each on its own page. *Discrete Series,* an object consonant with its own day, continues to be the most economical formal example of the correlation of a metonymic mode of language and a serial structure. Empirically true in its particulars, yet the whole a finite, closed system. When Oppen says, with all Objectivist sincerity, that he "was attempting to construct a meaning by empirical statements," that meaning is nothing but the form of the series itself.

Notes

1. Burton Hatlen and Tom Mandel, "Poetry and Politics: A Conversation with George and Mary Oppen," in *George Oppen: Man and Poet,* ed. Burton Hatlen (Orono, Maine: National Poetry Foundation, 1981), p. 41. The title of Williams's review of *Discrete Series,* to which I allude, is "The New Poetical Economy," reprinted in Hatlen on pp. 267-70 from *Poetry* 44 (July 1934). Further references to this volume are abbreviated *MP.*

2. *The Collected Poems of George Oppen* (New York: New Directions, 1975), p. 21. All poetry by Oppen is cited from this volume, abbreviated *CP.*

3. "George Oppen," in *The Contemporary Writer,* ed. L. S. Dembo and Cyrena N. Pondrom (Madison: University of Wisconsin Press, 1972), p. 174. First published in *Contemporary Literature* 10 (Spring 1969). Further references to this interview are abbreviated *CW.*

4. Rachel Blau DuPlessis, "George Oppen: 'What do we believe to live with?'" *Ironwood* 5 (1975): 65. Thomas Sharp also suggests the subway as a "prototype" for *Discrete Series,* but the Oppens, in conversation, were lukewarm to the idea (*MP* 277). Sharp nevertheless quotes a passage from Mary Oppen's autobiography *Meaning a Life* (Santa Barbara: Black

Sparrow Press, 1978) which concisely illustrates both the "serial" and the "discrete" aspects of subway transportation: "We didn't yet know the subway system [in New York, 1929], and we got off at stations at random just to see what was above ground. Once we stuck our heads out into a cemetery, another time we were on clay fields with standing pools of water, and once we were among giant apartment buildings in the Bronx, block after block" (p. 89).

5. *The Complete Poems and Selected Letters and Prose of Hart Crane,* ed. Brom Weber (Garden City, N.Y.: Anchor, 1966), pp. 110-11.

6. Charles Tomlinson, "An Introductory Note on the Poetry of George Oppen," *Ironwood* 5 (1975): 13. Harold Schimmel rebuts in favor of a "Bonnard bathroom nude" (*MP* 299-300), but his arguments for "Under arm" and "red globe" as the erotic glimpses of a keyhole peeper seem unnecessarily Freudian. Thomas Sharp attempts to confirm Tomlinson's suggestion of the elevator in conversation with the Oppens (*MP* 281). However, his claim that "with this knowledge, the poem gains for the present reader total clarity" reduces the poem to a riddle that one declares satisfactorily "solved" when one has "discovered" the referent. Such a poem—filled in and thrown out like the puzzle page of a daily newspaper—would be dispensable when the reader arrives at the "total clarity" of the referential "solution." Gilbert Sorrentino has suggested in a letter to me that the object may be "a signal stanchion on the New York subway system platform (no longer, I think, in use). The signals were meant to alert passengers as to the identity of the next arriving train (red and white were the 'colors' of the dead and departed Sea Beach Express). Each line had its own color code—two greens, the 4th Ave. local, etc. etc."

7. Louis Zukofsky, "Sincerity and Objectification," in *Poetry* 37 (February 1931): 273. In this special number edited by Zukofsky, the current first and third poems of *Discrete Series* appear in earlier versions, numbered 1 and 2, under the title "1930's." It is possible that "1930's" was a proto-title for the entire series. The decade, overburdening the single poem, becomes a more convincing referent for the thirty-one poems in a serial form. As Williams says, the Objectivist intends to make "an object consonant with his day."

8. Oppen, "The Mind's Own Place," *Montemora* 1 (Fall 1975): 133. First appeared in *KULCHUR* 10 in 1963.

9. In "Poetry and Politics: A Conversation with George and Mary Oppen," Mary claims, "We had no particular leanings toward the Communist Party—we were looking for someone who was active and who was doing something right now, and was something we could join. But we looked at the poets, we looked at the writers and we did not think that was any kind of art. Neither the paintings, the things that I was doing or—George can speak for himself—but we couldn't

enter into that sort of artistic world. It was propaganda art" (*MP* 33). And George has said, in "The Mind's Own Place," "There are situations which cannot honorably be met by art" (p. 136), explaining in part his twenty-five-year hiatus from poetry—to confront the Fascists in Germany, and to evade the McCarthy hearings by self-imposed exile to Mexico.

10. Oppen, "An Adequate Vision: A George Oppen Daybook," in the special Oppen issue of *Ironwood* 26 (1985): 24-25. Oppen has testified to his admiration of Bronk's work in several interviews; he refers to Bronk in the series "A Narrative" (*CP* 138).

11. William Bronk, *Life Supports* (San Francisco: North Point Press, 1981), pp. 43-44.

12. Charles Altieri, "The Objectivist Tradition," *Chicago Review* 30 (Winter 1979): 6.

13. William Carlos Williams, *Selected Essays* (1921; New York: New Directions, 1969), pp. 33-34.

14. In "George Oppen's Serial Poems," *Contemporary Literature* 29 (Summer 1988): 221-40, Alan Golding argues that Oppen must not be considered as a kind of "miniaturist" but as a poet whose work is characteristically in serial form. Golding is of course quite right in his assessment. He does very little, however, to distinguish between the several types of long forms: "Oppen did distinguished work in the genre of—call it what you will—the long poem, the serial poem, the poetic sequence. My point, then, is this: that to overlook Oppen's sequences *as sequences*—to ignore *why* Oppen works in this genre—is to misunderstand, by limiting, the nature of his achievement" (p. 222). As with other critics, Golding makes the mistake of blurring rather than distinguishing these types of the long form in contemporary poetry. Oppen's serial poems are clearly *not* sequences, and they should not be described as such. Similarly, he compares Oppen's technique to Creeley's, but refers to the latter's volume *Pieces* as a "sequence of fragments" (p. 235). Such a description hardly clarifies Creeley's distinct practice of seriality, though the comparison with Oppen stands.

15. Williams, *Selected Essays*, p. 129.

16. Hugh Kenner, *A Homemade World* (New York: Knopf, 1975), p. 169.

17. Kenner, *Homemade World*, p. 170.

18. Williams, *Imaginations* (1932; New York: New Directions, 1970), p. 288.

19. Kevin Power, "An Interview with George and Mary Oppen," *Montemora* 4 (1978): 187.

20. Oppen here slightly rephrases his definition of the discrete series, in a letter to Rachel Blau DuPlessis, quoted in her essay in *Ironwood* 5: 64.

21. Williams, *The Autobiography of William Carlos Williams* (New York: New Directions, 1967), pp. 264-65.

Marjorie Perloff (essay date 1991)

SOURCE: "Against Transparency: From the Radiant Cluster to the Word as Such," in *Radical Artifice: Writing Poetry in the Age of Media,* The University of Chicago Press, 1991, pp. 79-87.

[*In the following excerpt, Perloff considers Oppen's poetic diction within the context of the popular use of words and images in advertising.*]

Oppen's famous twenty-five-year silence (he published no book between *Discrete Series* [1934] and *The Materials* [1962] has often confounded readers: what can it mean, it is asked, to abandon one's chosen art for a quarter of a century? And did the poet's political activism (he worked for Communist party causes on and off for some twenty years) and his years of exile in Mexico reinforce or interfere with his poetics?[1] For my purposes here, the psychology of Oppen's silence is less important than what I take to be its paradoxically positive effect on the poetry. When Oppen resurfaced, Rip Van Winkle—like, in 1958, first in New York and later in San Francisco, he had missed the protracted controversy about the awarding of the Bollingen Prize to Pound for the *Pisan Cantos* in 1948—a controversy that triggered the larger debate about the relationship of poetry to knowledge, of the raw versus the cooked, of Olson's projective verse versus the "closed verse" of the "genteel" tradition. Largely detached from the various schools and having, in the intervening years, read more philosophy (especially Heidegger)[2] than the poetry of his contemporaries, Oppen may well have had less difficulty than, say, Williams, in coming to terms with a world increasingly characterized by what Charles Bernstein has called "imagabsorption"—the "*im-position* of the image on the mind" from without.[3] And indeed, judging from the various essay collections devoted to his work, Oppen's later books—*The Materials, This in Which* (1965), *Of Being Numerous* (1968)—have tended to speak to poets who were at least two, sometimes four, decades younger: Bruce Andrews, Donald Davie, Louise Gluck, Robert Hass, Michael Heller, Sharon Olds, Michael Palmer, John Peck, Rachel Blau duPlessis, Robert Pinsky, Ron Silliman, Gilbert Sorrentino, John Taggart, Eliot Weinberger.[4]

But then Oppen, even in his early poetry, displayed little predilection for "direct treatment of the thing," for the image as "radiant node or cluster."[5] Consider the third poem in *Discrete Series*:[6]

> Thus
> Hides the
>
> Parts—the prudery
> Of Frigidaire, of
> Soda-jerking——

Thus

Above the

Plane of lunch, of wives
Removes itself
(As soda-jerking from
the private act

Of
Cracking eggs);

big-Business

The early 1930s, when Oppen wrote this little poem, were the years in which the Frigidaire or General Electric refrigerator became a secular icon. "As a protector of health through the prevention of spoilage," writes Roland Marchand, "it served as a benevolent guardian of the family's safety. As the immediate source of a great variety of life-sustaining foods, it acquired the image of a modern cornucopia. No open refrigerator door in an advertising tableau ever disclosed a sparse supply of food. The gleaming white of the refrigerator's exterior suggested cleanliness and purity." Indeed, "the visual cliché of the entrancing refrigerator," wife and husband (the husband was never seen in the vicinity of a refrigerator without his wife), or wife and guests, rapturously contemplating its well-stocked shelves became, says Marchand, a "moment of secular epiphany."[7]

Oppen's little Frigidaire poem deconstructs such moments, not by writing a critique of the consumer culture that produces Frigidaires—that would be much too easy and uninteresting—but by rupturing the very sentence and phrasal units in which the image appears. Indeed, we never "see" the Frigidaire or the soda-jerk or the wives having lunch at the ground-floor soda fountain while big business is presumably conducted in the offices upstairs. "Thus / Hides the / Parts," the poem begins oddly. "Thus," as Harold Schimmel points out in his excellent essay on *Discrete Series,* surprises the reader by its formality, its "uncolloquial nature"; reappearing in line 6, again in isolated position, "Thus" functions, Schimmel notes, as an arrow, road sign, or mathematical symbol, that points us in a particular direction.[8] It is not a signifier pointing toward a particular signified but a relational term.

But what is it that "Thus / Hides the / Parts"? Oppen characteristically omits the subject noun or pronoun. Is it the Frigidaire itself, whose exterior "prudery" (its white walls and door) hides its motor. Or are the hidden parts the delectable food items placed in the refrigerator? Or do the lines refer to the soda-jerk who prudently cracks the eggs ahead of time and behind the scene (a "private act") so that his performance will appear more streamlined? Or to the "big-Business" of the last line, that hides by removing itself (line 9) from its own production as from the "Plane of lunch, of wives" below? The poem invites all these readings, but not to make a didactic point. For the poem itself "Hides / the parts," aligning words so as to create paragrams. "Parts—the prudery" suggests, by its allitera-

tion and word placement that prudery has something to do with hiding one's parts. "Of Frigidaire, of" provides the brand name with a frame that seems to limit its power. The line "Above the" sits above "Plane of lunch, of wives" as if the poet himself were stationed somewhere on the balcony, and "lunch" and "wives" are not properly nouns in apposition. The capitalization of "Plane" points back to the capitalized "Parts" (notice that Oppen doesn't automatically begin a line with a capital letter), and the lower-case "big" in "big-Business" forces us to look hard at that particularly hackneyed phrase.

However one interprets the poem, it is, finally, the "Thus" of lines 1 and 6 that remains most enigmatic. For Oppen never does explain *how* the "parts," whether of Frigidaires or of soda-jerking or of manufacturing, are "hidden." His interest is not to produce a clear visual image of a particular scene, a description of lunch at the office building soda fountain, but, on the contrary, to see how *words,* taken out of their normal syntactic contexts, can assume new meanings. "Thus / Hides the" in that "thus" contains and obscures the meaning of "the." "Thus / Above the" points to the hierarchy of words within the poem. The apposition of "Cracking eggs" and "big-Business" suggests that the "act / Of / Cracking eggs" *is* a big business. And so on.

Syntax, writes Oppen in his "Daybook" (the entries are undated): "a careful packing of a poem to avoid mere shuffling, a deadening, to avoid destroying a word by its relationships."[9] Which is to say by the wrong relationships. "Those who are not very concerned with art," writes Oppen, "want poems or pictures to record for them something they already know—as one might want a picture of a place he loves" (DBK 29). But, as he puts it, again in his "Daybook" (DBK 25), preparatory to its incorporation in the poem "Route": "Words cannot be wholly transparent. And this is the 'heartlessness' of words" (*Collected Poems* 186) [hereafter abbreviated as *GOCP*]. "Heartless" in the sense of being uncompromising, unwilling to engage in rituals of transcendence, of otherness. It is interesting to compare Oppen's refusal of transparency, his repeated insistence that "the word is a solid" (DBK 25), to Pound's 1915 definition of Image:

> The Image can be of two sorts. It can arise within the mind. It is then 'subjective.' External causes play upon the mind, perhaps; if so, they are drawn into the mind, fused, transmitted, and emerge in an Image unlike themselves. Secondly, the Image can be objective. Emotion seizing upon some external scene or action carries it intact to the mind; and that vortex purges it of all save the essential or dominant or dramatic qualities, and it emerges like the external original.[10]

"Purged" by the vortex, the Image, as Pound said elsewhere (LE 33), "stands clean," a substitute, as it were, for the "external original," which it resembles. It is this still-Modernist faith in the image as analogy that Oppen calls into question in the poems of the sixties that begin with *The Materials.* "Image of the Engine," one poem is called, but its descriptive Whitmanian opening soon dissolves into phrases like "What ends / Is that" (*GOCP* 20). In another poem (no. 21 of **"Of Being Numerous," *GOCP*** 162) that starts out as a quintessentially Objectivist lyric with its emphasis on thingness, on "the brick / In a brick wall / The eye picks / So quiet of a Sunday,"[11] Oppen abruptly "drops" the brick and, pointedly avoiding the pictorial or tactile, skips a line and places, all by itself, a proper name that may or may not be the "you" of lines 5–6:

> Here is the brick, it was waiting
> Here when you were born
>
> Mary-Anne.

The ordinary name Mary-Anne, three syllables bearing two short *a*'s surrounded by white space, has an odd opacity. For we don't know any more about Mary-Anne than we do about the brick: the name evokes no image, tells no story; indeed the address to Mary-Anne seems to interrupt the poet's rumination about the past and leave its meaning suspended.[12] What relatedness there is exists on the level of sound rather than meaning: *Mar*-y picks up the sound of "There" in line 1 so that anaphora brings us full circle: "There"—"Here"—"Here"—"Mar-y."

From Image to the "'heartlessness' of words": consider now what happens in a short poem from *The Materials* deceptively called **"The Hills"**:

> That this is I,
> Not mine, which wakes
> To where the present
> Sun pours in the present, to the air perhaps
> Of love and of
> Conviction.
>
>   As to know
> Who we shall be. I knew it then.
> You getting in
> The old car sat down close
> So close I turned and saw your eyes a woman's
> Eyes. The patent
> Latches on the windows
> And the long hills whoever else's
> Also ours.

(GOCP, 54)

The title **"The Hills"** leads us to expect some sort of description—an image, perhaps, of how "the hills" of childhood have changed ("Tintern Abbey") or of where the poet is stationed ("I stood tiptoe / Upon a little hill"), or of the relationship of the hilly landscape to the speaking subject, as in H.D.'s "The Helmsman":

> We wandered from pine-hills
> through oak and scrub-oak tangles
> we broke hyssop and bramble,
> we caught flower and new bramble-fruit
> in our hair: we laughed
> as each branch whipped back,
> we tore our feet in half buried rocks
> and knotted roots and acorn-cups.[13]

In Oppen's poem, such concretion is notably absent: the only adjective used to describe the "hills" is found in the penultimate line and it is hardly very descriptive: "the long hills." But then the whole poem has only four adjectives—"long," "present," "old," and "patent"—and no more than twelve nouns; it is composed primarily of deictics, the "little words I like so much" as Oppen called them,[14] as in that first unsparing and flatly monosyllabic line, "That this is I," followed enigmatically by the disclaimer "Not mine."

"That this is I, / Not mine, which wakes"—here the possibilities of syntax rather than of image or metaphor are put into play. In line 1, the dependent (dependent on what?) clause challenges the reader to fill in the gaps. For instance:

> I know that this is I.
> I can't believe that this is I.
> How strange that this is I.
> How ironic that this is I.
> I must face the truth that this is I.

And the next line can be read as follows:

>   It can't be mine, this body which is now waking up
>   to the morning
> sunshine.
>   It is not mine, this household now coming to life in
>   the morning
> sunshine.
>   It is not mine, the "I" which the sun awakes; I have
>   no control over
> my self.

And so on. This is not to suggest, however, that Oppen's lines don't "say" anything. For however one chooses to read these opening words, they convey a tone of extreme disorientation, as if their speaker were cut off, not only from others but from his own inner being. "That this is I"—four syllables with four stresses, like a monotonous drumbeat that demands to be heard, and which, for that matter, the poet instantly seems to retract with the words "Not mine." The abruptness of the opening suggests that the speaker is waking up in a strange place and that he has momentarily lost all sense of self and of bodily weight. The "present / Sun pours in the present": the repetition is not gratuitous, stressing as it does the recognition that this is indeed the light of common day, the harsh and full daylight. Nor is what awaits at all certain: the "air" is only "perhaps" (the word coming at the end of the long fourth line is emphatic) the air "Of love and of / Conviction." And anyway, love does not necessarily insure conviction or vice versa.

The opening of the second visual unit ("stanza" seems too strong for this irregular block of type) is almost as enigmatic. "As to know / Who we shall be" can mean "I am not so presumptuous as to know / Who we shall be." Or again it may be a question: "Who is so wise as to know / Who we shall be?" These deictics, in any case, now give way to a more traditional image: a memory, evidently, of the poet's beloved (or, more specifically, as we know from the other poems, his wife Mary) in the early days of their courtship, getting into his "old car" and sitting "close / So close I turned and saw your eyes a woman's / Eyes." The scene is hardly remarkable: one thinks of a dozen old films in which a lovely young woman gets into a man's car and looks into his eyes: Claudette Colbert, for example, flagging a ride with Clark Gable. Or the standard sixties ad in which the beautiful couple (the man of course at the wheel) is seen, driving their new Thunderbird through the green and verdant hills of a luscious America.

But just when the reader settles into the romance plot, something jars. The "woman's / Eyes" (the line break oddly separating the eyes from the rest of her person) are now placed in apposition to "The patent / Latches on the windows." What sort of collocation can this be? Latches are what lock the windows; patent latches are inscribed with their brand name; "patent" also connotes patent leather which is black and shiny. Thus the line "Eye. The patent" oddly relates Mary's eyes to black and shiny little machine parts with a brand name, parts that shut the speaking subject *inside* the machine itself. Somehow, although we don't know how, the memory has a painful edge; when the poem concludes, "And the long hills whoever else's / Also ours," the pleasure of return (here are the familiar hills!) remains muted.

If one knows Oppen's biography, **"The Hills"** can be read as an elegiac poem recounting the poet and his wife's return, after many years, to the hills of San Francisco where they had been young, a return that is bittersweet and fraught with memories of early love but also of constriction. But **"The Hills"** is not so much "about" this return as it is about the despair of not knowing what one once thought one knew. Just when "the little words" seem to be pointing toward *things*—"You getting in / The old car sat down close"—the syntax undermines their momentum. "The patent / Latches on the windows": suppose "patent" is read as a noun, "latches" as a verb. How, then, do we characterize the remembered car ride?

"The question 'What is a word really?'" says Wittgenstein in *Philosophical Investigations,* "is analogous to 'What is a piece in chess?'"[15] In following the Wittgensteinian precept that "the meaning of a word is its use in the language" (PI 43), that "naming" is at best "a *queer* connexion of a word with an object" (38), Oppen's work suggests that perhaps we have had, at least for the moment, a surfeit of luminous detail. . . .

Notes

1. See, for example, Tom Mandel, "Appendix to Poetry and Politics: A Conversation with George Oppen," in *George Oppen: Man and Poet,* ed. Burton Hatlen (Orono, ME: National Poetry Foundation, 1981), pp. 49–50; and, in the same collection, Burton Hatlen, "'Not Altogether Lone in a Lone Universe': George Oppen's *The Materials,*" pp. 325–58, esp. pp. 325–26. This collection is subsequently cited as GOMP.

2. *This in Which* (1965) has an epigraph from Heidegger, ". . . the arduous path of appearance." Oppen has commented on the importance of Heidegger, and particularly of *Being and Time,* in various interviews: see L. S. Dembo, "George Oppen: An Interview," *Contemporary Literature* 10 (Spring 1969): 168, subsequently cited as LSD; and Burton Hatlen and Tom Mandel, "Conversation with George Oppen," GOMP 34–35. For an excellent discussion of the Heidegger-Oppen relationship, see Randolph Chilton, "The Place of Being in the Poetry of George Oppen," GOMP 89-112.

   The influence of Kierkegaard and Maritain on Oppen has also been noted, and in recent years we have become more aware of the interesting relationship to Wittgenstein. See, for example, David McAleavey, "Clarity and Process: Oppen's *Of Being Numerous,*" GOMP 392-93; Burton Hatlen, "Zukofsky, Wittgenstein, and the Poetics of Absence," *Sagetrieb* 1 (Spring 1982): 63-93. Although, as the title indicates, this essay deals with Zukofsky rather than Oppen, the discussion of the Wittgensteinian refusal to relate words to things applies neatly to Oppen as well.

3. Charles Bernstein, *Content's Dream: Essays, 1975-1984* (Los Angeles: Sun & Moon Press, 1986), p. 90.

4. See the following: *Ironwood* (ed. Michael Cuddihy, Tucson, Arizona) has had three special Oppen issues: 5 (1975), 24 (1984), and 26 (1985). *Paideuma* (ed. Carroll F. Terrell, Orono, Maine) had a special Oppen issue: 10, no. 1 (Spring); this was followed by Burton Hatlen's *George Oppen: Man and Poet* (1981), which includes only a few of the *Paideuma* contributors and has extensive notes and annotated bibliography. The *Ironwood* issues are subsequently cited as IR; *Paideuma* is cited as P.

5. In "The New Political Economy," *Poetry* 44 (1934): 220–25; rpt. in GOMP 267–70, Williams praises the technical excellence of Oppen's poems in *Discrete Series* and comments on the poet's "plain words" and his "metric . . . taken from speech" (pp. 269–70). But the tone of the review, which sidetracks into a general attack on those who judge poetry according to its subject matter, suggests a certain perplexity on Williams's part, as if he wanted very much to praise the younger poet but didn't quite see what he was getting at. See, on this point, my *Dance of the Intellect* (Cambridge and New York: Cambridge University Press, 1985), pp. 119-34.

6. George Oppen, *The Collected Poems* (New York: New Directions, 1975), p. 4. This text is subsequently cited as *GOCP.*

7. Roland Marchand, *Advertising the American Dream: Making Way for Modernity, 1920-1940* (Berkeley and Los Angeles: University of California Press, 1985), pp. 270–72.

8. Harold Schimmel, "(On) *Discrete Series,*" GOMP 293-321, esp. p. 301.

9. "An Adequate Vision: A George Oppen Daybook," ed. Michael Davidson, in IR 26:5-31, esp. 29. This text is subsequently cited in the text as DBK.

10. "As for Imagisme" (1915), in SPR 374-75. In "George Oppen, *Discrete Series,* 1929-1934," GOMP 271-92, Tom Sharp cites this passage as evidence that Oppen's is best understood as the second or objective image (see pp. 272–73).

11. The first version of this poem (January 1959), recently published in "The Circumstances: A Selection from George Oppen's Uncollected Writing," ed. Rachel Blau duPlessis, *Sulfur* 25 (Fall 1989): 23–24, is called "The Town":

> There can be a brick in a brick wall
> The eye picks
> So empty on a Sunday.
> The silent signs.
>
>
> Quiet Sunday
> On the flatof the table
> The match box, there asmuch as anything.
>
>
> Handling baggage in leather gloves,
> A few years out of high school,
> A young man furious. The new wine.

Note that Oppen revises in the direction of ellipsis, abstraction, less figurative language and that "Mary-Anne" does not appear in the more imagistic early version at all.

12. See, on this point, the interesting discussion in Burton Hatlen, "Opening Up the Text: George Oppen's 'Of Being Numerous,'" IR 85: 274-75.

13. H.D., "The Helmsman," *Collected Poems, 1912–1944,* ed. Louis L. Martz (New York: New Directions, 1983), p. 6.

14. See LSD 163. In the poem "Psalm," which Oppen cites in this passage, we find the lines "The small nouns / Crying faith / In this in which the wild deer / Startle, and stare out"; see CP 78. This poem is frequently cited as evidence of Oppen's faith in the "small nouns," but the fact is, that as Oppen remarks in a number of places, nouns, like verbs, pose a problem for him. See, for example, Oppen, DBK 13: "Not sure I can count further on the nouns in an open voyage." And on the same page, we read: "the verbs, which I have never been able to hand," "the verb, the *ACT* of things—even as I say it, it seems to me that that necessarily involves failure."

15. Ludwig Wittgenstein, *Philosophical Investigations,* 3d ed., trans. G. E. M. Anscombe (New York: Macmillan, 1968), section 108. The numbers refer not to page but to section. Subsequently cited as PI.

Michael Heller (essay date 1993)

SOURCE: "Oppen and Stevens: Reflections on the Lyrical and the Philosophical," in *Sagetrieb,* Vol. 12, No. 3, Winter, 1993, pp. 13-32.

[*In the following analysis of the poetry of Oppen and Wallace Stevens, Heller explores the boundaries between poetry and philosophy.*]

> "If it were not for the Poetic or Prophetic character the Philosophic & Experimental would soon be at the ratio of all things, stand still unable to do other than repeat the same dull round over again.
>
> —Blake

It was on my way toward writing this paper that I encountered two essays in the Spring 1993 issue of the magazine *Common Knowledge,* one by Gary Morson entitled "Prosaic Bakhtin" and the other, "Toward An Avant-Garde *Tractatus*: Russell and Wittgenstein on War," by Marjorie Perloff. I will come to the Perloff essay in a moment, but first, I want to note that, according to Morson, Bakhtin, throughout his long intellectual participation in the thought of this century, insisted, everywhere in his work, that we regard an individual as always unfinished, unfinishable, that the other person in the world (including oneself) be understood as a project always still on the way to completion. And it is from this perspective that I would like to address the topics of the lyrical and philosophical.

Naturally, one begs the usual indulgence, that whenever these two words, lyrical and philosophical, are mentioned they must be heard or seen as though surrounded by quotation marks; further, that these quotation marks do not imply, at least on my part, any disagreement with current usage or definitions; rather, that I think we ought to regard these terms as linguistic or rhetorical pressures, words not pointing at objects but vectored with desires, with one's hopes and fears. We know, looking at either poetry or philosophy, that labels have become insufficient. When, for example, Perloff writes in her essay that the "peculiar strength" of Wittgenstein's *Tractatus* is "its failure to articulate the inner connection of its propositions," and that this is not a failure of philosophy but a show of "poetic power," the conflations of the philosophical with the lyrical seem only too evident. Indeed, one agrees with Perloff, only noting carefully that the operative words "strength," "failure," and "power," the vocabulary of her intention to find the "poetry" in the philosophy, are not necessarily those of Wittgenstein.

Taking for granted a certain rightness to Perloff's judgment, still, it is also possible for us to imagine Wittgenstein, that troubled and troubling figure who lies across so much of contemporary thought, almost hoping to "fail" at philosophizing in order that we may read what he has done as poetry. I am alluding here not only to Wittgenstein's scattered clues in letters and recorded statements, to his need for the writings of mystics such as Meister Eckhart and Kierkegaard, but to the constant testing and pressuring within the architecture of his "philosophical" thought as it tried to break through the barriers of logical positivism and, as well, the practice of German idealism. If we read Wittgenstein as a poet, it is not because of what he founds (because that is not poetry's business) but because of what he unfounds, what he demolishes as it stands in the way, not of further thought, but of a poetic or lyrical intrusion.

The "time of the chapels," as Tzvetan Todorov has called it, that obsessive worshipping at the shrine of the monoliths of discourse, if such singular obeisances ever existed: that time, for the moment at least, is decidedly over. But let us remember that for many twentieth-century poets, the chapels of discourse have often been heavy-handedly operative. Nietzsche had been premature in declaring God dead; there was Eliot, among many others, to take up His cause again. And then there were Pound, the Fugitives, the pre-World War II Objectivists such as Zukofsky or Oppen or Rakosi, all of whom had submitted poetic power to one omniscient principle or another, a principle which defined the world and held sway with the equivalence of a theological force. Our histories of modern and contemporary poetry demonstrate, even if in the marginalia of our discussions of craft and technique, how one poet after another spent his or her time in a chapel and on bended knee. Such histories will also, I'm sure, provide illustrations both of the stiff-necked and of the curiously pliable such as Stevens and Williams, and of those, again like Oppen and Rakosi, who resurrected themselves as poets in open air, so to speak, only by leaving the entombments of the chapel.

As with our intuitions concerning Wittgenstein, the most powerful and important of these unhousings and refusals, these apostasies and demolitions, strike me as belonging to the domain of the lyric. Put bluntly, the lyric I am speaking of here occurs not as some effusion of the soul or the private song of interiority but rather as an attempt to go public with an utterance when the environing philosophy hardens by becoming its overbearing attendants: discourse, authority, objectivity. At such moments, philosophy as we know it no longer squares with our experience. Suddenly this lack of "fit" is precisely what gives rise to the poet's lyric and, subversively, amounts to poetry's endless propensity not only for creating worlds but for criticizing those which exist. Further, following Yeats's distinction between imagination and rhetoric, I would call lyric's domain one which is created not by the will alone but by an act of receptivity or recognition.

In the unruly manners of my discussion here, I am lumping together discourse, logic, certain prose tendencies, rhetoric, as those families of tropes which inhabit the realm of the philosophical as they strive each in their own way toward positing a false self-sufficiency. One tendency of philosophical language, especially in its guise as syllo-

gism, as theory or argument, is to mask itself as science, to have the last word, to exploit the psychology of its own literalism. In this desperate act, language's self-referentiality and non-referentiality both amount to the same thing: the armor of imperviousness. The philosophical trope, in this sense, is always coercive. It gives up the power of human speech, of dialogue, in order to acquire the absolutized speech of a god or deity. Plato's ban is only an instance.

Every turn away from this coercive philosophical trope, every tear in its logic, whether by choice, by luck or indirection, is governed by some sort of return to the world or to the body. I am thinking not only of Stevens's well known *cri de coeur,* that the "greatest poverty is not to live in a physical world," but also of all of his and Oppen's registrations of the fact that the world and thought beat upon the body and make poetry's sound. This may also be part of the lesson of Wittgenstein's "failure." "The lie in modernist imagery," says W. R. Johnson in *The Idea of the Lyric,* "is that no one snaps the picture" (15). The Objectivists, Oppen in particular, sensed the bad faith in Imagism's idea of an uncritical, non-reflective, impersonal art. Perhaps they saw the Poundian (less so the Eliotic) notion of the "impersonal artist" as an overreaching or disguised falsity when it attempted to exclude rhetoric from the notion of lyric, when it posed as datum rather than voice. Oppen's difficulties with Williams's formulation of the poem as "a machine made of words" constitute another aspect of the critique of early imagist practice.

In thinking about early Oppen, one conjectures a problematic similar to Wittgenstein's relation to positivism—that the effect of the degraded Marxist thought under which he placed himself in the late 1920s and '30s was to let that thought impose itself as a totality, to make him mute. As I have written elsewhere ("Thirties Poetry and Poetics: Utopocalyptic Moments," forthcoming in *The Objectivist Nexus*), the broken forms of *Discrete Series* strike me as a resultant of a mind dealing with the potentials of its own imprisonment, of a situation where, faced with the hegemonic totality of Thirties Marxism, Oppen, as he put it in a letter in 1959, felt "at the time [the Thirties] a tremendous difficulty of honesty, the whole weight of sincerity [seeming] to rest on one's shoulders" (*The Selected Letters of George Oppen* 82) [hereafter abbreviated as *SL*]. "The 'Marxism' of *Discrete Series*," he tells the poet John Campbell in retrospect, "is, was felt as, the struggle against the loss of the commonplace." Let me quote from the poetry:

> Closed car—closed in glass—
> At the curb,
> Unapplied and empty:
> A thing among others
> Over which clouds pass and the
> 　　　alteration of lighting,
> An overstatement
> Hardly an exterior.
> Moving in traffic
> This thing is less strange—

Tho the face, still within it,
Between glasses—place, over which
        time passes—a false light.

[*Collected Poems* 6; hereafter abbreviated as *CP*]

As I read it, the minor increments of language of *Discrete Series* are not held together by a syntax of Marxist thought. They are, rather, an attempt under duress to adhere to Pound's imagist principles of a representable world of "natural" symbols and permanent metaphors. The isolated constellations, the word clusters of Oppen's poems, are the vestiges of a struggle to articulate this world against the negative repression of an ideology. The "commonplaces"— almost all of them the traces of sensory data awash in a matrix of questions and negative comments—are proffered as moments of difficult honesty, held out as almost bejewelled, pointillist—*and lyrical*—intelligences against the threats of ideological discursiveness. This is not a failure of poetic nerve but rather a refusal to place "perception" under the dominance of leftist "right thinking" or under a prescribed socialist realist poetics such as was employed in the pages of *The New Masses* and other Thirties journals of the Left.

Which brings us back to Perloff's instructive description. Wittgenstein's inability or reluctance to connect one proposition with another but rather to leave logical blanks in the spaces of his thought is deemed a "poetic power." We know, if we may speak of inclinations and pressures, that the philosophical tends toward form, that it must ultimately rest, not on personality, but on the idea that the sessions of thought are also instances of no one "snapping a picture," that at the closure of a philosophical argument, the rest is indeed silence. The author of a thought, by philosophy's law of generality, has been excluded. Certainly Wittgenstein seems to have held such an idea. He is reported to have lectured in Norman Malcolm's presence that

> [d]oubt, belief, certainty—like feelings, emotions, pain, etc—have certain characteristic facial expressions. Knowledge does *not* have a characteristic facial expression. There is the *tone* of doubt, but no tone of knowledge.
>
> (Malcolm 92)

In this view, it is only a weak and corrupt usage of philosophy to speak of Leibnitz's ideas or to say that "Kant proclaims." Where philosophy is writ large, there can be no idolatry of the personal kind.

If we look more closely, we can speculate on what troubled Wittgenstein—that, like Oppen later, he could no longer accept the rest or surcease provided by the strictures of form under which he was required to write. To the extent that one attempts to separate tone from knowledge, to deny the rhetorical force of knowledge (or, in Oppen's case, to deny the rhetorical or tonal dimension of imagism), this is to go against one's own self-knowledge. What burdened Wittgenstein was his un-saying, the si-lences which were more important than his utterances. Indeed, what he could not say or write to fit into the marked off or tabooed boundaries of the logical positivists both mocked and, at the same time, made "poetic" the rhetorical engines of the *Tractatus,* and later even the bewitching nets of the *Philosophical Investigations.* Somewhere, the self-sufficiency, the propositional intertextuality of the philosophy no longer assuaged. Wittgenstein wanted a philosophy of "kindness," he also told Norman Malcolm, not one of "truth," of instrumental reason. "All that philosophy can do," he was to write (and how much a poet's words these are), "is to destroy idols. And that means not making any new ones—say out of 'the absence of idols'" (Monk 325).

We remember that both Wittgenstein and Oppen gave up their intellectual labors for a time to work among the dispossessed and the poor, Wittgenstein as a hospital orderly and Oppen as a workers' organizer. These parallel *hegiras* may not so much represent interregnums in the processes of the mind as moments where lyric, where poetry's "own lack" (the term is Yves Bonnefoy's) can speak, can only go public through silence and gesture. Wittgenstein's ambivalent turn and return to philosophy, his giving away of his fortune, like Oppen's leaving and coming back to poetry, may have some base in what I might dare to call a "lyrical" action, the doing of an open-ended physical "kindness," a kind of gift act in another language outside the discursive practices of a world where most "speaking" has been materialized in power relations and imperialist philosophies. For Wittgenstein, as for Oppen—again, this is speculation—the return to intellectual labor may have been not a question of either/or, but an action taken within a deeper transmuted understanding of the power of language. And perhaps it is this new idea of language that lies behind such curious remarks in Wittgenstein's *Philosophical Investigations* as: "It is our *acting* which is at the base of the language-game."

What then of Oppen's reemergence from the shadows of Marxist philosophy and rhetoric? Thought and companionate lyric have a journey to make in Oppen, an odd trip from the fragmented utterances of the early *Discrete Series* through a twenty-year period of no utterance at all while Oppen worked as a labor organizer and then fled to Mexico with his wife during the McCarthy period of the early Fifties. Toward the end of the Fifties, while still in Mexico, and after a strange dream in which he imagined himself rusting, Oppen began to write poetry again. From this return to writing, came the poems of *The Materials* and *This In Which.* And then another, more internal, journey takes place toward a new kind of "fragmentation" found in the late books of *Seascape: Needle's Eye* and *Primitive.* It is this internal journey which concerns me here.

Oppen, as he begins to write poetry again, in a 1959 letter to his sister, June Oppen Degnan, establishes the grounds for his earlier abandonment of poetry: "Maybe I admire myself more however, for knowing what is one thing and what is the other and what are the levels of truth—that is to say, for simply not attempting to write communist verse. That is, any statement already determined before the verse." It is out of this understanding that he can now proceed, claiming his new intention: "Poetry has to be protean, the meaning must begin there," which is "to write one's perception, not argue one's belief." Here, Oppen invokes a phenomenological poetics which evolves over the reminder of his career from these early questions of mind and world to the more subtle complexities of language-in-the-world, of the holds on thought of the philosophical and the rhetorical. Throughout, philosophy is perceived as an ambivalent nemesis. "I do not care for 'systems,'" he writes in his journal; "what I read is the philosophy of the astonished" ["**The Philosophy of the Astonished**" 203; hereafter abbreviated as **POA**]. "Astonished" and not "astonishment"—as though to steer the world "philosophy" away from the notion of the conceptual and instead invoke something more intimate and personal, the singular body-as-witness to that "one moment of sincerity [that] threatens to disclose everything" (**POA** 208).

This is the drama of the staging of Oppen's poems in his reappropriation of poetic power as he begins to write again. Emblematic would be the imagery of return, the welcoming of contingencies in the charged vocabulary: "bequeathed," "inherited," "we were lucky," and so on, in "**Blood From The Stone**," which Oppen reported as the first poem he wrote after breaking silence (Dembo 189). But even more illustrative is such a poem as "**Image of the Engine**," in which mechanistic life and thought, "the machine involved in itself," is released into human and creative realms by recognition of powers and orders external to the self's solipsism: "also he has set the world / in their hearts," Oppen writes, and "they will find / in flood, storm, ultimate mishap . . . the heart thundering / absolute desire."

The world. As one takes up Oppen's later poetry, one sees that these words, "the world," do not so much refer to a place but to a kind of lyric intentionality, a site of excess in potential, one that both generates and holds together the fragmented, elliptical, and syntactically disjunctive character of the late poems.

"It is true I speak of a Realist poetry!" Oppen tells the French critic Serge Faucherau: "Realist in that it is concerned with a fact which it did not create" (Faucherau 80). Oppen's poetics, as he describes it in the interview, is concerned with confronting and breaking through discursive entrapment, with realizing what I would call a realist obligation, as in this passage from "**The Occurrences**": "[to] Move / with all one's force / Into the commonplace that pierces or erodes / / The mind's structure . . ." (**Collected Poems** 206). "Prosody," he writes, "sings / in the stones" (**CP** 221). "The middle voice," of **Myth of the Blaze,** for example, takes place within the interstices of the "magic of the dark grain of sand and eternity" (**CP** 252). Things and self are the entangled enabling conditions for this later poetry. This is an imagist legacy which has come a long

way, even through muteness, by keeping an almost affectionate and rigorous trust with a reality existing on its own terms, severed from our "use" of it, yet, paradoxically, brought into being only by an incarnated and fragmented speech.

In Oppen, then, astonishment, awe, the vocabulary of philosophical wonderment are entrained not to modalities of thought or to theories and syllogistic reasonings but to the phenomenological, to the meetings of signs and occurrences. "Belief also *happens* [space] conviction happens there is no free choice" (**POA** 206), he claims in the later notes, as though to define his own philosophizing as in no way related to the imperatives of logic and discourse. To remind us, as well, that not all fragmentariness is the same.

The boundary markers of this poetics are two-fold: on the one hand, a powerful belief in the generative power of language; on the other, the objectivist faith in the power of realism to rescue the sign from the arbitrariness of signification. Realism, for Oppen, occurs, as he writes earlier in "**Of Being Numerous,**" "where the known and the unknown touch" (**CP** 172). In one of his letters from 1967, Oppen refers to "the strange unbounded voice of a Wittgenstein" (**SL** 158). "We create order," he writes to himself in his notes, "and it cannot contain us" (**POA** 216). And there are moments, in both the poetry and the notebooks, where he sounds peculiarly like Wittgenstein at the boundary or like the religious mystics and philosophers who fed the thought of both writers: "I speak only of my experience and of course therefore above all of my emotions but there appears again and again the word *thing,* the profound word, the impenetrable word, the final word" (**POA** 206).

Admittedly, there is no pure philosophy and no pure poetry. Oppen's "profound, impenetrable, final word," as he formulates it in the passage above, would involve the appearance of a word beyond the will of our wording, an occurrence which neither philosophy nor poetics can predicate. I want to approach Oppen's poetics again, a bit circuitously by way of the writings of Paul Ricoeur. In his essay entitled "Phenomenology and Hermeneutics" in *Hermeneutics and the Human Sciences,* Ricoeur claims that "what is to be interpreted in the text is a proposed world which I could inhabit and in which I could project my inmost possibilities" (*HHS* 112).

Ricoeur posits here the possibility of the intersubjective realm, not as a structure but as a place of structuring, an arena of mental or psychic activity which on the level of the text, and consequently of the poetic image, can be likened to the phenomenological field. The poem, the text or image-in-language, is now a place inhabited by consciousnesses and can no longer be reduced to a fixed sign or a scientific datum. There is already, in the acknowledgment of a speaker, an excess, a supplementarity, an "unboundedness." The image no longer paints a pleasing picture on the page but is instead a place of tensions and resistances, of antipathies and sympathies.

In such a recognition, problems of referentiality and simple mimesis take a second place to the gestural powers of language, the as-if quality, the viability and possibility of the world proposed by the image. Certainly "representativeness" comes in by the back door, so to speak, because every image, while being a concretion of language and sight, is also a fulcrum for idealization and universalization. But, as we find in Oppen's later poetry, the very power of the image is in its ability to drive the wedge between our conceptions of the real and the ideal, to propose a structure in language that bridges these two realms (realms originally yoked by Blake, that most extraordinary necromancer of analogies) between the physicality of a word like "sand" and the impossible mentalizations aroused by a word like "eternity."

This power is explored in Ricoeur's study of meaning, *The Rule of Metaphor,* in particular the two adjacent sections entitled respectively, "The Work of Resemblance" and "Metaphor and Reference." Here, Ricoeur proceeds by radically inverting the usual direction of literary interpretation. Normative interpretation takes the image as a source of critical production. Since the image, although made of words, is mute or occasions a nearly infinite multiplicity of resonances (which amounts to the same thing), the interpreter must take the image in hand and generate explanations. Instead of moving (or ruling out moving) from the imaginary to the discursive, Ricoeur suggests that "the question remains whether one ought to or cannot attempt the reverse, and *proclaim the image to be the final moment of a semantic theory*" (*ROM* 207). Here, briefly, philosophy and poetry appear to be conjoined, only to be left behind in that final moment when all that can be said is the image itself.

Ricoeur carries the notion further in the section of *The Rule of Metaphor* entitled "Metaphor and Reference." Joining the idea, derived from linguistic and semantic philosophy, of the *text as work* with his considerations of the image drawn above, he states:

> My whole aim is to do away with [this] restriction of reference to scientific statements. . . . Just as the metaphorical statement captures its sense as metaphorical amidst the ruins of the literal sense, it also achieves its reference upon the ruins of what might be called (in symmetrical fashion) its literal reference.
>
> (*ROM* 221)

"The real," according to Oppen, "possesses an indestructible element, an irreducible element" (*POA* 218). In Ricoeur's words, poetic language has a similar unyielding quality; it is neither real nor unreal, neither literal nor metaphoric. It is as though Oppen's "profound word *thing*" were arrived at (were to "appear again," in Oppen's words) as shining splendor beyond either thought or lyric.

Walter Benjamin, perhaps with Baudelaire in mind, writing years before Ricoeur, and here remaining on the sociohistorical plane, echoes Ricoeur's proclamation of "the image" as the "final moment of a semantic theory." He tells us that "when thinking suddenly stops in a configuration pregnant with tensions, it gives that configuration a shock by which it crystallizes into a monad." This monad's power is "to blast a specific era out of the homogenous course of history . . . to redeem both past and present." Oppen, in his notes, has his own version of this redemptive process: "In meaning the world stops but is illumined" (*POA* 212). The poet in his poem-making constitutes what he calls the "Archangel of the moment" (*POA* 218). And while it is not the subject of this paper to enter into the political sociology of Oppen's return to poetry, it is worth reminding ourselves that it is archangels who are empowered to perform earthly good deeds, to be unacknowledged legislators, to make a difference.

Necessarily, I have been associating the philosophical with the coercive, with ideology and the lock-step of rhetoric. And, if we think of Oppen or Wittgenstein, it would seem that the function of the poem, if it has any for its reader, would be to interrupt or rupture this conceptual reading of the world. But poetry, too, is an aggression; its syntax or diction, its imaginative lulling to sleep of reason (Yeats's point), comprise a design upon us. At any moment, the poetic, like the philosophical, can exist as malevolent sclerosis. And it is lyric's function, in its dream of unboundedness, to break these sclerotic holds on our mind. In this sense, what I name as lyric remains the privileged moment of *both* philosophy and poetry because it opens again on the unconditioned, the unplanned testimony of a body in history, time and space.

Wittgenstein's philosophical "failure," which according to Perloff has led to an instance or show of poetic power, is an appearance of this dilemma in another form: the birth of a lyric moment in the exposure of the discontinuities of a thought process trying to complete itself. The discovery of a fictive dimensionality to the doing of philosophy reminds us that the recourse to definitions is often paved with bad or wrong-headed faith. And yet, something has happened here which is instructive: in watching a thinker come toward the boundary, the very brink of philosophical activity (this, in so many words, was Wittgenstein's project), it may be best to scrutinize, to witness, rather than label.

Jacques Derrida, in his essay "Force and Signification" in *Writing and Difference,* quotes Kant's useful formula for witnessing the imagination at work: "the freedom of the imagination consists precisely in the fact that it schematicizes without a concept" (Derrida 7). "Writing," Derrida continues further on, "is inaugural . . . [M]eaning present[s] itself as such at the point at which the other is found. . . . Thus, the notion of an Idea or 'interior design' as simply anterior to a work . . . is a prejudice . . . of the traditional criticism called *idealist*" (Derrida 11). What does the word "inaugural" suggest but that the act of writing initiates a new phase of consciousness? Derrida relates this aspect of writing to a metaphysics of absence and presence, the key to which resides in the Saussurean play of differences. Thus, his analysis is primarily given in semantic terms.

Bonnefoy, one of the most prescient of commentators on the poetry of Baudelaire and Mallarmé, provides something of an addition or corrective to Derrida's thought when he writes that we too easily connect poetic activity with "the flow of intertextuality or the play of *dif-férence*—and forget to examine the inscription of himself that the author tries to establish in the midst of the verbal turbulence" (Bonnefoy 163). A phenomenological consideration of poetic activity, such as Ricoeur's or Merleau-Ponty's, might well reflect the "inaugural" perspective of writing, less as a semantic function than as a description of the dynamics of encounter. Thinking of a host of lines and poetic compactions from Oppen's late poetry—for example these near-adjacent ones from *Primitive* [hereafter abbreviated as *P*]: "young workmen's loneliness on the structures has touched and touched the heavy tools" (*P* 22) or "I would go out past the axioms / of wandering" (*P* 23)—I find it hard to imagine how we could read him otherwise than as being so encountered, so inaugurated by his own thought. Which is why we cannot reduce the notion of the lyric in a poet like Oppen to a genre, to a text that can be compared to other "lyric" texts, but must instead see it as an instance of incarnated mind piercing through to what Oppen calls the "commonplace," his world, his "realist" reality.

It is in this spirit that I want to approach Steven's poetry. Already, we have come by way of Oppen's profound word "thing," by Ricoeur's reversal of interpretative momentum, to a phenomenology of signs that is impelled by thought, by culture, by the experience of the body.

Allen Grossman, in his remarkable study, *Summa Lyrica,* insists that "lyric begins with the rounding of linguistic man, with the 'I'," that "lyric . . . is the artistic form generated by the conditions and consequences of I-saying." This is an idea he takes from Emile Benveniste's well-known maxim: "Language is so organized that it permits each speaker to appropriate to himself an entire language by designating himself as *I*." Benveniste's thought here is especially intriguing, in a time when the "I" has been under attack in a number of guises ranging from the Foucauldian "death of the author" to the critical abuse (some of it surely justified) heaped on the so-called lyric voice, to the end of subjectivity and the recent preference in art (and its attendants in the academy) for surface rather than depth or interiority. Intriguing, because Benveniste suggests the positing of an "I" not as the ego-driven cipher of poststructuralist thought but rather as a figure of capaciousness, one that, because of language's ever-present availabilities, can see, via the individual's own receptivity, through and around the imprisoning engines of totalitarian and utopian thought. The office of the poet is, of course, to be seated as this linguistic man (or woman) that Grossman describes, to make "lyric . . . generated by the consequences and conditions of 'I-saying.'" So yes, Plato's banishment of the poets is not so much a moment in the history of ideas as it is, indeed, the constant parable of the relationship between the lyrical and the philosophical.

In our time, the keeper of this parable, its oracle and progenitor, has been Wallace Stevens. "Begin, ephebe," he writes in "Notes Toward A Supreme Fiction,"

> by perceiving the idea
> Of this invention . . .
>
> You must become an ignorant man again
> And see the sun again with an ignorant eye
> And see it clearly in the idea of it.
>
> (*CP* 380)

Here, in two primary tercets of "Notes," Stevens has unified the disparate ambitions of poetic willing so as not only to turn toward the world with the ignorant eye of the child, to recover it in the old discredited idea of the lyrical imagination as "childlike" and innocent, but to see as well how much this turn of the eye is itself an "idea." Innocence is lost or displaced in Stevens's thinking not to a weary, jaded maturity, but to the far more pervasive effect—perhaps it is the same thing—of its transformation from desire into concept.

Such a trope is perhaps the central one of many of Stevens's "horde of destructions," as he called them, repeated as both idea and *poesis* in the poetry and prose. For what the lines achieve is a peculiar doubling of innocence and knowledge; they remind us of poetry's inherent capaciousness and paradoxicality, its ability to contain both a thought and its other, or, in Stevens's words, to find in the poem that "the true imagination," as he puts it in *The Necessary Angel,* "is the sum of our faculties" (61). Stevens's achievement has a dynamic not unlike the later Oppen's yoking of thought and world—though, looking at Oppen's remarks on Stevens in the letters one suspects that he was somewhat blind to Stevens's realizations of that dynamic.

If Stevens, who comes earlier, sometimes appears to be more our contemporary than Oppen, it may well be that he inaugurates (to use Derrida's term) a mode of writing which already sees the fictive nature of the philosophical, which takes this fiction for granted, which loves the *jouissance* of rubbing one philosophical idea against another, and is unrelentingly skeptical of philosophy's urge toward certainties. Stevens makes the relationship of language to the philosophical immediately critical and parodistic. His poem "Connoisseur of Chaos," for example, begins with its initial mockery of the syllogism:

> A. A violent order is disorder; and
> B. A great disorder is an order. These
> Two things are one. (Pages of illustrations.)
>
> (*CP* 215)

But the poem is also a critique, directed at the mind's pressure toward totality, a rather more serious matter than mere satirization. This is something one hears in the poem's crisp sonorities: "opposite things partake of one, / At least that was the theory, when bishops' books / Resolved the world. We cannot go back to that" (215).

Admittedly, Stevens, by comparison with Oppen's always darkly dramatic and potentially inimical encounter with the agency of philosophy, indulges in a kind of shaking hands with buffoonery. On this basis, Stevens is the playful Socratic figure of the poem, a comedic parser—and debunker—of our thought systems. So much of Stevens—the *con brio* of his diction, the bright, clean spaciousness of the lines, which make them look like the most high-minded sky writing, this efflorescence, this overly strong sunlight—often hides the near ground and the close facticity of the poetry's deeper notes, the "intelligence of his despair," as he calls it in "Esthétique du Mal."

But we need to go only one more moment with the image of a mocking Socrates to see that Stevens's poetry throughout is, as in the *Apology* and *Crito,* also a re-annunciation of the figures of fate and tragedy. The sail of the vessel marking death is almost always on the horizon of its words. That is, foreshadowings of meaninglessness or dying have been preoccupations of Stevens's lyric/dialectic from the first. We find them, for example, in Peter Quince's *arpeggios,* where "in the muted night" Susannah "turned" to her dying, or in the "nothing"-ness of "The Snow Man." One could, indeed, "give pages of illustrations." The phenomenology of Stevens's poetics, the good-humored yet serious nature of the verbal play at the edge of thought, a dance on the rim of the logical abyss, is tinctured with mortality.

Fate, the truism goes, makes one "philosophical"; but do the deeper tonalities of Stevens, particularly in the late poetry, constitute the hold of a philosophy on his poetics, or are these tones already a more profound reach beyond the philosophical, as I've defined it here, into lyricism? For ultimately what strikes me as wedding all of Stevens's work into a unity is less a matter of stylistics or even its romantic preoccupations with death and non-meaning; rather, it is precisely the poem's engagement with the problematic which I have been addressing in this paper all along: that the poetry is occasioned by a break-down, in the margins, so to speak, of the means of philosophy. This is not the usual talk about the breakdowns of language, for Stevens's imagination has been, first to last, a transmigratory shuttle between the failed logic of the meditative mode and the uncapturable reality of common nouns such as "sky" and "moon" and "shadow" (what Oppen called, in his terms, a "taxonomy"). For Stevens, as he puts it in "The Figure of the Youth as Virile Poet" in *The Necessary Angel,* the poet "must get rid of the hieratic in everything that concerns him," that is, the tendency of the machinery of philosophy to establish and impose hierarchies and subordinations. "He must move constantly," Stevens continues, "in the direction of the credible. He must create his unreal out of what is real" (58).

What is generative of further and more complex poetry in Stevens comes to us as the disguise and the undoing of the disguise of the philosophical. Thus, he writes of the poet in the poem "Men Made Out of Words" as one whose fate is cast in "propositions torn by dreams," by "incantations" which "go public" by the way of language and so are necessarily—as poetry cannot *not* be—"eccentric." In "An Ordinary Evening in New Haven," he names this forever interruptive eccentricity as "Desire, set deep in the eye, behind all actual seeing." We keep "coming back and com-

ing back to the real," the poem insists (*CP* 471), to find in it all that is strangely liberating by the act of the poem: "The coming on of feasts and the habits of saints, / The pattern of the heavens and high, night air" (*CP* 472). Again, I find this geometry, in its admittance of incommensurable worlds, very much like Oppen's, as in this last section of "Ordinary Evening":

> The less legible meanings of sounds, the little reds
> Not often realized, the lighter words
> In the heavy drum of speech . . .
>
> Flickings from finikin to fine finikin . . .
>
> These are the edgings and inchings of final form,
> The swarming activities of the formulae
> Of statement, directly and indirectly getting at,
>
> Like an evening evoking the spectrum of violet,
> A philosopher practicing scales on his piano,
> A woman writing a note and tearing it up.
>
> It is not in the premise that reality
> Is solid. It may be a shade that traverses
> A dust, a force that traverses a shade.
>
> (*CP* 488-89)

"Poetry," Stevens has been warning us so often and in so many ways, "must resist the intelligence almost successfully." We must pay attention to its finikins as opposed to its premises. The armatures of philosophy, the stepladders of tradition (like Wittgenstein's ladder of thought) have no other purpose, Stevens seems to say, than to enable us to climb above them, to break free. It is not surprising then, that we find in Stevens's late poem, "The Sail of Ulysses," these lines which, as they run down the page, are entangled in the characteristics of both the philosophical and the lyric:

> . . . We come
> To knowledge when we come to life.
> Yet always there is another life,
> A life beyond this present knowing,
> A life lighter than this present splendor,
> Brighter, perfected and distant away,
> Not to be reached but to be known,
> Not an attainment of the will
> But something illogically received,
> A divination, a letting down
> From loftiness, misgivings dazzlingly
> Resolved in dazzling discovery.
> There is no map of Paradise.
>
> (*OP* 101-102)

Entangled, but finally released, for isn't the freedom sought here one that is "known" rather than "reached," "illogically received" rather than calculated, "dazzlingly resolved" in "misgivings"? Pound complained of having "no Aquinas map" but Stevens, with a kind of sweetness rarely found in Pound, only wants to throw the discursive or philosophical maps away.

Oppen, too, distrusts the road map unless it accidentally leads into the country of the astonished: "Belief also *happens* conviction happens," he reminds us. And so, possibly, where Stevens and Oppen come closest is in their sense, as Oppen put it, that "the entire Western philosophic tradition is also approach to mysteries" (**POA** 216). The only means to get out from under is poetry, glorious poetry, in the search for the mapless Paradise of mysteries.

I come back to Bakhtin, to his notion of unfinishability, by way of his late essay exploring the nature of the "dialogic," "The Problem of the Text." There, he reminds us that authorship is, in some way, the violation of the planes of discourse, and that such a transformation "always makes a departure beyond the boundaries of linguistics" (Bakhtin 119). "The *given* and the *created* in a speech utterance," he reflects, "always create something that never existed before, something absolutely new and unrepeatable, and, moreover, it always has some relation to value (the true, the good, the beautiful and so forth)" (Bakhtin 119-120). Stevens was acutely aware of this "departure"; for him, it occurred because, as he writes above, "there is always another life," one that is beyond the "premises," one that is mapless and suffused with desire. This sense of "another life" may be what Bakhtin meant when he refers in his writing to such words as "surplus" or "eventness." Lyric, the occasion for "I-saying," is here a gate, a means, an identity of an author and unbounded thought, thought which, as Oppen notes, "cannot contain us."

I return again to Wittgenstein, not because I have something unique to say about him, but because, like Nietzsche, he represents well-known and serious philosophy on the cutting edge. Imagine then a fantasy, that while completing this paper, I came upon the following, written by a Romanian literary critic, Folrep Eyrojram, in a 1953 work, *The Act of Radials*: "Wittgenstein's book-length poem, *Tractatus Logico-Philosophicus,* tends, occasionally, as though in a concession to our understanding, to resemble something like philosophy. Can it be that this seeming failure of poetic nerve is really an instance of philosophical strength?" (Eyrojram 83). All along, we have been thinking, like Ricoeur, that the text is "work," that the lyrical is rounded on the final inarticulateness of a philosophical motion.

But perhaps it may not at all be a case of what a work says to us, but rather of our disposition toward it. Both Oppen and Stevens frame their poems in a space of uncertainty, of not knowing, and it is this unknowing which is generative. But Wittgenstein also operated in a space of uncertainty. At one point he wrote:

> The real discovery is the one that makes me capable of stopping doing philosophy when I want to—the one that gives philosophy peace, so that it is no longer tormented by questions which bring *itself* into question. . . . But then we will never come to the end of our job! Of course not, because it has no end.
>
> (Monk 325)

Perhaps, whether we have mounted Wittgenstein's famous ladders or entered into the multivalent language of the poem, our one freedom occurs at the moment of closure, the one that gives either poetry or philosophy "peace."

Imagination's most potent dream is a silent one. Eyrojram, in this imagined essay, reminds us that the "silences," the ones Wittgenstein claimed to be of the utmost importance, are, after all, not really that silent.

Works Cited

Bakhtin, M. M. *Speech Genres & Other Late Essays.* Trans. Vern W. McGee. Ed. Caryl Emerson and Michael Holquist. Austin: U of Texas P, 1986.

Bonnefoy, Yves. *The Act and the Place of Poetry: Selected Essays.* Ed. John T. Naughton. Chicago: U of Chicago P, 1989.

Cuddihy, Michael, ed. *George Oppen: A Special Issue. Ironwood* 3.1 (1975).

Dembo, L. S. and Pondrom, Cyrena, eds. *The Contemporary Writer: Interviews with Sixteen Writers and Poets.* Madison: U of Wisconsin P, 1972.

Derrida, Jacques. *Writing and Difference.* Trans. Alan Bass. Chicago: U of Chicago P, 1978.

Eyrojram, Folrep. *The Act of Radials.* Trans. M. H. Elur. Brooklyn: Pulaski Street U P, 1955.

Faucherau, Serge. "Three Oppen Letters with a Note." *Ironwood* 3.1 (1975): 78-85.

Grossman, Allen. "Summa Lyrica." *Western Humanities Review* 44.1 (Spring 1990): 5-138.

Johnson, W. R. *The Idea of the Lyric.* Berkeley: U of California P, 1982.

Malcolm, Norman. *Ludwig Wittgenstein: A Memoir.* London: Oxford U P, 1962.

Monk, Ray. *Ludwig Wittgenstein: The Duty of Genius.* New York: Penguin, 1990.

Morson, Gary Saul. "Prosaic Bakhtin: *Landmarks,* Anti-Intelligentsialism, and the Russian Counter-Tradition." *Common Knowledge* 2.1 (Spring 1993): 35-74.

Oppen, George. *Collected Poems.* New York: New Directions, 1975.

——."The Philosophy of the Astonished." *Sulfur* 10.2 (Fall 1990): 202-20.

——.*Primitive.* Los Angeles: Black Sparrow P, 1978.

——.*The Selected Letters of George Oppen.* Ed. Rachel Blau DuPlessis. Durham; NC: Duke U P, 1990.

Perloff, Marjorie. "Toward an Avant-Garde *Tractatus:* Russell and Wittgenstein on War." *Common Knowledge* 2.1 (Spring 1993): 15-34.

Ricoeur, Paul. *Hermeneutics and the Human Sciences: Essays on Language, Action, and Interpretation.* Trans. John B. Thompson. Cambridge: Cambridge UP, 1981

——.*The Rule of Metaphor.* Trans. Robert Czerny with Kathleen McLaughlin and Job Costell, SJ: Toronto: U of Toronto P, 1977.

Stevens, Wallace. *Collected Poems.* New York: Knopf, 1973.

————.*The Necessary Angel.* New York: Vintage, 1965.

————.*Opus Posthumous.* New York: Knopf, 1989.

John Shoptaw (essay date 1993)

SOURCE: "Lyric Incorporated: The Serial Object of George Oppen and Langston Hughes," in *Sagetrieb,* Vol. 12, No. 3, Winter, 1993, pp. 105-24.

[*In the following essay, Shoptaw considers similarities between the work of Oppen and Langston Hughes, and their relation to the socio-economic cultures in which they were produced and which they reproduced in their poetry.*]

> Well, I can understand what people who object to taking a poem apart are saying. On the other hand, I don't think a poem is all that fragile.
>
> —George Oppen[1]
>
> Be nice to people on your way up because you'll meet' em on your way down.
>
> —attributed to Jimmy Durante

1. THE OBJECT OF THE POEM.

In 1968, long after the emergence of the objectivists, George Oppen explained that the "objectivist" poetics meant "the objectification of the poem, the making an object of the poem" (*D* 1968: 173). The objectified poem is designed to be not just a recognizable reproduction of, or a secondary commentary on, its object, but an object in its own right. The poem becomes an object by sticking to its subject, by refraining from predication: "I'm really concerned with the substantive, with the subject of the sentence, with what we are talking about, and not rushing over the subject-matter to make a comment about it" (*D* 1968: 174). It is important to note that Oppen does not rule out commentary or meaning, but instead resists the rush to judgment. As we shall see, this poetic slowdown, sabotaging the accelerated schedules of modern life, is key to the poem's resistance.

In his 1934 review of Oppen's **Discrete Series,** William Carlos Williams similarly maintained that the modern poem's significance, not its meaning but its importance, lies not "in what the poem says" but in "what the poem *is.*" Williams compared the new poem suggestively with a machine. No longer one among Word-worth's rocks and stones and trees, an objectified poem is a manufactured thing that works on its own. Its significant form is its "mechanical structure": "It is the acceptable fact of a poem as a mechanism that is the proof of its meaning and this is as technical a matter as in the case of any other machine."[2] What meaning (if any) a poem might have should derive not from the poet's personal response to the object but from the object itself. Oppen tried, accordingly, to dwell within a thing's implicit meaning: "The other point for

me, and I think for Louis [Zukofsky], too, was the attempt to construct meaning . . . from the imagist intensity of vision" (*D* 1968: 174).

But the meaning or significance of an object, as is clear from Oppen's poems, is not right there before one's eyes, like a vase of flowers. A thing is inextricable from the culture that produces or cultivates it; it is inseparable from its uses and the experience of its users. This inextricability is central to Zukofsky's definition of the "Objective" of poetry as the "Desire for what is objectively perfect, inextricably the direction of historic and contemporary particulars," particulars that may include "a thing or things as well as an event or a chain of events: i.e., an Egyptian pulled-glass bottle in the shape of a fish or oak leaves, as well as the performance of Bach's *Matthew Passion* in Leipzig, or the Russian revolution. . . ."[3] As these examples suggest, the object, which may be as aesthetically and technologically significant as an Egyptian bottle or as overwhelming as the Russian revolution, cannot be extracted from its mesh of productive circumstances. A "historic or contemporary" thing is also "inextricably" bound to its experience: *St. Matthew's Passion* in Bach's eighteenth-century Leipzig, as Zukofsky shows in *A 1,* is quite another thing from the formal affair two centuries later in a secular, concert-going New York's Carnegie Hall. It is this public and shared (or conflicting) experience which is the meaning inherent in the manifold thing and the objective of the modern poem.

Things aren't what they used to be. In the twentieth century, objects began to be mass-produced "by" (under the direction of, according to the nationalized formulas and specifications of) big corporations. A Frigidaire, to take one of Oppen's objects, is a replaceable, returnable item in an indefinite series. It isn't all there. To discover its "mechanism," you need to look not only inside but outside it, into its corporate structure. What do such corporate, serial things matter to us? How has modern urban experience changed as a result of these things? To what extent is New York, for instance, a corporate thing? What are corporate objectives? These are questions of implicit significance which the twentieth-century serial poem (with or without its serial numbers) raises by virtue of its own inextricably modern existence. I am taking as my object two modern lyric series, written in and about New York, Oppen's **Discrete Series** (1934) and Langston Hughes's *Montage of a Dream Deferred* (1951). I will read Oppen's and Hughes's serial poems not as individual things or perpetual motion machines but as products, the net result of various cultural and social forces and mechanisms. As opposed to close reading, the object of what I call "productive reading" is to seek a poem's significance by asking not only what it means or how it works but how it was produced, how it produces its own experience. Productive reading is thus necessarily at once historically and textually specific.

2. OPPEN'S *DISCRETE SERIES.*

In a 1965 letter to Rachel Blau DuPlessis, Oppen offered his clearest explanation of the concept behind the production of his first book, and added an illuminating example:

"Discrete Series—a series in which each term is empirically justified rather than derived from the preceding term. Which is what the expression means to a mathematician. . . . (I thought too late—30 years too late—that the flyleaf should have carried the inscription 14, 28, 32, 42 which is a discrete series: the names of the stations on the east side subway.)"[4] A series is "discrete" when its terms are not "found" by a mathematical rule but are locally and actually discovered. Each term in a discrete series is mathematically independent and isolated from its neighbors. Moreover, unlike a sequence ($1/2$, $1/4$, $1/8$, . . .), a series ($1/2 + 1/4 + 1/8 + . . . = 1$) is the finite or infinite sum of its terms, a challenging problem when the series obeys no rule. Oppen's "discrete series," a term which modernizes and opposes the traditionally romantic "lyric sequence," is an oxymoron, denominating an aggregate of unpredictable terms with a "cumulative" effect. A poem in Oppen's **Discrete Series** may be thought of as a representative sample of urban experience. Statistical techniques such as sampling were used increasingly in the 1920s to achieve synecdochically accurate descriptions of amazingly complex discrete series such as New York. But Oppen's example of the subway system (not a series but a sequence) shows how enmeshed the modern matter of "discrete" empirical existence really is. The Lexington Avenue subway stops do not follow a mathematical formula, but they do not occur in random isolation either. In fact, the intervals vary from five to ten blocks and were "arrived at" by virtue of pre-existing financial, transportation, and social networks (e.g., Grand Central Station at 42nd). So too, Oppen's own poetic series, though it does not follow a predictable narrative or logical sequence, adjusts itself to firmly and newly established objects, sites, situations, and experiences; his series is both under and out of his control.

My first stop in Oppen's **Discrete Series**[5] is an untitled, two-part poem (or two-poem part) distinguished, appropriately enough, by numbers:

1

White. From the
Under arm of T

The red globe.

Up
Down. Round
Shiny fixed
Alternatives

From the quiet

Stone floor . . .

2

    Thus
Hides the

Parts—the prudery
Of Frigidaire, of
Soda-jerking—

Thus

Above the

Plane of lunch, of wives
Removes itself
(As soda-jerking from
the private act

Of
Cracking eggs);

big-Business

Our initial experience of these poems, even before we begin to read them, is of their verticality. Like the other markedly vertical poem in Oppen's series, "Bolt / in the frame" (cf. "bolt upright"), which describes a housed ship, these scaled-down poems mimic a towering modern object, in this case the skyscraper. The technological breakthrough of the fireproofed, steel girder frame in the 1890s, which made possible the serial construction of skyscraping buildings floor by floor, led to a dramatic alteration of the New York cityscape. In fact, two of its dazzling new additions, the Chrysler Building (1930) and the Empire State Building (1931), were under construction at the same time as Oppen's series. The descriptive object of the first poem, an elevator (as several readers have remarked) with its white and red globes under a decorative T, signifying respectively Up and Down, was a necessary expedient for the new long-distance vertical travelling.[6] Oppen's comments on the poem thirty years later to Charles Tomlinson, one of his reviewers, train a distant light on this newfangled thing, "So familiar . . . that I don't think anyone was puzzled at the time. . . . The office building evoked by its lighting effects in those dim days, And its limited alternatives, the limited alternatives of a culture" (*The Selected Letters of George Oppen* 90) [hereafter abbreviated as *SL*]. The social analogy or metaphor of Oppen's poetic sample, as explicated in his letter, calls to mind the vertical figuration of economic status: the stock market is up (before the crash) or down, some people move uptown, while others have fallen down the (rotted) economic ladder. Oppen's orotund but ruptured Stevensian line "Down. Round" indicates just what is missing from this ride up and down the twentieth century: one cannot go sideways or around, cannot sidestep the system.

Although the elevator may have been a familiar object, its presence in poetry was less so. In a letter to his daughter, June Oppen Degnan, Oppen illustrates the "difficulty" of modern poetry with an allusion to his own poem: "It is difficult to say anything very specific by comparison to a rose, today, because the sentiment has been generalized to include too much. People surely do have reactions to things in their lives, but I think they are upset and distracted if you ask them to realize not how they feel about a rose, but how they feel waiting for an elevator" (*SL* 23-24). This description is instructive. We learn from it that the object of Oppen's poem is not the lighted elevator itself but the "objective" (intersubjective, familiar), discretely modern experience of waiting for the elevator to "o[p]pen." The poem's manufacturer has inscribed his own name, just audible in "Up / Down," on his scale model of this experience.[7]

The modern experience of waiting—frustrating, boring, distracting—breeds awareness of the system. Nobody likes to wait—least of all for the opportunity to continue waiting. Waiting commonly occurs at spatially and temporally indeterminate junctures, nodes, or backups in the system, making us question the system itself. What's taking it so long? There's got to be a better way. Let me out! The everyday critical, poetic consciousness brought on by waiting has attracted other urban poets writing in Oppen's wake. In "East Coker" (1940) T. S. Eliot finds the mystical "way down" in the experience of waiting in a suspended subway: "when an underground train, in the tube, stops too long between stations / And the conversation rises and slowly fades into silence." At such moments, Eliot advises passengers to "wait" without hope, love, or thought, so as to experience their temporary temporal derailment.[8] In "Melodic Trains" (1975) John Ashbery raises representative suspicions about the system's deregulated operating procedures: "Only the wait in stations is vague and / Dimensionless, like oneself. How do they decide how much / Time to spend in each? One begins to suspect there's no / Rule or that it's applied haphazardly."[9] Most recently, in a grumbling lyric interlude in *The Practice of Everyday Life,* the sociologist Michel de Certeau claims that waiting in a standing or moving train is a "travelling incarceration. Immobile inside the train, seeing immobile things slip by. What is happening? Nothing is moving inside or outside the train. The unchanging traveller is pigeonholed, numbered, and regulated in the grid of the railway car, which is a perfect actualization of the rational utopia."[10] Whether rational or haphazard, regulated or discrete, gaps in the system preoccupy its passengers. Poems likewise keep us waiting until their questions arrive.

What holds up "White" is its syntax. It doesn't take us long to sense its structural instability, which keeps us from travelling directly through it or from operating it smoothly. Since the "red globe," the inverted subject of the verbless sentence "From the / Under arm of T // The red globe." (to which we could supply the verb "depends," after its prototype, Williams's "so much depends," which also juxtaposes "red" and "white" but rural objects), follows the prepositional phrase "From . . . ," we would expect a corresponding "white globe" to follow from the parallel prepositional phrase, "From the quiet. . . ." But "White.", discretely isolated, is displaced from the bottom to the top of the poem. In its anticipated place we find elliptical dots, ticking like minutes or floors. The poem also has a few screws missing. Along with the expected key words "elevator" and "wait," Oppen has carefully removed any image of people waiting, or more precisely, he has removed them from the picture plane, situating them invisibly, along with us, before the unopen elevator and the unyielding poem. The punctuated "White." is an incomplete sentence but a complete (muttered or unspoken) utterance. Those

below, very likely on the ground "Stone floor," see "White," meaning Up, and think "Wait." Period. What else can you do? This particularly excruciating wait has several stages: first you wait for the elevator to stop elevating, then you wait for it to return to your floor, finally you climb in and wait for your destination, on another floor, before repeating the operation in reverse. "White." not only implies but echoes or encrypts the imperative "Wait." I call this kind of productive underwriting "cryptography," the unwritten words "crypt words," and their resonant traces "markers." Though missing from the poem, "wait" drives its productive malfunctioning.

In its earlier published form, in Zukofsky's Objectivist anthology in *Poetry* (February 1931), "Thus" (then symmetrically divided into a central quatrain and two surrounding quinzains) was ill-paired with the langorous Jamesian exercise "The knowledge not of sorrow," which now functions as a proem for the series. By contrast, "White," with its vertical object and objectification, makes such a good introduction to "Thus" that it seems likely it was written to order. On one occasion, Oppen wrote of them in series, sketching the second poem's undergirding syntax: "And its quiet / stone floor. From there to 'thus'— big business—'hides the parts.'"[11] The "deep structure" of Oppen's unstopped, scrambled poem goes something like this: Thus, prudishly, big business hides its private parts, removes itself, from view; thus (putting it empirically) the big-business husbands remove themselves by elevator from the mundane lunch-counter floor of their shopping wives. As with "White," "Thus" operates by ironic dislocations: "big-Business," the grammatical subject and poetic object, is deferred until the final, punch line while "private" and "from view" are removed entirely. Even so, the general social significance of this Depression-era lyric sample is clear enough to present-day readers. But the historical and textual specifics of Oppen's objectification are probably less so. To piece "Thus" together, after more than a half century of capitalist prudery, we need to know something of the contemporary relations between its partly visible parts—"big-Business," "Frigidaire," and "Soda-jerking."

When Oppen wrote "Thus," the term "big business" was relatively new (it came into currency around the turn of the century). His quirky punctuation of it, "big-Business," is significant: the inverted capitals mark a typographical pun on capital and the hyphenation incorporates two words into one conglomerate. The term referred to large combinations of businesses merging and acting together to corner markets and to influence governmental policy; one result was the series of business-friendly Republican Presidents in the 1920s (Harding, Coolidge, and Hoover) who ushered in the Depression. These combinations were "incorporated," a legal expedient whereby a corporate body maintained the privileges and immunities of a "private" citizen (this metaphor informs Oppen's "private act"). Corporations were both horizontal (buying up competitors and controlling prices) and, like "Thus," vertical (controlling the production process from the gathering and preparation of raw materials to manufacturing to marketing). With its self-interested philosophy of Social Darwinism, the sanctity of private (corporate) property, laissez-faire government policy, and labor efficiency, big business managed much of modern life in the United States.[12]

The challenge and potential of the corporate poetic object are evident in "Frigidaire," which in "Thus" names both an "individual" refrigerator (each goes by the same brand name) and the corporation. The Frigidaire Corporation, a subsidiary in the 1920s and 1930s of General Motors, was probably the largest manufacturer of refrigerators of its day, having sold its millionth in May 1929. Frigidaire's biggest sales were to other, often affiliated corporations. The advent of compact, inexpensive refrigerators in the 1920s, which enabled merchants to stock a full menu indefinitely and sell it anywhere (drug stores, cigar stores, hardware stores), assured the viability of Frigidaire.[13] The Crash presented only a temporary setback for the company; in 1931 its sales jumped nearly 40% over the previous year, an achievement made possible by an undercutting 10% price reduction.[14] Refrigerated soda fountains reproduced rapidly to become America's first fast-food chains. By the end of the 1920s, every sales counter had to have what Oppen calls a "plane of lunch."

A sense of the impact the soda fountain had on modern New York life is afforded by Eunice Fuller Barnard's 1930 feature in the *New York Times,* "Our Filling Station: The Soda Fountain."[15] Soda fountains, Barnard notes, have made American eating a public affair: "Three meals a day, once a function of hearth and home, and lately of the kitchenette and restaurant are passing before our unconsidering gaze to the nickeled and marbled purlieus of the soda fountain." For Barnard, the soda fountain embodies a democratic ideal of "Broker and stenographer" sharing a counter (if not employment opportunities), while "embryo financiers and literati who in an earlier generation would have been sharpening their wits against the boarding house beef-steak, now snatch their orange juice and soft-boiled eggs across the marble counter." These "soda-chains," as they were called, were run by national corporations, and were in effect a growing part of the new big-business service industry. Mesmerized by what Oppen elsewhere in *Discrete Series* calls "20th century chic and / efficiency" (5), and clearly taken by Frederick Winslow Taylor's enormously influential principles of scientific management (with efficiency experts and time-and-motion studies), Barnard marvels at the modern fountain: "It represents to date the ultimate economy of space and time. Mixing, cooking, refrigerating, eating, and dishwashing for hundreds of people . . . go on within a few square feet. Moreover, in the up-to-date soda dispensing chains the whole process is timed to the fraction of a second. . . . In fifteen minutes at the outside [the businessman] should have finished his lunch and be on the way back to the office." (In the accompanying behind-the-counter sketch, soda-jerking is performed with the precision of a ballet; the nearest jerker dispenses soda with his thumb while discreetly closing

what appears to be the refrigerator door with his toe.) Businessmen can thus manage their own time more efficiently: "What with this efficient shuttling process and a soda luncheonette in every office building, eating is all but done on the job." As modern eating is "scaled down" to "less than an hour a day," space too is conserved; whereas the Romans ate reclining on cushions, "today in our compressed and vertical cities dawns the new era of standing about the fountain." As in Oppen's compact poem, seating is limited. Modern women, increasingly present in midtown as consumers, also conserve corporate space, Barnard speculates, and seek out the fountain "for viands at once sweet and slenderizing."

The soda-jerker, often an itinerant worker in seasonal fountains around the nation, was himself a replaceable moving part. Barnard notes that soda-jerkers, more than "foreign-born" restaurant employees and cooks, were "at least 90 per cent American," and met "the fountain's traditional demands merely by being native-born, strong, quick, and what is known in the trade as clean-looking." Unfazed by these racist hiring practices, what Barnard balks at is the prohibition of the soda-jerker's flavorful style and lingo in which "'Burn one, and let it cackle,' is, for instance, the signal for an egg malted milk." She laments that "recently, . . . sundry of the so-called soulless corporations have been attempting to quell such fountain effervescence. . . . [The soda-jerker's] deportment and his syntax should conform to Chesterfieldian models." With their "drills in manners," their "decorous good morning," and their "standardized uniforms" and recipes, "the soda jerker's life is rapidly losing that abandon of self-expression once so characteristic of the profession."

What Oppen, with a non-Chesterfieldian parallelism, calls "the prudery / Of Frigidaire, of / Soda-jerking—" was closely monitored and controlled; reproduction was to proceed only along company lines. As Barnard notes, the rise of soda fountains coincided with Prohibition ("soda water" was also known as "sober water"); the drinks and behavior were healthy and brisk. To expose this prudery, revealing the "private parts" "under the counter" (two crypt phrases of "Thus"), is Oppen's object. If "Frigidaire" exemplifies this prudery, one reason is surely its resonance of "frigidity"—a pseudo-scientific corporate diagnosis of the 1920s (which Oppen seems to take at face value), applied to the lack of female sexual response. Present only in the infertile genitive "of wives," women in "Thus" are themselves objectified as consuming appendages of big business. In frustration over their frigidity, the soda-jerkers jerk soda ("jerk off" like "frig" had meant "masturbate" since the previous century). Oppen's ideological critique of the disembodied or sterile corporation is neither banal nor vague. At the base of the phallic tower, he focuses on the fount (the ground floor) of corporate "reproduction" (another productive crypt word here) where eggs are sprayed with fizz. This artificial insemination seems motivated in part by the proverb, best known in French, "On ne saurait faire une omelette sans casser des oeufs" ("if you want to make an omelette, you have to crack some eggs"; Oppen wrote *Discrete Series* partly in France). Oppen reproduces "oeufs" in the generative genitive "Of," with its ovular capital, isolated for cryptographic emphasis and hidden within cracked eggshell parentheses. The proverb has been taken to mean that making a living involves sacrifices and risks. But Oppen's music of construction, which opposes the sibilant fizz ("Thus," "Business") to the consonantal crack, adds a more violent sense to the corporate act of "Cracking eggs." "The ends justify the means" would be a good translation. What goes on under the counter, "the private act," is hidden from view; the split-level organization of the soda fountain reproduces the two-story architecture of fountain and tower.

In fact, the aggressive prudery of incorporation reproduces Oppen's objectivist poetics too closely for comfort. The poetics of discretion, efficiency, cleanness and neatness (Oppen called a bad line "muffed" and "messed"), and serial identity all find their counterparts in big business. Another, less pejorative word for "prudery" in "Thus" might be "discretion." "Discreet," like "discrete," derives from *discernere,* to distinguish an object from other objects, including oneself. Despite Oppen's insistence that objectivist poetics should not be confused with "the psychologically objective attitude" (*D* 1968: 173), this discernment requires objectivity. In "Thus," for instance, Oppen hides his private response, removes himself from our view. As postmodern poets struggle against the current of free-floating commodification, Oppen strives in "Thus" to distinguish his own poetics from the operations of big business. But how indeed can he or we distinguish objectivist from corporate discreetness? The answer in which I believe is that Oppen exposes big business's private parts and practices by openly hiding and displacing them. His poem may be efficient, it is not quickly digested. It keeps us waiting, thereby forcing us to question what lies behind (and outside) it. In a much later poem, **"The Building of the Skyscraper"** (131), locked in its own struggle against Sartrean nihilistic "vertigo," Oppen observes that "The steel worker on the girder / Learned not to look down, and does his work / And there are words we have learned / Not to look at, / Not to look for substance / Below them." We can no longer ignore or dismiss corporate technological life as unreal; it represents everyday experience for too many people. But neither can we afford not to look down or through the chic efficiency to the messy hidden productive parts; too many people are risked and sacrificed in the process.

3. HUGHES'S LOOSE CHANGE.

From the 1930s to the 1950s, George Oppen and Langston Hughes led different but strangely parallel lives. Both became involved with the Communist party in the 1930s, Oppen because of the Depression, Hughes because of the Scottsboro trial. Hughes continued writing poems in the 1930s, some hotly political, while Oppen, who couldn't reconcile political with poetic activity, stopped. Both poets

supported the 1948 presidential campaign of the Progressive candidate, Henry Wallace; both were hounded by anti-communists and investigated by the FBI.[16] Hughes, the more prominent writer, drew more high-level attention. In May 1948, months before he began writing *Montage of a Dream Deferred,* Hughes was attacked by name for his ironic poem "Goodbye Christ" in J. Edgar Hoover's essay, "Secularism-Breeder of Crime" (*R* 168). The Oppens went into exile in Mexico in 1950; Hughes testified in 1953 as a "cooperative witness" before the House Un-American Activities Committee. Under interrogation by Roy Cohn and Senator Joseph McCarthy, he proved a wily but sadly self-incriminating witness, refusing to disavow his political affiliations directly but disclaiming some of his earlier political poems (*R* 209-221). But already before the hearings, Hughes had been experimenting in a new, quickly changing poetics which would be harder for his censors to pin down.

Nearly thirty years after Oppen's lyric series, Hughes produced his own serial lyric, and first long poem, *Montage of a Dream Deferred.*[17] Like Thelonius Monk, Hughes breathlessly improvised his seventy-five page poem on the typewriter in the first week in September, 1948 (*R* 151). Dedicated to Fanny and Ralph Ellison (the latter a jazz musician), the series was scored on the apparently discrete schemes of cinema and jazz. By basing his poem on jazz progressions, Hughes was situating himself aesthetically as well as physically in his Harlem community. As he explains in his irrepressible authorial note, *Montage* should be listened to for its changes: "In terms of current Afro-American popular music and the sources from which it has progressed—jazz, ragtime, swing, blues, boogie-woogie, and be-bop—this poem on contemporary Harlem, like be-bop, is marked by conflicting changes, sudden nuances, sharp and impudent interjections, broken rhythms, and passages sometimes in the manner of the jam session, sometimes the popular song, punctuated by the riffs, runs, breaks, and disc-tortions of the music of a community in transition." For Hughes, the endlessly progressive variations of jazz composed an unrealized dream session: "To me jazz is a montage of a dream deferred. A great big dream—yet to come—and always *yet*—to become ultimately and finally true."[18] With its rapid breaks and casually jarring changes, Hughes's playing was likely to be discounted as experimental nonsense, as some of his previous poetry had been. In his Jesse B. Semple (or simply, Simple) column in the *Chicago Defender* (19 November 1949; written after the composition but before the publication of *Montage*), Hughes justified be-bop's "nonsense" as a highly significant (signifying) outlet of black urban pain. Simple derives the nonsense term "be-bop" from "the police beating Negroes' heads. . . . Every time a cop hits a Negro with his billy club, that old club says, 'BOP! BOP! . . . BE-BOP! . . . MOP! . . . BOP! . . . That's where Be-Bop came from, beaten right out of some Negro's head into them horns and saxophones and piano keys that plays it. Do you call that nonsense?"[19]

Hughes also synchronized his poem with a technique not drawn from his Harlem community, cinematic montage, a method of breaking up and slowing down the action by rapidly intercutting similar but unrelated images. Hughes implicitly likens montage to the rapid, uninterrupted transitions of jazz segues, as in the direction of one of the subsections of *Montage,* "Boogie segue to Bop." Hughes was well aware of the avant-garde and ideological history of montage. When he went to the Soviet Union in 1932 with a group of black artists to work on an ill-fated joint cinematic venture, *Black and White,* it was Sergei Eisenstein, whose *Battleship Potemkin* had appeared in 1925, who gave the party in the visitors' honor.[20] In the 1960s Oppen conceded that montage technique had also informed his **Discrete Series,** noting that one of its poems (**"Who comes is occupied"**) is "a sort of 'montage,' because there's just the city and I'm jumping around like the fashionable camera of that time" (*D* 1981: 201). While the jam session of dialogue and back talk most immediately distinguishes Hughes's "poems within a poem" from Oppen's relatively silent shots, *Montage* also exploits cinematic, visual effects, especially in the less emphatically rhythmic, elliptical, "slighter" poems, though these have received little attention.[21] But swift waters also run deep.

I will focus on the third of the six sections, or sessions, of *Montage,* "Early Bright" (running from "Flatted Fifths" to "Tag"), and on two of its poems in particular, "Tomorrow" (30) and "Cafe: 3 A.M." (32). Inverting the rural idiom "bright and early," Hughes's "early bright" is what his fellow native Missourians would call the middle of the night, illuminated in Harlem by a neon brightness, as he illustrates in "Neon Signs" (17):

> Spots where the booted
> and unbooted play
>
>   ∴
>
>   LENOX
>
>   ∴
>
>   CASBAH
>
>   ∴
>
>   POOR JOHN'S
>
>   ∴
>
> Mirror-go-round
> where a broken glass
> in the early bright
> smears re-bop
> sound

In "Neon Signs" each capitalized line stop is a night stop until the close, as the poem segues to be-bop. Rhythms return with the bopping "Mirror-go-round," in which a dance-hall mirror globe reflects the merry-go-round's carnival atmosphere. The word itself is "smeared" (in jazz terminology "smearing" means sliding or slurring one note into another). But in the late 1940s, a time of increasing redbaiting, the word also had more sinister connotations, as in "smear-sheet," an expression coined around the time *Montage* was published. Hughes's word-smearing is his

variation on cryptography, playing off-beat and sometimes dissonant harmonies over continuous melodies.

The dawn's own early bright is awaited in "Tomorrow":

> Tomorrow may be
> a thousand years off:
>
> TWO DIMES AND A NICKLE ONLY
>
>   says this particular
>   cigarette machine.
>
> Others take a quarter straight.
>
>   *Some dawns*
>   *wait.*

As Oppen did with "White" and "Thus," Hughes makes us wait, and think, for the poem to deliver. And as with Oppen's pair of poems, the rough outlines of the social message come through immediately: the "revolution" (the crypt word marked by "dawn") may be indefinitely deferred. But once again, the poem's productive specifics are less forthcoming. The opening clairvoyant couplet is itself dreamy; only the punctuating "off:" (instead of "a thousand years away . . ."), puts the present object in our way, or more accurately, a sign—not an invitation as in "Neon Signs" but a prohibition.

In 1948 this sign was, first of all, a sign of things to come. In August, around a month before Hughes began *Montage,* new cigarette taxes were being levied in New York and New Jersey, raising the price of a pack of cigarettes from 20¢ to 23¢. As a consequence, "cigarette vending machines," as the *New York Times* reported, "were being altered to operate on quarters."[22] Beyond hiking prices, this "particular" corporately jimmied machine will not take a "quarter," money of the same value but in a different form. That is, to use a pun encrypted here, it will not accept the revolutionary "change" of equal access. For that, you have to make change. While we wait, the Jim Crow smear dawns on us. In case it doesn't, Hughes gives us the unsmeared version of "TWO DIMES AND A NICKLE ONLY" further along in *Montage,* in "Freedom Train" (45): "I hope there ain't no Jim Crow on the Freedom Train, / No back door entrance to the Freedom Train, / No signs FOR COLORED on the Freedom Train, / No WHITE FOLKS ONLY on the Freedom Train." The machine's corporate prudery is color-coded. In an article entitled "My Most Humiliating Jim Crow Experience," Hughes recalls that while on a high school expedition to hear Sarah Bernhardt he and "a Polish-American" classmate went to eat in one of Cleveland's modern "self-service" cafeterias. Each boy loaded his tray with cheap dishes:

> But when the white woman looked at me and then down at my tray, I thought she would never stop striking the keys on the cash register. . . . Finally the cashier pulled out a check and flung it on my tray. It was *Eight Dollars and Sixty-Five Cents!*

My friend's check had been only about forty-five or fifty cents. I had selected about the same amount of food. I looked in amazement at the cashier.

"Why is mine so much?" I asked.

"That is just what you will pay if you eat in here," said the cashier.[23]

Hughes and his friend left the cafeteria, which he reports would be picketed in subsequent years. The "particular" machine of "Tomorrow," which like this cashier seems to "register" Hughes's color and charge him accordingly, is part of an encompassing capitalist system which reserves the right to refuse to wait on some. As with Oppen's perverse capitalization "big-Business," Hughes's capitalization makes us wait until we take in its Capital. When Mussolini's forces conquered Ethiopia in 1936, Hughes published a searing indictment in the *New Masses,* "White Man," which ended by capitalizing on a similar typography: "Is your name spelled / C-A-P-I-T-A-L-I-S-T? / Are you always a White Man? / Huh?"[24] In "Tomorrow," Hughes, himself a heavy smoker (*R* 148), denies us the deep-down satisfaction of the capitalist drag.

In the next line, Hughes talks back with a bounce: "Others take a quarter straight." But this isolated line defers its final meaning with a host of competing senses. The idiomatic use of "straight" here alters the no-nonsense streettalk, "He takes his liquor straight," with "quart" smeared into "quarter." But what kind of unmixed (segregated?) pleasure do these other machines promise? Getting "straight" can mean getting high or getting sober. A "straight" cigarette isn't rolled with marijuana—as it seems to be in Hughes's elliptical riddle-poem across the page, "Gauge" (31): "Hemp. . . . / A stick. . . . / A roach. . . . / Straw. . . ." Even so, "Tomorrow" might have ended with this snappy comeback, which resolves the poem syntactically and rhythmically. Instead, Hughes's last phrase quiets the poem down again and shifts printing keys: "*Some dawns / wait.*" Italics signify voices elsewhere in *Montage,* but these three spaced words, with a wait before "*wait,*" are uttered or played from out of nowhere. The dislocation is heightened by the deferred or supplemental syntax. We expect some contrastive syntax to structure "Tomorrow" such as "This particular machine . . . but others" or "Some . . . but others." In Hughes's brilliant mirror-go-round, "this . . . Others . . . Some dawns / wait" (cf. "Someday"), we are left waiting before the machine. But "Tomorrow," like Oppen's elevator, never comes.

At least since the end of World War II, another, underground meaning of "straight" has been "not gay."[25] This stray meaning from "Tomorrow" re-emerges in "Cafe: 3 A.M.":

> Detectives from the vice squad
> with weary sadistic eyes
> spotting fairies.
> *Degenerates,*
>
> some folks say.

> But God, Nature,
> or somebody
> made them that way.

> Police lady or Lesbian
> over there?

> *Where?*

As different as it seems (no trace of modern mass-marketing here, no speedy efficiency, no big-Business gleam, no segregated "democratic" counter[26]), Hughes's cafe is actually quite similar to Oppen's soda fountain. Both public eating places prohibit alcoholic consumption, Oppen's soda fountain after Prohibition and Hughes's cafe after the bars have closed (Hughes usually worked until dawn after leaving the bars; *R* 148). Moreover, both spots are smeared with "prudery," Oppen's in the name of efficiency, Hughes's in the name of normative morality. And as sexuality continues to manifest itself in different forms under Oppen's counter, in Hughes's cafe homosexuality removes itself from the vice squad's particular view. Rampersad, who finds no definitive evidence that Hughes was homosexual (*R* 149), neglects the testimony of poems such as "Cafe: 3 A.M." in which Hughes at the very least displays an uncanny discernment of an early bright atmosphere—at once charged with danger and dissipated with confusion. The dreamy sophistication of Hughes's be-bop verse is often overlooked. In the first poem in "Early Bright," "Flatted Fifths" (be-bop's dominant note), "Little cullud boys with beards," high on beer and jazz, suffer a "sea change": "at a sudden change" their drinks "become sparkling Oriental wines / rich and strange" and they appear transvested in "silken bathrobes with gold twines" (29). In this respect, Oppen's public place is as different from Hughes's as day from early bright.

"Cafe: 3 A.M." stages a McCarthy-era paranoid scene, infiltrated by an "enemy in our midst," where the lines of demarcation are smeared: white and black, day and night, male and female ("Police lady"), masculine and "fairy," straight and lesbian, undercover and closeted, informer and customer. Our eyes adjust more or less gradually to Hughes's critique: What's the difference between the "sadistic" detectives and the so-called "*Degenerates*"? Whose behavior is "straight" and whose is "crooked"? In "Passing" (57), Hughes looks wryly at those downtown blacks "who've crossed the line," who "miss you, / Harlem of the bitter dream, / since their dream has / come true." Sweet and bitter dreaming is still dreaming; and passing in the 1950s was also a nightly expedient. At the end of "Cafe: 3 A.M." the dialogue parts are confused: "Police lady or Lesbian / over there? // *Where?*" The final italicized question disorients the complicit, detecting reader. Where indeed are we in this open ending—in the night spot where nothing is spotted, in the invisible montage? In Hughes's surrealist subversion, the detectives aren't bopped back but put to sleep.

4. The Poem's Objective.

All four of the poems discussed above concern the pursuit of private happiness in public places, while none of them incorporates "I" or addresses "you." Hughes's as well as Oppen's serial poems might thus be termed objectivist; or they might be described as public, satirical, and political rather than private, romantic, and personal. This kind of description associates the subjective with what is inside—private, hidden, undemonstrable, possibly nonexistent—and the objective with what is outside—public, visible, verifiable, beyond question. An objectified poem, like an object in full view, would have nothing to hide. But as we have seen (and not seen), these eminently objective poems are just as elusive and idiosyncratic as any of their subjective predecessors. As with corporate things, their agency is dramatically and discreetly hidden and displaced.

What, then, is the objective, the point, of these urbane poems? How can they object to their incorporated mirror images? Enmeshed in history, these poems see through corporate networks without seeing to the end of them. They raise questions, about themselves and their objects, without laying them to rest. Unlike the increasingly instantaneous systems in which they find themselves, these serial poems keep their consuming readers waiting. Thus neither series is, nor can their "explications" be, a definitive exposé. What makes Oppen's **Discrete Series** and Hughes's *Montage of a Dream Deferred* inexhaustibly objective is the way they keep the prudish city's undersides plainly hidden, all the while showing that something else, some dawn or door, has not yet opened.

Notes

1. L. S. Dembo, "Oppen on his Poems," interview with George Oppen, *George Oppen: Man and Poet,* ed. Burton Hatlen (Orono: National Poetry Foundation, 1981) 212. Quotations from this interview, which was conducted in 1968, will be cited hereafter in the text as *D* 1981, to distinguish it from an earlier published portion of the interview, "George Oppen," *The Contemporary Writer: Interviews with Sixteen Novelists and Poets,* ed. L. S. Dembo and Cyrena N. Pondrom (Madison: U of Wisconsin P, 1972), which will be cited as *D* 1968. Burton Hatlen's invaluable collection of interviews and essays will be cited hereafter as *H.*

2. William Carlos Williams, "The New Poetical Economy," *Poetry* 44 (July 1934): 220-25; reprinted in H 267-70.

3. Louis Zukofsky, "Program: 'Objectivists' 1931," *Poetry* 37.5 (February 1931): 268. A revised version of the essay appears in Louis Zukofsky, *Prepositions: The Collected Critical Essays of Louis Zukofsky* (1967; Berkeley: U of California P, 1981) 12-18.

4. George Oppen, *The Selected Letters of George Oppen,* ed. Rachel Blau DuPlessis (Durham: Duke UP, 1990) 122. References to Oppen's letters are from this edition, noted hereafter in the text as *SL.*

5. George Oppen, *The Collected Poems of George Oppen* (New York: New Directions, 1975) 3-4.

6. My reading of Oppen's *Discrete Series* has benefited from several incisive and lively studies: Tom Sharp, "George Oppen, *Discrete Series,* 1929-1934," H 271-292; Harold Schimmel, "(On) Discrete Series," H 293-315; Marjorie Perloff, *Radical Artifice: Writing Poetry in the Age of Media* (Chicago: U of Chicago P, 1991) 79-92; Joseph M. Conte, *Unending Design: The Forms of Postmodern Poetry* (Ithaca: Cornell UP, 1991) 121-41.

7. Oppen began writing poetry again, after a twenty-eight year hiatus, after dreaming of an article entitled "How to Prevent Rust in Copper," a title in which he discerned his own somewhat tarnished name. See Mary Oppen, *Meaning a Life: An Autobiography* (Santa Barbara: Black Sparrow Press, 1978) 201.

8. T. S. Eliot, *The Complete Poems and Plays, 1909-1950* (New York: Harcourt Brace Jovanovich, 1971) 126-27.

9. John Ashbery, *Houseboat Days* (New York: Viking, 1977) 24.

10. Michel de Certeau, *The Practice of Everyday Life,* trans. Steven Rendall (Berkeley: U of California P, 1984) 111.

11. Oppen, *Letters* 90.

12. For a readable introduction to these matters, see Samuel Eliot Morison, Henry Steele Commager, William E. Leuchtenburg, *A Concise History of the American Republic,* 2nd ed. (New York: Oxford UP, 1983) 361-71, 577-600.

13. David M. Schwartz, "Life was sweeter, and more innocent, in our soda days," *Smithsonian* 17 (July 1986) 194.

14. *New York Times* 28 January 1928: 31; 17 May 1929: 36; 21 October 1930: 38; 16 June 1931: 15.

15. *New York Times* 2 February 1930: 5, 8, 20.

16. For a concise summary of Oppen's harassment by the FBI and fear of the HUAC, see DuPlessis's introduction to Oppen's *Selected Letters,* xiii-xvii. Hughes's political activities in the 1940s and after are examined in detail in Arnold Rampersad's invaluable biography, *The Life of Langston Hughes,* vol. 2 (New York: Oxford UP, 1988). References to Rampersad's biography are made in the text, abbreviated hereafter as *R.*

17. Langston Hughes, *Montage of a Dream Deferred* (New York: Holt, 1951). The poem is also included, without subsections, in Hughes's *The Collected Poems of Langston Hughes,* ed. Arnold Rampersad and David Roessel (New York: Knopf, 1994) 387-429.

18. Langston Hughes, "Jazz as Communication," *The Langston Hughes Reader* (New York: Braziller, 1981) 494.

19. Hughes's dialogue "Bop" may be found in Hughes's *The Best of Simple* (New York: Farrar Straus Giroux, 1990) 117-19.

20. Faith Berry, *Langston Hughes: Before and Beyond Harlem* (1983; New York: Citadel, 1992) 159.

21. For an engaging survey, see Onwuchekwa Jemie, "Jazz, Jive, and Jam," *Langston Hughes,* ed. Harold Bloom (New York: Chelsea House, 1989) 66-79.

22. *New York Times* 6 August 1948: 28.

23. Langston Hughes, *The Langston Hughes Reader* 488.

24. Hughes, *Collected Poems* 195.

25. See *Dictionary of American Slang,* ed. Harold Wentworth and Stuart Berg Flexner, 2nd ed. (New York: Crowell, 1975) 524.

26. Upon the publication in 1950 of his first compilation of "Simple" columns, Hughes complained in the *Chicago Defender* that "this gentleman of color . . . can't get a cup of coffee in a public place in the towns and cities where most of our American book reviewers live (unless it is a 'colored' place)" but "is, nevertheless, being most warmly received by white critics from Texas to Maine" (quoted in R 179).

Norman Finkelstein (essay date 1995)

SOURCE: "In the Realm of the Naked Eye: The Poetry of Paul Auster," in *Beyond the Red Notebook: Essays on Paul Auster,* edited by Dennis Barone, University of Pennsylvania Press, 1995, pp. 52-56.

[*In the following excerpt from a study of writer/poet Paul Auster, Finkelstein examines the Objectivists', and especially Oppen's, importance to Auster's poetics and worldview.*]

If Paul Auster's work were concerned only with the past or with the flickering self, it would not have achieved the tensile strength and jagged expressivity that mark it as among the best American writing of the last twenty years. In poetry especially, a concern solely for tradition or solely for the vicissitudes of the ego will severely limit a writer's range of expression. Even when such concerns are simply combined—as in the case of Robert Lowell, for example—one can expect only limited success. "Its past was a souvenir," Wallace Stevens says in "Of Modern Poetry"; and then, echoing Whitman, "It has to be living, to learn the speech of the place / It has to face the men of the time and to meet / The women of the time" (174-175). If such Romantic optimism, such broad extroversion, is less accessible in recent years, it is due to the equally Romantic pull of interiority, which becomes increasingly difficult to resist when the men and women of the time prove to be some-

what more banal than Stevens believed. Given such circumstances, modern lyric interiority risks triviality, as does a poetry devoted only to exteriors.

The objectivists are some of the few poets who manage to avoid this impasse. Scrupulously measuring even minimal encounters of self and world, and dedicated to finding the linguistic strategies necessary to render their measurements into a verse both abstract and sensual, poets such as Louis Zukofsky, Charles Reznikoff, and George Oppen become increasingly important to a younger generation that values integrity—in thought, in feeling, in craft—above all else. The objectivists share the general modern distrust of tradition, but grow strong through secret affinities to the past (Oppen, author of the paradigmatic **"Psalm,"** once admitted that Blake was more important to him than was W. C. Williams). These poets, paying such close and thoughtful attention to the present moment, in turn provide the new generation with links to a usable past. As Auster says in "The Decisive Moment," his essay on Reznikoff, "Each moment, each thing, must be earned, wrested away from the confusion of inert matter by a steadiness of gaze, a purity of perception so intense that the effort, in itself, takes on the value of a religious act" (*Art of Hunger* 36).

This piece, dated "1974; 1979," is written during the years when Auster's poetry is most strongly influenced by the objectivists. For Auster, Reznikoff's insistence on the poem as a "testimony" to the individual's perceptions of the world, or Oppen's belief that poetry should be a "test of truth," does indeed take on the value of a religious act. As the objectivists themselves understood, such a poetic both confirms and supplants an older form of devotional poetry, though as Harold Bloom often points out, it is difficult in this context to make a clear distinction between secular and religious literature. The older religious poem, at least in the Jewish tradition, is predicated on a preexisting text as a manifestation of transcendental presence, however remote. Frequently the poem is in some sense a midrash or commentary. In *Wall Writing* Auster subverts but still depends on this strategy, given the aura of some previously inscribed source or "prooftext" that hovers around many of the poems. But the devotional quality of the objectivist poem depends on a complete sense of absence, for only then can direct encounters with the material world take on the value previously reserved for encounters with mediating sacred texts. The poet is thus doubly exiled: from the homeland, to be sure, but from what George Steiner calls the homeland of the text as well. "For as long as he remains in the realm of the naked eye," Auster announces in *White Spaces,* "he continues to wander" (*Disappearances* 107).

This "realm of the naked eye" differs from the world of the original objectivists in that it is far more barren and rendered with greater abstraction. Like Auster's *In the Country of Last Things,* it is a realm in which objects seem to "disappear and never come back" (1). The glinting pieces of broken glass, the twigs and buds growing in urban lots, the sparrows and children hopping about the stoops and alleys—in short, all the reassuring materials of the objectivist lyric, quietly celebrated for their mere being—are gone. In *White Spaces,* all that is left is "a landscape of random impulse, of knowledge for its own sake—which is today a knowledge that exists, that comes into being beyond any possibility of putting it into words" (*Disappearances* 103-104). Speaking a language that is almost prior to language, a language of bare consciousness that methodically eschews the enumeration of objects, the poet, invoking the "invisible God of the Hebrews," states flatly that "It is sometimes necessary not to name the things we are talking about" (105).

Readers familiar with the tenets of objectivism may wonder how a poetry based upon acts of testimony and reportage can become transformed, in Auster's hands, into a poetry made out of "letters from nowhere, from the white space that has opened up in his mind" (106). What are these spaces into which the objective world has disappeared, and more importantly, how could the same impetus behind objectivism lead to such resolute unmaking? In fact, it is a logical progression. Objectivism, as these poets themselves came to understand it, is primarily concerned not with objects per se, but with a language of objectification derived dialectically from an honest apprehension of a subjective response to the world. The term that the objectivists so often privilege in discussing their work is *sincerity,* and it is sincerity as the force behind the poet's reportage that also operates in Auster's work. If a white space opens in the poet's mind, if he is continually faced with "the supreme indifference of simply being wherever we happen to be" (104), he must keep faith with himself by finding a discourse that will objectify even so subjective a state of experience. Furthermore, while Auster admires, perhaps even envies the objectivists' ability to give themselves (though not without a struggle) to the simple grace of the object world, he understands that he cannot give himself to the world in quite the same way. The quasi-religious optimism of the objectivists' careful gaze finally is remote from the bleaker perspective of Auster's naked eye.

A helpful comparison could be drawn between *Disappearances* (1975), the title sequence of Auster's volume, and the poetry of Oppen, especially ***Of Being Numerous*** (1968). Auster's poem bears the clear influence of Oppen's work from the sixties: the same dry, clipped phrasing; the deliberately measured lines of varied lengths, expressive of concerned mental activity; the uncanny abstraction in the face of what is obviously a wildly sprawling urban sensorium. Oppen's great theme, "the ship-wreck / Of the singular" (151), and the consequent social and political exploration "of being numerous," opens outward, despite his persistent skepticism and frequent horror, into a vision of community:

> Which is ours, which is ourselves,
> This is our jubilation
> Exalted and as old as that truthfulness
> Which illumines speech.
>
> (173)

Although the "meditative man" has been subsumed by the crowd, the potential for "clarity"—in poetry as much as in social existence—is preserved.

But in *Disappearances* (and the very title can be opposed to Oppen's precariously balanced but still hopeful ***Of Being Numerous***), although Auster acknowledges that he too is "beyond the grasp / of the singular," a brooding counternarrative develops:

> He is alive, and therefore he is nothing
> but what drowns in the fathomless hole
> of his eye,
>
> and what he sees
> is all that he is not: a city
>
> of the undeciphered
> event,
>
> and therefore a language of stones,
> since he knows that for the whole of life
>
> a stone
> will give way to another stone
>
> to make a wall
>
> and that all these stones
> will form the monstrous sum
>
> of particulars.
>
> (77-78)

The stones in the wall, the people of the city, produce "the monstrous sum / of particulars"—a horror of anonymous multiplication against which the poet can only oppose "his nostalgia: a man." Later in the poem, Auster, understanding his subjectivity is lost within such monstrosity, elaborates on his predicament:

> It is nothing.
> And it is all that he is.
> And if he would be nothing, then let him begin
> where he finds himself, and like any other man
> learn the speech of this place.
>
> (83)

Language may be our only recourse, but it does not offer the same regenerative promise of clarity as in Oppen's work. Auster's conclusions are more limited, tentative, guarded:

> . . . For the city is monstrous,
> and its mouth suffers
> no issue
> that does not devour the word
> of oneself.
>
> Therefore, there are the many,
> and all these many lives
> shaped into the stones
> of a wall,

and he who would begin to breathe
will learn there is nowhere to go
but here.

(85)

Here, not elsewhere: no longer a discourse of the other, Auster's poetry resignedly takes up residence in the familiar, for it has nowhere else to go. But if a primal rediscovery of self and world (however historically determined) offers his objectivist fathers renewed poetic opportunities, for Auster such chances have already been exhausted.

Michael Davidson (essay date 1997)

SOURCE: "Palmitexts: George Oppen, Susan Howe, and the Material Text," in *Ghostlier Demarcations: Modern Poetry and the Material Word,* University of California Press, 1997, pp. 64-93.

[*In the following excerpt, Davidson examines how Oppen's method of composition "built" his poems into objects.*]

Piling up pieces of paper to find the words

—George Oppen

In the previous chapter, I described how Gertrude Stein's most recalcitrant work reveals a social narrative in textual practices that would seem to serve entirely aesthetic ends. Those practices include her use of repetition, her deployment of social idiolects, her puns and pronominal play, her satirical use of canonical genres (play, sonnet, Bildungsroman), her flattened diction. What I have called "textual practices" Stein called "composition" to invoke both the evolving character of writing in time and the overall shape of the text. But perhaps we can see this social narrative in the physical page itself—not the published version of a text but the handwritten or typed manuscript on which the author first begins to compose. How does the materiality of the page interact with the materiality of social forms beyond the archive? What happens when the writer foregrounds manuscript and archive in the final published version? What is on the surface of the page?

To answer these questions we might turn to a page from the papers of George Oppen [. . .]. It is relatively free of penciled marks or emendations. Brief prose remarks are spaced at intervals, sometimes separated by typed underlining. At the top of the page is a short lyric entitled **"Rembrandt's Old Woman Cutting Her Nails"**:

An old woman
As if I saw her now
For the first time, cutting her nails
In the slant light

It is a poem whose brevity and economy embody many of the values one associates with Imagism and Objectivism. The only concession to a larger theme is the phrase beginning "As if," which introduces the absent poet, a third participant in the conversation between painter (Rembrandt) and old woman. This "As if" finds its visual correlative in the reference to "slant light," which hints at the indirect source of sight, mediated through a painter, a historical period, an aesthetic frame, a rhetorical displacement: "As if I saw her now."

Below the poem, perhaps serving as a commentary on it, is a prose remark, typed in caps:

WE HAVE A LONG TRADITION OF CONTEMPT FOR MATTER, AND HAVE CEASED TO NOTICE THAT ITS EXISTENCE—AND ONLY *ITS* EXISTENCE—REMAINS ABSOLUTELY UNEXPLAINED

To some extent this prose extends the poet's meditation on Rembrandt's design but shifts the emphasis from the painting's subject—the old woman—to its materiality, a shift that, as subsequent lines make clear, has distinctly existential implications:

We speak of people's death, except the deaths of the extremely old, as if they might have lived forever Of course they could not have, and therefore the difference between thirty years of life and seventy years does not in itself define tragedy

But the wives or husbands and parents and children!! That is, when the young die, there are the bereaved By the time the old man or woman dies, no one is bereaved? Dare we say that?

What began as a depiction of an old woman has now become an interrogation of the life beyond her. The author seems anxious to interpret the painting by understanding the world he shares with it, a world in which matter "matters." And to the degree that both painter and poet engage the problem of mortality, they share the same world. What links poet and painter, youth and age, painting and subject is care: "It would be hard for human nature to find a better ally in this enterprise than love," the poet quotes from *The Symposium.* But care alone is not enough; the material expression of that care, as presented in painting, poem, and prose, is the form that love takes. "Mankind is a conversation," and one might add that the page itself, in its wandering and questioning, is the material analog of that conversation.

This page by George Oppen, one of thousands like it among his papers housed at the Archive for New Poetry at the University of California, San Diego, represents a crucial problem for any consideration of literary genre: that of the poem's materiality, its existence as writing.[1] Once we have seen the poem in this context, it becomes difficult to isolate it from its written environment. Indeed, can we speak of "poetry" at all when so much of it is embedded in other quotations, prose remarks, and observations? Does Oppen's oeuvre end in the work we know as *The Collected Poems,* or does it end on the page where it began? I would like to take up some of these questions by thinking about the status of the manuscript page, not out of some antiquarian interest in early drafts but out of a concern for epistemological and social questions that lie at the heart of genre theory. For if genre implies a way of organizing knowledge, then to "think genericity" is to think thinking.

The question of genre in recent literary theory has most often taken the form of a debate over "new" genres (various forms of non-narrative prose, sound poetry, procedurally derived forms) or the rediscovery of previously marginalized genres (the manifesto, the fragment, the epistle). And while this discussion has had a useful taxonomic function, it has not addressed the issue of genericity itself, the degree to which modern and postmodern texts challenge notions of categorization altogether. It could be said that the current debate extends a more pervasive romantic skepticism over formal categories, manifesting itself on the one hand by a pursuit of some idealized, Mallarméan *livre* or on the other by a ruthless exhaustion of types through forms of appropriation, quotation, and parody.[2] It could equally be said that both positions rest on an opposition between literary and ordinary language that can be transcended only by exploiting the possibilities of the former to accommodate selective aspects of the latter.

The most significant critique of genericity has occurred within the context of poststructuralism with its emphasis on *écriture* as the recognition of difference (*différance*) within the linguistic sign. Literature ceases to be defined by its "signs of literariness" but rather by its intransitivity, its refusal of rhetorical and generic markers. This refusal is a deterritorializing gesture that displaces the authority of official print culture in favor of what Deleuze and Guattari (1991) have called a "minor literature." I would like to retain poststructuralism's emphasis on writing as trace, as inscription of an absence, but emphasize the material fact of that trace, an inscribing and reinscribing that, for lack of a better term, I have called a "palimtext." By this word I mean to emphasize the intertextual—and interdiscursive—quality of modern writing as well as its materiality. The palimtext is neither genre nor object but a writing-in-process. As its name implies, the palimtext retains vestiges of prior inscriptions out of which it emerges. Or, more accurately, it is the still-visible record of its responses to those earlier writings.

The palimtext is a kind of ruin that emerges in an era when ruins no longer signify lost plenitude. The modern ruin, as Walter Benjamin points out, is immanent in mass-produced commodities, an allegory of modern materiality's impermanence and ephemerality. Like the electric lights in Stein's Faust play, the modern commodity-as-ruin transforms the idea of illumination to a gaudy display, invented for maximum exposure and salability, not for the subtleties of chiaroscuro. Textual self-referentiality—the modern equivalent of the baroque allegorist's memento mori—becomes a recognition of transitoriness and ephemerality in a world committed to the illusion of progress and permanence. Baudelaire is Benjamin's example of the modern allegorical poet precisely because he first diagnoses the shock features of modern urban life—the juxta-

positions of dissimilar phenomena encountered among crowds in the city. The Paris of Baudelaire's poems "is a submerged city, more submarine than subterranean," and like the city the poet's lyrics are an archaeology of historical transformations and ruptures; they provide a "pictorial image of dialectics, the law of dialectics seen at a standstill" (*Reflections* 157).

It is this image of dialectics at a standstill that best describes the manuscripts of George Oppen, a poet whose lyricism has often been treated as the replacement or repression of his own political involvement. By looking at his manuscript page, we can test his avowed interest in separating art and politics by showing his poetry as a form of daily practice. Because Oppen's work so little challenges generic boundaries, his material text becomes important for reconsidering the authority of those boundaries. The image of historical rupture in the lyric also animates my understanding of more recent writers such as Susan Howe, whose self-conscious manipulation of the material features of the page attempts to animate voices that speak from the margins of American frontier ideology. In both poets, the material nature of the sign and its specifically social and discursive contexts become part of what Oppen called a "lyric reaction to the world."

"A LYRIC REACTION TO THE WORLD"

Poetry, according to Louis Zukofsky, "is precise information on existence out of which it grows" (*Prepositions* 28). It is seldom observed, however, that this growth begins and ends on a page. Traditional textual research has provided us with a methodology for investigating such materiality, but always with an eye toward some definitive version out of which to establish a copy text. As Jerome McGann points out, textual criticism has had until recently one end: "to establish a text which . . . most nearly represents the author's original (or final) intentions" (*Critique of Modern Textual Criticism* 15). That desire to recover the author in the work is part of a "paradigm which sees all human products in processive and diachronic terms" (119). Those intentions can be discovered by locating the last text upon which the author had a primary hand before it came under the influence of copy editors, compositors, and house style. The textual editor must master the corrupt text and delete any superfluous or extraneous material not directly related to the work in question. Genre becomes an ally in such mastery insofar as it provides a codified set of rhetorical and textual markers to which the text must ultimately conform. The editor's service to the author therefore is mediated by generic expectations.

Modern poets, in this context, are no different from previous generations in the way that they keep notebooks, use paper, and revise their work. But poets since Pound have incorporated the material fact of their writing into the poem in ways that challenge the intentionalist criteria of traditional textual criticism. At the same time that poets have foregrounded the page as a compositional field, they have tended to "think genericity" to an unprecedented degree, making the issue of formal boundaries a central fact of their poetics. Indeed, for many poets today it has become meaningless to speak of "the poem" but rather of "the work," both in the sense of oeuvre and of praxis. We can see the evolution of such a poetics not just in the writings of poets but in their papers and manuscripts that, in increasing numbers, have been deposited in academic libraries. What we see in such collections is the degree to which writing is archaeological, the gradual accretion and sedimentation of textual materials, no layer of which can ever be isolated from any other. George Oppen's page, to return to my initial example, is only one slice through a vast, sedimented mass that quite literally rises off the page, carrying with it the traces of prior writings. That page is part of a much larger conversation for which the published poem is a scant record.

One of the most important implications to be derived from studying the material text is the way that the page reinforces certain epistemological concerns, notably the idea that writing is a form of knowing. Robert Creeley's remark, "One knows in writing," Charles Olson's equation of logos and mythos (thought and saying), and Allen Ginsberg's poetics of spontaneity are but three examples of a pervasive attempt to ground thought not in reflection but in action (Creeley, "An Interview," 279; Olson, *The Special View of History* 20). George Oppen is no exception. In a letter to Rachel Blau DuPlessis, he speaks of the poem as a "process of thought" and then goes on to qualify this remark:

> but it is what I think. A poem which begins with an idea—a "conceit" in the old use of the term—doesn't learn from its own vividness and go on from there unless both terms of the conceit or one at least is actually *there.* I mean, had it begun from the parade, the experience of the parade and stuck to it long enough for the thing to happen it could have got one into the experience of being among humans—and aircraft and delivery trucks—?

("Letters to Rachel Blau DuPlessis" 121)

For Oppen the poem does not represent the mind thinking; it *is* the thinking itself, including its marginal references, afterthoughts, and postscripts. One may begin with a "conceit," but, if one attends to the "parade" of passing things, one will find oneself "among humans—and aircraft and delivery trucks." Like one of his favorite philosophers, Heidegger, Oppen understands that knowledge is gained not by bracketing experience but by finding oneself already in the world, engaged in human intercourse. The poet strives to reduce words to their barest signification, prior to their subordination to cognitive or rhetorical schemes.

The ideal of a poetry that no longer represents but participates in the process of thought is hardly new. It is part of the romantic movement's desire to escape forms of associationism and empiricism by a belief in the poem's creative nature. George Oppen is seldom mentioned in such contexts, but this is because we have tended to read his poetry through modernist spectacles. Critics have seen his work as the logical extension of certain Imagist principles involving "direct treatment of the thing" and economy of language. It is as though we have focused only on the first word in the title to his first book, *Discrete Series,* to the exclusion of the second. By doing so, we have reified the processual—and I would argue dialogical—nature of his thought in an ethos of the hard, objective artifact.[3] Such a reading is not surprising; many of Oppen's own comments speak of the poem as a discrete object among others, "a girder among the rubble," as he liked to quote from Reznikoff. This emphasis on the single poem is supported by his oft-stated desire to find the final real and indestructible things of the world, "That particle of matter, [which] when you get to it, is absolutely impenetrable, absolutely inexplicable" ("Interview" 163).

My contention is that, rather than being regarded as a series of single lyric moments, George Oppen's poetry should be seen as "a lyric reaction to the world," a fact that becomes dramatically evident once one looks at a page like the one described earlier ("Interview" 164). His poems represent the outer surfaces of a larger debate that appears fragmentarily in broken phrases, ellipses, quotations, and italics. We know, for example, that *Of Being Numerous* is constructed largely around quotations from Meister Eckhart, Kierkegaard, Whitehead, Plato, Whitman, as well as friends such as Rachel Blau DuPlessis, Armand Schwerner, and John Crawford, all of whom enter the poem silently in the form of inverted commas. And even where such obvious quotation does not occur, as in the poems from *Discrete Series,* Oppen's paratactic logic, truncated syntax, and ambiguous use of antecedents embody the shifting attentions of a mind dissatisfied with all claims to closure. Like the **"Party on Shipboard"** in that volume, Oppen's narrative movement is "Freely tumultuous" (*Collected Poems* 8).

This idea of poetry as a "lyric reaction" can be understood best by comparing a poem from *Of Being Numerous* with a page from which it emerged. In the fourth section of **"Route,"** we encounter the image of a sea anemone, which launches a series of observations on language:

> Words cannot be wholly transparent. And that is the "heartlessness" of words.
>
> Neither friends nor lovers are coeval . . .
>   as for a long time we have abandoned those in
>   extremity and we find it unbearable that we should
>   do so . . .
>
> The sea anemoine dreamed of something, filtering the
> sea
>   water thru its body,
>
> Nothing more real than boredom—dreamlessness, the
>   experience of time, never felt by the new arrival
>   never at the doors, the thresholds, it is the native
>
> Native in native time . . .

The purity of the materials, not theology, but to present
the circumstances

(Collected Poems 186)

"Route" deals with the difficulties of achieving clarity, the
lure of the finite and indestructible in a world of fluid
boundaries. The section quoted here appears to be a qualification of that clarity, an attempt to express the "heartlessness" of words when they refuse transparency.[4] This qualification takes the form of a meditation on boredom, a state
in which the world is reduced, as Oppen says, to "dream-
lessness." The reality of boredom is, as he says elsewhere,
"the knowledge of what *is*," a state in which things have
been divested of instrumental reason and may be encountered spontaneously, without reflection ("Interview" 169).
It is a state in which one is naturalized in one's environment, "Native in native time." Things have lost their novelty and may now be encountered ready-to-hand. This is a
far cry from modernist despair over *ennui* as expressed in
writers from Baudelaire to Eliot. In Oppen's version, boredom is the condition within which the "purity of the materials" may be experienced.[5]

The most confusing lines of this passage are those concerning the sea anemone. It is the only concrete image of
the section and so becomes all the more important in establishing exactly how Oppen understands boredom. On
the one hand, the sea anemone could represent a kind of
ultimate passivity in which the organism's whole existence
is conceived around "filtering the sea / water thru its body."
This interpretation would seem to be borne out by a brief
prose remark included among Oppen's papers:

> Boredom, the sense of lack of meaning—In the cities
> from the sense of being submerged in the flood of
> people, of not being able to see out, of being a passen-
> ger—In the small cities from the sense of shallowness,
> the shallowness of affairs———Actually, of nothing
> happening

Here boredom is compared to "being submerged in the
flood of people," a sort of urban analog to the anemone's
condition. On the other hand, because it is capable of
dreaming (at least in Oppen's version), the sea anemone
might represent the endurance of concern and novelty
against the deadening effects of routine. However the "conceit" is being used, Oppen is clearly trying to find an image of reduced nature, a biological reality that challenges
the theological and metaphysical. In its published version,
the image of the sea anemone cannot be interpreted symbolically; it is one of those "heartless" words that must be
interrogated over time and through the poem.

This refusal of the anemone to become symbol is all the
more evident when we look at a page upon which it makes
an earlier appearance. Unlike the final published version in
which all lines are relatively long, the typescript page contains a variety of prose and lined verse forms [. . .]. The
image of the sea anemone is contained in considerably
shorter lines and seems to respond to a previous prose remark:

Impossible to use a word without finally wondering
what one means by it. I would find that I mean nothing, that everything remained precisely as it was without the word, or else that I am naming absolute im-
plausibilities, which are moreover the worst of all
nightmares

The attempt to name, to "use a word without finally wondering what one means by it," leads to a cycle of repetition in which the only thing to say is that "we die":

> We die we die we die
>
> All there is to say
> The sea-anemeone dreamed of somethong
> No reason he should not
> Or each one does
> Filtering the sea water thru his body

I have retained Oppen's typos and misspellings to indicate
how, at least in his early writing of it, the sea anemone
was closely identified with the individual. The pronoun
"one" is hidden in the misspelled word "anemeone," and
"somethong" is explicitly developed in the penultimate
two lines (deleted from the published version). These two
lines also provide an alternate antecedent for "his" in the
final line, uniting anemone and human subject. Oppen
wants to link human mortality with that of other creatures—as if to say "each one of us is like the sea anemone,
living in a perpetual state of boredom, filtering the world
rather than reflecting upon it. In this state all we can say
of existence is that 'we die.'"

This existential fact is not alleviated by theological alternatives. In the published version, Oppen stresses "The purity of the materials, *not theology,* but to present the circumstances" (emphasis added), but in the typescript
version an attack on theology becomes the central feature,
directly linked to Oppen's concern with language: "Because some people wrote a book a long time ago, they
think they know what god is." This remark on the limitations of an authorizing logos is extended later in a definition of the trinity as "the man, the spirit, and the mystery. /
Which is man. And says nothing about god." In pencil,
Oppen has added "Job's God," a remark that may very
well have inspired the final remark: "an inconceivably brutal universe; it is possible that sea anemones dream continually." Clearly a logocentric world view is inadequate
to the brutality of the universe, a disparity given secular
force by the image of the anemone and salvific force by
the story of Job.

What we see in the typescript page but not in the published poem is the dialogue between individual sections,
each responding to and qualifying the previous. The sections are linked, one to the next, in a debate or argument
over the efficacy of language in a "brutal universe." Language is both the vehicle and the object of Oppen's speculations as he oscillates between competing propositions.
Such dialectical progress can be seen in the published version to be sure, but the page—with its spelling mistakes,

holograph emendations, and variable lineation—provides a "graphic" indication of how immediate and personal that progress is. Where the published page provides us with a series of more or less balanced (if truncated) prose statements on the theme of language, the typescript page provides us with the "graphic voice" out of which that theme emerges. The page shows Oppen grousing about difficulties of self-expression, the image of the sea-anemone serving as a satiric version of the poet himself dreaming in his watery environment. The sea anemone, rather than serving as an icon of either boredom or conscious reflection, is a term around which all other sections constellate. It does not "serve" the poet's purpose but gets in his way, forces him to ask each question anew.

The Archive

The varieties of intentions I have described on one page are repeated throughout Oppen's archive. Like the individual page, the archive returns a quality of voice and physicality to work that may seem, in its published version, hermetic and isolated. In terms that I have already employed, the archive revises generic expectations, turning lines of poetry into quotations, queries, and speculations. As this chapter's epigraph suggests, Oppen was engaged in "Piling up pieces of paper to find the words" that would ultimately become poems. The archive is the physical remains of that piling up and deserves to be described as a text in its own right.

As the onetime curator of the Archive for New Poetry, I had a unique chance to view Oppen's papers in their pristine state, before they were divided up into separate categories according to genre (manuscripts, notes, correspondence, daybooks, etc.). When I first opened the boxes in which the papers were sent, I was not prepared for the chaos that appeared. Where some archives come in folders or envelopes with dates or other identifying marks on them, Oppen's papers appeared as a great midden with shards of writing in every conceivable form, no one page related to the next. A page containing a verse from the early 1960s would be followed by a page with scribbles from his last days. Prose and poetry were interspersed with grocery lists, phone numbers, quotations from philosophers, observations on films, tables of contents from books (his own and others). Every conceivable type of paper had been used, from cheap, high-acid newsprint (seriously decaying and flaking) to letterhead bond. Writing had been performed equally by typewriter and pen, the former often heavily annotated by the latter. Occasionally, passages of particular importance had been circled by crayons or felt-tipped pencil. Each manuscript page was like the collection as a whole: a marvelously scribbled, jumbled, and chaotic written field.

Although the bulk of the collection consists of individual pages like those already discussed, there are numerous larger manuscripts made up of anything from two to several hundred pages. In some cases, these manuscripts consist of a final typed draft of poems for a book, but in most cases the gathering is simply a heterogeneous scatter of poems, jottings, and typings. The methods by which these groupings are held together deserve some comment. Oppen used a variety of fasteners—from safety pins, pieces of wire, and pipe cleaners to ring binders. The manuscript for the poem **"The Little Pin"** is held together, appropriately enough, by a little pin. Another batch of pages is held together by a nail driven through the upper left-hand corner into a piece of plywood. A better definition of Objectivism cannot be imagined.

Oppen's method of composition can be best glimpsed by considering what I will call his "palimpsestic" manuscripts: pages of individual poems onto which new lines or stanzas have been glued so that the revised draft seems to rise vertically off the page in a kind of thick, textual impasto. Rather than add new lines on fresh sheets of paper, he would build his poem on top of itself, adding new lines, in many cases ten or twelve pages thick. One such palimpsest, containing work from *The Materials,* appropriately enough given the title, is "built" out of a ring binder. On the front and back inside covers, Oppen glued the entire script for a reading given at the Guggenheim Museum, including his own interlinear commentary.[6] The binder's metal clasps hold part of a manila envelope (addressed to the Oppens in Brooklyn) to which other drafts and fragments are glued. The whole pile of pages is held together by pipe cleaners that are wrapped, at the top, around a number 2 pencil and a one-inch roundhead screw.[7]

My purpose in describing the material component of Oppen's work is to suggest the degree to which writing was first and foremost a matter of something ready-to-hand—as immediate as a coat hanger or piece of wire. The pipe cleaners, metal clasps, and glue are visible representations of those "little words" that Oppen liked so well, the basic materials of a daily intercourse. "Gone for Breakfast in Z coffee shop across the street," reads the back of one heavily scribbled folder, indicating that the recto of poetry easily became the verso of daily living. And just as he used whatever writing surface was nearby, so he drew upon the "signage" that surrounded him: newspapers, books, magazines, and, of course, conversations, parts of which can be found recorded through the collection. Oppen did not keep a separate notebook for poems and another for quotations and another for prose but, rather, joined all of them together in a continuing daybook.[8] One finds drafts of letters to friends on pages that contain the beginnings of poems. In many cases, a quotation from a newspaper would become the genesis of a poem, a poem the genesis for a prose commentary on an article in the newspaper.

This daily, unbound diary covers an extraordinary range of subjects: the youth culture of the 1960s, the civil rights movement, rock and roll, the poetics of Imagism, the work of John Berryman ("shameless but seductive"), Jung, the Vietnam War, the Altamont concert, Elizabeth Bishop's "The Fish" ("I had always thought 'o to be like the Chinook' was the silliest line ever written, but I see that it is not"), Charles Olson on PBS ("giving birth to the continent out of his head like Jove"), Plato, Hegel, and Marx. His comments on Robert Lowell's "Skunk Hour" are worth quoting in full:

> perhaps I simply do not understand the Christian sense of "sin." I do not understand a sin by which no one was injured. If the people in the love cars were embarrassed by his peeking, then it was a sin. If not, it was merely undignified.

Or his remarks on Pound:

> —and if Pound had walked into a factory a few times the absurdity of Douglas' theory of value, which Pound truculently repeats in the *Cantos* would have dawned on him—it sometimes pays to have a look And to keep still till one has seen.

Treated palimtextually, such remarks elucidate that trinity of concerns that informs Oppen's entire life: politics, epistemology, and poetics. The archive suggests that all three are inextricably united like those jerry-rigged manuscripts held together with pipe cleaners. As he meditated on contradictions in American politics, so he drafted poems; as he drafted poems, so he thought about the relationship of old age to love. The manuscripts do not suggest someone working toward the perfect lyric but one struggling for a vision of society in which the poem plays an instrumental role. To adapt a remark on the page mentioned earlier, Oppen "knows what he thinks but not what he will find."

Notes

1. All references to George Oppen's papers are to the George Oppen Manuscript Collection at the Mandeville Department of Special Collections, University of California, San Diego.

2. To be historically accurate, the debate over genres is no longer "current," important work by Marjorie Perloff, Linda Hutcheon, Brian McHale, David Antin, Ihab Hassan, and others having been conducted between 1970 and 1980. What has superseded debate over genre more recently has been a powerful "narrative turn," marked most dramatically by the work of Fredric Jameson but visible in current trends in cultural studies, new historicism, and postcolonial studies. I discuss this shift in chapter 5.

3. Exceptions to this rule of reading Oppen's work as discrete poems are Joseph Conte's chapter on Oppen in *Unending Design* and Alan Golding's essay on "George Oppen's Serial Poems."

4. In earlier drafts of the poem, section 4 directly follows those which, in the published version, conclude section 2: "I have not and never did have any motive of poetry / But to achieve clarity."

5. Eric Mottram glosses these lines as stating that "Knowledge of boredom becomes a philosophic tool to ascertain what the facts are" ("Political Responsibilities of the Poet" 151).

6. The unusual convention of providing an oral script for one's reading is sustained by Oppen's colleague Charles Reznikoff. In the latter's papers, also housed in the Archive for New Poetry, can be found several such scripts for various venues, accompanied by written "offhand remarks" to the audience. A visual record of such practices can be seen in a video made of Reznikoff's reading at San Francisco State University given in March 1973 and available through the Poetry Center, San Francisco State University, 1600 Holloway Ave., San Francisco, Calif., 94132, catalog number 36/28.

7. Many of the palimpsestic manuscripts had originally been pasted to the wall of Oppen's study, suggesting that he not only wrote *on* paper but lived quite literally *within* it.

8. I have edited a selection from Oppen's "daybooks" in *Ironwood* 26 (1985): 5-31. Excerpts appear, as well, in *Conjunctions* 10 (1987). Since many pages from his daybooks are early drafts of what became letters, it is worth looking at Rachel Blau DuPlessis's edition of *The Selected Letters of George Oppen*, which faithfully maintains the poet's spacing and typography.

Peter Nicholls (essay date 1997)

SOURCE: "Of Being Ethical: Reflections on George Oppen," in *Journal of American Studies,* Vol. 31, No. 2, August, 1997, pp. 153-70.

[In the following essay, Nicholls explores the meaning of "ethical" when applied to a state of "being-between" which Oppen's career and his poems both suggest he occupied.]

The poems of George Oppen continue to occupy a marginal place in most literary histories, even though his work encapsulates some of the major shifts in American writing between high modernism and contemporary Language poetry. In part this marginalization is due to the habit of tying Oppen to Louis Zukofsky's shortlived "Objectivist" tendency of the thirties. Oppen did indeed publish his first collection, *Discrete Series,* in 1934, and with a strong endorsement from Ezra Pound ("I salute a serious craftsman, a sensibility which is not every man's sensibility and which has not been got out of any other man's books").[1] Yet after this propitious start Oppen fell silent for twenty-five years, jettisoning poetry for politics. He and his wife Mary were members of the Communist Party between 1936 and 1941, their activities eventually attracting close scrutiny from the FBI.[2] In 1949, Oppen and his family opted for political exile in Mexico to avoid harassment. They would not return until 1958; only then did Oppen begin writing poetry again, initiating a sequence of major volumes, from *The Materials* (1962) to *Primitive* (1978).

The break in Oppen's literary career raises important questions about where we "place" his work historically, questions which are highlighted by the recent publication of two fat anthologies of twentieth-century American poetry. In Douglas Messerli's *From the Other Side of the Century,* for example, Oppen appears in the early pages in the company of fellow Objectivists like Louis Zukofsky, Lorine Niedecker, Carl Rakosi, and Charles Reznikoff. In Paul Hoover's *Postmodern American Poetry,* on the other hand, Objectivism is not represented at all, and the volume opens instead with work by Charles Olson and John Cage.[3] Clearly, Hoover sees writers like Oppen as contributors to an earlier modernism, whereas Messerli locates the original Objectivist group within the main line of innovation which runs from 1960 to 1990.

Of the two choices, Messerli's seems to me the better one. To begin with, there are the historical facts of publication: each of the poets I have named above was still bringing out collections in the seventies (Zukofsky, *80 Flowers,* 1978; Niedecker, *Blue Chicory,* 1976; Rakosi, *Ex Cranium Night,* 1975; Reznikoff, *Holocaust,* 1975; Oppen, *Primitive,* 1978), and this continued productivity to some extent compels us to reckon with a sort of double chronology. On the one hand, there is "Objectivism," a phase or tendency which is often (misleadingly) seen as merely an offshoot of Pound's Imagism; this is writing which develops its particular texture and perspectives from the experience of the Depression years. Then there is the later work which shows these writers offering an influential alternative to the so-called "personal" poetry of later decades.[4] The matter of designation—whether the Oppen-Zukofsky group were "modernists" or not—is not of especial importance in itself, but what does interest me is the intermediary position they now seem to occupy: *between* modernism and postmodernism, perhaps; a betweenness, at any rate, which seems highly characteristic of much of this writing at the level of both its formal and social ambitions.

As was clear in Zukofsky's own manifesto essay, "Sincerity and Objectification" (1931), Objectivism was (somewhat paradoxically in view of its name) a practice of writing which was ultimately concerned less with objects than with the "shape" of the poem and "the resolving of words and their ideation into structure."[5] What was objectified was the poem itself; as Zukofsky put it: "This rested totality may be called objectification—the apprehension satisfied completely as to the appearance of the art form as an object" (274).[6] The word Zukofsky had reluctantly chosen at editor Harriet Monroe's insistence would, however, continue to mislead; Oppen signalled the problem on several occasions:

> Several dozen commentators and reviewers have by now written on the assumption that the word "Objectivist" indicated the contributors' objective attitude to reality. It meant, of course, the poets' recognition of the necessity of form, the objectification of the poem.[7]

At first sight, this version of "objectification" may sound like just another formalism, but it actually entails a significant departure from Poundian modernism. As Rachel Blau DuPlessis observes, "This poetics . . . had an ethical dimension, for it began with the person, not the word, that

is, began with sincerity."[8] Pound's notion of "technique as a test of a man's sincerity" lay in the background,[9] though the absoluteness of that axiom would lead in *The Cantos* to the very different assumption that linguistic precision was *in itself* adequate proof of authorial honesty and sound judgement.[10] Oppen seems not to have been an avid reader of that poem, responding to its local felicities rather than to its grand ambition,[11] but, as one of his own poems, **"Of Hours,"** makes clear, the perceived failure of *The Cantos* and the tragedy of the life which sustained it came to represent one blind alley of a modernism disastrously wedded to a politics it hardly understood ("What is it you 'loved,'" asks Oppen of this finally "Unteachable" poet).[12] What had begun as unplanned adventure, an Odyssean "sailing after knowledge," mutated across the thirties into a vision which Pound habitually defined as "totalitarian."[13] Increasingly the poem concerned itself with definitions of just authority, even as the writing began to close down questions about its own judgemental legitimacy. Where the early *Cantos* had to some degree invited the reader's scepticism, now the poem began to demand a certain faith; and, as Pound began to discover in Mussolini a stronger, more authoritative self-image, so the poem acquired an intransigent, often hectoring tone.

It is important to appreciate the difference between the forms of objectification increasingly at work within Pound's poem and the kind of writing that Oppen and Zukofsky define as "Objectivism." In the latter case, as I have said, it is the poem that is objectified, whereas in one major strand of the earlier modernism—the strand represented by Pound, Eliot, Lewis, and Hemingway—it is "the world outside, the other [that] is always object."[14] In this aesthetic, the self's relation to the other is generally construed as one of domination, and is characterized by discontinuity and separateness. Successful individuation entails the establishing of boundaries which divide the self from others. Psychic maturity is associated with a break from the feminine and maternal which is now conceived as other and object. The modernist avant-garde we associate with the writers I have named thus has a strong agonistic component—aesthetic form is seen to be won from struggle, in the process of which a masterful and coherent self emerges over against the chaotic, purely appetitive forces of a decadent modernity.

The principal interest of Objectivism is arguably that it marked the point where a new generation of poets initiated a radical departure from these forms of objectification and from the politics they embodied. Pound's *Cantos* was thus, for this generation, a crucially ambiguous work, offering, on the one hand, an array of dazzlingly new formal devices while, on the other, exhibiting all the dangers of an increasingly pragmatic politics of mastery. As the poem moved into its late sequences—*Section: Rock-Drill* (1955) and *Thrones* (1959)—it must have seemed increasingly clear to those readers still in the dinghy astern that Pound was becoming more and more comfortable with an openly didactic mode. These late Cantos developed the mixed tones of the Pisan sequence, oscillating between the fragmentary and indeterminate, on the one hand, and the as-sertive, not to say imperative, habit on the other. In line with Pound's dependence on neo-Confucian texts like *The Sacred Edict of Kang H'si,* the rhetoric became increas-ingly paternalistic while the model of social order invoked was nakedly feudalistic. At this point, myth, politics, and ethics seemed to fold into one, a synthesis which could seem untroubling only in so far as it was projected back into an idyllic and remote past.

Almost from the first, Oppen was keen to dissociate the terms of Pound's synthesis of myth, politics, and ethics. The two poets' divergence in this respect is particularly striking given that both were drawn in different ways to a vision of social totality: Pound came to invest more and more heavily in a unitary model of social process—"The whole tribe is from one man's body," he declared in *Thrones*[15]—while Oppen returned again and again to the formal and conceptual problems of collective identity. Yet the divergence in their thinking was a telling one—not simply because Oppen went Left rather then Right, but be-cause he insisted on the rigorous separation of poetry from politics. Of twentieth-century American poets, Oppen was perhaps keenest to drive home that lesson in both his work and his life, as his long period of "silence" amply testifies.

For some critics, though, Oppen's political commitments cannot but be felt in the later work, and Burton Hatlen, among others, has made a strong case for the persistence of certain "Marxist" themes in these volumes.[16] Oppen himself, however, was adamant about the incompatibility of politics and poetry—not simply because the poetry of the Left had proved to be little more than sloganeering, but also because (as he put it in **"The Mind's Own Place"** [1963]), "the aesthetic . . . will be defined outside of any-body's politics, or defined wrongly," and "the poet, speak-ing as a poet, declares his political non-availability."[17] In comments like these, Oppen seems to look to "writing" or "poetry" as a sort of defence against a totalizing vision. "I was right," he concluded in a retrospective look at the thir-ties, "not to write bad poetry—poetry tied to a moral or a political (same thing) judgment."[18] And, in similar vein, he asserted that "art can no longer present a system, a be-lief,"[19] a view that led him to emphasize "Not . . . that I take truth to be a social virtue. I think very probably it is not. But I think it is poetic: I think really that nothing else is."[20] This "poetic" truth is hard to define, though we may take it that once again Oppen is trying to dissociate his own work from any taint of (Poundian) instrumentalism. "There are situations," he declares, "which cannot honor-ably be met by art, and surely no one need fiddle precisely at the moment that the house next door is burning."[21]

Does this divorce between aesthetics and politics distin-guish Oppen's work from high modernism, or does it actu-ally tie him more closely to it? Andrew Ross thinks the latter:

> Regardless of whether we might agree with Oppen that it is not a question of aesthetics, or "bad fiddling," his

final opinion—that "the question can only be whether one intends, at a given time, to write poetry or not"—would have to be regarded today as a superannuated one.[22]

Oppen's dissociation is by this account a modernist one, and he is thus to be distinguished from postmodern writers like the Language poets for whom poetry can become "po-litically sufficient in itself" (365). Ross is thinking of claims made by contemporary poets like Bruce Andrews for "writing *as* politics, not writing *about* politics. Asking: what is the *politics* inside the work, inside *its* work? In-stead of instrumentalized or instrumentalizing, this is a po-etic writing more actively *explanatory*."[23] Yet Oppen is wary of this word "political" and its tendency to cohabit with "truth"; for him, poetry has a different role to play:

> It is part of the function of poetry to serve as *a test of truth*. It is possible to say anything in abstract prose, but a great many things one believes or would like to believe or thinks he believes will not substantiate them-selves in the concrete materials of the poem. It is not to say that the poet is immune to the "real" world to say that he is not likely to find the moment, the image, in which a political generalization will prove its truth.[24]

Oppen thus warns us that poetry is not a purveyor of "truth," but rather that it submits "truth" to a kind of "test." Exactly what this "testing" might be becomes clearer if we consider politics not just as social action, but as also, in some sense, akin to Poundian myth in its aspiration to to-tality and "generalization."

The idea that poetic language may somehow refuse to "substantiate" such myths brings to mind Jean Luc Nan-cy's more recent account of writing as an "interruption" of myth. In *The Inoperative Community,* Nancy suggests that myth expresses a desire for communion—"fusion in a shared, immanent Being,"[25] the community that becomes "*a single* thing (body, mind, fatherland, Leader)" (xxxix); by way of contrast, Nancy proposes an idea of community based on "being *in* common" in which there is no single social identity, but rather an experience of "singularity" through which Being is understood as divided and shared (xxviii), what Nancy calls a "strange being-the-one-with-the-other to which we are exposed" (xxxix). It is literature which "puts into play nothing other than being *in* com-mon," concludes Nancy, and, more specifically, it is writ-ing which has the capacity to "interrupt" those fantasies of immanence and fusion which characterize the condition of myth: "once myth is interrupted, writing recounts our his-tory to us again" (69).[26]

Nancy's account has several points of connection with Op-pen's work. First, his notion of "being *in* common" stresses both "the impossibility either of an individuality, in the precise sense of the term, or of a pure collective totality" (6).[27] This refusal of the conventional polarity of indi-vidual and society parallels Oppen's evasion of the agonis-tic structure of the modernist avant-garde, with its tensed subject-object relation. It was this dimension of Pound's poetics which most troubled Oppen: "Pound's ego system, Pound's organization of the world around a character, a kind of masculine energy, is extremely foreign to me."[28] So, too, was the related sense of what Oppen termed "the closed universe, the closed self";[29] he would base his own work on a deliberately alternative model of subjectivity as "encountered, not found."[30] The encounter is somehow tentative because it is grasped as a movement or process, so, when Oppen recalled in an interview that "The first question at the time [the early thirties] in poetry was simply the question of honesty, of sincerity,"[31] the point was that a poetics founded on the (philosophically) simple recognition of actuality—"That it is"[32]—would ultimately concern itself with an equally "simple" and non-agonistic perception of social relationships. Viewed in these terms, poetry might offer a way of acknowledging the world and others without seeking to reduce them to objects of knowledge.

Such a poetics would be quite different from Poundian modernism. In eschewing "knowledge," for example, it would deprive us of any sense of context or ground, yielding instead, as Marjorie Perloff has remarked, a peculiar sense of disconnectedness.[33] Take the first poem of Oppen's major sequence, **"Of Being Numerous"**:

> There are things
> we live among "and to see them
> Is to know ourselves."
> Occurrence, a part
> Of an infinite series,
> The sad marvels;
>
> Of this was told
> A tale of our wickedness.
> It is not our wickedness.
>
> "You remember that old town we went to, and we sat
> in the ruined window, and we tried to imagine that we
> belonged to those times—It is dead and it is not dead,
> and you cannot imagine either its life or its death; the
> earth speaks and the salamander speaks, the Spring
> comes and only obscures it—"

(*Collected Poems* 147) [hereafter abbreviated as *CP*]

Disconnected, certainly: Perloff observes that "the number of prepositions and pronouns, taken together, is greater than that of nouns, adjectives, and verbs combined."[34] This unexpected displacement of emphasis gives the lines a curious feeling of provisionality; the thought is, we might say, precisely pre-positional, postponing any resolution or closing formulation.[35] The form of the writing thus enacts its main theme, which appears to be the inadequacy of narrative as explanation. So "occurrence," which here suggests a moment in which we grasp the connectedness of ourselves and the world, is placed over against the biblical "tale of our wickedness" which has tied humanity to a dogma of guilt and false humility (though "it is not our wickedness"). The past, in fact, escapes us—"you cannot imagine either its life or its death"—whereas the essentially non-narrative "series" offers us an opening into "presentness" rather than the dead weight of past experience.[36]

We may recall here that Oppen's first collection takes the title *Discrete Series* from mathematics as a way of deriving form from the praxis of perception rather than from any predetermined "rule":

> A pure mathematical series would be one in which each term is derived from the preceding term by a rule. A discrete series is a series of terms each of which is empirically derived, each one of which is empirically true. And this is the reason for the fragmentary character of those poems. I was attempting to construct a meaning by empirical statements, by imagist statements.[37]

One of Oppen's favourite examples of such a series was the sequence of stations on the New York subway (14, 28, 32, 42), a sequence expressing contiguity but no extrapolable logic.[38] Following this example, Oppen aimed to jettison narrative for what Derrida has aptly termed a "seriality without paradigm."[39] This takes us closer to one of the major themes of **"Of Being Numerous,"** which is that of the apparent unknowability of what is not the self: "the world, if it is matter, / Is impenetrable" (*CP*, 148). Like the city, which implies the individual's tie to place while all the time actually expressing only pure "flow" (*CP*, 149), the poem moves forward, bringing one thing within the field of another, but (in contrast to *The Cantos*) hesitating to insist on the meaningful connection between them. Hence, perhaps, the ambiguity which plays around the idea of "being numerous": have we "chosen the meaning / Of being numerous" (*CP*, 151) simply because of our bewilderment over "the shipwreck / Of the singular"? Or is Oppen suggesting that we have chosen merely the *meaning* of being numerous and not its reality? Readers have, reasonably enough, been so pleased to find a poet confronting this theme that they have tended to wish away ambiguity in order to discover a powerful sense of social collectivity here. Almost alone, Marjorie Perloff has read the poem more sceptically, observing that "A good deal has been written about Oppen's relationship to the masses, but at least in **"Of Being Numerous,"** the point is that there is no relationship."[40] In fact, she continues, the sequence exemplifies the poet's "withdrawal from human contact" (200); we are closer to the world of Beckett than to any kind of populist vision.

One can sympathize with Perloff's sceptical reading—after all, this does seem a poem which is often as concerned with the distances between people as it is with images of collective experience. Yet we should acknowledge, too, that the poem itself is sceptical about the power of such images, and this testifies not to some ill-concealed "alienation" on Oppen's part, but rather to his sense (comparable to Nancy's) of social being as both divided and shared. We may get closer to Oppen's meditation on this theme if we see it as primarily philosophical rather than political, and informed in part by the poet's enduring interest in the work of Heidegger. For, even in his first small volume of poems, *Discrete Series* (1934), where Oppen, looking back, discerned a clearly "Marxist" component,[41] the major question raised seems to relate to the attempt to see "humanity as a single thing," as Oppen later put it in relation to the poem called **"Party on Shipboard"** ("a statement, and a very clear one, of what I was going in search of when I quit writing"[42]).

Rather obviously, that poem turns on the relation of the particular to the universal, of the waves to the ocean as a whole:

> The shallow surface of the sea, this,
> Numerously—the first drinks—
> The sea is a constant weight
> In its bed.
>
> (*CP,* 8)

The transition between "this" and "numerously" (the old enigma of what is both one and many) pinpoints the principal dilemma of Oppen's work. "I try to get again to humanity as a single thing," he observes in the same letter, "as something like a sea which is a constant weight in its bed."[43] Yet that singleness and constancy is, like Pound's whole tribe sprung from one man's body, a mythic condition, and even in this early poem the vision of totality splinters before it can be fully grasped ("They pass, however, the sea / Freely tumultuous").

Reflecting on his early books, Oppen explained: "I had thought I could arrive at the concept of Being from an account of experience as it presents itself in its own terms."[44] Oppen had chosen, with Heidegger, "the arduous path of appearance," a decision with which he deliberately closed the way to any conception of Being as Platonic essence.[45] Instead, Being is characterized by what Heidegger calls a movement of "withdrawal" (*Zurückziehung*) by which it constantly retreats into individual beings.[46] That sense of withdrawal colours Oppen's handling of the concept of "humanity"; as he puts it in a letter glossing **"Of Being Numerous"**: "We *cannot* live without the concept of humanity . . . and yet we cannot escape this: that we *are* single. And face, therefore, shipwreck. And yet this, the tragic fact, is the brilliance of one's life."[47]

Even as we think the condition of "humanity," then, the collective reveals itself as a collection of singularities, and our only way out of a static ambiguity is to map the constant oscillation between these two conditions, their constant fading into each other.[48] This may help to explain Oppen's scepticism about narrative at the beginning of **"Of Being Numerous"** and, indeed, the otherwise puzzling reduction of "history" to a date "Frozen in the moonlight" in the second poem of the sequence (*CP,* 150). As Nancy puts it, when writing interrupts myth we may recover our history,

> But it is no longer a narrative—neither grand nor small—but rather an offering: a history is offered to us. Which is to say that an event—and an advent—is proposed to us, without its unfolding being imposed upon us. What is offered to us is that community is coming about, or rather, that something is happening to us in common. Neither an origin nor an end: something *in* common. Only speech, a writing—shared, sharing us.[49]

"Neither an origin nor an end"—Nancy's conception of the event (or advent) stresses the in-betweenness which is, for him, a condition of both authentic social relations and of the writing in which they are exemplified ("we would not write if our being were not shared," he observes [69]). The double condition of language, as both personal and collective, as opaque and transparent, embodies the interdependency of self and other: "But compearance is of a more originary order than that of the bond. It does not set itself up, it does not establish itself, it does not emerge among already given subjects (objects). It consists in the appearance of the *between* as such: you *and* I (between us)—a formula in which the *and* does not imply juxtaposition, but exposition" (29).[50] That idea of "exposition" by contiguity rather than juxtaposition-as-opposition (arguably the Poundian mode) seems very suggestive in view of Oppen's idea of "series" as a "cadence of disclosure." So, too, Nancy's sense that "something is happening to us in common" is close to Oppen's creation of an open syntax which constantly proposes relationships and shared experiences without formulating them absolutely. In place of Pound's increasingly didactic relation to the reader, we approach what Language poet Lyn Hejinian calls a "generative" as opposed to "directive" writing: "Reader and writer engage in a collaboration from which ideas and meanings are permitted to evolve."[51] And as Hejinian has said of Gertrude Stein: "it was not truth but understanding that was of value—a shift of emphasis, from perceived to perceiving, and thus to writing, in which acts of observation, as complex perception, take place."[52]

Many of these features can be seen together in **"Occurrences,"** a poem from the late collection *Seascape: Needle's Eye* (1972):

> Limited air drafts
> In the treasure house moving and the movements of
>   the living
> Things fall   something balanced   Move
> With all one's force
> Into the commonplace that pierces or erodes
>
> The mind's structure but nothing
> Incredible happens
> It will have happened to that other
> The survivor   The survivor
> To him it happened
>
> Rooted in basalt
> Night hums like the telephone dial tone blue gauze
> Of the forge flames the pulse
> Of infant
> Sorrows at the crux
>
> Of the timbers
> When the middle Kingdom
> Warred with beasts Middle Things the elves the
>
> Magic people in their world
> Among the plant roots   hopes
> Which are the hopes
> Of small self interest called

Superstition chitinous
Toys of the children wings
Of the wasp

(*CP,* 206)

I am not sure that I completely understand this poem, but nor am I sure that I am meant to. The syntax seems broken, precarious, though to describe it as "fragmented" would misleadingly assume a reconstitutable logic of propositions.[53] As is often the case in Oppen's work, the poem might be said to enact the inadequacy of thought, or at least to propose poetic form as a desirable substitute for more conventional habits of thinking. The difficulty of the text—registered emphatically in the lateral double spacing and in the characteristic ambiguity of line-endings[54]—dramatizes a resistance to thought and to dialectic, a resistance which the lacunary syntax of the poem seems to signal as that of language itself.

But what are these **"Occurrences"**? Oppen glosses the word in a letter as follows: "Occurrences—events the heavy events—and down or somewhere to the toys of everyday, small self-interest, the wings of the wasp."[55] The poem is caught between the large, catastrophic forces of "history," we might say, and the minute temporality of the "commonplace" and "everyday." Like many of Oppen's later poems, this one seems to be written in the shadow of the holocaust, though we deduce that rather obliquely, through references to the survivor and through images of estranged communication (the telephone dial) and the forge flaming. There is no collective pronoun in this poem, no "we" to alleviate the narrow perspectives of "small self interest." The "incredible" has happened to someone else, the survivor, and all that is left to do in the present is to "move" into the commonplace, as Oppen puts it, a move which in "piercing" or "eroding" the mind's structure will somehow open the sensibility to a sense of community with the experience of that survivor. Yet perhaps the main point of the poem is that such a relationship cannot be formulated directly or rhetorically. Nor can the wasp provide a reassuring image of the natural world, as it could momentarily for Pound at Pisa.[56] Instead, the anticipation of relationship is articulated through the hesitancy of the syntax, through ambiguity and apposition, through the heavily stressed and repeated "Of's—all elements which evoke relationship without reducing it to two terms, to a subject-object dualism.

This deliberate lack of closure is, for Oppen, a primary instance of poetry's difference from politics, placing the poem within that intermediary space of which Nancy speaks. To speak politically of the holocaust would be to move within the world of distinct positionalities and moral judgements, whereas these inchoate forms are meant to open up that space between "you *and* I," as Nancy puts it, in which the survivor's experience can be understood without being appropriated as part of "our" historical narrative. The lack of totalization here thus seems to suggest that poetry, in contrast to political discourse, can open relations which precede ideology and morality. As Oppen puts it in a prose section of the long poem **"Route"**:

We are brothers, we are brothers?—these things are composed of a moral substance only if they are untrue. If these things are true they are perfectly simple, perfectly impenetrable, those primary elements which can only be named.

(*CP,* 189)[57]

Naming, as Oppen makes clear in his interview with L. S. Dembo, entails "an act of faith" which testifies in turn to the "simplest" of theologies: "I do believe that consciousness exists and that it is consciousness of something, and that is a fairly complete but not very detailed theology, as a matter of fact."[58] This equation of "truth" with a non-moral impenetrability implies that the sense of commonness Oppen has in mind is one which is primary because it exists prior to social codes and prescriptions.

We may recall at this point a definition of "ethics" which has been much discussed in recent years. I am thinking of the work of Emmanuel Levinas, for whom the Western tradition, and especially the thought of Hegel, has been characterized by a pursuit of knowledge which seeks the subordination of objects and other people to its own power. Philosophy has not, according to this line of argument, been primarily concerned with the claims of other people, but rather with the capacity of the self to elide difference, to make the other like itself. Levinas's antidote to this tradition is what he calls "ethics," a relation which presupposes that the self comes into being only by first recognizing its responsibility to others. "Ethics" in this usage, then, denotes the claims of others rather than a body of moral rules and values.[59] In the words of Jean-François Lyotard, it entails "obligation without conditions."[60]

I am not suggesting, of course, that Oppen knew of Levinas's work, but only that this way of understanding "ethics" may help to elucidate Oppen's evolving poetic. Levinas's sense of a relation to the other as the quintessential expression of the ethical may define something in Oppen's writing which has strong social motivation but which is not, in his terms, "political" as such. At least, once we think of the ethical, in Levinas's sense, at least two consequences follow, both at odds with Poundian modernism. First, a poetics of "encounter" will assume that the domain of the ethical is also the domain of the ordinary and the everyday, of relationships expressing proximity rather than contemplative or legislative distance ("Near is / Knowledge," says Oppen in **"Of Being Numerous"** [*CP,* 176]). Second, the ethical subject is not only open, but vulnerable and in question. Levinas thus speaks of "the risky uncovering of oneself, in sincerity, the breaking up of inwardness and the abandon of all shelter, exposure to traumas, vulnerability."[61]

This way of understanding "sincerity," not as a question of truth, but rather as one of relation and exposure to the claims of others, has more than a little in common with Oppen's work. For "sincerity" is not so much a true account of one's inner feelings (manifest, then, Pound would say, in precise verbal formulation), as an acceptance of what *exceeds* the self. In Levinas's sense, this self is always unbounded, open to a perception of radical heterogeneity. As Maurice Blanchot nicely puts it, "the other withdraws me from what would make me unique,"[62] a view which accords with Oppen's own attempt to transcend what he calls, in **"Philai Te Kou Philai,"** "a ruined ethic / / Bursting with ourselves" (*CP*, 76). "The self," he warns us in **"World, World—,"** "is no mystery" (*CP*, 143) but there is instead "a force of clarity, it is / of what is not autonomous in us" (*CP*, 185). But what is "The act of being, / the act of being / More than oneself" (*CP*, 143)? Language which hovers on the brink of intelligibility, handing over to the "materials" of poetry rather than producing clear self-expression—this is perhaps one means of "being / More than oneself." But the difficulty lies in saying what that "more" exactly is, for this transcendence of self is toward something ultimately "impenetrable," to use Oppen's favourite word again. The idea of collective social being is in this sense "impenetrable," which is why its strongest expression will always be in the intermediary forms of poetry rather than in any kind of political discourse. As Oppen puts it in his interview with L. S. Dembo:

> we have a kind of feeling that the absolutely unitary is somehow absolute, that, at any rate, it really exists. It's been the feeling always that that which is absolutely single really does exist—the atom, for example. That particle of matter, when you get to it, is absolutely impenetrable, absolutely inexplicable.[63]

It is the idea of a related linguistic impenetrability or opacity which contemporary poets have discerned in this work. For many of the Language poets, it is in the recognition of language as a material and social medium that some sort of "ethical" frame for writing is to be found. Charles Bernstein, for example, assumes that "Language is the commonness in being," arguing that:

> The move from purely descriptive, outward directive, writing toward writing centred on its wordness, its physicality, its haecceity (thisness) is, in its impulse, an investigation of human self-sameness, of the place of our connection: in the world, in the word, in ourselves.[64]

Oppen, as we have seen, certainly moves toward this perception of writing as a kind of intermediary space in which a certain "connection" might be felt. Yet the temptation remains to speak *about* that connection, and as Bernstein notes acutely, Oppen's

> often claimed commitment to clarity, however qualified, annuls a number of possibilities inherent in his technique. . . . That is, he tends, at times, to fall back onto "clarity" as a self-justifying means of achieving resolution through scenic motifs, statement, or parable in poems that might, given his compositional techniques, outstrip such controlling impulses.[65]

Bernstein's observation invites us to read Oppen's work as a sort of hinge between modernism and something we may choose (or not) to call postmodernism. At some point in that trajectory, ideas of a "commonness" in language

underwent a drastic change; Oppen's poems are there to help us see how poets could begin to associate an "ethical" relation with a certain linguistic opacity.

Notes

1. Pound's "Preface" to *Discrete Series* is reprinted in *Paideuma*, 10. 1 (Spring 1981), 13.

2. See Rachel Blau DuPlessis, "Introduction" to *Selected Letters of George Oppen* (Durham and London: Duke University Press, 1990), xiv. See also Mary Oppen, *Meaning a Life: An Autobiography* (Santa Barbara: Black Sparrow Press, 1978).

3. Douglas Messerli ed. and introd., *From the Other Side of the Century: A New American Poetry 1960-1990* (Los Angeles: Sun & Moon Press, 1994); Paul Hoover, ed., *Postmodern American Poetry: A Norton Anthology* (New York and London: W. W. Norton, 1994).

4. The contrast is proposed in Jerome McGann, "Contemporary Poetry, Alternate Routes," *Critical Inquiry*, 13 (Spring 1987), 624-47. Bob Perelman, *The Marginalization of Poetry: Language Writing and Literary History* (Princeton: Princeton University Press, 1996), 40 also notes that in the seventies "The Objectivists were still active and were in fact a much stronger presence than they had been in prior decades."

5. Louis Zukofsky, "Sincerity and Objectification," *Poetry*, 37. 5 (February 1931), 273, 274.

6. For the counter-view, that Zukofsky's practice "exposes the object-status of the poem as a delusion," see Michael Davidson, "Dismantling 'Mantis': Reification and Objectivist Poetics," *American Literary History*, 3. 3 (Fall 1991), 522. I have suggested a qualification to Davidson's argument in "Lorine Niedecker: Rural Surreal," in Jenny Penberthy, ed., *Lorine Niedecker: Woman and Poet* (National Poetry Foundation: Orono, ME, 1996), 199-200.

7. Quoted in Serge Fauchereau, "Three Oppen Letters with a Note," *Ironwood*, 5 (1975), 79. The letter is dated 19 June 1966. Cf. Rachel Blau DuPlessis, ed., *Selected Letters*, 47: "'Objectivist' meant, not an objective viewpoint, but to objectify the poem, to make the poem an object. Meant form."

8. "Objectivist Poetics and Political Vision: A Study of Oppen and Pound," in Burton Hatlen, ed. and introd., *George Oppen: Man and Poet* (National Poetry Foundation: Orono, ME, 1981), 125. The essay provides a helpful assessment of the relation between the two poets.

9. *Literary Essays of Ezra Pound*, ed. T. S. Eliot (London: Faber and Faber, 1954), 9.

10. See my *Ezra Pound: Politics, Economics and Writing* (London: Macmillan, 1984), 100.

11. See, for example, *Selected Letters*, 249-50: "that the Cantos would benefit as poetry thru excision as dras-

tic as Pound's editing of *The Waste Land*—emerges as obviously true // I suspect we all admit to ourselves—or I will admit *for* myself that I read the Cantos in fragments as fragments. Despite the challenges of the scholars [.]"

12. George Oppen, *Collected Poems* (New York: New Directions, 1975), 210-12. Further references to this volume as *CP* will be given in the text.

13. See, for example, *Guide to Kulchur* (London: Peter Owen, 1938).

14. Jessica Benjamin, *The Bonds of Love,* 190. I have drawn on Benjamin's critique of this aspect of the Hegelian tradition in my extended account of this aesthetic in *Modernisms: A Literary Guide* (Berkeley and Los Angeles: University of California Press, 1995).

15. Ezra Pound, *The Cantos* (London: Faber and Faber, 1986), 722.

16. Burton Hatlen, "'Not Altogether Lone in a Lone Universe': George Oppen's *The Materials*", in *George Oppen: Man and Poet,* 326: "Oppen's later poetry represents, I believe, a systematic attempt to body forth certain political commitments (Oppen today calls his political position 'populism') in and through an uncompromisingly modernist poetic method."

17. "The Mind's Own Place," *Kulchur,* 3. 10 (1963), 8.

18. *Selected Letters,* 66.

19. Ibid, 68.

20. Ibid. 82.

21. "The Mind's Own Place," 8.

22. Andrew Ross, "The New Sentence and the Commodity Form: Recent American Writing," in Cary Nelson and Lawrence Grossberg, eds., *Marxism and the Interpretation of Culture* (Basingstoke: Macmillan, 1988), 362 (further references will be given in the text). Ross goes on to observe that "In modernism, the 'political' and the 'aesthetic' struggle for sovereignty over every last inch of cultural soil."

23. Bruce Andrews, "Poetry as Explanation, Poetry as Praxis," excerpted in Hoover, ed., *Postmodern American Poetry,* 669.

24. "The Mind's Own Place," 4 (my italics).

25. Jean Luc Nancy, *The Inoperative Community,* trans. Peter Connor (Minneapolis and Oxford: University of Minnesota Press, 1991), xxxiii. Further references will be given in the text.

26. Cf. Giorgio Agamben, *The Coming Community,* trans. Michael Hardt (Minneapolis and London: University of Minnesota Press, 1993), 86: "What the State cannot tolerate in any way . . . is that the singularities form a community without affirming an identity, that humans co-belong without any representable condition of belonging (even in the form of a simple presupposition)."

27. In an unpublished note, Oppen writes: "Numerous: not only that I could not see the individual merged in 'humanity,' but that I saw humanity no less helpless [deletion] than the individual." Quoted from the George Oppen Papers, Box 13, Folder 8, by kind permission of the Mandeville Special Collections Library, University of California at San Diego.

28. Interview with L. S. Dembo, *Contemporary Literature,* 10. 2 (Spring 1969), 170.

29. Letter to June Oppen Degnan, *Ironwood,* 26 (Fall 1985), 223. Oppen is glossing his allusion to the serpent Ouroboros in "A Narrative" (*CP,* 137).

30. Reinhold Schiffer, "Interview with George Oppen," *Sagetrieb,* 3. 3 (Winter 1984), 19: "one's subjectivity is also encountered, not found."

31. See "An Adequate Vision: A George Oppen Daybook," ed. Michael Davidson, *Ironwood,* 26 (Fall 1985), 17: "But Numerous actually takes more space for a simpler undertaking than *This in Which.* The relationship between things—the relationship between people; What it is rather than That it is. Surely simpler tho it is consciously played out against the background That it is. Which is of course why the poem could not be satirical." For a gloss on the title of *This in Which,* see Interview with L. S. Dembo, 163: "the nouns do refer to something; that it's there, that it's true, the whole implication of these nouns; that appearances represent reality, whether or not they misrepresent it: that this in which the thing takes place, this thing is here, and that these things do take place."

32. "An Adequate Vision," 17.

33. Marjorie Perloff, "The Shipwreck of the Singular: George Oppen's 'Of Being Numerous,'" *Ironwood,* 26 (Fall 1985), 193.

34. Perloff, ibid.

35. See also Paul Naylor, "The pre-position 'of,'" *Contemporary Literature,* 32 (Spring 1991), 100-15.

36. Referring to Maritain's *Creative Intuition in Art and Poetry,* Oppen remarks: "the word presentness: central to me too" (*Selected Letters,* 311). The prose section which concludes this first poem recalls Mary Oppen talking about Yves Bonnefoy's *On the Motion and Immobility of Douve* (see *Selected Letters,* 129).

37. Interview with L. S. Dembo, 161.

38. See *Selected Letters,* 122.

39. Jacques Derrida, "Living On: Borderlines," trans. James Hulbert, in Harold Bloom et al., eds., *Deconstruction and Criticism* (New York: Seabury Press, 1986), 130. For Oppen's negative view of "narrative," see, for example, *Selected Letters,* 19: "If the novel is dead it seems likely to me that people just can't bear narrative, with its implication of the incomprehensibility of time, of the non-existence of what's past, and such." See also ibid., 55-56: "Narra-

tive, which is everyone's art, and everyone's comfort, is wearing. There is no fact more obvious than that every life ends badly."

40. Perloff, "The Shipwreck of the Singular," 197.

41. See *Selected Letters,* 254: "The 'Marxism' of *Discrete Series* is, was felt as, the struggle against the loss of the commonplace." The last phrase was borrowed from Michael Heller (see ibid., 252-53).

42. *Selected Letters,* 111.

43. Ibid., 111.

44. Quoted ibid., 410 n. 29.

45. The phrase, from Heidegger's *Introduction to Metaphysics,* is used as an epigraph to Oppen's *This in Which* (1965). The matter of Oppen's interest in Heidegger, dating back to at least 1929, merits further attention. Some useful points are made in Randolph Chilton, "The Place of Being in the Poetry of George Oppen," in *George Oppen: Man and Poet,* 89-112.

46. See, for example, Krzysztof Ziarek, *Inflected Language: Toward a Hermeneutics of Nearness* (Albany, NY: SUNY Press, 1994), 28: "Being covers itself with beings, and in its retreat it becomes indistinguishable from beings, almost a being itself. This retreat is visible in the 'language of Being,' which continually missays and unsays Being, unable to escape describing it in the same syntactical and grammatical terms as entities."

47. *Selected Letters,* 263.

48. See *CP,* 141: "Tho I had hoped to arrive / at an actuality / In the mere number of us / And record now / That I did not."

49. Cf. Nancy, "Finite History," in David Carroll, ed., *The States of Theory: History, Art, and Critical Discourse* (Stanford, CA: Stanford University Press, 1994), 169: "History is not a narrative or a statement, but the announcement of a 'we' (history is writing in this sense)."

50. Cf. Jacques Derrida, "Living On: Borderlines," in Harold Bloom, et al. eds., *Deconstruction and Criticism* (London: Routledge and Kegan Paul, 1979), 167: "The word 'and' is to be understood in each case as a conjunction that does not join logically, for example in contradiction, nor according to chronology, succession or absolute simultaneity, nor according to some fundamental ontology."

51. Lyn Hejinian, "The Rejection of Closure," in Bob Perelman, ed., *Writing/Talks* (Carbondale and Edwardsville, IL: Southern Illinois University Press, 1985), 272.

52. Lyn Hejinian "Two Stein Talks," *Temblor,* 3 (1986), 129-30.

53. Cf. Kenneth Rexroth, "Introduction" to his *Pierre Reverdy: Selected Poems* (New York: New Directions, 1969), vi: "Eliot works in *The Waste Land* with fragmented and recombined arguments; Pierre Reverdy with dismembered propositions from which subject, operator and object have been wrenched free and re-structured into an invisible or subliminal discourse which owes its cogency to its own strict, complex and secret logic." See also my "Lorine Niedecker: Rural Surreal," 199.

54. See Charles Bernstein, "Hinge, Picture," *Ironwood,* 26 (Fall 1985), 240-42.

55. *Selected Letters,* 419 n. 52.

56. *The Cantos,* 546. In an unpublished note, Oppen writes: "pull down they [*sic*] vanity etc It's a remarkably bombastic ant but the wasp, whose head or tip . . . I think it is the great moment in Pound's writing, the great moment of the cantos." Quoted from the George Oppen Papers, Box 13, Folder 20, by kind permission of the Mandeville Special Collections Library, University of California at San Diego.

57. Oppen tended to reject "ethics" (meaning, for him, moralism) in favour of "ontology." See, for example, *Selected Letters,* 118-19, where Oppen notes of "Of Being Numerous" that there "I speak of the ontological not the ethical problem" (118). See also 119: "Atrocity becoming ordinary—worldly—despite the secular ethic, despite our fear of the disappearance of any ethic which is not based on an ontology and an eschatology. This is the meaning of 'crisis.'" In his interview with Oppen, Dembo observes that "for all your desire merely to report your feelings and to repudiate an ethical aim for your poetry, you do have strong ethical convictions to express. But, as you've said, the important thing is that the ethic be felt and not merely constructed" (174).

58. L. S. Dembo, Interview, 163.

59. See, for example, Jacques Derrida, "Violence and Metaphysics: An Essay on the Thought of Emmanuel Levinas," in *Writing and Difference,* trans. Alan Bass (London: Routledge and Kegan Paul, 1978), 111: "It is true that Ethics, in Levinas's sense, is an Ethics without law and without concept, which maintains its non-violent purity only before being determined as concepts and laws. This is not an objection: let us not forget that Levinas does not seek to propose laws or moral values, does not seek to determine *a* morality, but rather the essence of the ethical relation in general."

60. Jean-François Lyotard, *The Differend: Phrases in Dispute,* trans. Georges Van Den Abbeele (Manchester: Manchester University Press, 1988), 137.

61. Emmanuel Levinas, *Otherwise than Being Or Beyond Essence,* trans. Alphonso Lingis (The Hague: Martinus Nijhoff, 1981), 48, quoted in Gerald L. Bruns, "Dialogue and the Truth of Scepticism," *Religion and Literature,* 22. 2-3 (1990), 89. Bruns comments that "the ethical subject according to Levinas is no longer a propositional agent but is dialogically situated, that is, *in question.*"

62. Maurice Blanchot, *The Writing of the Disaster,* trans. Ann Smock (Lincoln and London: University of Nebraska Press, 1986), 13.

63. L. S. Dembo, 163.

64. Charles Bernstein, *Content's Dream: Essays 1975-1984* (Los Angeles, CA: Sun & Moon Press 1986) 32. Cf. ibid., 20: "political writing becomes disoriented when it views itself as description and not discourse; as not being *in* the world but *about* the world."

65. Charles Bernstein, "Hinge/Picture," 241.

Stephen Fredman (essay date 1999)

SOURCE: "'And All Now Is War': George Oppen, Charles Olson, and the Problem of Literary Generations," in *The Objectivist Nexus: Essays in Cultural Poetics,* edited by Rachel Blau DePlessis and Peter Quartermain, The University of Alabama Press, 1999, pp. 286-93.

[*In the following essay Fredman explores similarities in the poetry of Oppen and Charles Olson.*]

The convenient notion of literary generations has been an important part of the fictional structure of literary history, helping to separate it from history proper. In literary histories, we have used named generations as markers in the assembling of an orderly narrative of innovation, struggle, triumph, and succession. By means of this generational narrative, we have been able to tell ourselves stories about "literature," presenting it as a self-enclosed entity that constitutes its own world. Historical fact, though, can step in and disturb our recounting of these comforting tales of dynastic succession—as, for instance, when we notice that both Keats and Carlyle were born in 1795. We can take such a fact as a synecdoche for the plethora of historical facts that has troubled the generational narrative of romanticism and Victorianism and has caused a wholesale revision of views about nineteenth-century English poetry. "Romantic" and "Victorian" are not equivalent names, either, for "romantic," as a generational term, has been used traditionally to designate in English poetry the works of six men, while "Victorian" has been used in less generational and more historical senses to cover a larger period of time and a much greater diversity of writers.

For the poetry of the twentieth century, both poets and critics have been anxious to identify and promote literary movements and to give these movements generational characteristics. When poets invent a movement and ascribe certain qualities to it, critics often follow suit by grouping the poets together and by interpreting the poetry solely through the lens ground by the poets. In the cases of most of the poets of our century, we are just beginning to look at their writing from perspectives other than the generational ones they themselves supply. One way to resist enclosure in generational fictions is to explore the historical factors behind the invention by poets of specific generational narratives. For example, Lawrence Rainey has recently demonstrated two major personal and social exigencies behind Pound's promotion of imagism: the collapse of the means Pound had worked out to secure himself a livelihood, and his observation of Marinetti's spectacular success in commodifying futurism while in London in 1912-14. Discovering the efficacy of generational discourse for securing a hearing (and a living) for new writers, Pound then passed along this public-relations tip to other new poets. A full thirty pages of the Pound/Zukofsky correspondence are taken up with discussions in 1930 about how to position the "Objectivists" issue of *Poetry.* Charles Olson inaugurated another Poundian generation in 1950 with his platform essay for *Poetry New York,* whose composition occupies Olson and Robert Creeley for much of the first 220 pages of their correspondence. Generally, literary historians have been only too happy to follow the lead of these two aggressive forays into public relations (that is, Zukofsky's essays "Program: 'Objectivists' 1931" and "Sincerity and Objectification," and Olson's essay "Projective Verse") and have thereby presented Objectivism and Projectivism as two distinct and successive generations in American poetry. It is instructive to ponder how our received literary history might differ had L. S. Dembo not decided to make the reconstruction of Objectivism a central focus of his 1968 interviews with George Oppen, Carl Rakosi, Charles Reznikoff, and Louis Zukofsky, or had Donald Allen not featured Charles Olson, the Black Mountain poets, and "Projective Verse" as headliners for his 1960 anthology *The New American Poetry.* Such editorial contingencies often have everything to do with the creating of a literary history.

I would like to throw a wrench into the narrative of succession that posits an Objectivist generation, launched in 1931, followed by a Projectivist one, launched in 1950. The easiest way to do so is to introduce another historical fact: George Oppen and Charles Olson were born two years apart, in 1908 and 1910, respectively. Routinely, this potentially disturbing fact is glossed over by designating Oppen the youngest Objectivist and Olson the eldest Projectivist. This preserves the generational narrative, but at the cost of distorting the careers of these writers by framing them solely by the decades in which their generations came to light: we view Oppen as a man of the thirties, for whom the depression, populism, and communism are defining issues, and we view Olson as a man of the fifties, enmeshed in the cold war and the nascent counterculture. Such contexts demonstrably aid our understanding of these writers, but choosing to read their works exclusively through the concerns of one particular moment restricts our vision unnecessarily; in particular, such a way of reading blinds us to a number of similarities in the works of Oppen and Olson. To begin to rectify this situation, I would like to focus upon World War II as a defining influence upon both poets. World War II represents a moment between the thirties and the fifties, a moment whose impact has been remarkably poorly explored in our generation-bound history of American poetry.

In this century of horrors, World War II holds pride of place for Americans as the most devastating event, both for the numbers of Americans killed and for the difficulty of coping with the unthinkable destruction caused by the Holocaust and the Bomb. We must take this crucial era more fully into account in order to render an accurate history not just of the writing of that time but, in a larger sense, of the writing produced by those who lived through it. The two poets under consideration participated in the war in different but vitally consuming ways—George Oppen as a soldier, who was wounded fighting in France, and Charles Olson as a propagandist, working in Washington, D.C., for the Office of War Information. Right off the bat, thinking about Oppen in the context of the war allows him to escape from the tight little room we have designated as "Objectivism." In some measure, Hugh Kenner can be held responsible for constricting the dimensions of that room with his unfortunately memorable statement: "The Objectivists seem to have been born mature, not to say middle-aged" (*Homemade World* 169). This image of prematurely wizened poets—who felt, Kenner says, "that the arts ought not to exhilarate, save austerely, and moreover that in a gray time (1931) they had best be gray" (168)— contrasts vividly with Mary Oppen's portrait of George's energetic determination in 1944, when he entered the Army at age thirty-six: "he was overage for the draft, but he wanted to go. . . . He went in as a responsible Jew, who someone was trying to wipe out and he was not going to stand still" (Young 37). This hardly sounds like a man who, thirteen years before, had slipped into a premature middle age. Nor does the poetry Oppen wrote after the war—which includes all but his short, precocious first book—sit comfortably in the imagist tradition that Kenner has been so instrumental in delineating. In fact, the incredible pressure that Oppen exerts upon both language and thought brings him much closer to a younger European poet like Paul Celan (1920-70) than to Pound or Williams (both born in the 1880s). As a Jew whose military unit liberated a concentration camp, Oppen "certainly saw those horrors firsthand" (Young 37), so that the world of "that which happened" (Felstiner xvi), as Celan designates the Holocaust, was not at all distant from the threatened facticity of "this in which" (Oppen, *Collected Poems* 78) Oppen set his writing. Another crucially formative influence for both poets—one that the war complicated considerably for each of them—was the philosophy of Martin Heidegger. Both poets found decisive Heidegger's investigations of the relationship between language, thought, and being, yet each fought off the philosopher's dispassion in an effort to enunciate an ethic of caring appropriate to a devastated world.

Taking into account Oppen's experience of World War II and his connection to Heidegger, a strong case can be made for thinking of him as an existentialist rather than as an Objectivist—or else we must open our definition of Objectivism to include much more than the pallid epithet "second-generation imagism." One index of the difference it makes when we think of Oppen this way concerns his commitment to "the real" or "the actual." Is it enough to assume that these terms return to the imagist hygiene prescribing the accurate visual representation of things or that

they draw upon the impressionist equation of visual data with emotional states? During an interview with the Oppens in which Kevin Power engages them in a discussion of Camus, Sartre, and Heidegger (Power 196-97), he asks George to "talk about 'actualness' and how that enters the poem." George replies, "Well there's that prose section of Pierre Adam in **'Route'** when he tells me about his experience. I was conscious, when I wrote that, that any of the Existentialists could have written it. I wrote it, nevertheless, because it was actually what he said to me. Existential in the sense that you do what you do and that is the answer. . . . Simply that you are yourself" (197). The story Oppen alludes to was told to him in Alsace, where he was fighting in the Battle of the Bulge. Many Alsatian men, upon learning they had been drafted into the German army, dug themselves holes in the ground, in which they hid for as long as two or three years. When the Germans learned that men were in hiding, they made reprisals, killing family members and sending wives to the army brothels in Germany. Pierre fed and assisted the men in the holes. "Men would come to Pierre and they would say: I am thinking of making a hole. Pierre would say: yes. They would say then: but if I do they will kill my parents; or: they will take my wife and my children. Then Pierre would say, he told me: *if* you dig a hole, I will help you" (Oppen, *Collected Poems* 187-88).

For Oppen, this kind of terrifying existential choice defines the realm of "the actual." Such was the actuality French resistance fighters like Sartre and Camus faced, and it remained the (often unstated) background for their existential philosophies. In his essay "The Resistance," Charles Olson provides something like a gloss on Pierre Adam's story, asserting that the horrors of World War II have rendered the body as the only meaningful instrument of resistance: "When man is reduced to so much fat for soap, superphosphate for soil, fillings and shoes for sale, he has, to begin again, one answer. . . . It is his body that is his answer" (*Human Universe* 47). By bodily acts of resistance, such as those practiced by the Alsatians against the Nazis, Olson claims that human beings can learn to think concretely through the body rather than through the dangerous abstractions such as nation, race, and class. In "Causal Mythology" Olson avers, "I don't believe in cultures myself. I think that's a lot of hung up stuff like organized anything. I believe there is simply ourselves, and where we are has a particularity which we'd better use because that's about all we've got. . . . Put an end to nation, put an end to culture, put an end to divisions of all sorts" (*Muthologos* 94). This notion that large abstractions are dangerous and that what we think and do must be grounded instead in who we actually are jibes perfectly with Oppen's statement that his recounting of Pierre Adam's story was "Existential in the sense that you do what you do and that is the answer. . . . Simply that you are yourself."

Although Olson did not fight in the war, he read the daily dispatches in Washington, and they directed his thinking along lines that could also be called "existentialist." A pivotal example of such thinking occurs in the aphorism around which he organizes his "Causal Mythology" lecture: "That which exists through itself is what is called meaning" (*Muthologos* 72). This proposition can be read as a perfect synopsis of existentialist metaphysics and epistemology. When Olson delivered it at the Berkeley Poetry Conference in 1965, Oppen received a report from a friend. Writing back, Oppen comments: "Olson's [']that which seems to exist in itself we call meaning['] is a good statement of the thing—. . . That which exists of itself can not be explained it . . . cannot be analyzed, it is the object of contemplative thought, it is known by 'indwelling.' The Given. 'things explain each other / Not themselves'" (*Selected Letters* 115). The last phrase consists of two lines from Oppen's **"A Narrative"** (*Collected Poems* 134)—indicating that these two poets share a notion of resistance which extends from the political to the epistemological and is grounded in the inexplicable actuality of people and things. From this perspective, knowledge and action rest solely on individual responsibility, and yet they have ramifications for society at large. Both poets believe there is no substitute for the existential encounter; as Olson says in "Causal Mythology," "You're simply stuck with the original visionary experience of having been *you*, which is a hell of a thing" (*Muthologos* 72).

Prior to *The Maximus Poems,* Olson's poetry consistently weighs the effects upon thought and action of the devastation of World War II. For one thing, there is a recurrent preoccupation with the dead, as in the dreamworld of "As the Dead Prey Upon Us" or in the opening of "La Préface," an inaugural poem that portrays the concentration camps as the background to Olson's setting forth on a new poetry. No matter in what direction the poet sets out, the dead cannot be ignored:

> The dead in via
> in vita nuova
> in the way

Not only does the speaker find the way toward a new poetry (and a new life) blocked, but he must stop immediately to read what might be called "the writing on the wall":

> "I will die about April 1st . . ." going off
> "I weigh, I think, 80 lbs . . ." scratch
> "My name is NO RACE" address
> Buchenwald new Altamira cave
> With a nail they drew the object of the hunt.

> (*Collected Poems* 46)

The walls of the camp at Buchenwald provide a palimpsest upon which the new poetry will be inscribed. Changing the image but remaining focused upon the dead of World War II, Olson finds "among the DPs—deathhead / at the apex / of the pyramid" (46). This poem implies that for a postwar culture to emerge from the ashes and become capable of creating works of the first order, such as the cave art of Altamira or the pyramids, these new works must be conceived of as a kind of projective funerary art, for "We are born not of the buried but these unburied dead" (47). Likewise, Olson's most famous poem, "The Kingfishers," bases its exploration of primitive mysteries in Greece and Mexico upon a Heraclitean acknowledg-

ment of the universal condition of war. At one point, Olson turns from a depiction of "the priests / (in dark cotton robes, and dirty / their dishevelled hair matted with blood, and flowing wildly / over their shoulders)," urging the Mexicans to protect their gods against the invading Spaniards, to a general statement:

> And all now is war
> where so lately there was peace,
> and the sweet brotherhood, the use
> of tilled fields.

> (*Collected Poems* 89)

Out of a recognition that when "all now is war" everything has changed, and that what it means to be a human being is something new and newly terrifying, Oppen and Olson begin to write a new poetry. In locating a common ground for aspects of their poetry, I do not mean to suggest that the two worked in direct conjunction. Olson seems to have kept his distance from Oppen. In 1962 he wrote William Bronk: "I do know Oppen, and though some of my friends thought his review of *The Distances* and *Maximus from Dogtown* . . . was the old business of measuring me by Pound, and I thought myself he raced his motor on *Maximus from Dogtown,* I thought his picking 'The Satyrs' for a voice which was peculiarly my own, true enough. (I haven't yet seen his poems at all . . .)" (Butterick 495-96). In the review, Oppen states that "*Maximus from Dogtown* is obviously not part of Olson's best work," but he praises *The Distances:* "What is happening in these poems is that the poet is speaking: they are a discourse, always beautifully modeled and beautifully constructed" ("Three Poets" 330). Speaking to L. S. Dembo in 1968, Oppen says, "I've read a lot of Olson. I think 'In Cold Hell, In Thicket' is a very fine poem. I don't really like the *Maximus Poems* nor accept them at all" (Dembo and Pondrom 184). It is not at all surprising that two such ambitious poets would seek to circumscribe their points of contact.

Despite their uneasy accommodation to each other and the many differences in poetics and in personalities, some striking similarities in the work of Oppen and Olson appear when attention centers on the impact of World War II. For example, both poets engage extensively in practical politics, stretching back to the thirties, but after the war they leave political activism and begin to use poetry as a vehicle for a political thinking shot through with metaphysics and epistemology. This leads both poets to ponder deeply the relationship between the individual and the collectivity, between what Oppen calls "being singular" and "being numerous." In conjunction with the affirmation of resistant individuality noted earlier, both poets feel a newfound urgency to speak for the entirety of what Robert Duncan calls "the company of the living": Oppen's use of "we" throughout his central poem, **"Of Being Numerous,"** testifies to this desire, as do Olson's attempts to place the present at the crosshairs of time and space in *The Maximus Poems.* Ultimately, both poets adopt what might be called a wary prophetic stance, addressing the most pressing concerns of contemporary life in terms that do not rely upon the old rallying points of religion or nation. I say "wary" to mark the way in which both poets disavow received concepts, as though it were necessary not only to save the world but to reinvent the terms by which it is known. Formally, this wary prophetic stance results in truncations of both line and syntax; such formal disruptions insist that readers, too, practice vigilance against falling into the easy grooves that both poets roundly condemn. And stylistically, both poets oscillate between lyric and didactic modes of address, in order to keep knowledge existential and yet to demonstrate the social constituents of the personal.

If the historical connections between the works of George Oppen and Charles Olson are this strong, does it follow that we should discard completely generational terms like "Objectivism" and "Projectivism"? I don't think so. I am arguing not for the abolition of literary-historical terminology but rather for a more nuanced historicizing of poetry. Inevitably, this would involve exploring the historical exigencies that contribute to coining and maintaining generational terms like "Objectivism" and "Projectivism," just as much as it would necessitate a more careful historical placement of the works of individual poets and more specific comparisons of poets based upon their responses to particular circumstances. On the practical level, we certainly can do more than repeat the shopworn clichés that Objectivism is concerned with the "object" and Projectivism is a poetry of "process." Instead of remaining fixated on these shibboleths, why not return to the practice Louis Zukofsky recommended in 1931 as "thinking with the things as they exist" ("Sincerity and Objectification" 273)?

Works Cited

Butterick, George F. *A Guide to "The Maximus Poems" of Charles Olson.* Berkeley: U. of California P, 1978.

Dembo, L. S., and Cyrena N. Pondrom. *The Contemporary Writer: Interviews with Sixteen Novelists and Poets.* Madison: U. of Wisconsin P, 1972.

Kenner, Hugh. *A Homemade World: The American Modernist Writers.* New York: Morrow, 1975.

Olson, Charles. *Human Universe and Other Essays.* Ed. Donald M. Allen. New York: Grove, 1967.

———. *Muthologos: The Collected Lectures and Interviews.* Ed. George F. Butterick. Vol. 1. Bolinas: Four Seasons, 1978.

Oppen, George. *Collected Poems.* New York: New Directions, 1975.

———. *Selected Letters.* Ed. Rachel Blau DuPlesis. Durham:Duke UP, 1990.

———. "Three Poets." *Poetry* 100. 5 (1962): 329–33.

Power, Kevin. "An Interview with George and Mary Oppen." *Montemora* 4 (1978): 187-203.

Young, Dennis. "Conversation with Mary Oppen." *Iowa Review* 18.3 (1988): 18-47.

Zukovsky, Louis. "Sincerity and Objectification with Special Reference to the Work of Charles Reznikoff." *Poetry* 37. 5 (February 1931); 272–85.

FURTHER READING

Bibliography

McAleavy, David. "A Bibliography of the Works of George Oppen," in *Paideuma,* 10 (Spring 1981): 155-169.
A comprehensive listing of Oppen's work.

Biography

Oppen, Mary. *Meaning A Life,* Santa Barbara: Black Sparrow (1978), 213 p.
Mary Oppen traces courses through which she and her husband steered their life together.

Criticism

Hatlen, Burton, ed. *George Oppen: Man and Poet* Orono: National Poetry Foundation/University of Maine Press, 1981, 514 p.
A formidable collection of essays about Oppen with a copiously annotated bibliography.

Simpson, Louis. "Poetry in the Sixties B Long Live Blake! Down with Donne!" in *The New York Times,* Vol. CXIX, No. 40, 881 (December 28, 1969): VII. pp. 2, 18.
Includes Oppen in a discussion of poets and poetry of the 1960s.

Taggart, John. "Walk-Out: Rereading George Oppen," in *Chicago Review,* Vol. 44, No. 2, pp. 29-93.
A lyrical analytic speculation regarding Oppen's postulated Jewish identity problem, the effect on him of his Alzheimer's disease in his last years, and Mary Oppen's role in the preparation of his last volume of poetry.

Additional coverage of Oppen's life and career is contained in the following sources published by the Gale Group: *Contemporary Authors,* Vols. 13-16R, 113; *Contemorary Authors New Revision Series,* Vol. 8; *Contemporary Literary Criticism,* Vols. 7, 13, 34; and *Dictionary of Literary Biography,* Vols. 5, 165.

E. L. Thorndike
1874-1949

(Full name Edward Lee Thorndike) American psychologist and educator.

INTRODUCTION

Thorndike was a pioneer in American psychology and education theory. His research into reward and punishment in learning—known as connectionism—led to the widely used stimulus-response theories that followed, and he made many other significant contributions to his field.

BIOGRAPHICAL INFORMATION

Thorndike was born in Williamsburg, Massachusetts, in 1874. He received his bachelor's degree from Wesleyan University in 1895 and another B.A. from Harvard the following year, where he studied under William James. In 1897 he graduated with a master's degree from Harvard and then attended Columbia University, where he earned his Ph.D. in 1898. Thorndike served in the United States Army as chairman of the Committee on Classification of Personnel and as a member of the Advisory Board in the office of the surgeon general's Division of Psychology from 1917 to 1918. Thorndike had an extensive career in education, working as a professor at numerous colleges and universities between 1898 and 1949. He belonged to and served as president of many professional organizations, including the American Psychological Association, the American Association for the Advancement of Science, the American Association for Adult Education, and the Psychometric Society. He died in 1949.

MAJOR WORKS

Thorndike published more than five hundred books and articles, most of them reports of his own experiments. His doctoral thesis, "Animal Intelligence: An Experimental Study of Associative Processes in Animals" (1898), became one of his best-known works because of its groundbreaking research into the ways animals learn. In particular, Thorndike noted the importance of the completion of an act successfully followed by positive reinforcement, and he would later apply his findings to the learning patterns of humans in *Notes on Child Study* (1901) and *An Introduction to the Theory of Mental and Social Measurements* (1904). Thorndike's three-volume *Educational Psychology* (1913-14) became the standard in its field and ensured Thorndike's reputation as an eminent American

psychologist. In the years just prior to the First World War, Thorndike began writing and publishing a series of standardized educational and intelligence tests. During World War I he served on the committee that administered many similar tests to military personnel, and he published several studies on military psychology. Thorndike came to disagree with the common notion of an overall general factor of intelligence, positing instead his idea that there was a limitless number of measurably intelligent acts that may or may not overlap. His *Measurement of Intelligence* (1926) illustrates this theory and seeks to apply the tests Thorndike had used during the war to civilian children. In *Human Learning* (1931) and *The Fundamentals of Learning* (1932) Thorndike presented summarized versions of his experiments and beliefs. Articles published during the 1930s demonstrate the evolution of Thorndike's thoughts on the reward-and-punishment, or connectionism, system of learning. Punishment, Thorndike came to believe, served a lesser purpose and was chiefly useful in causing the subject to search for the correct answer; reward he found to be clearly superior in encouraging students to learn. In the

1940s Thorndike was mainly interested in language studies and the question of the influence of nature versus environment on human psychology.

CRITICAL RECEPTION

Thorndike had many critics during his lifetime, most of whom found the experimental situations he devised to be overly restrictive and his theories of learning to ignore the complexities of human behavior. But while more recent research into educational psychology has shifted significantly from Thorndike's interest in connectionism, Thorndike himself is recognized as having had a profound influence on twentieth-century learning theory.

PRINCIPAL WORKS

The Human Nature Club: An Introduction to the Study of Mental Life (nonfiction) 1901

Notes on Child Study (nonfiction) 1901

Educational Psychology (nonfiction) 1903

An Introduction to the Theory of Mental and Social Measurements (nonfiction) 1904

The Elements of Psychology (nonfiction) 1905

Principles of Teaching (nonfiction) 1906

Animal Intelligence: Experimental Studies (nonfiction) 1911

Individuality (nonfiction) 1911

Educational Psychology. 3 vols. (nonfiction) 1913-14

Educational Psychology: Briefer Course (nonfiction) 1914

Reading Scales (nonfiction) 1919

The Teacher's Word Book (nonfiction) 1921

The Psychology of Arithmetic (nonfiction) 1922

The Psychology of Algebra (nonfiction) 1923

The Measurement of Intelligence (nonfiction) 1926

Elementary Principles of Education [with A. I. Gates] (nonfiction) 1929

Human Learning (nonfiction) 1931

The Fundamentals of Learning (nonfiction) 1932

Predictions of Vocational Success (nonfiction) 1934

The Psychology of Wants, Interests, and Attitudes (nonfiction) 1935

The Teaching of Controversial Subjects (nonfiction) 1937

Education as Cause and Symptom (nonfiction) 1939

Your City (nonfiction) 1939

Human Nature and the Social Order (nonfiction) 1940

Man and His Works (nonfiction) 1943

Psychology and the Science of Education: Selected Writings [edited by Geraldine M. Jonchich] (nonfiction) 1962

CRITICISM

Henry Davidson Sheldon (review date 1904)

SOURCE: A review of *Educational Psychology,* in *The Dial,* Vol. XXXVI, No. 428, April 16, 1904, pp. 263-65.

[*In the following excerpt, Sheldon praises* Educational Psychology *but points out that progress in the field will be slow despite Thorndike's work.*]

Students of genetic psychology or child study have long been waiting for some well-organized general survey which should present in readable form the results of the many studies in this field. Prof. E. A. Kirkpatrick, in his *Fundamentals of Child Study,* has attempted to meet this demand and at the same time write a text-book for class use in normal schools and colleges. The larger half of his book is devoted to a discussion of the different human instincts from infancy to manhood; the author by this method avoids the necessity of marking off and characterizing the periods of growth. Aside from instincts, the subjects dealt with are physical growth and development, native motor activities and general order of development, development of intellect, heredity, individuality, abnormalities, and child study applied in schools. Appended to each chapter is a list of questions bearing on the text but not covered by it, designed to stimulate independent thought among the students. Each chapter also contains a bibliography, well adapted for class use, of the materials used. The general bibliography at the beginning of the book is by no means as judiciously selected, works of great value by such men as Preyer, Baldwin, Sully, and Compayré being mentioned by the side of Wiggin's *Children's Rights* and Du Bois's *Beckoning of Little Hands.* This, however, is a matter of small importance. Considering the difficulties of the subject, Professor Kirkpatrick's book must be pronounced a success of the first order. The author's thorough knowledge of psychology has protected him from crude generalizations; his sense of proportion is good; the material is well digested, and the practical suggestions that he ventures upon from time to time are useful. The book is well adapted to the serious lay reader, and at the same time is valuable to the student.

Prof. Irving King's *The Psychology of Child Development* covers the same ground as the work just spoken of, though from an entirely different standpoint; the aim in this case being not so much the organization of facts as the interpretation of the more fundamental phenomena. Professor King has a thesis to defend, which in brief is this: A great mistake has been made by Preyer and others in studying the mental life of children; this mistake consists in employing the mental processes or faculties of the adult as instruments in measuring and describing the child's intelligence. The true method is functional, it regards the child's experience as a unity and describes it as such instead of trying to discover the rudimentary beginnings of adult mental processes to single acts. In his application of this view to infancy and early childhood, Professor King has been successful in making the child's activity seem more intelligible than in the writings of any previous thinker. His thesis leads him to magnify the difference between the child and the adult mind, and to somewhat exaggerate the difficulties in the way of understanding children's ideas after the first three or four years. As a running commentary on the methods generally in use, this book will perform good service, its function being distinctly critical. No recent educational book gives more evidence of painstaking thought, of the careful consideration of a subject from a single point of view. It is an important contribution to the literature of the subject. There is a fairly representative but by no means complete bibliography in the appendix.

The third volume of the present group, that by Dr. E. L. Thorndike of Columbia on *Educational Psychology,* also discusses method in child study. It is a plea for more rigorously scientific standards and methods than those that have hitherto been largely employed. The volume consists of a summary and criticism of all the studies which the author considers sufficiently accurate to be of value. The territory covered is indicated by the following list of topics: the measurement of mental traits, the distribution of mental traits, the relationship between mental traits, original and acquired traits, mental inheritance, the influence of environment, the influence of special training upon general abilities, the influence of selection, the development of mental traits with age, sex difference, exceptional children, the relationship of mental and physical traits, and broader studies of human nature. The last chapter treats of the questionnaire method of investigation, which Dr. Thorndike condemns, carefully pointing out the abuses to which it is liable. There can be little question that this criticism is greatly needed; still if we are to throw out all data that cannot be tested by the methods of the exact sciences, progress is likely to be slow in all of the social disciplines for some time to come. Several sections of Professor Kirkpatrick's book show that in the hands of a thinker who knows and makes allowance for the limitations of the questionnaire and similar methods, results of significance can be achieved. . . .

The Dial (review date 1905)

SOURCE: A review of *Elements of Psychology* in, *The Dial,* Vol. XXXIX, No. 457, July 1, 1905, p. 19.

[*In the following review of* Elements of Psychology, *the critic praises the book but notes a lack of "desirable literary value and consistent exposition."*]

A text-book of *Elements of Psychology,* recently added to the considerable group that reflects the present-day interest in the subject, brings as its distinctive contribution the emphasis upon the practical reaction which the student is induced to make to the principles set before him. The author is Professor Thorndike, of the Teachers' College of Columbia University, who brings to his task vigor and in-

sight, as well as the practical temper of one engaged in training teachers. By the constant facing of questions and exercises, the student is compelled to assume an active attitude to the pages of his text, and to reinterpret in the light of experience and reflections the conclusions which are embodied in accepted psychological doctrine. Particularly for introductory study does this method possess advantages, although it inevitably deprives the text of a desirable literary value and consistent exposition. Admitting the pertinence of the method (and there are doubtless many classes in need of this form of stimulation), one obtains from a survey of the pages an impression of decided appreciation of the students' needs and shortcomings, and likewise of the probable success with which the work will meet the needs of the situation. The excellence and completeness of the chapters on the nervous system deserve special commendation. The book is published by A. G. Seiler, New York.

Margaret Floy Washburn (review date 1912)

SOURCE: A review of *Animal Intelligence: Experimental Studies,* in *The Journal of Philosophy,* Vol. 9, No. 7, March 28, 1912, pp. 193-94.

[*In the following review, Washburn praises* Animal Intelligence: Experimental Studies.]

All psychologists will be glad to have Thorndike's experimental work on the intelligence of animals brought together in this convenient form. The thesis on **"Animal Intelligence,"** which was for many of us the first intimation that a real science of comparative psychology was possible, has been for some time out of print. It is here reprinted, together with the paper on **"The Instinctive Reactions of Young Chicks,"** the **"Note on the Psychology of Fishes,"** and the monograph on **"The Mental Life of the Monkeys."** To these papers there have been added an introductory chapter, an essay on **"Laws and Hypotheses of Behavior,"** and one on **"The Evolution of the Human Intellect."**

It is the new chapters, of course, that demand discussion in the present review. Thorndike's experimental researches have now undergone the test of time, and their influence has been valuable enough to satisfy any worker in a scientific field: few doctors' theses, indeed, have been so fruitful as *Animal Intelligence.* The introductory chapter in the present book defends the study of behavior as opposed to that of "consciousness as such." The chapter on **"Laws and Hypotheses of Behavior"** proposes, as laws of behavior in general, that behavior is predictable, that "every response or change in response of an animal is the result of the interaction of its original knowable nature and the environment"; and the law of instinct, that "to any situation an animal will, apart from learning, respond by virtue of the inherited nature of its reception-, connection-, and action-systems." All learning can be brought under the law of effect, that "of several responses made to the same situation, those which are accompanied or closely followed by satisfaction to the animal will, other things being equal, be more firmly connected with the situation, so that, when it recurs, they will be more likely to recur;" the reverse being true of responses accompanied by discomfort; and the law of exercise, that "any response to a situation will, other things being equal, be more strongly connected with the situation in proportion to the number of times it has been connected with that situation and to the average vigor and duration of the connections. The satisfaction and discomfort mentioned in the law of effect are correlated with advantage and disadvantage, not necessarily to the organism as a whole, but to its neurones." Accessory conditions to the laws of effect and of exercise are the closeness with which the satisfaction is associated with the response, and "the readiness of the response to be connected with the situation." The chief point at which the reviewer would take issue with the author in this chapter concerns the relation between an act and the idea of an act. As is well known, Thorndike opposes the doctrine that an idea of a movement causes the movement. The reviewer, for whom this doctrine is one of the really valuable and fruitful discoveries of modern psychology, has long felt that its critics misunderstood the meaning of the term "movement idea," and the arguments put forward in the chapter under consideration confirm this opinion. Take for instance the following: "It is certain that in at least nine cases out of ten a response is produced, not by an image or other representation of it, but by a situation nowise like it or any of its accessories. Hunger and the perception of edible objects far outweigh ideas of grasping, biting, and swallowing as causes of the eating done in the world." It is surely sufficient to reply that the doctrine of the movement idea is applied to the perfecting of new responses, not to the performance of instinctive responses, and that of course even in new responses the place of the movement idea is commonly later taken by an associated idea or perception. "It is also certain," the author continues, "that the idea of a response may be impotent to produce it. I can not produce a sneeze by thinking of sneezing. And, of course, one can have ideas of running a mile in two minutes, jumping a fence eight feet high, or drawing a line exactly equal to a hundred millimeter line, just as easily as of running the mile in ten minutes, or jumping four feet. It is further certain that the thought of doing one thing very often results in the man's doing something quite different. The thought of moving the eyes smoothly without stops along a line of print has occurred to many people, who nevertheless actually did as a result move the eyes in a series of jumps with long stops." The sneeze, of course, as a reflex, may be left out of consideration; nobody ever claimed that movement ideas produced reflexes. As for the other instances adduced, it is sufficient to say that no one has ever had an idea of running a mile in two minutes, or of any of the other impossible feats mentioned, or of moving the eyes smoothly along a line of print. The ideas which people may have thus labeled would be revealed by even a moderate degree of introspective analysis to be ideas of movements that had actually been performed by the persons entertaining the ideas. A movement idea is the revival, without peripheral stimulation, of the sensations that resulted from the actual performance of the movement: if the movement has never been performed, its idea is impossible.

Further, Professor Thorndike appears to think that the admission of the law that the idea of a movement can cause the performance of the movement would add a third principle of learning to the laws of effect and exercise. It would never have occurred to the reviewer not to see in the law of the movement idea a striking instance of the law of effect. It is of course always understood that a movement idea will not produce the corresponding movement if it or any of the associated processes that may be substituted for it has been connected with sufficiently strong unpleasantness. Just as an outside stimulus that by virtue of an inherited nervous connection naturally produces a movement may cease to do so if the movement has unpleasant consequences, so may a movement idea lose its movement-generating power. And the movement idea is itself based on the most immediate effect of the movement; the sensations, kinesthetic and otherwise, that are aroused by the motor process as it takes place.

In the last chapter, on **"The Evolution of Human Intellect"** the writer points out that the superiority of the human mind consists in the power of analyzing situations, which, in turn, depends on "the increased delicacy and complexity of the cell structures in the human brain."

F. C. Bartlett (review date 1945)

SOURCE: A review of *Man and His Works*, in *Mind*, Vol. LIV, No. 213, January, 1945, pp. 161-71.

[*In the following review, Bartlett asserts that his impression of Thorndike as an ingenious researcher was confirmed after reading* Man and His Works.]

Professor Thorndike plunges at once into a discussion of Nature's gifts to Man [in ***Man and His Works***]. He prefers genetic language, and calls the gifts in which he is most interested 'genes'. Others have called them 'tendencies', 'predispositions', 'instincts', and even, sometimes, 'faculties'. Whatever name they are given they are always supposed to have some special concern with action. They are elements, or groups of elements, in the internal constitution of animals, including man, which require stimulation from outside to make them do anything, but which, so far as they themselves go, owe nothing else to the outside world. People who call them 'tendencies', or something like that, generally like to think of them as limited in number, and they often make short lists which somebody else at once begins to dispute. Thorndike, calling them 'genes', likes to think of them in their thousands, and this certainly avoids one rather fruitless squabble. He thinks of thousands of genes co-operating in thousands of ways. When I got to this point I wondered whether he also thought of them as fighting one another sometimes. For it appears to me that they do, and that this may be very important indeed. But the general drift of the whole book shows that he is all for co-operation and all against mutual interference, and that is certainly an admirable characteristic in him, though it may be held to limit his theories.

The genes are not only very numerous, but they do not operate as entities or fixed groups, and so allow for an immense variability in original behaviour; they are not modifiable from generation to generation; they require outside stimulation through the sense organs, and the ones that contribute most to the works of man are those which lie at the basis of speech and tool-using.

In all this there neither is nor pretends to be anything original. But there are some exceedingly ancient difficulties. The great bulk of man's behaviour now consists of learned activities. How, if there ever is a stage in which only genes are operative, does such learning begin? Thorndike does indeed contemplate certain types of gene-determined behaviour as 'insufficient'. It is not very clear for what they can be insufficient unless some additional assumptions are made about genes besides those that are mentioned. But in any case he uses the consideration, correctly, only to distinguish between behaviour which seems to express some 'general tendency' and behaviour which requires a specialised mechanism, both being equally and entirely gene-determined. He is "confident" that the genes "provide no direct and primary responses to any mental images, or ideas of concrete things, or judgments about them, much less to general or abstract ideas and judgments about them." Difficulties accumulate when he begins to talk about speech and tool-using: "Man by nature moves the tongue and other mouth parts to produce a great variety of sounds, and has pleasure in doing so. These movements, in connection with certain intellectual powers, can produce meaningful speech." The "certain intellectual powers" are a bit of a mystery. They come in with a bang, casting no shadow before them and bearing no credentials with them. They cannot be special genes because their objectives are just the sorts of things that no gene can do anything about. If they are to be accounted for at all, the conditions of their appearance must belong, so far as Thorndike is concerned, to a study of learning process.

To this study he devotes the second chapter, which is vital to very nearly everything else in the book. A man's mind is depicted as an extraordinarily elaborate network of connections. To describe anybody fully we have to make a list (Thorndike is fonder of lists than anybody else I have ever known. Pretty well all his experiments present people with lists. If he has any problem to solve he first makes a list. Most of his illustrations are enumerations. Therefore, perhaps, one should not be surprised to find that man himself is only a list) of all the situations "he might encounter and be sensitive to and lists of all the responses he might possibly make to each, and statements of the probability that any of the situations would evoke any of the responses in

that person". If S is situation and R response, a man is "the total of all his S-R probabilities", where "total" obviously means "list". It comes with a shock to find Thorndike roundly asserting that this is true, and all of the truth, whatever conceivable kind of theoretical foundation psychology may have. All that environment does is to change the values of the R probabilities up or down, and all the wrangles about different sorts of psychologies are quarrels about the number and character of the "forces" that do this.

Thorndike dubs his view "connectionist" and says its distinguishing feature is that it uses only two such "forces"— *repetition* and *reward.*

Fortunately Thorndike does not make much play with repetition. He says that strictly it ought to be called "occurrence", because the occurrence of any response very slightly increases the probability of its recurrence. In the setting of general theory provided, this does not come to much. For response, to Thorndike, is some sort of movement. The exercise of any sort of movement produces a degree of pleasure. Pleasure is a kind of reward, indeed the only basic kind there is. It seems as if "mere occurrence" can signify nothing at all, and as no carefully controlled experiments ever have demonstrated that sheer repetition is of any importance in learning, this need not occasion any worry. There is, then, one "force" only to account for learning, the "force" of reward.

Perhaps two of the many questions that can be asked at this point are the most interesting. How does reward work? and, Is Thorndike successful in his attempt to show that no other influence operates to promote and direct learning?

Thorndike's answer to the former question is perfectly definite. Reward works by strengthening connections, chiefly between the response and the situation to which the response is made, but also to a smaller degree, between that response and neighbouring situations. Any psychologically trained reader will know that Thorndike's conclusion is based upon many years of patient, ingenious and original experiment. All the experiments have a strong family likeness, and it is worth considering briefly the one described in this chapter.

A list of 135 words was made and to each word one of the numbers 1 to 5 was assigned, there being, of course, no reason inherent in the word why it should be attended by one number rather than another. The list was then read aloud to many and different kinds of auditors who were asked to guess and record the correct number in the case of every word. At irregular intervals the correct number of a particular word was also stated. If the subject happened by chance to have hit on the right number, this statement constituted his reward. Invariably, confirmed numbers reappeared in subsequent readings with a frequency much greater than could be accounted for by chance and the same numbers were also assigned to near-by words in the list more often than their random use would explain.

The conclusion seems plain and just. A connection between giving a particular number in response to special words has been strengthened by confirmation, or reward. Thorndike immediately generalises on a large scale. The normal man experiences confirming reactions in their dozens every minute of every working day. They all work the same way.

"To each phrase that I speak you respond by a certain meaning. If this meaning satisfies you by making sense the connection is confirmed. Similarly, in reading a page a satisfying flow of sense is confirmed step by step."

At this point it seemed to me that a simple trial of these views might be made. It could not by itself be conclusive but it might suggest whether further tests would be worth while, and how they might be planned. I read on to the end of the chapter and closed the book. Thorndike's exposition is beautiful in form. With very few exceptions I think I fully appreciated the meaning of the sentences and paragraphs, so that they were satisfying in that sense. In a great part I also approved the meaning so that a further, and perhaps a different sort of, satisfaction had been present. It seemed to me that if the connectionist theory is correct I ought to be able, to a considerable extent, to repeat the language, particularly if I could begin with a few "key" words. But no, nothing of the sort happened. I could write down the argument; and other people who had read it, or were familiar with it, could easily identify it as derived from Thorndike. But the words, the sequence, the style were different.

The truth is, I think, that a connectionist theory of learning seems to be adequate in proportion as the items of a situation are more separated and individualised than is usual in daily life, and the responses attached to them more arbitrary. In most learning experiments this is just what does happen, and when, as to an altogether preponderant extent in Thorndike's experiments, they consist of parallel lists, it happens in its most extreme form. The conclusion is concealed in the design of the experiment and not in the natural facts.

It is more difficult to state briefly how reward, in so far as it operates at all, does work. But it seems as if it must be *either* by strengthening specific connections *or* by stimulating a mass of material whose items may vary freely in sequence, form and individual characteristics while yet their general significance remains constant. The second kind of learning appears to be very much more frequent under everyday conditions than the first. Perhaps it might be urged that the second type is properly described as the sort of instance in which the odds against any particular response are extremely small, and those in favour of a large number of differing responses are about even. Very few psychologists would, I think, agree with that.

Is reward the only "force" operating in learning? This is a hard question to answer and though Thorndike's exposition seems to amount to a strong assertion that it is, I am still uncertain whether he really does think so. Partly this is due to the extreme ambiguity of the word "reward". Reward can, in fact, be applied to almost any state of mind that follows action, within, possibly, certain rather wide temporal limits. The only reward of truly gene-determined action is pleasure. But Thorndike says little about pleasure. The words he prefers are "confirming reaction", "satisfyingness" and even "belongingness". The trouble about all these is that they stand for objectives which, by his hypothesis, no genes can possibly deal with. Presumably the mysterious "intellectual powers" must come in again. Even on the gene level, pleasure is not the only reward. Thorndike specifically dissents from any theory of hedonistic selection. This suggests the view, with which, so far as I can gather, he would agree, that different groups of genes have different degrees of potency. In that case the genes will not only co-operate, they will also interfere with one another. Obviously, however, such conflict can do nothing to effect a change of the principle of solution from pleasure to, say, belongingness, unless it brings some new determinant on the scene. It may be that we are to suppose that when two sets of genes of differing potency collide, the "intellectual powers" are awakened, or, in some sense, originated. But Thorndike does not say so, and if he did he would have at least two kinds of reward, on two such different levels that nothing could combine them into one.

Apart from this it seems to me that "confirming reaction", "satisfyingness" and "belongingness" are genuinely different rewards, each appropriate to its own special circumstances and leading to different results.

What about punishment? Most people continue to think of this as having a genuine effect upon learning, different from that of "reward", negative in an immediate sense, though, according to some views, positive in a remote sense. In a connectionist theory, if this view is correct, punishment must first work either by preventing a connection from being made, or by weakening a connection that has already been made.

Thorndike, therefore, as most people will know, carried out a large number of multiple-choice experiments in human learning. The punishment he used was to tell his subjects when they made the "wrong" choices. "What was my surprise", he writes, "to find that a connection made and punished was more likely to be made again than if it had not been made at all!" He generalises that punishment has no direct effect in producing or tending to produce an avoiding reaction.

Once again, I believe, we have a result which is more a matter of the design of the experiment than of anything else. Thorndike's multiple choices were usually very numerous, far beyond what any normal person could take into his "span of apprehension". The mildness of the punishment may not be very important, for he analyses the results of a number of animal experiments and arrives at the same conclusion, when the punishment appears to have been anything but mild. But his method one way and another certainly reduced punishment to a sort of minimal significance. In some so far unpublished experiments carried out at the Cambridge Psychological Laboratory, Miss A. Dand repeated Thorndike's procedure, except that she reduced the number of choices to a range lying within or just within the "span of attention" of her subjects. A verdict "wrong" was as likely to be followed by the avoidance of a particular choice, as a verdict "right" was to be followed by the repetition of a particular choice.

More interesting was another experiment which at the moment can be described only in general terms. This involved a highly complex activity, depending on accurate visual perception of a moving pattern with many items, the exact location, or judgment, of a particular position within the pattern, and a timed movement requiring the co-ordinate activity of a number of muscle groups. Both experimenter and subject knew what it was desired to achieve, or learn. When the subject had done his best the experimenter knew how near he had come to a perfect performance. Neither knew just how the perfect performance could be achieved. There was a strong motive to learn, for in this case the success achieved meant life or death to a lot of people, if it could be transferred to a different but very similar situation outside the laboratory.

We took two sufficiently large groups, as equal as possible in all relevant respects. One we trained with persistent encouragement (or reward) and the other with persistent discouragement (or punishment). Both improved significantly at almost the same rate and to almost the same degree within the limits of the learning period assigned. And when the end was reached nobody knew by what precise sequence of processes it had been reached. Certainly it was not reached by going along any fixed chain of links with progressively strengthened or weakened connections. The final trials were with patterns which had never been seen before, and could not be dealt with simply by unrolling an established sequence. But they were dealt with by both groups, with a success that would have been totally impossible at the beginning of learning.

In fact, except perhaps in carefully selected cases, there seems to be something radically wrong with any theory which demands that the acquisition of skill must consist in establishing and strengthening links either between whatever is treated as a single situation and a single response, or between various items in the situation and a series of responses having a definite order. It is necessary to bring in order of sequence because if that is altered the links cannot possibly be the same links; and this is clearest of all in a view such as Thorndike's, according to which responses are fundamentally movements of some kind. Both these cases, however, the case of fixed single reaction, and that of fixed serial reactions, are uncommon except in specifically arranged experiment.

In normal times a man has two or three great-coats. Having learned to button up one of them he does not, when he puts on another for the first few times, have to learn in the same way to button that, though the buttons and the button-holes may vary widely in size, spacing, position and other respects. He has mastered the buttoning process, and will achieve it readily and with a minimum of conscious effort even though the movements and their connections differ from coat to coat. Similarly, in the second of the two experiments described above, the terminal response (usually considered to be particularly important in a connectionist theory) consists in pressing a morse key. But this can be done just as well by any finger of either hand, and what is often noticed is an inverse relationship between the frequency with which a particular movement has been used and the probability that that particular movement will immediately recur. Indeed, the very great difficulty of transferring a fixed series of responses from one situation to any like situation, which every experimental psychologist has come across, ought to make anybody suspect the adequacy of a simple connectionist theory.

I often think that those of us who live mainly in the psychological laboratory—as I do—would gain greatly if we sometimes relaxed into the arm-chair, and took a little more notice of the works of those who have been much less tied than we are to the limits of carefully invented situations. In learning, for example, we might well reflect again about Lloyd Morgan's notion of "persistency with varied effort" and the use made of it by G. F. Stout. It is true that both of them look upon the "varied effort" as particularly incidental to a stage of learning, and give less thought to the variation which remains a prominent characteristic of most forms of mastered skill. But if, with this principle in mind, we examine the daily practice of skills, whether of movements or of words, or of any other medium, we shall find that in mastery also, in the majority of instances, it is "varied effort" that more than anything else calls for explanation.

There seems nothing for it but to admit that in some way or another the details of whatever media are used in any form of acquired skill, including remembering, are organised into groups and have interconnections which may vary widely while yet the groups as a whole retain an identical functional significance. The man learns *what* to do and not strictly, except perhaps in very early stages or in specifically routinized cases, any one way of doing it. The link that is of real importance is the link between the situation and its predominant immediate demands, whether these demands are the expression of genes or groups of genes with differing potency, or are the objectives of what Thorndike calls "intellectual powers". This link can be strengthened or weakened, not only by reward or punishment, in the ordinary sense of these words, but also by many other determining conditions which it is the business of the psychologist to distinguish and study. As the steps towards attempted satisfaction of the demand are taken, various items from the organised groups of media that must be used, appear one after another. They vary freely in form, in number, in order and in qualitative character. Thus both the items which are connected and the sequence of connections may be different from one practice effort to another, and still more from one exercise of acquired skill to another of the same skill. So long as what were called the "demands of the situation" are met, the exact ways in which they are met are usually only very loosely controlled.

Is it possible to give any generalised account of why the same skill will go first along one pathway and then along another? I think it is, and I think that when Thorndike gets away from his experimental lists, with their limited and defined possibilities of "right" and "wrong", he indicates one of the leading clues. He says that genes, and gene groups, and their derivative "powers" must be regarded as having differing degrees of potency in any concrete situation. Presumably these relative potencies are inherent in the gene-determined organisation of the individual, but those of the derivative powers simply cannot be regarded as inherent in the same way. In this book, however, they are described as simply present and operating; there is nothing to show how they have been established, how they are related to the material environmental conditions in any case, and how, when they are active, their simultaneous operation, with differing temporary balance from case to case, helps to explain why the same skill takes now one course and now another.

Thorndike claims to use one other principle only. He does this when he is considering the understanding and utilisation of meanings as they have been expressed in continuous prose passages. He then says that besides "the principle of potencies or weights", we must use the principle that "the elements must be put and left in the right relations". Unfortunately the reader is left to put his own interpretation upon this, and given no clue beyond what he can gather from the context. From this it seems as if Thorndike considers that the same elements must be evoked in the same serial order as were present some time or, more likely, a large number of times before.

I suspect, however, that this second principle is a rather obscure way of stating whatever is involved in the notion of "belongingness", used in this book several times, but elaborated in other writings of our author. Now whatever else is true about "belongingness" it seems plain that it has the character of an abstract notion, and requires a proposition for its expression. It cannot therefore, as I have said already, be a part of man's endowment. The whole drift of Thorndike's discussion suggests that "belongingness" requires simply the reappearance of items and a sequence that have appeared before. In a very precise and literal sense perhaps this never occurs in the whole field of the phenomena of life. But we come nearest to it in the various forms of tropistic and reflex action and in rote recapitulation, the first being usually regarded as a part of endowment and the second as the simplest of all possible forms of learning. To take what may approximately happen at a very lowly level of behaviour as a sufficient model for all levels of action is, to my mind, a lamentable and fundamental mistake.

I have considered the theory of learning which is presented in this book at such length because it is vital for the greater part of the work, and also because Thorndike has, as I think, done better and more experiments on this topic than any other living psychologist. He may have oversimplified his explanation. He may appear to have only the three principles of reward, together with (in some cases) relative potencies, and the maintenance of "right relations", merely because he has squashed into these three others which are in fact incompatible with them. He may have overdone the fixed sequential characteristic of acquired skill. More than anybody else he has certainly proved that there is something which happens at the culmination of a series of responses which, working back upon the responses and their relations, makes it likely that what the responses achieve will be achieved with greater or less ease in the future. He has also demonstrated in several directions how and within what limits the retro-active influence works. It is, for example, still believed by many that a response to certain classes of situations may be left to become thoroughly established and then suddenly prevented by some drastic and dramatic punishment. Thorndike has shown that it is not so, and that a form of behaviour is not rendered more likely directly in proportion to the size of the reward or less likely directly in proportion to the severity of its punishment.

I should like to consider in detail the two brilliant, but, I think, theoretically unsatisfying chapters on the psychology of language. I should also like to linger over his discussions of Human Relations, Rulers and Ruled, and Laws and the Law. But the review is already very long and I will be content with a few remarks about the original and interesting contribution which this book makes to the Psychology of Welfare.

There are two main problems: the Welfare of Individuals and the Welfare of Communities. Both are approached in Thorndike's characteristic list-making manner. I propose to consider the second only.

Thorndike draws up "A bill of specification of a good life for a community". This contains seventy-two items. They all refer to life in the modern American city. The first thirty-seven items are crucial and their combined "score" constitutes what Thorndike calls the "G index of the general goodness of life in a city". The remaining items yield subsidiary information which, treated by a variety of statistical methods, may, Thorndike thinks, throw at least some light on what are the main conditions of social welfare. All of the first thirty-seven items can be given an objective expression. They are such features as "Infant death-rate reversed"; "Average salary of an elementary school teacher"; "*Per capita* public property minus public debt". A good many of the subsidiary items are difficult to measure, and some, like "Justice of voters to tax-payers", or "Intelligent sympathy of old with young", invite opinions merely.

Thorndike claims no finality for his list, and recommends anybody who thinks he can do better to try. It is certain that most people of his own level of culture and with his social background will accept the enumeration as on the whole just, and probably sufficient.

He now took 295 American cities of from 30,000 to 500,000 population and got the facts about them for all of the measurable items on his "bill", and opinions for all of the unmeasurable items. Any city that was as low in every item as the city that was lowest of the 295 would gain a G score of 0 and any city that was as high in each item as the city that was highest in the 295 in that item would gain a G score of 1541. The actual range in the case of these particular cities in the year 1930 was from about 300 to about 1100.

It is not possible here to consider the statistical methods used by Thorndike in his attempt to analyse his G score and to discover the conditions which make it high or low. Some of them may involve rather dubious assumptions about the distribution of the characters measured. Thorndike has, however, few peers in this field, and on the whole the work is meticulously careful as well as ingenious. The conclusion is that two groups of factors are more important than any others: the *per capita* income of a city's residents, and their level of intelligence, character and ideals. There is, naturally, something common to these two and there is an unnamed residue, probably, though Thorndike does not say so, specifically social in its character.

More interesting perhaps are the suggested negative conclusions. Apparently the welfare of a community, as measured in this way, has little or nothing to do with its size, and nothing at all with its wealth except in the form of the highest level of income for the greatest relative number of persons. The G score is not necessarily depressed in communities which have developed large scale mass production, or raised in those which maintain a large Church membership. There is no evidence that the political system, or form of government preferred, is of any particular importance.

Criticism is very easy. It will doubtless be said that the whole approach is superficial; that the "bill of specification" is highly selected and, in any case, can have regional and temporal significance only; that in the present state of record keeping even the most sharply defined of the measures used are bound to be highly approximate; that no amount of statistical manipulation can transform inaccurate data into accurate conclusions; that at best all that we are given are certain current and conventional standards of social welfare, together with a rough approximation to the degree in which these standards are attained in more or less comparable groups.

All these objections are valid. In particular Thorndike does often write as if he is making a genuine contribution to the ethics of social life, whereas all that he shows is that if certain social ideals are good, then these are likely to be approached in fact when certain aspects of training fundamental to them are vigorously developed, and certain others are given less than their common current consideration. This seems to me a great step forward. It means that when social welfare is being discussed, within the limits of the scheme we do know reasonably definitely what we are talking about, and it means that a way has been found of comparing communities which makes it possible, however tentatively and approximately, to range them in an order of achievement. Moreover, again within the limits of the method proposed, it indicates what can be done, especially by way of improving records, to make the ranking more certain and reliable. Between sixty and seventy years ago the first tentative efforts to measure individual intelligence level could have been criticised in much the same way as these proposals can be attacked now. It may be that Thorndike's courageous attempt to deal with the much more complex problem of the level of social welfare may have as great and as beneficial a development as has already been secured in the field of intelligence.

I began to read this book with a very lively regard for Professor Thorndike and his works. He has a long and enviable record of ingenious, simple, unconventional and well directed experimental achievement. There is, I fear, no getting away from the fact that many of his earlier publications, though they nearly always describe genuinely original work of very high quality, are over-long, wordy, detailed, and contain drawn-out dull passages. There are none of these here. He is summing up the main results of a life-time of research. He does it with remarkable economy and outstanding clarity. So I should like to set it down that I finished my reading with my regard for the author enhanced and my admiration raised to a higher level. It seemed to me to matter little that I could not agree with all his arguments. I knew what he was arguing about, and the whole work is written with that perfect honesty, simplicity and directness which are the marks of a master.

Simeon Potter (review date 1945)

SOURCE: A review of *Man and His Works,* in *The Modern Language Review,* Vol. 40, No. 3, July, 1945, pp. 149-50.

[*In the following review, Potter finds the lectures collected in* Man and His Works *"eminently readable: shrewd, witty and vivacious."*]

The William James Lectures, delivered recently at Harvard by Edward Lee Thorndike, have now been published in an attractive volume bearing the comprehensive title ***Man and His Works.*** These lectures are eminently readable: shrewd, witty and vivacious. Their themes range from the inherited causative agents or 'genes' of the mind to the laws of man's 'modifiability', human relations in general, and the psychology of government, punishment and welfare. Two lectures out of ten are devoted to the psychology of language. Seeing that they occupy a central position in this book (Chapters IV and V) and that they are from the pen of a world-famous experimentalist, we approach them with expectation. Most useful syntheses have recently been made by Thorndike's Transatlantic colleagues, Graff

(1932), Bloomfield (1933) and Gray (1939). A similar survey of linguistic psychology on a more general background would now be no less acceptable. These chapters do, indeed, give us much. Their intrinsic value lies in their application to human speech of the Thorndikian doctrine of *repetition* and *reward*. But they are otherwise disappointing and, digressive and trifling, they do not seem to fit well into the pattern of the book. There are, it is true, plenty of good things. Language, we are reminded, not only expresses, but also arouses, thoughts and feelings. It arouses movements. Chemistry and mathematics now have 'well-nigh perfect languages'. The equations of physics are 'the most pregnant sentences ever said or written about the physical world'. Language has infinite variety. A man can construct more declarative sentences about a blade of grass than there are blades of grass in the world. When, however, the author turns to discuss modern trends in semantics, he is content to refer to a single chapter in Bloomfield's *Language,* to some pages in Eisenson's *Psychology of Speech,* and to *The Meaning of Meaning* by Ogden and Richards. He does not mention de Saussure, Oertel, Nyrop, Delacroix, Brunot or Carnoy; nor does he point to the notable advances made in the closely related field of mathematical logic by Tarski and Carnap. The paragraphs on the origin of language are more interesting, for in them he expounds his own 'babble-babble', 'babble-by-luck' or 'babble-luck' theory with great clarity and precision, a theory 'relying on the miscellaneous vocal play of man instead of his alleged mimetic or emotional utterances'. The steps or stages are well portrayed: the aimless babble or prattle of 'primitive' man: the particular prattle with a chance association; the crude or 'beggarly' private language; then speech in the speaker-hearer relation. 'The normal operations of repetition and reward would lead men to the final two-way, give-and-take speech'. As one of many possible contributory factors in the origin or creation or birth of language (whatever precise significations may be attached to these expressions), this is all feasible. No fundamental fallacy can be detected in these deductions. The 'babble-luck' surmise is quite as good as any one of its congeners, whether 'bow-wow', 'ding-dong', 'pooh-pooh', 'yo-he-ho', 'sing-song' or 'ta-ta'. Whilst no longer holding to the rigid principle that all such speculations should be banned as unprofitable, many will nevertheless wish that so eminent an empiricist and statistician had produced something more definite from his rich store of experience, that he had expressed his views on some less speculative aspect of the *evolution* of language, and that he had written, however briefly, on the immediate and more urgent tasks which now confront the student of linguistic psychology.

Edward L. Thorndike (essay date 1949)

SOURCE: An introduction to *Selected Writings From A Connectionist's Psychology,* Appleton-Century-Crofts, Inc., 1949, pp. 1-11.

[*In the following introduction to* Selected Writings from a Connectionist's Psychology, *Thorndike provides an autobiographical account of his life and work.*]

I have no memory of having heard or seen the word *psychology* until in my junior year at Wesleyan University (1893-1894), when I took a required course in it. The textbook, Sully's *Psychology,* aroused no notable interest, nor did the excellent lectures of Professor A. C. Armstrong, though I appreciated and enjoyed the dignity and clarity of his presentation and admired his skill in discrimination and argument. These discriminations and arguments stimulated me very little, however, and this was later true also of the writings of Ward and Stout. There is evidently some lack in my equipment which makes me intolerant of critical studies unless fortified by new facts or decorated by a captivating style.

The candidates in a prize examination were required to read also certain chapters from James's *Principles.* These were stimulating, more so than any book that I had read before, and possibly more so than any read since. The evidence is three-fold. I bought the two volumes (the only book outside the field of literature that I voluntarily bought during the four years of college) and read all save parts of the most technical chapters. Though not, I hope, more impertinent than the average collegian, I reproached Professor Armstrong for not having given us James in place of Sully as our text. When, a year later, circumstances permitted me to study at Harvard, I eagerly registered for the course available under James.

During the first semester at Harvard (1895-1896) my program was half English, one-fourth psychology, and one-fourth philosophy, the last at the suggestion or requirement of Professor Royce. The subtlety and dexterity of Royce's mind aroused admiration tinged with irritation and amusement. Most of the students saw him as a prophet, but to me then he seemed too much a performer. Under no circumstances, probably, could I have been able or willing to make philosophy my business. Its stars shone brightly at Harvard in those years (1895-1897); Royce and Santayana were at or near their full glory, and Palmer was, as ever, the perfect expositor, but what I heard from them or about them did not attract me. Later I read the *Life of Reason* with extraordinary interest and profit, and learned to value the integrity and sincerity and impartiality of Dewey's writings on philosophy as well as on psychology and education; but in general my acquaintance with philosophy has been superficial and casual. Work in English was dropped in favor of psychology in the course of the first graduate year, and, by the fall of 1897, I thought of myself as a student of psychology and a candidate for the Ph.D. degree.

Münsterberg was in Germany from the fall of 1895 to the fall of 1897. During the second half of the period from 1895 to 1896, Mr. Hackett and I had made experiments in a course under the direction of Professor Delabarre, who had charge of the laboratory. During 1896-1897 I first attempted to measure the responsiveness of young children (3-6) to facial expressions or movements made unconsciously as in mind-reading experiments. I would think of one of a set of numbers, letters, or objects (I cannot now recall which or how many.) The child, facing me across a small table, would look at me and guess. If he guessed correctly, he received a small bit of candy. The children enjoyed the experiments, but the authorities in control of the institution would not permit me to continue them. I then suggested experiments with the instinctive and intelligent behavior of chickens as a topic, and this was accepted. I kept these animals and conducted the experiments in my room until the landlady's protests became imperative. James tried to get the few square feet required for me in the laboratory, and then in the Agassiz Museum. He was refused, and with his habitual kindness and devotion to underdogs and eccentric aspects of science, he harbored my chickens in the cellar of his own home for the rest of the year. The nuisance to Mrs. James was, I hope, somewhat mitigated by the entertainment to the two youngest children.

During the two years of study at Harvard, I had supported myself by acting as tutor to a boy. We roomed together, and the incessant companionship and responsibility was burdensome, though he was cheerful, coöperative, and fonder of me than I deserved, and though I learned much practical psychology and pedagogy from the experience. A year free from such labor seemed desirable, so I applied for a fellowship at Columbia. I received the appointment, and upon inquiry was informed by Professor Cattell that an extension of my work on the mental life of animals would be suitable for a doctor's thesis. I continued these experiments with chickens at my parents' home during the summer. I tried white rats also, but I was stupid in handling them and the family objected to the smell, so I let them go.

I came to New York, bringing in a basket my two most educated chickens, from whom I expected in due time a family which would enable me to test the influence of acquired mental traits upon inherited capacity, a foolish project in view of the slow breeding-rate of fowls. I also expected to test the permanence of their learning over a long interval, but never did, the first of a regrettable list of enterprises left incomplete.

Cattell was not only kind, but highly efficient, providing a room in the attic which was ample for my purpose, and giving, as always, sound advice. The freedom from work and worry for money was a great boon. The present policy of universities is to reduce grants for scholarships and fellowships relatively to the number of students, replacing them by loan funds, and this may be wise. But, so far as I can judge, scholarships at Harvard and a fellowship at Columbia increased my productive work in science by at least two years and probably improved its quality.

The motive for my first investigations of animal intelligence was chiefly to satisfy requirements for courses and degrees. Any other topic would probably have served me as well. I certainly had no special interest in animals and had never taken a course in biology until my last year of graduate work, when I worked hard at it and completed a minor for the doctor's degree. The work with monkeys,

from 1899 to 1901, was done from the mixture of duty, interest, and desire for good repute which motivates most scientific work. The extension of the fruitful experimental method to representative primates was obviously important. I would have gladly continued the work with the higher apes, but could not afford to buy or maintain them.

In the spring of 1898, I was offered two positions, one as a teacher of psychology in a normal school, the other at a much lower salary as a teacher of education in the College for Women of Western Reserve University. I chose the latter, partly because my brother expected to go there and partly because of the repute of Western Reserve. I spent the summer in reading the facts and important theories about education and teaching. This could then be done if the history of educational practices was omitted. After a year at Cleveland, I was given a trial at teaching psychology and child study at Teachers College, and there I have spent the past thirty-one years.

I have recorded my beginning as a psychologist in detail because it illustrates what is perhaps the most general fact about my entire career as a psychologist later; namely, its responsiveness to outer pressure or opportunity rather than to inner needs. Within certain limits set by capacity and interest I did in those early years and have done since what the occasion seemed to demand. Thus for various courses taught at Teachers College I wrote the *Elements of Psychology, Notes on Child Study, Educational Psychology* (in three editions, from 1903 to 1914), *An Introduction to the Theory of Mental and Social Measurements,* and *The Psychology of Arithmetic.* It has always seemed to me better for an instructor to present his contributions in black and white than to require the labor and risk the errors of note-taking. Thus I have made somewhat laborious researches on mental inheritance, individual and sex differences, memory, work, fatigue, interest, the interrelations of abilities, the organization of intellect, and other topics in educational psychology, because in each case the matter seemed important for theory or practice or both. I planned and directed the psychological work of the New York State Commission on Ventilation, prepared tests for the selection of clerical employees, and served on the Committee on Classification of Personnel in the Army and in various other enterprises because I was told by persons in whom I had confidence that it was in the line of duty. I have written textbooks for children to show that psychology does apply in detail to the work of the classroom. Thus, in 1919, at the request of the faculty of Columbia College, I undertook the responsibility of preparing annually an intelligence examination suitable for use in the selection and placement of freshmen; and in 1922, at the request of Justice Stone, then Dean of the Columbia Law School, I conducted a three-year investigation which resulted in the Capacity Test adopted in 1928 as a part of the system of selection of entrants to the Columbia Law School.

Obviously I have not "carved out my career," as the biographers say. Rather, it has been a conglomerate, amassed under the pressure of varied opportunities and demands.

Probably it would have been wiser to plan a more consistent and unified life-work in accord with interest and capacity, but I am not sure. Even in the case of great men, there is considerable evidence that the man's own interests and plans may not cause a better output than his responses to demands from outside. Under pressure, James wrote the *Principles* with wailing and gnashing of teeth to fulfill a contract with a publishing firm. *Pragmatism* and *The Will to Believe* were done when he was free to choose. An ordinary man of science has probably less reason to put his own plans above those which the world makes for him. So I do not complain of the restrictions imposed by the necessity of earning a living by various drudgeries to which I have been assigned. And I reproach myself only moderately for not having looked and thought longer before leaping to this, that, and the other job.

In the last dozen years I have been enabled by grants from the Carnegie Corporation to carry on two investigations which I did choose and plan, one on the fundamentals of measurement of intellect and capacity, the results of which appeared as *The Measurement of Intelligence,* the other on the fundamentals of learning, the results of which have appeared in *The Fundamentals of Learning* and in *The Psychology of Wants, Interests, and Attitudes.* These do seem to me by far the best work that I have done and I cannot help wondering what would have happened if similar support had been available in 1905 or 1915.

The impetuosity to which I have referred has influenced my work in detail. I often have to do corrective and supplementary experiments and discard work because in its course a better way is found.

Another weakness has been an extreme ineptitude and distaste for using machinery and physical instruments. Presumably my work would have been better, and certainly it would have *seemed* better, if I had been at home with apparatus for exposing, timing, registering, and the like.

The training which I have most keenly missed has been a systematic course in the use of standard physiological and psychological apparatus and extended training in mathematics. Perhaps the first would not have profited me much in view of my extreme incapacity. I did not lack capacity for mathematics and tried to remedy the second deficiency by private study, but something else always seemed more important. I managed to learn the essentials of statistical method somehow, and have handled some fairly intricate quantitative problems without, I think, making more than one mistake (which I was able to correct promptly at the suggestion of Dr. T. L. Kelley). I feel incompetent and insecure, however, in the abstract algebraic treatment of a quantitative problem and I am helpless when the calculus is necessary.

Young psychologists who share one or more of my disabilities may take comfort in the fact that, after all, I have done useful experiments without mechanical ability or training and have investigated quantitative relations with very meager knowledge of mathematics.

As personal features on the other side of the ledger I may put intelligence, good health, strong eyes, the interest in work and achievement which Veblen has called the "instinct of workmanship," impartiality, and industry. As environmental features I may note home life with parents of superior intelligence and idealism, many profitable courses at Wesleyan, Harvard, and Columbia, especially those in abnormal psychology with James, statistical methods with Boas, and neurology with Strong, university colleagues eminent in psychology and other fields, and the great body of published work in science.

The last is, of course, the most important. Though an investigator rather than a scholar, I have probably spent well over 20,000 hours in reading and studying scientific books and journals.

I have tried to make two lists, one of authors all or nearly all of whose writings I have read, and another of authors not included in the above to whom I owe valuable facts or suggestions. But the first list of thirty or so names grades off into the names of many more, much of whose writing I have read, and the second list, which is very long, cannot be accurate because of faults of memory. Therefore, I may note only that the writings of James and Galton have influenced me most, and that factual material seems to benefit me more than what is commonly called discussion and criticism. Although, as has been stated, my tendency is to say "Yes" to persons, my tendency seems to have been to say "No" to ideas. I have been stimulated to study problems to which Romanes, Wesley Mills, Stanley Hall, Alexander Bain, Kraepelin, Spearman, and others seemed to me to give wrong answers, more often than to verify and extend work which seemed sound. Of late years this negative or critical tendency seems to have weakened and given place to an interest in questions to which the answers are conflicting or inadequate, and in questions which have not even been faced.

Until the first World War I was able to keep fairly well informed of the findings of psychologists in respect to animal psychology, individual psychology, and educational psychology, but since 1917 I have been able only to follow specially important work and that which I had to know about in connection with my own researches. In spite of the saving of time due to the Psychological Abstracts, my reading is now less and less adequate each year.

I have a suspicion that our scientific code, which demands that an investigator should acquaint himself with everything, good, bad, and indifferent, that has been done on the problem which he is investigating, should be somewhat relaxed. Personally, I seem to have profited more from reading important books outside of the topics I had to investigate, and even outside of psychology, than from some of the monographs and articles on animal learning, intelligence tests, and the like, which our code required me to read.

We are especially urged in these psychological autobiographies to describe our methods of work, but I seem to have little or nothing useful to say in this regard. In the actual work of advancing knowledge of human nature we may use three methods. We may observe and think about the facts that come our way; we may deliberately gather by observation or experiment facts which we see can be got and which seem likely to be instructive; we may pose a question that we know is important and then do our best to get facts to answer it. I have done all three; most often the last. The most fruitful methods often come to mind late in the course of an investigation. When one does everything that he can think of, the doing often makes him think of something else. So the idea of the delayed-reaction experiment (which has proved the most valuable of my methods of studying animal mentality) came to me after two years of work with animals. So the idea that the difficulty of a task for intellect (or any other ability) can be measured only in the case of a task composed of enough elements to involve all of intellect (or of the ability, whatever it may be), and nothing but it, came only after thirty years of study of intellect, and over a year of special investigation of means of measuring difficulty for intellect.

Concerning conditions favorable and unfavorable to scholarly and productive work in science, I have little or nothing instructive to report. Peaceful successful work without worry has rarely tired me, though if I drop below a certain minimum amount of sleep, a headache results. Noise does not disturb me unless it is evidence of distress, as of a person or animal in pain. Surety of freedom from interruption is of course beneficial. Social intercourse except with intimate friends is fatiguing, and all forms of personal conflict, as in bargaining, persuading, or rebuking, are trebly so. Physical exercise is enjoyable, but not, so far I know, beneficial. A general background of freedom from regret and worry is almost imperative, and I early decided to spend so little and earn so much as to keep free from financial worries. In order to reduce one cause for worry, it has been my custom to fulfill my contractual obligations as a professor before doing anything else. The good opinion of others, especially those whom I esteem, has been a very great stimulus, though I have come in later years to require also the approval of my own judgment.

Since my own history is so barren of interest and instruction I may add a few notes of general observation. Excellent work in psychology can surely be done by men widely different in nature or training or both. James and Hall were essentially literary men, one with an extraordinary sense of fact, the other with extraordinary imagination and prophetic zeal. On the other hand, some of our present leaders were first trained in physics or engineering.

Excellent work can surely be done by men with widely different notions of what psychology is and should be, the best work of all perhaps being done by men such as Galton, who gave little or no thought to what it is or should be.

Excellent results have come from the successive widenings of the field of observation to include the insane, infants, and animals, and from the correlation of mental events with physiological changes. Should we not extend our observations to include, for example, history, anthropology, economics, linguistics, and the fine arts, and connect them with biochemistry and biophysics?

The above covers my work till 1934 or age 60. I now (1948) add notes about some activities since then which may be of interest to students of psychology.

It seemed to me that psychology should strive to become a basic science on which Anthropology, Sociology, Economics, Political Science, Law, Criminology, and Philanthropy could count for certain fundamental facts and principles, especially concerning human abilities and wants. With generous aid from the Carnegie Corporation, I spent much time from 1934 to 1940 working with a group of students of history and political science, lawyers, and psychologists who already had doctor's degrees and were given fellowships for two or more years. It was hoped that some of them would become leaders in making psychology a basic part of these special sciences: and perhaps some of them yet will. So far they have done many excellent things, but not that.

I myself wrote **Human Nature and the Social Order** (1940), stating some of the facts of psychology which students of these special sciences, especially of Economics, Political Science, Law, and Philanthropy, seemed to me to need to know. This book may yet be used by such students, but so far it has not. Their neglect of it does not seem to be due to any distrust of me; for articles by me on topics strictly within the fields of economics, political science, and law have been accepted by the *Quarterly Journal of Economics,* the *Harvard Business Review,* the *Public Administration Review,* and the *Columbia Law Review.* The distrust seems to be of psychology.

It seemed to me probable that sociology would profit by studying the differences of communities in the same way that psychology studies the differences of individuals. Therefore I collected nearly 300 items of fact concerning each of 310 cities, studied their variations and intercorrelations, computed for each city three scores for the general goodness of life for good people for each city (G), for the personal qualities of its residents (P), and for their per capita income (I), and studied the causes of the differences among cities in G. The resulting book, *Your City* (1939), has been welcomed by leaders in many cities and used as an aid to community improvement, but has had little influence upon either research or teaching by sociologists. However, I still think that a college course in sociology may profitably include the measurement of individual differences among communities and the causation of these differences as revealed by suitable correlational methods.

It had long seemed to me that both the science and the teaching of language deserved more attention from psychology than they were receiving. I had begun with the humble task of counting the frequencies of occurrence of English words, publishing the facts for a ten-million count in 1921 and an extension of it in 1931. Dr. Irving Lorge and I brought out a greatly extended and improved count in 1944, and a count of meanings (*A Semantic Count of English Words*) in 1938. From 1937 on I published ten articles reporting work on euphony, semantics, and other features of language.

Apart from these three divagations I continued to work on learning, interests, and individual differences and their causes, especially heredity, as previously.

It should perhaps be noted that I have spent much time and thought on educational science proper, as shown in various monographs and articles, most of them factual.

Geraldine M. Joncich (essay date 1962)

SOURCE: "Science: Touchstone for a New Age in Education," in *Psychology and the Science of Education: Selected Writings of Edward L. Thorndike,* edited by Geraldine M. Joncich, Bureau of Publications, Teachers College, Columbia University, 1962, pp. 1-26.

[*In the following essay, Joncich explains the revolutionary influence of Thorndike's scientific method of educational psychology.*]

I

Much has been written, both perceptive and foolish, of the influence of philosophy, politics, and business on education. Far too little, however, has been said of the influence of science. Yet science is probably the most significant fact of contemporary life, the force that best represents twentieth-century civilization. And the scientists who have concerned themselves with education have been among the most vigorous, able, and influential men of modern educational history.

Edward L. Thorndike epitomized the scientific impulse in education.[1] In his forty years as a professor at Columbia University's Teachers College, he played a leading part in shaping the ideas and practices of thousands of teachers and educational psychologists. He wrote more than five hundred articles, books, and monographs which spread his views on education and the results of his psychological experiments to every public and professional library in the nation.[2] His work, and that of his students and colleagues, was discussed in countless professional meetings, in scholarly and scientific gatherings, and in teacher-training classes. Coming to the field of educational psychology in its early, formative days, Thorndike was able to dominate its course to an extent hardly possible to one man today. Moreover, the overriding image Thorndike cast on the scientific movement in education was reinforced by his association with Teachers College. When Thorndike joined its faculty in 1899, that institution was becoming the nation's most influential center for training leaders in all aspects of education—teaching, school administration, psychology,

philosophy. Through its courses, various research institutes, and the writings of its faculty, Teachers College was a potent force. Speaking of Thorndike and Teachers College, its Dean, James Earl Russell, has written:

> In developing the subject of educational psychology and making it a fit study for students in all departments, Professor Thorndike has shaped the character of the College in its youth as no one else has done and as no one will ever again have the opportunity of doing.[3]

There were two corollary principles to which Thorndike subscribed: (1) Psychology no longer needed to be a branch of philosophy; it could become a rigorous science, adopting the appropriate methods of the physical sciences and worthy of the credentials of objectivity and verifiability. (2) Education could and must itself become scientific, aided by all the appropriate knowledge brought to it by the physical, biological, and social sciences—especially by psychology. Probably no other educational scientist, before or since, better embodied in his own work the range of scientific currents of his time.

There are, to be sure, other great names in the history of educational psychology.[4] Among psychologists the theory of evolution has possessed no more enthusiastic exponent than G. Stanley Hall, nor has psychology ever had a more articulate spokesman or a better student of his science than William James. Abroad, Johann Friedrich Herbart urged an education based on a truly scientific psychology early in the nineteenth century. There, too, the imagination of Sir Francis Galton, the experimental precision of Germany's Wilhelm Wundt, and the dedicated persistence of Alfred Binet in France are each unrivaled in the story of the relationship of the schools to the science of the mind.

Yet it was Thorndike who built a philosophy of educational science and a comprehensive system of psychology. Accepting Hall's zeal but rejecting his sentimentalism and anecdotal research methods, Thorndike sought to make Hall's child-study movement scientific. Inspired by James, his own teacher, he rejoiced in the experimental method of psychological research which James reported but refused to pursue. Possessed of the insights of Darwin and of the experimentalists Thorndike was able to move beyond Herbart. He escaped the trap of narrowed interests and restricted imagination which limited the scope of Wundt's own work. Taking Galton's statistical tools, he transformed and swelled Galton's own quixotic study of individual differences and Binet's intelligence test into the vast, systematic enterprise that became the "measurement movement" of twentieth-century social science.

Today we take our scientific developments increasingly for granted. Yet there is far less belief among contemporary scientists and social theorists in the nineteenth century's notion of science as a panacea for all the ills of human society. Evidence has mounted that possessing knowledge, *even when it is scientific knowledge,* does not necessarily make men either good or wise. An older faith and fervor have been blunted, alike by the accomplishments and failures of science.

How different it was in Thorndike's youth! He was born in Williamsburg, Massachusetts, in 1874, just fifteen years after Darwin published *Origin of Species.* This book represents a most portentous event, not only in the history of science, but for its effect upon every line of human activity.[5] Conservatively interpreted, the doctrine of evolution meant that man would inevitably evolve to higher levels, mentally, physically, and culturally. Thus, "to a whole generation in search of scientific assurance about the fate of man, this was a gospel of good cheer."[6] More radically, some took Darwinism as a mandate for deliberate social action. This interpretation meant that progress was not automatic but required the intervention of men. As the physical sciences had begun to reveal and to utilize the laws guiding the operation of the natural world, there arose the belief that the social sciences could know human nature and thereby direct the course of civilization. This view made science an ally of the social and political reform movement called Progressivism.[7] Since the progressives believed education to be a critical instrument in the building of a better world, the educational scientist who labored to discover psychological laws became a partner in the whole reform effort.

Because of Darwin animal psychology became an important avenue to knowledge about human behavior and learning. Thus, Thorndike's doctoral dissertation, a study of animal learning called **"Animal Intelligence,"** has become a benchmark in the development of educational psychology. In studying human mental life, Thorndike placed man squarely in the animal world. "Nowhere more truly than in his mental capacities is man a part of nature. Amongst the minds of animals that of man leads, not as a demigod from another planet, but as a king from the same race," he wrote.[8]

Darwinism represents one main stream flowing through Thorndike's work; another is experimentalism. Older psychology had been based on rational or empirical approaches. To define the principles of mental life one practiced introspection, examining one's own ideas and processes of thought. At best the earlier psychologists observed the behavior of others, trying to deduce objectively some general laws of human mental operations. It was not until 1879 that Wilhelm Wundt founded the world's first psychological laboratory, at the University of Leipzig. Thereafter, a score of American psychologists studied with Wundt, returning to establish psychological laboratories at various American universities and dedicating themselves to experimentalism in a new, scientific psychology. When a group of educators and psychologists interested in education met in Chicago in 1893, as part of the World's Columbian Exhibition, they called their gathering the Congress of Experimental Psychology in Education. This was but one indication of the growing identification of the new psychology with the concerns of schoolmen. By making animal psychology an experimental, laboratory science for the first time and by drawing educational inferences from his results, Thorndike joined the evolutionary and the experimental streams in the new, emerging educational psychology.

Early in his assault upon pedagogical views haunted by tradition and *a priori* principles, Thorndike wrote, "It is the vice or the misfortune of thinkers about education to have chosen the methods of philosophy or of popular thought instead of those of science."[9] What did Thorndike think science had to offer educators that was superior to philosophy, tradition, or opinion? For one thing, he contended that schools could be run more efficiently with the help of science. The efficiency motif was a timely argument around the turn of the century. On every side schoolmen were bombarded by shortages of money, space, and time—all of which raised questions of school efficiency. With respect to teaching methods, for example, Thorndike held that psychology could contribute to efficiency on two counts. First, methods should be made consonant with the child's nature and with the laws of learning, both of which psychology could study. In this way teaching would be facilitated, rather than obstructed, and efficiency would increase. Second, the results of learning—products like arithmetic examples, samples of handwriting, and test scores—could be used to evaluate the efficiency of a particular teaching method.

The identification of science with efficiency was widespread in those days, transcending the schools. With progressive views of politics came the call for "scientific city government." In business and industry it meant "scientific management." Among the military, the gigantic, pioneering efforts that resulted in the Army tests of World War I were an attempt to create an efficient system of classifying recruits.[10]

Science's claim to efficiency was by no means its only appeal to educators. The schools are notoriously subject to fads; and there was hope that science would give education a stability it could hardly otherwise possess, especially in a period of rapid social change. There was another, related task for science. It was widely assumed that the high prestige of science would minimize outside interference, that the indisputability of scientific "laws" would reserve educational control to educators trained in the principles and methods of a scientific pedagogy. This possibility was highly valued by the leaders of the rapidly professionalizing field of education in the early years of this century.

Through the activities of scientifically minded educators and educationally minded scientists like Thorndike, the old notion of teaching as an "art" was challenged by a new and far more rigorous definition of teaching as a "science." The effort to make education a science or, at least, to define the scientific areas which it might embrace, was international in scope. Ernst Meumann in Germany, Cyril Burt in England, Gabriel Compayré in France and, somewhat later, Jean Piaget in Switzerland were only a few of the prominent scientists participating in this enterprise. But the undoubted center of activity and enthusiasm was the United States, and Thorndike was in large part responsible.

Completely committed to the objectivity and precision of the scientific method, Thorndike was ultimately a visionary in his expectations for educational science, as the following statement testifies:

> Experiments measuring the effects of school subjects and methods seem pedantic and inhuman beside the spontaneous tact and insight of the gifted teacher. But his personal work is confined by time and space to reach only a few; their [experimental] results join the free common fund of science which increases the more, the more it is used, and lives forever.[11]

In his earliest speeches and writings Thorndike expressed the conventional view that, once the goals and objectives of education had been set forth, psychology was to determine the best means of insuring their fulfillment. After society had decided that arithmetic and citizenship should be part of the school curriculum, the scientific researcher would investigate, adjust, and appraise the most efficient way of arranging arithmetic skills and of determining how best to form habits of good citizenship. In his first psychology textbook, Thorndike stated that the question of aims was the province of ultimate values, to be judged by ideals and not by facts.[12] However, with his growing involvement in the scientific movement in education, and perhaps also reflecting the close alliance of educational science with the general reform movement which has come to be called progressive education, Thorndike gave science an increasingly greater part in goal-setting as well.

In the keynote article of the new *Journal of Educational Psychology* which he helped to found in 1910, Thorndike defined science's role with respect to aims as being twofold.[13] First, psychology could make already given aims better understood by defining, clarifying, and limiting them, by encouraging the statement of educational objectives as *exact changes in behavior* that education was to bring about. In this way a goal loosely stated as: "The school will teach children to write a legible and pleasing hand" would be restated as: "At the end of Grade 2 the average child will be able to write a sentence equal in quality to step 14 on a given standardized handwriting scale; at the end of Grade 3 he shall. . . ." Second, psychology could influence aims by enlarging and refining them, as in revealing facts of human nature that were previously unknown or which had been considered unimportant. By pushing into the unknown, psychology could help the schools to evolve as an ever more useful and vital social agency. In Thorndike's own work there is an excellent example of how educational psychology can enlarge the scope of education. His researches into the learning potential of adults were important in initiating and extending adult education programs through the public schools and in industry, an especially telling development in an age when Binet-type mental-age scales and the results of the Army tests supported popular opinion in the traditional view that childhood is the time for learning.

The distinction between the realms of fact and value narrowed as Thorndike's career progressed. Perhaps he fell victim to what John Stuart Mill long ago described as the inevitable temptation of the social scientist to become an adviser or even a policy maker. Thorndike came to believe that values were as much a fact of human nature as intelligence and, therefore, the province of the psychologist. Educational products and purposes must *both* be translated into quantitative statements.

Through his scientific studies of the curriculum and by means of the materials prepared for schools—textbooks, tests, and scales of achievement—Thorndike vitally influenced professional thinking about what education *should* do. Indeed, no pedagogical philosophizing can afford to ignore the ways in which the scientific movement helped to determine modern-day conceptions of educational purposes.

II

The scientific movement was a viable phenomenon, characterized by a plentitude of activity and enthusiasm. Its strength derived from the general aura of scientism in American social thought, especially after 1859, and from the reputation and vigor of many of its early advocates. As a figure in the movement, Thorndike exerted leadership on two fronts. His system of psychology became the dominant educational psychology. This was particularly true during the first two decades of the twentieth century, before the development of strong alternative "schools" of psychology, before Freudian and gestalt theories began to influence educational thought. Furthermore, his works inspired other developments in educational science, sometimes only tangentially related to psychology.[14] Most of these can be grouped together as aspects of the "measurement movement," the attempt to express the various dimensions of the educative enterprise in quantitative form.

Because Thorndike derived teaching procedures and the arrangement of subject matter from certain psychological "laws," a brief explication of his theories is in order. Thorndike's system of psychology is usually called Connectionism, or "stimulus-response psychology." Connectionism is Thorndike's version of the much older "Association" psychology, best represented by British theorists in the nineteenth century and the dominant explanation for mental phenomena of its day. Both terms—Connectionism and Associationism—reflect the view that thought or learning is the result of joining things together. This might be the association of ideas or the linking of a particular perception or sensation with some action. In Thorndike's terms learning is the forming of a bond between some response and a given stimulus; hence the term stimulus-response bond or, simply, S-R bond.

The major structure of Thorndike's psychological theory was laid down by the time he wrote his masterpiece, the three-volume *Educational Psychology.*[15] Constructed from certain long-established principles of Western psychology, it also reflected that uniquely American concern with the total behavior of the individual organism which began in the nineteenth century and went by the name of "functionalism." The "functionalist" preoccupied himself with how man functions, with behavior, rather than with the description or analysis of abstract mental states. Thorndike spoke of connections between a stimulus and some motor response (though it need not be an overt action), not about connections between one idea and another. To Thorndike there is a directness in connection-making with a minimum of mediation by ideas.[16]

Mind was described by Thorndike not as an extra-physical existence nor even as a distinct organ of the body. Rather, mind was a general term for "the sum total of connections between the situations which life offers and the responses which the man makes."[17] Out of the doctrine of evolution and his animal studies, Thorndike constructed a theory that defined intelligence as a quantity of specific elements. Probably following the reasoning of Herbert Spencer, he claimed that animals feel things in a gross, total response to a situation. However, man possesses the neurological capacity to select, to turn a complex impression into its many component parts. Being a highly active being, he is capable of experiencing a multitude of different details, abstracting and connecting them in ways which bring about the so-called "higher mental processes" characteristic only of human life. But "thinking" is simply having a number of particular impressions of the elements of a situation. Man's superiority to other animals, said Thorndike, lies in his greater ability to select and then to form connections.

In the same way, individual men differ intellectually from one another. This is the essence of Thorndike's quantitative theory of intelligence. It places man on a continuous line of evolutionary descent and intellectual advancement. It also furnishes a rationale for the intelligence test. Since men differ in intelligence through possessing greater or lesser numbers of connections, it is possible roughly to assess any one man's total by taking a carefully selected sample. Exposing an individual to a standardized test is this sampling process.

Properly speaking, there is no one "general intelligence" in Thorndike's view.[18] Rather, there exists a vast range of specific connections, some innate and unlearned and the rest the product of experience. Thorndike knew that the intelligence tests being constructed measured only a restricted range of types of connections, most particularly the verbal skills. He also registered an early warning against the fatalistic use of tests with children for whom they were inappropriate.[19] In constructing his own tests, Thorndike never claimed to be measuring "intelligence," but, instead, a statistically relevant sample of associations useful in predicting a person's ability to learn further, to form still more connections of the kinds which schools favor. Many educators were far less cautious in interpreting test results, however. By and large the abuses of test scores can be laid more to schoolmen who interpret tests than to the psychologists who construct them.

Throughout his career Thorndike faced the charge that his psychology was mechanistic, that it adequately explained only the most rote, automatic, and habitual kinds of learning. Connectionism was frequently grouped with the conditioned response psychology of the Russian, Ivan Pavlov.[20] Yet there were many ways in which Connectionist learning theory differed from Pavlovian conditioning. For one thing, Thorndike consistently preferred the inclusive term "situation" to the more restricted "stimulus." "The word situation . . . must be taken broadly," he wrote, for "the connection made is not necessarily with one particular circumstance or thing, but with the total state of affairs felt."[21] The child kept after school does not make a connection with the isolated stimulus, sight of confining walls, but rather with the situation, sight of confining walls plus feelings of hunger plus absence of campanions plus sound of companions at a distance, etc. These features of a total situation effect the response. Also, the response is neither simple nor unitary; a reaction is whatever is thought, or felt, or done as a result of the total state of affairs acting upon one. It is only for the purposes of scientific analysis, said Thorndike, that partialing-out or abstracting certain elements from a situation or a response is useful.

Since the school is concerned with learning, the connection or bond is of signal importance. Thorndike described the connection as a "tendency to respond" in a previously established way if the situation should be encountered again; thus it is the product of experience, of learning. He labeled all learned connections "habits," whether they are partially formed or strongly fixed and whether they refer to the tendency to put one's left shoe on first or to a liking for the music of Bartok. For this reason Thorndike called education the process of forming the habits desired by society. To his critics, many of whom defined habit much more narrowly, this made Thorndike the proponent of an education that would produce automatons, individuals whose behavior is narrowed, nonthinking, and drill-induced.

Psychologists participating in education's scientific movement were to provide educators with a knowledge of the laws by which connections are made and broken—the laws of learning. Thorndike postulated two major laws, the laws of Exercise and Effect. Of the two, the Law of Effect is more original with Thorndike, though it had clear antecedents in the work of earlier psychologists, especially in that of Britain's C. Lloyd Morgan.

The Law of Exercise is Thorndike's restatement of the old principle of frequency or repetition to explain the forming of an association. As Thorndike phrased it, when a connection is made between a situation and a response, the strength of the connection is increased as it is used or practiced or exercised. Thus, if a child says "apple" at every sight of that fruit, the tendency to say or think "apple" at its every future appearance will be increased. The latter Connectionism came to regard Exercise as less important, denying that *mere* repetition will tend to fix a connection. The Law of Effect became the central explanation of learning.

"When a modifiable connection between a situation and a response is made and is accompanied or followed by a satisfying state of affairs, that connection's strength is increased; when made and accompanied or followed by an annoying state of affairs, its strength is decreased."[22] This, formally stated, is Thorndike's Law of Effect. For education it means that the child should obtain pleasure or satisfaction or reward from his correct responses. Therefore, his lessons should enlist his interest and establish a desire for successful achievement in school. As an educational maxim this was not new; as a scientist's statement of psychological "law" this was Thorndike's bequest and represents the cornerstone of subsequent psychological interest in motivation in learning.[23] Being scientific, derived through experimental research, the Law of Effect was a decisive force in the arsenal of progressive education. It called forth a new scrutiny of rewards, punishments, and incentives in schools. It complemented the new concern with child nature and the factors of instinct and pupil activity which were being stressed by G. Stanley Hall and John Dewey among others.

While psychological research was carried on to determine the laws of human behavior, educational scientists also made broad-scale applications of measurement and statistics to other aspects of education. The school survey was among the most common and persisting of these efforts. To explain the schools' problems to a much interested public, to gain support for changes in curriculum and school organization, and to marshal reform interests in the schools, professional educators turned increasingly to the use of concrete facts and figures. Scores of school districts hired educational experts to survey the schools and their communities. Armed with the new language of statistics, professors of education and specialists in school administration crisscrossed the nation in the decades after 1910. Leading figures in the surveys, like George D. Strayer of Teachers College and Ellwood P. Cubberley of Stanford University, received their statistical training and their faith in the power of quantification in Thorndike's courses in educational measurement.

Related to the interest in numbers and the survey technique was the accompanying effort to construct a curriculum on scientific grounds. The first organized attempt was made by the Committee on the Economy of Time in Education appointed by the National Education Association in 1911. Then came the less systematized but more widespread practice of the 1920s and 1930s whereby individual school districts conducted curriculum studies, often with the counsel of outside experts. Thorndike's part was strong but indirect. He had been a member of an earlier national committee on tests and standards but he did not collaborate in the work of the Committee on the Economy of Time or in subsequent activities of the curriculum survey movement. Apart from training in the principles of educational measurement and in statistics, the debt of the curriculum-science enthusiasts to Thorndike was one of inspiration. Thorndike's studies of human nature, his researches into the learning process, his psychological analysis of subject matter fields, and his oft-expressed faith in science, generated a belief that a science of curriculum making was clearly possible.

The need for concerted study of the school curriculum came from several sides. For one thing, scholarship and discovery in a number of fields, especially the sciences, raised demands for a modernized curriculum. This was a much-trod plank in the platform of educational reform. The changing character of commercial and industrial life brought pressures to teach the skills required by an ever more specialized society. The upward extension of free, public schooling to include secondary education for all meant that a kind of education originally intended for college-bound youth needed to be altered. Describing this era, one of the active participants in the scientific movement said, "We discovered that the dragnet of compulsory education was bringing into our schools hundreds of children who were unable to keep step with their companions, and because this interfered with the ordinary administration of our school systems we began to ask why these children were backwards."[24] It was decided that part of the "backwardness" could be attributed to "nonessentials" in the curriculum. Thus, the Committee on the Economy of Time prepared its reports which outlined the minimum essentials of various school subjects. The Committee's fundamental assumption was that it is uneconomical to teach a child something he does not need to know, and that economy will result from the selection of only that knowledge which is directly serviceable.

The concern for relating the curriculum to the needs and abilities of a new kind of student cannot be separated from the desire of educational and social reformers that the school be made a more meaningful part of the lives of all children. For some this meant making the life of the society the curriculum of the schools. Equipped with standardized check lists and questionnaires, an army of investigators marched out in the scientific spirit to survey the community's ways of making a living and its habits of daily life. Responses were recorded, correlations were tabulated, and the results were translated into the lists of skills, habits, attitudes, and appreciations which were to be taught in particular school districts. Courses of study thus prepared appeared throughout the nation. Although the major enterprise of systematically surveying community life patterns declined in popularity after the 1930s, locally appointed curriculum committees operating from the same functionalist premises continued this work for at least two more decades. Finally, vocal criticism directed at the "life-adjustment" character of this method of deciding about school subjects led to varying alternative approaches.

Throndike stood at the very center of another phase of the scientific movement, the construction of tests and scales. Masses of achievement and intelligence tests were produced after 1910 and the output has never diminished. Today we are less familiar with the product scales which aroused so much interest in the early days of testing. Yet these measuring instruments, developed especially for handwriting, drawing, and composition, illustrate perfectly Thorndike's philosophy of scientific measurement. Consider his own handwriting scale as an example of the techniques he used. A large number of handwriting samples were arranged in a series of graded steps. Each step represented an improvement in some aspect of the quality of handwriting. The ranking-system—based on the pooled opinion of handwriting experts who had agreed on the arrangement—allowed a pupil's own writing to be compared to and matched with the samples of the scale.[25] This meant the pupil's writing *quality* could be assigned a *quantitative* value; that is, quality could be expressed in quantitative terms. Such scales represented the essence of Thorndike's belief that questions of quality are restatable in terms of quantity. Thus men do not differ by virtue of being heavy or lean, tall or short, wise or foolish, good or bad. These categories imply a qualitative distinction which Thorndike rejected. Rather, men differ in the *amount* of weight, height, intelligence, and virtue they exhibit. Therefore, where statements *in amount* are lacking, it is not because numbers furnish an inadequate language. Instead, said Thorndike, it is because our science is still very young.

III

There is general recognition of Thorndike as a figure in the scientific movement in education. His place in the history of psychology is even better known. However, it is noteworthy that Thorndike is not usually placed among the figures of the school reform movement of this century called progressive education, despite the many ways in which he furthered its goals.[26] It is no less interesting that latter-day critics of education do not list him among the culprits responsible for modern school practices although today's schools bear the clear imprint of educational science. Rather his more noisome detractors have identified themselves with the progressive education movement.[27] Some of the ways in which Thorndike belongs to and stands apart from the course of progressivism in American education are worthy of consideration.

Today, it is hardly possible to read an educational policy statement that does not mention individual differences. Whether the topic be the education of the gifted, the need for a "solid" curriculum, the expansion of higher education, or the improvement of mathematics teaching, there is implicit or explicit commitment to the proposition that the school must take account of individual differences. True, in more than two thousand years of recorded educational history there have been frequent, if sporadic, expressions of concern for individual differences. But it is only with the advent of modern psychology that the *facts* of human variation have been available, contributing to a radically altered conception of the school. Earlier psychology concerned itself with the mind in general, not with specific minds. Not until the work of Francis Galton and James M. Cattell was there sustained interest in individual minds. However, when psychology began to investigate the nature and extent of human variation in intellect and personality it did so with a vengeance and, again, the United States was the center of such study.

According to Thorndike, psychology must extend its restricted study of individual responses in reaction time and its perceptual acuity experiments to controlled investigation of the ways in which individual children and adults differ in native capacity and patterns of learning. Science must transform the sentimental and haphazard concern for the child, shown by the child-study societies, into systematic analyses of the school population. The long-standing American enthusiasm for rugged individualism must be sustained by a precise and accurate knowledge of the nation's human resources. Thorndike enlisted educational science on behalf of both an efficient treatment of the child as an individual and for general educational planning. His work on individual characteristics was climaxed by the third volume of *Educational Psychology* in 1914, the most complete and comprehensive treatise on the subject of its day.

Thorndike proposed several school measures that were compatible with progressive theory. First, he recommended that special provisions be secured for children at either extreme of the range of abilities. Second, he declared that attempts to bring all children "up to grade" were fallacious and impossible of realization; instead Thorndike showed that equal practice opportunities actually increased differences in achievement between children. Third, he gave scientific sanction to the modern pedagogical dictum that the teacher must discover where each child stands and lead him from there, that education must begin with and take its lead from human nature as individually expressed.

Determining the characteristics of human nature and how they are expressed in various children was not the stopping point in Thorndike's view, however. Aided by science, education must *change behavior.* The school was to *use* its knowledge of human nature to mold children in accord with social mandates. Thus did Thorndike differ from the Naturalists who preceded him. While Rousseau contended that education must be compatible with nature, the dictates were from nature and not from society or from reason. Hall, too, believed that the best education interferes least with nature. Thorndike would have no such neutral conceptions of the school. Like Dewey, but unlike some of the later progressives enamored of an image of a "child-centered" school, Thorndike denied that nature is inherently good; rather it is whatever man can make of it. "That the natural is the good is a superstition which psychology cannot tolerate. Still less, however, can psychology tolerate the superstition that there can be any foundation for educational achievement other than the best that human nature itself affords," he said.[28] And, again, "Original nature has achieved what goodness the world knows as a state achieves order, by killing, confining, or reforming some of its elements."[29]

Thorndike did not permit the facts of a gigantic and hitherto unrealized spectrum of human differences to lead him to lower his expectations of the schools. "I avoid nothing because it is difficult," he once said. The existence of a science is predicated on the belief in that regularity of action called "law," which science seeks to discover and explain. Thorndike was convinced that "it is folly to give up the attempt to get rational principles for teaching because the teacher's task varies with the individuals taught."[30]

Beyond describing individual differences, educational science sought to explain their cause. Thorndike early concluded that heredity is the major reason for human variation in intellect and character, that no other factor is more significant than innate and inherited inequalities in the capacity to learn. He denied John Locke's doctrine that at birth each child's mind is a white tablet to be written upon by experience alone. Instead, he argued that every child possesses a legacy of possibilities; and experience realizes these possibilities. Thorndike's formulation was opposed by most of the theorists of the progressive education movement who believed that education is the *source* of intelligence, that the schools could build intelligence in the society by making enriched and functional learnings available to all.[31] Thorndike seemed a determinist, since his theory meant that any individual's nature and future possibilities are predetermined by heredity and that he would modify and limit schooling on the basis of revealed differences. But Thorndike denied the accusation of determinism, holding that once educators clearly know the respective roles of heredity and environment, the responsibilities of the school—its limits and its options—could be set reasonably. We serve education better by understanding it than by praising it, he said in 1914.

Despite the energy and effort which Thorndike exerted to bring about improvements in the schools, his science was not satisfactory to those reformers who claimed that education's powers were well nigh limitless. His explanation of the sources of differences between men was unacceptable to those who believed that education can create a democracy of equals. For his part Thorndike rejected this progressive thesis as a sentimentalism and an obscurantism which permits laxity in school and society alike. In his St. Louis address to the American Association for the Advancement of Science in 1935 he said:

> Ethics, politics, and philanthropy have been guilty of neglecting individual differences, partly because doing so simplifies all problems, and partly because of the retention of theological and sentimental prejudices in favor of the similarity and equality of man.[32]

Although there was basic agreement between Thorndike and the educators of the progressive movement about the need to consider individual differences in school planning, their interpretation of these differences had to vary. They held fundamentally opposed philosophical views of the nature of man and society.

On other fronts, too, this incompatibility intruded. There was substantial initial agreement between Thorndike and the educational progressives about the subject matter of the curriculum; but differences concerning the nature of the mind and the learning process led to an eventual and irreconcilable quarrel. When a psychologist of Thorndike's stature said there is no such thing as general intelligence, he gave support to those wanting a broadened curriculum. He undermined the existing argument that the established sequence of studies was universally suitable when he described the mind as a myriad of specific connections and

not as a muscle which must be exercised on a classical core of subjects.

Thorndike's attack upon the ancient doctrine of formal discipline aroused considerable agitation in educational and psychological circles. Beginning with the Thorndike-Woodworth experiment in 1901, there arose continual discussion of the question: How much of what is learned in one situation is transferred to another?[33] The predominant view had been that certain subjects—particularly the more abstract studies such as mathematics—disciplined the mind, training its various faculties of memory, perception, and reasoning, so that the individual would be equipped in *any* future situation. This dogma of formal discipline said that transfer results from the strengthening of powers or faculties rather than from the usability of some particular content or method of study. Considerable skepticism existed among psychologists of the late nineteenth century, largely as a result of the theories of Herbart and the famous memory experiment of William James. There was also doubt among educators, but at the turn of the century, faculty psychology and formal discipline were still accepted guides to curriculum selection and teaching practice.

Thorndike entered the fray early. "Now surely the sensible way to reason is not to set up an abstract notion of a proper discipline and argue about whether different studies fulfill its qualifications," he wrote in 1899, "but to see empirically what the different studies give to their followers."[34] His first study found that practice in one kind of task, such as learning to estimate the area of a rectangle, did not result in improvement in estimating areas of differing shapes. His own later experiments corroborated these first results, showing little transfer to ease subsequent learning. What transfer did occur was attributed to the presence of common or identical elements in the two situations.[35] Although Thorndike later objected when others said that *no* transfer existed, he maintained that there was less harm in assuming too little transfer than in inferring that significant amounts occur.

The issue of transfer was not settled by Thorndike and the many other researchers who went to work on the question; and it is with us still. But the effect of the doubt cast by the transfer studies was critically important to the curriculum reform government. A review of the 1903 edition of Thorndike's ***Educational Psychology*** described the book as providing a "powerful argument to those who would adapt school programs to the needs of life as directly as possible."[36] The contention that the curriculum should be made up of subjects useful in life already existed, as an alternative to the dominant belief in the mental disciplinary value of certain other subjects. The function of psychology was to give the criterion of usefulness scientific support, and it did so beautifully. If transfer does not occur or if its effects are minimal, then subjects must be chosen for their direct utility in life, the argument ran. Since learning is specific the schools must provide direct experience with the skills and knowledges required by life. Proposals to teach by "problem" or "project" methods received support as well. Thorndike made numerous statements favoring a lifelike, concrete, and directly useful education. Progressive theorists like William Heard Kilpatrick used the language of Connectionist psychology, at least in the early days before rival psychologies emerged which were philosophically more compatible.

Among psychologists, Thorndike's formulation of the Law of Effect is considered one of his signal contributions to learning theory. It is especially paradoxical that educators have virtually ignored this contribution which has coincided so well with their own concern for pupil interests and with making learning satisfying and pleasurable. Rather they chose to attack him on the basis of the Law of Exercise. He was labeled a reactionary in education, a proponent of rote-learning and teaching by drill methods. This charge was made despite the fact that, from the beginning of his career, Thorndike made Exercise and Effect companion laws. Long before he renounced Exercise as a major law of learning in 1929, he stated that mere practice does not strengthen a connection and does not insure learning.

It is not because Thorndike's complete psychology was unavailable that it was misrepresented by many of the most influential educational leaders of his day. The reason may well be laid to Thorndike's consistent criticism of those who were entrapped by a teaching methodology which assumed that learning could be simply achieved, that schools operated on the reform principles of progressive education would make learning easy—indeed, almost automatic! There is no royal road to learning or teaching, Thorndike said. Schools with happy, unrestrained children studying vital problems and lifelike "units," would still require exacting teaching if real learning were to occur. Some of the educators who welcomed Thorndike's research on transfer of training were as guilty of a belief in automatic learning as the older proponents of formal discipline had been. They sometimes assumed that pleasant surroundings, a sympathetic teacher, movable furniture, and a serviceable curriculum would insure the rich learnings in which the founders of progressive education had believed. Thorndike's scientific training did not permit him to share this naïveté. In 1914 he told a group of educators:

> A child's mind is never a witch's pot to be set in action by educational incantations. Its defects are not curable by faith. To discipline it means to improve the specific habits. To develop it means to add bonds productive of desirable responses and to weaken the opposite.[37]

For his unflinching and unabashed use of terms like "habit," "repression," and "systematic practice" Thorndike was criticized. His views on heredity's limitations upon learning ability seemed too harsh to a nation proudly extending universal education upward and to a profession wanting to believe in no inherent limit on the school's power to build a better society. As the successful years of leadership early in the century passed, one by one, into the

1920s and 1930s and 1940s, Thorndike's pedagogy slid more and more from fashion. Yet in these same years the other achievements of the scientific movement were securely established in the schools. Still, it might be remembered that fashions in education, as elsewhere, often follow cyclical patterns. And, hopefully, it might once again be said of Thorndike's work, as he himself once said of science, that its ideals of accuracy and honesty are destined to live on, in honor.

Notes

1. Neither a biography of Thorndike nor comprehensive studies of his work exist. Among the more helpful accounts of his life and career are Robert S. Woodworth, *Biographical Memoir of Edward Lee Thorndike* (Washington, D.C.: National Academy of Sciences, 1950) and Florence L. Goodenough, "Edward Lee Thorndike, 1874-1949," *American Journal of Psychology,* LXIII (April 1950). Three issues of the *Teachers College Record* (Vol. XXVII, February 1926; XLI, May 1940; LI, October 1949) contain honorary essays written by Thorndike's colleagues and former students. A chapter is devoted to Thorndike in Merle Curti, *The Social Ideas of American Educators* (New York: Charles Scribner's Sons, 1935). See also parts of Harold Rugg, *Foundations for American Education* (Yonkers-on-Hudson, New York: World Book Company, 1947).

2. Bibliographies of Thorndike's published writings are printed in the three issues of the *Teachers College Record* mentioned, the earliest of which is an annotated listing.

3. James E. Russell, "Thorndike and Teachers College," *Teachers College Record,* XXVII (February 1926), p. 460.

4. The history of educational psychology is still unwritten. Useful general histories of psychology include Edwin G. Boring, *A History of Experimental Psychology,* 2d ed. (New York: Appleton-Century-Crofts, 1950); Gardner Murphy, *Historical Introduction to Modern Psychology,* rev. ed. (New York: Harcourt Brace and Company, 1949); Edna Heidbreder, *Seven Psychologies* (New York: D. Appleton-Century Company, 1933); J. C. Flugel, *A Hundred Years of Psychology,* 2d ed. (London: Gerald Duckworth and Company, 1953). Different in approach are Henry E. Garrett, *Great Experiments in Psychology* (New York: The Century Company, 1930), and Wayne Dennis, ed., *Readings in the History of Psychology* (New York: Appleton-Century-Crofts, 1948).

5. The impact of Darwinism on fields as different as architecture and religion, economics and anthropology, is ably shown in the collection of essays edited by Stow Persons, *Evolutionary Thought in America* (New York: George Braziller, 1956). See also Richard Hofstadter, *Social Darwinism in American Thought* (Philadelphia: University of Pennsylvania Press, 1944).

6. Henry Steele Commager, *The American Mind* (New Haven: Yale University Press, 1950), p. 86.

7. Lawrence A. Cremin in *The Transformation of the School* (New York: Alfred A. Knopf, 1961) shows this relationship not only in education but on the broad front of the social movement that was Progressivism.

8. "The Evolution of Human Intellect," *Popular Science Monthly,* LX (November 1901), p. 65.

9. *Educational Psychology* (New York: The Science Press, 1903), p. 164.

10. The general success of the Army program and the popular interest it aroused played no small part in furthering the use of tests in the public schools and colleges of the United States. The testing movement is the subject of Joseph Peterson, *Early Conceptions and Tests of Intelligence* (Yonkers-on-Hudson, New York: World Book Company, 1925); Frank N. Freeman, *Mental Tests: Their History, Principles and Applications,* rev. ed. (Boston: Houghton Mifflin Company, 1939); Florence L. Goodenough, *Mental Testing: Its History, Principles, and Applications* (New York: Rinehart and Company, 1949).

11. "Educational Diagnosis," *Science,* XXXVII (January 1913), p. 142.

12. *Educational Psychology* (New York: The Science Press, 1903), p. 163.

13. "The Contributions of Psychology to Education," *The Journal of Educational Psychology,* I (January 1910), pp. 5-6.

14. Various aspects of the scientific movement are treated in *The Scientific Movement in Education,* Thirty-seventh Yearbook of the National Society for the Study of Education, Part II (Bloomington, Illinois: Public School Publishing Company, 1938).

15. Volume I: *The Original Nature of Man*; Volume II: *The Psychology of Learning*; Volume III: *Mental Work and Fatigue and Individual Differences and Their Causes* (New York: Teachers College, Columbia University, 1913, 1914).

16. Although all contemporary psychology was to some extent behavioristic, the more radical theory was the Behaviorism of John B. Watson. He held that ideas do not exist, that mental life is nothing more than behavior. See *Psychology from the Standpoint of a Behaviorist* (Philadelphia: Lippincott and Company, 1919).

17. "The Foundations of Educational Achievement," National Education Association, *Addresses and Proceedings, 1914* (Ann Arbor, Michigan, 1914), p. 199.

18. Charles Spearman, a British psychologist, was the leader of the opposition to both the unitary view of a "general intelligence" and that of Thorndike, which Spearman labeled as "anarchic." Using mental tests and noting certain correlations of abilities, Spearman posited a type of two-factor theory: "g" is a factor which enters into the measurements of abilities of all kinds; "s" (for "specific") factors are wholly uncorrelated with "g," are essentially independent of one another, and are highly complex. See Charles Spearman, *The Abilities of Man, Their Nature and Measurement* (New York: The Macmillan Company, 1927).

19. "The Significance of the Binet-Simon Tests," *Psychological Clinic,* X (October 1916), pp. 121-123.

20. Pavlov's classical experiment featured the dog who was trained, or "conditioned," to salivate at the stimulus of a bell; originally the response of salivation was made only to the sight of meat powder.

21. *The Elements of Psychology* (New York: A. G. Seiler, 1905), p. 205.

22. *The Psychology of Learning, op. cit.,* p. 4.

23. This indebtedness is also mentioned in Ernest R. Hilgard, *Theories of Learning* (New York: Appleton-Century-Crofts, 1948), pp. 21ff.

24. Leonard Ayres, in National Education Association, *Addresses and Proceedings, 1911* (Winona, Minnesota, 1911), p. 245.

25. Thorndike was led to scale arrangements by the work of Fullerton and Cattell at the University of Pennsylvania in 1892. They showed that subjects made many errors in comparing a collection of 200 gray-colored strips, differing only slightly in brightness. But the strips could be arranged in order of brightness with considerable consistency. The average of the results of human arrangement compared very favorably with the results obtained by using an objective physical measurement such as that obtained by the use of a light meter.

26. One history of progressive education which assigns educational "science" a leading role is Cremin, *op cit.*

27. For evaluations from the progressive coterie at Teachers College see Harold O. Rugg and Ann Shumaker, *The Child-Centered School* (Yonkers-on-Hudson, New York: World Book Company, 1928); William H. Kilpatrick, *Remaking the Curriculum* (New York: Newson and Company, 1936); William H. Kilpatrick, ed., *The Educational Frontier* (New York: D. Appleton-Century Company, 1933). See also George S. Counts, *The American Road to Culture* (New York: John Day Company, 1930) and Boyd H. Bode, *How We Learn* (Boston: D. C. Heath and Company, 1940). Two dissertations by former students of Bode may be included: H. Gordon Hullfish, *Some Aspects of Thorndike's Psychology* (Columbus: Ohio State University Press, 1926) and Pedro T. Orata, *The Theory of Identical Elements* (Columbus: Ohio State University Press, 1928).

28. "The Foundations of Educational Achievement," *loc. cit.,* p. 105.

29. *Educational Psychology*, Vol. I: *The Original Nature of Man, op. cit.*, p. 293.

30. *The Principles of Teaching, op. cit.*, p. 84.

31. William C. Bagley, *Determinism and Education* (Baltimore: Warwick and York, 1925); John Childs, *Education and Morals* (New York: Appleton-Century-Crofts, 1950). Thorndike's conservative economic and political views are related to his position on heredity by Curti, *op. cit.*, p. 478.

32. The address was printed as "Science and Values," in *Science*, LXXXIII (January 1936), pp. 1-8.

33. The extent of this interest is recorded in many articles in educational and scientific journals for fully thirty years after 1901. See also Walter B. Kolesnik, *Mental Discipline in Modern Education* (Madison, Wisconsin: University of Wisconsin Press, 1958).

34. "Reading as a Means of Nature Study," *Education*, XIX (February 1899), p. 368.

35. An alternative explanation for transfer was the "generalization" theory of Charles H. Judd of the University of Chicago. Where transfer is absent or minimal, said Judd, it is because the original learning situation—especially the teaching method—did not promote the formation of generalizations which would be transferable to new situations. Among Judd's many writings is *Education as Cultivation of the Higher Mental Processes* (New York: Macmillan Company, 1936). Also see Orata, *op. cit.*

The protagonists of these two theories and their disciples engaged in sharp debate. Many educators accepted both explanations of transfer.

36. H. Austen Aikens, *Science*, XX (November 11, 1904), pp. 644-645.

37. "The Foundations of Educational Achievement," *loc. cit.*, p. 200.

Geraldine Joncich (essay date 1968)

SOURCE: "The Thesis: A Classic in Psychology," in *The Sane Positivist: A Biography of Edward L. Thorndike*, Wesleyan University Press, 1968, pp. 126-48.

[*In the following excerpt from her book* The Sane Positivist: A Biography of Edward L. Thorndike, *Joncich explicates the major points in Thorndike's thesis "Animal Intelligence" and discusses its reception in the academic community.*]

As the year 1898 opens, it finds Thorndike "covering yards of paper with ink." While his experimental work continues until mid-February, writing has already begun on the project conceived and begun at Harvard in 1896. "The title of my thesis," he writes Bess [Elizabeth Moulton] in March, is "Association in Animals." Before submitting the completed report to the Columbia faculty in April, however, he changes this to **"Animal Intelligence,"** subtitled "An Experimental Study of the Associative Processes in Animals."[1] The change is significant, for it represents the originality of Thorndike's conclusions; while his findings re-emphasize association as the mechanism of animal learning, at the same time they are used to deny other prevailing conceptions of animal "intelligence."

Throughout the thesis, learning—i.e. adaptive change in behavior—is explained as the forming and strengthening of associations between situations in which an animal finds itself and impulses to action. Although these associations later come to be called "connections" or "bonds" in Thorndike's "connectionism," his system is distinctly a latter-day association psychology, in the tradition of the British empiricists from the seventeenth century's John Locke through Bishop Berkeley to Alexander Bain.[2] William James taught a version of associationism, although one predictably less mechanical and deterministic than is Thorndike's.

For an associationist like Thomas Hobbes (1588-1679), thinking is solely the excitation of brain matter; desire and habit determine "trains of thought," which represent Hobbes' rudimentary concept of association. As with Locke, the senses are the only means of gaining those elements called ideas which, in turn and by reflection, give rise to ideas of greater complexity and abstractness. Combining several simultaneous experiences—later called "simultaneous association"—defines, in part, what Locke means by reflection. It was David Hume (1711-1776), however, who first promulgated laws describing the association of ideas: universal principles of human behavior which he considered parallels to the physicist's law of gravitation. According to Hume, association takes place in three ways: by similarity (an object perceived leads us to think of what it resembles); by contiguity (things experienced at the same place or time tend to become linked); and by causality (an experience is connected with its consequences), a principle later interpreted to be only a special form of association by contiguity.

In *Observations on Man* (1749) David Hartley goes further, to explain association principles through their supposed physiological correlates. His is a thoroughly mechanistic formulation: sensations cause vibrations in the brain, and when a sensation recurs, its vibration arouses that belonging to some other sensation previously associated with the first; what is experienced is the "idea" of the latter. Hartley also relates the operation of pleasure and pain to these same vibrations: limited vibration causes pleasure, excessive vibration induces pain. Since greater vibration strengthens associations, the implication is that painful experiences are better learned. Here is a nonempirical but physiological attempt to account for the associative process by recourse to pleasure and pain, but only after making them naturalistic or physicalistic concepts. James Mill, whose psychological writings were edited and republished in 1869 by his son, John Stuart Mill, and by Alexander Bain, offered another and equally mechanistic explanation for variations in the strength of associations: the frequency and vividness of the original stimuli or sensations.

This, briefly, comprises the associationist tradition by Darwin's time: a mind more or less passive to the mechanical operation of associative laws; consciousness sometimes stressed, more often minimized; ideas and sense impressions as the elements constituting mental life—the whole is the sum of its parts and no more. Also present in those British associationists identified with materialistic and utilitarian schools of philosophy is a motivational theory based upon a psychological hedonism: the will must choose pleasure-seeking responses.[3] If the psychologists of the classical associationist tradition sometimes disagree and if they are inconsistent by admitting certain nonassociation explanations, they resemble other and subsequent schools of psychological thought in this respect.

"Animal Intelligence" is more than associationism, however; it is association in animals and hence heir to Darwinism as well. Neither a love of animals nor an intrinsic, scientific interest in animal psychology motivated most studies of animal behavior after 1859—the year when Darwin published *Origin of Species* and climaxed decades of suggestion and speculation about the relatedness of all life and of the processes of variation and change in species.[4] *The Descent of Man* (1871) is Darwin's own extension of his conclusions about evolution to humans, wherein mental processes, too, have their prototypes in "lower" forms of life. So, writes Thorndike, "Comparative psychology wants first of all to trace human intellection back through the phylum to its origins." (p. 38).

A year before Thorndike's birth Louis Agassiz died, and with him ended America's scientific opposition to the general theory of evolution. Thereafter the ideological controversy recedes in importance, and the debate is marked by the accumulation of empirical evidence corroborating Darwin's thesis, by the wholesale conversion of the scientific community to evolutionism, and by the popularistic extension of various Darwinist principles and of the evolutionary outlook to fields beyond biology. The once firm belief in the immutability of species was broken by Darwin, as it had not been by the *Systema Natura* of Linnaeus or by Lamarck's *Philosophie Zoologique*. Also shaken were all manner of systems, and conservatives and liberals have been competing since in explaining their own political and economic interests by Darwinist concepts. Everywhere idealist philosophers have been challenged by an unsentimental naturalism, as the principles of the "survival of the fittest" and "struggle for existence" paint nature herself as cruel, wasteful, and indifferent. Man has become another mammal, a product of the natural selection of small, accidental variations in a world apparently bereft of beneficent design. Liberal theologians shun their fundamentalist peers and argue for the separation of theology from religion so that, if acceptance of evolution is destroying the former, it will not imperil the latter. Christianity is not the Bible's account in Genesis, writes Wesleyan's Billy Rice, willing to shuck Genesis in order to preserve Christ.

It is already certain that Darwinism is triumphant, even in the once orthodox colleges, this despite the last gasp of fundamentalist creationism which the Scopes Monkey trial of 1925 will represent. Nicholas Murray Butler rightly observes that "Every conception of the nineteenth century, educational as well as other, has been cross-fertilized by the doctrine of evolution."[5] The physical sciences earlier stimulated a "scientific" outlook in such subjects as history, economics, and philology. Now biology suggests additional concepts for the explanation of human phenomena. Historians, for example, may replace their catastrophic or heroic interpretations with those featuring slow, evolutionary forces and environmental adaptation.

Adaptation is a critical concept in evolutionary schemes: that species survives which best adjusts to an amoral environment, and within any given species superior individuals are those with the best genetic equipment in the competitive struggle to live and to produce viable young. Mental evolution, Thorndike concludes, leads toward the ability to form conceptions and to abstract general ideas; it merely represents, however, psychological power "naturally selected by reason of its utility" (pp. 81f). Over untold ages brain and nerve cells of increased refinement and neurological structures of greater complexity have evolved because humans, prototypes of humans, and possibly the primates who were thus equipped have enjoyed success in the struggle for survival. Anthropological grading of contemporary cultures from primitive to civilized is analogous to conceiving of physical and mental evolution as development along a continuum from the simpler to the more complex. Field studies of strange populations therefore, hold more than exotic interest, since the history of human society now is assumed to be visible. Similarly, child-study appears an avenue to understanding adult behavior. Thorndike suggests that his own research has application along these related lines.

> Very possibly an investigation of the history of primitive man and of the present life of savages in the light of the results of this research might bring out old facts in a new and profitable way. . . . [Another task is] to study the passage of the child-mind from a life of immediately practical associations to the life of free ideas; . . . [and] to find out how far the anthropoid primates advance toward a similar passage, and to ascertain accurately what faint beginnings or preparations for such advance the early mammalian stock may be supposed to have had.
>
> (p. 106)

Such lines of inquiry, however, are prone to the genetic fallacy to which Thorndike is not completely alert.[6] To assume that the simple is primitive, and that the complex and specialized are more "highly" evolved, accords with common sense and is not an easily challenged presumption. Attempts to deduce earlier stages as being simpler is also appealing, since the complex seems more understandable when seen as composed of simpler elements. This, however, confuses the temporal order, in which things have actually happened, with the logical order, in which we reconstruct that development. Yet, recorded history shows growth in the direction of simplicity as well as toward complexity. The view of man as a higher animal is simplistic too, since some lower forms demonstrate more specialized—and presumably more complex—features than does man. Actually, any particular species unevenly develops in characteristics and functions: some quite specialized, others more generalized, some evolved, others "primitive."

On this score Thorndike's **"Animal Intelligence"** does show some sophistication. At one point, partly to explain away imitative behavior in birds, he notes that evolution is not single-line development; birds, for one, represent an evolutionary dead end—"a specialization removed from the general course of mental development, just as the feathers or right aortic arch of birds are particular specializations of no consequence for the physical development of mammals" (p. 47). In his criticisms of such romantic super-Darwinists as G. Stanley Hall, he calls attention to evolution's complexity; at the same time he denies that scientific determinism is a resigned capitulation to natural forces:

> The best way with children may often be in the pompous words of an animal trainer, "to arrange everything in connection with the trick so that the animal will be compelled by the laws of his own nature to perform it."
>
> This does not at all imply that I think, as a present school of scientists seem to, that because a certain thing *has been* in phylogeny [in the evolutionary history of a given species] we ought to repeat it in ontogeny [the development of the individual organism]. Heaven knows that Dame Nature herself in ontogeny abbreviates and skips and distorts the order of the appearance of organs and functions, and for the best of reasons. We ought to make an effort, as she does, to omit the useless and antequated and get to the best and most useful as soon as possible; we ought to change what *is* to what *ought to be,* as far as we can.
>
> (p. 105)

Nature herself then furnishes a lesson of indeterminate growth, and Thorndike is critical both of the popular slogan—"ontogeny recapitulates phylogeny"—and of its use by the naturalist educator to mean that the child's experiences should be arranged to reproduce the "racial" (i.e. cultural) history of mankind.

In extending comparative psychology to cultural history, Thorndike is being frankly speculative. In one place he writes:

> If the method of trial and error, with accidental success, be the method of acquiring associations among the animals, the slow progress of primitive man, the long time between stone age and iron age, for instance, becomes suggestive. Primitive man probably acquired knowledge by just this process, aided possibly by imitation. At any rate, progress was not by seeing through things, but by accidentally hitting upon them. . . .

> I think it will be of the utmost importance to bear in mind the possibility that the present anthropoid primates may be mentally degenerate. Their present aimless activity and incessant, but largely useless curiosity may be the degenerated vestiges of such a well-directed activity and useful curiosity as led homo sapiens to important practical discoveries, such as the use of tools, the art of making fire, etc. It is even a remote possibility that their chattering is a relic of something like language, not a beginning of such. . . . A natural and perhaps sufficient cause of degeneracy would be arboreal habits. The animal that found a means of survival in his muscles might well lose the means before furnished by his brain.
>
> (pp. 105f)

During Thorndike's stay at Harvard, C. Lloyd Morgan lectured on the flight of birds at Harvard's Natural History and Zoölogical Club. The work of this Welshman, the world's most renowned comparative psychologist, was already known to Thorndike, for William James reported on Morgan's studies. And one of the purposes of Morgan's trip to America in 1896 was to meet with the like-minded Baldwin and McGill University's Wesley Mills for a symposium on emergent evolution.[7] A devoted Darwinist, Morgan nevertheless disavows the view of evolution as slow progress by minute changes through natural selection. He favors instead "emergent evolution": changes in mental processes, for example, suddenly erupting from unimportant and premature traits. This conception follows the French naturalist Lamarck (1744-1829) in asserting the inheritance of acquired characteristics, in that individual consciousness could develop traits and cause them to operate until the laws of natural selection could take over and fix them as genetically transmissible characteristics.

Possibly to forestall assumptions that a mental process had emerged in a species before it could definitely be proven, Morgan phrased what became known as "Morgan's Canon." As stated in 1894 this precept was: "In no case may we interpret an action as the outcome of the exercise of a higher psychical faculty, if it can be interpreted as the outcome of the exercise of one which stands lower in the psychological scale." Whether truly a law of parsimony or not, most psychologists consider it such.[8] Thorndike, however, calls Morgan's canon puzzling and of dubious practical value, and he faults him for violating his own principle by accepting imitation in animal learning, although one could explain most of Morgan's illustrations by the simple forms of the association mechanism. His own, he is sure, is an interpretation of animal intelligence more parsimonious and reductionist than anything yet seen anywhere in comparative psychology. What Thorndike and Morgan—whom he does call "the sanest writer on comparative psychology"—both seek is an end to prevailing anthropomorphic interpretations of animal psychology. In this search neither was totally successful. Morgan's own canon presumes that behavior is mentally determined; his "behavior scale" is a psychological scale ranging from less to more sentience, rather than one rooted in totally physiochemical processes in the manner of Jacques Loeb's "tropisms."

Similarly, while Thorndike writes that, "Most of my theorizing will be in the line of denying relatively high functions to animals" (p. 39), someone who presumes differences between the human and animal mind (as do Morgan and, more so, Thorndike) is anthropomorphizing as much as is the observer who presumes similarities (as George Romanes often does); the one is being romantic and the other idealistic.[9]

Before Darwin, naturalists had argued whether animals acted more by instinct or by reason. In so far as animal behavior was instinctive behavior, it was according to a divine plan; in so far as it was deemed rational, it led to anthropomorphic interpretations. Interest in instincts, however, has survived evolutionary repudiations of their divine origin as psychologists construct lists of inborn tendencies, hereditary associations, and instinctive responses. Evolutionists, seeking to bridge the gap between animals and humans, have reported "intelligence" in trick horses and household pets, identifying behavior which seemingly goes beyond instinct. Others besides Romanes are relating men to gorillas by scaling the gorilla up rather than bringing the gentleman down.[10] Because analogy from human experience springs so easily to mind, such terms as "curiosity," "affection," "suggestibility," and "anxiety" abound. Even Morgan concludes that "There can be little doubt that the song of the nightingale gives *pleasure* to the singer, and we may fairly presume that it gives pleasure to his mate."[11] It seems to Thorndike, instead, that man's prideful interest in himself causes him to observe animal behavior selectively, first to note "their wonderful performances which resemble our own" wonderful performances, and then to explain these in human terms. Moreover, he speculates that "The main reason why dogs seem to us so intelligent is . . . because, more than any other domestic animal, they direct their attention to us, to what we do, and so form associations connected with acts of ours" (p. 38).

Belief in a divine law presupposes the purposes of some divine plan; but while divine law was considered discernible to reason, it was not directly and reliably revealed to the senses. Evolutionary theory has meant a twofold change: belief in an orderly cosmos remains, but its laws are naturalized, and observation surpasses reason as a means of knowing in the organic sphere as it already had in the nonorganic realm. Optimism also flowers about this remarkable alteration in perspective. Celebrating the centenary of Darwin's birth, Thorndike will speak thus of it:

> No excuse is left for hoping and fearing instead of thinking—for teasing and bribing instead of working. Our intellects and characters are no more subjects for magic, crude or refined, than [are] the ebb and flow of the tides or the sequence of day and night. Thus, at last, man may become ruler of himself as well as of the rest of nature. For, strange as it may sound, man is free only in a world whose every event he can understand and foresee. Only so can he guide it. We are captains of our own souls only so far as they act in perfect law so that we can understand and foresee every response which we will make to every situation. Only so can we

> control our own selves. It is only because our intellects and morals—the mind and spirit of man—are a part of nature, that we can be in any significant sense responsible for them, proud of their progress, or trustful of their future.[12]

The earliest comparative psychologists were like the first child-study enthusiasts, confusing casually acquired anecdotes with scientific data. Their successors castigate such anecdotal evidence. As the first important comparative psychologist, George John Romanes (1848-1894) has received much of this censure. Of a wealthy Scottish family, Romanes traveled in England's foremost scientific circles, meanwhile devoting himself entirely to his animal studies. He collected systematic observations. He even conducted occasional experiments, teaching Sally, a chimpanzee at the London Zoo, how to count to five. He also put cats in sacks and released them far from home to check on the "homing instinct"; he reared animals in isolation to study their cries. His works are widely read, and his *Mental Evolution in Man: Origin of Human Faculty* is reportedly the most heavily marked volume in the library of the controversial psychopathologist, Sigmund Freud. Apparently, then, Romanes' reputation for unscientific anecdotalism stems primarily from a popularized account, *Animal Intelligence,* which he published in 1882, while his experimental work is underestimated by his critics.[13] It is not at all unlikely that Thorndike appropriated the title of Romanes' best-known work, so as to heighten the contrast between his own achievement and that of his precursors. Thorndike's thesis quotes Romanes at length, using selections which will illustrate "an attitude of investigation which this [my] research will, I hope, render impossible for any scientist in the future" (p. 40). Although Thorndike will conclude in later years that excellent work can be done by men with greatly differing views of what psychology should be, the one constant must be scrupulous observation—and on this score he finds Romanes deficient without equivocation.

A properly scientific attitude of investigation, contrary to popular opinion, is not one of neutrality; certain preconceptions about the natural order do exist beforehand, and these assumptions may change from one age of science to another. For modern science one such presumption is the postulate of consecutive change. Another, and older, conviction is that events are not random or even merely regular, but that they follow fixed laws or mechanisms. Explanatory paradigms and intellectual patternings set the limits of what the observer can accept as standing to reason or, in Copernicus' words, as "sufficiently absolute and pleasing to the mind." Hence, the mere accumulation of additional observations, or the development of more refined instruments of observations and measurement, does not necessarily define scientific advance; what is required is to make sense of data by applying more satisfactory explanatory principles—such as "inertia" in physics, "natural selection" in biology, or "association" in psychology.

Apprehending and organizing observations—the facts of experience—is not a function reserved and unique to the scientist; neither is theoretical knowledge exclusively his.

A whole range of matter-of-fact generalizations from experience (fire produces heat, water runs downhill, a thin edge cuts) belongs to even simple societies, although the explanation for these phenomena may not be matter of fact (as when fire is explained as a spirit). But where ornate, dramatic, and animistic explanatory schemes predominate, there science is small. Where events focus cultural attention on the province of matter-of-fact generalizations, science grows by new, internally consistent, theoretical formulations. It is not surprising, therefore, that impersonal interpretations of phenomena, modern norms, historically occur earlier in matter-of-fact fields closest to technology and commerce and last in such areas as ethics, politics, and economics.

Western science is only slowly accepting the idea of the relativism of truth and knowledge. In American academic circles in the 1890s positivism dominates, for knowledge is still considered "something firm"; everywhere the emphasis remains upon definitive studies, those which will not have to be repeated. Science is likened to a rising building or to an island growing into the sea of the unknown.[14] Facts are considered preeminent, and of almost magical power. The renowned chemist, Ira Remsen, says as much in 1902, at his inauguration as President of the Johns Hopkins University: "People do not know the facts, and therefore they disagree, and discuss, and get into all sorts of turmoil; whereas, if they had time enough and would use . . . scientific method . . . to find out what the facts actually are, half, yes, more than half of the bitter denunciations and discussions that we are all familiar with, would cease."[15] Such sentiments are widely shared among scientists. John M. Coulter, University of Chicago botanist, likens truth to an ear of corn: "The husks of human opinion that have been growing for generations about the facts of society must be stripped off and the facts laid bare."[16] This is positivism, and the attitude is hard to shake. Even at Harvard, Woodworth describes his friend Thorndike as already showing that "sane positivism" characteristic of his matured scientific philosophy.

During these, the waning years of the nineteenth century, scientific method means the natural sciences' combination of observation, experiment, and rational induction. Look and see is Thorndike's advice (p. 30): "If other investigators, if especially all amateurs who are interested in animal intelligence will take other cats and dogs, especially those supposed by owners to be extraordinarily intelligent, and experiment with them in this way" the questions will be answered. Nonetheless, among psychologists there is still intense debate about appropriate methods. Seven decades before Thorndike's birth, Johann Friedrich Herbart outlined a science of psychology which did not include experiment. Experimental work began, instead, with the psychophysicists, Gustav Fechner and Hermann von Helmholtz. In 1876 a chance exposure to Fechner's *Elements* inspired Hermann Ebbinghaus to test experimentally the associationist principle of frequency as a condition of learning and recall, thus extending experimentation to a problem clearly more "mental" than are those elaborately

instrumented investigations of visual perception and reaction time occupying such psychological laboratories as Wundt's.

Although the data of the natural sciences consist of observations, methodological debate makes exaggerated distinctions between observation and experiment. The degree to which the conditions of the observations are selected and manipulated determines how experimental is the observation. The major contribution of Ebbinghaus, for example, lies in his elaborate efforts to control factors, to eliminate potential sources of error, to measure his findings carefully—making his work a model of scientific exactitude in psychology.[17] On the other hand, comparative psychology uses the natural-history approach almost exclusively: field observations of behavior in ordinary, lifelike situations. Of course, the results are sometimes very good, for surely Darwin was a superb field observer.

Before Romanes, experiment in animal psychology received only sporadic attention, with the earlier work of Douglas Spalding (1840-1877) an isolated example—although one known to James, who thinks highly of his work.[18] Thorndike certainly knows of Sir John Lubbock's work on insects, and he uses some of his methods. While Morgan often criticized Romanes, he generally admires his work. Therefore, when he learns of Thorndike's experimental situations, he sees them as erring in the opposite direction: being "artificial" and furnishing an account of animal learning which exaggerates the roles of accident, random behavior, and other "non-intelligent" factors. In his *Animal Behavior* (1900) Morgan notes that Thorndike's animal subjects might be called instead his "victims." Such criticisms are typical of the objections of his generation of psychologists to experimental psychology, although Morgan goes even farther and faults the implications of observation itself. His own purposes, he continues, are both scientific and "psychological": to construct generalizations about mental evolution. "But, for me, the plain tale of behavior, as we observe and describe it, yields only, as I have put it, body-story and not mind-story. Mind-story is always 'imputed' insofar as one can put oneself in the place of another. And this 'imputation,' as I now call it, must always be hazardous." Morgan's solution is to check the plain tale of behavior by introspection: looking inward and examining one's own mental experiences. Introspection, which many of the younger psychologists think is murdered by such work as Thorndike's, lives on in such men as Morgan.

Introspection is like "philosophizing"; it is subjective and mere "saying so," hence untrustworthy. Thorndike's empiricist prejudices are already well developed. In a paper presented to Butler's seminar, **"The Psychology of Descartes"** (based, he writes to Bess, on "three fat volumes of an old seventeenth century philosopher who wrote in Latin and whom no one has been foolish enough to translate"), Thorndike reports that reading Descartes shows him anew how little psychology has shared in the progress of the natural sciences: "His [Descartes] physiological theories have all been sloughed off by science long ago. No one ever quotes him as an authority in morphology or physiology. . . . Yet his theory of the nature of the mind is still upheld by not a few, and the differences between his doctrines of imagination, memory, and of the emotions, and those of many present-day psychology books are comparatively unimportant."[19] In his research Thorndike found only one book about Descartes, that of Anton Koch (1881), that deals with his psychology apart from his philosophy. While Thorndike finds Koch's treatise detailed and useful, it fails on two counts: its critique is essentially philosophical, and it neglects the trends toward experimental and neurological researches, since it was written before 1880. Thorndike concludes that although Descartes himself had the "bad habit of settling new questions by some cut and dried principle previously settled, instead of by an independent investigation," he does uncover examples wherein Descartes "forsook fancies about specific soul faculties whenever he could lay his finger on a definite fact of physical connection." There was too little of this, however, for Descartes lived in a rationalistic, not an empirical age.

In treating the Cartesian handling of the question of the interaction of body and mind, Thorndike specifies his own requirements for resolving all such discussions:

> The real absurdity is to settle beforehand *what mind or matter can cause without empirical study of the phenomena of the connection of mind and body.* No one proves that causation is impossible between heterogeneous orders of being just by *saying so in a loud voice.* And the psychologist who affirms without other reason that because the mind moves the particles of the brain, it must be material, like a pumpkin, has a mind which is enough like a pumpkin to partially justify him.[20]

An exclusive devotion to empirical investigations is what Thorndike has set for himself. "You'd like to see the kittens open thumb latches, and buttons on doors, and pull strings, and beg for food like dogs and other such stunts" Thorndike writes to Bess, "me in the meantime eating apples and smoking cigarettes."[21] In his patient observations of the behavior of his animals, and in the painstaking recording of that behavior, Thorndike demonstrates what, more than anything else, augurs well for success as an experimentalist; it is the absence of this same trait, and a "chronic infirmity of will—the lack of a capacity for laborious routine"—that prevent William James from being a scientist. Where James cares about the particular, the personal, the clinical, the idiosyncratic, Thorndike does not; as a former student of Thorndike's will remark, he "didn't care a hoot" about the particular for, as a scientist looking for universal principles, he wants a general, a statistical finding.[22]

In **"Animal Intelligence,"** Thorndike describes his experimental equipment: assorted boxes, with various escape devices, for the cats and dogs and pens for the chicks. The pens are sometimes hardly more than books stood on end; but diagrams show them to be rudimentary mazes of the kind that will characterize countless investigations by sub-

sequent comparative psychologists. Some are more complex, with steps and inclined planes which the chicks must traverse to find food and society.

Bertrand Russell will, one day, facetiously observe that even the experimental animals of psychologists exhibit the national characteristics of their observers: animals studied by the Germans sit still and think, while American animals are active and energetic. Evolutionists, however, are generally interested in the organism's ability to adapt. Hence in Thorndike's most fundamental single investigation—in research which yields the outlines of a major, new theoretical system—he selects what appears on the face of it to be a merely pragmatic, and rather prosaic, situation: behavioral studies calling for response categories characteristic of the everyday activity of cats and dogs. This bent of evolution-marked social scientists toward adaptive behavior (and institutions) further obfuscates the already complex distinction between pure or basic science on the one hand and applied research on the other.

The old question of instinct versus reason is giving way somewhat to another: the respective roles of instinctive and learned responses. In the process the new psychology is moving away from intellectual to motivational processes. "Never will you get a better psychological subject than a hungry cat," Thorndike will remark (p. 30). Motivation, conscious and unconscious, is critical in this new learning psychology, and Thorndike is showing the way in making this question more explicit and more measurable both.

In his attempt to make sure that animal psychology goes along with the new psychology in its nonrationalistic, mechanistic bent, Thorndike begins with the hypothesis that "intellection," especially association by similarity, is probably absent in animals. He labels intelligence "a factor too vague to be very serviceable"; for it he substitutes "observed differences in vigor, attention, memory, and muscular skill" (p. 30). Emulating natural science—where every event in the universe is assumed to be causally determined—psychology presumes that every mental event is so ordered. Concepts like free will are becoming an abomination; yet, as William James maintains, even when psychologists deny freedom, they half believe and usually act as if it exists.[23] The same situation seems to pertain with other "mentalisms," and for Thorndike too.

In the concept of "impulse" **"Animal Intelligence"** encounters difficulty within a strictly mechanistic psychology. Impulse appears to be more than "response"; at times it assumes mentalistic overtones, and is never satisfactorily defined. Yet in 1898 he calls impulse "the *sine qua non* of the association" (p. 67), a position it will not have in later connectionism. It is only because sense impressions are associated with certain impulses that "a certain situation brings forth a certain act" (p. 73). If it is relatively easy to equate sense impression with "situation," does impulse mean "act," with the association being "a direct bond between the situation and the impulse"? Apparently not, since Thorndike also declares an impulse (or "innervation") "a necessary element in every association formed if that association leads to an act" (p. 71). Are impulses, then, to be considered elements in the association or agents or instrumental forces connecting the situation and some act? He explicitly differentiates impulse from instinct, partly on motivational grounds. Instinct is a reaction to a situation without experience, an unlearned response; an impulse, however, is not the motive to the act and not intended as the learned equivalent of instinct.

Thorndike introduces impulse in this way: "The word impulse is used against the writer's will, but there is no better . . . impulse means the consciousness accompanying a muscular innervation apart from that feeling of the act which comes from seeing oneself move, from feeling one's body in a different position, etc. It is the direct feeling of the doing as distinguished from the idea of the act done. . . . For this reason I say 'impulse and act' instead of simple 'act'" (p. 183f). The concept is not firmly grasped, however, for he writes variously of "impulsive struggles" and "non-successful impulses." At one place he writes that "Whether the impulse to struggle be due to an instinctive reaction to confinement or to an association, it is likely to succeed in letting the cat out of the box"; here impulse is a consequence of a learned or unlearned association. Impulse, then, sounds severally like motive, response, and something more than response.

Mechanism is somewhat circumscribed also when Thorndike calls attention a factor in quicker learning, as when a cat "merely happens to be attending to its paw" when it claws open a door; moreover, successful acts are the kinds which get attended to. Or, "Previous experience makes a difference in the quickness with which the cat forms the associations . . . [for] its tendency to pay attention to what it is doing gets strengthened" (p. 28). But why should attention facilitate association formation when mere success, nonconscious and nonideational, could be counted as sufficient explanation? Mentalism also hovers when Thorndike speaks of a torpid cat: "The absence of a fury of activity let him be more conscious of what he did do" (p. 27). If this implies reflection, however, Thorndike denies such an intention: "We must be careful to remember that when we say that the cat attended to what was said, we do not mean that he thereby established an idea of it" (p. 102).

Long before Thomas Hobbes constructed a psychological system using the pleasure-pain principle, certain philosophers were hedonists. An innovation came with Herbert Spencer, who "naturalized" hedonism by considering pain and pleasure as evolutionary adaptation for their control of learning and apart from any consciously sought end. Instead of justifying pleasure in terms of social ethics—Bentham's "greatest pleasure for the greatest number," for example—the evolutionist's system is a naturalistic ethics: there will be a correlation between those actions which give pleasure and those which promote survival. Rather than motives for action, pleasure and pain become agents

of reinforcement.[24] By 1898 Thorndike is actually closer to Spencer's views than he had been in 1895, when he wrote a paper at Wesleyan entitled **"A Review and Criticism of Spencer's *Data of Ethics.*"** Therein he criticized Spencer's presumption that "Deeds are not right or wrong but useful or harmful, according as they do or do not further happiness thro' furthering complete living, the chronological end of evolution." Spencer's description of the random behavior of an animal who by chance makes moves which result in pleasure clearly contributes to Thorndike's formulation in **"Animal Intelligence,"** although the source is left unacknowledged.[25]

While the term "trial-and-error learning" came from Morgan and Alexander Bain (1818-1903), who referred often to the "grand process of trial and error," the underlying concept is covered by Spencer's random behavior. Thorndike constantly returns to the role of chance to explain even the most seemingly intelligent animal behavior: "If *all* cats, when hungry and in a *small* box, will accidentally push the button that holds the door, an occasional cat in a *large* room may very well do the same. If three cats out of eight will accidentally press down a thumb-piece and push open a small door, three cats out of a thousand may very well open doors or gates in the same way" (p. 44).

On the physiological correlates of pleasure and pain, Thorndike uses the rudimentary theorizing employed in current writings: "The one impulse, out of many accidental ones, which leads to pleasure, becomes strengthened and stamped in thereby. . . . Futile impulses are gradually stamped out. . . . [Successful responses] represent the wearing smooth of a path in the brain, not the decisions of a rational consciousness" (p. 45). The origin of the term "stamping in" is obscure, but it is frequently found in psychological and physiological writings after about 1875. So diffused is the term that a Connecticut physician writes of memory in the *New Englander* magazine in 1880 that it comes with vibrations along nervous circuits that are "stamped in" to leave some sort of "residuum." Nerves which have participated in pleasure-inducing activities are, Spencer speculates, rendered "more permeable," so that when the appropriate situation recurs, that response is made more likely. In speaking of the tendency to perceive again what was previously perceived, James uses an analogy similar to one which Thorndike and many others employ: "The brain reacts by paths which the previous experiences have worn. . . ."[26]

That Thorndike comes to the Schermerhorn attic with intellectual luggage is clear. That he also comes with preconceptions of what empirical tests would reveal is as proper as it is inevitable: it is always man who frames the questions asked of nature, and the questions asked inevitably depend on prior theoretical considerations.[27] In **"Animal Intelligence"** Thorndike writes:

> So far I have given facts which are quite uninfluenced by a possible incompetence or prejudice of the observer. I may add that my observations of all these ani-

mals during the months spent with them failed to find any act that even seemed due to reasoning. . . . I should claim that the psychologist who studies dogs and cats in order to defend this "reason" theory is on the level of a zoologist who should study fishes with a view to supporting the thesis that they possessed clawed digits.

(p. 46)

Yet what Thorndike, like other scientists, looks for is evidence that will shape his ideas still further. Part of what is trimmed away by Thorndike when he scrutinizes the graphs plotting an animal's improvement in escaping from a box is the association of ideas. Classical associationism uses ideas as the units of association. William James accepted this even in his more parsimonious moments, writing that

> Compared with men, it is possible that brutes neither attend to abstract characters, nor have association by similarity. Their thoughts probably pass from one concrete object to its habitual concrete successor far more uniformly than is the case with us. In other words, their associations of ideas are almost exclusively by contiguity.[28]

Thorndike is convinced that he has "positive evidence that no power of inference was present" in his animal subjects. The proof comes primarily from the absence of sudden descents in his time curves, since

> if there were in these animals any power of inference, however rudimentary, however sporadic, however dim, there should have appeared among the multitude some cases where an animal seeing through the situation, knows the proper act, does it, and from then on does it immediately upon being confronted with the [same] situation. There ought, that is, to be a sudden vertical descent in the time curves.

(p. 45)

This means to him that the associative process operates without the intervention of ideas:

> The cat does not look over the situation, much less *think* it over, and then decide what to do. It bursts out at once into the activities which instinct and experience have settled on as suitable reactions to the situation *"confinement when hungry with food outside."* It does not ever in the course of its success realize that such an act brings food and therefore decide to do it and thenceforth do it immediately from *decision* instead of from impulse.

(p. 45)

Even those psychologists who doubt the existence of reasoning powers in animals do accept learning by imitation, since it is a reasonable alternative explanation of what appears to be intelligent behavior. Thorndike also rejects imitation, however, and reminds his readers that even in humans imitation may be "unthinking," as when a man shouts in a mob. Not once in animals does he see what he would call associations acquired by imitation; the burden of proof is passed to adherents of the a priori assertion which he declares imitation to be.

This thesis makes frequent references to previous investigations, as Cattell invariably requires of his students. Thorndike uses these references, however, as an excellent opportunity to dramatize, by contrast, the novelty of his conclusions and the originality of his methods. Not only are other psychologists mauled in **"Animal Intelligence"**; so also is that other class of "experts" in comparative psychology: animal trainers. Completed questionnaires were received from five trainers "of acknowledged reputation" who were asked such questions as: "If Dog B saw Dog A beg for food 10 or 20 times, would Dog B then do it?" and "If you wanted to teach a cat to escape from a box by pressing a thumb latch, would you push down the latch with the cat's paw or leave the cat inside until he'd taught himself?" Their answers usually supported imitation, although Thorndike finds discrepancies between what they professed to believe and what as practical men they claimed actually to do in the training of animals:

> I cannot find that trainers make any practical use of imitation in teaching animal tricks, and on the whole I think these replies leave the matter just where it was before. They are mere opinions—not records of observed facts. It seems arrogant and may seem to some unjustifiable thus to discard testimony, to stick to a theory based on one's own experiments in the face of these opinions.

(p. 64)

Evidence of a remarkable flair for the dramatic, the exotic, the clever, the attention-provoking statement or action appears in Thorndike's student days, and nowhere more clearly than in the thesis. He would be disappointed if **"Animal Intelligence"** failed to be received as highly original and controversial. The tone of the following statement recurs throughout:

> If I had wished to gain applause and avoid adverse criticism, I would have abstained from upholding the radical view of the preceding pages. At times it seems incredible to me that the results of my experiments should embody the truth of the matter that there should be no imitation. The theory based on them seems, even to me, too radical, too novel. It seems highly improbable that I should be right and all the others wrong. But I cannot avoid the responsibility of giving what seems to my judgment the most probable explanation of the results of the experiments; and that is the radical explanation already given.

(p. 64)

In another place (p. 104) he refers to a neurological theory as "mythology." And, on the role of language in distinguishing human from animal psychology, he writes bluntly: "When anyone says that language has been the cause of the change from brute to man, when one talks as if *nothing but it* were needed [to] turn animal consciousness into human, he is speaking as foolishly as one who should say that a proboscis added to a cow would make it an elephant" (p. 83).

Make no mistake: Thorndike deliberately, self-confidently asserts the uniqueness of both his methods and his interpretations, and with precious little genuine modesty. This effect is, if anything, exaggerated by his wry "tail-twisting" and sarcasm. Belying his later reputation for shyness and aversion to polemics, in 1898 he seeks attention as a young David goading the old Goliaths.

On January 24, 1898, the New York Academy of Sciences' section on Psychology and Anthropology provides Thorndike's first outside audience. He does not record the reaction of the members to his paper on **"Experiments in Comparative Psychology."**[29] His own expectations for the larger reaction are, however, recorded. While there may have been some of the posturing of a young man hoping to impress his girl with his brilliance and daring, Thorndike's letters to Bess are more than that. A few weeks after beginning to write the thesis, he jokes:

> On it (floor) and on the book case, thus emptied, are lots of little piles of thesis. On my chair is also thesis. I walk and sit on thesis. I haven't yet reached the stage where the bed has also to serve but expect by next week to sleep on thesis. It is fun to write all the stuff up and smite all the hoary scientists hip and thigh. I shall be jumped on unmercifully when the thing gets printed, if I ever raise the cash to print it. I shall probably take the thing up to Cambridge to get James to read it. If I do you'll have to clear your gang out.[30]

"My thesis is a beauty," he writes on March 12, "or would be if I felt good so that I could put ginger into writing it. I've got some theories which knock the old authorities into a grease spot." These same authorities certainly will taste the "ginger," since Columbia requires that theses be printed. Cattell has accepted Thorndike's article, **"Some Experiments on Animal Intelligence,"** for a June issue of *Science*. Moreover, Cattell again asks him to address the winter meeting of the American Psychological Association, and this time he consents. The report to Bess of his encounter there is brief but revealing: "New York wasn't much fun except that an oak read a long paper soaking my book and me right and left. I said a few modest words in reply which made a good impression and rather enjoyed the free advertising."[31]

Among the fifty-one members in attendance at the APA's most successful gathering yet are several old Wesleyan and Harvard associates: Armstrong and Judd, Delabarre and Dickinson Miller. More are strangers to Thorndike, and some of the older men probably feel about Thorndike as does young Lewis Terman, who compares Thorndike to Charles Spearman, a British psychologist whose "dogmatism and finality" are renowned:

> The impression which Thorndike made on me up to 1905 was somewhat similar, though less extreme. I could understand him better than I could understand Spearman, but my admiration of his independence was tempered a little by the cocksureness with which he tore into "established" psychological doctrine. For a youth still in his twenties, he seemed to me shockingly lacking in a decent respect for the opinions of mankind![32]

Following that meeting, McGill University's expert in animal psychology, Wesley Mills, publishes his critique of Thorndike and is answered in kind. "The oak who jumped on my thesis Christmas has published his article," Thorndike writes, "and I shall now jump on him. It is earnestly to be hoped that the advertisements thus afforded may make enough money for me for two or three drives this June."[33] Whether profitable in this way or not, the exchange is fascinating. Mills resents Thorndike's dismissal of all other comparative psychologists, and in words reminiscent of Terman's: "Dr. Thorndike has not been hampered in his researches by any of that respect for workers of the past of any complexion which usually causes men to pause before differing radically from them, not to say gleefully consigning them to the psychological flames." He disputes Thorndike's enthroning of observation, although he also complains that "We could have [from Thorndike] less rhetoric and more detail of observations." Well taken is his statement that "I venture to think that in all cases it is a question of whose eyes, or, in other words, the training those eyes have had, and still more of the intellect that passes judgment on what is seen."

The Thorndike rebuttal opens with a sarcastic apology for the unavoidable "personal tone" of his discussion, but "as Professor Mills had mentioned Dr. Thorndike twenty-nine times in his article, this reply will of necessity contain the word 'I' oftener than one would wish." His response to Mills' charge of "conceit" is blunt and characteristic:

> For psychological interpretations of the sort given by Romanes and Lindsay I certainly had and have no respect, though, of course, I esteem them for their zeal. But I cannot see that the presence or absence of megalomania in me is of any interest to comparative psychology. The monograph in question was not a presentation of personal opinion, but of certain facts, the accuracy of which, and of certain impersonal inductions and deductions, the logic of which, should be treated impersonally. The question is whether certain facts exist and what they mean and does not concern the individual psychology of any person.

The rest is given over to methodological quarrels, with a bow to Mills whose eminence made the reply necessary.

The reaction of the Columbia faculty is quick and positive. "My thesis is held in reverence at Columbia, I find," Thorndike notifies Bess.[34] Considering Cattell's great influence in the scientific world, it is a clear benefit to have his active support. Yet **"Animal Intelligence"** is, by itself, an undeniably important event: it is a substantive and methodological contribution of great moment. The Mills-Thorndike debate concerns fundamental research questions as well as personalities. Subsequent animal work—like that of Robert M. Yerkes, John B. Watson, and B. F. Skinner—will have in **"Animal Intelligence"** a touchstone immeasurably more significant than that which Thorndike had in Romanes, or even in Morgan. Very quickly this work earns for itself the description which Edinburgh University will bestow, formally, many years later: "a doctorate thesis entitled **'Animal Intelligence,'** which immediately took rank as a classic, and marks the real starting point of experimental animal psychology."[35]

Notes

1. Printed in *The Psychological Review, Monograph Supplements,* 2 (June, 1898), 109 pp. Also as *Columbia Contributions to Education,* vol. 4. Revised and expanded in 1911 (New York: Macmillan, 1911).

   Page numbers in parentheses refer to the first edition of *Animal Intelligence.*

2. On connectionism as an association system, see Ernest R. Hilgard, *Theories of Learning,* especially chapters 1, 2. Cf. Howard C. Warren, *A History of Association Psychology* (New York: Charles Scribner's Sons, 1921) and William James, *Psychology, The Briefer Course* (New York: Henry Holt, 1892), Chapter 7.

3. Robert C. Bolles, "Hedonism and the Law of Effect," unpublished MS, 1962. A much abridged and condensed version appears in Bolles' *Theory of Motivation* (New York: Harper & Row, 1967).

4. The intensity of the controversy following publication of *The Origin of Species* and the rapid conversion to Darwinism lend support to the interpretation that "An earlier generation had been storing the powder to be exploded in the battles of the '60's." W. Riley, *American Thought,* pp. 172ff. Cf. G. Himmelfarb, *Darwin,* esp. p. 423, and B. J. Lowenberg, *The Impact of the Doctrine of Evolution,* passim.

5. "Status of Education at the Close of the Century," National Education Association, *Addresses and Proceedings* (Chicago, 1900), p. 193.

6. M. R. Cohen and E. Nagel, *An Introduction to Logic and Scientific Method,* pp. 388ff.

7. *Science,* 3 (1896): 355, 409. Conwy Lloyd Morgan (1852-1936), mining engineer and metallurgist before reading Darwin, devoted the years after 1882 to questions of mental evolution. From 1884 to 1920 he was Professor of Geology and Zoology and Principal of University College, Bristol. Perhaps his most influential book was *An Introduction to Comparative Psychology* (London: Walter Scott, 1894, 1906).

8. One who does not is Philip H. Gray, "Morgan's Canon: A Myth in the History of Comparative Psychology," *Proceedings of the Montana Academy of Sciences,* 23 (1963): 219-224.

9. Gray, p. 222.

10. Hearnshaw, p. 95.

11. Quoted in Gray, p. 222.

12. "Darwin's Contributions to Psychology," *University of California Chronicle,* 12 (1909): 78.

13. The most sympathetic brief account of his work is probably that of Hearnshaw, pp. 92-95. On Freud's library, see D. Shakow and D. Rapaport, *The Influence of Freud,* p. 43.

14. Veysey, p. 597.

15. *Celebration of the 25th Anniversary of the Founding of the University and the Inauguration of Ira Remsen, LL.D., as President of the University* (Baltimore: Johns Hopkins Press, 1902), p. 122.

16. Quoted in Veysey, p. 601.

17. R. I. Watson, pp. 264-268.

18. Douglas Spalding, "Instinct with Original Observations on Young Animals," *Macmillan's Magazine,* 27 (February, 1873): 282-293. This is a study of instincts in chicks. See also J. B. S. Haldane, "Introducing Douglas Spalding," *British Journal of Animal Behavior,* 2 (January, 1954): p. 1; William James, *Psychology, The Briefer Course,* pp. 400ff.

19. "The Psychology of Descartes," The Columbia University Seminar in Philosophy, 1897-1898, p. 1, handwritten manuscript. Thorndike MSS. Thorndike undoubtedly was assisted in this paper by A. C. Armstrong's translation from the German of Richard Falckenberg's *History of Modern Philosophy* (New York: Holt, 1893).

20. Ibid., p. 66. (Italics in the original.)

21. Thorndike to EM, October 25, 1897.

22. Perry, I, p. 129; Augusta Bronner, in J. C. Burnham, *Oral History Interviews.*

23. Gordon W. Allport, Introduction to the Torchbook edition of William James' *Psychology, The Briefer Course* (New York: Harper & Row, 1961), pp. xiii, xx. (Originally published by Henry Holt, 1892.)

24. William James tends to view pain and pleasure not as original motives, but as "accompaniments" to action which modify and regulate that action; thoughts of pain and pleasure later "acquire themselves impulsive and inhibitory powers." *Psychology, The Briefer Course* (1961 edition), p. 311.

25. Thorndike's failure to acknowledge Spencer may reflect his age's extreme and irrational tendency to reduce Spencer's once admittedly over-inflated reputation. Cf. R. I. Watson, p. 296. Bolles (see footnote 3) "excuses" Thorndike, partly on the grounds that "he never gave credit to anybody."

26. Gray finds Spalding using the term "stamping in" in an article in 1873 and traces the German equivalent (*einzupragën*) through O. Heinroth and K. Z. Lorenz, who made it "imprinting." In Philip Howard Gray, "The Descriptive Study of Imprinting in Birds from 1873 to 1953," *Journal of General Psychology,* 68 (April, 1963): 333-346; for James' analogy to paths see his *The Briefer Course,* p. 196.

27. "We are here concerned not with prejudiced belief, but rather with preformed concepts." S. Toulmin, *Foresight and Understanding,* p. 101.

28. James, *The Briefer Course* (1961), p. 234. In 1913 Thorndike writes that the lower animals do occasionally show signs of ideas and of their influence upon behavior. *The Psychology of Learning*, p. 11.

29. "Records of Meetings," New York Academy of Sciences, *Annals*, 11 (January 18, 1899): 450; Thorndike to EM, January 23, 1898.

30. Thorndike to EM, February 26, 1898.

31. Thorndike to EM, January 6, 1899. Cf. "Proceedings of the Seventh Annual Meeting of the American Psychological Association," *American Psychological Review*, 6 (March, 1899): 146-179. At this meeting Thorndike was elected to membership and John Dewey to its presidency.

32. Terman, autobiography in Murchison, II, p. 319. Terman was still in school in 1898, graduating from Clark in 1903. He subsequently earned his greatest fame as the author of the Stanford Revision of the Binet intelligence scale and for the several-volume longitudinal study, *The Genetics of Genius*.

33. Thorndike to EM, May 8, 1899. For the debate, see Wesley Mills, "The Nature of Animal Intelligence and the Methods of Investigating It," *Psychological Review*, 5 (May, 1899): 262-274 and E. L. Thorndike, "A Reply to 'The Nature of . . . ,'" *Psychological Review*, 6 (July, 1899): 412-420.

34. Thorndike to EM, October 30, 1898.

35. Quoted in "Edinburgh Honors Professor Thorndike," *Columbia University Quarterly*, 28 (September, 1936): 227.

Geraldine Joncich Clifford (essay date 1968)

SOURCE: "E. L. Thorndike: The Psychologist as Professional Man of Science," in *Historical Conceptions of Psychology*, edited by Mary Henle, Julian Jaynes, and John J. Sullivan, eds., Springer Publishing Company, Inc., 1973, pp. 230-45.

[*In the following essay, which appeared in an unabridged form in* American Psychologist *in 1968, and was published in 1973 in* Historical Conceptions of Psychology, *Clifford discusses the ways in which Thorndike propelled the notion of psychologists and educators as scientists.*]

During the celebration of Thorndike's twenty-fifth year at Teachers College, Columbia psychologist James McKeen Cattell (1926) quoted William James to the effect that E. L. Thorndike, more than anyone else he knew, had that objectivity essential to scientific work. And the introduction that James wrote for Thorndike's *The Elements of Psychology* (1905) seemed to Cornell psychologist E. B. Titchener (1905) to be so extreme in its "unstinted praise" that he even questioned its tastefulness in his review of the book written for the prestigious British journal, *Mind*—a review so sarcastic that Cattell protested to the editors of *Mind*.[1]

Whether or not James' assessment is overly generous and uncritical in Thorndike's case, remains an open question. What appears a clear and indisputable fact is that James was expressing a judgment of Thorndike—one focusing upon his taste and temperament for scientific work—that precisely matched Thorndike's own self-image. Over his entire career Thorndike tried to guide his behavior by the "scientist" model, because this is what he wanted most to be, this is what he was convinced he could be, and this is what he thought he was.

As a professional man, Thorndike can be said to have occupied two other chairs: one is, of course, the psychologist's; he was also the educationist, concerned with professionalizing teaching and school management. Nevertheless, his position as professional scientist was the more important to him. It overrode both others because it incorporated both, while connecting him with a whole system of scientific expertise and its high prestige. There are innumerable indications of Thorndike's preference, but only one will be mentioned here. Note the character of Thorndike's response to Titchener's attack upon *The Elements of Psychology*. To Titchener's warning that his book would receive harsh words, Thorndike replied in July 1905:[2]

> I do, of course, regret if I have fallen in your estimation with respect to accuracy of scholarship. However I cherish hopes of rising again if you will read my *Measurements of Twins* (to be out soon) which is 75 pages of solid accuracy and of which there were 40 pages more accurate still but too expensive to print. I confess to two points of view—practical expediency in books for beginners and the limit of exactitude in contributions to my equals and superiors.

When the review finally appeared in the October 1905 issue of *Mind*, Thorndike wrote to Titchener his objections to the assault upon his scientific reputation.

Titchener's reply failed to assuage Thorndike's hurt and he wrote a final time, closing with a pious withdrawal to the scientific ethic of impersonality:

> I would rather make a million errors in names, dates, references and the like than make such insinuations as you made unless I knew absolutely that the impression they would leave was in exact accord with the fact. Nor would I make them unless there was some clear benefit to the science.
>
> However in my view of life it is all a small matter. The best thing about scientific work is that it may be impersonal. I do the best I can and if you think I misuse my time and effort so much the worse for me if you are right, and for you, if you are wrong. . . .
>
> Yours truly, Edward L. Thorndike

Obviously, science is not an impersonal activity; what Thorndike was expressing was an ethic and ideology enjoying wide acceptance among his professional associates. It is inconceivable, then, that a Thorndike would ever echo Freud's self-description (Jones, 1961): "I am not really a man of science, not an observer, not an experimenter, and not a thinker. I am nothing but by temperament a conquistador—an adventurer" (p. xi).

In an autobiographical sketch (Murchison, 1930), Thorndike attempted to adumbrate the more potent environmental forces operating upon him. He listed "home life with parents of superior intelligence and idealism," college and university study, colleagues eminent in psychology and other fields, and "the great body of published work in science. The last is of course the most important." "Though an investigator rather than a scholar, I have probably spent well over 20,000 hours in reading and studying scientific books and journals" (Jonçich, 1962, p. 33). As a scientist, however, the psychologist must first publish and only secondarily read, and Thorndike's own bibliography numbers over 500 items.

To recapitulate, there is in Thorndike that certainty that he (like any trained investigator of human behavior) has as his major professional identification that of scientist *sui generis,* and that his primary reference group is the whole community of science. The explanation of this certainty inheres, it seems, in the greater (and, by today's standards, remarkable) cohesiveness of the scientific community in the late nineteenth century—when Thorndike left Wesleyan University a graduate in the classics and opted for science by selecting psychology at Harvard and Columbia.[3] To sketch out an account that will explain this communality of science—using Thorndike for illustration—is the aim of the rest of this article. The responsible factors, in ascending order of importance, are (1) personalistic and sociological characteristics held in common by Thorndike's generation of scientists; (2) the recency and incompleteness of American science's attempts to professionalize itself; (3) the dominance of positivism; and (4) the messianic zeal of the "sciences of human nature," and especially of psychology.

PERSONAL AND BACKGROUND CHARACTERISTICS

In 1927, E. K. Strong asked Thorndike to take his Strong Vocational Interest Blank. His profile of scores showed a marked interest in the quantitative, a manipulative interest in ideas, a rather small interest in people, and a very low concern with objects. He shared most of the characteristics which Strong and later testers found associated with careers in mathematics and accounting, science and engineering. Had personality inventories been more widely applied to his generation, it seems more than likely that such a temperamental characteristic as Thorndike's preference for solitary work would have been found to have marked the whole scientific community then, as it does today. Lacking the evidence, however, we turn to factors of background—to find that psychologists typically shared common origins and a body of common experiences with the generality of other scientists.

Thorndike's may be called the "transitional generation" of men of science; they were the accommodation group, forced to adjust to an America in flux and tending to make similar decisions along similar career lines. They contrast significantly with scientists born before 1865 or so, men whose backgrounds and range of choices better describe them as the "security generation."

American science before the Civil War was peopled with amateurs and generalists, typically of the patrician class and overwhelmingly from New England. Even the young men joining Henry Rowland in creating the physics department at the new, innovative Johns Hopkins University were raised in comfort—the sons of well-to-do businessmen, prosperous farmers and lawyers, ministers of the older respectable Protestant denominations. They represented clerical and commercial New England, Yankee stock, a society that was passing away. They attended tiny, sectarian, static (even decadent) colleges, where it was an oddity if any of the professors wrote books; in a few cases they supplemented this with study in Germany or France. The technological boom following the Civil War carried virtually no concomitant emphasis on the basic sciences. In 1850, Harvard, the nation's best and strongest educational institution, had no laboratories for teachers or students in chemistry, not a single piece of apparatus, not even any lectures in the subject since Harvard's sole chemistry instructor had been hanged for murder the previous year (Beardsley, 1964). Columbia in the 1870s gave a little laboratory experience only in chemistry and then only to engineering students. When Michael Pupin left Columbia for graduate study in Europe's great centers of physics, he did so without any laboratory training behind him.

To contrast this earlier generation with the one coming immediately after Thorndike's is to suggest the magnitude of the challenge, and the exhilarating sense of opportunity, faced by his generation of transition. Later scientists may be termed the "generation of ambition," representing a markedly upward-mobile social group and magnetized by engineering. Thus, physicists embarking on careers in 1910 and after came less often from the homes of lawyers and ministers than from those of small businessmen and farmers, schoolteachers and white-collar workers; the rise in technical enrollments in public institutions and in the aggrandizing private universities evidences the fact that the middle class, the traditionally opportunity-minded class, was now using the nation's colleges.[4] As part of the shift to middle western origins, these scientists typically were public school, not private academy, products, whose collegiate educations—in state universities, technical schools, the weaker colleges—were succeeded, nearly invariably, by doctoral study in an American university. No longer was expensive foreign study necessary, since domestic programs multiplied with specialization, diversity, and the elective system, while the force of institutional imitation pushed even reluctant college administrations closer to the mainstream of a now securely technocratic society.

In 1884, Reverend Thorndike moved his family, including 10-year-old Edward, to Lowell, Massachusetts. For a community of 60,000 people, there were 30 churches, but it was the factory chimney, not the steeple, that dominated the Lowell skyline. Most scientists of Thorndike's generation still came from northeastern America, but their boyhoods were spent in similar mill-town surroundings, for when Thorndike entered college New England alone led every country in the world in the per capita value of its manufactures. Like his fellows in science, Thorndike was of Yankee stock, but the decline of the "old-English" strain was obvious, for the cities and mill towns attracted huge numbers of immigrants. In 1800, Everett's population was 90 percent of English ancestry; by Thorndike's time 25 percent were immigrants and another 25 percent were the children of immigrants.

Such population diversity, plus the secularizing influence of an urbanizing, industrializing economy, meant a less fundamentalistic, less secure Protestantism. This consequence was directly pertinent to our population of scientists, for the striking fact is that a clergyman's household, combined with a New England setting, was the best predictor of a future career in science. Indeed, among Americans born around 1870, as was Thorndike, the proportion which became notable and who were sons of clergymen was twice as large as the combined total coming from all the other professions.

Thorndike's was a day when organized religion was nonetheless steadily losing stature in the nation's social and intellectual life, when theology (like medicine) was becoming a specialized study and not a part of general education, when science was usurping its place in academic disputations and attracting college graduates away from ministerial careers. This was not, however, a day of atheism; most academic scientists of Thorndike's generation—while rejecting their fathers' careers and liberalizing their own confessional associations—were apparently quite sincere in professing Christianity *and* the new biology, geology, physics, psychology. Thorndike was atypical here because his conversion to science was preceded by his adopting an exclusively naturalistic view of man; he once called agnostics, like himself, "conscientious objectors to immortality." Yet, like certain other wayward sons of the clergy, he (guiltily perhaps) infused his work with messianic fervor, so that science itself took on a crusade-like character. Moreover, in contending that agnostic scientists usually rate very highly for their private and public virtues, Thorndike was expressing the common tendency of nineteenth-century science to moralize about its advancement. Indeed, there has been a pronounced tendency in America to moralize all activities, all knowledge! "The proper study of nature begets devout affection [and] a true naturalist cannot be a bad man," one reads in *Knickerbocker* magazine in 1845. Similarly, General Francis A. Walker, President of M.I.T., told a gathering in 1893 that the scientific men of America were surpassed, if indeed approached, by no other group in their "sincerity, simplicity, fidelity and generosity of character, in nobility of aims and earnestness of effort" (p. 20).

In Thorndike's youth, interest in science was so intense that *Popular Science Monthly* was an outstanding success in the magazine field, and the sale of Herbert Spencer's books in the United States exceeded 300,000 copies. Yet, while the *Atlantic Monthly* was telling its readers, in 1898, that "America has become a nation of science," Thorndike's generation of future scientists attended schools and colleges grossly deficient in science education. Had it not been for a handful of ambitious graduate schools, the doing of American science—as opposed to its dissemination—would have been delayed even more. Although historians of science disagree as to how poor American science actually was before 1900, scientists contemporary with Thorndike have described the available training as seriously retarded (Jonçich, 1966). Only at the university level were matters much improved. While Charles Judd was convinced enough of the still-present advantage of a German doctorate to borrow the fare from his hometown minister, students who chose Hopkins, Clark, Cornell, Chicago, or (like Thorndike) Harvard and Columbia were exposing themselves to Americanized versions of a German university—and with every expectation of adequate preparation.

Students in the physical and social sciences now accounted for a full half of American graduate enrollments. At Teachers College, Thorndike succeeded in teasing and prying—from an administration reluctant to support such "academical" pursuits—a succession of teaching and research assistants, research courses, and, finally, even a research institute in which he secluded himself for twenty years. He was securely within that first generation of academic science in the modern era.

THE PROFESSIONALIZATION OF SCIENCE

A common characteristic of turn-of-the-century science in America was its heavy academic involvement. Government science was small, and industrial laboratories were still in the future. Full-time research was more rare in the United States than in Europe; Germany, in 1913, had six times as many research men in proportion to population as did the United States. In 1910, Cattell calculated that barely 1,000 Americans were occupied with serious research, and then, on the average, for only half-time.

Academe was, moreover, a setting where generalists and generalism had long reigned, where the standard of the broadly learned scholar hung on into the modern age of specialism. Since the typical college remained small—about 150 students—the philosopher-generalist had an employment advantage over the psychologist-specialist. For example, he would teach more subjects and rarely hounded the president for research time, laboratory space, costly equipment. Small wonder that, in 1898, Thorndike contemplated medical studies, or even a second doctorate in psychology. For months his only offer of employment was from the Oshkosh (Wisconsin) State Normal School, and Teachers College would not even accept his offer to teach there at half pay!

With academic specialization still only emergent, conglomerate and ill-defined departments abounded—prolonging, however, the opportunity for intellectual communion among the disciplines. Thorndike took his own doctorate in Columbia's Department of Philosophy, Psychology, Anthropology, and Education. And it was via anthropology, for example, that psychologists first entered membership in the National Academy of Sciences.

Before scientists cut themselves off from one another by specialization, priority went to cutting themselves off from the public; that is, the first order of business was banding together to effect the tardy professionalization of science writ large. To become professionalized meant the erection of various barriers against amateurs, the untrained, the unorthodox, the exotic, the "merely interested."

One such structure was the degree barrier. University expansion—greatly facilitated by the benefactions of businessmen and by institutional competition—permitted formal graduate training in the sciences to become widespread enough to assist in the exclusion process. In fact, by the time the American Psychological Association celebrated its twenty-fifth anniversary, psychology had exceeded all the other sciences in the proportion of its members holding doctorates—84 percent (Cattell, 1917).

When a body of knowledge becomes esoteric, that is, unavailable to the general scholar, its possessors are isolated by a second barrier: the barrier of unintelligibility (Daniels, 1965). Before the Civil War, science principally meant astronomy, agronomy, and medicine, and was part of the general stock of knowledge; by 1860, however, chemistry, geology, and the natural history fields had advanced enough to wrest away the designation of "science," while proceeding into esoterica too rapidly to be captured by nonprofessionals. For a while popularizers pretended to bridge the widening chasm between the common man and the now uncommon knowledge, but by 1915 the once prosperous *Popular Science Monthly* was dropped by its publisher of forty-two years, in significant contrast to Cattell's other journal, *Science,* successful because its content was almost wholly professional.

Although the charter members of the American Psychological Association, founded in 1892, contained a goodly number of philosophers, the situation soon changed, and psychology's future as a science, empirical and experimental, was loudly trumpeted within this professional association. For this, James McKeen Cattell—Thorndike's mentor and colleague at Columbia—was in large measure responsible; no one else as vigorously boosted psychology, meanwhile reiterating its connections with the whole of science. Cattell was proud to have been the world's first (1888) to be titled "professor of psychology." His laboratory at the University of Pennsylvania was reportedly the first to conduct research while teaching experimental methods systematically to undergraduates. Between 1891 and 1917 Cattell built the nation's largest Ph.D. program at Columbia, himself supervising some 50 dissertations. He was the first psychologist elected to the National Academy of Sciences, in 1901, preceding even William James. Cattell was of that small group which established the Ameri-

can Psychological Association; he was its President in 1895, and edited *Psychological Review.* He induced the New York Academy of Sciences to establish a section for anthropology and psychology—where Thorndike first reported his findings from **"Animal Intelligence"** and several other critical researches, including the famous 1901 studies of transfer of training.

In 1900, Thorndike was assisting Cattell in the editorship of *Popular Science Monthly* and *Science* when he met biologist Jacques Loeb at the Marine Biological Laboratory at Woods Hole. As Thorndike recorded it, "Loeb . . . told me I was a damned fool, that I was spoiling myself and ought to be shut up and kept at research work." He decided that Loeb was "largely right," and dropped this sideline; nevertheless, even this brief editorial experience only reinforced Thorndike's sense of familiarity with, and participation in, the totality of American science.

Thorndike was much less the committee man, the organizational figure, than was Cattell; despite this, he also became conspicuous in scientific circles. He was the first of the younger experimental psychologists to be elected (1917) to the National Academy of Sciences and attended its sessions fairly often. Like the Academy's membership, the leadership of AAAS has been dominated by chemistry, physics, astronomy, and geology; half of its presidents to date have come from these fields. Still, in 1934 Thorndike was chosen President of AAAS; except for economist W. C. Mitchell in 1938, no other social scientist headed this professional organization for the whole body of scientists since Thorndike's tenure, until Don Price became President in 1966.

POSITIVISM—A COMMON MENTAL SET

In common with every working scientist, Thorndike constructed his experimental situations according to his own theoretical postulates; when possessed of even a rudimentary theory, he tried to test the predictions emanating from that theory. It is such choices of experimental situation that decrease the probability that one theorist will directly test the major premises of another's theory.[5] The collecting and interpreting enterprise itself, however, must conform to certain expectations held in common with other scientists, for science is in part an attitude of mind shared by all its practitioners—even when they are ill-put or loath to articulate it.

Speaking of their college days together, Thorndike's longtime friend and associate, Robert S. Woodworth (Murchison, 1932), said of him, "His sane positivism was a very salutary influence for a somewhat speculative individual like myself . . ." (p. 366). The modifier "sane" conforms to Thorndike's own self-perception of his moderate, "common-sensical" intellectual approach in the quest for natural laws. In 1941, in recommending Thorndike for the William James Lectureship, Edwin G. Boring[6] was impressed with his continued mental vigor, and described Thorndike's latest research as "a very elementary positivism but a very interesting approach in the way it works out." The modifier here, "elementary," undoubtedly reflects the progress of philosophical sophistication about scientific method over the intervening forty-five years.

Even before his conversion to psychology, Thorndike was victim of the optimistic and widespread assumptions of nineteenth-century positivism. Even his college literary exercises revealed a hard tone, a disdain for the sentimental, a total confidence in dispassionate analysis ("the emotionally indifferent attitude of the scientific observer," he called it), the surety of the existence of "truth" and its ineluctable serviceability. Nature is, above all, he wrote in his first article addressed to teachers (Thorndike, 1899), "*a thing to study, to know about, to see through*" (p. 61). He abhorred vagueness, and for indeterminacy he substituted positivism: things do not happen by mere chance in human life any more than in the fall of an apple or an eclipse of the moon; behind the seemingly endless variety of human affairs there are invariably acting laws which make possible the advance of human control by reason.

That knowledge is power, that truth can be known, that facts can be trusted—these approached copybook maxims in Thorndike's youth, and such ideas no less distinguished those inducted into science in its perhaps most optimistic age. Facts were considered prepotent, and fact-finding the essence of all scientific endeavors. This applied as well to the social sciences. In a college essay on the moral force of the realist school of fiction writing, Thorndike[7] opined: "Truth is only truth, I think, [and] knowledge of any fact, no matter how vile, cannot but be morally helpful if it is true in the perspective and import given to it." "Look and see" was his advice to all other investigators of animal intelligence. While he considered that school visitations (for the purpose of marrying theory to practice or for the demonstration of already known psychological principles) were a tedious, inefficient, and unnecessary expenditure of the time of an educational psychologist, he was willing even to go into a schoolroom if the purpose was collecting facts for science.

Academic circles in the late nineteenth century were strangers to scientific relativism. Instead, knowledge was considered something firm, and in all the disciplines the emphasis was upon the never again to be repeated, upon the definitive study. It is *not* that Thorndike craved certainty. The immaturity of science, even of parts of the "hard sciences," was an accepted—and acceptable—proposition. But that indeterminacy is an ultimate barrier of nature against science was not yet proposed and would never be tolerated by many of his age; that all the psychologist's concepts, as well as the physicist's time and space, probably apply only to the unsophisticated, commonplace experiences of daily life requires a philosophical reorientation too radical for a generation of positivists. What Thorndike accepted about the introspectionist—that is, his uncontrollable, unintentional, but inevitable distortion of the psychological data he reports—cannot be true of the behaviorist.

The perfect model of the certain, nearly finished (i.e., perfectly polished) science of Thorndike's day was physics: it was preeminently experimental, devoted to the collection of physical facts and the testing of hypotheses. All its great discoveries were presumed made, and its remaining task centered upon the making of measurements of already known phenomena and their statement in forms precise to the sixth decimal point (Kevles, 1964). Roentgen's animating report in 1895 of the X-ray did not end the impress of physics upon the whole scientific community, for physics stood best for the widespread faith in quantification. Clerk Maxwell had expressed it well: "We owe all the great advances in knowledge to those who endeavor to find out how much there is of anything." So did Lord Kelvin: "One's knowledge of science begins when he can measure what he is speaking about, and express it in numbers." How redolent of Thorndike's these words are, and where Thorndike thought himself most deficient was in his meager mathematical training.

The year Thorndike spent at Columbia University (1897-98) was its first year at the new Morningside Heights campus; no longer was the President's house home to both Pupin's electrical laboratory (in its cellar) and Cattell's laboratory (in its attic). Yet that spatial juxtaposition of physics and psychology had been an apt symbolization of a compatible methodological and conceptual "togetherness"—call it "reductionism" if you will—so evident in the 1890s. The laboratory was the destination of virtually every aspiring young scientist of the later nineteenth century. Botanists left their fields, even their herbaria, for the laboratory's dyes and microscopes. Many a psychologist developed his aggressively mechanical and materialistic visages in Germany's psychophysical and physiological centers. Albion Small (Small and Vincent, 1894) declared laboratory discipline essential to social science, calling research experience in physics, chemistry, and biology "ideal preparation for sociological research . . ." (p. 24).

When American students made "experiment" synonymous with "scientific," this was methodological reductionism; in conceiving of "mental atoms," the "conservation of psychic energy," or "the natural selection of cultures," this was theoretical or conceptual reductionism (Wolman, 1965). Reducing (i.e., taking over) Galileo's theory of falling bodies into Newton's theory of gravitation and mechanics was an early example entirely within the field of physics. More obvious and controversial is reductionism across the sciences—treating metabolic processes or the emotions entirely as chemistry, for instance. Breakthroughs in one science often precipitate or speed reductionism. Thus, chemistry assaulted the not so ancient distinction between organic and inorganic because chemical synthesis seemed to drive vitalism out of biology and physiology. Even the radical reductionist—accepting an identity of the subject matter as he does—leaves separate spheres for the different sciences, however, and John B. Watson distinguished between psychology and physiology by giving the former the organism's functions as a whole to deal with, and the latter its separated functions.

The science toward which most others gravitated was physics. Despite the power of physics, however, it is also necessary to recall that each science responded to the others' revolutions. Even before Darwin, for instance, there was sizable interest in all the sciences in the origins of matter. Franz Boas, who taught statistics to Thorndike, began as a physicist, proceeded to geography, and settled in anthropology; his reasons for abandoning physics were similar to the botanist's who left morphology for plant life history. Nicholas Murray Butler was largely correct in claiming that every strain of nineteenth-century thought had been cross-fertilized by the doctrine of evolution. Impersonal evolutionary forces and environmental adaptation furnished historiography with alternatives to catastrophic and heroic explanation. And conservatives and liberals alike rushed to buoy their political and economic preferences with Darwinism.

> The circle of the earth is long since complete, but in the presence of each man is an unexplored world—his own mind. There is no mental geography describing the contents of the mind, still less is there a mental mechanics demonstrating necessary relations of thought. Yet the mind is the beginning and the end of science. Physical science is possible because the mind observes and arranges, and physical science has worth because it satisfies mental needs.
>
> (Cattell, 1893, p. 779)

Such comfortable and familiar allusions as "mental geography" and "mental mechanics" came naturally to Cattell's pen. As the twentieth century advanced, however, they would become anathema to many behavioral scientists. Quantum mechanics, probabilistic physics, and the rediscovery of Mendel and the new genetics made nature appear more complex, even mysterious. "The range of the measurable is *not* the range of the knowable"—this was sociologist Robert A. MacIver's challenge to Thorndike across the Columbia campus. Pitirim Sorokin (1943) was a particularly acicular commentator upon such borrowings as "social distance" and "organizational equilibrium"; he held up for ridicule A. P. Weiss' definition of consciousness as "an electron-proton aggregation" (Sorokin, 1943, p. 27). In a similar manner, some social psychologists became wary of what seemed a psychobiologic dominance; they protested that special social-psychological laws preclude dependence upon generalizations drawn from individual behavioral systems. It was now heard that the social sciences are the sciences of culture, not of nature. By the time that Thorndike's mammoth ***Human Nature and the Social Order*** appeared in 1940, his was too simplistic and atomistic, too unified an application to interest most other social scientists.

The multiplication of "schools" and theories was fragmenting psychology also. Nevertheless Wolman (1965) may be correct that, even in 1965, at base most psychologists hope for the eventual reduction of psychological processes to the physicochemical sciences. At any rate, this seems true of Thorndike. He was early convinced of the unity of nature and that psychology must attain the certainty and exactness of the physical sciences, and could not do so without resting upon their foundations. In the last month of his life he said that he still wanted most in his lifetime to see demonstrated the fruitfulness, for the social arts and sciences, of the exacting sort of scientific procedures found in his youth only in the physical sciences.

THE MESSIANIC CHARACTER OF THE "NEW PSYCHOLOGY"

In his presidential address to the American Psychological Association in 1937, California's E. C. Tolman (1938) declared that—given psychology's inability even to predict the direction a rat would turn in a maze—he considered his science unready to furnish guidelines for human behavior. Thorndike's perceptions of both the possibilities and the actual achievements of psychology were considerably more immodest than Tolman's; he never lost much of that optimism, buoyancy, and sense of mission evident in the "new psychology" of the 1890s.

Fully accepting Karl Pearson's (1892) proposition, in *The Grammar of Science,* that science, rightly understood, is competent to solve all problems, Thorndike was understandably impatient with the backwardness of psychological knowledge, although not with its new aims. In a graduate seminar paper Thorndike noted with indignation:[8]

> [Descartes'] physiological theories have all been sloughed off by science long ago. No one ever quotes him as an authority in morphology or physiology. . . . Yet his theory of the nature of the mind is still upheld by not a few, and the differences between his doctrines of imagination, memory, and of the emotions, and those of many present-day psychology books are comparatively unimportant.

Not that this deplorable situation was all grim, however: a good opportunity for iconoclasm was made available, and Thorndike got much sheer delight from it in his early, "assertive years."[9] Of his thesis he wrote to his future wife, "It is fun to write all the stuff up and smite all the hoary scientists hip and thigh. I shall be jumped on unmercifully when the thing gets printed, if I ever raise the cash to print it."

Years later, when Thorndike himself was older and mellower and successful, he chided John B. Watson a little for that same mixture of scientific evangelism and iconoclastic sarcasm which colored his own beginnings: In a review of *Behavior,* Thorndike (1915) wrote: "For students of objective behavior to regard themselves as martyrs, heroes or prophets is now unnecessary" (p. 466).

The new psychology meant, in part, the eschewing of "armchair speculation," a cleaving from the humanities, a rejecting of philosophy. At times the philosophers seemed to assist the process. It was a philosopher who inducted Judd, Thorndike, Freeman, and W. F. Dearborn into psychology. And Princeton's philosopher President, James

McCosh, presumably an unregenerate conservative, wrote to James Mark Baldwin (1926) in Leipzig in 1884: "You may tell Professor Wundt that his works are known in this college to our best students . . . [and that] two years ago we had a Wundt Club which met to read the Mental Physiology" (pp. 199-200). From but four independent psychology departments in American universities in 1904, there were 34 a decade later.

The number of psychological laboratories increased rapidly. Between 1874 and 1904, 54 were established in North America. Even Titchener's group, espousing the unpopular method of introspection as a unique psychological tool and in self-imposed structuralist isolation from the main body of American psychologists, counted itself within the new psychology for its devotion to the laboratory. Cornell offered probably the nation's most stringent training, cultivated a highly technical vocabulary, conducted elaborately controlled investigations. Such among Titchener's students as Carl Seashore (Murchison, 1930b) thought Titchener's four-volume *Experimental Psychology* "the highest embodiment of the idea of intensive, fundamental drill exercises" (p. 262) and lamented when such stylized training and laboratory formalism fell away.

The new psychology had its skeptics, of course, including William James, America's best known philosopher and psychologist. Dispatching a copy of his *Measurements* to James, Thorndike warned him:[10]

> I am sending you a dreadful book which I have written, which is no end scientific but devoid of any spark of human interest. You must make all your research men read it, but never look within its covers yourself. The figures and curves and formulae would drive you mad.

James' response was cordial, tactful, affectionate:

> I open your new book with full feelings of awe and admiration for your unexampled energy. It was just the thing I hoped for when I was teaching psychology and wondered why no one wrote it. And now you are the man to have done it. I should think it would immediately be translated.

> I am glad I have graduated from the necessity of using that kind of thing any longer. I shall stick to "qualitative" work as more congruous with old age. Nothing like metaphysics for people in their dotage.

Thorndike well knew that his teacher thought America was already oversupplied with psychological laboratories, and that James doubted even the credibility of the "exact" sciences. James preferred, instead, "non-systems"—in an eternally pluralistic, liberal, permissive, open universe. Thorndike revered him above all other men, but the younger psychologists were so anxious to give scientific status to their work that James seemed an "irritating impressionist." Thorndike's own tolerance of James did not extend to G. Stanley Hall, however, and he never criticized or satirized anyone as severely as he did Hall. The

possibility that the pseudo-scientific pretensions of the child-study movement might be mistaken for educational psychology was too horrible to contemplate.

Hugo Münsterberg typified a different kind of skeptic. He dichotomized the art and the science of education, for instance, and doubted applied psychology's worth (especially for education). But Thorndike (1898b) answered: "Many things have been declared out of court . . . which the widening researches of matter-of-fact men have triumphantly reinstated" (p. 646). In 1918, speaking as a Vice-President of AAAS, Thorndike (1919) described applied psychology as "much more than cleverness and common sense. . . . It is scientific work, research on problems of human nature complicated by conditions of the shop or school or army, restricted by time and labor cost and directed by imperative needs. The secret of success in applied psychology or human engineering is [he concluded] *to be rigorously scientific*" (p. 60).

To explain the difficulties of behavioral research, Thorndike (1935) once used this illustration: "*Science* cannot roll identical villages down a depression again and again to test the laws of economics as *it* rolls ivory balls down an inclined plane to test the uniformity of the laws of motion" (p. 228). Such difficulties were not totally unappreciated in the larger scientific community either. It seemed to one American physicist (Crew, 1934) that "to tell the truth about an experiment in physics is child's play, compared with telling the truth about a man" (p. 331). Another observed that "physics is the simplest of all sciences, for the reason that all the rest are *physics-plus* . . ." (p. 23).[11]

Nevertheless, American psychology continued to be extremely active—and in the name of science. By 1913, *Who's Who in Science* (published in England) reported the United States was the most productive nation in psychological research, with 84 of the world's leading investigators (surpassing the combined totals of Germany, England, and France). Only here, among all the sciences, was America the world's leader. In 1931, at an international gathering of psychologists and educators, it was frequently remarked that America virtually owned psychometrics. As Thorndike (Monroe, 1931) protested to that assemblage, however, "it would be more in the interests of science and of our comfort" if standardized tests were *not* called "American examinations," since *"science is certainly not national and the only claim of Americans busy in that line is that they are trying to be scientific"* (p. 262, italics added).

As for himself, among all the congratulations showered upon him with his election to the presidency of the American Association for the Advancement of Science, none must have pleased Thorndike more than those words in the *New York Times* (January 13, 1934) editorial that said simply, "But first and last, he is a scientist."

Notes

1. Cattell to the editors, undated. Copy in unpublished Thorndike papers (not indexed), Montrose, New York.

2. Thorndike's replies to Titchener are located and indexed in the Titchener Papers, Cornell University, Ithaca, New York.

3. Just how much separatism has developed in this century is suggested in Higham (1966).

4. See Kevles (1964), Veysey (1965), and Visher (1939).

5. Because Thorndike believed learning to be grounded in trial-and-error behavior, he adopted puzzle-box techniques; because of his associationist theory, he employed word tests of paired associates. Where Thorndike constructed experimental situations to secure random responses, Köhler devised his to secure evidence of insight.

6. E. G. Boring, personal communication to Gordon Allport, May 2, 1941 Archives of the Psychology Department, Harvard University.

7. Student essays, in the collection of the Eclectic Society, Wesleyan University, Middletown, Connecticut.

8. "The Psychology of Descartes," 1898. In unpublished Thorndike papers, Montrose, New York.

9. E. L. Thorndike, personal communications to Elizabeth Moulton, February 26, 1898; March 12, 1898: January 6, 1899. In unpublished Thorndike papers, Montrose, New York.

10. E. L. Thorndike, personal communication to W. James, September 28, 1904. In Thorndike file, James Papers, Houghton Library, Harvard University. James' response (dated October 6, 1904) in unpublished Thorndike papers, Montrose, New York.

11. Daniel F. Comstock, "Autobiographical Notes." In Comstock Papers, Library, American Institute of Physics, New York City.

References

Baldwin, J. M. *Between two wars.* Vol. I. Boston: Stratford, 1926.

Beardsley, E. H. The rise of the American chemistry profession, 1850-1900. *University of Florida Monographs in Social Sciences,* No. 23, 1964.

Cattell, J. McK. The progress of psychology. *Popular Science Monthly,* 1893, *43,* 779-785.

Cattell, J. McK. Our psychological association and research. *Science,* 1917, *45,* 275-284.

Cattell, J. McK. Thorndike as colleague and friend. *Teachers College Record,* 1926, *27,* 461-465.

Crew, H. *Thomas Corwin Mendenhall.* Biographical Memoir, National Academy of Sciences, 1934.

Daniels, G. The process of professionalization in American science: The emergent period, 1820-1860. Paper presented at the meeting of the History of Science Society, San Francisco, December 1965.

Higham, J. The schism in American scholarship. *American Historical Review,* 1966, *72,* 1-21.

Jonçich, G. (Ed.) *Psychology and the science of education: Selected writings of Edward L. Thorndike.* New York: Teachers College, 1962.

Jonçich, G. Scientists and the schools of the nineteenth century: The case of American physicists. *American Quarterly,* 1966, *18,* 667-685.

Jones, E. *The life and work of Sigmund Freud.* (Abridged ed., by L. Trilling & S. Marcus) New York: Basic Books, 1961.

Kevles, D. J. The study of physics in America, 1865-1916. Unpublished doctoral dissertation, Princeton University, 1964.

Monroe, P. (Ed.) *Conference on examinations.* New York: Teachers College, 1931.

Murchison, C. (Ed.) *A history of psychology in autobiography.* Worcester, Mass.: Clark University Press, Vol. 1, 1930a; Vol. 2, 1932; Vol. 3, 1936.

Murchison, C. (Ed.) *Psychologies of 1930.* Worcester, Mass.: Clark University Press, 1930. (b)

Pearson, K. *The grammar of science.* New York: Scribners, 1892.

Small, A. W., & Vincent, G. E. *An introduction to the study of sociology.* New York: American Book, 1894.

Sorokin, P. A. *Sociocultural causality, space, time.* Durham: Duke University Press, 1943.

Thorndike, E. L. Animal intelligence. *Psychological Review Monographs,* No. 2, 1898. (a)

Thorndike, E. L. What is a physical fact? *Psychological Review,* 1898, *5,* 645-650. (b)

Thorndike, E. L. Sentimentality in science teaching. *Educational Review,* 1899, *17,* 57-64.

Thorndike, E. L. *The elements of psychology.* New York: A. G. Seiler, 1905.

Thorndike, E. L. Review of Watson's "Behaviorism." *Journal of Animal Behavior,* 1915, *5,* 462-470.

Thorndike, E. L. Scientific personnel work in the army. *Science,* 1919, *49,* 53-61.

Thorndike, E. L. The paradox of science. *Proceedings of the American Philosophical Society,* 1935, *75,* 287-294.

Titchener, E. B. Review of Thorndike's "The Elements of Psychology." *Mind,* 1905, *56,* 552-554.

Tolman, E. C. The determiners of behavior at a choice point. *Psychological Review,* 1938, *45,* 1-35.

Veysey, L. R. *The emergence of the American university,* Chicago: University of Chicago Press, 1965.

Visher, S. Distribution of the psychologists starred in the six editions of "American Men of Science." *American Journal of Psychology,* 1939, *52,* 278-292.

Walker, F. *Formal opening of the engineering and physics building.* Montreal: McGill University Press, 1893.

Wolman, B. (Ed.) *Scientific psychology.* New York: Basic Books, 1965.

Clarence J. Karier (essay date 1986)

SOURCE: "Edward L. Thorndike: Toward a Science of Psychology," in *Scientists of the Mind: Intellectual Founders of Modern Psychology,* University of Illinois Press, 1986, pp. 89-105.

[*In the following essay, Karier explores the larger cultural and ethical implications of Thorndike's focus on the science of education.*]

In one of his rare ventures into fictional writing, Edward L. Thorndike, America's most influential educational psychologist, wrote a very revealing morality play, *The Miracle.* In it he assumed the character of Dr. Richard Cabot, who, discoursing with a traditional clergyman, said:

> My God is all the good in all men. My God is the mother's courage in childbirth; the laborer doing an honest job; the citizen counting his own advantage less than the common weal; the little child, brave, just, and happy in his play; the father toiling to educate his children—all the good in all men. Your God is in heaven; my God is on earth. Your God made us; but we ourselves make my God. He is as great and wise and good as we choose to make him.
>
> My God does not hear prayers. Work for him.[1]

This God would play a most significant role throughout his adult life.

Thorndike was the son of a strong-willed, determined, Puritan woman, Abbie Ladd Thorndike, and an itinerant Methodist minister, Edward Robert Thorndike, who preached the gospel of Christ throughout Massachusetts. Reared in a controlled religious environment, his family instilled in him a respect for practical disciplined values for living, while he developed a general disinterest in music and theater and only a limited interest in books.[2] His background thus established the moral capital on which he drew throughout his professional career. However, by the time Thorndike graduated from Wesleyan and moved on to Harvard to continue his education with William James, he had begun to break away from the traditional faith of his father and mother. His new naturalistic faith was intimately tied to his career as an educational psychologist. He was convinced, as he stood in the dawning secular light of the twentieth century, that the "scientific" psychologist was destined to displace the traditional philosopher and theologian. His faith was to be a faith in empirical science. Unlike his father, he would preach the gospel of positivistic science, one that included not only a careful empirical description of what "is," but also a highly selec-

tive, relatively unexamined set of assumptions about what "ought" to be. Embedded in those assumptions were the ethical and ideological values that marked much of his work. Merle Curti notes that, "Despite Thorndike's predominant interest in applying the scientific method to education, his statement of general aims was determined by ethics. To make men 'want the right things, and to make them better able so to control all the forces of nature and themselves that they can satisfy these wants' is the basic doctrine of his educational philosophy."[3]

The "right" thing to do, according to Thorndike, "is the thing which a man who could foresee all the consequences of all acts, and who considered fairly the welfare of all men, would in that case choose."[4] This would be the role of empirical science. The purpose of education, then, was not only to help us see the truth but to help us want the right things. From Thorndike's perspective, "the aims of education as a whole are identical with those of morality."[5] He believed that science could be employed as an instrument to shape better human beings and ultimately a better social order. By "better" he did not necessarily mean a significantly different social system; rather, it was a matter of bringing our wants into line with the realities dictated by "truth." Hence, the more knowledge we have of the "truth," the better off we will be. Such knowledge leads to the satisfaction of human wants and, more importantly, "predisposes men against unsatisfiable wants—to know what the world really is prevents us from wanting what it cannot give. It leads to the satisfaction of all good wants—knowledge is power." The aim of education, Thorndike continued, should be "to cultivate good will to men and the higher or impersonal or unselfish pleasures, and to get rid of irrational wants—wants not fitted to the world in which we live."[6] The irrational wants cultivated by organized religions would thus fade away in the light of scientific knowledge.

Thorndike espoused that branch of Enlightenment thinking that, from Helvétius to Comte, conceived of the progress in scientific knowledge not in terms of freeing men from an oppressive system, but rather in terms of binding them to a more orderly system. He was very much a part of that positivistic tradition usually appearing on the conservative side of the social-economic ledger. In this chapter I will analyze Thorndike's major educational ideas and practices and consider the moral assumptions upon which many of his ideas were based, the social implication these ideas seemed to contain, as well as the impact his work had for educational thought and practice in the twentieth century.

In 1898, when William James introduced the term *pragmatism* to popular audiences at the University of California, his student Edward L. Thorndike (1874-1949) was completing his epoch-making dissertation, **"Animal Intelligence: An Experimental Study of Associative Processes in Animals."** It was quickly recognized as a landmark work in experimental psychology, and Thorndike's career sky-rocketed. Within a few years he was a full professor at Columbia University, with major interests in human learning and educational psychology. For almost half a century Thorndike held sway at Columbia, during which time he taught thousands of teachers and administrators, and published 50 books and 450 monographs and articles. His massive three-volume work entitled *Educational Psychology* (1913) set the tone for almost the next two decades. From his pen flowed a prodigious number of educational maxims, psychological laws, textbooks and scales of achievement for elementary, secondary, and college courses in varied fields, dictionaries for children in elementary and secondary schools, and teacher manuals. Because he wrote so many of the texts and tests used in elementary and secondary schools, his impact on American educational practice was both immediate and pervasive.

In 1901, in collaboration with Robert Woodworth, Thorndike published his now-famous paper on the transfer of training, in which he attempted to empirically refute the claims made by the exponents of the traditional doctrine of formal discipline. At a time when attacks on the classical languages were increasing at a feverish rate, the findings of Thorndike and Woodworth were received with great enthusiasm. Down through the years, the classicists had argued that the study of Greek and Latin was to be valued not so much for its specific content as for its power to develop the faculty of reasoning. The experiment of Woodworth and Thorndike appeared to demonstrate that specific ability did not transfer beyond the learning environment, except in those cases where the new conditions under which the ability was to be utilized were identical or closely identical to the original conditions under which the ability was learned.[7] Thorndike concluded that school subjects are to be valued for their specific content and not for any generalized disciplinary powers.[8] For the next thirty years, the battle would rage with relentless fury, until Greek was eliminated from the public school curriculum and Latin was reduced to an elective course. Not only the disciplinary value of studying these languages was lost, but also the intellectual stimulation of engaging many of the West's most profound thinkers. Although many factors contributed to the demise of the classics in American education, Thorndike's timely arguments were of major importance.[9]

The elimination of the classics from American public schools meant in the end, the elimination of the aim of classical education itself—to teach the "best that was thought and said in the past" and to ensure the development of independent thinkers, well equipped with all the necessary intellectual tools for formulating their own critical judgments. As this aim disappeared from the educator's rhetoric, it was replaced with discussions about individual differences and meeting individual needs in the name of social efficiency.

Throughout its history, the classical ideal existed as an elitist's educational achievement, never effectively translated into a system of mass schooling. What remains today of that classical system is to be found largely among America's elite prep schools. What eventually displaced it in America's public schools was a meritocratic system with an elitist principle as a cornerstone. That system required an intensive concern for individual differences, the measurement of those differences, and the development of educational experiences to ensure differential treatment. While the classical ideal had emphasized the education of the well-rounded individual for leadership, the new educational ideal emphasized a differential curriculum which presumed to prepare people for a variety of career roles. Designed mainly for the rapidly growing high school, the new education would prepare some people for the factory, some for the office, and others for college. In the name of individual differences, an educational tracking system was born, all in the name of social efficiency.

While John Dewey, George Herbert Mead, and others wrote and spoke of a new individualism arising out of the ruins of the older laissez-faire competitive system, and from time to time had their names evoked to support a given educational reform, the direct effect of their work on education in its broadest context was quite different. Dewey and Mead created a philosophy of new liberalism which tended to satisfy the ideological needs of the professional class, especially the social scientist; men like Thorndike, Lewis Terman, and others worked more directly with teachers to structure and develop the mainstream of thinking and practice in American public education. Although these two views never seemed to rest too comfortably with each other, in the end they both included the primary notion of a meritocratic society, namely, that somehow the meritorious must be allowed to lead. Questions about the role of the expert, the meaning of democracy, and the idea of freedom were crucial, however. In this regard, Dewey and Thorndike held significantly different opinions. For example, the role of the expert in Dewey's *The Public and Its Problems* is vastly different from the role of the expert in Thorndike's **"The Psychology of the Half-Educated Man."** In the former case, Dewey attempted to dissolve the role of the expert in an idealistically fluid community; in the latter case, Thorndike recommended outright public subservience to the expert: "Outside that field [our own expertise] the intelligent procedure for most of us is to refuse to think, spending our energy rather in finding the expert in the case and learning from him."[10] The differences between Thorndike and Dewey are very much a result of Mead's and Dewey's reconstruction of liberalism, and with it a new view of individualism. Thorndike's position on individualism remained similar in many respects to that of his mentor, William James. In the end it was the James-Thorndike brand of individualism that came to dominate much public school thought and practice in the twentieth century.

In certain striking respects, Thorndike modeled his professional career after that of his former teacher. Just as James's two-volume work on *The Principles of Psychology* (1890) dominated the field for two decades, so did Thorndike's three-volume work on educational psychology (1913). Both men found it necessary to condense these volumes into a single work—Thorndike called his *Educa-*

tional Psychology: Briefer Course (1914)—for teachers. Thorndike also used James's earlier work as the basis for his own thought. For example, moving from the James-Lange theory of bonds, Thorndike constructed his own theory of connectionism,[11] which gradually came to include various "laws of learning" based on a physiological conception of the nervous system. Thorndike's psychology, too, was replete with the conventional wisdom of the period, including the stereotyping of women and ethnic groups as well as races. Reminiscent of James's tendency to romanticize the condition of the worker, we find Thorndike suggesting, "Probably three out of four chauffeurs would really much rather drive a car than live as the King of England does."[12] His psychology also justified the competitive spirit of capitalism; although he did not suggest, as James had, that private property was an instinctive characteristic of human nature, he did find the "mastery and submissive" characteristic of the human species among their original endowment. While both men from time to time uttered certain criticisms of the social economic system, by and large they both not only accepted that system as given, but embraced many of the personal values that made it work. Again, even though he found certain educational problems with it, he, like his mentor, recognized the need for the "instinct of rivalry." Both men accepted the social class system and looked to the elite for leadership. Although it should be clear that James held a far broader view of reality, tolerating and incorporating many more subjective experiences within his psychology, much of Thorndike's empirical psychology is in line with James's. The spirit of capitalism is writ large across the value system of both men. Perhaps for this reason, more than any other, Thorndike's work proved to be so popular among practical-minded educators as well as philanthropic foundations.

In more ways than one, Edward Thorndike was a man of the hour, spearheading the Zeitgeist of his time. This Zeitgeist saw science as an instrument to organize the public school on the model of a business establishment.[13] George P. Strayer, a leader of the efficiency movement in education, stated: "all our investigations with respect to the classification and progress of children in the elementary schools, in high schools, and in higher education are based upon Professor Thorndike's contribution to the psychology of individual differences."[14]

In 1904 Thorndike published his *Introduction to the Theory of Mental and Social Measurements,* which made him a leader in the test and measurement movement. Many years later he chaired the Committee on Classification of Personnel of the United States Army, and for the first time group intelligence tests were introduced into American culture on a massive scale. In the post-World War I era, Thorndike's influence led to the use of various tests in business and industry, as well as in education. By serving on the National Research Council, he helped to develop the popular National Intelligence Test used in elementary schools. By 1926 he published *The Measurement of Intelligence,* dealing with the well-known CAVD test.

Throughout the 1920s and 1930s, Thorndike stood at the center of the storm raging over the meaning of intelligence as well as the nature-nurture argument. His response to both problems was consistent with his psychological conception of the individual.

As an evolutionist, Thorndike believed that "amongst the minds of animals that of man leads, not as a demigod from another planet, but as a king from the same race."[15] Because human minds were continuous with the minds of animals, the study of animal learning could provide a simplified key for understanding human intelligence. Such study led in part to his theory of *connectionism,* which "as conceived by Thorndike can be defined in rather simple terms. In all species of animals, including man, certain neurobiological connections of such a nature that the application of a given stimulus tends to elicit a particular type of response (S-R bonds) are found to exist. Some of these connections have already been established in the normal animal at the time of birth; others which he is potentially capable of forming, are acquired as a result of post-natal experiences."[16] Connections are "stamped in" by way of the law of *exercise* and the law of *effect.* The former implies that repetitions strengthen connections; the latter, that rewards also strengthen connections, while punishment weakens them. Later research by Thorndike and others seemed to indicate that punishment did not effectively weaken those connections, however.[17]

With the law of effect stripped of punishment, Thorndike evolved a theory of reinforcement, which B. F. Skinner eventually would develop more fully. Thorndike was, however, no Skinnerian, or even a Watsonian behaviorist. He disagreed with Watson as to the origin of differences among individuals. Both men were determinists, although Watson attributed individual differences to environment and Thorndike attributed them to heredity. As Joncich notes, "Thorndike early concluded that heredity is the major reason for human variation in intellect and character, that no other factor is more significant than innate and inherited inequalities in the capacity to learn."[18]

Throughout his life, Thorndike assumed a positive correlation between intellect, character, and wealth, and usually assumed that each was determined primarily by heredity. In this view we find something of the older Puritan doctrine of predestination of the elect. The God of nature had showered some people with the grace of intelligence, which somehow not only made them wiser but also morally better and richer. These were the elect who, in a really good society, would rule. Thorndike believed this could be proven quantitatively. These visible saints were not, however, just the pure products of natural evolution, somehow inevitably destined for sainthood, but also the products of what goodness had been achieved by people changing themselves. As Thorndike said: "original nature has achieved what goodness the world knows as a state achieves order, by killing, confining or reforming some of its elements. It progresses, not by *laissez faire,* but by changing the environment in which it operates and by renewedly changing itself in each generation." Man makes himself "civilized, rational and humane," to suit himself. "His nature is not right in his own eyes. Only one thing in it, indeed, is unreservedly good, the power to make it better. This power, the power of learning or modification in favor of the satisfying, the capacity represented by the law of effect, is the essential principle of reason and right in the world."[19] The power of God is thus in the world of the secular minister of science. According to Thorndike, "we ourselves make my God. He is as great and wise and good as we choose to make him. My God does not hear prayers. Work for him."[20]

Putting aside the traditional religious garb of his father, Thorndike donned what he believed to be the robe of the scientist: objective quantitative measurement. The major thrust of his thought and influence followed these lines. "Whatever exists at all exists in some amount,"[21] he asserted early in his career, and he spent the rest of his life trying to measure what existed. Curti correctly notes: "His influence in establishing and popularizing the fact-finding, statistical, and experimental technique in education has been immeasurable. Taking over the methods of the physical and natural sciences, and using the more quantitative devices of such pioneers as Pearson, Galton, Cattell, Rice, and Boas, Thorndike, together with Judd, revolutionized American educational technique."[22] Advising teachers to think in terms of measurable behavioral objectives,[23] and to conceive of learning as a stamping-in process, Thorndike went on to suggest that the new science of psychology might quantitatively determine not only the best methods to be used but the best objectives of education as well.[24] His unbounded faith in a quantitative science of education led him to define not only what is, but what ought to be, unrestrained by the fact that what he thought ought to be actually was predetermined by his personal values. Strangely enough, when Thorndike reported his experimental work with animal behavior, he tended to be quite circumspect; when he dealt with complex human social systems, however, he tended to speculate freely.[25] Many of his professional colleagues warned him that he moved too freely beyond his data. Curti observes: "One must question to what extent his social opinions are truly related, scientifically, to his experimental work, and to what extent they are determined by his own unconscious participation in the prejudices of our own time."[26]

For Thorndike, the role of the secular minister preaching a gospel of secularized Methodist values and that of a scientist constantly testing for truth, repeatedly came into conflict. The latter role usually was sacrificed at precisely those points where Thorndike's personal values were at stake. His attitudes toward the sexes, races, and lower classes bring this problem into sharper focus.

Thorndike believed that men were more variable, and thus we might find more genius among the male rather than the female of the species. He argued that while, in general, women may be as intelligent as men, and can usually profit from similar kinds of education, the variability factor accounts for the disproportionate number of men doing graduate work. Women, he believed, were instinctively different from men, which should be taken into account in the educational guidance and tracking of women toward their occupational destinies. While men were possessed of the instinct to fight and compete, women (or so he thought) were possessed of the instinct to nurse, to care for and fuss over others, to relieve, comfort, pet, coddle, console, and do for others.[27] Thus, men and women ought to receive a partially differentiated curriculum, which would channel women into those occupations appropriate to their nature, such as nursing, teaching, and medicine, while men would be channeled into the more competitive world of statesmanship, philosophy, and scientific research.[28] Just as the social inferiority of immigrants and blacks was embedded in the curricular content and practices of the school, so too was the inferior status of women.[29] Thorndike clearly played a significant role in establishing that content and encouraging those practices.

As an elitist, Thorndike supported the emergence of those characteristics in American education. He believed that progress depended not on the extension of culture to the masses, but rather on the education of the gifted elite. Repeatedly, he argued against the upward extension of the compulsory education law on the grounds that such attempts at further education of the mentally unfit were doomed to failure. His emphasis on individual differences and objective classification of students led to the logical conclusion of segregating, for educational purposes, the superior intellects, whom he believed to be of higher moral character and good will.

> But, in the long run, it has paid the "masses" to be ruled by intelligence. Furthermore, the natural processes which give power to men of ability to gain it and keep it are not, in their results, unmoral. Such men are, by and large, of superior intelligence, and consequently of somewhat superior justice and good will. They act, in the long run, not against the interests of the world, but for it. What is true in science and government seems to hold good in general for manufacturing, trade, art, law, education, and religion. It seems entirely safe to predict that the world will get better treatment by trusting its fortunes to its 95- or 99-percentile intelligences than it would get by itself. The argument for democracy is not that it gives power to all men without distinction, but that it gives greater freedom for ability and character to attain power.[30]

Thorndike was quite sure that "to him that hath a superior intellect is given also on the average a superior character." His own white middle-class values seemed obvious when he suggested that his scientific observations indicated that "the abler persons in the world in the long run are the more clean, decent, just, and kind."[31] He saw a positive correlation between moneymaking, intelligence, and moral character. In many ways, Thorndike was a twentieth-century example of the traditional spirit of capitalism which, from Benjamin Franklin to William Graham Sumner, equated virtue with wealth. The difference, however, was that he equated it "scientifically."

People were not, he believed, solely a product of their environment; moral and intellectual differences existed due to ancestry. Because "mental and moral inheritance from near ancestry is a fact," Thorndike was also sure that "racial differences in original nature are not mere myths."[32] He objectively tested black and white children and found that even though there was considerable overlap between the two races, the white pupils were demonstrably superior in scholarship. This, he concluded, was attributable to original nature, since "the differences in the environment do not seem at all adequate to account for the superiority of the whites."[33] Thorndike believed in the genetic superiority of whites over blacks, just as he firmly believed that the good society was ultimately a society ruled by the talented, morally righteous, and wealthy.

As a son of the Enlightenment, Thorndike believed in the progress of humanity through the manipulation and reform of social institutions. He carried the idea of social melioration and the perfectibility of humankind to one of its possible conclusions, eugenics, a movement he supported throughout his professional career. As he grew older, however, he tended to place greater emphasis on heredity and increasingly less on the importance of an improved environment. In his last major work he argued for the legal sterilization of those with low intelligence and morals, as well as those he called "dull or vicious epileptics and for certain sorts of dull and vicious sex perverts." He concluded: "By selective breeding supported by a suitable environment we can have a world in which all men will equal the top ten percent of present men. One sure service of the able and good is to beget and rear offspring. One sure service (about the only one) which the inferior and vicious can perform is to prevent their genes from survival."[34]

Thorndike included in his twenty-point program for social progress such advice as: society should practice scientific "eugenics"; "the able and good should acquire power"; and "quality is better than equality."[35] Interestingly, some thirty-three years earlier, Thorndike had attacked Lester Frank Ward's *Applied Sociology* for ignoring the Galton thesis which made ancestry so significant. Ward's egalitarianism, Thorndike surmised, was nothing more than a "defense of intellectual communism."[36] Throughout his life, Thorndike held fast to a conception of human nature which saw the individual as the product of biologic evolution, with some higher and others lower on the genetic scale. His massive studies of individual differences confirmed, for him and for others, that social and economic classes were largely caused by differences in inherited intelligence. Thorndike's original view of human nature was confirmed by the statistical charts of a lifetime of work. Humans could progress if they recognized the pernicious nature of Ward's egalitarianism and proceeded to practice eugenics to ensure the mental and moral best.

One of Thorndike's last major research projects was to develop a "G" scale for judging the value (goodness) of American cities and a "P" scale for judging the personal qualities of their inhabitants. He studied over 310 municipalities, compiling a list of more than three hundred criteria by which each city might be evaluated. "Among the three hundred items or features or traits there are thirty-seven, all or nearly all of which all reasonable persons will regard as significant for the goodness of life for good people in a city."[37] Of the thirty-seven criteria used, over twenty items deal with public and private value of property, size of income and expenditures, as well as the number of people who possess such items as automobiles, radios, and telephones. The "all reasonable persons" upon which he based his study were, it seems, highly materialistic, upper-middle-class people who valued their *Better Homes and Gardens, National Geographic,* and *Good Housekeeping* magazines.[38] Under the circumstances, it should come as no surprise that the ten cities rating the highest on the "G" scale were Pasadena, Montclair, Cleveland Heights, Berkeley, Brookline, Evanston, Oak Park, Glendale, Santa Barbara, and White Plains.[39] Thorndike found that the more black families a city contained, the lower the "G" and "P" ratings.[40] Thus, the cities with the least "goodness" were in the South: Augusta, Columbus, Meridian, High Point, Charleston, Savannah, and Durham.[41]

The important thing to do to improve a city, Thorndike argued, was to get "good" people to join the community and, most of all, to get "good" people who knew how to earn money—the more money the better.

> Cities are made better than others in this country primarily and chiefly by getting able and good people as residents—people who, for example, are intelligent, read books, do not contract syphilis, or commit murder, or allow others to do so, own their own homes, have telephones, and support doctors, nurses, dentists and teachers rather than lawyers and domestic servants. The second important cause of welfare is income. Good people, rich or poor, earning much or earning little, are a good thing for a city, but the more they have and earn the better. They and their incomes account for at least three-fourths, and probably more, of the differences of American cities in the goodness of life for good people.[42]

Since "good" cities are largely made up of high-income "good" people, the logical question to ask is how might the community manage to get more good people. Thorndike's answer: "The surest way to have good people is to breed them."[43] In the end, it was always a matter of sterilization of the unfit and breeding of the best.[44]

It should not go unnoticed that Thorndike found church memberships inversely related to his rating of the general goodness of life. He asked, "What are the churches doing with their prestige and power if they are neither helping the health and education and recreation of a community nor improving the personal qualities of its residents?" His response: "Unless the better communities under-report their church membership or the worse communities over-report theirs, we must suspect that the churches are clubs of estimable people and maintainers of traditional rites and ceremonies rather than powerful forces for human betterment."[45] Perhaps his own lifetime of success also had helped him to reach the conclusion that the work of the scientist, rather than that of the clergy, was a more powerful force for human betterment. From this perspective, he had chosen the right path.

Edward Thorndike objectified, standardized, and typed both the individual and society. He played a significant role, indirectly at least, in the "scientific management" movement in business, and directly in the efficiency movement in education. Through his many disciples, and his textbooks, tests, achievement scales, and teachers' manuals, he had a profound impact on American education. Perhaps more than any other single individual, he helped to structure American education in the twentieth century. Through his efforts, and the work of others, American school administrators, teachers, and curriculum experts learned how to regard their students objectively and quantitatively. The question of this standardization of the educational frontier enhanced social mobility or decreased it, and questions concerning the merits of the value system on which the standards were based proved to be embarrassing for many educators by the mid-twentieth century. As more and more people involved in education came to reject the possibility of a value-free science of education, a value-free science of testing, and a value-free system of public schooling, they, in turn, began to see the extent to which significant bias against racial and ethnic minorities, women, and the lower social-economic classes had been institutionalized in American education. Much of this institutionalized bias can be traced directly to the work of professional educators like Thorndike who embraced what they thought was an objective science of education and confused what is with what they thought ought to be.

The vast influence Thorndike exercised over American education may be accounted for in part by his own values, which were those of white middle-class America. At least as important, however, is the fact that his empirical findings were essentially what business-minded Americans wanted to hear. His positive correlations of wealth, morality, intelligence, and social power could ruffle no one on the upper end of the power structure. Nor, indeed, would a well-washed, growing, middle-class America be upset to learn that science substantiated the notion that "the abler persons in the world in the long run are the more clean, decent, just and kind." The conservative social values of Thorndike were clearly and fundamentally compatible with a business-minded, conservative, middle-class, racist-oriented America.

In the early years of this century, Max Weber, in a brilliant series of essays, called attention to the intimate relationship between the Protestant ethic and the spirit of capitalism. He discussed how, when Protestant views with respect to work, thrift, predestination, calling, elect, asceticism, and divine grace become secularized, they seemed to fit into and become part of the ideological structure of capitalism. Weber further explained how the work of John Wesley and Methodism contributed so much to the utilitarian ethic of the capitalistic system. Sometime after Friedrich Nietzsche announced to the world that "God is dead and we have killed him," Thorndike, the young son of a Methodist minister, no longer accepting the faith of his father, set forth to preach a new gospel of scientific education and psychology. Implicit in many of the most important doctrines he espoused were values drawn from the Methodist moral capital of his past. While the God of his father may have died, the values and ethics of his father were very much alive for him, as was the spirit of capitalism. As he put it: "My God does not hear prayers. Work for him." Edward L. Thorndike did.

Notes

1. In Geraldine Joncich, *The Sane Positivist: A Biography of Edward L. Thorndike* (Middletown, Conn.: Wesleyan University Press, 1968), p. 64. "The Miracle, A Play in Three Acts" was written "about 1920" but never published, according to archival sources cited by Joncich.

2. See ibid., p. 29.

3. Merle Curti, *The Social Ideas of American Educators* (Paterson, N.J.: Littlefield, Adams and Co., 1961), p. 464.

4. Edward L. Thorndike, *Education* (New York: Macmillan Co., 1912), p. 29.

5. Ibid.

6. Ibid., pp. 12, 13.

7. See Edward L. Thorndike and Robert S. Woodworth, "The Influence of Improvement in One Mental Function upon the Efficiency of Other Functions," *Psychological Review* 8 (1901): 247-61, 384-95, 553-64.

8. Charles H. Judd, at the University of Chicago, found a different alternative to Thorndike's explanation. He argued that when a subject is taught for "generalizations," these generalizations transfer; various experiments have since confirmed Judd's hypothesis. See Charles H. Judd et al., *Education as Cultivation of Higher Mental Processes* (New York: Macmillan Co., 1936). If we push Thorndike's thesis to its logical extreme, the formal school might best return to an apprenticeship system. For a critical appraisal of Thorndike's theory that only identical elements transfer, see Pedro T. Orata, *The Theory of Identical Elements* (Columbus: Ohio State University Press, 1928).

9. Whether the ready acceptance of Thorndike's work on this subject was due to the evidence he presented, or because he found what the culture wanted, is indeed a moot question. See Walter B. Kolesnik, *Mental Discipline in Modern Education* (Madison: University of Wisconsin Press, 1958).

10. See Edward L. Thorndike, "The Psychology of the Half-Educated Man," *Harper* 140 (Apr. 1920): 670.

11. See Edward L. Thorndike, *Educational Psychology*, 3 vols. (New York: Mason-Henry Press, 1913), 1:150-54.

12. Edward L. Thorndike, "The Psychology of Labor," *Harpers* 144 (May 1922): 800.

13. For one aspect of this development, see Raymond E. Callahan, *Education and the Cult of Efficiency* (Chicago: University of Chicago Press, 1962).

14. Quoted in Curti, *Social Ideas of American Educators,* p. 483.

15. Edward L. Thorndike, "The Evolution of the Human Intellect," *Popular Science Monthly* 60 (Nov. 1901): 65.

16. Florence L. Goodenough, "Edward Lee Thorndike, 1874-1949," *American Journal of Psychology* 63 (1950): 292.

17. Thorndike's connectionist view of human learning accounts for his persistent attitude that intelligence must not be viewed as general but as specific kinds of behavior. He attributed the quantitative speed of making these connections to heredity.

18. Geraldine M. Joncich, ed., *Psychology and the Science of Education: Selected Writings of Edward L. Thorndike,* Classics in Education, no. 12 (New York: Bureau of Publications, Teachers College, Columbia University, 1962), p. 21.

19. Thorndike, *Educational Psychology,* 1:281, 282.

20. Joncich, *Sane Positivist,* p. 64.

21. National Society for the Study of Education, *Seventeenth Yearbook* (Bloomington, Ill., 1918), part 2, p. 16.

22. Curti, *Social Ideas of American Educators,* p. 460.

23. See Edward L. Thorndike, "The Contributions of Psychology to Education," *Journal of Educational Psychology* 1 (Jan. 1910): 5-6.

24. In 1903 he admitted that the aim and goal of education was determined "not by facts but by ideals." It was not long, however, before he asserted that ideals and values were proper subjects of scientific investigation and control. See Robert Woodworth, "Edward Lee Thorndike (1874-1949)," *National Academy of Science* 27 (1952): 217.

25. I am indebted to Geoffrey Lasky for first calling my attention to this phenomenon in Thorndike's work.

26. Curti, *Social Ideas of American Educators,* p. 498.

27. See Edward L. Thorndike, *Educational Psychology: Briefer Course* (New York: Teachers College, Columbia University, 1914), pp. 340-51. This book was designed specifically for teachers.

28. See Edward L. Thorndike, *Individuality* (Boston: Houghton Mifflin Co., 1911), pp. 30-34.

29. See Clarence J. Karier, *Shaping the American Educational State* (New York: Free Press, 1975), chaps. 6, 7.

30. Edward L. Thorndike, "Intelligence and Its Uses," *Harpers* 140 (Dec. 1919-May 1920): 235.

31. Ibid., pp. 233, 235.

32. Thorndike, *Individuality,* pp. 40, 36.

33. Ibid., pp. 37-38.

34. Edward L. Thorndike, *Human Nature and the Social Order* (New York: Macmillan Co., 1940), pp. 455, 957. Readers here should be cautioned that if they are seeking a clear understanding of Thorndike's ideas on sterilization and eugenics, they ought to use this edition, not the edited and abridged version by Geraldine Joncich Clifford (Cambridge, Mass.: M.I.T. Press, 1969). The latter work omits many of Thorndike's more significant and revealing statements on the subject. The above quote from p. 455, for example, does not appear in the latter work.

35. Ibid., pp. 957-62.

36. Edward L. Thorndike, "A Sociologist's Theory of Education," *Bookman* 24 (1906-7): 294. See also Edward L. Thorndike, "Scientific Books," *Science* 24 (Sept. 1906): 299-301.

37. Edward L. Thorndike, *Your City* (New York: Harcourt, Brace and Co., 1939), p. 22.

38. Ibid., pp. 29-31.

39. See *Science News Letter* 35 (May 6, 1939): 284-85.

40. Thorndike, *Your City,* p. 77.

41. *Science News Letter,* p. 285.

42. Thorndike, *Your City,* p. 67.

43. Edward L. Thorndike, *144 Smaller Cities* (New York: Harcourt, Brace and Co., 1940), p. 91.

44. This position can also be found among his earlier works; see, for example, Edward L. Thorndike, "Eugenics: With Special Reference to Intellect and Character," *Popular Science Monthly* 83 (Aug. 1913): 125-38.

45. "Best Cities Distinguished by Dentists, Not Clergymen," *Science News Letter,* p. 284. It should be noted that Thorndike's finding—the prevalence of dentists over clergymen in the upper-class suburban communities—comes as no surprise. Lower-class people seldom can afford the luxury of dental care, whereas upper-middle-class people can. Furthermore, church attendance had been dropping off among the white upper-middle-class population during the 1930s.

Barbara Beatty (essay date 1998)

SOURCE: "From Laws of Learning to a Science of Values: Efficiency and Morality in Thorndike's Educational Psychology," in *American Psychologist,* Vol. 53, No. 10, October, 1998, pp. 1145-52.

[*In the following essay, Beatty discusses the ways in which Thorndike developed and then marketed his notions about using scientific methodology in educational psychology to create an empirical way of measuring morality and character.*]

In the first sentence of the expanded 1911 edition of *Animal Intelligence* Edward L. Thorndike listed "intellect" and "character" (Thorndike, 1911, p. 1) as the two topics of behavioristic psychology. Thorndike researched and reworked these themes throughout the successive phases of his long career. Following his path-breaking animal experiments, he found employment in teacher education. He briefly explored G. Stanley Hall's child study, but rejected developmentalism on intellectual, methodological, and moral grounds and began measuring individual differences. In the years before World War I, Thorndike combined learning theory, psychometrics, and applied research on school-related subjects to form a psychology of education. In the 1920s, he helped turn educational psychology into a mass-market industry and produced numerous commercially successful tests and textbooks. In the final phase of his career in the 1930s, Thorndike proposed a science of values and developed quantitative indices of moral and social goodness.

Thorndike's positing of intellect and character as the dual themes of behavioristic psychology reflected the unified view of truth and morality characteristic of nineteenth-century educational philosophy. Character education was one of the main goals of public schooling (Tyack & Hansot, 1982). Religious and intellectual knowledge were linked in higher education as well (Reuben, 1996). Darwin's theory of evolution threatened this unity of knowledge and morality, though Darwin was also interested in explaining altruism (see Curti, 1980; Fancher, 1996; Richards, 1987; Ross, 1991; Sulloway, 1998). The construction of an empirical science of psychology posed a particular challenge to traditional religious explanations of human thought and action. Despite these intellectual and cultural tensions, most turn-of-the-century psychologists continued to do research on both intellect and character and to see them as interrelated topics.

Psychologists in the Progressive Era were confronted with enormously difficult, contentious social issues. Rapid industrialization, urbanization, immigration, poverty, violent labor disputes, changing relations both between the sexes and within the family, and growing global unrest caused great dislocations and instability. Psychology was pulled out of philosophy to help explain, contain, cure, and control these social ills, especially in education (Danziger, 1990). Educators looked to psychologists for assistance in categorizing, socializing, and instructing the flood of immigrant and poor children entering urban schools (Brown, 1992; Chapman, 1988). Educational psychology arose in response to these practical educational needs, and as a means of professionalizing education and expanding the profession of psychology.

Thorndike's project of creating a science of education was not new. Earlier nineteenth-century attempts had included deriving pedagogy from classroom practice; from psychological philosophy, especially that of Herbert Spencer and Alexander Bain; and from European pedagogical theories such as those of Pestalozzi, Froebel, and Herbart (Roberts, 1968). G. Stanley Hall amassed survey data that he claimed constituted a scientific approach to the study of children and education (Ross, 1972; White, 1990; Zenderland, 1990). Psychological methods were also being used by educators outside of academia. But some psychologists, such as William James, were skeptical as to whether education could become a science (James, 1899; and see Beatty, 1996; Brown, 1992; Cahan & White, 1992; Cuban, 1993; Danziger, 1990; Kliebard, 1986; O'Donnell, 1985; White, 1991).

However different psychologists in the Progressive Era conceived of the relationship of science, education, and morality, most equated science and efficiency. They believed their research would aid in the creation of a more rational, orderly, beneficent society (see Callahan, 1963; Kloppenburg, 1986; Wiebe, 1967). G. Stanley Hall used developmentalism to guide educational, moral, and social decision making (Ross, 1972). John Dewey was also concerned with preventing waste and building intellect and character and attempted to merge education, morality, and society through metaphors of organic growth and democratic community (Cahan, 1992; Ryan, 1995). Thorndike used connectionist learning theory to operationalize the relationship of education, morality, and society. How did Thorndike deal with intangible issues in morality and social policy? How did Thorndike attempt to maximize both efficiency and morality? How did Thorndike evolve from thinking science was separate from human ideals to believing that science should help set moral and social goals?

STUDYING CHILDREN AND REJECTING
DEVELOPMENTALISM

Thorndike was initially drawn from animal psychology into education for professional reasons. Like other young psychologists who received doctorates around the turn of the century, he encountered a dearth of academic positions in psychology (Jonçich, 1968). Psychology enrollments grew more rapidly in the 1890s than did the demand for psychologists. As Hugo Münsterberg wrote in 1898 to James McKeen Cattell, "my elementary psychology course . . . has 360 students—what will this country do with all these psychologists?" (quoted in Brown, 1992, p. 65). The answer was that many of them, like Thorndike, would find jobs in child study and teacher education programs (Dewsbury, 1992; O'Donnell, 1985).

Thorndike's early publications, after *Animal Intelligence,* showed the influence of William James and G. Stanley Hall, two older psychologists who had written about education and morality. James's well-known interest in spirituality was evident in Thorndike's book *The Human Nature Club,* first published in 1900, which Thorndike hoped would sell as well as James's very successful *Talks to Teachers* (1899). Intended for a popular audience of high-school and teacher-education students and adults interested in self-education, *The Human Nature Club* was written in the form of a fictional dialogue among members of a study group. After conversations on Jamesian themes of sensation, attention, memory, emotions, and so on, the club turns to "deeper questions" of free will and immortality. A minister joins the group and expresses what Thorndike may have wished his own deeply religious, Methodist minister father might have said—that though the Bible taken "as a piece of history" provided "evidence for continuance of mental life apart from the body," the psychological ideas the group was discussing did not (Thorndike, 1901a, pp. 201-202). One of the characters paraphrases James's *Human Immortality,* saying that "nerve cells might be just the means for *transmitting* . . . thought and feelings, which might exist apart, but as light penetrates through transparent substances, so might they appear in connection with . . . human brains" (Thorndike, 1901a, p. 210). The debate concludes with the passage from Plato's *Apologia* in which Socrates goes to his death saying that whether or not there is an afterlife one must act on the basis of conscience (Thorndike, 1901a, pp. 212-213).

G. Stanley Hall's child study methodology was the topic of Thorndike's next major publication, and of some of his courses at Teachers College, where he was hired in 1899 as an instructor in genetic psychology. *Notes on Child Study,* which appeared in 1901, contained criticisms of Hall but sounded some typically Hallian moral and social themes. Thorndike recommended the morally beneficial effects of fresh air, exercise, and healthy companions. But he advocated athletic "games and social clubs . . . for girls as well as boys" (Thorndike, 1901b, p. 127), unlike Hall, who was notoriously anxious about preserving masculinity. Thorndike was particularly critical of Hall's untrammeled developmentalism. For Thorndike, the interesting aspect of studying children was not how they were developmentally the same, but how they were individually different. General statements about children "must be false," Thorndike wrote, "for no two children are alike mentally" (Thorndike, 1901b, p. 14). All statements about children were probabilities, Thorndike asserted, probabilities which could be stated with a level of statistical accuracy.

Thorndike knew that children were different from adults and included in his work a chart of children's developmental stages (Thorndike, 1901b, p. 13), but he thought these differences were incremental. Even reasoning, which Charles Judd championed as a qualitatively different kind of higher order process, was essentially incremental for Thorndike. Thorndike asserted that all the rudiments of rational thought were present by the time a child entered school "and in fact long before then" (Thorndike, 1901b, p. 86). The great importance of schooling was that it was one of the main ways children honed their reasoning. Step by step "little by little," Thorndike wrote, "through constant correction and revision," children gradually learned academic skills and knowledge, until they acquired "the usage of science or literature of educated people" (Thorndike, 1901b, p. 87). And step by step, Thorndike honed his own views on education, society, and morality.

Thorndike was vehemently opposed to Hall's notion that the school curriculum should follow nature and recapitu-

late the stages of human cultural development. Not only was Hall's developmentalism intellectually uninteresting and methodologically inexact, Thorndike thought it was immoral and potentially dangerous. Schooling should improve upon nature. Not everything in nature was good; there were base instincts as well as good ones. Educators should use the impulses of nature only if they "further the aims of education, . . . when they work toward moral ideals" (Thorndike, 1901b, p. 136). "What development is can never teach what it ought to be," Thorndike stated, condemning Hall for committing the naturalistic fallacy. "No word perhaps is a poorer synonym for 'the good' than 'the natural'" (Thorndike, 1901b, p. 136).

MEASURING INDIVIDUAL DIFFERENCES AND CONSTRUCTING EDUCATIONAL PSYCHOLOGY

Although Thorndike rejected Hall's developmentalism and genetic psychology, he did not reject the genetic component of individual differences. For Hall, genetic psychology meant the history of the development of the human race; for Thorndike, genetic psychology meant biologically inherited characteristics in individuals. Thorndike spent the next decade and a half constructing an empirical psychology of education based on connectionist learning theory, statistical analyses of inherited and acquired individual differences, and other school-related research. The broad range of topics in his research course, Psychology 13, reflected Thorndike's changing interests. The syllabus for the 1900-1901 academic year included "mental life of the primates," "verbal discrimination in young children," the "correlations between the mental functions involved in school subjects," and the value of spelling and Latin as formal disciplines (Thorndike, 1901c, p. 10).

Some of this new research resulted in the publication of a study on transfer of training which was as influential as Thorndike's earlier work on animal intelligence. In association with his Columbia University colleague Robert S. Woodworth, Thorndike collected and correlated data from experiments on adults' ability to recognize misspelled words, ascertain accurate weights, add numbers, and associate word opposites. After only a few months, Thorndike and Woodworth reported that there was relatively little transfer of training from one of these disparate mental skills to another. This finding, which appeared in *The Psychological Review* in 1901, provided what was seen as one of the first empirical refutations of the concept of mental discipline, the prevailing theory in which the mental effort of learning subjects such as Greek or Latin was thought to improve the powers of the mind generally and to aid in learning other subjects (Thorndike & Woodworth, 1901).

Thorndike and Woodworth's (1901) findings spurred the growth of educational psychology by pointing to the need for new studies on the learning of specific academic skills and subjects. As Thorndike and Woodworth concluded, the

next steps in the study of the interdependence of mental functions would seem to be the exact analysis of the influence of one on the other where such is present and the discovery of its amount and nature in cases of practical importance, for instance, in the case of the training given in school subjects.

(Thorndike & Woodworth, 1901, p. 563)

Although Thorndike remained personally ambivalent about doing school-based research and relied heavily on data gathered by his graduate students and other researchers, his work with Woodworth convinced him of the need for more experimental studies of school learning, and he did some research in schools during the early years of his career (Jonçich, 1968, p. 231).

Thorndike infused this school-related work with theories derived from his research on animals and statistical analyses of individual differences in humans. Here again his intellectual program, research agenda, and publications were influenced by the demands of his teaching responsibilities and desire for professional advancement. By 1902 he was teaching Education 3, "Applications of Psychology in Teaching," a required elementary education course with large enrollments, which he had petitioned dean James Russell that he be given to teach. He changed its title to "Educational Psychology" and added a graduate level course, Education 3, "Application of Psychological and Statistical Methods to Education" (Jonçich, 1968; Thorndike, 1901c).

As Thorndike focused more on statistical methodology, his work became increasingly filled with graphs, curves, and charts. This wealth of quantitative information was intended to help teachers and educational administrators deal with practical educational problems. For example, Thorndike studied the question of whether boys and girls should be educated differently, an issue about which G. Stanley Hall, Dr. Edward Clarke, and others had made a great deal of noise, even though coeducation had proceeded quietly in most American public schools (Tyack & Hansot, 1990). After analyzing empirical data, Thorndike stated that the "differences in ability" were "not of sufficient amount to be important in arguments concerning differentiation of the curriculum or of methods of teaching in conformity with sex differences" (Thorndike, 1903, p. 118).

Although Thorndike did not think there were significant sex differences in intellectual ability, he thought there was a strong genetic component to individual variation, including variation in morality. He published studies on heredity and on twins in 1903 and 1905, quoted Galton frequently, and thought intellect had such a high, fixed genetic component that, to be efficient, schools should group children into different classes and programs by ability. Thorndike's hard-nosed position on genetic limitations on human potential and the inefficiency of providing equal education to all children was to become one of the main, longstanding criticisms of his work (see Jonçich, 1962, 21-22). "It is wasteful," he wrote in the 1903 version of his *Educational Psychology,* "to attempt to create and folly to pretend to create capacities and interests which are assumed or de-

nied to an individual before he is born" (p. 44). Thorndike also thought there was a genetic component to morality. But in contrast to his views on intelligence, at this early stage in his career he felt that environmental influences had a greater impact on character than on intellect, a position he would later modify. "The important moral traits seem to be matters of the direction of capacities and the creation of desires and aversions by environment to a much greater extent than are the important qualities of intellect and efficiency" (Thorndike, 1903, p. 45).

Using empirical data to make specific educational decisions was the raison d'etre of Thorndike's educational psychology. He did not think there was, or ever could be, a grand, overarching theory of education. Nor was he interested in creating one. His goal was to measure individual and group differences and the myriad particularities of human learning. As he wrote in his 1903 *Educational Psychology,* "there is no chance for any simple general theory"; the "true general theory must be the helpless one that there can be no general theory" (p. 163). What educational psychology could do was more modest. It could provide educators with lots of detailed information. "Multiply the number of different changes desired by the number of different original natures to be changed and the resulting number of concrete problems will measure the number of separate concrete precepts which the art of education must include," he concluded, with a specificity that would carry over to his views on moral education and later attempts to measure morality (Thorndike, 1903, p. 163).

In the years before World War I Thorndike wrote about instructional methods and assessment and established educational psychology as an academic discipline. In his first pedagogical work, *The Principles of Teaching,* published in 1906, he applied his learning theory to classroom teaching. Designed as a text for Education A, the largest course at Teachers College, this widely used book combined summaries of basic psychology with practical exercises for student teachers. Thorndike emphasized throughout that there were no shortcuts to learning. "Each special task adds its mite to the general store." "Intellect and character" were strengthened "not by any subtle and easy metamorphosis, but the establishment of particular ideas and acts under the law of habit" (Thorndike, 1906, p. 247). In the chapter on moral training he included a long, convoluted quotation on the "good and efficient character" from his *Elements of Psychology,* which stated that character was in part dependent on "the presence of worthy ideals" (Thorndike, 1906, p. 179). He laboriously explained each step in the process of character formation and stated that although moral training in the school was more difficult than in the home, because of limitations of time, class size, and other curricular subjects, school education had "high moral value." Schools helped teach the everyday virtues, the small "ordinary moral acts" that Thorndike valued as much or more than dramatic moral choices (Thorndike, 1906, pp. 106, 192).

In the final chapter of *Principles of Teaching,* Thorndike stated the scientific creed of his educational psychology. The "scientific study of teaching," he said, rested on testing for results. "Testing the results of teaching and study is for the teacher what verification of theories is to the scientist,—the *sine qua non* of sure progress" (Thorndike, 1906, p. 264). "A true educational science . . . must be made up from the study of the particular facts in answer to thousands of different questions," Thorndike stated, and "must rest upon direct observations of and experiments on the influence of educational institutions and methods made and reported with quantitative precision" (Thorndike, 1906, p. 163). Without such meticulous testing, theories of education were mere speculation.

Thorndike knew the science of education was in its infancy and worried that its complexity and laboriousness might put many psychologists off. But he was firmly convinced that education could be made into a science and proceeded to do the organizational and professional work necessary to do so. In the lead article of the first issue of *The Journal of Educational Psychology,* which Thorndike founded in 1910, he presented an agenda for how psychology could contribute to education and vice versa. Psychology could make the goals of education clearer and more exact, could measure the probability that these goals were attainable, and could enlarge and refine the aims of education. It could also contribute to understanding the content and means of education and to improving of methods of teaching (Thorndike, 1910, pp. 5-7). Thorndike also thought that education could in turn help psychology. "The science of education can and will itself contribute abundantly to psychology" (Thorndike, 1910, p. 12). Psychology laboratories were not the only places where valid scientific research could be done. "School-room life itself is a vast laboratory in which are made thousands of experiments of the utmost interest to 'pure' psychology" (Thorndike, 1910, p. 12).

In *Education,* his book on educational philosophy, which was published in 1912, Thorndike set forth his utilitarian views on education, morality, and the behavioristic approach to moral education. In "the broad sense" morality was "simply such thought and action as promote the improvement and satisfaction of human wants." The "'right' thing to do," Thorndike said, was that "which a man who could foresee all the consequences of all acts, and who considered fairly the welfare of all men, would in that case choose." The "aims of education as a whole" were thus "identical with those of morality" (Thorndike, 1912, p. 29). Thorndike admonished teachers to model positive moral behavior, rather than talk about it. Using bullying as an example, he gave practical advice on what today would be called behavior modification techniques, in which undesirable behavior could be inhibited by being ignored, followed by "discomfort," or substituted with positive behavior (Thorndike, 1912, p. 200). With characteristic concern for efficiency, Thorndike advised that positive reinforcement was more effective than punishment. Associating "good responses" with "satisfaction is in general preferable to the elimination of bad responses by pain or deprivation." In situations where there were many possible responses punishment could be "very wasteful" (Thorndike, 1912, p. 201). Finding the right mixture of "incentives and deterrents" depended on the particular case and was "an intricate problem" (Thorndike, 1912, p. 202).

In his 1913-1914 magnum opus, *Educational Psychology,* Thorndike moved closer to a biological view of morality in which ideals were a product of evolution. Dedicated to the memory of William James, the three volumes dealt exhaustively with "man's original mental equipment—the inherited foundations of intellect, morals, and skill," "the laws of learning," and individual differences (Thorndike, 1913-1914, p. vii). Thorndike formalized his research on learning into his three famous laws, "the laws of Readiness, Exercise and Effect" (Thorndike, 1913-1914, p. 1). He now stated that although there was "warfare of man's ideals with his original tendencies," "ideals themselves came at some time from original yearnings in man" (1913-1914, V.I, p. 311). In his 1903 version of *Educational Psychology* Thorndike had still thought there were some intangible questions that could not be usefully addressed by facts. Answers to the question of the aim of education, for instance, of what "people ought to be," would come from "conceptions of ultimate values" and would be "judged not by facts but by ideals," (Thorndike, 1903, p. 163). A decade later, Thorndike's views on ideals were more genetic. And as his career progressed, there would be fewer reservations about questions which facts could not helpfully address or answer.

PUBLISHING TESTS AND TEXTS AND COMMERCIALIZING EDUCATIONAL PSYCHOLOGY

World War I provided confirmation of the usefulness of Thorndike's educational psychology and served as a catalyst for him to apply his research on a larger scale. The disappointing results of recruits' performance on the Army intelligence tests, which Thorndike had helped design and analyze, gave further impetus to the movement to develop widely available psychological products. Educational psychology boomed as a mass-market industry in the 1920s. In the years after the war, Thorndike produced a number of commercially successful school materials. In addition to the rating scales for handwriting, English composition, and drawing he had developed earlier, he created a word frequency book for teachers, dictionaries, and tests to measure oral and silent reading, geography, spelling, and other academic skills.

Thorndike became involved in commercial ventures that extended the influence of his work. Along with Cattell and Woodworth, he founded the Psychological Corporation in 1921 and standardized and copyrighted numerous educational and psychological tests. His most influential piece of curriculum "psychologizing" was his *Thorndike Arithmetics* series, published by Rand-McNally, (Thorndike, 1917, 1922) which sold extremely well and augmented his academic salary handsomely (Jonçich, 1968). These tests and texts were used throughout the United States and probably had more direct, lasting impact on children and schools than anything else Thorndike did.

Thorndike's educational products were successful in part because they were based on empirical research and appeared to be scientific. He claimed that the messiness of classroom teaching and learning could be transformed into a science; the mystique of science and his wealth of charts, curves, and statistics made his claims seem credible. Thorndike's products were also successful because they met educators' practical needs. His arithmetic books were easy for teachers to use and fit well with existing curricula and methods. His tests provided administrators with information on student achievement in a format that was useful and convincing for reporting purposes. And the standardized results of his assessments provided arguably fairer rationales for the selection functions society demanded of schools than did teachers' subjective ratings and grades.

True to his early rejection of developmentalism, Thorndike did not try to alter subject matter but accepted the traditional curriculum. His goals of making school curricula more rational and efficient and eliminating waste and redundancy were ideas that American teachers and parents could understand and accept. This public acceptance and commercial success, combined with the scientific "look" and usefulness of educational psychology, explains much about why Thorndike's methods won out over those of John Dewey (see Lagemann, 1989) and other more socially radical and child-centered educational philosophers and psychologists.

MEASURING MORALITY AND PROPOSING A SCIENCE OF VALUES

In the last phase of his career, Thorndike applied some of the methods of educational psychology to broad societal issues. Supported by a large grant from the Carnegie Corporation and by the staff and facilities of Columbia's Institute for Educational Research, he now had the time, resources, and inclination to focus on the social and moral questions that had been underlying themes throughout his earlier work. Although the Depression had shaken faith in the power of science to solve social problems, Thorndike remained a firm believer. He thought psychology could serve as the basic science for the rest of the social sciences (Jonçich, 1968) and began collecting data on industry, crime, labor, management, consumerism, government, law, economics, and all manner of other topics.

In *Your City* (1939), and other of the many studies that resulted from this enormous project, Thorndike went beyond measurement of specific facts to making normative and comparative evaluations of generic goodness. After statistical analyses of "over three hundred items of fact" on cities with populations of over 30,000 in 1930 (Thorndike, 1939, p. 21), he developed a "goodness" index based on 37 supposedly significant variables ranging from mortality rates, crime, home ownership, and teachers' salaries, to

"per capita park acreage" and circulation of *Better Homes, National Geographic, Good Housekeeping,* and *Literary Digest* (Thorndike, 1939, pp. 29-31). Aside from the almost comical subjectivity and class bias of some of Thorndike's variables, *Your City* shows how hard it was to do social science before the advent of computers and multivariate regression analysis.

Thorndike painstakingly calculated correlations among his variables and other statistics and reported his findings in detail. A "high percentage of Negro families," for instance, was "a bad sign" for a city's goodness index (Thorndike, 1939, p. 77). Not surprisingly, the cities with the lowest "G Scores" were in the South, although Woonsocket, Rhode Island, fared poorly as well. The highest scoring city was Pasadena, California (Thorndike, 1939, pp. 33-34). Thorndike then showed readers how they could measure their own cities, using a simple "ten-item city yardstick" that involved calculations such as obtaining the annual infant mortality rate, subtracting this number from 120, and multiplying the result by 2 (Thorndike, 1939, p. 153). Simplistic counting and numerology such as this was characteristic of the 1920s and 1930s, when statistical surveys were the rage in American education (see Lagemann, 1998). Thorndike's work provided the methodology for this kind of quasi-scientific research.

That Thorndike was trying to quantify a measure of goodness beyond a simple urban quality-of-life index was apparent in his last major book, *Human Nature and the Social Order,* which was published in 1940, the same year he resigned from the Teachers College faculty. Thorndike returned to some of the religious and moral questions he had dealt with in a lighter vein 40 years earlier in *The Human Nature Club.* On the question of the existence of life after death Thorndike now stated unequivocally that science was a more powerful explanatory system than religion. Although science could not provide information about the existence or nature of a "supernatural world," Thorndike argued that the value of believing in life after death should be viewed empirically and tested by its consequences. "If men had, during the past hundred years or thousand years, lived in the belief that the death of the body was the end of the person, who can be sure that they would have been less moral?" he asked. And in the future, would people be better off retaining traditional religious beliefs about immortality or by believing "that the fate of all men rested entirely with nature"? (Thorndike, 1940, p. 147). Thorndike thought answers to these and other "hard" questions should be determined by measuring the effects of such beliefs.

In *Human Nature and the Social Order,* Thorndike proposed the creation of a science of values that could inform moral and social decision making. He wanted to explore the "possibility and desirability of the existence of a natural science of values" that would "progress from and improve upon the best present opinions about what is good and what is bad by studying consequences of various conditions and events for the satisfaction of wants present and future" (Thorndike, 1940, p. 347). He rejected two other approaches to social valuation: religious and democratic methods. Thorndike said these "inferior procedures," trying "to discover what God's will is," and putting "it to a vote of all citizens, each being given equal weight" (Thorndike, 1940, p. 351), were problematic because they were not scientific. Science was Thorndike's religion. He did not approve of political or moral systems that did not maximize efficiency and rationality. "The God of science is revealed in reality, and science rebels against counting the votes of imbeciles and ignoramuses, who do not know what is for their own good, much less what is for the good of others" (Thorndike, 1940, p. 351). Unabashedly hereditarian and meritocratic, Thorndike thought more traditional, moral, political, and humanitarian views did not give enough weight to individual differences and was determined to find a scientific way to do so. "Ethics, politics and philanthropy have been guilty of neglecting individual differences, partly because doing so simplifies all problems, and partly because of the retention of theological and sentimental prejudices in favor of the similarity and equality of man" (Thorndike, 1940, p. 369).

Using methods similar to those he had used to assess handwriting and cities, Thorndike proposed a detailed, quantitative moral rating scale. This "system of weights" would combine both intellect and character and assign numerical scores for each. As on an intelligence test, an ordinary man would get a score of 100, while "Newton, Pasteur, Darwin, Dante, Milton, Bach, Beethoven, Leonardo da Vinci, and Rembrandt will count as 2000, and a vegetative idiot as about 1" (Thorndike, 1940, p. 372). Points would be added for "unselfishness, benevolence, and cooperativeness," exemplified by "Jane Addams, Madam Curie, Sidney and Beatrice Webb," and subtracted for "meaness and cruelty" (Thorndike, 1940, pp. 372-373). Young children would get extra points depending on their age, because they were "innocent," but no points were to be added for sex, family, wealth, or religious creed (Thorndike, 1940, p. 373). An individual child's score, however, was to be determined in part by those of her parents. Thus, "twenty-five percent of the plus or minus difference of his parents' average weight from 100 is combined with each child's intrinsic credit until the age of twenty-five" (Thorndike, 1940, p. 373). If a child's background was unknown, credits or penalties would be added "for being a member of a certain racial stock" (Thorndike, 1940, p. 373).

One of the most troubling aspects of this supposedly scientific moral weighting scale, other than its obvious racial bias and subjectivity, was Thorndike's belief that people who came out with high numbers were, and should be, more powerful. "Effective valuation," was "the total net result of the valuations of all the persons concerned, each weighted by the person's power" (Thorndike, 1940, p. 388). Thorndike was aware of the unfair, arbitrary, racist, and politically biased implications of disparities in power. He said, for instance, that a "magnate in business, government, the church, or literature" might see himself as "God, or God's special representative," and "grossly overrate the value" of his own wants, "or his family, or his church, or

his dogs, or white men, or artistic people, or thrifty people, or members of the Communist party" (Thorndike, 1940, p. 388). However because of his positivistic ideology, and possibly because of his own success in the business world, Thorndike accepted such power differentials as inevitable.

Nor was Thorndike able to resist the tendency to play God himself. His faith in the power of science and valuing of efficiency led him to espouse some highly undemocratic ideas. Like many other progressives, Thorndike supported eugenics and now proposed giving political power to the genetically more able (see Curti, 1980; Haller, 1984; Kevles, 1986). Thorndike had lectured on eugenics as early as 1913, but had stopped short of wholeheartedly recommending it (Thorndike, 1913). After more than 900 pages, the conclusion of *Human Nature and the Social Order* was an alarmingly simplistic list of 20 suggestions. Along with "increasing capital goods" and "the elimination of wars between and within nations," Thorndike recommended "better genes," "guidance by science," and a "national council of the able, good, and impartial endowed so as to be utterly their own masters" (Thorndike, 1940, pp. 957-961). Thorndike said he supported absolute meritocracy because quality "was better than equality" (Thorndike, 1940, p. 962). Despite the unreasonableness of some of these conclusions, his final recommendation was to have "Reasonable expectations" (Thorndike, 1940, p. 963).

Conclusion

When the state of the job market in psychology led Thorndike to shift his attention from animals to education, he maintained the nineteenth-century linkage between intellect and character. In *The Human Nature Club,* Thorndike questioned traditional religious views but allowed for the possibility of Jamesian spirituality. In *Notes on Child Study* he rejected Hall's developmentalism as uninteresting, inexact, and immoral and advocated differential rather than genetic psychology. In the first version of *Educational Psychology* Thorndike maintained that the moral aims of education should be determined by ideals, not facts, and that morality was more influenced by environment than intellect was. In *The Principles of Teaching* he described morality as a product of learning acquired through numerous specific connections. In the second version of *Educational Psychology* he stated a genetic view of the origins of ideals. At the end of his career, in *Human Nature and the Social Order,* he proposed a moral measurement system and advocated selective breeding to enhance individual and social goodness. Incrementally, like the connections in his theory of learning, Thorndike's explanations of morality became more efficiency-oriented, biologically-deterministic, and positivistic.

Most of Thorndike's early positions on education and morality were relatively conservative. Unlike some progressives, he did not challenge traditional assumptions about the content of curricula or the moral and political purposes of education. Thorndike transposed the culture of the laboratory onto the school. He created a seemingly empirical, marketable knowledge base for education that met the needs of psychologists and educators and responded to societal demands for order and efficiency. Thorndike's systematization and transformation of older, quasi-scientific theories of education to fit the emerging intellectual and methodological frameworks of experimentalism made educational psychology understandable and acceptable to academics (White, personal communication, November 11, 1997). Thorndike's regularization and rationalization of educational philosophies and instructional methods made educational psychology compatible with the "grammar of schooling" (Tyack & Cuban, 1995) and useful to schools and teachers. Thorndike's awareness and exploitation of the commercial possibilities of educational psychology established it in the economic sector and provided a profit motive which propelled further expansion of the field. Encouraged by this success and supported by a wealthy private foundation, Thorndike then applied his empirical methodology to a wide range of other social issues and attempted to measure moral worth, just as he had objectified, quantified, and commodified human learning.

It is not surprising that Thorndike's proposal for a science of values was not as successful as his educational psychology. It was subjective, unwieldy, and went against the grain of American religious and political traditions. But Thorndike should not be blamed if the thorniness of morality and politics proved unsuited to scientific analysis, or if traditional moral reasoning and democratic ethics did not diminish his satisfaction with what others might see as the troubling nature of many of his conclusions about moral and social values (Clifford, personal communication, January 14, 1998, p. 3). Most progressives believed unquestioningly in the ability of science to solve societal problems, and many supported eugenics. Few, if any, saw, or could be expected to foresee, the problematic consequences of some of their research and recommendations (see McCormick, 1990). If Thorndike was blinded by the precision of his statistics, so were many other psychologists and social scientists.

Character and intellect were pervasive topics in Thorndike's work and continued to be themes in behavioristic psychology, as the ideas of John Watson and books such as B. F. Skinner's *Walden Two* (1948) and *Beyond Freedom and Dignity* (1971), and Richard Hernstein and Charles Murray's *The Bell Curve* (1994) attest. Above all, however, Thorndike was a methodologist. He was an educational, moral, and social technician. Thorndike believed in lots of little measurements, not big theories. He excelled at doing exact, exacting analysis of data and reveled in work and findings other psychologists might have thought drudgery or minutia. Eagerness for "facts no matter how uninspiring," Thorndike wrote as the last sentence of **Human Nature and the Social Order,** would contribute more to "beneficent reforms" than "governments, churches, and social reformers in search of wholesale salvation" (Thorndike, 1940, p. 963).

References

Beatty, B. (1996). Rethinking the historical role of psychology in educational reform. In D. Olson & N. Torrance (Eds.), *The handbook of education and human development* (pp. 100-116). Oxford, England: Blackwell.

Brown, J. (1992). *The definition of a profession: The authority of metaphor in the history of intelligence testing, 1890-1930.* Princeton, NJ: Princeton University Press.

Cahan, E. D. (1992). Dewey and development. *Developmental Psychology, 28,* 205-214.

Cahan, E. D., & White, S. H. (1992). Proposals for a second psychology. *American Psychologist, 47,* 224-235.

Callahan, R. E. (1963). *Education and the cult of efficiency.* Chicago: University of Chicago Press.

Chapman, P. D. (1988). *Schools as sorters: Lewis M. Terman, applied psychology, and the intelligence testing movement.* New York: New York University Press.

Cuban, L. (1993). *How teachers taught: Constancy and change in American classrooms, 1880-1990.* New York: Teachers College Press.

Curti, M. (1980). *Human nature in American thought.* Madison: University of Wisconsin Press.

Danziger, K. (1990). *Constructing the subject: The historical origins of psychological research.* Cambridge, England: Cambridge University Press.

Dewsbury, D. A. (1992). Triumph and tribulation in the history of American comparative psychology. *Journal of Comparative Psychology, 106,* 3-19.

Fancher, R. E. (1996). *Pioneers of psychology* (3rd ed.). New York: Norton.

Haller, M. H. (1984). *Eugenics: Hereditarian attitudes in American life.* New Brunswick, NJ: Rutgers University Press.

Hernstein, R. J., & Murray, C. (1994). *The bell curve: Intelligence and class structure in American life.* New York: The Free Press.

James, W. J. (1899). *Talks to teachers.* New York: H. Holt.

Jonçich, G. M. (1962). Science: Touchstone for a new age in education. In G. M. Jonçich (Ed.), *Psychology and the science of education. Selected writings of Edward L. Thorndike* (pp. 1-26). New York: Bureau of Publications, Teachers College, Columbia University.

Jonçich, G. (1968). *The sane positivist: A biography of Edward L. Thorndike.* Middletown, CT: Wesleyan University Press.

Kevles, D. J. (1986). *In the name of eugenics.* New York: Knopf.

Kliebard, H. M. (1986). *The struggle for the American curriculum, 1893-1958.* Boston: Routledge & Kegan Paul.

Kloppenburg, J. T. (1986). *Uncertain victory: Social democracy and progressivism in European and American thought, 1870-1920.* New York: Oxford University Press.

Lagemann, E. C. (1989). The plural worlds of educational research. *History of Education Quarterly, 29,* 185-214.

Lagemann, E. C. (1998). Contested terrain: A history of education research in the United States, 1890-1990. *Educational Researcher, 26,* 9, 5-17.

McCormick, R. L. (1990). Public life in industrial America. In E. Foner (Ed.), *The new American history* (pp. 93-118). Philadelphia: Temple University Press.

O'Donnell, J. M. (1985). *The origins of behaviorism: American psychology, 1870-1920.* New York: New York University Press.

Reuben, J. (1996). *The making of the modern university: Intellectual transformation and the marginalization of morality.* Chicago: University of Chicago Press.

Richards, R. J. (1987). *Darwin and the emergence of evolutionary theories of mind and behavior.* Chicago: University of Chicago Press.

Roberts, J. R. (1968, Winter). The quest for a science of education in the nineteenth century. *History of Education Quarterly, 8,* 431-446.

Ross, D. (1972). *G. Stanley Hall: The psychologist as prophet.* Chicago: University of Chicago Press.

Ross, D. (1991). *The origins of American social science.* New York: Cambridge University Press.

Ryan, A. (1995). *John Dewey and the high tide of American liberalism.* New York: Norton.

Skinner, B. F. (1948). *Walden two.* New York: Macmillan.

Skinner, B. F. (1971). *Beyond freedom and dignity.* New York: Knopf.

Sulloway, F. J. (1998). Darwinian virtues. *New York Review of Books, XLV, 6,* 34-40.

Thorndike, E. L. (1901a). *The human nature club: An introduction to the study of mental life.* New York: Longmans, Green.

Thorndike, E. L. (1901b, June). Notes on child study [Monograph]. *Columbia University Contributions to Philosophy, Psychology, and Education, 8,* (Nos. 3-4). New York: Macmillan.

Thorndike, E. L. (1901c). The study of children. *Teachers College Record, 2,* 1-11.

Thorndike, E. L. (1903). *Educational psychology* New York: Lemcke & Buechner.

Thorndike, E. L. (1905). *The elements of psychology.* New York: A. G. Seiler.

Thorndike, E. L. (1906). *The principles of teaching, based on psychology.* New York: A. G. Seiler.

Thorndike, E. L. (1910). The contribution of psychology to education. *The Journal of Educational Psychology, 1,* 5-12.

Thorndike, E. L. (1911). *Animal intelligence.* New York: Macmillan.

Thorndike, E. L. (1912). *Education, a first book.* New York: Macmillan.

Thorndike, E. L. (1913, August). Eugenics. *Popular Science Monthly, 70,* 125-138.

Thorndike, E. L. (1913-1914). *Educational psychology.* New York: Teachers College Press.

Thorndike, E. L. (1917). *The Thorndike arithmetics, Books 1-3.* Chicago: Rand-McNally.

Thorndike, E. L. (1922). *The psychology of arithmetic.* New York: Macmillan.

Thorndike, E. L. (1939). *Your city.* New York: Harcourt, Brace.

Thorndike, E. L. (1940). *Human nature and the social order.* New York: Macmillan.

Thorndike, E. L., & Woodworth, R. S. (1901, May, July, November). The influence of improvement in one mental function upon the efficiency of the other. *Psychological Review, 8,* 247-261, 381-395, 556-564.

Tyack, D. B., & Cuban, L. (1995). *Tinkering toward utopia: A century of American public school reform.* Cambridge, MA: Harvard University Press.

Tyack, D. B., & Hansot, E. (1982). *Managers of virtue: Public school teachership in America, 1820-1980.* New York: Basic Books.

Tyack, D. B., & Hansot, E. (1990). *Learning together: A history of coeducation in American schools.* New Haven, CT: Yale University Press.

White, S. H. (1990). Child study at Clark University: 1894-1904. *Journal of the History of the Behavioral Sciences 24,* 131-150.

White, S. H. (1991). Three visions of a psychology of education. In L. T. Landesman (Ed.), *Culture, schooling, and psychological development* (pp. 1-38). Norwood, NJ: Ablex.

Wiebe, R. H. (1967). *The search for order, 1877-1920.* New York: Hill & Wang.

Zenderland, L. (1990). Education, evangelism, and the origins of clinical psychology: The child study legacy. *Journal of the History of the Behavioral Sciences, 24,* 152-165.

Donald A. Dewsbury (essay date 1998)

SOURCE: "Celebrating E. L. Thorndike a Century After *Animal Intelligence,*" in *American Psychologist,* Vol. 53, No. 10, October, 1998, pp. 1121-24.

[*In the following essay, Dewsbury provides an overview of Thorndike's life and career.*]

This is a year in which to celebrate the career of one of the most productive and influential of all American psychologists, Edward Lee Thorndike (1874-1949). It is the centenary of the publication of his doctoral dissertation, **"Animal Intelligence: An Experimental Study of the Associative Processes in Animals"** (E. L. Thorndike, 1898), a key work in shifting the focus of much thought about animal behavior and in the development of animal experimental psychology. However, Thorndike's influence was much wider than this. His animal research was confined primarily to the early years of his career. His work on psychometrics and educational psychology dominated most of his academic career and had considerable impact.

In the set of articles that follows, we explore various aspects of Thorndike's career. Rather than try to provide a comprehensive treatment, we deal in as much depth as possible in articles of this length with three divergent aspects of Thorndike's oeuvre. More comprehensive treatments of Thorndike's life and career can be found in the book-length biography of Jonçich (1968a), the autobiographical chapter of E. L. Thorndike (1936), or the articles by Gates (1949), Humphrey (1949), Goodenough (1950), Jonçich (1968b), R. L. Thorndike (1991), and Woodworth (1952).

Synopsis of the Life and Career of E. L. Thorndike

Thorndike was born in Williamsburg, Massachusetts, the second of four children, each of whom would have important academic careers. He received a bachelor of arts degree from Wesleyan University in 1895, a second bachelor of arts from Harvard University the next year, and a Harvard master of arts degree in 1897. Thorndike received his doctorate from Columbia University in 1897. His three-year career as a graduate student was a busy one. His interest in Harvard had been piqued by William James's (1890) *Principles of Psychology*. Thorndike began research at Harvard with studies of the facial expressions of young children in mind-reading experiments. When the university would not permit him to continue this line of work, he switched to animal research and studied the behavior of chickens, first in the room in which he lived, and later in the cellar of James's home. Granted a fellowship, Thorndike took himself and his two "most educated chickens" (E. L. Thorndike, 1936, p. 265) to Columbia University to complete graduate work under James McKeen Cattell. There he completed his dissertation work on animal intelligence. After a year on the faculty of Western Reserve University, Thorndike returned to the Teachers College at Columbia, where he spent the rest of his career.

As psychology was developing during the early years of the century, there was a greater demand for applied work than for work in animal intelligence (Dewsbury, 1992; O'Donnell, 1985) and Thorndike responded to the pressures and helped to develop the fields of applied psychology. Most of the remainder of his career was in educational psychology.

By the time Thorndike's career was over, his bibliography included some 508 titles, including over 50 books. This includes work in such diverse areas as animal learning and imitation, mental testing, educational psychology, children's dictionaries, and the relative evaluation of different cities as places to live.

Work in Animal Learning

In the field of animal learning, E. L. Thorndike's (1898) dissertation, which psychologists are celebrating this year, was followed up with several additional articles; the material from five articles was brought together with two original essays in *Animal Intelligence: Experimental Studies* (E. L. Thorndike, 1911). Thorndike's position, resulting from his experimental work, was that learning is the result of trial and error followed by accidental success. This process was most clearly illustrated by his classic studies of cats escaping from puzzle boxes. The successes led to a strengthening of connections, a process that Thorndike termed the *law of effect,* but that today, shorn of some terminology judged to be mentalistic, would be called *reinforcement.* Learning is gradual, not the result of understanding, reasoning, or insight. It does not require conscious processes: The greater the number of repetitions, the better the learning; this is Thorndike's law of exercise. Furthermore, all animals learn in fundamentally the same way. Differences among species are merely a matter of degree, not kind. Thorndike's thinking on this issue changed from 1898 to 1901 and 1911 as he came to think of human learning as more similar to that in other species than he had originally thought (see Bruce, 1997).

Thorndike's work was not without its problems. C. Lloyd Morgan, who inspired some of Thorndike's research, was critical of several aspects of Thorndike's formulation (Morgan, 1898). For instance, Morgan believed that Thorndike's experimental situation did not provide a good opportunity for reasoning to occur: "The conditions of his experiments were perhaps not the most conducive to the discovery of rationality in animals if it exist" (Morgan, 1898, p. 249). This theme was expanded by T. Wesley Mills (1899), who also believed that Thorndike gave his animals no opportunity to display reasoning; he wrote "as well enclose a living man in a coffin, lower him, against his will, into the earth, and attempt to deduce normal psychology from his conduct" (Mills, 1899, p. 266). This critique, in turn, led to a sharp reply from E. L. Thorndike (1899).

It was immediately apparent that Thorndike's work signaled a shift from speculation to experimentation under controlled conditions. Morgan (1898) applauded Thorndike's "experiment under conditions allowing for some control" (p. 249) and expressed "the hope that comparative psychology has passed from the anecdote stage to the higher plane of verifiable observation, and that it is rising to the dignity of science" (p. 250). At the same time, it appears that Thorndike's view that all species learn in roughly the same manner led animal psychologists to concentrate on a few species, such as laboratory rats, rather than develop a broader and more comprehensive science of behavior (but see Bruce, 1997).

WOODS HOLE[1]

An important influence on Thorndike's later work, deserving of further study, was the summers he spent in Massachusetts beginning in 1899 at the Marine Biological Station at Woods Hole. There, he met and interacted with such scientists as Robert Yerkes, Jacques Loeb, and Charles Otis Whitman.

Two of Thorndike's Woods Hole lectures were published (E. L. Thorndike, 1900a, 1900b). The second dealt with animal learning and the first with instinct. The instinct lecture followed Whitman's (1899) lecture, which is often considered to have provided the conceptual foundation for the development of European ethology. Thorndike accepted Whitman's arguments concerning the inherited nature of instinctive behavior, a notable event in the history of comparative psychology. Further, however, he cautioned that "since instinctive activities are the results of gradual development, they should be, not merely enumerated, described, and explained as to their utility, but also explained as to their development and relationships" (E. L. Thorndike, 1900b, p. 67). This passage is remarkable because it states concisely the issue that would divide many American comparative psychologists from European ethologists half a century later (e.g., Lehrman, 1953). The lecture also reflects the sympathy for evolutionary approaches that was characteristic of true comparative psychologists throughout the past 100 years.

In his work with human intelligence, Thorndike, like many of his contemporaries, was a strong hereditarian. It is likely that these Woods Hole experiences were important in shaping these views.

WORK IN EDUCATIONAL PSYCHOLOGY

Thorndike carried the same positivistic approach he had applied to research with nonhumans to his work with humans. One area of interest was in the famous transfer of training work done with Robert S. Woodworth (E. L. Thorndike & Woodworth, 1901). They studied the transfer of learning from one situation to another and concluded that the degree of positive or negative transfer was a function of the number of elements shared between the two situations. Extending this result led to a refutation of the belief that training in a narrow area, such as learning Latin or Greek, would benefit later performance in a wide variety of situations.

Thorndike's view of intelligence was consistent with that in animal learning. Thorndike "held that the only general ability was the ability to learn associations or connections. A higher level of ability simply depends on more numerous and more subtle connections" (Woodworth, 1952, p. 214).

Although he was not well trained in mathematics, Thorndike's approach to mental testing was a quantitative one. His *The Measurement of Intelligence* (E. L. Thorndike, Cobb, Woodyard, & staff, 1926) presented his CAVD scale based on completion, arithmetic, vocabulary, and directions. A total of 17 levels of difficulty were included. Thorndike thus promoted a doctrine of specificity of abilities and opposed Charles Spearman's construct of a general factor in intelligence (g). Thorndike viewed the correlations among tasks found by Spearman as due to the proportion of connections shared among tasks.

HUMAN LEARNING

Thorndike returned to the study of learning during the 1920s and 1930s (e.g., E. L. Thorndike, 1931, 1932). The positive effects of reward in the law of effect were confirmed but he revised his view that punishment led to a weakening of connections. Although punishment sometimes can be beneficial, he now believed that it worked mainly by causing the organism to shift its behavior to another response.

OTHER WORK

It is impossible to capture the range of Thorndike's interests in a short introduction. One systematic program was the investigation of the value of different cities as places in which good people might live (e.g., E. L. Thorndike, 1939). This effort is carried on by others today and causes a great flurry of publicity when the results are announced each year.

A major contribution was the production of English dictionaries written for school use with careful attention so that the words used in providing definitions would be those already familiar to the young readers (E. L. Thorndike, 1935). Similarly, he helped to develop mathematics textbooks with problems phrased in ways that would be easily understood by children (E. L. Thorndike, 1917). Thorndike's studies of word frequencies in the English language (e.g., E. L. Thorndike & Lorge, 1944) were of considerable help in such endeavors.

When Thorndike entered the field of vocational guidance (E. L. Thorndike, 1934), it was again with the goal of permitting solid decisions to be based on solid data. The results were generally disappointing, however (R. L. Thorndike, 1991).

WHAT KIND OF MAN?

Jonçich (1968a), following Robert Woodworth, entitled her biography of Thorndike *The Sane Positivist.* Clearly, Thorndike was that. He was a Progressive in a progressive era; he believed in the betterment of humankind and that empirical science provided the road to that betterment. Thorndike was a scientist first and foremost. He was not a visionary or a dreamer; he was not a planner. In the words of his son, "he was not by temperament a systematist but rather an empiricist, a conductor of investigations and an analyzer of data" (R. L. Thorndike, 1991, p. 140). He conducted experiments. He created situations in which experimental treatments would lead to fairly precise conclusions under controlled conditions. He then tried to apply his results in a no-nonsense manner to the alleviation of problems in society. As his son put it, "he applied a certain amount of formal psychology and a considerably larger dose of shrewd common sense to rationalizing instruction in a wide range of fields" (R. L. Thorndike, 1991, pp. 141-142). In a very American way, the line between theoretical and applied science was blurred. His positivism was "sane" in that it was reasoned, eclectic, useful, and down-to-earth.

Jonçich (1968b) treats him as "victim of the optimistic and widespread assumptions of nineteenth century positivism" (p. 440). "That knowledge is power, that truth can be known, that facts can be trusted—these approached copybook maxims in Thorndike's youth, and such ideas no less distinguished those inducted into science in its perhaps most optimistic age" (p. 440). Such sentiments are still present in parts of psychology, but many other parts have been strongly influenced by positions of relativism, postmodernism, and social constructionism. Adherents to such views would regard Thorndike's position as naive, but perhaps characteristic of the Progressivism of the time.

Physically, Thorndike was described as a bear of a man, but a man who was friendly, generous, and kind. He had a buoyant good humor and a sparkling wit. These made him a fine companion and teacher. In his younger days he was an avid tennis player. Outside of his academic life, he fit the role of a country gentleman (Gates, 1949). He was a workaholic largely because analyzing data was what he enjoyed more than anything else (R. L. Thorndike, 1991).

RECOGNITION

Edward L. Thorndike received many of the awards and other signs of recognition one would expect of a psychologist of his accomplishment and stature. He received honorary doctorates from Columbia University (1929), the University of Chicago (1932), the University of Athens, Greece (1937), the University of Iowa (1923), and the University of Edinburgh (1936). He received the Butler Medal from Columbia University in 1925. Thorndike was elected to the National Academy of Sciences in 1917 and the American Philosophical Society in 1932. He was elected a fellow of the American Academy of Arts and Sciences in 1934. He was elected a fellow in 1901, Vice President in 1902, and President in 1919-1920 of the New York Academy of Sciences; a Fellow in 1901, Vice President in 1911, and President in 1934 of the American Association for the Advancement of Science; President of the American Psychological Association in 1912; President of the Psychometric Society in 1936-1937; and President of the American Society for Adult Education in 1934-1935. In addition, he received various lectureships, election to various committees, and memberships in such organizations as Phi Beta Kappa, Sigma Xi, the British Psychological Society (honorary), the Leningrad Scientific-

Medical Pedological Society (honorary), and the Comenius Educational Association of Czechoslovakia (honorary) (Woodworth, 1952). . . .

Note

1. *Woods Hole* was spelled *Woods Holl* when Thorndike studied there. The titles of his publications from this period use the earlier spelling.

References

Bruce, D. (1997). Puzzling over animal intelligence. *Contemporary Psychology, 42,* 879-882.

Dewsbury, D. A. (1992). Triumph and tribulation in the history of American comparative psychology. *Journal of Comparative Psychology, 106,* 3-19.

Gates, A. I. (1949). Edward L. Thorndike 1874-1949. *Psychological Review, 56,* 241-243.

Goodenough, F. L. (1950). Edward Lee Thorndike: 1874-1949. *American Journal of Psychology, 63,* 291-301.

Humphrey, G. (1949). Edward Lee Thorndike, 1874-1949. *British Journal of Psychology, 40,* 55-56.

James, W. (1890). *Principles of psychology.* New York: Holt.

Jonçich, G. (1968a). *The sane positivist: A biography of Edward L. Thorndike.* Middletown, CT: Wesleyan University Press.

Jonçich, G. (1968b). E. L. Thorndike: The psychologist as professional man of science. *American Psychologist, 23,* 434-446.

Lehrman, D. S. (1953). A critique of Konrad Lorenz's theory of instinctive behavior. *Quarterly Review of Biology, 28,* 337-363.

Mills, W. (1899). The nature of intelligence and the methods of investigating it. *Psychological Review, 6,* 262-274.

Morgan, C. L. (1898). Animal intelligence: An experimental study. *Nature, 58,* 249-250.

O'Donnell, J. M. (1985). *The origins of behaviorism: American psychology, 1870-1920.* New York: New York University Press.

Thorndike, E. L. (1898). Animal intelligence: An experimental study of the associative processes in animals. *Psychological Review Monograph Supplement, 2,* 1-109.

Thorndike, E. L. (1899). A reply to "The nature of animal intelligence and the methods of investigating it." *Psychological Review, 6,* 412-420.

Thorndike, E. L. (1900a). The associative processes in animals. *Biological lectures from the Marine Biological Laboratory of Woods Holl 1899* (pp. 69-91). Boston: Ginn & Company.

Thorndike, E. L. (1900b). Instinct. *Biological lectures from the Marine Biological Laboratory of Woods Holl 1899* (pp. 57-67). Boston: Ginn & Company.

Thorndike, E. L. (1911). *Animal intelligence: Experimental studies.* New York: Macmillan.

Thorndike, E. L. (1917). *The Thorndike arithmetics, Books 1-3.* Chicago: Rand-McNally.

Thorndike, E. L. (1931). *Human learning.* New York: Century.

Thorndike, E. L. (1932). *The fundamentals of learning.* New York: Teachers College, Columbia University Press.

Thorndike, E. L. (1934). *Prediction of vocational success.* New York: Teachers College, Columbia University Press.

Thorndike, E. L. (1935). *Thorndike-Century junior dictionary.* Chicago: Scott Foresman.

Thorndike, E. L. (1936). Edward Lee Thorndike. In C. Murchison (Ed.), *A history of psychology in autobiography* (Vol. 3, pp. 263-270). Worcester, MA: Clark University Press.

Thorndike, E. L. (1939). *Your city.* New York: Harcourt Brace.

Thorndike, E. L., Cobb, M. V., Woodyard, E., & staff. (1926). *The measurement of intelligence.* New York: Teachers College, Columbia University Press.

Thorndike, E. L., & Lorge, I. (1944). *Teacher's wordbook of 30,000 words.* New York: Columbia University Press.

Thorndike, E. L. & Woodworth, R. S. (1901). The influence of one mental function upon the efficiency of other functions. *Psychological Review, 8,* 247-261, 384-395, 553-564.

Thorndike, R. L. (1991). Edward L. Thorndike: A professional and personal appreciation. In G. A. Kimble, M. Wertheimer, & C. White (Eds.), *Portraits of pioneers in psychology* (Vol. 1, pp. 139-151). Washington, DC: American Psychological Association.

Whitman, C. O. (1899). Animal behavior. *Biological lectures from the Marine Biological Laboratory of Woods Holl 1898* (pp. 285-338). Boston: Ginn & Company.

Woodworth, R. S. (1952). Edward Lee Thorndike 1874-1949. *Biographical Memoirs of the National Academy of Sciences of the United States of America, 27,* 209-237.

Bennett G. Galef, Jr. (essay date 1998)

SOURCE: "Edward Thorndike: Revolutionary Psychologist, Ambiguous Biologist," in *American Psychologist,* Vol. 53, No. 10, October, 1998, pp. 1128-34.

[*In the following essay, Galef argues that while Thorndike's contributions to the field of comparative psychology as an empiricist are invaluable, his misconceptions about biology remain damaging to his discipline.*]

Publication in June 1898 of Edward Thorndike's doctoral thesis, [*Animal Intelligence*], the first dissertation in psychology in which animals served as subjects, marked a turning point in the history of the study of behavior in North America. There can be little question that Thorndike knew that his thesis pointed the way to a new kind of behavioral research. As he wrote to his fiancée, Beth Moulton, a few months into drafting the final document, "My thesis is a beauty . . . I've got some theories which knock the old authorities into a grease spot" (quoted in Joncich, 1968, p. 146). Indeed, the opening chapter of Thorndike's dissertation was a breath of fresh air for a field in need of resuscitation.

THE REVOLUTIONARY PSYCHOLOGY OF E. L. THORNDIKE

COMPARATIVE PSYCHOLOGY IN THE VICTORIAN ERA

By the end of the 19th century, the literature in comparative psychology had become a morass of questionable anecdote and insupportable anthropomorphism (Galef, 1988a). The introduction to Thorndike's (1898) thesis called for rejection of the informal naturalism that had dominated the study of the behavior of animals for the preceding 100 years (Barber, 1980) and that was largely responsible for the disappointing state of comparative psychology at the turn of the century.

Throughout the 19th century, authors of volumes of natural history strove, as Charles Kingsley (1855) a successful author of the period, put it,

> [to bring] out the human side of science and [to give] seemingly dry disquisitions and animals of the lowest type, by little touches of pathos and humour, that living and personal interest, to bestow which is generally the function of the poet.
>
> (p. 160)

The need to tell engaging tales, rather than to provide objective description, shaped natural history books of the day. Public success often lay, then as now, in relating amusing animal anecdotes and in attributing human motives and human-like intelligence to almost any living creature.

There was, however, an important difference between 19th- and 20th-century publications in the field of animal behavior. In the 19th century, scientific publications were almost as rich in anthropomorphic interpretations of behavioral anecdotes as were books intended for the lay public. Even such distinguished journals as *Nature* accepted for publication letters similar to that excerpted below, describing the nesting behavior of a recently parturient cat that belonged to a Mr. Bidie. Mr. Bidie had returned from a journey, thus displacing from his quarters two young gentlemen who had been residing there in his absence and who had the nasty habit of teasing Mr. Bidie's recently parturient cat. Shortly after Mr. Bidie's return, the cat moved her kittens from a concealed nest to his dressing room. Mr. Bidie (1879) wrote to *Nature* to express his opinion that his cat's "train of reasoning seems to have been the following 'now that my master has returned, there is no risk of the kittens being injured . . . so I will take them out for my protector to see and admire'" (p. 96). Apparently, both Mr. Bidie and the editors of *Nature* took it for granted that progress in understanding the behavior of animals depended on chance observation of intriguing bits of behavior, putting one's self in the place of the animal, and then introspecting to discover the mental processes that might have led the animal to behave as it did. There was, initially, a scientific motivation for this anecdotalism and anthropomorphism. The debate between deists and evolutionists as to the origins of human mental faculties appeared to some participants to justify introspective interpretation of questionable evidence (Romanes, 1884). The rich intellectual and emotional lives thus attributed to animals provided a link between the minds of extant animals and humans that Darwin's theory of evolution appeared at the time to require. However, things had gone very far.

THE CRITIQUE

It is against this background of anecdotalism, anthropomorphism, introspectionism, and inference of motive and intelligence from informal observation that the first pages of Thorndike's (1898) thesis must be read. Even his title, "Animal intelligence," contains an implicit criticism of his contemporaries, Wesley Mills (1898), George Romanes (1882), and C. L. Morgan (1890), whose similarly titled books Thorndike (1898) ridiculed in the opening pages of his monograph.

> Most of the books do not give us a psychology, but rather a eulogy of animals. They have all been about animal intelligence, never about animal stupidity. . . . [They furnish] an illustration of the well-nigh universal tendency in human nature to find the marvelous wherever it can. . . . Thousands of cats on thousands of occasions sit helplessly yowling, and no one takes thought of it . . . but let one cat claw at the knob of a door supposedly as a signal to be let out, and straightway this cat becomes the representative of the cat mind in all the books . . . [the anecdotal school] has built up a general psychology from abnormal data. It is like an anatomy written from observations on dime-show freaks.
>
> (pp. 3-4, 152)

Thorndike's attack was unrelenting. He had no patience with the telling of tales, with what he called "the work of the anecdote school" (Thorndike, 1898, p. 29), nothing but contempt for a comparative psychology that ignored "the stupid and normal" (p. 25) and instead focused on "the intelligent and unusual" (p. 25). Thorndike was equally critical of inference from introspection as a means to understand the mental life of animals.

THE METHOD

If Thorndike had nothing to offer but criticism of his predecessors and contemporaries, he probably would (and should) have been ignored. However, Thorndike's (1898) dissertation also contained striking examples of an alternative strategy for studying not only comparative psychology but behavior generally.

Thorndike's methods are so widely used in the behavioral sciences today that it is difficult to imagine that they once needed a champion, but that they did, and their champion was Edward Thorndike. Thorndike insisted that the study of behavior be carried out in a systematic, quantitative fashion under controlled conditions so that the course of development of normal behavior in typical subjects could be described.

LEARNING BY TRIAL AND ERROR OR BY ASSOCIATION OF IDEAS

C. L. Morgan and Alexander Bain, like Thorndike, held the view that much of what animals learned they learned by trial and error. Late in the last century, there were even a few experiments conducted demonstrating trial-and-error learning. However, at the turn of the century, Thorndike, Romanes, Morgan, and many others believed, without experimental evidence, that animals could learn not only by trial and error but also by imitation and by having their limbs passively put through actions by a human trainer. Thorndike expected the experiments he undertook for his thesis to provide hard evidence in support of these widely held beliefs (Boakes, 1984), but he felt he "could do better than had been done" (as cited in Joncich, 1968, p. 89) in demonstrating such forms of learning.

Thorndike's methods for studying learning in animals derived from anecdotal reports by both Morgan (1894) and Romanes (1882) of dogs and cats that had learned to open garden gates. Morgan, for example, was convinced that his dog, Tony, had learned by trial and error to open the gate in Morgan's yard, though Morgan also credited animals with "intelligent inferences of wonderful accuracy and precision" when solving simple problems. Romanes (1882, p. 422) asserted that cats that had watched humans depress a latch with their thumbs and push on gates to open them were able to reason "if a hand can do it, why not a paw?" Clearly, in Romanes's view, an animal could be led to perform an act by associating the idea of the act (depressing the thumb latch and pushing the gate) with the idea of its consequences (escape from the confines of the yard). Thorndike preferred Morgan's trial-and-error learning to Romanes's association of ideas, but felt that careful experiments were needed to support either view of how animals learned to solve mechanical puzzles.

THE EXPERIMENTS

Thorndike's now-famous puzzle boxes (Thorndike, 1898), described in detail in Burnham (1972), were designed to permit repeated measurement of the speed with which cats, dogs, and (later) monkeys could learn to escape confinement and reach food by manipulating mechanical contrivances (levers, pulleys, treadles, etc.). The devices permitting escape were analogs of the latches on garden gates that the dogs and cats in Morgan's and Romanes's anecdotes had learned to open.

Thorndike's initial studies established normal latencies for hungry dogs and cats to escape from puzzle boxes and gain access to food. The gradual decrease across trials in these latencies convinced Thorndike that such learning involved a gradual increase in frequency of production of rewarded responses rather than an insightful association of ideas concerning escape and reward.

Thorndike hypothesized that placing an animal in a puzzle box elicited a set of activities reflecting both inherited tendencies and previous experiences of the animal. Eventually, and by accident, the animal performed an act that allowed it to escape from the apparatus and gain access to food, thus achieving "satisfaction." Over trials, and as the result of repeated success, the animal gradually came to associate the impulse for making a successful movement with the sensory stimuli provided by the box. The gradual decrease in latency to escape the box simply reflected the strengthening of the association between the situation of being in the box and the appropriate act. Thus, in Thorndike's view, the animal did not, as Romanes had proposed, perform an act resulting in release from constraint because it thought of the appropriate act and of the satisfaction that would result from performing that act. Rather, as the result of experiences of satisfaction following initial accidental performance of a response in a puzzle box, an animal simply came to feel like repeating that response when again placed in the same situation.

IMPLICATIONS

Thorndike's major theoretical contribution lay in the next step he took, one that provided experimental evidence contradictory to Romanes's (1882) view that animals learned to solve problems by associating ideas of actions and rewards. Thorndike argued that, if Romanes were correct, and associating the idea of an act with the idea of its outcome sufficed to produce the act, then learning an act ought to be facilitated by giving an animal the idea both of the appropriate act and of the satisfaction it could bring.

Thorndike explored several procedures that he felt should have facilitated learning, if associating the idea of an act with the idea of its outcome sufficed to produce learning. For example, if learning depended on the association of ideas, then animals that watched others perform acts that led to satisfaction should learn to perform those acts more rapidly than animals that did not have the opportunity to learn by observation. Similarly, if a passive animal was gently put through required movements and then allowed access to reward, it should, if the association of ideas underlies learning, produce the required movements more rapidly than an animal lacking such training. In both cases, the animal was presumed to have been given the opportunity to acquire the idea of the act, as well as of the pleasure that the act could produce. Thorndike found, to the contrary, that, when placed alone in an apparatus, neither animals that had been passively led to the correct act nor those that had observed others perform the correct act learned to escape more rapidly than did animals that had to learn without such tutoring. These unexpected failures to confirm the then universal belief that higher animals could learn by both imitation and passive movement of

their limbs shaped Thorndike's views on animal intelligence. The failures suggested to Thorndike that animals had a severely limited understanding of the world in which they lived. Animals might learn an association between a situation and what Thorndike called a "motor impulse." However, they learned such associations without awareness of the consequences of their acts; they could not learn to associate ideas of actions with ideas of their consequences. Occurrence of satisfying or dissatisfying events simply changed the probability that an animal would engage in any action by strengthening or weakening the connection between a situation and various motor acts. Thus, Thorndike provided both a novel and greatly simplified view of the mental life of animals and a set of tools for studying comparative psychology that was to prove astonishingly fruitful.

INNOVATIONS

In retrospect, it is hard to see the innovations in Thorndike's (1898) dissertation, because it all seems so straightforward and logical. However, at the turn of the century, Thorndike's work contained a set of methodological innovations that were to revolutionize the study of comparative psychology: A representative sample of subjects was examined in a carefully described, standardized situation. Quantitative measures of performance were made. Comparisons were made of the performance, in the standard situation, of groups of subjects that had received different treatments before testing. Interpretations of implications of different outcomes of these comparisons were arrived at before experiments were begun. Several different operations were used to address a single issue. The behavior of members of different species (dogs, cats, and monkeys) was measured in logically identical tasks. In summary, Thorndike developed a methodology suitable not only for experimental study of animal learning but for much of animal and human behavior as well.

Thorndike's views were not simply the expression of a prevailing zeitgeist. His ideas were, at first, viciously rejected by many of his contemporaries. In a lengthy review, Wesley Mills (1899) suggested that the unnatural methods Thorndike had used resulted in his studying starved, panic-stricken cats and dogs that had temporarily lost their normal wits, so that their intelligence was grossly underestimated. Linus Kline (1898-1899, p. 150) concluded a far briefer review with the suggestion that the chief value of Thorndike's thesis lay in its "testing a simple method whereby more of the facts of animal psychosis may be set forth." C. L. Morgan (1900) suggested that Thorndike's subjects would be better described as his victims. Opposition died down as the nature of Thorndike's work became better understood, and almost immediately, laboratories devoted to the experimental study of comparative psychology as advocated by Thorndike became established at Clark University, Harvard University, and the University of Chicago (Warden, 1927). Their descendants are still active today.

IMITATION LEARNING

In discussing the results of his dissertation research, Thorndike (1898, pp. 76-80) described a set of "pseudo-imitative" types of social learning that might be confused with true imitation (Galef, 1988b). One hundred years later, comparative psychologists are still trying to find situations where copying of the behavior of one animal by another can be attributed unequivocally to imitation rather than to one of the pseudo-imitative processes Thorndike described.

Thus, the results of Thorndike's (1898) thesis, as well as his methods, had sustained impact. In particular, his conclusion that animals could not learn by imitation, and its implication that animals did not learn by associating representations of acts and their consequences, were taken up as a challenge by succeeding generations of comparative psychologists. Thorndike's view provokes research to this day. Indeed, a century after Thorndike conducted his experiments on imitation learning in cats, dogs, and monkeys, the question of whether nonhuman vertebrates can truly imitate, in Thorndike's (1911, p. 173) sense of "learning to do an act from seeing it done," remains largely unanswered, though results of recent studies indicate that even parrots, Norway rats, and pigeons may be able to imitate simple acts (reviewed in Galef, 1998). Compelling demonstrations of learning by observation of complex, novel motor acts continues to elude researchers in the area (reviewed in Galef, 1998).

THE 1911 MONOGRAPH

During the decade following publication of Thorndike's dissertation in a *Psychological Review Monograph Supplement* in June 1898, Thorndike expanded his views on comparative psychology. In 1911 he published a new monograph on "animal intelligence," this one in book form. The book consisted of a reprinting of the 1898 thesis monograph; reprints of two other published, experimental papers; and two new essays in which Thorndike emphasized general, abstract laws of behavior derived from his experimental work. Although the principles were clear in the thesis of 1898, their first statement as general laws was in the 1911 publication.

The most enduring of Thorndike's laws, the law of effect, stated that an animal that made a response in a situation that was followed by satisfaction would be more likely to repeat that response in that situation. Conversely, an animal would be less likely to repeat responses made in a situation if those responses were followed by discomfort. This law of effect, together with the law of exercise (stating that, other things being equal, connections between situations and responses are strengthened by repetition) were to explain all learned behavior. Instinct simply provided the raw materials on which the laws of effect and exercise operated.

Thorndike argued further that, once the operations of the laws of effect and exercise were fully understood, the problem of learning would be solved: "the higher animals, including man, manifest no behavior beyond expectations from the laws of instinct, exercise and effect." (Thorndike, 1911, p. 274). By implication, experimental analysis of the effects of reward and punishment and of repetition carried out on the members of any species could yield laws of a general psychology of learning.

The central idea of the law of effect—that learning consists of the modification of response probabilities by their consequences—became a central assumption of B. F. Skinner's (1938) approach to the study of conditioning. The law of exercise was central to Watson's behaviorism. Equally influential was Thorndike's assertion that all of learning, both human and animal, could be understood in terms of a limited number of general principles that could be studied in any convenient situation and species. An ecological or phylogenetic framework was viewed as irrelevant to the field (Jenkins, 1979). Only in the last two decades, with the decline of neo-behaviorism and the growth, first of cognitive and then of Darwinian or evolutionary psychology, has there been a weakening of the commitment of students of animal learning to the notion that experimental analyses of effects of reward and punishment in any situation can yield general laws of learning.

As I show below, by the late 1960s, the study of animal learning had become so far removed from basic biological concerns that evidence of ecologically relevant, species-specific learning mechanisms was seen as a challenge to the viability of the entire enterprise (Rozin, 1977). Thorndike's approach to comparative psychology, although both innovative and heuristic, contained the seeds of its own destruction.

THE AMBIGUOUS BIOLOGY OF E. L. THORNDIKE

THORNDIKE, DARWIN, AND SPENCER

In the latter part of the 19th century, members of the scientific community entertained two incompatible views of phylogeny. According to Charles Darwin, at least in his earlier writings, speciation produced a great "tree of life" whose "green and budding twigs may represent existing species; and those produced during each former year may represent the long succession of extinct species." (Darwin, 1859, p. 120). On this view, the direct forebears of contemporary species, genera, and so on are to be found only as fossils entombed in the geological record. Extant species are related to one another not directly, as parents or grandparents are to their children and grandchildren, but as are cousins of varying degree.

Herbert Spencer (1855) proposed, as did Darwin, that life began on earth with a few simple forms. However, to Spencer, as to Lamarck before him, evolution meant steady linear progress from the simplest unicellular organisms to man. Gradual increase in physiological and neuroanatomical complexity as one ascended this *scala naturae* was a fundamental law of nature, and the increase in morphological complexity was reflected in increased sophistication of mind and behavior. "From the lowest to the highest forms of life, the increasing adjustment of inner to outer relations is one indivisible progression" (Spencer, 1855, p. 387).

The central problem with Spencer's (1855) approach is that it does not take into account the fact that extant species are not direct descendants of one another and, therefore, that any ranking with respect to complexity (whether of behavior or neuroanatomy) does not reflect historical relationships. The idea of ordering extant animals in terms of the complexity of their nervous systems and behavior surely did not originate with Spencer, but he was among those who provided a scientific, rather than theological, rationale for constructing a *scala naturae* or Great Chain of Being.

The distinction between Darwin's (1859) and Spencer's (1855) views of phylogeny is clear to the modern reader. It seems to have been less important to many working at the turn of the century.

Boakes (1984) reported that, while an undergraduate student at Wesleyan, Thorndike "was taught some psychology, read a great deal of Spencer and became inspired by James's Principles" (p. 68). Boakes does not, however, mention Thorndike's exposure to Darwin's thought. Boakes, I, and numerous others have read Thorndike as a proponent of Spencer's views. Clearly, the impression conveyed in Thorndike's 1911 monograph, which is far more accessible today than is Thorndike's 1898 publication in the *Psychological Review Monograph Supplement,* is that Thorndike had incorporated Spencer's (1855) rather than Darwin's (1859) view of phylogeny into his theorizing. For example, Thorndike (1911) wrote,

> there is, as we pass from the early vertebrates down to man, a progress in the evolution of the general associative process . . . It may be that the evolution of intellect has no breaks, that its progress is continuous from its first appearance to its present condition. . . . As we follow the development of animals in time, we find the capacity to select impulses growing. We find the associations thus made between situation and act growing in number, being formed more quickly, lasting longer and becoming more complex and more delicate.
>
> (pp. 285-287)

However, both Thorndike's (1898) thesis and some of his less frequently cited, early publications (1900, 1909) are far more Darwinian in flavor than is his 1911 monograph. The early papers make clear that Thorndike was widely read in Darwin's work and understood and accepted Darwin's views on phylogeny. As Thorndike (1898) stated in criticism of the views of a contemporary, "Since Hubrecht has shown how early the primate stock split off, it seems far-fetched to call a dog-mind and cat-mind an ancestor in any sense of the human" (p. 520). Similarly, in his thesis, Thorndike's thinking about phylogeny is clearly Darwinian rather than Spencerian. For example, Thorndike (1898, in Thorndike 1911) speculated, first that "the present an-

thropoid primates may be mentally degenerate;" second that "their chattering is a relic of something like language, not a beginning of such;" and third, that "comparative psychology should use the phenomenon of the monkey-mind of to-day to find out what the primitive mind from which man's sprung off was like" (p. 151).

Something changed Thorndike's thinking about phylogeny between 1898 and 1911. During the intervening years, Thorndike the animal psychologist became Thorndike the pedagogist, and Thorndike the Darwinian became Thorndike the Spencerian. In summary, in the end, Spencer's view of phylogeny eventually prevailed in Thorndike's thinking and led both Thorndike and many other comparative psychologists out of the mainstream of evolutionary thinking.

CONSEQUENCES

Thorndike's influence on later animal psychologists, particularly those interested in behavioral plasticity, shaped the future of much of the field. Thorndike (1911, pp. 286-287) wrote that his research with various animals showed a Spencerian progress in the general associative process that reflected a progressive increase in the "delicacy and complexity" of the "neurones" and the connections between them as "we pass from the early vertebrates down to man."

The notion that, as we move along the vertebrate series, associations are learned more rapidly and more lastingly because the brain is more complex is not without heuristic value. It underlies the work of Hebb (1949) and of Jerison (1973), both of whom hypothesized a relationship between various aspects of brain size or complexity and behavior. Hebb pointed to the change in the ratio of the volume of association areas and primary sensory areas as one moves from "lower" to "higher." He assumed that this change in relative size of brain areas was responsible for "the greater speed with which the 'lower' species could learn to respond selectively to the environment, and to the comparative simplicity of their behavior when it is fully developed" (p. 126). Jerison used mathematical techniques to demonstrate a progressive enlargement of the brain as one moves from lower to higher vertebrates, even when the corresponding general increase in body weight is taken into account. Bitterman's (1965, p. 408) demonstration of different patterns of learning as we "ascend the phyletic scale" also reflects the Spencer—Thorndike tradition in psychology.

The problem, of course, with all such work on progressive evolution of brain or behavior is, as Hodos and Campbell (1969) pointed out,

> the concept that all living creatures can be arranged along a continuous phylogenetic scale . . . is inconsistent with contemporary views of animal evolution . . . The widespread failure of comparative psychologists to take into account the zoological model of animal evolution when selecting animals for study and when inter-

preting behavioral similarities and differences has greatly hampered the development of generalizations with any predictive value.

(p. 337)

Although the doctrine of "levels" in the psychological capacities of animals (Schneirla, 1949) is evolutionary or comparative in the broadest sense of those terms, it is not historical, and for that reason it fails to make contact with much of mainstream biology.

Many comparative psychologists looked, as Thorndike (1911) seemed to be doing in his later work, for similarities and discontinuities in the mental abilities of distantly related species. However, those working, albeit some decades later, in what became the mainstream of biology were interested in comparisons of homologous characteristics in closely related species, and thus in tracing the actual phylogeny of behavior. This divergence in the approach of psychologists and biologists to the study of comparative behavior led one biologist, Konrad Lorenz, to remark in 1950 that there is "an American journal masquerad[ing] under the title of 'comparative' psychology, although, to the best of my knowledge, no really comparative paper ever has been published in it" (p. 240).

It is hard to imagine the extent to which important parts of animal psychology became divorced from other biological disciplines (see Dewsbury, 1984, for counter-examples). Examination of the indexes of texts used to teach me animal psychology some 30 years ago, when I was a graduate student, make the point. Maier and Schneirla's (1935) classic, *Principles of Animal Psychology* (of which I have the fondest memories), does not mention either Darwin or natural selection. The book does not contain a definition of *adaptation* in the biological sense; the term *evolution* appears only twice in 480 pages of text, and it is not used in a biological sense in either case. In Koch's (1959) edited text, *Psychology: A Study of a Science,* evolution is mentioned only in Hinde's (1959) chapter on ethology. Keller and Schoenfeld's (1950) *Principles of Psychology* never mentions Darwin, evolution, or adaptation, and Kimble's (1961) edition of *Hilgard and Marquis' Conditioning and Learning* gives Darwin only a paragraph and a footnote. By mid-century, the disassociation between the study of the psychology of animals derived from Thorndike's work and Darwinian biology was essentially complete. Large and very visible parts of comparative psychology had become abiological.

The pernicious effects of the disassociation of mainstream study of comparative psychology from mainstream evolutionary theory would not become apparent until the 1970s. However, the breach between animal psychology and biology played an important role in the eventual crisis of confidence in animal psychology (Beach, 1950; Lockard, 1971; Hirsch, 1987). Lack of an evolutionary perspective permitted various biological subdisciplines (e.g., behavioral ecology, sociobiology, Darwinian psychology) to become dominant in areas that were once the sole province of comparative psychologists.

CONCLUSION

As a consequence of Thorndike's influence, those trained in comparative psychology are still among the most experimentally sophisticated of animal behaviorists. As a second, though less desirable consequence of that same influence, many comparative psychologists have concentrated inordinately on problems of steadily diminishing interest to the larger community of animal behaviorists. The challenge is to preserve the first of Thorndike's legacies while breaking with the second.

References

Barber, L. (1980). *The heyday of natural history.* Garden City, NY: Doubleday.

Beach, F. A. (1950). The snark was a boojum. *American Psychologist, 5,* 115-124.

Bidie, G. (1879). Intellect in brutes. *Nature, 20,* 96.

Bitterman, M. E. (1965). Phyletic differences in learning. *American Psychologist, 20,* 396-410.

Boakes, R. (1984). *From Darwin to Behaviourism: Psychology and the minds of animals.* Cambridge, England: Cambridge University Press.

Burnham, J. C. (1972). Thorndike's puzzle boxes. *Journal of the History of the Behavioral Sciences, 8,* 159-167.

Darwin, C. (1859). *On the origin of species by means of natural selection.* London: Murray.

Dewsbury, D. A. (1984). *Comparative psychology in the twentieth century.* Stroudsberg, PA: Hutchison Ross.

Galef, B. G., Jr. (1988a). Evolution and learning before Thorndike: A forgotten epoch in the history of behavioral research. In R. C. Bolles & M. D. Beecher (Eds.), *Evolution and learning* (pp. 39-58). Hillsdale, NJ: Erlbaum.

Galef, B. G., Jr. (1988b). Imitation in animals: History, definition and interpretation of data from the psychological laboratory. In T. R. Zentall & B. G. Galef, Jr. (Eds.), *Social learning: Psychological and biological perspectives* (pp. 3-28). Hillsdale, NJ: Erlbaum.

Galef, B. G., Jr. (1998). Recent progress in studies of imitation and social learning in animals. In M. Sabourin, F. I. M. Craik, & M. Roberts (Eds.), *Advances in psychological science: Vol. 2. Biological and cognitive aspects* (pp. 275-300). London: Psychological Press.

Hebb, D. O. (1949). *The organization of behavior.* New York: Wiley.

Hinde, R. A. (1959). Some recent trends in ethology. In S. Koch (Ed.), *Psychology: A study of a science* (Vol. 2, pp. 561-610). New York: McGraw-Hill.

Hirsch, J. (1987). Comparative psychology—past, present, and future. *Journal of Comparative Psychology, 101,* 1-291.

Hodos, W., & Campbell, C. B. G. (1969). Scala naturae: Why there is no theory in comparative psychology. *Psychological Review, 76,* 337-350.

Jenkins, H. M. (1979). Animal learning and behavior theory. In E. Hearst (Ed.), *The first century of experimental psychology* (pp. 177-230). Hillsdale, NJ: Erlbaum.

Jerison, H. (1973). *Evolution of brain and intelligence.* New York: Academic Press.

Joncich, G. (1968). *The sane positivist: A biography of Edward L. Thorndike.* Middletown, CT: Wesleyan University Press.

Keller, F. S., & Schoenfeld, W. N. (1950). *Principles of psychology.* New York: Appleton-Century-Crofts.

Kimble, G. A. (1961). *Hilgard and Marquis' conditioning and learning.* New York: Appleton-Century-Croft.

Kingsley, C. (1855). *Glaucus; or the wonders of the shore.* Cambridge, England: Cambridge University Press.

Kline, L. W. (1898-1899). Animal intelligence: An experimental study of the associative process in animals, by E. L. Thorndike [monograph supplement 8 of the Psychological Review]. *American Journal of Psychology, 10,* 149-150.

Koch, S. (1959). *Psychology: A study of a science* (Vol. 2). New York: McGraw-Hill.

Lockard, R. B. (1971). Reflections on the fall of comparative psychology: Is there a message for us all? *American Psychologist, 26,* 168-179.

Lorenz, K. Z. (1950). The comparative method in studying innate behaviour patterns. *Symposium of the Society for Experimental Biology, 4,* 221-268.

Maier, N. R. F., & Schneirla, T. C. (1935). *Principles of animal psychology.* New York: McGraw-Hill.

Mills, W. (1898). *Animal Intelligence.* New York: Macmillan.

Mills, W. (1899). The nature of animal intelligence and the method of investigating it. *Psychological Review, 6,* 262-274.

Morgan, C. L. (1890). *Animal life and intelligence.* London: Edward Arnold.

FURTHER READING

Biography

Joncich, Geraldine. *The Sane Positivist: A Biography of Edward L. Thorndike.* Middletown, Conn.: Wesleyan University Press, 1968, 634 p.

Illustrated biography focusing on Thorndike's professional life.

Criticism

Goodenough, Florence L. "Edward Lee Thorndike: 1874-1949." *The American Journal of Psychology,* LXIII, No. 2 (April 1950): 291-301.

Obituary of Thorndike that provides an overview of his life, career, and major works.

Hilgard, Ernest R. "Thorndike's Connectionism." In *Theories of Learning,* 2nd ed., pp. 15-47. New York: Appleton-Century-Crofts, Inc., 1956.

Thorough examination of Thorndike's interpretation of connectionism.

Thorpe, Louis P. and Allen M. Schmuller. "Thorndike's Bond Hypothesis." In *Contemporary Theories of Learning,* pp. 45-84. New York: The Ronald Press Company, 1954.

Traces Thorndike's bond hypothesis back to the philosophy of Aristotle.

Additional coverage of Thorndike's life and career is contained in the following source published by the Gale Group: *Contemporary Authors,* Vol. 121.

How to Use This Index

The main references

Calvino, Italo
  1923-1985 .... **CLC 5, 8, 11, 22, 33, 39,
                          73; SSC 3**

---

list all author entries in the following Gale Literary Criticism series:

BLC = *Black Literature Criticism*
CLC = *Contemporary Literary Criticism*
CLR = *Children's Literature Review*
CMLC = *Classical and Medieval Literature Criticism*
DA = *DISCovering Authors*
DAB = *DISCovering Authors: British*
DAC = *DISCovering Authors: Canadian*
DAM = *DISCovering Authors: Modules*
      DRAM: Dramatists Module; MST: Most-Studied Authors Module;
      MULT: Multicultural Authors Module; NOV: Novelists Module;
      POET: Poets Module; POP: Popular Fiction and Genre Authors Module
DC = *Drama Criticism*
HLC = *Hispanic Literature Criticism*
LC = *Literature Criticism from 1400 to 1800*
NCLC = *Nineteenth-Century Literature Criticism*
NNAL = *Native North American Literature*
PC = *Poetry Criticism*
SSC = *Short Story Criticism*
TCLC = *Twentieth-Century Literary Criticism*
WLC = *World Literature Criticism, 1500 to the Present*

The cross-references

See also CANR 23; CA 85-88;
obituary CA116

---

list all author entries in the following Gale biographical and literary sources:

AAYA = *Authors & Artists for Young Adults*
AITN = *Authors in the News*
BEST = *Bestsellers*
BW = *Black Writers*
CA = *Contemporary Authors*
CAAS = *Contemporary Authors Autobiography Series*
CABS = *Contemporary Authors Bibliographical Series*
CANR = *Contemporary Authors New Revision Series*
CAP = *Contemporary Authors Permanent Series*
CDALB = *Concise Dictionary of American Literary Biography*
CDBLB = *Concise Dictionary of British Literary Biography*
DLB = *Dictionary of Literary Biography*
DLBD = *Dictionary of Literary Biography Documentary Series*
DLBY = *Dictionary of Literary Biography Yearbook*
HW = *Hispanic Writers*
JRDA = *Junior DISCovering Authors*
MAICYA = *Major Authors and Illustrators for Children and Young Adults*
MTCW = *Major 20th-Century Writers*
SAAS = *Something about the Author Autobiography Series*
SATA = *Something about the Author*
YABC = *Yesterday's Authors of Books for Children*

Literary Criticism Series
Cumulative Author Index

Akst, Daniel 1956- .... **CLC 109**
See also CA 161

Aksyonov, Vassily (Pavlovich)
1932- .... **CLC 22, 37, 101**
See also CA 53-56; CANR 12, 48, 77;
CWW 2

Akutagawa Ryunosuke 1892-1927 . **TCLC 16**
See also CA 117; 154; DLB 180

Alain 1868-1951 .... **TCLC 41**
See also CA 163

Alain-Fournier **TCLC 6**
See also Fournier, Henri Alban
See also DLB 65

Alarcon, Pedro Antonio de
1833-1891 .... **NCLC 1**

Alas (y Urena), Leopoldo (Enrique Garcia)
1852-1901 .... **TCLC 29**
See also CA 113; 131; HW 1

Albee, Edward (Franklin III) 1928- . **CLC 1,
2, 3, 5, 9, 11, 13, 25, 53, 86, 113; DA;
DAB; DAC; DAM DRAM, MST; DC
11**
See also AITN 1; AW; CA 5-8R; CABS 3;
CANR 8, 54, 74; CDALB 1941-1968;
DA3; DLB 7; INT CANR-8; MTCW 1, 2

Alberti, Rafael 1902-1999 .... **CLC 7**
See also CA 85-88; 185; CANR 81; DLB
108; HW 2

Albert the Great 1193(?)-1280 ...... **CMLC 16**
See also DLB 115

Alcala-Galiano, Juan Valera y
See Valera y Alcala-Galiano, Juan

Alcayaga, Lucila Godoy
See Godoy Alcayaga, Lucila

Alcott, Amos Bronson 1799-1888 .... **NCLC 1**
See also DLB 1, 223

Alcott, Louisa May 1832-1888 . **NCLC 6, 58,
83; DA; DAB; DAC; DAM MST, NOV;
SSC 27**
See also AAYA 20; AMWS 1; AW; CDALB
1865-1917; CLR 1, 38; DA3; DLB 1, 42,
79, 223, 239, 242; DLBD 14; JRDA;
MAICYA; SATA 100

Aldanov, M. A.
See Aldanov, Mark (Alexandrovich)

Aldanov, Mark (Alexandrovich)
1886(?)-1957 .... **TCLC 23**
See also CA 118; 181

Aldington, Richard 1892-1962 .... **CLC 49**
See also CA 85-88; CANR 45; DLB 20, 36,
100, 149

Aldiss, Brian W(ilson) 1925- . **CLC 5, 14, 40;
DAM NOV; SSC 36**
See also CA 5-8R; CAAS 2; CANR 5, 28,
64; DLB 14; MTCW 1, 2; SATA 34

Alegria, Claribel 1924- .... **CLC 75; DAM
MULT; HLCS 1; PC 26**
See also CA 131; CAAS 15; CANR 66, 94;
CWW 2; DLB 145; HW 1; MTCW 1

Alegria, Fernando 1918- .... **CLC 57**
See also CA 9-12R; CANR 5, 32, 72; HW
1, 2

Aleichem, Sholom **TCLC 1, 35; SSC 33**
See also Rabinovitch, Sholem

Aleixandre, Vicente 1898-1984
See also CANR 81; HLCS 1; HW 2

Alepoudelis, Odysseus
See Elytis, Odysseus
See also CWW 2

Aleshkovsky, Joseph 1929-
See Aleshkovsky, Yuz
See also CA 121; 128

Aleshkovsky, Yuz **CLC 44**
See also Aleshkovsky, Joseph

Alexander, Lloyd (Chudley) 1924- ... **CLC 35**
See also AAYA 1, 27; CA 1-4R; CANR 1,
24, 38, 55; CLR 1, 5, 48; DLB 52; JRDA;
MAICYA; MTCW 1; SAAS 19; SATA 3,
49, 81

Alexander, Meena 1951- .... **CLC 121**
See also CA 115; CANR 38, 70

Alexander, Samuel 1859-1938 .... **TCLC 77**

Alexie, Sherman (Joseph, Jr.)
1966- .... **CLC 96; DAM MULT**
See also AAYA 28; CA 138; CANR 95;
DA3; DLB 175, 206; MTCW 1; NNAL

Alfau, Felipe 1902-1999 .... **CLC 66**
See also CA 137

Alfred, Jean Gaston
See Ponge, Francis

Alger, Horatio, Jr. 1832-1899 .... **NCLC 8, 83**
See also DLB 42; SATA 16

Algren, Nelson 1909-1981 ..... **CLC 4, 10, 33;
SSC 33**
See also CA 13-16R; 103; CANR 20, 61;
CDALB 1941-1968; DLB 9; DLBY 81,
82; MTCW 1, 2

Ali, Ahmed 1908-1998 .... **CLC 69**
See also CA 25-28R; CANR 15, 34

Alighieri, Dante
See Dante

Allan, John B.
See Westlake, Donald E(dwin)

Allan, Sidney
See Hartmann, Sadakichi

Allan, Sydney
See Hartmann, Sadakichi

Allen, Edward 1948- .... **CLC 59**

Allen, Fred 1894-1956 .... **TCLC 87**

Allen, Paula Gunn 1939- .... **CLC 84; DAM
MULT**
See also AMWS 4; CA 112; 143; CANR
63; DA3; DLB 175; MTCW 1; NNAL

Allen, Roland
See Ayckbourn, Alan

Allen, Sarah A.
See Hopkins, Pauline Elizabeth

Allen, Sidney H.
See Hartmann, Sadakichi

Allen, Woody 1935- .... **CLC 16, 52; DAM
POP**
See also AAYA 10; CA 33-36R; CANR 27,
38, 63; DLB 44; MTCW 1

Allende, Isabel 1942- . **CLC 39, 57, 97; DAM
MULT, NOV; HLC 1**
See also AAYA 18; AW; CA 125; 130;
CANR 51, 74; CWW 2; DA3; DLB 145;
HW 1, 2; INT 130; MTCW 1, 2

Alleyn, Ellen
See Rossetti, Christina (Georgina)

Allingham, Margery (Louise)
1904-1966 .... **CLC 19**
See also CA 5-8R; 25-28R; CANR 4, 58;
DLB 77; MTCW 1, 2

Allingham, William 1824-1889 ...... **NCLC 25**
See also DLB 35

Allison, Dorothy E. 1949- .... **CLC 78**
See also CA 140; CANR 66; DA3; MTCW
1

Allston, Washington 1779-1843 .... **NCLC 2**
See also DLB 1, 235

Almedingen, E. M. **CLC 12**
See also Almedingen, Martha Edith von
See also SATA 3

Almedingen, Martha Edith von 1898-1971
See Almedingen, E. M.
See also CA 1-4R; CANR 1

Almodovar, Pedro 1949(?)- .... **CLC 114;
HLCS 1**
See also CA 133; CANR 72; HW 2

Almqvist, Carl Jonas Love
1793-1866 .... **NCLC 42**

Alonso, Damaso 1898-1990 .... **CLC 14**
See also CA 110; 131; 130; CANR 72; DLB
108; HW 1, 2

Alov
See Gogol, Nikolai (Vasilyevich)

Alta 1942- .... **CLC 19**
See also CA 57-60

Alter, Robert B(ernard) 1935- .... **CLC 34**
See also CA 49-52; CANR 1, 47

Alther, Lisa 1944- .... **CLC 7, 41**
See also CA 65-68; CAAS 30; CANR 12,
30, 51; GLL 2; MTCW 1

Althusser, L.
See Althusser, Louis

Althusser, Louis 1918-1990 .... **CLC 106**
See also CA 131; 132; DLB 242

Altman, Robert 1925- .... **CLC 16, 116**
See also CA 73-76; CANR 43

Alurista
See Urista, Alberto H.
See also DLB 82; HLCS 1

Alvarez, A(lfred) 1929- .... **CLC 5, 13**
See also CA 1-4R; CANR 3, 33, 63; DLB
14, 40

Alvarez, Alejandro Rodriguez 1903-1965
See Casona, Alejandro
See also CA 131; 93-96; HW 1

Alvarez, Julia 1950- .... **CLC 93; HLCS 1**
See also AAYA 25; AMWS 7; CA 147;
CANR 69; DA3; MTCW 1

Alvaro, Corrado 1896-1956 .... **TCLC 60**
See also CA 163

Amado, Jorge 1912- .... **CLC 13, 40, 106;
DAM MULT, NOV; HLC 1**
See also CA 77-80; CANR 35, 74; DLB
113; HW 2; MTCW 1, 2

Ambler, Eric 1909-1998 .... **CLC 4, 6, 9**
See also BRWS 4; CA 9-12R; 171; CANR
7, 38, 74; DLB 77; MTCW 1, 2

Amichai, Yehuda 1924-2000 .. **CLC 9, 22, 57,
116**
See also CA 85-88; 189; CANR 46, 60;
CWW 2; MTCW 1

Amichai, Yehudah
See Amichai, Yehuda

Amiel, Henri Frederic 1821-1881 .... **NCLC 4**

Amis, Kingsley (William)
1922-1995 ...... **CLC 1, 2, 3, 5, 8, 13, 40,
44, 129; DA; DAB; DAC; DAM MST,
NOV**
See also AITN 2; BRWS 2; CA 9-12R; 150;
CANR 8, 28, 54; CDBLB 1945-1960;
DA3; DLB 15, 27, 100, 139; DLBY 96;
INT CANR-8; MTCW 1, 2

Amis, Martin (Louis) 1949- .... **CLC 4, 9, 38,
62, 101**
See also BEST 90:3; BRWS 4; CA 65-68;
CANR 8, 27, 54, 73, 95; DA3; DLB 14,
194; INT CANR-27; MTCW 1

Ammons, A(rchie) R(andolph)
1926-2001 ...... **CLC 2, 3, 5, 8, 9, 25, 57,
108; DAM POET; PC 16**
See also AITN 1; CA 9-12R; CANR 6, 36,
51, 73; DLB 5, 165; MTCW 1, 2

Amo, Tauraatua i
See Adams, Henry (Brooks)

Amory, Thomas 1691(?)-1788 .... **LC 48**

Anand, Mulk Raj 1905- .. **CLC 23, 93; DAM
NOV**
See also CA 65-68; CANR 32, 64; MTCW
1, 2

Anatol
See Schnitzler, Arthur

Anaximander c. 611B.C.-c.
546B.C. .... **CMLC 22**

Anaya, Rudolfo A(lfonso) 1937- ...... **CLC 23;
DAM MULT, NOV; HLC 1**
See also AAYA 20; CA 45-48; CAAS 4;
CANR 1, 32, 51; DLB 82, 206; HW 1;
MTCW 1, 2

Andersen, Hans Christian
  1805-1875 .... **NCLC 7, 79; DA; DAB;
  DAC; DAM MST, POP; SSC 6**
  See also AW; CLR 6; DA3; MAICYA;
  SATA 100

Anderson, C. Farley
  See Mencken, H(enry) L(ouis); Nathan,
  George Jean

Anderson, Jessica (Margaret) Queale
  1916- .... **CLC 37**
  See also CA 9-12R; CANR 4, 62

Anderson, Jon (Victor) 1940- . **CLC 9; DAM
  POET**
  See also CA 25-28R; CANR 20

Anderson, Lindsay (Gordon)
  1923-1994 .... **CLC 20**
  See also CA 125; 128; 146; CANR 77

Anderson, Maxwell 1888-1959 .... **TCLC 2;
  DAM DRAM**
  See also CA 105; 152; DLB 7, 228; MTCW
  2

Anderson, Poul (William) 1926- .... **CLC 15**
  See also AAYA 5, 34; CA 1-4R, 181; CAAE
  181; CAAS 2; CANR 2, 15, 34, 64; CLR
  58; DLB 8; INT CANR-15; MTCW 1, 2;
  SATA 90; SATA-Brief 39; SATA-Essay
  106; SCFW 2

Anderson, Robert (Woodruff)
  1917- .... **CLC 23; DAM DRAM**
  See also AITN 1; CA 21-24R; CANR 32;
  DLB 7

Anderson, Sherwood 1876-1941 ..... **TCLC 1,
  10, 24; DA; DAB; DAC; DAM MST,
  NOV; SSC 1**
  See also AAYA 30; AW; CA 104; 121;
  CANR 61; CDALB 1917-1929; DA3;
  DLB 4, 9, 86; DLBD 1; GLL 2; MTCW
  1, 2

Andier, Pierre
  See Desnos, Robert

Andouard
  See Giraudoux, (Hippolyte) Jean

Andrade, Carlos Drummond de CLC 18
  See also Drummond de Andrade, Carlos

Andrade, Mario de 1893-1945 .... **TCLC 43**

Andreae, Johann V(alentin)
  1586-1654 .... **LC 32**
  See also DLB 164

Andreas-Salome, Lou 1861-1937 ... **TCLC 56**
  See also CA 178; DLB 66

Andress, Lesley
  See Sanders, Lawrence

Andrewes, Lancelot 1555-1626 .... **LC 5**
  See also DLB 151, 172

Andrews, Cicily Fairfield
  See West, Rebecca

Andrews, Elton V.
  See Pohl, Frederik

Andreyev, Leonid (Nikolaevich)
  1871-1919 .... **TCLC 3**
  See also CA 104; 185

Andric, Ivo 1892-1975 .... **CLC 8; SSC 36**
  See also CA 81-84; 57-60; CANR 43, 60;
  DLB 147; MTCW 1

Androvar
  See Prado (Calvo), Pedro

Angelique, Pierre
  See Bataille, Georges

Angell, Roger 1920- .... **CLC 26**
  See also CA 57-60; CANR 13, 44, 70; DLB
  171, 185

Angelou, Maya 1928- .... **CLC 12, 35, 64, 77;
  BLC 1; DA; DAB; DAC; DAM MST,
  MULT, POET, POP; PC 32**
  See also AAYA 7, 20; AMWS 4; AW; BW
  2, 3; CA 65-68; CANR 19, 42, 65;
  CDALBS; CLR 53; DA3; DLB 38;
  MTCW 1, 2; SATA 49

Anna Comnena 1083-1153 .... **CMLC 25**

Annensky, Innokenty (Fyodorovich)
  1856-1909 .... **TCLC 14**
  See also CA 110; 155

Annunzio, Gabriele d'
  See D'Annunzio, Gabriele

Anodos
  See Coleridge, Mary E(lizabeth)

Anon, Charles Robert
  See Pessoa, Fernando (Antonio Nogueira)

Anouilh, Jean (Marie Lucien Pierre)
  1910-1987 .... **CLC 1, 3, 8, 13, 40, 50;
  DAM DRAM; DC 8**
  See also CA 17-20R; 123; CANR 32;
  MTCW 1, 2

Anthony, Florence
  See Ai

Anthony, John
  See Ciardi, John (Anthony)

Anthony, Peter
  See Shaffer, Anthony (Joshua); Shaffer, Peter (Levin)

Anthony, Piers 1934- .... **CLC 35; DAM POP**
  See also AAYA 11; AW; CA 21-24R; CANR
  28, 56, 73; DLB 8; MTCW 1, 2; SAAS
  22; SATA 84

Anthony, Susan B(rownell)
  1916-1991 .... **TCLC 84**
  See also CA 89-92; 134

Antoine, Marc
  See Proust, (Valentin-Louis-George-Eugene-
)Marcel

Antoninus, Brother
  See Everson, William (Oliver)

Antonioni, Michelangelo 1912- .... **CLC 20**
  See also CA 73-76; CANR 45, 77

Antschel, Paul 1920-1970
  See Celan, Paul
  See also CA 85-88; CANR 33, 61; MTCW
  1

Anwar, Chairil 1922-1949 .... **TCLC 22**
  See also CA 121

Anzaldua, Gloria (Evanjelina) 1942-
  See also CA 175; DLB 122; HLCS 1

Apess, William 1798-1839(?) .... **NCLC 73;
  DAM MULT**
  See also DLB 175; NNAL

Apollinaire, Guillaume 1880-1918 .. **TCLC 3,
  8, 51; DAM POET; PC 7**
  See also CA 152; MTCW 1

Appelfeld, Aharon 1932- ... **CLC 23, 47; SSC
  42**
  See also CA 112; 133; CANR 86; CWW 2

Apple, Max (Isaac) 1941- .... **CLC 9, 33**
  See also CA 81-84; CANR 19, 54; DLB
  130

Appleman, Philip (Dean) 1926- .... **CLC 51**
  See also CA 13-16R; CAAS 18; CANR 6,
  29, 56

Appleton, Lawrence
  See Lovecraft, H(oward) P(hillips)

Apteryx
  See Eliot, T(homas) S(tearns)

Apuleius, (Lucius Madaurensis)
  125(?)-175(?) .... **CMLC 1**
  See also DLB 211

Aquin, Hubert 1929-1977 .... **CLC 15**
  See also CA 105; DLB 53

Aquinas, Thomas 1224(?)-1274 ..... **CMLC 33**
  See also DLB 115

Aragon, Louis 1897-1982 .. **CLC 3, 22; DAM
  NOV, POET**
  See also CA 69-72; 108; CANR 28, 71;
  DLB 72; GLL 2; MTCW 1, 2

Arany, Janos 1817-1882 .... **NCLC 34**

Aranyos, Kakay 1847-1910
  See Mikszath, Kalman

Arbuthnot, John 1667-1735 .... **LC 1**
  See also DLB 101

Archer, Herbert Winslow
  See Mencken, H(enry) L(ouis)

Archer, Jeffrey (Howard) 1940- ...... **CLC 28;
  DAM POP**
  See also AAYA 16; BEST 89:3; CA 77-80;
  CANR 22, 52, 95; DA3; INT CANR-22

Archer, Jules 1915- .... **CLC 12**
  See also CA 9-12R; CANR 6, 69; SAAS 5;
  SATA 4, 85

Archer, Lee
  See Ellison, Harlan (Jay)

Archilochus c. 7th cent. B.C.- .... **CMLC 44**
  See also DLB 176

Arden, John 1930- .... **CLC 6, 13, 15; DAM
  DRAM**
  See also BRWS 2; CA 13-16R; CAAS 4;
  CANR 31, 65, 67; DLB 13; MTCW 1

Arenas, Reinaldo 1943-1990 . **CLC 41; DAM
  MULT; HLC 1**
  See also CA 124; 128; 133; CANR 73; DLB
  145; GLL 2; HW 1; MTCW 1

Arendt, Hannah 1906-1975 .... **CLC 66, 98**
  See also CA 17-20R; 61-64; CANR 26, 60;
  DLB 242; MTCW 1, 2

Aretino, Pietro 1492-1556 .... **LC 12**

Arghezi, Tudor CLC 80
  See Theodorescu, Ion N.
  See also CA 167; DLB 220

Arguedas, Jose Maria 1911-1969 .... **CLC 10,
  18; HLCS 1**
  See also CA 89-92; CANR 73; DLB 113;
  HW 1

Argueta, Manlio 1936- .... **CLC 31**
  See also CA 131; CANR 73; CWW 2; DLB
  145; HW 1

Arias, Ron(ald Francis) 1941-
  See also CA 131; CANR 81; DAM MULT;
  DLB 82; HLC 1; HW 1, 2; MTCW 2

Ariosto, Ludovico 1474-1533 .... **LC 6**

Aristides
  See Epstein, Joseph

Aristophanes 450B.C.-385B.C. .... **CMLC 4;
  DA; DAB; DAC; DAM DRAM, MST;
  DC 2**
  See also AW; DA3; DLB 176

Aristotle 384B.C.-322B.C. ..... **CMLC 31; DA;
  DAB; DAC; DAM MST**
  See also AW; DA3; DLB 176

Arlt, Roberto (Godofredo Christophersen)
  1900-1942 .... **TCLC 29; DAM MULT;
  HLC 1**
  See also CA 123; 131; CANR 67; HW 1, 2

Armah, Ayi Kwei 1939- .... **CLC 5, 33, 136;
  BLC 1; DAM MULT, POET**
  See also BW 1; CA 61-64; CANR 21, 64;
  DLB 117; MTCW 1

Armatrading, Joan 1950- .... **CLC 17**
  See also CA 114; 186

Arnette, Robert
  See Silverberg, Robert

**Arnim, Achim von (Ludwig Joachim von
  Arnim)** 1781-1831 ..... **NCLC 5; SSC 29**
  See also DLB 90

Arnim, Bettina von 1785-1859 .... **NCLC 38**
  See also DLB 90

Arnold, Matthew 1822-1888 ..... **NCLC 6, 29,
  89; DA; DAB; DAC; DAM MST,
  POET; PC 5**
  See also AW; CDBLB 1832-1890; DLB 32,
  57

Arnold, Thomas 1795-1842 .... **NCLC 18**
  See also DLB 55

Arnow, Harriette (Louisa) Simpson
  1908-1986 .... **CLC 2, 7, 18**
  See also CA 9-12R; 118; CANR 14; DLB
  6; MTCW 1, 2; SATA 42; SATA-Obit 47

Arouet, Francois-Marie
See Voltaire
Arp, Hans
See Arp, Jean
Arp, Jean 1887-1966 .... **CLC 5**
See also CA 81-84; 25-28R; CANR 42, 77
Arrabal
See Arrabal, Fernando
Arrabal, Fernando 1932- ... **CLC 2, 9, 18, 58**
See also CA 9-12R; CANR 15
Arreola, Juan Jose 1918- .... **SSC 38; DAM MULT; HLC 1**
See also CA 113; 131; CANR 81; DLB 113; HW 1, 2
Arrian c. 89(?)-c. 155(?) .... **CMLC 43**
See also DLB 176
Arrick, Fran CLC 30
See also Gaberman, Judie Angell
Artaud, Antonin (Marie Joseph)
1896-1948 . **TCLC 3, 36; DAM DRAM; DC 14**
See also CA 104; 149; DA3; MTCW 1
Arthur, Ruth M(abel) 1905-1979 ..... **CLC 12**
See also CA 9-12R; 85-88; CANR 4; SATA 7, 26
Artsybashev, Mikhail (Petrovich)
1878-1927 .... **TCLC 31**
See also CA 170
Arundel, Honor (Morfydd)
1919-1973 .... **CLC 17**
See also CA 21-22; 41-44R; CAP 2; CLR 35; SATA 4; SATA-Obit 24
Arzner, Dorothy 1900-1979 .... **CLC 98**
Asch, Sholem 1880-1957 .... **TCLC 3**
See also CA 105; GLL 2
Ash, Shalom
See Asch, Sholem
Ashbery, John (Lawrence) 1927- .. **CLC 2, 3, 4, 6, 9, 13, 15, 25, 41, 77, 125; DAM POET; PC 26**
See also Berry, Jonas
See also AMWS 3; CA 5-8R; CANR 9, 37, 66; DA3; DLB 5, 165; DLBY 81; INT CANR-9; MTCW 1, 2
Ashdown, Clifford
See Freeman, R(ichard) Austin
Ashe, Gordon
See Creasey, John
Ashton-Warner, Sylvia (Constance)
1908-1984 .... **CLC 19**
See also CA 69-72; 112; CANR 29; MTCW 1, 2
Asimov, Isaac 1920-1992 ..... **CLC 1, 3, 9, 19, 26, 76, 92; DAM POP**
See also AAYA 13; AW; BEST 90:2; CA 1-4R; 137; CANR 2, 19, 36, 60; CLR 12; DA3; DLB 8; DLBY 92; INT CANR-19; JRDA; MAICYA; MTCW 1, 2; SATA 1, 26, 74; SCFW 2
Assis, Joaquim Maria Machado de
See Machado de Assis, Joaquim Maria
Astley, Thea (Beatrice May) 1925- .. **CLC 41**
See also CA 65-68; CANR 11, 43, 78
Aston, James
See White, T(erence) H(anbury)
Asturias, Miguel Ángel 1899-1974 .... **CLC 3, 8, 13; DAM MULT, NOV; HLC 1**
See also CA 25-28; 49-52; CANR 32; CAP 2; DA3; DLB 113; HW 1; MTCW 1, 2
Atares, Carlos Saura
See Saura (Atares), Carlos
Atheling, William
See Pound, Ezra (Weston Loomis)
Atheling, William, Jr.
See Blish, James (Benjamin)
Atherton, Gertrude (Franklin Horn)
1857-1948 .... **TCLC 2**
See also CA 104; 155; DLB 9, 78, 186; TCWW 2

Atherton, Lucius
See Masters, Edgar Lee
Atkins, Jack
See Harris, Mark
Atkinson, Kate CLC 99
See also CA 166
Attaway, William (Alexander)
1911-1986 .... **CLC 92; BLC 1; DAM MULT**
See also BW 2, 3; CA 143; CANR 82; DLB 76
Atticus
See Fleming, Ian (Lancaster); Wilson, (Thomas) Woodrow
Atwood, Margaret (Eleanor) 1939- ... **CLC 2, 3, 4, 8, 13, 15, 25, 44, 84, 135; DA; DAB; DAC; DAM MST, NOV, POET; PC 8; SSC 2**
See also AAYA 12; AW; BEST 89:2; CA 49-52; CANR 3, 24, 33, 59, 95; DA3; DLB 53; INT CANR-24; MTCW 1, 2; SATA 50
Aubigny, Pierre d'
See Mencken, H(enry) L(ouis)
Aubin, Penelope 1685-1731(?) .... **LC 9**
See also DLB 39
Auchincloss, Louis (Stanton) 1917- ... **CLC 4, 6, 9, 18, 45; DAM NOV; SSC 22**
See also AMWS 4; CA 1-4R; CANR 6, 29, 55, 87; DLB 2; DLBY 80; INT CANR-29; MTCW 1
Auden, W(ystan) H(ugh) 1907-1973 . **CLC 1, 2, 3, 4, 6, 9, 11, 14, 43, 123; DA; DAB; DAC; DAM DRAM, MST, POET; PC 1**
See also AAYA 18; AMWS 2; AW; CA 9-12R; 45-48; CANR 5, 61; CDBLB 1914-1945; DA3; DLB 10, 20; MTCW 1, 2
Audiberti, Jacques 1900-1965 .... **CLC 38; DAM DRAM**
See also CA 25-28R
Audubon, John James 1785-1851 . **NCLC 47**
Auel, Jean M(arie) 1936- .... **CLC 31, 107; DAM POP**
See also AAYA 7; BEST 90:4; CA 103; CANR 21, 64; DA3; INT CANR-21; SATA 91
Auerbach, Erich 1892-1957 .... **TCLC 43**
See also CA 118; 155
Augier, Emile 1820-1889 .... **NCLC 31**
See also DLB 192
August, John
See De Voto, Bernard (Augustine)
Augustine 354-430 .... **CMLC 6; DA; DAB; DAC; DAM MST**
See also AW; DA3; DLB 115
Aurelius
See Bourne, Randolph S(illiman)
Aurobindo, Sri
See Ghose, Aurabinda
Austen, Jane 1775-1817 ...... **NCLC 1, 13, 19, 33, 51, 81, 95; DA; DAB; DAC; DAM MST, NOV**
See also AAYA 19; AW 1; CDBLB 1789-1832; DA3; DLB 116
Auster, Paul 1947- .... **CLC 47, 131**
See also CA 69-72; CANR 23, 52, 75; DA3; DLB 227; MTCW 1
Austin, Frank
See Faust, Frederick (Schiller)
See also TCWW 2
Austin, Mary (Hunter) 1868-1934 . **TCLC 25**
See also Stairs, Gordon
See also CA 109; 178; DLB 9, 78, 206, 221; TCWW 2
Averroes 1126-1198 .... **CMLC 7**
See also DLB 115

Avicenna 980-1037 .... **CMLC 16**
See also DLB 115
Avison, Margaret 1918- .... **CLC 2, 4, 97; DAC; DAM POET**
See also CA 17-20R; DLB 53; MTCW 1
Axton, David
See Koontz, Dean R(ay)
Ayckbourn, Alan 1939- ...... **CLC 5, 8, 18, 33, 74; DAB; DAM DRAM; DC 13**
See also BRWS 5; CA 21-24R; CANR 31, 59; DLB 13; MTCW 1, 2
Aydy, Catherine
See Tennant, Emma (Christina)
Ayme, Marcel (Andre) 1902-1967 ... **CLC 11; SSC 41**
See also CA 89-92; CANR 67; CLR 25; DLB 72; SATA 91
Ayrton, Michael 1921-1975 .... **CLC 7**
See also CA 5-8R; 61-64; CANR 9, 21
Azorin CLC 11
See also Martinez Ruiz, Jose
Azuela, Mariano 1873-1952 . **TCLC 3; DAM MULT; HLC 1**
See also CA 104; 131; CANR 81; HW 1, 2; MTCW 1, 2
Baastad, Babbis Friis
See Friis-Baastad, Babbis Ellinor
Bab
See Gilbert, W(illiam) S(chwenck)
Babbis, Eleanor
See Friis-Baastad, Babbis Ellinor
Babel, Isaac
See Babel, Isaak (Emmanuilovich)
Babel, Isaak (Emmanuilovich)
1894-1941(?) .... **TCLC 2, 13; SSC 16**
See also Babel, Isaac
See also CA 104; 155; MTCW 1
Babits, Mihaly 1883-1941 .... **TCLC 14**
See also CA 114
Babur 1483-1530 .... **LC 18**
Baca, Jimmy Santiago 1952-
See also CA 131; CANR 81, 90; DAM MULT; DLB 122; HLC 1; HW 1, 2
Bacchelli, Riccardo 1891-1985 .... **CLC 19**
See also CA 29-32R; 117
Bach, Richard (David) 1936- .... **CLC 14; DAM NOV, POP**
See also AITN 1; BEST 89:2; CA 9-12R; CANR 18, 93; MTCW 1; SATA 13
Bachman, Richard
See King, Stephen (Edwin)
Bachmann, Ingeborg 1926-1973 .... **CLC 69**
See also CA 93-96; 45-48; CANR 69; DLB 85
Bacon, Francis 1561-1626 .... **LC 18, 32**
See also CDBLB Before 1660; DLB 151, 236
Bacon, Roger 1214(?)-1294 .... **CMLC 14**
See also DLB 115
Bacovia, George 1881-1957 .... **TCLC 24**
See also Bacovia, G.; Vasiliu, Gheorghe
See also DLB 220
Badanes, Jerome 1937- .... **CLC 59**
Bagehot, Walter 1826-1877 .... **NCLC 10**
See also DLB 55
Bagnold, Enid 1889-1981 ...... **CLC 25; DAM DRAM**
See also CA 5-8R; 103; CANR 5, 40; DLB 13, 160, 191; MAICYA; SATA 1, 25
Bagritsky, Eduard 1895-1934 .... **TCLC 60**
Bagrjana, Elisaveta
See Belcheva, Elisaveta
Bagryana, Elisaveta CLC 10
See also Belcheva, Elisaveta
See also CA 178; DLB 147
Bailey, Paul 1937- .... **CLC 45**
See also CA 21-24R; CANR 16, 62; DLB 14; GLL 2

Bashevis, Isaac
See Singer, Isaac Bashevis
Bashkirtseff, Marie 1859-1884 .... NCLC 27
Basho
See Matsuo Basho
Basil of Caesaria c. 330-379 .... CMLC 35
Bass, Kingsley B., Jr.
See Bullins, Ed
Bass, Rick 1958- .... CLC 79
See also CA 126; CANR 53, 93; DLB 212
Bassani, Giorgio 1916-2000 .... CLC 9
See also CA 65-68; CANR 33; CWW 2;
DLB 128, 177; MTCW 1
Bastos, Augusto (Antonio) Roa
See Roa Bastos, Augusto (Antonio)
Bataille, Georges 1897-1962 .... CLC 29
See also CA 101; 89-92
Bates, H(erbert) E(rnest)
1905-1974 . CLC 46; DAB; DAM POP;
SSC 10
See also CA 93-96; 45-48; CANR 34; DA3;
DLB 162, 191; MTCW 1, 2
Bauchart
See Camus, Albert
Baudelaire, Charles 1821-1867 . NCLC 6, 29,
55; DA; DAB; DAC; DAM MST,
POET; PC 1; SSC 18
See also AW; DA3
Baudrillard, Jean 1929- .... CLC 60
Baum, L(yman) Frank 1856-1919 ... TCLC 7
See also CA 108; 133; CLR 15; DLB 22;
JRDA; MAICYA; MTCW 1, 2; SATA 18,
100
Baum, Louis F.
See Baum, L(yman) Frank
Baumbach, Jonathan 1933- .... CLC 6, 23
See also CA 13-16R; CAAS 5; CANR 12,
66; DLBY 80; INT CANR-12; MTCW 1
Bausch, Richard (Carl) 1945- .... CLC 51
See also AMWS 7; CA 101; CAAS 14;
CANR 43, 61, 87; DLB 130
Baxter, Charles (Morley) 1947- .... CLC 45,
78; DAM POP
See also CA 57-60; CANR 40, 64; DLB
130; MTCW 2
Baxter, George Owen
See Faust, Frederick (Schiller)
Baxter, James K(eir) 1926-1972 .... CLC 14
See also CA 77-80
Baxter, John
See Hunt, E(verette) Howard, (Jr.)
Bayer, Sylvia
See Glassco, John
Baynton, Barbara 1857-1929 .... TCLC 57
See also DLB 230
Beagle, Peter S(oyer) 1939- .... CLC 7, 104
See also AW; CA 9-12R; CANR 4, 51, 73;
DA3; DLBY 80; INT CANR-4; MTCW
1; SATA 60
Bean, Normal
See Burroughs, Edgar Rice
Beard, Charles A(ustin)
1874-1948 .... TCLC 15
See also CA 115; 189; DLB 17; SATA 18
Beardsley, Aubrey 1872-1898 .... NCLC 6
Beattie, Ann 1947- ..... CLC 8, 13, 18, 40, 63;
DAM NOV, POP; SSC 11
See also AMWS 5; BEST 90:2; CA 81-84;
CANR 53, 73; DA3; DLBY 82; MTCW
1, 2
Beattie, James 1735-1803 .... NCLC 25
See also DLB 109
Beauchamp, Kathleen Mansfield 1888-1923
See Mansfield, Katherine
See also CA 104; 134; DA; DAC; DAM
MST; DA3; MTCW 2

Beaumarchais, Pierre-Augustin Caron de
1732-1799 . LC 61; DAM DRAM; DC 4
Beaumont, Francis 1584(?)-1616 .... LC 33;
DC 6
See also CDBLB Before 1660; DLB 58, 121
Beauvoir, Simone (Lucie Ernestine Marie
Bertrand) de 1908-1986 .... CLC 1, 2, 4,
8, 14, 31, 44, 50, 71, 124; DA; DAB;
DAC; DAM MST, NOV; SSC 35
See also AW; CA 9-12R; 118; CANR 28,
61; DA3; DLB 72; DLBY 86; MTCW 1,
2
Becker, Carl (Lotus) 1873-1945 ..... TCLC 63
See also CA 157; DLB 17
Becker, Jurek 1937-1997 .... CLC 7, 19
See also CA 85-88; 157; CANR 60; CWW
2; DLB 75
Becker, Walter 1950- .... CLC 26
Beckett, Samuel (Barclay)
1906-1989 .. CLC 1, 2, 3, 4, 6, 9, 10, 11,
14, 18, 29, 57, 59, 83; DA; DAB; DAC;
DAM DRAM, MST, NOV; SSC 16
See also AW; BRWS 1; CA 5-8R; 130;
CANR 33, 61; CDBLB 1945-1960; DA3;
DLB 13, 15, 233; DLBY 90; MTCW 1, 2
Beckford, William 1760-1844 .... NCLC 16
See also DLB 39,213
Beckman, Gunnel 1910- .... CLC 26
See also CA 33-36R; CANR 15; CLR 25;
MAICYA; SAAS 9; SATA 6
Becque, Henri 1837-1899 .... NCLC 3
See also DLB 192
Becquer, Gustavo Adolfo 1836-1870
See also DAM MULT; HLCS 1
Beddoes, Thomas Lovell
1803-1849 .... NCLC 3
See also DLB 96
Bede c. 673-735 .... CMLC 20
See also DLB 146
Bedford, Donald F.
See Fearing, Kenneth (Flexner)
Beecher, Catharine Esther
1800-1878 .... NCLC 30
See also DLB 1
Beecher, John 1904-1980 .... CLC 6
See also AITN 1; CA 5-8R; 105; CANR 8
Beer, Johann 1655-1700 .... LC 5
See also DLB 168
Beer, Patricia 1924- .... CLC 58
See also CA 61-64; 183; CANR 13, 46;
DLB 40
Beerbohm, Max
See Beerbohm, (Henry) Max(imilian)
See also BRWS 2
Beerbohm, (Henry) Max(imilian)
1872-1956 .... TCLC 1, 24
See also CA 104; 154; CANR 79; DLB 34,
100
Beer-Hofmann, Richard
1866-1945 .... TCLC 60
See also CA 160; DLB 81
Begiebing, Robert J(ohn) 1946- .... CLC 70
See also CA 122; CANR 40, 88
Behan, Brendan 1923-1964 ...... CLC 1, 8, 11,
15, 79; DAM DRAM
See also BRWS 2; CA 73-76; CANR 33;
CDBLB 1945-1960; DLB 13, 233;
MTCW 1, 2
Behn, Aphra 1640(?)-1689 .... LC 1, 30, 42;
DA; DAB; DAC; DAM DRAM, MST,
NOV, POET; DC 4; PC 13
See also AW; BRWS 3; DA3; DLB 39, 80,
131
Behrman, S(amuel) N(athaniel)
1893-1973 .... CLC 40
See also CA 13-16; 45-48; CAP 1; DLB 7,
44
Belasco, David 1853-1931 .... TCLC 3
See also CA 104; 168; DLB 7

Belcheva, Elisaveta 1893-1991 .... CLC 10
See also Bagryana, Elisaveta
Beldone, Phil "Cheech"
See Ellison, Harlan (Jay)
Beleno
See Azuela, Mariano
Belinski, Vissarion Grigoryevich
1811-1848 .... NCLC 5
See also DLB 198
Belitt, Ben 1911- .... CLC 22
See also CA 13-16R; CAAS 4; CANR 7,
77; DLB 5
Bell, Gertrude (Margaret Lowthian)
1868-1926 .... TCLC 67
See also CA 167; DLB 174
Bell, J. Freeman
See Zangwill, Israel
Bell, James Madison 1826-1902 ... TCLC 43;
BLC 1; DAM MULT
See also BW 1; CA 122; 124; DLB 50
Bell, Madison Smartt 1957- ...... CLC 41, 102
See also CA 111, 183; CAAE 183; CANR
28, 54, 73; MTCW 1
Bell, Marvin (Hartley) 1937- ...... CLC 8, 31;
DAM POET
See also CA 21-24R; CAAS 14; CANR 59;
DLB 5; MTCW 1
Bell, W. L. D.
See Mencken, H(enry) L(ouis)
Bellamy, Atwood C.
See Mencken, H(enry) L(ouis)
Bellamy, Edward 1850-1898 ...... NCLC 4, 86
See also DLB 12
Belli, Gioconda 1949-
See also CA 152; CWW 2; HLCS 1
Bellin, Edward J.
See Kuttner, Henry
Belloc, (Joseph) Hilaire (Pierre Sebastien
Rene Swanton) 1870-1953 ...... TCLC 7,
18; DAM POET; PC 24
See also AW 1; CA 106; 152; DLB 19, 100,
141, 174; MTCW 1; SATA 112
Belloc, Joseph Peter Rene Hilaire
See Belloc, (Joseph) Hilaire (Pierre Sebas-
tien Rene Swanton)
Belloc, Joseph Pierre Hilaire
See Belloc, (Joseph) Hilaire (Pierre Sebas-
tien Rene Swanton)
Belloc, M. A.
See Lowndes, Marie Adelaide (Belloc)
Bellow, Saul 1915- . CLC 1, 2, 3, 6, 8, 10, 13,
15, 25, 33, 34, 63, 79; DA; DAB; DAC;
DAM MST, NOV, POP; SSC 14
See also AITN 2; AW; BEST 89:3; CA
5-8R; CABS 1; CANR 29, 53, 95;
CDALB 1941-1968; DA3; DLB 2, 28;
DLBD 3; DLBY 82; MTCW 1, 2
Belser, Reimond Karel Maria de 1929-
See Ruyslinck, Ward
See also CA 152
Bely, Andrey TCLC 7; PC 11
See also Bugayev, Boris Nikolayevich
See also MTCW 1
Belyi, Andrei
See Bugayev, Boris Nikolayevich
Benary, Margot
See Benary-Isbert, Margot
Benary-Isbert, Margot 1889-1979 .... CLC 12
See also CA 5-8R; 89-92; CANR 4, 72;
CLR 12; MAICYA; SATA 2; SATA-Obit
21
Benavente (y Martinez), Jacinto
1866-1954 .... TCLC 3; DAM DRAM,
MULT; HLCS 1
See also CA 106; 131; CANR 81; GLL 2;
HW 1, 2; MTCW 1, 2

Benchley, Peter (Bradford) 1940- . **CLC 4, 8; DAM NOV, POP**
See also AAYA 14; AITN 2; CA 17-20R; CANR 12, 35, 66; MTCW 1, 2; SATA 3, 89

Benchley, Robert (Charles)
1889-1945 .... **TCLC 1, 55**
See also CA 105; 153; DLB 11

Benda, Julien 1867-1956 .... **TCLC 60**
See also CA 120; 154

Benedict, Ruth (Fulton)
1887-1948 .... **TCLC 60**
See also CA 158

Benedict, Saint c. 480-c. 547 .... **CMLC 29**

Benedikt, Michael 1935- .... **CLC 4, 14**
See also CA 13-16R; CANR 7; DLB 5

Benet, Juan 1927-1993 .... **CLC 28**
See also CA 143

Benet, Stephen Vincent 1898-1943 . **TCLC 7; DAM POET; SSC 10**
See also AW 1; CA 104; 152; DA3; DLB 4, 48, 102; DLBY 97; MTCW 1

Benet, William Rose 1886-1950 .... **TCLC 28; DAM POET**
See also CA 118; 152; DLB 45

Benford, Gregory (Albert) 1941- ..... **CLC 52**
See also CA 69-72, 175; CAAE 175; CAAS 27; CANR 12, 24, 49, 95; DLBY 82; SCFW 2

Bengtsson, Frans (Gunnar)
1894-1954 .... **TCLC 48**
See also CA 170

Benjamin, David
See Slavitt, David R(ytman)

Benjamin, Lois
See Gould, Lois

Benjamin, Walter 1892-1940 .... **TCLC 39**
See also CA 164; DLB 242

Benn, Gottfried 1886-1956 .... **TCLC 3**
See also CA 106; 153; DLB 56

Bennett, Alan 1934- .... **CLC 45, 77; DAB; DAM MST**
See also CA 103; CANR 35, 55; MTCW 1, 2

Bennett, (Enoch) Arnold
1867-1931 .... **TCLC 5, 20**
See also CA 106; 155; CDBLB 1890-1914; DLB 10, 34, 98, 135; MTCW 2

Bennett, Elizabeth
See Mitchell, Margaret (Munnerlyn)

Bennett, George Harold 1930-
See Bennett, Hal
See also BW 1; CA 97-100; CANR 87

Bennett, Hal CLC 5
See Bennett, George Harold
See also DLB 33

Bennett, Jay 1912- .... **CLC 35**
See also AAYA 10; AW; CA 69-72; CANR 11, 42, 79; JRDA; SAAS 4; SATA 41, 87; SATA-Brief 27

Bennett, Louise (Simone) 1919- ...... **CLC 28; BLC 1; DAM MULT**
See also BW 2, 3; CA 151; DLB 117

Benson, E(dward) F(rederic)
1867-1940 .... **TCLC 27**
See also CA 114; 157; DLB 135, 153

Benson, Jackson J. 1930- .... **CLC 34**
See also CA 25-28R; DLB 111

Benson, Sally 1900-1972 .... **CLC 17**
See also CA 19-20; 37-40R; CAP 1; SATA 1, 35; SATA-Obit 27

Benson, Stella 1892-1933 .... **TCLC 17**
See also CA 117; 155; DLB 36, 162

Bentham, Jeremy 1748-1832 .... **NCLC 38**
See also DLB 107, 158

Bentley, E(dmund) C(lerihew)
1875-1956 .... **TCLC 12**
See also CA 108; DLB 70

Bentley, Eric (Russell) 1916- .... **CLC 24**
See also CA 5-8R; CANR 6, 67; INT CANR-6

Beranger, Pierre Jean de
1780-1857 .... **NCLC 34**

Berdyaev, Nicolas
See Berdyaev, Nikolai (Aleksandrovich)

Berdyaev, Nikolai (Aleksandrovich)
1874-1948 .... **TCLC 67**
See also CA 120; 157

Berdyayev, Nikolai (Aleksandrovich)
See Berdyaev, Nikolai (Aleksandrovich)

Berendt, John (Lawrence) 1939- ...... **CLC 86**
See also CA 146; CANR 75, 93; DA3; MTCW 1

Beresford, J(ohn) D(avys)
1873-1947 .... **TCLC 81**
See also CA 112; 155; DLB 162, 178, 197

Bergelson, David 1884-1952 .... **TCLC 81**

Berger, Colonel
See Malraux, (Georges-)Andre

Berger, John (Peter) 1926- .... **CLC 2, 19**
See also BRWS 4; CA 81-84; CANR 51, 78; DLB 14, 207

Berger, Melvin H. 1927- .... **CLC 12**
See also CA 5-8R; CANR 4; CLR 32; SAAS 2; SATA 5, 88

Berger, Thomas (Louis) 1924- ... **CLC 3, 5, 8, 11, 18, 38; DAM NOV**
See also CA 1-4R; CANR 5, 28, 51; DLB 2; DLBY 80; INT CANR-28; MTCW 1, 2; TCWW 2

Bergman, (Ernst) Ingmar
1918-1997 .... **CLC 16, 72**
See also CA 81-84; CANR 33, 70; MTCW 2

Bergson, Henri(-Louis) 1859-1941 . **TCLC 32**
See also CA 164

Bergstein, Eleanor 1938- .... **CLC 4**
See also CA 53-56; CANR 5

Berkoff, Steven 1937- .... **CLC 56**
See also CA 104; CANR 72

Berlin, Isaiah 1909-1997 .... **TCLC 105**
See also CA 85-88; 162

Bermant, Chaim (Icyk) 1929-1998 ... **CLC 40**
See also CA 57-60; CANR 6, 31, 57

Bern, Victoria
See Fisher, M(ary) F(rances) K(ennedy)

Bernanos, (Paul Louis) Georges
1888-1948 .... **TCLC 3**
See also CA 104; 130; CANR 94; DLB 72

Bernard, April 1956- .... **CLC 59**
See also CA 131

Berne, Victoria
See Fisher, M(ary) F(rances) K(ennedy)

Bernhard, Thomas 1931-1989 ..... **CLC 3, 32, 61; DC 14**
See also CA 85-88; 127; CANR 32, 57; DLB 85, 124; MTCW 1

Bernhardt, Sarah (Henriette Rosine)
1844-1923 .... **TCLC 75**
See also CA 157

Berriault, Gina 1926-1999 .... **CLC 54, 109; SSC 30**
See also CA 116; 129; 185; CANR 66; DLB 130

Berrigan, Daniel 1921- .... **CLC 4**
See also CA 33-36R; CAAE 187; CAAS 1; CANR 11, 43, 78; DLB 5

Berrigan, Edmund Joseph Michael, Jr.
1934-1983
See Berrigan, Ted
See also CA 61-64; 110; CANR 14

Berrigan, Ted CLC 37
See also Berrigan, Edmund Joseph Michael, Jr.
See also DLB 5, 169

Berry, Charles Edward Anderson 1931-
See Berry, Chuck
See also CA 115

Berry, Chuck CLC 17
See also Berry, Charles Edward Anderson

Berry, Jonas
See Ashbery, John (Lawrence)
See also GLL 1

Berry, Wendell (Erdman) 1934- ... **CLC 4, 6, 8, 27, 46; DAM POET; PC 28**
See also AITN 1; CA 73-76; CANR 50, 73; DLB 5, 6, 234; MTCW 1

Berryman, John 1914-1972 ... **CLC 1, 2, 3, 4, 6, 8, 10, 13, 25, 62; DAM POET**
See also CA 13-16; 33-36R; CABS 2; CANR 35; CAP 1; CDALB 1941-1968; DLB 48; MTCW 1, 2

Bertolucci, Bernardo 1940- .... **CLC 16**
See also CA 106

Berton, Pierre (Francis Demarigny)
1920- .... **CLC 104**
See also CA 1-4R; CANR 2, 56; DLB 68; SATA 99

Bertrand, Aloysius 1807-1841 .... **NCLC 31**

Bertran de Born c. 1140-1215 .... **CMLC 5**

Besant, Annie (Wood) 1847-1933 ..... **TCLC 9**
See also CA 105; 185

Bessie, Alvah 1904-1985 .... **CLC 23**
See also CA 5-8R; 116; CANR 2, 80; DLB 26

Bethlen, T. D.
See Silverberg, Robert

Beti, Mongo CLC 27; BLC 1; DAM MULT
See also Biyidi, Alexandre
See also CANR 79

Betjeman, John 1906-1984 ...... **CLC 2, 6, 10, 34, 43; DAB; DAM MST, POET**
See also CA 9-12R; 112; CANR 33, 56; CDBLB 1945-1960; DA3; DLB 20; DLBY 84; MTCW 1, 2

Bettelheim, Bruno 1903-1990 .... **CLC 79**
See also CA 81-84; 131; CANR 23, 61; DA3; MTCW 1, 2

Betti, Ugo 1892-1953 .... **TCLC 5**
See also CA 104; 155

Betts, Doris (Waugh) 1932- ...... **CLC 3, 6, 28**
See also CA 13-16R; CANR 9, 66, 77; DLBY 82; INT CANR-9

Bevan, Alistair
See Roberts, Keith (John Kingston)

Bey, Pilaff
See Douglas, (George) Norman

Bialik, Chaim Nachman
1873-1934 .... **TCLC 25**
See also CA 170

Bickerstaff, Isaac
See Swift, Jonathan

Bidart, Frank 1939- .... **CLC 33**
See also CA 140

Bienek, Horst 1930- .... **CLC 7, 11**
See also CA 73-76; DLB 75

Bierce, Ambrose (Gwinett)
1842-1914(?) .... **TCLC 1, 7, 44; DA; DAC; DAM MST; SSC 9**
See also AW; CA 104; 139; CANR 78; CDALB 1865-1917; DA3; DLB 11, 12, 23, 71, 74, 186

Biggers, Earl Derr 1884-1933 .... **TCLC 65**
See also CA 108; 153

Billings, Josh
See Shaw, Henry Wheeler

Billington, (Lady) Rachel (Mary)
1942- .... **CLC 43**
See also AITN 2; CA 33-36R; CANR 44

Binyon, T(imothy) J(ohn) 1936- .... **CLC 34**
See also CA 111; CANR 28

Author Index

Bonnefoy, Yves 1923- .. **CLC 9, 15, 58; DAM MST, POET**
See also CA 85-88; CANR 33, 75; CWW 2; MTCW 1, 2

Bontemps, Arna(ud Wendell) 1902-1973 ..... **CLC 1, 18; BLC 1; DAM MULT, NOV, POET**
See also BW 1; CA 1-4R; 41-44R; CANR 4, 35; CLR 6; DA3; DLB 48, 51; JRDA; MAICYA; MTCW 1, 2; SATA 2, 44; SATA-Obit 24

Booth, Martin 1944- .... **CLC 13**
See also CA 93-96; CAAE 188; CAAS 2; CANR 92

Booth, Philip 1925- .... **CLC 23**
See also CA 5-8R; CANR 5, 88; DLBY 82

Booth, Wayne C(layson) 1921- .... **CLC 24**
See also CA 1-4R; CAAS 5; CANR 3, 43; DLB 67

Borchert, Wolfgang 1921-1947 .... **TCLC 5**
See also CA 104; 188; DLB 69, 124

Borel, Petrus 1809-1859 .... **NCLC 41**

Borges, Jorge Luis 1899-1986 ... **CLC 1, 2, 3, 4, 6, 8, 9, 10, 13, 19, 44, 48, 83; DA; DAB; DAC; DAM MST, MULT; HLC 1; PC 22, 32; SSC 4, 41**
See also AAYA 26; AW; CA 21-24R; CANR 19, 33, 75; DA3; DLB 113; DLBY 86; HW 1, 2; MTCW 1, 2

Borowski, Tadeusz 1922-1951 .... **TCLC 9**
See also CA 106; 154

Borrow, George (Henry) 1803-1881 .... **NCLC 9**
See also DLB 21, 55, 166

Bosch (Gavino), Juan 1909-
See also CA 151; DAM MST, MULT; DLB 145; HLCS 1; HW 1, 2

Bosman, Herman Charles 1905-1951 .... **TCLC 49**
See also Malan, Herman
See also CA 160; DLB 225

Bosschere, Jean de 1878(?)-1953 ... **TCLC 19**
See also CA 115; 186

Boswell, James 1740-1795 ...... **LC 4, 50; DA; DAB; DAC; DAM MST**
See also AW; CDBLB 1660-1789; DLB 104, 142

Bottomley, Gordon 1874-1948 ..... **TCLC 107**
See also CA 120; DLB 10

Bottoms, David 1949- .... **CLC 53**
See also CA 105; CANR 22; DLB 120; DLBY 83

Boucicault, Dion 1820-1890 .... **NCLC 41**

Boucolon, Maryse
See Conde, Maryse

Bourget, Paul (Charles Joseph) 1852-1935 .... **TCLC 12**
See also CA 107; DLB 123

Bourjaily, Vance (Nye) 1922- .... **CLC 8, 62**
See also CA 1-4R; CAAS 1; CANR 2, 72; DLB 2, 143

Bourne, Randolph S(illiman) 1886-1918 .... **TCLC 16**
See also CA 117; 155; DLB 63

Bova, Ben(jamin William) 1932- ...... **CLC 45**
See also AAYA 16; CA 5-8R; CAAS 18; CANR 11, 56, 94; CLR 3; DLBY 81; INT CANR-11; MAICYA; MTCW 1; SATA 6, 68

Bowen, Elizabeth (Dorothea Cole) 1899-1973 . **CLC 1, 3, 6, 11, 15, 22, 118; DAM NOV; SSC 3, 28**
See also BRWS 2; CA 17-18; 41-44R; CANR 35; CAP 2; CDBLB 1945-1960; DA3; DLB 15, 162; MTCW 1, 2

Bowering, George 1935- .... **CLC 15, 47**
See also CA 21-24R; CAAS 16; CANR 10; DLB 53

Bowering, Marilyn R(uthe) 1949- .... **CLC 32**
See also CA 101; CANR 49

Bowers, Edgar 1924-2000 .... **CLC 9**
See also CA 5-8R; 188; CANR 24; DLB 5

Bowie, David CLC 17
See also Jones, David Robert

Bowles, Jane (Sydney) 1917-1973 ..... **CLC 3, 68**
See also CA 19-20; 41-44R; CAP 2

Bowles, Paul (Frederick) 1910-1999 . **CLC 1, 2, 19, 53; SSC 3**
See also AMWS 4; CA 1-4R; 186; CAAS 1; CANR 1, 19, 50, 75; DA3; DLB 5, 6; MTCW 1, 2

Box, Edgar
See Vidal, Gore
See also GLL 1

Boyd, Nancy
See Millay, Edna St. Vincent
See also GLL 1

Boyd, William 1952- .... **CLC 28, 53, 70**
See also CA 114; 120; CANR 51, 71; DLB 231

Boyle, Kay 1902-1992 .... **CLC 1, 5, 19, 58, 121; SSC 5**
See also CA 13-16R; 140; CAAS 1; CANR 29, 61; DLB 4, 9, 48, 86; DLBY 93; MTCW 1, 2

Boyle, Mark
See Kienzle, William X(avier)

Boyle, Patrick 1905-1982 .... **CLC 19**
See also CA 127

Boyle, T. C.
See Boyle, T(homas) Coraghessan

Boyle, T(homas) Coraghessan 1948- .... **CLC 36, 55, 90; DAM POP; SSC 16**
See also BEST 90:4; CA 120; CANR 44, 76, 89; DA3; DLBY 86; MTCW 2

Boz
See Dickens, Charles (John Huffam)

Brackenridge, Hugh Henry 1748-1816 .... **NCLC 7**
See also DLB 11, 37

Bradbury, Edward P.
See Moorcock, Michael (John)
See also MTCW 2

Bradbury, Malcolm (Stanley) 1932-2000 .... **CLC 32, 61; DAM NOV**
See also CA 1-4R; CANR 1, 33, 91; DA3; DLB 14, 207; MTCW 1, 2

Bradbury, Ray (Douglas) 1920- ... **CLC 1, 3, 10, 15, 42, 98; DA; DAB; DAC; DAM MST, NOV, POP; SSC 29**
See also AAYA 15; AITN 1, 2; AMWS 4; AW; CA 1-4R; CANR 2, 30, 75; CDALB 1968-1988; DA3; DLB 2, 8; MTCW 1, 2; SATA 11, 64; SCFW 2

Bradford, Gamaliel 1863-1932 .... **TCLC 36**
See also CA 160; DLB 17

Bradford, William 1590-1657 .... **LC 64**
See also DLB 24, 30

Bradley, David (Henry), Jr. 1950- ... **CLC 23, 118; BLC 1; DAM MULT**
See also BW 1, 3; CA 104; CANR 26, 81; DLB 33

Bradley, John Ed(mund, Jr.) 1958- . **CLC 55**
See also CA 139

Bradley, Marion Zimmer 1930-1999 .... **CLC 30; DAM POP**
See also Chapman, Lee; Dexter, John; Gardner, Miriam; Ives, Morgan; Rivers, Elfrida
See also AAYA 9; AW; CA 57-60; 185; CAAS 10; CANR 7, 31, 51, 75; DA3; DLB 8; MTCW 1, 2; SATA 90; SATA-Obit 116

Bradstreet, Anne 1612(?)-1672 .... **LC 4, 30; DA; DAC; DAM MST, POET; PC 10**
See also AMWS 1; CDALB 1640-1865; DA3; DLB 24

Brady, Joan 1939- .... **CLC 86**
See also CA 141

Bragg, Melvyn 1939- .... **CLC 10**
See also BEST 89:3; CA 57-60; CANR 10, 48, 89; DLB 14

Brahe, Tycho 1546-1601 .... **LC 45**

Braine, John (Gerard) 1922-1986 . **CLC 1, 3, 41**
See also CA 1-4R; 120; CANR 1, 33; CD-BLB 1945-1960; DLB 15; DLBY 86; MTCW 1

Bramah, Ernest 1868-1942 .... **TCLC 72**
See also CA 156; DLB 70

Brammer, William 1930(?)-1978 ...... **CLC 31**
See also CA 77-80

Brancati, Vitaliano 1907-1954 .... **TCLC 12**
See also CA 109

Brancato, Robin F(idler) 1936- .... **CLC 35**
See also AAYA 9; CA 69-72; CANR 11, 45; CLR 32; JRDA; SAAS 9; SATA 97

Brand, Max
See Faust, Frederick (Schiller)
See also TCWW 2

Brand, Millen 1906-1980 .... **CLC 7**
See also CA 21-24R; 97-100; CANR 72

Branden, Barbara CLC 44
See also CA 148

Brandes, Georg (Morris Cohen) 1842-1927 .... **TCLC 10**
See also CA 105; 189

Brandys, Kazimierz 1916-2000 .... **CLC 62**

Branley, Franklyn M(ansfield) 1915- .... **CLC 21**
See also CA 33-36R; CANR 14, 39; CLR 13; MAICYA; SAAS 16; SATA 4, 68

Brathwaite, Edward (Kamau) 1930- ...... **CLC 11; BLCS; DAM POET**
See also BW 2, 3; CA 25-28R; CANR 11, 26, 47; DLB 125

Brautigan, Richard (Gary) 1935-1984 .... **CLC 1, 3, 5, 9, 12, 34, 42; DAM NOV**
See also CA 53-56; 113; CANR 34; DA3; DLB 2, 5, 206; DLBY 80, 84; MTCW 1; SATA 56

Brave Bird, Mary
See Crow Dog, Mary (Ellen)
See also NNAL

Braverman, Kate 1950- .... **CLC 67**
See also CA 89-92

Brecht, (Eugen) Bertolt (Friedrich) 1898-1956 .... **TCLC 1, 6, 13, 35; DA; DAB; DAC; DAM DRAM, MST; DC 3**
See also AW; CA 104; 133; CANR 62; DA3; DLB 56, 124; MTCW 1, 2

Brecht, Eugen Berthold Friedrich
See Brecht, (Eugen) Bertolt (Friedrich)

Bremer, Fredrika 1801-1865 .... **NCLC 11**

Brennan, Christopher John 1870-1932 .... **TCLC 17**
See also CA 117; 188; DLB 230

Brennan, Maeve 1917-1993 .... **CLC 5**
See also CA 81-84; CANR 72

Brent, Linda
See Jacobs, Harriet A(nn)

Brentano, Clemens (Maria) 1778-1842 .... **NCLC 1**
See also DLB 90

Brent of Bin Bin
See Franklin, (Stella Maria Sarah) Miles (Lampe)

Brenton, Howard 1942- .... **CLC 31**
See also CA 69-72; CANR 33, 67; DLB 13; MTCW 1

Breslin, James 1935-1996
See Breslin, Jimmy
See also CA 73-76; CANR 31, 75; DAM
NOV; MTCW 1, 2

Breslin, Jimmy CLC 4, 43
See also Breslin, James
See also AITN 1; DLB 185; MTCW 2

Bresson, Robert 1901(?)-1999 .... **CLC 16**
See also CA 110; 187; CANR 49

Breton, Andre 1896-1966 .. **CLC 2, 9, 15, 54;
PC 15**
See also CA 19-20; 25-28R; CANR 40, 60;
CAP 2; DLB 65; MTCW 1, 2

Breytenbach, Breyten 1939(?)- .. **CLC 23, 37,
126; DAM POET**
See also CA 113; 129; CANR 61; CWW 2;
DLB 225

Bridgers, Sue Ellen 1942- .... **CLC 26**
See also AAYA 8; AW; CA 65-68; CANR
11, 36; CLR 18; DLB 52; JRDA; MAI-
CYA; SAAS 1; SATA 22, 90; SATA-Essay
109

Bridges, Robert (Seymour)
1844-1930 ... **TCLC 1; DAM POET; PC
28**
See also CA 104; 152; CDBLB 1890-1914;
DLB 19, 98

Bridie, James TCLC 3
See also Mavor, Osborne Henry
See also DLB 10

Brin, David 1950- .... **CLC 34**
See also AAYA 21; CA 102; CANR 24, 70;
INT CANR-24; SATA 65; SCFW 2

Brink, Andre (Philippus) 1935- . **CLC 18, 36,
106**
See also CA 104; CANR 39, 62; DLB 225;
INT 103; MTCW 1, 2

Brinsmead, H(esba) F(ay) 1922- ...... **CLC 21**
See also CA 21-24R; CANR 10; CLR 47;
MAICYA; SAAS 5; SATA 18, 78

Brittain, Vera (Mary) 1893(?)-1970 . **CLC 23**
See also CA 13-16; 25-28R; CANR 58;
CAP 1; DLB 191; MTCW 1, 2

Broch, Hermann 1886-1951 .... **TCLC 20**
See also CA 117; DLB 85, 124

Brock, Rose
See Hansen, Joseph
See also GLL 1

Brodkey, Harold (Roy) 1930-1996 ... **CLC 56**
See also CA 111; 151; CANR 71; DLB 130

Brodsky, Iosif Alexandrovich 1940-1996
See Brodsky, Joseph
See also AITN 1; CA 41-44R; 151; CANR
37; DAM POET; DA3; MTCW 1, 2

Brodsky, Joseph CLC 4, 6, 13, 36, 100; PC 9
See also Brodsky, Iosif Alexandrovich
See also CWW 2; MTCW 1

Brodsky, Michael (Mark) 1948- .... **CLC 19**
See also CA 102; CANR 18, 41, 58

Brome, Richard 1590(?)-1652 .... **LC 61**
See also DLB 58

Bromell, Henry 1947- .... **CLC 5**
See also CA 53-56; CANR 9

Bromfield, Louis (Brucker)
1896-1956 .... **TCLC 11**
See also CA 107; 155; DLB 4, 9, 86

Broner, E(sther) M(asserman)
1930- .... **CLC 19**
See also CA 17-20R; CANR 8, 25, 72; DLB
28

Bronk, William (M.) 1918-1999 .... **CLC 10**
See also CA 89-92; 177; CANR 23; DLB
165

Bronstein, Lev Davidovich
See Trotsky, Leon

Brontë, Anne 1820-1849 .... **NCLC 4, 71**
See also DA3; DLB 21, 199

Brontë, Charlotte 1816-1855 ...... **NCLC 3, 8,
33, 58; DA; DAB; DAC; DAM MST,
NOV**
See also AAYA 17; AW; CDBLB 1832-
1890; DA3; DLB 21, 159, 199

Brontë, Emily (Jane) 1818-1848 ... **NCLC 16,
35; DA; DAB; DAC; DAM MST, NOV,
POET; PC 8**
See also AAYA 17; AW; CDBLB 1832-
1890; DA3; DLB 21, 32, 199

Brontës
See Brontë

Brooke, Frances 1724-1789 .... **LC 6, 48**
See also DLB 39, 99

Brooke, Henry 1703(?)-1783 .... **LC 1**
See also DLB 39

Brooke, Rupert (Chawner)
1887-1915 .... **TCLC 2, 7; DA; DAB;
DAC; DAM MST, POET; PC 24**
See also AW; BRWS 3; CA 104; 132;
CANR 61; CDBLB 1914-1945; DLB 19;
GLL 2; MTCW 1, 2

Brooke-Haven, P.
See Wodehouse, P(elham) G(renville)

Brooke-Rose, Christine 1926(?)- ...... **CLC 40**
See also BRWS 4; CA 13-16R; CANR 58;
DLB 14, 231

Brookner, Anita 1928- . **CLC 32, 34, 51, 136;
DAB; DAM POP**
See also BRWS 4; CA 114; 120; CANR 37,
56, 87; DA3; DLB 194; DLBY 87;
MTCW 1, 2

Brooks, Cleanth 1906-1994 . **CLC 24, 86, 110**
See also CA 17-20R; 145; CANR 33, 35;
DLB 63; DLBY 94; INT CANR-35;
MTCW 1, 2

Brooks, George
See Baum, L(yman) Frank

Brooks, Gwendolyn 1917-2000 . **CLC 1, 2, 4,
5, 15, 49, 125; BLC 1; DA; DAC;
DAM MST, MULT, POET; PC 7**
See also AAYA 20; AITN 1; AMWS 3; AW;
BW 2, 3; CA 1-4R; CANR 1, 27, 52, 75;
CDALB 1941-1968; CLR 27; DA3; DLB
5, 76, 165; MTCW 1, 2; SATA 6

Brooks, Mel CLC 12
See also Kaminsky, Melvin
See also AAYA 13; DLB 26

Brooks, Peter 1938- .... **CLC 34**
See also CA 45-48; CANR 1

Brooks, Van Wyck 1886-1963 .... **CLC 29**
See also CA 1-4R; CANR 6; DLB 45, 63,
103

Brophy, Brigid (Antonia)
1929-1995 .... **CLC 6, 11, 29, 105**
See also CA 5-8R; 149; CAAS 4; CANR
25, 53; DA3; DLB 14; MTCW 1, 2

Brosman, Catharine Savage 1934- ..... **CLC 9**
See also CA 61-64; CANR 21, 46

Brossard, Nicole 1943- .... **CLC 115**
See also CA 122; CAAS 16; CCA 1; CWW
2; DLB 53; GLL 2

Brother Antoninus
See Everson, William (Oliver)

The Brothers Quay
See Quay, Stephen; Quay, Timothy

Broughton, T(homas) Alan 1936- ..... **CLC 19**
See also CA 45-48; CANR 2, 23, 48

Broumas, Olga 1949- .... **CLC 10, 73**
See also CA 85-88; CANR 20, 69; GLL 2

Broun, Heywood 1888-1939 .... **TCLC 104**
See also DLB 29, 171

Brown, Alan 1950- .... **CLC 99**
See also CA 156

Brown, Charles Brockden
1771-1810 .... **NCLC 22, 74**
See also AMWS 1; CDALB 1640-1865;
DLB 37, 59, 73

Brown, Christy 1932-1981 .... **CLC 63**
See also CA 105; 104; CANR 72; DLB 14

Brown, Claude 1937- .... **CLC 30; BLC 1;
DAM MULT**
See also AAYA 7; BW 1, 3; CA 73-76;
CANR 81

Brown, Dee (Alexander) 1908- . **CLC 18, 47;
DAM POP**
See also AAYA 30; CA 13-16R; CAAS 6;
CANR 11, 45, 60; DA3; DLBY 80;
MTCW 1, 2; SATA 5, 110; TCWW 2

Brown, George
See Wertmueller, Lina

Brown, George Douglas
1869-1902 .... **TCLC 28**
See also CA 162

Brown, George Mackay 1921-1996 ... **CLC 5,
48, 100**
See also CA 21-24R; 151; CAAS 6; CANR
12, 37, 67; DLB 14, 27, 139; MTCW 1;
SATA 35

Brown, (William) Larry 1951- .... **CLC 73**
See also CA 130; 134; INT 133

Brown, Moses
See Barrett, William (Christopher)

Brown, Rita Mae 1944- .... **CLC 18, 43, 79;
DAM NOV, POP**
See also CA 45-48; CANR 2, 11, 35, 62,
95; DA3; INT CANR-11; MTCW 1, 2

Brown, Roderick (Langmere)
See Haig-Brown, Roderick (Langmere)

Brown, Rosellen 1939- .... **CLC 32**
See also CA 77-80; CAAS 10; CANR 14,
44

Brown, Sterling Allen 1901-1989 ...... **CLC 1,
23, 59; BLC 1; DAM MULT, POET**
See also BW 1, 3; CA 85-88; 127; CANR
26; DA3; DLB 48, 51, 63; MTCW 1, 2

Brown, Will
See Ainsworth, William Harrison

Brown, William Wells 1815-1884 ... **NCLC 2,
89; BLC 1; DAM MULT; DC 1**
See also DLB 3, 50

Browne, (Clyde) Jackson 1948(?)- ... **CLC 21**
See also CA 120

Browning, Elizabeth Barrett
1806-1861 ...... **NCLC 1, 16, 61, 66; DA;
DAB; DAC; DAM MST, POET; PC 6**
See also AW; CDBLB 1832-1890; DA3;
DLB 32, 199

Browning, Robert 1812-1889 . **NCLC 19, 79;
DA; DAB; DAC; DAM MST, POET;
PC 2**
See also AW; CDBLB 1832-1890; DA3;
DLB 32, 163

Browning, Tod 1882-1962 .... **CLC 16**
See also CA 141; 117

Brownson, Orestes Augustus
1803-1876 .... **NCLC 50**
See also DLB 1, 59, 73

Bruccoli, Matthew J(oseph) 1931- ... **CLC 34**
See also CA 9-12R; CANR 7, 87; DLB 103

Bruce, Lenny CLC 21
See also Schneider, Leonard Alfred

Bruin, John
See Brutus, Dennis

Brulard, Henri
See Stendhal

Brulls, Christian
See Simenon, Georges (Jacques Christian)

Brunner, John (Kilian Houston)
1934-1995 .... **CLC 8, 10; DAM POP**
See also CA 1-4R; 149; CAAS 8; CANR 2,
37; MTCW 1, 2; SCFW 2

Bruno, Giordano 1548-1600 .... **LC 27**

Brutus, Dennis 1924- .... **CLC 43; BLC 1;
DAM MULT, POET; PC 24**
See also BW 2, 3; CA 49-52; CAAS 14;
CANR 2, 27, 42, 81; DLB 117, 225

Conde (Abellan), Carmen 1901-
　See also CA 177; DLB 108; HLCS 1; HW 2
Conde, Maryse 1937- .... CLC 52, 92; BLCS;
　DAM MULT
　See also BW 2, 3; CA 110; CANR 30, 53,
　76; CWW 2; MTCW 1
Condillac, Etienne Bonnot de
　1714-1780 .... LC 26
Condon, Richard (Thomas)
　1915-1996 ...... CLC 4, 6, 8, 10, 45, 100;
　DAM NOV
　See also BEST 90:3; CA 1-4R; 151; CAAS
　1; CANR 2, 23; INT CANR-23; MTCW
　1, 2
Confucius 551B.C.-479B.C. .. CMLC 19; DA;
　DAB; DAC; DAM MST
　See also AW; DA3
Congreve, William 1670-1729 .... LC 5, 21;
　DA; DAB; DAC; DAM DRAM, MST,
　POET; DC 2
　See also AW; CDBLB 1660-1789; DLB 39,
　84
Connell, Evan S(helby), Jr. 1924- . CLC 4, 6,
　45; DAM NOV
　See also AAYA 7; CA 1-4R; CAAS 2;
　CANR 2, 39, 76; DLB 2; DLBY 81;
　MTCW 1, 2
Connelly, Marc(us Cook) 1890-1980 . CLC 7
　See also CA 85-88; 102; CANR 30; DLB
　7; DLBY 80; SATA-Obit 25
Connor, Ralph TCLC 31
　See also Gordon, Charles William
　See also DLB 92; TCWW 2
Conrad, Joseph 1857-1924 .... TCLC 1, 6, 13,
　25, 43, 57; DA; DAB; DAC; DAM
　MST, NOV; SSC 9
　See also AAYA 26; AW; CA 104; 131;
　CANR 60; CDBLB 1890-1914; DA3;
　DLB 10, 34, 98, 156; MTCW 1, 2; SATA
　27
Conrad, Robert Arnold
　See Hart, Moss
Conroy, Pat
　See Conroy, (Donald) Pat(rick)
　See also MTCW 2
Conroy, (Donald) Pat(rick) 1945- ... CLC 30,
　74; DAM NOV, POP
　See also Conroy, Pat
　See also AAYA 8; AITN 1; CA 85-88;
　CANR 24, 53; DA3; DLB 6; MTCW 1
Constant (de Rebecque), (Henri) Benjamin
　1767-1830 .... NCLC 6
　See also DLB 119
Conybeare, Charles Augustus
　See Eliot, T(homas) S(tearns)
Cook, Michael 1933-1994 .... CLC 58
　See also CA 93-96; CANR 68; DLB 53
Cook, Robin 1940- .... CLC 14; DAM POP
　See also AAYA 32; BEST 90:2; CA 108;
　111; CANR 41, 90; DA3; INT 111
Cook, Roy
　See Silverberg, Robert
Cooke, Elizabeth 1948- .... CLC 55
　See also CA 129
Cooke, John Esten 1830-1886 .... NCLC 5
　See also DLB 3
Cooke, John Estes
　See Baum, L(yman) Frank
Cooke, M. E.
　See Creasey, John
Cooke, Margaret
　See Creasey, John
Cook-Lynn, Elizabeth 1930- . CLC 93; DAM
　MULT
　See also CA 133; DLB 175; NNAL
Cooney, Ray CLC 62
Cooper, Douglas 1960- .... CLC 86
Cooper, Henry St. John
　See Creasey, John

Cooper, J(oan) California (?)- .... CLC 56;
　DAM MULT
　See also AAYA 12; BW 1; CA 125; CANR
　55; DLB 212
Cooper, James Fenimore
　1789-1851 .... NCLC 1, 27, 54
　See also AAYA 22; CDALB 1640-1865;
　DA3; DLB 3; SATA 19
Coover, Robert (Lowell) 1932- ...... CLC 3, 7,
　15, 32, 46, 87; DAM NOV; SSC 15
　See also AMWS 5; CA 45-48; CANR 3,
　37, 58; DLB 2, 227; DLBY 81; MTCW
　1, 2
Copeland, Stewart (Armstrong)
　1952- .... CLC 26
Copernicus, Nicolaus 1473-1543 .... LC 45
Coppard, A(lfred) E(dgar)
　1878-1957 .... TCLC 5; SSC 21
　See also AW 1; CA 114; 167; DLB 162
Coppee, Francois 1842-1908 .... TCLC 25
　See also CA 170
Coppola, Francis Ford 1939- ... CLC 16, 126
　See also CA 77-80; CANR 40, 78; DLB 44
Corbiere, Tristan 1845-1875 .... NCLC 43
Corcoran, Barbara 1911- .... CLC 17
　See also AAYA 14; CA 21-24R; CAAS 2;
　CANR 11, 28, 48; CLR 50; DLB 52;
　JRDA; SAAS 20; SATA 3, 77
Cordelier, Maurice
　See Giraudoux, (Hippolyte) Jean
Corelli, Marie TCLC 51
　See also Mackay, Mary
　See also DLB 34, 156
Corman, Cid CLC 9
　See also Corman, Sidney
　See also CAAS 2; DLB 5, 193
Corman, Sidney 1924-
　See Corman, Cid
　See also CA 85-88; CANR 44; DAM POET
Cormier, Robert (Edmund)
　1925-2000 .... CLC 12, 30; DA; DAB;
　DAC; DAM MST, NOV
　See also AAYA 3, 19; CA 1-4R; CANR 5,
　23, 76, 93; CDALB 1968-1988; CLR 12,
　55; DLB 52; INT CANR-23; JRDA; MAI-
　CYA; MTCW 1, 2; SATA 10, 45, 83
Corn, Alfred (DeWitt III) 1943- .... CLC 33
　See also CA 179; CAAE 179; CAAS 25;
　CANR 44; DLB 120; DLBY 80
Corneille, Pierre 1606-1684 ..... LC 28; DAB;
　DAM MST
Cornwell, David (John Moore)
　1931- .... CLC 9, 15; DAM POP
　See also le Carre, John
　See also CA 5-8R; CANR 13, 33, 59; DA3;
　MTCW 1, 2
Corso, (Nunzio) Gregory 1930-2001 . CLC 1,
　11; PC 33
　See also CA 5-8R; CANR 41, 76; DA3;
　DLB 5, 16; MTCW 1, 2
Cortazar, Julio 1914-1984 ... CLC 2, 3, 5, 10,
　13, 15, 33, 34, 92; DAM MULT, NOV;
　HLC 1; SSC 7
　See also CA 21-24R; CANR 12, 32, 81;
　DA3; DLB 113; HW 1, 2; MTCW 1, 2
Cortes, Hernan 1485-1547 .... LC 31
Corvinus, Jakob
　See Raabe, Wilhelm (Karl)
Corwin, Cecil
　See Kornbluth, C(yril) M.
Cosic, Dobrica 1921- .... CLC 14
　See also CA 122; 138; CWW 2; DLB 181
Costain, Thomas B(ertram)
　1885-1965 .... CLC 30
　See also CA 5-8R; 25-28R; DLB 9
Costantini, Humberto 1924(?)-1987 . CLC 49
　See also CA 131; 122; HW 1

Costello, Elvis 1955- .... CLC 21
Costenoble, Philostene 1898-1962
　See Ghelderode, Michel de
Cotes, Cecil V.
　See Duncan, Sara Jeannette
Cotter, Joseph Seamon Sr.
　1861-1949 ...... TCLC 28; BLC 1; DAM
　MULT
　See also BW 1; CA 124; DLB 50
Couch, Arthur Thomas Quiller
　See Quiller-Couch, SirArthur (Thomas)
Coulton, James
　See Hansen, Joseph
Couperus, Louis (Marie Anne)
　1863-1923 .... TCLC 15
　See also CA 115
Coupland, Douglas 1961- .... CLC 85, 133;
　DAC; DAM POP
　See also AAYA 34; CA 142; CANR 57, 90;
　CCA 1
Court, Wesli
　See Turco, Lewis (Putnam)
Courtenay, Bryce 1933- .... CLC 59
　See also CA 138
Courtney, Robert
　See Ellison, Harlan (Jay)
Cousteau, Jacques-Yves 1910-1997 .. CLC 30
　See also CA 65-68; 159; CANR 15, 67;
　MTCW 1; SATA 38, 98
Coventry, Francis 1725-1754 .... LC 46
Cowan, Peter (Walkinshaw) 1914- .... SSC 28
　See also CA 21-24R; CANR 9, 25, 50, 83
Coward, Noël (Peirce) 1899-1973 . CLC 1, 9,
　29, 51; DAM DRAM
　See also AITN 1; BRWS 2; CA 17-18; 41-
　44R; CANR 35; CAP 2; CDBLB 1914-
　1945; DA3; DLB 10; IDFW 3; MTCW 1,
　2
Cowley, Abraham 1618-1667 .... LC 43
　See also DLB 131, 151
Cowley, Malcolm 1898-1989 .... CLC 39
　See also AMWS 2; CA 5-8R; 128; CANR
　3, 55; DLB 4, 48; DLBY 81, 89; MTCW
　1, 2
Cowper, William 1731-1800 ..... NCLC 8, 94;
　DAM POET
　See also DA3; DLB 104, 109
Cox, William Trevor 1928- ... CLC 9, 14, 71;
　DAM NOV
　See also Trevor, William
　See also CA 9-12R; CANR 4, 37, 55, 76;
　DLB 14; INT CANR-37; MTCW 1, 2
Coyne, P. J.
　See Masters, Hilary
Cozzens, James Gould 1903-1978 . CLC 1, 4,
　11, 92
　See also CA 9-12R; 81-84; CANR 19;
　CDALB 1941-1968; DLB 9; DLBD 2;
　DLBY 84, 97; MTCW 1, 2
Crabbe, George 1754-1832 .... NCLC 26
　See also DLB 93
Craddock, Charles Egbert
　See Murfree, Mary Noailles
Craig, A. A.
　See Anderson, Poul (William)
Craik, Dinah Maria (Mulock)
　1826-1887 .... NCLC 38
　See also DLB 35, 163; MAICYA; SATA 34
Cram, Ralph Adams 1863-1942 ..... TCLC 45
　See also CA 160
Crane, (Harold) Hart 1899-1932 .... TCLC 2,
　5, 80; DA; DAB; DAC; DAM MST,
　POET; PC 3
　See also AW; CA 104; 127; CDALB 1917-
　1929; DA3; DLB 4, 48; MTCW 1, 2

Crane, R(onald) S(almon)
1886-1967 .... CLC 27
See also CA 85-88; DLB 63

Crane, Stephen (Townley)
1871-1900 .... TCLC 11, 17, 32; DA;
DAB; DAC; DAM MST, NOV, POET;
SSC 7
See also AAYA 21; CA 109; 140; CANR
84; CDALB 1865-1917; DA3; DLB 12,
54, 78

Cranshaw, Stanley
See Fisher, Dorothy (Frances) Canfield

Crase, Douglas 1944- .... CLC 58
See also CA 106

Crashaw, Richard 1612(?)-1649 .... LC 24
See also DLB 126

Craven, Margaret 1901-1980 .... CLC 17;
DAC
See also CA 103; CCA 1

Crawford, F(rancis) Marion
1854-1909 .... TCLC 10
See also CA 107; 168; DLB 71

Crawford, Isabella Valancy
1850-1887 .... NCLC 12
See also DLB 92

Crayon, Geoffrey
See Irving, Washington

Creasey, John 1908-1973 .... CLC 11
See also CA 5-8R; 41-44R; CANR 8, 59;
DLB 77; MTCW 1

Crebillon, Claude Prosper Jolyot de (fils)
1707-1777 .... LC 1, 28

Credo
See Creasey, John

Credo, Alvaro J. de
See Prado (Calvo), Pedro

Creeley, Robert (White) 1926- .. CLC 1, 2, 4,
8, 11, 15, 36, 78; DAM POET
See also AMWS 4; CA 1-4R; CAAS 10;
CANR 23, 43, 89; DA3; DLB 5, 16, 169;
DLBD 17; MTCW 1, 2

Crews, Harry (Eugene) 1935- ..... CLC 6, 23,
49
See also AITN 1; CA 25-28R; CANR 20,
57; DA3; DLB 6, 143, 185; MTCW 1, 2

Crichton, (John) Michael 1942- .... CLC 2, 6,
54, 90; DAM NOV, POP
See also AAYA 10; AITN 2; AW; CA 25-
28R; CANR 13, 40, 54, 76; DA3; DLBY
81; INT CANR-13; JRDA; MTCW 1, 2;
SATA 9, 88

Crispin, Edmund CLC 22
See also Montgomery, (Robert) Bruce
See also DLB 87

Cristofer, Michael 1945(?)- ... CLC 28; DAM
DRAM
See also CA 110; 152; DLB 7

Croce, Benedetto 1866-1952 .... TCLC 37
See also CA 120; 155

Crockett, David 1786-1836 .... NCLC 8
See also DLB 3, 11

Crockett, Davy
See Crockett, David

Crofts, Freeman Wills 1879-1957 .. TCLC 55
See also CA 115; DLB 77

Croker, John Wilson 1780-1857 .... NCLC 10
See also DLB 110

Crommelynck, Fernand 1885-1970 .. CLC 75
See also CA 189; 89-92

Cromwell, Oliver 1599-1658 .... LC 43

Cronin, A(rchibald) J(oseph)
1896-1981 .... CLC 32
See also CA 1-4R; 102; CANR 5; DLB 191;
SATA 47; SATA-Obit 25

Cross, Amanda
See Heilbrun, Carolyn G(old)

Crothers, Rachel 1878(?)-1958 .... TCLC 19
See also CA 113; DLB 7

Croves, Hal
See Traven, B.

Crow Dog, Mary (Ellen) (?)- .... CLC 93
See also Brave Bird, Mary
See also CA 154

Crowfield, Christopher
See Stowe, Harriet (Elizabeth) Beecher

Crowley, Aleister TCLC 7
See also Crowley, Edward Alexander
See also GLL 1

Crowley, Edward Alexander 1875-1947
See Crowley, Aleister
See also CA 104

Crowley, John 1942- .... CLC 57
See also CA 61-64; CANR 43; DLBY 82;
SATA 65

Crud
See Crumb, R(obert)

Crumarums
See Crumb, R(obert)

Crumb, R(obert) 1943- .... CLC 17
See also CA 106

Crumbum
See Crumb, R(obert)

Crumski
See Crumb, R(obert)

Crum the Bum
See Crumb, R(obert)

Crunk
See Crumb, R(obert)

Crustt
See Crumb, R(obert)

Cruz, Victor Hernandez 1949-
See also BW 2; CA 65-68; CAAS 17;
CANR 14, 32, 74; DAM MULT, POET;
DLB 41; HLC 1; HW 1, 2; MTCW 1

Cryer, Gretchen (Kiger) 1935- .... CLC 21
See also CA 114; 123

Csath, Geza 1887-1919 .... TCLC 13
See also CA 111

Cudlip, David R(ockwell) 1933- .... CLC 34
See also CA 177

Cullen, Countee 1903-1946 .... TCLC 4, 37;
BLC 1; DA; DAC; DAM MST, MULT,
POET; PC 20
See also AMWS 4; AW; BW 1; CA 108;
124; CDALB 1917-1929; DA3; DLB 4,
48, 51; MTCW 1, 2; SATA 18

Cum, R.
See Crumb, R(obert)

Cummings, Bruce F(rederick) 1889-1919
See Barbellion, W. N. P.
See also CA 123

Cummings, E(dward) E(stlin)
1894-1962 .... CLC 1, 3, 8, 12, 15, 68;
DA; DAB; DAC; DAM MST, POET;
PC 5
See also AW; CA 73-76; CANR 31; CDALB
1929-1941; DA3; DLB 4, 48; MTCW 1,
2

Cunha, Euclides (Rodrigues Pimenta) da
1866-1909 .... TCLC 24
See also CA 123

Cunningham, E. V.
See Fast, Howard (Melvin)

Cunningham, J(ames) V(incent)
1911-1985 .... CLC 3, 31
See also CA 1-4R; 115; CANR 1, 72; DLB
5

Cunningham, Julia (Woolfolk)
1916- .... CLC 12
See also CA 9-12R; CANR 4, 19, 36;
JRDA; MAICYA; SAAS 2; SATA 1, 26

Cunningham, Michael 1952- .... CLC 34
See also CA 136; CANR 96; GLL 2

Cunninghame Graham, R. B.
See Cunninghame Graham, Robert
(Gallnigad) Bontine

Cunninghame Graham, Robert (Gallnigad)
Bontine 1852-1936 .... TCLC 19
See also Graham, R(obert) B(ontine) Cun-
ninghame
See also CA 119; 184; DLB 98

Currie, Ellen 19(?)- .... CLC 44

Curtin, Philip
See Lowndes, Marie Adelaide (Belloc)

Curtis, Price
See Ellison, Harlan (Jay)

Cutrate, Joe
See Spiegelman, Art

Cynewulf c. 770-c. 840 .... CMLC 23

Czaczkes, Shmuel Yosef
See Agnon, S(hmuel) Y(osef Halevi)

Dabrowska, Maria (Szumska)
1889-1965 .... CLC 15
See also CA 106

Dabydeen, David 1955- .... CLC 34
See also BW 1; CA 125; CANR 56, 92

Dacey, Philip 1939- .... CLC 51
See also CA 37-40R; CAAS 17; CANR 14,
32, 64; DLB 105

Dagerman, Stig (Halvard)
1923-1954 .... TCLC 17
See also CA 117; 155

Dahl, Roald 1916-1990 ...... CLC 1, 6, 18, 79;
DAB; DAC; DAM MST, NOV, POP
See also AAYA 15; AW; BRWS 4; CA 1-4R;
133; CANR 6, 32, 37, 62; CLR 1, 7, 41;
DA3; DLB 139; JRDA; MAICYA;
MTCW 1, 2; SATA 1, 26, 73; SATA-Obit
65

Dahlberg, Edward 1900-1977 .. CLC 1, 7, 14
See also CA 9-12R; 69-72; CANR 31, 62;
DLB 48; MTCW 1

Daitch, Susan 1954- .... CLC 103
See also CA 161

Dale, Colin TCLC 18
See also Lawrence, T(homas) E(dward)

Dale, George E.
See Asimov, Isaac

Dalton, Roque 1935-1975
See also HLCS 1; HW 2

Daly, Elizabeth 1878-1967 .... CLC 52
See also CA 23-24; 25-28R; CANR 60;
CAP 2

Daly, Maureen 1921-1983 .... CLC 17
See also AAYA 5; AW; CANR 37, 83;
JRDA; MAICYA; SAAS 1; SATA 2

Damas, Leon-Gontran 1912-1978 .... CLC 84
See also BW 1; CA 125; 73-76

Dana, Richard Henry Sr.
1787-1879 .... NCLC 53

Daniel, Samuel 1562(?)-1619 .... LC 24
See also DLB 62

Daniels, Brett
See Adler, Renata

Dannay, Frederic 1905-1982 . CLC 11; DAM
POP
See also Queen, Ellery
See also CA 1-4R; 107; CANR 1, 39; DLB
137; MTCW 1

D'Annunzio, Gabriele 1863-1938 ... TCLC 6,
40
See also CA 104; 155

Danois, N. le
See Gourmont, Remy (-Marie-Charles) de

Dante 1265-1321 .... CMLC 3, 18, 39; DA;
DAB; DAC; DAM MST, POET; PC 21
See also AW; DA3

d'Antibes, Germain
See Simenon, Georges (Jacques Christian)

Danticat, Edwidge 1969- .... CLC 94, 139
See also AAYA 29; AW; CA 152; CANR
73; MTCW 1

Dobrolyubov, Nikolai Alexandrovich
1836-1861 .... **NCLC 5**

Dobson, Austin 1840-1921 .... **TCLC 79**
See also DLB 35; 144

Dobyns, Stephen 1941- .... **CLC 37**
See also CA 45-48; CANR 2, 18

Doctorow, E(dgar) L(aurence)
1931- .... **CLC 6, 11, 15, 18, 37, 44, 65,
113; DAM NOV, POP**
See also AAYA 22; AITN 2; AMWS 4;
BEST 89:3; CA 45-48; CANR 2, 33, 51,
76; CDALB 1968-1988; DA3; DLB 2, 28,
173; DLBY 80; MTCW 1, 2

Dodgson, Charles Lutwidge 1832-1898
See Carroll, Lewis
See also AW 2; CLR 2; DA; DAB; DAC;
DAM MST, NOV, POET; DA3; MAI-
CYA; SATA 100

Dodson, Owen (Vincent)
1914-1983 .... **CLC 79; BLC 1; DAM
MULT**
See also BW 1; CA 65-68; 110; CANR 24;
DLB 76

Doeblin, Alfred 1878-1957 .... **TCLC 13**
See also Doblin, Alfred
See also CA 110; 141; DLB 66

Doerr, Harriet 1910- .... **CLC 34**
See also CA 117; 122; CANR 47; INT 122

Domecq, H(onorio Bustos)
See Bioy Casares, Adolfo

Domecq, H(onorio) Bustos
See Bioy Casares, Adolfo; Borges, Jorge
Luis

Domini, Rey
See Lorde, Audre (Geraldine)
See also GLL 1

Dominique
See Proust, (Valentin-Louis-George-Eugene-
)Marcel

Don, A
See Stephen, SirLeslie

Donaldson, Stephen R. 1947- .. **CLC 46, 138;
DAM POP**
See also AAYA 36; CA 89-92; CANR 13,
55; INT CANR-13; SATA 121

Donleavy, J(ames) P(atrick) 1926- .... **CLC 1,
4, 6, 10, 45**
See also AITN 2; CA 9-12R; CANR 24, 49,
62, 80; DLB 6, 173; INT CANR-24;
MTCW 1, 2

Donne, John 1572-1631 .... **LC 10, 24; DA;
DAB; DAC; DAM MST, POET; PC 1**
See also AW; CDBLB Before 1660; DLB
121, 151

Donnell, David 1939(?)- .... **CLC 34**

Donoghue, P. S.
See Hunt, E(verette) Howard, (Jr.)

Donoso (Yanez), Jose 1924-1996 ... **CLC 4, 8,
11, 32, 99; DAM MULT; HLC 1; SSC
34**
See also CA 81-84; 155; CANR 32, 73;
DLB 113; HW 1, 2; MTCW 1, 2

Donovan, John 1928-1992 .... **CLC 35**
See also AAYA 20; AW; CA 97-100; 137;
CLR 3; MAICYA; SATA 72; SATA-Brief
29

Don Roberto
See Cunninghame Graham, Robert
(Gallnigad) Bontine

Doolittle, Hilda 1886-1961 . **CLC 3, 8, 14, 31,
34, 73; DA; DAC; DAM MST, POET;
PC 5**
See also H. D.
See also AMWS 1; AW; CA 97-100; CANR
35; DLB 4, 45; GLL 1; MTCW 1, 2

Dorfman, Ariel 1942- ...... **CLC 48, 77; DAM
MULT; HLC 1**
See also CA 124; 130; CANR 67, 70; CWW
2; HW 1, 2; INT 130

Dorn, Edward (Merton)
1929-1999 .... **CLC 10, 18**
See also CA 93-96; 187; CANR 42, 79;
DLB 5; INT 93-96

Dorris, Michael (Anthony)
1945-1997 .... **CLC 109; DAM MULT,
NOV**
See also AAYA 20; AW; BEST 90:1; CA
102; 157; CANR 19, 46, 75; CLR 58;
DA3; DLB 175; MTCW 2; NNAL; SATA
75; SATA-Obit 94; TCWW 2

Dorris, Michael A.
See Dorris, Michael (Anthony)

Dorsan, Luc
See Simenon, Georges (Jacques Christian)

Dorsange, Jean
See Simenon, Georges (Jacques Christian)

Dos Passos, John (Roderigo)
1896-1970 ... **CLC 1, 4, 8, 11, 15, 25, 34,
82; DA; DAB; DAC; DAM MST, NOV**
See also AW; CA 1-4R; 29-32R; CANR 3;
CDALB 1929-1941; DA3; DLB 4, 9;
DLBD 1, 15; DLBY 96; MTCW 1, 2

Dossage, Jean
See Simenon, Georges (Jacques Christian)

Dostoevsky, Fedor Mikhailovich
1821-1881 . **NCLC 2, 7, 21, 33, 43; DA;
DAB; DAC; DAM MST, NOV; SSC 2,
33, 44**
See also AW; DA3; DLB 238

Doughty, Charles M(ontagu)
1843-1926 .... **TCLC 27**
See also CA 115; 178; DLB 19, 57, 174

Douglas, Ellen CLC 73
See also Haxton, Josephine Ayres; Williamson, Ellen Douglas

Douglas, Gavin 1475(?)-1522 .... **LC 20**
See also DLB 132

Douglas, George
See Brown, George Douglas

Douglas, Keith (Castellain)
1920-1944 .... **TCLC 40**
See also CA 160; DLB 27

Douglas, Leonard
See Bradbury, Ray (Douglas)

Douglas, Michael
See Crichton, (John) Michael

Douglas, (George) Norman
1868-1952 .... **TCLC 68**
See also CA 119; 157; DLB 34, 195

Douglas, William
See Brown, George Douglas

Douglass, Frederick 1817(?)-1895 .. **NCLC 7,
55; BLC 1; DA; DAC; DAM MST,
MULT**
See also AMWS 3; AW; CDALB 1640-
1865; DA3; DLB 1, 43, 50, 79; SATA 29

Dourado, (Waldomiro Freitas) Autran
1926- .... **CLC 23, 60**
See also CA 25-28R; 179; CANR 34, 81;
DLB 145; HW 2

Dourado, Waldomiro Autran
See Dourado, (Waldomiro Freitas) Autran
See also CA 179

Dove, Rita (Frances) 1952- .... **CLC 50, 81;
BLCS; DAM MULT, POET; PC 6**
See also AMWS 4; BW 2; CA 109; CAAS
19; CANR 27, 42, 68, 76; CDALBS;
DA3; DLB 120; MTCW 1

Doveglion
See Villa, Jose Garcia

Dowell, Coleman 1925-1985 .... **CLC 60**
See also CA 25-28R; 117; CANR 10; DLB
130; GLL 2

Dowson, Ernest (Christopher)
1867-1900 .... **TCLC 4**
See also CA 105; 150; DLB 19, 135

Doyle, A. Conan
See Doyle, Arthur Conan

Doyle, Arthur Conan 1859-1930 .... **TCLC 7;
DA; DAB; DAC; DAM MST, NOV;
SSC 12**
See also Doyle, Sir Arthur Conan
See also AAYA 14; AW; CA 104; 122; CD-
BLB 1890-1914; DA3; DLB 18, 70, 156,
178; MTCW 1, 2; SATA 24

Doyle, Conan
See Doyle, Arthur Conan

Doyle, John
See Graves, Robert (von Ranke)

Doyle, Roddy 1958(?)- .... **CLC 81**
See also AAYA 14; BRWS 5; CA 143;
CANR 73; DA3; DLB 194

Doyle, Sir A. Conan
See Doyle, Arthur Conan

Doyle, Sir Arthur Conan
See Doyle, Arthur Conan
See also BRWS 2

Dr. A
See Asimov, Isaac; Silverstein, Alvin

Drabble, Margaret 1939- ...... **CLC 2, 3, 5, 8,
10, 22, 53, 129; DAB; DAC; DAM
MST, NOV, POP**
See also BRWS 4; CA 13-16R; CANR 18,
35, 63; CDBLB 1960 to Present; DA3;
DLB 14, 155, 231; MTCW 1, 2; SATA 48

Drapier, M. B.
See Swift, Jonathan

Drayham, James
See Mencken, H(enry) L(ouis)

Drayton, Michael 1563-1631 ..... **LC 8; DAM
POET**
See also DLB 121

Dreadstone, Carl
See Campbell, (John) Ramsey

Dreiser, Theodore (Herman Albert)
1871-1945 .... **TCLC 10, 18, 35, 83; DA;
DAC; DAM MST, NOV; SSC 30**
See also AW; CA 106; 132; CDALB 1865-
1917; DA3; DLB 9, 12, 102, 137; DLBD
1; MTCW 1, 2

Drexler, Rosalyn 1926- .... **CLC 2, 6**
See also CA 81-84; CANR 68

Dreyer, Carl Theodor 1889-1968 ...... **CLC 16**
See also CA 116

Drieu la Rochelle, Pierre(-Eugene)
1893-1945 .... **TCLC 21**
See also CA 117; DLB 72

Drinkwater, John 1882-1937 .... **TCLC 57**
See also CA 109; 149; DLB 10, 19, 149

Drop Shot
See Cable, George Washington

Droste-Hulshoff, Annette Freiin von
1797-1848 .... **NCLC 3**
See also DLB 133

Drummond, Walter
See Silverberg, Robert

Drummond, William Henry
1854-1907 .... **TCLC 25**
See also CA 160; DLB 92

Drummond de Andrade, Carlos
1902-1987 .... **CLC 18**
See also Andrade, Carlos Drummond de
See also CA 132; 123

Drury, Allen (Stuart) 1918-1998 .... **CLC 37**
See also CA 57-60; 170; CANR 18, 52; INT
CANR-18

Dryden, John 1631-1700 .... **LC 3, 21; DA;
DAB; DAC; DAM DRAM, MST,
POET; DC 3; PC 25**
See also AW; CDBLB 1660-1789; DLB 80,
101, 131

Duberman, Martin (Bauml) 1930- ..... **CLC 8**
See also CA 1-4R; CANR 2, 63

Dubie, Norman (Evans) 1945- .... **CLC 36**
See also CA 69-72; CANR 12; DLB 120

Du Bois, W(illiam) E(dward) B(urghardt)
1868-1963 ... **CLC 1, 2, 13, 64, 96; BLC 1; DA; DAC; DAM MST, MULT, NOV**
See also AMWS 2; AW; BW 1, 3; CA 85-88; CANR 34, 82; CDALB 1865-1917; DA3; DLB 47, 50, 91; MTCW 1, 2; SATA 42

Dubus, Andre 1936-1999 ..... **CLC 13, 36, 97; SSC 15**
See also AMWS 7; CA 21-24R; 177; CANR 17; DLB 130; INT CANR-17

Duca Minimo
See D'Annunzio, Gabriele

Ducharme, Rejean 1941- .... **CLC 74**
See also CA 165; DLB 60

Duclos, Charles Pinot 1704-1772 .... **LC 1**

Dudek, Louis 1918- .... **CLC 11, 19**
See also CA 45-48; CAAS 14; CANR 1; DLB 88

Duerrenmatt, Friedrich 1921-1990 ... **CLC 1, 4, 8, 11, 15, 43, 102; DAM DRAM**
See also CA 17-20R; CANR 33; DLB 69, 124; MTCW 1, 2

Duffy, Bruce 1953(?)- .... **CLC 50**
See also CA 172

Duffy, Maureen 1933- .... **CLC 37**
See also CA 25-28R; CANR 33, 68; DLB 14; MTCW 1

Dugan, Alan 1923- .... **CLC 2, 6**
See also CA 81-84; DLB 5

du Gard, Roger Martin
See Martin du Gard, Roger

Duhamel, Georges 1884-1966 .... **CLC 8**
See also CA 81-84; 25-28R; CANR 35; DLB 65; MTCW 1

Dujardin, Edouard (Emile Louis)
1861-1949 .... **TCLC 13**
See also CA 109; DLB 123

Dulles, John Foster 1888-1959 .... **TCLC 72**
See also CA 115; 149

Dumas, Alexandre (pere)
See Dumas, Alexandre (Davy de la Pailleterie)

Dumas, Alexandre (Davy de la Pailleterie)
1802-1870 ...... **NCLC 11, 71; DA; DAB; DAC; DAM MST, NOV**
See also AW; DA3; DLB 119, 192; SATA 18

Dumas, Alexandre (fils)
1824-1895 .... **NCLC 9; DC 1**
See also AAYA 22; DLB 192; EW 1

Dumas, Claudine
See Malzberg, Barry N(athaniel)

Dumas, Henry L. 1934-1968 .... **CLC 6, 62**
See also BW 1; CA 85-88; DLB 41

du Maurier, Daphne 1907-1989 .. **CLC 6, 11, 59; DAB; DAC; DAM MST, POP; SSC 18**
See also AAYA 37; BRWS 3; CA 5-8R; 128; CANR 6, 55; DA3; DLB 191; MTCW 1, 2; SATA 27; SATA-Obit 60

Du Maurier, George 1834-1896 ..... **NCLC 86**
See also DLB 153, 178

Dunbar, Paul Laurence 1872-1906 . **TCLC 2, 12; BLC 1; DA; DAC; DAM MST, MULT, POET; PC 5; SSC 8**
See also AMWS 2; AW; BW 1, 3; CA 104; 124; CANR 79; CDALB 1865-1917; DA3; DLB 50, 54, 78; SATA 34

Dunbar, William 1460(?)-1520(?) .... **LC 20**
See also DLB 132, 146

Duncan, Dora Angela
See Duncan, Isadora

Duncan, Isadora 1877(?)-1927 .... **TCLC 68**
See also CA 118; 149

Duncan, Lois 1934- .... **CLC 26**
See also AAYA 4, 34; AW; CA 1-4R; CANR 2, 23, 36; CLR 29; JRDA; MAICYA; SAAS 2; SATA 1, 36, 75

Duncan, Robert (Edward)
1919-1988 .... **CLC 1, 2, 4, 7, 15, 41, 55; DAM POET; PC 2**
See also CA 9-12R; 124; CANR 28, 62; DLB 5, 16, 193; MTCW 1, 2

Duncan, Sara Jeannette
1861-1922 .... **TCLC 60**
See also CA 157; DLB 92

Dunlap, William 1766-1839 .... **NCLC 2**
See also DLB 30, 37, 59

Dunn, Douglas (Eaglesham) 1942- .... **CLC 6, 40**
See also CA 45-48; CANR 2, 33; DLB 40; MTCW 1

Dunn, Katherine (Karen) 1945- .... **CLC 71**
See also CA 33-36R; CANR 72; MTCW 1

Dunn, Stephen 1939- .... **CLC 36**
See also CA 33-36R; CANR 12, 48, 53; DLB 105

Dunne, Finley Peter 1867-1936 ...... **TCLC 28**
See also CA 108; 178; DLB 11, 23

Dunne, John Gregory 1932- .... **CLC 28**
See also CA 25-28R; CANR 14, 50; DLBY 80

Dunsany, Edward John Moreton Drax Plunkett 1878-1957
See Dunsany, Lord
See also CA 104; 148; DLB 10; MTCW 1

Dunsany, Lord TCLC 2, 59
See also Dunsany, Edward John Moreton Drax Plunkett
See also DLB 77, 153, 156

du Perry, Jean
See Simenon, Georges (Jacques Christian)

Durang, Christopher (Ferdinand)
1949- .... **CLC 27, 38**
See also CA 105; CANR 50, 76; MTCW 1

Duras, Marguerite 1914-1996 . **CLC 3, 6, 11, 20, 34, 40, 68, 100; SSC 40**
See also CA 25-28R; 151; CANR 50; CWW 2; DLB 83; MTCW 1, 2

Durban, (Rosa) Pam 1947- .... **CLC 39**
See also CA 123

Durcan, Paul 1944- .... **CLC 43, 70; DAM POET**
See also CA 134

Durkheim, Emile 1858-1917 .... **TCLC 55**

Durrell, Lawrence (George)
1912-1990 .... **CLC 1, 4, 6, 8, 13, 27, 41; DAM NOV**
See also BRWS 1; CA 9-12R; 132; CANR 40, 77; CDBLB 1945-1960; DLB 15, 27, 204; DLBY 90; MTCW 1, 2

Dürrenmatt, Friedrich
See Duerrenmatt, Friedrich

Dutt, Toru 1856-1877 .... **NCLC 29**
See also DLB 240

Dwight, Timothy 1752-1817 .... **NCLC 13**
See also DLB 37

Dworkin, Andrea 1946- .... **CLC 43, 123**
See also CA 77-80; CAAS 21; CANR 16, 39, 76, 96; GLL 1; INT CANR-16; MTCW 1, 2

Dwyer, Deanna
See Koontz, Dean R(ay)

Dwyer, K. R.
See Koontz, Dean R(ay)

Dwyer, Thomas A. 1923- .... **CLC 114**
See also CA 115

Dybek, Stuart 1942- .... **CLC 114**
See also CA 97-100; CANR 39; DLB 130

Dye, Richard
See De Voto, Bernard (Augustine)

Dylan, Bob 1941- .... **CLC 3, 4, 6, 12, 77**
See also CA 41-44R; DLB 16

E. V. L.
See Lucas, E(dward) V(errall)

Eagleton, Terence (Francis) 1943- .. **CLC 63, 132**
See also CA 57-60; CANR 7, 23, 68; DLB 242; MTCW 1, 2

Eagleton, Terry
See Eagleton, Terence (Francis)

Early, Jack
See Scoppettone, Sandra
See also GLL 1

East, Michael
See West, Morris L(anglo)

Eastaway, Edward
See Thomas, (Philip) Edward

Eastlake, William (Derry)
1917-1997 .... **CLC 8**
See also CA 5-8R; 158; CAAS 1; CANR 5, 63; DLB 6, 206; INT CANR-5; TCWW 2

Eastman, Charles A(lexander)
1858-1939 .... **TCLC 55; DAM MULT**
See also AW 1; CA 179; CANR 91; DLB 175; NNAL

Eberhart, Richard (Ghormley)
1904- .. **CLC 3, 11, 19, 56; DAM POET**
See also CA 1-4R; CANR 2; CDALB 1941-1968; DLB 48; MTCW 1

Eberstadt, Fernanda 1960- .... **CLC 39**
See also CA 136; CANR 69

Echegaray (y Eizaguirre), Jose (Maria Waldo) 1832-1916 .... **TCLC 4; HLCS 1**
See also CA 104; CANR 32; HW 1; MTCW 1

Echeverria, (Jose) Esteban (Antonino)
1805-1851 .... **NCLC 18**

Echo
See Proust, (Valentin-Louis-George-Eugene-)Marcel

Eckert, Allan W. 1931- .... **CLC 17**
See also AAYA 18; CA 13-16R; CANR 14, 45; INT CANR-14; SAAS 21; SATA 29, 91; SATA-Brief 27

Eckhart, Meister 1260(?)-1327(?) ... **CMLC 9**
See also DLB 115

Eckmar, F. R.
See de Hartog, Jan

Eco, Umberto 1932- .... **CLC 28, 60; DAM NOV, POP**
See also BEST 90:1; CA 77-80; CANR 12, 33, 55; CWW 2; DA3; DLB 196, 242; MTCW 1, 2

Eddison, E(ric) R(ucker)
1882-1945 .... **TCLC 15**
See also CA 109; 156

Eddy, Mary (Ann Morse) Baker
1821-1910 .... **TCLC 71**
See also CA 113; 174

Edel, (Joseph) Leon 1907-1997 .. **CLC 29, 34**
See also CA 1-4R; 161; CANR 1, 22; DLB 103; INT CANR-22

Eden, Emily 1797-1869 .... **NCLC 10**

Edgar, David 1948- .. **CLC 42; DAM DRAM**
See also CA 57-60; CANR 12, 61; DLB 13, 233; MTCW 1

Edgerton, Clyde (Carlyle) 1944- ...... **CLC 39**
See also AAYA 17; AW; CA 118; 134; CANR 64; INT 134

Edgeworth, Maria 1768-1849 .... **NCLC 1, 51**
See also BRWS 3; DLB 116, 159, 163; SATA 21

Edmonds, Paul
See Kuttner, Henry

Edmonds, Walter D(umaux)
1903-1998 .... **CLC 35**
See also CA 5-8R; CANR 2; DLB 9; MAI-CYA; SAAS 4; SATA 1, 27; SATA-Obit 99

Edmondson, Wallace
See Ellison, Harlan (Jay)

Edson, Russell CLC 13
See also CA 33-36R

Erasmus, Desiderius 1469(?)-1536 ...... **LC 16**

Erdman, Paul E(mil) 1932- .... **CLC 25**
　　See also AITN 1; CA 61-64; CANR 13, 43, 84

Erdrich, Louise 1954- .... **CLC 39, 54, 120; DAM MULT, NOV, POP**
　　See also AAYA 10; AMWS 4; BEST 89:1; CA 114; CANR 41, 62; CDALBS; DA3; DLB 152, 175, 206; MTCW 1; NNAL; SATA 94; TCWW 2

Erenburg, Ilya (Grigoryevich)
　　See Ehrenburg, Ilya (Grigoryevich)

Erickson, Stephen Michael 1950-
　　See Erickson, Steve
　　See also CA 129

Erickson, Steve **CLC 64**
　　See also Erickson, Stephen Michael
　　See also CANR 60, 68

Ericson, Walter
　　See Fast, Howard (Melvin)

Eriksson, Buntel
　　See Bergman, (Ernst) Ingmar

Ernaux, Annie 1940- .... **CLC 88**
　　See also CA 147; CANR 93

Erskine, John 1879-1951 .... **TCLC 84**
　　See also CA 112; 159; DLB 9, 102

Eschenbach, Wolfram von
　　See Wolfram von Eschenbach

Eseki, Bruno
　　See Mphahlele, Ezekiel

Esenin, Sergei (Alexandrovich)
　　1895-1925 .... **TCLC 4**
　　See also CA 104

Eshleman, Clayton 1935- .... **CLC 7**
　　See also CA 33-36R; CAAS 6; CANR 93; DLB 5

Espriella, Don Manuel Alvarez
　　See Southey, Robert

Espriu, Salvador 1913-1985 .... **CLC 9**
　　See also CA 154; 115; DLB 134

Espronceda, Jose de 1808-1842 ..... **NCLC 39**

Esquivel, Laura 1951(?)- ... **CLC 141; HLCS 1**
　　See also AAYA 29; CA 143; CANR 68; DA3; MTCW 1

Esse, James
　　See Stephens, James

Esterbrook, Tom
　　See Hubbard, L(afayette) Ron(ald)

Estleman, Loren D. 1952- ..... **CLC 48; DAM NOV, POP**
　　See also AAYA 27; CA 85-88; CANR 27, 74; DA3; DLB 226; INT CANR-27; MTCW 1, 2

Euclid 306B.C.-283B.C. .... **CMLC 25**

Eugenides, Jeffrey 1960(?)- .... **CLC 81**
　　See also CA 144

Euripides c. 485B.C.-406B.C. .... **CMLC 23; DA; DAB; DAC; DAM DRAM, MST; DC 4**
　　See also AW; DA3; DLB 176

Evan, Evin
　　See Faust, Frederick (Schiller)

Evans, Caradoc 1878-1945 ... **TCLC 85; SSC 43**

Evans, Evan
　　See Faust, Frederick (Schiller)
　　See also TCWW 2

Evans, Marian
　　See Eliot, George

Evans, Mary Ann
　　See Eliot, George

Evarts, Esther
　　See Benson, Sally

Everett, Percival
　　See Everett, Percival L.

Everett, Percival L. 1956- .... **CLC 57**
　　See also Everett, Percival
　　See also BW 2; CA 129; CANR 94

Everson, R(onald) G(ilmour)
　　1903-1992 .... **CLC 27**
　　See also CA 17-20R; DLB 88

Everson, William (Oliver)
　　1912-1994 .... **CLC 1, 5, 14**
　　See also CA 9-12R; 145; CANR 20; DLB 212; MTCW 1

Evtushenko, Evgenii Aleksandrovich
　　See Yevtushenko, Yevgeny (Alexandrovich)

Ewart, Gavin (Buchanan)
　　1916-1995 .... **CLC 13, 46**
　　See also CA 89-92; 150; CANR 17, 46; DLB 40; MTCW 1

Ewers, Hanns Heinz 1871-1943 ..... **TCLC 12**
　　See also CA 109; 149

Ewing, Frederick R.
　　See Sturgeon, Theodore (Hamilton)

Exley, Frederick (Earl) 1929-1992 .... **CLC 6, 11**
　　See also AITN 2; CA 81-84; 138; DLB 143; DLBY 81

Eynhardt, Guillermo
　　See Quiroga, Horacio (Sylvestre)

Ezekiel, Nissim 1924- .... **CLC 61**
　　See also CA 61-64

Ezekiel, Tish O'Dowd 1943- .... **CLC 34**
　　See also CA 129

Fadeyev, A.
　　See Bulgya, Alexander Alexandrovich

Fadeyev, Alexander **TCLC 53**
　　See also Bulgya, Alexander Alexandrovich

Fagen, Donald 1948- .... **CLC 26**

Fainzilberg, Ilya Arnoldovich 1897-1937
　　See Ilf, Ilya
　　See also CA 120; 165

Fair, Ronald L. 1932- .... **CLC 18**
　　See also BW 1; CA 69-72; CANR 25; DLB 33

Fairbairn, Roger
　　See Carr, John Dickson

Fairbairns, Zoe (Ann) 1948- .... **CLC 32**
　　See also CA 103; CANR 21, 85

Fairman, Paul W. 1916-1977
　　See Queen, Ellery
　　See also CA 114

Falco, Gian
　　See Papini, Giovanni

Falconer, James
　　See Kirkup, James

Falconer, Kenneth
　　See Kornbluth, C(yril) M.

Falkland, Samuel
　　See Heijermans, Herman

Fallaci, Oriana 1930- .... **CLC 11, 110**
　　See also CA 77-80; CANR 15, 58; MTCW 1

Faludi, Susan 1959- .... **CLC 140**
　　See also CA 138; MTCW 1

Faludy, George 1913- .... **CLC 42**
　　See also CA 21-24R

Faludy, Gyoergy
　　See Faludy, George

Fanon, Frantz 1925-1961 ... **CLC 74; BLC 2; DAM MULT**
　　See also BW 1; CA 116; 89-92

Fanshawe, Ann 1625-1680 .... **LC 11**

Fante, John (Thomas) 1911-1983 ..... **CLC 60**
　　See also CA 69-72; 109; CANR 23; DLB 130; DLBY 83

Farah, Nuruddin 1945- .. **CLC 53, 137; BLC 2; DAM MULT**
　　See also BW 2, 3; CA 106; CANR 81; DLB 125

Fargue, Leon-Paul 1876(?)-1947 .... **TCLC 11**
　　See also CA 109

Farigoule, Louis
　　See Romains, Jules

Farina, Richard 1936(?)-1966 .... **CLC 9**
　　See also CA 81-84; 25-28R

Farley, Walter (Lorimer)
　　1915-1989 .... **CLC 17**
　　See also AW; CA 17-20R; CANR 8, 29, 84; DLB 22; JRDA; MAICYA; SATA 2, 43

Farmer, Philip Jose 1918- .... **CLC 1, 19**
　　See also AAYA 28; CA 1-4R; CANR 4, 35; DLB 8; MTCW 1; SATA 93

Farquhar, George 1677-1707 ... **LC 21; DAM DRAM**
　　See also DLB 84

Farrell, J(ames) G(ordon)
　　1935-1979 .... **CLC 6**
　　See also CA 73-76; 89-92; CANR 36; DLB 14; MTCW 1

Farrell, James T(homas) 1904-1979 . **CLC 1, 4, 8, 11, 66; SSC 28**
　　See also CA 5-8R; 89-92; CANR 9, 61; DLB 4, 9, 86; DLBD 2; MTCW 1, 2

Farren, Richard J.
　　See Betjeman, John

Farren, Richard M.
　　See Betjeman, John

Fassbinder, Rainer Werner
　　1946-1982 .... **CLC 20**
　　See also CA 93-96; 106; CANR 31

Fast, Howard (Melvin) 1914- .. **CLC 23, 131; DAM NOV**
　　See also AAYA 16; AW; CA 1-4R, 181; CAAE 181; CAAS 18; CANR 1, 33, 54, 75; DLB 9; INT CANR-33; MTCW 1; SATA 7; SATA-Essay 107; TCWW 2

Faulcon, Robert
　　See Holdstock, Robert P.

Faulkner, William (Cuthbert)
　　1897-1962 .... **CLC 1, 3, 6, 8, 9, 11, 14, 18, 28, 52, 68; DA; DAB; DAC; DAM MST, NOV; SSC 1, 35, 42**
　　See also AAYA 7; AW; CA 81-84; CANR 33; CDALB 1929-1941; DA3; DLB 9, 11, 44, 102; DLBD 2; DLBY 86, 97; MTCW 1, 2

Fauset, Jessie Redmon
　　1882(?)-1961 .... **CLC 19, 54; BLC 2; DAM MULT**
　　See also BW 1; CA 109; CANR 83; DLB 51

Faust, Frederick (Schiller)
　　1892-1944(?) .... **TCLC 49; DAM POP**
　　See also Austin, Frank; Brand, Max; Challis, George; Dawson, Peter; Dexter, Martin; Evans, Evan; Frederick, John; Frost, Frederick; Manning, David; Silver, Nicholas
　　See also CA 108; 152

Faust, Irvin 1924- .... **CLC 8**
　　See also CA 33-36R; CANR 28, 67; DLB 2, 28; DLBY 80

Fawkes, Guy
　　See Benchley, Robert (Charles)

Fearing, Kenneth (Flexner)
　　1902-1961 .... **CLC 51**
　　See also CA 93-96; CANR 59; DLB 9

Fecamps, Elise
　　See Creasey, John

Federman, Raymond 1928- .... **CLC 6, 47**
　　See also CA 17-20R; CAAS 8; CANR 10, 43, 83; DLBY 80

Federspiel, J(uerg) F. 1931- .... **CLC 42**
　　See also CA 146

Feiffer, Jules (Ralph) 1929- ..... **CLC 2, 8, 64; DAM DRAM**
　　See also AAYA 3; CA 17-20R; CANR 30, 59; DLB 7, 44; INT CANR-30; MTCW 1; SATA 8, 61, 111

Ford, Ford Madox 1873-1939 ... **TCLC 1, 15, 39, 57; DAM NOV**
See also Chaucer, Daniel
See also CA 104; 132; CANR 74; CDBLB 1914-1945; DA3; DLB 162; MTCW 1, 2

Ford, Henry 1863-1947 .... **TCLC 73**
See also CA 115; 148

Ford, John 1586-1639 .... **DC 8**
See also CDBLB Before 1660; DAM DRAM; DA3; DLB 58

Ford, John 1895-1973 .... **CLC 16**
See also CA 187; 45-48

Ford, Richard 1944- .... **CLC 46, 99**
See also AMWS 5; CA 69-72; CANR 11, 47, 86; DLB 227; MTCW 1

Ford, Webster
See Masters, Edgar Lee

Foreman, Richard 1937- .... **CLC 50**
See also CA 65-68; CANR 32, 63

Forester, C(ecil) S(cott) 1899-1966 ... **CLC 35**
See also CA 73-76; 25-28R; CANR 83; DLB 191; SATA 13

Forez
See Mauriac, Fran

Forman, James Douglas 1932- .... **CLC 21**
See also AAYA 17; AW; CA 9-12R; CANR 4, 19, 42; JRDA; MAICYA; SATA 8, 70

Fornés, María Irene 1930- . **CLC 39, 61; DC 10; HLCS 1**
See also CA 25-28R; CANR 28, 81; DLB 7; HW 1, 2; INT CANR-28; MTCW 1

Forrest, Leon (Richard) 1937-1997 .. **CLC 4; BLCS**
See also BW 2; CA 89-92; 162; CAAS 7; CANR 25, 52, 87; DLB 33

Forster, E(dward) M(organ) 1879-1970 ...... **CLC 1, 2, 3, 4, 9, 10, 13, 15, 22, 45, 77; DA; DAB; DAC; DAM MST, NOV; SSC 27**
See also AAYA 2, 37; AW; CA 13-14; 25-28R; CANR 45; CAP 1; CDBLB 1914-1945; DA3; DLB 34, 98, 162, 178, 195; DLBD 10; MTCW 1, 2; SATA 57

Forster, John 1812-1876 .... **NCLC 11**
See also DLB 144, 184

Forsyth, Frederick 1938- .... **CLC 2, 5, 36; DAM NOV, POP**
See also BEST 89:4; CA 85-88; CANR 38, 62; DLB 87; MTCW 1, 2

Forten, Charlotte L. **TCLC 16; BLC 2**
See also Grimke, Charlotte L(ottie) Forten
See also DLB 50

Foscolo, Ugo 1778-1827 .... **NCLC 8, 97**

Fosse, Bob **CLC 20**
See also Fosse, Robert Louis

Fosse, Robert Louis 1927-1987
See Fosse, Bob
See also CA 110; 123

Foster, Stephen Collins 1826-1864 .... **NCLC 26**

Foucault, Michel 1926-1984 .. **CLC 31, 34, 69**
See also CA 105; 113; CANR 34; DLB 242; GLL 1; MTCW 1, 2

Fouque, Friedrich (Heinrich Karl) de la Motte 1777-1843 .... **NCLC 2**
See also DLB 90

Fourier, Charles 1772-1837 .... **NCLC 51**

Fournier, Pierre 1916- .... **CLC 11**
See also Gascar, Pierre
See also CA 89-92; CANR 16, 40

Fowles, John (Philip) 1926- .. **CLC 1, 2, 3, 4, 6, 9, 10, 15, 33, 87; DAB; DAC; DAM MST; SSC 33**
See also BRWS 1; CA 5-8R; CANR 25, 71; CDBLB 1960 to Present; DA3; DLB 14, 139, 207; MTCW 1, 2; SATA 22

Fox, Paula 1923- .... **CLC 2, 8, 121**
See also AAYA 3, 37; AW; CA 73-76; CANR 20, 36, 62; CLR 1, 44; DLB 52; JRDA; MAICYA; MTCW 1; SATA 17, 60, 120

Fox, William Price (Jr.) 1926- .... **CLC 22**
See also CA 17-20R; CAAS 19; CANR 11; DLB 2; DLBY 81

Foxe, John 1517(?)-1587 .... **LC 14**
See also DLB 132

Frame, Janet **CLC 2, 3, 6, 22, 66, 96; SSC 29**
See also Clutha, Janet Paterson Frame

France, Anatole **TCLC 9**
See also Thibault, Jacques Anatole Francois
See also DLB 123; MTCW 1

Francis, Claude 19(?)- .... **CLC 50**

Francis, Dick 1920- .... **CLC 2, 22, 42, 102; DAM POP**
See also AAYA 5, 21; BEST 89:3; CA 5-8R; CANR 9, 42, 68; CDBLB 1960 to Present; DA3; DLB 87; INT CANR-9; MTCW 1, 2

Francis, Robert (Churchill) 1901-1987 .... **CLC 15**
See also CA 1-4R; 123; CANR 1

Frank, Anne(lies Marie) 1929-1945 . **TCLC 17; DA; DAB; DAC; DAM MST**
See also AAYA 12; CA 113; 133; CANR 68; DA3; MTCW 1, 2; SATA 87; SATA-Brief 42

Frank, Bruno 1887-1945 .... **TCLC 81**
See also CA 189; DLB 118

Frank, Elizabeth 1945- .... **CLC 39**
See also CA 121; 126; CANR 78; INT 126

Frankl, Viktor E(mil) 1905-1997 ...... **CLC 93**
See also CA 65-68; 161

Franklin, Benjamin
See Hasek, Jaroslav (Matej Frantisek)

Franklin, Benjamin 1706-1790 .. **LC 25; DA; DAB; DAC; DAM MST**
See also AW; CDALB 1640-1865; DA3; DLB 24, 43, 73

Franklin, (Stella Maria Sarah) Miles (Lampe) 1879-1954 .... **TCLC 7**
See also CA 104; 164; DLB 230; MTCW 2

Fraser, (Lady)Antonia (Pakenham) 1932- .... **CLC 32, 107**
See also CA 85-88; CANR 44, 65; MTCW 1, 2; SATA-Brief 32

Fraser, George MacDonald 1925- ...... **CLC 7**
See also CA 45-48, 180; CAAE 180; CANR 2, 48, 74; MTCW 1

Fraser, Sylvia 1935- .... **CLC 64**
See also CA 45-48; CANR 1, 16, 60; CCA 1

Frayn, Michael 1933- .... **CLC 3, 7, 31, 47; DAM DRAM, NOV**
See also CA 5-8R; CANR 30, 69; DLB 13, 14, 194; MTCW 1, 2

Fraze, Candida (Merrill) 1945- .... **CLC 50**
See also CA 126

Frazer, J(ames) G(eorge) 1854-1941 .... **TCLC 32**
See also BRWS 3; CA 118

Frazer, Robert Caine
See Creasey, John

Frazer, Sir James George
See Frazer, J(ames) G(eorge)

Frazier, Charles 1950- .... **CLC 109**
See also AAYA 34; CA 161

Frazier, Ian 1951- .... **CLC 46**
See also CA 130; CANR 54, 93

Frederic, Harold 1856-1898 .... **NCLC 10**
See also DLB 12, 23; DLBD 13

Frederick, John
See Faust, Frederick (Schiller)
See also TCWW 2

Frederick the Great 1712-1786 .... **LC 14**

Fredro, Aleksander 1793-1876 .... **NCLC 8**

Freeling, Nicolas 1927- .... **CLC 38**
See also CA 49-52; CAAS 12; CANR 1, 17, 50, 84; DLB 87

Freeman, Douglas Southall 1886-1953 .... **TCLC 11**
See also CA 109; DLB 17; DLBD 17

Freeman, Judith 1946- .... **CLC 55**
See also CA 148

Freeman, Mary E(leanor) Wilkins 1852-1930 .... **TCLC 9; SSC 1**
See also CA 106; 177; DLB 12, 78, 221

Freeman, R(ichard) Austin 1862-1943 .... **TCLC 21**
See also CA 113; CANR 84; DLB 70

French, Albert 1943- .... **CLC 86**
See also BW 3; CA 167

French, Marilyn 1929- .... **CLC 10, 18, 60; DAM DRAM, NOV, POP**
See also CA 69-72; CANR 3, 31; INT CANR-31; MTCW 1, 2

French, Paul
See Asimov, Isaac

Freneau, Philip Morin 1752-1832 ... **NCLC 1**
See also AMWS 2; DLB 37, 43

Freud, Sigmund 1856-1939 .... **TCLC 52**
See also CA 115; 133; CANR 69; MTCW 1, 2

Friedan, Betty (Naomi) 1921- .... **CLC 74**
See also CA 65-68; CANR 18, 45, 74; MTCW 1, 2

Friedlander, Saul 1932- .... **CLC 90**
See also CA 117; 130; CANR 72

Friedman, B(ernard) H(arper) 1926- .... **CLC 7**
See also CA 1-4R; CANR 3, 48

Friedman, Bruce Jay 1930- ...... **CLC 3, 5, 56**
See also CA 9-12R; CANR 25, 52; DLB 2, 28; INT CANR-25

Friel, Brian 1929- .... **CLC 5, 42, 59, 115; DC 8**
See also BRWS 5; CA 21-24R; CANR 33, 69; DLB 13; MTCW 1

Friis-Baastad, Babbis Ellinor 1921-1970 .... **CLC 12**
See also CA 17-20R; 134; SATA 7

Frisch, Max (Rudolf) 1911-1991 ... **CLC 3, 9, 14, 18, 32, 44; DAM DRAM, NOV**
See also CA 85-88; 134; CANR 32, 74; DLB 69, 124; MTCW 1, 2

Fromentin, Eugene (Samuel Auguste) 1820-1876 .... **NCLC 10**
See also DLB 123

Frost, Frederick
See Faust, Frederick (Schiller)
See also TCWW 2

Frost, Robert (Lee) 1874-1963 .. **CLC 1, 3, 4, 9, 10, 13, 15, 26, 34, 44; DA; DAB; DAC; DAM MST, POET; PC 1**
See also AAYA 21; CA 89-92; CANR 33; CDALB 1917-1929; CLR 67; DA3; DLB 54; DLBD 7; MTCW 1, 2; SATA 14

Froude, James Anthony 1818-1894 .... **NCLC 43**
See also DLB 18, 57, 144

Froy, Herald
See Waterhouse, Keith (Spencer)

Fry, Christopher 1907- .... **CLC 2, 10, 14; DAM DRAM**
See also BRWS 3; CA 17-20R; CAAS 23; CANR 9, 30, 74; DLB 13; MTCW 1, 2; SATA 66

Frye, (Herman) Northrop 1912-1991 .... **CLC 24, 70**
See also CA 5-8R; 133; CANR 8, 37; DLB 67, 68; MTCW 1, 2

Fuchs, Daniel 1909-1993 .... **CLC 8, 22**
See also CA 81-84; 142; CAAS 5; CANR
40; DLB 9, 26, 28; DLBY 93

Fuchs, Daniel 1934- .... **CLC 34**
See also CA 37-40R; CANR 14, 48

Fuentes, Carlos 1928- .. **CLC 3, 8, 10, 13, 22,
41, 60, 113; DA; DAB; DAC; DAM
MST, MULT, NOV; HLC 1; SSC 24**
See also AAYA 4; AITN 2; AW; CA 69-72;
CANR 10, 32, 68; CWW 2; DA3; DLB
113; HW 1, 2; MTCW 1, 2

Fuentes, Gregorio Lopez y
See Lopez y Fuentes, Gregorio

Fuertes, Gloria 1918-1998 .... **PC 27**
See also CA 178, 180; DLB 108; HW 2;
SATA 115

Fugard, (Harold) Athol 1932- . **CLC 5, 9, 14,
25, 40, 80; DAM DRAM; DC 3**
See also AAYA 17; CA 85-88; CANR 32,
54; DLB 225; MTCW 1

Fugard, Sheila 1932- .... **CLC 48**
See also CA 125

Fukuyama, Francis 1952- .... **CLC 131**
See also CA 140; CANR 72

Fuller, Charles (H., Jr.) 1939- .... **CLC 25;
BLC 2; DAM DRAM, MULT; DC 1**
See also BW 2; CA 108; 112; CANR 87;
DLB 38; INT 112; MTCW 1

Fuller, Henry Blake 1857-1929 .... **TCLC 103**
See also CA 108; 177; DLB 12

Fuller, John (Leopold) 1937- .... **CLC 62**
See also CA 21-24R; CANR 9, 44; DLB 40

Fuller, Margaret
See Ossoli, Sarah Margaret (Fuller marchesa
d')
See also AMWS 2

Fuller, Roy (Broadbent) 1912-1991 ... **CLC 4,
28**
See also CA 5-8R; 135; CAAS 10; CANR
53, 83; DLB 15, 20; SATA 87

Fuller, Sarah Margaret
See Ossoli, Sarah Margaret (Fuller marchesa
d')

Fulton, Alice 1952- .... **CLC 52**
See also CA 116; CANR 57, 88; DLB 193

Furphy, Joseph 1843-1912 .... **TCLC 25**
See also CA 163; DLB 230

Fussell, Paul 1924- .... **CLC 74**
See also BEST 90:1; CA 17-20R; CANR 8,
21, 35, 69; INT CANR-21; MTCW 1, 2

Futabatei, Shimei 1864-1909 .... **TCLC 44**
See also CA 162; DLB 180

Futrelle, Jacques 1875-1912 .... **TCLC 19**
See also CA 113; 155

Gaboriau, Emile 1835-1873 .... **NCLC 14**

Gadda, Carlo Emilio 1893-1973 .... **CLC 11**
See also CA 89-92; DLB 177

Gaddis, William 1922-1998 .. **CLC 1, 3, 6, 8,
10, 19, 43, 86**
See also AMWS 4; CA 17-20R; 172; CANR
21, 48; DLB 2; MTCW 1, 2

Gage, Walter
See Inge, William (Motter)

Gaines, Ernest J(ames) 1933- ...... **CLC 3, 11,
18, 86; BLC 2; DAM MULT**
See also AAYA 18; AITN 1; AW; BW 2, 3;
CA 9-12R; CANR 6, 24, 42, 75; CDALB
1968-1988; CLR 62; DA3; DLB 2, 33,
152; DLBY 80; MTCW 1, 2; SATA 86

Gaitskill, Mary 1954- .... **CLC 69**
See also CA 128; CANR 61

Galdos, Benito Perez
See Perez Galdos, Benito

Gale, Zona 1874-1938 .... **TCLC 7; DAM
DRAM**
See also CA 105; 153; CANR 84; DLB 9,
78, 228

Galeano, Eduardo (Hughes) 1940- . **CLC 72;
HLCS 1**
See also CA 29-32R; CANR 13, 32; HW 1

Galiano, Juan Valera y Alcala
See Valera y Alcala-Galiano, Juan

Galilei, Galileo 1564-1642 .... **LC 45**

Gallagher, Tess 1943- ...... **CLC 18, 63; DAM
POET; PC 9**
See also CA 106; DLB 212

Gallant, Mavis 1922- .. **CLC 7, 18, 38; DAC;
DAM MST; SSC 5**
See also CA 69-72; CANR 29, 69; CCA 1;
DLB 53; MTCW 1, 2

Gallant, Roy A(rthur) 1924- .... **CLC 17**
See also CA 5-8R; CANR 4, 29, 54; CLR
30; MAICYA; SATA 4, 68, 110

Gallico, Paul (William) 1897-1976 ..... **CLC 2**
See also AITN 1; CA 5-8R; 69-72; CANR
23; DLB 9, 171; MAICYA; SATA 13

Gallo, Max Louis 1932- .... **CLC 95**
See also CA 85-88

Gallois, Lucien
See Desnos, Robert

Gallup, Ralph
See Whitemore, Hugh (John)

Galsworthy, John 1867-1933 .... **TCLC 1, 45;
DA; DAB; DAC; DAM DRAM, MST,
NOV; SSC 22**
See also AW; CA 104; 141; CANR 75; CD-
BLB 1890-1914; DA3; DLB 10, 34, 98,
162; DLBD 16; MTCW 1

Galt, John 1779-1839 .... **NCLC 1**
See also DLB 99, 116, 159

Galvin, James 1951- .... **CLC 38**
See also CA 108; CANR 26

Gamboa, Federico 1864-1939 .... **TCLC 36**
See also CA 167; HW 2

Gandhi, M. K.
See Gandhi, Mohandas Karamchand

Gandhi, Mahatma
See Gandhi, Mohandas Karamchand

Gandhi, Mohandas Karamchand
1869-1948 .... **TCLC 59; DAM MULT**
See also CA 121; 132; DA3; MTCW 1, 2

Gann, Ernest Kellogg 1910-1991 ..... **CLC 23**
See also AITN 1; CA 1-4R; 136; CANR 1,
83

Garber, Eric 1943(?)-
See Holleran, Andrew
See also CANR 89

Garcia, Cristina 1958- .... **CLC 76**
See also CA 141; CANR 73; HW 2

Garcia Lorca, Federico 1898-1936 . **TCLC 1,
7, 49; DA; DAB; DAC; DAM DRAM,
MST, MULT, POET; DC 2; HLC 2;
PC 3**
See also Lorca, Federico Garcia
See also AW; CA 104; 131; CANR 81;
DA3; DLB 108; HW 1, 2; MTCW 1, 2

Garcia Marquez, Gabriel (Jose)
1928- .... **CLC 2, 3, 8, 10, 15, 27, 47, 55,
68; DA; DAB; DAC; DAM MST,
MULT, NOV, POP; HLC 1; SSC 8**
See also AAYA 3, 33; AW; BEST 89:1,
90:4; CA 33-36R; CANR 10, 28, 50, 75,
82; DA3; DLB 113; HW 1, 2; MTCW 1,
2

Garcilaso de la Vega, El Inca 1503-1536
See also HLCS 1

Gard, Janice
See Latham, Jean Lee

Gard, Roger Martin du
See Martin du Gard, Roger

Gardam, Jane 1928- .... **CLC 43**
See also AW; CA 49-52; CANR 2, 18, 33,
54; CLR 12; DLB 14, 161, 231; MAI-
CYA; MTCW 1; SAAS 9; SATA 39, 76;
SATA-Brief 28

Gardner, Herb(ert) 1934- .... **CLC 44**
See also CA 149

Gardner, John (Champlin), Jr.
1933-1982 ...... **CLC 2, 3, 5, 7, 8, 10, 18,
28, 34; DAM NOV, POP; SSC 7**
See also AITN 1; AMWS 5; CA 65-68; 107;
CANR 33, 73; CDALBS; DA3; DLB 2;
DLBY 82; MTCW 1; SATA 40; SATA-
Obit 31

Gardner, John (Edmund) 1926- ...... **CLC 30;
DAM POP**
See also CA 103; CANR 15, 69; MTCW 1

Gardner, Miriam
See Bradley, Marion Zimmer
See also GLL 1

Gardner, Noel
See Kuttner, Henry

Gardons, S. S.
See Snodgrass, W(illiam) D(e Witt)

Garfield, Leon 1921-1996 .... **CLC 12**
See also AAYA 8; AW; CA 17-20R; 152;
CANR 38, 41, 78; CLR 21; DLB 161;
JRDA; MAICYA; SATA 1, 32, 76; SATA-
Obit 90

Garland, (Hannibal) Hamlin
1860-1940 .... **TCLC 3; SSC 18**
See also CA 104; DLB 12, 71, 78, 186;
TCWW 2

Garneau, (Hector de) Saint-Denys
1912-1943 .... **TCLC 13**
See also CA 111; DLB 88

Garner, Alan 1934- ..... **CLC 17; DAB; DAM
POP**
See also AAYA 18; AW; CA 73-76, 178;
CAAE 178; CANR 15, 64; CLR 20; DLB
161; MAICYA; MTCW 1, 2; SATA 18,
69; SATA-Essay 108

Garner, Hugh 1913-1979 .... **CLC 13**
See also Warwick, Jarvis
See also CA 69-72; CANR 31; CCA 1; DLB
68

Garnett, David 1892-1981 .... **CLC 3**
See also CA 5-8R; 103; CANR 17, 79; DLB
34; MTCW 2

Garos, Stephanie
See Katz, Steve

Garrett, George (Palmer) 1929- .. **CLC 3, 11,
51; SSC 30**
See also AMWS 7; CA 1-4R; CAAS 5;
CANR 1, 42, 67; DLB 2, 5, 130, 152;
DLBY 83

Garrick, David 1717-1779 .... **LC 15; DAM
DRAM**
See also DLB 84

Garrigue, Jean 1914-1972 .... **CLC 2, 8**
See also CA 5-8R; 37-40R; CANR 20

Garrison, Frederick
See Sinclair, Upton (Beall)

Garro, Elena 1920(?)-1998
See also CA 131; 169; CWW 2; DLB 145;
HLCS 1; HW 1

Garth, Will
See Hamilton, Edmond; Kuttner, Henry

Garvey, Marcus (Moziah, Jr.)
1887-1940 ...... **TCLC 41; BLC 2; DAM
MULT**
See also BW 1; CA 120; 124; CANR 79

Gary, Romain CLC 25
See also Kacew, Romain
See also DLB 83

Gascar, Pierre CLC 11
See also Fournier, Pierre

Gascoyne, David (Emery) 1916- .... **CLC 45**
See also CA 65-68; CANR 10, 28, 54; DLB
20; MTCW 1

Gaskell, Elizabeth Cleghorn
1810-1865 .... **NCLC 5, 70, 97; DAB; DAM MST; SSC 25**
See also CDBLB 1832-1890; DLB 21, 144, 159

Gass, William H(oward) 1924- . **CLC 1, 2, 8, 11, 15, 39, 132; SSC 12**
See also AMWS 6; CA 17-20R; CANR 30, 71; DLB 2, 227; MTCW 1, 2

Gassendi, Pierre 1592-1655 .... **LC 54**

Gasset, Jose Ortega y
See Ortega y Gasset, Jose

Gates, Henry Louis, Jr. 1950- .... **CLC 65; BLCS; DAM MULT**
See also BW 2, 3; CA 109; CANR 25, 53, 75; DA3; DLB 67; MTCW 1

Gautier, Theophile 1811-1872 .. **NCLC 1, 59; DAM POET; PC 18; SSC 20**
See also DLB 119

Gawsworth, John
See Bates, H(erbert) E(rnest)

Gay, John 1685-1732 .. **LC 49; DAM DRAM**
See also DLB 84, 95

Gay, Oliver
See Gogarty, Oliver St. John

Gaye, Marvin (Penze) 1939-1984 ..... **CLC 26**
See also CA 112

Gebler, Carlo (Ernest) 1954- .... **CLC 39**
See also CA 119; 133

Gee, Maggie (Mary) 1948- .... **CLC 57**
See also CA 130; DLB 207

Gee, Maurice (Gough) 1931- .... **CLC 29**
See also CA 97-100; CANR 67; CLR 56; SATA 46, 101

Gelbart, Larry (Simon) 1928- .... **CLC 21, 61**
See also Gelbart, Larry
See also CA 73-76; CANR 45, 94

Gelbart, Larry 1928-
See Gelbart, Larry (Simon)

Gelber, Jack 1932- .... **CLC 1, 6, 14, 79**
See also CA 1-4R; CANR 2; DLB 7, 228

Gellhorn, Martha (Ellis)
1908-1998 .... **CLC 14, 60**
See also CA 77-80; 164; CANR 44; DLBY 82, 98

Genet, Jean 1910-1986 .. **CLC 1, 2, 5, 10, 14, 44, 46; DAM DRAM**
See also CA 13-16R; CANR 18; DA3; DLB 72; DLBY 86; GLL 1; MTCW 1, 2

Gent, Peter 1942- .... **CLC 29**
See also AITN 1; CA 89-92; DLBY 82

Gentile, Giovanni 1875-1944 .... **TCLC 96**
See also CA 119

Gentlewoman in New England, A
See Bradstreet, Anne

Gentlewoman in Those Parts, A
See Bradstreet, Anne

Geoffrey of Monmouth c.
1100-1155 .... **CMLC 44**
See also DLB 146

George, Jean Craighead 1919- .... **CLC 35**
See also AAYA 8; AW; CA 5-8R; CANR 25; CLR 1; DLB 52; JRDA; MAICYA; SATA 2, 68

George, Stefan (Anton) 1868-1933 . **TCLC 2, 14**
See also CA 104

Georges, Georges Martin
See Simenon, Georges (Jacques Christian)

Gerhardi, William Alexander
See Gerhardie, William Alexander

Gerhardie, William Alexander
1895-1977 .... **CLC 5**
See also CA 25-28R; 73-76; CANR 18; DLB 36

Gerstler, Amy 1956- .... **CLC 70**
See also CA 146

Gertler, T. **CLC 134**
See also CA 116; 121

Ghalib **NCLC 39, 78**
See also Ghalib, Hsadullah Khan

Ghalib, Hsadullah Khan 1797-1869
See Ghalib
See also DAM POET

Ghelderode, Michel de 1898-1962 ..... **CLC 6, 11; DAM DRAM**
See also CA 85-88; CANR 40, 77

Ghiselin, Brewster 1903- .... **CLC 23**
See also CA 13-16R; CAAS 10; CANR 13

Ghose, Aurabinda 1872-1950 .... **TCLC 63**
See also CA 163

Ghose, Zulfikar 1935- .... **CLC 42**
See also CA 65-68; CANR 67

Ghosh, Amitav 1956- .... **CLC 44**
See also CA 147; CANR 80

Giacosa, Giuseppe 1847-1906 .... **TCLC 7**
See also CA 104

Gibb, Lee
See Waterhouse, Keith (Spencer)

Gibbon, Lewis Grassic **TCLC 4**
See also Mitchell, James Leslie

Gibbons, Kaye 1960- .... **CLC 50, 88; DAM POP**
See also AAYA 34; CA 151; CANR 75; DA3; MTCW 1; SATA 117

Gibran, Kahlil 1883-1931 .... **TCLC 1, 9; DAM POET, POP; PC 9**
See also CA 104; 150; DA3; MTCW 2

Gibran, Khalil
See Gibran, Kahlil

Gibson, William 1914- .. **CLC 23; DA; DAB; DAC; DAM DRAM, MST**
See also AW; CA 9-12R; CANR 9, 42, 75; DLB 7; MTCW 1; SATA 66; SCFW 2

Gibson, William (Ford) 1948- ... **CLC 39, 63; DAM POP**
See also AAYA 12; CA 126; 133; CANR 52, 90; DA3; MTCW 1

Gide, Andre (Paul Guillaume)
1869-1951 . **TCLC 5, 12, 36; DA; DAB; DAC; DAM MST, NOV; SSC 13**
See also AW; CA 104; 124; DA3; DLB 65; MTCW 1, 2

Gifford, Barry (Colby) 1946- .... **CLC 34**
See also CA 65-68; CANR 9, 30, 40, 90

Gilbert, Frank
See De Voto, Bernard (Augustine)

Gilbert, W(illiam) S(chwenck)
1836-1911 .... **TCLC 3; DAM DRAM, POET**
See also CA 104; 173; SATA 36

Gilbreth, Frank B., Jr. 1911-2001 .... **CLC 17**
See also CA 9-12R; SATA 2

Gilchrist, Ellen 1935- ...... **CLC 34, 48; DAM POP; SSC 14**
See also CA 113; 116; CANR 41, 61; DLB 130; MTCW 1, 2

Giles, Molly 1942- .... **CLC 39**
See also CA 126

Gill, Eric 1882-1940 .... **TCLC 85**

Gill, Patrick
See Creasey, John

Gilliam, Terry (Vance) 1940- .... **CLC 21, 141**
See also Monty Python
See also AAYA 19; CA 108; 113; CANR 35; INT 113

Gillian, Jerry
See Gilliam, Terry (Vance)

Gilliatt, Penelope (Ann Douglass)
1932-1993 .... **CLC 2, 10, 13, 53**
See also AITN 2; CA 13-16R; 141; CANR 49; DLB 14

Gilman, Charlotte (Anna) Perkins (Stetson)
1860-1935 .... **TCLC 9, 37; SSC 13**
See also CA 106; 150; DLB 221; MTCW 1

Gilmour, David 1949- .... **CLC 35**
See also CA 138; 147

Gilpin, William 1724-1804 .... **NCLC 30**

Gilray, J. D.
See Mencken, H(enry) L(ouis)

Gilroy, Frank D(aniel) 1925- .... **CLC 2**
See also CA 81-84; CANR 32, 64, 86; DLB 7

Gilstrap, John 1957(?)- .... **CLC 99**
See also CA 160

Ginsberg, Allen 1926-1997 .... **CLC 1, 2, 3, 4, 6, 13, 36, 69, 109; DA; DAB; DAC; DAM MST, POET; PC 4**
See also AAYA 33; AITN 1; AMWS 2; AW; CA 1-4R; 157; CANR 2, 41, 63, 95; CDALB 1941-1968; DA3; DLB 5, 16, 169; GLL 1; MTCW 1, 2

Ginzburg, Natalia 1916-1991 .... **CLC 5, 11, 54, 70**
See also CA 85-88; 135; CANR 33; DLB 177; MTCW 1, 2

Giono, Jean 1895-1970 .... **CLC 4, 11**
See also CA 45-48; 29-32R; CANR 2, 35; DLB 72; MTCW 1

Giovanni, Nikki 1943- .... **CLC 2, 4, 19, 64, 117; BLC 2; DA; DAB; DAC; DAM MST, MULT, POET; PC 19**
See also AAYA 22; AITN 1; AW; BW 2, 3; CA 29-32R; CAAS 6; CANR 18, 41, 60, 91; CDALBS; CLR 6; DA3; DLB 5, 41; INT CANR-18; MAICYA; MTCW 1, 2; SATA 24, 107

Giovene, Andrea 1904- .... **CLC 7**
See also CA 85-88

Gippius, Zinaida (Nikolayevna) 1869-1945
See Hippius, Zinaida
See also CA 106

Giraudoux, (Hippolyte) Jean
1882-1944 .... **TCLC 2, 7; DAM DRAM**
See also CA 104; DLB 65

Gironella, Jose Maria 1917- .... **CLC 11**
See also CA 101

Gissing, George (Robert)
1857-1903 .... **TCLC 3, 24, 47; SSC 37**
See also CA 105; 167; DLB 18, 135, 184

Giurlani, Aldo
See Palazzeschi, Aldo

Gladkov, Fyodor (Vasilyevich)
1883-1958 .... **TCLC 27**
See also CA 170

Glanville, Brian (Lester) 1931- .... **CLC 6**
See also CA 5-8R; CAAS 9; CANR 3, 70; DLB 15, 139; SATA 42

Glasgow, Ellen (Anderson Gholson)
1873-1945 .... **TCLC 2, 7; SSC 34**
See also CA 104; 164; DLB 9, 12; MTCW 2

Glaspell, Susan 1882(?)-1948 . **TCLC 55; DC 10; SSC 41**
See also AMWS 3; AW 2; CA 110; 154; DLB 7, 9, 78, 228; TCWW 2

Glassco, John 1909-1981 .... **CLC 9**
See also CA 13-16R; 102; CANR 15; DLB 68

Glasscock, Amnesia
See Steinbeck, John (Ernst)

Glasser, Ronald J. 1940(?)- .... **CLC 37**

Glassman, Joyce
See Johnson, Joyce

Glendinning, Victoria 1937- .... **CLC 50**
See also CA 120; 127; CANR 59, 89; DLB 155

Glissant, Edouard 1928- . **CLC 10, 68; DAM MULT**
See also CA 153; CWW 2

Gloag, Julian 1930- .... **CLC 40**
  See also AITN 1; CA 65-68; CANR 10, 70
Glowacki, Aleksander
  See Prus, Boleslaw
Gluck, Louise (Elisabeth) 1943- .. **CLC 7, 22,**
    44, 81; DAM POET; PC 16
  See also AMWS 5; CA 33-36R; CANR 40,
    69; DA3; DLB 5; MTCW 2
Glyn, Elinor 1864-1943 .... **TCLC 72**
  See also DLB 153
Gobineau, Joseph Arthur (Comte) de
    1816-1882 .... **NCLC 17**
  See also DLB 123
Godard, Jean-Luc 1930- .... **CLC 20**
  See also CA 93-96
Godden, (Margaret) Rumer
    1907-1998 .... **CLC 53**
  See also AAYA 6; CA 5-8R; 172; CANR 4,
    27, 36, 55, 80; CLR 20; DLB 161; MAI-
    CYA; SAAS 12; SATA 3, 36; SATA-Obit
    109
Godoy Alcayaga, Lucila
    1899-1957 .... **TCLC 2; DAM MULT;**
    HLC 2; PC 32
  See also BW 2; CA 104; 131; CANR 81;
    HW 1, 2; MTCW 1, 2
Godwin, Gail (Kathleen) 1937- ..... **CLC 5, 8,**
    22, 31, 69, 125; DAM POP
  See also CA 29-32R; CANR 15, 43, 69;
    DA3; DLB 6, 234; INT CANR-15;
    MTCW 1, 2
Godwin, William 1756-1836 .... **NCLC 14**
  See also CDBLB 1789-1832; DLB 39, 104,
    142, 158, 163
Goebbels, Josef
  See Goebbels, (Paul) Joseph
Goebbels, (Paul) Joseph
    1897-1945 .... **TCLC 68**
  See also CA 115; 148
Goebbels, Joseph Paul
  See Goebbels, (Paul) Joseph
Goethe, Johann Wolfgang von
    1749-1832 ...... **NCLC 4, 22, 34, 90; DA;**
    DAB; DAC; DAM DRAM, MST,
    POET; PC 5; SSC 38
  See also AW; DA3; DLB 94
Gogarty, Oliver St. John
    1878-1957 .... **TCLC 15**
  See also CA 109; 150; DLB 15, 19
Gogol, Nikolai (Vasilyevich)
    1809-1852 . **NCLC 5, 15, 31; DA; DAB;**
    DAC; DAM DRAM, MST; DC 1; SSC
    4, 29
  See also AW; DLB 198
Goines, Donald 1937(?)-1974 . **CLC 80; BLC**
    2; DAM MULT, POP
  See also AITN 1; BW 1, 3; CA 124; 114;
    CANR 82; DA3; DLB 33
Gold, Herbert 1924- .... **CLC 4, 7, 14, 42**
  See also CA 9-12R; CANR 17, 45; DLB 2;
    DLBY 81
Goldbarth, Albert 1948- .... **CLC 5, 38**
  See also CA 53-56; CANR 6, 40; DLB 120
Goldberg, Anatol 1910-1982 .... **CLC 34**
  See also CA 131; 117
Goldemberg, Isaac 1945- .... **CLC 52**
  See also CA 69-72; CAAS 12; CANR 11,
    32; HW 1
Golding, William (Gerald)
    1911-1993 ..... **CLC 1, 2, 3, 8, 10, 17, 27,**
    58, 81; DA; DAB; DAC; DAM MST,
    NOV
  See also AAYA 5; AW; BRWS 1; CA 5-8R;
    141; CANR 13, 33, 54; CDBLB 1945-
    1960; DA3; DLB 15, 100; MTCW 1, 2
Goldman, Emma 1869-1940 .... **TCLC 13**
  See also CA 110; 150; DLB 221
Goldman, Francisco 1954- .... **CLC 76**
  See also CA 162

Goldman, William (W.) 1931- ...... **CLC 1, 48**
  See also CA 9-12R; CANR 29, 69; DLB
    44; IDFW 3
Goldmann, Lucien 1913-1970 .... **CLC 24**
  See also CA 25-28; CAP 2
Goldoni, Carlo 1707-1793 .... **LC 4; DAM**
    DRAM
Goldsberry, Steven 1949- .... **CLC 34**
  See also CA 131
Goldsmith, Oliver 1730-1774 . **LC 2, 48; DA;**
    DAB; DAC; DAM DRAM, MST, NOV,
    POET; DC 8
  See also AW; CDBLB 1660-1789; DLB 39,
    89, 104, 109, 142; SATA 26
Goldsmith, Peter
  See Priestley, J(ohn) B(oynton)
Gombrowicz, Witold 1904-1969 .... **CLC 4, 7,**
    11, 49; DAM DRAM
  See also CA 19-20; 25-28R; CAP 2
Gomez de la Serna, Ramon
    1888-1963 .... **CLC 9**
  See also CA 153; 116; CANR 79; HW 1, 2
Goncharov, Ivan Alexandrovich
    1812-1891 .... **NCLC 1, 63**
  See also DLB 238
Goncourt, Edmond (Louis Antoine Huot) de
    1822-1896 .... **NCLC 7**
  See also DLB 123
Goncourt, Jules (Alfred Huot) de
    1830-1870 .... **NCLC 7**
  See also DLB 123
Gontier, Fernande 19(?)- .... **CLC 50**
Gonzalez Martinez, Enrique
    1871-1952 .... **TCLC 72**
  See also CA 166; CANR 81; HW 1, 2
Goodman, Paul 1911-1972 ..... **CLC 1, 2, 4, 7**
  See also CA 19-20; 37-40R; CANR 34;
    CAP 2; DLB 130; MTCW 1
Gordimer, Nadine 1923- ...... **CLC 3, 5, 7, 10,**
    18, 33, 51, 70, 123; DA; DAB; DAC;
    DAM MST, NOV; SSC 17
  See also AW; BRWS 2; CA 5-8R; CANR 3,
    28, 56, 88; DA3; DLB 225; INT CANR-
    28; MTCW 1, 2
Gordon, Adam Lindsay
    1833-1870 .... **NCLC 21**
  See also DLB 230
Gordon, Caroline 1895-1981 . **CLC 6, 13, 29,**
    83; SSC 15
  See also CA 11-12; 103; CANR 36; CAP 1;
    DLB 4, 9, 102; DLBD 17; DLBY 81;
    MTCW 1, 2
Gordon, Charles William 1860-1937
  See Connor, Ralph
  See also CA 109
Gordon, Mary (Catherine) 1949- .... **CLC 13,**
    22, 128
  See also AMWS 4; CA 102; CANR 44, 92;
    DLB 6; DLBY 81; INT 102; MTCW 1
Gordon, N. J.
  See Bosman, Herman Charles
Gordon, Sol 1923- .... **CLC 26**
  See also CA 53-56; CANR 4; SATA 11
Gordone, Charles 1925-1995 .... **CLC 1, 4;**
    DAM DRAM; DC 8
  See also BW 1, 3; CA 93-96, 180; 150;
    CAAE 180; CANR 55; DLB 7; INT 93-
    96; MTCW 1
Gore, Catherine 1800-1861 .... **NCLC 65**
  See also DLB 116
Gorenko, Anna Andreevna
  See Akhmatova, Anna
Gorky, Maxim TCLC 8; DAB; SSC 28
  See also Peshkov, Alexei Maximovich
  See also AW; MTCW 2
Goryan, Sirak
  See Saroyan, William

Gosse, Sir Edmund (William)
    1849-1928 .... **TCLC 28**
  See also CA 117; DLB 57, 144, 184
Gotlieb, Phyllis Fay (Bloom) 1926- .. **CLC 18**
  See also CA 13-16R; CANR 7; DLB 88
Gottesman, S. D.
  See Kornbluth, C(yril) M.; Pohl, Frederik
Gottfried von Strassburg fl. c.
    1170-1215 .... **CMLC 10**
  See also DLB 138
Gould, Lois CLC 4, 10
  See also CA 77-80; CANR 29; MTCW 1
Gourmont, Remy (-Marie-Charles) de
    1858-1915 .... **TCLC 17**
  See also CA 109; 150; MTCW 2
Govier, Katherine 1948- .... **CLC 51**
  See also CA 101; CANR 18, 40; CCA 1
Goyen, (Charles) William
    1915-1983 .... **CLC 5, 8, 14, 40**
  See also AITN 2; CA 5-8R; 110; CANR 6,
    71; DLB 2; DLBY 83; INT CANR-6
Goytisolo, Juan 1931- .... **CLC 5, 10, 23, 133;**
    DAM MULT; HLC 1
  See also CA 85-88; CANR 32, 61; CWW
    2; GLL 2; HW 1, 2; MTCW 1, 2
Gozzano, Guido 1883-1916 .... **PC 10**
  See also CA 154; DLB 114
Gozzi, (Conte) Carlo 1720-1806 .... **NCLC 23**
Grabbe, Christian Dietrich
    1801-1836 .... **NCLC 2**
  See also DLB 133
Grace, Patricia Frances 1937- .... **CLC 56**
  See also CA 176
Gracian y Morales, Baltasar
    1601-1658 .... **LC 15**
Gracq, Julien CLC 11, 48
  See Poirier, Louis
  See also CWW 2; DLB 83
Grade, Chaim 1910-1982 .... **CLC 10**
  See also CA 93-96; 107
Graduate of Oxford, A
  See Ruskin, John
Grafton, Garth
  See Duncan, Sara Jeannette
Graham, John
  See Phillips, David Graham
Graham, Jorie 1951- .... **CLC 48, 118**
  See also CA 111; CANR 63; DLB 120
Graham, R(obert) B(ontine) Cunninghame
  See Cunninghame Graham, Robert
    (Gallnigad) Bontine
  See also DLB 98, 135, 174
Graham, Robert
  See Haldeman, Joe (William)
Graham, Tom
  See Lewis, (Harry) Sinclair
Graham, W(illiam) S(idney)
    1918-1986 .... **CLC 29**
  See also CA 73-76; 118; DLB 20
Graham, Winston (Mawdsley)
    1910- .... **CLC 23**
  See also CA 49-52; CANR 2, 22, 45, 66;
    DLB 77
Grahame, Kenneth 1859-1932 ...... **TCLC 64;**
    DAB
  See also AW 1; CA 108; 136; CANR 80;
    CLR 5; DA3; DLB 34, 141, 178; MAI-
    CYA; MTCW 2; SATA 100
Granovsky, Timofei Nikolaevich
    1813-1855 .... **NCLC 75**
  See also DLB 198
Grant, Skeeter
  See Spiegelman, Art
Granville-Barker, Harley
    1877-1946 .... **TCLC 2; DAM DRAM**
  See also Barker, Harley Granville
  See also CA 104

Hampton, Christopher (James)
1946- .... **CLC 4**
See also CA 25-28R; DLB 13; MTCW 1

Hamsun, Knut TCLC 2, 14, 49
See also Pedersen, Knut

Handke, Peter 1942- .... **CLC 5, 8, 10, 15, 38, 134; DAM DRAM, NOV**
See also CA 77-80; CANR 33, 75; CWW 2; DLB 85, 124; MTCW 1, 2

Handy, W(illiam) C(hristopher)
1873-1958 .... **TCLC 97**
See also BW 3; CA 121; 167

Hanley, James 1901-1985 ..... **CLC 3, 5, 8, 13**
See also CA 73-76; 117; CANR 36; DLB 191; MTCW 1

Hannah, Barry 1942- .... **CLC 23, 38, 90**
See also CA 108; 110; CANR 43, 68; DLB 6, 234; INT 110; MTCW 1

Hannon, Ezra
See Hunter, Evan

Hansberry, Lorraine (Vivian)
1930-1965 ..... **CLC 17, 62; BLC 2; DA; DAB; DAC; DAM DRAM, MST, MULT; DC 2**
See also AAYA 25; AMWS 4; BW 1, 3; CA 109; 25-28R; CABS 3; CANR 58; CDALB 1941-1968; DA3; DLB 7, 38; MTCW 1, 2

Hansen, Joseph 1923- .... **CLC 38**
See also Brock, Rose; Colton, James
See also CA 29-32R; CAAS 17; CANR 16, 44, 66; DLB 226; GLL 1; INT CANR-16

Hansen, Martin A(lfred)
1909-1955 .... **TCLC 32**
See also CA 167; DLB 214

Hanson, Kenneth O(stlin) 1922- .... **CLC 13**
See also CA 53-56; CANR 7

Hardwick, Elizabeth (Bruce)
1916- .... **CLC 13; DAM NOV**
See also AMWS 3; CA 5-8R; CANR 3, 32, 70; DA3; DLB 6; MTCW 1, 2

Hardy, Thomas 1840-1928 .. **TCLC 4, 10, 18, 32, 48, 53, 72; DA; DAB; DAC; DAM MST, NOV, POET; PC 8; SSC 2**
See also AW; CA 104; 123; CDBLB 1890-1914; DA3; DLB 18, 19, 135; MTCW 1, 2

Hare, David 1947- .... **CLC 29, 58, 136**
See also BRWS 4; CA 97-100; CANR 39, 91; DLB 13; MTCW 1

Harewood, John
See Van Druten, John (William)

Harford, Henry
See Hudson, W(illiam) H(enry)

Hargrave, Leonie
See Disch, Thomas M(ichael)

Harjo, Joy 1951- ...... **CLC 83; DAM MULT; PC 27**
See also CA 114; CANR 35, 67, 91; DLB 120, 175; MTCW 2; NNAL

Harlan, Louis R(udolph) 1922- .... **CLC 34**
See also CA 21-24R; CANR 25, 55, 80

Harling, Robert 1951(?)- .... **CLC 53**
See also CA 147

Harmon, William (Ruth) 1938- .... **CLC 38**
See also CA 33-36R; CANR 14, 32, 35; SATA 65

Harper, F. E. W.
See Harper, Frances Ellen Watkins

Harper, Frances E. W.
See Harper, Frances Ellen Watkins

Harper, Frances E. Watkins
See Harper, Frances Ellen Watkins

Harper, Frances Ellen
See Harper, Frances Ellen Watkins

Harper, Frances Ellen Watkins
1825-1911 ...... **TCLC 14; BLC 2; DAM MULT, POET; PC 21**
See also BW 1, 3; CA 111; 125; CANR 79; DLB 50, 221

Harper, Michael S(teven) 1938- ... **CLC 7, 22**
See also BW 1; CA 33-36R; CANR 24; DLB 41

Harper, Mrs. F. E. W.
See Harper, Frances Ellen Watkins

Harris, Christie (Lucy) Irwin
1907- .... **CLC 12**
See also CA 5-8R; CANR 6, 83; CLR 47; DLB 88; JRDA; MAICYA; SAAS 10; SATA 6, 74; SATA-Essay 116

Harris, Frank 1856-1931 .... **TCLC 24**
See also CA 109; 150; CANR 80; DLB 156, 197

Harris, George Washington
1814-1869 .... **NCLC 23**
See also DLB 3, 11

Harris, Joel Chandler 1848-1908 ... **TCLC 2; SSC 19**
See also AW 1; CA 104; 137; CANR 80; CLR 49; DLB 11, 23, 42, 78, 91; MAICYA; SATA 100

Harris, John (Wyndham Parkes Lucas) Beynon 1903-1969
See Wyndham, John
See also CA 102; 89-92; CANR 84; SATA 118

Harris, MacDonald CLC 9
See also Heiney, Donald (William)

Harris, Mark 1922- .... **CLC 19**
See also CA 5-8R; CAAS 3; CANR 2, 55, 83; DLB 2; DLBY 80

Harris, (Theodore) Wilson 1921- ..... **CLC 25**
See also BW 2, 3; CA 65-68; CAAS 16; CANR 11, 27, 69; DLB 117; MTCW 1

Harrison, Elizabeth Cavanna 1909-
See Cavanna, Betty
See also AW; CA 9-12R; CANR 6, 27, 85

Harrison, Harry (Max) 1925- .... **CLC 42**
See also CA 1-4R; CANR 5, 21, 84; DLB 8; SATA 4; SCFW 2

Harrison, James (Thomas) 1937- ...... **CLC 6, 14, 33, 66; SSC 19**
See also Harrison, Jim
See also CA 13-16R; CANR 8, 51, 79; DLBY 82; INT CANR-8

Harrison, Jim
See Harrison, James (Thomas)
See also TCWW 2

Harrison, Kathryn 1961- .... **CLC 70**
See also CA 144; CANR 68

Harrison, Tony 1937- .... **CLC 43, 129**
See also BRWS 5; CA 65-68; CANR 44; DLB 40; MTCW 1

Harriss, Will(ard Irvin) 1922- .... **CLC 34**
See also CA 111

Harson, Sley
See Ellison, Harlan (Jay)

Hart, Ellis
See Ellison, Harlan (Jay)

Hart, Josephine 1942(?)- .... **CLC 70; DAM POP**
See also CA 138; CANR 70

Hart, Moss 1904-1961 .... **CLC 66; DAM DRAM**
See also CA 109; 89-92; CANR 84; DLB 7

Harte, (Francis) Bret(t)
1836(?)-1902 ... **TCLC 1, 25; DA; DAC; DAM MST; SSC 8**
See also AMWS 2; AW; CA 104; 140; CANR 80; CDALB 1865-1917; DA3; DLB 12, 64, 74, 79, 186; SATA 26

Hartley, L(eslie) P(oles) 1895-1972 ... **CLC 2, 22**
See also CA 45-48; 37-40R; CANR 33; DLB 15, 139; MTCW 1, 2

Hartman, Geoffrey H. 1929- .... **CLC 27**
See also CA 117; 125; CANR 79; DLB 67

Hartmann, Sadakichi 1869-1944 ... **TCLC 73**
See also CA 157; DLB 54

Hartmann von Aue c. 1170-c. 1210 .... **CMLC 15**
See also DLB 138

Hartmann von Aue 1170-1210 ...... **CMLC 15**

Haruf, Kent 1943- .... **CLC 34**
See also CA 149; CANR 91

Harwood, Ronald 1934- .... **CLC 32; DAM DRAM, MST**
See also CA 1-4R; CANR 4, 55; DLB 13

Hasegawa Tatsunosuke
See Futabatei, Shimei

Hasek, Jaroslav (Matej Frantisek)
1883-1923 .... **TCLC 4**
See also CA 104; 129; MTCW 1, 2

Hass, Robert 1941- ... **CLC 18, 39, 99; PC 16**
See also AMWS 6; CA 111; CANR 30, 50, 71; DLB 105, 206; SATA 94

Hastings, Hudson
See Kuttner, Henry

Hastings, Selina CLC 44

Hathorne, John 1641-1717 .... **LC 38**

Hatteras, Amelia
See Mencken, H(enry) L(ouis)

Hatteras, Owen TCLC 18
See also Mencken, H(enry) L(ouis); Nathan, George Jean

Hauptmann, Gerhart (Johann Robert)
1862-1946 .... **TCLC 4; DAM DRAM; SSC 37**
See also CA 104; 153; DLB 66, 118

Havel, Václav 1936- ..... **CLC 25, 58, 65, 123; DAM DRAM; DC 6**
See also CA 104; CANR 36, 63; CWW 2; DA3; DLB 232; MTCW 1, 2

Haviaras, Stratis CLC 33
See also Chaviaras, Strates

Hawes, Stephen 1475(?)-1529(?) .... **LC 17**
See also DLB 132

Hawkes, John (Clendennin Burne, Jr.)
1925-1998 .. **CLC 1, 2, 3, 4, 7, 9, 14, 15, 27, 49**
See also CA 1-4R; 167; CANR 2, 47, 64; DLB 2, 7, 227; DLBY 80, 98; MTCW 1, 2

Hawking, S. W.
See Hawking, Stephen W(illiam)

Hawking, Stephen W(illiam) 1942- . **CLC 63, 105**
See also AAYA 13; BEST 89:1; CA 126; 129; CANR 48; DA3; MTCW 2

Hawkins, Anthony Hope
See Hope, Anthony

Hawthorne, Julian 1846-1934 .... **TCLC 25**
See also CA 165

Hawthorne, Nathaniel 1804-1864 ... **NCLC 2, 10, 17, 23, 39, 79, 95; DA; DAB; DAC; DAM MST, NOV; SSC 3, 29, 39**
See also AAYA 18; AW; CDALB 1640-1865; DA3; DLB 1, 74, 223

Haxton, Josephine Ayres 1921-
See Douglas, Ellen
See also CA 115; CANR 41, 83

Hayaseca y Eizaguirre, Jorge
See Echegaray (y Eizaguirre), Jose (Maria Waldo)

Hayashi, Fumiko 1904-1951 .... **TCLC 27**
See also CA 161; DLB 180

Haycraft, Anna (Margaret) 1932-
See Ellis, Alice Thomas
See also CA 122; CANR 85, 90; MTCW 2

Author Index

Hughes, Ted 1930-1998 . CLC **2, 4, 9, 14, 37, 119; DAB; DAC; PC 7**
See also Hughes, Edward James
See also AW; BRWS 1; CA 1-4R; 171; CANR 1, 33, 66; CLR 3; DLB 40, 161; MAICYA; MTCW 1, 2; SATA 49; SATA-Brief 27; SATA-Obit 107

Hugo, Richard F(ranklin) 1923-1982 .... CLC **6, 18, 32; DAM POET**
See also CA 49-52; 108; CANR 3; DLB 5, 206

Hugo, Victor (Marie) 1802-1885 .... NCLC **3, 10, 21; DA; DAB; DAC; DAM DRAM, MST, NOV, POET; PC 17**
See also AAYA 28; AW; DA3; DLB 119, 192; SATA 47

Huidobro, Vicente
See Huidobro Fernandez, Vicente Garcia

Huidobro Fernandez, Vicente Garcia 1893-1948 .... TCLC **31**
See also CA 131; HW 1

Hulme, Keri 1947- .... CLC **39, 130**
See also CA 125; CANR 69; INT 125

Hulme, T(homas) E(rnest) 1883-1917 .... TCLC **21**
See also CA 117; DLB 19

Hume, David 1711-1776 .... LC **7, 56**
See also BRWS 3; DLB 104

Humphrey, William 1924-1997 .... CLC **45**
See also CA 77-80; 160; CANR 68; DLB 212; TCWW 2

Humphreys, Emyr Owen 1919- .... CLC **47**
See also CA 5-8R; CANR 3, 24; DLB 15

Humphreys, Josephine 1945- ..... CLC **34, 57**
See also CA 121; 127; INT 127

Huneker, James Gibbons 1860-1921 .... TCLC **65**
See also DLB 71

Hungerford, Pixie
See Brinsmead, H(esba) F(ay)

Hunt, E(verette) Howard, (Jr.) 1918- .... CLC **3**
See also AITN 1; CA 45-48; CANR 2, 47

Hunt, Francesca
See Holland, Isabelle

Hunt, Howard
See Hunt, E(verette) Howard, (Jr.)

Hunt, Kyle
See Creasey, John

Hunt, (James Henry) Leigh 1784-1859 .... NCLC **1, 70; DAM POET**
See also DLB 96, 110, 144

Hunt, Marsha 1946- .... CLC **70**
See also BW 2, 3; CA 143; CANR 79

Hunt, Violet 1866(?)-1942 .... TCLC **53**
See also CA 184; DLB 162, 197

Hunter, E. Waldo
See Sturgeon, Theodore (Hamilton)

Hunter, Evan 1926- .... CLC **11, 31; DAM POP**
See also CA 5-8R; CANR 5, 38, 62; DLBY 82; INT CANR-5; MTCW 1; SATA 25

Hunter, Kristin (Eggleston) 1931- .... CLC **35**
See also AITN 1; AW; BW 1; CA 13-16R; CANR 13; CLR 3; DLB 33; INT CANR-13; MAICYA; SAAS 10; SATA 12

Hunter, Mary
See Austin, Mary (Hunter)

Hunter, Mollie 1922- .... CLC **21**
See also McIlwraith, Maureen Mollie Hunter
See also AAYA 13; AW; CANR 37, 78; CLR 25; DLB 161; JRDA; MAICYA; SAAS 7; SATA 54, 106

Hunter, Robert (?)-1734 .... LC **7**

Hurston, Zora Neale 1891-1960 .. CLC **7, 30, 61; BLC 2; DA; DAC; DAM MST, MULT, NOV; DC 12; SSC 4**
See also AAYA 15; AW; BW 1, 3; CA 85-88; CANR 61; CDALBS; DA3; DLB 51, 86; MTCW 1, 2

Husserl, E. G.
See Husserl, Edmund (Gustav Albrecht)

Husserl, Edmund (Gustav Albrecht) 1859-1938 .... TCLC **100**
See also CA 116; 133

Huston, John (Marcellus) 1906-1987 .... CLC **20**
See also CA 73-76; 123; CANR 34; DLB 26

Hustvedt, Siri 1955- .... CLC **76**
See also CA 137

Hutten, Ulrich von 1488-1523 .... LC **16**
See also DLB 179

Huxley, Aldous (Leonard) 1894-1963 .... CLC **1, 3, 4, 5, 8, 11, 18, 35, 79; DA; DAB; DAC; DAM MST, NOV; SSC 39**
See also AAYA 11; AW; CA 85-88; CANR 44; CDBLB 1914-1945; DA3; DLB 36, 100, 162, 195; MTCW 1, 2; SATA 63; SCFW 2

Huxley, T(homas) H(enry) 1825-1895 .... NCLC **67**
See also DLB 57

Huysmans, Joris-Karl 1848-1907 ... TCLC **7, 69**
See also CA 104; 165; DLB 123

Hwang, David Henry 1957- .. CLC **55; DAM DRAM; DC 4**
See also CA 127; 132; CANR 76; DA3; DLB 212; INT 132; MTCW 2

Hyde, Anthony 1946- .... CLC **42**
See also Chase, Nicholas
See also CA 136; CCA 1

Hyde, Margaret O(ldroyd) 1917- ..... CLC **21**
See also CA 1-4R; CANR 1, 36; CLR 23; JRDA; MAICYA; SAAS 8; SATA 1, 42, 76

Hynes, James 1956(?)- .... CLC **65**
See also CA 164

Hypatia c. 370-415 .... CMLC **35**

Ian, Janis 1951- .... CLC **21**
See also CA 105; 187

Ibanez, Vicente Blasco
See Blasco Iba

Ibarbourou, Juana de 1895-1979
See also HLCS 2; HW 1

Ibarguengoitia, Jorge 1928-1983 ...... CLC **37**
See also CA 124; 113; HW 1

Ibsen, Henrik (Johan) 1828-1906 ... TCLC **2, 8, 16, 37, 52; DA; DAB; DAC; DAM DRAM, MST; DC 2**
See also AW; CA 104; 141; DA3

Ibuse, Masuji 1898-1993 .... CLC **22**
See also CA 127; 141; DLB 180

Ichikawa, Kon 1915- .... CLC **20**
See also CA 121

Ichiyo, Higuchi 1872-1896 .... NCLC **49**

Idle, Eric 1943-2000 .... CLC **21**
See also Monty Python
See also CA 116; CANR 35, 91

Ignatow, David 1914-1997 .. CLC **4, 7, 14, 40**
See also CA 9-12R; 162; CAAS 3; CANR 31, 57, 96; DLB 5

Ignotus
See Strachey, (Giles) Lytton

Ihimaera, Witi 1944- .... CLC **46**
See also CA 77-80

Ilf, Ilya TCLC **21**
See also Fainzilberg, Ilya Arnoldovich

Illyes, Gyula 1902-1983 .... PC **16**
See also CA 114; 109; DLB 215

Immermann, Karl (Lebrecht) 1796-1840 .... NCLC **4, 49**
See also DLB 133

Ince, Thomas H. 1882-1924 .... TCLC **89**

Inchbald, Elizabeth 1753-1821 .... NCLC **62**
See also DLB 39, 89

Inclan, Ramon (Maria) del Valle
See Valle-Inclan, Ramon (Maria) del

Infante, G(uillermo) Cabrera
See Cabrera Infante, G(uillermo)

Ingalls, Rachel (Holmes) 1940- .... CLC **42**
See also CA 123; 127

Ingamells, Reginald Charles
See Ingamells, Rex

Ingamells, Rex 1913-1955 .... TCLC **35**
See also CA 167

Inge, William (Motter) 1913-1973 ..... CLC **1, 8, 19; DAM DRAM**
See also CA 9-12R; CDALB 1941-1968; DA3; DLB 7; MTCW 1, 2

Ingelow, Jean 1820-1897 .... NCLC **39**
See also DLB 35, 163; SATA 33

Ingram, Willis J.
See Harris, Mark

Innaurato, Albert (F.) 1948(?)- ... CLC **21, 60**
See also CA 115; 122; CANR 78; INT 122

Innes, Michael
See Stewart, J(ohn) I(nnes) M(ackintosh)

Innis, Harold Adams 1894-1952 .... TCLC **77**
See also CA 181; DLB 88

Ionesco, Eugene 1912-1994 ... CLC **1, 4, 6, 9, 11, 15, 41, 86; DA; DAB; DAC; DAM DRAM, MST; DC 12**
See also AW; CA 9-12R; 144; CANR 55; CWW 2; DA3; MTCW 1, 2; SATA 7; SATA-Obit 79

Iqbal, Muhammad 1877-1938 .... TCLC **28**

Ireland, Patrick
See O'Doherty, Brian

Irenaeus St. 130- .... CMLC **42**

Iron, Ralph
See Schreiner, Olive (Emilie Albertina)

Irving, John (Winslow) 1942- ... CLC **13, 23, 38, 112; DAM NOV, POP**
See also AAYA 8; AMWS 6; BEST 89:3; CA 25-28R; CANR 28, 73; DA3; DLB 6; DLBY 82; MTCW 1, 2

Irving, Washington 1783-1859 . NCLC **2, 19, 95; DA; DAB; DAC; DAM MST; SSC 2, 37**
See also AW; CDALB 1640-1865; DA3; DLB 3, 11, 30, 59, 73, 74, 186

Irwin, P. K.
See Page, P(atricia) K(athleen)

Isaacs, Jorge Ricardo 1837-1895 ... NCLC **70**

Isaacs, Susan 1943- .... CLC **32; DAM POP**
See also BEST 89:1; CA 89-92; CANR 20, 41, 65; DA3; INT CANR-20; MTCW 1, 2

Isherwood, Christopher (William Bradshaw) 1904-1986 ... CLC **1, 9, 11, 14, 44; DAM DRAM, NOV**
See also CA 13-16R; 117; CANR 35; DA3; DLB 15, 195; DLBY 86; MTCW 1, 2

Ishiguro, Kazuo 1954- . CLC **27, 56, 59, 110; DAM NOV**
See also BEST 90:2; BRWS 4; CA 120; CANR 49, 95; DA3; DLB 194; MTCW 1, 2

Ishikawa, Hakuhin
See Ishikawa, Takuboku

Ishikawa, Takuboku 1886(?)-1912 ... TCLC **15; DAM POET; PC 10**
See also CA 113; 153

Iskander, Fazil 1929- .... CLC **47**
See also CA 102

Isler, Alan (David) 1934- .... CLC **91**
See also CA 156

Leyner, Mark 1956- .... **CLC 92**
  See also CA 110; CANR 28, 53; DA3;
  MTCW 2

Lezama Lima, Jose 1910-1976 .... **CLC 4, 10, 101; DAM MULT; HLCS 2**
  See also CA 77-80; CANR 71; DLB 113;
  HW 1, 2

L'Heureux, John (Clarke) 1934- ...... **CLC 52**
  See also CA 13-16R; CANR 23, 45, 88

Liddell, C. H.
  See Kuttner, Henry

Lie, Jonas (Lauritz Idemil)
  1833-1908(?) .... **TCLC 5**
  See also CA 115

Lieber, Joel 1937-1971 .... **CLC 6**
  See also CA 73-76; 29-32R

Lieber, Stanley Martin
  See Lee, Stan

Lieberman, Laurence (James)
  1935- .... **CLC 4, 36**
  See also CA 17-20R; CANR 8, 36, 89

Lieh Tzu fl. 7th cent. B.C.-5th cent.
  B.C. .... **CMLC 27**

Lieksman, Anders
  See Haavikko, Paavo Juhani

Li Fei-kan 1904-
  See Pa Chin
  See also CA 105

Lifton, Robert Jay 1926- .... **CLC 67**
  See also CA 17-20R; CANR 27, 78; INT
  CANR-27; SATA 66

Lightfoot, Gordon 1938- .... **CLC 26**
  See also CA 109

Lightman, Alan P(aige) 1948- .... **CLC 81**
  See also CA 141; CANR 63

Ligotti, Thomas (Robert) 1953- ...... **CLC 44; SSC 16**
  See also CA 123; CANR 49

Li Ho 791-817 .... **PC 13**

Liliencron, (Friedrich Adolf Axel) Detlev von 1844-1909 .... **TCLC 18**
  See also CA 117

Lilly, William 1602-1681 .... **LC 27**

Lima, Jose Lezama
  See Lezama Lima, Jose

Lima Barreto, Afonso Henrique de
  1881-1922 .... **TCLC 23**
  See also CA 117; 181

Lima Barreto, Afonso Henriques de
  See Lima Barreto, Afonso Henrique de

Limonov, Edward 1944- .... **CLC 67**
  See also CA 137

Lin, Frank
  See Atherton, Gertrude (Franklin Horn)

Lincoln, Abraham 1809-1865 .... **NCLC 18**

Lind, Jakov **CLC 1, 2, 4, 27, 82**
  See also Landwirth, Heinz
  See also CAAS 4

Lindbergh, Anne (Spencer) Morrow
  1906-2001 .... **CLC 82; DAM NOV**
  See also CA 17-20R; CANR 16, 73; MTCW
  1, 2; SATA 33

Lindsay, David 1878(?)-1945 .... **TCLC 15**
  See also CA 113; 187

Lindsay, (Nicholas) Vachel
  1879-1931 . **TCLC 17; DA; DAC; DAM MST, POET; PC 23**
  See also AMWS 1; AW; CA 114; 135;
  CANR 79; CDALB 1865-1917; DA3;
  DLB 54; SATA 40

Linke-Poot
  See Doeblin, Alfred

Linney, Romulus 1930- .... **CLC 51**
  See also CA 1-4R; CANR 40, 44, 79

Linton, Eliza Lynn 1822-1898 .... **NCLC 41**
  See also DLB 18

Li Po 701-763 .... **CMLC 2; PC 29**

Lipsius, Justus 1547-1606 .... **LC 16**

Lipsyte, Robert (Michael) 1938- ..... **CLC 21; DA; DAC; DAM MST, NOV**
  See also AAYA 7; CA 17-20R; CANR 8,
  57; CLR 23; JRDA; MAICYA; SATA 5,
  68, 113

Lish, Gordon (Jay) 1934- ... **CLC 45; SSC 18**
  See also CA 113; 117; CANR 79; DLB 130;
  INT 117

Lispector, Clarice 1925(?)-1977 .... **CLC 43; HLCS 2; SSC 34**
  See also CA 139; 116; CANR 71; DLB 113;
  HW 2

Littell, Robert 1935(?)- .... **CLC 42**
  See also CA 109; 112; CANR 64

Little, Malcolm 1925-1965
  See Malcolm X
  See also BW 1, 3; CA 125; 111; CANR 82;
  DA; DAB; DAC; DAM MST, MULT;
  DA3; MTCW 1, 2

Littlewit, Humphrey Gent.
  See Lovecraft, H(oward) P(hillips)

Litwos
  See Sienkiewicz, Henryk (Adam Alexander
  Pius)

Liu, E 1857-1909 .... **TCLC 15**
  See also CA 115

Lively, Penelope (Margaret) 1933- .. **CLC 32, 50; DAM NOV**
  See also CA 41-44R; CANR 29, 67, 79;
  CLR 7; DLB 14, 161, 207; JRDA; MAI-
  CYA; MTCW 1, 2; SATA 7, 60, 101

Livesay, Dorothy (Kathleen)
  1909-1996 . **CLC 4, 15, 79; DAC; DAM MST, POET**
  See also AITN 2; CA 25-28R; CAAS 8;
  CANR 36, 67; DLB 68; MTCW 1

Livy c. 59B.C.-c. 17 .... **CMLC 11**
  See also DLB 211

Lizardi, Jose Joaquin Fernandez de
  1776-1827 .... **NCLC 30**

Llewellyn, Richard
  See Llewellyn Lloyd, Richard Dafydd Viv-
  ian
  See also DLB 15

Llewellyn Lloyd, Richard Dafydd Vivian
  1906-1983 .... **CLC 7, 80**
  See also Llewellyn, Richard
  See also CA 53-56; 111; CANR 7, 71;
  SATA 11; SATA-Obit 37

Llosa, (Jorge) Mario (Pedro) Vargas
  See Vargas Llosa, (Jorge) Mario (Pedro)

Lloyd, Manda
  See Mander, (Mary) Jane

Lloyd Webber, Andrew 1948-
  See Webber, Andrew Lloyd
  See also AAYA 1; CA 116; 149; DAM
  DRAM; SATA 56

Llull, Ramon c. 1235-c. 1316 .... **CMLC 12**

Lobb, Ebenezer
  See Upward, Allen

Locke, Alain (Le Roy) 1886-1954 . **TCLC 43; BLCS**
  See also BW 1, 3; CA 106; 124; CANR 79;
  DLB 51

Locke, John 1632-1704 .... **LC 7, 35**
  See also DLB 101

Locke-Elliott, Sumner
  See Elliott, Sumner Locke

Lockhart, John Gibson 1794-1854 .. **NCLC 6**
  See also DLB 110, 116, 144

Lodge, David (John) 1935- ...... **CLC 36, 141; DAM POP**
  See also BEST 90:1; BRWS 4; CA 17-20R;
  CANR 19, 53, 92; DLB 14, 194; INT
  CANR-19; MTCW 1, 2

Lodge, Thomas 1558-1625 .... **LC 41**
  See also DLB 172

Lodge, Thomas 1558-1625 .... **LC 41**

Loennbohm, Armas Eino Leopold 1878-1926
  See Leino, Eino
  See also CA 123

Loewinsohn, Ron(ald William)
  1937- .... **CLC 52**
  See also CA 25-28R; CANR 71

Logan, Jake
  See Smith, Martin Cruz

Logan, John (Burton) 1923-1987 .... **CLC 5**
  See also CA 77-80; 124; CANR 45; DLB 5

Lo Kuan-chung 1330(?)-1400(?) .... **LC 12**

Lombard, Nap
  See Johnson, Pamela Hansford

London, Jack **TCLC 9, 15, 39; SSC 4**
  See also London, John Griffith
  See also AAYA 13; AITN 2; AW; CDALB
  1865-1917; DLB 8, 12, 78, 212; SATA
  18; TCWW 2

London, John Griffith 1876-1916
  See London, Jack
  See also CA 110; 119; CANR 73; DA;
  DAB; DAC; DAM MST, NOV; DA3;
  JRDA; MAICYA; MTCW 1, 2

Long, Emmett
  See Leonard, Elmore (John, Jr.)

Longbaugh, Harry
  See Goldman, William (W.)

Longfellow, Henry Wadsworth
  1807-1882 .... **NCLC 2, 45; DA; DAB; DAC; DAM MST, POET; PC 30**
  See also AW; CDALB 1640-1865; DA3;
  DLB 1, 59, 235; SATA 19

Longinus c. 1st cent. - .... **CMLC 27**
  See also DLB 176

Longley, Michael 1939- .... **CLC 29**
  See also CA 102; DLB 40

Longus fl. c. 2nd cent. - .... **CMLC 7**

Longway, A. Hugh
  See Lang, Andrew

Lonnrot, Elias 1802-1884 .... **NCLC 53**

Lopate, Phillip 1943- .... **CLC 29**
  See also CA 97-100; CANR 88; DLBY 80;
  INT 97-100

Lopez Portillo (y Pacheco), Jose
  1920- .... **CLC 46**
  See also CA 129; HW 1

Lopez y Fuentes, Gregorio
  1897(?)-1966 .... **CLC 32**
  See also CA 131; HW 1

Lorca, Federico Garcia
  See Garcia Lorca, Federico

Lord, Bette Bao 1938- .... **CLC 23**
  See also BEST 90:3; CA 107; CANR 41,
  79; INT 107; SATA 58

Lord Auch
  See Bataille, Georges

Lord Byron
  See Byron, George Gordon (Noel)

Lorde, Audre (Geraldine)
  1934-1992 ... **CLC 18, 71; BLC 2; DAM MULT, POET; PC 12**
  See also Domini, Rey
  See also BW 1, 3; CA 25-28R; 142; CANR
  16, 26, 46, 82; DA3; DLB 41; MTCW 1,
  2

Lord Houghton
  See Milnes, Richard Monckton

Lord Jeffrey
  See Jeffrey, Francis

Lorenzini, Carlo 1826-1890
  See Collodi, Carlo
  See also MAICYA; SATA 29, 100

Lorenzo, Heberto Padilla
  See Padilla (Lorenzo), Heberto

Loris
See Hofmannsthal, Hugo von
Loti, Pierre TCLC 11
See also Viaud, (Louis Marie) Julien
See also DLB 123
Lou, Henri
See Andreas-Salome, Lou
Louie, David Wong 1954- .... CLC 70
See also CA 139
Louis, Father M.
See Merton, Thomas
Lovecraft, H(oward) P(hillips)
1890-1937 ...... TCLC 4, 22; DAM POP;
SSC 3
See also AAYA 14; CA 104; 133; DA3;
MTCW 1, 2
Lovelace, Earl 1935- .... CLC 51
See also BW 2; CA 77-80; CANR 41, 72;
DLB 125; MTCW 1
Lovelace, Richard 1618-1657 .... LC 24
See also DLB 131
Lowell, Amy 1874-1925 .... TCLC 1, 8; DAM
POET; PC 13
See also CA 104; 151; DLB 54, 140;
MTCW 2
Lowell, James Russell 1819-1891 ... NCLC 2,
90
See also AMWS 1; CDALB 1640-1865;
DLB 1, 11, 64, 79, 189, 235
Lowell, Robert (Traill Spence, Jr.)
1917-1977 .... CLC 1, 2, 3, 4, 5, 8, 9, 11,
15, 37, 124; DA; DAB; DAC; DAM
MST, NOV; PC 3
See also AW; CA 9-12R; 73-76; CABS 2;
CANR 26, 60; CDALBS; DA3; DLB 5,
169; MTCW 1, 2
Lowenthal, Michael (Francis)
1969- .... CLC 119
See also CA 150
Lowndes, Marie Adelaide (Belloc)
1868-1947 .... TCLC 12
See also CA 107; DLB 70
Lowry, (Clarence) Malcolm
1909-1957 .... TCLC 6, 40; SSC 31
See also BRWS 3; CA 105; 131; CANR 62;
CDBLB 1945-1960; DLB 15; MTCW 1,
2
Lowry, Mina Gertrude 1882-1966
See Loy, Mina
See also CA 113
Loxsmith, John
See Brunner, John (Kilian Houston)
Loy, Mina CLC 28; DAM POET; PC 16
See also Lowry, Mina Gertrude
See also DLB 4, 54
Loyson-Bridet
See Schwob, Marcel (Mayer Andre)
Lucan 120-200 .... CMLC 33
See also AW 33; DLB 211
Lucas, Craig 1951- .... CLC 64
See also CA 137; CANR 71; GLL 2
Lucas, E(dward) V(errall)
1868-1938 .... TCLC 73
See also CA 176; DLB 98, 149, 153; SATA
20
Lucas, George 1944- .... CLC 16
See also AAYA 1, 23; CA 77-80; CANR
30; SATA 56
Lucas, Hans
See Godard, Jean-Luc
Lucas, Victoria
See Plath, Sylvia
Lucian c. 125-c. 200 .... CMLC 32
See also DLB 176
Ludlam, Charles 1943-1987 .... CLC 46, 50
See also CA 85-88; 122; CANR 72, 86

Ludlum, Robert 1927-2001 .... CLC 22, 43;
DAM NOV, POP
See also AAYA 10; BEST 89:1, 90:3; CA
33-36R; CANR 25, 41, 68; DA3; DLBY
82; MTCW 1, 2
Ludwig, Ken CLC 60
Ludwig, Otto 1813-1865 .... NCLC 4
See also DLB 129
Lugones, Leopoldo 1874-1938 ...... TCLC 15;
HLCS 2
See also CA 116; 131; HW 1
Lu Hsun TCLC 3; SSC 20
See also Shu-Jen, Chou
Lukacs, George CLC 24
See also Lukacs, György (Szegeny von)
Lukacs, György (Szegeny von) 1885-1971
See Lukacs, George
See also CA 101; 29-32R; CANR 62; DLB
242; MTCW 2
Luke, Peter (Ambrose Cyprian)
1919-1995 .... CLC 38
See also CA 81-84; 147; CANR 72; DLB
13
Lunar, Dennis
See Mungo, Raymond
Lurie, Alison 1926- .... CLC 4, 5, 18, 39
See also CA 1-4R; CANR 2, 17, 50, 88;
DLB 2; MTCW 1; SATA 46, 112
Lustig, Arnost 1926- .... CLC 56
See also AAYA 3; CA 69-72; CANR 47;
CWW 2; DLB 232; SATA 56
Luther, Martin 1483-1546 .... LC 9, 37
See also DLB 179
Luxemburg, Rosa 1870(?)-1919 ..... TCLC 63
See also CA 118
Luzi, Mario 1914- .... CLC 13
See also CA 61-64; CANR 9, 70; CWW 2;
DLB 128
Lyly, John 1554(?)-1606 .... LC 41; DAM
DRAM; DC 7
See also DLB 62, 167
L'Ymagier
See Gourmont, Remy (-Marie-Charles) de
Lynch, David (K.) 1946- .... CLC 66
See also CA 124; 129
Lynch, James
See Andreyev, Leonid (Nikolaevich)
Lyndsay, Sir David 1485-1555 .... LC 20
Lynn, Kenneth S(chuyler) 1923- ...... CLC 50
See also CA 1-4R; CANR 3, 27, 65
Lynx
See West, Rebecca
Lyons, Marcus
See Blish, James (Benjamin)
Lyotard, Jean-Francois
1924-1998 .... TCLC 103
See also DLB 242
Lyre, Pinchbeck
See Sassoon, Siegfried (Lorraine)
Lytle, Andrew (Nelson) 1902-1995 ... CLC 22
See also CA 9-12R; 150; CANR 70; DLB
6; DLBY 95
Lyttelton, George 1709-1773 .... LC 10
Maas, Peter 1929- .... CLC 29
See also CA 93-96; INT 93-96; MTCW 2
Macaulay, Catherine 1731-1791 .... LC 64
See also DLB 104
Macaulay, (Emilie) Rose
1881(?)-1958 .... TCLC 7, 44
See also CA 104; DLB 36
Macaulay, Thomas Babington
1800-1859 .... NCLC 42
See also CDBLB 1832-1890; DLB 32, 55
MacBeth, George (Mann)
1932-1992 .... CLC 2, 5, 9
See also CA 25-28R; 136; CANR 61, 66;
DLB 40; MTCW 1; SATA 4; SATA-Obit
70

MacCaig, Norman (Alexander)
1910-1996 .... CLC 36; DAB; DAM
POET
See also CA 9-12R; CANR 3, 34; DLB 27
MacCarthy, Sir(Charles Otto) Desmond
1877-1952 .... TCLC 36
See also CA 167
MacDiarmid, Hugh CLC 2, 4, 11, 19, 63; PC
9
See also Grieve, C(hristopher) M(urray)
See also CDBLB 1945-1960; DLB 20
MacDonald, Anson
See Heinlein, Robert A(nson)
Macdonald, Cynthia 1928- .... CLC 13, 19
See also CA 49-52; CANR 4, 44; DLB 105
MacDonald, George 1824-1905 .... TCLC 9
See also CA 106; 137; CANR 80; CLR 67;
DLB 18, 163, 178; MAICYA; SATA 33,
100
Macdonald, John
See Millar, Kenneth
MacDonald, John D(ann)
1916-1986 .. CLC 3, 27, 44; DAM NOV,
POP
See also CA 1-4R; 121; CANR 1, 19, 60;
DLB 8; DLBY 86; MTCW 1, 2
Macdonald, John Ross
See Millar, Kenneth
Macdonald, Ross CLC 1, 2, 3, 14, 34, 41
See also Millar, Kenneth
See also AMWS 4; DLBD 6
MacDougal, John
See Blish, James (Benjamin)
MacDougal, John
See Blish, James (Benjamin)
MacEwen, Gwendolyn (Margaret)
1941-1987 .... CLC 13, 55
See also CA 9-12R; 124; CANR 7, 22; DLB
53; SATA 50; SATA-Obit 55
Macha, Karel Hynek 1810-1846 .... NCLC 46
Machado (y Ruiz), Antonio
1875-1939 .... TCLC 3
See also CA 104; 174; DLB 108; HW 2
Machado de Assis, Joaquim Maria
1839-1908 ..... TCLC 10; BLC 2; HLCS
2; SSC 24
See also CA 107; 153; CANR 91
Machen, Arthur TCLC 4; SSC 20
See also Jones, Arthur Llewellyn
See also CA 179; DLB 36, 156, 178
Machiavelli, Niccolò 1469-1527 ..... LC 8, 36;
DA; DAB; DAC; DAM MST
See also AW
MacInnes, Colin 1914-1976 .... CLC 4, 23
See also CA 69-72; 65-68; CANR 21; DLB
14; MTCW 1, 2
MacInnes, Helen (Clark)
1907-1985 .... CLC 27, 39; DAM POP
See also CA 1-4R; 117; CANR 1, 28, 58;
DLB 87; MTCW 1, 2; SATA 22; SATA-
Obit 44
Mackenzie, Compton (Edward Montague)
1883-1972 .... CLC 18
See also CA 21-22; 37-40R; CAP 2; DLB
34, 100
Mackenzie, Henry 1745-1831 .... NCLC 41
See also DLB 39
Mackintosh, Elizabeth 1896(?)-1952
See Tey, Josephine
See also CA 110
MacLaren, James
See Grieve, C(hristopher) M(urray)
Mac Laverty, Bernard 1942- .... CLC 31
See also CA 116; 118; CANR 43, 88;
INT 118

MacLean, Alistair (Stuart)
1922(?)-1987 .. **CLC 3, 13, 50, 63; DAM POP**
See also CA 57-60; 121; CANR 28, 61; MTCW 1; SATA 23; SATA-Obit 50; TCWW 2

Maclean, Norman (Fitzroy)
1902-1990 .... **CLC 78; DAM POP; SSC 13**
See also CA 102; 132; CANR 49; DLB 206; TCWW 2

MacLeish, Archibald 1892-1982 ... **CLC 3, 8, 14, 68; DAM POET**
See also CA 9-12R; 106; CANR 33, 63; CDALBS; DLB 4, 7, 45; DLBY 82; MTCW 1, 2

MacLennan, (John) Hugh
1907-1990 . **CLC 2, 14, 92; DAC; DAM MST**
See also CA 5-8R; 142; CANR 33; DLB 68; MTCW 1, 2

MacLeod, Alistair 1936- .... **CLC 56; DAC; DAM MST**
See also CA 123; CCA 1; DLB 60; MTCW 2

Macleod, Fiona
See Sharp, William

MacNeice, (Frederick) Louis
1907-1963 .... **CLC 1, 4, 10, 53; DAB; DAM POET**
See also CA 85-88; CANR 61; DLB 10, 20; MTCW 1, 2

MacNeill, Dand
See Fraser, George MacDonald

Macpherson, James 1736-1796 .... **LC 29**
See also Ossian
See also DLB 109

Macpherson, (Jean) Jay 1931- .... **CLC 14**
See also CA 5-8R; CANR 90; DLB 53

MacShane, Frank 1927-1999 .... **CLC 39**
See also CA 9-12R; 186; CANR 3, 33; DLB 111

Macumber, Mari
See Sandoz, Mari(e Susette)

Madach, Imre 1823-1864 .... **NCLC 19**

Madden, (Jerry) David 1933- .... **CLC 5, 15**
See also CA 1-4R; CAAS 3; CANR 4, 45; DLB 6; MTCW 1

Maddern, Al(an)
See Ellison, Harlan (Jay)

Madhubuti, Haki R. 1942- . **CLC 6, 73; BLC 2; DAM MULT, POET; PC 5**
See also Lee, Don L.
See also BW 2, 3; CA 73-76; CANR 24, 51, 73; DLB 5, 41; DLBD 8; MTCW 2

Maepenn, Hugh
See Kuttner, Henry

Maepenn, K. H.
See Kuttner, Henry

Maeterlinck, Maurice 1862-1949 ... **TCLC 3; DAM DRAM**
See also CA 104; 136; CANR 80; DLB 192; SATA 66

Maginn, William 1794-1842 .... **NCLC 8**
See also DLB 110, 159

Mahapatra, Jayanta 1928- .... **CLC 33; DAM MULT**
See also CA 73-76; CAAS 9; CANR 15, 33, 66, 87

Mahfouz, Naguib (Abdel Aziz Al-Sabilgi)
1911(?)-
See Mahfuz, Najib
See also BEST 89:2; CA 128; CANR 55; CWW 2; DAM NOV; DA3; MTCW 1, 2

Mahfuz, Najib **CLC 52, 55**
See also Mahfouz, Naguib (Abdel Aziz Al-Sabilgi)
See also DLBY 88

Mahon, Derek 1941- .... **CLC 27**
See also CA 113; 128; CANR 88; DLB 40

Mailer, Norman 1923- ... **CLC 1, 2, 3, 4, 5, 8, 11, 14, 28, 39, 74, 111; DA; DAB; DAC; DAM MST, NOV, POP**
See also AAYA 31; AITN 2; CA 9-12R; CABS 1; CANR 28, 74, 77; CDALB 1968-1988; DA3; DLB 2, 16, 28, 185; DLBD 3; DLBY 80, 83; MTCW 1, 2

Maillet, Antonine 1929- .. **CLC 54, 118; DAC**
See also CA 115; 120; CANR 46, 74, 77; CCA 1; CWW 2; DLB 60; INT 120; MTCW 2

Mais, Roger 1905-1955 .... **TCLC 8**
See also BW 1, 3; CA 105; 124; CANR 82; DLB 125; MTCW 1

Maistre, Joseph de 1753-1821 .... **NCLC 37**

Maitland, Frederic William
1850-1906 .... **TCLC 65**

Maitland, Sara (Louise) 1950- .... **CLC 49**
See also CA 69-72; CANR 13, 59

Major, Clarence 1936- . **CLC 3, 19, 48; BLC 2; DAM MULT**
See also BW 2, 3; CA 21-24R; CAAS 6; CANR 13, 25, 53, 82; DLB 33

Major, Kevin (Gerald) 1949- . **CLC 26; DAC**
See also AAYA 16; CA 97-100; CANR 21, 38; CLR 11; DLB 60; INT CANR-21; JRDA; MAICYA; SATA 32, 82

Maki, James
See Ozu, Yasujiro

Malabaila, Damiano
See Levi, Primo

Malamud, Bernard 1914-1986 .. **CLC 1, 2, 3, 5, 8, 9, 11, 18, 27, 44, 78, 85; DA; DAB; DAC; DAM MST, NOV, POP; SSC 15**
See also AAYA 16; AMWS 1; AW; CA 5-8R; 118; CABS 1; CANR 28, 62; CDALB 1941-1968; DA3; DLB 2, 28, 152; DLBY 80, 86; MTCW 1, 2

Malan, Herman
See Bosman, Herman Charles; Bosman, Herman Charles

Malaparte, Curzio 1898-1957 .... **TCLC 52**

Malcolm, Dan
See Silverberg, Robert

Malcolm X **CLC 82, 117; BLC 2**
See also Little, Malcolm
See also AW

Malherbe, Francois de 1555-1628 .... **LC 5**

Mallarme, Stephane 1842-1898 ...... **NCLC 4, 41; DAM POET; PC 4**

Mallet-Joris, Francoise 1930- .... **CLC 11**
See also CA 65-68; CANR 17; DLB 83

Malley, Ern
See McAuley, James Phillip

Mallowan, Agatha Christie
See Christie, Agatha (Mary Clarissa)

Maloff, Saul 1922- .... **CLC 5**
See also CA 33-36R

Malone, Louis
See MacNeice, (Frederick) Louis

Malone, Michael (Christopher)
1942- .... **CLC 43**
See also CA 77-80; CANR 14, 32, 57

Malory, Thomas 1410(?)-1471(?) .... **LC 11; DA; DAB; DAC; DAM MST**
See also AW; CDBLB Before 1660; DLB 146; SATA 59; SATA-Brief 33

Malouf, (George Joseph) David
1934- .... **CLC 28, 86**
See also CA 124; CANR 50, 76; MTCW 2

Malraux, (Georges-)Andre
1901-1976 .... **CLC 1, 4, 9, 13, 15, 57; DAM NOV**
See also CA 21-22; 69-72; CANR 34, 58; CAP 2; DA3; DLB 72; MTCW 1, 2

Malzberg, Barry N(athaniel) 1939- ... **CLC 7**
See also CA 61-64; CAAS 4; CANR 16; DLB 8

Mamet, David (Alan) 1947- .. **CLC 9, 15, 34, 46, 91; DAM DRAM; DC 4**
See also AAYA 3; CA 81-84; CABS 3; CANR 15, 41, 67, 72; DA3; DLB 7; MTCW 1, 2

Mamoulian, Rouben (Zachary)
1897-1987 .... **CLC 16**
See also CA 25-28R; 124; CANR 85

Mandelshtam, Osip
See Mandelstam, Osip (Emilievich)

Mandelstam, Osip (Emilievich)
1891(?)-1943(?) .... **TCLC 2, 6; PC 14**
See also CA 104; 150; MTCW 2

Mander, (Mary) Jane 1877-1949 ... **TCLC 31**
See also CA 162

Mandeville, John fl. 1350- .... **CMLC 19**
See also DLB 146

Mandiargues, Andre Pieyre de **CLC 41**
See also Pieyre de Mandiargues, Andre
See also DLB 83

Mandrake, Ethel Belle
See Thurman, Wallace (Henry)

Mangan, James Clarence
1803-1849 .... **NCLC 27**

Maniere, J.-E.
See Giraudoux, (Hippolyte) Jean

Mankiewicz, Herman (Jacob)
1897-1953 .... **TCLC 85**
See also CA 120; 169; DLB 26; IDFW 3

Manley, (Mary) Delariviere
1672(?)-1724 .... **LC 1, 42**
See also DLB 39, 80

Mann, Abel
See Creasey, John

Mann, Emily 1952- .... **DC 7**
See also CA 130; CANR 55

Mann, (Luiz) Heinrich 1871-1950 ... **TCLC 9**
See also CA 106; 164, 181; DLB 66, 118

Mann, (Paul) Thomas 1875-1955 ... **TCLC 2, 8, 14, 21, 35, 44, 60; DA; DAB; DAC; DAM MST, NOV; SSC 5**
See also AW; CA 104; 128; DA3; DLB 66; GLL 1; MTCW 1, 2

Mannheim, Karl 1893-1947 .... **TCLC 65**

Manning, David
See Faust, Frederick (Schiller)
See also TCWW 2

Manning, Frederic 1887(?)-1935 ... **TCLC 25**
See also CA 124

Manning, Olivia 1915-1980 .... **CLC 5, 19**
See also CA 5-8R; 101; CANR 29; MTCW 1

Mano, D. Keith 1942- .... **CLC 2, 10**
See also CA 25-28R; CAAS 6; CANR 26, 57; DLB 6

Mansfield, Katherine **TCLC 2, 8, 39; DAB; SSC 9, 23, 38**
See also Beauchamp, Kathleen Mansfield
See also AW; DLB 162; GLL 1

Manso, Peter 1940- .... **CLC 39**
See also CA 29-32R; CANR 44

Mantecon, Juan Jimenez
See Jimenez (Mantecon), Juan Ramon

Manton, Peter
See Creasey, John

Man Without a Spleen, A
See Chekhov, Anton (Pavlovich)

Manzoni, Alessandro 1785-1873 .... **NCLC 29**

Map, Walter 1140-1209 .... **CMLC 32**

Mapu, Abraham (ben Jekutiel)
1808-1867 .... **NCLC 18**

Mara, Sally
See Queneau, Raymond

Marat, Jean Paul 1743-1793 .... **LC 10**

Marcel, Gabriel Honore 1889-1973 . **CLC 15**
See also CA 102; 45-48; MTCW 1, 2

March, William 1893-1954 .... **TCLC 96**

Marchbanks, Samuel
See Davies, (William) Robertson
See also CCA 1

Marchi, Giacomo
See Bassani, Giorgio

Marguerite
See de Navarre, Marguerite

Margulies, Donald CLC 76
See also DLB 228

Marie de France c. 12th cent. - ..... **CMLC 8;
PC 22**
See also DLB 208

Marie de l'Incarnation 1599-1672 ...... **LC 10**

Marier, Captain Victor
See Griffith, D(avid Lewelyn) W(ark)

Mariner, Scott
See Pohl, Frederik

Marinetti, Filippo Tommaso
1876-1944 .... **TCLC 10**
See also CA 107; DLB 114

Marivaux, Pierre Carlet de Chamblain de
1688-1763 .... **LC 4; DC 7**

Markandaya, Kamala CLC 8, 38
See also Taylor, Kamala (Purnaiya)

Markfield, Wallace 1926- .... **CLC 8**
See also CA 69-72; CAAS 3; DLB 2, 28

Markham, Edwin 1852-1940 .... **TCLC 47**
See also CA 160; DLB 54, 186

Markham, Robert
See Amis, Kingsley (William)

Marks, J
See Highwater, Jamake (Mamake)

Marks-Highwater, J
See Highwater, Jamake (Mamake)

Markson, David M(errill) 1927- .... **CLC 67**
See also CA 49-52; CANR 1, 91

Marley, Bob CLC 17
See Marley, Robert Nesta

Marley, Robert Nesta 1945-1981
See Marley, Bob
See also CA 107; 103

Marlowe, Christopher 1564-1593 ...... **LC 22,
47; DA; DAB; DAC; DAM DRAM,
MST; DC 1**
See also AW; CDBLB Before 1660; DA3;
DLB 62

Marlowe, Stephen 1928-
See Queen, Ellery
See also CA 13-16R; CANR 6, 55

Marmontel, Jean-Francois 1723-1799 .. **LC 2**

Marquand, John P(hillips)
1893-1960 .... **CLC 2, 10**
See also CA 85-88; CANR 73; DLB 9, 102;
MTCW 2

Marques, Rene 1919-1979 ..... **CLC 96; DAM
MULT; HLC 2**
See also CA 97-100; 85-88; CANR 78;
DLB 113; HW 1, 2

Marquez, Gabriel (Jose) Garcia
See Garcia Marquez, Gabriel (Jose)

Marquis, Don(ald Robert Perry)
1878-1937 .... **TCLC 7**
See also CA 104; 166; DLB 11, 25

Marric, J. J.
See Creasey, John

Marryat, Frederick 1792-1848 .... **NCLC 3**
See also DLB 21, 163

Marsden, James
See Creasey, John

Marsh, Edward 1872-1953 .... **TCLC 99**

Marsh, (Edith) Ngaio 1899-1982 .... **CLC 7,
53; DAM POP**
See also CA 9-12R; CANR 6, 58; DLB 77;
MTCW 1, 2

Marshall, Garry 1934- .... **CLC 17**
See also AAYA 3; CA 111; SATA 60

Marshall, Paule 1929- .. **CLC 27, 72; BLC 3;
DAM MULT; SSC 3**
See also BW 2, 3; CA 77-80; CANR 25,
73; DA3; DLB 33, 157, 227; MTCW 1, 2

Marshallik
See Zangwill, Israel

Marsten, Richard
See Hunter, Evan

Marston, John 1576-1634 .... **LC 33; DAM
DRAM**
See also DLB 58, 172

Martha, Henry
See Harris, Mark

Martí (y Pérez), Jose (Julian)
1853-1895 ...... **NCLC 63; DAM MULT;
HLC 2**
See also HW 2

Martial c. 40-c. 104 .... **CMLC 35; PC 10**
See also DLB 211

Martin, Ken
See Hubbard, L(afayette) Ron(ald)

Martin, Richard
See Creasey, John

Martin, Steve 1945- .... **CLC 30**
See also CA 97-100; CANR 30; MTCW 1

Martin, Valerie 1948- .... **CLC 89**
See also BEST 90:2; CA 85-88; CANR 49,
89

Martin, Violet Florence
1862-1915 .... **TCLC 51**

Martin, Webber
See Silverberg, Robert

Martindale, Patrick Victor
See White, Patrick (Victor Martindale)

Martin du Gard, Roger
1881-1958 .... **TCLC 24**
See also CA 118; CANR 94; DLB 65

Martineau, Harriet 1802-1876 .... **NCLC 26**
See also AW 2; DLB 21, 55, 159, 163, 166,
190

Martines, Julia
See O'Faolain, Julia

Martinez, Enrique Gonzalez
See Gonzalez Martinez, Enrique

Martinez, Jacinto Benavente y
See Benavente (y Martinez), Jacinto

Martinez Ruiz, Jose 1873-1967
See Azorin; Ruiz, Jose Martinez
See also CA 93-96; HW 1

Martinez Sierra, Gregorio
1881-1947 .... **TCLC 6**
See also CA 115

Martinez Sierra, Maria (de la O'LeJarraga)
1874-1974 .... **TCLC 6**
See also CA 115

Martinsen, Martin
See Follett, Ken(neth Martin)

Martinson, Harry (Edmund)
1904-1978 .... **CLC 14**
See also CA 77-80; CANR 34

Marut, Ret
See Traven, B.

Marut, Robert
See Traven, B.

Marvell, Andrew 1621-1678 .. **LC 4, 43; DA;
DAB; DAC; DAM MST, POET; PC 10**
See also AW; CDBLB 1660-1789; DLB 131

Marx, Karl (Heinrich) 1818-1883 . **NCLC 17**
See also DLB 129

Masaoka Shiki TCLC 18
See also Masaoka Tsunenori

Masaoka Tsunenori 1867-1902
See Masaoka Shiki
See also CA 117

Masefield, John (Edward)
1878-1967 ..... **CLC 11, 47; DAM POET**
See also CA 19-20; 25-28R; CANR 33;
CAP 2; CDBLB 1890-1914; DLB 10, 19,
153, 160; MTCW 1, 2; SATA 19

Maso, Carole 19(?)- .... **CLC 44**
See also CA 170; GLL 2

Mason, Bobbie Ann 1940- ... **CLC 28, 43, 82;
SSC 4**
See also AAYA 5; AW; CA 53-56; CANR
11, 31, 58, 83; CDALBS; DA3; DLB 173;
DLBY 87; INT CANR-31; MTCW 1, 2

Mason, Ernst
See Pohl, Frederik

Mason, Lee W.
See Malzberg, Barry N(athaniel)

Mason, Nick 1945- .... **CLC 35**

Mason, Tally
See Derleth, August (William)

Mass, William
See Gibson, William

Master Lao
See Lao Tzu

Masters, Edgar Lee 1868-1950 .... **TCLC 2,
25; DA; DAC; DAM MST, POET; PC
1**
See also AMWS 1; AW; CA 104; 133;
CDALB 1865-1917; DLB 54; MTCW 1,
2

Masters, Hilary 1928- .... **CLC 48**
See also CA 25-28R; CANR 13, 47

Mastrosimone, William 19(?)- .... **CLC 36**
See also CA 186

Mathe, Albert
See Camus, Albert

Mather, Cotton 1663-1728 .... **LC 38**
See also AMWS 2; CDALB 1640-1865;
DLB 24, 30, 140

Mather, Increase 1639-1723 .... **LC 38**
See also DLB 24

Matheson, Richard Burton 1926- .... **CLC 37**
See also AAYA 31; CA 97-100; CANR 88;
DLB 8, 44; INT 97-100; SCFW 2

Mathews, Harry 1930- .... **CLC 6, 52**
See also CA 21-24R; CAAS 6; CANR 18,
40

Mathews, John Joseph 1894-1979 .. **CLC 84;
DAM MULT**
See also CA 19-20; 142; CANR 45; CAP 2;
DLB 175; NNAL

Mathias, Roland (Glyn) 1915- .... **CLC 45**
See also CA 97-100; CANR 19, 41; DLB
27

Matsuo Basho 1644-1694 .... **LC 62; DAM
POET; PC 3**

Mattheson, Rodney
See Creasey, John

Matthews, (James) Brander
1852-1929 .... **TCLC 95**
See also DLB 71, 78; DLBD 13

Matthews, Greg 1949- .... **CLC 45**
See also CA 135

Matthews, William (Procter, III)
1942-1997 .... **CLC 40**
See also CA 29-32R; 162; CAAS 18; CANR
12, 57; DLB 5

Matthias, John (Edward) 1941- .... **CLC 9**
See also CA 33-36R; CANR 56

Matthiessen, F(rancis) O(tto)
1902-1950 .... **TCLC 100**
See also CA 185; DLB 63

Matthiessen, Peter 1927- ... **CLC 5, 7, 11, 32,
64; DAM NOV**
See also AAYA 6; AMWS 5; BEST 90:4;
CA 9-12R; CANR 21, 50, 73; DA3; DLB
6, 173; MTCW 1, 2; SATA 27

Maturin, Charles Robert
1780(?)-1824 .... **NCLC 6**
See also DLB 178

Paretsky, Sara 1947- .. **CLC 135; DAM POP**
See also AAYA 30; BEST 90:3; CA 125;
129; CANR 59, 95; DA3; INT 129

Parfenie, Maria
See Codrescu, Andrei

Parini, Jay (Lee) 1948- .... **CLC 54, 133**
See also CA 97-100; CAAS 16; CANR 32,
87

Park, Jordan
See Kornbluth, C(yril) M.; Pohl, Frederik

Park, Robert E(zra) 1864-1944 ..... **TCLC 73**
See also CA 122; 165

Parker, Bert
See Ellison, Harlan (Jay)

Parker, Dorothy (Rothschild)
1893-1967 .... **CLC 15, 68; DAM POET;
PC 28; SSC 2**
See also CA 19-20; 25-28R; CAP 2; DA3;
DLB 11, 45, 86; MTCW 1, 2

Parker, Robert B(rown) 1932- .... **CLC 27;
DAM NOV, POP**
See also AAYA 28; BEST 89:4; CA 49-52;
CANR 1, 26, 52, 89; INT CANR-26;
MTCW 1

Parkin, Frank 1940- .... **CLC 43**
See also CA 147

Parkman, Francis, Jr. 1823-1893 .. **NCLC 12**
See also AMWS 2; DLB 1, 30, 186, 235

Parks, Gordon (Alexander Buchanan)
1912- .... **CLC 1, 16; BLC 3; DAM
MULT**
See also
See also AAYA 36; AITN 2; BW 2, 3; CA
41-44R; CANR 26, 66; DA3; DLB 33;
MTCW 2; SATA 8, 108

Parmenides c. 515B.C.-c.
450B.C. .... **CMLC 22**
See also DLB 176

Parnell, Thomas 1679-1718 .... **LC 3**
See also DLB 94

Parra, Nicanor 1914- ...... **CLC 2, 102; DAM
MULT; HLC 2**
See also CA 85-88; CANR 32; CWW 2;
HW 1; MTCW 1

Parra Sanojo, Ana Teresa de la 1890-1936
See also HLCS 2

Parrish, Mary Frances
See Fisher, M(ary) F(rances) K(ennedy)

Parson
See Coleridge, Samuel Taylor

Parson Lot
See Kingsley, Charles

Parton, Sara Payson Willis
1811-1872 .... **NCLC 86**
See also DLB 43, 74, 239

Partridge, Anthony
See Oppenheim, E(dward) Phillips

Pascal, Blaise 1623-1662 .... **LC 35**

Pascoli, Giovanni 1855-1912 .... **TCLC 45**
See also CA 170

Pasolini, Pier Paolo 1922-1975 .. **CLC 20, 37,
106; PC 17**
See also CA 93-96; 61-64; CANR 63; DLB
128, 177; MTCW 1

Pasquini
See Silone, Ignazio

Pastan, Linda (Olenik) 1932- .... **CLC 27;
DAM POET**
See also CA 61-64; CANR 18, 40, 61; DLB
5

Pasternak, Boris (Leonidovich)
1890-1960 .... **CLC 7, 10, 18, 63; DA;
DAB; DAC; DAM MST, NOV, POET;
PC 6; SSC 31**
See also AW; CA 127; 116; DA3; MTCW
1, 2

Patchen, Kenneth 1911-1972 .. **CLC 1, 2, 18;
DAM POET**
See also CA 1-4R; 33-36R; CANR 3, 35;
DLB 16, 48; MTCW 1

Pater, Walter (Horatio) 1839-1894 . **NCLC 7,
90**
See also CDBLB 1832-1890; DLB 57, 156

Paterson, A(ndrew) B(arton)
1864-1941 .... **TCLC 32**
See also CA 155; DLB 230; SATA 97

Paterson, Katherine (Womeldorf)
1932- .... **CLC 12, 30**
See also AAYA 1, 31; CA 21-24R; CANR
28, 59; CLR 7, 50; DLB 52; JRDA; MAI-
CYA; MTCW 1; SATA 13, 53, 92

Patmore, Coventry Kersey Dighton
1823-1896 .... **NCLC 9**
See also DLB 35, 98

Paton, Alan (Stewart) 1903-1988 ...... **CLC 4,
10, 25, 55, 106; DA; DAB; DAC; DAM
MST, NOV**
See also AAYA 26; AW; BRWS 2; CA 13-
16; 125; CANR 22; CAP 1; DA3; DLB
225; DLBD 17; MTCW 1, 2; SATA 11;
SATA-Obit 56

Paton Walsh, Gillian 1937- .... **CLC 35**
See also Walsh, Jill Paton
See also AAYA 11; AW; CANR 38, 83;
CLR 2, 65; DLB 161; JRDA; MAICYA;
SAAS 3; SATA 4, 72, 109

Paton Walsh, Jill
See Paton Walsh, Gillian

Patton, George S(mith), Jr.
1885-1945 .... **TCLC 79**
See also CA 189

Paulding, James Kirke 1778-1860 ... **NCLC 2**
See also DLB 3, 59, 74

Paulin, Thomas Neilson 1949-
See Paulin, Tom
See also CA 123; 128

Paulin, Tom CLC 37
See also Paulin, Thomas Neilson
See also DLB 40

Pausanias c. 1st cent. - .... **CMLC 36**

Paustovsky, Konstantin (Georgievich)
1892-1968 .... **CLC 40**
See also CA 93-96; 25-28R

Pavese, Cesare 1908-1950 .. **TCLC 3; PC 13;
SSC 19**
See also CA 104; 169; DLB 128, 177

Pavic, Milorad 1929- .... **CLC 60**
See also CA 136; CWW 2; DLB 181

Pavlov, Ivan Petrovich 1849-1936 . **TCLC 91**
See also CA 118; 180

Payne, Alan
See Jakes, John (William)

Paz, Gil
See Lugones, Leopoldo

Paz, Octavio 1914-1998 . **CLC 3, 4, 6, 10, 19,
51, 65, 119; DA; DAB; DAC; DAM
MST, MULT, POET; HLC 2; PC 1**
See also AW; CA 73-76; 165; CANR 32,
65; CWW 2; DA3; DLBY 90, 98; HW 1,
2; MTCW 1, 2

p'Bitek, Okot 1931-1982 .... **CLC 96; BLC 3;
DAM MULT**
See also BW 2, 3; CA 124; 107; CANR 82;
DLB 125; MTCW 1, 2

Peacock, Molly 1947- .... **CLC 60**
See also CA 103; CAAS 21; CANR 52, 84;
DLB 120

Peacock, Thomas Love
1785-1866 .... **NCLC 22**
See also DLB 96, 116

Peake, Mervyn 1911-1968 .... **CLC 7, 54**
See also CA 5-8R; 25-28R; CANR 3; DLB
15, 160; MTCW 1; SATA 23

Pearce, Philippa CLC 21
See Christie, (Ann) Philippa
See also CLR 9; DLB 161; MAICYA;
SATA 1, 67

Pearl, Eric
See Elman, Richard (Martin)

Pearson, T(homas) R(eid) 1956- .... **CLC 39**
See also CA 120; 130; INT 130

Peck, Dale 1967- .... **CLC 81**
See also CA 146; CANR 72; GLL 2

Peck, John 1941- .... **CLC 3**
See also CA 49-52; CANR 3

Peck, Richard (Wayne) 1934- .... **CLC 21**
See also AAYA 1, 24; CA 85-88; CANR
19, 38; CLR 15; INT CANR-19; JRDA;
MAICYA; SAAS 2; SATA 18, 55, 97;
SATA-Essay 110

Peck, Robert Newton 1928- .... **CLC 17; DA;
DAC; DAM MST**
See also AAYA 3; AW; CA 81-84, 182;
CAAE 182; CANR 31, 63; CLR 45;
JRDA; MAICYA; SAAS 1; SATA 21, 62,
111; SATA-Essay 108

Peckinpah, (David) Sam(uel)
1925-1984 .... **CLC 20**
See also CA 109; 114; CANR 82

Pedersen, Knut 1859-1952
See Hamsun, Knut
See also CA 104; 119; CANR 63; MTCW
1, 2

Peeslake, Gaffer
See Durrell, Lawrence (George)

Peguy, Charles Pierre 1873-1914 ... **TCLC 10**
See also CA 107

Peirce, Charles Sanders
1839-1914 .... **TCLC 81**

Pellicer, Carlos 1900(?)-1977
See also CA 153; 69-72; HLCS 2; HW 1

Pena, Ramon del Valle y
See Valle-Inclan, Ramon (Maria) del

Pendennis, Arthur Esquir
See Thackeray, William Makepeace

Penn, William 1644-1718 .... **LC 25**
See also DLB 24

PEPECE
See Prado (Calvo), Pedro

Pepys, Samuel 1633-1703 ..... **LC 11, 58; DA;
DAB; DAC; DAM MST**
See also AW; CDBLB 1660-1789; DA3;
DLB 101

Percy, Thomas 1729-1811 .... **NCLC 95**
See also DLB 104

Percy, Walker 1916-1990 .... **CLC 2, 3, 6, 8,
14, 18, 47, 65; DAM NOV, POP**
See also AMWS 3; CA 1-4R; 131; CANR
1, 23, 64; DA3; DLB 2; DLBY 80, 90;
MTCW 1, 2

Percy, William Alexander
1885-1942 .... **TCLC 84**
See also CA 163; MTCW 2

Perec, Georges 1936-1982 .... **CLC 56, 116**
See also CA 141; DLB 83

**Pereda (y Sanchez de Porrua), Jose Maria
de** 1833-1906 .... **TCLC 16**
See also CA 117

Pereda y Porrua, Jose Maria de
See Pereda (y Sanchez de Porrua), Jose
Maria de

Peregoy, George Weems
See Mencken, H(enry) L(ouis)

Perelman, S(idney) J(oseph)
1904-1979 .. **CLC 3, 5, 9, 15, 23, 44, 49;
DAM DRAM; SSC 32**
See also AITN 1, 2; CA 73-76; 89-92;
CANR 18; DLB 11, 44; MTCW 1, 2

Peret, Benjamin 1899-1959 .... **TCLC 20; PC
33**
See also CA 117; 186

Peretz, Isaac Loeb 1851(?)-1915 ... **TCLC 16;
SSC 26**
See also CA 109

Peretz, Yitzhkok Leibush
See Peretz, Isaac Loeb

Przybyszewski, Stanislaw
 1868-1927 .... **TCLC 36**
 See also CA 160; DLB 66
Pteleon
 See Grieve, C(hristopher) M(urray)
 See also DAM POET
Puckett, Lute
 See Masters, Edgar Lee
Puig, Manuel 1932-1990 .... **CLC 3, 5, 10, 28, 65, 133; DAM MULT; HLC 2**
 See also CA 45-48; CANR 2, 32, 63; DA3; DLB 113; GLL 1; HW 1, 2; MTCW 1, 2
Pulitzer, Joseph 1847-1911 .... **TCLC 76**
 See also CA 114; DLB 23
Purdy, A(lfred) W(ellington)
 1918-2000 .... **CLC 3, 6, 14, 50; DAC; DAM MST, POET**
 See also CA 81-84; 189; CAAS 17; CANR 42, 66; DLB 88
Purdy, James (Amos) 1923- .... **CLC 2, 4, 10, 28, 52**
 See also AMWS 7; CA 33-36R; CAAS 1; CANR 19, 51; DLB 2; INT CANR-19; MTCW 1
Pure, Simon
 See Swinnerton, Frank Arthur
Pushkin, Alexander (Sergeyevich)
 1799-1837 . **NCLC 3, 27, 83; DA; DAB; DAC; DAM DRAM, MST, POET; PC 10; SSC 27**
 See also AW; DA3; DLB 205; SATA 61
P'u Sung-ling 1640-1715 .... **LC 49; SSC 31**
Putnam, Arthur Lee
 See Alger, Horatio, Jr.
Puzo, Mario 1920-1999 .... **CLC 1, 2, 6, 36, 107; DAM NOV, POP**
 See also CA 65-68; 185; CANR 4, 42, 65; DA3; DLB 6; MTCW 1, 2
Pygge, Edward
 See Barnes, Julian (Patrick)
Pyle, Ernest Taylor 1900-1945
 See Pyle, Ernie
 See also CA 115; 160
Pyle, Ernie TCLC 75
 See also Pyle, Ernest Taylor
 See also DLB 29; MTCW 2
Pyle, Howard 1853-1911 .... **TCLC 81**
 See also AW; CA 109; 137; CLR 22; DLB 42, 188; DLBD 13; MAICYA; SATA 16, 100
Pym, Barbara (Mary Crampton)
 1913-1980 .... **CLC 13, 19, 37, 111**
 See also BRWS 2; CA 13-14; 97-100; CANR 13, 34; CAP 1; DLB 14, 207; DLBY 87; MTCW 1, 2
Pynchon, Thomas (Ruggles, Jr.)
 1937- ...... **CLC 2, 3, 6, 9, 11, 18, 33, 62, 72, 123; DA; DAB; DAC; DAM MST, NOV, POP; SSC 14**
 See also AMWS 2; AW; BEST 90:2; CA 17-20R; CANR 22, 46, 73; DA3; DLB 2, 173; MTCW 1, 2
Pythagoras c. 582B.C.-c. 507B.C. . **CMLC 22**
 See also DLB 176

Q
 See Quiller-Couch, SirArthur (Thomas)
Qian Zhongshu
 See Ch'ien Chung-shu
Qroll
 See Dagerman, Stig (Halvard)
Quarrington, Paul (Lewis) 1953- ..... **CLC 65**
 See also CA 129; CANR 62, 95
Quasimodo, Salvatore 1901-1968 ..... **CLC 10**
 See also CA 13-16; 25-28R; CAP 1; DLB 114; MTCW 1
Quay, Stephen 1947- .... **CLC 95**
 See also CA 189

Quay, Timothy 1947- .... **CLC 95**
 See also CA 189
Queen, Ellery CLC 3, 11
 See also Dannay, Frederic; Davidson, Avram (James); Deming, Richard; Fairman, Paul W.; Flora, Fletcher; Hoch, Edward D(entinger); Kane, Henry; Lee, Manfred B(ennington); Marlowe, Stephen; Powell, Talmage; Sheldon, Walter J.; Sturgeon, Theodore (Hamilton); Tracy, Don(ald Fiske); Vance, John Holbrook
Queen, Ellery, Jr.
 See Dannay, Frederic; Lee, Manfred B(ennington)
Queneau, Raymond 1903-1976 ..... **CLC 2, 5, 10, 42**
 See also CA 77-80; 69-72; CANR 32; DLB 72; MTCW 1, 2
Quevedo, Francisco de 1580-1645 .... **LC 23**
Quiller-Couch, SirArthur (Thomas)
 1863-1944 .... **TCLC 53**
 See also CA 118; 166; DLB 135, 153, 190
Quin, Ann (Marie) 1936-1973 .... **CLC 6**
 See also CA 9-12R; 45-48; DLB 14, 231
Quinn, Martin
 See Smith, Martin Cruz
Quinn, Peter 1947- .... **CLC 91**
Quinn, Simon
 See Smith, Martin Cruz
Quintana, Leroy V. 1944-
 See also CA 131; CANR 65; DAM MULT; DLB 82; HLC 2; HW 1, 2
Quiroga, Horacio (Sylvestre)
 1878-1937 .... **TCLC 20; DAM MULT; HLC 2**
 See also CA 117; 131; HW 1; MTCW 1
Quoirez, Francoise 1935- .... **CLC 9**
 See also Sagan, Francoise
 See also CA 49-52; CANR 6, 39, 73; CWW 2; MTCW 1, 2
Raabe, Wilhelm (Karl) 1831-1910 . **TCLC 45**
 See also CA 167; DLB 129
Rabe, David (William) 1940- .. **CLC 4, 8, 33; DAM DRAM**
 See also CA 85-88; CABS 3; CANR 59; DLB 7, 228
Rabelais, François 1494-1553 .... **LC 5, 60; DA; DAB; DAC; DAM MST**
 See also AW
Rabinovitch, Sholem 1859-1916
 See Aleichem, Sholom
 See also CA 104
Rabinyan, Dorit 1972- .... **CLC 119**
 See also CA 170
Rachilde
 See Vallette, Marguerite Eymery
Racine, Jean 1639-1699 . **LC 28; DAB; DAM MST**
 See also DA3
Radcliffe, Ann (Ward) 1764-1823 ... **NCLC 6, 55**
 See also DLB 39, 178
Radiguet, Raymond 1903-1923 ...... **TCLC 29**
 See also CA 162; DLB 65
Radnoti, Miklos 1909-1944 .... **TCLC 16**
 See also CA 118
Rado, James 1939- .... **CLC 17**
 See also CA 105
Radvanyi, Netty 1900-1983
 See Seghers, Anna
 See also CA 85-88; 110; CANR 82
Rae, Ben
 See Griffiths, Trevor
Raeburn, John (Hay) 1941- .... **CLC 34**
 See also CA 57-60

Ragni, Gerome 1942-1991 .... **CLC 17**
 See also CA 105; 134
Rahv, Philip CLC 24
 See also Greenberg, Ivan
 See also DLB 137
Raimund, Ferdinand Jakob
 1790-1836 .... **NCLC 69**
 See also DLB 90
Raine, Craig 1944- .... **CLC 32, 103**
 See also CA 108; CANR 29, 51; DLB 40
Raine, Kathleen (Jessie) 1908- ..... **CLC 7, 45**
 See also CA 85-88; CANR 46; DLB 20; MTCW 1
Rainis, Janis 1865-1929 .... **TCLC 29**
 See also Plieksans, Janis
 See also CA 170; DLB 220
Rakosi, Carl CLC 47
 See also Rawley, Callman
 See also CAAS 5; DLB 193
Ralegh, SirWalter (?)-
 See Raleigh, SirWalter
Raleigh, Richard
 See Lovecraft, H(oward) P(hillips)
Raleigh, SirWalter 1554(?)-1618 .. **LC 31, 39; PC 31**
 See also CDBLB Before 1660; DLB 172
Rallentando, H. P.
 See Sayers, Dorothy L(eigh)
Ramal, Walter
 See de la Mare, Walter (John)
Ramana Maharshi 1879-1950 .... **TCLC 84**
Ramoacn y Cajal, Santiago
 1852-1934 .... **TCLC 93**
Ramon, Juan
 See Jimenez (Mantecon), Juan Ramon
Ramos, Graciliano 1892-1953 .... **TCLC 32**
 See also CA 167; HW 2
Rampersad, Arnold 1941- .... **CLC 44**
 See also BW 2, 3; CA 127; 133; CANR 81; DLB 111; INT 133
Rampling, Anne
 See Rice, Anne
 See also GLL 2
Ramsay, Allan 1686(?)-1758 .... **LC 29**
 See also DLB 95
Ramuz, Charles-Ferdinand
 1878-1947 .... **TCLC 33**
 See also CA 165
Rand, Ayn 1905-1982 ...... **CLC 3, 30, 44, 79; DA; DAC; DAM MST, NOV, POP**
 See also AAYA 10; AMWS 4; AW; CA 13-16R; 105; CANR 27, 73; CDALBS; DA3; DLB 227; MTCW 1, 2
Randall, Dudley (Felker) 1914-2000 . **CLC 1, 135; BLC 3; DAM MULT**
 See also BW 1, 3; CA 25-28R; 189; CANR 23, 82; DLB 41
Randall, Robert
 See Silverberg, Robert
Ranger, Ken
 See Creasey, John
Ransom, John Crowe 1888-1974 .. **CLC 2, 4, 5, 11, 24; DAM POET**
 See also CA 5-8R; 49-52; CANR 6, 34; CDALBS; DA3; DLB 45, 63; MTCW 1, 2
Rao, Raja 1909- ..... **CLC 25, 56; DAM NOV**
 See also CA 73-76; CANR 51; MTCW 1, 2
Raphael, Frederic (Michael) 1931- ... **CLC 2, 14**
 See also CA 1-4R; CANR 1, 86; DLB 14
Ratcliffe, James P.
 See Mencken, H(enry) L(ouis)
Rathbone, Julian 1935- .... **CLC 41**
 See also CA 101; CANR 34, 73

Rattigan, Terence (Mervyn)
1911-1977 .... **CLC 7; DAM DRAM**
See also CA 85-88; 73-76; CDBLB 1945-
1960; DLB 13; IDFW 3; MTCW 1, 2

Ratushinskaya, Irina 1954- .... **CLC 54**
See also CA 129; CANR 68; CWW 2

Raven, Simon (Arthur Noel) 1927- .. **CLC 14**
See also CA 81-84; CANR 86

Ravenna, Michael
See Welty, Eudora

Rawley, Callman 1903-
See Rakosi, Carl
See also CA 21-24R; CANR 12, 32, 91

Rawlings, Marjorie Kinnan
1896-1953 .... **TCLC 4**
See also AAYA 20; AW; CA 104; 137;
CANR 74; CLR 63; DLB 9, 22, 102;
DLBD 17; JRDA; MAICYA; MTCW 2;
SATA 100

Ray, Satyajit 1921-1992 .. **CLC 16, 76; DAM MULT**
See also CA 114; 137

Read, Herbert Edward 1893-1968 ..... **CLC 4**
See also CA 85-88; 25-28R; DLB 20, 149

Read, Piers Paul 1941- .... **CLC 4, 10, 25**
See also CA 21-24R; CANR 38, 86; DLB
14; SATA 21

Reade, Charles 1814-1884 .... **NCLC 2, 74**
See also DLB 21

Reade, Hamish
See Gray, Simon (James Holliday)

Reading, Peter 1946- .... **CLC 47**
See also CA 103; CANR 46, 96; DLB 40

Reaney, James 1926- .. **CLC 13; DAC; DAM MST**
See also CA 41-44R; CAAS 15; CANR 42;
DLB 68; SATA 43

Rebreanu, Liviu 1885-1944 .... **TCLC 28**
See also CA 165; DLB 220

Rechy, John (Francisco) 1934- ...... **CLC 1, 7, 14, 18, 107; DAM MULT; HLC 2**
See also CA 5-8R; CAAS 4; CANR 6, 32,
64; DLB 122; DLBY 82; HW 1, 2; INT
CANR-6

Redcam, Tom 1870-1933 .... **TCLC 25**

Reddin, Keith CLC 67

Redgrove, Peter (William) 1932- . **CLC 6, 41**
See also CA 1-4R; CANR 3, 39, 77; DLB
40

Redmon, Anne CLC 22
See also Nightingale, Anne Redmon
See also DLBY 86

Reed, Eliot
See Ambler, Eric

Reed, Ishmael 1938- .. **CLC 2, 3, 5, 6, 13, 32, 60; BLC 3; DAM MULT**
See also BW 2, 3; CA 21-24R; CANR 25,
48, 74; DA3; DLB 2, 5, 33, 169, 227;
DLBD 8; MTCW 1, 2; TCWW 2

Reed, John (Silas) 1887-1920 .... **TCLC 9**
See also CA 106

Reed, Lou CLC 21
See also Firbank, Louis

Reese, Lizette Woodworth 1856-1935 . **PC 29**
See also CA 180; DLB 54

Reeve, Clara 1729-1807 .... **NCLC 19**
See also DLB 39

Reich, Wilhelm 1897-1957 .... **TCLC 57**

Reid, Christopher (John) 1949- .... **CLC 33**
See also CA 140; CANR 89; DLB 40

Reid, Desmond
See Moorcock, Michael (John)

Reid Banks, Lynne 1929-
See Banks, Lynne Reid
See also AW; CA 1-4R; CANR 6, 22, 38,
87; CLR 24; JRDA; MAICYA; SATA 22,
75, 111

Reilly, William K.
See Creasey, John

Reiner, Max
See Caldwell, (Janet Miriam) Taylor
(Holland)

Reis, Ricardo
See Pessoa, Fernando (Antonio Nogueira)

Remarque, Erich Maria
1898-1970 ... **CLC 21; DA; DAB; DAC; DAM MST, NOV**
See also AAYA 27; CA 77-80; 29-32R;
DA3; DLB 56; MTCW 1, 2

Remington, Frederic 1861-1909 ..... **TCLC 89**
See also CA 108; 169; DLB 12, 186, 188;
SATA 41

Remizov, A.
See Remizov, Aleksei (Mikhailovich)

Remizov, A. M.
See Remizov, Aleksei (Mikhailovich)

Remizov, Aleksei (Mikhailovich)
1877-1957 .... **TCLC 27**
See also CA 125; 133

Renan, Joseph Ernest 1823-1892 .. **NCLC 26**

Renard, Jules 1864-1910 .... **TCLC 17**
See also CA 117

Renault, Mary CLC 3, 11, 17
See also Challans, Mary
See also DLBY 83; GLL 1; MTCW 2

Rendell, Ruth (Barbara) 1930- . **CLC 28, 48; DAM POP**
See also Vine, Barbara
See also CA 109; CANR 32, 52, 74; DLB
87; INT CANR-32; MTCW 1, 2

Renoir, Jean 1894-1979 .... **CLC 20**
See also CA 129; 85-88

Resnais, Alain 1922- .... **CLC 16**

Reverdy, Pierre 1889-1960 .... **CLC 53**
See also CA 97-100; 89-92

Rexroth, Kenneth 1905-1982 .... **CLC 1, 2, 6, 11, 22, 49, 112; DAM POET; PC 20**
See also CA 5-8R; 107; CANR 14, 34, 63;
CDALB 1941-1968; DLB 16, 48, 165,
212; DLBY 82; INT CANR-14; MTCW
1, 2

Reyes, Alfonso 1889-1959 .. **TCLC 33; HLCS 2**
See also CA 131; HW 1

Reyes y Basoalto, Ricardo Eliecer Neftali
See Neruda, Pablo

Reymont, Wladyslaw (Stanislaw)
1868(?)-1925 .... **TCLC 5**
See also CA 104

Reynolds, Jonathan 1942- .... **CLC 6, 38**
See also CA 65-68; CANR 28

Reynolds, Joshua 1723-1792 .... **LC 15**
See also DLB 104

Reynolds, Michael S(hane)
1937-2000 .... **CLC 44**
See also CA 65-68; 189; CANR 9, 89

Reznikoff, Charles 1894-1976 .... **CLC 9**
See also CA 33-36; 61-64; CAP 2; DLB 28,
45

Rezzori (d'Arezzo), Gregor von
1914-1998 .... **CLC 25**
See also CA 122; 136; 167

Rhine, Richard
See Silverstein, Alvin

Rhodes, Eugene Manlove
1869-1934 .... **TCLC 53**

Rhodius, Apollonius c. 3rd cent.
B.C.- .... **CMLC 28**
See also DLB 176

R'hoone
See Balzac, Honor

Rhys, Jean 1894(?)-1979 ...... **CLC 2, 4, 6, 14, 19, 51, 124; DAM NOV; SSC 21**
See also BRWS 2; CA 25-28R; 85-88;
CANR 35, 62; CDBLB 1945-1960; DA3;
DLB 36, 117, 162; MTCW 1, 2

Ribeiro, Darcy 1922-1997 .... **CLC 34**
See also CA 33-36R; 156

Ribeiro, Joao Ubaldo (Osorio Pimentel)
1941- .... **CLC 10, 67**
See also CA 81-84

Ribman, Ronald (Burt) 1932- .... **CLC 7**
See also CA 21-24R; CANR 46, 80

Ricci, Nino 1959- .... **CLC 70**
See also CA 137; CCA 1

Rice, Anne 1941- .. **CLC 41, 128; DAM POP**
See also AAYA 9; AMWS 7; AW; BEST
89:2; CA 65-68; CANR 12, 36, 53, 74;
DA3; GLL 2; MTCW 2

Rice, Elmer (Leopold) 1892-1967 ...... **CLC 7, 49; DAM DRAM**
See also CA 21-22; 25-28R; CAP 2; DLB
4, 7; MTCW 1, 2

Rice, Tim(othy Miles Bindon)
1944- .... **CLC 21**
See also CA 103; CANR 46

Rich, Adrienne (Cecile) 1929- ... **CLC 3, 6, 7, 11, 18, 36, 73, 76, 125; DAM POET; PC 5**
See also AMWS 1; CA 9-12R; CANR 20,
53, 74; CDALBS; DA3; DLB 5, 67;
MTCW 1, 2

Rich, Barbara
See Graves, Robert (von Ranke)

Rich, Robert
See Trumbo, Dalton
See also IDFW 3

Richard, Keith CLC 17
See also Richards, Keith

Richards, David Adams 1950- .... **CLC 59; DAC**
See also CA 93-96; CANR 60; DLB 53

Richards, I(vor) A(rmstrong)
1893-1979 .... **CLC 14, 24**
See also BRWS 2; CA 41-44R; 89-92;
CANR 34, 74; DLB 27; MTCW 2

Richards, Keith 1943-
See Richard, Keith
See also CA 107; CANR 77

Richardson, Anne
See Roiphe, Anne (Richardson)

Richardson, Dorothy Miller
1873-1957 .... **TCLC 3**
See also CA 104; DLB 36

**Richardson (Robertson), Ethel Florence
Lindesay** 1870-1946
See Richardson, Henry Handel
See also CA 105; DLB 230

Richardson, Henry Handel TCLC 4
See also Richardson (Robertson), Ethel Flo-
rence Lindesay
See also DLB 197

Richardson, John 1796-1852 .... **NCLC 55; DAC**
See also CCA 1; DLB 99

Richardson, Samuel 1689-1761 ...... **LC 1, 44; DA; DAB; DAC; DAM MST, NOV**
See also AW; CDBLB 1660-1789; DLB 39

Richler, Mordecai 1931- ...... **CLC 3, 5, 9, 13, 18, 46, 70; DAC; DAM MST, NOV**
See also AITN 1; CA 65-68; CANR 31, 62;
CCA 1; CLR 17; DLB 53; MAICYA;
MTCW 1, 2; SATA 44, 98; SATA-Brief
27

Richter, Conrad (Michael)
1890-1968 .... **CLC 30**
See also AAYA 21; AW; CA 5-8R; 25-28R;
CANR 23; DLB 9, 212; MTCW 1, 2;
SATA 3; TCWW 2

Ricostranza, Tom
See Ellis, Trey

Riddell, Charlotte 1832-1906 .... **TCLC 40**
See also CA 165; DLB 156

Ridge, John Rollin 1827-1867 ...... NCLC 82;
DAM MULT
See also CA 144; DLB 175; NNAL

Ridgway, Keith 1965- .... CLC 119
See also CA 172

Riding, Laura CLC 3, 7
See also Jackson, Laura (Riding)

Riefenstahl, Berta Helene Amalia 1902-
See Riefenstahl, Leni
See also CA 108

Riefenstahl, Leni CLC 16
See also Riefenstahl, Berta Helene Amalia

Riffe, Ernest
See Bergman, (Ernst) Ingmar

Riggs, (Rolla) Lynn 1899-1954 ..... TCLC 56;
DAM MULT
See also CA 144; DLB 175; NNAL

Riis, Jacob A(ugust) 1849-1914 ..... TCLC 80
See also CA 113; 168; DLB 23

Riley, James Whitcomb
1849-1916 .... TCLC 51; DAM POET
See also CA 118; 137; MAICYA; SATA 17

Riley, Tex
See Creasey, John

Rilke, Rainer Maria 1875-1926 .. TCLC 1, 6,
19; DAM POET; PC 2
See also CA 104; 132; CANR 62; DA3;
DLB 81; MTCW 1, 2

Rimbaud, (Jean Nicolas) Arthur
1854-1891 . NCLC 4, 35, 82; DA; DAB;
DAC; DAM MST, POET; PC 3
See also AW; DA3

Rinehart, Mary Roberts
1876-1958 .... TCLC 52
See also CA 108; 166

Ringmaster, The
See Mencken, H(enry) L(ouis)

Ringwood, Gwen(dolyn Margaret) Pharis
1910-1984 .... CLC 48
See also CA 148; 112; DLB 88

Rio, Michel 19(?)- .... CLC 43

Ritsos, Giannes
See Ritsos, Yannis

Ritsos, Yannis 1909-1990 .... CLC 6, 13, 31
See also CA 77-80; 133; CANR 39, 61;
MTCW 1

Ritter, Erika 1948(?)- .... CLC 52

Rivera, Jose Eustasio 1889-1928 ... TCLC 35
See also CA 162; HW 1, 2

Rivera, Tomas 1935-1984
See also CA 49-52; CANR 32; DLB 82;
HLCS 2; HW 1; TCWW 2

Rivers, Conrad Kent 1933-1968 .... CLC 1
See also BW 1; CA 85-88; DLB 41

Rivers, Elfrida
See Bradley, Marion Zimmer
See also GLL 1

Riverside, John
See Heinlein, Robert A(nson)

Rizal, Jose 1861-1896 .... NCLC 27

Roa Bastos, Augusto (Antonio)
1917- .... CLC 45; DAM MULT; HLC 2
See also CA 131; DLB 113; HW 1

Robbe-Grillet, Alain 1922- .... CLC 1, 2, 4, 6,
8, 10, 14, 43, 128
See also CA 9-12R; CANR 33, 65; DLB
83; MTCW 1, 2

Robbins, Harold 1916-1997 .... CLC 5; DAM
NOV
See also CA 73-76; 162; CANR 26, 54;
DA3; MTCW 1, 2

Robbins, Thomas Eugene 1936-
See Robbins, Tom
See also CA 81-84; CANR 29, 59, 95;
DAM NOV, POP; DA3; MTCW 1, 2

Robbins, Tom CLC 9, 32, 64
See also Robbins, Thomas Eugene
See also AAYA 32; BEST 90:3; DLBY 80;
MTCW 2

Robbins, Trina 1938- .... CLC 21
See also CA 128

Roberts, Charles G(eorge) D(ouglas)
1860-1943 .... TCLC 8
See also CA 105; 188; CLR 33; DLB 92;
SATA 88; SATA-Brief 29

Roberts, Elizabeth Madox
1886-1941 .... TCLC 68
See also CA 111; 166; DLB 9, 54, 102;
SATA 33; SATA-Brief 27

Roberts, Kate 1891-1985 .... CLC 15
See also CA 107; 116

Roberts, Keith (John Kingston)
1935-2000 .... CLC 14
See also CA 25-28R; CANR 46

Roberts, Kenneth (Lewis)
1885-1957 .... TCLC 23
See also CA 109; DLB 9

Roberts, Michele (Brigitte) 1949- ..... CLC 48
See also CA 115; CANR 58; DLB 231

Robertson, Ellis
See Ellison, Harlan (Jay); Silverberg, Robert

Robertson, Thomas William
1829-1871 .... NCLC 35; DAM DRAM

Robeson, Kenneth
See Dent, Lester

Robinson, Edwin Arlington
1869-1935 ..... TCLC 5, 101; DA; DAC;
DAM MST, POET; PC 1
See also CA 104; 133; CDALB 1865-1917;
DLB 54; MTCW 1, 2

Robinson, Henry Crabb
1775-1867 .... NCLC 15
See also DLB 107

Robinson, Jill 1936- .... CLC 10
See also CA 102; INT 102

Robinson, Kim Stanley 1952- .... CLC 34
See also AAYA 26; CA 126; SATA 109

Robinson, Lloyd
See Silverberg, Robert

Robinson, Marilynne 1944- .... CLC 25
See also CA 116; CANR 80; DLB 206

Robinson, Smokey CLC 21
See also Robinson, William, Jr.

Robinson, William, Jr. 1940-
See Robinson, Smokey
See also CA 116

Robison, Mary 1949- .... CLC 42, 98
See also CA 113; 116; CANR 87; DLB 130;
INT 116

Rod, Edouard 1857-1910 .... TCLC 52

Roddenberry, Eugene Wesley 1921-1991
See Roddenberry, Gene
See also CA 110; 135; CANR 37; SATA 45;
SATA-Obit 69

Roddenberry, Gene CLC 17
See also Roddenberry, Eugene Wesley
See also AAYA 5; SATA-Obit 69

Rodgers, Mary 1931- .... CLC 12
See also CA 49-52; CANR 8, 55, 90; CLR
20; INT CANR-8; JRDA; MAICYA;
SATA 8

Rodgers, W(illiam) R(obert)
1909-1969 .... CLC 7
See also CA 85-88; DLB 20

Rodman, Eric
See Silverberg, Robert

Rodman, Howard 1920(?)-1985 .... CLC 65
See also CA 118

Rodman, Maia
See Wojciechowska, Maia (Teresa)

Rodo, Jose Enrique 1871(?)-1917
See also CA 178; HLCS 2; HW 2

Rodriguez, Claudio 1934-1999 .... CLC 10
See also CA 188; DLB 134

Rodriguez, Richard 1944-
See also CA 110; CANR 66; DAM MULT;
DLB 82; HLC 2; HW 1, 2

Roelvaag, O(le) E(dvart)
1876-1931 .... TCLC 17
See also Rolvaag, O(le) E(dvart)
See also CA 117; 171; DLB 9

Roethke, Theodore (Huebner)
1908-1963 .... CLC 1, 3, 8, 11, 19, 46,
101; DAM POET; PC 15
See also CA 81-84; CABS 2; CDALB 1941-
1968; DA3; DLB 5, 206; MTCW 1, 2

Rogers, Samuel 1763-1855 .... NCLC 69
See also DLB 93

Rogers, Thomas Hunton 1927- .... CLC 57
See also CA 89-92; INT 89-92

Rogers, Will(iam Penn Adair)
1879-1935 ..... TCLC 8, 71; DAM MULT
See also CA 105; 144; DA3; DLB 11;
MTCW 2; NNAL

Rogin, Gilbert 1929- .... CLC 18
See also CA 65-68; CANR 15

Rohan, Koda
See Koda Shigeyuki

Rohlfs, Anna Katharine Green
See Green, Anna Katharine

Rohmer, Eric CLC 16
See also Scherer, Jean-Marie Maurice

Rohmer, Sax TCLC 28
See also Ward, Arthur Henry Sarsfield
See also DLB 70

Roiphe, Anne (Richardson) 1935- .. CLC 3, 9
See also CA 89-92; CANR 45, 73; DLBY
80; INT 89-92

Rojas, Fernando de 1475-1541 .... LC 23;
HLCS 1

Rojas, Gonzalo 1917-
See also HLCS 2; HW 2

Rojas, Gonzalo 1917-
See also CA 178; HLCS 2

Rolfe, Frederick (William Serafino Austin
Lewis Mary) 1860-1913 .... TCLC 12
See also CA 107; DLB 34, 156

Rolland, Romain 1866-1944 .... TCLC 23
See also CA 118; DLB 65

Rolle, Richard c. 1300-c. 1349 ...... CMLC 21
See also DLB 146

Rolvaag, O(le) E(dvart)
See Roelvaag, O(le) E(dvart)

Romain Arnaud, Saint
See Aragon, Louis

Romains, Jules 1885-1972 .... CLC 7
See also CA 85-88; CANR 34; DLB 65;
MTCW 1

Romero, Jose Ruben 1890-1952 .... TCLC 14
See also CA 114; 131; HW 1

Ronsard, Pierre de 1524-1585 . LC 6, 54; PC
11

Rooke, Leon 1934- . CLC 25, 34; DAM POP
See also CA 25-28R; CANR 23, 53; CCA 1

Roosevelt, Franklin Delano
1882-1945 .... TCLC 93
See also CA 116; 173

Roosevelt, Theodore 1858-1919 ..... TCLC 69
See also CA 115; 170; DLB 47, 186

Roper, William 1498-1578 .... LC 10

Roquelaure, A. N.
See Rice, Anne

Rosa, Joao Guimaraes 1908-1967 ... CLC 23;
HLCS 1
See also CA 89-92; DLB 113

Rose, Wendy 1948- .. CLC 85; DAM MULT;
PC 13
See also CA 53-56; CANR 5, 51; DLB 175;
NNAL; SATA 12

Author Index

Sidney, Mary 1561-1621 .... **LC 19, 39**

Sidney, SirPhilip 1554-1586 . **LC 19, 39; DA; DAB; DAC; DAM MST, POET; PC 32**
See also CDBLB Before 1660; DA3; DLB 167

Siegel, Jerome 1914-1996 .... **CLC 21**
See also CA 116; 169; 151

Siegel, Jerry
See Siegel, Jerome

Sienkiewicz, Henryk (Adam Alexander Pius) 1846-1916 .... **TCLC 3**
See also CA 104; 134; CANR 84

Sierra, Gregorio Martinez
See Martinez Sierra, Gregorio

Sierra, Maria (de la O'LeJarraga) Martinez
See Martinez Sierra, Maria (de la O'LeJarraga)

Sigal, Clancy 1926- .... **CLC 7**
See also CA 1-4R; CANR 85

Sigourney, Lydia Howard (Huntley) 1791-1865 .... **NCLC 21, 87**
See also DLB 1, 42, 73, 239

Sigüenza y Gongora, Carlos de 1645-1700 .... **LC 8; HLCS 2**

Sigurjonsson, Johann 1880-1919 ... **TCLC 27**
See also CA 170

Sikelianos, Angelos 1884-1951 ...... **TCLC 39; PC 29**

Silkin, Jon 1930-1997 .... **CLC 2, 6, 43**
See also CA 5-8R; CAAS 5; CANR 89; DLB 27

Silko, Leslie (Marmon) 1948- .... **CLC 23, 74, 114; DA; DAC; DAM MST, MULT, POP; SSC 37**
See also AAYA 14; AMWS 4; AW; CA 115; 122; CANR 45, 65; DA3; DLB 143, 175; MTCW 2; NNAL

Sillanpaa, Frans Eemil 1888-1964 ... **CLC 19**
See also CA 129; 93-96; MTCW 1

Sillitoe, Alan 1928- ... **CLC 1, 3, 6, 10, 19, 57**
See also AITN 1; BRWS 5; CA 9-12R; CAAS 2; CANR 8, 26, 55; CDBLB 1960 to Present; DLB 14, 139; MTCW 1, 2; SATA 61

Silone, Ignazio 1900-1978 .... **CLC 4**
See also CA 25-28; 81-84; CANR 34; CAP 2; MTCW 1

Silone, Ignazione
See Silone, Ignazio

Silver, Joan Micklin 1935- .... **CLC 20**
See also CA 114; 121; INT 121

Silver, Nicholas
See Faust, Frederick (Schiller)
See also TCWW 2

Silverberg, Robert 1935- .... **CLC 7, 140; DAM POP**
See also AAYA 24; CA 1-4R, 186; CAAE 186; CAAS 3; CANR 1, 20, 36, 85; CLR 59; DLB 8; INT CANR-20; MAICYA; MTCW 1, 2; SATA 13, 91; SATA-Essay 104; SCFW 2

Silverstein, Alvin 1933- .... **CLC 17**
See also CA 49-52; CANR 2; CLR 25; JRDA; MAICYA; SATA 8, 69

Silverstein, Virginia B(arbara Opshelor) 1937- .... **CLC 17**
See also CA 49-52; CANR 2; CLR 25; JRDA; MAICYA; SATA 8, 69

Sim, Georges
See Simenon, Georges (Jacques Christian)

Simak, Clifford D(onald) 1904-1988 . **CLC 1, 55**
See also CA 1-4R; 125; CANR 1, 35; DLB 8; MTCW 1; SATA-Obit 56

Simenon, Georges (Jacques Christian) 1903-1989 .... **CLC 1, 2, 3, 8, 18, 47; DAM POP**
See also CA 85-88; 129; CANR 35; DA3; DLB 72; DLBY 89; MTCW 1, 2

Simic, Charles 1938- .... **CLC 6, 9, 22, 49, 68, 130; DAM POET**
See also CA 29-32R; CAAS 4; CANR 12, 33, 52, 61, 96; DA3; DLB 105; MTCW 2

Simmel, Georg 1858-1918 .... **TCLC 64**
See also CA 157

Simmons, Charles (Paul) 1924- .... **CLC 57**
See also CA 89-92; INT 89-92

Simmons, Dan 1948- .... **CLC 44; DAM POP**
See also AAYA 16; CA 138; CANR 53, 81

Simmons, James (Stewart Alexander) 1933- .... **CLC 43**
See also CA 105; CAAS 21; DLB 40

Simms, William Gilmore 1806-1870 .... **NCLC 3**
See also DLB 3, 30, 59, 73

Simon, Carly 1945- .... **CLC 26**
See also CA 105

Simon, Claude 1913- .... **CLC 4, 9, 15, 39; DAM NOV**
See also CA 89-92; CANR 33; DLB 83; MTCW 1

Simon, (Marvin) Neil 1927- ... **CLC 6, 11, 31, 39, 70; DAM DRAM; DC 14**
See also AAYA 32; AITN 1; AMWS 4; CA 21-24R; CANR 26, 54, 87; DA3; DLB 7; MTCW 1, 2

Simon, Paul (Frederick) 1941(?)- ..... **CLC 17**
See also CA 116; 153

Simonon, Paul 1956(?)- .... **CLC 30**

Simpson, Harriette
See Arnow, Harriette (Louisa) Simpson

Simpson, Louis (Aston Marantz) 1923- ...... **CLC 4, 7, 9, 32; DAM POET**
See also CA 1-4R; CAAS 4; CANR 1, 61; DLB 5; MTCW 1, 2

Simpson, Mona (Elizabeth) 1957- .... **CLC 44**
See also CA 122; 135; CANR 68

Simpson, N(orman) F(rederick) 1919- .... **CLC 29**
See also CA 13-16R; DLB 13

Sinclair, Andrew (Annandale) 1935- . **CLC 2, 14**
See also CA 9-12R; CAAS 5; CANR 14, 38, 91; DLB 14; MTCW 1

Sinclair, Emil
See Hesse, Hermann

Sinclair, Iain 1943- .... **CLC 76**
See also CA 132; CANR 81

Sinclair, Iain MacGregor
See Sinclair, Iain

Sinclair, Irene
See Griffith, D(avid Lewelyn) W(ark)

Sinclair, Mary Amelia St. Clair 1865(?)-1946
See Sinclair, May
See also CA 104

Sinclair, May **TCLC 3, 11**
See also Sinclair, Mary Amelia St. Clair
See also CA 166; DLB 36, 135

Sinclair, Roy
See Griffith, D(avid Lewelyn) W(ark)

Sinclair, Upton (Beall) 1878-1968 ..... **CLC 1, 11, 15, 63; DA; DAB; DAC; DAM MST, NOV**
See also AMWS 5; AW; CA 5-8R; 25-28R; CANR 7; CDALB 1929-1941; DA3; DLB 9; INT CANR-7; MTCW 1, 2; SATA 9

Singer, Isaac
See Singer, Isaac Bashevis

Singer, Isaac Bashevis 1904-1991 .. **CLC 1, 3, 6, 9, 11, 15, 23, 38, 69, 111; DA; DAB; DAC; DAM MST, NOV; SSC 3**
See also AAYA 32; AITN 1, 2; AW; CA 1-4R; 134; CANR 1, 39; CDALB 1941-1968; CLR 1; DA3; DLB 6, 28, 52; DLBY 91; JRDA; MAICYA; MTCW 1, 2; SATA 3, 27; SATA-Obit 68

Singer, Israel Joshua 1893-1944 .... **TCLC 33**
See also CA 169

Singh, Khushwant 1915- .... **CLC 11**
See also CA 9-12R; CAAS 9; CANR 6, 84

Singleton, Ann
See Benedict, Ruth (Fulton)

Sinjohn, John
See Galsworthy, John

Sinyavsky, Andrei (Donatevich) 1925-1997 .... **CLC 8**
See also Tertz, Abram
See also CA 85-88; 159

Sirin, V.
See Nabokov, Vladimir (Vladimirovich)

Sissman, L(ouis) E(dward) 1928-1976 .... **CLC 9, 18**
See also CA 21-24R; 65-68; CANR 13; DLB 5

Sisson, C(harles) H(ubert) 1914- .... **CLC 8**
See also CA 1-4R; CAAS 3; CANR 3, 48, 84; DLB 27

Sitwell, DameEdith 1887-1964 ...... **CLC 2, 9, 67; DAM POET; PC 3**
See also CA 9-12R; CANR 35; CDBLB 1945-1960; DLB 20; MTCW 1, 2

Siwaarmill, H. P.
See Sharp, William

Sjoewall, Maj 1935- .... **CLC 7**
See also Sjowall, Maj
See also CA 65-68; CANR 73

Sjowall, Maj
See Sjoewall, Maj

Skelton, John 1460-1529 .... **PC 25**

Skelton, Robin 1925-1997 .... **CLC 13**
See also Zuk, Georges
See also AITN 2; CA 5-8R; 160; CAAS 5; CANR 28, 89; CCA 1; DLB 27, 53

Skolimowski, Jerzy 1938- .... **CLC 20**
See also CA 128

Skram, Amalie (Bertha) 1847-1905 .... **TCLC 25**
See also CA 165

Skvorecky, Josef (Vaclav) 1924- ...... **CLC 15, 39, 69; DAC; DAM NOV**
See also CA 61-64; CAAS 1; CANR 10, 34, 63; DA3; DLB 232; MTCW 1, 2

Slade, Bernard **CLC 11, 46**
See Newbound, Bernard Slade
See also CAAS 9; CCA 1; DLB 53

Slaughter, Carolyn 1946- .... **CLC 56**
See also CA 85-88; CANR 85

Slaughter, Frank G(ill) 1908- .... **CLC 29**
See also AITN 2; CA 5-8R; CANR 5, 85; INT CANR-5

Slavitt, David R(ytman) 1935- ..... **CLC 5, 14**
See also CA 21-24R; CAAS 3; CANR 41, 83; DLB 5, 6

Slesinger, Tess 1905-1945 .... **TCLC 10**
See also CA 107; DLB 102

Slessor, Kenneth 1901-1971 .... **CLC 14**
See also CA 102; 89-92

Slowacki, Juliusz 1809-1849 .... **NCLC 15**

Smart, Christopher 1722-1771 .. **LC 3; DAM POET; PC 13**
See also DLB 109

Smart, Elizabeth 1913-1986 .... **CLC 54**
See also CA 81-84; 118; DLB 88

Smiley, Jane (Graves) 1949- ...... **CLC 53, 76; DAM POP**
See also AMWS 6; CA 104; CANR 30, 50, 74, 96; DA3; DLB 227, 234; INT CANR-30

Smith, A(rthur) J(ames) M(arshall) 1902-1980 .... **CLC 15; DAC**
See also CA 1-4R; 102; CANR 4; DLB 88

Smith, Adam 1723-1790 .... **LC 36**
See also DLB 104

Smith, Alexander 1829-1867 .... **NCLC 59**
See also DLB 32, 55

Stone, Zachary
   See Follett, Ken(neth Martin)
Stoppard, Tom 1937- ... **CLC 1, 3, 4, 5, 8, 15, 29, 34, 63, 91; DA; DAB; DAC; DAM DRAM, MST; DC 6**
   See also AW; BRWS 1; CA 81-84; CANR 39, 67; CDBLB 1960 to Present; DA3; DLB 13, 233; DLBY 85; MTCW 1, 2
Storey, David (Malcolm) 1933- . **CLC 2, 4, 5, 8; DAM DRAM**
   See also BRWS 1; CA 81-84; CANR 36; DLB 13, 14, 207; MTCW 1
Storm, Hyemeyohsts 1935- ..... **CLC 3; DAM MULT**
   See also CA 81-84; CANR 45; NNAL
Storm, Theodor 1817-1888 .... **SSC 27**
Storm, (Hans) Theodor (Woldsen) 1817-1888 .... **NCLC 1; SSC 27**
   See also DLB 129
Storni, Alfonsina 1892-1938 . **TCLC 5; DAM MULT; HLC 2; PC 33**
   See also CA 104; 131; HW 1
Stoughton, William 1631-1701 .... **LC 38**
   See also DLB 24
Stout, Rex (Todhunter) 1886-1975 ..... **CLC 3**
   See also AITN 2; CA 61-64; CANR 71
Stow, (Julian) Randolph 1935- ... **CLC 23, 48**
   See also CA 13-16R; CANR 33; MTCW 1
Stowe, Harriet (Elizabeth) Beecher 1811-1896 .... **NCLC 3, 50; DA; DAB; DAC; DAM MST, NOV**
   See also AMWS 1; AW; CDALB 1865-1917; DA3; DLB 1, 12, 42, 74, 189, 239; JRDA; MAICYA
Strabo c. 64B.C.-c. 25 .... **CMLC 37**
   See also DLB 176
Strachey, (Giles) Lytton 1880-1932 .... **TCLC 12**
   See also BRWS 2; CA 110; 178; DLB 149; DLBD 10; MTCW 2
Strand, Mark 1934- .... **CLC 6, 18, 41, 71; DAM POET**
   See also AMWS 4; CA 21-24R; CANR 40, 65; DLB 5; SATA 41
Stratton-Porter, Gene(va Grace) 1863-1924
   See Porter, Gene(va Grace) Stratton
   See also CA 137; DLB 221; DLBD 14; MAICYA; SATA 15
Straub, Peter (Francis) 1943- . **CLC 28, 107; DAM POP**
   See also BEST 89:1; CA 85-88; CANR 28, 65; DLBY 84; MTCW 1, 2
Strauss, Botho 1944- .... **CLC 22**
   See also CA 157; CWW 2; DLB 124
Streatfeild, (Mary) Noel 1897(?)-1986 .... **CLC 21**
   See also CA 81-84; 120; CANR 31; CLR 17; DLB 160; MAICYA; SATA 20; SATA-Obit 48
Stribling, T(homas) S(igismund) 1881-1965 .... **CLC 23**
   See also CA 189; 107; DLB 9
Strindberg, (Johan) August 1849-1912 .... **TCLC 1, 8, 21, 47; DA; DAB; DAC; DAM DRAM, MST**
   See also AW; CA 104; 135; DA3; MTCW 2
Stringer, Arthur 1874-1950 .... **TCLC 37**
   See also CA 161; DLB 92
Stringer, David
   See Roberts, Keith (John Kingston)
Stroheim, Erich von 1885-1957 ..... **TCLC 71**
Strugatskii, Arkadii (Natanovich) 1925-1991 .... **CLC 27**
   See also CA 106; 135
Strugatskii, Boris (Natanovich) 1933- .... **CLC 27**
   See also CA 106

Strummer, Joe 1953(?)- .... **CLC 30**
Strunk, William, Jr. 1869-1946 ...... **TCLC 92**
   See also CA 118; 164
Stryk, Lucien 1924- .... **PC 27**
   See also CA 13-16R; CANR 10, 28, 55
Stuart, Don A.
   See Campbell, John W(ood, Jr.)
Stuart, Ian
   See MacLean, Alistair (Stuart)
Stuart, Jesse (Hilton) 1906-1984 ... **CLC 1, 8, 11, 14, 34; SSC 31**
   See also CA 5-8R; 112; CANR 31; DLB 9, 48, 102; DLBY 84; SATA 2; SATA-Obit 36
Sturgeon, Theodore (Hamilton) 1918-1985 .... **CLC 22, 39**
   See also Queen, Ellery
   See also CA 81-84; 116; CANR 32; DLB 8; DLBY 85; MTCW 1, 2
Sturges, Preston 1898-1959 .... **TCLC 48**
   See also CA 114; 149; DLB 26
Styron, William 1925- .... **CLC 1, 3, 5, 11, 15, 60; DAM NOV, POP; SSC 25**
   See also BEST 90:4; CA 5-8R; CANR 6, 33, 74; CDALB 1968-1988; DA3; DLB 2, 143; DLBY 80; INT CANR-6; MTCW 1, 2
Su, Chien 1884-1918
   See Su Man-shu
   See also CA 123
Suarez Lynch, B.
   See Bioy Casares, Adolfo; Borges, Jorge Luis
Suassuna, Ariano Vilar 1927-
   See also CA 178; HLCS 1; HW 2
Suckling, Sir John 1609-1642 .... **PC 30**
   See also DAM POET; DLB 58, 126
Suckow, Ruth 1892-1960 .... **SSC 18**
   See also CA 113; DLB 9, 102; TCWW 2
Sudermann, Hermann 1857-1928 .. **TCLC 15**
   See also CA 107; DLB 118
Sue, Eugene 1804-1857 .... **NCLC 1**
   See also DLB 119
Sueskind, Patrick 1949- .... **CLC 44**
   See also Suskind, Patrick
Sukenick, Ronald 1932- .... **CLC 3, 4, 6, 48**
   See also CA 25-28R; CAAS 8; CANR 32, 89; DLB 173; DLBY 81
Suknaski, Andrew 1942- .... **CLC 19**
   See also CA 101; DLB 53
Sullivan, Vernon
   See Vian, Boris
Sully Prudhomme 1839-1907 .... **TCLC 31**
Su Man-shu .... **TCLC 24**
   See also Su, Chien
Summerforest, Ivy B.
   See Kirkup, James
Summers, Andrew James 1942- .... **CLC 26**
Summers, Andy
   See Summers, Andrew James
Summers, Hollis (Spurgeon, Jr.) 1916- .... **CLC 10**
   See also CA 5-8R; CANR 3; DLB 6
Summers, (Alphonsus Joseph-Mary Augustus) Montague 1880-1948 .... **TCLC 16**
   See also CA 118; 163
Sumner, Gordon Matthew .... **CLC 26**
   See also Sting
Surtees, Robert Smith 1805-1864 .. **NCLC 14**
   See also DLB 21
Susann, Jacqueline 1921-1974 .... **CLC 3**
   See also AITN 1; CA 65-68; 53-56; MTCW 1, 2
Su Shih 1036-1101 .... **CMLC 15**
Suskind, Patrick
   See Sueskind, Patrick
   See also CA 145; CWW 2

Sutcliff, Rosemary 1920-1992 .... **CLC 26; DAB; DAC; DAM MST, POP**
   See also AAYA 10; AW; CA 5-8R; 139; CANR 37; CLR 1, 37; JRDA; MAICYA; SATA 6, 44, 78; SATA-Obit 73
Sutro, Alfred 1863-1933 .... **TCLC 6**
   See also CA 105; 185; DLB 10
Sutton, Henry
   See Slavitt, David R(ytman)
Svevo, Italo .... **TCLC 2, 35; SSC 25**
   See also Schmitz, Aron Hector
Swados, Elizabeth (A.) 1951- .... **CLC 12**
   See also CA 97-100; CANR 49; INT 97-100
Swados, Harvey 1920-1972 .... **CLC 5**
   See also CA 5-8R; 37-40R; CANR 6; DLB 2
Swan, Gladys 1934- .... **CLC 69**
   See also CA 101; CANR 17, 39
Swanson, Logan
   See Matheson, Richard Burton
Swarthout, Glendon (Fred) 1918-1992 .... **CLC 35**
   See also AW; CA 1-4R; 139; CANR 1, 47; SATA 26; TCWW 2
Sweet, Sarah C.
   See Jewett, (Theodora) Sarah Orne
Swenson, May 1919-1989 ...... **CLC 4, 14, 61, 106; DA; DAB; DAC; DAM MST, POET; PC 14**
   See also AMWS 4; CA 5-8R; 130; CANR 36, 61; DLB 5; GLL 2; MTCW 1, 2; SATA 15
Swift, Augustus
   See Lovecraft, H(oward) P(hillips)
Swift, Graham (Colin) 1949- ...... **CLC 41, 88**
   See also BRWS 5; CA 117; 122; CANR 46, 71; DLB 194; MTCW 2
Swift, Jonathan 1667-1745 ..... **LC 1, 42; DA; DAB; DAC; DAM MST, NOV, POET; PC 9**
   See also AW; CDBLB 1660-1789; CLR 53; DA3; DLB 39, 95, 101; SATA 19
Swinburne, Algernon Charles 1837-1909 .... **TCLC 8, 36; DA; DAB; DAC; DAM MST, POET; PC 24**
   See also AW; CA 105; 140; CDBLB 1832-1890; DA3; DLB 35, 57
Swinfen, Ann .... **CLC 34**
Swinnerton, Frank Arthur 1884-1982 .... **CLC 31**
   See also CA 108; DLB 34
Swithen, John
   See King, Stephen (Edwin)
Sylvia
   See Ashton-Warner, Sylvia (Constance)
Symmes, Robert Edward
   See Duncan, Robert (Edward)
Symonds, John Addington 1840-1893 .... **NCLC 34**
   See also DLB 57, 144
Symons, Arthur 1865-1945 .... **TCLC 11**
   See also CA 107; 189; DLB 19, 57, 149
Symons, Julian (Gustave) 1912-1994 .... **CLC 2, 14, 32**
   See also CA 49-52; 147; CAAS 3; CANR 3, 33, 59; DLB 87, 155; DLBY 92; MTCW 1
Synge, (Edmund) J(ohn) M(illington) 1871-1909 . **TCLC 6, 37; DAM DRAM; DC 2**
   See also CA 104; 141; CDBLB 1890-1914; DLB 10, 19
Syruc, J.
   See Milosz, Czeslaw
Szirtes, George 1948- .... **CLC 46**
   See also CA 109; CANR 27, 61

von Hofmannsthal, Hugo
See Hofmannsthal, Hugo von

von Horvath, Odon
See Horvath, Oedoen von

von Horvath, Oedoen
See Horvath, Oedoen von
See also CA 184

von Liliencron, (Friedrich Adolf Axel) Detlev
See Liliencron, (Friedrich Adolf Axel) Detlev von

Vonnegut, Kurt, Jr. 1922- . **CLC 1, 2, 3, 4, 5, 8, 12, 22, 40, 60, 111; DA; DAB; DAC; DAM MST, NOV, POP; SSC 8**
See also AAYA 6; AITN 1; AMWS 2; AW; BEST 90:4; CA 1-4R; CANR 1, 25, 49, 75, 92; CDALB 1968-1988; DA3; DLB 2, 8, 152; DLBD 3; DLBY 80; MTCW 1, 2

Von Rachen, Kurt
See Hubbard, L(afayette) Ron(ald)

von Rezzori (d'Arezzo), Gregor
See Rezzori (d'Arezzo), Gregor von

von Sternberg, Josef
See Sternberg, Josef von

Vorster, Gordon 1924- .... **CLC 34**
See also CA 133

Vosce, Trudie
See Ozick, Cynthia

Voznesensky, Andrei (Andreievich) 1933- .... **CLC 1, 15, 57; DAM POET**
See also CA 89-92; CANR 37; CWW 2; MTCW 1

Waddington, Miriam 1917- .... **CLC 28**
See also CA 21-24R; CANR 12, 30; CCA 1; DLB 68

Wagman, Fredrica 1937- .... **CLC 7**
See also CA 97-100; INT 97-100

Wagner, Linda W.
See Wagner-Martin, Linda (C.)

Wagner, Linda Welshimer
See Wagner-Martin, Linda (C.)

Wagner, Richard 1813-1883 .... **NCLC 9**
See also DLB 129

Wagner-Martin, Linda (C.) 1936- .... **CLC 50**
See also CA 159

Wagoner, David (Russell) 1926- .... **CLC 3, 5, 15; PC 33**
See also CA 1-4R; CAAS 3; CANR 2, 71; DLB 5; SATA 14; TCWW 2

Wah, Fred(erick James) 1939- .... **CLC 44**
See also CA 107; 141; DLB 60

Wahloo, Per 1926-1975 .... **CLC 7**
See also CA 61-64; CANR 73

Wahloo, Peter
See Wahloo, Per

Wain, John (Barrington) 1925-1994 . **CLC 2, 11, 15, 46**
See also CA 5-8R; 145; CAAS 4; CANR 23, 54; CDBLB 1960 to Present; DLB 15, 27, 139, 155; MTCW 1, 2

Wajda, Andrzej 1926- .... **CLC 16**
See also CA 102

Wakefield, Dan 1932- .... **CLC 7**
See also CA 21-24R; CAAS 7

Wakoski, Diane 1937- ...... **CLC 2, 4, 7, 9, 11, 40; DAM POET; PC 15**
See also CA 13-16R; CAAS 1; CANR 9, 60; DLB 5; INT CANR-9; MTCW 2

Wakoski-Sherbell, Diane
See Wakoski, Diane

Walcott, Derek (Alton) 1930- .... **CLC 2, 4, 9, 14, 25, 42, 67, 76; BLC 3; DAB; DAC; DAM MST, MULT, POET; DC 7**
See also BW 2; CA 89-92; CANR 26, 47, 75, 80; DA3; DLB 117; DLBY 81; MTCW 1, 2

Waldman, Anne (Lesley) 1945- .... **CLC 7**
See also CA 37-40R; CAAS 17; CANR 34, 69; DLB 16

Waldo, E. Hunter
See Sturgeon, Theodore (Hamilton)

Waldo, Edward Hamilton
See Sturgeon, Theodore (Hamilton)

Walker, Alice (Malsenior) 1944- ... **CLC 5, 6, 9, 19, 27, 46, 58, 103; BLC 3; DA; DAB; DAC; DAM MST, MULT, NOV, POET, POP; PC 30; SSC 5**
See also AAYA 3, 33; AMWS 3; AW; BEST 89:4; BW 2, 3; CA 37-40R; CANR 9, 27, 49, 66, 82; CDALB 1968-1988; DA3; DLB 6, 33, 143; INT CANR-27; MTCW 1, 2; SATA 31

Walker, David Harry 1911-1992 ...... **CLC 14**
See also CA 1-4R; 137; CANR 1; SATA 8; SATA-Obit 71

Walker, Edward Joseph 1934-
See Walker, Ted
See also CA 21-24R; CANR 12, 28, 53

Walker, George F. 1947- . **CLC 44, 61; DAB; DAC; DAM MST**
See also CA 103; CANR 21, 43, 59; DLB 60

Walker, Joseph A. 1935- .... **CLC 19; DAM DRAM, MST**
See also BW 1, 3; CA 89-92; CANR 26; DLB 38

Walker, Margaret (Abigail) 1915-1998 .... **CLC 1, 6; BLC; DAM MULT; PC 20**
See also BW 2, 3; CA 73-76; 172; CANR 26, 54, 76; DLB 76, 152; MTCW 1, 2

Walker, Ted CLC 13
See also Walker, Edward Joseph
See also DLB 40

Wallace, David Foster 1962- ..... **CLC 50, 114**
See also CA 132; CANR 59; DA3; MTCW 2

Wallace, Dexter
See Masters, Edgar Lee

Wallace, (Richard Horatio) Edgar 1875-1932 .... **TCLC 57**
See also CA 115; DLB 70

Wallace, Irving 1916-1990 .... **CLC 7, 13; DAM NOV, POP**
See also AITN 1; CA 1-4R; 132; CAAS 1; CANR 1, 27; INT CANR-27; MTCW 1, 2

Wallant, Edward Lewis 1926-1962 ... **CLC 5, 10**
See also CA 1-4R; CANR 22; DLB 2, 28, 143; MTCW 1, 2

Wallas, Graham 1858-1932 .... **TCLC 91**

Walley, Byron
See Card, Orson Scott

Walpole, Horace 1717-1797 .... **LC 49**
See also DLB 39, 104

Walpole, Hugh (Seymour) 1884-1941 .... **TCLC 5**
See also CA 104; 165; DLB 34; MTCW 2

Walser, Martin 1927- .... **CLC 27**
See also CA 57-60; CANR 8, 46; CWW 2; DLB 75, 124

Walser, Robert 1878-1956 .... **TCLC 18; SSC 20**
See also CA 118; 165; DLB 66

Walsh, Gillian Paton
See Paton Walsh, Gillian

Walsh, Jill Paton CLC 35
See also Paton Walsh, Gillian
See also CLR 2, 65

Walter, Villiam Christian
See Andersen, Hans Christian

Wambaugh, Joseph (Aloysius, Jr.) 1937- .... **CLC 3, 18; DAM NOV, POP**
See also AITN 1; BEST 89:3; CA 33-36R; CANR 42, 65; DA3; DLB 6; DLBY 83; MTCW 1, 2

Wang Wei 699(?)-761(?) .... **PC 18**

Ward, Arthur Henry Sarsfield 1883-1959
See Rohmer, Sax
See also CA 108; 173

Ward, Douglas Turner 1930- .... **CLC 19**
See also BW 1; CA 81-84; CANR 27; DLB 7, 38

Ward, E. D.
See Lucas, E(dward) V(errall)

Ward, Mary Augusta 1851-1920 ... **TCLC 55**
See also DLB 18

Ward, Peter
See Faust, Frederick (Schiller)

Warhol, Andy 1928(?)-1987 .... **CLC 20**
See also AAYA 12; BEST 89:4; CA 89-92; 121; CANR 34

Warner, Francis (Robert le Plastrier) 1937- .... **CLC 14**
See also CA 53-56; CANR 11

Warner, Marina 1946- .... **CLC 59**
See also CA 65-68; CANR 21, 55; DLB 194

Warner, Rex (Ernest) 1905-1986 ...... **CLC 45**
See also CA 89-92; 119; DLB 15

Warner, Susan (Bogert) 1819-1885 .... **NCLC 31**
See also DLB 3, 42, 239

Warner, Sylvia (Constance) Ashton
See Ashton-Warner, Sylvia (Constance)

Warner, Sylvia Townsend 1893-1978 .... **CLC 7, 19; SSC 23**
See also CA 61-64; 77-80; CANR 16, 60; DLB 34, 139; MTCW 1, 2

Warren, Mercy Otis 1728-1814 ..... **NCLC 13**
See also DLB 31, 200

Warren, Robert Penn 1905-1989 .. **CLC 1, 4, 6, 8, 10, 13, 18, 39, 53, 59; DA; DAB; DAC; DAM MST, NOV, POET; SSC 4**
See also AITN 1; AW; CA 13-16R; 129; CANR 10, 47; CDALB 1968-1988; DA3; DLB 2, 48, 152; DLBY 80, 89; INT CANR-10; MTCW 1, 2; SATA 46; SATA-Obit 63

Warshofsky, Isaac
See Singer, Isaac Bashevis

Warton, Thomas 1728-1790 ..... **LC 15; DAM POET**
See also DLB 104, 109

Waruk, Kona
See Harris, (Theodore) Wilson

Warung, Price TCLC 45
See also Astley, William

Warwick, Jarvis
See Garner, Hugh
See also CCA 1

Washington, Alex
See Harris, Mark

Washington, Booker T(aliaferro) 1856-1915 ...... **TCLC 10; BLC 3; DAM MULT**
See also BW 1; CA 114; 125; DA3; SATA 28

Washington, George 1732-1799 .... **LC 25**
See also DLB 31

Wassermann, (Karl) Jakob 1873-1934 .... **TCLC 6**
See also CA 104; 163; DLB 66

Wasserstein, Wendy 1950- .. **CLC 32, 59, 90; DAM DRAM; DC 4**
See also CA 121; 129; CABS 3; CANR 53, 75; DA3; DLB 228; INT 129; MTCW 2; SATA 94

Waterhouse, Keith (Spencer) 1929- . **CLC 47**
See also CA 5-8R; CANR 38, 67; DLB 13, 15; MTCW 1, 2

Waters, Frank (Joseph) 1902-1995 .. **CLC 88**
See also CA 5-8R; 149; CAAS 13; CANR 3, 18, 63; DLB 212; DLBY 86; TCWW 2

Waters, Roger 1944- .... **CLC 35**

Watkins, Frances Ellen
See Harper, Frances Ellen Watkins

Watkins, Gerrold
See Malzberg, Barry N(athaniel)

Watkins, Gloria Jean 1952(?)-
See hooks, bell
See also BW 2; CA 143; CANR 87; MTCW 2; SATA 115

Watkins, Paul 1964- .... **CLC 55**
See also CA 132; CANR 62

Watkins, Vernon Phillips
1906-1967 .... **CLC 43**
See also CA 9-10; 25-28R; CAP 1; DLB 20

Watson, Irving S.
See Mencken, H(enry) L(ouis)

Watson, John H.
See Farmer, Philip Jose

Watson, Richard F.
See Silverberg, Robert

Waugh, Auberon (Alexander)
1939-2001 .... **CLC 7**
See also CA 45-48; CANR 6, 22, 92; DLB 14, 194

Waugh, Evelyn (Arthur St. John)
1903-1966 .. **CLC 1, 3, 8, 13, 19, 27, 44, 107; DA; DAB; DAC; DAM MST, NOV, POP; SSC 41**
See also AW; CA 85-88; 25-28R; CANR 22; CDBLB 1914-1945; DA3; DLB 15, 162, 195; MTCW 1, 2

Waugh, Harriet 1944- .... **CLC 6**
See also CA 85-88; CANR 22

Ways, C. R.
See Blount, Roy (Alton), Jr.

Waystaff, Simon
See Swift, Jonathan

Webb, Beatrice (Martha Potter)
1858-1943 .... **TCLC 22**
See also CA 117; 162; DLB 190

Webb, Charles (Richard) 1939- .... **CLC 7**
See also CA 25-28R

Webb, James H(enry), Jr. 1946- ...... **CLC 22**
See also CA 81-84

Webb, Mary Gladys (Meredith)
1881-1927 .... **TCLC 24**
See also CA 182; 123; DLB 34

Webb, Mrs. Sidney
See Webb, Beatrice (Martha Potter)

Webb, Phyllis 1927- .... **CLC 18**
See also CA 104; CANR 23; CCA 1; DLB 53

Webb, Sidney (James) 1859-1947 .. **TCLC 22**
See also CA 117; 163; DLB 190

Webber, Andrew Lloyd CLC 21
See also Lloyd Webber, Andrew

Weber, Lenora Mattingly
1895-1971 .... **CLC 12**
See also CA 19-20; 29-32R; CAP 1; SATA 2; SATA-Obit 26

Weber, Max 1864-1920 .... **TCLC 69**
See also CA 109; 189

Webster, John 1580(?)-1634(?) ... **LC 33; DA; DAB; DAC; DAM DRAM, MST; DC 2**
See also AW; CDBLB Before 1660; DLB 58

Webster, Noah 1758-1843 .... **NCLC 30**
See also DLB 1, 37, 42, 43, 73

Wedekind, (Benjamin) Frank(lin)
1864-1918 .... **TCLC 7; DAM DRAM**
See also CA 104; 153; DLB 118

Weidman, Jerome 1913-1998 .... **CLC 7**
See also AITN 2; CA 1-4R; 171; CANR 1; DLB 28

Weil, Simone (Adolphine)
1909-1943 .... **TCLC 23**
See also CA 117; 159; MTCW 2

Weininger, Otto 1880-1903 .... **TCLC 84**

Weinstein, Nathan
See West, Nathanael

Weinstein, Nathan von Wallenstein
See West, Nathanael

Weir, Peter (Lindsay) 1944- .... **CLC 20**
See also CA 113; 123

Weiss, Peter (Ulrich) 1916-1982 .. **CLC 3, 15, 51; DAM DRAM**
See also CA 45-48; 106; CANR 3; DLB 69, 124

Weiss, Theodore (Russell) 1916- ... **CLC 3, 8, 14**
See also CA 9-12R; CAAE 189; CAAS 2; CANR 46, 94; DLB 5

Welch, (Maurice) Denton
1915-1948 .... **TCLC 22**
See also CA 121; 148

Welch, James 1940- ..... **CLC 6, 14, 52; DAM MULT, POP**
See also CA 85-88; CANR 42, 66; DLB 175; NNAL; TCWW 2

Weldon, Fay 1931- . **CLC 6, 9, 11, 19, 36, 59, 122; DAM POP**
See also BRWS 4; CA 21-24R; CANR 16, 46, 63; CDBLB 1960 to Present; DLB 14, 194; INT CANR-16; MTCW 1, 2

Wellek, Rene 1903-1995 .... **CLC 28**
See also CA 5-8R; 150; CAAS 7; CANR 8; DLB 63; INT CANR-8

Weller, Michael 1942- .... **CLC 10, 53**
See also CA 85-88

Weller, Paul 1958- .... **CLC 26**

Wellershoff, Dieter 1925- .... **CLC 46**
See also CA 89-92; CANR 16, 37

Welles, (George) Orson 1915-1985 .. **CLC 20, 80**
See also CA 93-96; 117

Wellman, John McDowell 1945-
See Wellman, Mac
See also CA 166

Wellman, Mac CLC 65
See also Wellman, John McDowell; Wellman, John McDowell

Wellman, Manly Wade 1903-1986 ... **CLC 49**
See also CA 1-4R; 118; CANR 6, 16, 44; SATA 6; SATA-Obit 47

Wells, Carolyn 1869(?)-1942 .... **TCLC 35**
See also CA 113; 185; DLB 11

Wells, H(erbert) G(eorge)
1866-1946 . **TCLC 6, 12, 19; DA; DAB; DAC; DAM MST, NOV; SSC 6**
See also AAYA 18; AW; CA 110; 121; CDBLB 1914-1945; CLR 64; DA3; DLB 34, 70, 156, 178; MTCW 1, 2; SATA 20

Wells, Rosemary 1943- .... **CLC 12**
See also AAYA 13; AW; CA 85-88; CANR 48; CLR 16, 69; MAICYA; SAAS 1; SATA 18, 69, 114

Welty, Eudora 1909- ...... **CLC 1, 2, 5, 14, 22, 33, 105; DA; DAB; DAC; DAM MST, NOV; SSC 1, 27**
See also AW; CA 9-12R; CABS 1; CANR 32, 65; CDALB 1941-1968; DA3; DLB 2, 102, 143; DLBD 12; DLBY 87; MTCW 1, 2

Wen I-to 1899-1946 .... **TCLC 28**

Wentworth, Robert
See Hamilton, Edmond

Werfel, Franz (Viktor) 1890-1945 ... **TCLC 8**
See also CA 104; 161; DLB 81, 124

Wergeland, Henrik Arnold
1808-1845 .... **NCLC 5**

Wersba, Barbara 1932- .... **CLC 30**
See also AAYA 2, 30; AW; CA 29-32R, 182; CAAE 182; CANR 16, 38; CLR 3; DLB 52; JRDA; MAICYA; SAAS 2; SATA 1, 58; SATA-Essay 103

Wertmueller, Lina 1928- .... **CLC 16**
See also CA 97-100; CANR 39, 78

Wescott, Glenway 1901-1987 .. **CLC 13; SSC 35**
See also CA 13-16R; 121; CANR 23, 70; DLB 4, 9, 102

Wesker, Arnold 1932- ... **CLC 3, 5, 42; DAB; DAM DRAM**
See also CA 1-4R; CAAS 7; CANR 1, 33; CDBLB 1960 to Present; DLB 13; MTCW 1

Wesley, Richard (Errol) 1945- .... **CLC 7**
See also BW 1; CA 57-60; CANR 27; DLB 38

Wessel, Johan Herman 1742-1785 .... **LC 7**

West, Anthony (Panther)
1914-1987 .... **CLC 50**
See also CA 45-48; 124; CANR 3, 19; DLB 15

West, C. P.
See Wodehouse, P(elham) G(renville)

West, Cornel (Ronald) 1953- .... **CLC 134; BLCS**
See also CA 144; CANR 91

West, (Mary) Jessamyn 1902-1984 ... **CLC 7, 17**
See also AW; CA 9-12R; 112; CANR 27; DLB 6; DLBY 84; MTCW 1, 2; SATA-Obit 37

West, Morris L(anglo) 1916-1999 ..... **CLC 6, 33**
See also CA 5-8R; 187; CANR 24, 49, 64; MTCW 1, 2

West, Nathanael 1903-1940 .... **TCLC 1, 14, 44; SSC 16**
See also CA 104; 125; CDALB 1929-1941; DA3; DLB 4, 9, 28; MTCW 1, 2

West, Owen
See Koontz, Dean R(ay)

West, Paul 1930- .... **CLC 7, 14, 96**
See also CA 13-16R; CAAS 7; CANR 22, 53, 76, 89; DLB 14; INT CANR-22; MTCW 2

West, Rebecca 1892-1983 ... **CLC 7, 9, 31, 50**
See also BRWS 3; CA 5-8R; 109; CANR 19; DLB 36; DLBY 83; MTCW 1, 2

Westall, Robert (Atkinson)
1929-1993 .... **CLC 17**
See also AAYA 12; CA 69-72; 141; CANR 18, 68; CLR 13; JRDA; MAICYA; SAAS 2; SATA 23, 69; SATA-Obit 75

Westermarck, Edward 1862-1939 . **TCLC 87**

Westlake, Donald E(dwin) 1933- .... **CLC 7, 33; DAM POP**
See also CA 17-20R; CAAS 13; CANR 16, 44, 65, 94; INT CANR-16; MTCW 2

Westmacott, Mary
See Christie, Agatha (Mary Clarissa)

Weston, Allen
See Norton, Andre

Wetcheek, J. L.
See Feuchtwanger, Lion

Wetering, Janwillem van de
See van de Wetering, Janwillem

Wetherald, Agnes Ethelwyn
1857-1940 .... **TCLC 81**
See also DLB 99

Wetherell, Elizabeth
See Warner, Susan (Bogert)

Whale, James 1889-1957 .... **TCLC 63**

Whalen, Philip 1923- .... **CLC 6, 29**
See also CA 9-12R; CANR 5, 39; DLB 16

Literary Criticism Series
Cumulative Topic Index

This index lists all topic entries in Gale's *Classical and Medieval Literature Criticism, Contemporary Literary Criticism, Literature Criticism from 1400 to 1800, Nineteenth-Century Literature Criticism,* and *Twentieth-Century Literary Criticism.*

Topic Index

TCLC Cumulative Nationality Index

Gorky, Maxim **8**
Gumilev, Nikolai (Stepanovich) **60**
Gurdjieff, G(eorgei) I(vanovich) **71**
Guro, Elena **56**
Hippius, Zinaida **9**
Ilf, Ilya **21**
Ivanov, Vyacheslav Ivanovich **33**
Kandinsky, Wassily **92**
Khlebnikov, Velimir **20**
Khodasevich, Vladislav (Felitsianovich) **15**
Klimentov, Andrei Platonovich **14**
Korolenko, Vladimir Galaktionovich **22**
Kropotkin, Peter (Aleksieevich) **36**
Kuprin, Aleksander Ivanovich **5**
Kuzmin, Mikhail **40**
Lenin, V. I. **67**
Mandelstam, Osip (Emilievich) **2, 6**
Mayakovski, Vladimir (Vladimirovich) **4, 18**
Merezhkovsky, Dmitry Sergeyevich **29**
Pavlov, Ivan Petrovich **91**
Petrov, Evgeny **21**
Pilnyak, Boris **23**
Prishvin, Mikhail **75**
Remizov, Aleksei (Mikhailovich) **27**
Rozanov, Vassili **104**
Shestov, Lev **56**
Sologub, Fyodor **9**
Stalin, Joseph **92**
Tolstoy, Alexey Nikolaevich **18**
Tolstoy, Leo (Nikolaevich) **4, 11, 17, 28, 44, 79**
Trotsky, Leon **22**
Tsvetaeva (Efron), Marina (Ivanovna) **7, 35**
Zabolotsky, Nikolai Alekseevich **52**
Zamyatin, Evgeny Ivanovich **8, 37**
Zhdanov, Andrei Alexandrovich **18**
Zoshchenko, Mikhail (Mikhailovich) **15**

SCOTTISH

Barrie, J(ames) M(atthew) **2**
Bridie, James **3**
Brown, George Douglas **28**
Buchan, John **41**

Cunninghame Graham, Robert (Gallnigad) Bontine **19**
Davidson, John **24**
Frazer, J(ames) G(eorge) **32**
Gibbon, Lewis Grassic **4**
Lang, Andrew **16**
MacDonald, George **9**
Muir, Edwin **2, 87**
Sharp, William **39**
Tey, Josephine **14**

SLOVENIAN

Cankar, Ivan **105**

SOUTH AFRICAN

Bosman, Herman Charles **49**
Campbell, (Ignatius) Roy (Dunnachie) **5**
Mqhayi, S(amuel) E(dward) K(rune Loliwe) **25**
Plaatje, Sol(omon) T(shekisho) **73**
Schreiner, Olive (Emilie Albertina) **9**
Smith, Pauline (Urmson) **25**
Vilakazi, Benedict Wallet **37**

SPANISH

Alas (y Urena), Leopoldo (Enrique Garcia) **29**
Barea, Arturo **14**
Baroja (y Nessi), Pio **8**
Benavente (y Martinez), Jacinto **3**
Blasco Ibañez, Vicente **12**
Echegaray (y Eizaguirre), Jose (Maria Waldo) **4**
Garcia Lorca, Federico **1, 7, 49**
Jimenez (Mantecon), Juan Ramon **4**
Machado (y Ruiz), Antonio **3**
Martinez Sierra, Gregorio **6**
Martinez Sierra, Maria (de la O'LeJarraga) **6**
Miro (Ferrer), Gabriel (Francisco Victor) **5**
Ortega y Gasset, Jose **9**
Pereda (y Sanchez de Porrua), Jose Maria de **16**

Perez Galdos, Benito **27**
Ramoacn y Cajal, Santiago **93**
Salinas (y Serrano), Pedro **17**
Unamuno (y Jugo), Miguel de **2, 9**
Valera y Alcala-Galiano, Juan **10**
Valle-Inclan, Ramon (Maria) del **5**

SWEDISH

Bengtsson, Frans (Gunnar) **48**
Dagerman, Stig (Halvard) **17**
Ekelund, Vilhelm **75**
Heidenstam, (Carl Gustaf) Verner von **5**
Key, Ellen (Karolina Sofia) **65**
Lagerloef, Selma (Ottiliana Lovisa) **4, 36**
Soderberg, Hjalmar **39**
Strindberg, (Johan) August **1, 8, 21, 47**

SWISS

Ramuz, Charles-Ferdinand **33**
Rod, Edouard **52**
Saussure, Ferdinand de **49**
Spitteler, Carl (Friedrich Georg) **12**
Walser, Robert **18**

SYRIAN

Gibran, Kahlil **1, 9**

TURKISH

Sait Faik **23**

UKRAINIAN

Aleichem, Sholom **1, 35**
Bialik, Chaim Nachman **25**

URUGUAYAN

Quiroga, Horacio (Sylvestre) **20**
Sanchez, Florencio **37**

WELSH

Davies, William Henry **5**
Evans, Caradoc **85**
Lewis, Alun **3**
Machen, Arthur **4**
Thomas, Dylan (Marlais) **1, 8, 45, 105**

Nationality Index

TCLC-107 Title Index